HISTORICAL DICTIONARY
OF THE
U.S. AIR FORCE

Historical Dictionary
of the
U.S. Air Force

EDITED BY

Charles D. Bright

Robin Higham,
Advisory Editor

GREENWOOD PRESS

New York • Westport, Connecticut • London

Library of Congress Cataloging-in-Publication Data

Bright, Charles D.
    Historical dictionary of the U.S. Air Force / edited by Charles D.
    Bright.
        p.   cm.
    Includes bibliographical references and index.
    ISBN 0–313–25928–3 (alk. paper)
      1. United States. Air Force—History—Dictionaries. I. Title.
UG633.B75   1992
358.4′00973—dc20   91–25461

British Library Cataloguing in Publication Data is available.

Library of Congress Catalog Card Number: 91–25461
ISBN: 0–313–25928–3

First published in 1992

Greenwood Press, 88 Post Road West, Westport, CT 06881
An imprint of Greenwood Publishing Group, Inc.

Printed in the United States of America

The paper used in this book complies with the
Permanent Paper Standard issued by the National
Information Standards Organization (Z39.48–1984).

10 9 8 7 6 5 4 3 2 1

To

my Band of Brothers

of B–17F *Round Trip Ticket III*

Frank N. Carroll

Gilbert E. D'Alonzo

Wilbur T. Fowler

Paul B. Kessler

Ernest R. Martin

Sylvan H. Odegard

Marvin H. Price

Robert S. Shepherd, Jr.

Harry T. Welch

CONTENTS

Photographs appear following page xix.

PREFACE

The airplane has been the most important invention of the 20th century. Even before the century's midpoint, the airplane had changed the world economically and politically. Already in that short time, the first man-made vehicles had left the atmosphere and penetrated space using machinery that was, at least partly, a development of aviation. The major participant in these aerospace events was the U.S. Air Force (USAF) and its antecedents.

Preparing a one-volume historical dictionary of such an organization required me to make many personal judgments. My initial assessment of what should be included about battles, campaigns, concepts, individuals, organizations, equipment, legislation, and other matters ended with some 850 items. I then sought and received advice from contributors to this dictionary and other informed persons and settled upon the final result of 1,028 items. Errors of commission and omission in judgment are mine alone.

Space has been allocated to the subjects according to their relative importance to the U.S. Air Force. This determination was also mine, based on my experience as a former USAF officer and as a trained military historian, and I take full responsibility for it.

In many cases, topics can be identified by two or more names. Often is is not clear which name is the proper name and which is a common one. I have preferred the proper form unless it is relatively obscure; obscure proper names are cross-referenced to their common names.

I have simplified listings where possible. Airfields have single listings only. If one wants to find a listing for "Kelly Field" or "Kelly AFB," for example, one should look under "Kelly." Aircraft are listed by their most basic codes. For example, "C-47" includes the variants AC-47, EC-47, SC-47, and so forth. In cases where a designation or name of an aircraft or missile has changed over the years, the most recent is used. Thus, a "P-51" will be found under "F-51." Older designations are cross-referenced, as are the names of equipment.

In two cases, two significant but different aircraft have had the same designation; there were two B-26s and two O-1s. I have called one B-26 the B-26 Invader and the other the B-26 Marauder; I have called one O-1 Bird Dog and the other the O-1 Falcon. Smaller missiles are also listed under their model designations, such as AIM-4. Aircraft and missiles are cross-referenced if they have a name. Large missiles are listed under their names, such as Atlas, because their designations are rarely used. Operations and projects are listed under their most commonly used forms. These subjects may be found under their full titles, such as Operation Babylift, or by their names, such as Aphrodite.

An attempt was made to present parallel information on the characteristics of aircraft and missiles. However, not all information was available on some equipment, and sources sometimes disagreed. Relevance was often the test for inclusion. Dimensions have been rounded to the nearest inch or foot.

Abbreviations and acronyms in the U.S. Air Force are legion, and their use is common. For the most part, they are used in this book only after the full name has been used. The exceptions, because of overwhelming frequency, are:

USAF	U.S. Air Force
USAAF	U.S. Army Air Forces
USAAC	U.S. Army Air Corps
USAAS	U.S. Army Air Service
AB	Air Base
AFB	Air Force Base

Organizational changes have been frequent in the USAF and its antecedents. Even a list of all important organizations would be unmanageable. Except in special cases, only the current names of major air commands, air forces, separate operating agencies, and direct reporting units are described separately. Some important or famous units now extinct are included.

The USAF and its antecedents have now fought five wars and have about 800 aces. Coverage therefore had to be limited. I chose three criteria for inclusion: an arbitrary standard, fame, or special uniqueness. The arbitrary standard was 20 victories (half of top ace Richard Bong's total).

Just as the "Marseillaise" was said to be worth two divisions, I have included in the listed topics art, folklore, movies, novels, slang, songs, and television. I believe they fill a significant role in inspiring and defining an organization as large and historical as the USAF.

I wished to include more than I have been able to on the aerospace industry, which is inseparably linked to the USAF. Aerospace power includes civilian and industrial activities as well as military ones. The industry is worth as much space as the USAF, but it had to be largely sacrificed to achieve the primary aim of the book.

The primary aim of this book is to provide those who are already acquainted with the USAF a tool for investigating subjects with which they are not now familiar. For persons with only a slight knowledge of the USAF, the aim is to provide a base. In either case, the references listed with each topic are a guide to further sources. Titles of official histories are sometimes unclear when they are part of a series; if any such reference in this book is unclear, it can be looked up in Robin Higham, *Official Histories*, 1970. An asterisk following a name signals that there is an entry for it in this book.

The many contributors to this dictionary were asked to participate because they were historians or they possessed experience or unusual knowledge about a topic. For example, a winner of the Air Force Medal of Honor contributed the essay on that subject. The brief vitae of all of the contributors shows some of this expertise. I am most grateful to the contributors for their large share in this work. Unsigned entries were prepared by the editor.

I received much help aside from the contributions. Special thanks go to Robin Higham of Kansas State University, who served as special adviser, and Alice Price, Office of the Secretary of the Air Force, who provided information, negatives, and prints on USAF art. Especially useful help on topic selection was provided by Warren A. Trest, Air Force Historical Research Center; Roger Beaumont, Texas A&M University; and Alwyn T. Lloyd, The Boeing Company. Thanks go also to Mildred Vasan, Senior Editor, Social and Behavioral Services, and Penny Sippel, Production Editor, for Greenwood Press. Finally, thanks go to Heidi B. Parales for help in style.

ABBREVIATIONS

Some references are used often, and the following abbreviations are used:

AAHS Journal	*American Aviation Historical Society Journal.*
AF	*Air Force Magazine.*
AH	*Aerospace Historian.*
AWST	*Aviation Week & Space Technology.*
Berger, *USAF in SEA*	Carl Berger, ed., *The United States Air Force in Southeast Asia 1961–1973*, 1977.
Brown, *Eagles*	Jerold E. Brown, *Where Eagles Land: Planning and Development of U.S. Army Airfields, 1910–1941*, 1990.
C&C	*See* Craven and Cate in text.
DuPre, *USAF Bio.*	Flint O. DuPre, *U.S. Air Force Biographical Dictionary*, 1965.
Futrell, *Ideas*	Robert Frank Futrell, *Ideas, Concepts, Doctrine: Basic Thinking in the United States Air Force*, vol. 1, *1907–1960*, vol. 2, *1961–1984*, 1989.
Futrell, *USAF in Korea*	Robert F. Futrell, *The United States Air Force in Korea 1950–1953*, rev. ed., 1983.
Goldberg, *Hist. USAF*	Alfred Goldberg, ed., *A History of the United States Air Force*, 1957.
Gunston, *Airc. Arm.*	Bill Gunston, *The Illustrated Encyclopedia of Aircraft Armament*, 1988.
Gurney, *5 Down*	Gene Gurney and Mark P. Friedlander, Jr., *Five Down and Glory: A History of the American Air Ace*, 1958.
Hess, *Aces Album*	William N. Hess, ed., *The American Fighter Aces Album*, 1978.

Higham, *Air Pwr.*   Robin Higham, *Air Power: A Concise History*, 3d
                                      ed., 1988.

Higham, *Combat Airc.*   Robin Higham, Abigail Siddall, and Carol Williams,
                                      eds., *Flying Combat Aircraft of the USAAF-USAF*,
                                      3 vols., 1975, 1978, and 1981.

Knaack, *US Airc.*   Marcelle Size Knaack, *Encyclopedia of U.S. Air
                                      Force Aircraft and Missile Systems*, vol. 1, *Post–
                                      World War II Fighters 1945–1973*, 1978, vol. 2,
                                      Post–World War II Bombers 1945–1973, 1988.

Maurer, *Avn. in Army*   Maurer Maurer, *Aviation in the U.S. Army, 1919–
                                      1939*, 1987.

Mueller, *AFB*   Robert Mueller, *Air Force Bases*, vol. 1, *Active Air
                                      Force Bases within the United States of America on
                                      17 September 1982*, 1989.

Polmar, *SAC*   Norman Polmar, ed., *Strategic Air Command: Peo-
                                      ple, Aircraft, and Missiles*, 1979.

Ravenstein, *Org. USAF*   Charles A. Ravenstein, *The Organization and Li-
                                      neage of the United States Air Force*, 1986.

Roberts, *Dir. USAF*   Michael Roberts, *The Illustrated Directory of the
                                      United States Air Force*, 1989.

Swanborough, *US Mil. Airc.*   Gordon Swanborough and Peter M. Bowers, *United
                                      States Military Aircraft since 1909*, 1989.

Wagner, *Am. Planes*   Ray Wagner, *American Combat Planes*, 3d ed.,
                                      1982.

A BRIEF HISTORY OF THE U.S. AIR FORCE

The U.S. Army had an interest in aviation starting with observation balloons in the Civil War, used from 1861 to 1863. It continued with a financial grant to Samuel P. Langley* for an airplane during the Spanish-American War. However, history of the USAF only truly begins with the first of its five predecessor units.

AERONAUTICAL DIVISION, U.S. ARMY SIGNAL CORPS*

Despite the long-standing interest in aviation, the military usefulness of aviation was disputed in the early 20th century. It took intervention by President Theodore Roosevelt* to cause the Army to form the Aeronautical Division on 1 August 1907.

This organization's concern was to find out what the airplane could do. Reconnaissance* was the most likely use, but bombing was tried in 1911 and a machine gun was mounted in June 1912 to test the possibility of armed aircraft.

AVIATION SECTION, U.S. ARMY SIGNAL CORPS*

The rapid technological advances in aviation in its early years convinced some that aviation *might* prove useful for reconnaissance. So, on 18 July 1914, the Aviation Section was formed. Shortly thereafter the early events of World War I* confirmed the critical usefulness of aviation for reconnaissance.

The Aviation Section started with training. Its first battle operations were in the Mexican expedition of 1916,* but it performed poorly with its fragile elementary equipment. It was far behind its European counterparts. The section was faced with a herculean task when America entered World War I in 1917. By that time fighter* and bomber* operations, as well as reconnaissance, had proven to be important in the war. Now an enormous expansion was demanded of the section. There was a need to go, almost overnight, from a shoestring operation with obsolete aircraft to an effective force comparable to its German, British, and French counterparts. The American aircraft industry, which was just a shadow of those of the other great powers, was expected to produce clouds of modern aircraft.

Even though the job could not be done in the time demanded, the great expansion called for a more appropriate organization. The Signal Corps proved unable to manage two vast buildups.

U.S. ARMY AIR SERVICE*

On 24 May 1918, the USAAS was established. The fledgling air force mounted two great air offensives for the St. Mihiel* and Meuse-Argonne* campaigns before the war ended. However, the only American-built aircraft used in battle was the de Haviland DH-4,* which was an observation* and bomber aircraft. The other aircraft used by the USAAS were furnished by the British and French.

The accomplishments and the expansion can be well measured by the size of the air force throughout this period. It increased from 311 men in 1916 to 195,023 in 1918, a 627-fold increase.

The USAAS emerged from the war with competence in tactical operations,* an awareness of some ideas of strategic operations,* a large force of trained aircrews, and a dynamic combat leader and air power theorist in the person of Brigadier General William Mitchell.*

Mitchell forecast the preeminence of aerial operations in war and urged that America establish a separate and independent air force. He was confident that aviation would continue to make rapid technological progress and that its effectiveness and organization should be judged accordingly. A flamboyant and outspoken prophet, he took his case directly to the American people, in part via Mitchell's bombing tests on warships.* In addition, the USAAS tried to show the public the capabilities of the aircraft of the time by participating in air races, including the Schneider Cup race of 1925,* the nonstop transcontinental flight,* the dawn-to-dusk flight,* and the Round-the-World Flight of 1924.* The USAAS made efforts to improve aircraft quickly, as with the Barling bomber.* Unfortunately, in reality the USAAS was a skeleton force left after demobilization, flying obsolete aircraft held over from the war.

The impatient Mitchell seized upon the bungled flight of the naval airship USS *Shenandoah* in 1925 to direct the public's attention to the neglect and abuse of military aviation. Mitchell's court-martial failed to arouse general public support. However, together with the lamentations of the desperate American aircraft industry struggling with the aftereffects of demobilization, it caused the formation of the President's Aircraft Board.* The findings of the Morrow Board led to the Air Corps Act* of 1926. This act raised the status of the air service to an Army branch and directed a five-year plan for its and the industry's recovery.

U.S. ARMY AIR CORPS*

The USAAC was established on 2 July 1926. It continued to try to develop better aircraft, to demonstrate the ability of air power through spectacular flights, and, through its Air Corps Tactical School,* to find the most effective doctrine* to follow in a future war. Its leaders followed a more quiet and patient course than Mitchell's, while still aiming at an independent and separate air force.

The continued rapid technological advance of aviation, together with the adoption of a doctrine based on strategic operations, gave the USAAC hope it could soon perform as it had planned should war come. Despite continued insistence by the Army that it be a tactical service in support of the ground forces, the USAAC was permitted to form the General Headquarters Air Force* in 1935. That was the seed of a strategic operations air force.

The Munich agreement of 1938 and the first campaigns of World War II* showed the dominance of air power in military and naval operations. The airmen were once again called upon to change from a small to a great organization. They had been a service neglected by the executive and legislative branches of the federal government and by the American public, virtually confined to the continental United States, using obsolete and obsolescent aircraft. They grew into a first-rate air force conducting global operations. Before this rearmament had progressed far, the importance of air power dictated higher organizational stature for the airmen.

U.S. ARMY AIR FORCES*

The USAAF came into being on 20 June 1941 and had autonomous status within the Army. It needed to expand into an even larger service than was used in World War I. Soon the USAAF was active around the world, conducting strategic, tactical, and airlift operations.*

A new prophet, Major Alexander P. de Seversky,* carried the USAAF message to the American people with his best-selling book, *Victory Through Air Power*, which was followed by an influential movie based on the book. Coming after the impressive accomplishments of the Luftwaffe and the Royal Air Force (RAF), de Seversky succeeded in gaining the public support for air power that Mitchell had failed to achieve.

The experience and the forced draft of a hard-fought war led to changes in doctrine and to sweeping development of improved aircraft to exploit fully aviation's technological revolution. Strategic operations were modified and tactical and airlift operations were greatly advanced. The USAAF, with its allies, achieved air supremacy and conducted effective strategic, tactical, and airlift operations campaigns in all theaters of war. Measuring the extent of the expansion, again with personnel, the service went from 23,455 persons in 1939 to 2,372,292 in 1944, a 101-fold increase.

In the end, the USAAF used only two B-29s* with nuclear weapons* to precipitate Japan's surrender in August 1945. The airmen now had the power to break nations, and the deterrence of war was feasible.

Following the war, the air force was again demobilized to a shadow of its former self. However, public and political support for a separate and independent air force had become irresistible because of the USAAF's war record and demonstrated power.

U.S. AIR FORCE*

Nearly 30 years after Billy Mitchell's vain attempts, the USAF finally became a military service equal to the Army and Navy on 18 September 1947. Mitchell was the prophet and spiritual leader, but the founding fathers of the USAF, whose efforts date back to the USAAC, were General of the Air Force H. H. Arnold;* Generals Ira C. Eaker,* George C. Kenney* and Carl A. Spaatz;* Lieutenant Generals Frank M. Andrews* and Harold L. George;* and Major Generals Benjamin D. Foulois,* Hugh J. Knerr,* and Robert Olds.*

The USAF was able to rebuilt from its shrunken condition after demobilization by way of the President's Air Policy (Finletter) Commission* of 1947, the Cold War,* and the Korean War.* The Commission addressed the status of the USAF and the aircraft industry in a parallel with the President's Aircraft Board of 1925. The commission endorsed an American defense based primarily upon nuclear-armed, intercontinental bomber* strategic operations. This became a grand strategy of massive retaliation.

Unexpectedly, the importance of the USAF and its airlift capability was soon demonstrated in the Cold War's Berlin Airlift* of 1948 to 1949. The operation showed the humanitarian and political power of the USAF by supplying a great city entirely by air and frustrating Soviet objectives. Humanitarian missions continued to be important as USAF airlift abilities grew in later years. The Berlin Airlift also showed the need for the North Atlantic Treaty Organization* (NATO), which was formed in April 1949 before the end of the air bridge. The USAF has been a key element in NATO ever since.

Another great test soon faced the USAF with the Korean War, which ran from 1950 to 1953. This time tactical operations had to be revitalized from a neglected state. The USAF had mistakenly underrated wars that were less than total, because it had believed that forces able to win an unlimited war would be used to win a limited one. Those holding this idea failed to foresee the domestic U.S. political factors that developed in modern limited wars. Also, the nuclear bomber force was still being built in 1950. The USAF's strategic operations against the Korean irrigation dams target system* and the threat of them against Manchuria led the enemy to accept truce terms.

After the Korean War, the USAF was prepared for and faced continuing threats of limited war with its tactical forces, and there were changes in the 1950s in the strategic operations situation. The U.S. nuclear monopoly ended, and the USSR developed delivery systems using both bombers and ballistic missiles.*

Until the end of the 1950s the main threat was bombers, so the USAF had to develop an air defense capability together with Canada in a North American Aerospace Command,* or NORAD. During the Truman* and Eisenhower* administrations, from 1948 to 1960, the USAF received priority over the other services. It has not had this status since the Kennedy administration began in 1961.

In the 1960s, the strategic situation shifted mainly to the potential use of ballistic missiles. Since both superpowers—the United States and the USSR— had these weapons for which there was no adequate defense, the grand strategy changed to mutual assured destruction (MAD). The Cuban crisis of 1962* illustrated the change.

From 1948 to 1965, an effective leader dominated the USAF. General Curtis E. LeMay* molded the USAF to his vision and made it a more traditional military service.

Soon after the USAF was formed, a continuing revolution in reconnaissance began. First there was the U-2,* which was able for years to fly over the USSR with impunity. Then the Mach 3 SR-71* came into service. In the 1960s satellite reconnaissance became operational. In addition, important progress was made in electronic reconnaissance.

In 1965, another land war in Asia began with the Vietnam War.* This war was conducted by the USAF under highly restrictive rules. For years, only abridged tactical operations were conducted, and the USAF's strategic bombers were adapted to tactical use. Forbidden to blockade the enemy, the USAF and U.S. Navy were unable to stop the aggression and supplies from the north despite elaborate technological innovations. In the spring of 1972, this changed and the USAF and Navy were allowed to blockade the enemy. On 18 December, the USAF was permitted to conduct a strategic operations campaign with its B-52s* designed to cause North Vietnam to agree to a peace. It was called Linebacker* II. One month later, on 23 January 1973, an accord was reached between the United States and North Vietnam, ending U.S. operations.

Since the Vietnam War, the USAF has continued modernization of its forces, including the U.S. Air Force Reserve* (USAFR) and Air National Guard* (ANG). This modernization is aimed at maintaining a globally ready force with equipment and training superior to that of any potential enemy. The modernization has also included an emphasis on countering enemy radar* and sensors by stealth* while improving the USAF's own detectors. By improving its own power, the USAF has contributed to the effectiveness of the aerospace industry and the airlines; the synergism has further increased U.S. aerospace power. That power was spectacularly demonstrated in the Iraq crisis of 1990* and Iraq War* of 1991. USAF air power was the main ingredient in one of the most lopsided victories in history.

With its deterrent power and its ability to wreak destruction should peace break down, the USAF has become an important part of U.S. society and the greatest air force in history.

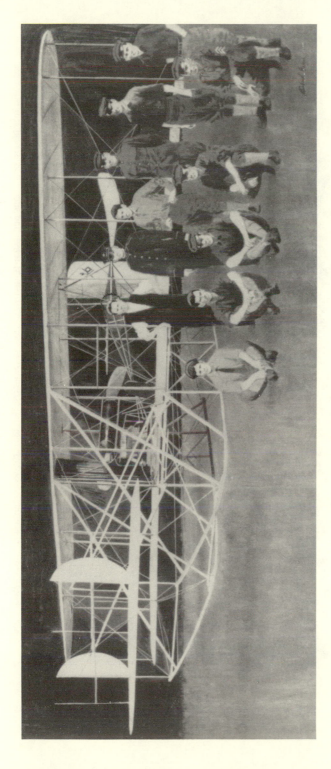

Photo 1. "The Entire Air Force, 1910" by Richard Green. This painting includes the first plane of the Aeronautical Division, U.S. Army Signal Corps, built by the Wright Brothers. Its crew is (back row, left to right): civilian O. G. Simmons, First Lieutenant Benjamin D. Foulois, and four enlisted men including Private Glenn R. Madole, Private Kinsey, and Private William C. Abolin. In the front row are Private Felix Clarke, Sergeant Stephen J. Idzorek, Private R. W. Brown, Corporal Vernon L. Burge, and Sergeant Herbert Marcus. The USAF has come far in the subsequent eight decades. (Courtesy U.S. Air Force Art Collection.)

Photo 2. The P-12, a beautiful example of the biplane design, served the USAAC outstandingly in the 1920s and 1930s. The pilot is Captain Ira C. Eaker, one of the founding fathers of the USAF. This 26 February 1929 photo shows a uniform of the horse-era style that Brigadier General William Mitchell had succeeded in replacing the choke collar with a soft one. The Sam Browne belt and riding boots were not very popular with airmen by the early 1930s. (Courtesy USAF.)

Photo 3. An unusual view of the B-17. Shown is the Boeing Aircraft Company's school for USAAC and USAAF mechanics in Seattle, Washington, in the 1940s. It demonstrates that the industrial contribution to aerospace power lies not just in the design and production of equipment, but also in training for the vital maintenance function. The B-17 served mostly in Europe, where it was the main part of the strategic operations* force which caused the collapse of German armament production in World War II.* (Courtesy The Boeing Company.)

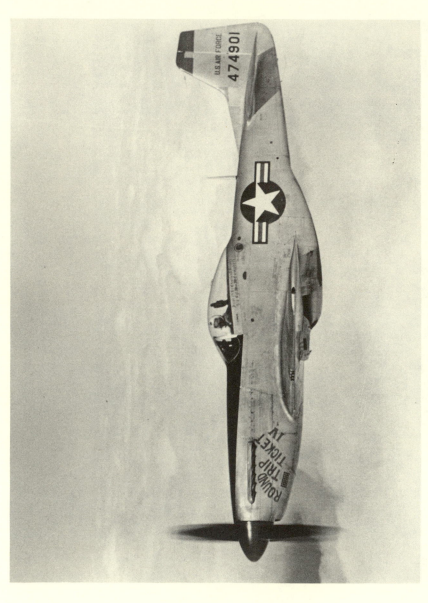

Photo 4. The Editor's F-51D. The F-51 was the best piston-engined fighter in World War II and a critical contributor to the USAAF's attainment of air superiority over Germany itself in early 1944. This victory meant Germany had lost the war. This 1952 photo illustrates USAF nose art. Also note that the pilot's and crew chief's names are on the canopy base. (Courtesy Daniel R. Rhodes.)

Photo 5. The famous *Enola Gay* B-29. It was one of only two B-29s whose nuclear weapon strategic operations precipitated Japan's conditional surrender to end World War II. Previously other B-29s had devastated the country in the strategic campaign against Japan, including mining operations that wrought havoc with transportation. Later the B-29 contributed to deterrence of the USSR in the Cold War and to strategic and tactical operations in the Korean War. In 1953 the threat of B-29 strategic operations against Manchuria was an incentive for Red China to accept United Nations (UN) terms for peace. (Courtesy The Boeing Company. Photo by Peter M. Bowers.)

Photo 6. On 14 October 1947, the USAF's X-1 was the first plane to exceed Mach 1. Captain Charles E. "Chuck" Yeager was the pilot. This photo of the X-1 Team shows (back row, left to right) Captains Yeager and Jackie L. Ridley. The front row (left to right) shows the X-1 ground crew, Merle Woods, Jack Russell, and Garth Dill. Behind the men is the X-1, named *Glamorous Glennis*, and its carrier stage B-29. (Courtesy USAF.)

Photo 7. "Armament Crews Loading F-51s in Korea" by Francis Beaugureau. Aerospace power is impossible without its logistics train of supply and maintenance. In the Korean War, the USAF's now-obsolete air superiority fighters, like the F-51, and bombers performed the attack function well, leading to communist acceptance of United Nations (UN) peace terms. In the Vietnam War, USAF attack planes played the major role in Linebacker 1, which defeated a North Vietnamese field army. In the Iraq War, USAF attack planes were the principal factor in air power's destruction of the entrenched Iraqi army. (Courtesy U.S. Air Force Art Collection.)

Photo 8. The sleek F-84. Obsolete in the Korean War, the F-84 pioneered jet-attack operations in that conflict. It was the main aircraft used for the strategic operations against the Korean irrigation dams target system. This action probably induced the North Koreans to accept United Nations (UN) peace terms. Note the early aerial refueling equipment on the wing-tip fuel tanks for use with the probe and drogue method. (Courtesy USAF.)

Photo 9. Major Robert M. "Bob" White with the X-15 aerospace aircraft. On 17 July 1962, Major White was the first to pilot an airplane in space, flying at an altitude of 314,750 feet. He was also the first man to fly faster than Mach 4, 5, and 6. (Courtesy USAF.)

Photo 10. "Launching an Atlas ICBM" by Ralph Iligan. The first application of space power was the ballistic missile. Beginning with the Atlas, ICBMs have formed one of the USAF's two legs of America's deterrent triad. The policy of deterrence probably won the Cold War and prevented a major war for over four decades. (Courtesy U.S. Air Force Art Collection.)

Photo 11. The fabulous SR-71 is the most technologically advanced aircraft ever built. It gave the USAF great reconnaissance capability. The crewman on the left is unknown; on the right is Colonel Thomas J. Keck. Notice the aircrew's dress for flight on the threshold of space. (Courtesy USAF.)

Photo 12. Aerial refueling of a B-52 by a KC-135 using a flying boom. Aerial refueling gives the USAF worldwide operational capability. The B-52 has been most of the airplane part of the deterrence triad for decades, and it takes part in the control of the seas. It was B-52s that conducted the strategic operations of Linebacker II, which led North Vietnam to begin peace-talks in January 1973. B-52s were also used for attack operations in the Vietnam and Iraq wars. (Courtesy The Boeing Company.)

Photo 13. Mrs. Barbara Bush escorts Armenian patients from on-board a Military Airlift Command C-141 transport. This action was in the long-standing tradition of humanitarian operations conducted globally by the USAF. (Courtesy USAF.)

Photo 14. "Global Power" by Dean Fausett. This painting illustrates the global reach of the USAF's modern jet fighters, bombers, tankers, transports, and attack planes. Eight decades of aerospace technological advances in range, payload, speed, and aerial refueling provide the means to apply USAF aerospace power for military or humanitarian operations worldwide within hours. (Courtesy U.S. Air Force Art Collection.)

HISTORICAL DICTIONARY
OF THE
U.S. AIR FORCE

A

A-1 SKYRAIDER

The U.S. Navy ordered a new dive- and torpedo-bomber from the Douglas Aircraft Company in 1944. Originally designated XBT2D-1, it went into production as the AD-1. Production ended in 1957.

Some were taken out of storage in 1963, rebuilt, and assigned to the Air Force Special Warfare Center at Eglin* AFB. By this time, they were designated A-1s. Twenty-five of them, A-1Es, were sent to the Vietnam War* in 1964 by Secretary of Defense (SECDEF) Robert S. McNamara.* They were to replace the USAF's* Farm Gate* B-26 Invaders* and T-28s.* The B-26s and T-28s had already seen much service when they were sent to Vietnam in 1961, and, when a second T-28 shed its wings, McNamara wanted them retired as worn out. The A-1E was seen by some as a very effective attack* aircraft because it was rugged, could carry 6,500 pounds of external ordnance, and could loiter in a combat area for a long time. These qualities account for a USAF nickname of "Flying Dumptruck." It had increasing difficulty with flak* and surface-to-air missiles* (SAM) during combat in Vietnam. By the end of the 1960s, the USAF had retired its A-1s. The USAF A-1s were also nicknamed "MiG-Killer," "Spad,"* and "Super Spad."

Characteristics: engine, Wright R-3350–26WA of 2,700 horsepower; span, 51 feet; length, 39 feet; height, 16 feet; maximum weight, 24,872 pounds; top speed, 365 miles per hour; ceiling, 25,000 feet; range, over 2,700 miles; total ordnance, 8,000 pounds.

References. Primary: Higham, *Combat Airc.*, vol. 2. Secondary: "A Gallery of USAF Weapons," *AF*, September 1969, p. 198. Gordon Swanborough and Peter M. Bowers, *United States Navy Aircraft since 1911*, 2d ed., 1976. Wagner, *Am. Planes.*

A-7 CORSAIR II

The U.S. Navy sought a replacement for its A-4 in 1963. The Vought Division of the LTV Corporation won the design competition with an adaptation of its Navy F-8. In the Vietnam War,* the U.S. Army pressed the USAF* to use specialized attack* airplanes instead of fighters* for close air support of ground forces. The USAF bowed to the pressure and chose to buy A-7s. The USAF wanted a more powerful engine than the Navy's, and its versions, the A-7D and A-7K, first flew in 1968. Service operations began in 1970. Production ended in 1976, when the USAF had received 459.

The USAF's A-7s only entered the Vietnam War in 1972, yet they flew 12,928 sorties and were highly effective. Only four A-7s were lost in battle. The USAF's A-7s were nicknamed "Little Hummer" and "Short Little Ugly F——," or "SLUF."

Characteristics: engine, Allison TF41-A-1 turbofan of 14,500 pounds thrust; span, 39 feet; length, 46 feet; height, 16 feet; gross weight, 42,000 pounds; top speed, 698 miles per hour; range with external tanks, 2,871 miles; ordnance, 15,000 pounds.

References. Primary: Higham, *Combat Airc.*, vol. 2. Thomas G. Ryan, "That Super-Accurate SLUF," *AF*, March 1972, pp. 27–32. Secondary: John L. Frisbee, "How the A-7D Rewrote the Book in Southeast Asia," *AF*, August 1973, pp. 30–36. Bill Gunston, *Attack Aircraft of the West*, 1974. Richard G. Head, "The Air Force A-7 Decision; The Politics of Close Air Support," *AH*, December 1974, pp. 218–24. Wagner, *Am. Planes*.

See also Howze Board; McNamara, Secretary Robert S.

A-10 THUNDERBOLT II

The Fairchild Republic Company designed the A-10 as a close air support attack* aircraft. The USAF* was looking for an "A-X" with great destructive power against surface targets, especially tanks. It also wanted ruggedness and range. The A-10 won the flying competition in 1972 against the Northrop Corporation's entry, the A-9. A notable feature was the tank-killer GAU-8* gun. The A-10 entered operational service in 1977, and production ended in 1984 after 713 were built. A-10As participated in the Grenada incident* in 1983. In the Iraq War* in 1991 the A-10 had a field day against the enemy. For example, on a single day two A-10s operating as a team demolished 23 tanks.

In 1990, the USAF had 600 in service and scheduled them for retirement in 1994, but Congress passed a law requiring their transfer to the U.S. Army and Marine Corps. The USAF was charged with continued logistical support of them. Congress intended this as a test of the concept of taking the close air support (CAS) mission away from the USAF. The A-10's nicknames were "Hog," "Porker," "SLAT" (Slow, Low, Aerial Target), "Thud II," and "Warthog."

Characteristics: engines, two General Electric TF34-GE-100 turbofans with 9,065 pounds of thrust each; span, 58 feet; length, 53 feet; height, 15 feet; gross weight, 50,000 pounds; combat speed, 439 miles per hour; range, 288 miles; ordnance, 16,000 pounds.

References. Primary: John F. Gulick, "The A-10 Does It Better," *AF*, July 1976, pp. 75–79. Secondary: Jim Beavers, "The A-10—Monstrosity with a Mission," *AF*, February 1980, pp. 66–70. Futrell, *Ideas*, vol. 2. Bill Gunston, *Attack Aircraft of the West*, 1974. Susan H. H. Young, "Gallery of USAF Weapons," *AF*, May 1990, p. 146.

See also F-16.

A-12 SHRIKE

The USAAC* sought an all-metal attack* monoplane in 1930 and got it in the A-8, A-10, and A-12 Shrike. Produced by the Curtiss Aeroplane and Motor Company, Inc., it first flew in 1931 and entered service in 1932. The USAAC's 46 Shrikes were an important type in the 1930s and served until 1942.

Characteristics: engine, Wright R-1820–21 of 670 horsepower; span, 44 feet; length, 32 feet; height, 9 feet; gross weight, 5,756 pounds; top speed, 177 miles per hour; service ceiling, 15,150 feet; range, 510 miles; bombs, 400 pounds.

References. Walter M. Jefferies, Jr., and Kenn C. Rust, "The Curtiss Shrikes," *AAHS Journal*, Summer 1965, pp. 129–39. Swanborough, *US Mil. Airc.* Wagner, *Am. Planes*.

A-16. *See* F-16.

A-17

Manufactured by Northrop Aircraft, Inc., the A-17 was the principal USAAC* attack* plane in the years just before World War II.* Developed from the Gamma and Delta types, an attack prototype was finished in 1933. It was designated the YA-13. Re-engined, it became the XA-16. Yet another engine was tried, and it became the A-17. It entered active service in 1935 and the total bought was 241. In 1940 some were sold to Britain and France.

Characteristics (A-17A): engine, Pratt & Whitney R-1535–13 with 825 horsepower; span, 48 feet; length, 32 feet; height, 12 feet; gross weight, 7,543 pounds; top speed, 220 miles per hour; service ceiling, 19,400 feet; range, 732 miles; bombs, 400 pounds.

References. Swanborough, *US Mil. Airc.* Wagner, *Am. Planes*.

A-20 HAVOC

More A-20s were built than any other USAAC* or USAAF* aircraft with the A, attack,* designation. Those services received 7,230. U.S. allies received an additional 155. The large number reflects the model's success. The Douglas Aircraft Company's famous Ed Heinemann began design work on the A-20 in 1937. British and French rearmament resulted in production orders in 1938, and the USAAC ordered some in 1939. The A-20 was the first plane to fight in Europe as part of the USAAF, arriving in 1942. It served in the Fifth Air Force* (5AF) in the Pacific, and the Ninth* and Fifteenth* in Europe. Variants include the F-3 for reconnaissance* and the P-70 interceptor.* Plans for an O-53 for observation* were never completed. Production ended in 1944. Its nickname was "Flying Pike."

Characteristics (A-20K): engines, two Wright R-2600–29 with 1,700 horsepower each; span, 61 feet; length, 48 feet; height, 18 feet; gross weight, 21,264 pounds; top speed, 329 miles per hour; service ceiling, 28,250 feet; range, 1,060 miles; ordnance, 2,600 pounds.

References. Gregory A. Moreira, "An A-20 Pilot," *AAHS Journal*, Summer 1970, pp. 94–101. Swanborough, *US Mil. Airc.* Wagner, *Am. Planes*.

A-26 INVADER. *See* B-26 Invader.

A-36. *See* F-51.

A-37. *See* T-37.

AA (ANTIAIRCRAFT). *See* flak, surface-to-air missiles.

AAA (ANTIAIRCRAFT ARTILLERY). *See* flak, surface-to-air missiles.

AABNCP. *See* E-4.

AAC. *See* U.S. Army Air Corps; Alaskan Air Command.

AACS. *See* Air Force Communications Command.

AAFES. *See* Army and Air Force Exchange Service.

AAS. *See* U.S. Army Air Service.

ABC-1. *See* AWPD-1.

AC. *See* U.S. Army Air Corps; aviation cadet.

AC&W. *See* aircraft control and warning.

ACCOUNTING AND FINANCE CENTER. *See* U.S. Air Force Accounting and Finance Center.

ACE

The USAF* has produced about 800 aces and many of them were among the best in history. The word *ace* is derived from the pre–World War I* French colloquialism *as*, denoting an athletic champion. By 1915, the French applied the word to any pilot* who had shot down ten or more enemy aircraft. Germany followed this trend, calling its best *experten*, or experts. Brigadier General Hugh M. Trenchard,* head of Britain's Royal Flying Corps (RFC), at first refused to use the distinction because of his emphasis on teamwork. Later, Trenchard was forced to acknowledge his fighter* pilots as aces, partly to raise morale in Britain. America's late entry into World War I caused it to reduce the number of aerial kills from ten to five to produce its share of aces.

Five confirmed kills became the standard qualification for ace status through the 1980s. Fighter pilots think the title "ace" should apply only to them. The three top USAF aces of all time are Major Richard I. Bong,* Major Thomas B. McGuire, Jr.,* and Colonel Francis S. Gabreski.*

References. Ian Parsons, *The Encyclopedia of Air Warfare*, 1975. Raymond F. Toliver and Trevor J. Constable, *Fighter Aces of the U.S.A.*, 1979.
See also gunner; weapon system operator.

Ronald W. Yoshino

ACT OF 18 JULY 1914

This act is generally recognized as the one establishing the second forerunner of the USAF, * the Aviation Section* of the U.S. Army Signal Corps. The act was first presented to Congress in August 1913, but debate over certain provisions of the bill delayed passage until the following year. It limited personnel strength to 60 officers and 260 enlisted men, established flying pay formulas, and defined the aeronautical ratings of Military Aviator* and Junior Military Aviator.

References. Carroll V. Glines, *The Compact History of the United States Air Force*, 1963. Goldberg, *Hist. USAF*.

D. K. Vaughan

ACT OF 3 APRIL 1939

Alarmed at the role of air power in the Munich agreement of 1938, President Franklin D. Roosevelt* recognized the need for a stronger USAAC.* He asked some military advisers for a plan for 10,000 USAAC planes. Major General H. H. Arnold* told Roosevelt that an air force needed more than aircraft. The number of aircraft was reduced to 6,000 to provide money for men and bases. Roosevelt's message to Congress, on 12 January 1939,* was aimed at putting the plan into effect.

Congress quickly responded with the act of 3 April 1939. The act enabled the USAAC to buy 3,251 planes, which would triple its inventory over that of early 1939. The 1939 act was the first step in the USAAC's mobilization and modernization for World War II.* The obvious support of the president and Congress caused the U.S. Army to reduce limitations imposed on its air arm. There were two main changes in the Army restrictions. First, the USAAC was no longer confined in its planning to the defense of America's land territories, but could now include the Western Hemisphere. The second change was related to the first. The Army's ban on buying long-range four-engined bombers was lifted to give the USAAC the means for hemispheric defense. This important act opened the way for the effective global USAAF* of a few years later.

References. Goldberg, *Hist. USAF*. Maurer, *Avn. in Army*.
See also Army-Navy agreements of 1931 and 1938.

ACTS. *See* Air Corps Tactical School.

AD. *See* division.

ADC. *See* Aerospace Defense Command.

ADIZ. *See* Air Defense Identification Zone.

ADM-20 QUAIL

First known as the GAM-72, this unique missile was used only on the B-52.*
Produced by the McDonnell Aircraft Corporation, the Quail first flew in 1958
and entered service in 1960. It was retired in 1978. The purpose of the ADM-
20, or Air/Decoy/Missile, was to mimic in every way a B-52 bomber penetrating
enemy air space. Four could be carried in the forward bomb bay. Upon release,
the Quail would fly its own course while duplicating a B-52's radar* or infrared
signature. It had no warhead.

Characteristics: engine, General Electric J85 turbojet with an infrared burner
to enhance its temperature; span, 6 feet; length, 13 feet; top speed, Mach 0.9;
range, up to 400 miles.

References. David A. Anderton, *Strategic Air Command: Two-thirds of the Triad*. c.
1974. Walter Boyne, *Boeing B-52*, 1981. Polmar, *SAC*. Kenneth P. Werrell, *The Evolution of the Cruise Missile*, 1985.

Philip Long

ADVANCED AIRBORNE NATIONAL COMMAND POST. *See* E-4.

ADVANCED MEDIUM-RANGE AIR-TO-AIR MISSILE. *See* AIM-120.

ADVANCED MEDIUM STOL TRANSPORT (AMST)

The AMST was first conceived during the USAF's* Project Forecast, a 1964
study evaluating the possibilities for more effective application of science and
technology. In 1970 the Tactical Air Command* (TAC) established a requirement
for an AMST for its tactical airlift* forces. It was needed to beef up theater
distribution systems with a transport* that could carry "outsize" cargo as did
the new C-5,* that would be jet powered, that would have a short takeoff and
landing (STOL) capability for short European runways, and that would have
large cargo capacity. The requirement included a 3,600-nautical-mile range, 14-
ton payload, and the ability to use a 2,000-foot-long runway and to cruise at
Mach 0.75. It was to be the next generation combat airlifter and successor to
the aging C-130s* which were first used in the 1950s.

Development began in 1971 when Congress appropriated the first $6 million
for a competitive AMST program. The following year the secretary of defense
(SECDEF) authorized the USAF to award contracts to The Boeing Company
and the McDonnell Douglas Corporation for the initial designs of the AMST
prototype. The designs by these two firms eventually were built as the YC-14
of Boeing and YC-15 of McDonnell in 1975. The USAF held a "fly-off" of
the two aircraft in 1976 and 1977. Based upon these tests, the USAF issued a
proposal instruction package (PIP) to both Boeing and McDonnell on 16 September 1977. The idea was to have both contractors merge the best attributes
of the YC-14 and YC-15 and work toward an AMST Cooperative Development
Program.

However, the AMST program was already under fire from several quarters.
It was not included in the president's budget for fiscal year (FY) 1979 when the

budget was compiled in December 1977. In the weaker-kneed defense environment of the Carter administration, the AMST program finally met its demise. On 31 October 1979, the SECDEF, in a meeting with USAF officials, canceled the AMST program. It was replaced with a new airlift concept, the C-X transport. This new airlifter, larger than the C-141* but smaller than the C-5, was to possess both a strategic and tactical ability. This program emerged in the early 1980s as the C-17.*

References. *Pedigree of Champions: Boeing since 1916*, 5th ed., 1984. George M. Watson, Jr., *The Advanced Medium Short Take-Off and Landing Transport and the Implication of the Minimum Engineering Development Program*, n.d. Bill Yenne, *McDonnell Douglas: A Tale of Two Giants*, 1985.

Roger D. Launius

ADVANCED RANGE INSTRUMENTATION AIRCRAFT. *See* C-18 for EC-18B variant.

ADVANCED TACTICAL FIGHTER (ATF)

In 1979 the USAF* began a review of future fighter designs. It was gravely concerned about increasingly sophisticated Soviet fighters, the MiG-23 and Su-24 at that time. Both were using larger engines and carrying improved avionics and weapons. Furthermore, Soviet air defenses in the West were formidable. By 1986, they had 10,000 radar* sites, 12,000 flak* guns, and 4,600 surface-to-air missiles* (SAM). This hardware was backed by budgets and industries that beat American SAM production by a 15-to-one ratio. The USAF's Scientific Advisory Board* (SAB) investigated fighter designs for up to and beyond the year 2000. The SAB decided that what the radical jumps in technology needed was beyond existing means. In 1982 the SAB opted to incorporate into the ATF some advanced technical systems still under development and to set a completion goal of the end of the decade.

The ATF was expected to exceed all similar craft in all aspects of flying, including sustained supersonic flight, extreme maneuverability, and short takeoff and landing (STOL) capabilities. Plans sought "self-repairing flight control systems" able to compensate for battle damage while flying. Stealth,* or low sensor detection, requirements were to affect components with perhaps 50 percent of the craft made of composites like graphite epoxy. A trade-off was to be made between optimum flying performance and stealth requirements. Engines were to have about 32,000 pounds of thrust with demands for 40 to 60 percent fewer parts, 60 percent fewer specialized tools for maintenance, and 150 percent longer component life spans than existing engines.

Seven companies sought the contract. A team of Lockheed, Boeing, and General Dynamics was to develop the YF-22A. A team of Northrop and McDonnell Douglas was to develop the YF-23A. Each team won identical $691 million contracts in 1986. Rockwell International and Grumman Aerospace were eliminated from the competition. Pratt & Whitney* and General Electric* developed the YF119 and YF120 engines, respectively. Two prototypes of each airframe were to be built, each with a different engine. The first flights were made in 1990 and tests were scheduled to last into 1991. The winning airframe and engine combination were to cost, in 1985 dollars, $35 million each. Plans expected production of 72 ATFs a year until 750 had been built.

References. "The Advanced Tactical Fighter Program: Affordability and National Security," *Vital Speeches of the Day*, 22 May 1986, pp. 596–99. "Air Force Requests Proposals for Advanced Tactical Fighter," *AWST*, 14 October 1985, pp. 24–25. "First Team Forms to Prepare Proposals for ATF Competition," *AWST*, 7 July 1986, p. 20. "The $40 Billion Dogfight," *Forbes*, 4 May 1987, pp. 35–38. "Lockheed Reorganizes Advanced Tactical Fighter Effort," *AWST*, 21 December 1987, p. 29. "USAF Awards ATF Contract to Lockheed, Northrop," *AWST*, 10 November 1986, pp. 18–19. "USAF Extends Deadline for ATF Validation Proposals," *AWST*, 16 December 1985, p. 24.

See also Air Force 2000.

Ronald W. Yoshino

ADVISERS. *See* Military Assistance Program.

AECP. *See* Officer Candidate School; Officer Training School.

AERIAL GUNNER. *See* Movies.

AERIAL MINING. *See* mining.

AERIAL REFUELING

This is an in-flight system of transferring fuel from one aircraft to another to extend the range or endurance of the recipient plane. The use of aerial refueling has extended the range of the USAF* to global operations.

Increasing the fuel supply of an aircraft to extend the range creates new limitations. The increase in weight ultimately raises the fuel consumption rate so high that no more range is achieved. In order to stretch aircraft range to the ultimate, which is global, aviation needed solutions from new power sources or from outside the aircraft. Possible solutions were nuclear-powered aircraft, forward bases, and aerial refueling. The attempt at a nuclear-powered aircraft, the X-6,* was technologically impractical in its time. Forward bases have the severe handicap of dependence upon political agreement with a host country.

Experiments were conducted between World Wars I* and II* in aerial refueling by the USAAS* and USAAC.* The method used was to lower a fuel hose by hand from a tanker* to the receiving aircraft. This was a clumsy technique unsuitable for high-performance aircraft.

After World War II, the USAF adopted the British-developed probe-and-drogue system. It uses a hose reeled out from a tanker. The receiver plane hooks up by inserting a probe into a funnel-like device at the end of the hose. This system has been used by smaller aircraft. A telescoping, flying boom for the tanker, which permits large amounts of fuel to be transferred quickly to big aircraft, was developed by the Boeing Company. Since then, the USAF has used aircraft specialized as tankers. *See* B-29, B-50, C-10, C-97, C-130, and C-135.

References. David Anderton, *Strategic Air Command: Two-thirds of the Triad*, c. 1974. Billy R. Gibson, "Casey Lowers the Boom," *AH*, Summer 1968, pp. 12–17. Alwyn T. Lloyd, *B-29 in Detail & Scale*, part 2, 1987. Randal E. Morger, "Tankers for a Thirsty Fleet," *AF*, June 1986, pp. 74–80. Albert W. Schinz, " 'Ho-Hum' Fighter In-Flight Refueling—Not So!" *AH*, September 1984, pp. 174–76.

AEROMEDICAL EVACUATION

Evolving from humble beginnings, aeromedical evacuation ensures American service members the best medical care in the world and is a great humanitarian resource.

World War I* fostered airplane ambulances out of necessity. Many student pilots were crashing in remote locations, making immediate attention through conventional medical recovery operations next to impossible. In February 1918, a JN* Jenny was modified to carry a patient in a semireclining position in the rear cockpit. This arrangement made the first military aeromedical evacuation flight in the United States. By the fall of 1918, air ambulances were used at six fields.

The need for air ambulances grew after the war as cross-country flying increased. The types of aircraft used varied widely. The USAAC* used the B-18,* C-9 (a Ford trimotor, not to be confused with the C-9A* Nightingale), and C-39 in the years immediately before World War II.* In that war, aeromedical evacuation became a necessity. There were limited medical facilities in Alaska, Africa, India, and China. Physicians, acting on their own, began to evacuate the sick and wounded in transport* planes that had flown in troops and supplies. The USAAF's air surgeon, Brigadier General David N. W. Grant, became responsible for developing an aeromedical evacuation system. C-46,* C-47,* and C-54* aircraft were used. The evacuation units lacked a unified command and were parceled out to the theaters of operation. Aeromedical evacuation became widely recognized as the best way to transport casualties great distances, and more than 1.3 million patients were airlifted in the war.

In 1946, the Air Transport Command (ATC) assumed responsibility for aeromedical evacuation in the United States. In 1948 the ATC's successor organization, the Military Air Transport Service (MATS), extended aeromedical evacuation to its airlift mission. MATS' intertheater air evacuation became so efficient and beneficial that the Department of Defense (DoD), in 1949, designated airlift as the primary means of transporting patients. The Korean War* affirmed the concept of aeromedical evacuation. Most aeromedical airlift moved casualties requiring specialized treatment or lengthy recovery from Korean air bases to Japan, and the on to America, if needed. By the end of the war, 311,000 casualty movements were made. The speed of airlift, as well as advances in medicine, reduced the deaths from 45 per 1,000 in World War II to 25 in the Korean War.

In 1954 the C-131, a variant of the civil Convair 240 or 340, began aeromedical operations in the continental United States (CONUS). Unlike other aircraft, it was designed for the mission. For intertheater airlift, MATS used C-97s,* C-118s, and C-121s.*

In the Vietnam War,* C-118s and C-130s* evacuated patients to hospitals within Vietnam and then, if needed, to other hospitals in the Pacific Command (PACOM). At first, C-135s* flew casualties to the United States. They could carry 44 litter and 54 ambulatory patients. The C-135 could fly from Yokota* AB, Japan, to Travis* AFB, California, in nine hours, while propeller aircraft had taken 42 hours for the same flight. In July 1965, the Military Airlift Command* (MAC) replaced the C-135s with C-141s,* which could carry 80 litter patients. More than 405,000 Vietnam casualty movements were recorded between 1965 and 1973. During the war, only 1 percent of America's wounded died after reaching a medical facility. In the wake of Vietnam War reassessments, the USAF* placed all theater aeromedical resources under the MAC.

In 1990 the worldwide aeromedical evacuation system maintained its readiness by airlifting service people and their dependents to military treatment centers. C-9As performed most of these airlifts. The C-141 performed airlifts between theaters, and the C-130 did combat airlift.

References. Berger, *USAF in SEA*. Robert F. Futrell, *Development of Aeromedical Evacuation in the United States Air Force, 1909–1960*, 1961. Cecil L. Reynolds, *MAC Aeromedical Evacuation Support of Southeast Asia, 1964–1971*, 1972.

See also flight nurse; helicopters; Iraq War; rescue.

Betty Raab Kennedy

AERONAUTICAL DIVISION, U.S. ARMY SIGNAL CORPS

The first antecedent organization of the USAF* was the Aeronautical Division of the Army's Signal Corps. It was established on 1 August 1907. Captain Charles deForest Chandler* was placed in charge and was assigned two enlisted men, one of whom soon deserted. Until 1911 the division was primarily concerned with balloon activities. The unit was chronically underfunded until it was replaced in July 1914 by the newly formed Aviation Section of the U.S. Army Signal Corps.*

References. Carroll V. Glines, *The Compact History of the United States Air Force*, 1963. Goldberg, *Hist. USAF*. Juliette A. Hennessy, *The United States Army Air Arm April 1861 to April 1917*, 1985.

D. K. Vaughan

AEROSPACE CORPORATION. *See* think tanks.

AEROSPACE DEFENSE COMMAND (ADC)

ADC, originally the Air Defense Command, was for many years a major command of the USAF.* It was established in 1946. From 1948 to 1951, its mission was assumed by the Continental Air Command.* Reestablished in 1951 as a major command, it was redesignated as the Aerospace Defense Command in 1965.

Although cooperation with Canada on the air defense of North America began in 1951, a formal organization was not in place for this effort until 1957. In that year the predecessor of the North American Aerospace Defense Command* (NORAD) began operation, with ADC as a part of it. ADC's units were reduced over time as its tasks were transferred to the Air National Guard* and the USAF Reserve.* ADC was inactivated in 1980, and most of its remaining assets were divided between the Tactical and Strategic Air Commands.*

References. "Aerospace Defense Command," *AF*, May 1979, pp. 66–67. Goldberg, *Hist. USAF*. Ravenstein, *Org. USAF*.

See also aerospace defense operations.

AEROSPACE DEFENSE OPERATIONS

The British in World War I* faced the threat of the first important air strategic operations,* so they established the first extensive air defense operations. By contrast, the Americans in France used only fighter* patrols searching for enemy aircraft* and balloon and ground observers who reported aircraft movements.

By 1933 the USAAC* had plans for patrols out to 300 miles beyond U.S. coasts and wanted long-range bombers* to strike any hostile forces there. However, the USAAC soon decided that offensive aviation would provide the best defense.

The Battle of Britain showed the usefulness of defensive aviation and the shortcomings of offensive aviation of the time. As a result, the USAAC formed an Air Defense Command in 1940. But efforts to make this an adequate system before the raid on Pearl Harbor* failed through complacency and indifference. Pearl Harbor changed that frame of mind quickly. On 9 December 1941, President Franklin D. Roosevelt* warned that an attack could be mounted against U.S. coastal areas.

A Japanese submarine fired 13 shells into an oil refinery on the California coast on 23 February 1942. During the next two nights there was a succession of air defense alerts in Los Angeles, and, on the second night, flak* batteries opened fire amid a confusion of reports. This "Battle of Los Angeles" reflected inexperience, poor equipment and organization, and hysteria.

Over time a true air defense system was set up by the USAAF,* consisting of four elements under a central control. The first was detection, using radar* and ground observers. The second was issuing air raid warnings and ordering the use of smoke generation to obscure possible targets. The third was radio control of fighters to intercept enemy airplanes. The fourth was control of searchlights, barrage balloons, and flak. This system demanded cooperation among the USAAF, the Army, and civilian defense agencies.

The basic system of World War II was modernized to deal with technological changes: ballistic and cruise missiles,* long-range radar, reconnaissance* satellites, jet fighters, computers, electronic warfare,* air interceptor missiles* (AIM), and surface-to-air missiles* (SAM). Air defense was transformed into aerospace defense. The first warning of a ballistic missile attack may be detected by satellites and confirmed by the Ballistic Missile Early Warning System* (BMEWS). Other radars were designed to detect submarine-launched ballistic missiles. There were also the traditional radar nets to defend against aircraft, plus the E-3s* Airborne Warning and Control System* (AWACS) which can detect low-flying objects. The next major change in the technology could be the Strategic Defense Initiative* (SDI).

References. Primary: C. L. Chennault, "The Role of Defensive Pursuit," unpub., 1935. Secondary: "Aerospace Defense Command," *AF*, May 1979, pp. 66–67. C&C, vols. 1 and 6. Goldberg, *Hist. USAF*. Donald C. Latham, "The Strategic Defense Triad," *AF*, April 1988, pp. 88–91.

See also air base defense; North American Aerospace Defense Command.

AEROSPACE INDUSTRY

The aerospace industry is the arsenal of democracy for the United States and its allies' aerospace power.* It is roughly as old as the USAF.* The USAF has relied upon private industry, and not government arsenals, for its equipment. This system has contributed to the success of the USAF.

There have been roughly 80 American companies that have supplied airframes to the USAF and 15 engine manufacturers. The great airframe company names have been the Bell Aircraft Corporation, The Boeing Company, Consolidated Vultee Aircraft Corporation (Convair), Curtiss-Wright Corporation, Douglas Aircraft Company, Fairchild Industries, General Dynamics Corporation, Lockheed Aircraft Corporation, McDonnell Aircraft Corporation, McDonnell Douglas Corporation, Glenn L. Martin Company, Inc., Martin Marietta Aerospace, North American Aviation, Inc., Northrop Corporation, Republic Aviation Corporation, Rockwell International Corporation, and Seversky Aircraft Corporation. The great engine company names have been Continental Motors Corporation, Curtiss-Wright Corporation, General Electric Company, General Motors Corporation's Allison Division, and United Technologies Corporation's Pratt & Whitney Division.

The industry struggled until America's entry into World War I.* Then it was asked to produce 20,000 planes. By 1918 it had expanded to a capacity of 14,500 aircraft per year. It had also developed the world's best trainer, the JN* Jenny, and two useful engines, the Curtiss OX-5* and the Liberty.* Most aircraft of this era had a frame of wood or steel tubing covered with fabric or plywood.

After the war, military contracts ended for an industry that had expanded greatly with private financing. To make matters worse, government surplus aircraft and engines flooded the market. The industry was also criticized because it produced military goods, and there were allegations of wartime profiteering. In the late 1920s, there was some recovery because of the Air Corps Act,* Air Mail Act, Air Commerce Act, and the popularity of Charles A. Lindbergh.*

The depression severely damaged the industry, which did not truly recover until the British and French rearmed in the late 1930s and bought U.S. aircraft. Some developments helped in this period. There was a technological revolution; higher-powered engines had been developed, making dramatic economical improvements. Airplanes now could be made of stressed-skin aluminum and could be equipped with flaps, retractable landing gear, variable speed propellers, superchargers, radios, instruments for blind flying, and anti-icing systems. These improvements pressured the military to reequip, and the deadly airmail flights of 1934* showed it was necessary. Modern airliners appeared and, with government subsidies, a practical airline system provided some sales.

World War II* showed that air superiority* was a prerequisite for victory. The industry expanded explosively, and, to prevent a postwar debacle such as had followed World War I, the growth was heavily government-financed. During the four years ending in June 1936, the USAAC* received an average of only 132 aircraft per year. Yet more than 95,000 warplanes were built in the United States in 1944, and more than 250,000 were built from 1940 through 1944. In 1944, aircraft was the largest industry in the United States.

The end of World War II brought another collapse as military surplus aircraft and engines again flooded the market. Then a series of developments caused demand for the industry's products again. Coach fares and more economical piston-engined airliners enabled the airlines to compete with surface transport. The jet engine, with its enormous increase in productivity, made the piston-engined airplane virtually obsolete. The jetliner eclipsed surface transport, and U.S. industry produced the world's best airliners. The domestic airlines reequipped, and the export sales of U.S. jetliners became so large that they became a major favorable factor in the U.S. trade balance. The Cold War* and the Korean* and Vietnam* Wars required military preparedness. The intercontinental ballistic missile* (ICBM) became practical, and the United States sought a leadership role in space exploration.

In 1990 the industry had overcapacity, which is an expense of readiness for war. Another major problem for the industry is the cyclic nature of its businesses. As the United States has been alternately fearful and complacent, the industry has gone through boom and bust cycles in its military sales. The airliner business is also cyclic. When they do not counterbalance each other, cycles limit the ability of the industry to perform and make its products more costly than they should be.

References. Charles D. Bright, *The Jet Makers: The Aerospace Industry from 1945 to 1972*, 1978. "50th Anniversary Issue," a special issue of *Flying*, September 1977, pp. 240–47. Irving Brinton Holley, Jr., *Buying Aircraft: Matériel Procurement for the Army Air Forces*, 1964. John B. Rae, *Climb to Greatness: The American Aircraft Industry, 1920–1960*, 1968. Herman O. Stekler, *The Structure and Performance of the Aerospace Industry*, 1965.

AEROSPACE POWER

Aerospace power is the ability to conduct military, commercial, or humanitarian operations through air and space. If it is done properly, it is the supreme expression of military mobility and hitting power, which makes it enormously effective. Aerospace power has military and civil components. Military aerospace force is the overt expression of power. It must be of adequate size, security, and quality so it can project power through aerospace defense, strategic, tactical, and airlift operations.* Clear distinctions cannot always be made among these categories. Civil aviation and private space capabilities directly reinforce the military means. The USAF* is the principal means by which the United States exerts military aerospace power.

The civil component of aerospace power embraces an entire nation. There must be will and understanding by the political leadership. An aerospace industry* with the latest technology and the immediate capacity to produce and to expand must exist. The population must be large, enterprising, vigorous, and knowledgeable about aerospace power. Landmass and physical resources, or access to them, must be adequate. There must be an effective network of airfields and support facilities. Without a sufficient civil component, the military part will be impotent regardless of its appearance.

References. Charles D. Bright, *The Jet Makers: The Aerospace Industry from 1945 to 1972*, 1978. Dennis M. Drew, ''We Are an Aerospace Nation,'' *AF*, November 1990, pp. 32–36. Higham, *Air Pwr.* Jerry D. Page and Royal H. Roussel, ''What *Is* Air Power?'' *Air University Quarterly Review*, Summer 1955, pp. 2–9.

AF. *See* U.S. Air Force.

AFA. *See* Air Force Association.

AFAA. *See* Air Force Audit Agency.

AFAFC. *See* U.S. Air Force Accounting and Finance Center.

AFB. *See* air force bases.

AFCC. *See* Air Force Communications Command; Air Force Combat Command.

AFCOMS. *See* Air Force Commissary Service.

AFCPMC. *See* Air Force Civilian Personnel Management Center.

AFCS. *See* Air Force Communications Command.

AFCSTC. *See* Air Force Cost Center.

AFDW. *See* Air Force District of Washington.

AFESC. *See* Air Force Engineering and Services Center.

AFHF. *See* Air Force Historical Foundation.

AFHRC. *See* U.S. Air Force Historical Research Center.

AFIA. *See* Air Force Intelligence Agency.

AFISC. *See* Air Force Inspection and Safety Center.

AFLC. *See* Air Force Logistics Command.

AFLSC. *See* Air Force Legal Services Center.

AFMEA. *See* Air Force Management Engineering Agency.

AFMPC. *See* Air Force Military Personnel Center.

AFNEWS. *See* Air Force News Center.

AFOMS. *See* Air Force Office of Medical Support.

AFOSI. *See* Air Force Office of Special Investigations.

AFOSP. *See* Air Force Office of Security Police.

AFOTEC. *See* Air Force Operational Test and Evaluation Center.

AFR. *See* U.S. Air Force Reserve.

AFROTC. *See* Air Force Reserve Officer Training Corps.

AFSC. *See* Air Force Systems Command.

AFSPACECOM. *See* Air Force Space Command.

AFTAC. *See* Air Force Technical Applications Center.

AGENT ORANGE. *See* Operation Ranch Hand.

AGGRESSOR. *See* Red Flag.

AGM. *See* air-to-ground missile.

AGM-12 BULLPUP

The AGM-12 came out of a Korean War* requirement for a standoff bomb to keep aircraft out of flak* range. Built by the Martin Marietta Corporation, it entered service in 1959. The missile comprised a solid propellant rocket engine, a 250-pound warhead and a roll-stabilized airframe. The operator controlled it by keeping tracking flares mounted on the missile's rear in his gunsight and using a small joy stick for four axis movements. Almost immediately, a storable liquid propellant rocket replaced the solid, which increased the range. The next version was the AGM-12C. It used a semiarmor piercing warhead and an enlarged engine for more range. The AGM-12D could use either a nuclear or conventional warhead. A final version was the AGM-12E with an antipersonnel warhead.

The AGM-12 series enjoyed huge success with more than 75,000 being built in the United States and other countries. It was cheap and effective, but by the Vietnam War* it was obsolescent. Its weight and size limited the maneuverability of the carrier, and its guidance range was short. It has been replaced by the AGM-65* Maverick.

Characteristics (AGM-12C): diameter, 18 inches; length, 14 feet; weight, 1,800 pounds; speed, Mach 1.8; range, 10 miles.

References. Gunston, *Airc. Arm.* Norman Friedman, *U.S. Naval Weapons*, 1983. *See also* AZON, RAZON, and TARZON.

Philip Long

AGM-28 HOUND DOG

First called the GAM-77, the AGM-28 was an early cruise missile* built by North American Aviation, Inc. Two could be carried under the wings of B-52* aircraft. The flight path could be varied from ground level to 55,000 feet using the on-board inertial guidance system. The warhead was a W-28 thermonuclear weapon of about one megaton yield. The missile had several interesting features. The engines were used to help the B-52 take off, and the missile fuel tanks were then topped off in flight from the mother aircraft. The missile guidance system could be used for navigation if there was a failure in the aircraft systems. The AGM-28 went into service in 1960 and was retired in 1976.

Characteristics: engine, Pratt & Whitney J52-P-3 turbojet of 7,500 pounds thrust; diameter, 28 inches; span, 12 feet; length, 43 feet; weight, 10,140 pounds; top speed, Mach 2.1; range, 700 miles.

References. Walter Boyne, *Boeing B-52*, 1981. Chuck Hansen, *U.S. Nuclear Weapons*, 1988. Polmar, *SAC*. Kenneth P. Werrell, *The Evolution of the Cruise Missile*, 1985.

Philip Long

AGM-45 SHRIKE

The AGM-45 was the first antiradar* missile to be widely used. It was made by the Naval Weapons Center. Broadly based on the AIM-7,* the missile began service on F-105G* Wild Weasels* in 1965 during the Vietnam War.* The seeker used a receiver tuned to known enemy radar frequencies. When the seeker picked up a transmission, the missile could be fired. Early versions of this missile had many problems and went through many changes and upgrades. Thirteen separate seeker heads were available with each tuned to a specific radar frequency. The USAF* bought AGM-45s until 1978, when 12,000 had been received. It was still in service in 1990.

Characteristics: engine, Rocketdyne Mk 39 Mod 7 or Aerojet Mk 53 solid rocket; span, 3 feet; length, 10 feet; diameter, 8 inches; weight, 400 pounds (145-pound warhead); range, up to 25 miles.

References. Larry Davis, *Wild Weasel: The SAM Suppression Story*, 1986. Gunston, *Airc. Arm.* Lon O. Nordeen, Jr., *Air Warfare in the Missile Age*, 1985. Susan H. H. Young, "Gallery of USAF Weapons," *AF*, May 1990, p. 157.

Philip Long

AGM-65 MAVERICK

The AGM-65 is an air-to-ground missile* in wide use in the USAF* and other air forces around the free world. It has been made by the Hughes Missiles Systems Group of General Motors and Raytheon Company. It was used in combat by the Israelis during the Yom Kippur War in 1973 and by the United States during the March 1986 Libyan raid* and in 1988 against the Iranian navy during the Gulf crisis. With more than 100,000 made or on order, the AGM-65 will be widely used until after the turn of the century.

It came in five basic varieties. The *A* version used a shaped charge warhead and television guidance. The pilot acquired the target and aligned the crosshairs of the seeker head using his on-board television display. When fired, the missile homed on the area delineated by the crosshairs. The *B* version, also with a shaped charge, had an upgraded seeker section with magnification ability. The *C* version was not produced. The *D* version, with a shaped charge warhead, was especially modified to use the Low-Altitude Navigation and Targeting Infrared System for Night* (LANTIRN) night sight fitted on the F-16* and the A-10.* The *E* version used a laser head with a heavyweight, or penetrator, warhead. The *F* version also used the heavyweight warhead and had an infrared head. The *G* version uses infrared and improved flight controls. *D*s and *G*s are still in production.

Characteristics (AGM-65A): engine, Thiokol TX-481 solid rocket; span, 28 inches; length, 8 feet; diameter, 1 foot; weight, 462 pounds; range, up to 14 miles.

References. John T. Correll, "The Many Battles of Maverick," *AF*, March 1983, pp. 98–103. Larry Davis, *Wild Weasel: The SAM Suppression Story*, 1986. Gunston, *Airc. Arm.* Susan H. H. Young, "Gallery of USAF Weapons," *AF*, May 1990, p. 157.

Philip Long

AGM-69 SHORT-RANGE ATTACK MISSILE (SRAM)

The AGM-69 is a supersonic air-to-surface missile made by The Boeing Company. A General Precision/Kearfott inertial system provided the guidance. The missile was designed to provide B-1Bs,* B-52s,* and the FB-111s (*see* F-111) with the capability to neutralize enemy defenses such as surface-to-air missiles* (SAM) and to strike heavily defended and mobile targets. It is armed with a nuclear weapon.* A total of 1,500 AGM-69s were ordered by the USAF,* and the production period spanned 1971 to 1975.

Characteristics: engine, Lockheed LPC-415 solid two-pulse rocket; diameter, 17 inches; length, 14 feet; weight, 2,208 pounds; top speed, up to Mach 2.5; range, 100 miles at high altitude, 35 miles at low altitude.

References. Alwyn T. Lloyd, *B-52 Stratofortress in Detail & Scale*, 1988. U.S. Air Force Fact Sheet 86–6, "AGM-69 Short-Range Attack Missile," December 1986. Susan H. H. Young, "Gallery of USAF Weapons," *AF*, May 1990, p. 156.

Alwyn T. Lloyd

AGM-78 STANDARD ANTIRADIATION MISSILE (Standard ARM)

The AGM-78 was built by General Dynamics Corporation and went into production in 1968. It was carried on USAF* Wild Weasel* aircraft. It used the same seeker as the AGM-45* and had the same problems, so a Maxson broadband seeker head was developed to give the missile the capability to attack not only surface-to-air missile* (SAM) radars* but any transmitter. The AGM-78 was never made in large numbers and was retired in 1986.

Characteristics: engine, Aerojet-General Mk 27 Mod 4 solid rocket; span, 42 inches; length, 15 feet; diameter, 13 inches; weight 1,356 pounds; top speed, Mach 2; range, 15 miles.

References. Christopher Campbell, *Air Warfare: The Fourth Generation*, 1984. Gunston, *Airc. Arm.* Susan H. H. Young, "Gallery of USAF Weapons," *AF*, May 1985, p. 164.

Philip Long

AGM-84A-1 HARPOON

The AGM-84 is an all-weather, over-the-horizon, antiship missile made by the McDonnell Douglas Corporation. It was originally designed for the U.S. Navy. It can be launched by surface ships, submarines, and aircraft. The missile has a sea-skimming cruise trajectory, terminal-active radar* guidance, electronic countermeasures (ECM), and a warhead designed to assure survivability and effectiveness.

During the mid–1980s, the Strategic Air Command* (SAC) tested the missile at Mather* AFB and adopted it. Consequently, SAC is able to work with the Navy in control of the seas well beyond the range of other aircraft. Only the B-52G* can carry the AGM-84.

Characteristics: engine, Teledyne J402-CA-400 turbojet of 660 pounds of thrust; diameter, 13 inches; length, 13 feet; weight, 1,145 pounds; speed, high subsonic; range, over 57 miles.

References. Alwyn T. Lloyd, *B-52 Stratofortress in Detail & Scale*, 1988. Jeffrey P. Rhodes, "SAC's Sea Patrol," *AF*, October 1987, pp. 48–54. John W. R. Taylor, *Jane's All the World's Aircraft*, 1986. U.S. Air Force Fact Sheet 88–12, "AGM-84A-1 Harpoon Missile," July 1988. Susan H. H. Young, "Gallery of USAF Weapons," *AF*, May 1990, pp. 157–58.

Alwyn T. Lloyd

AGM-86B AIR-LAUNCHED CRUISE MISSILE (ALCM)

The AGM-86B was designed and made by The Boeing Company. It is equipped with a nuclear warhead and is part of the strategic triad.* It has a high degree of flexibility for target attack and, when used in combination with other forces, can dilute an enemy's forces and complicate its defense problem. Both B-1Bs* and B-52s* can carry it. Production of 1,715 missiles spanned 1980 to 1986. When launched, the missile's wings and vertical tail pop out, its engine inlet pops up, and the engine ignites. A Litton inertial navigation unit uses contour matching, allowing the missile to fly complicated routes.

Characteristics: engine, Williams Research Corporation F107-WR-100 turbofan of 600 pounds thrust; span, 12 feet; length, 21 feet; diameter, 2 feet; weight, 3,150 pounds; speed, 550 miles per hour; range, over 1,500 miles.

References. Alwyn T. Lloyd, *B-52 Stratofortress in Detail & Scale*, 1988. Patricia R. Rogers, "ALCM in Its Second Operational Year," *AF*, February 1984, pp. 46–48. U.S. Air Force Fact Sheet 87–23, "AGM-86B Air Launched Cruise Missile," June 1987. Susan H. H. Young, "Gallery of USAF Weapons," *AF*, May 1990, p. 156.

Alwyn T. Lloyd

AGM-88A HIGH-SPEED ANTIRADIATION MISSILE (HARM)

Made by Texas Instruments, Inc., the AGM-88A is an antiradar missile used to destroy enemy acquisition and fire control radar.* The HARM was first used in combat against radar transmitters during the 1986 Libyan raid.*

The missile has three modes of operation. The first is self-protection. The seeker detects emissions of a known enemy radar frequency, programs the data into the missile brain, and signals the pilot* when the missile can be fired. In flight, the AGM-88 follows the radar beam back to its source. If the target radar is switched off, the on-board control system will still guide the missile to its target. The second mode is for a target of opportunity. Even when a radar transmitter is turned off, the seeker can still lock on to certain secondary transmissions associated with radar equipment, and the missile can be fired at these targets. The last mode is preprogrammed. The missile is fired blindly at known enemy transmitters. If no target is transmitting, the missile self-destructs. If a target does transmit, the missile homes on it as in the first mode.

Characteristics: engine, Thiokol smokeless solid rocket; span, 4 feet; length, 14 feet; diameter, 10 inches; weight, 805 pounds; speed, over Mach 2; range, over 10 miles.

References. Larry Davis, *Wild Weasel: The SAM Suppression Story*, 1986. "Electronic Warfare," a special issue of *AWST*, 11 September 1989, pp. 69–70. Gunston, *Airc. Arm.* Jeffrey P. Rhodes, "Slam 'Em and Jam 'Em," *AF*, June 1989, pp. 50–56. Susan H. H. Young, "Gallery of USAF Weapons," *AF*, May 1990, p. 158.

Philip Long

AGM-129A ADVANCED CRUISE MISSILE (ACM)

The General Dynamics Corporation's AGM-129A is a development of the earlier AGM-109 Tomahawk. The ACM has been engineered for extreme evasion of radar,* or stealth.* It probably has a lower radar cross section than any other flying vehicle. Range and maneuverability have been enhanced with a low wing loading. New internal software and hardware have been fitted. It uses a W-80 warhead with about the same size and weight as that of the AGM-109. The

AGM-129 is a very formidable weapon. It is impossible to detect and is capable of delivering a 200-kiloton weapon within a few yards after a flight of more than 1,550 miles.

Characteristics: engine, Williams International F112 turbofan.

References. Gunston, *Airc. Arm*. Susan H. H. Young, "Gallery of USAF Weapons," *AF*, May 1990, p. 156.

Philip Long

AGM-130. *See* GBU-15.

AGM-131A SHORT-RANGE ATTACK MISSILE (SRAM II)

Made by The Boeing Company, SRAM II is in development as a replacement of the AGM-69* SRAM missile. The missile is to be carried in rotary launchers on B-1s,* B-2s,* and B-52s* to suppress enemy defenses ahead of a manned penetrating bomber.* Improvements consist of a new longer-ranged engine, a ring laser inertial guidance system, and radar* resistance, or stealth,* design. The size is smaller than the AGM-69, and the weight is about 1,540 pounds.

References. Gunston, *Airc. Arm*. Susan H. H. Young, "Gallery of USAF Weapons," *AF*, May 1990, p. 156.

Philip Long

AGM-136A TACIT RAINBOW

The contractor for the AGM-136A is Northrop Ventura, and the weapon is complementary to the AGM-88A.* The AGM-136A is an antiradiation cruise missile* under development. The method of operation is for the missile to be fired blindly over enemy territory. It will then fly a circuit guided by its on-board system while recording the location of enemy transmissions. At the end of its reconnaissance,* the missile decides which recorded target is most valuable. It homes in on that one, even if the transmitter is turned off. The missile is to be very flexible in its operation and should ensure that no enemy radio transmitter is safe in wartime. However, in 1990 AGM-136A had difficult technical problems.

Characteristics: engine, Williams International J-400–44404 turbofan; span, 5 feet; length, 8 feet; diameter, 27 inches; weight, 1,268 pounds; range, 56 miles.

References. Gunston, *Airc. Arm*. "Pentagon to Review Funding, Scheduling for Tacit Rainbow," *AWST*, 19 September 1988, pp. 64, 66. Susan H. H. Young, "Gallery of USAF Weapons," *AF*, May 1990, p. 158.

Philip Long

AGM-142A HAVE NAP

This is a program of buying some Israeli Popeye guided missiles,* which were ordered in 1988. The Popeye is guided by television and has given B-52Gs* a standoff capability with conventional explosives.

Characteristics: engine, solid fuel rocket; span, 5 feet; length, 19 feet; diameter, 21 inches; weight, 3,300 pounds; range, 50 miles; warhead, 1,975 pounds.

References. John D. Morocco, "Have Nap Offers Stand-off Capability for B-52s in Mideast," *AWST*, 3 September 1990, p. 35. Susan H. H. Young, "Gallery of USAF Weapons," *AF*, May 1990, p. 158.

AIM. *See* air interceptor missile.

AIM-4 FALCON AND SUPER FALCON

The AIM-4 was originally designated as a guided aircraft rocket, GAR-1. It was the first air-launched guided missile in the world to enter service. It was a product of the Hughes Aircraft Company, which also designed the matching aircraft fire control systems. It became operational in 1956 on F-89* and F-102* interceptors.* The original version used semiactive radar homing (SARH), a system that rode a radar* beam from the launching aircraft to the target airplane. This version was soon followed by the AIM-4B with infrared (IR) homing guidance. The missile had minor improvements in range and accuracy through a series ending in the AIM-4G Super Falcon. The first major change was the fitting of a much larger engine and a nuclear warhead to make the AIM-26. The same missile had a version with a large high-explosive warhead. When the F-106* left active service in 1988, the Falcons also were retired.

A final proposed version had been the AIM-47. This long-range model was the proposed armament of the F-108 and the YF-12A, but when the aircraft programs were canceled, so was the proposed missile.

Characteristics (AIM-4G): engine, Thiokol two-stage solid rocket, with 6,000 pounds thrust in the first stage; span, 2 feet; length, 7 feet; diameter, 7 inches; weight, 145 pounds; top speed, Mach 2.5; range, 7 miles.

References. Gunston, *Airc. Arm.* Bill Yenne, *The History of the US Air Force*, 1984. Susan H. H. Young, "Gallery of USAF Weapons," *AF*, May 1988, p. 188.

Philip Long

AIM-7 SPARROW

The Sparrow was the radar*-guided component of the U.S. Navy's missile program of the 1950s. The basic missile was also used for the AGM-45* Shrike and the ship-launched RIM-7H NATO Sea Sparrow. AIM-7s were in wide use in 1990 in all U.S. services and 11 foreign countries. The AIM-7 was made by Raytheon Company and General Dynamics Corporation. The AIM-7A and all versions other than the *B* have used semiactive radar homing (SARH) for guidance. SARH uses a radar beam from the launch aircraft to "paint" the target airplane, and the missile follows the beam. The AIM-7B was to use an active radar on board the missile, but the version was canceled when it proved impossible to fit the radar into the missile. The AIM-7C, Sparrow III, entered USAF* service on the F-4C* in 1960. Current production is of the AIM-7M which will probably be the last version, as the replacement AIM-120* should soon enter service.

Characteristics (AIM-7F): engine, Hercules Mk 58 Mod O rocket; span, 3 feet; length, 12 feet; diameter, 8 inches; weight, 504 pounds; top speed, over Mach 3.5; range, over 25 miles.

References. Christopher Campbell, *Air Warfare: The Fourth Generation*, 1984. Norman Friedman, *U.S. Naval Weapons*. 1983. Gunston, *Airc. Arm.* Susan H. H. Young, "Gallery of USAF Weapons," *AF*, May 1990, p. 157.

Philip Long

AIM-9 SIDEWINDER

The Sidewinder is the most important air-to-air missile ever built. More than 150,000 have been made. It is used by all U.S. services and 32 foreign countries. The USSR has copied it directly as their AA-2 Atoll. It was originally developed by the U.S. Navy as a heat-seeking guided missile version of the five-inch high-velocity aircraft rocket* (HVAR). The contractors are the Raytheon Company and General Dynamics Corporation. The Sidewinder has four fixed fins at the rear and four triangular moveable guidance fins near the nose. It has four main parts: a seeker head, a control system, a warhead, and an engine. The first successful test of the Sidewinder took place in 1953, and it entered service the same year. It soon was popular, in part because its price was 3,000 1960 dollars.

The AIM-9 is simple to carry and to fire with little extra wiring or support equipment required from the aircraft. It can be used on fighters,* helicopters,* and patrol planes. The pilot merely selects the Sidewinder setting on his armament switch, places the target in his sight, and fires when he hears the missile "growl" in his headset. The missile needs no further outside guidance. This fire-and-forget feature has been a great selling point of the Sidewinder.

It has undergone many improvements. There have been 14 variants through the AIM-9R. Although the 38-year-old Sidewinder is expected to be replaced, with the planned AIM-132 Advanced Short-Range Air-to-Air Missile (AS-RAAM), development on the AIM-9 continues. The Sidewinder should be an effective weapon well into the 21st century.

Characteristics (AIM-9M): engine, Thiokol Hercules Mk Mod 11 solid rocket; span, 25 inches; length, 10 feet; diameter, 5 inches; weight, 191 pounds; top speed, over Mach 2; range, over 10 miles.

References. Norman Friedman, *U.S. Naval Weapons*, 1983. Gunston, *Airc. Arm.* Lon O. Nordeen, Jr., *Air Warfare in the Missile Age*, 1985. Robert L. Shaw, *Fighter Combat: Tactics and Maneuvering*, 1985. Susan H. H. Young, "Gallery of USAF Weapons," *AF*, May 1990, p. 157.

Philip Long

AIM-26. *See* AIM-4.

AIM-120 ADVANCED MEDIUM-RANGE AIR-TO-AIR MISSILE (AM-RAAM)

The AIM-120 is a replacement for the AIM-7.* It is intended to give the F-15* and F-16* an all-weather strike ability. Designed in 1981 and built by Hughes Aircraft Company, it was to be lighter, smaller, and cheaper than the AIM-7.

It was also to have higher speed, an ability to engage multiple targets, electronic countermeasures (ECM), increased range, and easier maintenance. The missile is initially guided by radar* from the launching aircraft. After an inertial mid-course correction, an on-board active radar seeker takes control. This permits the aircraft to maneuver without losing control of the missile. Cost overruns and other troubles almost caused cancellation of the program several times, but production has begun with the expectation of a long, useful life for the weapon.

Characteristics: span, 25 inches; length, 12 feet; diameter, 7 inches; weight, 340 pounds; cruise speed, about Mach 4; range, about 31 miles.

References. Gunston, *Airc. Arm.* Edward H. Kolcum, "AMRAAM Testing Advances to Complex Combat Modes," *AWST*, 22 August 1988, pp. 36–37. Edgar E. Ulsamer, " 'Brilliant' Weapons Gather Momentum," *AF*, August 1988, pp. 79–80. Susan H. H. Young, "Gallery of USAF Weapons," *AF*, May 1990, p. 157.

Philip Long

AIR-2A GENIE

This air intercept rocket (AIR) was not a guided missile in the truest sense. Genie was a Douglas Aircraft Company project beginning in 1955. The missile was a rocket mated with a W-25 nuclear warhead. All control was by a Hughes Aircraft Company fire control system in the launching F-106.* The system would acquire the target, compute a launch point and flight time, program the missile's timer, warn the pilot* to arm the warhead, and fire the missile at the correct time. The F-106 would then take evasive action from the warhead detonation. A training version of the missile, the ATR-2A, used a spotting charge warhead. Genie went out of service when the F-106 was retired in 1988, but the engines and airframes have been used since for several other projects.

Characteristics: engine, Thiokol SR49-TC-1 solid rocket with 36,000 pounds of thrust; span, 40 inches; length, 10 feet; diameter, 17 inches; weight, 820 pounds; top speed, Mach 3; range, 6 miles.

References. Gunston, *Airc. Arm.* Susan H. H. Young, "Gallery of USAF Weapons," *AF*, May 1985, pp. 162–63.

Philip Long

AIRACOBRA. *See* P-39.

AIRACOMET. *See* P-59.

AIRACUDA. *See* FM-1.

AIR BASE. *See* air force bases.

AIR BASE DEFENSE

The surest way to destroy an air force is to hit it on the ground where it is most vulnerable. Air base defenses are the methods and resources necessary to prevent this destruction.

Although USAAS* leaders recognized the importance of air base defense in France during World War I,* no serious threats to airdromes ever materialized. Thus base security measures never progressed beyond a rudimentary guard system. After World War I,* the Army's air base defense doctrine was based on the experience in France, so little actual effort to plan for a systematic air base defense took place.

One of Germany's strategies in World War II* was to destroy enemy air power on the ground. To counteract this threat, Allied forces formed flak* and ground defense units for air bases before May 1940, but they were inadequate. It was not until after the Pearl Harbor* raid that U.S. air base defense policies emerged. On 12 February 1942, the Army approved 53,299 men for the USAAF* for air base defense units. Designed to defend primarily against local ground attacks, these units were armed with rifles, machine guns, and 37mm cannon.

In 1943, the inactivation of these units began. By this time, the widening Allied control of the air and ground had largely removed the necessity for tight air base security. At the end of World War II, air base defense forces were demobilized and much of the expertise of the function was rapidly lost. In 1947, the Army and the USAF* agreed that each would take care of its own facilities, including air base defense.

The Korean War* refocused concern on the air base defense issue. The USAF began a buildup of ground combat units for this purpose. These security forces grew from 10,000 men in July 1950 to 39,000 in December 1951. Armored cars, machine guns, recoilless rifles, and other infantry weapons were procured.

By 1953, it was decided that air base defense would be an emergency task, and the USAF would not prepare for sustained ground fighting. The defense units were made up of airmen not directly linked to air operations and were organized and equipped like infantry. The Air Police, today called the Security Police, formed the cadre for these forces, and they were commanded by the base commander or provost marshal. The USAF had a foundation in doctrine, manpower, equipment, and training for an organic air base defense capability. However, this program fell victim to demobilization after the Korean War, a new national strategy, and revised intelligence estimates. Little planning and organization took place during the remainder of the 1950s.

Many of the issues came into focus again in the Vietnam War.* Here the threats were almost all from ground forces, usually guerrillas or sappers, and air base defense procedures developed accordingly. The first action came early on 1 November 1964 when enemy forces struck Bien Hoa* Air Base in South Vietnam. The enemy positioned six 81mm mortars about 1,300 feet north of the field and fired some 80 rounds onto parked aircraft and troop billets. The enemy then withdrew undetected and unmolested. Four U.S. military advisers were killed and 30 were wounded. Twenty B-57s* were hit and five of them were destroyed. After this, U.S. aerial forces increasingly became targets. Through 1973 there were 475 enemy attacks on U.S. airfields, resulting in U.S. losses of 898 aircraft damaged and 155 service people killed.

To counter these attacks, forces were deployed to Vietnam to secure airfields. The first force, the 9th Marine Expeditionary Brigade, landed at Da Nang* Air Base in March 1965. U.S. Army and Air Force air base defense units followed soon thereafter. These units fought the threats of sabotage, ground attack, sapper infiltration, and shelling by standoff weapons. Actually, sabotage was little used and ground attacks by battalion-sized forces took place only twice. Sapper raids posed a more serious threat, but, in terms of numbers and damage, standoff rocket and mortar fire presented the greatest hazard. The air base defense forces were partially successful in countering these threats. From 1969 on, attacks decreased every year until the United States withdrew. Casualties and aircraft losses registered similar declines. Yet, USAF bases in Vietnam were always vulnerable to raids. Since the Vietnam War, the USAF has maintained an air base defense force built along the lines employed in that war.

References. Berger, *USAF in SEA.* John T. Correll, "Fighting under Attack," *AF*, October 1988, pp. 50–55. Roger P. Fox, *Air Base Defense in the Republic of Vietnam, 1961–1973*, 1979. John F. Kreis, *Air Warfare and Air Base Air Defense 1914–1973*, 1988. Curtis E. LeMay, *Mission with LeMay: My Story*, 1965.

Roger D. Launius

AIRBORNE WARNING AND CONTROL SYSTEM (AWACS)

The employment of College Eye* EC-121 (*see* C-121) aircraft in Southeast Asia provided the first battlefield experience with airborne radar* platforms in a tactical command and control environment. During this era, the EC-121 evolved from the *D* model used primarily by the Air Defense Command for airborne early warning and control to the more advanced *T* model retrofitted as an airborne surveillance and control system (ASACS). The next milestone was an operational AWACS, which was reached in March 1977 when the USAF* received the first production model of the E-3* Sentry aircraft.

The E-3 was a modified version of the commercial Boeing 707 airframe with a rotating radar dome installed. It added a new dimension to the all-weather surveillance, command, control, and communications capabilities of the United States and North Atlantic Treaty Organization* (NATO) tactical and air defense forces. A marked improvement over ground-based radar systems which were confused by ground clutter, the Sentry's radar provided coverage from the earth's surface into the stratosphere, over land or water, more than 200 miles out for low-flying targets and farther for those at high altitudes. The command, control, and communications equipment on the E-3 was superior to that carried on the EC-121s. In its air defense role, the E-3 could detect, identify, and track hostile aircraft far from the boundaries of the United States and of NATO countries, and it could direct friendly interceptors* to those targets. It gave tactical air commanders information relative to gaining and maintaining control of the air battle, as well as for interdiction, reconnaissance,* airlift operations,* and close support of friendly forces.

As of 1990, the USAF had 34 E-3s assigned to the 552nd Airborne Warning and Control Division at Tinker* AFB, Oklahoma, with some of these aircraft assigned to other locations in the United States and overseas. NATO was acquiring 18 E-3s. Production was scheduled to end in 1991. In 1991, E-3s had their first test in battle in the Iraq War* and performed well.

References. Futrell, *Ideas*. Jerold R. Mack and Richard M. Williams, "552d Airborne Early Warning and Control Wing in Southeast Asia," *Air University Review*, November–December 1973, pp. 70–78. U.S. Air Force Fact Sheet, "Airborne Warning and Control System," March 1985.

Warren A. Trest

AIR COMMANDOS. *See* Cochran, Colonel Philip G.; Farm Gate; Twenty-Third Air Force.

AIR CORPS. *See* U.S. Army Air Corps.

AIR CORPS ACT

The Air Corps Act of 1926 is one of the most significant pieces of legislation in the history of the USAF.* It resulted from the recommendations of the President's Advisory Board.* The USAAS* was raised to a corps and renamed the U.S. Army Air Corps* (USAAC). The law created a new assistant secretary of war (for air), included air sections in the general staff, and added two general officers as assistant chiefs of the Air Corps. The status of airmen was raised by permitting temporary promotions for USAAC officers, using Reserve officers on extended active duty and giving additional pay to air mechanics.

The heart of the act was a five-year program to expand the USAAC from 919 to 1,650 officers, from 8,725 to 15,000 enlisted men, and from 1,254 to 1,800 aircraft. Funds were needed to fill the program, but money problems began when both Presidents Calvin Coolidge and Herbert Hoover sought economies in government, especially with the onset of the Great Depression. The USAAC got 45 percent of the monies it believed were needed for the expansion, and the program was not completed in the five years. At its end, in 1931, the USAAC had 1,254 officers, 13,060 enlisted men, and 1,709 planes. The numbers do not tell the whole story, for the quality of the airplanes was much improved. The five-year program fell short of its objectives, but it did represent substantial improvements for the service.

References. Goldberg, *Hist. USAF*. Maurer, *Avn. in Army*.

AIR CORPS TACTICAL SCHOOL (ACTS)

World War I* caught the Aviation Section of the U.S. Army Signal Corps* unprepared, and the section's subsequent expansion demanded a rationalizing institution. Traditionally, the Army provided each branch with a service school. The resultant USAAS* School was authorized on 25 February 1920 and sited at Langley* Field, Virginia. It was charged with surveying the service's growth, extracting lessons learned from World War I, and teaching those lessons to air officers. One year later (1921) the Army renamed it the Air Service Field Officers School. It was retitled again as the Air Service Tactical School on 8 November

1922. After the passage of the Air Corps Act* in 1926, the center got yet another name, the Air Corps Tactical School (ACTS). In 1931 it moved to Maxwell* Field, Alabama.

There the ACTS attracted many of the forward thinkers in the USAAC.* Officers like Lieutenant Colonel Harold L. George,* Major Donald Wilson, and Lieutenants Kenneth N. Walker and Haywood S. Hansell* elaborated the concept of daylight strategic operations.* Their ideas did not go unchallenged. From 1932 to 1936, Captain Claire L. Chennault* fought the "bomber* invincibility" school, arguing that timely fighter* interception could thwart unescorted bombing attacks. Bad health and unpopularity led to his retirement in 1936. From then until 1942 the concept of strategic bombing, which had been forged at ACTS, was taught to its students. Many of them would lead USAAF* operations in World War II.*

With wartime expansion of the USAAC, Maxwell Field became headquarters for the Southeast Training Center, and the last ACTS class graduated on 9 October 1942. The ACTS's insignia and functions were assumed by the Army Air Forces School of Applied Tactics at Orlando, Florida. By 1945 this school had been redesignated the A.A.F. Center and was moved back to Maxwell Field as a major command of the USAAF. On 12 March 1946, the A.A.F. Center became the Air University.*

References. Primary: John D. Barker, "History of the Air Corps Tactical School," c. 1931. Thomas D. Milling, "The Air Service Tactical School," 1924. Secondary: Robert T. Finney, *History of the Air Corps Tactical School, 1920–1940*, 1955. Charles A. Ravenstein, *Organization of the Air Force*, 1982. Joe Gray Taylor, "They Taught Tactics!" *AH*, Summer 1966, pp. 67–72.

Ronald W. Yoshino

AIR CORPS TRAINING CENTER

The Air Corps Training Center was a vital stage in the building of the modern USAF.* When the USAAC* was established and expanded under the Air Corps Act,* there was a need for an enlarged training program. Flight training* was reorganized, and Brigadier General Frank P. Lahm* was put in command. Initially, Lahm oversaw the Primary Flying School and the School of Aviation Medicine, both at Brooks* Field, Texas, and the Advanced Flying School at Kelly* Field, Texas. An additional primary school was at March* Field, California.

Lahm soon wanted all flying training concentrated at one airfield and preferred it be located near San Antonio, Texas. This was not a new idea; it had been suggested as early as 1913. Construction began in 1929 on Randolph* Field. In 1931, the primary schools moved on to the field and the base became headquarters for the Air Corps Training Center. Randolph became known as "The West Point of the Air." The advanced school, however, stayed at Kelly. This system could handle 550 pilots per year.

The expansion of the USAAC in 1938 and later required training far beyond that level. Arrangements were made with civilians in the contract primary flight training* scheme. Also, other USAAC bases began flying training, and the Air Corps Training Center emphasized the training of instructor pilots. In 1940 the expansion led to reorganization. Under the Training and Operations Division of the Office, Chief of Air Corps, were three Air Corps Training Centers. These were the Southeast, Gulf Coast, and West Coast Centers. Their headquarters were at Maxwell* Field, Alabama; Randolph* Field; and Moffett Field, California; respectively.

References. C&C, vol. 6. Maurer, *Avn. in Army. The Official Pictorial History of the AAF*, 1947. "U.S. Army Air Forces," a special issue of *Flying and Popular Aviation*, September 1941, p. 70–71, 140, 144, 146–50.

AIRCRAFT BOARD. *See* Aircraft Production Board.

AIRCRAFT CONTROL AND WARNING (AC&W)

This is a system that uses radar* to detect and follow aircraft for air defense purposes. Warnings are issued if needed, and active air defense forces are mobilized and controlled to engage the enemy. It was first developed from 1936 to 1940 by the British Royal Air Force (RAF). The First Air Force* (1AF) provides air defense for the continental United States (CONUS) under the North American Aerospace Defense Command* (NORAD).

References. Goldberg, *Hist. USAF*. "Tactical Air Command," *AF*, May 1989, pp. 90–91. Woodford Agee Heflin, ed., *The United States Air Force Dictionary*, 1956. *See also* aerospace defense operations.

AIRCRAFT INDUSTRY. *See* aerospace industry.

AIRCRAFT PRODUCTION BOARD

This board (also called the Aircraft Board) was established in May 1917 to coordinate aircraft and engine designs for the U.S. Army and Navy and to assist in overcoming production difficulties associated with the urgent weapons buildup after the United States entered World War I.* The functions of the board were derived from two preceding organizations, the National Advisory Committee for Aeronautics (NACA) of 1915 (now the National Aeronautics and Space Administration* [NASA]) and the Joint Army and Navy Technical Air Craft Board, established in early 1917.

Because the United States had no aircraft industry to speak of and severely limited production capacity, board members consisted almost exclusively of automobile production executives. The board was headed by Howard E. Coffin,* vice president of the Hudson Motor Car Company. In an attempt to facilitate production, the board opted for the development of the Liberty engine,* derived from an automotive design, and the de Haviland DH-4,* a British two-place reconnaissance* and bombing aircraft. The board was the subject of congressional inquiry in the spring of 1918 after aircraft production had fallen far short of overly optimistic initial forecasts.

References. Benedict Crowell, *America's Munitions: 1917–1918*, 1919. I. B. Holley, Jr., *Ideas and Weapons: Exploitation of the Aerial Weapon by the United States during World War I*, 1953. Arthur Sweetser, *The American Air Service: Its Difficulties, Its Failures and Its Achievements*, 1919.

D. K. Vaughan

AIR DEFENSE COMMAND. *See* Aerospace Defense Command.

AIR DEFENSE IDENTIFICATION ZONE (ADIZ)

An ADIZ is the airspace over a designated geographic area in which the rules for flight are designed to identify an aircraft as friendly or hostile. It is a buffer zone to give air defense forces the depth needed to prevent surprise and to take effective action if it is appropriate. An ADIZ may cover coastal waters, an appropriate American landmass, or neighboring foreign territory. American AD-IZs, first called air defense zones, were established in early 1942.

References. Goldberg, *Hist. USAF*. Woodford Agee Heflin, ed., *The United States Air Force Dictionary*, 1956.

AIR DIVISION. *See* division.

AIR DOCTRINE. *See* doctrine.

AIR FORCE. *See* U.S. Air Force.

AIR FORCE

An air force is an organizational level that is subordinate to an operational* or support command.* It is superior to a division.* It equates to an army. Some air forces are numbered, such as Fifth Air Force.* The number should be spelled out for formal usage, but Arabic numerals can be used informally, such as 5AF. Numbered air forces are usually operational organizations. There have been 23 numbered air forces. Some air forces have been named, such as the Crew Training Air Force.* Named air forces have been both operational and support organizations. There have been 13 named air forces. The first air force unit was in the USAAC* and was named the General Headquarters Air Force.* In the USAAF,* numbered air forces were major commands.*

References. Woodford Agee Heflin, ed., *The United States Air Force Dictionary*, 1956. Ravenstein, *Org. USAF*.

AIR FORCE

Hollywood's Jack Warner wanted to make a special film about the USAAF.* The product was *Air Force* of 1943. Dudley Nichols wrote the story with inputs from USAAF Captain Samuel Triffy and Hollywood director Howard Hawks. Set in the Pacific war, *Air Force* is about one B-17* and its crew. The film was one of ten movies* in 1943 that made the most money, and it won an Oscar.

Air Force was the most important fictional movie about the USAAF made during World War II.*

References. James H. Farmer, *Celluloid Wings*, 1984. Bruce W. Orriss, *When Hollywood Ruled the Skies*, 1984. Lawrence Howard Suid, *Air Force*, 1983.

AIR FORCE. *See* novels.

AIR FORCE ACADEMY. *See* U.S. Air Force Academy.

AIR FORCE ACCOUNTING AND FINANCE CENTER (AFAFC). *See* U.S. Air Force Accounting and Finance Center.

AIR FORCE ASSOCIATION (AFA)

Founded on 4 February 1946, the AFA is an international nonprofit, nonpolitical organization of 200,000 members and patrons. It supports a strong national defense posture for the security and peace of the nation and the free world, and it is dedicated to the application of aerospace technology for the betterment of mankind. It has chapters in all 50 states and in Europe and the Far East so it can contribute to community understanding of the USAF.* It has around 300 industrial associates and publishes *Air Force Magazine* (*AF*). In 1990, the AFA was strong and continuing in its established traditions.

The AFA has a spiritual founder, Major General William Mitchell,* the prophet of American air power. After World War I,* he tried to achieve an adequate U.S. air arm in two ways: by convincing his superiors in the government and by taking his case to the people. Mitchell's court martial in 1925 signaled his failure with U.S. leaders, but he continued taking his case to the people. One of the ways he tried to do this was by founding an Air Force Association in 1926, but it did not last long. Mitchell knew the vital need for public understanding and support for what was to become the aerospace power* of the United States.

One of the USAF's founding fathers, General of the Air Force H. H. Arnold,* conceived and became the founder of the modern AFA. In April 1945 he saw that an independent civilian organization would be needed to sustain adequate air power. Later, he asked Major General Edward P. "Ted" Curtis, who was leaving the service, to organize such a group. By February 1946, 20 years after Mitchell's abortive attempt, there were temporary officers selected, including James H. Doolittle* as president. In 1947, the first convention was held in Columbus, Ohio. Membership was more than 126,000, and an independent USAF was in the offing.

In the AFA's first eight years, membership and finances were a problem, as membership fell to 35,000. However, during those years a building process was proceeding that eventually produced growth and an effective organization. A key to AFA's success was James H. "Jim" Straubel. He was the editor and publisher of *AF* from 1941 to 1945, when the periodical was an official publication of the USAAF.* After the war, he entered paperback book publishing, but soon returned to the magazine when it became the AFA's organ. *AF* proved to be the AFA's means to solvency in the early years. In 1948, Straubel became AFA's executive director until his retirement in 1980.

Annual conventions have been important to the AFA. Other activities are also helpful. An educational affiliate, the Aerospace Education Foundation, seeks to educate youth and the general public about key aerospace issues through myriad programs in support of the AFA mission. The AFA sponsors comprehensive briefings by key USAF and Department of Defense (DoD) leaders at national symposia across the country. The AFA has an Outstanding Airman of the Air Force program to help ensure that superior airmen are recognized annually.

References. Primary: Air Force Association Field Operations Guidebook, 1988. John F. Loosbrock, "Jim Straubel: The Man Who Put AFA Together and Made It Work," *AF*, September 1980, pp. 34–40. James H. Straubel, "AFA's Early Days," *AF*, September 1981, pp. 52–69, and *Crusade for Air Power: The Story of the Air Force Association*, 1982. Secondary: "Through Ten Years," *AF*, August 1956, pp. 42–51, 68.

AIR FORCE AUDIT AGENCY (AFAA)

This separate operating agency* (SOA) evaluates operational, support, and financial responsibilities for USAF* management. It is headquartered at Norton* AFB, California, and the auditor general of the Air Force reports directly to the secretary of the Air Force.* The agency became an SOA in 1971. It has three directorates: Acquisitions and Logistics Audit, Financial and Support Audit, and Field Activities. The agency has about 950 personnel.

References. "Air Force Audit Agency," *AF*, May 1990, pp. 98–99. Ravenstein, *Org. USAF*. Roberts, *Dir. USAF*.

AIR FORCE BASES (AFB)

An AFB is a major installation of the USAF* on U.S. soil. It usually has a runway, shops, warehouses, offices, and dormitories. On foreign soil such an installation is called an air base (AB). The USAF also has minor installations, often without a runway. On U.S. soil they are called air force stations (AFS); abroad they are called air stations (AS). AFBs were usually called fields before the USAF was established.

From the beginning the locations were selected by factors influencing military flying, such as climate, weather, terrain, field elevation, remoteness, and defensive operations. The principal modifying factor in location has been politics. An example is the old service joke that Georgia would sink into the Atlantic were one more military installation located there. The result of all factors is that the Sun Belt, and not the Snow Belt, contains most USAF facilities. The locations have had significant social and economic effects upon the United States. In 1990, the USAF had 129 major and 27 minor installations, not counting those of the Air National Guard* and the USAF Reserve.*

References. Brown, *Eagles*. "Guide to Major Air Force Installations Worldwide," *AF*, May 1990, pp. 122–33. Gilbert S. Guinn, "A Different Frontier: Aviation, the Army Air Forces, and the Evolution of the Sunshine Belt," *AH*, March 1982, pp. 34–45.

AIR FORCE CIVILIAN PERSONNEL MANAGEMENT CENTER (AFCPMC)

Established in 1986 as a direct reporting unit* (DRU), the AFCPMC is at Randolph* AFB, Texas. It was previously designated the Office of Civilian Personnel Operations. The center's mission is to manage and support U.S. and foreign civilian personnel programs and information systems. This affects 250,000 people. The center has two divisions: Integrated Systems and Career Management.

References. "AF Civilian Personnel Management Center," *AF*, May 1990, p. 117. Roberts, *Dir. USAF*.

See also civilians employed by the USAF.

AIR FORCE COMBAT COMMAND (AFCC)

The AFCC was a short-lived unit in the USAAF.* It was established on 20 June 1941 to take over the combat readiness duties of the General Headquarters (GHQ) Air Force* and was abolished on 2 March 1942 by War Department Circular 59. Initially, the AFCC controlled the continental air forces, made up of four groups,* over which the GHQ Air Force had jurisdiction since 1935. By March 1942, however, the groups under AFCC had been assigned to other units: one to the Eastern Defense Command, the second and third to unit training agencies, and the fourth to the Western Defense Command.

References. C&C, vol. 1. Mark Watson, *Chief of Staff: Prewar Plans and Preparations*, a vol. of *United States Army in World War II*, 1949.

Lester H. Brune

AIR FORCE COMMISSARY SERVICE (AFCOMS)

The AFCOMS mission is to supply food to the USAF.* It was established as a separate operating agency* (SOA) in 1976. The next year it was placed under the Air Force Engineering and Services Agency and lost its SOA status. It regained SOA status in 1978. It is headquartered at Kelly* AFB, Texas. AF-COMS provides food to both its dining facilities and its commissary resale stores. This commissary benefit is believed to be the second most important nonpay benefit to USAF people, being almost as important as medical benefits. Thus AFCOMS is a major factor in retaining career people in the service. AFCOMS has roughly 1,100 military and 9,000 civilian personnel, and it supports more than 115 troop facilities and 145 commissaries.

References. "Air Force Commissary Service," *AF*, May 1990, pp. 99–100. Jules E. Dubois, "Commissaries Serve the Families," *AF*, August 1982, pp. 40–41. Roberts, *Dir. USAF*. U.S. Air Force Fact Sheet 87–32, "Air Force Commissary Service," August 1987.

AIR FORCE COMMUNICATIONS COMMAND (AFCC)

Modern warfare requires rapid communications with all units. The USAF* began operating globally during World War II.* The confluence of these factors has raised communications to the status of a major command* (MAJCOM).

Experience with the Alaskan flight of 1934* led to the establishment of the Army Airways Communication System (AACS) in 1938. Its mission was to provide communication between ground stations and flyers along the airways, to disseminate weather information, and to provide air traffic control. AACS started with three officers, 300 enlisted men, and 33 stations. In 1941, the expansion into global operations led the AACS first to provide communications over the North Atlantic. By 1945, effective AACS communications were provided worldwide, and the organization was a MAJCOM in the USAAF.* It has eight wings and 49,400 people at 819 stations.

Peacetime brought demobilization and a drastic reduction in strength so that it lost MAJCOM status. With a name change to Airways and Air Communications Service (AACS), it became subordinate to the Air Transport Command (ATC). The Berlin Airlift* was a great challenge and opportunity for the AACS, and the service was vital to the success of the operation. Shortly thereafter, a second challenge came with the support required for the Korean War,* including the Korean Airlift.*

Rapid advances in communications technology occurred from the beginning of this organization. A key element in the progress was automation. In 1961, the organization was restored to MAJCOM status as the Air Force Communications Service (AFCS) to unify communications management. In 1979 the organization assumed its current name. In 1990 the AFCC had its headquarters at Scott* AFB, Illinois, and had 55,000 people in 700 units at 430 locations in the United States and 26 foreign countries. Its tasks now include computer support for the USAF. The technology of communications is now so advanced that it can be abused through micromanagement.

References. "Air Force Communications Command," *AF*, May 1990, pp. 62–63. Roberts, *Dir. USAF*. Thomas S. Snyder, ed., *The Air Force Communications Command 1938–1986: An Illustrated History*, 2d ed., 1986.

AIR FORCE COMMUNICATIONS SERVICE. *See* Air Force Communications Command.

AIR FORCE COST CENTER (AFCSTC)

The AFCSTC is a direct reporting unit* (DRU) established in 1985. Its mission is to use cost and economic analysis for new techniques, automated models, and data bases. These tools are used to estimate costs of acquisition, operation, and support of weapons systems. Three divisions make up the center: Acquisition, Operation and Support, and Information Systems.

Reference. "Air Force Cost Center," *AF*, May 1989, pp. 124, 127.

AIR FORCE COUNCIL

The council, established in 1951, serves the chief of staff of the Air Force* by recommending actions and policies. This relieves the chief of detailed work. The chief appoints the members. The council also gives policy guidance to the Air Staff* and monitors the ability of the USAF* to discharge its mission. The council is chaired by the vice chief of staff.

References. Goldberg, *Hist. USAF*. Woodford Agee Heflin, ed., *The United States Air Force Dictionary*, 1956. L. F. Loesch and C. R. Low, "Air Force Headquarters: Its Mission and Organization," *Air University Quarterly Review*, Summer 1956, pp. 102, 107–9. U.S. Air Force Fact Sheet 89–05, "Organization of the United States Air Force," February 1989.

AIR FORCE, DEPARTMENT OF THE. *See* Department of the Air Force.

AIR FORCE DISTRICT OF WASHINGTON (AFDW)

The AFDW is a direct reporting unit* (DRU). It is a showcase organization that supports USAF* activities in and near the capital. It has its headquarters at Bolling* AFB, District of Columbia, and was established in 1985. The AFDW acts as a housekeeping unit, and it conducts ceremonies. It includes the USAF Honor Guard and USAF Band.*

References. "Air Force District of Washington," *AF*, May 1986, p. 139, and May 1990, pp. 118–19. Roberts, *Dir. USAF*.

AIR FORCE ENGINEERING AND SERVICES CENTER (AFESC)

This separate operating agency* (SOA) was established in 1977 as the Air Force Engineering and Services Agency. It was given its current name in 1978, and it is based at Tyndall* AFB, Florida. The agency helps major commands and Air Force installations in the operation and maintenance of facilities.

References. "Air Force Engineering and Services Center," *AF*, May 1990, p. 100. Ravenstein, *Org. USAF*. Roberts, *Dir. USAF*.

AIR FORCE HISTORICAL FOUNDATION (AFHF)

The AFHF was founded in 1953 at Maxwell* AFB, Alabama, at the suggestion of General Hoyt S. Vandenberg* as a nonprofit corporation and has ever since enjoyed the endorsement of the chief of staff of the Air Force.* Its original purpose, as stated in an early issue of its journal, centered on the idea that a civilization cannot endure if it is weak in belief and courage. Early trustees included Major Alexander P. de Seversky;* Major General Benjamin D. Foulois;* and Generals Ira C. Eaker,* Carl A. Spaatz,* and Nathan F. Twining* among others. Of the original Editorial Board, Major General Ramsay D. Potts, Jr., was still serving as publisher in 1990. The journal *Airpower Historian* was established in 1954, first in 6-by-9-inch format and then in 1961 in an 8½-by-11-inch format. Major General Orville A. Anderson served as editor until his death in 1965. Then Brigadier General Dale O. Smith took over. By 1966 the journal appeared out of Bolling* AFB, Washington, D.C.

The foundation always had more ideas than assets. In spite of a long and distinguished list of trustees, it lacked consistent focus. As a result, in 1969 it was decided that *Aerospace Historian* or *AH* (so renamed in 1965) should fold. But a committee headed by Lieutenant General A. P. Clark and Colonel Eldon Downs, editor of the *Air University Review*, was able to persuade President James A. McCain of Kansas State University (KSU), Manhattan, Kansas, that the journal was worth saving. A team of Ramsay Potts, president of AFHF, Jack Loosbrock, publisher of *Air Force Magazine* (*AF*), and Professor Robin Higham of KSU worked to make *AH* self-supporting from 1970 to 1988. General Eaker headed the new Editorial Advisory Board composed equally of USAF* officers and scholars. After many years, KSU gave notice in 1987 that it would not manage the journal beyond the last issue of 1988. The foundation then decided to revitalize itself, raise money, and take the renamed *Air Power History* back to Washington, D.C. in 1989.

In the 1980s the AFHF began a program of publishing historical studies such as *A Few Great Captains* and *Forged in Fire*, both by DeWitt S. Copp.

References. See the reports of annual meetings of the AFHF that appeared in either the December or March issues of *AH*.

Robin Higham

AIR FORCE INSPECTION AND SAFETY CENTER (AFISC)

The AFISC is a separate operating agency* (SOA), and its mission is to evaluate the fighting and management effectiveness of the USAF.* It began as the Office of the Inspector General in 1948 and became an SOA in 1971. It is headquartered at Norton* AFB, California, to be near the aircraft industry. The agency has four directorates. One evaluates operational readiness and management. Another manages all USAF safety programs except nuclear, which is the responsibility of a third directorate. A fourth inspects medical facilities.

References. "Air Force Inspection and Safety Center," *AF*, May 1990, pp. 100–101. Roberts, *Dir. USAF*. U.S. Air Force Fact Sheet 86–25, "Air Force Inspection and Safety Center," August 1986.

AIR FORCE INTELLIGENCE AGENCY (AFIA)

The AFIA is a separate operating agency* (SOA) with its headquarters in Washington, D.C. Originally designated the Air Force Intelligence Service (AFIS), it was established in 1972. The AFIA provides the Air Staff* and USAF* units with help in the use of intelligence. It collects, processes, analyzes, and disseminates information.

References. "Air Force Intelligence Agency," *AF*, May 1990, pp. 101–2. Ravenstein, *Org. USAF*. Roberts, *Dir. USAF*.

AIR FORCE LEGAL SERVICES CENTER (AFLSC)

The AFLSC is a separate operating agency* (SOA) and was established in 1978. It is headquartered in Washington, D.C., and its mission is to provide specialized civil and military legal service to the USAF.* The Air Force judge advocate general is commander of the AFLSC. The AFLSC provides civil law functions through six staff units: Claims and Tort Litigation Staff, General Litigation Division, Contract Law Division, Environmental Law Division, Patents Division, and the Preventive Law and Legal Assistance Office. Military justice is administered by the Court of Military Review, Military Justice Division, Defense Services Division, Trial Judiciary Division, Government Trial and Appellate Counsel Division, and the Clemency, Corrections, and Officer Review Division.

References. "Air Force Legal Services Center," *AF*, May 1990, p. 102. Roberts, *Dir. USAF*. U.S. Air Force Fact Sheet 87–31, "Air Force Legal Services Center," July 1987.

AIR FORCE LOGISTICS COMMAND (AFLC)

The mission of this major command is the adequate logistical support of the USAF.* The AFLC accomplishes its mission through buying, supplying, transporting, and by maintaining equipment.

The original organization for this command, established in 1921, was the USAAS's* Property, Maintenance and Cost Compilation Office located at Fairfield Army Air Depot, Ohio. During World War II* the AFLC's antecedent was the Air Service Command (ASC). After the war, it was renamed the Air Materiel Command (AMC). It became the AFLC in 1982.

The AFLC is headquartered at Wright-Patterson* AFB (W-P AFB), Ohio. Under it are five large industrial-type activities called Air Logistic Centers. These specialize in different weapons systems, with each providing USAF-wide support. The centers are Ogden at Hill* AFB, Utah; Oklahoma at Tinker* AFB, Oklahoma; San Antonio at Kelly* AFB, Texas; Sacramento at McClellan* AFB, California; and Warner Robins at Robins* AFB, Georgia.

The command also has ten specialized units. One is the Aerospace Guidance and Meteorology Center, Newark Air Force Station, Ohio, which repairs guidance and navigation systems. Another is the Air Force Acquisition Logistics Division, W-P AFB, which ensures that USAF equipment will be effective in battle. A third is the Air Force Contract Maintenance Center at Wright-Patterson AFB. The Cataloging and Standardization Center, Battle Creek, Michigan, catalogs data on all items used by the USAF. The International Logistics Center, W-P AFB, gives support for foreign nations under assistance programs. The Logistics Management Systems Center, also at W-P AFB, manages dataprocessing capabilities.

The Logistics Operations Center, W-P AFB, insures that USAF weapons systems are ready and supported. The Aerospace Maintenance and Regeneration Center, Davis-Monthan* AFB, Arizona, is the USAF's "boneyard," which stores, reclaims, or disposes of aircraft and missiles not needed. The USAF Museum* is at W-P AFB.

The AFLC's work is indispensable to the continued combat readiness of the USAF. In 1992, the AFLC is scheduled to merge with the Air Force Systems Command* (AFSC) to become the Air Force Materiel Command (AFMC).

References. Primary: Fred J. Dau, "Air Force Supply—1952–1959," *AH*, March 1982, pp. 26–30. James R. McCarthy, "A Quarter Century of Air Force Maintenance," *AH*, March 1982, pp. 48–55. Secondary: "Air Force Logistics Command," *AF*, May 1990, pp. 63–64. Bernard J. Termena et al., *Logistics: An Illustrated History of AFLC and Its Antecedents, 1921–1981*, 1981. U.S. Air Force Fact Sheet 86–12, "Air Force Logistics Command," April 1986. Lois E. Walker and Shelby E. Wickham, *From Huffman Prairie to the Moon: The History of Wright-Patterson Air Force Base*, 1982.

AIR FORCE MANAGEMENT ENGINEERING AGENCY (AFMEA)

The AFMEA was originally activated as a separate operating agency* (SOA) in 1975. Its mission is to improve the use of manpower in the USAF* and to ensure the implementation of the Management Engineering Program (MEP). It is headquartered at Randolph* AFB, Texas. Through this agency the USAF seeks optimum productivity from its people. In addition, the MEP determines wartime manpower needs.

References. "Air Force Management Engineering Agency," *AF*, May 1990, pp. 102, 105. Ravenstein, *Org. USAF*. Roberts, *Dir. USAF*.

AIR FORCE MATERIEL COMMAND. *See* Air Force Logistics Command; Air Force Systems Command.

AIR FORCE MEDAL OF HONOR

The Medal of Honor is the highest award for bravery in the United States. It is presented to its recipient by a high official, usually the U.S. president, "in the name of the Congress." For this reason, it is sometimes erroneously called the Congressional Medal of Honor. Fifty-eight men have won the Air Force Medal of Honor.

In 1861 and 1862 there was much thought in Washington, D.C., concerning the need to recognize the deeds of U.S. servicemen who were distinguishing themselves. Senator James W. Grimes of Iowa took the lead as chairman of the Senate Naval Committee and introduced a bill to create a Navy decoration. It passed Congress and was signed by President Abraham Lincoln on 21 December 1861. Action on an Army decoration was started when Senator Henry Wilson of Massachusetts introduced a Senate resolution for "medals of honor" to enlisted men of the Army. It became law on 12 July 1862. An act of 3 March 1863 extended its provisions to include officers. An act of 10 August 1956 codified prior laws and added the awarding of such decorations to members of the USAF.*

The Air Force decoration is similar in design to that of the Army, except that it is the same size as the Navy's. It is suspended from the ribbon by a bar with the word *VALOR* on it. Below the bar is a cluster of lightning bolts coming from behind a set of wings.

Generally, it may be awarded for personal bravery or self-sacrifice above and beyond the call of duty. The recipient must be a member of the U.S. armed forces in military action against a foreign enemy or be serving with a friendly foreign force in action against an opposing armed force when the United States is not a belligerent.

Not all acts of extraordinary courage or service deserve a Medal of Honor. Yet all of them need recognition and degrees of valor can be determined. The problem of recognition of lesser deeds was solved over time by a system of decorations arranged in an ascending order with the Medal of Honor as the supreme award.

References. Committee on Veterans' Affairs, U.S. Senate, *Medal of Honor Recipients 1863–1978*, 1979. "Decorations," *The Encyclopedia Americana International Edition*, vol. 8, 1989.

Joe M. Jackson

AIR FORCE MILITARY PERSONNEL CENTER (AFMPC)

The AFMPC is a separate operating agency* (SOA) composed of about 2,000 military and civilian persons. The agency is responsible for placing people of appropriate skills into USAF* units. The center was relocated in 1963 to Randolph* AFB, Texas, from Washington, D.C.

The AFMPC brings new personnel onto active duty, classifies them, and assigns them to a unit for training or service. Supporting these functions requires management of promotions, retentions, separations from the service, retirements, and casualty services. To help with morale, the center is also responsible for recreational facilities.

References. "Air Force Military Personnel Center," *AF*, May 1990, pp. 105–6. Bruce D. Callander, "Half a Million Destinies," *AF*, July 1987, pp. 92–94. Roberts, *Dir. USAF*. U.S. Air Force Fact Sheet 86–27, "Air Force Military Personnel Center," September 1986.

AIR FORCE NEWS CENTER (AFNEWS)

The AFNEWS, formerly called Air Force Service Information and News Center (AFSINC), is a separate operating agency* (SOA) and was established in 1978. The agency provides public affairs services for the USAF* and information for its people. It is headquartered at Kelly* AFB, Texas. AFNEWS has four elements: Army and Air Force Hometown News Service, Air Force Broadcasting Service, Air Force Office of Youth Relations, and Directorate of Internal Information.

References. "Air Force News Center," *AF*, May 1990, p. 106. Roberts, *Dir. USAF*. U.S. Air Force Fact Sheet 87–7, "Air Force Service Information and News Center," January 1987.

AIR FORCE OFFICE OF MEDICAL SUPPORT (AFOMS)

This office directs health care support for the USAF.* It is a separate operating agency* (SOA) headquartered at Brooks* AFB, Texas. AFOMS assists the Air Force surgeon general by preparing plans, programs, policies, studies, and practices for health care. It is organized into two parts. One is the Directorate of Health Care Support, composed of a Medical Facilities Division, Biometrics

Division, Medical Logistics Division, and Medical Service Information Systems Division. The other part is the Professional Affairs Activities composed of the Health Promotion Program, Family Advocacy Program, and the Air Force Radioisotope Committee.

References. "Air Force Office of Medical Support," *AF*, May 1990, p. 106. Michael B. Perini, "Medical Readiness Is Looking Up," *AF*, July 1984, pp. 108, 109. Roberts, *Dir. USAF*. U.S. Air Force Fact Sheet 86–26, "Air Force Office of Medical Support," August 1986.

AIR FORCE OFFICE OF SECURITY POLICE (AFOSP)

The AFOSP, a separate operating agency* (SOA), was established in 1979. It sets USAF* policy for security, law enforcement (police), air base ground defense, information security, and small arms training and maintenance. It is headquartered at Kirtland* AFB, New Mexico.

References. "Air Force Office of Security Police," *AF*, May 1990, pp. 107–8. Ravenstein, *Org. USAF*. Roberts, *Dir. USAF*.

AIR FORCE OFFICE OF SPECIAL INVESTIGATIONS (AFOSI)

Tasked with counterintelligence and criminal investigation responsibilities, the AFOSI is charged with determining the facts. It is not an action activity. It is a separate operating agency* (SOA) headquartered at Bolling* AFB, Washington, D.C.

The USAF* had long faced hostile intelligence activities but had no centralized agency for response until the AFOSI was established in 1948. It became an SOA in 1971. The agency won the Air Force Outstanding Unit Award in 1956, 1965, 1976, and 1983.

References. "Air Force Office of Special Investigations," *AF*, May 1990, p. 108. Phil Lacombe, "After the Bad Guys," *AF*, April 1982, pp. 80–86. Stanley Levine, "Reservists as Blue-Suit Sleuths," *AF*, July 1984, pp. 104–5. Roberts, *Dir. USAF*. U.S. Air Force Fact Sheet 86–34, "Air Force Office of Special Investigations," October 1986.

AIR FORCE ONE. *See* presidential airlift.

AIR FORCE OPERATIONAL TEST AND EVALUATION CENTER (AFOTEC)

AFOTEC manages the USAF's* operational test and evaluation (OT&E) function. In 1990, it was headquartered at Kirtland* AFB, New Mexico, with five detachments ranging from Edwards* AFB, California, to Kapaun Administrative Annex, Germany, and more than 24 test teams. The test teams are formed wherever and whenever needed. AFOTEC also exercised control over people from other commands and services and received specialized scientific and technical support from several civilian contractors. AFOTEC may be involved with a weapon system all the way from the drawing board to the flight line.

The USAF established AFOTEC in 1974 as the Air Force Test and Evaluation Center. The word *operational* was added in 1983. As a separate operating agency* (SOA), AFOTEC's mission is independently to test and evaluate major weapons and other systems under the most realistic conditions possible. Its evaluations help determine production decisions for new systems and help make improvements to existing ones. AFOTEC also monitors and advises on hundreds of other operational tests conducted by major commands and participates in multiservice and joint test and evaluation (JT&E).

The questionable performance of many weapon systems used in the Vietnam War* was a major reason the Department of Defense (DoD) had the services establish OT&Es. The USAF created AFOTEC after studies indicated the need for objective operational testing as early as possible in the acquisition process. Before AFOTEC, the only Air Force operational testing unit had been the Air Proving Ground Command,* which existed in various forms from 1941 to 1957. This command, unfortunately, tested only equipment in production. Production decisions had already been made based upon contractor testing and those of the developmental commands. This system emphasized meeting specifications and engineering criteria rather than rigorously testing under realistic field conditions. Between 1974 and 1988, AFOTEC conducted hundreds of OT&E programs involving about 95 major systems ranging from fighters* to satellite communications networks.

References. "Air Force Operational Test and Evaluation Center," *AF*, May 1990, pp. 108, 111. Roberts, *Dir. USAF*. U.S. Air Force Fact Sheet 87–6, "Air Force Operational Test and Evaluation Center," January 1987.

Lawrence R. Benson

AIR FORCE ORGANIZATION ACT OF 1951

The National Security Act of 1947* did not provide a statutory basis for the USAF's* composition and organization. Previously, Congress had provided a statutory basis for the U.S. Army and Navy. The act of 1951 completed statutory provisions for the USAF. The act specified the USAF's internal organization and the responsibilities of the secretary of the Air Force.*

Reference. Goldberg, *Hist. USAF*.

AIR FORCE RESERVE (AFR). *See* U.S. Air Force Reserve; Air National Guard.

AIR FORCE RESERVE OFFICER TRAINING CORPS (AFROTC)

The AFROTC has been an indispensable source of commissioned officers for the USAF.* It has been under the Air Training Command* (ATC) since 1978. It began as the Air Reserve Officer Training Corps in 1920. After World War II,* Air ROTC units were established at 78 colleges and universities. The ROTC Vitalization Act of 1964 set up a two-year senior program, scholarships, and a junior program. Women have been enrolled in the corps since 1969.

The senior program had units at 152 colleges and universities in 1987. Such units can accommodate students from nearby schools that lack a program. The total enrollment of these units averages 25,000 persons. Subject matter in the senior program includes a general military course, field training, management, communication skills, and defense policy. Scholarships are available for science and engineering students. The faculty is made up of USAF officers. Corps cadets may join the Arnold Air Society, an honorary professional and service organization. The society has an auxiliary, the Angel Flight.

In 1987 the junior program had units at 296 high schools in the United States and at some U.S. military dependents' schools in Guam and Europe, for a total enrollment of about 41,000 cadets. The junior program features leadership training and aerospace science. The faculty is retired USAF commissioned and noncommissioned officers.

References. William P. Schlitz, "AFROTC Bounces Back," *AF*, January 1984, pp. 68–72. U.S. Air Force Fact Sheet 87–24, "Air Force Reserve Officer Training Corps," May 1987.

AIR FORCES ICELAND

Iceland occupies a key geographic position in relation to North Atlantic air and sea routes. Air power, operating out of Iceland, can command the air and the sea in the area.

The Air Forces Iceland is the smallest named air force.* It was first established in 1952 as the Iceland Air Defense Force and was under the Military Air Transport Service (MATS). It became the Air Forces Iceland in 1960 and was assigned to the Air Defense Command (ADC). It was placed under the Tactical Air Command* (TAC) in 1979. In 1990 it was assigned to the First Air Force.*

References. Ravenstein, *Org. USAF*. "Tactical Air Command," *AF*, May 1990, p. 89.

AIR FORCE SPACE COMMAND (AFSPACECOM)

AFSPACECOM is a major command* (MAJCOM) of the USAF,* established in September 1982. It is the Air Force component of the U.S. Space Command. Its mission is to support U.S. defense satellites and forces in space. It is also charged with giving warning of a missile or space-based attack, as well as countering enemy space systems during conflicts. The USAF has operated space systems since the 1960s. Over the years these systems have grown in number and importance. The command was formed to provide appropriate control of these activities. AFSPACECOM has three wings* and operates facilities with about 8,500 USAF and 5,500 contractor personnel. It is headquartered at Peterson* AFB, Colorado.

References. "Air Force Space Command," *AF*, May 1990, pp. 65–66. Roberts, *Dir. USAF*. Edgar Ulsamer, "Space Command: Setting the Course of the Future," *AF*, August 1982, pp. 48–55. U.S. Air Force Fact Sheet 88–13, "Air Force Space Command," July 1988.

AIR FORCE SYSTEMS COMMAND (AFSC)

A major command* (MAJCOM), the AFSC advises the leadership of the USAF* on the scientific and technical options available for its aerospace equipment needs. To do this, the AFSC manages an array of research and development

(R&D), test and evaluation (T&E), and acquisition resources. Its headquarters is at Andrews* AFB, Maryland.

The AFSC was originally established in January 1950 as the Research and Development Command (RDC). It was a direct outgrowth of the USAAF's* experience in World War II.* The USAAF's leaders had been alarmed because many of the innovations that threatened to revolutionize war had either originated or been perfected abroad. These were radar,* jets, ballistic missiles,* and nuclear weapons.* Even the USAAF's traditional equipment, except for heavy bombers, had been inferior to those of other powers at the beginning of the war.

Although the AFSC was a product of World War II, its heritage went back to the United States's entry into World War I.* Behind the Europeans in equipment, the U.S. Army established the functional antecedent to the AFSC near Dayton, Ohio, at McCook Field in October 1917. After the war, McCook became famous as the Engineering Division of the USAAS.* However, the USAAC's* Materiel Division managed procurement and industrial war planning as well as supply and maintenance. By 1946 the old Materiel Division had been transformed into the Air Materiel Command (AMC).

The proper scope and organization for post–World War II R&D provoked heated debate in the USAAF. Some leaders realized that, although they had headed the world's largest air force when Japan surrendered, most of it had become obsolete. The USAAF attempted to settle the organizational issue by creating an Air Staff* office to direct R&D while the AMC continued its daily management of the function. A small group of technically minded officers led by Lieutenant General Donald L. Putt and some allies outside the USAAF, including Lieutenant General James H. Doolittle,* eventually convinced General Hoyt S. Vandenberg,* chief of staff of the Air Force* (1948–1953), to put more emphasis on R&D. This led to the establishment of the RDC.

The RDC was renamed the Air Research and Development Command (ARDC) in September 1950. It launched many ambitious programs in the 1950s. Technical innovation and risk taking were encouraged. The explosion of the first Soviet hydrogen bomb in 1953 and reports that the USSR was ahead of the United States in developing intercontinental ballistic missiles* sparked a crash effort to catch up. In 1954 Brigadier General Bernard A. Schriever* was selected to run the successful USAF Atlas* missile program. In early 1961 the Soviets placed their first manned orbiter in space. Then Deputy Secretary of Defense Roswell L. Gilpatrick told the USAF it would lose the coveted military space R&D mission unless it overhauled its organization. There had been a sharp rivalry between the ARDC and the AMC because of overlapping responsibilities and different worldviews. In April 1961, the ARDC was redesignated the AFSC and given the weapons procurement and production functions from the AMC. The AMC was renamed the Air Force Logistics Command* (AFLC), which was to focus on supply and depot maintenance activities. Ironically, Secretary of Defense (SECDEF) Robert S. McNamara* soon reduced the authority of the AFSC by removing much of it to the Office of the Secretary of Defense (OSD). From 1969 to 1970, Melvin Laird, then SECDEF, restored a larger role to the service.

During the Vietnam War,* the AFSC concentrated on finding quick solutions to the war's needs. Electronic warfare,* gunships,* precision-guided munitions, forward-looking infrared* (FLIR) sensors, and the defense meteorological satellite program were some AFSC projects. Since the end of the Vietnam War, weapons modernization and acquisition reform have been the major trends for the AFSC. The pace of weapons development escalated in the 1980s as the Reagan administration rearmed the United States. There was an effort to reform weapons acquisition, but the AFSC was troubled by the trend toward congressional micromanagement of the details of acquisition programs. Thus, AFSC activities not only became based upon military requirements and technical opportunities but were influenced by social, political, and economic forces in American life.

In 1991 the decision was made to reverse the judgments of 1950 and 1961 and recombine the AFLC and the AFSC into an Air Force Materiel Command (AFMC) in 1992. It was believed that this would improve the development and procurement of weapons systems.*

References. Primary: Air Force Regulation 23–8, "Organization and Mission—Field. Air Force Systems Command," 10 February 1986. Charles J. Gross interview of Lieutenant General Donald L. Putt, 30–31 March 1987. Charles J. Gross and Walter L. Kraus interview of General Robert T. Marsh, July 1984–July 1985. Secondary: "Air Force Systems Command," *AF*, May 1990, pp. 66–67. Michael H. Gorn, *Vulcan's Forge: The Making of an Air Force Command for Weapons Acquisition, 1950–1986*, 1986. Charles J. Gross, Perry D. Jamieson, and Walter L. Kraus, "AFSC: A Short History," 1987.

See also National Aeronautics and Space Administration; Scientific Advisory Board.

Charles J. Gross

AIR FORCE TECHNICAL APPLICATIONS CENTER (AFTAC)

AFTAC is a direct reporting unit* (DRU) and is responsible for the U.S. Atomic Energy Detection System (USAEDS). It was first established as the 1035th USAF Field Activities Group in 1959. It was redesignated as the 1035th Technical Operations Group in 1972. It was redesignated AFTAC and made a DRU in 1980. It is headquartered at Patrick* AFB, Florida. AFTAC's task is to detect events and determine if they are nuclear. Its special missions have included tracking matter that resulted from the 1986 Soviet Chernobyl accident.

References. "Air Force Technical Applications Center," *AF*, May 1990, pp. 119–120. Ravenstein, *Org. USAF*. Roberts, *Dir. USAF*.

AIR FORCE 2000

The advent of "smart bombs" raised the question of whether manned or unmanned weapon delivery systems would be better. This developed into some disputes between the U.S. Army and the USAF.* AirLand Battle, an Army study in 1982, predicted a struggle for the airspace above the battlefield to be fought with smart weapons and lasers from hovercraft, remotely piloted vehicles, and missiles. Shortly after AirLand Battle was released, it was modified by the Army with its Light Infantry concept. The USAF also produced a study in 1982, called Air Force 2000. The USAF's study foresaw an expansion of the air superiority* struggle into space. An Advanced Tactical Fighter* (ATF) was expected to be the means to conduct operations against surface forces. Thus, the Army foresaw unmanned systems, and the USAF predicted manned ones. Out of these studies have come the Army's Joint Tactical Missile System (JTACMS) and the USAF's Joint Surveillance Target Attack Radar System* (Joint STARS).

References. A. J. Bacevich, *The Pentomic Era: The U.S. Army between Korea and Vietnam*, 1986. Christopher Campbell, *Air Warfare: The Fourth Generation*, 1984. Futrell, *Ideas*, vol. 2.

AIR INTERCEPTOR MISSILE (AIM)

AIMs are now the primary weapon of aerial combat. They are made with three different types of guidance systems. Infrared (IR) systems home in on the heat of an enemy airplane and can be fired and forgotten. IR guidance is generally effective in short-range dogfighting. Early versions could only be fired toward the rear of the target and have been known to chase the sun or heat sources on the ground. The second type is the semi-active radar* homing (SARH) guidance system. The launching aircraft "paints" the target with a radar beam and then fires the missile. The missile rides the beam to the target. Some versions have a small on-board radar for terminal guidance. These missiles are long-range but require the pilot* to keep the enemy target in his sights for a time, which is unsafe during battle. If the pilot breaks the beam, missile lock-on may be lost.

The third guidance method is on-board radar. The pilot acquires the target, fires the missiles, and the missile radar guides it to the target. This system has the most range. The AIM-54 Phoenix, a Navy missile, will intercept at over 100 miles range. However, missiles using a large and powerful radar are big, heavy, and expensive. AIMs permit operations in depth. Fighters can carry simultaneously long-range radar missiles, short-range IR missiles, and guns for close engagement.

References. Frank Barnaby, *The Automated Battlefield*, 1986. Christopher Campbell, *Air Warfare: The Fourth Generation*, 1984. Robert L. Shaw, *Fighter Combat: Tactics and Maneuvering*, 1985.

Philip Long

AIR-LAUNCHED CRUISE MISSILE (ALCM). *See* AGM-86B.

AIRLIFT OPERATIONS

Airlift operations involve the application of large transport* airplanes or helicopters,* often specially designed for military use, to move people, equipment, and supplies. Within the Department of Defense (DoD), the Military Airlift Command* (MAC) is the single manager for airlift. There is both strategic and tactical airlift.* Strategic airlift involves transporting resources from the United States to overseas theaters and back. Tactical airlift is the movement of forces and supplies within theaters of operation and rescue.* Airlift operations can involve noncombat logistical transport between two locations or can be done in battle. In a combat environment there may be landings, airdrops, or air pickups.

Airlift operations have been a part of USAF* planning since World War II,* when its importance was proven. To accomplish this central mission, MAC has used C-5,* C-130,* and C-141* transports and HH-3 (*see* H-3) and HH-53 (*see* H-53) helicopters since the 1960s.

References. Ray L. Bowers, *Tactical Airlift*, 1983. Futrell, *Ideas*, vol. 1. House of Representatives, Committee on Armed Services, Research and Development Subcommittee, *Hearings on the Posture of Military Airlift*, 1975. Charles E. Miller, *Airlift Doctrine*, 1988.

Roger D. Launius

AIRLIFT RODEO. *See* competitions.

AIRLINES

U.S. airlines form a strong reserve of the USAF's* air power. Their many experienced aircrews, high-capacity modern airliners, and skilled mechanics are a great reservoir of talent and equipment. An important factor is their continuous high usage and global exercise of their resources.

The United States had the first airline using airplanes. (A German airline used dirigibles.) It ran from Tampa to St. Petersburg, Florida, in 1914. This brief start was followed by a 12-year gap. The Contract Mail Act of 1925 took the federal government out of the business of flying the mail. By 1926, 16 airlines, using 300 aircraft, sprang up to fly the mail. The Air Commerce Act of 1926 started government regulation of the industry. In May 1930, Postmaster General Walter Folger Brown called a conference of the larger airlines. At this so-called Spoils Conference, Brown used his contracting power to align the airlines and routes to his vision for commercial aviation. Alleged corruption led to an uproar and, in 1934, an unhappy President Franklin D. Roosevelt* ordered the Army's airmail flights of 1934.* The resulting disaster exposed the USAAC's* sad state after long neglect. Even though Brown was proven innocent by congressional hearings, the allegations and the USAAC's failure to carry the mail efficiently led to the Air Mail Act of 1934.

That act increased government regulation of the airlines and punished the existing ones, resulting in a different airline industry. The new industry was allowed no connections with aircraft manufacturers. This period of turbulence coincided with the technological revolution in aircraft structures leading to the first modern airliner, the Model 247 of the Boeing Division, United Aircraft & Transport Corporation. It was quickly followed by the greatly superior Douglas Aircraft Company's DC-1 and then the DC-3. With the DC-3, airlines could operate profitably under the existing government subsidies. With profitability came expansion. The Civil Aeronautics Act of 1938 was designed to spur further airline growth and to increase government regulation.

After Pearl Harbor,* President Roosevelt wanted to nationalize the airlines but was talked out of it. The airlines shrank during World War II* as their resources were partly mobilized for air power. Some airliners were taken into military service, production was switched to military transports, some aircrews moved into the services, and nonwar transportation was discouraged. Improved transports, like the DC-4 (C-54) and Lockheed Aircraft Corporation's Constellation (C-69), were built during the war and became available as cheap military surplus when peace returned. The Berlin Airlift* (1948–1949) provided improved traffic control methods, and coach fares were introduced. The airlines improved and grew despite boom and bust cycles in the industry.

In 1958, a great breakthrough occurred with the availability of the first U.S. jetliner, the Boeing Airplane Company's 707. The jet engine brought a revolutionary advance in airliner economy and convenience, and the airlines began to dominate passenger transportation. A deadly airliner accident in 1958 led to yet more government regulation with the creation of the Federal Aviation Authority (FAA).

The adverse effects of all this regulation were highly visible in the 1970s and led to the Airline Deregulation Act of 1978. The act kept safety regulation but opened routes and fares to free market economics. The result was yet another revolution for the airlines. Initially, many new companies entered the industry, resulting in price wars. The long-term effects included a great expansion, more people flying more often, and the bankruptcy of inefficient airlines. In 1971, the airlines were still elitist. Less than half of all Americans had flown. By 1989, three-quarters had flown, and more than one-fifth were flying at least three times a year. Airline traffic receipts rose from $33 billion in 1979 to $50 billion in 1987. Also, the airline accident rate was cut in half during deregulation.

The U.S. airlines had 5,660 multiengine aircraft at the end of 1988, a good measure of their contribution to U.S. air power. This resource is organized to support U.S. air power by the Civil Reserve Air Fleet* (CRAF). In addition, the airlines have cooperated with the USAF in training and facility support.

References. R.E.G. Davies, *Airlines of the United States since 1914*, rev. ed., 1982. "50th Anniversary Issue," a special issue of *Flying*, September 1977, pp. 216–30. Higham, *Air Pwr*. Phil Lacombe, "The Air Force and the Airlines," *AF*, February 1985, pp. 92–96. Christopher Winans and Jonathon Dahl, "Airlines Skid on Bad Moves, Bad News," *The Wall Street Journal*, 20 September 1989, p. B1.

AIRMAIL FLIGHTS OF 1934

U.S. Army aviation became involved with airmail on two major occasions: the airmail service by the Army in 1918* and the time of alleged scandal in the airmail division of the U.S. Post Office in 1934. The 1934 venture highlighted the USAAC's need for better equipment and helped generate more funds during the next several years.

After World War I, Brigadier General William Mitchell* and other advocates of a united air service proposed taking over the airmail as a means of peacetime preparedness. Although the Post Office rejected these efforts, it cooperated with the USAAS* in preparing air routes across the nation. In 1934, President Franklin D. Roosevelt* canceled private airmail contracts because of allegations that the

Post Office negotiated contracts that gave a favored few airline companies government subsidies and profits. Roosevelt's decision to cancel the contracts required the Post Office to ask the USAAC* to carry the mail. On 9 February, Major General Benjamin D. Foulois,* chief of the Air Corps, agreed to do so with ten day's preparation.

In retrospect, Foulois' desire to demonstrate the Air Corps' ability left him too little time to prepare men and equipment for their duties. Lack of funds had left the USAAC with less than the best aircraft and instrument equipment for flying in all types of weather. As a result, during its five months of operations the USAAC experienced great difficulty. During the period from midnight on 19 February to 9 March, five pilots were killed on airmail operations and six others were injured seriously. Roosevelt's opponents in the commercial aviation industry, such as Edward V. Rickenbacker,* accused the government of "legalized murder," and the ensuing publicity made the USAAC operations appear disastrous. Yet, with little preparation, the USAAC operated the airmail for 78 days, flew more than one and one-half million miles, carried 777,000 pounds of mail, completed 75 percent of its flights, and claimed not to lose a single letter.

References. Primary: Ross G. Hoyt, "Neither Snow, Nor Rain, Nor Gloom of Night," *AF*, January 1978, pp. 58–64. Secondary: DeWitt S. Copp, *A Few Great Captains*, 1980. Eldon W. Downs, "Army and the Airmail, 1934," *Air Power Historian*, January 1962, pp. 35–51. William M. Leary, *Aerial Pioneers: The U.S. Air Mail Service, 1918–1927*, 1985.

See also airlines.

Lester H. Brune

AIRMAIL SERVICE BY THE ARMY IN 1918

Airmail service was established by the Aviation Section, U.S. Army Signal Corps* on 15 May 1918. President and Mrs. Woodrow Wilson attended the inaugural flight. The Army officials were embarrassed when the aircraft engine failed to start because the airplane had not been refueled. Lieutenant George L. Boyle finally departed the old polo grounds on the banks of the Potomac in Washington, D.C., with a load of mail intended for Philadelphia and New York City. Unfortunately, Boyle was an inexperienced pilot who had never flown cross-country in the Washington to Philadelphia area, and he headed south instead of north. After he landed in a farmer's field in southern Maryland, the mail was placed on a train for Philadelphia. The pilot on the second leg, Lieutenant Paul Culver, flew the Philadelphia mail to New York.

Although approval for the start of airmail service had been given on 1 March 1918, the Army men involved did not learn about it until 3 May. The officer in charge was Major Reuben Fleet, later to found and head Consolidated Aircraft Corporation, who had been recommended for the job by Colonel H. H. Arnold.* The short notice gave Fleet little time to build a system. First, a suitable aircraft had to be found. Fleet ordered from the factory six JN* Jennys to be specially built. Second, Fleet had to find three suitable airfields and settled on Belmont

Racetrack, Long Island, the polo grounds in Washington, D.C., and a field outside Philadelphia near Bustleton. Third, Fleet requested four veteran Army pilots. The Post Office requested that novice pilots Boyle and Lieutenant James C. Edgerton be assigned, for they were relatives of high-ranking people associated with the Post Office. Boyle was subsequently reassigned, but Edgerton flew the route like a veteran.

The Army operated the airmail system successfully for three months without suffering a major accident or serious injury. Captain Benjamin B. Lipsner, an able administrator, was in charge of the operation. It included civilian pilots, many of whom were recruited from the military. On 29 August, the Army was relieved of its airmail duties. Lipsner then resigned from the Army and worked for the Post Office as superintendent of the airmail. The Army flew the airmail only once thereafter, in the airmail flights of 1934,* from 19 February to 10 March. In that time ten USAAC* aviators lost their lives trying to fly the airmail in severe winter weather.

References. Joe Christy, *American Aviation: An Illustrated History*, 1987. Edith Dodd Culver, *Tailspins: A Story of Early Aviation Days*, 1986. C. V. Glines, "The Day the Airmail Started," *AF*, December 1989, pp. 98–101.

D. K. Vaughan

AIRMAN EDUCATION AND COMMISSIONING PROGRAM. *See* Officer Candidate School; Officer Training School.

AIR MATERIEL COMMAND. *See* Air Force Logistics Command.

AIR MATERIEL FORCE, EUROPEAN AREA

This named air force* was established as the Air Materiel Force, Europe, in 1954 under the U.S. Air Forces in Europe* (USAFE). Its headquarters was at Wiesbaden, Germany. It was redesignated as the Air Materiel Force, European Area, under the Air Materiel Command (AMC) in 1956. The headquarters moved to Chateauroux Air Station, France, in 1958. It was inactivated in 1962. At one time, this air force had three large depots, at RAF Burtonwood, England; Chateauroux; and Nouasseur, French Morocco. These large depots were primarily supply organizations but did some maintenance. There were five other air depots at the time in Britain, France, and Libya. Improved distribution systems eliminated the need for these huge depots.

References. Ravenstein, *Org. USAF*. Bernard J. Termena et al., *Logistics: An Illustrated History of AFLC and Its Antecedents, 1921–1981*, c. 1981.

AIR MATERIEL FORCE, PACIFIC AREA

This named air force* was established as the Far East Air Service Command in 1944 with headquarters at Brisbane, Australia. It was under the Far East Air Forces (FEAF). It became the Pacific Air Service Command, U.S. Army, in 1946, and the Far East Air Materiel Command in 1947. In those years it changed locations many times until reaching Tachikawa Air Base, Japan. It was redesignated as the Far East Air Logistics Force in 1952. In 1955 it became the Air Materiel Force, Pacific Area, under the Air Materiel Command (AMC). It moved to Wheeler* AFB, Hawaii, in 1957, and back to Tachikawa AB in 1960. It was inactivated in 1962. This air force had two main locations, Tachikawa AB and Clark* AB, Philippines. Improving supply distribution methods eliminated the need for these huge depots.

References. Ravenstein, *Org. USAF*. Bernard J. Termena et al., *Logistics: An Illustrated History of AFLC and Its Antecedents, 1921–1981*, c. 1981.

AIR NATIONAL GUARD (ANG)

The ANG, also called the Air Guard, is administered by the National Guard Bureau, a joint bureau of the USAF* and U.S. Army in Washington, D.C. The ANG is a war reserve force for the federal government and a humanitarian force for aid in case of natural or man-caused civil emergencies in the states. When not federalized, which is to be mobilized into federal service, the ANG units are under the command of the state governors but have peacetime assignments to ten USAF major air commands* (MAJCOM) to assure their war readiness.

The ANG is roughly as old as the USAF; in 1909 the Missouri National Guard established a 15-man aero unit. The first air units to be federalized were called for the Mexican expedition of 1916.* Between World War I* and World War II,* the National Guard air squadrons increased from 2 in 1921 to 28 by 1941, while personnel rose from 110 to 3,426. These squadrons had an observation aviation* mission. Federalizing the guard squadrons began in 1940. By 1942, the USAAF* began to replace the obsolete observation aircraft with fighter,* attack,* and bomber* airplanes. Overseas movements began the same year. Inactivation of the Guard squadrons began in 1945.

The postwar ANG had staffing, equipment, and financial problems, but it was to prove effective in 1950 when the United States became involved in the Korean War.* Beginning in October, a total of 66 ANG squadrons were federalized. The ANG provided a major contribution to the strength of the USAF in the war. In the Vietnam War* the ANG contributed to the Vietnam Airlift.* Thirteen fighter squadrons were federalized in the USS *Pueblo* crisis. All mobilized units had returned to the states by 1969.

In 1974, the ANG became part of the Total Force Policy.* From 1946 to 1981, the ANG grew from 1 to 91 mission squadrons and from 108 to 98,293 personnel. In 1990 the ANG had 92 percent of the USAF interceptors,* 50 percent of the reconnaissance* force, 55 percent of the attack* aircraft, 38 percent of tactical airlift,* 24 percent of air superiority* fighters, 19 percent of aerial refueling* capability, 33 percent of air rescue* capability, and 6 percent of strategic airlift capability. The ANG also had units to provide support missions, including tactical control units, combat information, installation engineers, weather, and aircraft control and warning.* The personnel strength of the ANG in 1990 was 116,000. The ANG played an important role in the Iraq crisis of 1990–1991* and the Iraq War (1991).*

References. Primary: John B. Conaway, "The Global Guard," *AF*, September 1985, pp. 53–55, and "Soul of the Guard," *AF*, September 1984, pp. 93–95. Secondary: "Air National Guard," *AF*, May 1990, pp. 114–15. René Francillon, *The Air Guard*, 1982. Charles Joseph Gross, *Prelude to the Total Force: The Air National Guard 1943–1969*, 1985. U.S. Air Force Fact Sheet 86–22, "Air National Guard," July 1986.

AIR POLICE. *See* Air Force Office of Security Police.

AIR POWER. *See* aerospace power.

AIRPOWER JOURNAL

This periodical has been the professional journal of the USAF* since its beginning in 1987. The *Airpower Journal* succeeded the *Air University Quarterly Review* and the *Air University Review*, which were the USAF professional journals from 1947 to 1987. The name was changed in 1963 when the *Review* became a bimonthly publication. The *Review* contained feature-length articles on strategy, the role of air power, geopolitics, and military professionalism. In the late 1950s an emphasis on new technology and aviation concepts was added, reflecting the rapid technological changes in the military. By the 1960s a large number of management articles began to appear as well as entire issues devoted to specific topics. These "theme" issues included such topics as missile development, man-in-space, and logistics. By the early 1970s, politico-military issues and international relations began to dominate the article selection. Especially noteworthy in the *Review* was the coverage of the Korean* and Vietnam* Wars. The Korean coverage emphasized the use of air power in that conflict, including excellent photographic coverage. The Vietnam articles reflected the problems of dealing with insurgencies, the methods the USAF used in counterinsurgency, and the politico-military issues in the war.

In addition to the English-language edition, the *Review* was printed in Spanish and Portuguese beginning in 1949. These issues were distributed primarily to Latin America. The *Air University Review* ceased publication with the January–March 1987 issue.

The focus of the *Airpower Journal* is the operational level of war, emphasizing air power. As such it publishes articles on all aspects related to the leadership, training, maintenance, administrative and logistical support, and employment of combat power. The majority of authors are active-duty USAF officers. There are also occasional articles by civilian military experts, foreign military personnel, and people from other U.S. military services. The *Journal* is a function of the Airpower Research Institute, a part of the Center for Aerospace Doctrine, Research and Education, located at Maxwell* AFB, Alabama. In addition to the

English version, editions are published in Spanish and Portuguese on a biannual basis.

Michael A. Kirtland

AIR PROVING GROUND COMMAND

This organization was, at times, a major command* (MAJCOM). It was established originally as the Army Air Forces School of Applied Tactics (AAF-SAT) in 1942 at Orlando, Florida. It was redesignated as the AAF Tactical Center in 1943, AAF Center in 1945, AAF Proving Ground Command in 1946, and Air Proving Ground Command later in 1946. In 1945 it was moved to Eglin* Field, Florida. It was again redesignated Air Proving Ground in 1948 as part of the Air Materiel Command (AMC), ceasing to be a MAJCOM. Within months it was again a MAJCOM and resumed the name of Air Proving Command in 1951. In 1957 it was redesignated Air Proving Ground Center, lost MAJCOM status, and went under the Air Research and Development Command (ARDC). It became the Armament Development and Test Center in 1968 and the Armament Division in 1979.

During World War II* the center had 8,000 square miles near Orlando available for its activities. It trained cadres from operational units to form new units. It also conducted more than 40 short courses in subjects such as tactical inspection, combat intelligence, and photo interpretation. By mid–1944 it had trained more than 35,000 persons. The center also tested new tactics and techniques. By mid–1944 about 500 tactical tests had been made. After the war, testing continued under simulated battle conditions. The tests included flying and maintenance circumstances.

References. *AAF: A Directory, Almanac and Chronicle of Achievement*, 1944. Goldberg, *Hist. USAF*. Ravenstein, *Org. USAF*.

AIR RESCUE. *See* rescue.

AIR RESEARCH AND DEVELOPMENT COMMAND. *See* Air Force Systems Command.

AIR RESERVE PERSONNEL CENTER (ARPC)

The ARPC is a special operating agency* (SOA). It was established as the Air Reserve Records Center in 1956 and was activated in 1957 under the Continental Air Command* (CONAC). It was redesignated as the ARPC in 1965. When CONAC was inactivated in 1968, the ARPC became an SOA. In 1978 it was reassigned to the U.S. Air Force Reserve* (USAFR) and lost its SOA status until 1983. It is headquartered in Denver, Colorado. The ARPC performs personnel support for the mobilization and demobilization of the Air National Guard* (ANG), USAFR, and retired members of those organizations.

References. "Air Reserve Personnel Center," *AF*, May 1990, pp. 111–12. Ravenstein, *Org. USAF*. Roberts, *Dir. USAF*.

AIR RESERVE TECHNICIAN PROGRAM

This program was implemented in 1958 as a means of improving the combat readiness of U.S. Air Force Reserve* (USAFR) units. Before that time the USAF* had tried various management systems for the administration and training of USAFR units, but none had been satisfactory. Air Reserve Technicians are key full-time civilian employees of the USAFR units who are also members of the unit. Among other jobs, they occupy commander, operations, and maintenance positions. In addition to training their fellow reservists on weekends and on active duty, they provide the units an administrative continuity that had been lacking. In 1988 there were about 8,000 Air Reserve Technicians authorized in the USAFR, and three-fourths of them worked in aircraft maintenance.

Reference. U.S. Air Force Fact Sheet 86–29, "United States Air Force Reserve," September 1986.

Gerald T. Cantwell

AIR SERVICE COMMAND. *See* Air Force Logistics Command.

AIR SERVICE TACTICAL SCHOOL. *See* Air Corps Tactical School.

AIRSHIPS. *See* lighter-than-air.

AIR STAFF

The Air Staff is a headquarters group that advises and assists the top leadership of the USAF:* the secretary of the Air Force,* the under secretary and assistant secretaries of the Air Force, and the chief of staff of the Air Force.* It consists of the chief of staff, vice chief of staff, assistant vice chief of staff, up to four deputy chiefs of staff, and others as assigned. The Air Staff was created along with the USAAF* and began functioning in 1942.

References. Primary: Laurence F. Kuter, "The General vs. the Establishment: General H. H. Arnold and the Air Staff," *AH*, December 1974, pp. 185–89. Secondary: Goldberg, *Hist. USAF*. Woodford Agee Heflin, ed., *The United States Air Force Dictionary*, 1956. L. F. Loesch and C. R. Low, "Air Force Headquarters: Its Mission and Organization," *Air University Quarterly Review*, Summer 1956, pp. 102–9. U.S. Air Force Fact Sheet 89–05, "Organization of the United States Air Force," February 1989.

AIR STATION. *See* air force bases.

AIR SUPERIORITY

In 1984, the USAF* created a broad air superiority doctrine. "Aerospace" forces suggest a war in space, conventional air operations, and the doctrines governing those possibilities. Wherever the conflict, air superiority is the first priority of the USAF. It is to be obtained through either strategic or tactical operations.* The purpose of such operations is to deny the enemy use of its own air space, while allowing U.S. aircraft the freedom to accomplish their tasks. Control can be temporary or, less likely, permanent.

Air superiority, in its modern sense, arose from USAF fighter* experiences in World War II.* The evolution of the strategic operations concept during the 1930s denied the need for fighter protection of bombers,* thus consigning the U.S. pursuit aviation arm to a point defense mission. World War II increasingly drove home the need to control the skies so that both aerial and surface missions could be accomplished. In the European theater of operations (ETO), air superiority over battlefields was won as early as 1943. Air superiority over the heart of Germany was won in March 1944 by long-range fighters like the F-51.* They not only intercepted enemy aircraft attempting to hit U.S. bombers but also swept ahead of the bomber stream and destroyed German fighters on or near airfields. In the Pacific area, the USAAF* used fighter escort* with bomber missions to reduce and then eradicate enemy airfields, clearing the way for subsequent invasion. The U.S. Navy fighters gained temporary air superiority over scattered Japanese-held islands and then shattered local enemy air units. Air superiority over the heart of Japan itself was won in the spring of 1945 by F-51s operating from Iwo Jima.

In both the Korean War* and the Vietnam War,* U.S. air power flew against weaker enemy flying arms and obtained air superiority by compelling communist forces to fight for their own air space and defend their military assets. In each war, this gave friendly surface forces freedom of action, unaffected by hostile air interference.

Given increasingly deadly antiaircraft capabilities and the rising costs of airplanes, debate continues on where and what craft best fits the air superiority role. One school contends that the mission can be accomplished on the forward edge of battle by tactical strikes of more numerous but less expensive aircraft. The other suggests the more traditional deep penetration attack against enemy airfields and staging areas. This would require fewer, highly sophisticated fighters capable of surviving in a high-threat environment. Recent designs suggest a balanced force capable of both approaches, but in the Iraq War* the traditional deep penetration gave the USAF air superiority after only a few hours of action.

References. Thomas H. Greer, *The Development of Air Doctrine in the Army Air Arm, 1917–1941*, 1955. Richard H. Kohn and Joseph P. Harahan, *Air Superiority in World War II and Korea*, 1983. Albert F. Simpson, "Tactical Air Doctrine: Tunisia and Korea," *Air University Quarterly Review*, Summer 1951, pp. 4–20. U.S. Air Force, *Basic Aerospace Doctrine of the United States Air Force*, Air Force Manual 1–1, 1984. William D. White, *U.S. Tactical Air Power: Missions, Forces, and Costs*, 1974.

See also political air superiority; Red Flag.

Ronald W. Yoshino

AIR-TO-AIR MISSILE. *See* air interceptor missile; AIM-4; AIM-7; AIM-9; AIM-120; AIR-2A.

AIR-TO-GROUND MISSILE (AGM)

AGMs are a class of aircraft-launched missiles designed for the destruction of surface or subsurface targets. They are composed of an engine, control surfaces, a warhead, a fuzing and firing section, and a guidance and control unit.

The AGM was another development of German science during World War II,*
but the United States was not far behind with its AZON* missiles. Modern
defenses against warplanes suggest that attack* from a distance by AGMSs will
be the preferred method for the foreseeable future.

AGMs can best be described by their guidance methods. Large cruise missiles*
use inertial guidance with or without mid-course correction for sea targets or
inertial and map matching for land targets. Tactical missiles use several guidance
systems. One of the most common is energy homing that targets emissions from
enemy radios or radars.* Television guidance is frequently used. An on-board
missile camera acquires the target and the operator can either guide it manually
or let it guide itself to the target. Infrared is another common method, either as
a straight heat seeker or as a thermal imaging system. Heat seekers home in on
the heat emitted by objects. Thermal imaging is similar to television guidance,
except that the image on the screen is taken from the heat of the target, not the
light reflected from it. Infrared is very useful in the adverse weather normally
encountered over western Europe. The last system in common use is radar with
an on-board system to pick out the target. It is used, with or without mid-course
correction, on antiship missiles. AGMs may use multiple guidance systems,
sometimes interchangeably, on the same missile to meet different target and
weather conditions.

The warhead carried depends on the target. Large missiles use either nuclear
or high-explosive devices. Antitank missiles use a shaped charge warhead. Antipersonnel and material (APAM) and antipersonnel (APER) missiles have high-
explosive, incendiary, or chemical warheads and are used against targets such
as bunkers, soft-skinned vehicles, and infantry.

References. Bill Gunston and Lindsay Peacock, *Fighter Missions*, 1989. Kenneth P.
Werrell, *The Evolution of the Cruise Missile*, 1985.

See AGM-12; AGM-28; AGM-45; AGM-65; AGM-69; AGM-78; AGM-84A-1; AGM-
86B; AGM-88A; AGM-129A; AGM-131A; AGM-136A.

Philip Long

AIR TRAINING COMMAND (ATC)

In 1943, the major command* (MAJCOM) now recognized as the ATC came
into existence with the merger of the Technical Training and Flying Training
Commands. Born of necessity to save manpower, the command became responsible for all training from classification center through pilot and technical
schools. The command appeared "full grown" in World War II* with more
than a million men and 600 training installations. Command headquarters shifted
at various times from Ft. Worth, Texas, to bases at Barksdale,* Louisiana;
Scott,* Illinois; and finally to Randolph* Field, Texas, where it remains today.
Its mission and strength have fluctuated, depending upon the era. Basically,
however, the ATC provided new people in the USAF* with what they needed
of military, technical, flight training,* and precommissioning education. The
ATC's motto is "the first command," because it is the initial organization that
every person entering the USAF experiences.

In 1990, the ATC included six technical training centers; six pilot* training bases and advanced navigation at a seventh; survival training conducted in various locations; training units at some 90 locations; and headquarters of the Air Force Reserve Officer Training Corps* (AFROTC) at Maxwell* AFB, Alabama. The command not only recruits through its Air Force Recruiting Service but follows each recruit through a six-week basic military training course at Lackland* AFB, Texas. It provides technical training with some 350 specialties available in more than 3,000 formal training courses. The command is responsible for some fairly diversified activities including a corrections and rehabilitation program at Lowry* AFB, Colorado, and an integrated on- and off-duty education effort that leads to an associate degree in applied science. At Sheppard* AFB, Texas, medical services training is conducted with departments in dentistry, medicine, nursing, biomedical science, and health services administration. Other functions include occupational analysis, to ensure that airman promotion tests identify the most qualified for promotion, and teaching the English language to foreign students.

References. "Air Training Command," *AF*, May 1990, pp. 68–69. Lloyd H. Cornett, Jr., "Air Training Command Organization: A 30-Year View 1943–1974," unpub. ms., 1974. John T. Correll, "Tradition and Change in ATC," *AF*, December 1988, pp. 40–44. U.S. Air Force Fact Sheets 83–34, 85–6, and 88–3, "Air Training Command," October 1983, April 1985, and February 1988.

Lloyd H. Cornett, Jr.

AIR TRANSPORT COMMAND (ATC). *See* Military Airlift Command.

AIR UNIVERSITY (AU)

Headquartered at Maxwell* AFB, Alabama, this unique major command* (MAJCOM) has served as the USAF's* center for professional military education since its activation in 1946. It has evolved as a leader in researching and managing designated fields of aerospace study and in developing and testing USAF doctrine, concepts, and strategy. The command's specialized and degree-granting programs have given the USAF more than 40 years of academic growth in the scientific, technological, managerial, and other professional disciplines. About 12,000 military and civilians complete resident AU classes annually, with thousands more completing nonresident seminar and correspondence courses.

AU's schools are centered at Maxwell, where it administers the Air War College (AWC) for senior officers, the Air Command and Staff College (AFSC) for mid-career officers, and Squadron Officer School for company grade officers. The command also has the Center for Professional Development (CPD); the Center for Aerospace Doctrine, Research, and Education (CADRE); the Air University Library (AUL); and the USAF's support for the Civil Air Patrol* (CAP) at Maxwell. The Extension Course Institute (ECI) and the Air Force Senior Noncommissioned Officer Academy operate from nearby Gunter* AFB, Alabama. The Air Force Institute of Technology (AFIT), another dimension of AU, is at Wright-Patterson* AFB, Ohio.

A primary goal of AU's diverse mission is to advance the war-fighting knowledge of the USAF. In addition to its air warfare curriculum, the command has been a key participant in efforts to preserve and evaluate the USAF's combat experience in both the Korean War* and the Vietnam War.* Of particular value was project Corona Harvest's* comprehensive, USAF-wide program of documenting and examining the role of air power in Southeast Asia. Recent contributions to the USAF's war-fighting skills have come from such programs as the chief of staff of the Air Force*–directed Senior Officer Employment Course, developed and offered by the CADRE staff at Maxwell, and the new Air Force Wargaming Center (AFWC), also managed by CADRE. The Air Power Institute under CADRE conducts an ongoing program to research and publish professional studies on low-intensity conflict and nuclear deterrence and war-fighting issues. There is also a newly created Combat Employment Institute which conducts courses in combined air warfare and contingency and wartime planning.

References. Air University Fact Sheet, December 1987. "Air University," *AF*, May 1990, pp. 72–73. Futrell, *Ideas*, vol. 2. U.S. Air Force Fact Sheet 88–1, "Air University," January 1988.

Warren A. Trest

AIR UNIVERSITY QUARTERLY REVIEW. See Airpower Journal.

AIR UNIVERSITY REVIEW. See Airpower Journal.

AIR WAR PLANS DIVISION (AWPD)
The initial task of the AWPD was the formulation of AWPD-1,* the "air war plan that defeated Germany." The AWPD was established on 20 June 1941 as part of the Air Staff* under Army Regulation (AR) 95–5,* which created the USAAF.* The first chief of AWPD was Colonel Harold L. George,* who had been chief of the Bombardment Section of the Air Corps Tactical School.* Although neither AR 95–5 nor the Marshall Reorganization of 2–9 March 1942 gave AWPD autonomy, for practical purposes AWPD became the agency for USAAF plans and, after 1942, the Army War Plans Division made ground forces plans.

References. Primary: Haywood S. Hansell, Jr., *The Air War Plan That Defeated Germany*, 1972. Secondary: C&C, vol. 1.

Lester H. Brune

AIRWAYS AND AIR COMMUNICATIONS SERVICE. *See* Air Force Communications Command.

AIR WEATHER SERVICE
This subordinate unit of the Military Airlift Command* (MAC) provides worldwide weather services to the USAF,* U.S. Army, and other agencies. Weather has always been a factor in military operations, but it is a crucial one in aerial activities. This was recognized in 1937 when the War Department transferred weather support of its aviation from the Signal Corps to the USAAC.*

Its importance is shown by its global World War II* operations, when, at one time, it had 900 locations with 19,000 personnel. In 1946, the service became part of the Air Transport Command (ATC), the antecedent organization of MAC. In 1989 it had about 5,000 personnel at more than 260 locations.

References. Primary: Robert Lee Clark, "Flight into Camille," *AH*, June 1982, pp. 74–80. Secondary: John F. Fuller, "Weather and War," *AH*, March 1976, pp. 24–27. "Military Airlift Command," *AF*, May 1990, pp. 76, 78. U.S. Air Force Fact Sheet 87–21, "Air Weather Service," April 1987.

ALASKAN AIR COMMAND (AAC)

The AAC had its genesis in World War II.* The Alaskan Air Force was activated at Elmendorf* Field, Alaska, in January 1942. In February it was redesignated the Eleventh Air Force* (11AF) and served in the offensive to liberate the Aleutians* from the Japanese. It attacked the Kuril Islands, and both during the war and later formed part of the defense of Alaska. In December 1945, the AAC was formed from the 11AF. It is interesting to note that a new 11AF was formed as part of the Air Defense Command (ADC) and assigned to the new AAC from 1946 to 1948. In 1990, the AAC reverted again to being the 11AF. The AAC's motto was "Top Cover for America."

The AAC was a major command* (MAJCOM). It provided air defense to part of North America under the North American Aerospace Defense Command* (NORAD). It had three AFBs in Alaska: Elmendorf, Eielson,* and Shemya.* Its fighters* operated out of Alaskan forward fields at King Salmon and Galena airports. Galena is the fighter base on U.S. soil that was closest to the USSR. The AAC operated a long-range intercept with teams consisting of two F-15s,* an E-3A,* and a KC-135 (*see* C-135). They routinely intercepted Soviet bombers* probing U.S. airspace. In addition, aircraft control and warning* (AC&W) squadrons were on the Alaskan west coast and strategically placed in the interior.

The AAC had operational control of C-130s,* HC-130s, and HH-3s (*see* H-3) used in the region by the Military Airlift Command* (MAC). An AAC Rescue Coordination Center directed USAF,* Army, Air National Guard (ANG),* and Civil Air Patrol* (CAP) aircraft for search and rescue* and emergency evacuation missions. A combat support group in the AAC provided air liaison officers and forward air controllers* (FAC) in support of Army operations. Several joint exercises have been conducted in Alaska annually. The terrain and environment are similar to that found in 65 percent of the USSR, all of Siberia, much of Red China, and North Korea. The AAC supported these exercises.

In the event of a natural disaster, emergency, or hostilities other than aerospace defense, the AAC commander reported to the Joint Chiefs of Staff (JCS) through the Joint Task Force (JTF). Normally, the AAC commander headed the JTF, which is composed of all U.S. forces stationed in Alaska. The commander in chief of the U.S. Readiness Command at MacDill* AFB, Florida, delegated the responsibility for developing the JTF-Alaska plan to the AAC. In 1990 the AAC reported to the Alaskan Command. This is a subordinate command reporting to

Pacific Air Forces* (PACAF). In this role, the Alaskan Command augmented the war-fighting capabilities of PACAF.

References. "Alaskan Air Command," *AF*, May 1990, pp. 73–74. John Haile Cloe and Michael F. Monaghan, *Top Cover for America: The Air Force in Alaska 1920–1983*, 1984. Craig Covault, "Alaskan Air Command," *AWST*, 8 May 1988, pp. 34–55; 16 May 1988, pp. 50–57; and 23 May 1988, pp. 34–42. Maurer Maurer, *Air Force Combat Units of World War II*, 1983. U.S. Air Force Fact Sheet 87–28, "Alaskan Air Command," July 1987.

Alwyn T. Lloyd

ALASKAN FLIGHT OF 1934

Ten B-10* bombers* flew a round trip of 7,360 miles from Washington, D.C., to Fairbanks, Alaska, and returned, the outstanding flight of the year 1934. While USAAC* leaders hoped the flight would counteract the unfavorable publicity of the airmail flights of 1934,* the official mission was to photograph 23,000 acres of Alaska for suitable landing areas, to design emergency plans to defend Alaska, and to demonstrate frontier defense by aviation.

The flight was led by Lieutenant Colonel H. H. Arnold,* but the success can also be attributed to his executive officer, Major Hugh J. Knerr.* Knerr prepared the planes for the trip at Wright Field, Ohio. Most of the B-10s had been modified for airmail use and had to revert to original status, while several had to be readied to carry necessary photographic equipment. The entire trip went unusually well. The planes left on 9 July and arrived in Fairbanks on 24 July. In Alaska there was a delay due to weather that was bad for photography. The photo equipment had been shipped overland, and, after being mounted on three planes, three days were spent photographing the surrounding regions. The return began on 16 August. Arnold scheduled a 980-mile flight across the Pacific Ocean from Juneau, Alaska, to Seattle, Washington, an event criticized by Navy officers who claimed USAAC planes had no missions beyond 100 miles of the coastline. The Pacific trip succeeded and on 20 August the planes arrived home at Bolling* Field, where a crowd of dignitaries awaited them.

Although the flight received excellent publicity for the USAAC and aviation, it had an unfortunate postscript when many of the 14 officers on the trip blamed Arnold for the War Department's failure to recognize their achievement properly. Arnold received the MacKay Trophy for leading 1934's greatest aviation feat, but the U.S. Army brass hats made the event an "official failure." Fearing a revival of a "Mitchell*-like" attack on Army and Navy leaders, Chief of Staff General Douglas MacArthur rejected Arnold's recommendation that all officers on the flight receive the Distinguished Flying Cross (DFC). MacArthur allowed only one commendation letter, and that was for Arnold. Arnold appealed the decision but was turned down again.

Arnold's efforts remained in secret files for more than 30 years while most of the Alaskan flight officers blamed him for their lack of recognition. It did not help when MacArthur's successor, General Malin Craig, awarded Arnold a DFC. In 1971, Knerr applied to the USAF* Board for the Correction of Military

Records to recognize the Alaskan flight for all involved officers. Knerr submitted declassified documents on the 1934 events, but the board denied his appeal. Knerr died in 1971 before the board ruled.

References. Primary: Hugh J. Knerr, "Washington to Alaska and Back: Memories of the 1934 U.S. Air Corps Test Flight," *AH*, April 1972, pp. 20–24. Secondary: DeWitt S. Copp, *A Few Great Captains: The Men and Events That Shaped the Development of U.S. Air Power*, 1980. Murray Green, "The Alaskan Flight of 1934—A Spectacular Official Failure," *AH*, March 1977, pp. 15–19.

See also Alaskan Air Command; Army-Navy agreements of 1931 and 1938.

Lester H. Brune

ALBATROSS. *See* U-16.

ALCM. *See* AGM-86B.

ALCONBURY. *See* RAF Alconbury.

ALDRIDGE, SECRETARY EDWARD C., JR., "PETE" (1938–   )

Appointed 17th secretary of the Air Force* (SAF) (1986–1988), Aldridge's distinguished career in aerospace industry and government made him uniquely qualified to serve the USAF* during a time of accentuation in strategic modernization programs and in mutual force reductions between the United States and the USSR.

Aldridge joined the Department of Defense (DoD) as an operations research analyst in 1967, rising quickly to the position of director of the Strategic Defense Initiative* (SDI), where he also served as an adviser to the Strategic Arms Limitation Talks (SALT) in Helsinki, Finland, and Vienna, Austria. He previously held managerial positions with the Douglas Aircraft Company's Missile Space Division in Santa Monica, California, and in Washington, D.C. In 1972 he left government to become a senior manager with LTV Aerospace Corporation, returning the next year as senior management associate in the Office of Management and Budget, Executive Office of the President. The following year, Aldridge was selected as deputy assistant secretary of defense for strategic programs, then became a principal adviser to the secretary of defense (SECDEF) in the planning and program evaluation of U.S. military forces and support structure. Aldridge reentered private industry in 1977 as vice president of the National Policy and Strategic Systems Group for the System Planning Corporation in Arlington, Virginia. He was responsible for the corporation's study and analysis activities in the areas of strategic and conventional forces and long-range strategic planning.

In August 1981, he became under secretary of the Air Force with responsibility for guiding and directing USAF space programs, including launch and on-orbit operations, and planning for future space capabilities. His expert handling of these responsibilities completed Aldridge's grooming for the appointment as SAF. His knowledge of the strategic modernization program and its "obvious influence" on nuclear arms negotiations was crucial for today's and tomorrow's USAF. This modernization, which stressed the full complement of B-1* bombers,* Peacekeeper* intercontinental ballistic missiles* (ICBM), and future systems like the B-2,* was endangered by stringent budgets imposed in the final months of the Reagan* administration. Aldridge's priorities during this period of stress was to keep the USAF from being badly damaged, while insuring that readiness was maintained at current or improved levels. He stated his first leadership priority was to improve the USAF quality of life, concluding that this was essential to the retention of an able force. Budget cuts demanded that the force be reduced, but Aldridge promised that the end result would be a ready and modern USAF.

References. Primary: "Airman's Interview," *Airman*, April 1988, pp. 8, 9. Secondary: James W. Canan, "Storm Flags on the Budget Front," *AF*, January 1988, pp. 98–104. U.S. Air Force Biography, "Edward C. Aldridge, Jr.," June 1986.

Warren A. Trest

ALEUTIANS

Battle operations in the Aleutians lasted 15 months and were the only ones on North American soil in World War II.* The climate and weather of the area were a special challenge to the USAAF,* being the worst for flying in the world. Strong winds, cold temperatures, frequent precipitation, and fog were normal problems. The USAAC* had long believed Alaska was a critical location, as shown by the Alaskan flight of 1934,* but there were almost no airfields until 1941. The Aleutian campaign brought the USAF* to Alaska to stay. In 1990, the Eleventh Air Force* (11AF) had three major bases there, including Shemya* AFB in the Aleutians.

On 3 June 1942, the Japanese struck at Dutch Harbor, in the Aleutians, as a diversion from their move against Midway Island. A few days later they seized Attu and Kiska Islands. To attack these Japanese garrisons, airfields were built on Adak and Amchitka Islands. An air and sea blockade of the Japanese bases was undertaken. The USAAF designated its units as the 11AF.

In May 1943 Attu was retaken. Airfields were then built on Attu and Shemya Islands, and the 11AF made the first attacks on Japanese territory since the Doolittle raid on Tokyo.* The targets were in Paramushiro in the Kuril Islands, and 1,500 sorties were flown against that area by the end of the war. The Japanese evacuated Kiska before the Americans landed to retake it. The USAAF operated P-38s,* P-39s,* P-40s,* B-17s,* B-18s,* B-24s,* and B-26 Marauders* in the campaign. The 11AF flew about 4,000 combat sorties and dropped 3,500 tons of bombs. It lost 40 planes in battle and 174 otherwise, mostly to unfavorable weather. Its top strength was 359 planes. About 70 Japanese aircraft were destroyed in the air and on the ground.

References. C&C, vols. 1 and 4. John L. Frisbee, "The Forgotten Front," *AF*, February 1984, pp. 96–101. Brian Garfield, *The Thousand-Mile War: World War II in Alaska and the Aleutians*, 1969.

ALLEN, GENERAL LEW, JR. (1925–   )

Allen was the tenth chief of staff of the Air Force* (1978–1982). During his tenure, the AGM-86* and F-16* entered service, the B-1B* program began, and the Air Force Space Command* (AFSPACECOM) was created.

Born in Gainesville, Texas, he was a 1946 U.S. Military Academy (USMA) graduate, attended the University of Illinois for graduate training in nuclear physics, and received a master of science degree in 1952 and a doctorate in 1954. He was then assigned to the Los Alamos Scientific Laboratory of the Atomic Energy Commission (AEC), where he served as a physicist in the test division. Allen conducted experiments relating to the physics of thermonuclear weapons design and to the effects of high-altitude nuclear detonations on ballistic missile* defense. He has held the following positions: vice chief of staff, 1978; commander, Air Force Systems Command* (AFSC), 1977–1978; director, National Security Agency; chief, Central Security Service; deputy to director of central intelligence for the intelligence community, 1973; chief of staff, AFSC, 1973; director of special projects, with additional duty as deputy commander for satellite programs, Space and Missiles Systems Organization (SAMSO); and assistant to director of space projects, Office of the Secretary of the Air Force,* Los Angeles, 1970–1971. Following retirement from the USAF in 1982, he became director of the Jet Propulsion Laboratory (JPL) in Pasadena, California.

References. Primary: USAF Oral History Interview K239.0512–1694, 8–10 January 1986, USAFHRC/OH, Maxwell AFB, Alabama. Secondary: Air Force Pamphlet (AFP) 31–1, Roster of Retired General Officers, 1987. Futrell, *Ideas*, vol. 2. U.S. Air Force Biography, Secretary of the Air Force, Office of Information, 1978. Bill Yenne, *The History of the US Air Force*, 1984.

James C. Hasdorff

ALLISON ENGINES

James Allison founded the Allison Engineering Company in the early 1920s. At first, the firm modified Liberty engines.* The company started development of its own in-line engine in the 1930s. Before the engine was completed, the firm was sold to Edward V. Rickenbacker.* In turn, Rickenbacker sold it to General Motors, where it became the Allison Division. Later the name was changed to Detroit Diesel Allison Division. The new engine became the effective V-1710. It was reaching final development at a time when the USAAC* decided that in-line engines would have less drag than radials and so would be preferable engines for fighters.* Rated at 1,250 horsepower, the V-1710 was used for the F-51,* F-82,* P-38,* P-39,* P-40,* and P-63.* Allison has continued to compete in the manufacture of aircraft engines into the jet age. Its turbojet J-35 was used in F-84s* and F-89s.* The J-35 had thrust from 4,000 to over 5,400 pounds. Its J-71, with 10,000 pounds of thrust, was used in the B-66.* Its TF-41, with 14,500 pounds of thrust, powers the A-7.* Allison's most successful engine has been the turboprop T-56 of 4,050 horsepower used in the C-130.*

References. Stanley W. Kandebo, "Allison Plans Flight Tests of Turboprop GMA 2100," *AWST*, 19 February 1990, pp. 36–37, 39. "50th Anniversary Issue," a special issue of *Flying*, September 1977, pp. 241–47. James E. Knott, "They Pulled 'em Through," *AH*, Autumn 1969, pp. 48–51. Herschel Smith, *Aircraft Piston Engines: From the Manly Balzer to the Continental Tiara*, corrected ed., 1986.

ALL-WEATHER FIGHTER. *See* interceptor.

ALL-WEATHER FLYING CENTER (AWFC)

The ability to fly in all types of weather has always been a USAF* need. In 1946, the AWFC was established at Clinton County Army Air Field in Wilmington, Ohio. It was operated by the All Weather Flying Division of the Air Materiel Command (AMC). The center moved to Wright-Patterson* AFB in 1949 and disbanded in 1953. Techniques were developed by flying through and around storms. The tests were conducted until 1949 in conjunction with the National Weather Service and the National Advisory Committee for Aeronautics (NACA). A daily all-weather airline operation was flown between Clinton County and Andrews* AFB, Maryland, during 1948. A complete record of the weather and its effects upon flyability and scheduling was made.

References. Primary: Unit History, "AWFC at Clinton County AAFld, AFSHRC," 1949. Secondary: F. Barrows Colton, "New Frontier in the Sky," *National Geographic*, September 1946, pp. 387–88. Alwyn T. Lloyd, *B-17 Flying Fortress in Detail & Scale*, part 3, 1986.

Alwyn T. Lloyd

ALTUS AIR FORCE BASE

This base in Oklahoma was established in 1942 for flight training* because of its favorable weather. Called Altus Army Air Field (AAF), a basic class was graduated every four and one-half weeks. At the end of World War II,* Altus was declared surplus, made inactive, and became Altus Municipal Airport. Because of the Korean War,* it was reactivated on 1 August 1953 for the Tactical Air Command* (TAC). The 63rd Troop Carrier Wing, operating T-11 and C-47* aircraft in support of U.S. Army airborne and combat supply, was based there. Late in 1953, the Strategic Air Command* (SAC) took over the base and assigned to it the 96th Bombardment Wing.

On 1 July 1968, the SAC tuned over host responsibilities for the base to the Military Airlift Command* (MAC), which transferred its strategic airlift training unit to Altus from Tinker* AFB. Since then the 443rd Military Airlift Wing, flying both C-5* and C-141* transport aircraft, has continued to provide specialized training for MAC crews.

References. Mueller, *AFB*. Charles A. Ravenstein, *Air Force Combat Wings: Lineage and Honors Histories, 1947–1977*, 1984. Esther B. Renfro, *A History of Altus Air Force Base, 1942–1988*, 1988. Roberts, *Dir. USAF*.

Roger D. Launius

AMC. *See* Air Force Logistics Command.

AMERICAN BALLOON BUSTER, THE. *See* Luke, Second Lieutenant Frank, Jr.

AMERICAN-BRITISH-CANADIAN PLAN 1 (ABC-1). *See* AWPD-1.

AMERICAN VOLUNTEER GROUP (AVG)

In the winter of 1940–1941, President Franklin D. Roosevelt* authorized the formation of a covert U.S. air force to fight for China in the Sino-Japanese War. Two fighter* groups and one medium bomber* group were planned. To equip the first of these, 100 Tomahawk IIB fighters, equivalent to the USAAC's* P-40C,* were diverted from British order. One hundred U.S. military pilots* and 200 technicians resigned to accept private employment with the AVG. Under the command of a retired USAAC officer, Captain Claire L. Chennault,* the 1st AVG trained in neutral Burma but did not see combat until after the Japanese breakout in December 1941. With the United States at war, the follow-on groups were canceled and Chennault's volunteers were celebrated as "Flying Tigers" by journalists hungry for good news. They played a major part in the defense of Burma until the Allied rout in May 1942 and in holding western China until reinforcements reached the Chungking government later that year. Formally disbanded on 4 July 1942, the AVG was merged into the 23rd Pursuit Group of the USAAF.* Only five pilots accepted induction in China, though many later rejoined the military, including Medal of Honor winners James Howard of the USAAF and Gregory "Pappy" Boyington of the U.S. Marine Corps.

The Tigers were credited with destroying 297 Japanese aircraft at a cost of 23 men killed or captured. Recent research indicates that the AVG's victories were considerably inflated, but it remains the only Allied fighting unit to have compiled a winning record against the Japanese armed forces in the winter of 1941–1942. The AVG finally achieved veteran status in 1991.

References. Charles Bond and Terry Anderson, *A Flying Tiger's Diary*, 1984. Martha Byrd, *Chennault*, 1987. Daniel Ford, *Flying Tigers: Claire Chennault and the American Volunteer Group*, forthcoming. Japanese Defense Agency, *Nampo shinko rikugun koku sakusen*, 1970.

See also Fourteenth Air Force.

Daniel Ford

AMRAAM. *See* AIM-120.

AMST. *See* Advanced Medium STOL Transport.

ANDERSEN AIR FORCE BASE

A historic airfield, Andersen is on Guam. It was named for Brigadier General James Roy Andersen, who died in an aircraft accident in 1946. Work on it began in late 1944 while the area still abounded with Japanese corpses. Its first name was North Field. In February 1945, B-29* operations against Japan were begun from it by the 314th Bombardment Wing (Very Heavy). Twenty years later, in 1965, Arc Light* operations began out of Andersen with B-52s.* Operations were continuing in 1970, when Eighth Air Force* (8AF) headquarters was moved from Westover AFB, Massachusetts, to Andersen. In 1972, B-52s from the base participated in Linebacker* II. Vietnam War* operations ended in 1973, and, in 1975, BAF headquarters moved out of Andersen. In 1990, Andersen was a Pacific Air Forces* (PACAF) base having the 43rd Bomb Wing with B-52s and KC-135s (see C-135).

References. C&C, vols. 5 and 7. "Guide to Major Air Force Installations Worldwide," *AF*, May 1989, p. 152. Polmar, *SAC*. Roberts, *Dir. USAF*.

ANDREWS, LIEUTENANT GENERAL FRANK M. (1884–1943)

Andrews was one of the great founding fathers of the USAF.* His career ended tragically in a 1943 plane crash. He was inducted into the National Aviation Hall of Fame in Dayton, Ohio, in 1986.

Born in Nashville, Tennessee, and a U.S. Military Academy (USMA) graduate in 1906, he served as a cavalry officer before entering the air service in 1917. After pilot* training, he spent World War I* as a training officer in the United States. During the 1920s he had a number of routine postings. By the end of the decade, Andrews had graduated from both the Air Corps Tactical School* (ACTS) and the Command and General Staff School. Andrews rose to prominence in the 1930s. After a staff tour in Washington, D.C., he attended the Army War College there, graduating in 1933. He commanded the 1st Pursuit Group at Selfridge* Field, Michigan, until his 1934 recall to Washington, D.C., to help draft plans for the new General Headquarters Air Force* (GHQ Air Force). In 1935, Andrews was promoted two grades to brigadier general and took command of the GHQ Air Force, the USAAC's* only independent combat unit.

As GHQ Air Force commander, Andrews told his subordinates that deeds rather than words would win the argument for independence. His airmen drew public attention to military aviation in a number of exercises, including the 1938 mock attack by B-17s* in the *Rex* interception.* Andrews saw the B-17 as the key to developing a strategic operations* force. His advocacy of the four-engined bomber* over the B-18* cost him an appointment as chief of the USAAC. In 1939 he was exiled to a minor post in San Antonio, Texas, in his permanent grade of colonel. His exile was short-lived. General George C. Marshall, the new U.S. Army chief of staff, brought him to Washington, D.C., as assistant chief of staff for operations and training. Here Andrews presided over the prewar expansion and training of both ground and air forces. He left this post in 1941 and served successively as commander of the Panama Canal Air Force, the Caribbean Defense Command, and the European theater of operations.

References. Primary: Ira Eaker, "Lt. Gen. Frank M. Andrews," *AF*, September 1980, pp. 102–4. Secondary: John L. Frisbee, *Makers of the United States Air Force*, 1987. Maurer, *Avn. in Army*. Mark S. Watson, *Chief of Staff: Prewar Plans and Preparations*, in the series *United States Army in World War II*, 1950.

John R. Reese

ANDREWS AIR FORCE BASE

Andrews was first established as Camp Springs Army Air Field (AAF), Maryland, in 1942. Only 12 miles east of Washington, D.C., its reason for existence in World War II* was air defense of the capital. It became operational in 1943 with F-47* fighters.* It was named for the late Lieutenant General Frank M. Andrews* in 1945.

Andrews has served largely as a headquarters base since then. Its operational capacity was curtailed following World War II, and it successively served between 1945 and the present as the home of the Continental Air Command* (CONAC), Strategic Air Command* (SAC), Military Air Transport Service (MATS), and the Air Force Systems Command* (AFSC), still there in 1990. In 1961 the last of the special air mission (SAM) units supporting the president and high government executives transferred there from Washington National Airport. A year later all fixed wing flying activities were transferred from nearby Bolling* AFB. In 1963, the Navy's special air missions moved from Anacostia, D.C., to Andrews. Since that time, Andrews has become firmly established as the main aerial port of entry for foreign military and government officials en route to or from the United States.

Currently, Andrews is the headquarters of the 89th Military Airlift Wing, which provides special mission support to the nation's leaders. Its three flying squadrons operate several different types of executive aircraft. The main one is the VC-25A (*see* C-25) known as Air Force One, which supports the presidential airlift.* The 4,322-acre base is the workplace for more than 24,000 military and civilian employees. It has more than 20 separate Military Airlift Command* (MAC) units, the host organization, and 30 tenant units.

References. Raymond D. Baker, *Flight of Excellence: A Chronology of SAM FOX, A 40th Anniversary*, 1988. "Guide to Major Air Force Installations Worldwide," *AF*, May 1990, p. 122. Mueller, *AFB*. Roberts, *Dir. USAF*.

Roger D. Launius

ANG. *See* Air National Guard.

ANGLE OF ATTACK. See novels.

ANTIAIRCRAFT (AA) (AAA). *See* flak.

ANTISUBMARINE COMMAND. *See* Army Air Forces Antisubmarine Command.

APHRODITE

The increasing rate of fire from the German V-1 "buzz bombs," and the great difficulties experienced in striking their large launching sites composed of huge reinforced concrete structures in 1944, prompted General Carl A. Spaatz* to order experiments with radio-controlled heavy bombers.* A small group of worn-out Eighth Air Force* (8AF) B-17s,* called BQ-7s for the project, and U.S. Navy Liberators, or PB4Ys, was assembled for Operation Aphrodite. Other code names for it were Batty, Castor, Orphan, and Weary-Willie. The plane interiors were stripped and filled with about 20,000 pounds of Torpex explosive. A plane's pilot* was to take off, climb to altitude, turn over control of the plane to an escort radio controller aircraft, and then bail out. The use of Aphrodite appeared moot in September 1944 when the Allied armies overran the V-1 launching sites.

Still, Aphrodite remained under consideration for much of the rest of World War II.* General of the Army H. H. Arnold,* for example, thought that large numbers of these weapons could be used as U.S. buzz bombs to attack German cities. The British chief of the Air Staff and the War Cabinet were reluctant to endorse the project because of the ability of the Germans to retaliate in kind. In any case, the aircraft were hard to control and were inaccurate. Navy Lieutenant Joseph Kennedy, brother of the future president, was accidentally blown up while flying an Aphrodite aircraft. Only a small number of missions were flown and those were against such targets as Helgoland and Oldenburg, Germany.

References. C&C, vol. 3. Conrad Crane, "The Strange Career of WEARY WILLIE," *AH*, September 1988, pp. 200–208. Alwyn T. Lloyd, *B-17 Flying Fortress in Detail & Scale*, part 3, "More Derivatives," 1986. Ronald Schaffer, *Wings of Judgement*, 1985. Kenneth P. Werrell, *The Evolution of the Cruise Missile*, 1985.

W. A. Jacobs

APPROPRIATIONS ACT OF 24 JULY 1917

This act was the funding approval by Congress for the establishment of American air power in World War I.* Funding was for a total of $640 million, at that time the largest sum of money appropriated by Congress for a single purpose. The funds were authorized for the development of flying fields in the United States and for the construction of ample aircraft to equip as many as 345 combat squadrons.* Unfortunately, aircraft production capabilities were woefully inadequate to deliver such a large number of aircraft. By the end of the war, only 45 combat squadrons had reached the front lines, mostly equipped with foreign-built aircraft.

References. Primary: Benedict Crowell, *America's Munitions; 1917–1918*, 1919. Secondary: Goldberg, *Hist. USAF*. James J. Hudson, *Hostile Skies: A Combat History of the American Air Service in World War I*, 1968. Arthur Sweetser, *The American Air Service*, 1919.

D. K. Vaughan

ARC LIGHT

This was the overall term for B-52* operations in the Vietnam War.* Beginning in June 1965, B-52Ds and B-52Fs flew sorties out of Guam and Thailand. It had not been expected that B-52s would ever drop conventional, or high-explosive, bombs,* so the aircraft had to be modified for a larger payload. This was called project Big Belly, and the B-52's capacity was enlarged to almost 30 tons of bombs. Arc Light operations were carpet bombings of enemy bases, concentrations, and supply lines. They were called aerial excavations by soldiers. During the battle at Khe Sanh,* South Vietnam, for example, B-52s dropped almost 60,000 tons of bombs on enemy supplies and concentrations. The B-52s were also used in the famous Linebacker* II operations. Arc Light ended in August 1973, after 126,615 sorties.

References. David A. Anderton, *Strategic Air Command: Two-thirds of the Triad*, 1974. Berger, *USAF in SEA*. Walter Boyne, *B-52: A Documentary History*, 1981. Donald J. Mrozek, *Air Power and the Ground War in Vietnam: Ideas and Actions*, 1988. Polmar, *SAC*.

Frank L. Goldstein contributed to this entry.

ARDC. *See* Air Force Systems Command.

AREAS AND REGIONS

Areas have been USAF* units similar to divisions.* Regions have been similar to wings.* They have usually been used in relation to a geographic zone, such as the Ogden Air Material Area, now named the Ogden Air Logistics Center, and the Central Air Force Reserve Region. The terms have been falling into disuse.

Reference. Ravenstein, *Org. USAF*.

ARGUMENT

This was the code name of a plan developed in November 1943 to counter the growing power of the German fighter* force. It involved an all-out attack on the German aircraft industry target system* by the Eight and Fifteenth Air Forces* (8AF and 15AF).

Essential for the success of such a coordinated attack was a realistic appraisal of the potentially high cost involved due to the absence of effective fighter escort.* It was assumed that these anticipated losses could only be justified by highly successful results. The success of the plan was likewise dependent upon excellent weather conditions over central Europe for an entire week. Similarly, satisfactory conditions would be needed for safe takeoff and landing of bombers* from eastern England and southern Italy. Argument was carried out in the battle known as the "Big Week*" and marked the beginning of the decline in the Luftwaffe's fighter forces.

References. C&C, vols. 2 and 3. DeWitt S. Copp, *Forged in Fire: Strategy and Decisions in the Air War over Europe 1940–45*, 1982.

Gilbert E. D'Alonzo

ARIA. *See* C-18.

ARIZONA COWBOY, THE. *See* Luke, Second Lieutenant Frank, Jr.

ARMED RECONNAISSANCE, OR ARMED RECCE. *See* reconnaissance; tactical operations.

ARMSTRONG, LIEUTENANT GENERAL FRANK A., JR. (1902–   )

Armstrong has been immortalized as Brigadier General Frank Savage, the hero of the novel *Twelve O'Clock High.** This is high tribute.

Armstrong was born in Hamilton, North Carolina, and graduated from Wake Forest College in 1923. He entered the USAAC* as a flying, or aviation, cadet* and received his pilot* wings in 1929. He had mostly flying assignments until, as a lieutenant colonel, he became operations officer of the VIII Bomber Command, later the Eighth Air Force* (8AF), in England. He also held B-17* group and wing command positions. These included the 97th and 306th Bombardment Groups (Heavy). On 17 August 1942, he led the first U.S. heavy bomber* attack on continental Europe. In 1943 he led the first such attack against a target in Germany. It was on these command and operational experiences that *Twelve O'Clock High* is based.

In 1943 he returned to the United States, and in 1945 he took the 315th Bombardment Wing to the war against Japan. This enabled Armstrong to lead both the first and the last USAAF* heavy bomb operations in World War II.* After the war, he led a flight from Japan to Washington, D.C., nonstop. In 1952 he became commander of the Second Air Force,* in 1956 commander of the Alaskan Air Command* (AAC), and, in the same year, commander of the Alaskan Command, a unified command.* He retired in 1961. The record shows that Armstrong was a superb battle commander, so it is fitting that he be remembered best in connection with *Twelve O'Clock High*.

References. DuPre, *USAF Bio.* "The 40th Anniversary of the USAF," a special issue of *AH*, September 1987, p. 207–8. Brent L Gravatt and Francis H. Ayers, Jr., "The Fireman: *Twelve O'Clock High* Revisited," *AH*, September 1988, pp. 204–8.

ARMY AIR CORPS (AAC). *See* U.S. Army Air Corps.

ARMY AIR FORCE BAND. *See* Miller, Major (Alton) Glenn.

ARMY AIR FORCES (AAF). *See* U.S. Army Air Forces.

ARMY AIR FORCES ANTISUBMARINE COMMAND (AAFAC)

Few people are aware of the AAFAC and the USAF's mission to help with command of the seas. The AAFAC, created to counter the U-boat threat, was established and activated at New York City in October 1942. It was the first

USAAF* organization to have a headquarters within the continental United States (CONUS) and to have a major operational mission. The AAFAC operated from four continents with the following areas of operation: the north and middle Atlantic Ocean from Newfoundland to Trinidad, and the Bay of Biscay and the approaches to North Africa. Seven types of aircraft were employed by the AA-FAC: A-20s,* A-29s, B-17s,* B-18s,* B-24s,* B-25s,* and B-34s. The B-24 was by far the most effective aircraft of the time for this mission. Training was conducted from Langley* Field, Virginia. New radar* equipment and tactics were developed and proven. During the AAFAC's brief period of operation, the percentage of U-boats sunk by air action rose from 10 to 50 percent. The command was officially credited with sinking ten German U-boats. Its most effective unit was the 480th Antisubmarine Group which operated out of Port Lyautey, French Morocco.

The U.S. Navy's interest in heavy flying boat patrol bombers was waning, and it looked with much interest at the USAAF's successful Antisubmarine Command. In a major wartime trade, the Navy relinquished the Boeing Aircraft Company plant in Renton, Washington, which was built by the Navy for the production of the PBB-1 Sea Ranger. In return, the Navy received some B-24s, B-25s, and B-34s right off the assembly lines; some B-24s out of the USAAF inventory; and a major plum, the antisubmarine mission. This trade gave the USAAF a fourth plant for building B-29s.* The AAFAC disbanded in August 1943, after only ten months of existence.

However, in 1986, the USAF* reentered the antisubmarine task as part of its mission to help control the seas. For the whole mission, the USAF uses B-52Gs* equipped with AGM-84* Harpoons.

References. *AAF: A Directory, Alamanc and Chronicle of Achievement*, 1944. C&C, vols. 1 and 2. Robert L. Curtis, John Mitchell, and Martin Copp, *Langley Field, the Early Years 1916–1946*, 1977. Alwyn T. Lloyd, *B-24 Liberator*, 1989. Maurer Maurer, *Air Force Combat Units of World War II*, 1983.

See also mining; Strategic Air Command.

Alwyn T. Lloyd

ARMY AIR SERVICE. *See* U.S. Army Air Service.

ARMY AIRWAYS COMMUNICATION SYSTEM. *See* Air Force Communications Command.

ARMY AND AIR FORCE AUTHORIZATION ACT OF 1950

This act, passed on 10 July 1950, provided the first legal definition for USAF* composition. It allowed the USAF to have 502,000 officers and men and 24,000 aircraft. This size was in accordance with the airmen's belief that a 70-group air force* was needed to carry out the USAF's mission. The act was passed only days after the Korean War* had begun. On 3 August, Congress suspended the strength limitations of the act to permit expansion for the Korean War.

References. Goldberg, *Hist. USAF*. *United States Code*, Title 10.

ARMY AND AIR FORCE EXCHANGE SERVICE (AAFES)

The AAFES is a joint organization of the U.S. Army and the USAF.* It provides competitive and convenient goods and services to active duty, qualified reserve, retired people, and their families. It is a worldwide organization with headquarters in Dallas, Texas.

Until 1889, peddlers, called sutlers, sold personal items to soldiers. Lack of competition meant they were often able to sell inferior products at excessive prices. In 1889 the War Department authorized canteens, and local units ran them. In 1941, the Army Exchange Service was established with Post Exchanges (PX) to take care of the global operations. As a result of the independence of the USAF, the organization became the AAFES in 1948 with Base Exchanges (BX) for the airmen.

The head of the AAFES is a general officer responsible to a board of directors. The board is selected by the secretaries of the Army and the Air Force.* The AAFES is basically operated by 65,000 civilians, who are paid from AAFES income. It is organized in the continental United States (CONUS) into five exchange regions and one distribution region. Headquarters for overseas exchanges are in Munich, Germany, and Honolulu, Hawaii. The AAFES operates nearly 16,000 facilities, and annual sales exceed $4.9 billion. Profits are given to the Army and USAF to be used for morale, welfare, and recreation; this money is usually spent on libraries, gyms, hobby shops, recreational areas, and athletic equipment.

Reference. U.S. Air Force Fact Sheet 86–35, "Army and Air Force Exchange Service," October 1986.

ARMY-NAVY AGREEMENTS OF 1931 AND 1938

The U.S. Army and Navy long shared the responsibility for defending U.S. seacoasts. In 1918 the USAAS* began to consider coastal defense against a seaward attack. Defensive measures included patrolling, defending the shoreline, and spotting for the Army's coast defense artillery. This was estimated to require 15 squadrons of aircraft and ten balloon companies.

In protecting its share of the mission, the Army objected to Navy adoption of land-based aircraft for coastal defense. Secretary of War Patrick J. Hurley asked President Herbert Hoover to stop the Navy's moves to procure such aircraft and bases. In 1931, General Douglas MacArthur and Admiral William V. Pratt, the chiefs of their services, formulated an agreement designed to end the discord. It limited naval aviation to functions associated with forces afloat. The USAAC* then proceeded with plans for coastal defense, including attacking hostile ships. The coastal defense mission also gave the USAAC a basis for seeking long-range bombers* for strategic operations.* Thus the USAAC's plans were to include the use of the General Headquarters Air Force.* This was at a time when the Army considered only defensive operations. Pratt retired in 1933. His successor, Admiral William H. Stanley, ended the agreement. The Navy then developed land-based aircraft, hoping to assume all aerial coastal defense operations.

A joint Army-Navy exercise in 1937 took place off the California coast. Representing an enemy fleet was the target ship USS *Utah*. USAAC B-10s* and B-17s* successfully intercepted the *Utah** at 250 miles at sea and simulated attacks, scoring hits. In 1938, the USAAC played a liner as an approaching enemy fleet. This was the *Rex* interception.* B-17s caught the *Rex* while still 700 miles at sea.

Shortly after the *Rex* incident, the Army limited the USAAC to operations within 100 miles of the shore. There have been assertions by high-ranking USAAC officers that the Navy originated this limit, but no written documentation has been found. Thus, there may not have been an Army-Navy agreement in 1938, even an oral one. However, the USAAC believed there was one. Only four years later the USAAF* would be conducting transatlantic operations against the German navy through its Army Air Forces Antisubmarine Command* (AA-FAC).

The agreements may seem amusing today because the USAF* applies aerospace power globally, but they were important in their own time under different policies and technology.

References. DeWitt S. Copp, *A Few Great Captains: The Men and Events That Shaped the Development of U.S. Air Power*. 1980. Futrell, *Ideas*. Maurer, *Avn. in Army*.

ARMY REGULATION 95–5 (AR 95–5)

This order of 20 June 1941 created the USAAF,* a milestone on the road to an independent air force. After September 1939, President Franklin D. Roosevelt* and Secretary of War Henry Stimson believed that aviation had a vital role in warfare. In March 1941, Stimson told his new assistant secretary of war for air,* Robert A. Lovett,* to streamline the Army air organization. On Lovett's recommendation, AR 95–5 created the USAAF whose commander reported directly to the Army chief of staff. In addition, General Headquarters Air Force* (GHQ Air Force) functions were transferred to the Air Force Combat Command.* Major General H. H. Arnold* became chief, later commanding general, of the USAAF and had an Air Staff* to assist him.

The USAAF's autonomy was enhanced further by War Department Circular 59 of 2 March 1942, effective 9 March 1942. As part of General George Marshall's reorganization of General Headquarters, Circular 59 abolished the Office of Chief of the Air Corps and made the USAAF, Army Ground Forces, and Army Service Forces coordinate commands under the chief of staff. The Air Force Combat Command* was abolished because its four continental forces had been assigned to defense or training duties. Arnold retained control over combat functions because, in addition to being commanding general of the USAAF, he was deputy chief of staff and served on both the Joint Chiefs of Staff and the Combined Chiefs of Staff.

As Craven and Cate* indicate, USAAF officers were schooled to avoid the term *independent air force*, although for practical purposes the USAAF now had equal status with the Army and Navy.

References. C&C, vol. 1. Mark S. Watson, *Chief of Staff: Prewar Plans and Preparations*, a vol. of *United States Army in World War II*, 1950.

Lester H. Brune

ARMY REORGANIZATION ACT OF 1920. *See* National Defense Act of 1920.

ARNHEM, NETHERLANDS. *See* Market.

ARNOLD, GENERAL OF THE AIR FORCE H. H. "HAP" (1886–1950)
Arnold is one of the greatest military leaders and managers in U.S. history. More than anyone else, he was the father of the USAF* as an organization. His vision directly shaped important events in the growth of U.S. air power. His success in leading the puny, pygmy USAAC* of 1938 into the world-shaking, giant USAAF* of 1945, a transformation taking only seven years, is an accomplishment of the first order.

Born in Gladwyne, Pennsylvania, and a 1907 graduate of the U.S. Military Academy (USMA), he was a pioneer airman who was taught to fly by the Wright brothers.* In 1912 he won the first MacKay Trophy ever awarded for a reconnaissance* flight. In 1935 he won a second one for personally organizing and leading the Alaskan flight of 1934.* The flight consisted of ten B-10* bombers* that made a record round-trip flight from Washington, D.C., to Fairbanks, Alaska. In February 1935, Arnold was jumped two grades to brigadier general and put in command of the 1st Wing of the General Headquarters Air Force* (GHQ Air Force) at March* Field, California. He encouraged development of the B-17* and B-24* four-engined bombers and insisted on the precision training of crews.

In January 1936, Arnold became assistant to the chief of the Air Corps in Washington, D.C., and in September 1938 was promoted to major general and appointed chief of the Air Corps. His title was changed to chief of the Army Air Forces in June 1941, and he was promoted to lieutenant general in December. With Colonel Ira C. Eaker,* he wrote *Winged Warfare* (1941) and *Army Flyer* (1942). When the War Department General Staff was organized in March 1942, Arnold became commanding general of Army Air Forces. During World War II,* he directed air activities for the nation's global struggle, and under him the air arm grew from 22,000 officers and men to nearly 2,500,000 and from 3,900 planes to 75,000.

Because of Arnold's respect and appreciation for science and engineering, he carefully guided the development, procurement, and production of equipment. Arnold also knew when to be tough. As an example, in 1943, when Arnold finally accepted the need for a long-range, air superiority* fighter,* he *demanded* it. The Engineering Branch at Wright-Patterson* Field, Ohio, did not believe the type could be built despite Alexander de Seversky's* demonstration of one in 1938 and the Japanese A6M Reisen (Zero) fighter. Arnold got his fighters, and his action was a decisive factor in the defeat of Germany and Japan.

Arnold made contributions to the Argentia and Casablanca Conferences that were critical to U.S. and USAAF interests. He would not accept priorities for the Royal Air Force (RAF) at the expense of the USAAF at the Argentia meeting. At Casablanca he saved USAAF plans to strike at German industry instead of following Winston Churchill's desire for the United States to join the RAF in attacking cities.

Arnold was promoted to general in March 1943 and to the five-star grade of general of the Army, equivalent to the foreign grade of field marshall, in December 1944.

Arnold suffered a heart attack in 1945 as the war drew to a close, and he retired in June 1946, after earning most of the nation's highest honors. In May 1949, Arnold was appointed the first general of the Air Force, a five-star grade, by Congress. He was inducted into the National Aviation Hall of Fame in Dayton, Ohio, in 1967. His name is perpetuated at the Arnold Engineering Development Center* at Arnold* AFB, Tennessee, and with the Arnold Air Society of the Air Force Reserve Officer Training Corps* (AFROTC).

References. Primary: H. H. Arnold, *Global Mission*, 1949. Ira C. Eaker, "Hap Arnold: The Anatomy of Leadership," *AF*, September 1977, pp. 83–86, 91–92. Secondary: Thomas M. Coffey, *HAP: The Story of the U.S. Air Force and the Man Who Built It—General H. "Hap" Arnold*, 1982. DeWitt S. Copp, *A Few Great Captains: The Men and Events That Shaped the Development of U.S. Air Power*, 1980, and *Forged in Fire: Strategy and Decisions in the Air War over Europe 1940–45*, 1982. DuPre, *USAF Bio*.

James C. Hasdorff

ARNOLD AIR FORCE BASE

Named for General of the Air Force H. H. Arnold,* this base was activated in 1950. It is an Air Force Systems Command* (AFSC) facility near Manchester, Tennessee, and the site of the Arnold Engineering Development Center.*

References. "Guide to Major Air Force Installations Worldwide," *AF*, May 1990, p. 122. Roberts, *Dir. USAF*.

ARNOLD ENGINEERING DEVELOPMENT CENTER (AEDC)

Located at Arnold* AFB, Tennessee, this organization originally was the Air Engineering Development Division, established as a separate operating agency* (SOA) in 1950. In 1951 it lost its SOA status as it was reassigned to the Air Research and Development Command (ARDC), now named the Air Force Systems Command* (AFSC). Later in the same year, the unit took its current name in honor of General of the Air Force H. H. Arnold.* The AEDC has been important in USAF equipment development.

Its genesis was the great advances in aviation and space technology made by Germany in World War II.* Arnold wanted to improve U.S. efforts to prevent falling behind again. A step in this direction was the work of Dr. Theodore von Karman* and the Scientific Advisory Board.* They advanced the idea of building the world's foremost wind tunnel facility. The idea bore fruit as the AEDC, with the original facilities costing $100 million. The AEDC now occupies more than

40,000 acres and has wind tunnels, engine test cells, space chambers, and ballistic ranges.

References. Napoleon B. Byars, "Big Wind at Tullahoma," *AF*, January 1985, pp. 78–82. Michael H. Gorn, *Harnessing the Genie: Science and Technology Forecasting for the Air Force, 1944–1986*, 1988. Ravenstein, *Org. USAF*.

ARPC. *See* Air Reserve Personnel Center.

ART

The art collection of the USAF* was started in 1950. Soon thereafter the U.S. Army transferred 800 of its paintings that related to the USAF in World War II.* By 1988 the collection included more than 7,000 works of art—paintings, drawings, sketches, and sculptures. The works have been donated to the USAF, and most are on exhibit to the public. They can be seen at the Pentagon in Washington, D.C., the U.S. Air Force Academy,* Colorado Springs, Colorado; the U.S. Air Force Museum,* Wright-Patterson* AFB, Ohio; and the Air University,* Maxwell AFB, Alabama. USAF art provides a unique yet traditional way to define and explain the service.

References. John Blake, *Aviation Art*, 1987. James J. Hagerty and Warren Reiland Smith, *The U.S. Air Force: A Pictorial History in Art*, 1966. William S. Phillips, "Aviation Art—One Man's Philosophy," *AH* September 1986, pp. 155–57. Secretary of the Air Force Office of Public Affairs, Community Relations, Art and Museum Branch brochure, "United States Air Force Art Collection," n.d.

ASC. *See* Air Force Logistics Command.

ASSISTANT SECRETARY OF WAR FOR AIR

This position was established by the Air Corps Act* of 1926, giving U.S. Army aviation direct access to the secretary of war.

President Calvin Coolidge appointed Frederick Trubee Davison to this position, which he retained until January 1933. President Franklin D. Roosevelt* did not appoint a successor. Although some USAAC* airmen thought the office of assistant secretary was a waste of funds, preferring that the chief of Air Corps report directly to the secretary of war, Ira Eaker* believed Davison did the best possible job. Davison was a wealthy New York politician who had been interested in aviation since his college days when he organized a Yale Aviation Unit. He tried hard to get as much funding as possible for the USAAC at a time when Army and Navy appropriations were meager. Because neither Coolidge nor President Herbert Hoover would fully fund the five-year aircraft program, Davison's best efforts achieved little toward obtaining the 1,800 modern aircraft that the act authorized.

References. DeWitt S. Copp, *A Few Great Captains: The Men and Events That Shaped the Development of U.S. Air Power*, 1980. Edwin H. Rutkowski, *The Politics of Aviation Procurement, 1926–1934*, 1966.

Lester H. Brune

ASTRONAUTS

Astronaut is the U.S. term for a person who piloted or served as a crew member aboard a flight into space, defined as 50 miles above the surface of the earth. U.S. astronauts have participated in the X-15,* Mercury, Gemini, Apollo, Apollo-Soyuz, Skylab, and Space Shuttle programs. Two other programs, the joint USAF* and National Aeronautics and Space Administration* (NASA) X-20* and the Department of Defense Manned Orbiting Laboratory, failed to reach operational status.

In December 1958, President Dwight Eisenhower* decided only military test pilots would be eligible to become astronauts. Of the first group of seven project Mercury astronauts, three were USAF pilots: Gordon Cooper, Virgil I. "Gus" Grissom, and Donald "Deke" Slayton. Since then the eligibility requirements have steadily evolved, but USAF personnel continue to play a major role in the U.S. space program. As of 1985, NASA had selected 103 astronauts from military ranks, with 48 of them coming from the USAF. Eight civilian astronauts had also served in the USAF prior to joining the astronaut corps.

Although the entire astronaut program has changed greatly since 1958, it is possible to generalize about the selection and training of astronauts. As might be expected, the selection process is an exhaustive one. Initially, NASA screens all applicants' records for the proper education and experience. For example, the project Mercury astronauts had to be less than 40 years old, have a bachelor's degree in engineering or its equivalent, be a graduate of test pilot school, and be a qualified jet pilot with at least 1,500 hours of flying time. After meeting these basic criteria, the candidates submitted to a barrage of testing, including physical fitness, psycho-physiological stress, and clinical examinations, from blood to X-rays. NASA relaxed the physical standards slightly, in 1978, for mission specialists.

The astronaut training program is no less rigorous; it generally consists of academics and procedures and mission training. The academics may consist of everything from basic mechanics and aerodynamics to meteorology and physiology. NASA's intent is to help the astronauts understand as much as possible about their vehicle and their operational environment. Procedures training takes place on a wide variety of devices and in a wide range of locales. NASA adapted much of its program from earlier USAF training techniques and devices. Some of the training devices used over the years include various means of simulating weightlessness, practicing lunar landings, and simulating different flight conditions. Procedures training also involves egress and survival training in an effort to enable the astronauts to cope with any eventuality. Mission training familiarizes the astronauts with a specific vehicle and prepares them to execute the mission's flight plan, whether walking on the moon or conducting experiments aboard the Shuttle.

References. Richard Hirsch and Joseph John Trento, *The National Aeronautics and Space Administration*, 1973. U.S. Congress, House, Committee on Science and Technology, *Astronauts and Cosmonauts: Biographical and Statistical Data*, 1985. U.S. Congress, Senate, Committee on Aeronautical and Space Sciences, *Manned Space Flight Program of the National Aeronautics and Space Administration: Projects Mercury, Gemini, and Apollo*, 1962.

Brian J. Nichelson

AT-6. *See* T-6.

ATB. *See* B-2.

ATC. *See* Air Training Command; Military Airlift Command.

ATF. *See* Advanced Tactical Fighter.

ATLANTIC, BATTLE OF THE. *See* Army Air Forces Antisubmarine Command; B-24.

ATLAS

This was the United States' first intercontinental ballistic missile* (ICBM)— a successful combination of a long-range missile with a nuclear warhead. Atlas *A*, *B*, and *C* versions were for testing only, but the *D*, *E*, and *F* were the operational models. Long out of service, a few remain for use as space launch vehicles. The Atlas was designated SM-65 and then redesignated HGM-19.

The Atlas was built by the General Dynamics Corporation and was operational in the USAF* from 1958 to 1965. The basic missile consisted of three major sections: the propulsion system, propellant tank, and reentry vehicle. The propulsion system was unique among large missiles, consisting of two boosters, a single sustainer engine, and two small vernier rockets to provide final "trim" velocity. Because the boosters were jettisoned shortly after lift-off, the Atlas was nicknamed the "stage-and-a-half" missile. To save weight, the 60-foot propellant tank was made of stainless steel thinner than a dime, with no internal framework. It had to be kept pressurized for the missile to keep its shape. The engines burned RP-1, a kerosene-like fuel, with liquid oxygen. The reentry vehicle contained the thermonuclear warhead. As with most large missiles, this could be replaced by a satellite payload.

Atlas missile squadrons were deployed at a number of bases, beginning in 1960. These included Altus* AFB, Oklahoma; Dyess* AFB, Texas; Fairchild* AFB, Washington; Forbes and Schilling AFBs, Kansas; Francis E. Warren* AFB, Wyoming; Lincoln and Offutt* AFBs, Nebraska; Plattsburgh* AFB, New York; and Walker AFB, New Mexico. Deployment was complete by December

1962. Obsolescence was equally rapid, and the last of the active Atlas squadrons had been inactivated in 1965.

The Atlas boasted an impressive number of "firsts." Because of its light weight, it was the first, and so far the only, missile in the world able to insert *itself* into satellite orbit. It became the first ICBM to reach a 9,000-mile range. It was the first U.S. rocket to be integrated into high-energy space missions and, as the booster for project Mercury, launched the first American astronauts into orbit.

Characteristics (Atlas *E*, *F*): engines, two LR105 boosters of 150,000 pounds thrust each, and one North American Rocketdyne LR89 sustainer of 57,000 pounds thrust; length, 75 or 83 feet; diameter, 10 feet; weight, 260,000 pounds; range, 11,500 miles.

References. John L. Chapman, *ATLAS: The Story of a Missile*, 1960. *From Snark to Peacekeeper: A Pictorial History of Strategic Air Command Missiles*, Office of Historian, SAC, Offutt AFB, Nebraska, 1990. Jacob Neufeld, *Ballistic Missiles in the United States Air Force 1945–1960*, 1990. Polmar, *SAC*. Don Smith, "The Bird in the Other Room," *AF*, September 1972, pp. 140–44.

Raymond L. Puffer

ATOMIC BOMB. *See* nuclear weapons.

ATTACK

Attack is the function of causing damage to an enemy surface or subsurface target. Usually the presence of enemy forces near a front or sea action is involved. Other names for this activity include strike, close air support (CAS), battlefield air interdiction (BAI), and interdiction. It is part of tactical operations.*

Attack also is used as the designator for an aircraft specialized for the attack function, as with the A-10.* This designator was used in the USAAS,* USAAC,* USAAF,* and USAF* from 1924 to 1948. It was revived in 1962 as part of the common designator system for the armed forces introduced that year. The attack function has also been carried out in the USAF and its antecedents by aircraft called fighter-bombers and light and medium bombers. Regular fighters* and bombers* are also used. Other services have also used the term *dive bomber*.

The USAAS first performed large-scale attack operations in the St. Mihiel* and Meuse-Argonne* campaigns in World War I.* Thereafter the U.S. Army regarded tactical operations and observation aviation* as the proper roles for aircraft. Aerial firepower provided unique fire support to soldiers on the battlefield. This gave the Army an understandably large appetite for it. However, it is not a top USAF priority, and this caused a rancor that still exists.

The Army, having almost always operated under conditions of air superiority,* has downgraded the importance of aerial combat and has wanted airmen to concentrate on attack aviation with specialized aircraft. On the other hand, the USAF has found that very few specialized attack aircraft have been able to live in the air against enemy air superiority fighters. Thus, the USAF has seen the air superiority task as having first priority and as being the most difficult of all air tasks, and it has regarded specialized attack aircraft as a dangerous diversion of resources. The USAF has preferred to use its air superiority fighters for the attack role when they can be spared from the battle for control of the air.

For the USAF, the problem with the specialized attack airplane includes the characteristics sought by the Army. The Army wants attack planes that can carry massive ordnance loads. The resultant weight inhibits survivability against air or ground hostile action. The Army also wants an umbrella of attack aircraft over its battlefields. This means an ability to "loiter" on call, or to fly in one area for hours. Again, such a capability inhibits survivability against a competent enemy since it means added weight and predictable behavior in battle. The USAF also regards it as a waste of valuable aircraft and crews. When advocates of the Army view admire the A-1* for its "six hours of loiter," advocates of the USAF view note that hours of use are wasted with no results.

Loiter over a fast-moving armor spearhead is justifiable because of the critical need to keep the tanks moving. But loiter over a static or quiet front line means taking resources away from better uses, in the USAF view. The USAF prefers that sporadic, or unpredictable, Army contingencies be served by the diversion of sorties planned for or launched against lesser priority targets or by a few air superiority fighters on ground alert for such emergencies. An air superiority fighter assures that the reaction time will be short.

The USAF believes that a supply of attack firepower at the level desired by the Army results in abusive demand and waste.

References. Thomas H. Greer, *The Development of Air Doctrine in the Army Air Arm 1917–1941*, 1985. Richard P. Hallion, *Strike from the Sky: The History of Battlefield Air Attack 1911–1945*, 1989. Richard G. Head, "The Air Force A-7 Decision; The Politics of Close Air Support," *AH*, December 1974, pp. 218–24. Jeffrey P. Rhodes, "Improving the Odds in Ground Attack," *AF*, November 1986, pp. 48–52. John Schlight, *The War in South Vietnam: The Years of the Offensive 1965–1968*, 1988. Albert F. Simpson, "Tactical Air Doctrine: Tunisia and Korea," *Air University Quarterly Review*, Summer 1951, pp. 4–20.

See also Coningham, Air Marshal Sir Arthur; Howze Board.

AU. *See* Air University.

AUDIT AGENCY. *See* Air Force Audit Agency.

AU REVIEW. *See Airpower Journal.*

AVENGER. *See* GAU-8.

AVG. *See* American Volunteer Group.

AVIANO AIR BASE

A U.S. Air Forces in Europe* (USAFE) main operating base in support of the North Atlantic Treaty Organization* (NATO), this base is near Aviano, in north Italy. USAFE began to use the field in 1966.

References. "Guide to Major Air Force Installations Worldwide," *AF*, May 1990, p. 122. Roberts, *Dir. USAF*.

AVIATION ARMOR. *See* flaksuits.

AVIATION CADET (AC)

The aviation cadet program was the source of most rated officers, those qualified to perform a flying aeronautical skill, until the late 1950s. Originally called flying cadet, the program started during World War I* in an effort to build up the nation's air arm. The term was often used to denote a pilot* cadet, but in its correct application it included persons in cadet training to become rated officers.

When the United States entered the war in 1917, it had 65 rated pilots and two flying schools. By the end of the war, more than 10,000 pilots had been trained on 41 American bases or by allies in Europe and Canada. To qualify as a flying cadet, an applicant had to be under 25 years of age, have two to three years of college, and be athletic, honest, and reliable. This was a fry cry from the extensive battery of physical, mental, and psychological tests required in later years.

Although the cadet program ended with the Armistice, Congress ordered its resumption in 1919 but limited the number on active duty to 1,300. Austerity hit the air arm in the 1920s, however, and in 1926 the authorized number of cadets on duty had dropped to 196. During this period, a cadet who earned his wings could either serve out his three-year commitment or take a discharge and enter the Officers' Reserve Corps as a second lieutenant. In 1929, during the five-year expansion program, the law was changed and cadets were required to serve three years, one in flight training* and two either as a reserve second lieutenant on active duty or as a regular Army officer. The term *flying cadet* was changed to *aviation cadet* in 1941, just prior to the enormous expansion of the cadet program during World War II.* Although the cadet program normally required at least two years of college, this was reduced to a high school diploma during the war. At the close of the war, aviation cadet training stopped, and it was not until 1948 that it began again at the modest rate of 5,000 pilots per year.

With the start of the Korean War,* flying quotas again began to rise. Although the educational requirement for the cadet program was again lowered to a high school diploma, more and more commissioned officers began entering flying training. Although the flying training was similar, these students were not cadets; they had received their commission through the Air Force Reserve Officer Training Corps* (AFROTC). When the U.S. Air Force Academy* (USAFA) graduated its first class in 1959, the number of AFROTC and USAFA graduates entering pilot and navigator* training increased, until in 1961 aviation cadet pilot training was discontinued. In 1965 aviation cadet navigator training ended. Since the end of the aviation cadet program, there have been several proposals to revive it, but none have been approved. A college degree remains the prerequisite for entry into pilot or navigator training.

References. Primary: Bruce D. Callander, 'The Aviation Cadets,'' *AF*, November 1990, pp. 98–101. History, Army Air Forces Training Command, 7 July 1939–V-J Day (ATC History Office, Randolph AFB, Texas). Secondary: C&C, vol. 6. Maurer Maurer, *Final Report and a Tactical History*, vol. 1 of *The U.S. Air Service in World War I*, 1978. Maurice G. Stack, "The Aviation Cadet Program in Retrospect," *Air University Review*, July–August 1965, pp. 78–90.

Thomas A. Manning

AVIATION MEDICINE

Solving the biological and psychological problems of aviation and space flight is necessary for operating in air and space. The solution relates to the selection and treatment of crews, to vehicle and equipment design, and to the transporting of patients by air. USAF* physicians specializing in aviation medicine have the title of flight surgeon.

The first U.S. efforts to manage aviation medicine were made by Colonel Theodore C. Lyster of the Aviation Section of the U.S. Army Signal Corps* in 1917. During World War I,* civilians were recruited to be "flight surgeons." In 1918, a Medical Research Laboratory at Hazelhurst Field, New York, was established to do research into aviation medicine. In 1919, after the loss of the wartime physicians, the USAAS* began to train Army physicians at Hazelhurst but ended research. By July 1921, the USAAS had graduated 46 flight surgeons. Their task was to prevent aircraft accidents for medical reasons; they performed physical examinations, monitored flyers, and participated in accident investigations. In 1922, the laboratory became the School of Aviation Medicine at Mitchel* Field, New York. It went back to doing research as well as training; it investigated deafness, better goggle lenses, and the effects of cold and low oxygen pressure at high altitudes. In 1926 the school moved to Brooks* Field, Texas, to improve the practicality of its work by being near pilot* flight training.* After Randolph* Field, Texas, opened, the school moved there. To become a flight surgeon, a physician took a three- to four-month course to become a medical examiner and normally practiced a year as an examiner before receiving the rating of flight surgeon.

In 1944, the school took over a course in aeromedical evacuation* and specialized training of USAAF* nurses. After World War II,* research work was conducted at the Aero Medical Laboratory at Wright-Patterson* AFB, Ohio; at the Air Force Flight Test Center, Edwards* AFB, California; and at Holloman* AFB's Air Development Center, New Mexico. For a global USAF* flying jets in combat, aviation medicine included research on oxygen use, decompression, fatigue, noise, in-flight food, bail out, survival, safety harnesses and clothing, and high temperatures. The training time for examiner's became nine weeks. In 1990, the school returned to Brooks and was part of the Air Force Systems Command* (AFSC).

References. C&C, vol. 6. Goldberg, *Hist. USAF*. Woodford Agee Heflin, ed., *The United States Air Force Dictionary*, 1956. Maurer Maurer, *Avn. in Army*, and ed., *The*

U.S. Air Service in World War I, vol. 4, 1979. Douglas Robinson, *The Dangerous Sky: A History of Aviation Medicine*, 1973.

AVIATION OFFICER, AMERICAN EXPEDITIONARY FORCES (AEF)

Although the position of aviation officer in the AEF was in existence for only about three months, its establishment was one of the first steps in the creation of a separate military air arm for the United States.

The position was established by General John J. Pershing* shortly after his appointment as commander in chief of the AEF on 26 May 1917. The same day he assumed those duties, Pershing appointed Major T. F. Dodd as his aviation officer. Dodd's appointment marked the first time that aviation activities were considered separate from Signal Corps affairs. Although the Signal Corps remained the parent organization in the United States, in France the two organizations were treated separately. When Lieutenant Colonel William Mitchell* arrived in Europe in June 1917, he replaced Dodd. Eventually the position was upgraded when the Office of the Chief of Air Service* was established on 3 September 1917.

References. I. B. Holley, Jr., *Ideas and Weapons*, 1983. James J. Hudson, *Hostile Skies: A Combat History of the American Air Service in World War I*, 1968. Maurer Maurer, *The U.S. Air Service in World War I*, 4 vols., 1978–79.

D. K. Vaughan

AVIATION SECTION, U.S. ARMY SIGNAL CORPS

This organization was the first discrete Army unit to be devoted exclusively to aviation and aviation-related activities. Derived from the older Aeronautical Division of the U.S. Signal Corps,* it was established by the act of 18 July 1914* and continued unchanged until 21 May 1918, when President Woodrow Wilson placed it under the dual control of the War Department's Bureau of Aircraft Production* and the Division of Military Aeronautics.*

On 27 August 1918, Wilson again reorganized the unit, calling it the U.S. Army Air Service,* (USAAS) and placing it under the control of the second assistant secretary of war, John D. Ryan.*

References. Goldberg, *Hist. USAF*. Juliette A. Hennessy, *The United States Army Air Arm April 1861 to April 1917*, 1985.

D. K. Vaughan

AVIATION STUDENT

This was a USAAC* grade created in 1941. Its purpose was to enable enlisted men to take the aircrew training of an aviation cadet* without a reduction in pay and allowances. Commissioned officers taking the training retained their grade but were distinguished by the category "student officer."

Reference. *AAF: A Directory, Almanac and Chronicle of Achievement*, 1944.

AWACS. *See* Airborne Warning and Control System.

AWFC. *See* All Weather Flying Center.

AWPD. *See* Air War Plans Division.

AWPD-1

Known as the "air war plan that defeated Germany," this document was prepared in August 1941 by the USAAF's newly created Air War Plans Division* (AWPD). It became part of the Joint Board of the Army and Navy report on war plans to President Franklin D. Roosevelt* on 11 September 1941.

On 9 July 1941, Roosevelt asked the War and Navy Departments to prepare estimates of the overall requirements to defeat potential enemies of the United States. This request resulted from meetings between U.S. and British officials from January to March 1941 which had formed the American-British-Canadian plan 1 (ABC-1) for cooperation in defeating the Axis powers. ABC-1 correlated with the Joint Board's Rainbow 5 war plan establishing the contingency strategy to defeat Germany first while adopting a strategic defensive against Japanese forces in the Pacific.

Following the appointment of Colonel Harold L. George* as director of AWPD in June 1941, the AWPD staff was eager to apply the strategic operations* concepts which George and other officers taught at the Air Corps Tactical School* during the 1930s. An AWPD committee consisting of George, Lieutenant Colonel Kenneth Walker, and Majors Laurence S. Kuter* and Haywood S. Hansell, Jr.,* gathered data from various offices and wrote AWPD-1 between 4 and 11 August 1941.

Although the plan included air divisions to defend the Western Hemisphere and to help the defensive against Japan, AWPD-1 focused on an aviation bombardment offensive against Germany and the territory it occupied. That was to be followed, if necessary, by tactical operations* in invading Europe, an event anticipated for April 1944.

AWPD-1 included details for mobilization and for the type of targets to hit. It called for aircraft production and personnel training to expand the USAAF* to 98 tactical groups with 6,834 planes in the European area and the Suez. Target objectives in German-held areas would be electric power grids, transportation facilities, and oil industries. After destroying these targets, bombing of urban areas would break down German morale. Other vital raids would be on German airfields and aircraft plants to neutralize the enemy's air force.

Despite previous German and British experience in losing bombers* to fighters* during daylight operations, AWPD-1 conjectured that U.S. bombers had sufficient speed, defensive firepower, and high-altitude flight ability to penetrate deeply into Germany during daytime. Nevertheless, the plan recommended development of an armored escort fighter with long-range capability in the event that German defenses proved to be too strong. Although the plan stated that a land campaign might not be necessary because of air power's ability, it provided for tactical forces to work with the Army in a final assault on Germany.

In brief, AWPD-1 outlined air power methods to apply a bomber offensive against Germany. The plans were approved by the Army War Plans Division as reported to President Franklin D. Roosevelt. Later, AWPD-1 became the basis for AWPD-42 and the Combined Bomber Offensive* used in Europe after 7 December 1941.

References. Primary: Haywood S. Hansell, Jr., *The Air War Plan That Defeated Germany*, 1972. Secondary: C&C, vol. 1. Ray S. Cline, *Washington Command Post: The Operations Division*, a vol. in the series *United States Army in World War II*, 1961. James K. Gaston, *Planning the American Air War: Four Men and Nine Days in 1941*, 1982.

See also German aircraft industry target system; German oil industry target system; German transportation target system; U.S. Strategic Bombing Survey.

Lester H. Brune

AZON, RAZON, AND TARZON

These were the first types of remotely guided munitions used operationally by the USAAF* and the USAF.* *AZON* stood for "azimuth only," a radio-controlled bomb* that could be turned laterally during its descent. Thus it would be useful only against such long axis targets as railway lines and bridges. In subsequent models, RAZON and TARZON, the angle of attack could be raised and lowered, *R* standing for range. TARZON alluded to the powerful, fictional Tarzan character. All were marked by tail flares and visually tracked.

German glide bomb successes against Allied fleets in the invasion of Italy in 1943 stimulated AZON production and deployment. About 3,000 AZONs were used in Europe and the Mediterranean. AZON was unpopular with some aircrews because controller aircraft had to keep them in sight all the way to the target. Commanders insisted AZONs be used only as part of larger conventional missions, and AZON hits on point targets sometimes were credited to free-fall bombs. Some scientists felt such obstructionism stemmed from the threat that improved accuracy raised to the image of mass bomber* formations which underlay air power advocates' claim to increased resources and a separate air force. That was not the case, however, for in Southeast Asia, some 500 AZONs were used to knock out 27 bridges, many of them untouched by repeated free-fall bombing attacks. After World War II,* AZON and TARZON, along with plans for other "smart weapons" systems, such as television-guided glide bombs and radar*-controlled ramjet missiles, were shelved as part of demobilization.

In the Korean War,* in late 1950, analysis of Far East Air Forces* (FEAF) bombing efforts revitalized remotely guided glide bomb technology, first in the form of RAZON, for range-azimuth, 1,000- and 2,000-pound bombs. Although less than half of the first batch responded to control due to storage decay and technical teething problems, 331 dropped by the 13th Bomb Group destroyed 15 bridges—double the effectiveness of free-fall bombs. In December 1950, the six-ton TARZON, derived from the Royal Air Force's (RAF) Tallboy, entered service. After initial hitches, TARZON's performance exceeded conventional bombing tenfold; 28 dropped and six targets destroyed. After detection of fuzing safety defects and exhaustion of FEAF's target inventory, TARZONs were withdrawn from operations.

References. Roger A. Beaumont, "Rapiers versus Clubs: The Fitful History of 'Smart Bombs,' " *Journal of the Royal United Services Institute*, December 1982, pp. 56–61. Joseph C. Boyce, *New Weapons for Air Warfare*, 1947. Harold B. Hinton, *Air Victory: The Men and the Machines*, 1948. Alwyn T. Lloyd, *B-29 Superfortress in Detail & Scale*, part 2, "Derivatives," 1987.

Roger A. Beaumont

B

B-1 LANCER**

The B-1B was in 1990 the USAF's* latest bomber* in service designed to fulfill all strategic operations* at intercontinental ranges. It was produced by the Rockwell International Corporation and was an outgrowth of the Advanced Manned Strategic Aircraft (AMSA) project. It was a follow-on design to the defunct B-70.* While the requirement had existed since 1961, the political climate was not right until 1970, when funding became available for full-scale development.

Four B-1As were built, with a first flight in 1974. A total of 244 B-1As were to be built; however, in a surprise move, President Jimmy Carter canceled the program in 1979. With a change in administration, the program was reinstated in 1982, making this the only major defense program to be canceled and reinstated. The result was that the taxpayer received 100 instead of 200 airplanes for the same price.

The reinstated airplane, the B-1B, was changed to a subsonic, low-level penetrator. Its justification was a stopgap between the B-52* and the B-2.* The latter, not the B-1B, was intended to exploit known technology fully. The B-1B was under cost and ahead of schedule during its production. The first flight was in 1984, active service began in 1985, and production ended in 1988. B-1Bs are in four Strategic Air Command* (SAC) wings. The press and political opposition battered the airplane for its early deficiencies; however, most of these problems were resolved. Most were no different than those encountered on previous airplanes. There was one important problem that continued: the defensive avionics system that was the most complex ever designed. The crews can work around the difficulties manually. Three possible causes have been considered: (1) the initial specification was too restrictive, (2) not enough time was spent on it, and (3) not enough airplanes were available in the test phase. Four B-1Bs were used for the tests, and earlier programs had more planes for the purpose. Rockwell named the aircraft "Centurian." The USAF nicknames are "Bone" (from B-One), "The Jet," and "Lawn Dart."

Characteristics (B-1B): engines, four General Electric F101-GE-102 turbofans of 30,780 pounds thrust in afterburner each; span, variable 78 to 137 feet; length, 147 feet; height, 34 feet; gross weight, 477,000 pounds; top speed, 792 miles per hour; service ceiling, 60,000 feet; range, 4,755 miles; ordnance, 42,000 pounds.

References. James W. Canan, "The Magnificent B-1B," *AF*, November 1984, pp. 58–65. Futrell, *Ideas*, vol. 2. Knaack, *US Airc.*, vol. 2. Don Logan and Jay Miller, *Rockwell International B-1A/B*, 1986. Swanborough, *US Mil. Airc.* Susan H. H. Young, "Gallery of USAF Weapons," *AF*, May 1990, p. 141.

**The P-43* was also named Lancer.

Alwyn T. Lloyd

B-2

Work on stealth* ideas began at the Northrop Corporation in the 1960s, and development of the Advanced Technology Bomber (ATB), now the B-2, started in the late 1970s. It is a multirole bomber* intended to complement or replace the ancient B-52* and interim B-1.* Northrop is the prime contractor with The Boeing Company and the Vought Company, a subsidiary of LTV Corporation, as major subcontractors.

The B-2 uses the traditional Northrop flying wing design and has a two-man crew. It is designed to use the AGM-129,* nuclear weapons,* and bombs.* The first flight took place in 1989, and it is expected to enter active service in the 1990s. In 1989 the USAF* planned to buy 132 B-2As. The 1989 estimates of the cost of the bomber ranged from one-half to one billion dollars each, depending on whether Congress stretches development or production and how many are built. Stretch-outs and low production numbers could make it the most expensive plane in USAF history. It appeared it might even be canceled as some congressmen and media have been arguing that the B-2 had no mission; the same argument was used to prevent buying B-17s* in 1938. Its nickname is "Batmobile."

Characteristics: engines, four General Electric F118-GE-100 turbofans of 19,000 pounds thrust each; span, 172 feet; length, 69 feet; height, 17 feet; top speed, subsonic; range, intercontinental; ordnance, 40,000 pounds.

References. Ted Coleman, *Jack Northrop and the Flying Wing: The Story behind the Stealth Bomber*, 1988. Jeffrey P. Rhodes, "On Stealthy Wings," *AF*, February 1989, pp. 43–46. William B. Scott, Michael A. Dornheim, and Bruce A. Smith, "B-2 First Flight," *AWST*, 24 July 1989, pp. 22–28. Swanborough, *US Mil. Airc.* Susan H. H. Young, "Gallery of USAF Weapons," *AF*, May 1990, pp. 141–42.

B-9

This was the first all-metal monoplane bomber* made for the USAAC.* It was built by the Boeing Division of the United Aircraft & Transport Corporation and was based upon the commercial Model 200 Monomail. The first flight was in 1931. According to USAAC test pilots, one of whom was James H. Doolittle,* it had inferior performance primarily because it was underpowered. Yet the B-9's speed was five miles per hour higher than that of contemporary fighters,* resulting in the development of a new line of fighters with superior performance. It did not enter active service.

Characteristics (Y1B-9A): engines, two Pratt & Whitney R-1860–11 of 600 horsepower each; span, 77 feet; length, 52 feet; height, 12 feet; gross weight, 14,320 pounds; top speed, 188 miles per hour; service ceiling, 20,750 feet; range, 540 miles; bombs, 2,260 pounds.

References. Peter M. Bowers, *Boeing Aircraft since 1916*, 1989. Swanborough, *US Mil. Airc.* Wagner, *Am. Planes*.

Alwyn T. Lloyd

B-10

The Glenn L. Martin Company built for the USAAC* a series of twin-engined bombers* that were all metal and had retractable landing gear. These aircraft succeeded with the concepts that were introduced in the Boeing B-9* and became the first mass-produced, all-metal bombers for the USAAC. The series was the B-10, B-12, and B-14. The B-10 was faster than any fighter* aircraft in the USAAC in 1932. Two prototypes were produced, an XB-10 and a YB-10. These were followed by a pair of B-10s, a YB-10A, and 103 B-10As. Glenn L. Martin received the Collier Trophy in 1932 for developing the B-10. The B-10B, the main version, began production in 1934. B-12s and a single XB-14 had different engines. Export versions were sold beginning in 1936 and saw combat.

Characteristics (B-10B): engines, two Wright R-1820–33 of 775 horsepower each; span, 71 feet; length, 45 feet; height, 15 feet; gross weight, 16,400 pounds; top speed, 213 miles per hour; service ceiling, 24,200 feet; range, 1,240 miles; bombs, 2,260 pounds.

References. Primary: Dale O. Smith, "But for the Captains," *AF*, March 1985, pp. 130–31. Secondary: Lloyd S. Jones, *U.S. Bombers 1928–1980s*, 4th ed., 1984. Swanborough, *US Mil. Airc.* Wagner, *Am. Planes*.

Alwyn T. Lloyd

B-15

In 1933, the USAAC* determined a need for a bomber* that could strike targets as far away as Alaska and Hawaii. The Boeing Division of the United Aircraft & Transport Corporation and the Glenn L. Martin Company submitted designs for this project, designated XLRB-1. Boeing's Model 294 was ordered in 1935 as the XB-15, and it first flew in 1937. For its day, it was the largest and most heavily armed U.S. bomber. Many of its design concepts were incorporated into the later Model 299 which became the B-17.* Being underpowered, it was unsuitable as a bomber and was converted to transport* use as the XC-105 in 1943.

Characteristics: engines, four Pratt & Whitney R-1830–11 of 1,000 horsepower each; span, 149 feet; length, 88 feet; height, 18 feet; gross weight, 70,706 pounds; top speed, 200 miles per hour; service ceiling, 18,900 feet; range, 5,130 miles.

References. Peter M. Bowers, *Boeing Aircraft since 1916*, 1989. Lloyd S. Jones, *U.S. Bombers 1928–1980s*, 4th ed., 1984. Swanborough, *US Mil. Airc.*

Alwyn T. Lloyd

B-17 FLYING FORTRESS

If one had to choose one airplane to represent the USAF,* it would have to be the beautiful, majestic "Fort." The B-17 became America's first bomber* for strategic operations* and paved the way for all subsequent U.S. heavy bombardment airplanes, in addition to establishing The Boeing Company as the preeminent designer of large aircraft. It had the distinction of being the first U.S. four-engined monoplane bomber. It proved the practicality of high-altitude flight with large loads, long range, and high speeds. It was as fast as contemporary fighter* planes. It was famous for its ruggedness and for its steadiness as a gun and bomb aiming platform. Coupled with the Norden bombsight,* the B-17 proved the concept of daylight precision bombardment. General Carl A. Spaatz* believed World War II* could not have been won without the B-17.

Boeing's Model 299 was built for entry into the USAAC* multiengine bomber competition of 1934. The key designers were Clairmont L. "Claire" Egtvedt, vice president of engineering, and Edward C. Wells. Boeing's competitors used two-engined designs—a mistake. The prototype B-17 first flew in 1935. In its tests it set many speed and payload records. On its nonstop flight to Wright Field for the competitive flights, it flew 2,000 miles at an average ground speed of 252 miles per hour, another record. Some B-17s, known as Fortress Is, entered combat with the Royal Air Force (RAF) operating from England. The first U.S. ones in battle were flying into Hawaii during the raid of 7 December 1941. Early combat showed the need for greatly increased armament. In the Eighth Air Force* (8AF), 26 bomb groups used the B-17. Another six groups flew it in the Mediterranean theater. The B-17 was better suited than the alternative B-24* to operations in Europe (rather than the Pacific). The ranges needed in Europe were not as long as those needed in the Pacific. But the main reason for its European success was that the B-17 could fly the tightest formations at high altitude. This made it more formidable against enemy fighters, a greater threat in Europe than in the Pacific, and it produced superior bomb patterns. The B-17 was also superbly rugged, which meant fewer losses to fighters and flak.*

A total of 12,731 B-17s were produced by Boeing, the Douglas Aircraft Company, and the Vega Aircraft Corporation, a subsidiary of the Lockheed Aircraft Corporation. Variants included the CB-17G, VB-17G, and C-108 transports;* F-9 reconnaissance;* TB-17G trainer; QB-17 and DB-17 for testing; and SB-17G "Dumbo" for rescue.* The XB-38 used liquid-cooled engines, the B-40 was a bomber escort, and BQ-17s were flying bombs for Aphrodite.* The variants show the design's flexibility. No USAF airplane has been more beloved by its crews. Its nicknames, besides "Fort," were "Big A— Bird" and "The Queen," given with affection.

Characteristics (B-17G): engines, four Wright R-1820–97 of 1,200 horsepower each; span, 104 feet; length, 74 feet; height, 19 feet; gross weight, 65,500 pounds; top speed, 287 miles per hour at 25,000 feet; service ceiling, 35,600 feet; range with three tons of bombs, 2,000 miles; maximum bombs, 17,600 pounds.

Movies: *Air Force*,* 1943. *Memphis Belle*,* 1944 and 1990.

References. Primary: Higham, *Combat Airc.*, vol 3. Robin Stoddard, "Flying the B-17 'Sally B,' " *AF*, September 1981, pp. 98–105. Secondary: Peter M. Bowers, *Boeing Aircraft since 1916*, 1989. Roger A. Freeman, *B-17 Fortress at War*, 1977. Alwyn T. Lloyd, *B-17 Flying Fortress in Detail & Scale*, vols. 1, 2, and 3, 1980, 1983, and 1986. W. L. White, *Queens Die Proudly*, 1943.

Alwyn T. Lloyd

B-18 BOLO

In 1934 the USAAC* sought a bomber* with double the bomb load and the range of the B-10.* The Douglas Aircraft Company tried to get the contract with a plane based upon its highly successful DC-2 airliner. The competition was a Glenn L. Martin Company Model 146 and an aircraft that became the Boeing Aircraft Company's B-17.* The USAAC's desires were overriden by the U.S. Army, and the Douglas design was selected for production as the B-18. With a buy of 217, the B-18 became, at the time, the USAAC's most common bomber. Production ended in 1940. There were 33 stationed in Hawaii at the time of the Pearl Harbor* strike, and many were destroyed. The USAAF* replaced them in bomber units as soon as possible with B-17s, and then 122 were used in anti-submarine patrols. The B-18s sank two U-boats, and a U-boat shot down a B-18. Two B-18s were converted to a transport* variant, the C-58.

Characteristics (B-18A): engines, two Wright R-1820–53 of 850 horsepower each; span, 90 feet; length, 58 feet; height, 15 feet; gross weight, 27,673 pounds; top speed, 215 miles per hour at 10,000 feet; service ceiling, 23,900 feet; range, 1,150 miles; bombs, 6,500 pounds.

References. Primary: Higham, *Combat Airc.*, vol. 3. Secondary: Swanborough, *US Mil. Airc.* Wagner, *Am. Planes*.

B-19

The sole XB-19 was designed and built by the Douglas Aircraft Company. Work began in 1935 as part of the USAAC's* investigation of long-range bomber* possibilities after aviation's technological revolution. It first carried the designation XBLR-2 and flew in 1941 as the largest U.S. airplane until the B-36.* It had the same model engines that would later be used on the B-29.* It was underpowered and spent its career in flight testing and as a transport.* The valuable test results were used in the design of the B-29 and B-36. Its nickname was "Douglas Flying Behemoth."

Characteristics: engines, four Wright R-3350–5 of 2,000 horsepower each; span, 212 feet; length, 132 feet; height, 42 feet; gross weight, 140,000 pounds; top speed, 224 miles per hour; service ceiling, 39,000 feet; range, 7,710 miles; bombs, 37,100 pounds.

References. René J. Francillon, *McDonnell Douglas Aircraft since 1920*, vol. 1, 1988.

Dan Goss, "Douglas XB-19," *United States Air Force Museum Friends Bulletin*, Summer 1989, pp. 14–19. Lloyd S. Jones, *U.S. Bombers 1928–1980s*, 4th ed., 1984. Swanborough, *US Mil. Airc.*

Alwyn T. Lloyd

B-24 LIBERATOR

The Consolidated Aircraft Corporation's B-24 was America's second bomber* for strategic operations.* It was built in larger numbers than any other combat aircraft except the German Bf 109. There were 18,482 produced by five manufacturers for the USAAF* and the British Empire, the latter receiving 2,445. In addition, 774 were made for the U.S. Navy, making a grand total of 19,256 aircraft. The British and the Navy, as well as the USAAF, were interested in the B-24 because it was superb for controlling the seas. It can be said that the Liberator was the single most responsible factor in the demise of the U-boat threat in the Atlantic, which meant the defeat of the German navy.

The airplane was built around the innovative Davis airfoil, a high-aspect wing with a high camber. Its distinctive twin tails made the plane slightly unstable and difficult to fly in formation. The resultant overboosting by its pilots led to an abnormally high failure rate for its engines. The last derivative, the Navy's PB4Y-2 Privateer, had a single tail. The airplane was originally conceived for the French. When France surrendered in 1940, the orders were diverted to the British. The first ones were identified as LB-30s, the *LB* standing for licensed-built. The Royal Air Force (RAF) Coastal Command employed these aircraft for maritime reconnaissance,* sea interdiction, and antisubmarine operations. Later B-24s were employed by the Army Air Forces Antisubmarine Command* and the U.S. Navy for antisubmarine work.

B-24s were not well liked in the European theater because of the difficulty in mixing formations of B-24s with B-17s.* Their performance was not compatible. Also, there was a need for tight formations over Germany. B-17 crews said, half in jest, that their best escort was B-24s because the latter attracted German fighters* away from B-17s. The B-24 did much better in the Mediterranean theater and performed superlatively in the Pacific theater. Variants of the B-24 were the F-7 for photo reconnaissance,* the C-87 Liberator Express and CB-24 transport,* B-41 Escort and C-109 tanker.* A number of B-24s were modified for electronic warfare.* In the Pacific theater, these aircraft, flying singly at low level at night, had a remarkable success rate. They paved the way for today's radar* bombing systems. The name *Liberator* was not bestowed by the British. It came about through a contest held at Consolidated. It was affectionately nicknamed "Lib" and not so affectionately "B Dash Crash."

Characteristics (B-24M): engines, four Pratt & Whitney R-1830–65 of 1,200 horsepower each; span, 110 feet; length, 67 feet; height, 18 feet; gross weight, 64,500 pounds; top speed, 300 miles per hour at 30,000 feet; service ceiling, 28,000 feet; range, 2,100 miles; bombs, 8,800 pounds.

References. Primary: William Carigan, *AD LIB: Flying the B-24 LIBERATOR in World War II*, 1988. Secondary: Alan G. Blue, *The B-24 Liberator*, 1976. Martin Bowman,

The *B-24 Liberator 1939–1945*, 1980. Alwyn T. Lloyd, *Liberator—America's Global Bomber*, 1990. Swanborough, *US Mil. Airc.*

Alwyn T. Lloyd

B-25 MITCHELL

The B-25 was one of the most outstanding bombers* ever used by the USAF.* It is appropriate that a great bomber and ship killer was named in honor of Brigadier General William "Billy" Mitchell.* The B-25 is one of only two USAF aircraft named for a person. Fame came quickly to it when it was used in April 1942 for the historic Doolittle raid on Tokyo,* taking off from the USS *Hornet.*

Work on the medium bomber began in 1938 by North American Aviation, Inc., as a speculation designated NA-40–1. Its first flight was in 1939. The USAAF* accepted 9,815 B-25s, but it never had more than 2,700 at any one time during World War II* because of the numbers supplied to others, including the U.S. Marine Corps. Nearly 11,000 were built, and they served globally. Active service on antisubmarine patrol began in 1941 from McChord* Field, Washington, and a Japanese submarine was sunk by one on Christmas Eve of that year. In 1942 some went into service with the Royal Air Force (RAF), Brazil, and the Soviets. The Dutch also bought the plane, but some of theirs were diverted to the USAAF to operate out of the Philippines before the U.S. evacuation.

Some extra armament, including a 75mm field gun in a few, was added to make the B-25 into a ship killer. The field gun proved unsatisfactory, but the B-25J with 14 fixed forward-firing 50-caliber guns was highly successful in the role. In March 1943, B-25s with ten forward-firing guns and 500-pound bombs played a big role, without any battle losses, in the near annihilation of a Japanese convoy in the Battle of the Bismarck Sea.* Their superb flying qualities enabled them to serve not only in battle but for transports,* for utility work, and as pilot* trainers. They were used as pilot trainers from 1943 to 1959. The B-25's qualities led to extensive postwar civilian service. Its variants were the F-10 reconnaissance* model and the TB-25 trainer. The Mitchell was a pilot's favorite, and it was nicknamed "Billy's Bomber" and "The Sweetheart of the Services."

Characteristics (B-25J): engines, two Wright R-2600–92 of 1,700 horsepower each; span, 68 feet; length, 53 feet; height, 16 feet; gross weight, 35,000 pounds; top speed, 272 miles per hour at 13,000 feet; service ceiling, 24,200 feet; range, 1,350 miles; bombs, 3,000 pounds.

References. Primary: John "Hank" Henry, "The Battle at Ormac Bay," *AH*, June 1976, pp. 86–89, 92–93. Higham, *Combat Airc.*, vol. 1. Secondary: Swanborough, *US Mil. Airc.* Wagner, *Am. Planes.*

B-26 INVADER

The B-26 was one of the most successful USAF* and Douglas Aircraft Company planes. It served the United States in three wars, from 1944 to 1969. It was loved by pilots* because it was responsive, easy to fly, and had high performance in its early days. Although it had two engines, it was agile and had speed approaching that of piston-engined fighters.* Its qualities have made it a favorite for various civil uses.

In 1940 the USAAC* sought a fast light bomber* that could also do precision bombing at medium heights. Douglas's candidate, the XA-26, first flew in 1942. When it entered active service in 1944 it was heavily armed and armored. Some versions had a Plexiglas nose for a bombardier,* while others had a "hard" nose, without Plexiglas and filled with guns. After World War II,* it was the main bomber of the new Tactical Air Command* (TAC). In 1948 the plane was redesignated the B-26 when the newly independent USAF eliminated the hated attack,* or *A*, designator. By that time the B-26 Marauder* was out of active service.

Third Bomb Wing Invaders flew the first USAF bombing strike in the Korean War.* Thereafter the B-26s were used extensively in the war, mostly on night interdiction missions. They flew 60,096 B-26 and 11,944 RB-26 sorties. Fifty-six were lost to enemy action in the war. Meanwhile, B-26s returned to Europe to support the North Atlantic Treaty Organization* (NATO). B-26s in the 1950s flew more heavily loaded than did those in World War II. In Korea the B-26s were able to mass 16 50-caliber machine guns to fire forward. The Third Bomb Wing also flew the last mission of the war.

Invaders were sent to the Republic of Vietnam in 1961 as part of Farm Gate* and stayed until 1964 when they were withdrawn as worn out. Rebuilt as B-26K Counter Invaders, they returned to Southeast Asia to operate out of Thailand until 1969. In 1967 the Thailand-based B-26s were redesignated A-26As to meet host nation treaty requirements.

B-26 Invader variants include CB-26B and VB-26B transports,* TB-26B and TB-26C trainers, and FA-26Cs and RB-26s for reconnaissance.* Total production was 2,446. B-26s served the U.S. Navy, Britain, France, Indonesia, Laos, Latin American countries, Portugal, Saudi Arabia, and Turkey. Its nicknames were "Li'l Hummer" and "Li'l Racer."

Characteristics (B-26C): engines, two Pratt & Whitney R-2800–79 of 2,000 horsepower each; span, 70 feet; length, 51 feet; height, 19 feet; gross weight, 37,740 pounds; top speed, 372 miles per hour at 10,000 feet; service ceiling, 20,450 feet; radius of action, 892 miles with 4,000 pounds of payload.

References. Primary: Chester L. Blunk, *"Every Man a Tiger: The 731st USAF Night Intruders over Korea*, 1982. Michael J. C. Roth, "NIMROD—King of the Trail," *AF*, October 1971, pp. 30–34. Secondary: René J. Francillon, *McDonnell Douglas Aircraft since 1920*, vol. 1, 1988. Knaack, *US Airc.*, vol. 2. Allan R. Scholin, "On the Graveyard Shift," *AF*, September 1973, pp. 102–6. Swanborough, *US Mil. Airc.*

B-26 MARAUDER

This medium bomber* started with a poor reputation, but it performed magnificently in Europe and it has been highly regarded ever since.

The Glenn L. Martin Company was awarded a contract for it in 1939. The design featured the highest wing loading for a U.S. Army plane up to that time.

The first flight was in 1940, and it entered active service in 1941. Wing loading was demanding of inexperienced pilots* who were the norm in the USAAC* in 1941. The aircraft soon was branded "A Plane a Day in Tampa Bay," "Baltimore Whore," "Widow Maker," and "Flying Prostitute" (no visible means of support). Wing area and span were increased on some models to make the plane more forgiving of mistakes, but by then enough weight was added to restore the high wing loading, and there was no trouble. The pilots' experience level had risen.

Marauders served in New Guinea,* at the Battle of Midway, in the Aleutians,* in North Africa, and in Western Europe. Production ended in 1945. The number accepted by the USAAF* was 5,157. The only variant was the AT-23, or TB-26, used for towing targets by both the USAAF and the U.S. Navy.

Characteristics (B-26G): engines, two Pratt & Whitney R-2800–43 of 2,000 horsepower each; span, 71 feet; length, 56 feet; height, 20 feet; gross weight, 38,200 pounds; top speed, 283 miles per hour at 5,000 feet; service ceiling, 19,800 feet; range, 1,100 miles; bombs, 4,000 pounds.

References. Primary: J. K. Havener, " 'Mediums Were Also Out,' " *AH*, December 1982, pp. 218–25. Higham, *Combat Airc.*, vol. 1. Donald J. Mrozek et al., eds., *Martin Marauder and the Franklin Allens: A Wartime Love Story*, 1980. Secondary: John L. Frisbee, "Marauders at Midway," *AF*, April 1986, p. 140. Swanborough, *US Mil. Airc.*

B-29 SUPERFORTRESS

On 6 August 1945, a B-29 named *Enola Gay** dropped the "Little Boy" nuclear weapon* on Hiroshima, Japan. Three days later a B-29 named *Bock's Car* dropped the "Fat Boy" on Nagasaki, Japan. On 16 August Emperor Hirohito ordered a Japanese cease-fire. Only two B-29s in a special strategic operations* bombing campaign had forced the end of the greatest war in history without invasion of the enemy country.

In 1939 the USAAC* wanted a super bomber* capable of speeds of 400 miles per hour, a 5,333-mile range, and a one-ton payload for half the range. These specifications resulted in the Boeing Aircraft Company's B-29, Lockheed Aircraft Corporation's B-30, Douglas Aircraft Company's B-31, and Consolidated Aircraft Corporation's B-32.* The B-30 and B-31 never left the drawing boards.

Boeing's concept was to propel a mass twice the speed and weight of the B-17.* The engines available would yield only 2,000 horsepower each, so reducing drag was the only way to get the desired performance. Aerodynamic improvements, better propellors, cabin pressurization for higher altitudes, Fowler flaps, and remote gun sighting stations were the means to achieve the design goals. Even before the first flight, Boeing had a contract for 14 YB-29s for test and 250 B-29s for production. The B-32 was continued as a hedge. The demand for B-29s was so great that four plants were needed: Boeing Renton in Washington, Boeing Wichita in Kansas, Martin Omaha in Nebraska, and Bell Marietta in Georgia. A total of 3,965 B-29s were produced.

Throughout its career, the engines caused the most grief to the B-29. Numerous refinements were made to reduce those problems. A massive effort, known as "The Battle of Kansas," worked out bugs in manufacturing, training, and testing. Never before had so complex a weapon system moved from drawing boards to full-scale production without an extensive flight test program. Problems found were sent to Boeing for design changes. Variants included SB-29 for rescue;* WB-29 for weather reconnaissance; F-13, FB-29, and RB-29 for reconnaissance;* CB-29 and VB-29 for transport;* KB-29 for aerial refueling;* and TB-29 for target towing.

The Twentieth Air Force* (20AF) was established just for the B-29s. Other air forces* were under U.S. Army theater commanders, but the 20AF reported directly to General of the Army H. H. Arnold.* The XX Bomber Command, part of the 20AF, was in India. Its first raid was on Bangkok, Thailand. To strike in the strategic campaign against Japan,* the 20AF had to move its own supplies into China for staging. The first target struck in Japan was the steel plant in Yawata.

When the Marianas Islands* were captured in the summer of 1944, a new unit, the Twenty-First Air Force* (21AF), was formed. It also was under Arnold. Initially led by Major General Haywood S. Hansell, Jr.,* it struck Japan for the first time on 24 October 1944. Hansell was soon replaced by Major General Curtis E. LeMay* who changed the strategic operations* tactics from high-altitude precision bombing to low-level area raids. They continued to 14 August 1945 and Arnold said more than 60 Japanese cities were hit. Most of Japan's heavy industries were destroyed and many Japanese leaders credit the B-29s with reducing Japan's industrial capacity by 50 percent.

During the Berlin Airlift,* the Strategic Air Command* (SAC) deployed B-29s to England as a show of force. The Soviets knew the aircraft could carry nuclear weapons but did not know that these particular airplanes were not so equipped. B-29s were in combat a second time in the Korean War* from 1950 to 1953.

Characteristics (B-29B): engines, four Wright R-3350 of 2,200 horsepower each; span, 141 feet; length, 99 feet; height, 30 feet; gross weight, 137,500 pounds; top speed, 364 miles per hour at 25,000 feet; service ceiling, 32,000 feet; range, 4,200 miles; bombs, 20,000 pounds.

Movies: *Above and Beyond*, 1953. *The Beginning or the End*, 1947. *Enola Gay*, 1980. *Wild Blue Yonder*, 1952.

References. Primary: Higham, *Combat Airc.*, vol. 1. Curtis E. LeMay and Bill Yenne, *Superfortress: The Story of the B-29 and American Air Power*, 1988. Secondary: Steve Birdsall, *Saga of the Superfortress: The Dramatic Story of the B-29 and the Twentieth Air Force*, 1980. Alwyn T. Lloyd, *B-29 Superfortress in Detail & Scale*, part 1, "Production Versions," 1983, and part 2, "Derivatives," 1987. Swanborough, *US Mil. Airc.*

See also B-50.

Alwyn T. Lloyd

B-32 DOMINATOR

In 1940 prototypes of this aircraft, also called Terminator, were ordered from the Consolidated Aircraft Corporation as a hedge against failure of the B-29* design. The B-29 was ordered at the same time. The first flight of the B-32, a twin-tailed aircraft, took place in 1942, and production was ordered in 1943.

Deliveries of a single-tailed version began in 1944. By then the B-29 was a success. The B-32 was criticized as too heavy, as having shoddy production workmanship, and as having an inadequate view for the bombardier.* The total built was 115, and 1,588 aircraft were canceled. Fifteen B-32s went into battle in the Pacific in 1945. One of them shot down the last Japanese aircraft destroyed in combat by Americans.

Characteristics: engines, four Wright R-3350–23 of 2,200 horsepower each; span, 135 feet; length, 82 feet; height, 33 feet; gross weight, 100,000 pounds; top speed, 357 miles per hour; service ceiling, 30,700 feet; range, 2,400 miles with ten tons of bombs.

References. Primary: Higham, *Combat Airc.*, vol. 2. Secondary: Swanborough, *US Mil. Airc.* Wagner, *Am. Planes.* John Wegg, *General Dynamics Aircraft and Their Predecessors*, 1990. William T. Y'Blood, "The Second String," *AAHS Journal*, Summer 1968, pp. 80–92.

B-35 AND B-49

The genesis for these Northrop Aircraft, Inc., "Flying Wings" can be traced back to 1923, when John K. "Jack" Northrop tinkered with the idea while employed by the Douglas Aircraft Company. In 1939 he was president and chief engineer of his own firm, Northrop. His prototype flying wing design, the N-1M, first flew in 1940. Intrigued by the concept, the USAAF* ordered four 7,100-pound flying scale models of the wings. These were followed by a pair of XB-35s and 13 YB-35s. A contract for 200 B-35As, to be produced by the Glenn L. Martin Company, was canceled.

A pair of YB-35s were converted into YB-49s, originally to be YB-35Bs, with the replacement of the reciprocating engines with turbojets buried in the wing. An order for 30 RB-49s was placed in 1948, canceled in 1949, and replaced with an order to convert nine YB-35s into YRB-49s. These later aircraft had four turbojets in the wing and two in external pods. In 1948 the second YB-49 was lost in a crash near Muroc AFB which killed the pilot,* Captain Glen Walter Edwards. Muroc was renamed Edwards* AFB in his honor.

Serious stability problems occurred during a protracted flight test program, so the USAF* canceled further development of the planes in 1950. According to the USAF, a B-29* could achieve bomb-run stability within 45 seconds, whereas the B-49 required up to four minutes. In addition, the USAF stated that the circular bombing error of the B-49 was twice that of a B-29. Pilots had difficulty holding a steady course, constant airspeed, or altitude unless the airplane was flown by autopilot. However, Jack Northrop contended that the stability problems could be solved with a little more time. The B-2* and F-117,* which use flying wing structures, give credence to his view. There is conjecture that the B-49 program was ended for political pork barrel reasons so that the Consolidated-Vultee Aircraft Corporation's (Convair) B-36* could be produced. Program termination occurred soon after Jack Northrop refused to have his design worked on by Convair.

All remaining aircraft, albeit one, were immediately scrapped. The last YRB-49A was flown to Northrop's Ontario International Airport where it is believed to have remained in storage for 18 months before being reclaimed by the USAF and scrapped in 1953. The careers of the B-2 and F-117 may give the final verdict on the Northrop Flying Wings.

Characteristics (YRB-49A): engines, six Allison J-35-A-21 turbojets of 5,600 pounds thrust each; span, 172 feet; length, 53 feet; gross weight, 206,000 pounds; top speed (YB-49), 520 miles per hour.

References. Primary: Ted Coleman, *Jack Northrop and the Flying Wing: The Story Behind the Stealth Bomber*, 1988. Secondary: Lloyd S. Jones, *U.S. Bombers 1928–1980s*, 4th ed., 1984. Knaack, *US Airc.*, vol. 2. Swanborough, *US Mil. Airc.*

Alwyn T. Lloyd

B-36 PEACEMAKER

This Consolidated-Vultee Aircraft Corporation design was a landmark airplane. It was the first intercontinental bomber,* able to carry any weapon in the U.S. arsenal to targets at distances of 3,100 to 3,900 miles. Thus it was the principal means of deterrence from 1948 to the late 1950s.

Work on it began in 1941; however, the demands of World War II* kept it from coming to fruition for almost five years. Its first flight took place in 1946. Its design competitor was the XB-35.* The defensive armament at first was just short of awesome. A total of 16 20mm cannon were carried in pairs mounted in six retractable turrets, a tail turret, and a nose mount. The B-36B carried 9,200 rounds of ammunition. Performance was improved with the B-36D, which added four jet engines in pods to the original six piston engines. When it was learned that Soviet fighters* could reach 50,000 feet, many B-36s were stripped of all armament except tail guns, and the crew was reduced from 15 to nine. These aircraft, known as B-36J Featherweights, were able to reach altitudes approaching 55,000 feet. F-86* pilots who tried to engage B-36s in mock battle respected the bomber.*

The B-36 was so large and heavy it was limited to a small number of bases, and it was a maintenance nightmare. While it was operational during the Korean War,* it never fired a shot in anger. Its active service ended in 1959 after jet bombers had taken over the deterrence mission. A total of 385 B-36s and RB-36s were built. One airframe was also built as the sole XC-99 transport which ferried engines for the B-36 fleet. One became the X-6.* Its nicknames were "Aluminum Overcast" and "Magnesium Overcast."

Characteristics (B-36J): engines, six Pratt & Whitney R-4360–53 of 3,800 horsepower each and four General Electric J47-GE-19 turbojets of 5,200 pounds thrust each; span, 230 feet; length, 162 feet; height, 47 feet; gross weight, 410,000 pounds; top speed, 411 miles per hour at 36,400 feet; service ceiling, 39,900 feet; range, 6,800 miles with five tons of bombs.

Movie: *Strategic Air Command*,* 1955.

References. Primary: Harry E. Goldsworthy, "B-36 Peacemaker," *AH*, December 1983, pp. 261–67. Secondary: Meyers Jacobson and Ray Wagner, *B-36 in Action*, 1980. Lloyd S. Jones, *U.S. Bombers 1928–1980s*, 4th ed., 1984. Knaack, *US Airc.*, vol. 2. Swanborough, *US Mil. Airc.* John Wegg, *General Dynamics Aircraft and Their Predecessors*, 1990.

　　See also B-36 controversy; fighter conveyor; Tom-Tom.

Alwyn T. Lloyd

B-36 CONTROVERSY

Also called "Revolt of the Admirals," the B-36 controversy represented an interservice dispute unprecedented in scope and bitterness. It was spurred by the April 1949 cancellation by Secretary of Defense (SECDEF) Louis A. Johnson* of the 65,000-ton supercarrier USS *United States*, the U.S. Navy's hope to get an air strategic operations* mission. Cedric Worth, a civilian assistant to the secretary of the Navy, released to the press an anonymous document charging that fraud riddled the USAF* procurement of the B-36* bomber* and that the aircraft was, in reality, a "billion-dollar blunder." The statement expressed the Navy's dissatisfaction with the severe budget cuts of President Harry S Truman's* administration and its exclusion from the air strategic operations proposed as the primary means of waging war against the USSR.

The publicity generated by Worth's document prompted an investigation by the House Armed Services Committee headed by Congressman Carl Vinson. A session held in August 1949 examined the allegations of corruption leveled against Johnson and the USAF. The hearings found not a trace of evidence to support the allegations.

A second session in October focused on a Navy challenge to the theory of strategic operations. During the hearings, teams of Navy technical experts questioned the ability of the B-36 to accomplish its mission while senior Navy leaders, including Chief of Naval Operations Admiral Louis Denfield, Admiral Arthur W. Radford, and retired Fleet Admiral Chester W. Nimitz, attacked the assumptions behind USAF strategic bombardment. An unstated situation was an internal struggle within the Navy over its roles and missions. Leading the defense of the concept, Chairman of the Joint Chiefs of Staff (JCS) General of the Army Omar N. Bradley and Chief of Staff of the Air Force Hoyt S. Vandenberg* cited the success of the USAAF* during World War II.* After rounds of heated testimony, the committee refrained from attempting to resolve professional military disagreements and, therefore, proposed no interference with the B-36 program.

Ironically, the outbreak of the Korean War* silenced many Navy critics of strategic operations when expanded budgets permitted funding of new supercarriers and the Navy got its own air strategic operations ability.

References. Primary: U.S. Congress, House, Committee on Armed Services, *Investigation of the B-36 Bomber Program*, 81st Cong., 1st sess., 1949. U.S. Congress, House, Committee on Armed Services, *The National Defense Program: Unification and Strategy*, 81st Cong., 1st sess., 1949. Secondary: Kenneth O. Condit, *The History of the Joint Chiefs of Staff, 1947–1949*, vol. 2, unpub. JCS report. Paul Y. Hammond, *Super Carriers and the B-36 Bombers: Appropriations, Strategy, and Politics*, 1963. Herman S. Wolk, "Revolt of the Admirals," *AF*, May 1988, pp. 62–67.

John T. Farquhar

B-40. *See* B-17; fighter escort.

B-41. *See* B-24; fighter escort.

B-45 TORNADO

The North American Aviation, Inc., B-45 was the United States's first production jet bomber* and the first tactical operations* aircraft able to use nuclear weapons.*

Work on it began in 1945 before the end of World War II.* Basically, it was a piston engine–era design incorporating jet engines. In 1947 the aircraft made its maiden flight. Its active service was from 1948 to 1958. The total number built was 143. Besides the RB-45 for reconnaissance,* variants included the JB-45C for testing and the DB-45 for director aircraft in guided missile* development.

B-45s were assigned to the Tactical Air Command* (TAC) while a few RB-45Cs found their way into the Strategic Air Command* (SAC). B-45s saw operational service in England. Three RB-45s flew combat missions in the Korean War.* They were used within MiG-15 operating areas in 1951. After two narrow escapes from MiGs, the second time despite F-84* escorts, the RB-45s were withdrawn from MiG flying areas.

In 1950, the first aerial refueling of a jet aircraft was achieved when an RB-45C was refueled by a KB-29P (*See* B-29). The Mackay Trophy for 1952 was awarded to the crew that flew an RB-45C nonstop from Elmendorf* AFB, Alaska, to Yokota* AB, Japan. This first nonstop transpacific flight was made possible by two refuelings from KB-29Ps.

Characteristics (B-45C): engines, four General Electric J47-GE-13/15 turbojets of 5,200 pounds thrust each; span, 89 feet; length, 75 feet; height, 25 feet; gross weight, 112,952 pounds; top speed, 579 miles per hour at sea level; service ceiling, 43,200 feet; range, 1,910 miles; bombs, 22,000 pounds.

References. Lloyd S. Jones, *U.S. Bombers 1928–1980s*, 4th ed., 1984. Knaack, *US Airc.*, vol. 2. Swanborough, *US Mil. Airc.*

Alwyn T. Lloyd

B-47 STRATOJET

A reliable three-man medium-range bomber,* the B-47 paved the way for an all-jet strategic operations* force and the B-52.* During its career, the B-47 was never called upon to deliver bombs in anger, serving as a nuclear-armed deterrent in the Cold War.*

In 1944, military requirements were issued that led four companies to enter designs in a competition for a jet-engined bomber. These were the North American Aviation, Inc., B-45,* Consolidated-Vultee Aircraft Corporation (Convair) XB-46, Boeing Aircraft Company B-47, and Glenn L. Martin Company XB-48. The B-47 won because its bomb bay could carry the large nuclear weapons* of the time.

The maiden flight was in 1947. Two prototypes were followed by nine B-47As and some B-47Bs which were thrust into a major evaluation program of 3,096 hours of wind tunnel time and five years of flying before this advanced airplane was ready for active service. Several modifications included the addition of aerial refueling* equipment and external fuel tanks. As with the B-17* and B-29,* the need for B-47s was so great that both the Douglas Aircraft Company and the Lockheed Aircraft Company were called in to help produce and maintain the 2,040 airplanes produced, including 287 photo reconnaissance* RB-47s. Uniquely, this large airplane could use the Low-Altitude Bombing System* (LABS). The only B-47s to operate outside of the USAF* were one bailed to the Royal Canadian Air Force (RCAF) for engine tests and a pair flown by the U.S. Navy for electronic warfare* testing. From 1963 to 1965 the B-47s were phased out of active service when the Strategic Air Command* (SAC) was directed to rely more on ballistic missiles.*

Characteristics (B-47E-II): engines, six General Electric J47-GE-25 turbojets of 6,000 pounds thrust each; span, 116 feet; length, 110 feet; height, 28 feet; gross weight, 206,700 pounds; top speed, 606 miles per hour at 16,300 feet; service ceiling, 40,500 feet; range, 4,000 miles; bombs, 20,000 pounds.

Movie: *Strategic Air Command,** 1955.

References. Primary: Higham, *Combat Airc.*, vol. 2. Dennis K. McDaniel "The B-47 from the Backseat, SAC from the Bottom—One Pilot's Account," *AH*, March, 1987, pp. 38–45. Secondary: Peter M. Bowers, *Boeing Aircraft since 1916*, 1989. Knaack, *US Airc.*, vol. 2. Alwyn T. Lloyd, *B-47 Stratojet in Detail & Scale*, 1986.

Alwyn T. Lloyd

B-49. *See* B-35.

B-50 SUPERFORTRESS

The Boeing Aircraft Company's B-50 served as an interim bomber* in the Strategic Air Command* (SAC) until the advent of the B-47.*

While similar in appearance to the B-29,* and first designated the B-29D, the B-50 was 75 percent different. It was designated B-50 in December 1945. The troublesome engines on the B-29 were replaced by more powerful ones, the largest reciprocating engines to enter mass production. The vertical tail was made five feet higher for more control during an engine-out condition, and a new type of propellor was used. Its systems and performance were considerably different. Aircrews who treated it as another version of the B-29 were in for a surprise. Of the 370 B-50s produced, from 1945 to 1953, three bomber types and one trainer type (TB-50) were built. From these airplanes sprang a number of conversions for reconnaissance* (RB-50s), weather reconnaissance (WB-50), tankers* (KB-50), and testing (DB-50). KB-50Js had two General Electric J-47 turbojets of 5,200 pounds thrust added to increase their speed for refueling jet aircraft. It is strange that the B-50 did not see combat in the Korean War.* B-50s did see combat as KB-50s in the Vietnam War* in 1964 and 1965. At this time the KB-50s were being retired.

Characteristics (B-50D): engines, four Pratt & Whitney R-4360 of 3,500 horsepower each; span, 141 feet; length, 99 feet; height, 33 feet; gross weight, 173,000 pounds; top speed, 380 miles per hour at 25,000 feet; service ceiling, 36,700 feet; range, 4,900 miles; bombs, 20,000 pounds.

References. Peter M. Bowers, *Boeing Aircraft since 1916*, 1989. Knaack, *US Airc.*, vol. 2. Alwyn T. Lloyd, *B-29 Superfortress in Detail & Scale*, part 3, "More Derivatives," 1989.

See also Lucky Lady.

Alwyn T. Lloyd

B-52 STRATOFORTRESS

In active service since 1955, older than many of its crews, and projected to soldier on into the 21st century, the B-52 has been the USAF's* most significant bomber* except for the B-17.* The B-52 has made an important contribution through deterrence to the long peace with the USSR. Also, its special strategic operations* campaign of Linebacker* II, or "The 11 Days' War," in 1972 forced the North Vietnamese back to peace talks and to the end of the Vietnam War.*

The Boeing Aircraft Company's B-52 was developed as the outgrowth of a major program review to enhance the B-36.* A preliminary design contract was awarded in 1946. At two points in time, once when the B-49* was being considered and the other when the YB-36C was proposed, the B-52 almost met its demise. Boeing took a four-engined turboprop design to Wright Field in 1948 but was influenced by Colonel Henry E. "Pete" Warden, the Air Materiel Command's (AMC) chief of bomber development, to consider turbojets instead. Over a single weekend in a Dayton, Ohio, hotel room, the Boeing people changed their design to a swept-wing, eight-engined turbojet bomber. The sketchy proposal was accepted by the AMC. Where the B-17 had required 153,000 engineering hours, 3 million were expended on the B-52. The prototype YB-52 made its inaugural flight in 1952. More than three years of flight testing of 15 aircraft were required before the first B-52 was delivered to the Strategic Air Command* (SAC) in 1955. Since then, this airplane has become the SAC's primary strategic bomber and the only recallable force in the U.S. nuclear triad.*

During its service in the Vietnam War,* the B-52 proved its mettle in conventional war. The enemy feared it more than any other weapon because it rained bombs from high altitudes and destroyed bunkers in Arc Light* operations. It was called upon again for the attack* function in the Iraq War.*

Originally conceived as a high-altitude bomber, it has changed into a low-altitude penetrator as well to deal with radar* and surface-to-air missiles* (SAM).

This move into the rigors of turbulent air had a deleterious effect on the aircraft's structure. Yet numerous upgrades in structure and system have kept these venerable airplanes in service longer than any other combat airplane. Some B-52Gs were modified to carry the AGM-84* Harpoon in support of the mission to control the seas. A total of 744 were built. In 1990 about 260 B-52Gs and B-52Hs were still in service with the SAC. No B-52 has been in the service of any other nation. Its nicknames are "BUFF," or "Big Ugly Fat F———," "Coconutknocker," and "Monkeyknocker." The latter two are from the Vietnam War.

Characteristics (B-52G): engines, eight Pratt & Whitney J57-P-43W turbojets of 11,200 pounds thrust each; span, 185 feet; length, 158 feet; height, 41 feet; gross weight, 480,000 pounds; top speed, 660 miles per hour at 20,000 feet; service ceiling, 55,000 feet; range, 10,000 miles; ordnance, 40,000 pounds.

Movie: *Bombers B-52*, 1957.

References. Primary: Ronald C. Elsdon, "B-52G: Mastering the Magnificent Monster," *AF*, November 1974, pp. 46–51. Victor B. Putz, "The Last B-52 Mission from Guam," *AF*, June 1974, pp. 49–54. Secondary: Walter Boyne, *Boeing B-52: A Documentary History*, 1981. Knaack, *US Airc.*, vol. 2. Alwyn T. Lloyd, *B-52 Stratofortress in Detail & Scale*, 1988, and "B-52: 35 Years Young," *AAHS Journal*, Summer 1988, pp. 106–13.

See also AGM-28; AGM-69; AGM-86B; Skybolt.

Alwyn T. Lloyd

B-57 CANBERRA

The Glenn L. Martin Company's B-57 was derived from the English Electric Company's Canberra B.Mk.2. This made it the only non-U.S. design that saw USAF* service after World War II.*

The B-57 was intended as a replacement for the B-26 Invader.* B-57As had the British side-by-side seating; the B-57B used tandem seating. Martin designed a rotary bomb bay with an integral door in place of the British clamshell doors. The B-57A first flew in 1953, and active service began in 1954. Under a program called Tropic Moon III, 16 B-57Bs were converted to B-57Gs for night intruder operations. They had low-light-level television, a new weapons delivery computer, and a new navigation system. Eleven of the aircraft saw combat in the Vietnam War.* The B-57C was a trainer and some were redesignated TB-57C. The B-57E was a tow target aircraft.

The RB-57D for reconnaissance* had a wingspan of 105 feet with an area of 1,500 square feet. A pair of 10,500-pound thrust engines were installed. The B-57D could fly above 70,000 feet. Structural problems with the wings and mission equipment failures accounted for 20 unsatisfactory out of 22 attempted sorties in June 1957. These shortcomings were corrected. The Strategic Air Command* (SAC) flew them along the borders of and over communist nations for several years. The General Dynamics Corporation improved on the RB-57D by conversions to the RB-57F. New wings of 122-feet span were installed. New Pratt & Whitney engines* of 16,000 pounds of thrust were used along with two

2,900-pound thrust auxiliary engines. The RB-57F had a range of 2,560 miles. Both the SAC and the Air Weather Service* (AWS) operated these aircraft, the former for passive reconnaissance and the latter for air sampling as part of the nuclear test program.

Some B-57Es were converted into EB-57Es for aerospace defense electronic warfare.* Martin built 403 B-57s, comprised of 8 B-57As, 202 B-57Bs, 38 B-57Cs, 68 B-57Es, 67 RB-57As, and 20 RB-57Ds. The B-57 left active service in the Air National Guard* (ANG) in 1982. Its nickname was "Cranberry."

Characteristics (B-57B): engines, two Wright J65-W-5F turbojets of 7,200 pounds thrust each; span, 64 feet; length, 66 feet; height, 16 feet; gross weight, 58,800 pounds; top speed, 598 miles per hour at 2,500 feet; service ceiling, 40,100 feet; range, 2,300 miles; bombs, 9,200 pounds.

References. Primary: Higham, *Combat Airc.*, vol. 2. Secondary: Lloyd S. Jones, *U.S. Bombers 1928–1980s*, 4th ed., 1984. Knaack, *US Airc.*, vol. 2. Swanborough, *US Mil. Airc.*

Alwyn T. Lloyd

B-58 HUSTLER

In 1951 the Consolidated-Vultee Aircraft Corporation (Convair) presented plans to the USAF* for a delta wing bomber.* It competed as the XB-58 against a Boeing Airplane Company design numbered XB-59. Convair's proposal was chosen in 1952, and the first flight was in 1956. Operational service of the USAF's first supersonic bomber began in 1960 with the Strategic Air Command* (SAC). Even though it was a bomber, it set 19 official world speed and altitude records.

There was one variant, the TB-58A trainer. Despite its high performance and popularity with aircrews, the B-58 ceased service in 1970 because it was a medium, and not a heavy, bomber. In addition, it was difficult to maintain. Its nickname was "Delta Queen."

Characteristics: engines, four General Electric J79-GE-5B turbojets with 15,500 pounds thrust each in afterburner; span, 57 feet; length, 97 feet; height, 31 feet; gross weight, 163,000 pounds; top speed, 1,321 miles per hour; combat ceiling, 64,800 feet; combat radius, 1,750 miles.

References. Primary: Higham, *Combat Airc.*, vol. 1. Secondary: Jennifer Harper, "Supersonic Hustler," *AF*, August 1982, pp. 62–63. Knaack, *US Airc.*, vol. 2. Swanborough, *US Mil. Airc.* John Wegg, *General Dynamics Aircraft and Their Predecessors*, 1990.

B-66 DESTROYER

The Douglas Aircraft Company converted the B-66 from the U.S. Navy's A3D Skywarrior to meet a USAF* requirement for a light bomber* and for reconnaissance.* While similar in appearance, the two aircraft were vastly different in detail because of the numerous changes needed to alter a naval to a USAF aircraft. The first flight was in 1954 and many technical problems were found. It entered service in 1956 and was retired by 1975. The production run for the aircraft was 5 RB-66As, 145 RB-66Bs, 72 B-66Bs, 36 RB-66Cs, and 36 WB-66Ds for weather reconnaissance. Two WB-66Ds were converted to X-21As to test laminar flow control systems.

The B-66 did not serve well in the bomber role, but, with modifications to EB-66, it performed invaluable electronic warfare* services in the Vietnam War.* Its most important use was to counter surface-to-air missiles* (SAM) and flak.* RB-66s and EB-66s were also operational with U.S. Air Forces in Europe* (USAFE) units. Its nickname was "Sooie" for its sluggishness on takeoff.

Characteristics (B-66B): engines, two Allison J71-A-13 turbojets of 10,000 pounds thrust each; span, 73 feet; length, 75 feet; height, 24 feet; gross weight, 83,000 pounds; top speed, 594 miles per hour at 36,000 feet; service ceiling, 40,900 feet; range, 1,500 miles; bombs, 15,000 pounds.

References. René J. Francillon, *McDonnell Douglas Aircraft since 1920*, vol. 1, 1988. René J. Francillon and Mike Roth, *Douglas B-66 Destroyer*, 1988. Lloyd S. Jones, *U.S. Bombers 1928–1980s*, 4th ed., 1984. Knaack, *US Airc.*, vol. 2. Swanborough, *US Mil. Airc.*

Alwyn T. Lloyd

B-70 VALKYRIE

North American Aviation, Inc., designed and built two XB-70 prototypes for a line of aircraft envisioned as replacing the B-52s.* Development began when the Boeing Airplane Company, working with the Rand Corporation, presented the USAF* with a study on a new intercontinental bomber* able to carry both conventional and nuclear weapons.* A competitive North American proposal was selected in 1957. Salient features of the XB-70 were its distinctive shape and the fuselage made from steel and titanium. Use of the latter material set the United States in the forefront of aeronautical technology worldwide. Another innovation was brazed stainless steel honeycomb sandwich skin which also incorporated titanium alloys. This huge delta wing aircraft used an innovative droop in the elevons so they could also serve as flaps. In supersonic flight the outboard wing panels drooped for added longitudinal stability.

Numerous technical hurdles in materials, together with escalating costs, resulted in extensions and, finally, to loss of the program in 1962. Also, there were well-grounded doubts that a high-altitude bomber* generating great heat could operate in an era of air interceptor missiles* (AIM) and surface-to-air missiles* (SAM).

Work continued for test purposes with two XB-70s. The first flight of one was in 1964. The second aircraft attained Mach 3 on its maiden flight in 1966, but soon, in 1966, tragedy struck. At an altitude of 25,000 feet, an accompanying F-104* collided with an XB-70, resulting in the loss of both aircraft and crew. With one remaining aircraft, the XB-70 program was ended. In 1967 this aircraft was transferred to the National Aeronautics and Space Administration* (NASA) for research for a U.S. supersonic transport* (SST) program. Before year's end, it was retired to the U.S. Air Force Museum,* Wright-Patterson* AFB, Ohio.

Characteristics: engines, six General Electric YJ93–3 turbojets of 28,000 pounds thrust each; span, 105 feet; length, 186 feet; gross weight, 521,056 pounds; top speed, Mach 3 at 70,000 feet; service ceiling, above 70,000 feet; range, 3,414 miles; ordnance, 65,000 pounds.

References. Lloyd S. Jones, *U.S. Bombers 1928–1980s*, 4th ed., 1984. Knaack, *US Airc.*, vol. 2.

Alwyn T. Lloyd

BAKER BOARD

Former Secretary of War Newton D. Baker chaired this committee, which investigated U.S. Army aviation in 1934. It concurred with the Drum Board* Report which recommended an increased USAAC* strength of 2,320 aircraft, provided it was not at the expense of the rest of the Army's units. The Baker Board Report became the basis of the Federal Aviation Commission* Report after the secretary of war told the commission that the War Department favored the Baker Board program.

Although the Baker Board recommended creation of the General Headquarters Air Force* (GHQ Air Force), James H. Doolittle,* a civilian who was a former test pilot for the USAAC, filed a minority report which advocated either a separate air force or a USAAC with its own budget and a staff separate from the Army's General Staff.

References. Maurer, *Avn. in Army*. Chase C. Mooney, *Organization of Military Aeronautics, USAF Historical Study*, no. 25, unpub. study, Air University, Maxwell AFB, Alabama, 1944. John F. Shiner, *Foulois and the U.S. Army Air Corps*, 1983.

Lester H. Brune

BALLISTIC MISSILE EARLY WARNING SYSTEM (BMEWS)

This is the radar* system deployed in the late 1950s and early 1960s at Thule,* Greenland (Site I); Clear, Alaska (Site II); and Fylingdales, England (Site III). It can detect, track, and predict the impact points of intercontinental ballistic missiles* (ICBMs) launched from the USSR against Canada and the United States and Soviet intermediate range ballistic missiles (IRBMs) launched against Britain. BMEWS has proved to be an efficient and effective system.

The major impetus for the deployment of BMEWS was the Soviet launch and orbit of Sputnik I in October 1957. This concrete demonstration of Soviet ballistic missile capability prompted the USAF* to issue a General Operational Requirement (GOR) for a Ballistic Missile Defense System in November 1957. It called for the design, development, and deployment of a system like BMEWS, thus providing sufficient warning time to enable Air Defense Command (ADC) interceptors* and Strategic Air Command* (SAC) bombers* to become airborne and scatter to preselected dispersal bases.

Following swift Department of Defense (DoD) and congressional approval, Congress appropriated funds for construction of the Thule site in January 1958. Four months later, Secretary of Defense (SECDEF) Neil H. McElroy authorized the USAF to construct both the Thule and Clear sites as well as the BMEWS display facility in the North American Air Defense (NORAD) and Air Defense

Command (ADC) Combat Operations Center (COC) at Cheyenne Mountain*
AFB, Colorado.

Construction at Thule commenced in May. It had four giant scanner search
radars, each 165 feet high and 400 feet long; and one tracking radar, a rotating
84-foot antenna enclosed in a 140-foot diameter radome for protection against
the elements. BMEWS Site I achieved Initial Operational Capability (IOC) on
1 October 1960. On 5 October 1960, this system gave a false alert of a Soviet
missile attack; it had detected, in fact, the rising moon. It attained full automatic
operation on 31 January 1961. Work on the site at Clear, 60 miles southwest
of Fairbanks, Alaska, began in 1958. The Clear site used three scanner search
radars. IOC was reached on 30 September 1961, with full automatic operation
achieved on 31 December 1961. Construction of Site III started in late 1960.
The site was composed of three tracking radars. It reached IOC in September
1963, followed four months later with the attainment of full automatic operation.

Through instantaneous and redundant communications links, the three-site
BMEWS was connected to the NORAD COC; the SAC headquarters at Offutt*
AFB, Nebraska; the Pentagon in Washington, D.C.; and the Royal Air Force
(RAF) Fighter Command in Stanmore, England.

References. David A. Anderton, *Strategic Air Command: Two-thirds of the Triad*,
1974. David Bellin and Gary Chapman, eds., *Computers in Battle—Will They Work?*
1987. Robert Jackson, *Strike Force: The USAF in Britain since 1948*, 1986. Radio
Corporation of America (RCA), BMEWS Final Program Report, Moorestown, New
Jersey, 1964.

E. Michael Del Papa

BALLISTIC MISSILES

Ballistic missiles are most important to the USAF,* as they make up one-
third of the triad.* They are unmanned, ground-launched vehicles that follow
suborbital paths to their targets after their engines are shut down. They consist
of a rocket engine, fuel, oxidizer, guidance system, and warhead. Those that
can travel maximum distances are called intercontinental ballistic missiles
(ICBMs), and those of lesser range are called intermediate-range ballistic missiles
(IRBMs). Ballistic missiles without warheads are often used as boosters for space
vehicles. The USAF's ballistic missiles have included the Atlas,* Jupiter,* Minuteman,* Thor,* and Titan.* Under development are the Peacekeeper* and the
Small ICBM.*

In 1929 the German army wanted to circumvent the Versailles Treaty limitations on its artillery. A project was set up to develop missiles as long-range
projectiles, and space travel enthusiasts were recruited to aid in the work. In a
remarkably short development time, the V-2, or A-4, became the first man-made
vehicle to enter outer space. This event took place in October 1942.

The technical and military success of the V-2 led to USAAF* and U.S. Army
experimentation after World War II.* The guidance systems of that time made
the ballistic missile less effective than bombers* even should a fission nuclear
weapon* be used, and the USAAF stopped funding research on its ballistic

missile, Atlas, in 1947. Fortunately, the contractor, Consolidated-Vultee Aircraft Corporation (Convair), continued research with its own money on Atlas.

In 1953 the advent of the thermonuclear, or hydrogen, bomb made the IRBM and ICBM feasible. The USSR, the U.S. Army, and the USAF began a development race on ballistic missiles. The USAF effort was made under the leadership of Major General Bernard A. Schriever.* By 1957, the USAF's private contractors were ahead of the Army's arsenals, and all ballistic missiles of more than 200 miles range were assigned to the USAF in the Wilson memorandum* of 26 November 1956.

References. "The Air Force Ballistic Missile," a special issue of *Air University Quarterly Review*, Summer 1957. Futrell, *Ideas*, vol. 2. Harry E. Goldsworthy, "ICBM Site Activation," *AH*, September 1982, pp. 154–61. John T. Greenwood, "The Air Force Ballistic Missile and Space Program (1954–1974)," *AH*, December 1974, pp. 190–205. Jacob Neufeld, *Ballistic Missiles in the United States Air Force, 1945–1960*, 1990.

BALLOONS. *See* lighter-than-air.

BANDS. *See* U.S. Air Force Band.

BAN U-TAPAO AB. *See* U-Tapao Royal Thai Air Force Base.

BARBER, COLONEL REX T. *See* Lanphier, Colonel Thomas G., Jr.

BARCAP. *See* MiGCAP.

BARCUS, LIEUTENANT GENERAL GLENN O. (1903–   )

Barcus was most noted for his analysis of Korean War* operations and was highly decorated. He was born in Genoa, Illinois, and graduated from the University of Illinois in 1924. He accepted a reserve commission but did not enter active duty. He entered flight training* and graduated in 1927. He was then assigned to the 1st Pursuit Group and in 1928 became a flight instructor. In 1935 he became commander of the 35th Pursuit Squadron at Langley* Field, Virginia, and attended the Air Corps Tactical School* in 1939. In 1942 he became commander of the I Fighter Command at Mitchel* Field, New York, and in 1944 commander of the 64th Fighter Wing at Naples, Italy. In 1945 he commanded the XII Tactical Air Command in France. Later he was commander of the Twelfth and First Air Forces* (12AF and 1AF).

In June 1952, Barcus became commander of the Fifth Air Force* (5AF) engaged in the Korean War.* In 1954 he assumed command of the Air Training Command* (ATC). Then he was commander of the Northeast Air Command* (NEAC). His last post was chief of staff of the U.S. European Command (EUCOM). He retired in 1960.

References. Primary: Barcus, Glenn O., Lt. Gen., Oral History Interview by Lt. Col. John N. Dick, Jr., 10–13 August 1976, Number USAFHRC 239.0512.908, USAF Historical Research Center, Maxwell AFB, Alabama. Secondary: DuPre, *USAF Bio*. Futrell,

USAF in Korea. War Department Biography, "Glenn Oscar Barcus," 18 December 1945.

Lloyd H. Cornett, Jr.

BARKSDALE AIR FORCE BASE

This Strategic Air Command* (SAC) base is in Bossier City, Louisiana. The field was activated in 1933 and named for Lieutenant Eugene H. Barksdale, who died in an aircraft accident in 1926. It was intended as a base for defense of the Gulf Coast. In the 1930s fighter* and attack* units occupied the base. It was under the General Headquarters Air Force* (GHQ Air Force) from 1935 to 1940. Antisubmarine operations and training were conducted from the field during World War II.* It became an SAC base in 1949 and headquarters for the Second Air Force* (2AF). At first it had B-47s* and KC-97s (*see* C-97). It had B-52s* beginning in 1960. In 1990 it had the headquarters for the Eighth Air Force* (8AF) and the 2nd Bomb Wing with B-52G, KC-135 (*see* C-135) and KC-10 (*see* C-10) aircraft on the field.

References. "Guide to Major Air Force Installations Worldwide," *AF*, May 1990, p. 122. Mueller, *AFB*. Roberts, *Dir. USAF*.

BARLING BOMBER

After World War I,* the USAAS* tried to build a heavy bomber.* It hoped to have equipment to match Brigadier General William Mitchell's* vision of a superbomber for strategic operations.* Work by the USAAS's Engineering Division began in 1920 under Walter H. Barling. He designed a triplane that was the largest plane made in the United States up to that time. It was built by the Witteman-Lewis Company. It was designated XNBL-1 for "Night Bombardment—Long-distance." The first flight was in 1923. It proved to be underpowered and had structural problems. It was flown until 1925, setting duration and altitude records for payloads. It was scrapped in 1928. Aviation technology was not far enough advanced for the concept. Fulfillment would come after another two decades.

Characteristics: engines, six Liberty of 520 horsepower each; span, 120 feet; length, 65 feet; gross weight, 42,569 pounds; top speed, 95 miles per hour; range, 335 miles.

References. Maurer, *Avn. in Army. The Official Pictorial History of the AAF*, 1947. Swanborough, *US Mil. Airc.* Earl H. Tilford, Jr., "The Barling Bomber," *AH*, June 1979, pp. 91–97.

BARREL ROLL

During the protracted Vietnam War,* U.S. airmen flew combat missions over northern Laos in support of forces loyal to the Royal Laotian Government (RLG). These operations, which often were overshadowed by the more intensive air campaigns in North and South Vietnam and in the Laotian panhandle, were called Barrel Roll. They started in June 1964 after Pathet Lao and North Vietnamese forces violated the Geneva Accords of 23 July 1962 by attacking pro-

RLG Neutralist positions on the Plain of Jars, and they ended nearly nine years later, in April 1973, when the United States quit its military commitment.

The air war in northern Laos was interwoven with the overall pattern of U.S. air power in Southeast Asia (SEA), but there were exceptional political circumstances surrounding Barrel Roll operations that set them apart. Although the Seventh Air Force* (7AF) commander controlled the fighters* operating in Barrel Roll, the U.S. ambassador at Vientiane virtually ran his own special air war in Laos. U.S. fighter sorties supported both the Royal Laotian Army and Neutralist troops, but they were flown primarily in support of the Central Intelligence Agency (CIA)–trained Meo tribesmen led by Major General Vang Pao, whose irregular army did much of the fighting and operated under the direct control of the U.S. embassy. Air support was provided at the embassy's request. The ambassador had the final word on what could and could not be done in the area. His major adviser on the use of air power was the U.S. air attaché who selected targets and proposed the forces to be employed. This presented special problems for the 7AF commander and the units under his control.

In his 1985 book, *Air Power in Three Wars*, General William W. Momyer* wrote of the problems arising from the embassy's incessant demands for more air power than was available for the Barrel Roll area. The embassy wanted a wing dedicated solely to the support of the ground war in northern Laos. Momyer explained that this proposed fragmenting of air power would have deprived other battlefield commanders of air support for emergencies. As elsewhere in SEA, the war in northern Laos was seasonal, and the theaterwide demands on air power were greater during the dry season offensives than during the monsoon lulls. The benefits derived from the 7AF's ability centrally to shift air power in SEA to where the need was greatest was revealed in Laos after the bombing halt against North Vietnam led to increased military pressure against Vang Pao's forces on the Plain of Jars. The rapid massing of air power by the 7AF commander was the key to Vang Pao's survival, just as it was for the U.S. forces during the siege at Khe Sanh* in South Vietnam.

The control of air power in Barrel Roll remained a sensitive political issue between the 7AF and the embassy for the duration of the conflict. There was usually enough air support available though, and it often meant the difference between victory and defeat for the friendly Laotian troops fighting numerically superior enemy forces.

References. Primary: Richard S. Drury, *My Secret War*, 1979. Secondary: Berger, *USAF in SEA*. John Morrocco, *Rain of Fire: Air War, 1969–1973*, a vol. of *The Vietnam Experience*, 1985.

Warren A. Trest

BARRIERS CAP (BARCAP). *See* MiGCAP.

BASE. *See* air force bases.

BATTY. *See* Aphrodite.

BEALE AIR FORCE BASE

Named for Indian agent Brigadier General Edward F. Beale, this former U.S. Army camp was acquired by the USAF* in 1951. Near Marysville, California, it is a Strategic Air Command* (SAC) base. Once used by heavy bombers,* tankers,* and Titan* Is, in 1990 it had headquarters of the 14th Air Division and the 9th Strategic Reconnaissance Wing (SRW) on base with KC-135s (*see* C-135), T-38s,* and TR-1s.

References. "Guide to Major Air Force Installations Worldwide," *AF*, May 1990, p. 122. Mueller, *AFB*. Roberts, *Dir. USAF*.

BELL AIRCRAFT CORPORATION. *See* aerospace industry; FM-1; P-39; P-59; P-63; X-1; X-2.

"BENNY." *See* Foulois, Major General Benjamin D.

BENTWATERS. *See* RAF Bentwaters.

BERGSTROM AIR FORCE BASE

This field was activated in 1942 near Austin, Texas, and its original name was Del Valle Army Air Base. A Tactical Air Command* (TAC) base, it was named for Captain John A. E. Bergstrom who died at Clark* Field, Philippines, 8 December 1941, as a result of a Japanese air attack.* During World War II* it was under the I Troop Carrier Command and trained units for airborne operations. After the war it became a strategic fighter* field with F-84s.* When the Strategic Air Command* (SAC) ended the use of fighters, it became a heavy bomber* and tanker* base with B-52s* and KC-135s (*see* C-135) from 1958 to 1966. In 1967 it became a TAC field with headquarters of the Twelfth Air Force* (12AF) and reconnaissance* aircraft. In 1990 it had headquarters of the Tenth Air Force* (10AF) and the 12AF and the 67th Tactical Reconnaissance Wing (TRW) with RF-4Cs (*see* F-4).

References. "Guide to Major Air Force Installations Worldwide," *AF*, May 1990, p. 122. Mueller, *AFB*. Roberts, *Dir. USAF*.

BERLIN, GERMANY

As a target of U.S. attack, Berlin was included in part of a plan drafted by the Eighth Air Force* (8AF) in November 1943. The plan, known as Argument,* called for a series of air attacks* on the German aircraft industry target system* making fighters.* To carry out this operation, a period of clear weather for at least a week was needed. Such a period was predicted to begin on 20 January 1944, and the plan was put into operation at that time. Six days later, it was terminated because of deteriorating weather conditions. Overall, the bombing results were not as successful as anticipated, and this period of Argument became known as the Big Week.* These missions did not produce all of the desired results, but they did pave the way for many future raids in Berlin as elsewhere in Germany. They showed the enemy that no city was safe from daylight precision bombing, and the Luftwaffe knew it could no longer stand up to the superior U.S. fighters.

Although no missions were flown to Berlin during Big Week, the strategic importance of ''Big B,'' as Berlin came to be called, still remained. Berlin, the headquarters and capital of the German Third Reich, became the ultimate target of the U.S. Strategic Air Forces in Europe* (USSTAF). The German high command was most fearful of the precision daylight bombing of strategic targets in and around Berlin and the disillusioning effect it would have on the German people. ''Big B'' as a target was one location the Luftwaffe would fiercely defend, regardless of the consequences.

The first opportunity to resume Argument with an attack on Berlin presented itself on 3 March, but the weather proved worse than predicted and the mission was recalled. On 4 March, this happened again, but one wing of 31 bombers* did not get the recall message and bombed the city. This was a significant mission; first, it was the first time Berlin was bombed in daylight and, second, the bombers had fighter escort* all the way. On 6 March more than 830 heavy bombers headed for Berlin, and fierce enemy fighter opposition was met to and from the target. Flak* was extremely intense and exceptionally accurate. Partial overcast conditions hampered the bombing and most of the bombs were scattered over a wide land area. Of the force dispatched, 630 bombers reached Berlin, and 69 bombers and 11 fighters were lost. Another 105 bombers were severely damaged, of which three had to be scrapped. This was and is the highest single-day loss for any U.S. armed force in aerial combat. Bomber gunners* claimed 97 enemy aircraft* destroyed, and friendly fighters claimed another 82. It was a loss rate the Luftwaffe could not sustain.

Less than 48 hours later, General Carl A. Spaatz* sent 600 bombers back to Berlin. Weather conditions were better and bombing results were good. Enemy fighter opposition was light, but flak was again intense and accurate. Thirty-seven bombers were lost. On 9 March the 8AF bombed by radar* and lost nine bombers. The weather on 22 March appeared good enough for a return. For the sixth time in less than three weeks the 8AF set out for Berlin, but weather forced bombing by radar again. Of 669 bombers, 12 were lost to flak or collision. Thereafter, Berlin continued to be a lucrative target.

References. Primary: Dale O. Smith, ''With the 384th to Big B,'' *AH*, June 1984, pp. 121–24. Secondary: C&C, vol. 3. Jeffrey Ethell and Alfred Price, *Target Berlin: Mission 250: 6 March 1944*, 1981. Roger A. Freeman, *The Mighty Eighth: Units, Men and Machines*, 1970. Edward Jablonski, *Target Germany*, vol. 1 of *Air War: Wings of Force*, 1979.

Gilbert E. D'Alonzo

BERLIN AIRLIFT, OR OPERATION VITTLES

The Berlin Airlift was one of the greatest achievements of the USAF* and showed the usefulness of aerospace power* in peacetime.

By 22 June 1948, the USSR imposed a land blockade of U.S., British, and

French occupation areas of Berlin,* Germany. This forced the Western Allies to choose between evacuating Berlin, using military force, or supplying West Berlin by air. The decision made was to try airlift operations.* This posed a formidable task for the West's resources. The adverse factors were that West Berlin had, first, more than two million inhabitants and, second, much inclement weather. A third factor was that only the Americans had much air transport,* and it was too few in numbers for the task, it was obsolescent, and it had low capacities.

There were favorable factors. First, the distances involved were short, ranging between 274 and 563 miles round-trip. Second, life in postwar Germany was very austere at this time, which meant that the supply requirements were estimated to be only about 4,500 tons per day. Third, the USAF had a large pool of highly experienced, competent pilots* from World War II.* Fourth, the USAF had the excellent experience of the wartime air bridge from India to China called "The Hump."* Fifth, the airlift generated enthusiastic support from the West and from the Germans. Sixth, the U.S. Air Forces in Europe* (USAFE) had a determined commander, Major General Curtis E. LeMay.*

At the beginning, the USAF had to improvise from its immediate resources in Europe. The first day's operations, on 26 June, delivered 80 tons of milk, flour, and medicine. By 20 July, with reinforcements from the United States, there were 54 C-54s* and 105 C-47s* delivering a maximum of 1,500 tons per day. The British could add another 750 tons per day. By 30 July, there were additional reinforcements and an airlift commander who had participated in the Hump, Major General William H. Tunner.* The U.S. air bridge became an operation using U.S. Army and Navy resources as well as the USAF's.

By September, the small and obsolescent C-47s had been replaced by C-54s. The peak number of C-54s used for the airlift reached 319, of which 225 were in operation in Europe. The rest were undergoing maintenance or conducting training.

The heavy traffic and unfavorable weather made severe demands upon aircraft controlling. The greatest hazard was fog. Ground-Controlled Approach* (GCA) was used for landing guidance. An interval of three minutes between GCA approaches was achieved. Ground operations were also emphasized. The turn-around time for loading aircraft was reduced to one hour and 25 minutes, and unloading in Berlin took only 49 minutes. In October, the city's daily requirement estimate was raised to 5,620 tons, of which two-thirds was coal. This total tonnage included the supplies needed to sustain industry. In April 1949, a record 12,941 tons was brought in on one day. The USSR's land blockade had been frustrated, and on 12 May the Soviets canceled it. The United States had delivered, 1,783,000 tons, at a cost of 31 U.S. lives lost in 12 accidents.

The Berlin Airlift demonstrated the application of nonviolent military means to achieve political ends. Its by-products were: First, invaluable experience was gained in conducting transport operations which could be applied to civil as well as to military uses. Second, it was learned that cargo aircraft with larger capacities was desirable.

The lessons learned in the Berlin Airlift were soon needed for the Korean Airlift.*

References. Primary: Gail S. Halvorsen, *The Berlin Candy Bomber*, 1990. Secondary: D. M. Giangreco and Robert E. Griffin, *Airbridge to Berlin: The Berlin Crisis of 1948, Its Origins and Aftermath*, 1988. Goldberg, *Hist. USAF*. Higham, *Air Pwr*. Roger D. Launius, "The Berlin Airlift: Constructive Air Power," *Air Power History*, Spring 1989, pp. 8–22, and "Lessons Learned, Berlin Airlift," *Air Power History*, Spring 1989, p. 23. Roger D. Launius and Coy F. Cross II, *MAC and the Legacy of the Berlin Airlift*, 1989.

See also Berlin Airlift Task Force; Combined Airlift Task Force; Operation Little Vittles.

BERLIN AIRLIFT TASK FORCE

On 1 July 1948, only seven days following the Soviet blockade of Berlin,* Germany, the Airlift Task Force Provisional was created as a temporary unit. Commanded at first by Brigadier General Joseph Smith, on 29 July Major General William H. Tunner,* formerly deputy commander of operations for the Military Air Transport Service (MATS), arrived. The organization consisted at first of a small headquarters element, but it expanded on 29 July when the 7499 Air Division was created. The operating units in the early days were the 60th Troop Carrier Group with C-47s* at Wiesbaden* AB, the 61st Troop Carrier Group with C-47s at Rhein-Main* AB, and a provisional C-54* Troop Carrier Group at Rhein-Main made up of aircraft from other theaters. All of these units flew from their home bases to Berlin's Tempelhof* Airport. On 5 August the 1421st Maintenance Squadron (Provisional) began operations at Oberpfaffenhofen Air Depot, Germany.

Tonnage records grew virtually every day. On 7 July the first 1,000-ton day was logged. On 20 July, it was 1,500 tons. On 26 August, the total past 100,000 tons. The Berlin Airlift Task Force ceased to exist on 14 October 1948 when the Combined Airlift Task Force* was created to merge U.S. and British efforts to supply Berlin. The Berlin Airlift Task Force showed the ability of the USAF quickly to mobilize effectively to meet an unexpected major contingency.

References. Richard Collier, *Bridge across the Sky: The Berlin Blockade and Airlift, 1948–1949*, 1978. W. Phillips Davison, *The Berlin Blockade: A Study in Cold War Politics*, 1978. Roger D. Launius and Coy F. Cross II, *The Berlin Airlift and the MAC Connection*, 1989. Office of MAC History, *The Berlin Airlift: A Brief Chronology*, 1988.

Roger D. Launius

BGM-109G GRYPHON GROUND-LAUNCHED CRUISE MISSILE (GLCM)

The General Dynamics Corporation's BGM-109 is a small cruise missile* with a W-80 warhead of 200 kilotons yield. The small size, mobility, and accuracy of the BGM-109 make it one of the most feared modern weapons.

The missile is issued as a complete round sealed in a tube, and no maintenance is required for several years. The launching vehicle is a semitrailer with four missile tubes. During times of crisis, units deploy throughout Europe on the road network. Upon receiving launch notification, the vehicle elevates the front of the tubes to clear the vehicle cab and a small solid fuel booster fires the missile through the tube. Upon reaching the correct altitude, the booster falls off, the wings and tail unfold, the engine scoop deploys, and the engine starts. Guidance is by a combination of inertial and map matching.

Characteristics: engine, Williams F107 turbojet of 600 pounds thrust; unfolded wingspan, 100 inches; diameter, 21 inches (to fit a standard torpedo tube); length, 252 inches; weight, 3,181 pounds; range, 2,000 miles.

References. Norman Friedman, *U.S. Naval Weapons*, 1985. Chuck Hansen, *U.S. Nuclear Weapons*, 1988. Susan H. H. Young, "Gallery of USAF Weapons," *AF*, May 1990, p. 156.

Philip Long

BIEN HOA AIR BASE

This AB was northeast of Saigon, South Vietnam. USAF* operations from it began in late 1961 with Farm Gate* using C-47s,* B-26 Invaders,* and T-28s.* By 1964 there were O-1 Bird Dogs,* 50 A-1Es,* and 18 B-57s* as well. In November 1964 a mortar shelling destroyed five B-57s. In 1965 F-100s* replaced the B-57s. Late that year F-5s* and AC-47s were added. In 1966 the A-1s moved out, and A-37s moved in the the next year. By 1973 Bien Hoa had been phased out as a major USAF AB.

References. Berger, *USAF in SEA*. John Schlight, *The War in South Vietnam: The Years of the Offensive 1965–1968*, 1988.

BIG B. *See* Berlin, Germany.

BIG BELLY. *See* Arc Light.

BIG EYE. *See* C-121; College Eye.

BIG FRIENDS. *See* "little friends."

BIG WEEK

Big Week began the operation known by the code name of Argument.* Planned by the Eighth Air Force* (8AF), Argument called for the destruction of the German aircraft industry target system.* The plan required at least a full week of clear weather over Central Europe and satisfactory takeoff and landing conditions for eastern England and southern Italy. Big Week was ended by inclement weather before the objectives could be obtained. Despite this, Big Week was not a failure. In addition to the damage inflicted on factories and the destruction of aircraft on the ground, the Luftwaffe lost many experienced pilots who were desperately needed. The USAAF* attained air superiority* over Germany during Big Week and never relinquished it to the Luftwaffe for the duration of the war.

On 19 February 1944, the weather section of the U.S. Strategic Air Forces in Europe* (USSTAF) predicted the conditions needed. The USSTAF commander, Lieutenant General Carl A. Spaatz,* made the decision to begin the assault. From 20 to 25 February, more than 3,300 heavy bombers* of the 8AF and another 500 of the Fifteenth Air Force* (15AF) unloaded 10,000 tons of bombs* over Germany. The losses were 226 heavy bombers, 28 fighters,* and an estimated 600 enemy aircraft.* Flying in support of USSTAF, the Ninth Air Force* (9AF) flew many diversionary missions. The Royal Air Force (RAF) Bomber Command flew more than 2,300 sorties at night, dropping 9,200 tons of bombs and losing 157 bombers.

The targets were bombed with greater intensity than ever before, crippling production of aircraft. However, German production actually increased after several months in response to careful planning by Otto Sauer, who was in charge of manufacturing operations.

References. C&C, vol. 3. DeWitt S. Copp, *Forged in Fire: Strategy and Decisions in the Air War over Europe 1940–1945*, 1982. Glenn Infield, *Big Week!* 1974. Edward Jablonski, *Target Germany*, vol. 1 of *Air War: Wings of Fire*, 1971. Christopher Shores, *Duel for the Sky*, 1985.

Gilbert E. D'Alonzo

"BILLY." *See* Mitchell, Major General William.

BINGHAM, MAJOR HIRAM (1875–1956)

This former Yale University professor directed the Schools of Aeronautics in World War I.* Bingham's program and his schools met their challenge.

Bingham earned a Ph.D. from Harvard University in 1905. He taught at Princeton University and Johns Hopkins University as well as at Yale. Bingham anticipated the U.S. entry into the war and joined the Connecticut National Guard as a captain in 1916. He also appreciated the importance of aviation and learned to fly early in 1917. When the United States went to war, a large expansion in the air arm was needed. It was believed that the quickest and best way to handle the ground school phase of flight training* would be through the nation's colleges and universities. Bingham was eminently qualified to head this effort. By the end of May 1917, Bingham had established schools at six leading educational institutions: at the universities of California, Cornell, Illinois, Ohio State, and Texas and at the Massachusetts Institute of Technology (MIT). Princeton University and the George Institute of Technology were added later. Until the end of the program, a few weeks after the Armistice, these schools received 22,689 cadets and graduated 17,540.

References. Primary: Hiram Bingham, "Building America's Air Army," *National Geographic*, January 1918, pp. 48–86, and *An Explorer in the Air Service*, 1920. Secondary: Daniel Cohen, *Hiram Bingham and the Dream of Gold*, 1984. James J. Hudson, *Hostile Skies: A Combat History of the American Air Service in World War I*, 1968.

James J. Hudson

BIRD DOG. *See* O-1.

BIRD OF PARADISE

This aircraft flew from California to Hawaii in one of the record-setting flights made by the USAAC* to prove the usefulness of aviation. Such a flight had been first proposed to the USAAS* in 1919 by First Lieutenant Lester J. Maitland.* He asked again in 1924. By that time, First Lieutenant Albert F. Hegenberger* was making the same request. The flight, with Maitland and Hegenberger as pilot and copilot in a Fokker C-2 built by the Atlantic Aircraft Corporation, was approved pending successful tests in 1926.

On 28 June 1927 their plane, named *Bird of Paradise*, took off from Oakland Municipal Airport, California. The key to success in flying to the remote islands was the navigation done by Hegenberger. During the day the crew checked its position with steamships and at night by celestial navigation. They arrived before daybreak and stayed in the air until daylight permitted a visual landing at Wheeler* Field. They landed after nearly 26 hours in the air. The *Bird* had been the first to make the flight.

The idea of a flight to Hawaii took fire after Charles A. Lindbergh's* achievement of flying from New York City to Paris, France. Four days later, James D. Dole, of the Hawaiian Pineapple Company, offered a $25,000 prize for a comparable flight to Hawaii from the mainland. The race for the Dole prize was run in August 1927. There were 14 entrants. Eight took off, four turned back, two crashed at sea, and two reached Hawaii. It was no easy flight for the time.

Maitland and Hegenberger's flight was not a stunt. They had carefully prepared it for years, and those preparations contributed to mastery of long-distance flights.

References. William J. Horvat, "Bird of Paradise," *AH*, Summer 1968, pp. 27–31. Maurer, *Avn. in Army*.

BISMARCK SEA, BATTLE OF THE

In this battle, with suitable tactics and training, the Fifth Air Force* (5AF) demonstrated Brigadier General William Mitchell's* old theory of aerial dominance over the seas.

By early 1943 Japanese expansive power in the Pacific had been broken. Defeats at Midway, New Guinea,* Guadalcanal,* and in the Aleutians* forced the enemy into retreat and consolidation. This was no more apparent than in the southwest Pacific theater where twin U.S. drives moved to isolate the bastion of Rabaul,* New Britain. General Douglas MacArthur's New Guinea campaign was poised to take Lae on the northeastern coast, blocking Japanese lines of communication with New Britain to the east. To counter this threat, two new divisions arrived from Asia to be part of the Eighteenth Army, and one of them, the 51st, was to sail from New Britain to Lae with Lieutenant General Adachi Hatazo in command. The move had additional urgency because the manpower at Lae had been unable to dislodge Australians at nearby Wau airstrip, giving the Allies air cover over Lae and Salamaua further down the coast.

Antishipping strikes by U.S. airmen in and around Guadalcanal gave the Japanese concern, so 100 Japanese fighters* were to fly cover for the convoy. Flak* ships were provided on a one-to-one ratio: eight destroyers for seven transports and one special service vessel. Preemptive air attacks* were planned for Allied airfields within range of the convoy's track, and the entire operation awaited a tropical weather front for a shield. Finally, the men and supplies were divided into self-contained units and parceled out to the ships so the loss of one vessel would not wipe out all key men or equipment. The convoy weighed anchor on 28 February.

The 5AF's Lieutenant General George C. Kenney* had been warned as early as 19 February of Japanese attempts to reinforce Lae. His staff drew up three plans, the first of which posited a direct line to Lae bringing the convoy within reach of the 5AF's whole strike force, including his ship-killing bombers,* A-20s* and B-25s.* Throughout the war, high-altitude antishipping attacks by heavy bombers netted few results, yet the airborne destruction of enemy naval units remained a priority task in the southwest Pacific. During the winter of 1942–1943, Kenney ordered experiments in low-level strikes by his medium bombers. The key lay in the ability to suppress the flak from escort vessels. Major Paul I. Gunn* and North American Aviation, Inc., field representative Jack Fox rigged eight extra 50-caliber guns in the nose of a B-25. When added to the twin gun top turret, the B-25 could lay down a withering fire aimed at clearing destroyer decks. Then, at 150 feet above the water, the bombers could skip bomb* the ships at the waterline. A five-second delayed-action fuse enabled the bomber to pass over the ship before detonation. The tactic had been practiced and perfected by the time the convoy approached.

On 1 March B-24s made contact with the convoy and began shadowing it. A raid by eight B-17s did not find the convoy. The next day the unescorted B-17s struck from 6,500 feet. This and two other heavy bomber raids sank two transports by nightfall. The Battle of the Bismarck Sea had begun.

On 3 March the convoy was within range of the medium bombers. An early raid by Royal Australian Air Force (RAAF) Beauforts achieved nothing. A follow-on attack, supported by B-17s, strafed and scattered the convoy. Then 13 B-25s bombed conventionally from medium altitude, followed immediately by low-level B-25s. Dispersed, and seeing only the higher bombers, the Japanese were shocked by the B-25 gunships, two to a target, that attacked from 500 feet or less. The Americans wreaked terrible damage with their guns before bombing. RAAF A-20s and 5AF B-17s and B-25s continued medium-altitude attacks that added to the destruction. On 4 March, the bombers dispatched a wounded destroyer. For several days afterward, medium bombers ranged the area of the battle, strafing Japanese survivors. Effective fighter cover had been provided by 5AF P-38s,* at a cost of three aircraft. Bomber losses were one B-17 and one B-25. Allied fighters and bombers claimed to down 50 to 60 enemy aircraft.*

It was, however, the Lae convoy that suffered most: all seven transports and the special service ship were sunk, as were four of the eight destroyers. More than 3,664 soldiers and sailors perished. The Japanese never again sent a convoy within range of U.S. air power. Supplying New Guinea was reduced to barges and luggers from New Britain, a method that could not sustain Japanese units.

References. C&C, vol. 4. Lawrence Cortesi, *The Battle of the Bismarck Sea*, 1967. Paul S. Dull, *A Battle History of the Imperial Japanese Navy (1941–1945)*, 1978. John Miller, Jr., *Cartwheel: The Reduction of Rabaul*, 1959.

Ronald W. Yoshino

BITBURG AIR BASE

After the North Atlantic Treaty Organization* (NATO) was formed, the United States built a series of bases to French specifications in the Rhineland. They were claimed to be a gift to France, which aspired to have its border on the Rhine River. As the bases were finished, some U.S. Air Forces in Europe* (USAFE) units moved westward out of their former Luftwaffe fields and into them. The 36th Tactical Fighter Wing (TFW) moved out of Fuerstenfeldbrueck AB and into Bitburg AB, Germany, in 1952. The 36th Wing was still there in 1990. Over the years a series of fighter* aircraft from F-84s* to F-15s* occupied the AB. The 36th and Bitburg AB have been a key part of NATO's defenses since 1952.

References. "Guide to Major Air Force Installations Worldwide," *AF*, May 1990, p. 122. Roberts, *Dir. USAF*. Michael Skinner, *U*S*A*F*E: A Primer of Modern Air Combat in Europe*, 1988.

BLACKBIRD. *See* SR-71.

BLACK WIDOW. *See* P-61.

BLAKESLEE, COLONEL DONALD J. M. (1918–)

This ace* with 15 victories commanded the Eighth Air Force's* (8AF) 4th Fighter Group, one of the two most famous fighter* units in the USAAF,* using F-47s* and F-51s.* It was called the "Blakesleewaffe." Blakeslee flew more than 400 sorties and fought the Luftwaffe longer than any other American. He logged more than 1,000 hours of combat. As a battle leader, he was in action for three and one-half years.

A native of Fairport Harbor, Ohio, he joined the Royal Canadian Air Force (RCAF) and arrived in England in 1941. He joined No. 121 Squadron, Royal Air Force (RAF), an Eagle Squadron,* and became its second commander. In 1942 the Eagle Squadrons were merged into the USAAF. Blakeslee is renowned as a battle commander. On one strike against Berlin,* Germany, he commanded in battle nearly 800 fighters of the 8AF Fighter Command. In 1950 he received the Mackay Trophy.

References. Roger A. Freeman, *The Mighty Eighth: Units, Men and Machines*, 1970. Gurney, *5 Down*. Grover C. Hall, Jr., *Death Squadron*, 1946.

BLESSE, MAJOR GENERAL FREDERICK C., "BOOTS" (1921–)

Blesse is the sixth-ranking U.S. jet ace* with ten victories and the author of the famous "No Guts, No Glory," an essay on air superiority* tactics.

Blesse was borne in Colon, Panama Canal Zone, and graduated from the U.S. Military Academy (USMA) in 1945. He flew his first operational tour* in the Korean War* in F-51s* and F-80s.* On his second tour, flying F-86s,* he shot down nine MiG-15s and one La-9. In 1955 he won all six individual trophies in the World Wide Gunnery Championship meet, a record that has not been equaled. He flew 157 sorties in the Vietnam War,* of which 109 were over

North Vietnam. He flew 6,500 hours in fighters,* 650 of which were combat hours. Blesse retired from the USAF* in 1975.

References. Primary: Frederick C. Blesse, *Check Six*, 1987. Secondary: DuPre, *USAF Bio*. Hess, *Aces Album*. Mike Spick, *The Ace Factor*, 1988.

BLIND FLYING. *See* instrument flying.

BMEWS. *See* Ballistic Missile Early Warning System.

BODY ARMOR. *See* flaksuit.

BOEING COMPANY, THE. *See* aerospace industry; B-9; B-15; B-17; B-29; B-47; B-50; B-52; C-25; C-97; C-135; C-137; E-3; E-4; E-8A; flying boom; H-21; IM-99; Minuteman; P-12; P-26; Peacekeeper; Small Intercontinental Ballistic Missile.

BOLLING, COLONEL RAYNAL C. *See* Bolling Mission.

BOLLING AIR FORCE BASE
Constructed in 1918, this airfield was named for Colonel Raynal C. Bolling of the Bolling Mission.* The base was used between the world wars for proficiency flying of staff officers and for pioneer flights. In 1940 the older part of the field was transferred to the U.S. Navy, which had been a tenant since 1918. The Navy area was then named Anacostia Naval Air Station. World War II* meant a great expansion as Bolling supplied air transport for officials, provided local air defense, and trained men. In 1948 its organization changed its name from Bolling Field Command to Headquarters Command, USAF.* Flying into and out of Bolling began to be restricted in the late 1940s for security of the Capitol and because of increasing commercial activity. All fixed-wing flying ended in 1962, and helicopters left in 1968. In 1990 Bolling belonged to the Air Force District of Washington.*

References. "Bolling Air Force Base: A Brief History," *AH*, June 1972, pp. 90–93. Brown, *Eagles*. "Guide to Major Air Force Installations Worldwide," *AF*, May 1990, p. 122. Mueller, *AFB*. Roberts, *Dir. USAF*.

BOLLING MISSION
Headed by Major Raynal C. Bolling, a long-time civilian leader in aviation, the Bolling Mission, especially selected by the Aircraft Production Board,* was sent to Europe in June 1917. The task was to study aircraft design and production facilities in France, Italy, and England. Its principal objectives were to (1) establish free exchange of rights to manufacture aviation material, (2) send sample airplanes and engines to the United States, (3) prepare for the purchase of planes for the United States, (4) train personnel in Europe, and (5) assist the U.S. air service of the Allied forces by allocation of raw material.

As a result of the mission's findings, the aircraft production authorities decided to build training aircraft initially and buy fighters* from the British and French. Fighter designs changed rapidly and needed to be built close to the fighting front. The French agreed in the summer of 1917 to produce for the United States about 6,000 planes, chiefly Nieuports,* Spads,* and Breguets,* plus engines, and to deliver by July 1918. Americans flew those aircraft and the British-built Sopwith Camels. American plane builders concentrated on building trainers and de Haviland DH-4s.* Eventually, the United States placed the British Handley-Page and Italian Caproni bombers* in production, but only the DH-4s were produced in quantity. Perhaps the greatest U.S. production success was the Liberty engine.*

Brigadier General Benjamin D. Foulois* made Bolling chairman of the Joint Army and Navy Aircraft Committee in the fall of 1917 but relieved him of the job in January 1918 when Bolling recommended that the committee be abolished because it served no useful purpose. Shortly thereafter, Bolling requested permission to prepare himself for work at the front with one of the fighting air units, and he was given a roving commission. To make a firsthand study of the combat situation, Bolling drove from one unit to another. In March 1918, he and his driver inadvertently approached too near the German lines at Amiens and were ambushed and killed.

References. Futrell, *Ideas*, vol. 1. Goldberg, *Hist. USAF*. James J. Hudson, *Hostile Skies: A Combat History of the American Air Service in World War I*, 1968. Theodore Macfarlane, *Wings of War*, 1920.

James J. Hudson

BOLO. *See* B-18; Operation Bolo.

BOMARC. *See* IM-99.

BOMBARDIER

The bombardier operates bombing equipment. In the technology of World War II,* the bombardier was vital to USAAF* success and had an aeronautical specialist rating. His aircrew tasks were to locate and identify targets and to drop bombs. With the Norden bombsight,* the bombardier controlled the bomber* during the "bomb run," or aiming period. Bombardiers also served as flexible gunners.* Bombardier training in World War II took 20 weeks, involving gunnery school, 120 hours in practice bomb runs, and 718 hours of ground school. Graduates received at least the grade* of flight officer. The training schools for bombardiers were established in 1941. By 1945, more than 45,000 men had become bombardiers. Two bombardiers won the Air Force Medal of Honor,* Lieutenants Jack Mathis and David R. Kingsley. Both decorations were awarded posthumously. Dan Devine, the Notre Dame football coach, was a bombardier. The USAF's* bombardiers have formed the Bombardiers Alumni Association.

Movie: *Bombardier*, 1943.

References. Primary: Michael J. Nisos, "The Bombardier and His Bombsight," *AF*, September 1981, pp. 106–10, 113. Secondary: *AAF: A Directory, Almanac and Chronicle* *of Achievement*, 1944. Bruce D. Callander, "Bombardier," *AF*, December 1990, pp. 76–80. John Steinbeck, *Bombs Away: The Story of a Bomber Team*, 1942.

BOMBER

A bomber is an aircraft designed to drop bombs.* The type is currently divided into three categories. A light bomber, one with a gross weight of under 100,000 pounds, flies its bomb load for an operating radius under 1,150 miles. There is no clear distinction between attack,* dive bomber, and light bomber aircraft. A medium bomber, with a gross weight of 100,000 to 250,000 pounds, carries its bomb load over a radius of 1,150 to 2,875 miles. A heavy bomber's gross is more than 250,000 pounds and has a radius over 2,875 miles.

The characteristics of these terms have changed over time as technology has improved, and the terms are now used less than before. Generally, the heavy bomber is considered the big punch of air power intended for strategic operations.* The smaller bombers are associated with tactical operations.* During World War II,* the category of Very Long Range (VLR), or Very Heavy Bomber, was given to the B-29* and B-32* because they exceeded the payload and range capabilities of the B-17* and B-24* heavy bombers. In the Korean War,* the B-29 was redesignated as a medium bomber.

In 1990, the B-1* and B-52* were heavy bombers, the FB-111 version of the F-111* was a medium bomber, and the A-7* and A-10* were light bombers.

References. Ernest J. Gentle and Lawrence W. Reithmaier, eds., *Aviation/Space Dictionary*, 6th ed., 1980. Woodford Agee Heflin, ed., *The United States Air Force Dictionary*, 1956. "The Strategic Bomber," *Air University Quarterly Review*, Summer 1955, pp. 88–137.

Alwyn T. Lloyd

BOMBERS B-52. See movies.

BOMBING. *See* doctrine; strategic operations.

BOMBING COMPETITION. *See* competitions.

BOMBING HALTS

The periodic bombing halts that President Lyndon B. Johnson* (LBJ) ordered during the Rolling Thunder* campaign against North Vietnam were intended to signal the U.S. government's willingness to negotiate a political settlement of the Vietnam War.*

After the first pause of about a week, in May 1965, LBJ approved a longer standdown of just over a month, beginning on Christmas Eve 1965. He periodically approved other pauses in the bombing to permit observance of the Vietnamese new year, called Tet, and other holidays.

From the North Vietnamese response to the bombing halts, it may be concluded that they saw such gestures as merely more signs of U.S. vacillation. Predictably, the North Vietnamese took advantage of the respites to rebuild their military strength and to heighten their infiltration activity southward.

LBJ's decision to cease all bombardment of the north on 1 November 1968 was not only a response to the political pressures at home against the bombing but also a recognition of the graduated escalation campaign's failure to weaken North Vietnam's resolve to pursue armed aggression against South Vietnam.

References. Berger, *USAF in SEA*. Larry Berman, *Lyndon Johnson's War: The Road to Stalemate in Vietnam*, 1989. Mark Clodfelter, *The Limits of Air Power: The American Bombing of North Vietnam*, 1989.

Warren A. Trest

BOMBS

The classic "iron bomb" is a streamlined case filled with high explosive (H.E.) and dropped from aircraft. The body is normally made of forged steel and machined to engineered dimensions. The filler H.E. is melted and poured into the case. Nose and tail holes are then cut into the H.E. and fuze wells fitted. The bomb and fuze combination must be more than 90 percent reliable and yet be able to be dropped safely when required.

The U.S. military had no standard bomb when it entered World War I,* and copies of British and French bombs were used. These were not completely satisfactory, so the U.S. Army produced new forms during the interwar period. These later bombs were satisfactory, and production rationalization during World War II* led to a joint Army-Navy (A/N-M) series. They were available in sizes from 100 to 10,000 pounds and were used until the early days of the Vietnam War.*

Although fine for low-speed, propellor-driven planes, the drag of the World War II-era bombs was excessive for jet aircraft. This caused the USAF* to develop two demolition bombs with less drag, the 759-pound M-117 and the 3,000 pound M-118, to supplement the older series. The iron bombs in standard use in 1988 were a Navy series in 250- to 2,000-pound sizes. These were the only H.E. bombs in production and were used by all U.S. services and most of the free world.

A development beyond the iron bomb is the "smart bomb," or precision-guided munition (PGM). These are iron bombs fitted with a kit in the field. A guidance section is fitted to the nose with a television or laser guidance (LGB) system; the tail is fitted with fins and a power supply. Sometimes enlarged fins or winglets are used to extend the bomb's range. Smart bombs have proven in combat to be both more accurate and safer for the pilot.*

There are many specialty types of bombs. Armor- and semiarmor-piercing bombs are for use against large ships and other protected targets. Light case bombs having a large H.E. load are used for blast effect on buildings. Antipersonnel fragmentation bombs are made with a thin case and then wound with a heavy square section spring. Very heavy deep penetration bombs in 11,000-, 22,000-, and 44,000-pound sizes were invented by Sir Barnes Wallis in England during World War II and were used on highly resistant targets such as U-boat pens and dams. During the Vietnam War,* the BLU-82 "Cheeseburger" was dropped from the rear door of C-130s* to clear helicopter* landing zones in the jungle. It weighed 15,000 pounds and had a main charge of 12,600 pounds of ammonium nitrate slurry. Another class of specialized bombs are the four and one-half pound incendiaries, with liquid, magnesium, or thermite fillings. These were very effective against cities during World War II and are still kept in inventory. The tactic of using detonation bombs to blow off roofs and penetrate walls followed by incendiaries to ignite flammables is especially effective against industrial targets.

Other examples of special-purpose bombs include cluster bombs, white phosphorous smoke bombs, and photoflash bombs. Practice bombs simulate all conventional and special weapons and come in sizes from four pounds to more than a ton. Practice bombs normally carry a spotting charge for target marking.

References. *Air Force Technical Order 60A-2-1-11*, vol. 2, 28 May 1947. Christopher Chant, *Encyclopaedia of Modern Aircraft Armament*, 1988. Gunston, *Airc. Arm.*

See also Azon, Razon, and Tarzon; glide bombs; nuclear weapons; Paveway I, II, and III laser-guided bombs; retarded bombs; target-marking munitions.

Philip Long

BOMBSIGHT. *See* Norden bombsight.

BONG, MAJOR RICHARD I. (1920–1945)

Bong is America's ace* of aces with 40 victories. He won every possible USAAF* decoration. In 1986 he was inducted posthumously into the National Aviation Hall of Fame in Dayton, Ohio.

Bong grew up on a farm in Poplar, Wisconsin. In 1941 he became a flying, or aviation, cadet* and graduated as a fighter* pilot* in 1942. He was assigned to fly P-38s* with the 35th Fighter Group and was an ace by January 1943. He then was sent to the 49th Fighter Group and had 21 victories by November 1943, when he went home on leave. He was put on the operations staff at headquarters of the Fifth Air Force* (5AF) when he returned to New Guinea. In April 1944 he again went home, this time with 28 victories and a promotion to major. In the United States he took a course in aerial gunnery and then returned to the Pacific. He scored another 12 victories in his next 30 sorties.

Bong received the Air Force Medal of Honor* from General of the Army Douglas MacArthur in December 1944 and was taken out of combat to return to the United States. He married and then was assigned as a test pilot for jets. In August 1945 he died in the crash of an F-80* after takeoff near Burbank, California.

References. Primary: George C. Kenney, *Dick Bong: Ace of Aces*, 1960. Secondary: DuPre, *USAF Bio.* Gurney, *5 Down.* Hess, *Aces Album.*

"BOOM." *See* Trenchard, Marshall of the Royal Air Force Lord Hugh M.

"BOOTS." *See* Blesse, Major General Frederick C.

BOOTSTRAP. *See* Operation Bootstrap.

BORAH, SENATOR WILLIAM E. (1865–1940)

This influential Idaho Republican was chairman of the Senate Foreign Relations Committee during most of the 1920s. He became a proponent of aviation as a coast defense weapon able to make practical the concepts of isolationism he advocated. He staunchly opposed the U.S. Navy's attempts to construct a large offensive naval force to control the Pacific Ocean. To support his opposition, Borah adopted Brigadier General William Mitchell's* early ideas for using the Army air arm in coastal defense.

In 1920–1921, Borah opposed the Navy's budget for a 48-battleship fleet by arguing that battleships might be obsolete. Borah had contact with both Mitchell and Rear Admiral William F. Fullam, who believed that airplanes and submarines would replace battleships in the future. Borah's speeches used Mitchell's claim that the United States could buy 1,000 aircraft for the price of one battleship. In early 1921, Borah used such arguments to persuade Congress to reduce naval appropriations and to call for a naval disarmament conference. When Congress debated the 1938 Vinson Naval Act and the 1939 Army aircraft bills proposed by President Franklin D. Roosevelt* (FDR), Borah led the isolationist faction that sought to limit the Navy to coastal defense and lauded an air force to defend the Western Hemisphere.

Borah's opinions on aviation represented an idea for using U.S. aircraft to avoid the collective security concepts of Woodrow Wilson and FDR. As aviation progressed steadily toward long-range aircraft, the air weapon could be conceived either as fostering international cooperation or providing a superior method for acting unilaterally if other nations hesitated to cooperate with the United States. Borah represented the latter view.

References. Primary: William Borah, radio speech of 25 March 1939, *Vital Speeches*, 15 April 1939, p. 399, and "Roosevelt's National Defense Program," *Congressional Digest*, March 1938, pp. 69–74. Secondary: Lester H. Brune, "Borah and Airplanes," *Idaho Yesterdays*, 1968. Robert James Maddux, *William E. Borah and American Foreign Policy*, 1969.

Lester H. Brune

BOYINGTON, COLONEL GREGORY. *See* American Volunteer Group.

BQM-34. *See* unmanned aerial vehicles.

BREGUET 14

Until U.S.-built de Haviland DH-4* "Liberty Planes" became available in August 1918, the USAAS* used French Breguet 14s and Salmson* 2A-2s for observation* and bomber* aircraft in France. The Breguet 14 was a 1917 design of the Société des Avions Louis Breguet. The 14A was for observation and the 14B for bombing. The 14B was an unusual aircraft with a bolted aluminum fuselage frame, negatively staggered wings, and automatic wing flaps. The USAAS used 229 14As, 47 14Bs, and 100 14E trainers.

Characteristics (14A): engine, Renault V-12 of 300 horsepower or Fiat of 285 horsepower; span, 47 feet; length, 29 feet; gross weight, 3,771 pounds; top speed, 129 miles per hour.

References. Swanborough, *US Mil. Airc.* Wagner, *Am. Planes.*

BRERETON, LIEUTENANT GENERAL LEWIS H. (1890–1967)

Brereton distinguished himself as a combat leader in both world wars. Born in Pittsburgh, Pennsylvania, he was a 1911 graduate of the U.S. Naval Academy (USNA). During World War I* he commanded the 12th Aero Squadron, one of the first U.S. flying units on the front. Brereton became chief of aviation for the 1st Army Corps in July 1918, took command of the Corps Observation Wing prior to the St. Mihiel campaign,* and in October 1918 became operations officer on Brigadier General William Mitchell's* staff of the American Expeditionary Forces' (AEF) Air Service. When the war ended, Brereton was appointed chief of staff of the Headquarters Air Service of the Third Army. Upon his return to the United States in February 1919, he became chief of operations in the USAAS* in Washington, D.C. He then held a variety of positions.

Brereton was commander of the Far East Air Force in the Philippines when World War II* began, and he lost most of his B-17* bombers* apparently without warning, while they were on the ground at Clark* Field shortly after hostilities started. Following the withdrawal from the Philippines, he became commander in chief of the Allied Air Forces on the staff of General Sir Archibald Wavell, in Java, in addition to his duties as commander of the Fifth Air Force* (5AF). In March 1942 he organized and commanded the Tenth Air Force* (10AF) in India, and in June he became commander of the Middle East Air Force, which later became the Ninth Air Force* (9AF). In August he became commanding general of the First Allied Airborne Army. He served in this post until the war ended. Brereton served the secretary of war from 1946 to 1947 and then became the chairman of the Military Liaison Committee to the U.S. Atomic Energy Commission. He retired in 1948.

References. Air Force Pamphlet (AFP) 31–1, "Roster of Retired General Officers," 1987. DuPre, *USAF Bio.* Robert P. Fogerty, *Biographical Study of USAF General Officers, 1917–1952*, vol. 1, n.d.

James C. Hasdorff

BRETT, LIEUTENANT GENERAL GEORGE H. (1886–1963)

Brett was chief of the Air Corps and commander of the Caribbean Defense Command during World War II.*

From Cleveland, Ohio, he graduated from Virginia Military Institute in 1909 and was commissioned a second lieutenant in the Philippine Scouts in 1910. In 1915 he began his aviation career, taking pilot* flight training* at San Diego

Signal Corps Aviation School,* California, graduating the next year. Brett served for 18 months at Air Service Headquarters in France during World War I* and rose to the grade of major. His postwar assignments included commander of Crissy Field, California, and Selfridge* Field, Michigan; instructor at Command and General Staff School; chief of staff of the General Headquarters Air Force* (GHQ Air Force); and chief of the Materiel Division at Wright Field.

In May 1941, Brett became chief of the Army Air Corps. He was promoted to lieutenant general in 1942 and became deputy supreme commander of the Allied forces in the southwest Pacific. In November 1942 he became commanding general of the Caribbean Defense Command, and in May 1945 took on the additional duty of commanding general of the Panama Canal Department. He retired in 1946.

References. Air Force Pamphlet (AFP) 31–1, "Roster of Retired General Officers," 1987. DuPre, *USAF Bio.* Robert P. Fogerty, *Biographical Study of USAF General Officers, 1917–1952*, vol. 1, n.d.

James C. Hasdorff

BROOKS AIR FORCE BASE

Brooks is an Air Force Systems Command* (AFSC) facility in San Antonio, Texas. The field was activated in 1917 and named for Cadet Sidney J. Brooks, Jr., who died in an aircraft accident. The field was a balloon and airship school from 1919 to 1923 and a primary flight training* school from 1922 to 1931. The School of Aviation Medicine arrived in 1926, and advanced flight training began in 1941. Brooks trained observers* from 1940 until such training was regarded as obsolete in 1943. Flying operations ceased in 1960. In 1990 the Human Systems Division of the AFSC was based on the field.

References. "Guide to Major Air Force Installations Worldwide," *AF*, May 1990, p. 122. Mueller, *AFB*. Roberts, *Dir. USAF*.

BROUGHTON, COLONEL JACKSEL M. "JACK" (1925–)

Broughton was a fighter* pilot* with a distinguished career until he acted to protect some subordinates from what he believed was unjustified punishment. Out of the USAF,* he wrote two critical and influential books, *Thud Ridge* (1969) and *Going Downtown: The War against Hanoi and Washington* (1988). Broughton's books portray the vivid reality of the Vietnam War* and express views common to USAF fighter pilots.

He graduated from the U.S. Military Academy (USMA) in 1945. He flew 114 combat sorties in the Korean War* in F-80s* and F-84s* and later was a leader of the Thunderbirds* aerial demonstration team. In the Vietnam War he served as the deputy commander of the 355th Tactical Fighter Wing (TFW), flying F-105s.* There he was decorated with the Air Force Cross and was recommended for a second.

In 1967 two of his pilots, in fear for their lives, shot back at gunners on the Soviet ship *Turkestan*. Because the *Turkestan* was in Haiphong* harbor, they had violated political air superiority* given to the enemy. Knowing they faced punishment for this act, the pilots lied. Broughton destroyed evidence that might have been adverse to protect his pilots. He was court-martialed and he then retired.

References. Primary: Chuck Yeager and Leo Janos, *Yeager: An Autobiography*, 1985. Secondary: John L. Frisbee, "Thud Ridge: A Legacy and a Legend," *AF*, October 1986, p. 108. R. Bradford McMahon, "The *Turkestan* and *Mikhail Frunze* Incidents," *The Retired Officer*, April 1988, pp. 28–32, and "The Vietnam War's Lingering Consequences," *The Retired Officer*, May 1988, pp. 22–26.

BROWN, GENERAL GEORGE S. (1918–1978)

General Brown was the eighth chairman of the Joint Chiefs of Staff (JCS), from 1974 to 1978, and the second USAF* officer to hold the position. Brown was also the eighth chief of staff of the Air Force,* from 1973 to 1974. Within military circles, he was highly respected for his success in combat and qualities of leadership, especially professionalism and loyalty to subordinates. In 1985 he was inducted posthumously into the National Aviation Hall of Fame in Dayton, Ohio.

A 1941 U.S. Military Academy (USMA) graduate, he flew combat missions with B-24s* in the Eighth Air Force's* (8AF) 93rd Bomb Group and subsequently directed operations for the 2nd Air Division. He distinguished himself in the August 1943 raid on Ploesti,* Romania.

After World War II,* he served in the Air Training Command* (ATC) and then in the Continental Air Command* (CONAC). In 1950 he took command of the 62nd Troop Carrier Group at McChord* AFB, Washington, with responsibility for airlift to Korea. He made the transition to fighters* in 1951, taking command of the 56th Fighter Interceptor Wing (FIW) at Selfridge* AFB, Michigan. Then he moved to the Korean War* as assistant director and later director of operations of the Fifth Air Force* (5AF) from 1952 to 1953. He commanded the 3525 Pilot Training Wing at Williams* AFB, Arizona, from 1953 to 1956.

Upon graduation from the National War College in 1957, he was appointed executive to the chief of staff of the Air Force, General Thomas D. White.* In 1959 he became military assistant to the secretary of defense, serving under Thomas S. Gates, Jr., and Robert S. McNamara* in the Eisenhower* and Kennedy* administrations. In 1963 he commanded the Eastern Transport Air Force at McGuire* AFB, New Jersey, and the next year the Joint Task Force 2, a JCS unit responsible for testing weapons systems for all services at Sandia AFB, New Mexico. In 1966 he became assistant to the chairman of the JCS, General Earle Wheeler. In 1968 he commanded the Seventh Air Force* (7AF) in the Vietnam War.* In 1970 he became commander of the Air Force Systems Command* (AFSC) until named chief of staff in 1973. His confirmation hearings became controversial because of the 7AF's role in the secret Cambodian operations.* He served as chairman of the JCS until his death from cancer. While he was chairman, Brown's comments about Jewish influence in banking and newspapers were criticized for ethnic stereotyping.

References. Primary: Edgar Puryear, Jr., oral history interviews K239.0512–1375 through K239.05132–1525, donated to the USAF Historical Research Center. Secondary: Futrell, *Ideas*, vol. 2. Lawrence J. Korb, *The Joint Chiefs of Staff: The First Twenty-Five Years*, 1976. Edgar F. Puryear, Jr., *George S. Brown, General, U.S. Air Force, Destined for Stars*, 1983. Claude Witze, ''USAF's New Leaders,'' *AF*, September 1973, pp. 58–59.

Maurice Maryanow

BROWN, SECRETARY HAROLD (1927–   )

Brown was the eighth secretary of the Air Force, from 1965 to 1969. In this position he emphasized both technological and human concerns.

He graduated from Columbia University in 1945 and held a Phi Beta Kappa key. He stayed at Columbia for an M.A. in 1946 and a Ph.D. in physics in 1949. Brown was a researcher at the University of California Radiation Laboratory in Berkeley, California, from 1950 to 1952 and at the E. O. Lawrence Radiation Laboratory in Livermore, California, from 1952 to 1960. He worked on developing weapons at Livermore with Dr. Edward Teller, the principal man in the development of thermonuclear devices. He was a member of the Polaris Steering Committee from 1956 to 1958. Then he became a member of the Air Force Scientific Advisory Board* from 1958 to 1961 after serving the board as a consultant for two years. In 1960 he became Livermore's director.

In 1961 he became the Department of Defense's (DoD) director of defense research and engineering (DDR&E). At that time this was the third highest position in the DoD. In 1965 he became secretary of the Air Force (SAF). On this Pentagon tour, Brown was heavily involved in strategic operations* systems. He presided over the introduction of Minuteman* II and the development of Minuteman III. He helped kill the B-70* because he preferred the B-1.* He also helped kill the X-6* and X-20.* For tactical operations* he advocated more airlift, including the C-5* and C-9,* and modernization of fighters* which helped lead to the F-111* and F-15.* He pushed for improvements in the U.S. Air Force Reserve* (USAFR) and the Air National Guard* (ANG). He also promoted arms limitation negotiations. Brown was noted for talking with enlisted airmen and noncommissioned and junior officers to enhance the human side of the USAF. He also established a reputation for rough treatment of senior officers who disagreed with him.

Brown became president of the California Institute of Technology following his stint as SAF. In 1969 he was a delegate to the Strategic Arms Limitation Talks (SALT I). He published an attack on the use of multiple independently targetable reentry vehicles* (MIRV) and antiballistic missile (ABM) systems while supporting SALT I and II.

Brown returned to the DoD as President Jimmy Carter's secretary of defense (SECDEF) from 1977 to 1981, the 14th in the post. Brown immersed himself in minutiae and showed no grand plans. This was inevitable because Carter acted as his own SECDEF. Carter's principal concern was to decrease defense spending. Carter overruled Brown and canceled the B-1 almost as soon as he was president. Soon Carter had disapproved the FB-111 (*see* F-111), delayed the Peacekeeper* (MX), and canceled the Advanced Medium STOL Transport* (AMST) and clean, or neutron, nuclear weapon* development. Brown's tenure as SECDEF was undistinguished but understandable in the climate in which he worked.

References. Futrell, *Ideas*, vol. 2. Richard A. Stubbing, *The Defense Game*, 1986. Jim Taylor, "Harold Brown—Fourteenth Secretary of Defense," *AF*, February 1977, pp. 22–25.

BROWNING MACHINE GUNS

John M. Browning (1855–1926) is considered the greatest firearms designer of all time. His gas-operated machine gun was adopted by the United States in 1896, and his 50-caliber M-2 machine gun is still in production.

The Colt-Browning model 1895 "potato digger" was updated by the Marlin-Rockwell Corporation in 1917, and an air-cooled version was adopted by the U.S. Army for aviation use as Model 1918, M-1. Almost 40,000 were made, and it served as the standard aircraft gun until the larger M-2 Browning gun was adopted in 1930. In World War I,* General of the Armies John J. Pershing,* commander of the American Expeditionary Force (AEF), wanted a more powerful cartridge so the 30 caliber was scaled up to 50 caliber and evolved into the M-2.

The definitive M-2 was put into production and served until the obsolescence of all airborne rifle caliber machine guns during World War II.* This model served as the standard for fixed, turret, and flexible mounts on nearly all U.S. aircraft in World War II. In 1945 the faster speeds of the new jet aircraft posed a requirement for a higher rate of fire, and the AN/M-3 was developed and replaced the M-2 for aviation use.

References. John Browning and Curt Gentry, *John M. Browning, American Gunmaker*, 1964. George M. Chinn, *The Machine Gun*, 1st and 5th eds., 1951 and 1987. W.H.B. Smith, *Small Arms of the World*, 8th ed., 1966.

Philip Long

BT-13 AND BT-15 VALIANT

Pilot* flight training* in World War II* was done in three stages: primary, basic, and advanced. The aircraft used in the basic stage was almost entirely the BT-13 and the similar BT-15. The BT-13 began as a private venture by Vultee Aircraft, Inc., with the company designation of Model 54. The USAAC* ordered it into production in 1939. Vultee's production outstripped Pratt & Whitney engine* manufacture for the plane, so a Wright engine* was adapted and those using it were designated BT-15s. BT-13s were also bought by the U.S. Navy. Some officers believed the Valiant was unsatisfactory because it was too easy to fly. In 1945 this view prevailed and the USAAF* replaced its BTs with the T-6,* at that time designated the AT-6. The BT was nicknamed "Bee Tee" and "Vultee Vibrator."

Characteristics (BT-13): engine, Pratt & Whitney R-985-AN-1 of 450 horsepower; span, 42 feet; length, 29 feet; height, 12 feet; gross weight, 4,496 pounds; top speed, 180 miles per hour; service ceiling, 21,650 feet; range, 725 miles.

References. Primary: Higham, *Combat Airc.*, vol. 3. Secondary: Swanborough, *US Mil. Airc.* John Wegg, *General Dynamics Aircraft and Their Predecessors*, 1990.

"BUD." *See* Mahurin, Colonel Walker M.

BULGE, BATTLE OF THE

There is a continuing interest in this battle because of its great drama. It has far greater importance as illustrative of the plus and minus effects of air power at this time in history.

German plans rested upon surprise, attacking U.S. divisions that needed a rest and neutralizing air power. The German army field commanders demanded Luftwaffe assistance. That help was deceptively promised to them. Luftwaffe resources amounted to less than 1,400 operational aircraft manned by poorly trained crews in the West, and the Americans and British held air superiority.* The German high command hoped for bad weather to eliminate air power as a factor.

Allied aerial reconnaissance* and ground intelligence reported the German buildup. It is not clear, then, why the German attack was a complete surprise. From 16 to 23 December 1944, the weather virtually shut down air operations and the Germans came close to a breakthrough. They might have succeeded had their fuel supplies not been critically low despite stockpiling for the offensive. This fuel shortage can be attributed to strategic operations* previously conducted against the German oil industry and transportation target systems.*

The flying weather that began on 24 December was called "victory weather" and enabled the fury of the Eighth and Ninth Air Forces* (8 and 9AF), with the British Second Tactical Air Force, to fall on the German supply lines and troops. The favorable weather lasted until 31 December when German defeat was assured. From 26 to 31 December, the 8AF bombers* dropped 14,177 tons of bombs* on transportation centers supporting the German army. Sixty-three bombers and 23 fighters* were lost and 128 German fighters were claimed as destroyed. The 9AF, with two additional fighter groups of the 8AF, flew 10,305 sorties from 23 to 31 December. They dropped 6,969 tons of bombs and claimed 264 enemy aircraft* destroyed at a loss of 158 U.S. planes. They estimated they had destroyed 2,323 motor transports, 207 armored units, 173 gun positions, 620 railroad cars, 45 locomotives, and 7 bridges.

References. C&C, vol. 3. Roger A. Freeman, *The Mighty Eighth: Units, Men and Machines*, 1970.

BULLPUP. *See* AGM-12.

BUREAU OF AIRCRAFT PRODUCTION

This agency was formed from the earlier Equipment Division of the U.S. Army Signal Corps by President Woodrow Wilson on 21 May 1918. It was an attempt to regularize control of aircraft production after the outcry against the

Aircraft Production Board* established in the summer of 1917. Under the secretary of war, the bureau was headed by John D. Ryan,* former president of Anaconda Copper Company. The Division of Military Aeronautics* was also established on 21 May, and, although the bureau and the division were then recognized as together constituting the USAAS,* the formal unification of the two did not occur until 27 August.

References. Primary: Benedict Crowell, *America's Munitions; 1917–1918*, 1919. Secondary: Futrell, *Ideas*, vol. 1. Goldberg, *Hist. USAF*. I. B. Holley, Jr., *Ideas and Weapons*, 1953.

D. K. Vaughan

BUSHEY PARK

This was the headquarters site of the Eighth Air Force* (8AF) from early 1942 to January 1944. It was in the southwest London suburbs, England. The code name was Widewing. In January 1944 the site became the headquarters of the U.S. Strategic Air Forces in Europe* (originally USSAFE, later USSTAF). The headquarters of the 8AF then operated from High Wycombe* Abbey School, code name Pinetree, the former headquarters of VIII Bomber Command of the 8AF.

References. Primary: James Parton, *"Air Force Spoken Here": General Ira Eaker and the Command of the Air*, 1986. Secondary: C&C, vols. 1, 2, and 3.

W. A. Jacobs

C

C-5 GALAXY

The Lockheed Aircraft Corporation's gigantic C-5 transport,* with its tremendous payload capability, was developed in the 1960s in response to the unprecedented airlift demands of the time. Then the world's largest aircraft, it became operational with the Military Airlift Command* (MAC) in 1969. The C-5s became important for the efficiency of the Vietnam Airlift* and were instrumental in the Israeli Airlift of 1973. Without the C-5s Israel probably would have lost the Yom Kippur War. The C-5A's success led to 50 C-5Bs, a modernized version, to be bought from 1985 to 1989. Its nickname is "Fat Albert."

The C-5 was especially important for the airlifts because it could carry virtually any equipment in the U.S. Army's inventory at intercontinental ranges and jet speeds. It could, for instance, handle such bulky items as the 74-ton mobile scissors bridge. In its test program, the C-5 airdropped 80 tons in four equal units in a single pass over a drop zone (DZ). It also could be loaded and unloaded simultaneously at the front and rear cargo openings and had the ability to "kneel down" to facilitate loading directly from truck bed levels. A wing modification program in 1987 extended the C-5 service life by 30,000 flying hours, ensuring it would operate into the 21st century.

Since the early 1970s the C-5 has been a mainstay of MAC. Most operations have been routine, but some are more noteworthy. The C-5s were instrumental for the defense of South Vietnam in the 1972 aggression by North Vietnam. Along with C-141s* and commercial carriers, C-5s moved 3,195 personnel and 1,600 tons of cargo from the United States to Vietnam during nine days in May. In the Israeli Airlift, MAC delivered 22,395 tons of supplies from about 20 locations in the continental United States (CONUS) in 567 aircraft missions over a distance of 7,420 miles. By comparison, the USSR provided the Arabs with 15,000 tons in 40 days in 935 aircraft missions over a distance of 1,950 miles. C-5As participated in the Grenada incident.* In 1988 a C-5 airlift took an

Archimedes screw to Alaska to aid in the rescue of two whales caught in the ice. In 1990–1991 C-5s contributed much to the Iraq crisis* and Iraq War* airlifts.

Characteristics (C-5A): engines, four General Electric TF39-GE-1 turbofans of 41,000 pounds of thrust each; span, 223 feet; length, 248 feet; height, 65 feet; gross weight, 769,000 pounds; top speed, 571 miles per hour; service ceiling, 34,000 feet; range with maximum payload of 220,000 pounds, 3,435 miles.

References. Berger, *USAF in SEA*. Dick J. Burkard, *Military Airlift Command Historical Handbook, 1941–1984*, 1984. "The C-5 Galaxy: Special Reports," *AF*, April 1968, pp. 64–104. René J. Francillon, *Lockheed Aircraft since 1913*, 1987. Swanborough, *US Mil. Airc*.

                                                                    Roger D. Launius

C-7 CARIBOU

De Haviland Aircraft of Canada began design of a DHC-4 in 1956 as a "Twin Otter." It was deliberately designed for military use in the hope of selling it to the U.S. Army. The Army did buy it in 1957 as a short takeoff and landing (STOL) transport* designated as the YAC-1. Its first flight was in 1958. Eventually 159 were bought. In 1962 the designation was changed to CV-2. The Army intended to use the CV-2 for tactical airlift* to areas close to land battles. But as its gross weight was 26,000 pounds, the Department of Defense (DoD) held that its capability overlapped USAF* responsibilities; so in 1967 the remaining 134 aircraft were transferred to the USAF and redesignated as C-7s.

The C-7 served well in the Vietnam War.* It was used mainly for carrying administrative material and for emergency deliveries of cargo under weather and hostile fire situations unsuitable for other planes. Thus it was usually used for airlift to Special Forces camps. The C-7 had favorable flying characteristics and was rugged. The USAF lost only eight to enemy action by the time C-7 operations in Vietnam ended in 1972. The C-7s ended active service in 1983.

Characteristics (C-7A): engines, two Pratt & Whitney R-2000–7M2 of 1,450 horsepower each; span, 96 feet; length, 73 feet; height, 32 feet; top speed, 216 miles per hour; service ceiling, 27,700 feet; range, 1,400 miles; payload, 32 combat troops.

References. Ray L. Bowers, *Tactical Airlift*, 1983. Swanborough, *US Mil. Airc*.

See also Pace-Finletter memorandum of 4 November 1952; separation from the U.S. Army; Wilson memorandums.

C-9 NIGHTINGALE

In 1967 the USAF* adapted the McDonnell Douglas Corporation's DC-9 as an aeromedical evacuation* aircraft designated C-9A. It entered active service in 1968 and was named for Englishwoman Florence N. Nightingale. A total of 21 C-9As were bought. Three additional were bought as VC-9Cs to serve as very important persons (VIP) transports* and presidential airlift.*

Characteristics (C-9A): engines, two Pratt & Whitney JT8D-9 turbofans of

14,500 pounds thrust each; span, 93 feet; length, 119 feet; height, 28 feet; gross weight, 108,000 pounds; top speed, 575 miles per hour; range, over 2,000 miles; payload, 40 litter patients.

References. René J. Francillon, *McDonnell Douglas Aircraft since 1920*, vol. 1, 1988. Swanborough, *US Mil. Airc.*

C-10A EXTENDER

In the 1970s the USAF* studied the possibility of using commercial airliners as tankers* and transports* for greater capacity per aircraft, and it was decided that the use of a converted airliner would provide worldwide access to spare parts and maintenance. The project was called Advanced Tanker/Cargo Aircraft (ATCA). The McDonnell Douglas Corporation's DC-10–30CF was selected in 1977. The first flight took place in 1980, and active service began in 1981 as the KC-10A. Fifty-nine were built.

Characteristics: engines, three General Electric CF6–50C2 turbofans of 52,500 pounds thrust each; span, 165 feet; length, 182 feet; height, 58 feet; gross weight, 590,000 pounds; cruise speed, Mach 0.825; service ceiling, 42,000 feet; range, 4,370 miles; payload, 169,000 pounds.

References. Charles E. Bailey, "The Maturing of the KC-10," *AF*, May 1983, pp. 52–55. William B. Scott, "Air Force to Retrofit KC-10s with Air Refueling Pods," *AWST*, 13 November 1989, pp. 36–37, 39, 42. Susan H. H. Young, "Gallery of USAF Weapons," *AF*, May 1990, p. 153.

C-17A

The McDonnell Douglas Corporation's C-17A was in 1990 a transport* under development. It was intended to carry outsize cargo for intercontinental distances and operate out of small airfields. The plan called for 210 C-17As to be built.

Characteristics (performance estimated): engines, four Pratt & Whitney F117-PW-100 turbofans of 40,700 pounds thrust each; span, 165 feet; length, 175 feet; height, 58 feet; gross weight, 580,000 pounds; cruising speed, 518 miles per hour; range with payload of 167,000 pounds, 2,765 miles.

References. "McDonnell Douglas Striving to Achieve C-17 Goals," *AWST*, 3 December 1990, pp. 36–37, 39, 46–51. Jeffrey P. Rhodes, "The First C-17," *AF*, August 1988, pp. 54–59. Swanborough, *US Mil. Airc.* Susan H. H. Young, "Gallery of USAF Weapons," *AF*, May 1990, p. 153.

C-18

These transports* were originally Boeing Airplane Company's Model 707–323Cs operated by American Airlines. After purchase, the USAF* used the eight aircraft as C-18As for training and support missions. Conversion of them to the EC-18B Advanced Range Instrumentation Aircraft (ARIA) was made by installing mission equipment from the C-135* variant, EC-135N ARIA, so they could serve as voice and telemetry links for the space program. Two aircraft were modified again to EC-18Cs for the Joint STARS mission and then redesignated as E-8As.* Another two aircraft were converted to a cruise missile* control mission and were designated as EC-18Ds.

Characteristics: *see* C-137.

References. Peter M. Bowers, *Boeing Aircraft since 1916*, 1989. Alwyn T. Lloyd, *Boeing 707 and AWACS in Detail & Scale*, 1987. Swanborough, *US Mil. Airc.* Susan H. H. Young, "Gallery of USAF Weapons," *AF*, May 1990, p. 151.

Alwyn T. Lloyd

C-25

Based upon The Boeing Company's E-4B,* a pair of Boeing 747–200 transports* were selected to replace the aging VC-137C (*see* C-137) aircraft serving as "Air Force One" for presidential airlift.* The first VC-25A was delivered in 1990. The pair will be based at Andrews* AFB, Maryland. Unlike the VC-137, the VC-25A is equipped for aerial refueling.* It has accommodations for 80 passengers and a crew of 23 and does not need foreign support for fuel or food.

Characteristics: engines, four General Electric CF6–80C2B1 turbofans of 56,750 pounds thrust each; span, 196 feet; length, 231 feet; height, 63 feet; maximum takeoff weight, 800,000 pounds; speed, 600 miles per hour; service ceiling, over 45,000 feet; unrefueled endurance, 12 hours.

References. Peter M. Bowers, *Boeing Aircraft since 1916*, 1989. "First of Two New Presidential Aircraft Makes Initial Flight," *AWST*, 5 February 1990, p. 81. Swanborough, *US Mil. Airc.*

Alwyn T. Lloyd

C-46 COMMANDO

Intended as an airliner when it was designed by the Curtiss-Wright Corporation in 1937, it first flew in 1940. The designers tried to make a 36-passenger aircraft, which was a four-engine load in 1937, that would use only two engines. They succeeded in this highly efficient goal. With the coming of World War II,* the USAAC* had the design converted to a military transport.* The first production aircraft was delivered in 1942, but subsequent airplanes were delayed by engineering problems. In all, the USAAF* bought 3,144. The C-46 was respected by its aircrews.

The C-46 had a larger payload and more ability to operate at higher altitudes than had the C-47,* so it was used in the Pacific theaters and was also important to the success of the "Hump" Airlift.* In the Korean War* the C-46 was used from 1950 to 1953. The USAF* sought to retire the C-46s before the end of the war, but Brigadier General Chester E. McCarty succeeded in keeping them because of their demonstrated reliability. This workhorse airplane was "retired" in 1960, but in 1954 the USAF had started its Logistic Airlift (LOGAIR) to speed high-priority materiel shipments. It kept title to many C-46s and they soldiered on under contract in the LOGAIR system. In 1962 they were used again in Southeast Asian operations, and only finally withdrawn in 1969. Their nickname was "Ol' Dumbo."

Characteristics (C-46A): engines, two Pratt & Whitney R-2800–51 of 2,000 horsepower each; span, 108 feet; length, 76 feet; height, 22 feet; gross weight, 56,000 pounds; top speed, 269 miles per hour at 15,000 feet; service ceiling, 27,600 feet; range, 1,200 miles; payload, 10,000 pounds.

References. Primary: Higham, *Combat Airc.*, vol. 1. Secondary: Peter M. Bowers, *Curtiss Aircraft 1907–1947*, 1979. H. L. "Duffy" Buller, "The C-46 and C-47 in CBI Operations," *AH*, pp. 80–83. Futrell, *USAF in Korea*. Swanborough, *US Mil. Airc.*

C-47 SKYTRAIN

The C-47 was the military variant of the Douglas Aircraft Company's DC-3 transport,* first flown in 1935. One of the great aircraft of all time, it was the backbone of the USAAF's* airlift capability in World War II* and saw continuous service through the 1960s with the USAF.*

More than 10,000 were built in 25 different models with specifically designed features. This versatility resulted in the variants AC-47 gunship;* EC-47 for electronic warfare* navigator* training; HC-47, or SC-47, for rescue;* RC-47 for reconnaissance;* TC-47 for training; and VC-47 for staff transportation. It did special operations, towed gliders, and did a myriad of other specialized tasks. Other variants were designated C-49, C-50, C-51, C-52, and C-53. In recognition of its importance, General of the Army Dwight D. Eisenhower* called the C-47 one of the four weapons, along with the bazooka, jeep, and atomic bomb, that most helped to win World War II.

The C-47 entered service in the USAAF in 1941 and was as widely deployed as the Allied air forces. It was among the first types of aircraft delivered by the Air Corps Ferrying Command (ACFC) across the North Atlantic Ferry Route to Britain in 1942, and it took an active part in the early stages of the "Hump" Airlift* between India and China. With the formation of the Air Transport Command (ATC) on 1 July 1942, the C-47 became the workhorse airlifter of the fleet. In the same year the C-47 was incorporated into the Troop Carrier Command and participated in *all* of the major airborne operations of the war. It served well as a paratroop platform and glider tug in virtually all tactical airlift* operations. For example, in the first 50 hours of Operation Overlord,* C-47s dropped the bulk of 60,000 paratroopers and their equipment behind German lines.

When the Military Air Transport Service (MATS) was formed in 1948, 239 C-47s were in it. C-47s were the first aircraft used in the Berlin Airlift.* The C-47 also was used in the Korean War* with Combat Cargo Command. It was operational in the Vietnam War* in the early 1960s as a general airlifter, and in 1965 its use as a gunship* began. Known as "Dragon," "Dragonship," "Puff the Magic Dragon," and "Spooky," the AC-47 was enormously successful until it and the regular C-47 were retired from USAF service in 1969. A favorite with pilots, C-47s were nicknamed "Dizzy Three," "Douglas Racer," "Dowager Duchess," "Goon," "Gooney Bird," "Grand Old Lady," "Old Methuselah," "Placid Plodder," and "The Three."

Characteristics: engines, two Pratt & Whitney R-1830–92 of 1,200 horsepower each; span, 95 feet; length, 63 feet; height, 17 feet; gross weight, 31,000 pounds; top speed, 230 miles per hour at 8,800 feet; service ceiling, 24,000 feet; range, 1,600 miles; payload, 10,000 pounds.

References. Primary: Higham, *Combat Airc.*, vol. 1. Secondary: Jack S. Ballard, *Development and Employment of Fixed-Wing Gunships, 1962–1972*, 1982. Dick J. Burkard, *Military Airlift Command: Historical Handbook 1941–1984*, 1984. Henry M. Holden, "Douglas DC-3—Wings of the World," *AAHS Journal*, Winter 1985, pp. 242–59, and Spring 1986, pp. 26–43. Swanborough, *US Mil. Airc.*

Roger D. Launius

C-54 SKYMASTER

The C-54 was one of the great transports* in USAF* history, being a key to the success of the Berlin* and Korean* Airlifts.

The aircraft was originally designed by the Douglas Aircraft Company to be the commercial DC-4A, planned for transcontinental airline operations. The USAAF* requisitioned those in production in 1942 and designated them C-54s. Soon the USAAF ordered cargo versions, and Douglas expanded its production facilities to build more C-54s in Chicago. In World War II* the type flew 79,642 ocean crossings with the loss of only three aircraft, one of which was intentionally lost in a test. The C-54 flew operations globally and was the first transport to fly the North Atlantic routinely. Thus, it was one of the land aircraft that demonstrated that flying boats were obsolete. Presidents Franklin D. Roosevelt* (FDR) and Harry S Truman* (HST) used a C-54 for presidential airlift,* and the first was named *The Sacred Cow* by the press. The USAAF bought 1,163 C-54s in the war. In 1947 a modified C-54 flew an automated flight from Newfoundland to England with pilots* aboard as monitors only.

There were 319 used for the Berlin Airlift (1948 to 1949), out of 400 in active service. Thirty-eight of them were stripped so they could carry coal and were designated as C-54Ms. The first U.S. aircraft lost in the Korean War* was a C-54 which was strafed while it was on Kimpo* airfield. Some C-54s were modified to fly wounded in aeromedical evacuation* from Japan to the United States in the Korean Airlift and were redesignated as MC-54Ms. Other variants include SC-54D and HC-54D for rescue,* JC-54s for recovery of missile nose cones, AC-54D and EC-54D for the Airways and Air Communications Service (AACS), VC-54s for personnel transports, and TC-54Ds for trainers. A C-54 using Allison V-1710–131 engines was designated the XC-114 and, later, the XC-116.

Characteristics: engines, four Pratt & Whitney R-2000–7 of 1,290 horsepower each; span, 118 feet; length, 94 feet; height, 28 feet; gross weight, 62,000 pounds; top speed, 265 miles per hour; service ceiling, 22,000 feet; range, 3,900 miles; payload, 50 troops.

References. Primary: Higham, *Combat Airc.*, vol. 1. Secondary: René J. Francillon, *McDonnell Douglas Aircraft since 1920*, vol. 1, 1988. Swanborough, *US Mil. Airc.*

C-82 PACKET

The Fairchild Engine and Airplane Corporation's C-82 was designed to meet a 1941 USAAF* requirement for a military freighter that would afford a large, uninterrupted cargo hold with direct access for ground-level loading. This was a first in design, and it was the only plane designed in World War II* specifically as a military transport.* The first flight was in 1944, and 100 were ordered. They arrived too late for use in the war. A total of 220 were built between 1945 and 1948. Most served for tactical airlift* in the Tactical Air Command* (TAC). Its excessive nose-high attitude during drops obscured the pilots'* view, and the USAAF ordered extensive redesign. The result was the C-119.* The C-82 had the nickname "Crowd Killer."

Characteristics: engines, two Pratt & Whitney R-2800–85 of 2,100 horsepower each; span, 106 feet; length, 77 feet; height, 26 feet; gross weight, 54,000 pounds; top speed, 248 miles per hour at 17,500 feet; service ceiling, 21,200 feet; range, 1,920 miles.

References. Goldberg, *Hist. USAF*. Swanborough, *US Mil. Airc.*

Alwyn T. Lloyd

C-97 STRATOFREIGHTER

The KC-97 performed an important role in the USAF* by providing the first complete aerial refueling* service in support of global operations.

The Boeing Airplane Company's C-97 was an outgrowth of its B-29* and B-50.* The first flight was in 1944. It served in the Military Air Transport Service (MATS) as a C-97 transport* including MC-97s for aeromedical evacuation,* and the Strategic Air Command* (SAC) used KC-97s as tankers.* All of the tankers were equipped with the new Boeing "flying boom"* for aerial refueling. C-97s were the first large aircraft assigned to the Air National Guard* (ANG). During the 1960s ANG KC-97Gs were converted into KC-97Ls, featuring the addition of two pod-mounted General Electric J-47 turbojet engines. The initiative for this redesign came from First Lieutenant Phillip A. Meyer. The change enabled the KC-97s to refuel jet aircraft better by flying at a higher speed, and so they were used until 1977. The ANG also used HC-97s for rescue* operations.

Characteristics (KC-97G): engines, four Pratt & Whitney R-4360–59B of 3,500 horsepower each; span, 141 feet; length, 117 feet; height, 38 feet; gross weight, 175,000 pounds; top speed, 375 miles per hour; operating ceiling, 30,200 feet; range, 4,300 miles; payload, 96 troops.

References. Peter M. Bowers, *Boeing Aircraft since 1916*, 1989. James L. Delaney, "The KC-97L: Evolution of the Air Guard's Six-Engine Tanker," *AH*, December 1982, pp. 265–68. Swanborough, *US Mil. Airc.*

Alwyn T. Lloyd

C-119 FLYING BOXCAR

The C-119 served the USAF* for long, but it had a checkered career. The Fairchild Engine and Airplane Corporation's C-119 was a direct follow-on to the C-82.* It was ordered into production based upon analysis and without the confidence of wind tunnel and flight test data. A total of 979 were built, of which Kaiser Manufacturing Corporation made 200. The USAF contract with Kaiser resulted in much bickering between the companies over engineering data and finances. In the end, Kaiser developed its own engineering changes, thereby compromising interchangeability. When Kaiser did not pay Fairchild for the data that they did not get, the USAF paid Fairchild. There were bitter allegations over Kaiser's delayed production schedule and higher costs, leading to a congressional investigation. Kaiser's defense prevailed, but the company left the aerospace industry* as a result. Relations between Fairchild and the USAF were damaged by this episode.

The C-119 proved itself in the Korean War* in paratroop drops and aerial resupply. The most notable mission was in support of the U.S. Marine Corps (USMC) in the Chosin Reservoir* area. A bridge was dropped from C-119s which enabled cutoff troops to break out. Its second conflict was the Vietnam War.* Twenty-six were converted into AC-119G gunships* with four GAU-2 7.62mm gatling guns. Another 26 AC-119Ks mounted two M-61s* and had a pair of General Electric J85 turbojets of 2,850 pounds of thrust each mounted in pods under the wings. They received the nicknames of "Stinger" and "Shadow" and were interim aircraft between the AC-47 (*see* C-47) and AC-130 (*see* C-130) gunships.

While the USAF experienced continuous problems with the C-119, the U.S. Air Force Reserve* (USAFR) used it for a long time and turned it into a viable transport.* Its nicknames included "Crowd Killer" and "Dollar 19."

Characteristics (C-119G): engines, two Wright R-3350–89A with 3,500 horsepower each; span, 109 feet; length, 87 feet; height, 27 feet; gross weight, 72,700 pounds; top speed, 281 miles per hour at 18,000 feet; service ceiling, 21,580 feet; range, 1,630 miles; payload, 62 troops.

References. Jack S. Ballard, *Development and Employment of Fixed-Wing Gunships 1962–1972*, 1982. Robert J. Lessels, "Shadow Gunships in Southeast Asia," *AF*, November 1971, pp. 38–40. Swanborough, *US Mil. Airc*.

Alwyn T. Lloyd

C-121 CONSTELLATION

Commercial transports* were requisitioned directly from the production lines after Pearl Harbor,* and so the long USAF* career of the Lockheed Aircraft Corporation's Constellation began. Those used in World War II* were designated C-69s and active service began in 1943. They were all sold as surplus after the war.

The USAF ordered copies of the improved L-749 Constellation in 1948, designating them as C-121As and VC-121As. Their intended use was for passengers, including presidential airlift,* and their designations were ultimately changed to PC-121As. As North Atlantic Treaty Organization* (NATO) commander, Dwight D. Eisenhower* used one named *Columbine*, and as president he used another, *Columbine II*. General of the Army Douglas MacArthur used one named *Bataan*. A bigger model, the C-121C, was adapted to use in airborne early warning air defense operations, designated later as RC-121C, then TC-121C, and finally EC-121C. These aircraft entered active service in 1953 and patrolled the waters off the Pacific and Atlantic coasts. Thirty EC-121s served in the Vietnam War* as College Eye* aircraft.

The Constellation ended active service in 1979. Its nicknames include "Connie," "Humpback," "Lockheed Flying Speedbrake," and "Swineicus Subsonicus."

Characteristics (C-121G): engines, four Wright R-3350–91 of 3,250 horsepower each; span, 123 feet; length, 116 feet; height, 25 feet; gross weight, 145,000 pounds; top speed, 368 miles per hour at 20,000 feet; service ceiling, 22,300 feet; range, 2,100 miles.

References. Primary: Higham, *Combat Airc.*, vol. 3. Secondary: Swanborough, *US Mil. Airc.*

C-123 PROVIDER

A longtime workhorse of the USAF,* this light transport* was built by the Fairchild Engine and Airplane Corporation. It was an outgrowth of the XG-20 assault glider designed by Chase Aircraft Company, Inc. The first flight was in 1949. A contract was filled for five C-123Bs in 1952. The Kaiser Manufacturing Corporation acquired a majority interest in Chase in 1953 and received a contract for 300. The contract was canceled after the turbulent affair of Kaiser production of the C-119.* Fairchild assumed production responsibility and produced 302 airplanes. Two YC-123s were produced by the Stroukoff Aviation Corporation. In 1957 Fairchild added two turbojets in wingtip pods, and the new model was designated C-123J. The *J*s were used to support distant early warning line* (DEW Line) installations. The C-123K had two wing-mounted turbojets in pods. Many C-123Bs and C-123Ks served in the Vietnam War* for airlift and other missions, NC-123Ks for night reconnaissance,* UC-123Ks for defoliant spraying, and a VC-123K for General William Westmoreland's personal transport. Active service for the C-123 ended in 1986.

Characteristics (C-123B): engines, two Pratt & Whitney R-2800–99W of 2,300 horsepower each; span, 110 feet; length, 76 feet; height, 34 feet; gross weight, 60,000 pounds; top speed, 245 miles per hour; service ceiling, 29,000 feet; range, 1,470 miles; payload, 61 troops.

References. Swanborough, *US Mil. Airc.* Susan H. H. Young, "Gallery of USAF Weapons," *AF*, May 1986, p. 151.

Joe M. Jackson

C-124 GLOBEMASTER II

This airplane was among the first of the heavy lift transports* perceived in 1949 as necessary for global military mobility. The C-124 performed such airlift operations* and, in addition, was involved in many humanitarian missions* to sites of natural or man-caused disasters.

It was a double-decked evolution from the C-74 Globemaster, and it first flew in 1949. It was designed and built by the Douglas Aircraft Company, and deliveries began in 1950. It was a low-wing monoplane with clamshell-type nose cargo doors. Ramps allowed easy access for many diverse types of vehicles, and a fuselage elevator, aft of the main landing gear, permitted loading of bulk cargo with relative ease. The main deck could be converted into a two-deck configuration which allowed the airlifting of up to 200 fully equipped soldiers.

Production ended in 1955 after 447 had been built. Most C-124s were transferred to the U.S. Air Force Reserve* (USAFR) or Air National Guard* (ANG) by 1970 and were subsequently released from service by mid–1974. The C-124 was known far and wide affectionately, and not so affectionately, as "Old Shakey" because the airframe had a characteristic vibration. It was also called "The Aluminum Cloud," "Aluminum Overcast," and "The Flying Reynolds Wrap."

Characteristics (C-124C): engines, four Pratt & Whitney R-4360–63A of 3,800 horsepower each; span, 174 feet; length, 130 feet; height, 48 feet; gross weight, 194,500 pounds; top speed, 271 miles per hour; service ceiling, 18,400 feet; range, 4,030 miles with 26,375 pounds of payload.

References. Ray L. Bowers, *Tactical Airlift*, 1983. Futrell, *Ideas*, vol. 2, and *USAF in Korea*. Swanborough, *US Mil. Airc.*

David H. Anderson

C-130 HERCULES

A legend in its own time, the appropriately named Hercules has been one of the principal transports* of the USAF* since the 1950s. The Lockheed Aircraft Corporation's design has proven itself remarkably adaptable to a wide variety of uses. It entered active service in 1951, was still being made in 1990, and may still be in production in the 21st century. More than 1,800 have been built, with 900 bought by the USAF, and it is flown by the U.S. Navy and the air forces of 45 other nations. It may surpass the C-47* in reputation.

The C-130 quickly became the workhorse of tactical airlift* operations in the Vietnam War.* Beginning in 1965 USAF leaders put the Hercules under the Pacific Air Forces* (PACAF) to provide much of the airlift in Southeast Asia (SEA). It had a critical role in tactical operations* there until 1975, when it was used in the evacuation of Americans and some South Vietnamese from Saigon.

A key aspect of its role in SEA was support of ground forces. For instance, the 173rd Airborne Brigade, 101st Airborne Division, made an airmobile assault on an airstrip 40 miles east of Bien Hoa* AB in November 1965. Within an hour of the assault, the first C-130s delivered troops and cargo. Another example was the aerial resupply of Khe Sanh.* This support was indispensable to the successful resistance by the garrison. Between 21 January and 8 April 1968, C-130s flew 496 airdrop, 67 low-altitude parachute extraction system (LAPES), and 273 landing missions to deliver some 12,400 tons of supplies. Between 1965 and 1973 USAF C-130s moved more than five million tons of passengers and cargo in SEA. The USAF lost 53 C-130s doing this, with more than half the losses in the North Vietnam offensives of 1967 and 1968. C-130s operated during the Grenada* and Panama* incidents. In 1990–1991, the C-130 was still the tactical airlift operations workhorse of the USAF for the Iraq crisis* and Iraq War,* and the EC-130H was used as well.

Variants include Tanker* KC-130s; the AC-130A Spectre* for attack;* DC-130As, first called GC-130As, for drone launching; EC-130H Compass Call for electronic warfare;* HC-130Hs for rescue;* JC-130s for tracking missiles and recovering satellites; LC-130Hs for Arctic and Antarctic operations; MC-130E Combat Talon for special operations; NC-130s for flight testing; RC-130As for reconnaissance;* TC-130As for training; and WC-130s for weather reconnaissance. Its nicknames include "Herk," "Herky Bird," and "Hog."

Characteristics (C-130H): engines, four Allison T56-A-15 turboprops of 4,910 horsepower each; span, 133 feet; length, 98 feet; height, 38 feet; gross weight, 175,000 pounds; top speed, 386 miles per hour; service ceiling, 33,000 feet; range, 2,745 miles; payload, 92 troops.

References. Primary: M. E. Morris, *C-130: The Hercules*, 1989. David K. Vaughan, "Flying the C-130 Hercules in Vietnam," *AH*, June 1985, pp. 74–81. Secondary: Joseph Earl Dabney, *Herk: Hero of the Skies*, 1979. Sam McGowan, *The C-130 Hercules: Tactical Airlift Missions, 1956–1975*, 1988. Swanborough, *US Mil. Airc.*

See also The Four Horsemen; humanitarian operations.

Roger D. Launius

C-131. *See* T-29.

C-133 CARGOMASTER

The USAF* decided in 1952 to try the turboprop engine for a heavy strategic airlift operations* aircraft. A Douglas Aircraft Corporation proposal was accepted in 1953 as the C-133. No prototypes were built for test, and it went directly into production in 1954. The first flight was in 1956, and active service began in 1957. The C-133 had a large hold able to carry Atlas,* Jupiter,* and Titan* missiles. A total of 50 C-133s were bought. The large turboprop engine proved to be less effective than the turbofan for transports.* This, together with metal fatigue problems, ended the C-133's service in 1971.

Characteristics (C-133A): engine, four Pratt & Whitney T34-P-7WA turboprops of 6,500 horsepower each; span, 180 feet; length, 158 feet; height, 48 feet; gross weight, 275,000 pounds; top speed, 331 miles per hour; range, 3,975 miles with 47,000 pounds payload.

References. René J. Francillon, *McDonnell Douglas Aircraft since 1920*, vol. 1, 1988. Swanborough, *US Mil. Airc.*

C-135 AND KC-135 STRATOLIFTER AND STRATOTANKER

The workhorse of USAF* aerial refueling* for global operations has been the KC-135. It has been one of the USAF's great airplanes of all time.

The Boeing Airplane Company's C-97* design was expanded for a better tanker.* In a private venture, Boeing changed the straight wing piston engine design into a swept wing jet. So promising was the design that the USAF ordered an enlarged version as a tanker. The KC-135 made its maiden flight in 1954, and deliveries were made between 1954 and 1967. The Boeing-designed "flying boom"* for aerial refueling is installed on it. While seven versions were made by Boeing, the C-135 is a versatile airframe that has been developed over the years into almost 40 variants through modifications. Besides transports* and tankers, they are RC-135, reconnaissance;* EC-135, airborne command posts; EC-135Y, testing; and TC-135, trainer. The only export version was the C-135F for France. Of 820 built, 732 were tankers.

In 1989, 594 KC-135s were still in service and should remain active well into the 21st century. KC-135s were worked hard in 1990–1991 for the Iraq crisis* and Iraq War.* All of the U.S. Air Force Reserve* (USAFR) and Air National Guard* (ANG) KC-135s have been retrofitted with Pratt & Whitney JT8D turbofans taken from retired Boeing 707s and redesignated as KC-135Es. This results in about 20 percent improved performance. Strategic Air Command* (SAC) KC-135As are being retrofitted with General Electric-SNECMA CFM56 high bypass fanjets as KC-135Rs, giving a 50 percent improvement in performance. Its nicknames are "Flying Gas Station," "GLOB" (Ground Loving Old Bastard), "Stratobladder," and "Tank."

Characteristics (KC-135A): engines, four Pratt & Whitney J57-P-59W turbojets of 11,200 pounds of thrust each; span, 131 feet; length, 136 feet; height, 38 feet; gross weight, 297,000 pounds; top speed, 585 miles per hour at 30,000 feet; service ceiling, 50,000 feet; range, 1,150 miles with 120,000 pounds payload.

References. Primary: Higham, *Combat Airc.*, vol. 2. Secondary: Peter M. Bowers, *Boeing Aircraft since 1916*, 1989. Alwyn T. Lloyd, "Versatility Unlimited—The Boeing KC-135 Story," *Air International*, part 1, November 1980, pp. 220–26, 236–38, part 2, December 1980, pp. 271–76, 291–95; and "30 Years Young—The KC-135 Celebrates 30 Years of Flight," *AAHS Journal*, Fall 1987, pp. 172–81. Swanborough, *US Mil. Airc.*

Alwyn T. Lloyd

C-137 AND VC-137

In 1959 this became the first jet aircraft to be used for the "Air Force One" presidential airlift* role. The VC-137A was the Boeing Airplane Company's Model 707–153. Two EC-137Ds were built as full-scale development aircraft for the Airborne Warning and Control System* (AWACS) program. These were subsequently converted to E-3As.*

Characteristics (VC-137C): engines, four Pratt & Whitney JT3D turbofans of 18,000 pounds thrust each; span, 146 feet; length, 153 feet; height, 42 feet; gross weight, 325,000 pounds; top speed, 627 miles per hour; service ceiling, 42,000 feet; unrefueled endurance, six hours.

References. Peter M. Bowers, *Boeing Aircraft since 1916*, 1989. Alwyn T. Lloyd, *Boeing 707 and AWACS in Detail & Scale*, 1987. Swanborough, *US Mil. Airc.*

Alwyn T. Lloyd

C-141 STARLIFTER

The C-141 transport* has been the mainstay of the Military Airlift Command's* (MAC) strategic airlift operations* fleet since the mid–1960s and has been a major contributor to the successful resupply of U.S. forces globally.

It was the first jet specifically designed as a strategic airlifter, and it became operational in 1965. By the end of production in 1968, 284 had been made. It can carry 67,620 pounds of payload for 4,000 miles or 20,000 pounds nonstop from California to Japan at 506 miles per hour. By comparison, its predecessor C-124* could carry 50,000 pounds for 1,000 miles or 25,000 pounds for about 2,300 miles at 230 miles per hour.

The USAF* used the C-141 as the workhorse of the Vietnam Airlift.* On several occasions, the USAF was called upon to deploy major U.S. Army units. The first rushed the 3rd Brigade from Hawaii to Pleiku, Vietnam, some 6,000 miles, in late 1965. MAC's C-141s bore the brunt of this activity flying, with C-133s,* 231 sorties in 26 days and moving 3,000 troops and 4,700 tons of equipment. At the height of the airlift, a C-141 or C-133 took off from Hickam* AFB every three hours.

MAC's C-141s carried out the first redeployments from Vietnam in 1969, flying 15,446 troops and 47.5 tons of materiel. In other withdrawals, C-141s responded similarly. In the Grenada incident* of 1983, MAC airlifted 15,374 tons of cargo and 35,911 passengers in 991 missions, 653 of which were flown by C-141s. MAC also evacuated 709 U.S. noncombatants in 16 C-141, one C-5,* and two C-130* missions.

From 1977 to 1982 the C-141s were refurbished, "stretched" by more than 23 feet to increase payload, and were made capable of aerial refueling.* The resulting C-141Bs have an expected service life of 45,000 flying hours. In 1982 the C-141 fleet had a collective five million flying hours, but its extended operational life is projected to last until the 21st century unless its extensive use in 1990–1991 for the Iraq crisis* and Iraq War* forces reappraisal. Its nicknames are "StarLizard" (when camouflaged) and "T-Tailed Mountain Magnet."

Characteristics (C-141B): engines, four Pratt & Whitney TF33-P-7 turbofans of 21,000 pounds thrust each; span, 160 feet; length, 168 feet; height, 39 feet; gross weight, 343,000 pounds; top speed, 571 miles per hour at 25,000 feet; service ceiling, 41,600 feet; range, 2,927 miles with 94,508 pounds of payload.

References. Primary: Higham, *Combat Airc.*, vol. 2. Secondary: Dick J. Burkard, *Military Airlift Command Historical Handbook, 1941–1984*, 1984. William Head, *Reworking the Workhorse: The C-141B Stretch Modification Program*, Office of History, Robins AFB, Georgia. Harold H. Martin, *Starlifter: The C-141, Lockheed's High Speed Flying Truck*, 1972. Swanborough, *US Mil. Airc.*

Roger D. Launius

CADET. *See* aviation cadet.

CALDWELL, CYRIL C. (1892–unknown)

Caldwell was an influential author from the late 1920s to the mid–1950s. He wrote for such magazines as *Aero Digest*, *Air Progress*, *American Aviation*, *Flying*, and *New Outlook*. He was the author of *Air Power and Total War* (1943).

Born in Britain, he was a Royal Flying Corps (RFC) pilot in World War I* and later, in the United States, a test and an airline pilot.* He predicted the targetting of civilians, the use of incendiary bombs, and a carrier task force–based U.S. Navy. He advocated targets like electrical power, depots, bridges, and a nation's will to fight. He criticized the ground force–oriented U.S. Army General Staff, naval spokesmen who believed the battleship to be immune to air assault, unescorted bombers,* and precision bombing. He also thought Giulio Douhet* was a brilliant neurotic who wrote childish scenarios.

Reference. DeWitt S. Copp, *A Few Great Captains: The Men and Events That Shaped the Development of U.S. Air Power*, 1980.

Roger A. Beaumont

CALL TO GLORY. *See* television.

CAMBODIAN OPERATIONS

In early 1969, the North Vietnamese launched a nationwide assault on South Vietnam. U.S. Army General Creighton W. Abrams, commander of the U.S. Military Assistance Command, Vietnam (MACV), asked President Richard M. Nixon for permission to use B-52s* to bomb the North Vietnam rear bases in Cambodia. Nixon agreed and directed the bombings be kept secret. B-52s flew 4,308 night sorties and dropped 120,578 tons of bombs between 18 March 1969 and 26 May 1970. In August 1969, a new Cambodian government appealed for international assistance to remove the 40,000 North Vietnamese troops. In April 1970, in response to another Cambodian government request for help, U.S. and South Vietnamese soldiers went into Cambodia to destroy the North Vietnamese. The USAF* provided attack* support.

After ground forces withdrew in June, the USAF and South Vietnamese air and ground units supported the Cambodians against communist military forces. These operations continued after the cease-fire in Vietnam in 1973. Airmen considered the support successful, including defeat of communist forces attempting to take the capital city, Phnom Penh in the summer of 1973. Congress opposed the attack operations and passed legislation halting them on 15 August 1973. The USAF continued airlift operations* of supplies for a period of time after that date. The communist forces were victorious in 1975 and started a genocide which killed more than one million Cambodians.

References. Berger, *USAF in SEA*. Ray L. Bowers, *Tactical Airlift*, 1983. Donald J. Mrozek, *Air Power and the Ground War in Vietnam*, 1988.

CAMPBELL, CAPTAIN DOUGLAS (1896–1990)

Campbell was the first U.S.-trained pilot* to become an ace.* He left Harvard University to join the Aviation Section of the U.S. Army Signal Corps* in 1917. He learned to fly at Issoudon,* France, and became a member of the 94th Aero Squadron.* On 14 April 1918 he shot down the second victory of the Aviation Section while flying a Nieuport 28.* He became an ace on 31 May. He was wounded in battle on 5 June after six victories and did not recover before the end of World War I.* After the war he left the service and retired in 1939 as a vice president of Pan American Grace Airways.

References. Hess, *Aces Album*. Quentin Reynolds, *They Fought for the Sky*, 1957.

CAM RANH BAY AIR BASE

There was an inadequate number of airfields available in the Republic of South Vietnam in 1965. A new field for jets at Cam Ranh Bay, on the country's east coast midsection, was built for the USAF* by the end of the year. In early 1966, four squadrons of F-4s* began operations from it. Later, C-7s,* C-118s, and C-9s* were added. In 1972 the USAF moved out.

References. Berger, *USAF in SEA*. John Schlight, *The War in South Vietnam: The Years of the Offensive 1965–1968*, 1988.

CANBERRA. *See* B-57.

CANIFF, MILTON (1907–1988)

Caniff was a newspaper cartoonist whose *Terry and the Pirates* (1934–1946) and *Steve Canyon* (1947–1988) played a major role in shaping the public image of the USAAF* and USAF* from early World War II* to the 1960s. No cartoonist in the "Golden Age" of newspaper strips (1930–1955) had more effectively blended literature and art or been more imitated, and no other artist had more influence on mass audiences in presenting his image of American air power.

Besides the strips above, he drew *The Gay Thirties* (1932–1933), *Dickie Dare* (1933–1934), and *Male Call* (1942–1945). With Noel Sickles, who drew the aviation strip *Scorchy Smith*, he introduced a heavily shadowed style emulated by many artists. His friends in aviation, especially Frank Higgs and USAF Colonel Philip G. Cochran,* aided him with background details.

After the U.S. entry into World War II, his main character, Terry Lee, was portrayed taking flight training* in China, and the panel in which the Cochran-based character "Flip" Corkin gave Terry a lecture on the traditions of the service was frequently reprinted. His characters of the Dragon Lady and "Hot Shot" Charlie became popular cultural clichés. *Terry* and *Male Call*, the latter drawn for servicemen only and the royalties donated to service charities, were the main featured strips in the service newspaper *Stars and Stripes*. They portrayed servicemen sympathetically and in a positive vein.

In 1947, he began *Steve Canyon*. Its main character, a veteran of the USAAF's Air Transport Command (ATC), first ran a charter service and, later, like Terry after the war, became an intelligence officer.

Caniff's role in shaping the self-image of U.S. military professionals became a matter of debate as Cold War* attitudes came under criticism in the Vietnam War* era. Caniff's patriotism and occasionally lurid portrayal of violence led to cancellation by many papers. He was accused of being a propagandist for the USAF, a role he did not mind playing, having much regretted being 4-F (unfit for service) in World War II.

He did many artistic services for the USAF over the years, and he received many honors from his peers in the cartooning world and from the USAF. At the time of his death, he was viewed in France as a maestro of the new art form of *bandes desinées*.

References. Shel Dorf, *Milton Caniff's America: Reflections of a Drawing Board Patriot*, 1987. Maurice Horn, ed., *The World Encyclopedia of Comics*, 1976. Rich Marschall and John Paul Adams, *Milton Caniff: Rembrandt of the Comic Strip*, 1981. Peter Poplaski, ed., *Male Call by Milton Caniff*, 1987. Arn Saba, "I'm Just a Troubador Singing My Supper," *The Comics Journal*, May 1986, pp. 60–72, 75–88, and 91–102.

Roger A. Beaumont

CANNON. *See* GAU-8; 20mm guns.

CANNON, GENERAL JOHN K. (1892–1955)

Cannon was a World War II* combat commander in the Mediterranean theater and commander of the Tactical Air Command* (TAC). Cannon AFB* in New Mexico is named in his honor.

Born in Salt Lake City, Utah, he graduated from Utah Agricultural College in 1914 and became an officer in the Infantry Reserve in 1917. He took flight training* from 1921 to 1922. There followed a variety of positions until 1941 when he became chief of staff of the First Air Force* (1AF).

He was commanding general of the 12th Air Support Command for the Western Task Force in the invasion of French Morocco in 1942. He became deputy commanding general of the Allied Tactical Air Force for the Sicilian and Italian campaigns. In 1943 he became commanding general of the Twelfth Air Force* (12AF) and the Mediterranean Allied Tactical Air Command. He was responsible for all air operations in the invasion of southern France in August 1944. In March 1945 he was named air commander-in-chief of all Allied air forces in the Mediterranean theater; in May 1945 he became commanding general of the USAAF* in Europe. In 1946 he became commanding general of the Air Training Command* (ATC). He was commanding general in 1948 of the U.S. Air Forces in Europe* (USAFE) and in 1951 of TAC. He retired in 1954.

References. Air Force Pamphlet (AFP) 31–1, "Roster of Retired General Officers," 1987. DuPre, *USAF Bio*. Robert P. Fogerty, *Biographical Study of USAF General Officers, 1917–1952*, vol. 1, n.d.

James C. Hasdorff

CANNON AIR FORCE BASE

This Tactical Air Command* (TAC) field is near Clovis, New Mexico. It was activated in August 1942 and named Clovis. During World War II* it trained men for heavy bombardment, weather, and weather reconnaisance* tasks. It became a fighter* base in 1953 and was renamed Cannon AFB in 1957 in honor of General John K. Cannon.* In 1990 the 27th Tactical Fighter Wing (TFW) was on the base flying F-111Ds.*

References. "Guide to Major Air Force Installations Worldwide," *AF*, May 1990, p. 122. Mueller, *AFB*. Roberts, *Dir. USAF*.

CAP. *See* Civil Air Patrol; MiGCAP.

CARIBOU. *See* C-7.

CARPET BOMBING. *See* tactical operations.

CARSWELL AIR FORCE BASE

Near Fort Worth, Texas, Carswell was activated in 1942 and is under the Strategic Air Command* (SAC). Its previous names were Tarrant Field and Griffiss AFB. During World War II* the base trained pilots* in medium and heavy bombers.* In 1948 it was given its current name in honor of Major Horace S. Carswell, Jr., of Fort Worth. He was a B-24* pilot killed in a crash landing in China in 1944. He received the Air Force Medal of Honor* posthumously. This base is the only one with its namesake interred on the field. In 1948 the USAF's* first B-36* was delivered to the 7th Bomb Group on the base. B-52s* and B-58s* arrived in 1958. In 1990 the 7th was still there with B-52s and KC-135s (*see* C-135).

References. "Guide to Major Air Force Installations Worldwide," *AF*, May 1990, p. 122. Mueller, *AFB*. Roberts, *Dir. USAF*.

CASABLANCA CONFERENCE

This conference of Allied heads of government and their military advisers was held at Anfa Camp outside of Casablanca, Morocco, in January 1943. The Casablanca Conference's decisions were fundamental to the conduct of the rest of World War II* in the air. At a news conference held jointly with Prime Minister Winston Churchill, President Franklin D. Roosevelt* (FDR) announced that the principal war aim of the Allied powers was the unconditional surrender of Germany and Japan.

The conferees reaffirmed the Germany-first concept and approved in principle U.S. offensive plans in the Pacific with forces already allocated. It also issued the first directive for an Allied strategic operations* campaign. Later called the Combined Bomber Offensive* (CBO), the campaign was governed by this and succeeding directives issued by the combined chiefs of staff until the end of World War II in Europe. Thus, the conference approved the concept of U.S. daylight bombing as a complement to the Royal Air Force (RAF) Bomber Command's night strikes. In addition, the combined chiefs reorganized the command structure in the Mediterranean theater, placing all air forces under a single officer, Air Marshal Sir Arthur Tedder. The Northwest African Air Forces (NAAF) command went to Major General Carl A. Spaatz,* under whom U.S. and British units were grouped together in Allied operational air forces: tactical, strategic, and coastal.

References. DeWitt S. Copp, *Forged in Fire: Strategy and Decisions in the Air War over Europe 1940–1945*, 1982. Michael Howard, *Grand Strategy*, vol. 4, 1970.

W. A. Jacobs

CASF. *See* Composite Air Strike Force.

CASSINO, ITALY

The bombing of Cassino illustrated that air power can be misused. After ground assaults failed on the German lines at Cassino, the USAAF* was ordered to bomb the Abbey of Monte Cassino, overlooking the battlefield, in the belief that the structure was being used militarily by the enemy. On 15 February 1944, 142 heavy and 112 medium bombers* dropped 576 tons of bombs on the historical abbey. A subsequent ground effort failed again to break the German line.

Then British Field Marshals Sir Henry Wilson and Sir Harold Alexander, U.S. Army General Mark Clark, and USAAF General H. H. Arnold* all believed that a maximum bomb effort on the city of Cassino would lead to a breakthrough on the ground. The USAAF's Lieutenant General Ira Eaker,* commander in chief of the Mediterranean Allied Air Forces, and Brigadier General Gordon P. Saville,* deputy commander of the XII Air Support Command, were skeptical of the project and objected to it. They thought the Germans could not be destroyed in their positions and that the bomb craters produced would prevent the use of tanks in a ground drive. They did not convince their superiors.

On 15 March, 275 heavy and about 200 medium bombers dropped more than 1,000 tons of 1,000-pound bombs. An artillery barrage followed. Next an assault was made by soldiers. The infantry was hindered by rubble and the tanks were delayed by the craters. Advances were made but the assault had to end on the 23rd. The bombardment was not as skillful as possible and the ground effort had flaws, but these did not cause the failure. The USAAF had done its assigned tasks of smashing the abbey and the city, but these acts did not kill the defenders, proved counterproductive for the war, and destroyed a famous landmark.

References. C&C, vol. 3. DeWitt S. Copp, *Forged in Fire: Strategy and Decisions in the Air War over Europe 1940–1945*, 1982.

CASTLE, BRIGADIER GENERAL FREDERICK W. (1908–1944)

Castle was an Air Force Medal of Honor* recipient in World War II.* Merced Army Air Field, California, was redesignated Castle* Field in his honor.

He was born in Manila, Philippines, and was a 1930 graduate of the U.S. Military Academy (USMA). Castle was one of eight officers selected to accompany Major General Ira C. Eaker* to England to form the Eighth Air Force* (8AF). He took command of the 94th Bomb Group in June 1943. As a new brigadier general, and on his 30th bombing sortie, he was killed on 24 December 1944 while leading an air division* of B-17s* over Liege, Belgium. En route to the target his plane lost an engine, forcing him out of formation. His crippled plane was immediately hit by German fighters.* Since Castle was over friendly troops he refused to jettison his bombs, and he remained at the controls until members of the crew could escape. Only Castle and the pilot* were unable to escape before the plane exploded.

References. Air Force Pamphlet (AFP) 31–1, "Roster of Retired Officers," 1987. DuPre, *USAF Bio*. John L. Frisbee, "The Quiet Hero," *AF*, March 1988, p. 107.

James C. Hasdorff

CASTLE AIR FORCE BASE

In 1941 the USAAF* began basic flight training* at an airfield at Merced, California. After processing 8,699 students, training ended in 1945. The next year the airfield was named in honor of Brigadier General Frederick W. Castle,* an Air Force Medal of Honor* winner, who died in action over Belgium in 1944. Six months later the base was inactivated. The field was reactivated in 1955 to become the first to operate B-52s.* In 1990, this Strategic Air Command* (SAC) base was the site of training of B-52 and KC-135 (*see* C-135) crews by the 93rd Bomb Wing.

References. "Guide to Major Air Force Installations Worldwide," *AF*, May 1990, pp. 122–23. Mueller, *AFB*. Harold P. Myers, "Castle Air Force Base," *AH*, June 1984, pp. 107–20. Roberts, *Dir. USAF*.

CASTOR. *See* Aphrodite.

CATCH-22

This 1961 novel* by Joseph Heller has had the greatest literary influence on the public with regard to the USAF.* How badly it has unfairly damaged the image of the USAF is immeasurable, but it must be large. In its first 25 years, *Catch–22* sold eight million copies. This black comedy is regarded by many as the definitive exposé of the institutions of the military and of free enterprise. Its main character is Captain "Yo-Yo" Yossarian, a bombardier* in B-25s* in the Mediterranean theater. Yossarian wants to stop flying combat, but "Catch–22" prevents him from doing so. "Catch–22" is a rule that contains conditions that prevent a solution, and the novel's title has entered the language. Yossarian finds a solution outside of the rule; he deserts. In 1970 the novel was made into a movie* with the same title. Faithful to the novel, the film was not a success because the power of the novel is in its literary style.

References. "The 40th Anniversary of the USAF," a special issue of *AH*, September 1987, p. 211.

CBI. *See* China-Burma-India theater.

CBO. *See* Combined Bomber Offensive.

CENTER

A center is a USAF* organizational unit that performs a specialty mission. Centers usually do training or development and have a single location. Centers may be subordinate to a major command* (MAJCOM) or may be directly under headquarters of the U.S. Air Force. Examples of centers are the Arnold Engineering Development Center* and the Keesler Technical Training Center.

References. Woodford Agee Heflin, ed., *The United States Air Force Dictionary*, 1956. Ravenstein, *Org. USAF*.

CENTRAL AIR DEFENSE FORCE

This organization was one of three air defense forces in the continental United States (CONUS). It was established in 1951 and assigned to the Air Defense Command. It was inactivated in 1960.

References. Goldberg, *Hist. USAF*. Ravenstein, *Org. USAF*.

CESSNA AIRCRAFT COMPANY. *See* O-1 Bird Dog; T-37.

CG-4 AND CG-15 HADRIAN. *See* G-4 and G-15.

CHAFF

Chaff consists of thin metallic strips. It is dropped from aircraft as a countermeasure to radar.* It reflects radar transmissions, resulting in confusing signals on radar receivers. Chaff varies in length to counter different radar frequencies.

References. Ernest J. Gentle and Lawrence W. Reithmaier, eds., *Aviation/Space Dictionary*, 6th ed., 1980. Woodford Agee Heflin, ed., *The United States Air Force Dictionary*, 1956.

CHAIN LIGHTNING. *See* movies.

CHANDLER, COLONEL CHARLES DEFOREST (1878–1939)

Charles deForest Chandler was the USAF's* first commander as leader of the Aeronautical Division of the U.S. Army Signal Corps* when it was established in 1907. He was commissioned in the Signal Corps in 1898.

Born in Cleveland, Ohio, he qualified as a balloon pilot* in 1907, dirigible pilot in 1909, and aeroplane pilot in 1911 and was awarded the Military Aviator* rating in 1912. He was in charge of the Signal Corps' aviation schools at College Park,* Maryland, and Augusta, Georgia. Later he commanded the 1st Aero Squadron* at Texas City, Texas, in 1913, and established the Army's balloon school at Fort Omaha, Nebraska. Chandler replaced Captain Frank P. Lahm* as head of the Balloon Section of the American Expeditionary Force (AEF) in November 1918. Chandler retired in 1920.

References. Primary: Charles deForest Chandler and Frank P. Lahm, *How Our Army Grew Wings: Airmen and Aircraft before 1914*, 1943. Secondary: Juliette A. Hennessy, *The United States Army Air Arm April 1861 to April 1917*, 1985. Maurer Maurer, *The*

U.S. Air Service in World War I, 4 vols., 1978 and 1979. *Who Was Who in America*, 1943.

D. K. Vaughan

CHANUTE AIR FORCE BASE

This third oldest active USAF* base was established as Rantoul Aviation Field, Rantoul, Illinois, in 1917. Later in the year it was renamed for Octave Chanute, an aviation pioneer. The base has long performed much of the vital task of technical training for the USAF.

It did flight training* for pilots* in World War I.* In 1921 the USAAS* Mechanics School was transferred to it. In 1922, photography and communications were also transferred in, with the three schools forming the Air Service Technical School. From 1922 to 1938 Chanute did the only technical training for the small air arm. It became a major training center in World War II,* and 200,000 students passed through its courses. Pilot training returned in 1943 with B-17s* and B-25s.* The base had another resurgence for technical training in the Korean War.* Since then Chanute has continued as one of the USAF's technical training bases, and, in 1990, its unit was named Chanute Technical Training Center. Chanute is scheduled to be closed in 1993 to save money.

References. Brown, *Eagles*. Mueller, *AFB*. Roberts, *Dir. USAF*. Thomas S. Snyder, *Chanute Field: The Hum of the Motor Replaced the Song of the Reaper, 1917–1921* (Chanute Historical Monograph), 1975. Donald O. Weckhorst and Morris E. Oursler, *The Seventy-Year History of Chanute AFB, 1917–1987* (Chanute Historical Monograph), 1987.

Thomas A. Manning

CHARLESTON AIR FORCE BASE

Named for the adjacent city in South Carolina, the base began as the Municipal Airport in 1941. It first served as a training base and for air defense forces. In 1945 it became an aerial port of embarkation for the Air Transport Command (ATC). In 1946 it became inactive. It was reactivated in 1953 and assigned to the Tactical Air Command* (TAC), with interceptors* on it. It was transferred to the Military Air Transport Service (MATS) in 1955. From it airlift operations* were conducted to European, Caribbean, and African ports. C-141s* arrived in 1966 and the base unit became the 437th Military Airlift Wing. C-5s* operated from the base from 1970 to 1973. In 1990, the 437th still had the host responsibilities for the field and flew C-141s.

References. Mueller, *AFB*. Charles A. Ravenstein, *Air Force Combat Wings: Lineage and Honors Histories, 1947–1977*, 1984. Roberts, *Dir. USAF*.

Roger D. Launius

CHASAN DAM. *See* Korean irrigation dams target system.

CHASE AIRCRAFT COMPANY. *See* C-123.

CHECO. *See* Contemporary Historical Examination of Current Operations.

CHENNAULT, LIEUTENANT GENERAL CLAIRE L. (1890–1958)

One of the USAF's* greats, Chennault was controversial and iconoclastic, the leading champion of fighters,* commander of the American Volunteer Group* (AVG), and commanding general of the Fourteenth Air Force* (14AF). He was posthumously inducted into the National Aviation Hall of Fame in Dayton, Ohio, in 1972.

Chennault entered the infantry as a first lieutenant in 1917. He transferred to the Signal Corps and became a pilot* in 1919. As a pursuit squadron commander, Chennault developed a lifelong interest in fighter strategy and tactics. After graduating from the Air Corps Tactical School* (ACTS) in 1931, Chennault remained as an instructor until 1936. While there, he vehemently opposed the "new orthodoxy" of strategic operations;* this earned him the enmity of his peers, the ACTS' "bomber* mafia." Chennault emphasized the fighter and its unique role in air superiority.* His influential text, *The Role of Defensive Pursuit* (unpublished), also advocated, in an era without radar,* a defensive warning net based on a network of trained spotters. The spotters would visually direct fighters against the enemy en route to the target. His system worked with mixed results in China in World War II.* Chennault's gruff personality diluted the impact of his innovative ideas. Physically exhausted and unpopular, he retired as a captain in 1937.

Late the same year Madame Chiang Kai-shek hired him to organize and train for the Republic of China. Chennault recruited in the United States for his AVG, famous as the "Flying Tigers." The AVG began operations in December 1941. In seven months they shot down 299 Japanese aircraft with a loss of 32 planes and 19 pilots. Chennault used an air guerrilla hit-and-run strategy with his P-40s* which were inferior to the Japanese fighters. In April 1942 Chennault returned to U.S. service as a colonel but was soon promoted to equal his Chinese grade of brigadier general. In July he became commanding general of the USAAF* in China, and the AVG became the 23rd Fighter Squadron. In March 1943 he was promoted to major general and became commander of the 14AF. The 14AF supported General Joseph Stillwell's ground forces, and Chennault's tactical leadership was outstanding. However, Chennault's logistics limitations made him more of a thorn in the Japanese side than anything else. Chennault complained about the lack of support he was getting, and he tended to deal directly with Generalissimo Chiang Kai-shek and President Franklin D. Roosevelt* (FDR). This earned him the distrust of Generals of the Army George Marshall and H. H. Arnold.* Chennault retired from the USAAF in October 1945.

From 1946 to 1950 he vigorously supported Chiang against the communists. He organized Chinese National Relief and the Civil Air Transport, of which he was president. In 1958, the USAF bestowed upon him the honorary grade of lieutenant general nine days before his death from cancer.

References. Primary: Claire L. Chennault, *Way of a Fighter*, 1949. Robert Lee Scott, Jr., *Flying Tiger: Chennault of China*, 1959. James H. Straubel, ed., *Air Force Diary: 111 Stories from the Official Service Journal of the USAAF*, 1947. Secondary: Martha Byrd, *Chennault: Giving Wings to the Tiger*, 1987.

Peter R. Faber

CHEYENNE MOUNTAIN AIR FORCE BASE

Six miles south of Colorado Springs, Colorado, this is an Air Force Space Command* (AFSPACECOM) facility. It was activated in 1966 and is named for its location which is mostly within the mountain. In 1990, the North American Aerospace Defense Command* (NORAD) Command Center, the AFSPACE-COM operations center, and the 3rd Space Support Wing were based there.

References. "Guide to Major Air Force Installations Worldwide," *AF*, May 1990, p. 123. Roberts, *Dir. USAF*.

CHICKASAW. *See* H-19.

CHICKSANDS. *See* RAF Chicksands.

CHIEF OF AIR SERVICE

This position was instituted by General John J. Pershing* in September 1917 when he called upon Brigadier General William L. Kenly* to establish a command and staff organization responsible for the development and implementation of the U.S. Army air arm forces. In November 1917, Brigadier General Benjamin D. Foulois* replaced Kenly, who returned to the United States to head the Division of Military Aeronautics.* In May 1918 Pershing appointed Brigadier General Mason M. Patrick* to replace Foulois, who became chief of Air Service for the First Army. After World War I,* the Office of the Chief of Air Service returned to the United States, where it supervised the activities of the USAAS* under the direction of the civilian office of the director of the Air Service.* During the war, no such position had existed within the United States. After the war, the post of chief of the Air Service was held by Major General Charles T. Menoher* until 1921, when he was replaced by Patrick.

References. Goldberg, *Hist. USAF*. I. B. Holley, Jr., *Ideas and Weapons*, 1953.

D. K. Vaughan

CHIEF OF STAFF, U.S. AIR FORCE

This officer is the head of the USAF,* a position created by the National Security Act of 1947.* The chief of staff, a USAF general, is appointed by the president for, usually, four years. The chief of staff is a member of the Joint Chiefs of Staff (JCS) and the Armed Forces Policy Council. This officer is a military adviser to the president, National Security Council, secretary of defense (SECDEF), and secretary of the Air Force* (SAF). This administrative post is responsible for the preparation of the USAF for military operations, so the incumbent presides over the Air Staff.*

References. Ravenstein, *Org. USAF*. U.S. Air Force Fact Sheet 89–05, "Organization of the United States Air Force," February 1989.

CHINA-BURMA-INDIA THEATER (CBI)

USAAF* operations in the CBI were distinguished by great achievements with minimum resources.

In 1942 the Japanese conquered Burma, cutting off overland communication with China. Important opposition came only from the American Volunteer Group* (AVG, or "Flying Tigers") under Brigadier General Claire L. Chennault.* In July the AVG was absorbed into the USAAF and, in time, became the Fourteenth Air Force* (14AF). A new USAAF unit had already been established in India for the theater, the Tenth Air Force* (10AF). The USAAF began to supply China from the air, forming the "Hump" Airlift.*

The CBI had low priority on USAAF resources, but the 14 and 10AFs were aggressive despite operating on a shoestring. The 14AF struck Shanghai and Japanese shipping and gave the Chinese armies attack* support. The 10AF carried out attack sorties in Burma and airlift operations* which made it possible to defend Imphal, India, from a Japanese offensive in 1944. Other airlift sustained long-range ground offensives in Burma. Late in 1944, the British launched a campaign to retake Burma. The 10AF provided attack and airlift support. By 1945, the Anglo-American Combat Cargo Task Force was supplying 356,000 soldiers by air. It was a different story in China in 1944. A Japanese offensive drove the 14AF far back into the hinterland. In 1945, a counteroffensive by the Chinese regained lost ground.

References. Primary: Winton R. Close, "B-29s in the CBI—A Pilot's Account," *AH*, March 1983, pp. 6–14. John G. Martin, *It Began at Imphal: The Combat Cargo Story*, 1988. William H. Tunner, *Over the Hump: The Story of General William H. Tunner, the Man Who Moved Anything Anywhere, Anytime*, 1964. Secondary: C&C, vols. 1, 4, and 5. Goldberg, *Hist. USAF*.

See also Matterhorn.

CHINA DOLL. *See* movies.

CHOSIN RESERVOIR, KOREA

The relief of U.S. Army and Marine (USMC) units at Chosin was remarkable and unique in USAF* airlift operations* history.

The first Red Chinese offensive in the Korean War* drove the Army and USMC into retreat. In early December 1950, the soldiers south of the Chosin Reservoir at Hagaru-ri and Koto-ri were cut off front and rear by the Chinese. The Far East Air Forces* (FEAF) Combat Cargo Command airlifted food, ammunition, and other supplies to them. In a week, the airlift, using C-47s,* brought in 274 tons of supplies and flew out 4,689 casualties and sick. The USAF offered to airlift out the beleaguered men, but they declined and said they wanted to fight their way out. Their principal problem was that the Chinese had blown up a bridge four miles south of Koto-ri. The bridge had spanned a 1,500-foot-deep gorge. If the bridge could not be replaced, the men would have to leave their vehicles and heavy equipment and cross the gorge on foot. USMC commander Major General Oliver P. Smith asked for an M-2 treadway bridge to be airlifted to the men.

Each packaged bridge span weighed two tons. Four spans were needed to span the gorge. No one had ever before dropped such an object from a transport.* A test drop was made unsuccessfully. Without time for further tests, larger parachutes were attached and the eight spans to be dropped were loaded into eight C-119s.* On 7 December the spans were released over an unmarked drop zone. One fell onto Chinese-held ground and one was damaged in landing.

The soldiers used the bridge and broke out. For 13 days they had depended upon an improvised airlift. The bridge drop was the only one that has been made in history. With 313 C-47 and C-119 sorties, 1,580 tons of supplies and equipment were provided. For their part in the successful evacuation, the 314th Troop Carrier Group, the 21st Troop Carrier Squadron, and the 801st Medical Air Evacuation Squadron were awarded Distinguished Unit Citations.

References. Futrell, *USAF in Korea*. Robert Jackson, *Air War over Korea*, 1973.
See also Korean electrical power target system.

CHRISTENSEN, COLONEL FRED J., JR. (1921–   )

Christensen, from Waterton, Massachusetts, won 20.5 aerial victories, putting him 14th on the list of all-time USAF* aces.* He became an officer and pilot* through the aviation cadet* program, graduating in 1942. He was in battle in Europe, mostly in the 56th Fighter Group of the Eighth Air Force* (8AF). Christensen flew 107 combat sorties of 300 hours in F-47s.* Christensen ran out of fuel returning from an escort sortie on 30 December 1943 and crashed. He walked away from it unhurt. On July 7 1944, at Gardelegen, Germany, Christensen shot down six Ju 52 transports* out of a landing pattern. The Germans reported the incident and said the transport pilots were women, but this is not believed to be true. After World War II,* Christensen left the USAAF* and joined the Massachusetts Air National Guard (ANG) as commander of the 102nd Fighter Group.

References. DuPre, *USAF Bio*. Roger A. Freeman, *The Mighty Eighth: Units, Men and Machines*, 1970.

CHRISTMAS BOMBINGS. *See* Linebacker; Vietnam War.

"CHUCK." *See* Yeager, Brigadier General Charles E.

CIM-10. *See* IM-99.

CIVIL AIR PATROL (CAP)

The CAP is an example of the value and contribution of civilian activities to aerospace power.* It is a volunteer organization that includes private fliers and planes. It began on 1 December 1941 as part of the Office of Civilian Defense. The CAP was made a USAAF* auxiliary organization by Executive Order on

29 April 1943 and helped with the national manpower shortage of that year by allowing 15-year-olds to learn about flying. During World War II* this included principles of flight, navigation, weather, code, aircraft identification, military and physical training, and first aid. The CAP started with 40,000 cadets.

The CAP made a significant contribution to the United States's antisubmarine campaign. From March 1942 to August 1943, it flew 24 million miles and reported 173 submarines. It was credited with sinking or damaging two. It found 91 vessels in distress, 363 sailors from sunken ships, and 17 mines. Other contributions included airlift, searching for lost aircraft, and patrol of the Mexican border.

In 1948 the CAP became an auxiliary of the USAF* with its headquarters at Maxwell* AFB, Alabama. It is still an early training ground for aviation, and its main nontraining activities are search and rescue* operations and local disaster relief. Most cadets are juniors and seniors in high school. The age limit for a cadet is 21.

References. *AAF: A Directory, Almanac and Chronicle of Achievement*, 1944. Hap Harris, "Civil Air Patrol," *AH*, Winter 1966, pp. 185–88. Frank Lowry, "Civil Air Patrol: Three Who Were There," *AH*, December 1981, pp. 268–74. James A. McDonnell, Jr., "Civil Air Patrol: Yesterday, Today, and in 2003," *AF*, March 1983, pp. 118–22.

CIVILIAN PERSONNEL MANAGEMENT CENTER. *See* Air Force Civilian Personnel Management Center.

CIVILIAN PRIMARY FLIGHT TRAINING. *See* contract primary flight training.

CIVILIANS EMPLOYED BY THE USAF

Most people perceive a military service to be composed of persons in uniform. Yet a third of the USAF* has been composed of people who wore mufti. The one-third figure has long been fairly stable.

The heavy reliance on civilians derives from the USAF's nature as an organization using advanced technologies. This is most visible in the extensive use of civilians in the Air Force Logistics Command* (AFLC). Also, most AFBs have at least 500 civilians. It has been the desire of Congress to have military jobs done by civilians unless the work is hazardous or involves overtime pay.

References. Ed Gates, "The Civilian Third of the Total Force," *AF*, November 1977, pp. 80–81. "The Quiet Crisis in Civilian Personnel," *AF*, July 1989, pp. 60–63.

See also Air Force Civilian Personnel Management Center.

CIVIL RESERVE AIR FLEET (CRAF)

A unique and significant part of the nation's military mobility force, CRAF augments the USAF's* organic airlift resources with commercial transports.* It illustrates an important civil component of aerospace power.

It arose during the early 1950s as a formal contractual framework so commercial air carriers would respond to an emergency. It was traceable to the

Brewster Board and the President's Air Policy Commission,* both of which investigated, among other issues, the strategic mobility of the USAF. In part, attention was directed toward airlift operations* as a result of performance in the Berlin and Korean Airlifts.* Their reports documented that the military had insufficient resources to meet contingencies and should plan for civil augmentation. Based on these recommendations, the Department of Defense (DoD) and the Department of Commerce signed a memorandum of understanding that established CRAF.

Under CRAF, participating air carriers voluntarily commit aircraft and personnel to support defense when DoD airlift requirements exceed the capability of the USAF. In return, the USAF ensures CRAF participants receive airlift contracts with the DoD. The Defense Air Transportation Administration (DATA) of the Department of Commerce took on the management of CRAF in 1952.

Since the early period, CRAF participants could be phased into operations by stages, ranging from the most minor to the most serious military emergencies. These stages have been viewed as a means of tailoring the civil and military airlift force to meet the contingency at hand. The airlines have committed their aircraft to the appropriate stages by annual contract with the Military Airlift Command* (MAC). MAC would schedule and control the aircraft missions.

The 1963 CRAF contained 342 aircraft, most of them the most modern available in the industry. In 1988 CRAF had 27 carriers with 324 aircraft in the long-range international fleet, 17 in the short-range international force, 36 for the domestic field, and 11 for the Alaskan theater. These recent numbers included a large number of Boeing 747s and other types of large transports.

The CRAF was not used until the Iraq crisis of 1990.* From August through November, more than 55 cargo and passenger transports flew more than 1,230 sorties. They moved 126,451 passengers and 25,226 tons of cargo, 60 percent and 20 percent of the total airlift. The entire airlift had flown 1.67 billion ton miles, which compares to 697.5 million ton miles for the Berlin Airlift.

References. Futrell, *Ideas*, vol. 2. Phil Lacombe, "The Air Force and the Airlines," *AF*, February 1985, pp. 92–96. James Ott, "Desert Shield Deployment Tests CRAF's Viability," *AWST*, 10 December 1990, pp. 31–32. Frederick C. Thayer, Jr., *Air Transport Policy and National Security: A Political, Economic, and Military Analysis*, 1965.

Roger D. Launius

CLARK AIR BASE

One of the great USAF* ABs, Clark is located 50 miles north of Manila, Philippines, and is a Pacific Air Forces* (PACAF) field. Named to honor Captain Harold M. Clark, a U.S. Army pilot* killed in a plane crash in Panama, Clark opened in 1919. Its first unit was the 3rd Aero Squadron equipped with de Haviland DH-4s.* For years Clark remained a lonely outpost, equipped with obsolete aircraft.

In the summer of 1941 new USAAF* units with modern aircraft began to arrive. By December it had the 19th Bombardment Group with B-17s* and B-18s* and the 24th Pursuit Group with P-35s* and P-40s.* Subordinate units were at Del Monte field in northern Mindanao; at nearby Del Carmen, now Basa AB; at Iba in Zambales; and at Nichols Field, now Villamor AB, in Manila.

Five and one-half hours after Pearl Harbor,* waves of Japanese aircraft struck all of the fields, except Del Monte, destroying almost all of the U.S. aircraft on the ground. Major General Lewis H. Brereton* had wanted to launch a preemptive strike against Formosa, but General Douglas MacArthur insisted upon waiting until the Japanese made an overt move. When that act came, it devastated U.S. air power in the Far East. Thereafter, U.S. and Philippine troops remained virtually at the mercy of the Japanese who had air superiority.* Most of the airmen survivors took part in the defense of Bataan, surrendered with Army Lieutenant General Jonathon Wainwright, and suffered through the Death March and incarceration in the concentration camps at O'Donnell and Cabanatuan. USAAF strikes against Clark in the U.S. return began in late 1944. After very stiff resistance, the Japanese evacuated it in January 1945.

The Thirteenth Air Force* (13AF) took up permanent residency in 1947. During the Korean War* and the Vietnam War,* Clark served as the logistics hub for funneling personnel and materiel to U.S. forces. In 1973, Clark became the first stop for prisoners of war (POW) (Vietnam)* repatriating in Operation Homecoming. Two years later it served the same role for orphan children (Operation Babylift)* and other allied persons (Operation New Life) being evacuated from Southeast Asia. In the February 1986 revolution against President Ferdinand E. Marcos, rebel pilots* flew to Clark for safety. It was to Clark that Marcos and his entourage fled, and the Military Airlift Command* (MAC) flew them to Guam and Hawaii. In the Philippines incident of 1989,* USAF* F-4s* from Clark supported President Corazon Aquino's defense in the sixth coup attempt against her.

In 1990, besides Headquarters, 13AF, Clark had the 3rd Tactical Fighter Wing (TFW) with F-4s and the 353rd Special Operations Wing of MAC.

References. Walter D. Edmonds, *They Fought with What They Had*, 1951. "Guide to Major Air Force Installations Worldwide," *AF*, May 1990, p. 123. Roberts, *Dir. USAF*. David L. Rosmer, *An Annotated Pictorial History of Clark Air Base: 1898–1986*, 13th Air Force Office of History, 1986.

David L. Rosmer

CLAY, GENERAL LUCIUS D., JR. (1919–   )

Clay, a 1942 graduate of the U.S. Military Academy (USMA), served in Europe with the 344th Bombardment Group during World War II* before embarking on many important assignments. He was the commander of the North American Air Defense Command* (NORAD) and commander of the Aerospace Defense Command (ADC) from 1973 to 1975. His previous assignments include commander of the Seventh Air Force* (7AF) and deputy commander for air operations of the Military Assistance Command, Vietnam (MACV) from 1970 to 1971. He was commander of the Pacific Air Forces* (PACAF) from 1971 to 1973.

References. Primary: U.S. Air Force Oral History Interview K239.0512–1829, 15–17 August 1988, USAFHRC/OH, Maxwell AFB, Alabama. Secondary: Air Force Pamphlet (AFP) 31–1, "Roster of Retired General Officers," 1987. U.S. Air Force Biography, Secretary of the Air Force, Office of Information, 1974.

James C. Hasdorff

CLOSE AIR SUPPORT. *See* attack; tactical operations.

CLUSTER BOMBS. *See* bombs.

COBRA. *See* St. Lo, France.

COCHRAN, COLONEL JACQUELINE "JACKIE" (unknown–1980)

Cochran was a world-renowned aviator and director of the Women Airforce Service Pilots* (WASP). In 1971 she was inducted into the National Aviation Hall of Fame in Dayton, Ohio.

She began flying in 1932 and after only three weeks of flying training obtained her pilot's* license. She continued her flying and competed successfully in numerous air races, becoming the second woman to win the Bendix Trophy in 1938.

In 1939 she publicly suggested that a large number of women be recruited and trained to fly military aircraft. Major General H. H. Arnold,* Chief of the Air Corps, advised that no immediate action be taken on her suggestion; he advised that she recruit American women volunteers for Britain's Air Transport Auxiliary (ATA) to give her invaluable experience should the need arise within the USAAC* for a women's component. Britain agreed and Cochran became chief of the 25 American women volunteers serving in the ATA.

In October 1942, Arnold directed the inauguration of a training program to produce 500 women ferry pilots, and Cochran was appointed director of Women's Flying Training. Within three days 50 women had been interviewed, and 40 were accepted and sent for training at Howard Hughes Airport in Houston, Texas. The next month Arnold wanted all future training to qualify women pilots for most noncombat flying jobs. This meant even larger numbers of women trainees. In February 1943, a new school for women pilots opened at Avenger Field in Sweetwater, Texas. By June, Cochran was appointed special assistant and director of women pilots within the USAAF.* Cochran and Nancy Harkness Love* were rivals. Cochran sponsored women who were not already pilots, while Love advocated existing women professional pilots. On 5 August 1943, the new official title for all women pilots serving with the USAAF became WASP. In 1944, citing the combat situation, the USAAF announced that WASP would be deactivated that December.

Cochran became a lieutenant colonel in the U.S. Air Force Reserve* (USAFR) and continued to break aviation records. In 1953, she broke the sound barrier at a speed of 652.337 miles per hour. She won the Harmon Trophy for 1937 through 1950 and for 1953. She was president of the Fédération Aéronautique

International from 1958 to 1959. In 1964 she flew an F-104* at a record-shattering 1,429.2 miles per hour (Mach 2). Cochran ran a successful cosmetics and perfume company and was a director of Northeast Airlines. In 1953 and 1954 she was "Business Woman of the Year."

References. Primary: Chuck Yeager and Leo Janos, *Yeager: An Autobiography*, 1985. Secondary: C&C, vol. 7. DuPre, *USAF Bio*. RitaVictoria Gomez, *A History of Women in the Air Force*, forthcoming. "Jacqueline Cochran—1907[sic]–1980," *AF*, September 1980, p. 31.

See also de Seversky, Major Alexander P.

RitaVictoria Gomez

COCHRAN, COLONEL PHILIP G. (1910–1979)

Cochran was the prototype for one of the best-known comic strip characters of World War II.* His casual, wise-cracking style reflected the USAAF* image of youthfulness, modernism, pragmatism, and energy. With John Alison, he founded and then commanded the 1st Air Commando Group (1st A.C.G.) in Burma.

From Pennsylvania, Cochran graduated from Ohio State University in 1934. He became a pilot* and officer in the USAAC* in 1935. In 1942 he commanded a green unit assigned to the Desert Air Force and soon developed a reputation of aggressiveness and creativity. He reformed elements of two disorganized squadrons* after the debacle at Kasserine Pass. After 60 sorties, he returned to the United States to find he was a celebrity. His friend Milton Caniff,* the cartoonist, had used him as the model for "Flip" Corkin in the strip *Terry and the Pirates*. *Terry* was the most sophisticated of newspaper adventure strips at the peak of that popular cultural genre.

In late 1943, General H. H. Arnold* sent him to the China-Burma-India theater* (CBI) to command U.S. air elements supporting the British. Colonels Cochran and Alison formed the 1st A.C.G. with its combat aircraft under the former and supply under the latter. The unit operated with minimal red tape, lean logistical support, informality, and little inter-Allied friction. It carried out 14 glider* landings in Burma. One, in March 1944, deployed a large "Chindit" force deep inside Japanese lines. The 1st A.C.G. flew 10,000 sorties, evacuated almost 2,000 casualties, and dropped 750 tons of bombs and over 1,200 tons of supplies. The 1st A.C.G. used mainly liaison aircraft* and made limited use of helicopters.*

Cochran's postwar civilian activities included radio announcing, Hollywood stunt flying, and various business enterprises. His persona was used by Caniff for "General Philerie" in the strip *Steve Canyon*.

References. Primary: U.S. Air Force Oral History Interview K239.0512–876, 20–21 October 1975 and 11 November 1975, USAFHRC/OH, Maxwell AFB, Alabama. Secondary: "Col. Philip G. Cochran, War Hero and Model for 2 Cartoon Figures," *New York Times*, 27 August 1979, p. L. Luigi Rossetto, "The First Air Commandos," *AH*, March 1982, pp. 2–12. Dave Schreiner, " 'Just Another Damn Hero': WWII and Col.

Philip G. Cochran,'' *Steve Canyon*, no. 17, 1986, pp. 32–44. Lowell Thomas, *Back to Mandalay*, 1951.

See also Twenty-Third Air Force.

Roger A. Beaumont

COFFIN, HOWARD E. (1873–1937)

Coffin was chairman of the Aircraft Production Board* in 1917–1918. A graduate engineer from the University of Michigan, he was vice president and consulting engineer of the Hudson Motor Car Company from 1910 to 1930. On the Aircraft Board, Coffin was credited with standardizing aircraft and aircraft engine production techniques, primarily of the de Haviland DH-4* and the Liberty engine.* Some critics, including later General of the Air Force H. H. Arnold,* claimed Coffin and other board members did not fully consider the actual operating requirements of aviation personnel in their technical decisions. Coffin was also a member of the President's Aircraft Board* in 1925 which was formed to respond to issues Brigadier General William Mitchell* raised prior to his court-martial later that year.

References. I. B. Holley, Jr., *Ideas and Weapons*, 1953. *Who Was Who in America*, 1943.

D. K. Vaughan

COLD WAR (1947–1990?)

Perhaps some day the term *Great Peace* may be used instead of *Cold War* because of the decades of European peace achieved.

The United States, the strongest military power in history at the time, demobilized as soon as World War II* ended. Within a few months the USAAF* did not have a single squadron* ready for battle. The USSR retained a massive army and air force, with the latter designed for tactical operations.* It held a line across Central Europe from Stettin to Trieste, and Winston Churchill called it an Iron Curtain in 1946, and the term stuck. By conquest or political gift, an additional hundred million people had been included in the Soviet Empire's open-air prison. The only free area left was the enclave of West Berlin.

Their new territories in Central Europe showed the Soviets the effects of strategic operations.* The USSR began an intensive effort to develop a strategic operations capability. It built Tu-4s, which were direct copies of captured U.S. B-29s.* It began work on intercontinental bombers* using jet technology, nuclear weapons,* and ballistic missiles.* It also began work on an air defense system to protect the fatherland from strategic operations. In 1949, it had an excellent interceptor* in the MiG-15, which was such an excellent design it could also serve as an air superiority* fighter.* The USSR went beyond creating an independent air force; it established three. They are the air force, or Voyenno-Vozdushnyye Sily (VVS); air defense, or Voyska Protivio-Vozdushnoy Oborony (VPVO); and strategic rocket force, or Raketnyye Voyska Strategicheskovo Naznacheniya (RVSN). The USSR has an air arm in its navy but not in its army. It kept over one million soldiers in the occupied countries of Eastern Europe.

The free world became alarmed at the possibilities of further Soviet expansion, especially after the threatened takeover of Greece and West Berlin and communist armed victory in mainland China. The United States, the only power able to resist the USSR militarily, was unwilling to defend itself through land power, because that would require it to become a garrison state. It chose instead to give first priority to deterrence through air power strategic operations. It also followed a foreign policy of containment and tried to forge a series of military alliances around the USSR starting with the North Atlantic Treaty Organization* (NATO) in 1949. This was called the Truman Doctrine. U.S. naïveté after its isolationism had ended, and it had a Christian view of rightness to moderate the perceived evil of global monolithic communism. There were those who saw the United States as the bellicose creator of the Cold War, blaming U.S. adoption of nuclear weapons as the root cause of all problems.

Throughout the Cold War it was only the U.S. strategic forces that could counterbalance the Soviet strategic forces and great superiority in land armies and tactical air forces. The Korean War* showed a need for U.S. land, sea, and tactical operations air forces to help contain communist aggrandizement by limited wars.

Soviet attainment of bomber,* nuclear weapon, and ballistic missile strategic operations capabilities enabled the USSR to threaten directly the continental United States (CONUS). The Soviet orbiting of an artificial earth satellite in 1957 and the Cuban crisis of 1962* were overt expressions of that power. The loss of a U-2* in 1960 showed that Soviet air defenses had become formidable, and USAF* bombers switched from high- to low-altitude techniques. The strategic operations capabilities of the two superpowers led to a Balance of Terror, with neither nation possessing survivability in a total war.

Soviet expansionism continued with client or allied governments established in Afghanistan, Angola, Cambodia, Cuba, Ethiopia, Laos, Nicaragua, and Vietnam. The United States tried unsuccessfully to resist the aggression in the Vietnam War* by fighting a land war. In 1990, there was evidence that the USSR had held and was holding U.S. prisoners of war (POW) from the Korean and Vietnam Wars along with persons kidnapped in the Cold War and fliers lost over or near Soviet territory.

Suddenly, in 1989, there was a wave of rebellions against communist governments following the conspicuous economic and human failures of socialism which had been weakening the USSR. These events gave rise to the possibility that the threat of a major war was diminished so much that the Cold War might be nearly over, decisively won by the West's policy of deterrence and containment and its superior economic and political systems. If ended, it was because of internal changes in the USSR and not in the United States. U.S. nuclear weapons then appeared to be inconsequential as a cause for the Cold War.

References. David A. Anderton, *History of the U.S. Air Force*, 1989. Charles D. Bright, *The Jet Makers: The Aerospace Industry from 1945 to 1972*, 1978. Goldberg, *Hist. USAF*. Higham, *Air Pwr*.

COLLEGE EYE

This was the code name for USAF* EC-121s (*see* C-121) employed as airborne command and control center (ABCCC) platforms in Southeast Asia (SEA). These "ultra-sophisticated, electronic-laden" aircraft were sent to the Vietnam War* zone in early 1965 to overcome deficiencies in ground-based radar* coverage and tactical air control capabilities. They added greater flexibility to the out-country air war by enabling successive Seventh Air Force* (7AF) commanders to exercise more complete control of attack* forces operating over North Vietnam and the Gulf of Tonkin. Initially, the EC-121 task force in SEA was called "Big Eye." The name was changed to "College Eye" in March 1967.

After the task force's arrival, all operations above the 20th parallel had the support of an EC-121 orbiting over the Gulf of Tonkin. Interconnected with the forward radar and tactical control units on the ground and to the Navy's Carrier Task Force 77 (CTF 77) systems, the EC-121 operating over the gulf primarily monitored and communicated information concerning enemy air activity. Later, another EC-121 began orbiting over northern Laos to track and warn strike aircraft when they were in danger of violating Red China's airspace. Among other duties, College Eye crews frequently assisted in searching for downed pilots* and in locating tankers* for emergency aerial refueling.*

References. Primary: Donald E. Born, " 'Triple Nickel' and 'College Eye,' " *United States Air Force Museum Friends Bulletin*, Winter 1987–88, pp. 20–29. William W. Momyer, *Air Power in Three Wars*, 1985. Secondary: Berger, *USAF in SEA*. R. Frank Futrell et al., *Aces and Aerial Victories*, 1976.

Warren A. Trest

COLLEGE PARK, MARYLAND

College Park was the site of the first military flight training* school in the United States, directed by the Wright brothers.* The War Department contract with the Wrights for an airplane required them to teach two officers to fly the plane. A large pasture near the then Maryland Agricultural College was chosen as the site. Between 8 October and 2 November 1909, Wilbur Wright trained Lieutenants Frank P. Lahm* and Frederick E. Humphreys. Lieutenant Benjamin D. Foulois* also received his first flying lessons with Wilbur. The College Park field continued to be used for training Wright pilots* for several more years. In 1912 two fatal accidents killed four men. Training of Wright pilots at College Park ceased soon after.

References. Primary: C. DeF. Chandler and Frank P. Lahm, *How Our Army Grew Wings: Airmen and Aircraft before 1914*, 1943. Benjamin D. Foulois, *From the Wright Brothers to the Astronauts*, 1968. Secondary: Tom D. Crouch, *The Bishop's Boys: A Life of Wilbur and Orville Wright*, 1989. C. V. Glines, "Eighty Years at College Park," *AF*, January 1990, pp. 98–99.

Patrick B. Nolan

COLUMBUS AIR FORCE BASE

This Air Training Command* (ATC) field near Columbus, Mississippi, was established in 1941 and is named for the city. During and after World War II* it was a flight training* base for pilots.* In 1955 it became a Strategic Air

Command* (SAC) field, supporting heavy bombers* and aerial refueling* tankers. In 1969 the field returned to flight training, this time for fighter* pilots with its 14th Flying Training Wing (FTW) using T-37s* and T-38s.*

References. "Guide to Major Air Force Installations Worldwide," *AF*, May 1990, p. 123. Mueller, *AFB*. Roberts, *Dir. USAF*.

COMBAT AIR PATROL (CAP). *See* MiGCAP.

COMBAT AMERICA. *See* movies.

COMBAT BOX

This term was Eighth Air Force* (8AF) parlance to denote a concentrated formation of bombers* flown as a single unit to and from the target. The term could be applied to squadron* up through wing* formations. In 1944 the term was most commonly applied to a group* box: a formation of 27 to 36 aircraft. The box was wedge-shaped seen from above and with staggered high, lead, and low units seen from the front. The box proved to be the best compromise bomber formation for defense against fighters* and for bombing effectiveness. The principal man to develop it was Colonel Curtis E. LeMay.*

References. Primary: Curtis E. LeMay, *Mission with LeMay: My Story*, 1965. Secondary: Roger A. Freeman, *Mighty Eighth War Manual*, 1984.

W. A. Jacobs

COMBAT CARGO. *See* tactical airlift.

COMBAT LANCER. *See* F-111.

COMBAT SKYSPOT

This was a bombing system used by B-52s* in the Vietnam War,* introduced in 1966. It consisted of ground radar* units using MSQ-77 sets, which directed bombers toward the target and advised the aircrew when to drop the bombs.* The system reduced the time to prepare for a sortie, allowed effective diversions to different targets, and could operate under adverse weather conditions. Combat Skyspot radars were able to cover nearly all of the battle zones in Southeast Asia (SEA). It showed its effectiveness at Khe Sanh* by placing devastating B-52 bomb loads only 328 yards from U.S. ground troops.

References. Berger, *USAF in SEA*. René J. Francillon, *Vietnam: The War in the Air*, 1987.

COMBAT TALON. *See* C-130.

COMBINED AIRLIFT TASK FORCE (CATF)

Early in the Berlin Airlift* the Royal Air Force (RAF) attached three representatives to the USAF's* Berlin Airlift Task Force* (Provisional). Although the efforts of the two nations to resupply blockaded Berlin,* Germany, were separate from 26 July through 14 October 1948, they worked closely with functional managers to coordinate their airlifts carefully. On the latter date the RAF was incorporated more directly when the United States and Britain created the CATF. There was a single commander, USAF Major General William H. Tunner,* with RAF Air Commodore J. W. F. Merer as his deputy.

The CATF operated until September 1949. After the Soviets reopened surface transportation in May 1949, it was no longer needed. It continued operations during the summer to protect against relations with the USSR souring again and to lay in a surplus of goods in Berlin.

References. Richard Collier, *Bridge across the Sky: The Berlin Blockade and Airlift, 1948–1949*, 1978. W. Phillips Davison, *The Berlin Blockade: A Study in Cold War Politics*, 1978. Roger D. Launius and Coy F. Cross II, *The Berlin Airlift and the MAC Connection*, 1989. Office of MAC History, *The Berlin Airlift: A Brief Chronology*, 1988.

Roger D. Launius

COMBINED BOMBER OFFENSIVE (CBO)

Otherwise known as Pointblank or the Eaker Plan, named for Major General Ira C. Eaker,* the CBO was the linking of the British Royal Air Force (RAF) Bomber Command operations with those of the USAAF* in Europe. The goal of the CBO was the devastation of German industry. The USAAF was to strike precision targets by day, and the RAF was to bomb areas at night. This was also called round-the-clock bombing. The decision to create the CBO was arrived at during the Casablanca Conference,* and its beginning is considered to be June 1943.

From June 1943 to the spring of 1944, the CBO was directed at the German aircraft industry target system* as a prerequisite to Operation Overlord,* the ground invasion of western Europe. Thus, strategic operations* were subordinated to the projected land campaign. Nevertheless, major strategic operations efforts were directed unsuccessfully at the German ball bearing industry target system* and the German oil industry target system* in the Schweinfurt,* Germany, and Ploesti,* Romania strikes. In 1943 the USAAF found it could not gain superiority* over the Luftwaffe without long-range fighters.*

The arrival of those fighters and their use in early 1944 effected victory over the Luftwaffe and air superiority for the USAAF. On D-Day the German commander of air defenses in the invasion area had only 80 operational aircraft available. The CBO was a partial success.

References. C&C, vols. 2 and 3. Goldberg, *Hist. USAF*.

COMISO AIR BASE

Comiso AB is part of Italy's Magliocco Air Base near Comiso, Italy, on Sicily. It is a U.S. Air Forces in Europe* (USAFE) field and was established in 1983. The USAF* unit on it in 1990 was the 487th Tactical Missile Wing (TMW) which used the BGM-109.*

References. ''Guide to Major Air Force Installations Worldwide,'' *AF*, May 1990, p. 123. Roberts, *Dir. USAF*.

COMMAND DECISION

William Wister Haines' novel* about the Eighth Air Force* (8AF) in World War II* was published in 1947. The story is about a decision with a dilemma. The decision maker could strike at Germany's production of jet fighters* while the factories can be destroyed. To do so would probably cause such horrendous bomber* losses as to result in a cessation of U.S. strategic operations.* The alternative course of action could avoid the losses now and so ensure continuation of strategic operations for the immediate future. The risk in this was the probability of losing air superiority* to the German jets later. *Command Decision* was made into both a successful play and movie,* which starred Paul Kelly and Clark Gable,* respectively.

References. James H. Farmer, *Celluloid Wings*, 1984. "The 40th Anniversary of the USAAF," a special issue of *AH*, September 1987, p. 207. Bruce W. Orriss, *When Hollywood Ruled the Skies*, 1984.

COMMANDO. *See* C-46.

COMMANDO BOLT. *See* Commando Hunt.

COMMANDO HUNT

President Lyndon B. Johnson's (LBJ) decision to end all bombing of North Vietnam in November 1968 resulted in greater concentration of the U.S. air effort against infiltration over the Ho Chi Minh trail* through Laos. This effort, which began immediately after the bombing halt* and continued through 1972, was carried out in a succession of intensified campaigns known as Commando Hunt.

Initially confined to the Steel Tiger* sector of southern Laos contiguous to South Vietnam, Commando Hunt operations eventually were extended into other areas such as the points of entry into Cambodia and South Vietnam. The primary objectives of these campaigns were to destroy supplies moving down the trail and to tie down enemy manpower, but they were also a test of the Igloo White* infiltration detection system that was introduced into Southeast Asia (SEA) in 1967.

The USAF* planned and conducted the Commando Hunt operations, which included increased U.S. Navy and Marine Corps (USMC) fighter* sorties, and provided the bulk of air resources. The operations included an array of attack* and reconnaissance* aircraft directed by forward air controllers* (FAC), B-52s,* C-130* airborne command and control centers, and AC-47 (*see* C-47), AC-119 (*see* C-119), and AC-130 (*see* C-130) gunships.* Attacks in support of Igloo White were called Commando Bolt. General William W. Momyer, commander of the Seventh Air Force* (7AF) from 1966 to 1968, said the best truck-killing weapon in the war was the AC-130. The AC-119, which joined Commando Hunt in 1969, proved adept. Along with C-123s* equipped with bomblet canisters, the gunships were the mainstay of the early Commando Hunt campaigns, but enemy air defenses soon made some interdiction areas impractical for the slower aircraft.

The bombing halt facilitated enemy movement south; the construction of a petroleum, oil, and lubricants (POL) pipeline into the southern Laotian panhandle; and the strengthening of flak* at key points along the trail. By 1971 the North Vietnamese had moved surface-to-air missiles* (SAM) into Laos to help defend the trail, a move that was facilitated by the fact that the weapons were no longer required to defend North Vietnam. Adding F-4* fighters with guided weapons gave a new dimension to the interdiction efforts, but, as was often found in Vietnam, a crafty and determined enemy was not long confounded by new technology.

There were estimates, perhaps inflated, that more than two-thirds of the enemy's supplies were destroyed before they reached the battlefields in South Vietnam, but the North Vietnamese were still able to move enough supplies to mount repeated offensives and, eventually, to win the war.

References. Primary: William W. Momyer, *Air Power in Three Wars*, 1985. Secondary: Berger, *USAF in SEA*. Futrell, *Ideas*, vol. 2. John Morrocco, *Rain of Fire: Air War, 1969–1973*, a vol. of *The Vietnam Experience*, 1985.

Warren A. Trest

COMMISSARY SERVICE. *See* Air Force Commissary Service.

COMMUNICATIONS COMMAND. *See* Air Force Communications Command.

COMPASS CALL. *See* C-130.

COMPETITIONS

Units of the USAF* hold tournaments in which organizations and individuals compete over their skills. These competitions are intended as a training substitute for the pressures of war, as a means of raising proficiency, and for raising morale.

The demobilizations after World War II* disrupted training because of the manning, supply, and administrative problems created. General George C. Kenney,* the head of the Strategic Air Command* (SAC), decided to hold a bombing tournament to spur interest in regaining proficiency in that skill. It was held at Castle* AFB, California, in June 1948. Thirty B-29* crews from ten groups* participated. The event became annual and was first called the SAC Bombing Competition. Now it is called Proud Shield. Navigation competition began in 1951, reconnaissance* in 1952, aerial refueling* in 1959, electronic countermeasures and munitions loading in 1961, and Olympic Arena for missiles in 1967. The Tactical Air Command* (TAC) conducts tournaments. The air superiority* competition is biennial and called William Tell. A separate tournament, called Gunsmoke, is run biennially for attack.* TAC runs a third tournament for reconnaissance in tactical operations* called Reconnaissance Air Meet (RAM). The Military Airlift Command* (MAC) conducts an annual competition for tactical airlift* called the Airlift Rodeo.

These tournaments have their critics who say they generate more gamesmanship and showmanship than combat readiness to the overall detriment of units. They have said that resources have been poured into selected crews at the expense of all other crews. To reduce this practice, Proud Shield now selects at random some participating crews a week before the tournament.

References. Gail F. Phillips, "Photo Finish," *AF*, December 1988, pp. 98–103. Polmar, *SAC*. Jeffrey P. Rhodes, "Airlift Rodeo," *AF*, September 1987, pp. 142–44, 147–48, 151–52; "On Target," *AF*, January 1988, pp. 58–63, 66–67, 69; "Up to the Test," *AF*, February 1988, pp. 52–58; and "The Sharpshooters of William Tell," *AF*, February 1989, pp. 68–73.

COMPOSITE AIR STRIKE FORCE (CASF)

The CASF was a mobile strike force of fighter,* reconnaissance,* airlift,* and command and control elements capable of worldwide deployment for tactical operations.* Vigorously supported by General Otto P. Weyland,* commander of the Tactical Air Command* (TAC), the CASF concept was developed in the early 1950s in response to the continued threat of limited wars. The CASF was to be capable of deploying rapidly to areas of imminent or actual hostilities, keeping the Strategic Air Command* (SAC) and theater forces free to counter the Soviet nuclear weapons* threat. In July 1955 the headquarters of the U.S. Air Force* authorized TAC to activate the Nineteenth Air Force* (19AF) at Foster AFB, Texas. Though assigned no units, the 19AF planned the deployment and employment of the CASF. Units from TAC's Ninth Air Force* (9AF) and Twelfth Air Force* (12AF), organized into "packages," would be released to 19AF control when a CASF was deployed.

The CASF concept stimulated USAF* developments in fighter aerial refueling,* tactical airlift* and other airlift operations,* worldwide command and control, joint service operations, and mobility logistics. CASFs were deployed for the first time in 1958 to Turkey and the Far East. Though the 19AF was deactivated in 1973 and unified commands have taken over most of the command and control functions, TAC still operates and trains under the CASF concept.

References. Primary: Harry Viccellio, "The Composite Strike Force 1958," *Air University Quarterly Review*, Summer 1958, pp. 3–17. O. P. Weyland, "Tactical Airpower—Worldwide," *AF*, July 1955, p. 41. Secondary: Futrell, *Ideas*, vol. 1.

See also U.S. Central Command Air Forces.

Budd A. Jones, Jr.

CONINGHAM, AIR MARSHAL SIR ARTHUR "MAORI" (1895–1948)

Coningham conceived of and proved the modern form of a tactical air control system* in North Africa during World War II.* The experience demonstrated the superiority of centralized tactical operations* command and convinced the U.S. Army to adopt it.

In the early 20th century century two major new mobile systems entered war, armor and aircraft. One result was uncertainty over the optimal degree of centralization in control of mobile weapons. For armor, some believed the 1940 Battle of France settled the issue. The German centralized-armor blitzkrieg army routed the French though the French had superiority in both quality and quantity of armor but had decentralized it. The Germans thought centralization of armor was important to the battle results, and they centralized armor into organizations as large as army groups.

For aircraft, the founding of the Royal Air Force (RAF) in 1918 was some recognition of centralized control. In the United States this came partly when the General Headquarters Air Force* (GHQ Air Force) was formed in 1935. Attack* operations continued to be decentralized for both services into World War II.

"Maori," pronounced "Mary," Coningham was from New Zealand. He became air officer commanding (AOC) of the Air Headquarters of Western Desert in October 1941 under Air Chief Marshal Sir Arthur W. Tedder, air commander-in-chief of the Mediterranean Air Command. Earlier, the British Eighth Army had decided that its 1941 defeat in the desert was caused by Luftwaffe air superiority.* Coningham took command in time to lead during a new British offensive named Crusader. This time the RAF had air superiority, so when Crusader failed it could not be attributed to German control of the air. The Army believed that the RAF had deliberately not supported the soldiers, and the RAF attributed the campaign failure to Army trepidation and incompetence. Coningham had seen, however, problems in the existing organization. At this time the Army got a new commander, Lieutenant General Bernard L. Montgomery. Coningham persuaded Montgomery to adopt a new arrangement. His plan was to have the air and army commanders and staff collocated and to cooperate as equals in the daily assignment of tactical operations. Coningham's principles for the use of his forces were flexibility, mobility, and concentration—all based primarily upon air superiority. When the new centralized system went into use in the Battle of El Alamein, Montgomery and Coningham were pleased with the results.

Later in the west, the British First Army and the American II Corps landed in North Africa and drove toward Tunisia. The tactical operations were provided by the RAF's Eastern Air Command and the USAAF's* Twelfth Air Force* (12AF). The air units were under the control of ground commanders. For the Americans this organization was enshrined in War Department Field Manual 31–35 (9 April 1942), *Aviation in Support of Ground Forces*, which directed decentralized control down to the small army unit level. The ground commanders exercised their authority. They hoarded their air power and used aircraft as protective umbrellas. There was little satisfaction with the military results at this time, which climaxed in the defeat at Kasserine Pass.

In February 1943, Coningham installed his organization. Lieutenant General Dwight D. Eisenhower,* commander in chief of the Allied forces, reported that results improved immediately. By late April the Allies had air superiority. In July 1943 there was a new U.S. Army Field Manual, 100–20, *Command Employment of Air Power*, which adopted Coningham's concepts. They were used successfully until the end of World War II.

Since that war there has continued to be a body of opinion that decentralized air power under minor army unit commanders works best for attack, but the USAF* continues to believe in Coningham's concepts.

References. C&C, vol. 2. Richard P. Hallion, *Strike from the Sky: The History of Battlefield Air Attack 1911–1945*, 1989. Daniel R. Mortensen, *A Pattern for Joint Operations: World War II Close Air Support, North Africa*, 1987. Vincent Orange, *Coningham: A Biography of Air Marshal Sir Arthur Coningham*, 1990. Albert F. Simpson, "Tactical Air Doctrine: Tunisia and Korea," *Air University Quarterly Review*, Summer 1951, pp. 4–20.

See also Howze Board.

CONSOLIDATED AIRCRAFT CORPORATION. *See* B-24; PT-1.

CONSOLIDATED-VULTEE AIRCRAFT CORPORATION. *See* aerospace industry; Atlas; B-24; B-32; B-36; B-58; BT-13; F-102; F-106; T-29.

CONSTELLATION. *See* C-121.

CONTEMPORARY HISTORICAL EXAMINATION OF CURRENT OPERATIONS (CHECO)

Born of the USAF's* desire to document and analyze operations in Southeast Asia (SEA), CHECO began in 1962. Its original name was Current Historical Evaluation of Counterinsurgency. Conceived and nurtured by the USAF Historical Program, it aimed to provide interpretive studies. Originally managed from the USAF Historical Division at Maxwell* AFB, Alabama, CHECO was responsive to the Air Staff* in Washington, D.C.

The first efforts produced a five-volume narrative of the early USAF experience in the Vietnam War,* a study that proved useful to the Air Staff. In 1965 responsibility for CHECO moved to the director of plans of the Air Staff, and the charter changed to the application of USAF doctrine,* concepts, and policy as events happened. In 1970, CHECO moved again, this time to the Office of Air Force History, a new unit. By the end of the war, CHECO had produced a thoroughly documented file of 218 special studies. CHECO became institutionalized with the command history functions in the Pacific Air Forces* (PACAF), the U.S. Air Forces in Europe* (USAFE), and the USAF Historical Research Center* (USAFHRC) at Maxwell AFB.

References. Warren A. Trest, "Projects CHECO and CORONA HARVEST: Keys to the Air Force's Southeast Asia Memory Bank," *AH*, June 1986, pp. 114–20.
See also Corona Harvest.

Lloyd H. Cornett, Jr.

CONTINENTAL AIR COMMAND (CONAC)

CONAC was activated in 1948 as a major command* (MAJCOM) designed to replace the Tactical Air Command* (TAC) and Air Defense Command (ADC). CONAC also controlled all U.S. Air Force Reserve* (USAFR) units because they had tactical operations* or air defense missions. TAC was reestablished as a MAJCOM after the Korean War* began in 1950. ADC was reestablished as a MAJCOM in 1951. After this, CONAC administered the Air National Guard* (ANG) and the USAFR. CONAC was inactivated in 1968.

References. Goldberg, *Hist. USAF*. Ravenstein, *Org. USAF*.

CONTRACT MAINTENANCE

This is the maintenance of materiel performed under contract by commercial organizations, including prime, or original, contractors either on a one-time or on a continuing basis. Contract maintenance has been a long-standing requirement of the USAF,* supplementing its own organic program. It is an example of the contribution of industry and civil aviation to aerospace power.*

Before World War II,* major aircraft maintenance was performed by air depots. The huge expansion of the USAAF* after Pearl Harbor* resulted in an expanded maintenance role for the Air Service Command (ASC), which operated the air depots. As a result, the ASC began contracting out to airlines and other civilian concerns to supplement depot maintenance.* Contract maintenance ended after the war. The USAF began contract maintenance again in the late 1940s, and by 1954 it was a normal procedure. It began overseas when USAF depots there were deactivated in the late 1950s. Examples of it are maintenance of B-52s* by The Boeing Company and of F-4s* in Korea by Korean Air Lines.

The advent of ballistic missiles* led to contractor support until the Air Materiel Command (AMC) could provide better support at lower cost. For example, the Martin-Marietta Company performed maintenance on its Titan* II missile.

In 1971 the Department of Defense (DoD) ordered that no more than 70 percent of mission-essential maintenance, excluding major items, should be done organically, and the depots should use at least 85 percent of their capacity. The Competition in Contracting Act of 1984 presumes that private contractors can perform jobs more cheaply.

USAF policy is to rely on contract maintenance whenever possible; however, there is still a vital need to maintain skilled airmen and the physical resources to meet wartime situations.

References. Primary: Air Force Regulation (AFR) 66–14, "The US Air Force Equipment Maintenance Program," 15 December 1986. Secondary: C&C, vol. 6. Hill AFB,

History of Ogden Air Logistics Center, 1988. Bernard J. Termena et al., *Logistics: An Illustrated History of AFLC and Its Antecedents, 1921–1981*, 1981.

P. *Susan Weathers and Charles G. Hibbard*

CONTRACT PRIMARY FLIGHT TRAINING

The USAF* used contract flight training* as an integral part of the pilot* training system during World War II* and the Korean War.* It was critical to the explosive expansion in the number of pilots required by the wars. Though private contractors provided several types of flight training, primary was the most important form. From 1939 to 1945 and again from 1950 to 1960, contract schools effectively monopolized primary pilot training. It is an example of the vital contribution of civil components to aerospace power.*

In 1939 the USAF selected nine civilian flying schools to supplement its own. A total of 64 eventually conducted primary training in World War II, graduating 250,000 students. The deep disarmament after World War II, the outbreak of the Korean War, and plans to expand the USAF from 48 to 95 operational wings caused the USAF to again resort to contract pilot training. It opened nine schools between December 1950 and October 1951. Four of them were closed in the late 1950s due to declining pilot production goals. The remaining five closed in 1960 and contract primary training ended. In this period, contract schools trained 44,949 students.

There was a mass closure of military pilot training bases in 1961 which resulted from a reevaluation that consolidated all phases of flight training on one base. Until this change, each phase was given on a different base. Using different bases meant that contractors could operate very cheaply compared to the USAF. Consolidation reduced USAF overall costs by using fewer bases and by decreasing moves by personnel in training.

Introduction of the T-37* also made contract training less desirable. Unlike previous primary trainers, the T-37 had at least some of the characteristics of first-line aircraft. The experience gained by the primary instructor pilots thus became more readily transferable to operational aircraft, making the USAF reluctant to divert valuable flying hours to civilian instructors.

The two changes, consolidation and the T-37, reinforced the USAF's major objection to contract training: training a military pilot was a military function. Military instructor pilots were considered essential to providing the environment needed to develop an individual commitment to the military profession. Contract training therefore was acceptable to the USAF only when the demand for pilots was so urgent that degraded military training had to be tolerated.

References. Primary: Don J. Armand, "Pilot Training—WWII: Primary Training 21 May 1943–29 July 1943," *Friends Journal*, Fall 1990, pp. 40–45. Secondary: C&C, vol. 6. Headquarters Air Training Command Studies, "A Comparative Study of Civilian Contract Operated and Military Operated Flying Training Schools within ATC," 26 May 1959, and "Consolidation of Preflight, Primary and Basic Pilot Training," vols. 1 to 4, January 1960. Barry H. Nickle, *Contract Flying Training in Air Training Command,*

1939–1980, an Air Training Command Historical Monograph, 1981. Stanford Research Institute Report, "Analysis of Training Methods for the United States Air Force," July 1949.

Thomas A. Manning

CONVAIR. *See* aerospace industry; Atlas; B-24; B-32; B-36; B-58; BT-13; F-102; F-106; T-29.

CORONA HARVEST

Not entirely satisfied with the total relevance of the Contemporary Historical Examination of Current Operations* (CHECO), the USAF* sought another instrument, Corona Harvest, to document lessons learned in Southeast Asia (SEA). Corona Harvest was originally named Loyal Look. Both projects became mutually supportive, although CHECO got its limited studies directly from the theater while Corona Harvest sought data on every aspect of the air efforts. While there were similarities, there were also vast differences. CHECO had limited resources, while Corona Harvest had the direct interest of the Air Staff,* and the steering committee chairman was the vice chief of staff of the USAF.

Corona Harvest wound down in the early 1970s and never completed its goal of determining the effectiveness of air power in SEA. For one thing, there was no viewing of enemy documents. Nevertheless, such goals as documenting the USAF's role, identifying and defining conceptual, operational, and doctrinal lessons were realized. Thus the USAF had documents on which to determine how well it supported national policy. Out of the project, the Air University* (AU) was able to prepare a final report for 1954 to 1969 of 11 volumes complemented with 16 volumes from a Pacific Air Forces* (PACAF) study group. In 1974 General William W. Momyer* evaluated the documentary sources resulting in another 21 reports. They identified lessons learned in hopes of improving future operations.

Overall, the USAF more than realized its investment in time, manpower, and money. Countless documents rest in the repository of the U.S. Air Force Historical Research Center* (AFHRC) at Maxwell* AFB, Alabama.

References. Futrell, *Ideas*, vol. 2. Warren A. Trest, "Projects CHECO and CORONA HARVEST: Keys to the Air Force's Southeast Asia Memory Bank," *AH*, June 1986, pp. 114–20.

Lloyd H. Cornett, Jr.

CORSAIR II. *See* A-7.

CRAF. *See* Civil Reserve Air Fleet.

CRAVEN AND CATE (C&C)

Wesley Frank Craven and James Lea Cate edited the seven-volume official history entitled *The Army Air Forces in World War II*. The work covered the USAF* in its greatest war when it had the most personnel ever and the most challenging tasks. The work was regarded early with some skepticism because the editors were medieval specialists, but it has gained in stature over the years.

Professor Craven was the head of the USAAF's* Operational History Branch and had been on the faculty of New York University and Princeton University. Professor Cate was head of the Strategic Bombardment Section of the USAAF's Historical Office until 1944 and then was historical officer of the Twentieth Air Force* (20AF). Later he was a history professor at the University of Chicago.

Volume 1, *Plans and Early Operations January 1939 to August 1942* (1948), covered the early history of the USAF, the effects and response of it to the period before the United States entered the war, and the first months of the war.

The war in Europe comprised volume 2, *Europe: Torch to Pointblank August 1942 to December 1943* (1949), and volume 3, *Europe: Argument to V-E Day January 1944 to May 1945* (1951). Volume 2 discussed Operation Torch,* early strategic operations,* and preparations for Operation Overlord.* Volume 3 covered Operation Overlord and continued operations in Italy.

The war in the Pacific theaters was the subject of the next two volumes. Volume 4, *The Pacific: Guadalcanal to Saipan August 1942 to July 1944* (1950), covers the southwest Pacific and the China-Burma-India theater* operations. Matterhorn,* Burma, the Philippines campaign, and the strategic campaign against Japan* are in volume 5, *The Pacific: Matterhorn to Nagasaki June 1944 to August 1945* (1953).

Procuring the equipment and training the men for the great mobilization are related in volume 6, *Men and Planes* (1955). Volume 7, *Services around the World* (1958), is about the supporting resources: airlift operations,* civil engineers, weather service, aviation medicine,* rescue,* and women—all needed for mobilization and global air operations.

CRAWFORD, ROBERT. *See* U.S. Air Force Song, The.

CREW TRAINING AIR FORCE (CREW TAF)

This named air force* was one of three of its time in the Air Training Command* (ATC). It was established in 1952 and had its headquarters at Randolph* AFB, Texas. Crew TAF took rated men and trained them for battle in particular aircraft. The command was inactivated in 1957 as the flow of students had declined greatly with the end of the Korean War.*

References. Goldberg, *Hist. USAF*. Ravenstein, *Org. USAF*.

CROSSROADS. *See* Operation Crossroads.

CROWELL COMMISSION

This was a 1919 War Department commission whose report was one of the few from 1919 to 1925 to urge the U.S. government to give immediate attention to building the nation's aviation capabilities.

Headed by Assistant Secretary of War Benedict Crowell, it was appointed by Secretary of War Newton Baker to study aviation's future. Consisting of representatives of the aviation industry and the U.S. Army and Navy, the group traveled to Europe for data and conducted investigations at home. Its report went to Baker in August 1919, but he did not release it until the news had leaked to the *New York Times*. Many scholars claim the Crowell Report was suppressed by Baker. The *Times* described the report, lauded it, and related Baker's objection to a unified air arm. The report urged government support for aviation to make it a more attractive private investment opportunity. The report said aviation growth would enable the nation to prepare for future aerial defense requirements by enhancing U.S. commercial and transportation abilities via airways. Finally, it said that a unified air service might be the best way to assure the proper development of the nation's air security, emphasizing air superiority.*

Baker's opposition to the report reflected the general attitude of most high-ranking Army and Navy officials in 1919. Captain Henry C. Mustin, the Navy's representative, filed a minority opinion stating that the Navy must control naval aviation. General of the Armies John J. Pershing's* World War I* report wanted Army aviation to be subordinate to ground combat command.

References. Primary: "Crowell Report" in U.S. Congress, House, *United Air Service. Hearings before the Subcommittee of the Committee on Military Affairs*, 66 Cong., 2nd sess., 1920. Secondary: Maurer, *Avn. in Army*. Chase C. Mooney, *Organization of Military Aeronautics, 1907–1935*, USAF Historical Study, #25, unpub., in Air University Library, Maxwell AFB, Alabama.

Lester H. Brune

CRUISE MISSILE

Cruise missiles are small unpiloted jet- or rocket-propelled aircraft with folding wings and fins, capable of being tube-launched or dropped from aircraft. The presence of these weapons will affect the strategic balance of the world for the foreseeable future.

Their ancestry reaches back to World War I* and to World War II's* German V-1 "buzz bomb" through the U.S. TM-61* missile of the 1950s and 1960s to the modern AGM-86* ALCM. Modern cruise missiles have changed the face of war. They fly at very low level through any programmed course, are a difficult target to detect and destroy, and are accurate. A small nuclear weapon*–tipped missile that can be fired from a pickup truck, fly thousands of miles, and then hit its target within a yard or two is a potent weapon indeed.

References. Frank Barnaby, *The Automated Battlefield*, 1986. Polmar, *SAC*. Kenneth P. Werrell, *The Evolution of the Cruise Missile*, 1985.

Philip Long

CUBAN CRISIS OF 1962

This was in international crisis threatening nuclear war in which the USAF* was prominently involved.

U.S. and Cuban relations deteriorated rapidly after dictator Fidel Castro moved toward the Soviet sphere of influence beginning in 1959. In mid–1962 the Soviets turned toward the goal of making Cuba an advanced base in the Western Hemisphere. There was a dramatic increase in military technicians in and shipments to Cuba. There were three major offensive weapons systems unloaded: Mobile Medium-Range Ballistic Missiles (MMRBM), Intermediate-Range Ballistic Missiles (IRBM), and IL-28 bombers.* The Strategic Air Command's* (SAC) U-2* reconnaissance* planes discovered deployed MMRBMs around San Cristobal, southwest of Havana. In all, the Soviets planned and started construction on nine launch sites. President John F. Kennedy* (JFK) directed low-altitude reconnaissance flights, a task done by USAF Tactical Air Command* (TAC) RF-101s (*see* F-101) and U.S. Navy F8Us. Tension mounted as the USSR's Nikita Khrushchev vehemently denied the presence of the systems and JFK was positive that the photographic evidence could not be dismissed. JFK addressed the nation over radio and television on 22 October, saying he had decided upon a military "quarantine" to become effective on 24 October.

The USAF began readying its forces for any eventuality, including nuclear strikes. TAC deployed forces to bases in Florida, and SAC and the Air Defense Command (ADC) dispersed their resources. The USAF moved U.S. Marines (USMC) into Guantanamo naval base. SAC continued sea and land reconnaissance to determine construction progress and the location of Soviet vessels on their way to Cuba. The quarantine went into effect as scheduled with 18 Soviet vessels headed toward Cuba. The U.S. Navy stopped and boarded some and permitted those that passed inspection to proceed. JFK's warnings, which earlier had fallen on deaf ears, finally roiled Khrushchev when followed up by military activity. Khrushchev chose to move away from the specter of conflict. He acceded to U.S. demands on 28 October, and the tension began to subside. Continued reconnaissance found the Soviets hard at work bulldozing the missile sites, dismantling the missiles, and transporting them to nearby ports. The 42 IL-28s shipped to Cuba were returned. Departing Soviet ships were stopped on the high seas by U.S. Navy surface ships where both visual and helicopter* inspection took place. Soviet crewmen pulled back tarpaulins and broke open crate ends to expose the departing weapons. The United States followed the Soviet ships' return across the Atlantic.

More than 400 reconnaissance flights had been made. The USAF played major reconnaissance and airlift operations roles, called up some U.S. Air Force Reserves* (USAFR), and deployed air defense, tactical, and strategic forces ready for any contingency.

References. David A. Anderton, *History of the U.S. Air Force*, rev. ed., 1989. Cuban Chronology, DOD Special Cuban Briefing, 6 February 1963, 108, 29 April 1986 "Special Cuban Briefing by Honorable Robert S. McNamara," SECDEF State Department Auditorium, 5 P.M., 6 February 1963 (USAFHRC K160.052–1). Department of State, "The US Response to Soviet Military Buildup in Cuba" (pamphlet). President Kennedy Reports to the People, 22 October 1962 (in Inter-America Series 80, GPO, USAFHRC K146.2–16). Futrell, *Ideas*, vol. 2.

Lloyd H. Cornett, Jr.

CURTISS, GLENN H. (1878–1930)

A pioneer aviator and inventor and a major contributor to military aviation, Curtiss was born and spent much of his career in Hammondsport, New York. Following his death, the federal government awarded him posthumously the Distinguished Flying Cross (DFC) for his services to U.S. aviation. In 1964 he was inducted into the National Aviation Hall of Fame in Dayton, Ohio.

His interest in aviation was aroused by Thomas Scott Baldwin, the pioneer dirigible balloonist, who began working with Curtiss on the first U.S. Army dirigible. It was tested and flown at Fort Meyer, Virginia, in 1905 with Curtiss as engineer and Baldwin as pilot. He soon joined with Alexander Graham Bell, Thomas E. Selfridge,* and others in the Aerial Experiment Association (AEA). The most notable invention of the AEA was the aileron, an improvement on the "wing warping" technique used by the Wright brothers,* which allowed for greater lateral stability and turning control.

Curtiss began to manufacture and sell airplanes. He opened a flying school in San Diego, California, in 1911 where he trained Army and Navy officers. In 1913 this became the Signal Corps Aviation School,* the first Army permanent aviation school. Curtiss's most important contribution to aviation was his work on taking off and landing on water. With World War I* came mass production. Curtiss built more than 5,000 of his JN* type of plane, which evolved into the most useful and respected training aircraft of the war, known to an entire generation of airmen as the "Jenny." After the war, Curtiss left active participation in the aviation industry.

References. Louis Casey, *Curtiss: The Hammondsport Era, 1907–1915*, 1981. Alden Hatch, *Glenn Curtiss: Pioneer of Naval Aviation*, 1942. Cecil R. Roseberry, *Glenn Curtiss: Pioneer of Flight*, 1972.

Patrick B. Nolan

CURTISS JENNY. *See* JN "Jenny."

CURTISS OX-5

This engine was famed as the power plant for the Curtiss JN* "Jenny," the training aircraft flown by almost all U.S.-trained aviators in World War I.* The OX-5 was the most widely produced of the OX models, which had been derived from the Model O, and from the Model L before that. The OX-5 employed eight cylinders in a V-type water-cooled arrangement. Its predecessor, the Model L, was rated at 80 horsepower (HP) at 1,500 revolutions per minute (RPM). The OX-5 was rated at 90 HP at 1,200 RPM and weighed about 400 pounds. Although it was reasonably reliable for the time, it frequently failed. Late models of the JN, the JN-6, were powered by the 150 HP Hispano-Suiza engine. The OX-5 powered other types of aircraft in the 1920s.

References. Glenn D. Angle, ed., *Aerosphere 1939*, 1940. James C. Fahey, ed., *U.S. Army Aircraft, 1908–1946*, 1946. Herschel Smith, *Aircraft Piston Engines: From the Manly Balzer to the Continental Tiara*, 1981.

D. K. Vaughan

D

DACT. *See* dissimilar aerial combat tactics.

DA NANG AIRPORT
This fortified airfield was on the coast in the northern part of South Vietnam. In 1963 the USAF* had a squadron* of C-123s* there. They left in 1967 and were replaced with C-130s.* In 1965 F-100s* and F-104s* arrived, and the field became a staging base for strikes on North Vietnam. As the Vietnam War* intensified, the F-100s and F-104s moved out and F-102s* and B-57s* moved in. The B-57s left and F-4s* arrived in 1966. In 1973 the USAF moved out.
References. Berger, *USAF in SEA.* John Schlight, *The War in South Vietnam: The Years of the Offensive 1965–1968,* 1988.

DAVIS, LIEUTENANT GENERAL BENJAMIN O. (1912–)
No officer did more than Davis to further the cause of integration of blacks within the USAF.* Son of the first black U.S. Army general, and born in Washington, D.C., he was the first black to graduate from the U.S. Military Academy (USMA) in the 20th century and the first black general in the USAF.
Responding to pressure from the black press and the National Association for the Advancement of Colored People (NAACP) in the presidential campaign of 1940, President Franklin D. Roosevelt* (FDR) ordered flight training* opened to blacks. In 1941, the segregated Tuskegee Army Air Field began training pilots.* Captain Davis entered with the first class. Davis became commander of the 99th Pursuit Squadron, and he took the unit to war in North Africa. The black squadron* was not treated with respect. Davis's approach to this problem was for the unit not to protest but to act with dignity and do its job well. The 99th, and Davis's next command, the 332nd Fighter Group, proved themselves beyond doubt. After World War II,* Davis's segregated units continued to show high performance. Citing the demonstrated ability, Davis urged integration in the USAF, and it was so ordered by General Hoyt S. Vandenberg* in 1949.

Davis then held several important commands and staff positions, such as deputy chief of staff for operations in headquarters of the U.S. Air Forces in Europe* (USAFE), until he retired in 1970. He later served as assistant secretary of transportation (environment, safety, and consumer affairs) in the Nixon administration.

References. DuPre, *USAF Bio*. John L. Frisbee, ed., *Makers of the United States Air Force*, 1987. Lawrence J. Paszek, "Separate, But Equal? The Story of the 99th Fighter Squadron," *AH*, September 1977, pp. 135–45. William P. Schlitz, "From Tuskegee to Space," *AF*, February 1983, pp. 74–79.

DAVIS, LIEUTENANT COLONEL GEORGE A., JR. (1920–1952)

Davis received the Air Force Medal of Honor* for action in the Korean War.* Only four men were so honored in that war. He scored 21 aerial victories, 7 in World War II* and 14 in the Korean War. Thus he is one of a small group of fighter* pilots* who attained ace* status in two wars. His score ranks him 16th on the list of all-time USAF* aces, a distinction shared with Colonel John J. Voll* and Colonel William T. Whisner.*

He was born in Dublin, Texas. He joined the USAAF* as an aviation cadet* in 1942 and became an officer and pilot the same year. In 1943 he joined the 342nd Fighter Squadron, 348th Fighter Group, flying F-47s* in New Guinea.* He returned to the United States in March 1945 after 266 combat sorties. In 1951 he was in Korea as commander of the 334th Fighter Interceptor Squadron flying F-86s.* He gained his first victory over a MiG-15 on 27 November. On 30 November he shot down three Tu-2 bombers* and one MiG-15 on one sortie. On 10 February 1952, he and his flight* attacked 12 MiG-15s. Davis scored two victories and was then shot down himself. He received his Medal of Honor posthumously for this action.

References. DuPre, *USAF Bio*. John L. Frisbee, "MiG Hunter," *AF*, May 1984, p. 207. Futrell, *USAF in Korea*. Hess, *Aces Album*.

DAVIS-MONTHAN AIR FORCE BASE

This field at Tucson, Arizona, was established in 1925 and named for Second Lieutenants Samuel H. Davis and Oscar Monthan. Davis was killed in 1921 when he was a passenger in a JN* crash. Monthan died in a Martin bomber* accident in 1924. In World War II* the field was first a training field for B-24s* and later for B-29s.* The mothballing of aircraft on the base began in 1945, and in 1989 it had all such USAF* planes. B-47* and KC-97 (*see* C-97) operations began in 1954, Titan* IIs in 1960. In 1990 it was a Tactical Air Command* (TAC) base with headquarters of the 836th Air Division and the 355th Tactical Training Wing (TTW) for A-10* combat crew training. It also had the 602nd Tactical Air Control Wing (TACW) with OA-10 and OV-10* aircraft.

References. "Guide to Major Air Force Installations Worldwide," *AF*, May 1990, p. 123. Mueller, *AFB*. Roberts, *Dir. USAF*.

DAWN-TO-DUSK FLIGHT

The first dawn-to-dusk flight across the United States was made by the USAAS* to show the military potential of the airplane. Using a Curtiss Aeroplane and Motor Company, Inc., PW-8, Lieutenant Russell L. Maughan flew 2,670 miles from New York City, New York, to San Francisco, California, on 23 June 1924. Five stops were required in this flight of 21 hours and 48 minutes. Upon arrival, Maughan handed the mayor of San Francisco a copy of the *New York Times* which had been printed that day.

References. *The American Heritage History of Flight*, 1962. Goldberg, *Hist. USAF*. Maurer, *Avn. in Army*.

Alwyn T. Lloyd

DAY FIGHTER. *See* fighter.

D-DAY. *See* Operation Overlord.

DE HAVILAND DH-4

When the United States entered World War I,* its military aviation was in a deplorable state because of official neglect, and this caused the U.S. aircraft industry to be ineffective. Although the U.S. potential to be a first-class air power was obvious, there was little time to save the Allies from possible defeat. The decision was made to build European types of aircraft in U.S. factories as the best approach to the challenge.

The Bolling Mission* selected several foreign designs, but the United States succeeded in building in quantity only the de Haviland 4 (DH-4). When selected, the DH-4 was an obsolescent observation aviation* design of the British from 1916. For the U.S. version a new engine, the famous Liberty,* was rushed into development. In an era when the term *Liberty* was overused—such as calling sauerkraut "Liberty Cabbage—the name "Liberty Plane" was officially applied to the U.S. design. That name was not popularly adopted. The Standard Aircraft Company, Dayton-Wright Company, and General Motors Corporation built 4,846 all-told, but design problems became apparent when the American DH-4s arrived in France. They sometimes caught fire in level, normal flight, which led to the nickname "Flaming Coffins." The pilot* and the observer* were separated by the fuel tank. This made it difficult for the aircrew to cooperate, especially under fire, and the tank normally crushed and killed the pilot in crashes. The DH-4 was nose-heavy and had a tendency to nose over in landing. The design problems were corrected in the DH-4B, but none saw combat. The U.S. Army in France lost 33 DH-4s in battle and 249 in accidents, while claiming 45 enemy aircraft* destroyed.

After the war ended, the overseas DH-4s were burned in France which led to accusations of a "Billion Dollar Bonfire." The U.S. government neglected military aviation again, although funds were provided to rebuild the remaining "Flaming Coffins" to make them safer. DH-4s then performed well in active service until 1931.

Characteristics (DH-4B): engine, Liberty of 416 horsepower; span, 42 feet; length, 30 feet; height, 10 feet; gross weight, 4,595 pounds; top speed, 118 miles per hour; service ceiling, 12,800 feet; endurance, 3.25 hours; bombs, 1,200 pounds.

References. Primary: Higham, *Combat Airc.*, vol. 3. Secondary: Swanborough, *US Mil. Airc.* Ray Wagner, *Am. Planes.*

DELTA DAGGER. *See* F-102.

DELTA DART. *See* F-106.

DEMOBILIZATION OF 1945 TO 1947

The United States demobilized after World War II* much as it had done after previous wars. The USAAF* had 2,253,000 men on the day Japan surrendered. There were only 890,000 by the end of 1945, and 450,000 in February 1946. In May 1947, the figure was 303,000. Thus the USAAF had shrunk to 13 percent of its wartime strength. By 1947 the air power that had ruled the global skies in early 1945 had only skeletal forces left overseas in occupation of Germany and Japan. Such a demobilization could only take place with the belief that nothing threatened the United States. Immediately after World War II it was believed in the armed services that any future use of U.S. military power would be as part of a United Nations operation.

With Britain exhausted and U.S. power disbanded, the USSR did not fully demobilize and proceeded to consolidate its conquests in Europe and abetted communist rebellions in Greece and Turkey. On 12 March 1947, President Harry S Truman* (HST) announced a U.S. policy of containment of the USSR backed by the USAAF with nuclear weapons.* The 18 months of illusions, complacency, and demobilization had ended.

References. David A. Anderton, *History of the U.S. Air Force*, rev. ed., 1989. C&C, vol. 7. Goldberg, *Hist. USAF.*

See also Cold War.

DEPARTMENT OF DEFENSE TOTAL FORCE POLICY. *See* Total Force Policy.

DEPARTMENT OF THE AIR FORCE

This organization provides civilian administrative control over the USAF.* It supervises the maintenance and improvement of the USAF. The department is responsible to the Office of the Secretary of Defense (OSD).

The department was established by the National Security Act of 1947,* which also set up the Department of Defense (DoD), the Joint Chiefs of Staff (JCS), and the other military departments for the U.S. Army and Navy. The powers of the DoD were made weak deliberately, and those of the military departments were much as they had been as Departments of War and Navy.

In 1958, President Dwight D. Eisenhower* changed the power structure with the Reorganization Act. The military secretaries were shorn of operational control of the services, and the chain of command ran from the secretary of defense (SECDEF) to U.S. military commanders. However, the act caused little change in actual practice until Robert S. McNamara* became SECDEF in 1961. McNamara vigorously applied his powers under the 1958 act. Since McNamara, the great power of the OSD has continued, and, with one exception, the military departments have had little influence. That exception was the Department of the Navy under Secretary John Lehman. Lehman had a political power base, and his department acted more as those of old.

References. Goldberg, *Hist. USAF*. Richard Halloran, *To Arm a Nation: Rebuilding America's Endangered Defenses*, 1986. Edward N. Luttwak, *The Pentagon and the Art of War: The Question of Military Reform*, 1985.

DEPOT MAINTENANCE

A USAF* depot is used for major overhaul or rebuild work on equipment and for storing material.

The service had its first three maintenance depots during World War I.* They were located at Dallas, Texas; Indianapolis, Indiana; and Montgomery, Alabama. Between the wars, there were large repair depots at Fairfield, Ohio; Middletown, Pennsylvania; San Antonio, Texas; and San Diego, California. The San Diego depot moved to Sacramento, California, shortly before World War II.*

The USAAC* and USAAF* established seven more depots in the United States during the war at Mobile, Alabama; Ogden, Utah; Oklahoma City, Oklahoma; Rome, New York; San Bernardino, California; Spokane, Washington; and Warner Robins, Georgia. Since World War II, the USAF has gradually consolidated this structure to Hill* AFB, Utah; Kelly* AFB, Texas; McClellan* AFB, California; Robins* AFB, Georgia: Tinker* AFB, Oklahoma; and Wright-Patterson* AFB, Ohio.

References. "Air Force Logistics Command," *AF*, May 1989, pp. 65–67. Douglas Baldwin, "Revolution in the Hangar," *AF*, April 1990, pp. 78–82. Woodford Agee Heflin, ed., *The United States Air Force Dictionary*, 1956. Bernard J. Termena et al., *Logistics: An Illustrated History of AFLC and Its Antecedents, 1921–1981*, 1981.

See also inspect and repair as necessary.

DESERT SHIELD. *See* Iraq crisis of 1990–1991.

DESERT STORM. *See* Iraq War.

DE SEVERSKY, MAJOR ALEXANDER P. (1894–1974)

One of the greatest contributors to American aerospace power,* de Seversky was both theorist and successful practitioner. He was inducted into the National Aviation Hall of Fame in Dayton, Ohio, in 1970.

As an imperial Russian navy fighter* pilot,* he lost a leg in action but returned to combat. He became an ace* with 13 victories. When Russia made peace, he offered his services to the U.S. government. He became an adviser to Brigadier

General William Mitchell* during Mitchell's bombing tests on warships.* After becoming a U.S. citizen, he was commissioned a major in the USAAC* Reserve. In 1931 he founded the Seversky Aircraft Corporation. The renamed organization continued into 1990 as a part of Fairchild Industries, Inc. De Seversky functioned as president, designer, and chief test pilot. He was an inventor holding patents. The automatic pilot was developed from his work with Elmer Sperry on gyroscopic flight instruments.

In the 1930s de Seversky believed in turbosupercharged, radial-engined, long-range fighters. In 1938 he went to the Office of the Chief of the Air Corps to show how he could increase fighter ranges. The USAAC was not interested. De Seversky's company used its own funds to prove his concept with a modified P-35.* De Seversky himself demonstrated its range by flying nonstop between New York City, New York, and Los Angeles, California, and between New York and Havana, Cuba. He set records doing so. The USAAC dismissed his flights because of his great skills as a pilot. In response, de Seversky hired a young and relatively unknown woman, Jacqueline Cochran,* to fly a Seversky plane nonstop from Los Angeles to Cleveland, Ohio. In doing so, she won the Bendix Race. The USAAC was unmoved until it was made desperate by the Luftwaffe in 1943, and it then launched its crash program to get a long-range fighter, the F-51B.*

De Seversky's last design contribution, working with the great engineer Alexander Kartveli, was the P-43* Lancer. The P-43 was the first fighter with a turbosupercharged radial engine, and it led to the famous F-47.* After several years of red ink, the 1939 Seversky board of directors fired de Seversky for emphasizing research and development over production.

He then set his air power views down in his famous book, *Victory through Air Power* (1942). Walt Disney made a movie from it with the same title in 1943. The book and the movie strongly influenced the U.S. public to the great benefit of the USAAF.* He wrote two more best-selling books on his aerospace views: *Air Power: Key to Survival* (1950) and *America: Too Young to Die!* (1961).

References. Futrell, *Ideas*, vol. 1. Edward T. Maloney, *Sever the Sky: Evolution of Seversky Aircraft*, 1979. Joshua Stoff, *The Thunder Factory: An Illustrated History of the Republic Aviation Corporation*, 1990. John F. Whiteley, "Alexander deSeversky [*sic*]," *AH*, September 1977, pp. 155–57.

DESTROYER. *See* B-66.

DEW LINE. *See* distant early warning line.

DIR. *See* inspect and repair as necessary.

DIRECTOR OF AIR SERVICE AND ASSISTANT SECRETARY OF WAR

This position was established by President Woodrow Wilson on 27 August 1918 in an effort to provide leadership to the USAAS.* The USAAS had been established on 21 May 1918 in two separate organizations, the Bureau of Aircraft

Production* and the Division of Military Aeronautics.* Wilson appointed John D. Ryan, who had been head of the Bureau of Aircraft Production, as the new director and assistant secretary. The new position elevated the importance of the aeronautical branch of the Army but kept it under civilian control, forestalling any movement to establish it as a separate agency.

References. Goldberg, *Hist. USAF*. James J. Hudson, *Hostile Skies: A Combat History of the American Air Service in World War I*, 1968.

D. K. Vaughan

DIRECT REPORTING UNITS (DRU)

DRUs are USAF* organizations that are specialized and have limited missions. Size is not a factor in designating a DRU. A DRU that does not relate to a major command* (MAJCOM) or separate operating agency* (SOA) reports directly to the headquarters of the USAF. This gives the Air Staff* more authority over a DRU than over an SOA. Examples of DRUs are the Air Force Civilian Personnel Management Center* (AFCPMC) and the U.S. Air Force Academy* (USAFA).

References. Ravenstein, *Org. USAF*. U.S. Air Force Fact Sheet 89–05, "Organization of the United States Air Force," February 1989.

DIRIGIBLES. *See* lighter-than-air.

DISASSEMBLE, INSPECT, AND REPAIR (DIR). *See* inspect and repair as necessary.

DISSIMILAR AERIAL COMBAT TACTICS (DACT)

One of two ways that fighter* pilots* can be trained is by pitting identical types of aircraft against each other in mock battle. The outcome in such a case depends almost entirely upon pilot, or "stick and rudder," skills. The other way is to engage different types of aircraft, or to simulate this, which is closer to true battle.

The second method, begun by aerial warfare's first important tactician, Germany's Hauptmann Oswald Boelcke in World War I,* was given the name DACT in 1967 as part of a new formal training program. In 1971 the USAF* and U.S. Navy cooperated in their DACT. F-106s* were used in the training for a few years and resulted in the temporary use of the name "College Dart" for the program.

Aerial Combat Tactics is a Navy term. The comparable USAF term is Air Combat Maneuvers (ACM). The early 1970s DACT evolved into the USAF's Red Flag* and the Navy's "Top Gun" training.

References. Primary: Donald D. Carson, "Dissimilar Aerial Combat Tactics—New Techniques in Battle Training," *AF*, March 1973, pp. 56–61. Secondary: Robert L. Shaw, *Fighter Combat: Tactics and Maneuvering*, 1985. Mike Spick, *The Ace Factor: Air Combat & the Role of Situational Awareness*, 1988.

DISTANT EARLY WARNING LINE (DEW LINE)

The DEW Line was part of a buildup for the air defense of North America and was to be a line of radar* stations running along the 69th parallel of the continent for 3,000 miles. Construction of it was approved by President Harry S Truman* (HST) in 1952. There was opposition to it. Comparisons were made to France's Maginot line, arguments were made over costs, and personal attacks were made on both proponents and opponents. It was 1954 before the issue was settled in favor of the proposal, and the line became operational in 1957. In 1990 the line was still in service watching the airspace north of the continent. It was undergoing a modernization program begun in 1987. This included converting some radar sites to Minimally Attended Radars and adding new sites to the line.

References. "Alaskan Air Command," *AF*, May 1990, p. 74. Futrell, *Ideas*, vol. 1. Goldberg, *Hist. USAF*. Roberts, *Dir. USAF*.

DIVE BOMBER. *See* attack.

DIVISION

A division is a USAF* unit which may be numbered or named. The term has been used since World War II.* Numbered air or aerospace divisions use Arabic numbers, as in 7th Air Division. They may be under an operational major command* (MAJCOM) or an air force.* Usually they have wings* as subordinate units. A named division is a unit in a large support command and is a significant part of that command. An example is the Electronic Systems Division of the Air Force Systems Command* (AFSC). There have been exceptions to the support role such as the Southern Air Division, at one time an operational unit of the Tactical Air Command* (TAC). The term *division* is also used for offices within a headquarters organization, separate operating agency* (SOA), or direct reporting unit* (DRU).

References. Ernest J. Gentle and Lawrence W. Reithmaier, eds., *Aviation/Space Dictionary*, 6th ed., 1980. Woodford Agee Heflin, ed., *The United States Air Force Dictionary*, 1956. Ravenstein, *Org. USAF*.

DIVISION OF MILITARY AERONAUTICS

This organization was established by President Woodrow Wilson on 21 May 1918, at the same time the Bureau of Aircraft Production* was established. The two agencies, both under the War Department, were recognized as constituting the new USAAS.* No overall chief of the Air Service* was appointed until August, when the president established the position of director of Air Service and assistant secretary of war.* The first head of the division was Major General William L. Kenly,* who had just returned from France where he had been first chief of the Air Service, American Expeditionary Force (AEF), from September to November of 1917.

References. Goldberg, *Hist. USAF*. James J. Hudson, *Hostile Skies: A Combat History of the American Air Service in World War I*, 1968.

D. K. Vaughan

DOCTRINE

Military doctrine may be described as distilled experience and generalized rules for employment, suggesting but not mandating what has been found to be the "best way" to accomplish the mission. Doctrine is developed not only to provide helpful guidelines on the application of force in combat but also to suggest the "way to go" across the whole spectrum of military activities, contracting, research and development, personnel, planning, and the like. Official doctrine is promulgated in manuals under the imprimature of the chief of staff of the Air Force,* after prolonged study of the historical record of operating experience. At the same time, a substantial body of informal doctrine flourishes within the services, experience that is absorbed by direct observation or passed on by word of mouth without ever being written down or officially sanctioned. The reason doctrine is suggestive rather than obligatory is that environmental changes often are thought to invalidate yesterday's sound solution; this is especially apparent where rapid technological change seems abruptly to alter the situation.

Doctrine should not be confused with the term *concept*. Concepts are suggestions, working hypotheses, ideas proposed for testing. Only when a concept has successfully withstood repeated trials does it become a candidate for adoption as official doctrine. So too, the term *principle* should not be used interchangeably with doctrine. Doctrines must be changed as innovations and other external factors invalidate former practice; in contrast to this, principles represent aspects of doctrine that are so enduring, so general, so abstract, that they have become almost axiomatic, such as the principles of war. Where doctrine can be laid down or discarded by fiat, a principle cannot, any more than the principle of gravity could be discarded.

The air arm of the U.S. Army was slow to develop an effective organization for studying past experience to devise doctrine. As a consequence, the full potential of the air weapon was not exploited for many years. Because airplanes in their crude early years had sharply limited lifting capacity, they were primarily visualized as observation aviation.* As such they were assigned to the Signal Corps, a service rather than a combat arm. Although the experience of the USAAS* in World War I* revealed much about the combat potential of aircraft, by far the greater part of that experience was with observation aircraft, the fighters* needed to protect them, and with planes devoted to attack.* The Air Service in France had only the most rudimentary scope of strategic operations.* As a consequence, senior army officials emerged from the war with a mind-set that favored tactical operations* but regarded strategic bombardment as unproven. This mind-set largely persisted in the upper echelons of the Army throughout the period between the two wars. Official doctrine reflected the thinking of the senior leadership, and as a consequence the aircraft procured for the Army were heavily weighted in favor of observation and fighter planes.

The creation of the USAAC* as a combat arm in 1926, with a substantially strengthened Air Corps Tactical School* (ACTS), provided an organizational vehicle for the serious study of doctrine, at least on a part-time basis, by members of the faculty. Their informal and unofficial formulations laid the groundwork for the strategic bombardment doctrine that dominated the acquisition of aircraft during World War II.* Subsequently, a change in Army leadership, more receptive to air arm ideas, authorized wider autonomy for a USAAF* and eventually led to a separate USAF.* Once established as an autonomous organization, the Air Force created a specialized agency for doctrine. Even after decades of cooperation, however, the procedures for devising doctrine remain far from fully perfected.

References. Dennis M. Drew, "Of Leaves and Trees: A New View of Doctrine," *Air University Review*, July 1982, pp. 40–48. Futrell, *Ideas*, 2 vols. I. B. Holley, Jr., "The Doctrinal Process: Some Suggested Steps," *Military Review*, April 1979, pp. 2–13. Dale O. Smith, *U.S. Military Doctrine: A Study and Appraisal*, 1955.

Irving Brinton Holley, Jr.

DOMINATOR. *See* B-32.

DON'T TOUCH ME

In 1951 a skilled author, MacKinlay Kantor, produced an accurate novel* about the USAF* in the Korean War.* Most of the story concerns itself with ground rather than flying activities. With families living on a base in Japan and the men fighting in Korea, the novel explores the ramifications of a commuter war on the people involved.

Reference. "The 40th Anniversary of the USAF," a special edition of *AH*, September 1987, pp. 209–10.

DOOLITTLE, GENERAL JAMES H. "JIMMY" (1896–)

Lieutenant Colonel Doolittle led the Doolittle raid on Tokyo* in World War II* and received the Air Force Medal of Honor* for that valor. He was a leading USAAF* commander throughout the war. He helped organize the Air Force Association* (AFA) and was its first president. He was inducted into the National Aviation Hall of Fame in Dayton, Ohio, in 1967. In 1985 Congress made him the first Reserve officer to be promoted to full general.

Born in Alameda, California, he enlisted in the Aviation Section of the U.S. Army Signal Corps* in 1917 and became a pilot.* From 1918 to 1930 he served as a flight leader and gunnery instructor, took the USAAS* mechanical school and aeronautical engineering courses, represented his service in record-setting cross-country flights and in air races, and earned a doctorate in aeronautics from the Massachusetts Institute of Technology (MIT). He won the Schneider Cup race of 1925* and received the Mackay Trophy. His notoriety during this period stemmed primarily from newsreel footage of the hair-raising but winning maneuvers he used in air races, executing daredevil dives at breakneck speeds while clearing turning-point pylons by only a whisker. In addition, he helped develop instrument flying* techniques, performing himself the first complete sortie in a covered cockpit. For this, he received the Harmon Trophy.

In 1930, Doolittle resigned his active-duty commission to manage the Aviation Department of the Shell Oil Company but retained his Reserve commission to serve periodically as a test pilot. Although continuing to race and fly goodwill tours, his primary prewar achievement was promoting the development of 100-octane aviation fuel, vital to the coming war effort.

Returning to active duty in 1940, Doolittle worked on the conversion of automobile plants to produce aircraft; traveled and assembled intelligence on foreign air forces; and, with promotion to lieutenant colonel, took up duties at the headquarters of the USAAF* culminating in the organization, planning, and leadership of his famous raid.

After duty in the Eighth Air Force* (8AF), Doolittle commanded the Twelfth Air Force* (12AF) in North Africa and then all North African Strategic Air Forces, advancing to major general. After a brief assignment as Fifteenth Air Force* (15AF) commander, he was promoted to lieutenant general and, in January 1944, command of the 8AF, in which he served in both European and Pacific theaters until the war ended.

Following the war, Doolittle left active duty but served with distinction on government commissions and boards, employing innovative approaches to such topics as officer-enlisted relationships, military justice, and air safety.

References. DeWitt S. Copp, *Forged in Fire: Strategy and Decisions in the Air War over Europe 1940–45*, 1982. Carroll V. Glines, *Jimmy Doolittle: Daredevil Aviator and Scientist*, 1972, and "Jimmy Doolittle: Master of the Calculated Risk," *The Retired Officer*, July 1988, pp. 46–48, 50, 52. Lowell Thomas and Edward Jablonski, *Doolittle: A Biography*, 1976.

Thomas C. Blow II

DOOLITTLE RAID ON TOKYO

On 18 April 1942, Lieutenant Colonel James H. Doolittle* led the first U.S. air strike against the Japanese home islands, hitting the capital and four other cities. The action was hailed as a great psychological victory by Americans. In addition, what the Japanese propagandists called a "do-little" raid did much to polarize Japanese military thought. To prevent at all costs a recurrence and to strike back for the sake of national honor, an assault on Midway Island was approved. Due to a combination of surprise, poor luck, and poorer cypher security, the overextended Japanese would lose four aircraft carriers and a devastatingly critical number of their experienced pilots.*

Sixteen modified B-25* bombers* carried out the raid, launching from the deck of the aircraft carrier USS *Enterprise*, while 650 to 700 miles from Japan. This novel and unexpected ploy allowed the *Enterprise*, the accompanying carrier *Hornet*, and supporting task force to escape counterattack after detection by the outer ring of Japan's sampan-and-gunboat warning system. President Franklin

D. Roosevelt* (FDR), partially for security reasons, stated the raid had come from "Shangri-La," a fictional paradise.

Although detection dictated an early launch and a daylight strike, the low-altitude penetration route, combined with poor interceptor* tactics of airborne fighters,* allowed all but one of the bombers, which jettisoned its load while under pursuit, to reach and bomb their targets: factories, shipyards, oil refineries, and arsenals. Subsequently, all but one of the planes had enough fuel, aided by a fortuitous tailwind, for the longer leg to landing bases in China. The other plane landed in the USSR. The planned recoveries in China went awry. Darkness, plus the lack of radio aids to navigation, forced the crews to parachute or crash-land. Two crews became prisoners of war (Japan)* and suffered execution or starvation and neglect. The remainder were smuggled out of Japanese-held China by, in many cases, only the narrowest of margins. The Japanese, incensed and ashamed that their native land and emperor had been laid open to attack, subsequently staged a bloody, retributive campaign in which an estimated quarter million Chinese soldiers and civilians were killed.

Movie: Thirty Seconds over Tokyo, 1944.

References. Mitsuo Fuchida and Masatake Okumiya, *Midway: The Battle That Doomed Japan*, 1955. Carroll V. Glines, *The Doolittle Raid*, 1988. Lowell Thomas and Edward Jablonski, *Doolittle: A Biography*, 1976.

Thomas C. Blow II

DOUGLAS, SECRETARY JAMES H. (1899–1988)

Douglas was the fifth secretary of the Air Force,* serving from 1957 to 1959. His strength and contribution was his capacity for mediation, particularly in resolving civilian with military viewpoints.

Born in Cedar Rapids, Iowa, he was a second lieutenant in the U.S. Army in 1918. Douglas graduated from Princeton University in 1920, studied at Corpus Christi College, Cambridge, England, and Harvard Law School in 1924. He was assistant secretary of the treasury from 1932 to 1933 and otherwise practiced law until World War II.* During the war he rose from major to colonel in the USAAF* and finished as chief of staff of the Air Transport Command (ATC). After the war he returned to the practice of law. From 1953 to 1957 Douglas was under secretary of the Air Force. After serving as secretary, he was deputy secretary of defense until 1961.

References. DuPre, *USAF Bio.* Goldberg, *Hist. USAF.*

DOUGLAS AIRCRAFT COMPANY. *See* aerospace industry; A-1; A-20; B-19; B-26 Invader; B-66; C-47; C-54; C-124; C-133; O-2; Skybolt; Thor.

DOUGLAS WORLD CRUISER. *See* Round-the-World Flight of 1924.

DOUHET, MAJOR GENERAL GIULIO (1869–1930)

An Italian army air power theorist, Douhet was second only to Brigadier General William Mitchell* in influence on the USAF's* founders. Douhet was brilliant. Before World War I* he foresaw the usefulness of the airplane and the mechanization of armies. A poet and playwright, he was able to express well his ideas. This irritated his superiors, for they had chosen the dirigible as the future vehicle of aviation and still believed in the horse. Although Douhet was not a pilot,* he commanded Italy's first aviation battalion. His unauthorized ordering of a three-engined bomber* gave his superiors the excuse to transfer him to the infantry. Then Douhet saw the weaknesses in the Italian army and wrote a memorandum detailing them and forecasting military reverses. As with critic Mitchell, Douhet was court-martialed. Douhet's punishment was worse, for he was imprisoned for a year. The Italian army's later performance confirmed Douhet's evaluation, which made him even less popular with the brass.

Douhet's famous book on air power, *The Command of the Air*, appeared in 1921, with a second edition in 1927. Douhet saw air power as the key to victory in war, with surface forces playing a subordinate and defensive role. While the army and navy held the line, the victorious nation would first achieve air superiority,* or command of the air. This would enable the nation to smash its opponent's entire nation in total war and break the enemy's will to fight. Douhet saw the bomber, a variant of which he called a "battleplane," as the main instrument in achieving air superiority and the destruction of the enemy nation. Thus, he underrated the fighter* plane.

Douhet's views were highly influential in Europe and with the USAAC* and helped form the latter's doctrines and policies. At least to an extent, his vision was realized in the Korean* and Vietnam* Wars where armies ended up holding their positions while air power forced the final decision. The Iraq War* of 1991 further demonstrated the validity of some of his views.

References. Primary: Giulio Douhet, *The Command of the Air*, 2d ed., 1927, translated by Dino Ferrari, 1942. Secondary: DeWitt S. Copp, *A Few Great Captains: The Men and Events That Shaped the Development of U.S. Air Power*, 1980. Futrell, *Ideas*, vol. 1. Thomas H. Greer, *The Development of Air Doctrine in the Army Air Arm 1917–1941*, 1985. Daird Nevin, *Architects of Air Power*, 1981, a vol. in the series *The Epic of Flight*.

DOUMER BRIDGE. *See* Paul Doumer bridge.

DOVER AIR FORCE BASE

This AFB was first established just ten days after Pearl Harbor* and is named for nearby Dover, Delaware. It was originally built to be a municipal airport. The first unit assigned was a federalized Air National Guard* (ANG) squadron* which began flying antisubmarine patrols with its O-27s. For the rest of World War II* it was a field for coastal patrol and F-47* training and for preseparation processing at the end of the war. It was inactivated between 1946 and 1951.

Upon its reactivation it was assigned to the Air Defense Command (ADC). In 1952 it was assigned to the Military Air Transport Service (MATS) and became a major port of embarkation for the European theater with the 1607th Air Transport Wing using C-54s,* followed by C-124s* in 1957. In 1966, MATS became the Military Airlift Command* (MAC), and the 1607th became the 436th Military Airlift Wing. Indicative of its importance, in 1971 Dover AFB became the first active airlift unit to receive the C-5.* In 1990 it was the largest airlift aerial port on the East Coast.

References. "Guide to Major Air Force Installations Worldwide," *AF*, May 1990, p. 123. Mueller, *AFB*. Roberts, *Dir. USAF*.

Roger D. Launius

DRAGONSHIP. *See* gunship.

DRESDEN, GERMANY

Dresden is the old capital of the Kingdom of Saxony and is on the Elbe River. It is also famous in history for the raids made on it in February 1945, which resulted in controversy over the civilians killed.

On the night of 13 February 1945, just over 770 Royal Air Force (RAF) bombers* delivered an area bombing strike in two waves, the first of which succeeded in starting a firestorm near the city center. On 14 February, 311 Eighth Air Force* (8AF) bombers delivered a partly visual, partly radar* guided strike. As Dresden had only been lightly hit before and had had little military significance, it was not well equipped with shelters, nor was its fire-fighting organization prepared to deal with a major raid. Dresden was also, at the time of the raids, crammed with refugees from the east. Casualty estimates have ranged from 35,000 to 135,000 civilians. Scholarly opinion now favors the lower figure.

The raids were controversial almost immediately and remain so. They were entirely consistent with existing policy and practice and were the result of decisions made at the highest levels. The RAF had been hitting German cities in this manner from a very early date in the war. At this stage of the war, more than half of all USAAF* bomb tonnage dropped on Germany was aimed with the aid of radar; the bomb fall of a USAAF raid delivered through more than five-tenths cloud on radar was usually quite similar to a successful RAF area assault. The only difference between the two was in the choice of aiming points. For Dresden, the RAF chose a sports stadium near the center of the city, and the 8AF fixed upon the rail marshaling yards.

The raid on Dresden followed, but should be considered part, of a mid-January series of strikes aimed at eastern German cities, including Berlin,* Leipzig, and Chemnitz. The target priorities agreed by the U.S. and British air commanders were, in order, oil, communications, and blind area strikes. Largely as a result of deliberations in the British Air Staff and a strong intervention from the prime minister, on 27 January 1945 the Air Ministry ordered the Bomber Command to hit the eastern German cities as soon as possible to aid the Soviet advance. Consultation was undertaken with the U.S. commander, Lieutenant General Carl A. Spaatz,* on the following day. Since he had already ordered a major raid on Berlin, he agreed to coordinate the U.S. effort with the RAF. This agreement was apparently discussed informally by the Combined Chiefs of Staff during their meeting at Malta, and U.S. participation was confirmed on 2 February. Two days later, during an early plenary session of the Yalta conference, the Red

Army deputy chief of staff put forward a request for air strikes on German eastern rail communications. This was consistent with U.S. and British decisions already taken. The actual timing of the raids was, as always, in the hands of the operational commanders: Lieutenant General James H. Doolittle,* commanding general of the 8AF, and Sir Arthur Harris, air officer commanding in Chief (AOC-in-C) of the Bomber Command.

References. C&C, vol. 3. Melden Smith, Jr., ''The Bombing of Dresden Reconsidered: A Study in Wartime Decision-Making,'' Boston University Ph.D. diss., 1971. Charles Webster and Noble Frankland, *Annexes and Appendices*, vol. 4 of *The Strategic Air Offensive against Germany*, 1961.

W. A. Jacobs

DRONE. *See* unmanned aerial vehicles.

DROP TANKS

Disposable, external fuel cells had been experimented with during World War I* but did not come into common use until the 1920s. They have been important to the range of aircraft, especially fighters.*

By 1924, USAAS* fighters regularly employed 20- and 50-gallon drop tanks in cross-country and ferrying operations. The 1929 Air Corps Tactical School* (ACTS) fighter text outlined their employment; drop tanks were to be used on outbound flights and released upon running dry or contact with hostile aircraft.

The use of drop tanks declined in the 1930s because of several nontechnical factors. Misuse brought criticisms of dangers in landing with them and reduced flight performance. Chiefly, however, drop tanks faded because of the rise of the strategic operations* bombing concepts. Long-legged fighter performance threatened the burgeoning ''bomber* invincibility'' theory that posited unescorted bombers striking selected targets. Pursuit aviation doctrine,* including drop tanks for longer range, was reduced to a defensive role after the retirement in 1936 of Captain Claire L. Chennault,* the fighter arm's chief advocate.

World War II's* global scope renewed USAAF* interest in drop tanks. Initially they were used in ferrying operations to Europe. In the Pacific theater the fighters' radius of action was extended by using 165-gallon external fuel cells by 1943. In the European theater the USAAF was slower to use them, partly because Europe was seen as the main testing ground for the strategic operations* theory. Heavy bomber losses to Luftwaffe interceptors* in the summer and fall of 1943 brought increased use of drop tanks and, when melded to the P-38,* F-47,* and F-51,* gave the USAAF a viable long-range fighter capability.

Drop tank employment continued thereafter. The Korean War* was in the jet age, with aircraft consuming fuel at so great a rate that external cells had to be used. F-86s* carried two 120-gallon tanks on their sorties to MiG Alley,* while jet fighter bombers such as the F-80* used oversized wing-tip ''Misawa'' tanks. Range continued to dictate fighter ability through the Vietnam War.* During raids on North Vietnam drop tanks and aerial refueling* were used.

In 1990 external fuel cells continued to rule fighter range, but increasingly sophisticated airframes demanded drop tanks to match. The F-15E* points to possible future paths with its conformal fuel tanks. An aerodynamically shaped cell is placed on each side of the fighter and is not released in combat. On the tanks, hard points for armament stores emphasize their permanent attachment to the craft. The conformal cells indicate their shape does not appreciably decrease performance or sacrifice weapon numbers while extending combat range.

References. Primary: Clayton Bissell, "Brief History of the Air Corps and Its Late Development," 1927, p. 16. U.S. Army Air Corps, *Pursuit–1929*, 1929. Secondary: Goldberg, *Hist. USAF*. Benjamin S. Kelsey, *The Dragon's Teeth?: The Creation of United States Air Power for World War II*, 1982.

Ronald W. Yoshino

DR. STRANGELOVE OR: HOW I LEARNED TO STOP WORRYING AND LOVE THE BOMB

This 1964 movie* had a screenplay by Stanley Kubrick, Peter George, and Terry Southern. It was based upon the 1958 novel* *Red Alert* by Peter Bryant. The movie significantly altered the plot of *Red Alert*. *Dr. Strangelove* was a black comedy starring Peter Sellers and George C. Scott, and it enjoyed a high degree of success. Like *Fail-Safe*,* it envisioned a failure of the USAF's* safeguards against accidental war. The film has a special horror, a doomsday bomb to destroy the human species. There is no doubt that this fictional movie badly hurt the popular image of the USAF.

References. Primary: Peter George, *Dr. Strangelove or: How I Learned to Stop Worrying and Love the Bomb*, 1963. Secondary: "The 40th Anniversary of the USAF," a special edition of *AH*, September 1987, p. 212.

DRUM BOARD

Major General Hugh A. Drum headed a War Department committee in 1934 whose recommendation to create the General Headquarters Air Force* (GHQ Air Force) gave limited autonomy to a centralized air group for offensive air missions.

The board originated partly because President Franklin D. Roosevelt* (FDR) decided not to appoint another assistant secretary of war for air* and partly because Chief of Staff General Douglas MacArthur and Chief of Naval Operations Admiral William V. Pratt made an agreement on coast defense jurisdiction which gave Army aviation a primary role in defending land bases.

Known officially as the Special Committee on the War Department on the Employment of the Army Air Corps, the board produced a report that pleased the airmen by recommending the GHQ Air Force. It displeased them by reporting that the USAAC* must be under firm Army control, because it was believed not possible for any foreign nation to cross the Atlantic or Pacific Oceans to hit vital U.S. targets.

References. C&C, vol. 1. DeWitt Copp, *A Few Great Captains: The Men and Events That Shaped the Development of U.S. Air Power*, 1980. Futrell, *Ideas*, vol. 1.
See also Army-Navy agreements of 1931 and 1938.

Lester H. Brune

DUGAN, GENERAL MICHAEL J. "MIKE" (1937–   )

Dugan was the 13th chief of staff of the Air Force* and the first to be fired from the position. He served less than three months, from July into September 1990. His firing received approval in the government and media, yet Dugan was a highly popular and respected officer. He was compared to General of the Army Omar N. Bradley by Secretary of the Air Force* (SAF) Donald B. Rice.* Dugan wanted more openness in the government, and, after the Iraq crisis of 1990–1991* began, he discussed with the press the role of air power should there be a war. Dugan was a proponent of air power's capabilities. Secretary of Defense (SECDEF) Richard B. Cheney then fired Dugan, saying he did not understand the situation in the crisis and had made inappropriate statements. Dugan's predecessor, General Larry D. Welch,* had been out of favor with Cheney because of his views on ballistic missiles* expressed to Congress. The Iraq War* of 1991 lent validity to Dugan's views.

Dugan graduated from the U.S. Military Academy (USMA) and became a pilot* in 1959. He flew A-1s* in the Vietnam War* from 1964 to 1967 and was wounded. Then he served on the Air Staff* until 1977, when he entered the Tactical Air Command* (TAC), staying until 1986. He again served in the Air Staff from 1986 to 1989, when he became commander in chief of the U.S. Air Force in Europe* (USAFE).

References. "Aerospace World," *AF*, November 1990, p. 20. Julie Bird, "The Making of a Chief of Staff," *Air Force Times*, 13 August 1990, pp. 12–13, 16, and "Dugan's Downfall," *Air Force Times*, 1 October 1990, pp. 14–15, 46. Gerald F. Seib and Bob Davis, "Air Force Chief Is Fired after Disclosing Classified Data, Using 'Poor Judgement,' " *Wall Street Journal*, 18 September 1990, pp. A3, A6.

DURANDAL. *See* runway cratering munitions.

DYESS AIR FORCE BASE

This field is near Abilene, Texas, and is named for Lieutenant Colonel William E. Dyess. In 1943 his P-38* caught fire over a heavily populated area in California and he died when he deliberately crashed on a vacant lot to ensure he would not endanger others' lives. The base was named for him in 1956; previously it was named for Abilene. The field was established in 1942. During World War II* it was used for fighter* pilot* training. The base was inactive from 1946 to 1955. Then it was used for B-47s* and KC-97s (*see* C-97) until 1962, when B-52s* and KC-135s (*see* C-135) arrived. C-130s* arrived in 1963, and B-1s* arrived in 1985. Dyess was the first AFB to have an operational B-1 wing. In 1990 it was a Strategic Air Command* (SAC) installation with the 96th Bomb

Wing and the 463rd Tactical Airlift Wing. Its aircraft were B-1s, KC-135s, C-130Hs, and T-38s.*

   References. "Guide to Major Air Force Installations Worldwide," *AF*, May 1990, p. 123. Mueller, *AFB*. Roberts, *Dir. USAF*.

DYNA-SOAR. *See* X-20.

E

E-3 SENTRY (AWACS)

The E-3 was based on the Boeing Airplane Company's Model 707–300 and was designed to replace the EC-121 (*see* C-121). Its mission is as an Airborne Warning and Control System* (AWACS), which includes early warning surveillance of aircraft and missiles and control of interceptors* and fighters.* It is distinguishable by its rotodome, or radome, a dielectric housing for its antenna. Testing began with a pair of EC-137Ds (*see* C-137). A total of 34 E-3As were delivered to the USAF* between 1977 and 1984. Improved USAF and North Atlantic Treaty Organization* (NATO) aircraft are designated as E-3Cs. The E-3 had its first test in battle in the Iraq War* and performed well.

Characteristics: *see* C-137.

References. Peter M. Bowers, *Boeing Aircraft since 1916*, 1989. Alwyn T. Lloyd, *Boeing 707 and AWACS in Detail & Scale*, 1987. Garry Mitchelmore, "Big World of the Sentry," *AF*, June 1984, pp. 70–74, 77. Lawrence A. Skantze, "How the E-3A Gives the Big Battle Picture," *AF*, July 1977, pp. 58–62, 65. Swanborough, *US Mil. Airc.*

Alwyn T. Lloyd

E-4

In 1973, The Boeing Company's Model 747–200 was selected for the Advanced Airborne National Command Post (AABNCP) to provide an airborne communications link between the U.S. National Command Authority and the forces of the USAF,* and U.S. Navy and Army. Hence the E-4 is the vehicle for the Post Attack Command and Control System* (PACCS). The first three were E-4As. Re-engined and with the capability for aerial refueling* added, they became E-4Bs.

Characteristics (E-4B): engines, four General Electric F103-GE-100 turbofans of 52,500 pounds thrust each; for other characteristics, *see* VC-25A in C-25.*

References. Peter M. Bowers, *Boeing Aircraft since 1916*, 1989. Swanborough, *US Mil. Airc.* Susan H. H. Young, "Gallery of USAF Weapons," *AF*, May 1990, p. 148.

Alwyn T. Lloyd

E-8A JOINT STARS

Two EC-18Ds (*see* C-18) were modified for the Joint Surveillance and Target Attack Radar System (Joint STARS) mission and redesignated E-8As. The modifications were extremely expensive. The first flight was in 1988.

Joint STARS is a USAF* and U.S. Army mission. The equipment includes multimode side-looking airborne radar* (SLAR) which can operate synthetic aperture radar* (SAR) to detect parked vehicles, especially tanks and armored personnel carriers. SLAR can also switch from doppler to SAR to detect slow-moving vehicles. Once targets are found while an E-8 flies behind U.S. lines, Joint STARS directs attacks* by using the Joint Tactical Information Distribution System* (JTIDS). The E-8 expects to find vehicle targets as far as 180 miles behind a front line. The E-8 airplane should be an excellent means to provide global mobility for Joint STARS. Testing of the E-8 should be finished in 1991, and, if successful, plans have been made to build 22 of them. The E-8 was rushed to the Iraq War* in 1991 and did so well that much further testing may not be needed.

Characteristics: *see* C-137.

References. Peter M. Bowers, *Boeing Aircraft since 1916*, 1989. Robert S. Dudney, "The Battle Vision of Joint STARS," *AF*, June 1989, pp. 42–45. Alwyn T. Lloyd, *Boeing 707 and AWACS in Detail & Scale*, 1987. Swanborough, *US Mil. Airc.* Susan H. H. Young, "Gallery of USAF Weapons," *AF*, May 1990, p. 148.

See also Air Force 2000; follow-on forces attack strategy.

Alwyn T. Lloyd

EAGLE. *See* F-15.

EAGLE CLAW. *See* Iran hostage rescue mission.

EAGLES. *See* novels.

EAGLE SQUADRONS

Some Americans volunteered to help Britain in World War II* as some had to help France in World War I's* Lafayette Escadrille.*

Charles Sweeny, a U.S. soldier of fortune, talked to Premier Edouard Daladier of France in November 1939. He proposed a new Lafayette Escadrille to be called the Eagle Flying Corps. The French were uninterested until the German offensive began in the spring of 1940. Sweeny claimed to have recruited 35 Americans who were in Paris when the French government fled the city. Five of them escaped to England and joined the Royal Air Force (RAF) in July 1940. Sweeny decided to switch plans to a U.S. squadron in the RAF and persuaded Britain's Air Council to support his ideas.

Sweeny began recruiting in the United States and found a competitor. The Royal Canadian Air Force (RCAF) had set up the Clayton Knight Committee. Knight was a famous aviation artist. At the time, it was illegal to recruit, but legal to accept, Americans for service in a foreign war. The Knight Committee processed 49,000 applicants and accepted 6,700 from 1941 to 1942, as U.S. authorities did not vigorously enforce the law.

Some Sweeny recruits were assigned to form No. 71 (Eagle) Squadron (RAF) at RAF Church Fenton, England, on 19 September 1940. The squadron went into action in the spring of 1941. A second squadron, No. 121, was formed in May 1941 and began combat operations three months later. A third and last squadron, No. 133, was formed in August and went into battle in October, when the squadrons converted from Hawker Hurricanes to Supermarine Spitfires. The three squadrons were transferred to the USAAF's* 4th Fighter Group in September 1942.

The motivation of the men of the Eagle Squadrons was more adventure than idealism. They created no special problems for the British and performed similarly to other RAF units.

References. Primary: William R. Dunn, *Fighter Pilot: The First American Ace of World War II*, 1982, and "The Ace," *AF*, September 1976, pp. 75–78, 81–82. Secondary: Earl Boebert, "The Eagle Squadrons," *AAHS Journal*, Spring 1964, pp. 3–20. James Saxon Childers, *War Eagles: The Story of the Eagle Squadron*, 1943. Gurney, *5 Down*. John Rawlings, *Fighter Squadrons of the RAF*, 1976.

EAGLESTON, COLONEL GLENN T. (1921–1991)

This ace* was the top-scoring pilot* of the Ninth Air Force* (9th AF) and ranks 19th among USAF* aces of all time with 20.5 victories. He commanded the highest-scoring USAAF* squadron in Europe, the 353rd Fighter Squadron of the 354th Fighter Group.

From Farmington, Utah, Eagleston entered the USAAC* in 1940. He became a pilot* in 1942 from the aviation cadet* program and began combat in December 1943 with the 354th in England. Eagleston was leading that group at 25,000 feet in October 1944 when it was hit by an estimated 100 German Bf 109s. The group had 48 planes. The ensuing dogfight took place from altitude down to the ground and lasted for one-half hour. The group destroyed 23 Bf 109s with the loss of two F-51s* and one pilot. Eagleston had three of the victories. He commanded the 4th Fighter Group in the Korean War* and shot down two MiG-15s.

References. DuPre, *USAF Bio*. Gurney, *5 Down*. Hess, *Aces Album*.

EAKER, GENERAL IRA C. (1896–1987)

Eaker was one of the great pioneers in air power and a founder of the USAF.* He commanded the Eighth Air Force* (8AF) in England during World War II.* Eaker* AFB has been named to honor him. He was inducted into the National Aviation Hall of Fame in Dayton, Ohio, in 1970.

Eaker was born in Field Creek, Texas, and graduated in 1917 from South-eastern Normal School in Oklahoma. He became an officer and pilot* before the Armistice. He joined the Air Staff* in time for Colonel William Mitchell's* court-martial in 1925 and assisted in Mitchell's defense. In the 1920s, Eaker became a good friend of Majors H. H. Arnold* and Carl A. Spaatz* and flew on the *Question Mark.** Eaker earned a degree in journalism from the University of Southern California in 1934 and attended the Air Corps Tactical School* (ACTS). With Arnold he wrote *Winged Warfare* (1941) and *Army Flyer* (1942).

He succeeded Spaatz as commander of the 8AF in 1942 and was in charge when the deep penetration strikes began on the enemy's homeland. Heavy losses were suffered in unescorted, daylight heavy bomber* raids to places like Schweinfurt* and Regensberg. By December 1943, measures had been taken to provide for future fighter escort.* Generals Eisenhower and Spaatz returned to England from the Mediterranean in the same month. They named Major General James H. Doolittle* to command the 8AF and sent Eaker to head the Mediterranean Allied Air Forces, in theory a promotion. Eaker led his air forces through the taking of Rome, the invasion of southern France, the shuttle missions to the USSR, and raids on southern Germany and Ploesti, Romania.*

Eaker became deputy commanding general of the USAAF* early in 1945 when Arnold's health was failing. He held the same post when Spaatz succeeded Arnold and through the legislative battles for and the initial organization of the USAF. He retired in 1947 to become a vice president for the Hughes Tool Company. Later he returned to Washington, D.C., to be active in air power affairs through prolific writing and speaking. He was promoted to general in 1985 while retired.

References. Primary: James Parton, *"Air Force Spoken Here": General Ira Eaker and the Command of the Air*, 1986. Secondary: DeWitt S. Copp, *A Few Great Captains: The Men and Events That Shaped the Development of U.S. Air Power*, 1980. David R. Mets, *Master of Airpower: General Carl A. Spaatz*, 1988.

David R. Mets

EAKER AIR FORCE BASE

This field, near Blytheville, Arkansas, was named for the city after its establishment in 1942. In 1988 it was renamed to honor General Ira C. Eaker.* The base conducted flight training* during World War II.* Advanced and instrument flying* was done through 1943, women transport* pilot* training in 1944, and tactical airlift* combat crew training in 1945. The field was inactivated in 1945. It was reactivated in 1955 with Tactical Air Command* (TAC) B-57s.* In 1958 the base went to the Strategic Air Command* (SAC) for B-52s* and KC-135s (*see* C-135) and in 1990 the 97th Bomb Wing was there.

References. "Guide to Major Air Force Installations Worldwide," *AF*, May 1990, p. 123. Mueller, *AFB*. Roberts, *Dir. USAF*.

EASTERN AIR DEFENSE FORCE

This named air force* was established in 1949 with headquarters at Mitchel* AFB, New York, under the Continental Air Command* (CONAC). Its purpose was the air defense of the continental United States (CONUS). Its headquarters moved to Stewart AFB, New York, in 1950, and it was reassigned to the Air Defense Command (ADC) in 1951. It was inactivated in 1960 when ADC eliminated the air force level of organization within the command.

References. Goldberg, *Hist. USAF*. Ravenstein, *Org. USAF*.

EASTERN TRANSPORT AIR FORCE. *See* Twenty-First Air Force.

EBERLE BOARD

This was a special naval board, headed by Rear Admiral Edward W. Eberle, which studied the effects of aviation on the U.S. Navy. It was convened as a result of Brigadier General William Mitchell's* charges that aviation required a united air service because it would become the primary defense weapon and as a result of naval air enthusiasts' belief that aviation should be developed for a larger role in future naval warfare. In January 1925, it reported to the secretary of the Navy that existing battleship plans were correct. It denied Mitchell's claims and said that aviation had no significant influence on the Navy. The board concluded that a Washington Treaty–type battleship with flak,* and crewed to repair damage, would be secure against sinking by bombs.*

References. Primary: *Eberle Board Hearings* and *Report*, portfolio in National Archives Reference Group 80, File S and C, 111–12. Secondary: Archibald D. Turnbull and Clifford L. Lord, *History of United States Naval Aviation*, 1949.

Lester H. Brune

EC-18B ARIA. *See* C-18.

"EDDIE." See Rickenbacker, Captain Edward V.

EDWARDS AIR FORCE BASE

Near Rosamond, California, Edwards is the home of the USAF* Flight Test Center (AFFTC) and the National Aeronautics and Space Administration's* (NASA) Ames-Dryden Flight Research Facility. It is assigned to the Air Force Systems Command* (AFSC). It was established in 1933 as a bombing and gunnery range and became the Muroc Army Air Base in 1942. During World War II* it provided final training for combat aircrews and the testing of experimental aircraft. In October 1942, a P-59A* took off from Muroc's lake bed and the United States entered the jet age.

On 14 October 1947, Muroc's Captain Charles E. Yeager* made the first supersonic flight in history, flying the X-1* at Mach 1.06. In 1948, Captain Glen W. Edwards lost his life flying the experimental YB-49 (*see* B-35 and B-49), and the base was renamed in his honor in 1949. The AFFTC was formally established in 1951. Since World War II, virtually every aircraft proposed for the USAF has been tested at Edwards. From it the first flights above 100,000, 200,000, and 300,000 feet have been made, as well as the first ones past Mach 1 through 6. It was the landing site for the first winged aerospace vehicle, the shuttle *Columbia*, in 1981.

References. "Guide to Major Air Force Installations Worldwide," *AF*, May 1990, p. 123. Richard P. Hallion, *Test Pilots: The Frontiersmen of Flight*, 1981, and *On the Frontier: Flight Research at Dryden, 1946–1981*, 1984. T. R. Milton, "Airing It Out at Edwards," *AF*, April 1987, pp. 92–97. Mueller, *AFB*.

James O. Young

EGLIN AIR FORCE BASE

Eglin is near the cities of Niceville and Valparaiso, Florida, and is an Air Force Systems Command* (AFSC) base. It was established in 1935 and originally called Valparaiso Bombing and Gunnery Base. It was renamed in 1937 for Lieutenant Colonel Frederick I. Eglin who died in an aircraft accident earlier the same year. In 1942 the field changed from a range to a flight testing base. In 1990 Eglin was, in land area, the largest air base outside the communist bloc. Its area was roughly two-thirds that of Rhode Island. Its main units were the Air Force Munitions System Division, Air Force Armament Laboratory, 33rd Tactical Fighter Wing, and the Tactical Air Warfare Center.

References. "Guide to Major Air Force Installations Worldwide," *AF*, May 1990, p. 123. Mueller, *AFB*. Roberts, *Dir. USAF*.

See also Hurlburt Field.

EIELSON AIR FORCE BASE

This base is 26 miles from Fairbanks, Alaska, and was initially named, in 1943, Mile 26 Satellite Field. It was renamed in 1948 in honor of Colonel Carl B. Eielson, a bush pilot* pioneer and member of the National Guard who died in an airplane crash in 1929. In 1927 Eielson had been the first to fly from Alaska to Spitsbergen, Norway. The field's first important mission was to stage Strategic Air Command* (SAC) bombers* and tankers. In 1980 it received A-10s.* In 1990, it was a Pacific Air Forces* (PACAF) base with the 343rd Tactical Fighter and 6th Strategic Reconnaissance Wings flying A-10s and RC-135s (*see* C-135).

References. "Guide to Major Air Force Installations Worldwide," *AF*, May 1990, p. 123. Mueller, *AFB*. Roberts, *Dir. USAF*.

18 SEPTEMBER 1947. *See* separation from the U.S. Army.

EIGHTEENTH AIR FORCE (18AF)

This numbered air force* was established in 1951 and was first designated as the Eighteenth Air Force (Troop Carrier). That same year the troop carrier term was dropped from its name. It was under the Tactical Air Command* (TAC). The 18AF had a training mission, but it also did airlift operations.* In 1954 it took French paratroops to Indochina for the battle at Dien Bien Phu. In 1955, 40 C-124s* moved a regimental combat team from Fort Campbell, Kentucky, to Japan and returned a team to Fort Bragg, North Carolina. At the time, this was the longest big airlift ever run. In its first five years, the 18AF flew more than 391 million passenger miles and 241 million ton miles. Originally based at Donaldson AFB, South Carolina, it moved to Waco, Texas, in 1957. It was inactivated in 1958.

References. Goldberg, *Hist. USAF*. Ravenstein, *Org. USAF*.

EIGHTH AIR FORCE (8AF)

The 8AF is the most famous of all USAF* air forces* because it spearheaded the USAAF* strategic operations* against Germany in World War II.* This, the USAAF believed at the time, would demonstrate the efficacy of strategic operations.

The organization began as the VIII Bomber Command in January 1942 in the United States. In the spring of 1942 it moved to England and began combat operations in August. It was redesignated as the 8AF in February 1944. Its most famous commanders in England were Major General Ira C. Eaker* (February–December 1943) and Lieutenant General James H. Doolittle* (January 1944–May 1945). Its bombers* were B-17s* and B-24s*

The 8AF did not show conclusively that strategic operations would win a war without the use of land power. A U.S. Strategic Bombing Survey* done after the war either proves or disproves the concept, depending upon the viewpoint of the reader. The supporters say that (1) the 8AF was ordered to digress repeatedly from strategic operations for tactical operations,* (2) 75 percent of its bombs were dropped only after U.S. and British armies were already back on the western part of the continent, (3) its efforts constituted a front in itself, (4) the only possible German answer to the bombing was the self-defeating dispersal, or forced inefficiency, of industry, (5) the German oil and transportation target systems* were destroyed and Germany's collapse soon followed, (6) the dispersal of German industry made its vulnerable transportation system an Achilles heel and guaranteed defeat, and (7) the policy of unconditional surrender prevented a rational and early German suit for peace.

The other view says that strategic operations had a fair test and that (1) the German ball bearing and aircraft industries' target systems* dispersed and remained effective though impaired, (2) success was not possible because of the weather alone, and (3) the Germans did not sue for peace until their armies were annihilated.

The 8AF had a Fighter Command which built up to 15 fighter groups* flying F-47s,* F-51s,* and P-38s.* More than any other organization, the 8AF's long-range fighters achieved air superiority* and credit for smashing the Luftwaffe. The 8AF's fighters destroyed 9,275 German aircraft and produced 261 aces,* far more than any other of the USAAF's air forces. Of these aces, 24 had 15 or more victories.

As the spearhead in the war against Germany, the 8AF received priorities in men, equipment, and publicity. This caused many to call it, in admiration, "The Big League," and others to nickname it, in derision, "The Hollywood Air Force."

The 8th moved to Okinawa,* Ryukyu Islands, in 1945 and to MacDill* Field,

Florida, in 1946 to serve the Strategic Air Command* (SAC). In 1946 it moved to what is now Carswell* AFB, Texas, and in 1955 it moved to Westover AFB, Massachusetts.

The 8AF moved to Andersen* AFB, Guam, in April 1970, and absorbed the headquarters of the 3rd Air Division. The 8AF then conducted B-52* and KC-135 (*see* C-135) operations in the Vietnam War.* In 1972 the Linebacker* I and II operations were performed. B-52 operations in Southeast Asia (SEA) ended in August 1973. In 1975, the 8AF moved to Barksdale* AFB, Louisiana, and absorbed the functions of the Second Air Force* (2AF). In 1990, the 8AF directed the 7th, 12th, and 45th Air Divisions and 12 wings.*

Movies: *Combat America*, 1943; *Memphis Belle*, 1944 and 1990; *Command Decision*, 1948; *Twelve O'Clock High*, 1949.

References. Primary: Curtis E. LeMay, *Mission with LeMay: My Story*, 1965. Secondary: C&C, vols. 2 and 3. Roger A. Freeman, *The Mighty Eighth: Units, Men and Machines*, 1970, *Mighty Eighth War Diary*, 1981, and *Mighty Eighth War Manual*, 1984. Polmar, *SAC*.

See also Eighth Air Force Historical Society.

EIGHTH AIR FORCE HISTORICAL SOCIETY

One million Americans have served in the Eighth Air Force* (8AF), the most people ever associated with a single military unit. Of those, 350,000 served in World War II.* The 8AF suffered half of the USAAF* casualties, 47,000, of whom 26,000 died. Men in the 8AF won 17 Air Force Medals of Honor,* 220 Distinguished Service Crosses (DSC), 850 Silver Stars, 7,000 Purple Hearts, 46,000 Distinguished Flying Crosses (DFC), and 442,300 Air Medals. It is no wonder that the men formed a historical society.

Under the leadership of the late Lieutenant Colonel John H. Woolnough, the 8th AF Clearinghouse was formed to reunite veterans of the 8AF with their units and buddies. The *8th AF NEWS* evolved from the Clearinghouse in 1975. Soon after, a reunion of 8AF veterans was planned, and the planners expanded their interests to a society. The Eighth Air Force Historical Society (8th AFHS) was established on 15 May 1975 and is located at 711 South Smith Avenue, St. Paul, Minnesota 55107. It has continued the *8th AF NEWS*. In 1990 it had 15,000 members.

References. John H. Woolnough, ed., *The First Five Years of the 8th AF NEWS*, 1981, *Stories of the Eighth*, 1983, and *The Second Five Years of the 8th AF NEWS 1980–1984*, 1985.

EISENHOWER, PRESIDENT DWIGHT D. "IKE" (1890–1969)

In his message to Congress on 10 April 1953, Eisenhower, the 34th U.S. president, asked for changes in the management of national defense. Instead of having an individual member of the Joint Chiefs of Staff head a unified command,* Eisenhower chose to have the service secretary head it. Also, the secretary of defense (SECDEF) was given nine assistants. These changes greatly increased the power of the SECDEF and civilian control of the services.

Ike also sought a "new look" in defense and a capacity for the United States to be ready for both a general and a limited war. The latter was called a one-and-one-half-war grand strategy. In addition, Ike wanted the most power at the least cost, expressed as "more bang for the buck." Contrary to popular opinion, nuclear forces are cheaper than conventional. So Ike's policy meant nuclear weapons* were for both general and limited war. For general war, the use of nuclear weapons was called "massive retaliation." Since the USAF* has had, in the main, most of the delivery systems for nuclear weapons, it received higher priority than the other military services in this administration. For example, in 1957 the USAF received about half of the obligational authority.

References. Futrell, *Ideas*, vols. 1 and 2. Goldberg, *Hist. USAF*. Alfred F. Hurley and Robert C. Ehrhart, *Air Power and Warfare*, 1979. Jacob Neufeld, *Ballistic Missiles in the United States Air Force 1945–1960*, 1990. Russell P. Strange, "The Supra-Staffs," *Air University Quarterly Review*, Spring 1955, pp. 118–22.

See also Kennedy, President John F.; Operation Vulture.

ELDORADO CANYON. *See* Libyan raid.

ELECTRONIC COUNTERMEASURES (ECM). *See* electronic warfare.

ELECTRONIC RECONNAISSANCE. *See* electronic warfare.

ELECTRONIC SECURITY COMMAND (ESC)

The ESC is a major command* (MAJCOM) responsible for USAF* electronic warfare* capabilities. This involves disrupting enemy communications and electronics systems, intelligence, and securing the USAF's* operations from enemy electronics interference. The ESC is headquartered at Kelly* AFB, Texas. The original name of the organization was the Air Force Security Group, established in 1948 in Arlington, Virginia. Later in the same year it became a MAJCOM as the USAF Security Service. It moved to Brooks* AFB, Texas, in 1949, and to Kelly in 1953. It was redesignated as the ESC in 1979. In 1990, ESC had three air divisions* in San Antonio, Texas; Ramstein* AB, Germany; and Hickam* AFB, Hawaii. It had two centers* in San Antonio and six wings* in the United States, Germany, and the United Kingdom.

References. "Electronic Security Command," *AF*, May 1990, pp. 74–76. Ravenstein, *Org. USAF*. Roberts, *Dir. USAF*. U.S. Air Force Fact Sheet 87–40, "Electronic Security Command," October 1987.

ELECTRONIC WARFARE

Electronics is beginning to dominate equipment and tactics. Electronic warfare is using electromagnetic means to exploit a military situation or to deny such resources to the enemy. It includes several specialties.

Electronic countermeasures (ECM) are measures to prevent or reduce enemy use of electromagnetic energy. Electronic counter-countermeasures (ECCM) are actions taken to secure the effective use of one's own electromagnetic resources.

Electronic deception includes radiation, reradiation, alternation, absorption, or reflection of electromagnetic means to mislead the enemy. Electronic intelligence is the collection and processing of information about the enemy. Electronic jamming is radiation, reradiation, or reflection with the goal of disrupting enemy electronic devices. Electronic reconnaissance is the pursuit of electronic intelligence.

This form of warfare began with the use of radio in World War I.* It greatly increased in World War II* with radar,* chaff* or "window," jamming, GEE,* identification friend or foe* (IFF), LORAN (long-range navigation), and radio proximity fuses.* There was another large increase in the Vietnam War* when developments included College Eye,* Combat Skyspot,* Igloo White,* some smart bombs, and Wild Weasel.*

Since the Vietnam War, still more emphasis has been placed on electronic warfare. A new aircraft designator, *E*, has come into use with the E-3,* E-4,* and E-8.* Other aircraft heavily using electronics include unmanned aerial vehicles* (UAVs). Computers have advanced far in increased usefulness. Also, sensors have been emphasized in concepts such as the follow-on forces attack* (FOFA) strategy. There is no sign of a slackening in the increased use of electronic warfare.

References. Frank Barnaby, *The Automated Battlefield*, 1986. Christy Campbell, *Weapons of War*, 1983. Richard S. Friedman et al., *Advanced Technology Warfare*, 1985. Ernest J. Gentle and Lawrence W. Reithmaier, eds., *Aviation/Space Dictionary*, 6th ed., 1980. George B. Harrison, "The Electronics of Attrition," *AF*, January 1991, pp. 68–71.

ELEMENT

An element is an informal subunit of USAF* organization able to operate by itself. Principally it has been half of a flight* of fighter* aircraft, or two airplanes in formation: a leader and a wingman, or follower. German Leutnant Werner Moelders and his pilots* devised these tactics in the Spanish Civil War.

The element is a team. Usually the element leader is the attacker and destroyer. This requires concentration on position relative to the enemy and aiming the armament. The wingman performs the vital role of the eyes of the element, watching the situation in the entire sky and informing the leader of any threats. The wingman flies formation loosely enough to stay with the leader and still observe everything. If the flight has broken up, the two aircraft in each element may stop flying in formation. They then maneuver as would a flight of two elements. Experienced fighter pilots fly as flight or element leaders, and novices fly as wingmen.

References. Primary: James P. Coyne, "Twos," *AF*, April 1986, pp. 66–67, 69, 71–72, 75. John E. Johnson, *Full Circle*, 1964. Robert L. Shaw, *Fighter Combat: Tactics and Maneuvering*, 1985. Secondary: Woodford Agee Heflin, ed., *The United States Air Force Dictionary*, 1956. Ravenstein, *Org. USAF*.

ELEVENTH AIR FORCE (11AF)

This numbered air force* began as a named one, the Alaskan Air Force, in January 1942. Only one month later it was redesignated as the 11AF. It defended Alaska during World War II* and conducted the USAAF's* operations in the Aleutians.* It was redesignated the Alaskan Air Command* (AAC) in 1945. A new unit was designated the 11AF in June 1946 and assigned to the Air Defense Command (ADC). Its primary task was U.S. Air Force Reserve* (USAFR) training. In 1948 it was inactivated. In 1990 the 11AF was reactivated, replacing the AAC.

References. C&C, vols. 1 and 4. Brian Garfield, *The Thousand-Mile War: World War II in Alaska and the Aleutians*, 1969. Maurer Maurer, ed., *Air Force Combat Units of World War II*, 1983. Ravenstein, *Org. USAF*.

ELLIS, GENERAL RICHARD H. (1919–1989)

Ellis was commander in chief of the Strategic Air Command* (CINCSAC) and director of the Joint Strategic Planning Staff from 1977 to 1981. His other major assignments included commander of the Allied Air Forces Central Europe (AAFCE) and commander in chief of the U.S. Air Forces in Europe* (CINCUSAFE) from 1975 to 1977 and vice chief of staff of the USAF* from 1973 to 1975.

During World War II,* he served in New Guinea* and the Philippines. A pilot* and later a group* commander, he flew more than 200 combat sorties, including a famous one extending the range of the A-20* for attacks* on Japanese shipping. After the war, he left active service and graduated from the Dickinson School of Law in Carlisle, Pennsylvania. Recalled to active duty in 1950, he served in the Tactical Air Command* (TAC), North Atlantic Treaty Organization* (NATO), Air Staff,* and joint staff duties. He held command positions in Japan, the United States, and Europe.

He became CINCSAC shortly after President Jimmy Carter canceled the B-1* program. Ellis advocated a modernization program including the interim FB-111 (*see* F-111) and the long-term B-2.* In 1982, President Ronald Reagan* appointed him ambassador and commissioner on the U.S.-Soviet Standing Consultative Commission. Ellis worked on arms control matters until his death.

References. Primary: Strategic Air Command, *The Words and Writings of Richard H. Ellis, General, United States Air Force*, 4 vols., 1981. U.S. Air Force Oral History Interview K239.0512–1764, 17–21 August 1987, USAFHRC/OH Maxwell AFB, Alabama. Secondary: C&C, vol. 5. Futrell, *Ideas*, vol. 2. U.S. Air Force Biography, Secretary of the Air Force Office of Information, 1980.

Maurice Maryanow

ELLSWORTH AIR FORCE BASE

This base is near Box Elder, South Dakota, and is the largest Strategic Air Command* (SAC) field. It was established in 1942 and named in 1953 for Brigadier General Richard E. Ellsworth, who had died that year in an RB-36 (*see* B-36) crash. Previously it was named Rapid City and Weaver AFB. During

World War II* the field was used for heavy bomber* training. After the war it was used by bombers, reconnaissance* aircraft, and ballistic missiles.* In 1990 it had the headquarters of the 12th Air Division, 28th Bombardment Wing, 99th Strategic Weapons Wing, and the 44th Strategic Missile Wing. It was equipped with B-1Bs,* B-52Hs,* and Minuteman* IIs.

References. "Guide to Major Air Force Installations Worldwide," *AF*, May 1990, p. 123. Mueller, *AFB*. Roberts, *Dir. USAF*.

ELMENDORF AIR FORCE BASE

This Pacific Air Forces* (PACAF) base is near Anchorage, Alaska. It was established in 1940 and named for Captain Hugh M. Elmendorf, who died in 1933 while flight testing a P-25. In World War II,* it was important to the Eleventh Air Force* (11AF). Since the war, it has primarily been an air defense field. In 1990, it had the headquarters of the Alaskan North American Aerospace Defense Command (NORAD) Region, the 21st Tactical Fighter Wing, 11th Tactical Control Wing, and 1931st Communications Wing. Its aircraft were F-15s,* C-12s, and C-130s.*

References. "Guide to Major Air Force Installations Worldwide," *AF*, May 1990, p. 123. Mueller, *AFB*. Roberts, *Dir. USAF*.

EMMONS, LIEUTENANT GENERAL DELOS C. "LUCKY" (1888–1965)

Emmons is important for his contributions to the USAF* in its formative years. Born in Huntington, West Virginia, he became an officer of Infantry in 1909 following graduation from the U.S. Military Academy (USMA). In 1916 he was assigned to the Aviation Section of the U.S. Army Signal Corps* for pilot* training. After several assignments he was appointed in 1927 as executive officer in the Office of the Chief of the Air Corps. The next year he became executive officer for the assistant secretary of war for air* until 1931. In 1936 he was assigned to March* Field, California, as commander of the First Wing; in 1939 he was made commanding general of the General Headquarters Air Force* (GHQ Air Force) at Langley* Field, Virginia. In 1941 he became chief of the Air Force Combat Command.* He retired in 1948.

References. Air Force Pamphlet 31–1, "Roster of USAF Retired General Officers," 1987. *Biographical Study of USAF General Officers 1917–1952*, vol. 1, n.d. DeWitt S. Copp, *A Few Great Captains: The Men and Events That Shaped the Development of U.S. Air Power*, 1980. DuPre, *USAF Bio*. Maurer, *Avn. in Army*.

Steven K. Yates

ENEMY AIRCRAFT

Enemy aircraft are commonly referred to, for clarity in air defense control shorthand language, as *bandits*; by national origin, *Germans*; by type, *Zeroes*; or, in combat reports, as *e/a*.

In World War I,* Americans fought against imperial German aircraft, especially Albatross Models D-III and D-Va and the Fokker D-VII, arguably the best fighter* of the war.

During World War II,* the USAAF* flew against a wide variety of German Luftwaffe aircraft. In western Europe this meant Messerschmitt Bf 109s; Focke Wulf Fw 190s and the "long nose" variant, Ta 152s; and Messerschmitt Me 262 jet fighters, nicknamed "Schwalbe" or "Swallow." In the Mediterranean area, Americans also faced the Italian Regia Aeronautica's Macchi C.202 Folgore.

In the Pacific, the imperial Japanese navy fielded various types of Mitsubishi A6M2 Reisen Zero-sen fighters with the Allied name of "Zeke." By late 1943 there was the Kawanishi N1K15 Shiden, or "George," and its 1944 variant N1K2 Shiden-Kai, as well as the Mitsubishi J2M3 Raiden, or "Jack." The Mitsubishi G4M Type 1 Attack Bomber Hamaki, or "Cigar," was a long-range bomber* used from the Aleutians to Australia. Its official Allied name was "Betty," but its vulnerable fuel tanks earned it the nickname "Flying Lighter." Effective early in the war, it was the most used Japanese bomber. The imperial Japanese army air arm early depended upon the Nakajima Ki–43–1 Hayabusa, called "Oscar." In 1943 came the Kawasaki Ki–61–1 Hein, or "Tony"; the Nakajima Ki–84 Hayate, or "Frank"; and the Nakajima Ki–44 Shoki, or "Tojo" fighters.

In the Korean War,* the pilots* of the North Korean and Red Chinese armies flew Soviet-designed aircraft. In 1950 to 1952 the North Koreans used old planes like the Ilyushin Il–10 configured as a fighter and the Yakolev Yak–9. In November 1950 the Chinese committed the modern Mikoyan-Gurevich MiG-15, called "Fagot" by the West, and sometimes flown by Soviet pilots. It intercepted United Nations (UN) planes and ushered in jet combat. From Manchurian sanctuaries north of the Yalu River, part of political air superiority,* high-flying MiGs challenged the UN fliers. After hard fighting, the U.S. F-86s* defeated the MiGs with a 10-to-1 kill ratio.

The Vietnam War* was again primarily a jet war with the North Vietnamese army using the Mikoyan-Gurevich MiG-21 "Fishbed" as its first line of defense, supplemented at lower altitudes with older MiG-15s and MiG-17 "Frescoes." In the Iraq War* of 1991 air superiority* was gained in hours by the USAF,* and enemy aircraft had no significant role in the conflict.

References. Enzo Angelucci, *The Rand McNally Encyclopedia of Military Aircraft, 1914–1980*, 1980. J. M. Bruce, *War Planes of the First World War*, 3 vols., 1965–1969. C&C, vols. 1–5. René J. Francillon, *Japanese Aircraft of the Pacific War*, 1979. Peter Gray and Owen Thetford, *German Aircraft of the First World War*, 1962.

Ronald W. Yoshino

ENGINEERING AND SERVICES CENTER. *See* Air Force Engineering and Services Center.

ENGLAND AIR FORCE BASE

This Tactical Air Command* (TAC) base was begun in 1941 near Alexandria, Louisiana. It was known as Alexandria until 1955, when it was named in honor of Lieutenant Colonel John B. England. A World War II* ace* with 19 victories,

England was killed in 1954 in an F-86* in France when he turned to avoid a barracks area while landing in fog. He had been a commander of the 389th Fighter Bomber Squadron, a unit once stationed at Alexandria. From its activation in 1943 until 1946, the field was used for B-17* and B-29* training. In 1946 TAC inactivated the base, and civilians used it until 1950. It was then used by the Air National Guard* (ANG). The USAF* returned in 1953. In 1990, England was the home of the 23rd Tactical Fighter Wing flying A-10s.*

References. "Guide to Major Air Force Installations Worldwide," *AF*, May 1990, p. 123. Mueller, *AFB*. Official USAF History, England AFB, 1989. Roberts, *Dir. USAF*.

David L. Rosmer

ENOLA GAY. *See* movies; Tibbets, Brigadier General Paul W., Jr.

EVEREST, BRIGADIER GENERAL FRANK K., JR., "PETE" (1920–   )

Everest is famous for his test pilot* work, especially with the X-2.* Retired from the USAF,* Everest was inducted into the National Aviation Hall of Fame in Dayton, Ohio, in 1989.

From Fairmont, West Virginia, he entered the USAAF* as an aviation cadet* in 1942. He flew an operational tour in the Mediterranean area and shot down two German aircraft. In 1944 he was commander of a fighter* squadron* in China, where he scored four victories over Japanese aircraft. He was shot down and became a prisoner of war in May 1945. After World War II* he became a test pilot at Edwards* AFB. Besides the X-2, Everest flew the XF-92, X-1,* X-3, X-4, X-5,* and XB-52 (*see* B-52). He set a world's speed record of 755 miles per hour flying a YF-100 (*see* F-100) in 1953. Piloting an X-2 he attained 1,957 miles per hour, an unofficial record, and was then called "the fastest man alive."

References. Primary: Frank K. Everest, Jr., *The Fastest Man Alive*, 1958. Secondary: DuPre, *USAF Bio*.

EXECUTIVE ORDER 9877, 26 JULY 1947

This document completed the administrative actions needed to unify the armed forces and to establish the USAF.*

President Harry S Truman* (HST) wanted the U.S. Army and Navy to agree on unification in 1946. The details were worked on by Major General Lauris Norstad,* USAAF* director of plans and operations, and Admiral Forrest Sherman, deputy chief of naval operations, under the guidance of Secretary of War Robert P. Patterson and Secretary of the Navy James V. Forrestal. Norstad and Sherman's work spelled out service roles and missions and arrangements for joint commands in Europe and the Far East.

On 16 January 1947, Patterson and Forrestal gave HST agreements for legislation and for a draft executive order on roles and missions. In the opinion of General of the Army Dwight D. Eisenhower,* as Army chief of staff, and General Carl A. Spaatz,* commanding general of the USAAF, the legislation needed to state principles and not roles and missions—hence the need for two actions, legislation and executive order.

The proposed legislation became the National Security Act of 1947.* It went into effect on 26 July 1947, and HST concurrently issued Executive Order 9877. The order included provisions for air superiority,* strategic and tactical operations,* airlift operations,* air defense, and assistance to the Army and Navy.

References. Goldberg, *Hist. USAF.* Herman S. Wolk, "The Birth of the US Air Force" *AF*, September 1977, pp. 68–72, 75–78, and "The Establishment of the United States Air Force," *AF*, September 1982, pp. 76–80, 83–84, 87.

EXPLORER I **AND** *II*. *See* lighter-than-air.

EXTENDER. *See* C-10A.

F

F-4 PHANTOM II

The F-4 dominated the USAF's* fighter* forces for two decades, the 1960s and 1970s. It was the USAF's primary air superiority* fighter of the Vietnam War.* The F-4 was also noteworthy as a U.S. Navy aircraft the USAF was ordered to buy.

It began in 1953 as a proposed Navy attack* plane, the McDonnell Aircraft Corporation's AH-1. In 1955 the proposal changed to an interceptor,* the F4H-1 Phantom II. Its first flight was in 1958 and production began in 1959. The F-4 soon set 21 world records, including a speed of Mach 2.57, or 1,606 miles per hour.

Secretary of Defense (SECDEF) Robert S. McNamara* believed that weapon costs could be substantially cut by reducing specialization. Common aircraft between the services and multipurpose planes would help gain this goal, and the USAF was ordered to buy the Phantom II. The nature of the plane made this decision fairly amenable to the USAF. It was a heavy, multiengine aircraft that was not out of line with USAF tradition, and it had remarkable performance for these characteristics.

The USAF first designated it as the F-110A and YRF-110A. In line with McNamara's wishes, the USAF and Navy adopted a single designation system in 1962, and the Phantom II became the F-4. The Navy used F-4As and F-4Bs while the USAF had F-4Cs and RF-4Cs, which had only minor changes from the As and Bs.

The F-4C entered USAF service in 1963; the RF-4C entered service in 1965. The addition of armament computers resulted in the F-4D. The F-4C went to the Vietnam War, and its first victories were two MiG-17s shot down with AIM-9s* in 1965. Battle experience showed a need for guns. Mounting the guns externally reduced the F-4's performance so much that the F-4E was developed with an internal M-61A1* gun. Battle also revealed other flaws. The F-4, a big target, was vulnerable to flak.* Visibility was poor from the rear cockpit, and its engines gave out much black smoke, making it highly visible to the enemy. The final version was the F-4G, a Wild Weasel* aircraft. The USAF bought 2,640 F-4s. Besides the Navy, the F-4 was used by 11 foreign countries. Production ended in 1981 after 5,057 F-4s had been built.

In battle, USAF F-4s destroyed 107.5 enemy aircraft consisting of 33.5 obsolete MiG-17s, 8 obsolescent MiG-19s, and 66 modern MiG-21s. Up to 1 January 1972, F-4 losses were 362. Most were lost to ground fire. The heavy, multipurpose-type fighter had again been a disappointment in aerial combat, and the USAF started work on the F-15* to replace the F-4 in the air superiority task.

Popular with its pilots, the F-4's nicknames in the USAF were "Double Ugly," "Old Smokey," "Rhino," and "St. Louis Slugger." In 1990 the USAF, the U.S. Air Force Reserve* (USAFR), and the Air National Guard* (ANG) still had hundreds of F-4s in service, primarily for the attack role. Some participated in the Philippines incident of 1989,* and F-4Gs and RF-4Cs were used in the Iraq War* of 1991.

Characteristics (F-4E): engines, two General Electric J79-GE-17A turbojets of 17,900 pounds thrust each in afterburner; span, 39 feet; length, 63 feet; height, 16 feet; gross weight, 61,795 pounds; top speed at 40,000 feet, around Mach 2.0; range with military load, 700 miles; external stores, 16,000 pounds.

References. Primary: Henry E. Bielinski, "The F-4E—A Pilot's View," *AF*, November 1972, pp. 34–39. Higham, *Combat Airc.*, vol. 2. Secondary: Knaack, *US Airc.*, vol. 1. Swanborough, *US Mil. Airc.* Wagner, *Am. Planes*. Susan H. H. Young, "Gallery of USAF Weapons," *AF*, May 1990, pp. 142–43.

F-5 FREEDOM FIGHTER

The F-5 was built by the Northrop Aircraft Corporation to be a lightweight and economical fighter.* It had single- and two-seat versions. It played an important role in USAF* training and in allowing many nations to develop modern air forces and ease the transition to new-generation fighters. A related design was the T-38.*

The F-5's maiden flight was in 1959, and that was the start of a line of fighters that would be built into the 1980s. Early USAF versions were the F-5A, nicknamed "Tiger," the F-5B trainer, and the RF-5A for reconnaissance.*

The USAF used a squadron* of F-5s in 1965 for evaluation in the Vietnam War* under the Skoshi** Tiger program. It was found to be capable of high sortie rates with solid combat effectiveness. However, because of the plane's low payload and short range, the USAF did not buy the F-5 for its multipurpose fighter forces. The tests did show the F-5 would be ideal for nations with small force needs.

In 1970 the F-5E Tiger II won the competition for the International Fighter Aircraft (IFA). The IFA was to replace earlier F-5s. The entire F-5 series was one of the most successful export fighter programs, because it sold to 31 countries. The F-5 had a low price often subsidized by the Military Assistance

Program* (MAP) and easy maintenance, and training was provided by the USAF at Williams* AFB, Arizona.

The USAF used F-5Es and F-5F trainers for dissimilar aerial combat tactics* (DACT) for itself and for other air forces. F-5 Aggressor squadrons were placed with the Pacific Air Forces* (PACAF), the Tactical Air Command* (TAC), and the U.S. Air Forces in Europe* (USAFE). The F-5 was an excellent simulator of the USSR's export MiG-21. In 1988 the F-16* began to replace the F-5 in this role. The F-5s had served superbly, but Soviet aircraft had improved greatly and the F-5 no longer matched their performance. Also, the F-5 was developing structural problems from the long years of hard use in mock combat.

Characteristics (F-5E): engines, two General Electric J85-GE-21B turbojets of 5,000 pounds thrust each in afterburner; span, 27 feet; length, 47 feet; height, 13 feet; gross weight, 24,722 pounds; top speed, Mach 1.64; service ceiling, 51,800 feet; combat radius, 656 miles; external stores, 7,000 pounds.

References. Primary: Higham, *Combat Airc.*, vol. 2. Secondary: *Jane's All the World's Aircraft*, 1971–72, 1974–75, and 1983–84. John W. R. Taylor, ed., *Combat Aircraft of the World*, 1969.

See also Red Flag.

**This Japanese is misspelled and misinterpreted. The Americans intended it to mean "little."

George W. Hawks, Jr.

F-15 EAGLE

The McDonnell Aircraft Corporation's F-15 was selected in 1969 to be the USAF's* air superiority* fighter.* The F-15 had an advantage over most fighters until the late 1970s when aircraft such as the MiG-29 Fulcrum were fielded.

The F-15A through F-15D have a large doppler radar,* a large thrust-to-weight ratio, and high maneuverability. These features allow long-range detection of adversaries and great capability in a dogfight. The *A* and *C* models are single-seat, and the *B* and *D* are two-seat. Each can carry four AIM-7s,* four AIM-9s,* and an internal M-61A1* gun. They also have an excellent attack* capability, but this was not exploited until emphasis was placed on the Rapid Deployment Joint Task Force (RDJTF) during the Carter administration from 1977 to 1980.

The F-15E was developed primarily as a two-seat attack plane, a replacement for, or complement of, the F-111* in long-range interdiction. It entered service in 1988. It uses the Low-Altitude Navigation and Targeting Infrared System for Night* (LANTIRN) with radar to attack targets at night and under overcasts. The F-15E can carry all the air superiority weapons of other F-15s. F-15s performed well for the USAF in the Iraq War* of 1991. F-15 nicknames are "Aluminum Overcast," "Big Bird," "Great Bird Rodan," and "Tennis Court" (for its big size).

The F-15 has been exported to three countries. It was flown in battle during the 1982 Israeli invasion of Lebanon, and Tsvah Hagana Le Israel/Heyl Ha'Avir

(Israeli air force) F-15s contributed to shooting down more than 100 Syrian aircraft without any losses.

Characteristics (F-15C): engines, two Pratt & Whitney F100-PW-100 turbofans of 23,830 pounds thrust each in afterburner; span, 43 feet; length, 64 feet; height, 18 feet; gross weight, 68,000 pounds; top speed, 1,650 miles per hour above 36,000 feet; service ceiling, over 60,000 feet; range, over 3,000 miles with no weapons; external stores, 24,500 pounds.

References. Primary: Higham, *Combat Airc.*, vol. 3. Steve Ritchie, "An Eagle for All Arenas," *AF*, November 1983, pp. 43–49. Secondary: Jeff Ethel, *F-15 Eagle*, 1981. *Jane's All the World's Aircraft*, 1988–89. Lon O. Nordeen, Jr., *Air Warfare in the Missile Age*, 1985.

George W. Hawks, Jr.

F-16 FIGHTING FALCON

This aircraft is the USAF's* current hope for the air superiority* task, and it has been adapted for air defense and attack.*

Because of the disappointing results for the USAF of the air superiority battles of the Vietnam War,* a Request for Proposals (RFP) was made in January 1972 for a Lightweight Fighter (LWF) program to replace the heavy F-4.* The General Dynamics Corporation's Model 401, or YF-16, won a competition against The Boeing Company's 908–909, Lockheed Corporation's CL-1200 Lancer, Northrop Corporation's YF-17, and Vought Corporation's Model V-1100. The first flight was in 1974, when it was called the Air Combat Fighter (ACF) instead of LWF.

A popular design, it was soon selected by other nations to replace their aged F-104s.* Active service in the USAF began in 1979. By 1988 there had been many improvements to it, including the Multinational Staged Improvement Program (MSIP), use of two different engines, better avionics, new missiles, and the Low-Altitude Navigation and Targeting Infrared System for Night* (LANTIRN). A version called Agile Falcon, or MSIP IV, is in development. The planned total buy by the USAF was 2,609. More than 1,100 are to be used by 16 other countries and the U.S. Navy. In 1990, the USAF's attack variant was to be designated A-16 and was to replace the A-10.* The F-16 saw action in the Iraq War.* The F-16's nicknames are "Electric Jet," "Lawn Dart," "Little Hummer," and "Viper."

Characteristics (F-16C): engine, General Electric F110-GE-100 or Pratt & Whitney F100-PW-220 turbofan with 29,000 pounds thrust in afterburner; span, 33 feet; length, 49 feet; height, 17 feet; gross weight, 37,500 pounds; top speed, over Mach 2 at 40,000 feet; service ceiling, above 50,000 feet; radius of action, more than 575 miles; external stores, 12,000 pounds.

References. Primary: Wayne C. Edwards, "The F-16: Not Like Any Other," *AF*, August 1980, pp. 34–39. Don McMonagle, "Pilot Report: AFTI/F-16," *AF*, April 1985, pp. 68–73. Secondary: Swanborough, *US Mil. Airc.* John Wegg, *General Dynamics*

Aircraft and Their Predecessors, 1990. Susan H. H. Young, "Gallery of USAF Weapons," *AF*, May 1990, pp. 143–44.

See also General Electric Company engines; Pratt & Whitney engines.

F-22. *See* Advanced Tactical Fighter.

F-23. *See* Advanced Tactical Fighter.

F-47 THUNDERBOLT

The F-47 made a significant contribution to the downfall of the Luftwaffe, the destruction of the German transportation target system,* and the defeat of the German and Japanese armies. More F-47s were built, 15,579, than any other USAAF* fighter,* and this is an indicator of its value. F-47 groups* were never less than 40 percent of the total fighter groups overseas in 1944 and 1945, another indicator.

Early developments in World War II* showed the USAAC* leaders that their disdain for and neglect of air superiority* fighters had been a terrible error. A crash effort was made to get a satisfactory fighter, and the USAAC found it in the Thunderbolt. At a conference in June 1940 where the USAAC's needs were explained, the chief designer of the Republic Aviation Corporation, Alexander "Sasha" Kartveli, began work on the F-47, originally P-47, on the back of an envelope. The F-47's design concepts began with Kartveli's P-35,* developed by the Seversky Aircraft Corporation under the leadership of Major Alexander P. de Seversky.* The first flight of the F-47 was in 1941. The keys to its success were its engine, a turbosupercharger, and rugged structure.

It entered active service in 1942 and began combat in May 1943 operating from England in the Eighth Air Force* (8AF). Its use spread to the Pacific war and to the Fifteenth Air Force* (15AF) in Italy. The Royal Air Force (RAF) and the USSR were given hundreds. Production ended in 1945. In World War II, USAAF F-47s flew 545,575 sorties and shot down 3,752 enemy aircraft,* with a loss of 824 in aerial battles. Its record was a victory rate of 4.6 to 1, an air superiority fighter indeed. Thunderbolts also destroyed or damaged 9,000 locomotives, 86,000 pieces of rolling stock, 68,000 trucks, 6,000 tanks and armored cars, and 60,000 horse-drawn vehicles. Its overall loss rate was a very low 0.7 percent.

After the war, a few F-47s went to the Air National Guard* (ANG) and the air forces of small nations. After the Korean War* started, the USAF* federalized some ANG F-47s back into service in the continental United States (CONUS), but they were soon retired as more jet fighters were produced. The F-47 influenced successor designs: F-84,* F-105,* and A-10.* Loved by its pilots, the F-47 had many nicknames: "Big Ugly," "Bucket of Bolts," "Cast Iron Beast," "Jug," "Repulsive Scatterbolt," "Seven-Ton Milk Bottle," "T-bolt," and "Thunder Mug." Jug was from "Little Brown Jug" and not from "juggernaut." The F-47 even caused a nickname to be given to its builder: the "Republic Locomotive Works and Iron Foundry."

Characteristics (F-47N): engine, Pratt & Whitney R-2800–77 of 2,800 horsepower; span, 43 feet; length, 36 feet; height, 15 feet; gross weight, 20,700 pounds; top speed, 467 miles per hour at 32,500 feet; service ceiling, 43,000 feet; range, 800 miles; ordnance, 2,000 pounds.

Movie: *Thunderbolt*, 1945.

References. Primary: William R. Dunn, "P-47—The Beautiful Beast," *AF*, September 1975, pp. 91–94, 97–98. Higham, *Combat Airc.*, vols. 2 and 3. Secondary: William Green, *Famous Fighters of the Second World War*, 1957. Len Morgan, *The P-47 Thunderbolt*, 1963. Swanborough, *US Mil. Airc.*

F-51 MUSTANG

This airplane is generally regarded as the best piston-engined air superiority* fighter* of World War II.*

In April 1940, Britain asked North American Aviation, Inc., to produce P-40s* for it. The company made a counterproposal of an improved design, and a first flight was quickly made in October 1940. Production aircraft delivery began in April 1941, and combat operations with the Royal Air Force (RAF) began in May 1942. Production for the USAAF* began in July 1942 as the P-51 Apache. Up to this time the airplane had an Allison engine. In the summer of 1942, it was proposed that the new Rolls Royce Merlin 65 engine be used. The adopted version, the P-51B Mustang, made its first flight in May 1943. A fuel tank was added behind the cockpit, which badly unbalanced the plane. However, that tank, together with two external drop tanks,* gave the P-51B the ability to fly deep into German airspace. The plane began operations in December 1943 and soon was a principal participant in the early 1944 air battles that defeated the Luftwaffe over Germany. Further improvements resulted in the P-51D, the main version.

This superb fighter was used extensively in western Europe, Italy, East Asia, and the Pacific. From Iwo Jima, the P-51s could operate over Japan. In Europe, from 1942 to 1945, P-51s scored 4,950 aerial victories and destroyed 4,131 aircraft on the ground while suffering 2,520 lost in battle. Variants in World War II were A-36 attack* and F-6 reconnaissance* aircraft. The A-36 saw combat in Sicily and Italy. After the war, P-51s and F-6s, redesignated F-51 and RF-51, continued to serve in the USAF.* The plane went back into combat in the Korean War* in an attack role.

Production totaled 14,490 of one of the most beloved fighters ever built. Nicknames for it were "Peter-Dash-Flash," "Spam Can," and " 'Stang." The affection and high performance has kept about 200 flying in civilian hands. It has become the dominant air racer since its military service ended.

Characteristics (F-51D): engine, Packard Merlin V-1650–7 of 1,300 horsepower; span, 37 feet; length, 32 feet; height, 12 feet; gross weight, 11,600 pounds; top speed, 437 miles per hour at 25,000 feet; service ceiling, 41,900 feet; range, 950 miles; ordnance, 2,000 pounds.

References. Primary: Higham, *Combat Airc.*, vol. 2. Secondary: Robert C. Burkholder, "New Thoughts on the Old Mustang," *AF*, June 1972, pp. 66–68. Jeffrey Ethell,

Mustang: A Documentary History of the P-51, 1981. Len Morgan, *The P-51 Mustang*, 1963. Swanborough, *US Mil. Airc*. Wagner, *Am. Planes*.
  See also F-82.

F-80 SHOOTING STAR, T-33, AND F-94 STARFIRE

The F-80 was a remarkable aircraft. It was the USAAF's* first operational jet fighter,* was transformed into the first effective jet trainer and then into an interceptor,* and caused the founding of the Lockheed Aircraft Corporation's famous "Skunk Works" development team.

In 1943, the USAAF was gravely concerned about intelligence reports on German jet fighters, especially since the first U.S. attempt at one, the P-59,* had been inadequate. Clarence L. "Kelly" Johnson of Lockheed proposed to develop the XP-80 in 180 days, using the Skunk Works concept of protecting engineers and craftsmen from military and company interference in their design and work. The prototype XP-80 was ready for testing within 139 days from the time work began on it. The first flight was in January 1944. With a new engine, production began in 1945 but the plane did not see combat in World War II.*

F-80s did see much service in the Korean War.* An F-80 destroyed a MiG-15 in November 1950. This is believed to be the first air battle between jet fighters in which one was shot down. By this time, however, the F-80 was obsolete as an air superiority* fighter. It shot down 37 enemy aircraft,* including six MiG-15s, but six were also lost to MiG-15s. It served primarily in attack* and reconnaissance* roles in the war. It flew 98,515 sorties. Aside from aerial battle, 366 were lost. F-80s flew 37 percent of fighter sorties, but its losses were 25 percent. Its monthly sortie rate was 28.5. For comparison, the F-51's* was 25.5, the F-84's* and F-86's* were 25, and the B-26 Invader's* was only 17. The F-80 ended active service in 1955 after 1,731 of all types had been accepted. The F-80's variants included the RF-80, or FP-80 and F-14, for reconnaissance; the T-33, or TF-80C and RT-33, for training; QF-80 drones and DF-80 directors; and the F-94 Starfire interceptor.*

The T-33 proved to be the main aircraft of the series. In 1947 Lockheed stretched an F-80C's fuselage for a second cockpit. The T-33 proved to be a wonderful trainer. Lockheed built 5,691 of them over 11 years, Canadair built 656 and called them CL-30 Silver Stars, and Kawasaki of Japan built 210. Of the Lockheed-built aircraft, 699 went to the U.S. Navy and 1,058 to the Military Assistance Program* (MAP). The T-33 probably has been flown by more military pilots* in the free world than any other aircraft. The T-33 left active service in the USAF* in 1988; it had been used for a remarkable 41 years. The reliable T-33 was a favorite among pilots. Its nicknames were "Lockheed Racer," "T-Bag," and "T-Bird."

The identical airplane that had been stretched from an F-80C into a T-33 was modified again in 1949 to become the first F-94 Starfire. It was a radar- and afterburner-equipped interceptor originally designated as the F-97A. Production began in 1949, and active service began in 1950. Beginning in 1951, F-94s served in the Korean War. F-94s were used to protect B-29s* in battle. In the presence of F-94s the enemy usually abandoned its efforts. The Starfires claimed four victories with one lost to enemy action. A total of 28 F-94s were lost between January 1952 and the end of the war. The USAF retired them in 1959, and they served another year in the Air National Guard* (ANG). A total of 854 were built for the USAF.

Characteristics (T-33): engine, General Electric J33-A-35 turbojet of 4,600 pounds thrust; span, 39 feet; length, 38 feet; height, 11 feet; gross weight, 11,965 pounds; top speed, 543 miles per hour at 25,000 feet; service ceiling, 47,500 feet; endurance, over three hours.

References. Primary: Douglas C. Conley, "USAF Series T-33A Aircraft," *AH*, September 1977, pp. 168–72. Higham, *Combat Airc.*, vols. 1 and 2. Secondary: Rhodes Arnold, *Shooting Star T-Bird & Starfire: A Famous Lockheed Family*, 1981. Knaack, *U.S. Airc.*, vol. 1. Swanborough, *US Mil. Airc.* E. T. Wooldridge, Jr., *The P-80 Shooting Star: Evolution of a Jet Fighter*, 1979.

F-82 TWIN MUSTANG

Without question, the F-82 was the most unusual Mustang variant. Developed by North American Aviation, Inc., as a very long range fighter escort* for the Pacific area, it had two engines, two pilots, and a large fuel capacity. Originally it had two standard F-51* fuselages, the right and left wing panels joined by a new center section and tailplane. The F-82 was the last piston-engined fighter* produced in quantity for the USAF.*

In 1946 the USAAF* ordered 250 Twin Mustangs, of which 100 would be P-82E escorts and 150 would be P-82F and P-82G interceptors.* Though based on the original F-51, these were, in truth, entirely new airplanes. Instead of using a pair of F-51 fuselages and outer wing sections as planned, the P-82 was six feet longer and incorporated new technological changes. They became F-82s in 1948. An F-82G, flown by Lieutenant William G. Hudson, scored the first aerial victory during the Korean War.* In this same engagement fellow pilots* scored two other victories, all without loss.

Characteristics (F-82G): engines, two Allison V-1710–143/145 of 1,600 horsepower each; span, 52 feet; length, 42 feet; height, 14 feet; gross weight, 25,891 pounds; top speed, 461 miles per hour at 21,000 feet; service ceiling, 38,900 feet; range, 2,240 miles; ordnance, 2,000 pounds.

References. Primary: "Air War over Korea 1950–53," a special issue of *Air Classics*, 1980, pp. 48–55. Secondary: Jeffrey L. Ethell et al., *The Great Book of World War II Airplanes*, 1984. Knaack, *U.S. Airc.*, vol. 1. Swanborough, *US Mil. Airc.*

Joe M. Jackson

F-84 THUNDERJET, THUNDERSTREAK, AND THUNDERFLASH

The F-84 did much to pioneer the operation of jet fighters* in the USAF.* It was a leader in developing jet attack* operations, fighter aerial refueling,* fighter nuclear weapons* delivery, zero launch,* and parasite fighters. It was probably the airplane most experimented with in USAF history.

The Republic Aviation Corporation needed to apply the jet engine to a successor to its F-47,* and design work began in 1944. The ideas were for a basically state-of-the-art design for piston-engined fighters including a straight wing, concepts which were to limit badly the plane's performance. The USAAF* ordered production in 1945, and the first flight took place in 1946. It set a U.S. speed record of 611 miles per hour the same year. Active service of the F-84 Thunderjet began in 1947. F-84s went into combat in the Korean War.* At first they were assigned as fighter escort* to protect B-29s* from MiG-15s. The MiG proved so superior to the F-84 in battle that the Thunderjet had to be relegated to the attack role. The F-84s were the main effort in the great strikes in 1953 on the Korean irrigation dams target system.* F-84s flew 86,400 sorties in the war, dropping 55,987 tons of bombs. There were 122 lost to flak.*

In 1950 the development of F-84 nuclear weapon delivery systems was begun, and the airplane became the first fighter with that ability in 1952. The F-84 also pioneered aerial refueling methods for fighters and was the first fighter to make long transoceanic flights by that means. A total of 4,457 straight-wing F-84 Thunderjets were built, with 2,036 going to U.S. allies.

In 1949, Republic started to improve the F-84 by adopting a swept wing. The first flight, under the designation YF-96A, was in 1950. The USAF asked that it be re-engined and changed the designation to F-84F Thunderstreak. Active service began in 1954. A total of 2,711 were made, of which 1,301 went to North Atlantic Treaty Organization* (NATO) air forces. The General Motors Corporation built 599 F-84Fs. A variant was the RF-84F Thunderflash, which first flew in 1952. Production of the RF-84F was 718, of which 386 were given to other air forces. Other variants were the JF-84F as a tanker* for RF-84Fs and the XF-84H, or XF-106, which used a turboprop engine.

In 1953, 25 RF-84Fs were modified with a retractable hook so they could be suspended on a trapeze beneath B-36* bomb bays as a parasite. This was called the fighter conveyor* (FICON) project. The 25 were designated first as GRF-84Fs and then as RF-84Ks. F-84Bs, redesignated EF-84Bs, were experiments for another form of parasite fighter escort, being attached to the wingtips of an EB-29A in project Tom-Tom.* F-84s were nicknamed ''Ground-Loving Whore,'' ''Hog,'' ''Lead Sled,'' ''Lieutenant Eater,'' and ''Mechanics' Nightmare.'' The F-84Fs were also called ''Super Hog.''

Characteristics (F-84G): engine, Allison J35-A-29 turbojet with 5,600 pounds thrust; span, 36 feet; length, 38 feet; height, 13 feet; gross weight, 23,525 pounds; top speed, 622 miles per hour; service ceiling, 40,500 feet; range, 2,000 miles; ordnance, 2,000 pounds.

References. Primary: Higham, *Combat Airc.*, vols. 1 and 2. Secondary: ''Air War over Korea 1950–1953,'' a special issue of *Air Classics*, 1980, pp. 8–9, 86–97. T. E. Baines, ''The 'Hog[F-84F]': A USAF Fighter That Never Fought,'' *AH*, September 1972, pp. 132–36. Futrell, *USAF in Korea.* Swanborough, *US Mil. Airc.*

F-85. *See* fighter conveyor.

F-86 SABRE

The F-86 has a secure place in U.S. history. Before the Korean War* the Americans and British believed they had the best jet fighters* in the world. When war broke out they soon learned, in dismay and panic, that the Soviet MiG-15 was greatly superior to their vaunted F-80s,* F-84s,* U.S. Navy fighters, and Gloster Meteors. Only the F-86 could stand up to the MiG-15 when the communists tried to seize air superiority* in Korea. Without the F-86, events in Korea would have been drastically and unfavorably different. It is even possible the war would have been lost quickly. It is fitting that this great airplane, the Sabre, was beautiful and flew so well it has been called the best pilot's* airplane ever.

The F-86 began as North American Aviation, Inc.'s design NA-140 in 1945, designated the XP-86. Like the F-84 it started as a piston-engine era–type design with a straight wing for a jet-engined craft. Wind tunnel tests showed this design would fly slower than the F-84. These results occasioned a review of captured German aerodynamics research that included wind tunnel reports on a proposed swept-wing version of the Messerschmitt Me 262. A new Sabre design using the German wing was developed, and the first flight was in 1947. An F-86 flew faster than Mach 1 in 1948, the first U.S. fighter to do so.

The F-86 entered service in 1949. The F-86E was produced in 1950 and was the first with a "flying tail," a radical new power-driven system that moved the entire horizontal surface and was a key to the F-86's battle successes. The F-86A was rushed into action in Korea in December 1950 to counter the MiG-15's challenge, which had been sweeping the air of F-51s* and F-80s. The MiGs were superior at high altitude; the F-86 was superior at lower altitudes. This is reflected in a wartime USAF song* about "MiGs jumping off the moon." The F-86 had an inherent disadvantage because its six Browning machine guns* were often inadequate for jet-age dogfight ranges, although the MiG's larger caliber guns had a slow rate of fire. The MiGs also had the great advantage of political air superiority.* A prime USAF advantage was in its veterans of World War II* who could make full use of the excellent qualities of the F-86, even though some MiGs had experienced Soviet pilots. By the truce in 1953, the F-86s had flown 87,177 sorties and shot down 792 MiGs for 78 lost in air battle, a superb 10-to-1 kill ratio.

The F-86's performance was so high it was first believed by those who did not fly it that it could not perform the attack* function. This was totally wrong. It did well in that role; Sabres dropped 7,508 tons of bombs and 148 tons of napalm and fired 270 rockets in the war. In 1949 the F-86 was drastically altered into an interceptor.* First designated the XF-95, it had radar,* an afterburner, and 24 2.75-inch rockets for armament. It was soon redesignated as the F-86D, or Sabre Dog. Active service began in 1953, which was over two yeare behind schedule because of fire-control problems and production difficulties with its engine. Other variants of the Sabre were RF-86s for reconnaissance,* TF-86s for training, DF-86s for drone direction, and QF-86s for testing.

The USAF bought 5,893 F-86s for itself and 460 for other countries. Production ended in 1956, active service in the USAF in 1960, and service in the Air National Guard* (ANG) in 1965. The Canadair Ltd. firm in Canada built its own "CL-13" Sabres, designated F-86E-6 by the Americans. It used the Avro Canada Orenda engine. It was built to provide the British Commonwealth with a modern swept-wing fighter. For this reason, Australia also built Sabres.

Characteristics (F-86F): engine, General Electric J47-GE-27 turbojet with 5,970 pounds thrust; span, 37 feet; length, 38 feet; height, 15 feet; gross weight, 17,000 pounds; top speed at sea level, 690 miles per hour; service ceiling, 50,000 feet; range, 1,270 miles; ordnance, 2,000 pounds.

References. Primary: Higham, *Combat Airc.*, vol. 1. Secondary: Maurice Allward, *F-86 Sabre*, 1978. Knaack, *U.S. Airc.*, vol. 1. Swanborough, *US Mil. Airc.* Ray Wagner, "MiG-15," *AH*, March 1988, pp. 45–54.

F-89 SCORPION

This airplane was the USAF's first multiseat, all-weather jet interceptor.* Northrop Aircraft, Inc., proposed the concept for it in 1945. The first flight was in 1948, and production began in 1949. Production ended in 1956 after 1,052 had been built. The F-89 had a long history of problems, and it was replaced as soon as possible with the greatly superior F-102.* It entered active service in 1951 and left active service with the USAF in 1960 and with the Air National Guard* (ANG) in 1968. The F-89 engines had low ground clearance; ingestion of debris from the ground led to the nicknames of "World's Largest Vacuum Cleaner" and "FOD Vacuum" (FOD stands for "foreign object damage"). It also was called "Stanley Steamer" for its big wheels.

Characteristics (F-89D): engines, two Allison J35-A-35 turbojets with 7,200 pounds thrust each in afterburner; span, 60 feet; length, 54 feet; height, 18 feet; gross weight, 42,241 pounds; top speed, 636 miles per hour at 10,600 feet; service ceiling, 49,200 feet; ferry range, 1,370 miles.

References. Primary: Higham, *Combat Airc.*, vol. 1. Secondary: Knaack, *US Airc.*, vol. 1. Swanborough, *US Mil. Airc.*

F-94. *See* F-80.

F-100 SUPER SABRE

North American Aviation, Inc., began speculation design work in January 1951 on a successor to its great F-86* Sabre. The USAF* ordered production in November. It was designated F-100, and this caused talk about "Century Series" fighters* as something new and exciting. A prototype, the YF-100, was flown at supersonic speed on its first flight in 1953. Later that year it set a world speed record of 755 miles per hour. It was the first USAF fighter to reach supersonic speeds in level flight.

It entered service in 1955 but soon had to be modified because of yaw stability problems. In 1956 the F-100 was adopted by the Thunderbirds* air show team and served until 1968. The F-100 was used in Southeast Asia (SEA) beginning in 1962 but was not used in the Vietnam War* until 1965, and then in the attack* role. It was withdrawn from SEA in 1971 and from USAF service in 1972 but remained in the Air National Guard* (ANG) until 1978. The USAF bought 2,294, with 45 given to the Military Assistance Program* (MAP). Throughout its long service, it was plagued with maintenance problems. Of 476 F-100Cs, 85 suffered major accidents. Of 1,274 F-100Ds, more than 500 were lost in accidents; in one year, 50 F-100Ds were lost in action. One-fourth, 74, of the F-100Fs were lost in accidents. The F-100's nicknames were "Hun," "Lead Sled," and "Silver Dollar."

Characteristics (F-100D): engine, Pratt & Whitney J57-P-21A turbojet of 17,000 pounds thrust in afterburner; span, 39 feet; length, 47 feet; height, 15 feet; gross weight, 34,832 pounds; top speed, 864 miles per hour; service ceiling, 39,600 feet; radius of action, 530 miles; external stores, 7,040 pounds.

References. Primary: Higham, *Combat Airc.*, vol. 3. Secondary: Knaack, *U.S. Airc.*, vol. 1. Swanborough, *US Mil. Airc.* Wagner, *Am. Planes.*

F-101 VOODOO

The McDonnell Aircraft Corporation began design work on a long-range fighter escort* in 1945. Two prototypes, an XF-88 and XF-88A, were built and flight testing began in 1948. A shortage of funds canceled the project in 1950.

In 1951, desire for an escort for the B-36* revived the program. New engines were available, and the altered design became the F-101 and RF-101. The Strategic Air Command* (SAC) lost interest in it in 1954 because the B-47* was in quantity production and escorts were not envisioned with that bomber,* but the Tactical Air Command* (TAC) then showed a desire for it. The first flight was in 1954, and in 1957 an F-101C set a world speed record of 1,207 miles per hour. Production of the RF-101 and an interceptor* version began in 1957. The F-101 was the first 1,000-mile-per-hour airplane to go into production in the United States. RF-101s served in the Vietnam War.* They were able to avoid the MiG-17s but not the MiG-21s. The plane had an important instability problem; it would pitch nose up in a tight turn, so it was not battleworthy. The F-101s were retired by the USAF in 1966, and the RF-101s in 1970. It was nicknamed "One-Oh-Wonder."

Characteristics (F-101B): engines, two Pratt & Whitney J57-P-55 turbojet engines of 14,500 pounds thrust each in afterburner; span, 40 feet; length, 67 feet; height, 18 feet; gross weight, 46,500 pounds; top speed, 1,220 miles per hour at 40,000 feet; service ceiling, 52,000 feet; range, 2,800 miles.

References. Paul D. Stevens, "RF-101s in Southeast Asia," *AAHS Journal*, Winter 1969, pp. 282–89. Swanborough, *US Mil. Airc.* Wagner, *Am. Planes.*

F-102 DELTA DAGGER

One of the most popular and successful interceptors* ever built, the F-102 had a difficult development. Americans were very interested in the advanced aeronautical research done by Germany up to the end of World War II.* One of the promising lines of work was in delta-shaped wings done by Dr. Alexander Lippisch. He helped the Consolidated-Vultee Aircraft Corporation (Convair) build the XF-92A in 1948. It was intended to be a Mach 1.5 fighter* and it was the first powered delta-winged aircraft to fly in the United States. Design work on the F-102 as an enlarged F-92 began in 1950. The first flight took place in 1953, and the speed was greatly below expectations. It took extensive redesign to correct the problems, with the biggest change being adoption of the "area rule" developed by Richard Whitcomb of the National Advisory Committee for Aeronautics (NACA). This change involved lengthening the fuselage and pinching in its waist, called a "coke-bottle" shape. The redesign caused severe financial troubles. In an effort to reduce procurement* costs, the USAF* tried to build the F-102 "concurrently." In other words, production tooling was made during the designing. The redesign required expensive retooling.

Flight tests of the redesigned YF-102 were supersonic and satisfactory otherwise. Production of this first interceptor of the USAF to have armament of only guided and unguided missiles began in 1953. It entered service in 1956. Production ended in 1958 after 1,000 had been built. The F-102 was sent to serve in the Vietnam War* in 1962 and was withdrawn in 1969. It flew in air defense and some combat air patrols (CAP) for B-52s.* A proposed F-102B was redesignated the F-106* because of the large number of changes to be made. The only variant built was the trainer TF-102, nicknamed "Tub" for its tubby cockpit. It trained prospective B-58* pilots* as well as F-102 pilots. Six F-102s were converted to drones as QF-102s or PQM-102s. The F-102 was nicknamed "The Deuce."

Characteristics (F-102A): engine, Pratt & Whitney J57-P-23A turbojet of 16,000 pounds thrust in afterburner; span, 38 feet; length, 68 feet; height, 21 feet; gross weight, 31,276 pounds; top speed, 780 miles per hour at 36,000 feet; combat ceiling, 51,800 feet; radius of action, 651 miles.

References. Knaack, *U.S. Airc.*, vol. 1. Swanborough, *US Mil. Airc.* Wagner, *Am. Planes.* John Wegg, *General Dynamics Aircraft and Their Predecessors*, 1990.

F-104 STARFIGHTER

Fighter* pilots* considered the F-104 to be the best fighter of its time. The Korean War* gave the USAF* concern about its poor showing in air superiority* fighters. In 1953 a letter contract was given the Lockheed Aircraft Corporation for a light-weight, advanced fighter. The company's C. L. "Kelly" Johnson developed the F-104 out of the F-90 and X-3 designs. The first flight was in 1954, and entry into service was in 1958. The same year, the F-104 was the first plane in history to hold three key world records simultaneously. It set a speed record of 1,404.19 miles per hour, an altitude record of 91,249 feet for a ground-launched plane, and time-to-climb records.

The USAF used only four squadrons* of F-104s for the air superiority role, and four squadrons served as interceptors.* Almost immediately after entering service, F-104s were sent to Taiwan to cool the Formosa crisis of 1958.* In

1960, after only two years of service, the Air Defense Command (ADC) gave away its F-104 squadrons to the Air National Guard* (ANG). After another year, three of those squadrons were federalized and moved to Europe for service in the Berlin crisis of 1961. In 1962, one of the federalized squadrons was converted to C-97s,* and the two others returned to service in the ADC. Soon the F-104s were called upon again to confront the potential enemy in the Cuban crisis of 1962.* From 1965 to 1967 F-104s served in the Vietnam War,* and the planned retirement of the fighter had to be postponed five years until 1967. The service record of the F-104 in the USAF shows the paradox of the leader's dislike for the airplane and dependence upon its effectiveness.

Variants of the F-104 included 24 used as target drones and three test aircraft designated NF-104A. The latter had a rocket engine added and reached an altitude of 120,000 feet in 1963. Other variants included the RF-104G for reconnaissance,* TF-104G trainer, F-104J for Japan, and CF-104 for Canada. The USAF accepted 663 F-104s, 296 for its own use and the rest for other air forces. F-104s were used by 15 foreign countries, and more than 2,500 were produced. The reborn Luftwaffe, with a gap of many years of experience with high-performance aircraft, had a tragic accident rate with its F-104Gs. F-104 nicknames were "Missile with a Man in It," "Widow Maker," "Zip," and "Zipper." Its pilots loved it.

Characteristics (F-104C): engine, General Electric J79-GE-11A turbojet with 15,800 pounds thrust in afterburner; span, 22 feet; length, 55 feet; height, 14 feet; gross weight, 23,590 pounds; top speed, 1,450 miles per hour; service ceiling, 58,000 feet; radius of action, 306 miles; ordnance, 2,000 pounds.

References. Primary: Higham, *Combat Airc.*, vol. 3. Secondary: Peter R. Foster, *F-104 Starfighter*, 1987. Knaack, *U.S. Airc.*, vol. 1. Swanborough, *US Mil. Airc.* Wagner, *Am. Planes*.

F-105 THUNDERCHIEF

In 1951 the Republic Aviation Corporation proposed the F-105 to the USAF* as a successor to the F-84F.* The development went slowly, with the first flight in 1955. It entered service in 1958, and production ended in 1964 after a total of 833 built.

The F-105 went into battle in the Vietnam War* in 1965. It flew more sorties into North Vietnam and suffered more combat losses than any other USAF aircraft, a reflection of the fact that it was a workhorse. It had superior speed at low altitudes, was rugged, and carried heavy payloads for great distances. With some exaggeration, there was a claim of as much payload for it as for a ten-man B-17* of World War II* and as much weight, but with only a crew of one or two. The USAF shot down 137 enemy aircraft in North Vietnam, and F-105s received credit for 28 of them, all obsolete MiG-17s. The obese airplane could not maneuver well in battle and was vulnerable to air superiority* fighters* and to flak.* It was less vulnerable to surface-to-air missiles* (SAM). The longer the F-105 was in service, the more it was praised, and that praise became high indeed.

Its nicknames were "Hyper-Hog," "Iron Butterfly," "Lead Sled," "The Nickel," "One-Man Air Force," "Republic Iron and Steel Works," "Squash, or Squat, Bomber" (it could destroy targets by "sitting on them"), "The Thud," "Thunderthud," "Triple Threat" (three ways it could kill its pilot), and "Ultra-Hog."

Characteristics (F-105D): engine, Pratt & Whitney J75-P-19W turbojet with 24,500 pounds thrust in afterburner; span, 35 feet; length, 64 feet; height, 20 feet; gross weight, 52,500 pounds; top speed, Mach 1.11 at sea level; combat ceiling, 49,000 feet; range, 2,000 miles; external stores, over 14,000 pounds.

References. Primary: Jack Broughton, *Thud Ridge*, 1969, and *Going Downtown: The War against Hanoi and Washington*, 1988. Don Carson, "Flying the Thud," *AF*, April 1974, pp. 18–23. Higham, *Combat Airc.*, vol. 1. Secondary: Knaack, *US Airc.*, vol. 1. Swanborough, *US Mil. Airc.*

F-106 DELTA DART

In the early 1950s there were development problems with the Consolidated-Vultee Aircraft Corporation's (Convair) F-102.* The changes needed became so extensive that their product became the F-106 in 1956. The Delta Dart was designed to be an all-weather supersonic interceptor* to operate with the Semi-automatic Ground Equipment* (SAGE) System. After SAGE was deactivated, the F-106 operated with the Joint Surveillance System* (JSS).

The first flight was in 1956 and production continued through 1960. In 1959 it set an official world speed record of 1,525.9 miles per hour. A total of 340 were made, and it was outstanding for its role. It was in service from 1959 to 1988, which shows its greatness. The pilots* called it, simply, the "Six," or "Sixshooter" when it had a gun pod.

Characteristics: engine, Pratt & Whitney J75-P-17 turbojet with 24,500 pounds thrust in afterburner; span, 38 feet; length, 71 feet; height, 20 feet; gross weight, 39,195 pounds; top speed, 1,327 miles per hour at 35,000 feet; service ceiling, 45,000 feet; combat radius, 730 miles.

References. Primary: Donald D. Carson, "Flying the Six," *AF*, October 1973, pp. 38–44. Higham, *Combat Airc.*, vol. 1. Secondary: Knaack, *US Airc.*, vol. 1. Swanborough, *US Mil. Airc.* John Wegg, *General Dynamics Aircraft and Their Predecessors*, 1990.

F-111

Despite troubles and hostility in its development, the F-111 became an effective and important airplane. In the late 1950s the USAF* saw great potential in the variable-sweep wing. Fully extended, the wing would provide the best range; fully swept, the best speeds. Therefore, some historically contradictory characteristics could be combined in one aircraft. This revolutionary new technology and two other factors resulted in the most controversial fighter* in USAF history. One factor was Secretary of Defense (SECDEF) Robert S. McNamara's* insistence that the USAF and the U.S. Navy use common aircraft. The second was McNamara's desire to micromanage military procurement.*

The F-111 started as the Tactical Fighter Experimental (TFX). McNamara overrode the services' choice of a Boeing Company design and ordered development of a General Dynamics Corporation proposal. As often happens with advanced technology, weight soon became a problem. It became so severe that the Navy version could not land on carriers and was abandoned. Amid much public criticism, Congress conducted an investigation of the TFX. The first flight took place in 1964, and the F-111A entered service in 1967. Its combat debut in the Vietnam War,* called Combat Lancer, resulted in excessive losses. The problems causing the losses were found and corrected.

By this time a variant was under development, the FB-111A. It was intended to be an interim strategic operations* bomber* because of slow progress on the Advanced Manned Strategic Aircraft (AMSA), or B-1.* The 76 FB-111As went into service in 1969. Another variant is the EF-111A Raven, an electronics warfare*–equipped F-111A. It became operational in 1983. This type of aircraft was important in the 1986 Libyan raid.* F-111s and EF-111s were used in the Iraq War* of 1991. The F-111 has the nicknames of "Aardvark," "Flying Edsel," "Swinger," "Switchblade," "Switchblade Edsel," " 'Vark," and "Widow Maker." The EF-111A has been nicknamed "Electronic Fox" and "Spark 'Vark."

Characteristics (F-111A): engines, two Pratt & Whitney TF30-P-3 turbofans of 18,500 pounds thrust each in afterburner; span, 32 feet to 63 feet; length, 74 feet; height, 17 feet; gross weight, 92,500 pounds; top speed, Mach 2.5 at 40,000 feet; service ceiling, over 60,000 feet; range, over 3,800 miles on internal fuel.

References. Primary: Higham, *Combat Airc.*, vol. 1. William R. Liggett, "FB-111 Pilot Report," *AF*, March 1973, pp. 30–37. Secondary: Knaack, *US Airc.*, vol. 1. Jeffrey P. Rhodes, "Slam 'Em and Jam 'Em," *AF*, June 1989, pp. 50–56. Swanborough, *US Mil. Airc.*

See also instrument flying.

F-117

The F-117 resulted from a project started in 1978 at the Lockheed Corporation's "Skunk Works." It was to adapt to fighters* the radar* and other sensor-avoidance technologies, popularly called "stealth,"* being developed.

The F-117's operational use is expected to be low-altitude attack* using air-to-surface missiles. It is not an air superiority* fighter. It is a single-seat, two-engined plane with a highly swept wing and forked tail. F-117As saw battle when at least two of them spearheaded the U.S. effort in the Panama incident of 1989.* They attacked flak* batteries at Rio Hata to clear the way for the USAF's* C-130s* bringing in U.S. Army Rangers. The F-117 was used in the Iraq War* and was a key to destroying Iraqi air defense facilities. Its nicknames are "Black Jet," "F-19," "Frisbee," and "Nighthawk."

Characteristics (estimated): span, 66 feet; length, 60 feet; height, 13 feet; gross weight, 42,000 pounds.

References. Michael A. Dornheim, "USAF/Lockheed F-117A Has High Wing Sweep But Low Wing Loading," *AWST*, 1 May 1989, p. 27. Roy T. Harris, Jr., "Out of the Clouds," *The Wall Street Journal*, 27 December 1989, pp. A1, A8. William B. Scott,

"USAF Expands Use of F-117A, Adds More Daytime Flights," *AWST*, 1 May 1989, pp. 24–26. Swanborough, *US Mil. Airc.*

See also B-2.

FAC. *See* forward air controller.

FACE OF A HERO. *See* novels.

FAIL-SAFE

This novel* by Eugene Burdick and Harvey Wheeler appeared in 1962. The title is the name of a system that is designed to counteract failure within itself. The story's plot is of the breakdown of the USAF's* system to prevent accidental war, resulting in the inadvertent destruction of Moscow by U.S. bombers.* With full knowledge that this was a mistake, the U.S. president and Soviet dictator agree that the USAF will obliterate New York City as fair compensation. It is done. This cynical horror novel was appropriate to the period of the 1960s and became a best-seller. It was then made into a 1964 movie* of the same name, with the screenplay by Walter Bernstein.

References. "The 40th Anniversary of the USAF," a special issue of *AH*, September 1987, pp. 211–12.

FAIRCHILD, GENERAL MUIR S. "SANTY" (1894–1950)

An important strategist, Fairchild served as vice chief of staff of the Air Force from 1948 to 1950. Born in Bellingham, Washington, Fairchild enlisted in 1916, became a flying cadet in 1917, and an officer and pilot* in 1918. He then flew combat in bombers.* After World War I* he held mostly engineering positions until he attended the Air Corps Tactical School* (ACTS) in 1934–1935. In 1936 he became an instructor at Maxwell* Field, Alabama, where he immersed himself in strategic studies. In World War II* Fairchild was in the Plans Division of the USAAC* at first. Then he received a key assignment to the Joint Strategic Survey committee. In this position he was able to advance his concepts on the use of air power. In early 1944, he conceived the idea that became the U.S. Strategic Bombing Survey* (USSBS). After the war, General Carl S. Spaatz* asked him to found the Air University* (AU).

References. Primary: Haywood S. Hansell, Jr., "Gen. Muir S. Fairchild: Strategist, Statesman, Educator," *AF*, January 1979, pp. 72–74. Secondary: DuPre, *USAF Bio.* Futrell, *Ideas*, vol. 1. Kenneth Schaffel, "Muir S. Fairchild: Philosopher of Air Power," *AH*, September 1986, pp. 165–71.

FAIRCHILD AIR FORCE BASE

This Strategic Air Command* (SAC) field is near Spokane, Washington. It was established in 1942 and was named for General Muir S. Fairchild* in 1950. Previously it had been called Galena Field and Spokane AFB. During World War II* the base was a logistics depot and overhauled 13,000 aircraft engines. It was adapted to support B-29s* in 1947, B-36s* in 1952, and B-52s* and KC-

135s (see C-135) in 1958. From 1960 to 1970 it was an Atlas* base. In 1990 it had the 92nd Bomb Wing and the 3636th Combat Crew Training Wing. Its aircraft were B-52s and KC-135s.

References. "Guide to Major Air Force Installations Worldwide," *AF*, May 1990, p. 123. Mueller, *AFB*. Roberts, *Dir. USAF*.

FAIRCHILD INDUSTRIES. *See* aerospace industry; C-82; C-119; C-123.

FAIRCHILD REPUBLIC. *See* A-10.

FAIRFORD. *See* RAF Fairford.

FALAISE-ARGENTAN, FRANCE

Air power and the USAAF* showed what could be done to concentrated and exposed ground forces at the Falaise-Argentan pocket and gap. The action led to the collapse of the German defenses in Normandy.

The German army launched an assault toward Avranches on 7 August 1944 in an attempt to upset the invasion of Normandy. In the preceding days the weather had inhibited flying and the Germans hoped these conditions would persist. The Americans expected the German drive and were ready for it. The assault went poorly from the start. On the first day of fighting the weather improved. By 1300 hours the attacks* by Allied fighters* and U.S. heavy bombers* had stopped the German advance.

Adolf Hitler allowed a retreat by 11 August. The British army hit the Germans from the north and the Americans from the south so that a pocket began to form. There was a narrow escape gap open to the Germans at Falaise-Argentan. They rushed to the roads to escape through the gap, and Allied fighters had exposed targets. On 14 August the Germans being strafed on one road waved white flags and were herded by U.S. fighters to U.S. lines for imprisonment. The German road columns became a traffic jam of destroyed or immobile vehicles by 17 August and were systematically annihilated. The gap was closed on 21 August. In the gap and pocket were left thousands of dead Germans and draft animals along with hundreds of tanks and other vehicles. Those shattered German forces that had escaped fled eastward. General Dwight D. Eisenhower* saw the killing fields and said only Dante would have the ability to describe the carnage.

References. C&C, vol. 3. Goldberg, *Hist. USAF*. Richard P. Hallion, *Strike from the Sky: The History of Battlefield Air Attack 1911–1945*, 1989.

FALCON. *See* AIM-4.

FALCON AIR FORCE BASE

This field is near Colorado Springs, Colorado, and is an Air Force Space Command* (AFSPACECOM) facility. The base was activated in 1985. In 1990 the 2nd Space Wing was operating there. It is also a Strategic Defense Initiative* (SDI) National Test Facility.

References. "Guide to Major Air Force Installations Worldwide," *AF*, May 1990, p. 123. Roberts, *Dir. USAF*.

FAR EAST AIR FORCE. *See* Fifth Air Force; Pacific Air Forces.

FAR EAST AIR FORCES. *See* Pacific Air Forces.

FARM GATE

Farm Gate's deployment moved the USAF* from a purely advisory capacity into a limited combat role in Vietnam. On 11 October 1961, President John F. Kennedy* (JFK) ordered a combat detachment of conventional aircraft to South Vietnam to help counter the growing insurgency there. Known as Farm Gate, this detachment was formed from the 4400th Combat Crew Training Squadron, an air commando unit named Jungle Jim,* which was activated at Eglin* AFB, Florida, six months earlier. Farm Gate had four RB-26s (*see* B-26 Invader), four SC-47s (*see* C-47), eight T-28s,* and 155 officers and airmen. They began arriving at Bien Hoa* AB in November 1961. The primary job was to train South Vietnamese, but they also began flying limited combat missions soon after arrival. Intended to destroy Viet Cong lifelines and support bases, such missions entailed photo reconnaissance,* surveillance, interdiction, and attack.*

By January 1963, Farm Gate resources had increased to 19 B-26 invaders,* six C-47s* and HC-47s (*see* C-47), 13 T-28s, four U-10s, and 275 men, while operations had expanded to other South Vietnamese bases. The detachment was renamed the 1st Air Commando Squadron. The squadron's B-26s and T-28s were replaced by A-1Es* in May–June 1964. In October 1964, a second Farm Gate squadron, the 602nd Fighter Commando Squadron, was organized. With the deployment of this second squadron, the USAF was moving toward the first stage of its buildup in South Vietnam.

References. Ray L. Bowers, *The United States Air Force in Southeast Asia: Tactical Airlift*, 1983. Robert F. Futrell, *The United States Air Force in Southeast Asia: The Advisory Years to 1965*, 1981.

Warren A. Trest

FATE IS THE HUNTER

This best-seller of 1961 is the autobiography of Ernest K. Gann, who was an airline pilot* and World War II* flyer in the USAAF's* Air Transport Command (ATC). In *Fate*, Gann told it like it was. He knows flying and can tell a great story. Gann is the author of several popular novels* about aviation: *Blaze of Noon* (1946), *The High and the Mighty* (1953), *In the Company of Eagles* (1966), *Band of Brothers* (1973), and *The Aviator* (1981). The first two and the last of these novels, as well as part of *Fate*, were made into movies.

Reference. "Aviation History—The State of the Art," a special issue of *AH*, March 1984, pp. 71, 73.

FCRC. *See* think tanks.

FEAF. *See* Pacific Air Forces.

FECHET, MAJOR GENERAL JAMES E. "JIM" (1877–1948)

Fechet was second chief of the Air Corps, serving from 1927 to 1931. He put priority on flight training* and worked to create Randolph* Field, Texas, as a great pilot* training center.

Fechet was born in Fort Ringgold, Texas, and enlisted in the U.S. Army in 1898. He served in various ground positions until 1917. In that year he became commanding officer of the Signal Corps' flying schools at Belleville, Illinois, and Arcadia, Florida. In 1918 he became commanding officer of Kelly* Field, Texas. In 1920 he went to Washington, D.C., for duty in the office of the Chief of Air Service.* In 1924 he became commandant of the Advanced Flying School at Kelly Field. Fechet was appointed assistant chief of the Air Corps in 1925 and, in 1927, chief of the Air Corps.

References. Primary: Ira C. Eaker, "Maj. Gen. James E. Fechet: Chief of the Air Corps, 1927–1931," *AF*, September 1978, pp. 94–97, and "Toward the Sound of the Guns," *AH*, Summer 1967, pp. 69–76. Secondary: Air Force Pamphlet 31–1, "Roster of USAF Retired General Officers," 1987. *Biographical Study of USAF General Officers, 1917–1952*, vol. 1, n.d. DuPre, *USAF Bio*.

Steven K. Yates

FEDERAL AVIATION COMMISSION

Also known as the Howell Commission, this presidential group disappointed advocates of an independent air force because it simply confirmed the findings of two War Department committees, the Drum Board* and the Baker Board.* This commission was authorized by the Air Mail Act of 12 June 1934 and appointed by the president in July. Its chairman was Clark Howell. It originated as a consequence of the problems the USAAC* had in the airmail flights of 1934* and reported in January 1935.

Although the Howell Commission traveled extensively and conducted hearings that included testimony from William Mitchell* and other airmen desiring changes in the nation's aviation organization, the committee accepted the War Department's notice that the Drum and Baker boards findings represented official policy based upon necessary data. Thus, while the Howell Report recommended formation of a General Headquarters Air Force* (GHQ Air Force) and a USAAC strength of 2,320 planes, it affirmed the need to keep the USAAC under Army control, acting as an adjunct of ground forces in coastal defense duties.

References. Primary: *Federal Aviation Commission Report*, Senate Document No. 15, 74th Cong., 1st sess., 1935. U.S. Federal Aviation Commission, *Public Hearings of the Commission*, Reporters minutes in 9 volumes, 1935. Secondary: Futrell, *Ideas*, vol. 1.

Irving Brinton Holley, Jr., *Buying Aircraft: Matériel Procurement for the Army Air Forces*, 1964.

Lester H. Brune

FEDERAL CONTRACT RESEARCH CENTERS. *See* think tanks.

FEINSTEIN, CAPTAIN JEFFREY S. *See* weapon system operator.

FICON. *See* fighter conveyor.

FIELD MAINTENANCE

The maintenance provided by wing* organizations is called field maintenance. It usually consists of the replacement of parts or subassemblies. Those include fuel, electrical, avionics, engine, hydraulic, in-flight refueling, ejection seats, wheels, tires, and the airframe itself. Field maintenance is an intermediate level of maintenance between that done in depots and operational or organizational maintenance* squadrons.*

As aircraft became more complex in the 1960s the USAF* responded by increased centralization of the management of maintenance and specialization of mechanics' skills. The computer played an increasing role in these changes. In 1989 a major effort was made to reduce failure rates and to simplify maintenance. It was called Reliability and Maintainability 2000 (R&M 2000).

References. Primary: James R. McCarthy, "A Quarter Century of Air Force Maintenance," *AH*, March 1982, pp. 48–55. Secondary: "Billy Mitchell's Feelings about the Man in the HBT Suit," *AF*, August 1956, p. 242. Ernest J. Gentle and Lawrence W. Reithmaier, eds., *Aviation/Space Dictionary*, 6th ed., 1980. Peter Grier, "R&M Is Serious Stuff," *AF*, November 1989, pp. 96–100. Woodford Agee Heflin, ed., *The United States Air Force Dictionary*, 1956.

FIFTEENTH AIR FORCE (15AF)

This numbered air force* was established in November 1943 in Tunisia and was assigned to the Mediterranean theater of operations (MTO). Previously its resources had been called the XII Bomber Command. It moved to Bari, Italy, a month later. Its purpose was to conduct strategic operations.*

The 15AF hit a dozen factories in the Big Week,* flying 500 sorties. By July 1944 it had almost 1,000 heavy bombers,* but it lost 318 that same month. It bombed southern France in preparation for the U.S. invasion there in August 1944. It conducted a campaign against Ploesti,* Romania, an important part of the German oil industry target system.* The 15AF had almost stopped the refinery by the time Romania surrendered in August. The 15AF's first commander, from 1943 to 1944, was the famous Major General James H. Doolittle.* Another significant World War II* commander was Major General Nathan F. Twining,* from 1944 to 1945. The 15AF was inactivated in Italy in September 1945 and reactivated in 1946 in the United States. It was then assigned to the Strategic Air Command* (SAC). In 1990 it was headquartered at March* AFB, California, and it was composed of the 1st Strategic Aerospace, the 3rd, 14th, 40th, and 57th Air Divisions; and eight separate wings.*

References. C&C, vols. 2 and 3. Maurer Maurer, ed., *Air Force Combat Units of World War II*, 1983. Ravenstein, *Org. USAF*. "Strategic Air Command," *AF*, May 1990, pp. 83–85.

FIFTH AIR FORCE (5AF)

This numbered air force* was activated in September 1941 as the Philippine Department Air Force, redesignated as the Far East Air Force in October, and again renamed as the 5AF in February 1942. What was left of it, after the initial fighting, retreated to Australia. In January 1942, it was sent to Java for combat. It was reorganized in September 1942 to command all USAAF* units in Australia and New Guinea.* The 5AF's record is probably second only to the Eighth Air Force* (8AF) as a USAF* combat air force.

The 5AF's first tasks were to destroy the Japanese air resources at Buna and Lae, New Guinea. The greatest need was for air superiority,* and the addition of P-38s* provided the means. The next tasks were tactical airlift* to supply the ground offensives in New Guinea and to command the seas to cut off Japanese reinforcements. The Battle of the Bismarck Sea* reduced the Japanese to using barges instead of ships. In October 1943, progress made Rabaul,* New Britain, the next objective. By December, the 5AF had air superiority over New Britain. The Thirteenth Air Force* (13AF) and the U.S. Navy had contributed to this result. By the summer of 1944 the Americans had finished their bypass campaign in New Guinea. The pattern had been for the 5AF to attack* the next Japanese stronghold to be taken, followed by naval bombardment and then landings.

The 5AF began an air campaign against the Japanese in Mindinao in August in preparation for retaking the Philippines.* After the Battle of Leyte* Gulf the Navy had to withdraw its carriers, and the air defense of the invasion beachhead was left to the 5AF. By the end of 1944 the 5AF had shot down 314 enemy aircraft* over Leyte with a loss of only 16. Air actions soon ended with the Japanese airmen crushed, and the 5AF did attack* work for the rest of the Philippine campaign. The 5AF moved on to Okinawa* when fields were available. From those bases it conducted operations against Japanese shipping, the China coast, and Kyushu until the end of World War II.*

After the war, the 5AF became the USAF part of the occupation of Japan. When the Korean War* broke out, the 5AF moved to South Korea and conducted the tactical operations* in that war. In 1990 the 5AF was under the Pacific Air Forces* and headquartered at Yokota* AB, Japan. Under it was the 313th Air Division and two separate wings.*

Its famous commanders were Major General Lewis H. Brereton,* 1941 to 1942; Lieutenant General George C. Kenney,* 1942 to 1944; Lieutenant General Ennis C. Whitehead,* 1944 to 1945; Major General Kenneth B. Wolfe,* 1945 to 1948; Major General Thomas D. White,* 1948; Lieutenant General Earle E. Partridge,* 1948 to 1951; and Lieutenant General Glenn O. Barcus,* 1952 to 1953.

References. C&C, vols. 1, 4, and 5. Futrell, *USAF in Korea*. Maurer Maurer, ed., *Air Force Combat Units of World War II*, 1983.

50,000 AIRPLANES. *See* Roosevelt message of 16 May 1940.

FIGHTER

This is an aircraft designed primarily to hunt down and destroy other airplanes of any type in flight. The essence of the fighter and the fighter pilot* is to take the offensive. Thus it is the means and key to achieving air superiority.* It can also hit any surface target. The fighter pilot is considered the elite of aviators.

Americans in the USAAS* called this type "pursuit aviation," adapted from the French *Avion de Chasse*, for pursuit or hunt airplane, reflected in the designator *P*. Sometimes the Americans and British used the word *scout*, a holdover from the days when the only military function of airplanes was reconnaissance.* The British primarily used the word *fighter*, and this term was used increasingly by Americans. After World War II,* the term *fighter* was formally adopted by the USAF,* hence the designator *F*. Beginning in World War II and until the Vietnam War,* when electronic warfare* was mostly limited to interceptors,* the air superiority airplane was often called a "day fighter." The Germans, like the French, have used the most definitive term, *Jagd*, which means "pursuit" or "hunt."

Although fighters have grown large and sophisticated since their 1915 introduction into the German army air service with Anthony Fokker's E-1, they possess commonalities. Among fighter traits are a design emphasis on speed; acceleration; high altitude; high rate of climb; range; forward-firing, hard-hitting firepower; and maneuverability. These call for low weight, hence usually one engine and a crew of one. Occasionally, a well-designed fighter with two engines or a crew of two has been successful.

References. Primary: Robert L. Shaw, *Fighter Combat: Tactics and Maneuvering*, 1985. Edward H. Sims, *Fighter Tactics and Strategy 1914–1970*, 1972. Secondary: Richard P. Hallion, *Rise of the Fighter Aircraft 1914–1918*, 1984. Mike Spick, *Modern Fighter Combat*, 1987. Jack K. Sun, "Fighter Armament of World War II," *AH*, June 1981, pp. 74–82.

See also ace; attack; fighter escort; Iraq War; Korean War; Red Flag; tactical operations; Vietnam War; World War I; World War II; all entries for aircraft designators *F* and *P*.

Ronald W. Yoshino

FIGHTER ATTACK. *See* movies.

FIGHTER BOMBER. *See* attack.

FIGHTER CONVEYOR (FICON)

In World War II* strategic operations* could not be carried out without air superiority* or fighter escort.* Thus, the development of the first intercontinental bomber,* the B-36,* had to address a need for fighter* protection, and the main problem was the escort's range.

In 1944 the solution was envisioned to be an unmanned aerial vehicle* (UAV) to be carried in the B-36's bomb bay and radio-controlled in battle. Development led to a preference for a manned fighter able to engage repeated enemy assaults. The McDonnell Aircraft Corporation designed the XF-85 Goblin in 1945 to be used for this purpose. The first flight of the XF-85 was in 1948. Test drops of it were made from a B-29.* It was abandoned because of technical and funding difficulties. There were also second thoughts about the uncertainty of recovery of the fighter during battle and that destruction of the bomber* before or after launch meant the loss of both aircraft and crews together.

The concept was switched to carrying a parasite RF-84 (*see* F-84) in an RB-36 (*see* B-36). The RF-84 would be released 800 to 1,000 miles from the bomber's target to photograph and return to the RB-36. An alternative was for the parasite to perform an attack* role. The first flight was made in 1952 with an RB-36D and F-84E. The flight tests went well and only minor modifications to the aircraft were needed. The first GRB-36D carrier and GRF-84F were delivered in 1955. The designator of the latter was changed to RF-84K. The Strategic Air Command* (SAC) used 10 GRB-36Ds and 25 RF-84Ks in the 99th Heavy Strategic Reconnaissance Wing. The FICON aircraft were removed from active service in 1957 following the retirement of the B-36Ds. Aerial refueling* proved to be the best solution for fighter range.

References. Larry Davis and David Menard, *F-84 Thunderjet in Action*, 1983. Knaack, *US Airc.*, vols. 1 and 2.

See also Tom-Tom.

FIGHTER ESCORT

This is protection for other types of aircraft by air superiority* fighters.* It has played a significant role in the history of the USAF,* because it broke the back of the Luftwaffe in 1944 and enabled the USAAF* to conduct strategic operations.*

The USAAS* provided fighter escort in 1918 when its observation aviation* performed an attack* function. When bomber* ranges were extended after World War I,* several questions were addressed. One was, is fighter escort necessary? The USAAC's* answer was that bomber speeds and massed defensive firepower in a formation made escort unnecessary. Another question was, is an air superiority fighter capable of flying as far as a bomber's radius of action? The USAAC's answer was no, despite Major Alexander P. de Seversky's* demonstrations that it was practical. A third question was, can a large, heavy, multiplace airplane, such as the FM-1,* perform the escort function? The USAAC leadership believed it could despite criticism of the view by Army fighter pilots.* A fourth question was, should fighter escort be close or not? Close escort means flying fighters only in the immediate vicinity of the aircraft they are defending—that is, operating an offensive weapon in a defensive manner. Soldiers erroneously believe they get the best protection from a fighter directly overhead, and bomber pilots believe the same. If the fighters are not tied to the bombers, they can be used offensively and go on the hunt over an area. This permits destruction of the enemy before the bombers can be hit. The bomber pilots running the USAAC believed in close escort.

The British and Germans learned quickly in World War II* that bombers in daylight suffered prohibitive losses from air superiority fighters. Their bombers fled to the cover of night. The USAAF still tried its unescorted ideas without success. Then the Americans tried the multiplace approach by converting B-17s* and B-24s* into flying gun platforms. Instead of carrying bombs, more guns were added and these aircraft, designated B-40 and B-41, were placed on the perimeter of the bomber formations. Their clumsiness and ineffectiveness made matters worse. Then the USAAF began a crash program for a long-range air superiority fighter. This was long after the USAAF in 1941 had encountered the best air superiority fighter in the world, which was also long-range, the Japanese Mitsubishi A6M Reisen, or "Zero." The USAAF found its fighter in the F-51* by adding internal fuel and external drop tanks.* The new model F-51s, helped by F-47s* and P-38s* with drop tanks, reduced bomber losses to an acceptable level by close escort. The F-47 was a descendent of de Seversky's long-range fighter.

Next the USAAF did what no other air service had done; it allowed its fighter escort to operate offensively in area escort. This permitted the fighters to do more than protect the bombers; they hit enemy aircraft wherever they could be found, in the air and on the ground, in "fighter sweeps." Soon the Luftwaffe was reduced to hiding and hit-and-run tactics even in the heart of German airspace. The Americans had achieved air superiority. Some believe the Luftwaffe could have countered the F-51 with better fighter dispositions and tactics to force the Americans to drop their tanks early in flight.

The USAAF and USAF continued to provide for fighter escort after the war. New methods were tried for greater range, because jet fuel consumption was much higher than piston engines at the time. The trials were with fighter conveyor* (FICON), Tom-Tom,* and aerial refueling.* The last has proven to be the best solution. The Strategic Air Command* (SAC) had fighter escort wings* until 1957, when bomber tactics switched from high altitude to low. At low altitudes, the bombers hope to evade fighters by avoiding detection.

Close escort was tried and failed again in the Korean War.* Area escort was not possible because the Chinese had been given political air superiority* with a Manchurian sanctuary. The result was that the USAF bombers fled to the cover of night operations. The use of B-52s* in the Vietnam War's* Linebacker* II called for fighter escort, and it was used successfully. Both close and area were used, supported by aerial refueling. Fighter escort was often called MiGCAP* in the Vietnam War.

References. Primary: Adolf Galland, *The First and the Last: The Rise and Fall of the German Fighter Forces, 1938–1945*, translated by Mervyn Savill, 1954. Secondary: Bernard Boylan, *Development of the Longrange Escort Fighter*, 1955. C&C, vol. 3. Futrell, *Ideas*, vol. 1. Thomas H. Greer, *The Development of Air Doctrine in the Army Air Arm 1917–1941*, 1985.

FIGHTER-INTERCEPTOR. *See* interceptor.

FIGHTER OPERATIONS. *See* attack; fighter; fighter escort; interceptor; tactical operations.

FIGHTER SQUADRON. See movies.

FIGHTER SWEEP. *See* fighter escort; tactical operations; World War II.

FIGHTING FALCON. *See* F-16.

FINLETTER, SECRETARY THOMAS K. (1893–1980)
   Finletter was the second secretary of the Air Force* (SAF), serving from 1950 to 1953, including during the Korean War.* His outstanding contribution to the USAF* was as chairman of the President's Air Policy Commission* of 1947. The commission's report was made in 1948 and recommended an expanded USAF to provide the most economical and effective basis for national defense and to help the struggling aircraft industry. The recommendations, in large measure, were adopted.
   He was from Philadelphia, Pennsylvania, and graduated from the University of Pennsylvania in 1915. Finletter was a captain of field artillery in World War I.* He received an LL.B. in 1920. He was chief of the Economic Cooperation Administration's mission to Britain before he became SAF. In the Kennedy* administration he was permanent representative to the North Atlantic Treaty Organization* (NATO).
   References. Primary: President's Air Policy Commission, *Survival in the Air Age*, 1948. Secondary: "Aerospace World," *AF*, June 1980, p. 31. DuPre, *USAF Bio*. Futrell, *Ideas*, vol. 1.

FINLETTER COMMISSION. *See* President's Air Policy Commission.

FIREBEE. *See* unmanned aerial vehicles.

1ST AERO SQUADRON
   This was the first U.S. squadron* to reach Europe in World War I.* It had only a little experience in the Mexican expedition of 1916* against Pancho Villa and arrived in France under the command of Captain Ralph Royce on 3 September 1917. After training at French flying schools, equipped with Spad two-seaters, the squadron received further training for observation aviation.* It was sent to the Toul sector on 4 April 1918, and on 15 April, its pilots* flew their first reconnaissance* mission over the lines. A few weeks later it was joined by the 12th and 88th Aero Squadrons and became a part of the 1st Corps Observation Group. For about three months it was very active in the Toul, Pont-à-Mousson, St. Mihiel* area. When the Germans began their big push in the Chateau-Thierry

sector in June and July of 1918, it, along with the 12th and 88th and the pursuit squadrons in the Toul area, was transferred to the Marne region.

In September it was shifted back to the St. Mihiel front and operated rather effectively as General John J. Pershing's* troops demolished the German forces between the Moselle and Meuse rivers. This campaign lasted from 12 to 15 September. The Meuse-Argonne* campaign opened on 26 September and lasted until the war ended on 11 November. During this operation the 1st Aero Squadron performed very well. No less than 45 squadrons of observation, pursuit, and bombing were involved.

During the war the 1st Aero Squadron scored 13 victories, 17 airmen were killed, nine were wounded, and five others became prisoners of war (Germany)* or were missing in action.

References. Goldberg, *Hist. USAF*. James J. Hudson, *Hostile Skies: A Combat History of the American Air Service in World War I*, 1968. Aaron Norman, *The Great Air War*, 1968. Paul M. Schmidt, "Being 1st Is Being Best," *AH*, December 1977, pp. 206–10.

James J. Hudson

FIRST AIR FORCE (1AF)

This numbered air force* began as the Northeast Air District in 1940. It was redesignated as the 1AF in 1941 and was headquartered at Mitchel* Field, New York. In World War II* it trained new units and replacements for units in combat and provided air defense for the eastern coast until 1943. In 1946 its headquarters moved to Fort Slocum, New York, and it was assigned to the Air Defense Command (ADC). It was placed under the Continental Air Command* (CONAC) in 1948 and moved back to Mitchel in 1949. It was discontinued in 1958. It was reactivated in 1966, again assigned to ADC, and headquartered at Stewart AFB, New York. It was inactivated in 1969 and reactivated again in 1986 and headquartered at Langley* AFB, Virginia, with assignment to the Tactical Air Command* (TAC). Its commanders included Major General Ralph Royce (1943) and Major General Glenn O. Barcus* (1949–1950). In 1990, the 1AF supervised two air divisions,* Air Forces Iceland,* and the USAF Air Defense Weapons Center.

References. C&C, vols. 1 and 6. Maurer Maurer, *Air Force Combat Units of World War II*, 1983. Ravenstein, *Org. USAF*. "Tactical Air Command," *AF*, May 1990, pp. 88–89.

FIRST AVIATION OBJECTIVE

Formulated in June 1940, this was the USAAC's* initial objective toward the 50,000 aircraft called for by President Franklin D. Roosevelt's (FDR) message of 16 May 1940.*

The plan called for a 54-group force consisting of 4,000 planes, 16,800 officers, 187,000 enlisted men, and 15,000 aviation cadets.* Like other goals for the Army's air arm, it was revised before being fulfilled. It was replaced in

October 1941 by a Second Aviation Objective.* FDR's 50,000 goal was a psychological one and not practical given U.S. aircraft production capacity.

The First Aviation Objective should not be confused with "first aviation strength," which, during World War II,* meant the normal number of planes for a combat group under AWPD-1.*

References. C&C, vol. 1. Futrell, *Ideas*, vol. 1. Irving Brinton Holley, Jr., *Buying Aircraft: Matériel Procurement for the Army Air Forces*, 1964.

Lester H. Brune

FLAK

This is an anagram from the German *Fl*ieger *A*bwehr *K*anone, or antiflyer gun. It was first used in World War I* and is now a generic term for all gun-fired antiaircraft weapons. Usually, flak has been placed in either a nation's air force or army. In the United States, it has always been part of the U.S. Army despite the fact that the USAF* has been responsible for air defense. Flak will be an integral part of air war for the foreseeable future, because surface-to-air missiles* (SAM) made high-altitude flight more dangerous, spurring warplanes to fly at lower altitudes.

Flak is commonly divided into heavy, medium, and light. Heavy flak was artillery of 75mm to 150mm and was made obsolete by SAM. Medium flak is automatic cannon from 30mm to 57mm, usually radar* controlled, and mounted in multiples on a wheeled or tracked chassis. Light flak is of two varieties: (1) machine guns of 7.62mm to 14.5mm, free mounted on nearly all military vehicles as secondary armament; and (2) the larger 15mm to 30mm automatic cannon used for close-in defense of airfields and other military targets. They combine an extremely rapid rate of fire, high mobility, high lethality, and low cost. In the Vietnam War,* USAF* fixed-wing aircraft losses were 112 to SAM and 1,406 to flak.

References. Primary: Curtis E. LeMay, *Mission with LeMay: My Story*, 1965. Robert L. Shaw, *Fighter Combat: Tactics and Maneuvering*, 1985. Secondary: Futrell, *Ideas*, vol. 1. Lon O. Nordeen, Jr., *Air Warfare in the Missile Age*, 1985. Kenneth P. Werrell, *Archie, Flak, AAA and SAM*, 1988.

Philip Long

FLAKSUITS

Body armor has been used by military services for thousands of years. After a lapse, it was restored to use with the infantry helmet in World War I.* An armored flying helmet was under development at the end of that war. Flaksuits have been important at times since then. It appears that flaksuits will continue to be important.

A study by the USAAF* in World War II* found that 70 percent of its casualties were caused by low-velocity objects. By the time of the study some aircrews had already begun wearing the M1 infantry helmet. Colonel Malcolm Grow, the U.S. Army Medical Corps, and the Eighth Air Force* (8AF) advocated flaksuits as well. In October 1942 Lieutenant General Carl A. Spaatz,* commander of the 8AF, ordered tests for suits. The experimental armor was a success and, in 1943, the new 8AF commander, Major General Ira C. Eaker,* ordered enough armor to equip all the bombers* used on operations. The suits included specialized helmets, vests, aprons, and groin armor. By the end of the war, a million units of armor had been made. Studies indicated that the flaksuits reduced casualties by 58 percent.

This success of the USAAF led to the postwar development of body armor for the U.S. Army, Navy, and Marine Corps. However, USAF* interest in flaksuits faded, and aircraft designers had a trend to reduce the alternative of armor built into the planes. The need for renewed attention to armor became evident in the Vietnam War.* Initially, World War II flaksuits were found in storage and shipped to Vietnam. The tropical climate and lower altitudes flown in the new war created great discomfort when aircrews wore the suits created for the cooler European war. The solution to the problem was to make flaksuits out of new materials, and ceramic composites proved satisfactory.

References. William A. Cohen, "The Case for Body Armor," *AF*, March 1972, pp. 52–55. Martin J. Miller, Jr., "The Armored Airmen: World War II U.S. Army Air Force Body Armor Program," *AH*, March 1985, pp. 27–32. Joshua Stoff, "American Aviators in Armor," *AAHS Journal*, Spring 1987, pp. 34–41.

FLAMING DART

This was the code name for the first reprisal air strikes against North Vietnam in which USAF* aircraft participated. U.S. Navy carriers launched the initial strikes above the 17th parallel on 5 August 1964, in retaliation for the North Vietnamese strikes on the destroyers USS *Maddox* and *C. Turner Joy* in the Gulf of Tonkin.** The Navy's operation, called Pierce Arrow, failed to deter more hits against U.S. installations in South Vietnam. After the Viet Cong killed eight Americans and wounded more than 100 in assaults near Pleiku on 7 February 1965, President Lyndon B. Johnson* (LBJ) approved additional reprisal strikes known as Flaming Dart I. Adverse weather delayed USAF and Vietnamese air force (VNAF) participation, so Navy fighters made the first bombing runs on 7 February, hitting North Vietnamese army barracks at Dong Hoi. The next afternoon, a force of 28 VNAF A-1s,* accompanied by 20 USAF F-100s* flying flak* suppression sorties, bombed barracks at Chap Le.

Again, LBJ's warning that the air strikes were in retaliation for assaults against U.S. interests, not an intention to widen the war, went unheeded. Enemy forces struck again on 10 February at Qui Nhon, killing more than 20 Americans. LBJ ordered a third air strike, Flaming Dart II, against North Vietnam, which was carried out by the USAF, Navy, and VNAF aircraft against barracks at Chanh Hoa and Vit Thu Lu on 11 February. Undeterred, the enemy announced it would continue to target, at will, U.S. military installations in South Vietnam. There was a 19-day pause before LBJ ordered a resumption of air strikes against North Vietnamese targets. The Rolling Thunder* campaign against North Vietnam began on 2 March, replacing Flaming Dart.

References. Berger, *USAF in SEA*. William W. Momyer, *Air Power in Three Wars*, 1985.
**Questions remain about the North Vietnamese action.

Warren A. Trest

FLIGHT

This is the second smallest operational flying unit and is composed of four aircraft. Often used in fighter* aviation, flights have two elements,* each featuring a leader and a wingman. Three to four flights form a squadron.* A flight is also a subordinate administrative unit of a squadron. Finally, the term is also used for some units used in parades and for honors ceremonies.

In 1915, during World War I,* the German army air arm initiated elements, later joined into flights for mutual protection and concentration of force. The Allies followed, and formations grew steadily larger with squadron and, by 1918, wing*-size engagements occurring over the Western Front.

Flights remained a standard subunit in the interwar years. The modern "finger four" formation, composed of two Rotten, or elements, evolved in the Luftwaffe during the Spanish Civil War. That configuration, or Schwarm, was so named because the aircraft in the formation resembled the tips of splayed fingers of a horizontally held hand. The primary tactician who devised this formation was Oberst, then Leutnant, Werner Moelders, a great ace* with 115 victories.

Eventually adopted by most air forces during World War II,* the flight soldiered on through the Korean War.* There, the USAF* fought communist MiG-15s along the Yalu River. The distance from South Korean airfields proved so great that the USAF F-86s* wasted no fuel in forming into squadrons. Instead, they flew directly to areas of battle in flights of four, to be joined at five-minute intervals by other F-86 flights. The World War II "finger four" formation evolved during the Korean War because of increases in fighter speeds and deadlier hostile air defenses. The result was a more flexible flight, the "fluid four." By 1988 the element had returned as the basic combat unit, using a series of highly versatile two-craft configurations referred to as "loose deuce" or "fluid two" formations.

References. Primary: J. E. Johnson, *The Story of Air Fighting*, 1985. Robert L. Shaw, *Fighter Combat: Tactics and Maneuvering*, 1985. Edward H. Sims, *Fighter Tactics and Strategy, 1914–1971*, 1972. Secondary: Woodford Agee Heflin, ed., *The United States Air Force Dictionary*, 1956.

Ronald W. Yoshino

FLIGHT ENGINEER

This is an aircrew member responsible for an aircraft's engines, systems, fuel control, and ground servicing. The specialty has been needed only on the largest planes.

When the USAAF* procured the B-29,* it believed the airplane needed three pilots* to control it. The division of labor was to use two to control the flying and one to run the mechanical systems. In the B-29 this third man sat behind the copilot facing a panel of instruments, switches, and levers. At first, qualified pilots were used for this task, but pilots resented the status so much that the arrangement did not work. In 1945 the USAAF made the flight engineer an aeronautical rating of its own and enrolled aviation cadets* and aviation students* in a training program. The course taught field maintenance* and the flying and mechanical characteristics of the airplane.

As time went on, engines increased in power, so fewer of them were needed for large aircraft. Also, the jet engine required less active control and automatic controls increased. The result was much less need for third pilots; none was used in the B-47,* for example.

References. C&C, vol. 6. Ernest J. Gentle and Lawrence W. Reithmaier, eds., *Aviation/Space Dictionary*, 6th ed., 1980.

FLIGHT NURSE (FN)

The development of aeromedical evacuation* naturally led to FNs to provide critical care for patients aboard aircraft. Formal integration of nurses into evacuation squadrons* and training began in 1942 at the School of Air Evacuation at Bowman Field, Kentucky. Hospital nurses had to apply to be an FN, which required the same physical examination as other aircrew. Training lasted eight weeks and included aircraft emergencies and survival after crashes. The first class graduated in February 1943. FNs went wherever there were USAAF* units, and the USAAF had 500 FNs in 1944. By then, aeromedical practices had become fairly standard. Each aircraft had one or two FNs and a Medical Corps enlisted technician team to perform care. The isolation of the teams and patients meant that the nurses and technicians had greater responsibilities than ground counterparts.

The Korean War* saw an expansion in FNs to keep pace with increased aeromedical evacuation. The USAF* evacuated 311,673 sick and wounded in the war.** Aeromedical evacuation was improved and expanded again in the Vietnam War,* with 406,022 patients carried with no accidents. In early 1968, the USAF had 409 FNs in the Far East alone. Comparison with the 1944 roll shows the increased usefulness of aeromedical evacuation and its FNs.

Movie: *Flight Nurse*, 1953.

References. Berger, *USAF in SEA*. C&C, vol. 7. Futrell, *USAF in Korea*.

**This figure includes multiple movements made for some patients.

FLIGHT NURSE. *See* movies.

FLIGHT SURGEON. *See* aviation medicine.

FLIGHT TRAINING

Pilot* training began on 8 October 1909, when two U.S. Army Signal Corps lieutenants, Frank P. Lahm* and Frederic E. Humphreys, began instruction under the Wright brothers.* It is one function that has remained vital to the USAF.*

Between 1911 and 1913, College Park,* Maryland, was the site of flying training except in winter. When College Park closed, training moved to the San Diego Signal Corps Aviation School* in California. When the United States declared war in 1917, new airfields opened until there were 27 in the United States and 16 in Europe. Flight training was divided into three phases: ground, primary, and advanced. Primary allowed flying, or aviation, cadets* to earn their ratings, or wings, in six to eight weeks. It took 40 to 50 flying hours, usually in the JN.* Most advanced training was done overseas where appropriate types of aircraft and experienced instructors were available. Some cadets won their wings overseas. More than 10,000 pilots were trained in the war. The years between the wars were difficult for air power. In the 1930s the USAAC* trained, on average, little more than 200 pilots per year.

World War II* quickly changed the tempo. The entrance requirements for cadets were lowered, and flight training, which had taken a year, was cut to seven months. Training was given in three phases: primary, basic, and advanced. Training took about 250 flying hours. At the height of the training, in 1943, the USAAF* operated 56 primary, 30 basic, and 33 advanced flying schools across the country. The principal aircraft used were the PT-17 (*see* PT-13) for primary, the BT-13* for basic, and the T-6* for advanced. Between 1939 and 1945, more than 193,000 pilots were graduated.

Flight training dwindled to next to nothing in the demobilization after the war, but the Cold* and Korean* Wars greatly expanded training. By mid–1953, the USAF had a program to graduate about 7,000 pilots per year through 1956 using 27 flying schools.

A major change in flight training occurred in 1959 when the USAF shifted from a specialized to a generalized system. Rather than select students for either single-engine (preparing for fighters*) or multiengine (preparing for bomber* and transport*) training, each pilot now went through the same undergraduate pilot training (UPT) and was considered universally assignable. Although the USAF had formerly believed fighter pilots were different from bomber and transport pilots, it denied any difference in 1959. In 1980, the USAF decided that it would return to specialized pilot training in the early 1990s when a multiengined trainer would be available.

The late 1970s saw the introduction of an instrument flying* simulator to reduce flying hours in UPT from 210 to 170 in a 49-week course. By 1988, however, flying hours had increased to 190, and the course was extended to 52 weeks. From most of the 1960s through the 1980s, the USAF used two trainers, the T-37* for primary and the T-38* for basic. The T-37 had replaced the T-34, and the T-38 had replaced the T-33. At the end of the 1980s, the USAF was conducting flight training at five bases, while a sixth base conducted Euro-NATO Joint Jet Pilot Training (ENJJPT) for both USAF and North Atlantic Treaty Organization* (NATO) pilots.

Movies: *West Point of the Air*, 1935. *I Wanted Wings*, 1941. *Winning Your Wings*, 1942.

References. Primary: Slim Connors, "The Satisfactions of a T-38 Instructor Pilot," *AF*, January 1981, pp. 58–62. James R. Patterson, "Hand Your Spurs to the Crew Chief," *AF*, September 1977, pp. 94–102. Secondary: C&C, vol. 6. Goldberg, *Hist. USAF*. John Steinbeck, *Bombs Away: The Story of a Bomber Team*, 1942.
See also Air Corps Training Center.

Thomas A. Manning

FLIR. *See* forward-looking infrared.

FLYING BOOM

During the late 1940s, the Strategic Air Command* (SAC) and the Boeing Aircraft Company developed a hose aerial refueling* method which was adapted from the British Flight Refueling Limited system. Aircraft modified into tankers* to use this probe-and-drogue* system were designated as KB-29Ms (*see* B-29). While this system worked, it was slow and extremely tedious in hookup and was slow in fuel transfer rates; the hose itself required a low airspeed. Boeing set out to develop a new method, using a flying boom.

The flying boom system consists of a tanker with a telescoping boom and a receiver aircraft with a fixed receptacle. The boom, mounted under the aft fuselage, is lowered and the receiver moves into a precontact position. After the receiver has stabilized its formation flying with the tanker, it moves forward into the refueling position, using an alignment stripe and director lights under the tanker for reference. After the receiver is in the refueling position, the boom operator extends the boom and guides its nozzle into the receptacle on the receiver. The boom operator controls the "flight" of the boom by means of a pair of "ruddevators" which are mounted on the aft end of the fixed portion of the boom. The boom may be moved vertically and through 17 degrees of azimuth. Boom extension is about 18 feet at full travel. During the refueling operation, the boom operator controls the boom hookup, while the crew on the tanker flight deck controls the rate of fuel transfer.

The Boeing flying boom system entered service in 1950 and has been used on the KB-29P, KC-97 (*see* C-97), and KC-135 (*see* C-135) tankers. An adapter may be installed on the KC-135 boom to refuel U.S. Navy and Marine aircraft which use the probe-and-drogue system. The McDonnell Douglas Corporation developed a larger boom, capable of increased fuel transfer rates, for use on its KC-10 (*see* C-10).

References. Knaack, *US Airc.*, vol. 2. Alwyn T. Lloyd, *B-29 Superfortress in Detail & Scale*, part 2, "Derivatives," 1987.

Alwyn T. Lloyd

FLYING CADET. *See* aviation cadet.

FLYING FORTRESS. *See* B-17.

FLYING TIGERS. *See* American Volunteer Group.

FLYING TIGERS. *See* movies.

FLYING TRAINING AIR FORCE (FLY TAF)

This named air force* was established in 1951. It was organized at James Connally AFB, Texas, and assigned to the Air Training Command* (ATC). It moved to Randolph* AFB, Texas, in 1957, and was discontinued in 1958. Fly TAF was created to decentralize supervision. It trained men to become pilots,* navigators,* and radar* observers. Trying to meet the USAF's* great demands for aircrews for the Korean War,* it gave retraining to U.S. Air Force Reserve* (USAFR)–rated aircrews recalled to active duty and aircrew training in the B-47.* The workload became too great for Fly TAF in 1952 and training for rated men was put under a new air force, the Crew Training Air Force* (Crew TAF). When the Korean War was over and training demands were down, Fly TAF absorbed Crew TAF in 1957.

References. Goldberg, *Hist. USAF*. Ravenstein, *Org. USAF*.

FLYING WING. *See* B-35.

FM-1 AIRACUDA

The designation *FM* meant fighter,* multiplace. The Bell Aircraft Corporation's FM-1 was the only airplane so designated. Although only 12 were built, the FM-1 is significant because of the concepts it displayed.

The USAAC* requested a long-range interceptor* in 1935 for defense against four-engine bombers.* Bell and the Lockheed Aircraft Corporation produced two-engine designs armed with cannon. Bell won a contract for a prototype of its unique aircraft. The engines were pushers, and there was a gunner* armed with a 37mm and .30-caliber gun forward of each engine. There were also .50- and .30-caliber guns in the fuselage; the FM-1 could carry 20 bombs of 17 or 30 pounds each. This heavy, clumsy airplane proved grossly deficient in speed, climb rate, maneuverability, and ceiling. It was not much faster than the bombers of the day and would have been unable to live in the air if enemy bombers had a fighter escort* of minimal competence. It would have had the same failing had it been used as an escort. The aircraft displayed a lack of appreciation of the requirements for air superiority.*

Characteristics: engines, two Allison V-1710–13s of 1,150 horsepower each; span, 70 feet; length, 46 feet; gross weight, 18,000 pounds; top speed, 270 miles per hour at 12,600 feet.

References. Swanborough, *US Mil. Airc.* Wagner, *Am. Planes*.

FOFA. *See* follow-on forces attack strategy.

FOLKLORE, MYTHS, AND SUPERSTITIONS

The USAF* is old enough to have some folklore, myths, and superstitions. One bit of lore is about tough General Curtis E. LeMay* smoking one of his cigars, for which he was famous. On this occasion he was in a hangar, a ''no smoking'' area, and he assured someone worried about fire that ''it wouldn't dare.'' This old story was included in the movie *Strategic Air Command** in altered form. Another tale told is that lowering one's landing gear in battle was a signal to the enemy of surrender. One day, as a story goes, a 100th Bomb Group B-17* used this signal to trick and trap German fighters* and shot one down. Thereafter, it was said, the Luftwaffe made a special effort to destroy a formation of the 100th, leaving only one B-17 to return home to spread the word.

One superstition involves mounting one's aircraft from the left side, as one would mount a horse. This practice is not limited to the USAF. In combat it was considered proper and lucky to neither volunteer for a sortie nor try to evade one, expressed as ''don't choose 'em and don't refuse 'em.'' If one returned safely from a combat sortie, it was considered prudent to try to do each subsequent sortie in the same way—wear the same articles of clothing, do the same acts, and so on. It was considered bad luck to display a record of one's combat sorties.

USAF folklore has included ''Roger Rudder,'' a ubiquitous pilot reminiscent of the civilian ''John Doe.'' Rudder's grade was usually lieutenant or colonel.

References. Bob Stevens, ''*There I Was . . . Flat on My Back*,'' 1975, and *If You Read Me, Rock the Tower!* 1980.

FOLLOW-ON FORCES ATTACK STRATEGY (FOFA)

Warsaw Pact strategy before 1990 called for beginning hostilities in Europe with a sudden thrust of massed armor and artillery. This first strike force would be from troops already in place in the lands bordering those in the North Atlantic Treaty Organization* (NATO). The second wave would consist of troops from the European USSR, and the third and successive groups would be from second- and third-line divisions brought up to strength with reservists recalled to duty.

FOFA is to be the NATO defense against such an assault. The strategy calls for attack* on the aggressor in depth before it can deploy its numerically superior forces in battle. Thus the plan involves attacking the follow-on units while they are in transit and some distance from the front. Because Warsaw Pact forces make nearly all long-distance troop and supply movements by rail, they are particularly vulnerable to attack by aircraft at choke points such as bridges, bypasses, and rail marshaling yards. If enough forces and supplies can be destroyed or delayed, NATO will have time to mobilize its reserves to push the invaders back to their own territory.

This interdiction plan is not entirely new. What makes FOFA different from prior plans is its reliance on sensors to find targets as much as 180 miles behind the front and the use of precision-guided munitions for the attack. There is some concern that FOFA sensors and homing devices may be misled by decoys and other countermeasures, as was the case with the Igloo White* system of the Vietnam War.* Sensors and homing devices can be made to distinguish between tricks and the real targets, but with the severe drawbacks of increased complexity and weight.

References. Peter Adams, "Soviets Aim to Counter NATO Attack Strategy," *Air Force Times*, 30 October 1989, p. 25. James W. Canan, "NATO on the Upbeat," *AF*, September 1984, pp. 134–47. Sam Cohen and David M. Abshire, "Can Smart Bombs Save the West?" *The Wall Street Journal*, 21 June 1989, p. A20. Jacquelyn K. Davis, "Europe's Edgy Approach to Strategy," *AF*, December 1985, pp. 82–84, 87–88. John J. Fialka, "Tricky Targets," *The Wall Street Journal*, 17 February 1989, pp. A1, A7. *See also* Air Force 2000; E-8A.

Philip Long

FONDA, JANE. *See* prisoners of war (North Vietnam).

FORMING OF USAF. *See* separation from the U.S. Army.

FORMOSA CRISIS OF 1958

In August 1958, the United States faced a crisis that loomed large in its political maneuvering with the communists. The USAF* was a principal means to support U.S. policy in this confrontation.

Shortly before, U.S. forces had been poised halfway around the world in the Middle East. The desire to divert world attention from this area may have been a major factor in the Formosa situation. Other factors included communist Chinese frustration at the Republic of China's reconnaissance* flights over it, and its bid for a seat in the United Nations which, in turn, carried with it recognition as the legitimate government of China. Whatever the underlying motives, the communist Chinese threatened to "liberate" the island of Taiwan.

Strikes in the Taiwan Straits, historically known in the West by the Portuguese name of Formosa, were largely directed against the offshore islands of Big and Little Quemoy. The communists had been conducting intermittent shelling of the area since the early 1950s. The intensity of the shelling increased markedly in August 1958. Most feared the shelling was a prelude to the invasion of Taiwan itself. U.S. policy, often vague in the area, appeared to hold fast in the face of Red Chinese and Soviet threats against both the Formosa Straits and the Middle East. As the shelling went on, the Joint Chiefs of Staff (JCS) ordered U.S. Navy carriers, Marines, and the USAF to deploy to Taiwan.

A Composite Air Strike Force* (CASF) began deployment on 29 August. The CASF, named X-Ray Tango, consisted of two F-100,* two F-101,* and two C-130* squadrons and one B-57* squadron. It was ready for battle in Taiwan on 12 September. Already in place was a TM-61C* squadron in southern Taiwan. In September, when the Red Chinese tightened the blockade, the United States announced it would fight for Taiwan, and supply was done by the USAF's Military Air Transport Service (MATS). In October, 12 USAF F-104s* were rushed to Taiwan. The Republic of China engaged the Red Chinese in air combat and had an 11-to-1 kill ratio over their adversaries. By month's end, the Reds had fired 384,000 projectiles into the Quemoys and had attempted one invasion. U.S. officials held firm to help the Republic, and typhoons Helen and Ida hampered military activity.

Red China announced a week's cease-fire for 6 October and then extended it for two weeks. On 18 October, the communists announced they would shell only on even-numbered days if the United States did not violate a 12-mile area declared by Peking. This marked the end of a need for U.S. forces, and they returned to the United States. More than a half million shells had been fired into the Quemoys, several air battles had occurred, and the Republic of China had held firm.

References. Primary: Air University, "Project File—Informal Project: A Study of the 1958 Taiwan Straits Crisis," June 1959 (unpub. ms. in USAFHRC K239.0429–10). Department of Defense, *Annual Report of the Secretary of Defense ... July 1, 1958 to June 30, 1959*. Arthur C. O'Neill, "History of the Fifth Air Force in the Taiwan Strait Crisis of 1958," 31 December 1958 (unpub. ms. in USAFHRC K730.04–16). Jacob Van Staaveren, "Air Operations in the Taiwan Crisis of 1958" (USAF Historical Division, Liaison Office, November 1962). Secondary: Thomas A. Bailey, *A Diplomatic History of the American People*, 10th ed., 1980. Futrell, *Ideas*, vol. 1.

Lloyd H. Cornett, Jr.

FORRESTAL, SECRETARY JAMES V. (1892–1949)

Forrestal played a key role in the establishment of the Department of Defense (DoD) and in the formation of the roles and missions of the USAF.*

Until his government service, he was an investment banker. His involvement with the USAF began in 1944 when he was under secretary of the Navy and testified to the House of Representatives Select Committee on Postwar Military Policy. He expressed skepticism about a DoD at that time. In the summer of 1945, as secretary of the Navy, Forrestal opposed a separate air force. In 1946, President Harry S Truman* (HST) acted as a mediator between Forrestal and Secretary of War Robert P. Patterson. The Navy's main concerns involved losing direct access to the president. Compromises resulted in the National Security Act of 1947* under which Forrestal became the first secretary of defense (SEC-DEF).

There was strife between the USAF and the Navy over the budget after the DoD was formed. The core of the difficulties was over strategic operations.* Both services wanted to conduct them, and there had not been enough funds for both. Forrestal's response was to mediate new agreements on all roles and missions. The Key West and Newport Conferences of 1948* were held with the Joint Chiefs of Staff (JCS). They awarded strategic operations to the USAF and control of the seas to the Navy. The missions were not compartmented, as the Navy was to assist the USAF in strategic operations, and the USAF to assist the Navy in control of the seas.

Unfortunately, the agreements did not end the budget struggles. Under Forrestal's successor, Louis A. Johnson,* the dissension became highly acrimonious in the B-36 controversy* of 1949. Nevertheless, the broad forms of the agreements of 1948 are still in evidence.

References. Goldberg, *Hist. USAF*. David R. Mets, *Master of Airpower: General Carl A. Spaatz*, 1988. Herman S. Wolk, "The Birth of the U.S. Air Force," *AF*,

September 1977, pp. 68–72, 75–78, and "The Establishment of the United States Air Force," *AF*, September 1982, pp. 76–80, 83–84, 87.

48-GROUP AIR FORCE. *See* 70-group air force.

FORWARD AIR CONTROLLER (FAC)

A FAC is a fighter* or attack* pilot* who controls or assists aircraft by radio from an advanced ground or air position in attacks on enemy surface forces. He helps the strike aircraft find and assess the target, determine the approach, provide for flak* suppression, and evaluate attack results. The FAC is an outgrowth and modernization of the fire control and assistance in the older observer* function.

The early fighting in World War II* showed that the older concepts of observation aviation* were no longer viable. The modern FAC function was started by the Royal Australian Air Force (RAAF) in the New Guinea* campaign using the Commonwealth Boomerang, a specialized aircraft for the purpose. The USAAF* began to use the L-5 liaison aircraft* for FACs in Italy in 1944 and called the system "Horsefly." FACs were important in keeping armored spearheads moving in later campaigns.

The USAF* used FACs much more in the Korean War.* They began to work almost immediately after the war started. The airborne FACs used L-5s and L-17s but soon encountered North Korean Yak fighters. T-6s* were brought in with the hope that they would stand some chance of surviving the presence of enemy aircraft.* The T-6s, the FACs, and their squadron were soon called "Mosquitoes." It was not long before the USAF established air superiority,* but the T-6s continued to be used for the FACs. When the front line became fairly stable, the T-6s became more vulnerable to ground fire and less useful.

FACs also played an important role in the Vietnam War,* operating in South Vietnam where the USAF had air superiority. FACs demonstrated the continued high value of daytime visual reconnaissance* in the war. As an example, from January through April 1966, USAF 0-1 Bird Dogs* flew 26,000 sorties, and 60 percent were for reconnaissance.

After both World War II and the Korean War, the FAC function was allowed to deteriorate. For the immediate future, should the U.S. Army be called upon to fight with U.S. air superiority, the record indicates that the FAC will continue to prove useful.

References. Primary: Douglas K. Evans, "Reinventing the FAC: Vietnam, 1962," *AF*, February 1980, pp. 71–75. Marshall Harrison, *A Lonely Kind of War: Forward Air Controller, Vietnam*, 1989. Secondary: Futrell, *USAF in Korea*. Richard P. Hallion, *Strike from the Sky: The History of Battlefield Air Attack 1911–1945*, 1989. John Schlight, *The War in South Vietnam: The Years of the Offensive 1965–1968*, 1988.

FORWARD-LOOKING INFRARED (FLIR)

The ability of aircraft to do effective reconnaissance* was demonstrated in World War I* and has continued to be important ever since. The aircraft's ability to do effective attack* was proven in World War II.* The main defense against these capabilities has been for the enemy to flee to the cover afforded by night-time.

In the Vietnam War,* intensive effort began to remove this impediment to reconnaissance and attack. FLIR was first used in the Vietnam War because of the potential infrared had for nighttime vision. FLIR equipment was costly and bulky at that time. Also, it used cryogenic cooling which required frequent servicing.

Development of this equipment has continued. By 1989 FLIR had been improved and incorporated into a system called Falcon Eye. The system was intended for battlefields and nearby target location and attack, while the Low-Altitude Navigation and Targeting Infrared System for Night* (LANTIRN) is for deep interdiction and precision operations. Tests in 1989 indicated a favorable potential for the new system.

References. Bruce D. Nordwall, "Signal Processing and VHSIC Transforming Reconnaissance," *AWST*, 7 September 1987, pp. 68–69. William B. Scott, "Falcon Eye Flir, GEC Helmet Aid F-16 Mission Flexibility," *AWST*, 17 April 1989, pp. 34–36, 41, 45–47.

FOULOIS, MAJOR GENERAL BENJAMIN D. "BENNY" (1879–1967)

Foulois was third chief of the Air Corps, serving in difficult times, from 1931 to 1935. He believed in an independent air arm and worked for its creation. Foulois was inducted into the National Aviation Hall of Fame in Dayton, Ohio, in 1963.

Born in Washington, Connecticut, Foulois enlisted in the U.S. Army Engineers in 1898. He participated in the Philippine campaigns and became an officer in 1901. In 1908 he joined the Signal Corps. Foulois operated the first dirigible of the federal government and taught himself to fly airplanes after obtaining an instruction manual from the Wright brothers.* In 1910 he was assigned the Army's first airplane and became the service's only pilot,* instructor, and observer.* In 1911 he designed the first radio receiver ever used on an airplane. He pioneered air reconnaissance* and developed methods for tactical operations.* From assignments to the San Diego Signal Corps Aviation School* in California and Galveston, Texas, he became commander of the 1st Aero Squadron.* Foulois led the 1st Aero Squadron in the Mexican expedition of 1916.* In 1917 he went to Washington, D.C., as chairman of the Joint Army-Navy Technical Aircraft Committee. He was a captain in May 1917 and a brigadier general in July of that year. Assigned to France, he was named chief of Air Service* for the American Expeditionary Force (AEF). In 1919 he reverted to the grade of major.

In 1927 Foulois was promoted from lieutenant colonel to brigadier general again and assigned as assistant to the chief of the Air Corps. In 1931 he commanded the annual USAAC* exercises and was awarded the Mackay Trophy for his performance.

While he was chief of the Air Corps, Foulois struggled with the Army and Navy over the coastal defense mission and established the General Headquarters

Air Force* (GHQ Air Force). He erred in believing that the USAAC could do
the airmail flights of 1934.* Congressional displeasure over negotiated procurement contracts and hostility from some congressmen led him to retire in 1935.

References. Primary: Benjamin D. Foulois and Carroll V. Glines, *From the Wright
Brothers to the Astronauts: The Memoirs of Major General Benjamin D. Foulois*, 1968.
Ira C. Eaker, " 'The Little Big One' or 'The Last of the First,' " *AH*, December 1970,
pp. 140–43. Secondary: DeWitt S. Copp, *A Few Great Captains: The Men and Events
That Shaped the Development of U.S. Air Power*, 1980. DuPre, *USAF Bio*. Maurer, *Avn.
in Army*. John F. Shiner, *Foulois and the Army Air Corps*, 1983.

See also Army-Navy agreements of 1931 and 1938.

Steven K. Yates

FOUR HORSEMEN, THE

This famous demonstration team was unique in the equipment it used. The
first C-130* Hercules were delivered to the 463rd Troop Carrier Wing (TCW)
of the Tactical Air Command* (TAC) at Ardmore AFB, Oklahoma, in December
1956. For the first time, USAF* transport* pilots* had a high-performance
aircraft in contrast to their earlier lumbering planes.

The 774th Troop Carrier Squadron (TCS), the "Green Weasel" unit of the
463rd, was at Fort Campbell, Kentucky, shortly thereafter to drop troops. Four
C-130s made short interval takeoffs and low formation flights down the runway
during a break in the drops. The pilots then formed an unofficial aerial demonstration team. They called it formally "Hercules and the Four Horsemen"
and informally "Thunderweasels." The latter obviously linked the name of the
USAF's Thunderbirds* with the squadron nickname. They are best known as
"The Four Horsemen." When the 314th TCW at Sewart AFB, Tennessee, was
to receive its C-130s, the Horsemen were sent to demonstrate the Hercules.

The USAF allowed the team to perform in Europe and the Far East. Application
was made for official status, but this was denied and the group could not continue.

References. Sam McGowan, *The C-130 Hercules: Tactical Airlift Missions, 1956–
1975*, 1988.

FOURTEENTH AIR FORCE (14AF)

This numbered air force* was activated in 1943 in Kunming, China. It was
made up of President Franklin D. Roosevelt's* (FDR) former covert force, the
American Volunteer Group* (AVG), called the "Flying Tigers" by the press,
plus reinforcing units.

The 14th was small for an air force. It had low USAAF* priority because its
mission was defensive, yet it was nearly all the Allied air strength in China.
Despite its limited resources, it struck at Shanghai and Japanese shipping off
the China coast. The Japanese retaliated to this thorn in their side with a ground
offensive in the spring of 1944, driving the Chinese army back and capturing
some air bases. Two Chinese divisions were flown back into China from Burma
by the USAAF in December 1944, and a successful counteroffensive was

launched in May 1945, for which the 14AF provided tactical operations.* Its famous commander from 1943 to 1945 was Major General Claire L. Chennault.*

The 14AF moved to the United States in December 1945 and was inactivated from January to May 1946. Then it was assigned to the Air Defense Command (ADC) and, in 1948, to the Continental Air Command* (CONAC) at Orlando AFB, Florida. Its mission from 1946 to 1960 was to supervise activities of the U.S. Air Force Reserve* (USAFR) and Air National Guard* (ANG). The 14AF was inactivated in 1960 and reactivated again in 1966 at Gunter* AFB, Alabama, again as part of the ADC. It moved to Colorado Springs, Colorado, in 1968, and was renamed the Fourteenth Aerospace Force. In 1976 it moved to the USAFR at Dobbins AFB, Georgia, and again was designated as the 14AF.

References. "Air Force Reserve," *AF*, May 1990, pp. 112–13. C&C, vols. 4 and 5. Maurer Maurer, *Air Force Combat Units of World War II*, 1983. Ravenstein, *Org. USAF*.

FOURTH AIR FORCE (4AF)

This numbered air force* was activated as the Southwest Air District at March* Field, California, in 1940, and redesignated the 4AF in 1941 and moved to Hamilton Field, California. It provided air defense for the western continental United States (CONUS) and trained new units until 1943. Thereafter, it trained replacements for combat units. Its most famous commander was Major General George C. Kenney* in 1942. It was assigned to the Air Defense Command (ADC) in 1946 and to the Continental Air Command* (CONAC) in 1948. It was inactivated in 1960 and reactivated under ADC in 1966, still at Hamilton. Again it was inactivated in 1969 and activated in 1976 at McClellan* AFB, California, and assigned to the U.S. Air Force Reserve* (USAFR). In 1990 its status had not changed and it still had seven wings* under it.

References. "Air Force Reserve," *AF*, May 1990, pp. 120–21. C&C, vols. 1 and 6. Maurer Maurer, *Air Force Combat Units of World War II*, 1983. Ravenstein, *Org. USAF*.

FRANCIS E. WARREN AIR FORCE BASE

This base near Cheyenne, Wyoming, was occupied by the USAAF* in 1947. Formerly Fort Francis E. Warren, it was named for Wyoming's first U.S. senator and a Civil War Medal of Honor winner. At first it was in the Air Training Command* (ATC) with an Aviation Engineering School and then a Technical School in 1948. In 1958 it became a Strategic Air Command* (SAC) base with Atlas* and, in 1962, Minuteman* missiles. In 1990 it was the home of the 90th Strategic Missile Wing (SMW) and was designated a future Peacekeeper* missile base.

References. "Guide to Major Air Force Installations Worldwide," *AF*, May 1990, p. 123. Mueller, *AFB*. Roberts, *Dir. USAF*.

G

G-4 AND G-15 HADRIAN

After the successful Luftwaffe use of gliders* for vertical envelopment in 1940, the U.S. Army adopted the idea in 1941. Several competitive designs were considered, and the Waco Aircraft Company was selected to build a CG-3 trainer and CG-4 for tactical airlift.* The *CG* designation stands for "cargo glider." Testing began in 1942, and production was done by 16 firms. The CG-4 was made of wood and metal and had two pilots.* It carried 15 equipped soldiers, a jeep and four soldiers, or a 75mm howitzer and its crew. An improved version was designated CG-15. There were 13,906 CG-4s and 427 CG-15s built. The CG-4 was used in Sicily, Burma, Operation Overlord,* the landings in southern France, Operation Market,* and the Rhine crossing. The *CG* designation was changed to *G* in 1948. Modern tactical airlift planes and helicopters* are better for the task than are gliders, which are no longer used.

Characteristics (G-4A): span, 84 feet; length, 48 feet; height, 13 feet; gross weight, 7,500 pounds; top speed, 120 miles per hour.

References. Higham, *Combat Airc.*, vol. 1. Secondary: Gerard M. Devlin, *Silent Wings: The Saga of the U.S. Army and Marine Combat Glider Pilots during World War II*, 1985. Swanborough, *US Mil. Airc.*

"GABBY." *See* Gabreski, Colonel Francis S.

GABLE, MAJOR CLARK "THE KING" (1901–1960)

The leading Hollywood star at the time, Gable enlisted in the USAAF* as a private in 1942. The USAAF quickly used Gable's popularity for recruiting purposes. He was sent to Officer Candidate School* (OCS) and was commissioned a second lieutenant. In 1943, Gable participated in making a recruiting film about the OCS named *Wings Up*. Next, the USAAF wanted a film to attract men to become gunners.* Gable was sent to gunnery school and earned his wings in 1943. He arrived in the Eighth Air Force* (8AF) in April 1943 with six men to make the next film. Gable flew five combat sorties in five months and was under fighter* assaults on three occasions. The film he produced was *Combat America* (1943), but it was upstaged in movie theaters by another USAAF picture, the *Memphis Belle** (1944). After the war, Gable portrayed an 8AF commander in the movie *Command Decision** (1948).

References. Roger A. Freeman, *Mighty Eighth War Diary*, 1981. Charles A. Watry and Duane L. Hall, *Aerial Gunners: The Unknown Aces of World War II*, 1986.

GABRESKI, COLONEL FRANCIS S. "GABBY" (1919–)

Having the most victories, 37.5, of any living American, he is the third-ranking U.S. ace* of all time as well as the leading ace of the Eighth Air Force* (8AF). In 1978, he was elected to the National Aviation Hall of Fame in Dayton, Ohio.

He was born in Oil City, Pennsylvania, and entered the USAAC* as an aviation cadet* in 1940. He became a pilot* in 1941. He was at Wheeler* Field, Hawaii, during the attack* on Pearl Harbor.* From 1942 to 1943 he served in England as liaison officer to the Polish air force in exile and flew 13 combat sorties in Supermarine Spitfires. Next he served with the 56th Fighter Group in the 8AF. On 22 May 1944, he scored four victories. After he had flown 166 sorties, with 500 hours in combat, and scored 31 victories, he hit the ground while strafing on 20 July 1944. He was a prisoner of war (Germany)* until May 1945.

He left the USAAF* in 1946 to work for the Douglas Aircraft Company. Gabreski went back into the USAAF in 1947 and graduated from Columbia University. He became deputy commander of the 4th Fighter Interceptor Wing in 1950 during the Korean War.* Later, in 1951, he became commander of the 51st Fighter Wing. He flew F-86s* and had 6.5 victories over MiG-15s. Gabreski retired from the USAF* in 1967 and became president of the Long Island Railroad and an executive of the Grumman Corporation.

References. DuPre, *USAF Bio.* Gurney, *5 Down.* Hess, *Aces Album.* Edward H. Sims, *American Aces in Great Fighter Battles of World War II*, 1958.

GABRIEL, GENERAL CHARLES A. (1928–)

Gabriel was the eleventh chief of staff of the Air Force,* serving from 1982 to 1986. He emphasized quality of life for USAF* people, force modernization, and joint work with the U.S. Army.

He was born in Lincolnton, North Carolina, and graduated from the U.S. Military Academy (USMA) in 1950. He flew 100 combat sorties in the Korean War* in F-51s* and F-86s* and was credited with shooting down two MiG-15s. In 1970, he flew 152 combat reconnaissance* sorties in the Vietnam War* as an F-4* wing* commander. He was USAF deputy for operational forces and deputy director of operations (1972–1975); deputy chief of staff for operations, plans, and readiness for the Tactical Air Command* (TAC) (1975–1977); deputy commander in chief of U.S. Forces Korea and deputy commander in chief of the United Nations Command (1977–1979); USAF deputy chief of staff for operations, plans, and readiness (1979–1980); and commander in chief of the U.S. Air Forces in Europe* (CINCUSAFE) and commander of Allied Air Forces Central Europe (1980–1982).

References. Air Force Pamphlet 31-1, "Roster of Retired General Officers," 1987. Futrell, *Ideas*, vol. 2. *United States Military Academy Register of Graduates*, 1802–1988. U.S. Air Force Biography, Secretary of the Air Force, Office of Information, 1984. Bill Yenne, *The History of the US Air Force*, 1984.

Steven K. Yates

GALAXY. *See* C-5.

GAM-77. *See* AGM-28.

GAR-1 FALCON. *See* AIM-4.

GATHERING OF EAGLES, A

This 1963 movie* was the last one to glorify USAF* bomber* aircraft. The plot originated with Sy Bartlett, who produced the movie, but the screenplay was by Robert Pirosh. Bartlett was a co-author of *Twelve O'Clock High*,* and *A Gathering* is a variant on the plot of the earlier story. A B-52* wing* fails its Operational Readiness Inspection (ORI), and the primary blame lies with the deputy commander. A new wing commander is assigned, and he corrects the wing's faults. Although successful, the film fell far short of *Twelve O'Clock High*.

Reference. "The 40th Anniversary of the USAF," a special issue of *AH*, September 1987, p. 212.

GAU-8 30MM AVENGER

This gun is a large seven-barrel rotary cannon weighing 3,700 pounds and firing at 2,100 or 4,200 rounds per minute. It is mounted in the A-10* and is capable of penetrating tank armor at battle ranges. It is a continuation of the very successful series of Gatling guns built by the General Electric Company. It uses a drum magazine holding more 1,100 rounds and a linkless feed system. GAU-13, a lightweight four-barrel version, is available for underwing carriage on aircraft. The cartridges are of three types: PGU-13 High-Explosive Incendiary, PGU-14 Armor-Piercing Incendiary, and PGU-15 Target Practice.

References. George M. Chinn, *The Machine Gun*, 5th ed., 1987. Ian V. Hogg, *Jane's Directory of Military Small Arms Ammunition*, 1985.

Philip Long

GBU-15 AND AGM-130

The *G*uided *B*omb *U*nit–15 is a modular kit built by the Rockwell International Corporation and is used to make an ordinary Mk–84 bomb* into a guided weapon. The front section has a fuze, an adapter, and target detector using television or imaging infrared. The rear section has a data link, control set, power supply, and autopilot. A set of four canard fins and four larger tail fins with movable control surfaces complete the GBU. The bomb is launched toward the target and then controlled by a data link from the aircraft. Upon target acquisition, the missile may be guided to the target by the aircraft or the on-board homing feature. The AGM-130 is derived from the GBU-15. The major difference is the addition of two long-burning rocket engines strapped on to the outside. This increases the range. The AGM-130 is more aerodynamic with minor changes in the fins.

References. Gunston, *Airc. Arm.* Jeffrey P. Rhodes, "Improving the Odds in Ground Attack," *AF*, November 1986, pp. 48–52. Edgar Ulsamer, "The Steady Evolution in Armaments," *AF*, December 1985, pp. 72–81. U.S. Air Force Fact Sheet 88–22, "GBU-15," November 1988. Susan H. H. Young, "Gallery of USAF Weapons," *AF*, May 1990, p. 158.

Philip Long

GCA. *See* ground-controlled approach.

GCI. *See* ground-controlled interception.

GEE, OBOE, AND GEE-H

Initially conceived by the British in 1938, GEE was an aid to navigation widely employed by the Royal Air Force (RAF), Eighth Air Force* (8AF), and Fifteenth Air Force* (15AF).

GEE was based on the technical ability to measure accurately the time taken by a transmitted radio pulse to reach a receiver. GEE used three ground stations arrayed in a triangle. The accuracy decreased as the range from the stations increased. Originally, it was hoped to use GEE as a blind-bombing aid, but it was not accurate enough. The Germans began to jam the transmissions, which restricted the usefulness to navigation over Britain and the North Sea. The 8AF decided that GEE was sufficiently valuable to equip the whole of its bomber* force with it. It was most helpful to the 8AF in assembling its large and complicated formations in difficult weather and as a homing aid.

Oboe was a British blind-bombing radar* device using different principles. It had two ground transmitters that orally guided bomber pilots.* A "Cat" transmitter kept the bomber on track to the target, and a "Mouse" transmitted time to the target and gave the bomb release order. The signals went at a tangent to the earth, so the range was limited. The 8AF was at first enthusiastic about Oboe, but its limited range and British concerns with secrecy caused the 8AF to transfer its Oboe equipment to the Ninth Air Force* (9AF) in early 1944. It proved highly useful for medium bombers in unfavorable weather.

GEE-H acted as "Oboe in reverse," for the transmitters were in the aircraft. Experimental missions were flown in the first half of 1944. The advance of the Allied armies in August put targets out of range of the ground stations. The ground stations moved forward in September, and the 8AF then used the equipment on a significant scale.

References. Roger A. Freeman, *Mighty Eighth War Manual*, 1984. Gordon Musgrove, *Pathfinder Force*, 1976, and *Operation Gomorrah*, 1981. Charles Webster and Noble Frankland, *The Strategic Air Offensive against Germany*, vols. 1 and 4, 1961.

W. A. Jacobs

GENERAL AVIATION. *See* aerospace power; Civil Air Patrol.

GENERAL DYNAMICS CORPORATION. *See* aerospace industry; Atlas; B-58; F-16; F-102; F-106; F-111; T-29.

GENERAL ELECTRIC COMPANY ENGINES

General Electric (GE) has been a great provider of jet engines to the USAF,* which has made the company a vital part of the U.S. aerospace power.*

Germany and Britain developed jet engines in the 1930s. The United States had nothing as late as 1941. Major General H. H. Arnold* persuaded the British to give the United States a copy of its engine, designed by Sir Frank Whittle. Arnold selected GE to copy the engine for the United States, although the company had not been making aircraft engines. The jet engine is a turbine, so electric generator manufacturers were a natural choice to develop the new form of power. GE's long experience with turbosuperchargers, developed by Dr. Sanford A. Moss, and high-temperature materials contributed to the firm's selection by Arnold. GE's turbosuperchargers were essential to the success of the B-17,* and the USAAC* ordered them put into key aircraft in World War II:* the B-24,* B-29,*, F-47,* and P-38.*

GE's first engines, based upon Whittle's, used centrifugal flow of air. However, the axial-flow jet engine, developed in 1939 by the Junkers Engine Company in Germany, was a more efficient design with greater potential for higher power. Once German knowledge was available, GE began work in 1946 on its axial-flow J47 engine with thrust of around 5,000 pounds. Production began in 1948, and it was used in the B-36,* B-47,* and F-86.* The success of the engine is shown by its production rate of 975 per month from 1953 to 1954. GE next developed the J73, an extension of the J47. It was the first GE engine to be tested with an afterburner. It was soon outdated, however, and it powered only the F-86H.

Design began in 1951 on the next engine, the highly successful J79. This was the first engine that Gerhard Neumann, a German immigrant, influenced, principally by his variable stator. The J79 was the first turbojet to be relatively economical on fuel. It was a Mach 2 engine with around 16,000 pounds of thrust in afterburner, and it powered the B-58,* F-4,* and F-104.* GE had built 17,000 J79s by the end of the 1970s. The company began to develop small jet engines in 1953. Its J85 powered the F-5,* T-37,* and business jets.

Boeing Airplane Company and Douglas Aircraft Company began work on jetliners in the 1950s. GE's rival of that time, the Pratt & Whitney (P&W) Division of United Aircraft Corporation, got the business of both airframe companies. GE turned to the late entrant in jetliners, the General Dynamics Corporation (GD). GD was too late to sell many jetliners despite fine designs, and GE lost $150 million in this failure. GE was shut out of the jetliner market through the 1960s.

Then the company won a USAF competition to design a high bypass, or turbofan, engine to be designated the TF39. The new engine was to power the giant C-5,* and this meant GE had a new means to get into the jetliner market. Boeing selected the TF39 for its Model 747. A version was selected for the McDonnell Douglas Corporation's DC-10 and Airbus Industrie's A300 as the jetliner manufacturers began to offer engine options to the airlines. GE won almost 25 percent of the free world's new orders. GE's participation in the jetliner business enables it to compete to power military transports.*

P&W's F100 was chosen to engine the F-15* and F-16,* while GE's F101 was selected for the B-1.* When the F100 had technical problems that P&W could not solve, GE proposed an alternative engine. Then strikes at subcontractor plants caused F100 engine shortages for the USAF. GE received a contract to develop the F101X for use in fighters* in 1979. The B-1 had a rebirth in 1981 which meant that a GE derivative of its engine would be much less expensive because of economies of scale. In the same year, successful flight tests of the F101 showed the engine had great promise. The USAF formally endorsed competition for its F-16 engine contract by sharing procurement between GE and P&W in 1984. The F101 was redesignated the F110. When the competition was being considered by the USAF, the F100 became much improved.

Since then, the USAF has continued to sponsor competition in engine procurement. Both GE and P&W are competing to power the Advanced Tactical Fighter* (ATF) with their YF120 and YF119s. The main feature of GE's YF120 is that it has the fuel economy of a turbofan at subsonic speeds while behaving like a turbojet at supersonic speeds.

References. Primary: Gerhard Neumann, *Herman the German*, 1984. Secondary: F. Clifton Berry, Jr., "The Push for Fighter Engines," *AF*, January 1990, pp. 74–79. Walter J. Boyne and Donald S. Lopez, *The Jet Age: Forty Years of Jet Aviation*, 1979. Robert W. Drewes, *The Air Force and the Great Engine War*, 1987. William Schoneberger et al., eds., *Seven Decades of Progress: A Heritage of Aircraft Turbine Technology*, 1979.

GENERAL HEADQUARTERS AIR FORCE (GHQ AIR FORCE)

The GHQ Air Force was a step in the direction of an independent air mission and organization. Officially established on 1 March 1935, the GHQ Air Force had been proposed as a means for the USAAC* to obtain a separate mission for reconnaissance* and bombardment directly under the U.S. Army chief of staff. Its chief responsibility would be tactical training and combat readiness for an offensive aviation force to find and attack* any invader as far from U.S. territory as possible.

Originally suggested by Major General Mason M. Patrick* to the Lampert Committee* as early as 1925, the GHQ Air Force (Provisional) was set up in January 1933 to experiment with this force in operating directly under the army commander as defined in a chief of staff letter. In October 1933, the Drum

Board* recommended establishment of the GHQ Air Force and, in May 1934, Secretary of War George Dern appointed Major General Frank M. Andrews* to plan its organizational details. In December 1934, Andrews became commanding general of the GHQ Air Force. Tactical operations* units from nine corps areas were assigned to it, which was headquartered at Langley* Field, Virginia. Three wings* were at Langley; three at Barksdale* Field, Louisiana; and three at March* Field, California.

At best, GHQ Air Force was a compromise designed to keep the air arm under Army command. Andrews and other airmen hoped it would permit Army aviation to make some progress in obtaining independent bombing missions and to justify development of long-range bomber* aircraft. To some degree these hopes were attained, but problems arose regarding the practical fulfillment of a separate air mission and the fact that the air arm lacked a central command. The latter organizational problem arose because the chief of the Air Corps continued to be responsible for supplies, training, and doctrines while the GHQ Air Force commander had charge of crew training, tactics, and combat readiness. It became obsolete as an organization in the expansion of World War II* and ended in 1941.

References. Primary: H. H. Arnold, *Global Mission*, 1948. Secondary: DeWitt S. Copp, *A Few Great Captains: The Men and Events That Shaped the Development of U.S. Air Power*, 1980. C&C, vol. 1. John L. Frisbee, "The GHQ Air Force," *AF*, September 1983, pp. 161–66. Futrell, *Ideas*, vol. 1.

See Air Force Combat Command.

Lester H. Brune

GENTILE, MAJOR DON S. "GENTLE" (1920–1951)

This pilot* scored 19.83 aerial victories in World War II,* making him the all-time 22nd-ranking USAF* ace.*

From Piqua, Ohio, he joined the Royal Canadian Air Force (RCAF) in 1940 after being turned down by the USAAC.* He was sent to England in 1942 to be an instructor. He was reassigned to one of the Eagle Squadrons,* No. 133, the same year. Soon he transferred to the 4th Fighter Group of the Eighth Air Force* (8AF). He flew Supermarine Spitfires until 1943, when the group got F-47s* and then F-51s* in 1944. The F-51 was the plane for Gentile. Between 3 March and 8 April 1944 he shot down 15.5 enemy aircraft.* He shot down two or three every time he was in battle during this period. He and Captain John T. Godfrey, an ace with 18 aerial victories, formed a famous element.* Gentile was sent home in June 1944 to sell war bonds. He flew as a test pilot at Wright-Patterson* AFB, Ohio, later. He died in a T-33 accident in 1951.

References. DuPre, *USAF Bio*. Gurney, *5 Down*. Grover C. Hall, Jr., *Death Squadron*, 1978. Hess, *Aces Album*. Mark M. Spagnuolo, *Don S. Gentile, Soldier of God and Country*, 1986.

"GENTLE." *See* Gentile, Major Don S.

GEORGE AIR FORCE BASE

Established near Victorville, California, in 1941, it was called Victorville until 1950 when it was named for Brigadier General Harold H. George. A World War I* ace,* George died in an aircraft accident near Darwin, Australia. The field was used for advanced flight training* in World War II.* Then it stored surplus aircraft from 1945 to 1948. Next it was a training field for F-51s* and F-86s.* In 1954, it was the first to have F-100s.* The base has been in the Tactical Air Command* (TAC) since 1951. In 1990 it had the headquarters of the 831st Air Division, the 35th Tactical Fighter Wing (TFW) with F-4Es,* and the 144th Fighter Interceptor Wing (FIW). The 35th TFW did training for the Luftwaffe as well as for the USAF.* The base was scheduled to close in December 1992.

References. "Guide to Major Air Force Installations Worldwide," *AF*, May 1990, pp. 123–24. Mueller, *AFB*. Roberts, *Dir. USAF*.

GEORGE, LIEUTENANT GENERAL HAROLD L. (1893–1986)

George was a major catalyst in the development of U.S. air power. He was a seminal force in shaping the strategic operations* concepts, doctrines, and plans used by the USAAF* in World War II.* In addition, he transformed the Air Transport Command (ATC), forerunner of the Military Airlift Command* (MAC), into a force capable of global mobility.

Born in Somerville, Massachusetts, he earned his commission and wings with the Aviation Section of the U.S. Army Signal Corps* in 1918 and flew bomber* sorties in the Meuse-Argonne campaign.* He participated in Mitchell's bombing tests on warships* and took his enthusiasm for Brigadier General William Mitchell's* theories to the Air Corps Tactical School* (ACTS). The ACTS was a hotbed of doctrinal thinking at Maxwell* Field, Alabama. As chief of the Bombardment Section (1932–1934) and director of the Department of Air Tactics and Strategy (1934–1936), he helped shape a new strategy for U.S. air power: precision daylight bombing to conduct strategic operations.

George had the opportunity to translate theory into practice when he became assistant chief of the Air Staff* for war plans in 1941. With a small cadre of former ACTS instructors, George created AWPD-1,* the bomber-oriented plan the USAAF would later use against Germany. In 1942, Lieutenant General H. H. Arnold* directed George to head the Ferrying Command. His charter was to make air transportation global. He and his deputy, Brigadier General C. R. Smith, the former president of American Airlines, took a command with only 130 transports* and 11,000 people and turned it into the ATC with more than 3,000 aircraft and 300,000 people by war's end. Starting under dangerous circumstances, air transoceanic travel became routine. Through George's guidance, air movement had become strategic, reaching anywhere it was needed. George retired in 1946.

References. John L. Frisbee, ed., *Makers of the United States Air Force*, 1987. Futrell, *Ideas*, vol. 1.

Peter R. Faber

GERMAN AIR ATTACK OF 1 JANUARY 1945

Adolf Hitler conceived the idea of a mass surprise strike at Allied air power on the ground early on the morning of New Year's Day of 1945. It was an attempt at a "Great Blow" as seen by Reichsmarschall Hermann Goering. It became a German tactical victory, but a strategic defeat. The Luftwaffe could not afford the irreplaceable losses of either fighters* or pilots.* It expended its last reserves of fighters and interceptors.*

For the effort, the Luftwaffe was able to muster 650 Fw 190s, 450 Bf 109s, and a few jets. The force was to hit the Allied airfields in Belgium, northern France, and the Netherlands. Goering made visits to his units to urge the pilots to hit hard. He labeled this attack Operation Bodenplatt (Ground Slab). The flights to the targets were made at low level, and complete surprise was achieved. At Brussels-Evere field the Luftwaffe caught hundreds of Allied aircraft lined up. Only a few Supermarine Spitfires were able to get into the air, and more than 100 Allied aircraft were destroyed. The results at Eindhoven field were similar, and the British lost a wing each of Spitfires and Hawker Typhoons. The raid cost the British 120 aircraft and the Americans 36. Allied operations were disrupted for a week. The Germans lost more than 100 planes in the air and to flak* and nearly another 200 which returned but were unrepairable.

References. C&C, vol. 3. John Killen, *A History of the Luftwaffe*, 1986.

GERMAN AIRCRAFT INDUSTRY TARGET SYSTEM

The German aircraft industry, including its subsidiaries, was about 40 percent of the total German war production and involved nearly two million workers. It was one of the major targets of strategic operations* throughout World War II.*

The industry was designed with an eye toward protection from air strikes. New plants were located in the hinterland and in suburban areas where concealment was possible. Buildings were separated and civil air raid precautions were provided. The industry was heavily defended by flak* and fighters.* Prewar planning emphasized a large overcapacity to insure maximum use in times of emergency.

From the summer of 1941 to the spring of 1943, occasional strikes against the industry resulted in little damage, but enough that the Germans initiated a dispersal program. Heavy raids in the second half of 1943 forced a program of compulsory dispersion in February 1944. The Allied Casablanca Conference* Directive of 21 January 1943 gave the air industry second priority to submarine construction. By 10 June 1943, with the issuance of the Pointblank Directive, or the Combined Bomber Offensive* (CBO) as it was titled, the German aircraft industry and fighter strength were listed as objectives before all other target systems. Included in this definition were supporting systems such as the airframe plants and the ball bearing industry. The aircraft industry retained top priority among strategic targets until June 1944, when the USAAF* had won air superiority* over the hinterland. Then the oil and transportation systems succeeded to this position.

Allied strikes on the German air industry were some of the largest and bloodiest of the war, yet results were mixed. German production peaked in 1944, falling off sharply afterward. The major direct effect of the attacks on the air industry was to force the Luftwaffe, especially its air superiority* fighters, into combat, which eventually caused its defeat by attrition.

References. Primary: Albert Speer, *Inside the Third Reich: Memoirs*, translated by Richard and Clara Winston, 1970. *The United States Strategic Bombing Survey*, vol. 1, 1976. Secondary: C&C, vol. 2. Williamson Murray, *Luftwaffe*, 1985. Anthony Verrier, *The Bomber Offensive*, 1968.

Edward L. Homze

GERMAN BALL BEARING INDUSTRY TARGET SYSTEM

This industry was heavily concentrated around Schweinfurt,* producer of half of Germany's ball bearings. Because of its concentration and vulnerability, it received high priority in the Allied Combined Bomber Offensive* (CBO). The British, early in 1943, ranked it second in their bombing priorities, and the CBO plan of 18 May 1943 listed it as a third priority. Raids against the industry were associated with the general assault against the German air industry.

The first heavy strikes by the Eighth Air Force* (8AF) occurred on 17 August and 14 October 1943 against Schweinfurt. Production was sharply reduced, but the cost to the Allied air forces was such that no follow-up strikes occurred until fighter escort* was available.

From August 1943 until December 1944, the industry was hit by more than 11,000 tons of bombs.* Schweinfurt received almost two-thirds of the tonnage. Despite the heavy damage inflicted, vigorous German countermeasures, dispersion and purchases from Sweden and Switzerland, prevented the Allies from achieving their strategic objectives.

References. Primary: Haywood S. Hansell, Jr., *The Air Plan That Defeated Hitler*, 1972. *The United States Strategic Bombing Survey*, vol. 1, 1976. Secondary: C&C, vol. 2.

Edward L. Homze

GERMAN OIL INDUSTRY TARGET SYSTEM

The Allies considered this a critical bottleneck of the German war economy during World War II.* With little natural oil except from Romania and Hungary, Germany relied on synthetic oil plants for most of its supply. Although the industry was a high-priority target, the main blows came only after Operation Overlord,* when the Luftwaffe's defensive strength was sharply reduced. The oil and transportation systems became the principal targets in the summer of 1944. Their destruction by January 1945 meant the end of the Third Reich.

The earliest U.S. raids against the industry occurred on 1 August 1943 by the Fifteenth Air Force* (15AF) operating from African and Italian bases and were aimed at the Romanian refinery at Ploesti.* Suffering heavy losses, the striking forces were able to reduce output only temporarily. Starting in April 1944, renewed raids by larger forces against Ploesti began to obtain results. By October, output was knocked out. The raids against the synthetic plants began in May 1944 and then, after an interval to support Overlord, were renewed in June 1944. The Germans used desperate measures to protect, repair, and disperse the industry, but to no avail. By January 1945 production was down to 15 percent of capacity, where it remained until April.

Shortages of oil reduced training, operations, and deployment of German forces. An additional dividend from the oil raids was a massive reduction in the synthetic nitrogen and methanol supply used in both explosives and synthetic rubber. Raids against the oil and transportation systems represented major victories of strategic operations.*

References. Primary: Haywood S. Hansell, Jr., *The Air Plan That Defeated Hitler*, 1972. *The United States Strategic Bombing Survey*, vol. 1, 1976.

Edward L. Homze

GERMAN TRANSPORTATION TARGET SYSTEM

The largest and most diffused target system in the German war economy during World War II* was the excellent railway system. It, augmented by inland waterways that carried a quarter of the freight, used coal for fuel. Highway transport was insignificant, less than 3 percent. Raids on the system were intimately woven with attack,* as in the interdiction bombing of the railways before Operation Overlord.* The system was not made top priority until March 1945.

During most of the war, the system was subordinate to other objectives or it was a target of opportunity. Starting in September 1944, the system within the Reich was subject to increasingly heavy raids culminating in the spring of 1945, when it became virtually the only target left. By the end of the war, 32.1 percent of the total bomb* tonnage dropped by the USAAF* and the Royal Air Force (RAF) was aimed at the land transportation system. Its destruction marked the end of industrial production and operations by the German armed forces.

References. Primary: Albert Speer, *Inside the Third Reich: Memoirs*, translated by Richard and Clara Winston, 1970. Secondary: C&C, vol. 3. Alfred Mierzejewski, *Allied Air Power and the German War Economy, 1944–1945*, 1988. Hans Rumpf, *The Bombing of Germany*, 1963.

Edward L. Homze

GHQ AIR FORCE. *See* General Headquarters Air Force.

GIB. *See* weapon system operator.

GLIDE BOMBS

Glide bombs are a type of guided bomb* that has fins or wings fitted to extend its range. The fittings are usually supplied as a kit composed of the parts that are to be assembled onto a bomb by squadron* ordnance personnel. Gliding gives extended range and thus safety to the launching aircraft. Bombs, such as the GBU-15,* can be launched at any altitude or attitude, acquire the target, and use one of two modes of guidance—either from aircraft or an on-board guidance system. Glide bombs are simple, cheap, and highly accurate. Glide bombs were introduced by the Germans to attack* Allied vessels off the Anzio beachhead, Italy, in January 1944.

Reference. Gunston, *Airc. Arm.*

See also AZON, RAZON, and TARZON.

Philip Long

GLIDERS

Between the world wars, military people were intrigued by the idea of "vertical envelopment," soldiers using the air to strike behind enemy lines. Three means were considered: landing transports,* paratroops, and gliders. On 10 May 1940, the Luftwaffe showed the idea of the glider was practical. It used nine gliders to carry soldiers inside Belgium's Fort Eben Emael. The fort, considered impregnable from ground assault, was taken.

The USAAC* saw two advantages to the glider: (1) without engines and accessories it could be built cheaply en mass, and (2) it could be used at night and achieve surprise by descending in silence. The USAAF* trained 5,000 glider pilots.* By the end of 1944, the idea of a specialized glider pilot was dropped because experience with them was unsatisfactory. Thereafter, transport pilots were used. The first USAAF use of gliders was in the invasion of Sicily in July 1943. From Tunisia, 106 American C-47s* towed U.S. gliders with British pilots and soldiers. For Operation Overlord,* 100 gliders took off on 5 June 1944. They landed under fire on small landing zones (LZ) containing obstructions. More landed with reinforcements on 6 June and 7 June, landing in a battle area. It had been well done. Gliders were also used in Europe in the assault on the south of France and in Market.* In Burma, gliders were used as early as March 1944. By the end of 1944, there were more than 300 G-4* gliders in the China-Burma-India theater* (CBI).

World War II* was the heyday of the glider, and the principal USAAF glider was the G-4. Improvements in transports and the development of the helicopter* provided better means for vertical envelopment. Gliders remained in the USAF* until 1955.

References. Primary: H. H. Arnold and Ira C. Eaker, *Winged Warfare*, 1941. Higham, *Combat Airc.*, vol. 1. Secondary: C&C, vols. 2–6. Gerard M. Devlin, *Silent Wings: The Saga of the U.S. Army and Marine Combat Glider Pilots during World War II*, 1985.

See also C-123; tactical airlift.

GLOBEMASTER II. *See* C-124.

GOC. *See* Ground Observer Corps.

GODDARD, BRIGADIER GENERAL GEORGE W. (1889–1987)

Goddard was a brilliant inventor in the field of photography. His contributions to reconnaissance* and peacetime mapping are immense, and he was inducted into the National Aviation Hall of Fame in Dayton, Ohio, in 1976. Goddard served the USAF* on active duty for 45 years.

A native of Tunbridge Wells, England, he immigrated to the United States and enlisted in the Aviation Section of the U.S. Army Signal Corps* in 1917. He became a pilot* and officer in 1918 and then was trained in photography at Cornell University. He quickly instituted improvements and caught the attention of Colonel Edward Steichen, the famous photographer, who helped him. Between World Wars I* and II,* Goddard took photographs that are familiar to many people: those of Mitchell's bombing tests on warships,* scenes from the Alaskan flight of 1934,* and the *Rex* interception.* Goddard managed the photographic survey done in the Alaskan flight.

He antagonized his superiors in two actions. The first act was when, on his own initiative during the presidential campaign in 1940, he showed President Franklin D. Roosevelt* (FDR) a fancy color portrait of the Roosevelt family. The second act was when he fell in love, divorced his first wife, and married his new love. General H. H. Arnold* considered this improper conduct. Had these incidents not happened, Goddard probably would have attained a higher grade.

His principal invention was the continuous strip system which produces sharp photos from 40,000 feet altitude and also at 50 feet while moving at 500 miles per hour. Strip photography produced the famous pictures of Soviet ballistic missiles* in Cuba in 1962. It also proved crucial in the reconnaissance flights in preparation for Operation Overlord* and for the invasion of Okinawa.* He had four other photographic inventions.

References. Primary: George W. Goddard, *Overview: A Life-long Adventure in Aerial Photography*, 1969, and "The Unexplored Philippines from the Air: Map-Making over Jungle Lands Never Before Seen by White Men," *National Geographic*, September 1930, pp. 311–43. Secondary: DeWitt S. Copp, *A Few Great Captains: The Men and Events That Shaped the Development of U.S. Air Power*, 1980. Murray Green, "George Goddard: Father of U.S. Aerial Reconnaissance," *The Retired Officer Magazine*, March 1990, pp. 30–32, 34, 36–37.

GOLDWATER, SENATOR BARRY M. (1909–   )

Goldwater rose to be a major general in the U.S. Air Force Reserve* (USAFR). With his experience in the USAFR and his capacity as an influential U.S. senator, he affected the USAF* in large measure. In 1982 he was inducted into the National Aviation Hall of Fame in Dayton, Ohio.

From Phoenix, Arizona, he became an officer in the Infantry Reserve in 1930. He was called to active duty in 1941 and won his pilot's* wings in 1942. He took part in the only flight of F-47s* across the North Atlantic. He was chief pilot for the Air Transport Command (ATC), serving in the Azores, Morocco, and India. Goldwater left active duty in 1945 but served in the Air National

Guard* (ANG) and USAFR, becoming a major general in 1962. He has flown 50 types of aircraft, including bombers* and fighters.*

Goldwater was elected to the Senate in 1952 and was the Republican candidate for president in 1964. The Democratic party portrayed him as a hawk at a time of popular concern over greater U.S. involvement in resisting North Vietnamese aggression. Also, he was accused of being trigger-happy on nuclear weapons,* as shown in Bill Moyers' "girl with a daisy" television commercial. He did not run for the Senate in 1964 but returned in 1968 and became chairman of the Senate Armed Services Committee. The committee often restores budget cuts that the House Armed Services Committee is prone to make. As a senator, Goldwater was a leading critic of Secretary of Defense (SECDEF) Robert S. McNamara's* approach to management of the armed forces. He was also disenchanted with SECDEF Caspar Weinberger. Goldwater took important and critical positions on failures within the Congress and the Department of Defense (DoD) on national defense. A product of his views was the important Goldwater-Nichols Act of 1987 that increased the power of the chairman of the Joint Chiefs of Staff (JCS). He retired in 1987.

References. Primary: Barry M. Goldwater, *Goldwater*, 1988. Secondary: DuPre, *USAF Bio*. Richard Halloran, *To Arm a Nation: Rebuilding America's Endangered Defenses*, 1986. *Who's Who in America, 1989–1990*.

GOODBYE, MICKEY MOUSE

This 1982 novel* about F-51* pilots* in the air superiority* battles of early 1944 over Germany is by Len Deighton. Deighton skillfully depicts the USAF* at this place and time of history.

Reference. "The 40th Anniversary of the USAF," a special issue of *AH*, September 1987, p. 213.

GOODFELLOW AIR FORCE BASE

"Goodbuddy" AFB is near San Angelo, Texas, and is an Air Training Command* (ATC) facility. It was established as the San Angelo Air Corps Basic Flying School in 1940 and got its current name in 1941 in honor of Second Lieutenant John J. Goodfellow, Jr., of San Angelo, a fighter* pilot* who died in action in 1918. Flight training* was conducted at the field until 1975. Since then, technical-cryptological training for the military services has been conducted there. In 1990, the Goodfellow Technical Training Center and the 3480th Technical Training Wing (TTW) were based there.

References. "Guide to Major Air Force Installations Worldwide," *AF*, May 1990, p. 124. Mueller, *AFB*. Roberts, *Dir. USAF*.

GOODWILL FLIGHT TO SOUTH AMERICA

In February 1938 the USAAC* was offered an excellent opportunity to demonstrate its long-range flying capabilities. In a goodwill gesture, the State Department requested that a flight be made to Buenos Aires, Argentina, to honor the inauguration of President Roberto M. Ortiz.

Lieutenant Colonel Robert Olds,* 2nd Bomb Group (BG) commander, led the mission. Six B-17s* flew from Langley* Field, Virginia, to Miami, Florida, and then flew a second leg of 2,695 miles to Lima, Peru. The third leg, which took the planes to Buenos Aires, was 2,200 miles. Olds delivered a letter from President Franklin D. Roosevelt* (FDR) to Ortiz. The aircraft then flew over the city as part of the inaugural ceremonies. For their achievements, Olds was awarded the Distinguished Flying Cross (DFC) and the 2nd BG the Mackay Trophy.

References. Primary: Curtis E. LeMay, *Mission with LeMay: My Story*, 1965. Secondary: Peter M. Bowers, *Fortress in the Sky*, 1976. Maurer, *Avn. in Army*.

Alwyn T. Lloyd

GORRELL, COLONEL EDGAR S. "NAP" (1891–1945)

Gorrell was the principal collector of historical material on the air service in World War I.* Born in Baltimore, Maryland, he graduated from the U.S. Military Academy (USMA) in 1912. Three years later, he learned to fly at the San Diego Signal Corps Aviation School,* California, and served with the 1st Aero Squadron* during the Mexican expedition of 1916.* He earned a master's degree in aeronautical engineering at the Massachusetts Institute of Technology (MIT) and was assigned as an intelligence officer in the Aeronautical Division of the U.S. Army Signal Corps* in Washington, D.C. In June 1917 he joined the Bolling Mission.* Later he became chief of the Technical Section of the air service of the American Expeditionary Force (AEF) and served as aviation officer at general headquarters of the AEF. He was a strong advocate of strategic operations.*

In December 1918 he was made chief historian of the USAAS,* and during the next several months he and his staff collected documents and histories from USAAS organizations. This collection, known as the "Gorrell History," was housed in the National Archives in Washington, D.C. Although a hodgepodge of histories, combat reports, rosters, letters, cablegrams, statistical studies, pictures, and charts with little organization, the collection is one of the most valuable resources for the study of the air service in World War I.

References. Goldberg, *Hist. USAF*. James J. Hudson, *Hostile Skies: A Combat History of the American Air Service in World War I*, 1968. Maurer Maurer, *The U.S. Air Service in World War I*, 4 vols., 1978 and 1979.

James J. Hudson

GRADES

Grades have been relatively stable in the air arm; however, they have changed from the USAAF* in World War II,* mostly because of separation from the U.S. Army.*

1990 Grade	1990 Title	1944 Title
O-10	General	General
O-9	Lieutenant General	Lieutenant General
O-8	Major General	Major General

O-7	Brigadier General	Brigadier General
O-6	Colonel	Colonel
O-5	Lieutenant Colonel	Lieutenant Colonel
O-4	Major	Major
O-3	Captain	Captain
O-2	First Lieutenant	First Lieutenant
O-1	Second Lieutenant	Second Lieutenant
		Warrant Officer (Chief)
		Warrant Officer (Junior Grade)
		Flight Officer
E-9	Chief Master Sergeant	
E-8	Senior Master Sergeant	
E-7	Master Sergeant	Master Sergeant
E-6	Technical Sergeant	Technical Sergeant
E-5	Staff Sergeant	Staff Sergeant
E-4	Sergeant	Sergeant
E-4	Senior Airman	
E-3	Airman First Class	Corporal
E-2	Airman	Private First Class
E-1	Airman Basic	Private

References. *AAF: A Directory, Almanac and Chronicle of Achievement*, 1944. "USAF Grade and Insignia," *AF*, May 1990, p. 40.

GRAND FORKS AIR FORCE BASE

This Strategic Air Command* (SAC) field, near Grand Forks, North Dakota, is on land donated to the USAF* by the citizens of Grand Forks. The facility was established in 1956. From 1957 to 1961, it was an interceptor* base with the Air Defense Command (ADC). In 1963, Grand Forks became a SAC base. Minuteman* II missiles were there from 1966 to 1974, followed by Minuteman IIIs. In 1990, it had headquarters of the 42nd Air Division, the 319th Bomb Wing (BW) with B-1s* and KC-135Rs (*see* C-135), and the 321st Strategic Missile Wing (SMW) with Minuteman IIIs.

References. "Guide to Major Air Force Installations Worldwide," *AF*, May 1990, p. 124. Mueller, *AFB*. Roberts, *Dir. USAF*.

GREELY, MAJOR GENERAL ADOLPHUS W. (1844–1935)

Greely was the chief signal officer of the U.S. Army from 1887 to 1906 and established the first balloon section in 1892. He arranged for the Army to provide $50,000 to Samuel P. Langley* in 1898 in support of efforts to build a heavier-than-air flying machine. Public outcry caused the Army to withdraw support after the machine, the Aerodrome A, fell into the Potomic River during launch in the fall of 1903.

Greely was dynamic and colorful. He began his military career as a private in the Union Army during the Civil War. He was instrumental in the installation of telegraph lines and equipment across the United States and in numerous other countries. He participated in polar exploration efforts, the most notable of which occurred in 1881, when he and his party of 25 reached latitude 83 north, the farthest north any party had traveled, and discovered new land north of Greenland.

References. Primary: William Mitchell, *General Greely: The Story of a Great American*, 1936. Secondary: Carroll V. Glines, *The Compact History of the United States Air Force*, 1963. Juliette A. Hennessy, *The United States Army Air Arm April 1861 to April 1917*, 1985. A. N. Marquis, *Who Was Who in America*, 1943.

D. K. Vaughan

GREENHAM COMMON. *See* RAF Greenham Common.

GREENLAND. *See* North Atlantic air bases; Thule Air Base.

GRENADA INCIDENT

The invasion of Grenada, Operation Urgent Fury, by the United States and some allies, was a minor campaign. However, it was important in terms of aerospace power* because of the threat posed by Grenada's pro-Cuban government and its geographic position. Its location, with an airfield under Cuban construction which was capable of serving Soviet military aircraft, was dangerous for its neighbors and the Panama Canal.

The USAF* task was mostly to provide airlift operations,* and it committed C-5As,* C-130s,* and C-141s.* Tactical operations* were to be conducted by AC-130Hs, E-3As,* EC-130s, F-15s,* KC-10s (*see* C-10), and MC-130s. These aircraft came from units of the Military Airlift Command* (MAC), the Strategic Air Command* (SAC), and the Tactical Air Command* (TAC).

USAF operations began on 23 October 1983 with surveillance of the Caribbean by E-3As. In the afternoon, President Ronald Reagan* gave the order to start the invasion. The first aircraft to reach the island was an AC-130 which did reconnaissance* and was subjected to flak* fire. Rangers were dropped from MC-130s, while AC-130s strafed flak, mortars, and trenches. When the airfield was secured, C-130s began to land under fire to unload, while AC-130s cleared the way for the Rangers. Late in the day, C-5s and C-141s brought in infantry. The next day, 26 October, AC-130s supported the rescue of U.S. medical students from the campus at Grand Anse. The evacuation of people, including the students, began the next day as airlift operations became routine. Hostilities officially ended on 2 November, and the first large joint and combined U.S. operation after the Vietnam War* had ended well against weak opposition. There had been problems with communications and controversy over the amount of freedom the media had.

The most significant aspect of the Grenada incident is that it was the first time since the era of Secretary of Defense (SECDEF) Robert S. McNamara* that commanders on the scene operated without micromanagement by the Office of the Secretary of Defense (OSD).

References. Primary: U.S. Congress, House Committee on Armed Services, *Lessons Learned as a Result of the U.S. Military Operations in Grenada*, 98th Cong., 2d Sess., 24 January 1984. Secondary: Daniel P. Bolger, *Americans at War: 1975–1986, An Era of Violent Peace*, 1988. James W. Canan, "Blue Christmas Coming Up," *AF*, January 1984, pp. 78–81. Stephen Harding, *Air War Grenada*, 1984. Edward N. Luttwak, *The Pentagon and the Art of War: The Question of Military Reform*, 1985.

GRIFFISS AIR FORCE BASE

Near Rome, New York, this is a Strategic Air Command* (SAC) facility. It was established in 1942 and was known as Rome until 1948. Then it was named in honor of Lieutenant Colonel Townsend E. Griffiss. Flying from the USSR to England in 1942, Griffiss's aircraft was mistaken for an enemy and shot down by the Royal Air Force (RAF). During World War II,* Griffiss provided depot maintenance* for aircraft engines. After the war it did development work. KC-135s (*see* C-135) were based there in 1959 and B-52s* in 1960. SAC took over the base in 1970. In 1990 its main units were the 416th Bomb Wing with B-52s and KC-135s, the Rome Air Development Center of the Air Force Systems Command* (AFSC), and headquarters of the 24th Air Division of the Tactical Air Command* (TAC).

References. "Guide to Major Air Force Installations Worldwide," *AF*, May 1990, p. 124. Mueller, *AFB*. Roberts, *Dir. USAF*.

GRISSOM AIR FORCE BASE

Grissom AFB is near Kokomo, Indiana. Originally, it was a U.S. Navy base, then the USAF Storage Branch from 1951 to 1954, and then Bunker Hill AFB from 1954 to 1968. It was named in 1968 to honor the USAF's* Virgil I. "Gus" Grissom, one of the original seven astronauts.* He died in the Apollo spacecraft fire in 1967. It is a Strategic Air Command* (SAC) base. From 1954 to 1957, the Tactical Air Command* (TAC) used the field. After SAC took over, Grissom had B-47s* and B-58s.* In 1990 it was used primarily by the 305th Air Refueling Wing (ARW) with EC-135s and KC-135s (*see* C-135).

References. "Guide to Major Air Force Installations Worldwide," *AF*, May 1990, p. 124. Mueller, *AFB*. Roberts, *Dir. USAF*.

GROUND-CONTROLLED APPROACH (GCA)

GCA is a navigational system for low-visibility landings. It was one of several ideas for that need. GCA won the competition in large measure because it requires no new equipment on board the airplane and no special training for the pilot.* GCA was one of the most important innovations in navigation of World War II.* The GCA system locates its client aircraft by ground-based radar* at about 30 miles from the runway. GCA controllers then guide the aircraft by radio communication until the plane can be landed visually.

GCA went into service in 1944. President Harry S Truman* (HST) gave the prestigious Collier Trophy to its inventor, Dr. Luis W. Alvarez, in 1946. The Berlin Airlift* was GCA's greatest single triumph. Without GCA, the air bridge could not have been sustained through Berlin's inclement winter weather. GCA enabled its command, now called the Air Force Communications Command* (AFCC), to claim it enabled planes to fly when the birds walked. The importance of GCA never diminished. It supported each successive airlift. In the Vietnam War* it was adapted to guide transports* to make air drops of cargo.

References. Ray L. Bowers, *Tactical Airlift*, 1983. Thomas S. Snyder, ed., *The Air Force Communications Command: 1938–1986; An Illustrated History*, rev. ed., 1986.

GROUND-CONTROLLED INTERCEPTION (GCI)

GCI uses ground-based facilities to guide fighters* or interceptors* to the engagement of enemy aircraft* based upon information from radar.* Originally, GCI referred to the radar system itself. In the summer of 1940, the British developed a radar scope for GCI called a plan position indicator (PPI), which appeared to the operator as similar to a map of the area and showed aircraft as spots of light on the map. This permitted efficient guidance for friendly aircraft toward the enemy planes and, under the control of a skilled and knowledgeable operator, could provide an initially advantageous position for the friendly aircraft from which to strike.

The United States had no such equipment or system at Pearl Harbor* in December 1941. The British Royal Air Force (RAF) sent Robert Watson-Watt, the famous scientific adviser on telecommunications to the Air Ministry, to the United States to help. His report spurred the USAAF* to catch up. In the early days a Ground Observer Corps* (GOC) supplemented the ground radar. Radar improvements after World War II* reduced the usefulness of a GOC. In 1951, airborne early warning and control (AEW&C) systems came into USAF* service to provide the supplement of greater surveillance, especially out to sea. The modern form of AEW&C is the Airborne Warning and Control System* (AWACS).

References. C&C, vol. 1. Futrell, *USAF in Korea*. Bill Gunston, *Night Fighters: A Development and Combat History*, 1976. Woodford Agee Heflin, ed., *The United States Air Force Dictionary*, 1956.

GROUND OBSERVER CORPS (GOC)

The GOC reported to the USAAF* on airborne aircraft to aid in the identification and location of enemy airplanes for air defense purposes. The observers were normally civilian volunteers, sometimes called aircraft spotters.

The USAAF had 4,000 observer stations on the East Coast and 2,400 on the West Coast in late 1941. Exercises testing the network proved disappointing. In July 1942 a formal organization was created, the AAF Ground Observer Corps. The number of stations on the East Coast was increased to 9,000, and 3,000 were added along the Gulf Coast. In 1943, the USAAF estimated that 1,500,000 citizens had served as observers. The GOC members were initially enthusiastic but lacked training and equipment, and their calls tended to overload the Ground-

Controlled Intercept (GCI) centers. The boredom of long vigils and lack of enemy strikes lowered morale, reductions began in 1943, and the system closed in 1944. Improvements in radar should reduce or eliminate any future need for the revival of a GOC.

References. C&C, vols. 1 and 6. Woodford Agee Heflin, ed., *The United States Air Force Dictionary*, 1956.

GROUP

A group is a USAF* unit, usually intermediate between a wing* and squadrons.* Groups normally are numbered using up to three Arabic digits. There are a few with unusual missions that are named groups, such as the Orientation Group. Groups may have operational or support missions. When under a wing, each group will carry the wing's number followed by its task before the word *group*. Thus, the 28th Bomb Wing's subordinate units would be the 28th Bomb Group, 28th Maintenance and Supply Group, 28th Administrative Group, and so forth. In the USAAF* a group was roughly equivalent to a USAF wing.

References. *AAF: A Directory, Almanac and Chronicle of Achievement*, 1944. Woodford Agee Heflin, ed., *The United States Air Force Dictionary*, 1956. Ravenstein, *Org. USAF*.

GRUMMAN AIRCRAFT ENGINEERING CORPORATION. *See* U-16.

GUADALCANAL

The USAAF* supported the U.S. Navy's landings and beachhead at Guadalcanal Island in the Solomons by flying reconnaissance* sorties with B-17s.* The B-17s also struck at the Japanese navy's efforts in late August 1942 to reinforce the enemy garrison. Soon thereafter, the 67th Fighter Squadron had some P-400s on Henderson Field on the island. The P-400s were Royal Air Force (RAF) Airacobras, or variants on the P-39,* repossessed from the British, and were of such low performance they could only do the attack* function. Later, some P-39s joined the 67th, and B-17s operated out of Henderson for a period of time. At one point, C-47s* were used to supply the field with gasoline. B-17s participated in the Battle of Santa Cruz Islands in October, but without effect except for reconnaissance. In November the USAAF could supply some P-38s* for Henderson. At last the USAAF had a fighter* able to contest the Japanese. A final enemy thrust at Guadalcanal was repulsed. USAAF B-17s scored hits in this action on the battleship *Hiei* and a troop transport. Guadalcanal was won, but the USAAF contribution was minor, a reflection of its weakness in the Pacific area in 1942.

References. Primary: James H. Straubel, ed., *Air Force Diary: 111 Stories from the Official Service Journal of the USAAF*, 1947. Secondary: C&C, vol. 4.

GUAM. *See* Andersen AFB; Marianas Islands.

GUARD OF HONOR

One of the more important novels* about the USAF* is *Guard of Honor* (1948) by James Gould Cozzens. It won a Pulitzer Prize and was one of five Book-of-the-Month works by Cozzens. The story is of USAAF* administration and concerns the interactions between career and citizen airmen, whites and blacks, airmen and civilians, men and women, and bosses and subordinates.

References. John Chamberlin, "Retrieval of a Gifted Writer from Undue Obscurity," *The Wall Street Journal*, 16 June 1983, p. 20. "The 40th Anniversary of the USAF," a special issue of *AH*, September 1987, p. 208. David K. Vaughan, *The Literature of Flight*, 1982.

GULF WAR. *See* Iraq War.

GUNN, COLONEL PAUL I. "PAPPY" (1900–1957)

Gunn was a legendary USAAF,* U.S. Navy, and civilian pilot* who, as chief "gadgeteer" of General George C. Kenney's* Fifth Air Force* (5AF), was largely responsible for many key aircraft modifications and new tactics. These were highly important to air power's success in supporting General Douglas MacArthur's drives during World War II.*

Born in Quitman, Arkansas, he joined the Navy in 1917 and served 20 years. He completed naval flight training* in 1925 and quickly developed a reputation as an outstanding pilot and incomparable storyteller. When he retired from the Navy as a chief petty officer, he moved his family to the Philippines where he became superintendent of maintenance for Philippine Air Lines.

After Pearl Harbor* the airline was absorbed into the USAAF, and Gunn became a captain. Leaving his family behind, he went to the 5AF in Australia to become engineering officer for the 3rd Attack Group. It was here that his reputation for improvisation began with his modifications to the A-20.* Installing two 450-gallon fuel tanks and four extra fixed .50-caliber machine guns, he turned a mediocre plane into one of the 5AF's most potent weapons. Turning his talents to the B-25C,* he modified it with eight fixed .50s. He also developed the low-altitude skip bombing* tactic for use against ships. Using Gunn's planes and tactics, a squadron* sank four cargo ships and two destroyers in 15 minutes in the Battle of the Bismarck Sea.* Until the end of the war he continued to work wonders with limited resources. He left active duty in 1946 and returned to his family in the Philippines and started another airline. He was killed in an aircraft accident north of Manila.

References. Primary: George C. Kenney, *The Saga of Pappy Gunn*, 1959. Secondary: DuPre, *USAF Bio*.

Budd A. Jones, Jr.

GUNNER

In 1912 Captain Charles DeForest Chandler* of the Aeronautical Division of the U.S. Army Signal Corps* fired a machine gun from an airplane while Lieutenant DeWitt Milling was the pilot.* The flight, at College Park,* Maryland, was to test the feasibility of firing a gun from a plane, making Chandler the USAF's* first gunner.

Soon after World War I* began, aircraft were armed with gunners using flexible gun mounts. When the fixed-gun fighter* was developed, it became the best way to strike at another aircraft or a surface target. Nevertheless, defensive gunners were effective. The observer* in observation aviation* had single or twin machine guns in a flexible mount. Bombers* had gunners fore, aft, and sometimes below for defense. Since almost all guns of the time were .30 caliber, a defending gunner was not badly outclassed by the most common fighters, which had two fixed guns. The fighter did have the advantage that the plane's forward speed added to the velocity of its bullets.

Between the world wars aircraft increased in speed and operating altitudes, presenting difficulties for the open-cockpit gunner who stood in the slipstream. Shields were tried, but the solution had to be enclosing the gunner inside, whether with a turret or window as in the B-17G.* The use of much heavier fighter armament in World War II* made the single .30-caliber flexible gun ineffective. The answer was multiple-gun turrets, power turrets, the Browning* .50-caliber gun and 20mm cannon, computing sights, and remotely controlled turrets. Although the massed firepower of a large bomber formation was formidable, the fighter still had an advantage, especially in a head-on assault. Attacking from the front with heavier weapons and higher closure speeds, the fighter also faced fewer defensive guns.

The head-on pass was an answer to other problems the fighter faced which were aggravated after World War II. As bombers operated at higher altitudes, the speed and maneuverability advantages of the fighter were reduced. The pursuit curve, or the natural path required of the fighter in a gun pass on another airplane when deflection is a factor, became much less practical. Yet, higher speeds in aircraft made the head-on approach increasingly difficult with the limited range of aerial guns, so the tail chase finally became necessary.

Still, when the bomber was piston-engined, such as a B-29* which operated from 20,000 to 30,000 feet, and encountered a jet fighter with heavy guns, such as the MiG-15, the fighter had an advantage. Going higher, as with the piston- and jet-engined B-36,* and with all jet power, as with the B-47* and B-52,* kept bomber gunnery defense viable for a time because these conditions meant tail chases.

The advent of the afterburner and the air interceptor missile* (AIM) restored a large speed advantage to the fighter and opened up ranges. With ranges of the AIM-4*- and AIM-7*-type missiles, a gunnery defense of aircraft has become a minor function. Bomber defense now must primarily rely upon evading detection, electronic warfare,* and devices to frustrate infrared guidance systems.

The heyday of the gunner was World War I, but he was still highly effective in World War II, when the USAAF* trained 297,000 men in gunnery schools. More men did flexible gunnery as navigators* and bombardiers.* Many gunners did double duty as flight engineers* and radio operators. Six Hollywood star actors flew in the USAAF as gunners. Radio operator gunners were Charlton Heston, Walter Matthau, and Slim Pickens (Louis Bert Lindley, Jr.). Plain gunners were Sabu Dastagir, Norman Fell, and Clark Gable.*

Gunners, who have a defensive task, have fewer chances than fighter pilots* to destroy enemy aircraft.* Nevertheless, the USAAF had some high-scoring gunners:

	Victories
Staff Sergeant Donald Crossley	12
Master Sergeant Michael Arooth	9
Technical Sergeant Arthur P. Benko	9
Staff Sergeant Benjamin F. Warmer	9
Technical Sergeant Thomas Dye	8

Sergeants Benko and Warmer each were given credit for seven on a single day. Some people think gunners with credit for five enemy aircraft should be called aces;* other people do not.

Movies: *Aerial Gunner*, 1943; *The Rear Gunner*, 1942.

References. Primary: George K. Bernhard, Jr., "Close Encounter of a B-17 Gunner," *AH*, June 1982, pp. 106–10. Secondary: C&C, vol. 6. Georgia Maddox Engle, "B-52 Tailgunner—Last of a Dying Breed," *AH*, December 1983, pp. 268–70. John Steinbeck, *Bombs Away: The Story of a Bomber Team*, 1942. Charles A. Watry and Duane L. Hall, *Aerial Gunners: The Unknown Aces of World War II*, 1986.

See also weapon system operator.

GUNS. *See* Browning machine guns; GAU-8 30mm Avenger; Lewis gun; M-61; 20mm guns; Vickers gun.

GUNSHIP

In 1971, General John D. Ryan,* chief of staff of the Air Force,* said the USAF* gunship was one of the better developments of the Vietnam War.* The USAF term *gunship* refers to its fixed-wing, side-firing aircraft. Other services identify different weapons systems as "gunships." In Commando Hunt* operations, the advanced gunships became known as the best truck killers available. General William H. Momyer* thought so; he also believed the gunship with sensors was the best means for support of a night battle by either air or ground weapons in Southeast Asia (SEA).

An old concept, the lateral firing gunship idea was resurrected within the Tactical Air Command* (TAC) during the limited war fervor of the early 1960s. Modified C-47s* fitted with M-61* 7.62mm miniguns and flare dispensers for night operations were the first of the genre to be tested in combat, staging from Bien Hoa* AB in December 1964. The advantages they provided in being able to loiter over targets, to change firing patterns readily, to correct malfunctions in flight, and to deliver an intense volume of ordnance rapidly and accurately proved ideal for fire support missions in South Vietnam and contiguous battle-fields where defensive fire was not prohibitive. Test missions continued out of Bien Hoa until November 1965 when the 4th Air Commando Squadron arrived at Tan Son Nhut* AB, outside Saigon, with a complement of 20 AC-47s (*see* C-47) called "Spooky," "Puff," and "Dragonship." The latter two terms were derived from a popular song of the period, "Puff the Magic Dragon." The plane quickly became one of the most dependable weapon systems available for the defense of hamlets and forts. The AC-47s and follow-on-type gunships were vital additions for other tactical operations* such as close air support, armed reconnaissance,* and interdiction. Advanced gunships, the AC-119 (*see* C-119) and AC-130 (*see* C-130), were introduced into combat after the SEA conflict escalated.

References. David A. Anderton, *History of the U.S. Air Force*, rev. ed., 1989. Jack S. Ballard, *Development and Employment of Fixed-Wing Gunships, 1962–1972*, 1982. William Head, "AC-47 Gunship Development," *Air Power History*, Fall 1990, pp. 37–46.

See also Spectre.

Warren A. Trest

GUNSMOKE. *See* competitions.

GUNTER AIR FORCE BASE

Originally Montgomery Municipal Airport, Alabama, Gunter was taken over by the USAAC* in its expansion of basic flying training* in 1940. It was renamed for William A. Gunter, a former mayor of Montgomery who was an advocate of air power. Flying operations ceased in 1945. The field was near Maxwell* AFB and, after the war, Gunter became an Air University* base. In 1990 the principal units at Gunter were headquarters of the Computer Systems Division, Air Force Communications Command* (AFCC); and the Air Force Logistics Management Center, Air Force Logistics Command* (AFLC).

References. "Guide to Major Air Force Installations Worldwide," *AF*, May 1990, p. 124. Mueller, *AFB*. John H. Napier III, "The Military, Montgomery, and Maxwell," *AH*, December 1977, pp. 192–93. Roberts, *Dir. USAF*.

GUY-IN-BACK. *See* weapon system operator.

GUY NAMED JOE, A. *See* movies.

H

H-3 JOLLY GREEN GIANT

The USAF* borrowed three U.S. Navy HSS-2s in 1962 to supply Texas Towers.* Their usefulness led to an order later that year from the Sikorsky Aircraft Division of the United Aircraft Corporation for a CH-3C long-range transport* version. Its first flight was in 1963.

Later, a rescue* version, the HH-3E, was bought. It had armor, aerial refueling* capability and armament and could use fuel drop tanks.* It was highly useful in the Vietnam War,* and the airmen affectionately called it "Jolly Green Giant," which became its official name. Two H-3s made the first helicopter* nonstop transatlantic flight in 1967, a distance of 4,270 miles. A third version was the VH-3A used for presidential airlift.*

Characteristics (HH-3A): engines, two General Electric T58-GE-5 turboshafts of 1,500 horsepower each; rotor diameter, 62 feet; length, 73 feet; height, 18 feet; gross weight, 22,050 pounds; top speed, 164 miles per hour; service ceiling, 13,600 feet; range, 760 miles with external fuel; payload, 5,000 pounds.

References. Swanborough, *US Mil. Airc.* Susan H. H. Young, "Gallery of USAF Weapons," *AF*, May 1990, p. 154.

H-19 CHICKASAW

The Sikorsky Aircraft Division of United Aircraft Corporation designed the H-19 in 1948 as a utility helicopter.* The first flight was in 1949, and active service began in 1951. Most H-19s served with the Military Air Transport Service (MATS) for rescue* operations and were designated SH-19s. In 1952, H-19s began rescue work in the Korean War.* They, and other rescue aircraft, saved 170 USAF* airmen who went down in enemy territory. This was 10 percent of total losses. The H-19 left active service in 1967.

Characteristics (H-19B): engine, Wright R-1300-3 of 800 horsepower; rotor diameter, 53 feet; length, 42 feet; height, 13 feet; gross weight, 7,900 pounds; top speed, 112 miles per hour; range, 360 miles; payload, 10 troops.

References. Futrell, *USAF in Korea*. James T. Stewart, ed., *Airpower: The Decisive Force in Korea*, 1957. Swanborough, *US Mil. Airc*.

H-21 WORKHORSE

The first tandem-rotor helicopter* for the USAF* was the H-21 from the Piasecki Helicopter Corporation. It was an adaptation of the U.S. Navy's HRP-2 and was ordered in 1949. Its first flight was in 1952. Its first service was in rescue* with the Military Air Transport Service (MATS) as the SH-21B. In 1953 it became a tactical airlift* transport.* A similar model was bought by the U.S. Army. In 1962 the H-21 was redesignated as the CH-21, and the SH-21B changed to the HH-21B. It was retired in the early 1970s. The H-21's nickname was "The Flying Banana."

Characteristics: engine, Wright R-1820–103 of 1,425 horsepower; rotor diameter, 45 feet; length, 86 feet; height, 15 feet; gross weight, 13,300 pounds; top speed, 131 miles per hour; service ceiling, 9,450 feet; payload, 20 troops.

Reference. Swanborough, *US Mil. Airc*.

H-53 SUPER JOLLY

As the USAF* gained experience in the Vietnam War,* it wanted a better rescue* aircraft than the HH-3A (*see* H-3). The requirements were called Combat Aircrew Rescue Aircraft (CARA). CARAs were to be available near the borders of North Vietnam to pick up aircrews that were shot down. The USAF found that its needs could be filled by the U.S. Marine Corps CH-53A Sea Stallion, made by the Sikorsky Aircraft Division of the United Aircraft Corporation. Its characteristics were similar to the HH-3A but on a larger scale with the addition of ejection seats and more modern avionics. The first flight of the HH-53B Super Jolly was in 1967, and it entered active service the same year.

Higher-powered engines were used for the HH-53C, which was designed to stand by for rescue during the Apollo launches and to recover military satellites from the Pacific Ocean. The HH-53C was also used as a transport* for large payloads. A variant was the MH-53H, bought in 1979. It was intended to have a better night and weather capability, called Pave Low II. The MH-53H used forward-looking infrared* (FLIR) designed for special operations. In 1986, work began to modify HH- and CH-53Bs and –53Cs to MH-53Js with Pave Low III Enhanced, which included terrain-following and terrain-avoidance radar.* Deliveries of these began in 1987.

Characteristics (HH-53C): engines, two General Electric T64-GE-7 turboshafts of 3,925 horsepower each; rotor diameter, 72 feet; length, 88 feet; height, 25 feet; gross weight, 42,000 pounds; top speed, 186 miles per hour; service ceiling, 18,550 feet; range, 540 miles; payload, including external, 20,000 pounds.

References. Swanborough, *US Mil. Airc*. Susan H. H. Young, "Gallery of USAF Weapons," *AF*, May 1990, pp. 154–55.

H-60G PAVE HAWK

Short of rescue* helicopters,* the USAF* began buying U.S. Army UH-60A Black Hawks in 1982 as MH-60Gs. The manufacturer, Sikorsky Aircraft, a division of United Technologies Corporation, modified the helicopter for USAF work. Its specialty is low-altitude rescue operations, either day or night, under marginal weather conditions.

Characteristics: engines, two General Electric T700-GE-700 turboshafts of 1,560 horsepower each; rotor diameter, 54 feet; length, 50 feet; height, 17 feet; gross weight, 20,250 pounds; top speed, 184 miles per hour; service ceiling, 19,000 feet; range with external tanks, 1,380 miles; payload, 14 troops.

References. George C. Larson, "A Legacy for the Night Hawk," *AF*, February 1984, pp. 102–4. Susan H. H. Young, "Gallery of USAF Weapons," *AF*, May 1990, p. 155.

HADRIAN. *See* G-4.

HAGUE COMMISSION TO REGULATE AERIAL WARFARE

Representing the signatory nations of the Five Power Treaty of the Washington Naval Conference* signed in 1922, a Special Jurist Commission met at The Hague from 1922 to 1923. Although its proposals were never ratified, the commission recommended rules to regulate aerial bombardment and to forbid "terror bombing" of civilian populations.

The five powers, Britain, France, Italy, Japan, and the United States, agreed to form the commission because the conference's Special Subcommittee on Aircraft could not agree on rules for aerial bombing and radiotelegraphy. The clause forbidding terror bombing gained much attention in 1923 because fears of aerial bombing of civilians had been present ever since H. G. Wells' science fiction novels described such operations. Moreover, aviation theorists such as Giulio Douhet* believed aerial bombing would break a nation's will to resist. Following the Hague Commission's report, the U.S. State Department tried to obtain a treaty based on the report. Of the other nations, only Japan agreed. In 1928, the State Department placed the report in its dead file.

References. Lester H. Brune, "An Effort to Regulate Aerial Bombing: The Hague Commission of Jurists, 1922–1923," *AH*, September 1982, pp. 183–85. Morton W. Royse, *Aerial Bombardment and the International Regulation of Warfare*, 1928.

Lester H. Brune

HAHN AIR BASE

This field is in West Germany, near Sohren, and was activated in 1951. The U.S. Air Forces in Europe* (USAFE) began operations from this base in 1953. Hahn was built under the same circumstances as Bitburg* AB. Its location made it the worst airfield of the series for flying because its field elevation and its cloudy and rainy climate is very unfavorable for flight operations. The 50th Tactical Fighter Wing (TFW) has been based at Hahn since it opened. It has had fighters* from the F-86* to the F-16.*

References. Primary: Chuck Yeager and Leo Janos, *Yeager: An Autobiography*, 1985. Secondary: "Guide to Major Air Force Installations Worldwide," *AF*, May 1990, p. 124. Roberts, *Dir. USAF*. Michael Skinner, *U*S*A*F*E: A Primer of Modern Air Combat in Europe*, 1988.

HAIPHONG, VIETNAM

This was the main seaport for North Vietnam in the Vietnam War.* It was a principal facility for war supplies for the North. For nearly all the war, it was declared a sanctuary for the enemy by Presidents Lyndon B. Johnson* (LBJ) and Richard M. Nixon. This was done to avoid antagonizing neutrals and North Vietnam's allies.

Nixon finally allowed a blockade of Haiphong and other ports, including mining,* in May 1972. In October Nixon again gave the enemy sanctuary in an effort to gain the foe's goodwill in the Paris peace talks. The talks soon stalled and Linebacker* II was authorized with the main targets of Hanoi* and Haiphong. Within Haiphong, the specific targets were the rail yards, port facilities, and oil and munitions storage. The North Vietnamese fought back with everything they had. They used up most of their flak* and surface-to-air missiles* (SAM), and their fighters* were overwhelmed. In the last days of the campaign, there was no damage to the USAF.*

The bombers* had devastated their targets. The North Vietnamese became conciliatory and the assault was called off on 28 December after 11 days. A cease-fire was signed in Paris on 23 January 1973.

References. Primary: Karl J. Eschmann, *Linebacker: The Untold Story of the Air Raids over North Vietnam*, 1989. Secondary: Berger, *USAF in SEA*, 1977. Futrell, *Ideas*, vol. 2.

HANOI, VIETNAM

Not only was this city the North Vietnamese capital, it was the most important economic and transportation hub in the country. Like Haiphong,* it was given sanctuary status by Presidents Lyndon B. Johnson* (LBJ) and Richard M. Nixon to show goodwill to the enemy. This political air superiority* enabled North Vietnam to have secure air defense installations around Hanoi, including five air bases.

The North Vietnamese broke off peace negotiations in Paris on 13 December 1972. Nixon decided on air raids with Linebacker* II to pressure the enemy to negotiate, and Hanoi was struck heavily beginning on 18 December. The damage caused to the rail system, storage facilities, and electric power was significant. Other targets were radio communications installations, military airfields, surface-to-air missile* (SAM) sites, and bridges. These latter targets were hurt, but not as much as the former. The campaign ended on 28 December.

Following Linebacker II, the North Vietnamese returned to the peace talks. The talks then made rapid progress and a cease-fire was agreed upon by 23 January. It would be difficult to argue that there was no relation between Linebacker II and the resumption of the peace talks.

References. Primary: Karl J. Eschmann, *Linebacker: The Untold Story of the Air Raids over North Vietnam*, 1989. Secondary: David A. Anderton, *History of the United States Air Force*, rev. ed., 1989. Berger, *USAF in SEA*.

HANOI HILTON. *See* prisoners of war (North Vietnam).

HANOI JANE. *See* prisoners of war (North Vietnam).

HANOVER STREET. *See* movies.

HANSCOM AIR FORCE BASE

This AFB is 18 miles northwest of Boston, Massachusetts, and is the location of the Electronic Systems Division (ESD) of Air Force Systems Command* (AFSC). ESD is responsible for the acquisition of Command, Control, Communications and Intelligence (C3I) systems for the USAF* as well as systems for other military services and other federal organizations. It is home to the Massachusetts Institute of Technology (MIT) Lincoln Laboratory, a Federal Contract Research Center (FCRC), or think tank,* with expertise in air defense. It is also home to the Air Force Geophysics Laboratory (AFGL).

Ground breaking for Boston Auxiliary Airport was in 1941. P-40s* arrived in 1942. The field was renamed Laurence G. Hanscom Field in 1943 shortly after Hanscom, a respected journalist and aviation enthusiast, was killed in an airplane accident. By the end of World War II,* MIT had acquired a preeminent position in electronics research. In the next decade the Boston suburbs had a vigorous growth in the electronics industry. Thus, the area had advantages for research facilities. In 1951, the Air Force Cambridge Research Center (AFCRC), now the AFGL, was located on the base. In the same year the decision was made to locate the Lincoln Laboratory there. In 1957 the Air Force Systems Management Office (AFSMO), now the ESD, was formed.

References. E. Michael Del Papa, *Fact Sheets: The Naming of Hanscom Air Force Base*, *Operational History of Hanscom Air Force Base*, *The Electronic Systems Division Story*, n.d. E. Michael Del Papa and Mary P. Warner, *A Historical Chronology of Hanscom AFB, 1941–1986*, 1987, and *A Historical Chronology of the Electronic Systems Division, 1947–1986*, 1987. Mueller, *AFB*.

E. Michael Del Papa

HANSELL, MAJOR GENERAL HAYWOOD S., JR., "POSSUM" (1903–1988)

Hansell was an important and influential planner and conductor of strategic operations.* Born into a family with a long tradition of U.S. Army service, he turned down an appointment to the U.S. Military Academy (USMA) to attend the Georgia Institute of Technology. Restless as an engineer, he enrolled as a flying, or aviation, cadet* in 1928. He became a pilot* and regular officer in 1929. He was an original member of the USAAC's* first aerial demonstration team, Captain Claire L. Chennault's* "Three Men on the Flying Trapeze." In 1931 he attended the Air Corps Tactical School* (ACTS) and caught the eye of Lieutenant Colonel Harold L. George,* chief of the ACTS' Bombardment Section. Hansell became an instructor and active member of the ACTS' "bomber mafia." He was a staunch advocate of strategic operations without fighter escort.*

Major Hansell went to work in the Air War Plans Division* (AWPD) of the Air Staff* in 1941. Hansell and three other former ACTS instructors and bomber* enthusiasts, George, Lieutenant Colonel Ken Walker, and Major Laurence S. Kuter,* devised AWPD-1.* That was the blueprint for strategic operations to weaken the German war machine and thus topple the Nazi state. The plan called for 3,800 bombers to hit 154 targets for a period of six months to destroy Germany's vital economic centers. After Pearl Harbor,* Hansell led the revision of AWPD-1 into a more precise plan, AWPD-42, and contributed to the development of a plan for the Combined Bomber Offensive* (CBO) used in Europe. In 1943, Brigadier General Hansell successfully commanded B-26 Marauder* and B-17* wings in Europe.

His success earned him the chance to lead the new XXI Bomber Command in the Pacific theater. On 24 November 1944, his B-29s* took off from the Marianas* and made their first raid on Tokyo in the strategic campaign against Japan.* However, high-altitude precision daylight bombing proved indecisive over Japan. Hansell was replaced by Major General Curtis E. LeMay,* who introduced the devastating strategy of low-level incendiary bombing. He retired in 1946 but was recalled in 1951 to serve as chief of the USAF Military Defense Assistance Program until 1955.

References. Primary: Haywood S. Hansell, Jr., *The Air Plan That Defeated Hitler*, 1972, and *The Strategic Air War against Germany and Japan*, 1986. Secondary: John L. Frisbee, "The Loneliness of Command," *AF*, July 1983, p. 77. Futrell, *Ideas*, vol. 1. Barry D. Watts, *The Foundations of U.S. Air Doctrine*, 1984.

Peter R. Faber

"HAP." *See* Arnold, General of the Air Force H. H.

HARM. *See* AGM-88A.

HARPOON. *See* AGM-84A-1.

HAT-IN-THE-RING SQUADRON. *See* 94th Aero Squadron.

HAVE NAP. *See* AGM-142A.

HAWK. *See* P-1; P-36.

HEADQUARTERS COMMAND, USAF

This major command* (MAJCOM) was first called the Bolling* Field Command in 1946. Its mission was to provide support functions. It was redesignated as the Headquarters Command in 1958. It was inactivated in 1976, and its tasks were divided between the Military Airlift Command* (MAC) and the 1947th Administrative Support Group. The 1947th was later redesignated as the 1947th Headquarters Support Group.

References. "Headquarters Command, USAF," *AF*, May 1976, p. 68. Ravenstein, *Org. USAF*.

HEAVY PRESS PROGRAM

In occupied Germany, the USAAF* found enormous, heavy presses used for aircraft production. The USAF* envisioned such presses as ideal for the jet age because they could extrude large airframe components and so would be particularly useful in mass production. A program to sponsor aircraft industry adoption of such presses was begun and some were acquired. Before it was completed, the view prevailed that aircraft would never again be built in the numbers used in World War II.*

Reference. Charles D. Bright, *The Jet Makers: The Aerospace Industry from 1945 to 1972*, 1978.

HEGENBERGER, MAJOR GENERAL ALBERT F. (1895–1983)

Hegenberger, with First Lieutenant Lester J. Maitland,* was the first to span the Pacific from California to Hawaii. In 1927, in a Fokker trimotor named *Bird of Paradise*,* the two flew 2,418 miles nonstop in 25 hours and 50 minutes, for which they received the Mackay Trophy. In 1976 Hegenberger was inducted into the National Aviation Hall of Fame in Dayton, Ohio.

He was born in Boston, Massachusetts, and attended the Massachusetts Institute of Technology (MIT) for three years before enlisting in the Aviation Section of the U.S. Army Signal Corps* in 1917. He served for many years as an engineering officer at McCook Field, Ohio, and was responsible for the development and improvement of various aircraft navigational instruments. In 1935, Hegenberger was awarded the Collier Trophy for personally performing the first all-instrument flight with equipment he had invented for this purpose. He served in the Pacific theater during World War II.* Afterward he was chief of the Special Weapons Group and assistant to the chief for atomic energy at headquarters of the USAF.* This group was credited with detecting the first Soviet atomic bomb test in 1949, for which Hegenberger received a second Legion of Merit. He retired in 1949.

References. Primary: U.S. Air Force Oral History Interview K239.0512–854, 11–12 February 1976, USAFHRC/OH, Maxwell AFB, Alabama. Secondary: Air Force Pamphlet 31–1, "Roster of Retired General Officers," 1987. *Biographical Study of USAF General Officers, 1917–1952*, vol. 1, n.d. DuPre, *USAF Bio*.

James C. Hasdorff

HELICOPTERS

These aircraft depend upon rotary rather than fixed wings and carry the designation of *H*. They can hover, take off and land vertically, and fly diagonally, but they are very limited in speed, service ceiling, range, and instrument flying.*

They have been very vulnerable to fighters,* flak,* and missiles. Thus, they have been highly limited unless they operated under air superiority.* The USAF* uses helicopters primarily for rescue* but also as minor transports* or for attack* or tactical airlift* in special situations.

References. Primary: Higham, *Combat Airc.*, vol. 3. Secondary: Frederic A. Bergerson, *The Army Gets an Air Force: Tactics of Insurgent Bureaucratic Politics*, 1980. Futrell, *Ideas*, vol. 2. Ernest J. Gentle and Lawrence W. Reithmaier, eds., *Aviation/Space Dictionary*, 6th ed., 1980. Susan H. H. Young, "Gallery of USAF Weapons," *AF*, May 1990, pp. 154–55.

See also Howze Board; *Mayaguez* incident; Son Tay prison raid; Vietnam War.

HELLENIKON AIR BASE

This U.S. Air Forces in Europe* (USAFE) base near Athens, Greece, has a support mission. It is named for a nearby town. It began operating in 1947. In 1990 its unit was the 7206th Air Base Group.

References. "Guide to Major Air Force Installations Worldwide," *AF*, May 1990, p. 124. Roberts, *Dir. USAF*.

HENDERSON FIELD. *See* Guadalcanal.

HERBICIDES. *See* Operation Ranch Hand.

HERCULES. *See* C-130.

HICKAM AIR FORCE BASE

This field in Hawaii was named in 1935 after Lieutenant Colonel Horace M. Hickam, who was killed in an aircraft accident in Texas in 1934. Hickam-based units have played an important role in every major conflict in which the United States has been engaged since the base was built. For U.S. interests, Hickam is one of the most vital links with all nations in the Pacific region, an area of increasing importance.

During the Japanese raid on Pearl Harbor,* Hickam aircraft and facilities were heavily damaged from strafing and bombing strikes. The base was attacked at the same time as the fleet to suppress U.S. air defense. On 7 December 1941, Hickam suffered 121 killed, 37 missing, and 274 wounded. Aircraft losses were severe with 157 of 231 destroyed or damaged. Hickam became a major staging base for forces used to prosecute World War II* in the Pacific, and the Korean* and Vietnam* Wars.

In 1957 Pacific Air Forces* (PACAF) headquarters was established at Hickam. As the air component of the Pacific Command (PACOM), it has been responsible for planning, conducting, and coordinating offensive and defensive air operations. The area of responsibility stretched roughly from the West Coast of the United States to the East Coast of Africa.

References. Primary: Harold S. Kaye, "Hickam Field, 7 December 1941—The First U.S. Army Air Corps [*sic*] Flying Fortress (B-17D) Combat Mission in World War II,"

AH, December 1966, pp. 218–27. Secondary: Kevin K. Krejcarek, ed., *Hickam, The First Fifty Years*, 1985. Mueller, *AFB*. William B. Murphy, "Beginnings of Hickam Field," *AAHS Journal*, Winter 1965, pp. 288–90.

George W. Hawks, Jr.

HIGH-VELOCITY AIRCRAFT ROCKET (HVAR)

The development of the HVAR has been followed by a host of folding-fin aircraft rockets like the AIM-4* family.

The USAAF's* interest in aircraft rockets began in 1942. Initially, efforts concentrated on adapting existing ground-force rockets to aircraft, but this proved unsatisfactory. The first product was the 4.5-inch forward-firing aircraft rocket, and tests proved it could be fired from a P-40.* However, the missile and its three-tube clusters had unsatisfactory accuracy and drag qualities.

The USAAF turned to fin-stabilized rockets developed by the U.S. Navy working with the National Defense Research Committee (NDRC) and the California Institute of Technology (CIT). The USAAF requested the five-inch HVAR, or "Holy Moses." It used a newly designed engine containing solventless, extruded fuel with a cruciform cross section. The USAAF first used HVAR on F-47s* in mid-July 1944 at St. Lo,* France. So successful were the strikes that HVARs were next used in support of the breakthrough in Brittany late in July. They also played a key part in halting the German offensive in August at Mortain. The HVAR was also used in the Pacific theater and Korean War.*

Characteristics: length, 72 inches; diameter, 5 inches; weight, 140 pounds; top speed, 938 miles per hour.

References. Primary: Case History of Aircraft Rockets (History Division, Air Technical Service Command, Wright Field, December 1945—USAFHRC 202.4–19). Secondary: Norman Friedman, *US Naval Weapons*, 1985. J. D. Gerrard-Gough and Albert B. Christman, *History of the Naval Weapons Center, China Lake, California*, vol. 2, 1978.

Lloyd H. Cornett, Jr.

HIGH WYCOMBE, ENGLAND

This town in south Buckinghamshire was near the headquarters of the VIII Bomber Command of the USAAF's* Eighth Air Force* (8AF). The headquarters itself was in the Wycombe Abbey School for Girls. In January 1944 the abbey became the headquarters for the 8AF. The headquarters was often referred to by its code name of Pinetree or as High Wycombe.

References. Primary: James Parton, *Air Force Spoken Here*, 1986.

W. A. Jacobs

HILL AIR FORCE BASE

Near Ogden, Utah, this field was activated in 1940 and named after Major Ployer P. Hill, a test pilot killed in the crash of the Boeing Aircraft Company's Model 299, the B-17* prototype, in 1935. Ogden Air Depot has operated the base for major supply and maintenance for northwestern United States. Minor aircraft maintenance began in 1941 and overhaul of B-17s in 1942. In 1943 an assembly line for B-24s* was opened. In the Korean War,* Ogden began overhauling B-26 Invaders* and B-29s.* Maintenance of the F-84* and F-89* began in 1953, and the F-101* and F-102* in 1957. Ogden became system manager of the F-4* in 1962 and of the F-16* in 1976. Ogden also has supported missiles: the Snark* beginning in 1954, IM-99* in 1957, Minuteman* in 1959, Titan* II in 1965, and Peacekeeper* in 1975.

References. Roger D. Launius, ''A Case Study in Civil-Military Relations: Hill Air Force Base and the Ogden Business Community, 1934–1945,'' *AH*, September 1988, pp. 154–63. Mueller, *AFB*. Kenneth L. Patchin, ed., *History of Hill Air Force Base*, 1981. P. Susan Weathers, *Chronology Ogden Air Logistics Center, Hill Air Force Base, Utah, 1976–1985*, 1986.

Charles G. Hibbard

HILL, COLONEL DAVID L. "TEX" (1915–   )

Hill scored 18 victories, 12 with the covert American Volunteer Group* (AVG) and six with the USAAF.*

Hill was born in Kwangju, Korea, and graduated from Austin College, Texas. He became a U.S. Navy pilot* and joined the AVG in 1941. After the USAAF took over the AVG, he commanded the 23rd Fighter Group. He led the first U.S. attack* on Formosa. The raid shot down seven Japanese aircraft and destroyed 35 on the ground with no losses. He returned to the United States in 1944 to command the 412th Fighter Group. The 412th was the United States' first jet group using first P-59s* and then F-80s.* After World War II,* he served in the Air National Guard* (ANG) and U.S. Air Force Reserve* (USAFR).

References. DuPre, *USAF Bio*. Gurney, *5 Down*. Hess, *Aces Album*.

HIROSHIMA AND NAGASAKI, JAPAN

These are the only locations against which nuclear weapons* have been used. Their bombing by two B-29s* precipitated Japan's surrender in World War II.*

President Harry S Truman* (HST) made the decision for the raids. The Japanese were warned and given peace terms well before the strikes. General Carl A. Spaatz* issued an order on 3 August to drop the first bomb as soon as the weather was suitable. Hiroshima, an industrial city, was first choice as a target. It had not been bombed before as it had been reserved as a nuclear target. The raiding force consisted of the B-29 *Enola Gay* carrying the bomb, named *Little Boy*, and two B-29s for observation. The commander was Colonel Paul W. Tibbetts,* and the unit was the 509th Composite Group. The bomb was dropped on 6 August, and the only hostile actions were a few flak* shells.

Afterward, HST again warned Japan. No reply had been received by 9 August, so the second bomb was used. At the time, the United States had made only two bombs. The target was to be Kokura with Nagasaki as a second choice. Nagasaki had been bombed during the war, but only lightly. Kokura had cloud cover, but a visual strike was possible at Nagasaki because of a hole in the clouds. Major Charles W. Sweeney commanded the B-29 *Bock's Car*, which dropped the second bomb named *Fat Man*.

At Hiroshima there was no air raid alert as an all-clear had been called 45 minutes earlier. In addition, the absence of actual strikes on Hiroshima had made the citizens complacent. Thus, the bomb burst on an unprotected city. The most dense parts of the city had 4.7 square miles destroyed. It is believed that 71,000 people died and 68,000 were injured out of a population of 345,000. More than 40,000 buildings, about 81 percent of the city, were destroyed. The people of Nagasaki were also casual despite an air raid alarm. It had 1.45 square miles destroyed. The Japanese said 23,700 were killed, 1,900 missing, and 23,300 injured out of a population of 270,000. The world would never be the same again.

References. Primary: Curtis E. LeMay and Bill Yenne, *Superfortress: The Story of the B-29 and American Air Power*, 1988. Secondary: C&C, vol. 5. Gordon Thomas and Max Morgan Witts, *Enola Gay*, 1977.

HO CHI MINH TRAIL

Named for the dictator of North Vietnam, the trail was basically a series of supply lines ranging from foot trails to truck and river routes leading from North Vietnam to South Vietnam. The trails also ran through Laos and Cambodia. It was also known as the Viet Cong Infiltration Route.

The trail had three main routes, each being used for a specific purpose. The Laos route was for trucks carrying supplies and some people from the north through Nape and Mu Gia passes. The Dong Hoi trail was for people. After training at Xuan Mar, troops were trucked to below Dong Hoi, crossed into Laos, and then went on foot to South Vietnam. The Cambodian portion was mainly for supplies and used both trucks and boats. The Laos portion of the trail was far more hazardous for Allied interdiction efforts than those sections inside South Vietnam. In Laos, flak* was intense, the terrain was very mountainous, maps were poor, and weather was difficult. In addition, few airmen shot down in Laos ever returned.

References. Primary: Michael J. C. Roth, "NIMROD—King of the Trail," *AF*, October 1971, pp. 30–34. Secondary: Berger, *USAF in SEA*. Futrell, *Ideas*, vol. 2. Richard H. Kohn and Joseph P. Harahan, eds., *Air Interdiction in World War II, Korea, and Vietnam*, 1986. Donald J. Mrozek, *Air Power and the Ground War in Vietnam: Ideas and Actions*, 1988.

See also Igloo White; Linebacker; Rolling Thunder; Vietnam War.

Frank L. Goldstein

HOLLOMAN AIR FORCE BASE

A Tactical Air Command* (TAC) base, this field in New Mexico was activated in 1942 as the Alamogordo Bombing and Gunnery Range. It was named in 1948 for Colonel George V. Holloman, a pioneer of instrument flying* and guided missiles.* Holloman died in a B-17* accident on Formosa in 1946. During World War II,* the base trained bomber* crews. It began experimental work on missiles in 1947 and other test work later. Fighters* were based there beginning in 1963, and tactical operations* training started in 1977. In 1990, it had the headquarters of the 833rd Air Division, the 49th Tactical Fighter Wing (TFW), and the 479th Tactical Training Wing (TTW). The 49th used F-15s,* and the 479th flew AT-38s (*see* T-38).

References. "Guide to Major Air Force Installations Worldwide," *AF*, May 1990, p. 124. Mueller, *AFB*. Roberts, *Dir. USAF*.

HOMESTEAD AIR FORCE BASE

Adjacent to Homestead, Florida, this base was begun in the late 1930s as a Pan American World Airways training base for flying-boat pilots.* In early 1942 it was released to the federal government for use as a stopover for aircraft being ferried to the Caribbean and North Africa. In 1943 USAAF* training began for C-46,* C-54,* and C-87 aircrews. By 1945 it was the largest four-engine training operation in the USAAF, but a severe hurricane led to a decision to close the field. In 1955 it was reactivated as headquarters for the Strategic Air Command's* (SAC) 823rd Air Division equipped with B-47s.* B-52s* replaced the B-47s in 1960. The 31st Tactical Fighter Wing (TFW) moved to Homestead in response to the Cuban missile crisis of 1962* and was still there in 1990. In 1968 the Tactical Air Command* (TAC) assumed control of the field. In 1981, base units started training in F-4s,* and in 1985 it became an operational base again with F-16s.*

References. "Guide to Major Air Force Installations Worldwide," *AF*, May 1990, p. 124. Mueller, *AFB*. Official History, Homestead AFB, Florida, 31 TFW Public Affairs Office, 1989. Roberts, *Dir. USAF*.

David L. Rosmer

HOUND DOG. *See* AGM-28.

HOWARD AIR FORCE BASE

In the Republic of Panama, Howard AFB represents USAF* operations in Latin America. The field began as a military post in 1928, and USAAC* use started in 1939. It was named for Major Charles H. Howard. In 1990 it had the headquarters of the 830th Air Division and the 24th Composite Wing with C-22As and C-130Es.* It was assigned to the Twelfth Air Force* (12AF) and the Tactical Air Command* (TAC).

References. "Guide to Major Air Force Installations Worldwide," *AF*, May 1990, p. 124. Roberts, *Dir. USAF*.

HOWELL COMMISSION. *See* Federal Aviation Commission.

HOWZE BOARD

In 1962 several factors led Secretary of Defense (SECDEF) Robert S. McNamara* to form the Army Tactical Mobility Requirements Board, usually called the Howze Board after its chairman, Lieutenant General Hamilton H.

Howze, director of Army aviation and a proponent of Army air power. The principal factor was that Army aviators manipulated McNamara into asking for the board. Another factor was the traditional USAF*-Army argument over attack* aviation. A third was McNamara's receptiveness to and sympathy for Army views. A fourth factor was the top defense priority given to the USAF since 1948. A fifth was the growing advocacy of greater use of the helicopter* by its partisans.

The helicopter advocates had already begun surreptitious tests and saw it as the answer to the Army's attack desires, as providing the dispersion and mobility sought for nuclear warfare, and as an ideal cargo and strike vehicle for anti-guerrilla operations. The John F. Kennedy* (JFK) administration was stressing antiguerrilla warfare.

The Howze Board was charged with examination of the Army's aviation concepts and organization and was made up of men sympathetic to Army air power. It recommended a major test of the helicopter as a battlefield transport* and attack craft. Its members believed the helicopter would enhance infantry, cavalry, artillery, and supply branches. This vertical assault concept was called airmobile operations. McNamara supported most of the board's views, and the "air assault division" was tested and approved in 1964. It was 100 percent air transportable. An ordinary infantry division was to have 101 helicopters, and an air assault division was to have 459.

The concept was given the test of battle in the Vietnam War,* mainly by the 101st Airborne Division. There were usually a limited number of adequate landing zones (LZ) near any enemy base that could be used by a formation of helicopters. The North Vietnamese used this knowledge, the number of the noisy incoming helicopters, a count of the artillery hanging from the helicopters, and U.S. Army preparation of an LZ to locate the planned LZ and to know the strength of the assault. The enemy commanders then usually had the time to decide whether to prepare an ambush or to retreat. The enemy could avoid contact by retreating only six miles from an LZ because that was the range of the 105mm howitzers airlifted by the helicopters.

The vertical assault, intended as an offensive weapon, thus often became a defensive operation after landing or after it failed to contact the enemy. Helicopter losses became heavy; one was lost for every 7.9 combat sorties between 1966 and 1971. The helicopter introduced other unexpected problems. It enabled senior commanders, nicknamed "flying squad leaders," to oversupervise or micro-manage small units while above them. Company commanders were diverted from command to give radio reports required by the senior officers.

The Army had 4,000 helicopters in South Vietnam in 1971. Thus the Howze Board strongly influenced the conduct of the Vietnam War, including the USAF role since the Army undertook much of its own attack operations. The board was also a factor in the continuing pressure by the Army to induce the USAF to adopt specialized attack aircraft. This pressure resulted in the USAF procurement of the A-7* and A-10.*

References. Frederic A. Bergerson, *The Army Gets an Air Force: Tactics of Insurgent Bureaucratic Politics*, 1980. Futrell, *Ideas*, vol. 2. James William Gibson, *The Perfect War: Technowar in Vietnam*, 1986. Richard G. Head, "The Air Force A-7 Decision; The Politics of Close Air Support," *AH*, December 1974, pp. 218–24.

See also C-7; Pace-Finletter memorandum of 4 November 1952; separation from the U.S. Army.

H2S. *See* Pathfinder Force.

H2X. *See* Pathfinder Force.

HU-16. *See* U-16.

"HUB." *See* Zemke, Colonel Hubert A.

HUGHES, JUSTICE CHARLES EVANS (1862–1948)

Hughes headed the presidential investigating committee established by Woodrow Wilson in response to charges of wrongdoing made against the Aircraft Production Board* of 1917–1918. The committee found no evidence of graft, corruption, or sabotage, but it strongly criticized the lack of direction, inexperience, and conflicts of interest among board members. Wilson eventually shifted the responsibility for aircraft production oversight to the Bureau of Aircraft Production,* one of the two agencies making up the USAAS.*

Hughes had been an associate justice of the Supreme Court and was the Republican candidate for president in 1916. Later he was secretary of state for Presidents Warren Harding and Calvin Coolidge.

References. Goldberg, *Hist. USAF*. A. N. Marquis, *Who Was Who in America*, vol. 2, 1950.

D. K. Vaughan

HUGHES COMMITTEE. *See* Hughes, Justice Charles Evans.

HUMANITARIAN OPERATIONS

Armed forces exist to protect citizens by dealing with violence from a hostile enemy or domestic disorder. Preparedness for this mission enables the military to have a high capability to protect and help people in emergencies. With air power this usually involves airlift operations* and rescue,* but it also can involve reconnaissance* and weapons. The capability for humanitarian service is a major contribution of the USAF* to the United States and the world.

The humanitarian capability was recognized early for the airplane with the advent of aeromedical evacuation.* In 1919 the USAAS* began aerial reconnaissance patrols to spot forest fires. The USAAC* performed the first large relief airlift in 1929 to help the victims of a flood in Alabama. In 1935 the USAAC bombed lava flows to protect Hilo, Hawaii, during an eruption by the volcano Mauna Loa. In 1939, the B-15* flew relief supplies to Chile for earthquake victims. As World War II* wound down, the USAAF* dropped badly needed food to the Dutch and evacuated prisoners of war.

The Berlin Airlift* of 1948–1949 was probably the greatest demonstration of the power of airlift for humanitarian ends. Since then, such operations have nearly become routine as the USAF has responded with relief to floods, earthquakes, and hurricanes. One of the most recent examples was the April 1989 delivery of equipment to fight the 3,000 square miles of oil slick resulting from the grounding of the Exxon *Valdez* tanker near Valdez, Alaska. From the patrols of 1919, the USAF has progressed to fighting forest fires by dropping retardant on the blazes.

Military technology today can predict disasters and not simply ameliorate them after the fact. Prediction can mean more effective action than just response, because it can provide loss containment or even prevention. The technology for this is multisensor reconnaissance linked to computers. For example, it is now known that the use of existing reconnaissance photographs could have warned of the flood disasters in the spring of 1983 by analysis of the snow pack. The floods cost 156 lives and more than $1 billion in property damage. The cost of preventive analysis would have been $5 million. Reconnaissance after a disaster can also provide valuable information for improving responses.

Similarly, the enormous power of nuclear weapons* and ballistic missiles* represents a threat to the continued existence of the human species. Yet this technology may also provide the opportunity to prevent extinction. There is no guarantee that there will never again be a collision of the earth with another large cosmic body. Such an accident could cause great loss of life and damage, and a sufficiently large body might cause the loss of all human life. Nuclear weapons and missiles provide the potential to deflect a large object on a collision course with the earth.

References. Andrew J. Birtle, "The Battle against Mauna Loa: The Use of Air Power to Protect Life and Property in Hawaii," *AH*, September 1988, pp. 181–89. Dino Brugioni, "New Roles for Recce," *AF*, October 1985, pp. 94–96, 99–101. Maurer, *Avn. in Army*. Harold F. Nufer, "Operation Chowhound: A Precedent for Post–World War II Humanitarian Airlift," *AH*, March 1985, pp. 2–9. Jeffrey P. Rhodes, "Giving Smokey a Hand," *AF*, October 1989, pp. 66–71.

"HUMP" AIRLIFT, THE

In World War II,* the United States had to furnish enough supplies to keep the Chinese fighting, not only for China's sake but also to provide bases for a future assault on Japan. When Japan closed the Burma Road, the only route into China was by air. This airlift probably kept China in the war and helped to defeat Japan. It was the pioneer effort for strategic airlift operations,* which have proven of immense value to the United States.

The airlift route began below sea level at Dinjan, India, passed over a series of mountains 14,000 to 16,000 feet high, and ended at Kunming, China, at an altitude of 6,200 feet. It was named the "Hump" for the rugged terrain over which it crossed. That terrain was only one of the hazards of "Flying the Hump." Aircrews often encountered the dilemma of extreme turbulence at minimum altitudes and icing conditions above. From May to November, monsoons dropped an average of 200 inches of rain on the route and runways. When the rains let up, the Japanese fighters* could find easy prey. Flying the "Hump" was probably the most hazardous 500 miles of air transport in the world. Yet the importance of the route overshadowed its hazards.

In its first month of operation, July 1942, C-47* transports* of the Tenth Air Force* (10AF) delivered 85 tons of cargo. There was a shortage of planes, crews, support equipment, supplies, and experience. By the end of 1942, responsibility for it went to the Air Transport Command (ATC), which set up an India-China Division (ICD). By April 1943, Brigadier General Claire L. Chennault* had to suspend operations because he lacked supplies. President Franklin D. Roosevelt* (FDR) then ordered tonnage to reach 7,000 by July and 10,000 by September. July set a new record, but it was 3,451 tons. Dangerous night flying was introduced to meet goals, and the 10,000-ton mark was reached in December. The accident rate reflected the dangers. There were 155 accidents with 168 deaths between June and December, an undesirable accident rate of two per 1,000 flying hours.

In September 1944, Brigadier General William H. Tunner* became ICD commander. He achieved increased tonnage with fewer losses. In July 1945, his crews carried a record 71,042 tons with an accident rate of 0.358 per 1,000 hours. The "Hump" ended in November 1945. It had hauled 650,000 tons of gasoline, ammunition, men, and other supplies. Tunner claimed airlift could move anything to anywhere.

References. Primary: William H. Tunner, *Over the Hump: The Story of General William H. Tunner, the Man Who Moved Anything Anywhere, Anytime*, 1964. Secondary: C&C, vols. 1–2 and 4–7. Bliss K. Thorne, *The Hump: The Great Military Airlift of World War II*, 1965.

Coy F. Cross II

HUNTERS, THE

The Korean War* ended in 1953, and the best novel* about its fighter* pilots* battling the communist MiG-15s appeared in 1956. Written by James Salter, it accurately portrayed the USAF's* air superiority* struggle of that time. A movie version followed quickly. Salter's story was greatly altered in the movie, and the film did not do well.

References. William Dowie, "A Final Glory: The Novels of James Salter," *College English*, January 1988, pp. 74–88. "The 40th Anniversary of the USAF," a special issue of *AH*, September 1987, p. 210.

HURLBURT FIELD

Hurlburt Field, or Eglin* Air Force Auxiliary Field No. 9, is at Valparaiso, Florida. Eglin was activated in 1935 as the Valparaiso Bombing and Gunnery Base, used for a proving ground for aircraft, armament, accessories, and operational techniques. In 1941, the USAAC* built nine auxiliary bases. In 1944, Field No. 9 was named in honor of First Lieutenant Donald W. Hurlburt who died in 1943 while taking off from Eglin. After it was a proving ground, Hurlburt became an IM-99* site and then home of the Special Air Warfare School. In 1990 it was a Military Airlift Command* (MAC) base with headquarters of the Twenty-Third Air Force* (23AF) and the 1st Special Operations Wing using MC-130Es (*see* C-130), AC-130Hs (*see* C-130) and MH-53Js (*see* H-53).

References. "Guide to Major Air Force Installations Worldwide," *AF*, May 1990, p. 124. Mueller, *AFB*. Roberts, *Dir. USAF*.

Coy F. Cross II

HUSTLER. *See* B-58.

HVAR. *See* high-velocity aircraft rocket.

HYDROGEN BOMB. *See* nuclear weapons.

I

ICBM. *See* ballistic missiles.

ICELAND. *See* Air Forces Iceland; North Atlantic air bases.

IDENTIFICATION FRIEND OR FOE (IFF)

An early problem with radar* was distinguishing on the screen between friendly and hostile aircraft. The British devised a radio transmitter for friendly aircraft that could send coded signals when a ground station asked for them. The USAAF* tried IFF first in B-17s* in Europe, and the use became widespread in World War II* and after. The equipment is useful for identifying any aircraft for air traffic control. In the 1980s, IFF had even greater usefulness for the USAF* because of the need for target identification for beyond-visual-range (BVR) missiles.

References. C&C, vol. 1. Bill Gunston, *Night Fighters: A Development and Combat History*, 1976. Michael B. Perini, "Telling Ours from Theirs," *AF*, June 1985, pp. 80–83.

IFF. *See* identification friend or foe.

IGLOO WHITE

One of several nicknames for the anti-infiltration detection system used in the Vietnam War,* Igloo White was the most famous. The system was an outgrowth of the Jason Division* report. Sponsored and ordered by Secretary of Defense (SECDEF) Robert S. McNamara,* Igloo White was a system of sensors that were scattered into the jungle to detect enemy troop movements and supply routes. The sensors were designed to relay their information through airborne EC-121R (*see* C-121) aircraft to a large computer center at Nakhon Phanom* Royal Thai AFB. This was called the Infiltration Surveillance Center (ISC). The whole system cost $2.5 billion. Igloo White was part of the whole interdiction campaign called Commando Hunt.*

The sensors used several means to detect the presence of the enemy. One means was to measure vibrations caused by movement. Another was to pick up noises such as engines, talking, or other sounds associated with movement. Others detected heat or urine. Some sensors took the form of spikes that embedded themselves in the ground and that had their antennas disguised as weeds. Others were dropped by parachute and were designed to be caught in trees. The information provided by the sensors was to be intelligence and to show where there was sufficient concentrations for mining* or attack.*

Igloo White went into operation in 1967. The enemy quickly learned of the system because they saw the parachutes used. The enemy also quickly had effective countermeasures. The acoustic detection devices were covered or tape recorders were placed near them to deceive. The vibration detectors lent themselves to providing misleading information. A single truck could be operated near one for a time, giving the impression of much activity.

Despite Igloo White's failure, McNamara insisted the system be continued. When it could do so, the USAF* installed infrared sensors on board its aircraft, and these worked much better.

References. David A. Anderton, *History of the U.S. Air Force*, rev. ed., 1989. Berger, *USAF in SEA*. James William Gibson, *The Perfect War: Technowar in Vietnam*, 1986. Richard H. Kohn and Joseph P. Harahan, eds., *Air Interdiction in World War II, Korea, and Vietnam*, 1986.

"IKE." *See* Eisenhower, President Dwight D.

IM-99 BOMARC

The IM-99, or CIM-10, was an interceptor* missile produced in the late 1950s to complement manned interceptors. It is a unique weapon in USAF* history.

A joint study, starting in 1950 between the Boeing Airplane Company and the University of Michigan's Aeronautical Research Center, resulted in this program and the missile's name. The Bomarc was an outgrowth of the earlier Ground-to-Air-Pilotless Aircraft (GAPA) program conducted from 1946 to 1950. It was developed under the weapons systems concept. The first flight was in 1959, when the IM-99 scored a direct hit on a QF-80 (*see* F-80) drone that was 100 miles away at missile launch. Bomarc entered active service the same year in Air Defense Command (ADC) bases along the eastern seaboard and in the Midwest. The Royal Canadian Air Force (RCAF) had two squadrons of them. There were 28 XIM-99As, 269 IM-99As, and 301 IM-99Bs built. It was retired in the early 1970s. The IM-99 was intended to be effective against either a massed bomber* raid or individual strikes over a wide area. It was to provide a defense in depth and to destroy hostile bombers before they did harm. The IM-99 was controlled by Semiautomatic Ground Environment* (SAGE) and homed on its target with on-board radar.* A nuclear weapon* could be carried, and the IM-99 had radio proximity fuzes.*

Characteristics (IM-99B): engines, one Thiokol solid rocket of 50,000 pounds thrust and two Marquardt ramjets of 12,000, pounds thrust each; span, 18 feet; length, 45 feet; height, 10 feet; gross weight, 16,000 pounds; top speed, over Mach 2; ceiling, 80,000 feet; range, over 400 miles.

References. Goldberg, *Hist. USAF.* Charles E. Minihan, "The BOMARC Weapon System," *Air University Quarterly Review*, Summer 1962, pp. 56–75. *Pedigree of Champions: Boeing since 1916*, 1977. Robert Redding and Bill Yenne, *Boeing: Planemaker to the World*, 1983. John W. Sheehan, Jr., "The CIM-10 Bomarc," *United States Air Force Friends Bulletin*, Summer 1989, pp. 24–32.

Alwyn T. Lloyd

INCIRLIK AIR BASE

A U.S. Air Forces in Europe* (USAFE) facility near Ankara, Turkey, it was activated in 1954. Before the installation was built, the area was a fig orchard, or *incirlik* in Turkish. The 39th Tactical Group was on it in 1990 and had been there since 1966.

References. "Guide to Major Air Force Installations Worldwide," *AF*, May 1990, p. 124. Roberts, *Dir. USAF*.

INDEPENDENT AIR FORCE. *See* doctrine; National Security Act of 1947.

INDEPENDENT MISSION. *See* doctrine; General Headquarters Air Force; Twentieth Air Force.

INFILTRATION SURVEILLANCE CENTER. *See* Igloo White.

INSIGNIA

Military aircraft have been marked with a national insignia from early times. In the United States there have been many changes in insignia carried by USAF* aircraft.

The first insignia was used in the Mexican expedition of 1916* and was unofficial. It was a red star, sometimes on a white circle. After U.S. entry into World War I,* in May 1917, an official insignia was adopted. It was a white star inside a blue circle, with a red disk in the center of the star. The plane's rudder carried vertical red, white, and blue stripes. Brigadier General William Mitchell* changed the insignia in 1918 to a roundel with a white disk inside a larger blue ring, with that inside a still larger red ring. The rudder was unchanged. This was adopted to have an insignia similar to that used by the Allies. In 1919, the 1917 insignia was readopted. From 1927 to 1940, the rudder marking became a vertical blue stripe forward and horizontal alternating red and white stripes aft.

At war in 1942, the red disk in the star was removed to avoid confusion with Japanese insignia. An unofficial variant used in 1942 added a narrow yellow ring outside the blue field. In 1943, white rectangles, or wings, were added at the side to increase insignia visibility. A red stripe ran around the outside of the insignia. Almost immediately, the red stripe was replaced by a blue one. Red was restored in 1947, when a horizontal red stripe was added in the middle of the rectangle. The Vietnam War,* and the advent of better air defense weapons, led to decreased visibility of the insignia for security. It was reduced greatly in size, and the colors were changed to gray or black on combat aircraft.

References. Jeffrey P. Rhodes, "Stars on the Wing," *AF*, June 1987, pp. 78–83. Charles G. Worman, " 'They've Got Your Number,' " *AH*, Spring 1969, pp. 21–26. Bill Yenne, *The History of the US Air Force*, 1984.

INSPECT AND REPAIR AS NECESSARY (IRAN)

In late 1950, the stress placed on the USAF* to provide combat-ready aircraft quickly and a growing shortage of experienced technicians caused the Air Materiel Command (AMC), now the Air Force Logistics Command* (AFLC), to review its repair policies. Those policies dated from early in World War II,* when the disassemble, inspect, and repair (DIR) system was adopted. DIR's concept was to repair aircraft and parts to look "like new."

A new approach came from the Warner Robins Air Materiel Area (WRAMA) at Robins* AFB, Georgia, and it was adopted in July 1953. It incorporated the experience of the Korean War* and was called IRAN. In the new system, items were repaired as necessary. Planes and equipment were cycled through depots at set intervals. Upon inspection, only items that needed repair received attention. IRAN meant aircraft could be returned to service quicker. At WRAMA, 572 aircraft, mostly B-29s,* B-36s,* and F-86s,* were processed in the last half of 1953. By contrast, 382 had been processed in the first half.

Despite its success in reducing repair time, problems still existed. IRAN initially required completely new work books and codings to comply with new technical orders. A continuing effect was that IRAN required better judgment by line inspectors. IRAN proved less effective than anticipated, and major changes were made in 1958. The flow of airplanes was changed to be based upon agreements between the AMC and the operating commands, and only stipulated work was done. Actual repairs became the responsibility of operating units, and the AMC did modification and modernization of aircraft, such as the C-141B* Stretch Modification Program.

In 1974, the AFLC renamed its depots Air Logistics Centers and replaced IRAN with programmed depot maintenance (PDM) to anticipate repairs rather than wait for needs to appear.

References. R. W. Barnwell, *The History of the Warner Robins Air Materiel Area*, Warner Robins ALC Office of History, 1954. B. Lewis Brinson et al., *A Pictorial History of Robins Air Force Base, Georgia*, 1982. William Head, *Reworking the Workhorse* and *A Chronological History of the Warner Robins Air Logistics Center and Robins Air Force Base, Georgia, 1936–1986*, Warner Robins ALC Office of History, 1987. Woodford Agee Heflin, ed., *The United States Air Force Dictionary*, 1956.

See also depot maintenance.

William Head and Diane Truluck

INSPECTION AND SAFETY CENTER. *See* Air Force Inspection and Safety Center.

INSTRUMENT FLYING

A heavier-than-air object must continuously exert force against gravity to fly and must use forces to change direction. This means the only reliable human sense that can be used to control an aircraft is sight, which is usually useless in clouds and at night. The only substitute for sight is instrumentation to inform the pilot* of his position in relation to the earth. Flight in clouds and at night, therefore, is instrument, or blind, flying.

Because clouds and night are frequent conditions, aviation has struggled to overcome these limits from the beginning. The USAAC* was a leader in solving this problem of flight. Experimentation began in 1926, and the USAAC gave facilities and men at Mitchel* Field, New York, for the Daniel Guggenheim Fund for Promotion of Aeronautics to set up a Full Flight Laboratory. On 24 September 1929, First Lieutenant James H. Doolittle* made the first complete flight on instruments. First Lieutenant Albert F. Hegenberger* carried on the research after Doolittle resigned from the USAAC. The means used to attack the problem were navigation aids and gyroscopic instruments. The work of Doolittle and Hegenberger did not solve all the problems of instrument flying, but it did provide a partial solution. The USAAC set up training and standards for instrument flying proficiency and adopted the Link trainer* after the airmail flights of 1934.*

The USAAC and USAAF* entered World War II* with a fair mastery over instrument flying. During the war, training in instrument flying was greatly improved and expanded. Takeoffs were possible when cloud ceilings were at least 1,000 feet above the ground and visibilities were at least one and one-fourth miles. It should be noted that these standards considered that nearly all USAAF pilots were inexperienced in their craft. At the same time, USAAF pilots were flying the "Hump"* day and night in an area where weather conditions were severe.

The development of Ground-Controlled Approach* (GCA) made the Berlin Airlift* possible. The operation was an all-weather one in an area where the winter climate makes flying very difficult. Many, including the Soviets, did not believe the USAF* could do the job.

GCA represented one of the earlier radar* and electronic approaches to the problems of nonvisual flying. In 1972 and 1973, the F-111* demonstrated the extent of progress by conducting all-weather and night operations against the enemy in the Vietnam War.* The F-111s, called "smart planes" because of this capability, flew 4,000 sorties with only six lost. It is now doubted that any were lost to weather or night flying conditions. The only known cause of the losses was surface-to-air missiles* (SAM). The enemy called the F-111 "Whispering Death."

This progress holds hope for complete mastery over clouds and night, the importance of which to air power and the USAF cannot be overestimated.

References. Bill Gunston, *F-111*, 1978. Maurer, *Avn. in Army*.

INTER-ALLIED BOMBING FORCE. *See* Inter-Allied Independent Air Force.

INTER-ALLIED INDEPENDENT AIR FORCE

The Allied Supreme War Council drew up a plan in August 1918 for an Inter-Allied Independent Air Force, also called Inter-Allied Bombing Force. This organization was intended to conduct strategic operations* when there was no need for tactical operations.* This limit was imposed by Marshal Ferdinand Foch, generalissimo of the Allied forces. The war ended before the force could become operational. The significance of this force to the USAF* is that it was the first recognition by the U.S. Army that strategic operations could be useful. Had the force been used, it might have strongly influenced the status of the Army's airmen after the war.

References. Goldberg, *Hist. USAF*. I. B. Holley, Jr., *Ideas and Weapons*, 1983.

INTERCEPTION OF THE USS *UTAH*

This incident strengthened the USAAC's* case that bombers* could be effective in defending the United States. In August 1937, the 2nd Bomb Group was in a joint U.S. Army-Navy exercise off the coast of California. The War Department stated the exercise was to test bombing methods rather than effects. The target ship USS *Utah*, part of a 12-ship task force, was the objective.

Navy reconnaissance* reported the position of the task force which was concealed by fog. A one-degree error in that reported position of the ships precluded Army bombers from finding the target. The Army was ordered to await a new report the following morning before taking off. Instead, the airmen took off to begin a search. The captain of the *Utah* broke radio silence in the belief that the exercise had been terminated for the day. Using a course set by First Lieutenant Curtis E. LeMay,* the lead navigator,* the aircraft spotted the *Utah* within 15 minutes and began a mock attack* from an altitude of 600 feet. There were numerous misses, but several bombs found their mark.

On the following morning, some B-10s* spotted the fleet in clear weather and bombed from 12,000 feet. Six minutes later, B-17s* attacked the task force. To this day, the Navy has this incident classified as "Secret."

References. Primary: Curtis E. LeMay, *Mission with LeMay: My Story*, 1965. Secondary: H. H. Arnold, *Global Mission*, 1949. Maurer, *Avn. in Army*.

See also Army-Navy agreements of 1931 and 1938; *Rex* interception.

Alwyn T. Lloyd

INTERCEPTOR

This is an airplane operated to identify and destroy hostile aircraft. Interceptor qualities usually include high rate of climb and short endurance. An air superiority* fighter* can usually perform this function.

However, the need to intercept under all conditions, in clouds and at night, led to specialized aircraft. Such aircraft were also called "night fighters" and "all-weather fighters." Usually the need for the specialty was to find and destroy bombers.* The addition of equipment and crew to master night and weather often added so much weight that the specialized interceptor could not stay alive against air superiority fighters. It is important not to confuse these types of aircraft and functions.

The idea of an interceptor became important in the 1930s, particularly for the air defense problems faced by Britain at that time. The light Supermarine Spitfire was designed during this period to be an interceptor and became one of the best air superiority fighters in World War II.* For the most part, however, many believed interceptors would require two or more engines. This was especially true in the USAAC* and led to relatively heavy aircraft such as the FM-1* and P-38.* The obese FM-1 was a complete failure, and the lighter P-38 was marginally inferior to the best and lighter single-engine air superiority fighters. When bombers fled to the safety of clouds or night in World War II, specialized interceptors were built with heavy radar* and electronic equipment and crewmen to operate the gear. The USAAF's* first was the P-61.*

After World War II, the USAAF and the USAF* made a major commitment to a long series of heavy interceptors, the F-82,* F-89,* F-86D,* F-94, F-102,* and F-106.* They were designed to protect against the threat of Soviet bombers in the skies over the United States where enemy air superiority fighters would not be a problem. Since those series ended with the F-106, the night and all-weather task has been given to the F-4* and F-15E.* Note the use of the common F designator for both air superiority and interceptor types of aircraft.

References. Primary: C. L. Chennault, *The Role of Defensive Pursuit*, unpub., 1935. Secondary: Ernest J. Gentle and Lawrence W. Reithmaier, eds., *Aviation/Space Dictionary*, 6th ed., 1980. Bill Gunston, *Night Fighters: A Development and Combat History*, 1976. Bill Gunston and Lindsay Peacock, *Fighter Missions*, 1989. Knaack, *US Airc.*, vol. 1.

INTERCONTINENTAL BALLISTIC MISSILE. *See* ballistic missiles.

INTERCONTINENTAL BOMBER

The intercontinental bomber is an aircraft that can fly from one continent to another, bomb a target, and return without landing en route. Originally, it was to operate without aerial refueling,* because the technique did not exist.

Airmen have always sought increased range, but events triggered this concept of the ultimate range. Germany controlled the continent of Europe, and a strong possibility existed that the British Isles would fall to the Reich in 1941. The USAAF* believed it faced a possible need to bomb Europe from North America. This was expressed as an August 1941 requirement for a bomber* to fly at 275 miles per hour for 4,000 miles with five tons of bombs* at up to 45,000 feet and then return. Development began that year. In 1943 the possibility arose of needing such an airplane to raid the Japanese homeland. For years, some engineers believed such an aircraft could not be built because of the weight of the fuel needed. The Consolidated-Vultee Aircraft Corporation succeeded, however, with its B-36.*

The Germans, faced with the same basic problem, took a different approach. Drs. Eugen Saenger and Irene Bredt worked on a project called the "Antipodal Bomber." The bomber was to weigh 200,000 pounds, have a top speed of 13,596 miles per hour, a bomb load of 660 pounds, and a range of 14,596 miles. It was to be launched from a 1.8-mile track by a booster rocket. It was to rise out of the atmosphere and get its desired range by skipping on the air as a flat stone does across water. After bombing, it was to glide to and land in friendly territory. After the war, this vision was altered and became a USAF* project, the X-20.*

In the immediate postwar world, the USAAF could not rely on bases overseas, so work continued on the B-36. Aggressive Soviet moves on West Berlin in 1948, which led to the Berlin Airlift,* confirmed the need for an intercontinental bomber; the USAF has believed in the usefulness of one ever since.

References. Woodford Agee Heflin, ed., *The United States Air Force Dictionary*, 1956. Knaack, *US Airc.*, vol. 2. Jay Miller, *The X-Planes*, rev. ed., 1988. Swanborough, *US Mil. Airc.*

INTERDICTION. *See* tactical operations.

INTERMEDIATE-RANGE BALLISTIC MISSILE. *See* ballistic missiles.

INTERNMENT IN NEUTRAL COUNTRIES. *See* neutral countries.

INVADER. *See* B-26 Invader.

IRAKLION AIR BASE

This AB is on the island of Crete, Greece, and is assigned to the U.S. Air Forces in Europe* (USAFE). It is named for the capital of Crete. The base was activated in 1954 and has had the 7276th Air Base Group (ABG) on it since 1978.

References. "Guide to Major Air Force Installations Worldwide," *AF*, May 1990, p. 124. Roberts, *Dir. USAF*.

IRAN. *See* inspect and repair as necessary.

IRAN HOSTAGE RESCUE MISSION

In April 1980 an attempt to rescue* the U.S. hostages in Iran, called Eagle Claw, proved most embarrassing to the armed forces of the United States. The hostages were seized along with the U.S. Embassy in Tehran in November 1979. For months thereafter, Secretary of Defense (SECDEF) Harold Brown* and the Joint Chiefs of Staff under General David C. Jones* made rescue plans. In April, President Jimmy Carter authorized an attempt.

The miniscule task force that had been planned included four armed forces, U.S. Air Force,* Army, Navy, and Marine Corps, made up into a new unit. The command structure was a holdover from the Vietnam War.* It ran from

Washington, D.C., through an intermediate command post in Egypt under an Army general. The task force itself had an Army commander with troops, a Navy commander with helicopters,* a USAF commander with transports,* and a landing zone (LZ) commander. On the mission there was confusion at the intermediate staging point in Iran, called "Desert One." The result was a collision that cost necessary equipment and eight lives. Only then was the on-scene commander given the authority to make an important decision: to withdraw.

This mission was in striking contrast to the efficiency of the earlier Israeli rescue of hostages from Entebbe airfield in Uganda. There was much criticism of the mission from Israelis and others associated with special operations work.

References. Charlie A. Beckwith, *Delta Force*, 1983. Daniel P. Bolger, *Americans at War: 1975–1986, An Era of Violent Peace*, 1988. Edward N. Luttwak, *The Pengaton and the Art of War: The Question of Military Reform*, 1985. Paul B. Ryan, *The Iranian Rescue Mission: Why It Failed*, 1985.

See also Twenty-Third Air Force.

IRAQ CRISIS OF 1990–1991

In the summer of 1990, Congress was creating demobilizational instability to achieve what it and others called a "peace dividend." This was based upon Congress's perceptions of Soviet intentions and not capabilities, upon a belief there was no prospect of a major war despite warnings about the volatile Middle East, and no cuts in the pork barrel. A demobilization loomed on the scale of those after the United States's large wars.

This process was rudely interrupted in August by Iraqi aggression against and conquest of Kuwait, which posed a threat to Saudi Arabia. President George Bush mounted a massive transfer of U.S. military forces into Saudi Arabia and the Persian Gulf called Operation Desert Shield. The stated reasons included Saudi security; restoration of the Kuwaiti monarchy; the accusation that Iraq's dictator, Saddam Hussein, was another Adolf Hitler and had to be halted; protecting oil sources desired by the industrial nations; preventing Iraq from becoming a nuclear weapons* power; shoring up the U.S. economy through spending; and the belief that the United States should deter aggression in general. Bush received support for his actions from the United Nations (UN) and individual nations that formed a coalition with the United States and established an embargo on Iraq. Nearly all the forces moved to the scene were American, which included 230,000 persons of the defensive land power of the U.S. Army and offensive air power of the USAF* and the U.S. Navy. An important element in the buildup was the biggest airlift ever involving the USAF, U.S. Air Force Reserve* (USAFR), and the Civil Reserve Air Fleet* (CRAF).

The independent Iraqi air force, Al Quwwat al-Jawwiya al-Iraqiya, was believed in 1989 to have 40,000 men; about 230 air superiority* fighters,* including modern Soviet types; air interceptor missiles* (AIM); and air-to-ground missiles* (AGM). The Iraqi army had almost one million men, with many veterans of its war with Iran; nearly 6,000 tanks, nearly all Soviet built; and surface-to-air missiles* (SAM), mostly of Soviet origin.

In September, the chief of staff of the Air Force,* General Michael J. Dugan* was fired for allegedly failing to understand the crisis and for making inappropriate statements. He had said that air power was the only suitable method to use in case of war and that the targets should be Baghdad and Hussein. Two days after the U.S. national elections in November, another 200,000 Americans were added to the force. These were mostly offensive-style land forces drawn from the defense of Western Europe. The U.S. draft was not activated, however.

The USAF's airlift operations* had been spectacular. By the end of November, the airlift, including the CRAF, had flown 1.67 billion ton miles. By contrast, the Berlin Airlift* flew 697.5 million ton miles. There had been 717 cargo missions flown and 432 passenger missions flown. Of the passenger flights, the average loads were 292 persons per sortie. The top number of transports* used in a day was 50. In January 1991, the crisis became the Iraq War.*

References. *Air Force Times*, August 1990 through January 1991. *AWST*, *Persian Gulf War: Assessing the Victory*, 1991. Thomas B. Allen, et al. *War in the Gulf*, 1991. Walter J. Boyne, *Gulf War: A Comprehensive Guide to People, Places & Weapons*, 1991. Norman Friedman, *Desert Victory: The War for Kuwait*, 1991.

IRAQ WAR (1991)

This was an air war fought for limited goals, and it was spectacularly successful. It showed the global effectiveness of the USAF,* the domination by air superiority* of war, the importance of stealth* and precision-guided munitions, and what can be done with a trained, volunteer force of professionals.

It was named Operation Desert Storm and was conducted by a coalition of airmen from the United States, Britain, France, Italy, Kuwait, Qatar, and Saudi Arabia. The U.S. air weapon included the USAF and U.S. Army, Navy, and Marine Corps air forces. The USAF had half the combat aircraft in the coalition and 10 percent of the personnel in the U.S. Central Command.

Some favorable important factors included the continuation by President George Bush of President Ronald Reagan's* policy that the field commander, in this case U.S. Army General H. Norman Schwarzkopf, should make the battle decisions. Politicians did not overtly intervene in the details of conducting the war. In contrast to the Korean* and Vietnam* Wars, air power had centralized control. It was under USAF Lieutenant General Charles A. Horner. Political air superiority* was not given to the enemy as had been done in the Korean and Vietnam Wars. This time, the United States did not fight a land war in Asia. In large measure, the war was fought by the United States with weapons untried in mass use, and they vindicated the research, development, and procurement of the past three decades. For years, the media and many in Congress claimed the weapons used in this war would prove inept and constituted a horrendous waste. However, the much criticized Reagan rearmament provided the people and materiel muscle for the war; the United States had spent money and not lives. The war was conducted under the principle of strike hard and fast and not by flexible response and gradual escalation. The Army's Patriot antiballistic missile's* performance indicated that the Strategic Defense Initiative* (SDI) may be less difficult technically to achieve than has been expected.

There were factors that were unfavorable from an airman's standpoint. The air war was conducted under ground officers. One commentator on television* said this was like asking your gardener to be the cook. As has happened repeatedly in wars, air power was diverted from productive military operations to serve political purposes. In the Iraq War, this consisted of searching for the militarily ineffective but psychologically disturbing Scud ballistic missiles.*

During the Iraq crisis* of 1990–1991, it was reiterated that a war would employ all armed services, implying amphibious and blitzkrieg methods. Schwarzkopf said the amphibious possibility was deliberate misinformation for the enemy. The United Nations (UN) set a 15 January 1991 deadline for Iraq to meet UN terms. On 20 December 1990, the coalition deputy commander, Army Lieutenant General Calvin A. H. Waller, told the media that the land forces would not be ready for the deadline. This caused consternation in the Bush administration, but Waller, unlike USAF General Michael J. Dugan,* was not fired. Just before Christmas, Schwarzkopf confirmed Waller's estimate. After the war, it was acknowledged the ground forces were not ready for an offensive until mid-February. Thus, the Iraq War was not deliberately fought as an air war but was forced to be one by the UN deadline, by Army unreadiness, and by the expressed U.S. public and congressional concern over another bloody ground war.

Iraq is mostly a desert country, so it should be vulnerable to strategic operations* against its water supplies, food, transportation, and armed forces. A desert presents the most favorable climate and terrain conditions for air operations. The Army, which should and does think in terms of land power, chose to direct the air war against Iraq's armed forces. In other words, it chose to strike against Iraq's strength instead of its weakness, which is just what Iraq's dictator, Saddam Hussein, wished. Iraq's army, the fourth largest in the world and favored by Hussein over his airmen, had prepared Maginot line–type forward defenses in the south, with a mobile reserve Republican Guard in the rear. Many Iraqis were war veterans. The Iraqis had religious and nationalist incentives to fight but had the drawback that Hussein used fear for discipline.

The air-only phase of the campaign, planned to last the 30 days until the Army was ready, began with a coalition effort to attain air superiority. The Al Quwwat al-Jawwiya al-Iraqiya, or Iraq air force (IAF), was the sixth largest air service in the world with about 1,000 first-class aircraft. The Iraq army had 17,000 surface-to-air missiles* (SAM) and more than 9,000 flak* units. Radar* and ground-controlled interception* (GCI), built by the French, were modern. A coalition surprise strike was made in the darkness of three o'clock in the morning of 17 January—a unique way for starting a war, before the customary dawn. The IAF was a day-flying air force, and the coalition had its air superiority in a matter of hours. Raids were made on the air defense system, including radar and the command and communications facilities. The USAF's F-117* was a key element in these operations despite the fact that it made up only 2.5 percent of the combat aircraft. It attacked 31 percent of the targets hit on the opening day of the war. In the war, no F-117 was shot down or sustained battle damage. Thirty-five enemy aircraft* were shot down in the war, of which the USAF had 31 kills. Most USAF victories were won with the AIM-7.* The IAF did not shoot down a single coalition aircraft. A factor in the campaign was the ability of weapons to penetrate the IAF's aircraft shelters, and an estimated 141 planes were destroyed this way. The only significant action by the IAF was that 122 of its planes fled to Iran and were interned. No Iraqi plane crossed the coalition's front line.

Raids were made on Iraq's factories for chemical and biological weapons and on electric power. These strikes were followed by interdiction. By the end of the war, out of 54 bridges, 40 were down and 10 were damaged. There were indications that the interdiction was not as vigorously pursued as airmen wanted, because the fliers were diverted early to destroy the Iraqi army. The USAF attacked 10,000 vehicles, and it dropped leaflets telling Iraqis that materiel was the target and suggesting that the men get away from equipment. Leaflets also said the USAF would not attack men walking northward. USAF B-52Gs* made raids from distant bases to hit the Iraqi army, although they lacked the Big Belly punch used in the Vietnam War's Arc Light* and Linebacker* operations. Coalition airmen were believed to be destroying 100 tanks a day in this effort, which was so successful it caused the Army to delay the ground effort from the planned 30 to 39 days to gain more destruction of the Iraqi army.

On 23 February, a ground offensive was launched instead of having air power finish the job. Bush may have been forced into this step by a Soviet peace initiative that threatened to thwart UN and U.S. goals. The Iraq "Maginot line" was assaulted, but the main effort was a bypass drive further north using vertical envelopment and armor. The Republican Guard tried to counterattack but was quickly crushed by air and land power. The Iraqi army, rendered impotent by air power, collapsed and disintegrated. Iraqis fleeing in vehicles from Kuwait City were trapped by airmen in a great traffic jam and then slaughtered. The greatest problem the coalition ground forces encountered, in what was called a clean-up operation, was managing 62,000 prisoners of war (POW) who surrendered in 100 hours.** Some Army men said their operations against the Iraqi army were as easy as clubbing baby seals. The estimate of Iraqis killed in the war was 100,000. Iraq accepted UN terms on 27 February.

General Merrill A. McPeak,* chief of staff of the Air Force,* said proudly the coalition had flown 109,876 sorties, of which the USAF had flown 59 percent and had 37 percent of the battle losses. The minor USAF losses were 14 aircraft, three men killed in action (KIA), five killed not in action, four prisoners of war (POWs), and 20 missing. The POWs may have been mistreated. There had been 88,500 tons of ordnance used by U.S. airmen, and the USAF had released 74 percent of it. Of the precision weapon tonnage, the USAF had released 90 percent. McPeak said this was the first time air power had defeated a field army. His remark could be challenged by citing the events of Falaise-Argentan,* France;

Linebacker I; and the surrender of German Generalleutnant Eric Elster's Foot March Group South at Beaugency, France, on 16 September 1944. Elster's force was made up of 754 officers, 18,850 men and two women. What was more significant was that air power defeated an entrenched army.

The USSR's Mikhail Gorbachev used the Iraq War to screen his use of military force against Lithuania as Nikita Khrushchev had covered his attack on Hungary by the Suez War of 1956.

References. Primary: Department of Defense News Briefing (with General Merrill A. McPeak), 15 March 1991. Secondary: Walter J. Boyne, *Gulf War: A Comprehensive Guide to People, Places & Weapons*, 1991. "How We Won," *Air Force Times*, 11 March 1991, pp. 4, 6, 8, 14–16, 30. *AWST, Persian Gulf War: Assessing the Victory*, 1991. Norman Friedman, *Desert Victory: The War for Kuwait*, 1991.

**It is difficult to surrender to a flying aircrew, and hundreds of Iraqi soldiers had surrendered in the first 39 days, doing so by crossing the lines.

IRBM. *See* ballistic missiles.

IRON BOMB. *See* bombs.

IRON HAND

This was the code name in the Vietnam War* for tactical operations* to identify, find, and destroy air defense systems using radar.* This included both surface-to-air missile* (SAM) and radar-controlled flak* sites. Iron Hand consisted of hunter-killer teams with various combinations of aircraft. The first fighter* aircraft to be modified with missile radar detection equipment was the F-100F,* called Wild Weasel* I. The F-105* was the second. Iron Hand performance improved with the introduction of the AGM-45* missile and the faster two-seat F-105F. The AGM-45 rode the radar beam down to the source and destroyed it.

References. Primary: Higham, *Combat Airc.*, vol. 1. Secondary: Berger, *USAF in SEA*. Larry Davis, *Wild Weasel: The SAM Suppression Story*, 1986.

Frank L. Goldstein

ISSOUDON, FRANCE

About 1,000 U.S. flying, or aviation, cadets,* most of them honor graduates of U.S. preflight ground schools, were sent to Issoudon for flight training* in the fall of 1917. Because this facility in central France was still under construction and proper aircraft was unavailable, the cadets waited months to start training. Called upon to perform construction duties and a variety of menial tasks, the cadets became known as the "Million Dollar Guard" who were paid $100 per month. At the rate at which training was proceeding then, it would have required ten months or more to place them all in primary flying schools.

At times there was near mutiny. Brigadier General Mason M. Patrick,* chief of Air Service* for the American Expeditionary Force (AEF), said only the quality of the men prevented a complete breakdown of morale. Some cadets were moved to St. Maixent, France, to a camp from which they went to schools as vacancies occurred.

As these cadets slaved in the mud of Issoudon and St. Maixent awaiting their chance to climb into the cockpit, their morale received another blow. Cadets who had remained in the United States arrived in France as officers, having received commissions upon completion of preliminary training in the United States. To correct this injustice, the War Department, on the advice of the AEF, commissioned all cadets with the grade and rank they would have held had they been commissioned at their graduation from ground school.

In the spring and summer of 1918 the Issoudon program was finally completed. Several of its schools were equipped with the Penguin, a trainer with clipped wings. Within a short time, 23-meter Nieuports arrived, quickly followed by 18- and 15-meter versions. Several hundred pilots were soon able to join combat units. Many of the new graduates were assigned as instructors. One of these was Major Carl A. Spaatz,* who later flew combat in the St. Mihiel* campaign and briefly in the Meuse-Argonne.*

References. Goldberg, *Hist. USAF*. James J. Hudson, *Hostile Skies: A Combat History of the American Air Service in World War I*, 1968. Maurer Maurer, *The U.S. Air Service in World War I*, vol. 1, 1978.

See also Tours, France.

James J. Hudson

I WANTED WINGS. See movies.

J

JABARA, COLONEL JAMES (1923–1966)

Jabara was America's first jet ace* and second in total victories in the Korean War.* Born in Muskogee, Oklahoma, he entered the aviation cadet* program in 1942. He became a commissioned pilot* in 1943. Jabara flew two combat tours in Europe in F-51s,* one with the Ninth Air Force* (9AF) and one with the Eighth Air Force* (8AF). He flew a total of 108 sorties and was credited with one and one-half victories. He went to Korea in 1950 to serve with the 4th Fighter Interceptor Wing (FIW) of the Fifth Air Force* (5AF) flying F-86s.* After six jet victories, he returned to the United States in 1951 for assignment to headquarters of the USAF.* He requested a second tour in Korea and achieved another nine victories. In 1964 he assumed command of the 4540th Combat Crew Training Group (CCTG) at Luke* AFB, Arizona. The group trained Luftwaffe and other foreign pilots in the F-104G.* Jabara died in an automobile accident.

References. Primary: James Jabara, "We Fly MIG [sic] Alley," *AF*, September 1972, pp. 108–12. Secondary: DuPre, *USAF Bio*. Gurney, *5 Down*. Hess, *Aces Album*.

"JACK." *See* Broughton, Colonel Jacksel M.

"JACKIE." *See* Cochran, Colonel Jacqueline.

JAPAN AIR DEFENSE FORCE

This named air force* of the USAF* was established in 1952 to replace the 314th Air Division. It was under the Far East Air Forces (FEAF). After World War II,* the Fifth Air Force* (5AF) was the occupying air force in Japan. The 5AF moved to Korea in 1950 to conduct operations in the war there. The Japan Air Defense Force was organized to defend Japan while the 5AF was in Korea. It was discontinued in 1954.

References. Futrell, *USAF in Korea*. Goldberg, *Hist. USAF*. Ravenstein, *Org. USAF*.

JASON DIVISION

Intelligence analyses had indicated in the Vietnam War* that U.S. attacks* on the oil supplies within North Vietnam would not stop that nation's aggression. When intelligence reports on Operation Rolling Thunder* appeared to confirm the predictions of the analyses, Secretary of Defense (SECDEF) Robert S. McNamara* asked for an assembly of scientists to review bombing operations in North Vietnam. This group was the Jason Division of the Institute for Defense Analysis.

The report of the division in September 1966 agreed with the intelligence analyses. The report also said that air power would be ineffective against North Vietnam because the agricultural country was simply a conduit for supplies acquired from the USSR and Red China. The report added that North Vietnam's resource of underemployed manpower made that conduit nearly invulnerable. In addition, it maintained that air attacks induced a popular resolve to intensify the war effort.

The expectation, therefore, was that the division would recommend one of these options: (1) U.S. withdrawal from the war, (2) a cessation of all air attacks on the North, (3) a blockade of the influx of war supplies to the conduit, or (4) shifting the attack to the agricultural base as the USAF* did in attacking the Korean irrigation dams target system.* Instead, the report proposed a new method of attacking the conduit. The recommendation was neither for nuclear weapons* to clear jungle and create obstructions, nor harassing chemicals, nor a mirror in space to remove nighttime darkness. It was to create a gigantic electronic barrier along the demilitarized zone. The electronic devices would be sensors of heat and noise. Aircraft would then attack based on information from the sensors— in other words, Igloo White.* That system was ordered by the SECDEF, but it failed.

A year later the division gave the SECDEF another study. It said air power had not weakened the resolve of North Vietnam and could not do so. Some believe now that Linebacker* II showed this later report to be in error.

References. David A. Anderton, *History of the U.S. Air Force*, rev. ed., 1989. James William Gibson, *The Perfect War: Technowar in Vietnam*, 1986.

JB-2 LOON

The JB-2 was a direct copy of the German V-1 "buzz bomb" and was an important step in the introduction of cruise missiles* into the USAF.* The USAAF* started the JB-2 project in 1944. The Willys-Overland Company was given a contract to make up to 50,000. This number was cut back after war's end, and the JB-2 did not see battle. The missile was redesignated the KUW-1 utility drone and used for testing only. The U.S. Navy used some and called the JB-2 the "Loon." The term became commonly used for the missile. The JB-2 was a small airplane powered by a pulsejet engine and had a 2,000-pound warhead.

References. Norman Friedman, *U.S. Naval Weapons*, 1983. Kenneth P. Werrell, *The Evolution of the Cruise Missile*, 1985.

Philip Long

"JENNY." *See* JN.

JET PILOT. *See* movies.

"JIM." *See* Fechet, Major General James E.

"JIMMY." *See* Doolittle, General James H.; Stewart, Brigadier General James.

JN "JENNY"

A truly historic airplane for the United States, this Curtiss Aeroplane and Motor Company, Inc., plane was ordered by the Aviation Section of the U.S. Army Signal Corps* in 1916 to be a trainer. It was soon used in the observation aviation* role in the Mexican expedition of 1916.* It trained 90 percent of U.S. pilots* in World War I.* More than 8,000 were made by Curtiss and others. There was a Canadian version built for the U.S. Army by the Canadian Aeroplane Corporation. These were designated as JN-4 Can, for "Canadian," and were nicknamed "Canucks."

After the war, hundreds of Jennies were sold to the public, and prices fell as low as $50 for each one. Jennies were used extensively by private owners especially for barnstorming and air shows. Thus they did much to popularize aviation in the 1920s, but their numbers on the used market made it very difficult for the U.S. aircraft industry to survive.

Characteristics (JN-4D): engine, Curtiss OX-5* of 90 horsepower; span, 44 feet; length, 27 feet; height, 10 feet; gross weight, 2,130 pounds; top speed, 75 miles per hour; service ceiling, 8,000 feet; range, 250 miles.

References. Robert B. Casari, *The Curtiss Jennies*, vol. 3 of *The World War I Production Program*, part 2 of *Encyclopedia of U.S. Military Aircraft*, 1975. F. G. "Jerry" Phillips, "An Ode to 'Jenny' " *AH*, December 1977, pp. 217–21. Swanborough, *US Mil. Airc.*

JOHNSON, COLONEL GERALD R. (1920–1945)

Johnson was the fourth-highest-scoring USAAF* fighter* ace* in the Pacific theater with 22 aerial victories. He is the 11th-ranking USAF* ace of all time, an honor he shares with Colonel Neel E. Kearby* and Lieutenant General Jay T. Robbins.* At one time, a USAF base in Japan was named for him, Johnson AB near Tokyo.

He was born in Kenmore, Ohio, and became an aviation cadet* in 1941. He became a commissioned pilot* the same year. In 1942 he flew 58 combat sorties in the Aleutians* and returned to the United States in the same year. In 1943 he joined the 9th Fighter Squadron of the 49th Fighter Group of the Fifth Air Force* (5AF). In one action in October, 1943, he led eight P-38s* against 20

Mitsubishi A6M Reisen (Zero) fighters and 20 Aichi D3A (Val) bombers.* Johnson destroyed one Zero and two Vals. In December 1944 with a flight* of four P-38s, he engaged and shot down three Nakajima Ki-43 Hayabusa (Oscar) fighters. Later he found six Nakajima Ki-49 Donryu (Helen) heavy bombers and shot down one. Johnson became the commander of the 49th.

After World War II, Johnson commanded Atsuga Airfield, Japan. On an administrative flight in a B-17* he lost his communications in bad weather. He gave his parachute to a passenger who had none. He tried to land but failed and died in the crash.

References. Primary: Gurney, *5 Down*. Secondary: DuPre, *USAF Bio*. Hess, *Aces Album*.

JOHNSON, SECRETARY LOUIS A. (1891–1966)

In 1949, Johnson succeeded James A. Forrestal to become the second secretary of defense (SECDEF). As an economy measure, he canceled the 65,000-ton supercarrier USS *United States*, the U.S. Navy's hope for a share in the U.S. strategic operations* mission. This unexpected measure on 23 April 1949 ignited the B-36* controversy,* also called the "revolt of the admirals."

Although a successful lawyer, World War I* veteran, and former national commander of the American Legion, Johnson may have owed his position to his role as chief fund-raiser for the 1948 Harry S Truman* (HST) election campaign. Nevertheless, Johnson relentlessly pursued HST's goals of military unification, efficiency, and budget control.

Johnson wholeheartedly supported the USAF* view of the B-36 as the key to an effective, affordable defense. Although a series of congressional hearings exonerated his reputation in the bitter interservice dispute over the B-36, the secretary's abrasive manner and controversial actions weakened his position with HST. The B-36 controversy overshadowed his role during other major crises, including the first Soviet explosion of a nuclear weapon* in 1949, the "loss" of China to Mao's communists, and the Korean War.* Frustrated by interservice quarreling and angered by Secretary of State Dean Acheson's policies, Johnson resigned at HST's request on 19 September 1950. He returned to the practice of law.

References. Kenneth O. Condit, *1947–1949*, vol. 2 of *The History of the Joint Chiefs of Staff*, unpub. JCS report, Modern Military Records Branch, National Archives, Washington, D.C., n.d. Robert J. Donovan, *Tumultuous Years: The Presidency of Harry S Truman 1949–1953*, 1982. Roger R. Trask, *The Secretaries of Defense: A Brief History 1947–1985*, 1985.

John T. Farquhar

JOHNSON, PRESIDENT LYNDON B. (LBJ) (1908–1973)

The 36th president, LBJ was important to the status and operations of the USAF* in the Vietnam War.* When LBJ became president and commander in chief, he kept President John F. Kennedy's* (JFK) defense team in office. LBJ initially admired and respected Secretary of Defense (SECDEF) Robert S.

McNamara* for his brilliance, decisiveness, and centralized management. Along with McNamara, LBJ accepted U.S. Army General Maxwell Taylor's strategies of flexible response and gradual escalation for war. The Vietnam War was a disliked burden for LBJ. He would have much preferred it go away so he could devote full time to his beloved "Great Society" and "War on Poverty." He often referred to Vietnam as the "other war."

During the war, LBJ and McNamara, in weekly meetings in the White House, set USAF targets, aircraft armament, and tactics without participation by active-duty officers. LBJ was proud that, as he put it, the airmen could not attack* an outhouse without his permission. In late 1967, LBJ became disappointed with McNamara as it did not appear the war was being won. McNamara was out as SECDEF by February 1968. The public reaction to North Vietnam's Tet offensive in January 1968 drove LBJ out of the 1968 presidential race.

References. Primary: Jack Broughton, *Going Downtown: The War against Hanoi and Washington*, 1988. Secondary: Larry Berman, *Lyndon Johnson's War: The Road to Stalemate in Vietnam*, 1989. David Halberstam, *The Best and the Brightest*, 1969. Robin Higham, ed., *Intervention or Abstention: The Dilemma of American Foreign Policy*, 1975.

JOHNSON, LIEUTENANT COLONEL ROBERT S. (1920–)

Johnson is the fourth U.S. ace* of all time with 28 victories in F-47s.* Born in Lawton, Oklahoma, he became an aviation cadet* in 1941. He became a pilot* and officer in 1942. Combat began for him in 1943 in the 61st Fighter Squadron, 56th Fighter Group, Eighth Air Force* (8AF). He flew 91 combat sorties, finishing in 1944. After combat, he toured the United States with top ace Richard I. Bong.* Then he was commander of an F-47 operational training unit until the end of World War II.* Johnson worked for Republic Aviation Corporation from 1945 to 1964 and then joined the Penn Mutual Life Insurance Company. He was president of the Air Force Association* (AFA), serving twice, 1949–1950 and 1950–1951.

References. Primary: Robert S. Johnson, *Thunderbolt!* 1958. Secondary: DuPre, *USAF Bio.* Gurney, *5 Down.* Hess, *Aces Album.* Edward H. Sims, *American Aces in Great Fighter Battles of World War II*, 1958.

JOINT CHIEFS OF STAFF (JCS) MEMORANDUM OF 22 JANUARY 1964

The USAF* studied the use of air power in Indochina (later Vietnam) in 1954. It concluded air power could help an army, but difficulties would include a lack of targets. A study that year by the JCS, NSC-68, came to a similar conclusion, noting that communists' supplies came from outside the country. In 1954, the president was Dwight D. Eisenhower,* the secretary of defense (SECDEF) was Charles E. Wilson, the chairman of the JCS was Admiral Arthur W. Radford, and the chief of staff of the Air Force* was General Nathan F. Twining.*

Nine years later, in November 1963, President Lyndon B. Johnson* (LBJ) asked the JCS to plan for increased covert operations against North Vietnam and for activities inside Laos to inhibit the flow of North Vietnamese forces southward. The JCS responded in January 1964. Its memo advocated the commitment of U.S. ground forces to Vietnam and Laos, large raids by commandos, mining* the seas, more reconnaissance* over Laos and Cambodia, and bombing operations against North Vietnam. At this time, the SECDEF was Robert S. McNamara,* the chairman of the JCS was U.S. Army General Maxwell D. Taylor, and the chief of staff of the Air Force was General Curtis E. LeMay.* LeMay has said since that he was against the use of a land army.

The memo of 1964 represented huge and significant shifts of view from 1954, though there had been little change in North Vietnam. The changes must have been primarily because of differences in the leaders involved. Such a change was important to the subsequent U.S. actions in Southeast Asia (SEA) and, therefore, to the USAF.

References. David A. Anderton, *History of the U.S. Air Force*, rev. ed., 1989. Robert F. Futrell, *The Advisory Years to 1965*, 1981.

See also Jason Division; Linebacker; 94-target plan; Vietnam War.

JOINT CHIEFS OF STAFF (JCS) SPECIAL COMMITTEE FOR REORGANIZATION OF NATIONAL DEFENSE

This committee was an important factor in the creation of an independent USAF.* In addition, the broad framework for the modern U.S. defense organization can be seen in the recommendations of this committee.

When, in May 1944, it was possible to visualize the end of World War II,* there was concern that the postwar armed forces organization reflect the lessons of the war. The JCS appointed a committee to consider the matter. It was composed of U.S. Army and Navy officers. It was given a specific charge to recommend the continuation of War and Navy Department; or War, Navy, and Air Departments; or a Department of Defense. The committee deliberated for ten months, visited every theater of operations, and interviewed 56 Army and Navy officers.

Its report was submitted in March 1945. It recommended a single Department of Armed Forces with three branches. The committee said the large autonomous USAAF* had evolved through experience. To calm Navy fears for its future, the committee recommended the Navy keep its air force and the Marine Corps. It also suggested the Army keep aviation directly related to ground requirements.

The Navy was not mollified. One naval officer, the committee chairman, Admiral J. O. Richardson, submitted a minority report opposing both a single department and an independent air force. The Navy feared the power of a single man over all services, a "supersecretary." It also feared it would some day lose its air force and Marines, that its long status as the priority service would be lost, and that its needs would be determined by people unfamiliar with sea power. Ultimately, two of the Navy's fears were realized. Secretary of Defense (SECDEF) Robert S. McNamara* would become the first "supersecretary," and under Presidents Harry S Truman* (HST) and Dwight D. Eisenhower, the USAF became the priority service.

References. Goldberg, *Hist. USAF*. Herman S. Wolk, "The Birth of the US Air Force," *AF*, September 1977, pp. 68–72, 75–78, and "The Establishment of the United States Air Force," *AF*, September 1982, pp. 76–80, 83–84, 87.

JOINT STARS. *See* E-8A.

JOINT STRATEGIC TARGET PLANNING STAFF (JSTPS)

The JSTPS is part of the Joint Chiefs of Staff (JCS). It is responsible for keeping a National Strategic Target List with a Single Integrated Operational Plan (SIOP) for the U.S. armed forces to conduct strategic operations.*

For a few years after their development, nuclear weapons* could be delivered against the USSR's land mass only by the Strategic Air Command* (SAC). The reliance on nuclear strategic operations received priority in the defense of the United States, so the other military services sought to develop such capability. In the 1950s this was achieved by the U.S. Navy's submarine-launched ballistic missiles* and by its tactical operations* forces. There was an obvious need to make all strategic operations planning fit together.

The JSTPS was established to do so in 1960. The commander of SAC is its director, and a naval officer is the deputy director. All U.S. services are represented on the staff together with theater commands and North Atlantic Treaty Organization* (NATO) commands. The JSTPS is located in SAC headquarters at Offutt* AFB, Nebraska.

References. David A. Anderton, *Strategic Air Command: Two-thirds of the Triad*, 1974. J. C. Hopkins, *The Development of Strategic Air Command 1946–1981 (A Chronological History)*, 1982. Polmar, *SAC*. Bill Yenne, *S*A*C: A Primer of Modern Strategic Airpower*, 1981.

JOINT SURVEILLANCE AND TARGET ATTACK RADAR SYSTEMS.
See E-8A.

JOINT SURVEILLANCE SYSTEM (JSS)

The JSS is an air defense surveillance and control system developed and deployed in the 1970s and early 1980s. It is a replacement for the Semiautomatic Ground Environment* (SAGE), Back-Up Interceptor Control (BUIC) systems for the continental United States (CONUS) and Canada, and the manual ground environment system in Alaska and Hawaii.

It has eight Region Operations Control Centers (ROCC). There are four in CONUS operated by the Tactical Air Command* (TAC), two in Canada operated by Canadians, one in Alaska operated by the Eleventh Air Force* (11AF), and one in Hawaii operated by the Pacific Air Forces* (PACAF). In addition there are 86 sensor sites and a System Support Element (SSE).

Each ROCC contains computers, displays, and communications and is at a base able to support E-3s,* facilitating transition of command and control from the ROCC to the E-3s. The sensor sites furnish the ROCCs with automated surveillance. The SSE provides maintenance and training support for ROCC hardware, software, firmware, and personnel.

The USAF* forecast that the replacement of SAGE, BUIC, and manual systems with JSS would result in an overall yearly savings of about $100 million in radar* operations and support costs.

References. Electronic Systems Division News Releases 76–29 and 76–464, 30 January and 28 October 1976. *Joint Surveillance System (JSS) Program Summary*, 31 March 1979 and n.d. "Tactical Air Command," *AF*, May 1984, pp. 120–22.

E. Michael Del Papa

JOINT TACTICAL INFORMATION DISTRIBUTION SYSTEM (JTIDS)

JTIDS, under development, seeks to provide a jam-resistant, secured source of navigation, identification, and communication for North Atlantic Treaty Organization* (NATO) arms.

In combat aircraft, forward-sweeping radar* has provided limited information in both distance and scope. JTIDS displays give a 360-degree picture of air activity at distant ranges and can identify hostile aircraft beyond visual range (BVR) and authorize an attack on them. JTIDS also allows its aircraft to approach hostile planes without using radar, eliminating warning by radar-triggered threat indicator devices.

The cockpit displays show the user aircraft in the center of a circle. A cathode ray tube identifies and color codes all friendly, unknown, and hostile aircraft and gives the altitude and direction of each. Superimposed on the screen are relevant national boundaries, "safe" air transit corridors, and friendly free-fire zones. Also shown is the radar coverage of the user and his wingman; enemy planes already targeted by friendly forces; and the altitude, speed, and estimated type of enemy aircraft* if highlighted with a cursor.

References. "Air Force Expanding Capabilities of McDonnell Douglas F-15 Fighter," *AWST*, 14 October 1985, p. 67. Shelford Bidwell, ed., *World War 3*, 1978. "JTIDS-Equipped F-15s to Provide Pilots with Battle Situation Display," *AWST*, 9 December 1985, pp. 100–101. Mike Spick, *An Illustrated Guide to Modern Fighter Combat*, 1987.

Ronald W. Yoshino

JOLLY GREEN GIANT. *See* H-3.

JONES, GENERAL DAVID C. (1921–)

Jones was the ninth chairman of the Joint Chiefs of Staff (JCS) from 1978 to 1982, the third USAF* officer to hold that position. He was also the ninth chief of staff of the Air Force* from 1974 to 1978 and a central figure in important defense reorganizations.

Born in Aberdeen, South Dakota, he was commissioned through the aviation cadet* program in 1943, so he was only the second chief who did not attend the U.S. Military Academy (USMA). The earlier was General Curtis E. LeMay.* Jones was a flying instructor in World War II.* Thus, he was the first chief who had not seen battle in that war. He flew more than 300 combat hours in B-29s* in the Korean War.* After his service in Korea, he was an operations planner and then an aide to LeMay at headquarters of the Strategic Air Command* (SAC). After graduation from the National War College in 1960, he went to the Air Staff* where he worked on the B-70.* In 1969 he became commander of the Second Air Force* (2AF) at Barksdale* AFB, Louisiana, and became commander in chief of the U.S. Air Forces in Europe* (CINCUSAFE) in 1971.

As USAF chief of staff and a supporter of the B-1* program, he was a controversial figure in public discussions. Nevertheless, he accepted President Carter's decision to cancel it. He called for force improvements, with emphasis on the Airborne Control and Warning System* (AWACS). As chairman of the JCS he favored the Strategic Arms Limitations Talks (SALT) and the Panama Canal Treaty of 1978 and oversaw JCS responses to regional crises, including the Soviet invasion of Afghanistan and the Iran hostage rescue mission.*

He has been closely associated with significant organizational changes. He moved headquarters of the USAFE from Lindsey* to Ramstein* AB, reduced the size of numbered air forces,* and secured the North Atlantic Treaty Organization* (NATO) agreement to create Allied Air Forces Central Europe (AAFCE) to direct allied tactical operations.* He eliminated the Aerospace Defense Command* (ADC) and consolidated many agencies under the Military Airlift Command* (MAC). While chairman of the JCS, he proposed several measures to strengthen the role of the JCS. After his retirement in 1982, he continued this work. Many of his ideas were incorporated into the Goldwater*-Nichols Act of 1987.

References. Primary: David C. Jones, "What's Wrong with Our Defense Establishment?" *New York Times Magazine*, 7 November 1982, pp. 38, 41, 42, 70, 73, 74, 76, 78, 80–83. U.S. Air Force Oral History Interview K239.0512–1664, October 1985, January and March 1986, USAFHRC/OH, Maxwell AFB, AL. Secondary: "Revamping the Pentagon's 'Corporate Board,' " *Congressional Quarterly*, 24 August 1985. John B. Taylor, "The Uncommon Jones," *Airman Magazine*, March 1975, pp. 20–25. U.S. Air Force Biography, Secretary of the Air Force Office of Information, 1979. Bill Yenne, *The History of the US Air Force*, 1984.

Maurice Maryanow

JSS. *See* Joint Surveillance System.

JSTPS. *See* Joint Strategic Target Planning Staff.

JTIDS. *See* Joint Tactical Information Distribution System.

JUNGLE JIM

This operation was established as the 4400th Combat Crew Training Squadron (Jungle Jim) at Eglin* AFB, Florida, in April 1961. Its purpose was to prepare forces to fight guerrilla war. It attracted highly motivated airmen who were qualified to conduct air commando operations. President John F. Kennedy* (JFK) authorized deployment of a Jungle Jim detachment to South Vietnam for training purposes in October 1961. It was based at Bien Hoa* AB. It had 151 officers and men, eight T-28s,* four SC-47s (*see* C-47) and four RB-26s (*see* B-26 Invader). All aircraft carried Vietnamese air force (VNAF) markings. In Vietnam, the detachment was called Farm Gate.*

References: Berger, *USAF in SEA.* Robert F. Futrell, *The Advisory Years to 1965,* 1981.

Frank L. Goldstein

JUPITER

The Jupiter* ballistic missile* was involved in a conflict over missions between the USAF* and the U.S. Army. When nuclear weapons* were developed, the Army began planning to use them. Its first step was with nuclear artillery. A 280mm gun was developed for this, but it had a range of only 17 miles. The Army wanted to hit further, and it wanted nuclear weapons to end its reliance on the USAF for heavy firepower.

The Army turned to the ballistic missile to reach its goal. It first developed the Corporal missile with a range of 75 miles. The next step was the Redstone with a range of 240 miles, followed in the early 1950s by a crash program for an intermediate-range ballistic missile (IRBM) named Jupiter, with a range of nearly 2,000 miles, which first flew in 1957. The USAF saw these programs as a challenge to its mission, agreed upon at the Key West and Newport Conferences of 1948,* as 50 miles beyond the front line. The Army defended its work by asserting the USAF had not satisfactorily supported the ground forces in the past and would not do so in the future. In addition, the Army said it wanted a weapon to use regardless of the weather and that a missile was simply a technical extension of artillery. The USAF was bothered that the Jupiter could be used for strategic operations,* which challenged the USAF's mission further than the tactical operations* argument. Secretary of Defense (SECDEF) Charles E. Wilson ruled in favor of the USAF in 1956, limiting the Army to missiles of less than 20 miles range. The Army petitioned Wilson's successor, Neil H. McElroy, for more range and was given 500 miles in 1957. SECDEF Robert S. McNamara* cut it back to 200 miles.

The Jupiter was developed by the Army's arsenal system under Dr. Wernher von Braun's formerly German team. It was built by the Chrysler Corporation in an Army arsenal. The U.S. Navy was ordered to adapt Jupiter for launching from ships and, if possible, from submarines. The Navy had great difficulty with using a large liquid-fueled missile on board ships and switched to the solid-propellant Polaris. After Wilson's decision, the Jupiters, numbering 60, were transferred to the USAF's Strategic Air Command* (SAC) because of their range. From 1960 to 1965, the USAF installed them in Italy and Turkey for service with the North Atlantic Treaty Organization* (NATO). They were operational from 1960 to 1965.

Characteristics: engine, North American Aviation, Inc., Rocketdyne S-3 with 150,000 pounds thrust; diameter, 105 inches; length, 60 feet; weight, 110,000 pounds; range, 1,976 miles.

References. Michael H. Armacost, *The Politics of Weapons Innovation: The Thor-Jupiter Controversy*, 1969. A. J. Bacevich, *The Pentomic Era: The US Army between Korea and Vietnam*, 1986. *From Snark to Peacekeeper: A Pictorial History of Strategic Air Command Missiles*, Office of Historian, SAC, Offutt AFB, Nebraska, 1990. Jacob Neufeld, *Ballistic Missiles in the United States Air Force 1945–1960*, 1990. Polmar, *SAC*.

See also Wilson memorandums.

JUST CAUSE. *See* Panama incident of 1989.

K

KADENA AIR BASE

This airfield is near Naha, on the island of Okinawa, 400 miles south of the main islands of Japan. It is a Pacific Air Forces* (PACAF) base and is named for a nearby city. Kadena had been a Japanese airfield before it was taken by the U.S. Army in April 1945. Within a month the USAAF* was operating from it, and bombers* arrived in a few weeks. When the Korean War* began, Kadena was the site of headquarters for the Twentieth Air Force* (20AF). Within days, the 19th Bombardment Group arrived from Guam and went into action against the North Koreans. Two more bomb* groups followed, and B-29* operations continued through the war. B-52s* were based there and flew Arc Light* missions in the Vietnam War.* Kadena also had KC-135 (see C-135) tankers* to support the B-52s and tactical operations.* In 1990, Kadena had the headquarters of the 313th Air Division, the 18th Tactical Fighter Wing (TFW) using F-15s,* and the 376th Strategic Wing with KC-135s and RC-135s (see C-135).

References. Berger, *USAF in SEA*. C&C, vol. 5. Futrell, *USAF in Korea*. "Guide to Major Air Force Installations Worldwide," *AF*, May 1990, p. 124. Roberts, *Dir. USAF*.

KAYDET. *See* PT-13.

"K.B." *See* Wolfe, Lieutenant General Kenneth B.

KC-10. *See* C-10.

KC-135. *See* C-135 and KC-135 Stratolifter and Stratotanker.

KEARBY, COLONEL NEEL E. (1911–1944)

This ace* won the Air Force Medal of Honor* and had 22 aerial victories. He is tied for eleventh-ranking USAF* ace of all time with Colonel Gerald R. Johnson* and Lieutenant General Jay T. Robbins.*

Kearby was from Arlington, Texas, and graduated from the University of Texas at Austin in 1937. From college he became an aviation cadet.* In 1938 he became a pilot* and an officer. He had a series of fighter* assignments until, in 1942, he became commander of the 348th Fighter Group. He took the 348th, with F-47s,* to the Fifth Air Force* (5AF) in the South Pacific in 1943. Kearby was a leader who flew often in battle. While he was leading a flight* on 11 October 1943, a Mitsubishi A6M Reisen (Zero) was sighted, and Kearby shot it down. Then 36 enemy fighters and 12 bombers* were engaged and Kearby shot down another Zero and two Mitsubishi A6M3 Reisen (Hamp) fighters. Next the flight fought two Kawasaki Ki-61 Hien (Tony) fighters. Kearby destroyed both, his fifth and sixth victories for the day. For this action, Kearby won the Medal of Honor.

He was made commander of the 309th Bomb Wing. On 5 March, on a sortie to Wewak, New Guinea,* he shot down a Japanese bomber and was then shot down himself by a Nakajima Ki-43 Hayabusa (Oscar).

References. DuPre, *USAF Bio*. John L. Frisbee, "Giant in a Jug," *AF*, August 1987, p. 105. Gurney, *5 Down*. Hess, *Aces Album*.

KEEP 'EM FLYING. See movies.

KEESLER AIR FORCE BASE

This field was established in 1941 in Biloxi, Mississippi. It was named for Second Lieutenant Samuel R. Keesler, Jr., an observer* whose plane was shot down in 1918 after Keesler shot down an enemy aircraft.* The base belongs to the Air Training Command* (ATC). Keesler has been used for training in aircraft maintenance, radar,* computers, aircraft weapons, avionics, communications, and personnel and other administration.

References. Brown, *Eagles*. "Guide to Major Air Force Installations Worldwide," *AF*, May 1990, p. 124. Mueller, *AFB*. Roberts, *Dir. USAF*.

KELLY AIR FORCE BASE

One of the most historic of AFBs, and the oldest one in continuous service, Kelly was established in 1917 as the Aviation Camp at Fort Sam Houston, San Antonio, Texas. It was soon named in honor of Second Lieutenant George M. Kelly who was the first air force pilot* to die in a military aircraft accident. The field belongs to the Air Force Logistics Command* (AFLC). In World War I* it conducted flight training* for pilots. Briefly, in 1920–1921, it stopped flight training and taught aircraft maintenance. Advanced fighter* and bomber* training started in 1921, and observation aviation* training started in 1922. A gunnery school was established in 1941. In 1943 it became a major air logistics facility.

In 1990 it had headquarters of the San Antonio Air Logistics Center, which provided logistics management, procurement, and distribution functions together with depot maintenance.*

Movie: *I Wanted Wings*, 1941.

References. Brown, *Eagles*. "Guide to Major Air Force Installations Worldwide," *AF*, May 1990, pp. 124, 126. Mueller, *AFB*. Roberts, *Dir. USAF*.

KELSEY, BRIGADIER GENERAL BENJAMIN S. (1906–1981)

Kelsey was a key research and development leader in the USAF.* He joined the USAAC* in 1929. During the 1930s he was chief of the Fighter Project Branch at Wright Field, Ohio, where he tested several new aircraft including the P-38.* Kelsey went to London, England, in 1940 as the assistant military attaché for air to observe the aviation side of World War II.* In 1942 he led the first ferry flight of fighters* across the North Atlantic to England and became deputy chief of staff of the IX Fighter Command. Later, he was chief of the Operational Engineering Section of the Eighth Air Force* (8AF). His principal assignment after the war was as deputy director of research and development in the Air Staff's* Office of the Chief of Staff for Development.

References. Primary: Benjamin S. Kelsey, *The Dragon's Teeth? The Creation of United States Air Power for World War II*, 1982. Secondary: Air Force Pamphlet 31–1, "Roster of Retired General Officers." Department of Defense, Office of Public Information, Press Branch Biography.

Steven K. Yates

KENLY, MAJOR GENERAL WILLIAM L. (1864–1928)

Kenly was the first head of the USAAS.* He was born in Baltimore, Maryland, graduated from the U.S. Military Academy (USMA) in 1889, and was commissioned in the artillery. Shortly before U.S. entry into World War I,* he attended the San Diego Signal Corps Aviation School* in California. He went overseas at the head of an artillery unit but was soon appointed as General John J. Pershing's* chief of Air Service.* As such he presided over Colonel Raynal Bolling, who was in charge of air service affairs in the rear, and Brigadier General William Mitchell,* who was in command at the front. He was relieved by Brigadier General Benjamin Foulois* in November 1917. He went back to the artillery before returning to the United States early in 1918 to become the chief of the Division of Military Aeronautics, or head of the USAAS, for the rest of the war. Since aircraft procurement* was then under a civilian agency, Kenly was mainly responsible for personnel acquisition and training. The war ended before he could have a great effect upon these programs, and the rest of his service was occupied with the rapid demobilization of USAAS men coming back from Europe. He retired in 1919.

References. DuPre, *USAF Bio*. Goldberg, *Hist. USAF*. *Who's Who in America*, vol. 2, 1920.

David R. Mets

KENNEDY, PRESIDENT JOHN F. (1917–1963)

President Dwight D. Eisenhower* sponsored a grand strategy in which the U.S. Army and Navy, and U.S. allies, provided the United States with a shield, and the USAF* had the sword of nuclear weapons.* This gave the USAF priority among the services. Maxwell Taylor, a retired Army general, disagreed with this strategy and his influential book, *The Uncertain Trumpet*, was published in 1959. It advocated a strategy of "flexible response," which could mean using the Army instead of nuclear weapons. In addition, he recommended military commitments be made in a gradual escalation of force. JFK, the 35th president, embraced Taylor's concepts and adopted them as grand national strategy. Taylor was recalled from retirement to become chairman of the Joint Chiefs of Staff (JCS). He implemented his strategy under Secretary of Defense (SECDEF) Robert S. McNamara* who agreed with him. Taylor's ideas stood Eisenhower's strategy on its head. The USAF and its nuclear weapons became the nation's shield and the Army its sword. This ended the USAF's priority status.

JFK's relations with the USAF were never warm. He appointed General Curtis E. LeMay* to be chief of staff of the Air Force,* but this might have been for political reasons. JFK and the outspoken LeMay never got along. It may be indicative of JFK's attitude toward air power that he authorized the Central Intelligence Agency's Bay of Pigs invasion with an inadequate provision for air participation. Then, during operations, he personally ordered that no air support be given to the rebels. In addition, JFK ended "Net Evaluation" briefings, given to assess the current chances of a nuclear war, after hearing only one. Early in JFK's administration, word spread throughout the USAF that JFK, upon being shown a nuclear weapon on a routine visit to an AFB, became emotionally upset. JFK also sponsored an idea to have the defense of Europe rest upon a fleet of surface ships called the "Multilateral Force" (MLF). The MLF would be jointly controlled by the United States and the North Atlantic Treaty Organization* (NATO) with each ship's crew to be multinational. In Europe, doubt grew that the United States would ever use nuclear weapons in the defense of Europe under any circumstances. If true, this would have meant a Soviet nonnuclear attack could have conquered Europe.

JFK and Taylor thought their strategies and concepts were particularly effective for a guerrilla war. Thus, in another reversal of Eisenhower's policies, JFK was becoming deeply involved in Indochina when he died. Soon President Lyndon B. Johnson* (LBJ), McNamara, and Taylor would apply the new strategy to a conflict in the area.

References. Thomas M. Coffey, *Iron Eagle: The Turbulent Life of General Curtis LeMay*, 1986. Futrell, *Ideas*, vol. 2. David Halberstam, *The Best and the Brightest*, 1969. William J. Rust, *Kennedy in Vietnam*, 1985. Richard A. Stubbing, *The Defense Game*, 1986.

See also presidential airlift; Vietnam War.

KENNEY, GENERAL GEORGE C. (1889–1977)

Kenney earned notoriety as an innovative troubleshooter and as General Douglas MacArthur's air commander in the Pacific theater during World War II.* He also was the first commander of the Strategic Air Command* (SAC). In 1971, he was inducted into the National Aviation Hall of Fame in Dayton, Ohio.

He was born in Yarmouth, Nova Scotia, and attended the Massachusetts

Institute of Technology (MIT). He worked as an engineer until enlisting in the Aviation Section of the U.S. Army Signal Corps* in June 1917 as a flying, or aviation, cadet.* In November, he was assigned to Issoudon,* France, for advanced flight training.* Afterward he joined the 91st Aero Squadron, which he eventually commanded. In the 91st, Kenney flew 75 combat sorties in the Toul and Meuse-Argonne* sectors and shot down two enemy aircraft.* Kenney had a unique capacity for technical and conceptual innovation. His attempts to find lost U.S. soldiers while flying at treetop level inspired him to develop ideas for low-level strikes. Other innovations of his included mounting machine guns on a plane's wings instead of the cowling to increase the rate of fire, bulletproof glass to protect pilots,* power turrets in bombers,* improved oxygen systems, parachute bombs* for low-level raids, and "skip-bombing"* to improve strikes on ships.

He became an advocate of attack* aviation while at the Air Corps Tactical School* (ACTS) from 1927 to 1929. In addition, he championed an independent air force while he was in the Plans Division of the Chief of the Air Corps from 1933 to 1935. He flew in the lead B-17* in the *Rex* interception.* After a series of jobs from 1940 to 1942 as Lieutenant General H. H. Arnold's troubleshooter, he became commander of the Fifth Air Force* (5AF) and all Allied air forces in the southwest Pacific. As MacArthur's air commander, his responsibilities included interdicting Japanese supply lanes and supporting MacArthur's island-hopping strategy. For three years, air power became an integral part of MacArthur's campaigns, as in the Battle of the Bismarck Sea,* where Kenney's plan sank 16 Japanese ships.

After the war, he led SAC. Additional responsibilities and a misplaced trust in his vice commander caused Kenney to neglect combat crew training. He was replaced by Major General Curtis E. LeMay.* His last command was of the Air University,* and he retired in 1951.

References. Primary: George C. Kenney, *General Kenney Reports*, 1949. Secondary: DeWitt S. Copp, *A Few Great Captains: The Men and Events That Shaped Development of U.S. Air Power*, 1980. Stanley L. Falk, "General Kenney, the Indirect Approach, and the B-29s," *AH*, September 1981, pp. 146–55. John L. Frisbee, ed., *Makers of the United States Air Force*, 1987. Herman S. Wolk, "The Other Founding Father," *AF*, September 1987, pp. 164–73.

Peter R. Faber

KEYSTONE BOMBER

This biplane, used by the USAAS* and USAAC* from 1923 to 1933, was important because its operations provided testing and experience that contributed to the USAAC concepts of strategic operations.* The first model, the single-engined Huff-Daland and Company, Inc., XLB-1, was unsatisfactory. It was modified to twin engines and numbered XLB-3. Before delivery, the firm was reorganized and became the Keystone Aircraft Corporation. Changes were made in the airframe and types of engines for variant models XLB-5 through LB-14.

The designation *LB*, for "light bomber,"* was dropped in 1930 and later variations of this airplane were B-3A, B-4A, and B-6A.

Characteristics (LB-6): engines, two Wright R-1750–1 Cyclones of 536 horsepower each; span, 75 feet; length, 43 feet; height, 18 feet; gross weight, 13,440 pounds; top speed, 114 miles per hour; service ceiling, 11,650 feet; range, 632 miles; bombs, 2,000 pounds.

References: Primary: Haywood S. Hansell, Jr., "The Keystone Bombers: Unhonored and Unloved," *AF*, September 1977, pp. 130–36. Secondary: Jon R. Donnelly, "Last of the Keystones," *AF*, July 1984, pp. 100–102. Swanborough, *US Mil. Airc.*

KEY WEST AND NEWPORT CONFERENCES OF 1948

When the USAF* became independent in 1947, it seemed the National Security Act of 1947* and Executive Order 9877 of 26 July 1947* had delineated roles and missions of the services satisfactorily. As time passed, new questions arose about the use and user of air power. The questions resulted from the desires of each service to have and use air power, because each saw an increasing usefulness for air operations. The budget struggles brought the questions into sharp focus.

The primary acrimony was between the USAF and the U.S. Navy. The Navy disparaged heavy bombers* and planned to build supercarriers to conduct strategic operations.* The USAF believed the carriers could not perform strategic operations satisfactorily. Questions also existed between the USAF and the U.S. Army. The Army claimed the air defense mission as part of its historical coastal defense task. With a recognition that Soviet bombers could soon threaten the continental United States (CONUS) by using a great circle approach, air defense was a prospective budgetary plum. Differences also arose over which service would have ballistic missiles.*

To try to settle these issues, Secretary of Defense (SECDEF) James V. Forrestal* called for conferences with the Joint Chiefs of Staff (JCS) to be held in Key West, Florida, in March 1948. More meetings were held in Newport, Rhode Island, the following August. The conferences reached an agreement that the USAF had primary responsibility for strategic operations and the Navy for control of the seas. In addition, each would seek assistance from the other in discharging its primary responsibility. The air defense mission was given to the USAF, but, strangely, the Army got a "function" of organizing, equipping, and training air defense units.

The conferences did not end the acrimony. In 1949, the USAF and Navy differences exploded in the B-36 controversy.* The Army sought to use the vagueness of the air defense agreements. It argued it had been given all ground-based air defense systems. The advent of surface-to-air missiles* (SAM) led to a squabble over control of them in the 1950s. SECDEF Charles E. Wilson* gave to the Army SAMs with ranges up to 100 miles and to the USAF those with more than 100. This gave the victory to the Army, since SAMs with a range of over 100 miles have not been built, unless one considers the IM-99* to be one.

The USAF and Army ballistic missile mission dispute began in 1953 when the Army developed the Corporal missile with a 75-mile range, although the USAF had responsibility for everything over 50 miles beyond the battleline. Wilson's decision in 1956 gave all ballistic missiles of over 20 miles range to the USAF. This was not final. Ultimately, SECDEF Robert S. McNamara* changed it to 200 miles.

References. A. J. Bacevich, *The Pentomic Era: The US Army between Korea and Vietnam*, 1986. Futrell, *Ideas*, vol. 1. Goldberg, *Hist. USAF*.

See also aerospace defense; attack; Jupiter; Pace-Finletter memorandum of 4 November 1952; separation from the U.S. Army; Wilson memorandums.

KHAM DUC AIRLIFT EVACUATION

The evacuation of the Allied garrison at the Kham Duc mountain post on 12 May 1968 was one of the most spectacular operations of the Vietnam War.* As early as April 1968, intelligence began to observe signs that this Special Forces Camp near the Laotian border was being threatened, as Khe Sanh* had been threatened. On 10 May the Allies found themselves under intense artillery, mortar, and recoilless rifle assault. The losses that day, the prospects for increased enemy activity, and the camp's vulnerability caused General William West-moreland, commander of the U.S. Military Assistance Command, Vietnam (MACV), to order evacuation. Through 12 May U.S. Army and Marine helicopters* airlifted out survivors, while air attack* held off the enemy. A C-130* and a C-123* took out a few in the morning. In the afternoon, three C-130s came in, but only one made a successful landing and evacuation. Late in the afternoon, three more C-130s brought out the last of the garrison. Of the 1,500 evacuated, the USAF* brought out more than 500, nearly all in the last crucial minutes before the camp fell.

Yet, one final evacuation took place. A C-130 brought in a three-man USAF control team to coordinate the additional pullout. By the time the team realized all had already left, the C-130 had taken off. To rescue this team from the enemy-controlled camp, a C-123 landed and took off under intense fire and successfully rescued them. For his valor, the C-123 pilot,* Lieutenant Colonel Joe M. Jackson, received the Air Force Medal of Honor.*

References. Alan L. Gropman, *Airpower and the Airlift Evacuation of Kham Duc*, 1979. Donald K. Schneider, *Air Force Heroes in Vietnam*, USAF Southeast Asia Monograph Series, vol. 7, 1979.

Roger D. Launius

KHE SANH, SOUTH VIETNAM

Khe Sanh is located in the extreme north of what was South Vietnam. A battle was fought there in early 1968 that resembled the famous French Dien Bien Phu defeat in 1954. At Khe Sanh, however, U.S. air power reversed the result, smashing two North Vietnamese divisions in the action.

Khe Sanh was a U.S. Marine Corps (USMC) enclave with 6,000 men, including South Vietnamese Rangers. By the end of 1967, it was facing two full North Vietnamese divisions, one of which had participated at Dien Bien Phu.

The enemy force was 20,000 men strong. Expecting an assault, Lieutenant General William W. Momyer,* commander of the Seventh Air Force* (7AF), tried to unify the air support under himself. The U.S. Navy would not agree, and so the area around this small camp had to be divided into zones with some assigned to the Navy and others to the USAF for Operation Niagara. Air operations began on 22 January 1968. The USAF used Combat Skyspot* so the weather would not stop operations. The Marines were totally dependent upon airmen for supplies and fire support. On 24 January the enemy took an outpost and began steady bombardment with mortars, missiles, and artillery. It also began tunneling toward the camp and moved into an assault position.

On 30 January, the enemy launched its Tet offensive throughout South Vietnam in hopes of igniting a general rebellion. The North Vietnamese got no support from the population in the South, and the 7AF maintained an undiminished support of Khe Sanh while fully supporting the U.S. Army's counteroffensive against the enemy.

In February the enemy bombardment became intense enough to endanger the supply transports that were landing. On 10 February a Marine C-130* was destroyed, and C-130 supply was switched to air drop. The one lost C-130 burned and was shown repeatedly in U.S. television accounts, giving the impression of heavy aircraft losses. Fighters* were used to attack* close to the Marines and B-52s* for more distant targets. Enemy attempts to use flak* were suppressed and became ineffective. Although assault trenches reached almost to the camp, the enemy never launched a serious attempt to overrun it. This is the best indicator of the results achieved by the USAF. In mid-March the enemy retreated and overland communications were restored to the enclave.

U.S. and South Vietnamese casualties in the battle were 1,800; the enemy's were estimated at 10,000, or half of its force. USAF losses totaled three C-123s.* Khe Sanh did divert enough USAF effort to allow the North Vietnamese to build up men and supplies for an offensive in May. In addition, the divided control of air operations reduced effectiveness until March when the Navy agreed to the USAF doctrine of unified control. General William C. Westmoreland, commander of the U.S. Military Assistance Command, in Vietnam (MACV), believed the B-52s were the key to the U.S. victory.

An argument has been made that Khe Sanh was a North Vietnamese victory. The basis for the claim is that the North's objective was to distract American attention away from the nearby Ho Chi Minh trail.* This was intended to mask the surge of resources sent southward for the Tet offensive. The Americans expected Tet but were surprised at its size. If the North's goal was truly a diversion, and not a repeat of Dien Bien Phu, Khe Sanh could be regarded as a communist victory won at a high cost in men. A problem with this argument concerns the times of the Khe Sanh and Tet battles.

References. Primary: John L. Cirofici, "CCT at Khe Sanh," *Air Power History*, Spring 1990, pp. 47–52. Secondary: Berger, *USAF in SEA*. Ray L. Bowers, *Tactical Airlift*, 1983. William H. Greenhalgh, Jr., "AOK Airpower over Khe Sanh," *AH*, March

1972, pp. 2–9. John Schlight, *The War in South Vietnam: The Years of the Offensive 1965–1968*, 1988.

KIMPO AIR BASE

Kimpo AB, or K-14, at Seoul, South Korea, figured prominently for the USAF* in the Korean War.* For months, fewer than 100 F-86s* of the 4th Fighter Interceptor Wing (FIW) at Kimpo dominated around 400 MiG-15s of the enemy.

Shortly after the war began, Kimpo was used by the USAF to evacuate Americans. Eight North Korean Il-10 Stormovik attack* planes tried to destroy the transports* on 27 June 1950. Kimpo was being defended by four F-80s,* which quickly shot down four Il-10s. The rest fled. These were the first victories for USAF jets and were scored by Captain Raymond E. Schillereff and Lieutenants Robert H. Dewald and Robert E. Wayne. It was Wayne who scored twice. On 29 June, B-29s* bombed the airfield when it was in enemy hands. The B-29s were hit by three fighters* and shot down one Yak without loss.

In September, an airlift into recaptured Kimpo began. In October, the 51st FIW moved in. In December, the 4th arrived at Kimpo with a new fighter for the war, the F-86. In January 1951, a Chinese offensive forced a second evacuation of Kimpo, but it was recaptured in February. The 8th Fighter Bomber Wing (FBW) moved in by June, but it was replaced by the 4th again in August. After the war, the USAF used Kimpo as a major base until the end of the 1960s.

References. "Air War over Korea 1950–1953," a special issue of *Air Classics*, 1980, pp. 64–73. Futrell, *USAF in Korea*.

KINCHELOE, CAPTAIN IVEN C., JR. (1928–1958)

Kincheloe is famed for his flights in the X-2.* At one time there was an AFB near Kinross, Michigan, named for him. The Society of Experimental Test Pilots (SETP) established a special award for outstanding test pilots and named it the Iven C. Kincheloe Memorial Award.

Kincheloe was from Detroit, Michigan, and graduated from Purdue University, having studied mechanical and aeronautical engineering. He entered the USAF* through the Air Force Reserve Officers Training Corps (AFROTC) in 1949. He became a pilot* in 1950. He flew 30 combat sorties in F-80s* and 101 in F-86s* with the 4th and 51st Fighter Wings in the Korean War.* This ace* scored ten aerial victories. In 1955 he started test flying at Edwards* AFB in California. In 1956 he set a world record altitude of 126,200 feet in an X-2 for which he received the Mackay Trophy. In 1958 he died in an F-104* accident.

References. DuPre, *USAF Bio*. Richard P. Hallion, *Test Pilots: The Frontiersmen of Flight*, 1981. Jay Miller, *The X-Planes*, rev. ed., 1988.

"KING, THE." *See* Gable, Major Clark.

KINGCOBRA. *See* P-63.

KINGPIN. *See* Son Tay prison raid.

KIRTLAND AIR FORCE BASE

This Military Airlift Command* (MAC) facility is near Albuquerque, New Mexico, and was first established in 1941 as the Albuquerque Army Air Base. It became the home of the 19th Bombardment Group. Its name was changed in 1942 to honor Colonel Roy C. Kirtland, who had been the oldest military pilot in the USAAF.* During World War II* it was used principally for bombardier* training and graduated thousands. At the end of the war the field was inactivated for a short time.

In 1946 it began to play a key role in nuclear weapons* development and testing. The Air Materiel Command (AMC) used it as a site for supporting nearby Sandia Field, currently part of Kirtland, which was the home of much scientific and technical research on the weapons. In 1977 the base was transferred to MAC. In 1990 it had the 1606th Air Base Wing with more than 100 tenant units, many of them still dedicated to weapons development and testing. Also on the base was the 1550th Combat Crew Training Wing for special operations training. Other units included the Air Force Contract Management Division, the Air Force Office of Security Police,* and the Air Force Operational Test and Evaluation Center.* Parts of the field are used for civilian flying.

References. Don E. Alberts and Allan E. Putnam, *A History of Kirtland Air Force Base, 1928–1982*, Kirtland AFB, New Mexico: Office of History, 1606 ABW, 1982. Mueller, *AFB*. Gerald D. Nash, ed., *Urban West*, 1979. Charles A. Ravenstein, *Air Force Combat Wings: Lineage and Honors Histories, 1947–1977*, 1984.

Roger D. Launius

K. I. SAWYER AIR FORCE BASE

This Strategic Air Command* (SAC) base is near Marquette, Michigan. It was activated in 1959 and named for Kenneth I. Sawyer, a county road commissioner who planned the airport in 1941. At first, the field was under the Air Defense Command (ADC) and had a Semiautomatic Ground Environment* (SAGE) facility. B-52s* and KC-135s (*see* C-135) were based there beginning in the 1960s. In 1990 it had the 410th Bomb Wing still using B-52s and KC-135s.

References. "Guide to Major Air Force Installations Worldwide," *AF*, May 1990, p. 126. Mueller, *AFB*. Roberts, *Dir. USAF*.

KNERR, MAJOR GENERAL HUGH J. (1887–1971)

This officer had an important role in sponsoring USAF* bombardment aviation. Born in Fairfield, Iowa, Knerr began his career as an ensign in the U.S. Navy after graduating from the U.S. Naval Academy (USNA) in 1908. Interested in flying, he transferred to the Aviation Section of the U.S. Army Signal Corps* in 1916 and became a pilot.* Knerr was commanding officer of the 2nd Bombardment Group from 1927 to 1930. He became chief of the Field Services Section of the Aircraft Materiel Division at Wright Field, Ohio, from 1930 to

1935. He then held his most influential position, chief of staff of the General Headquarters Air Force* (GHQ Air Force), until 1938. He was retired as a colonel in 1939 because of his insistent support for bombardment aviation, which was against official policy. In addition, there was personal animosity by Major General H. H. Arnold* stemming from the Alaskan flight of 1934.* He was recalled to active duty in 1942 as deputy commander of the Air Service Command. He thereafter held a variety of command and staff positions until retiring in 1950.

References. Primary: Hugh J. Knerr, "Washington to Alaska and Back: Memories of the U.S. Air Corps Test Flight," *AH*, April 1972, pp. 20–24. Secondary: C&C, vol. 1. DeWitt S. Copp, *A Few Great Captains: The Men and Events That Shaped the Development of U.S. Air Power*, 1980. John L. Frisbee, ed., *Makers of the United States Air Force*, 1987. Murray Green, "Maj. Gen. Hugh J. Knerr, Hard Campaigner for Airpower," *AF*, October 1978, pp. 90–92.

Steven K. Yates

KNUDSEN, LIEUTENANT GENERAL WILLIAM S. (1879–1948)

Knudsen contributed greatly to aircraft production, a critical factor in generating the air power needed for World War II.* He was from Denmark and rose to the presidency of General Motors Corporation. Famous for his ability to get production done, he was appointed a lieutenant general and director of production in the Office of the Under Secretary of War in 1942. In 1944 he was made director of Army Air Forces Materiel and Services at Patterson Field, Ohio. He returned to private industry in 1945.

References. C&C, vol. 6. DuPre, *USAF Bio.* Irving Brinton Holley, Jr., *Buying Aircraft: Matériel Procurement for the Army Air Forces*, 1964.

KORAT ROYAL THAI AIR FORCE BASE

In August 1964, as one result of the Gulf of Tonkin incident, eight F-105s* moved from Yokota* AB to Korat. More followed from McConnell* AFB, and Korat became a primary base for attacks* on North Vietnam. The 6234th Tactical Fighter Wing (TFW) was organized at Korat in April 1965. A year later it was redesignated the 388th TFW. The fighters* used were first F-105s and later F-4s.* The 388th left Korat in July 1973, and the field ceased to be a major USAF* base in 1975.

References. Berger, *USAF in SEA*. René J. Francillon, *Vietnam: The War in the Air*, 1987. Jerry Scutts, *Wrecking Crew: The 388th Tactical Fighter Wing in Vietnam*, 1990.

KOREAN AIRLIFT

This action set the pattern for airlift operations* on a large scale for overseas wars and furthered tactical airlift* concepts. When the United States became involved in the Korean War,* Major General William H. Tunner* and his staff relied on their experience with the "Hump"* Airlift in the World War II* and the Berlin Airlift* in 1948 to 1949. They established the Combat Cargo Command (CCC) of the Far East Air Forces at Ashiya AB, Japan, in August 1950. For the Korean Airlift, the Military Air Transport Service (MATS) maintained the longest air supply route ever flown to that time. It carried troops and supplies from the United States, either from Seattle, Washington, to Anchorage, Alaska, across the Aleutian Islands to Japan; or San Francisco, California, to Hawaii to Midway Island to Wake Island to Japan. From Japan the CCC shuttled the men and equipment to Korea in tactical airlift.

Vital cargo traveled back over the routes. Before the war, MATS provided aeromedical evacuation* for about 350 patients a month from Japan to the United States. From June 1950 to July 1953, MATS flew 43,196 casualties back to the United States for further medical treatment.

References. Primary: William H. Tunner, *Over the Hump: The Story of General William H. Tunner, the Man Who Moved Anything Anywhere, Anytime*, 1964. Secondary: Futrell, *USAF in Korea*.

Coy F. Cross II

KOREAN ELECTRICAL POWER TARGET SYSTEM

After armistice talks had been stalled for about a year, the Far East Air Forces (FEAF) proposed to strike North Korea's hydroelectrical power complex to raise the cost to the enemy of prolonging the war. On 11 June 1952, U.S. Army General Mark W. Clark, commander in chief of the United Nations Command (UNC) and Far East Command, approved.

From 23 to 27 June, strikes were made on the Sui-ho, Chosin, Fusen, and Kyosen power complexes by Fifth Air Force* (5AF) and U.S. Navy aircraft. The 5AF flew 730 attack* and 238 air superiority* sorties with no losses. The Navy flew 546 sorties and lost two aircraft to flak.* It had been feared the enemy would use its 250 MiG-15s based near Sui-ho for defense, but it did not. About 160 MiGs took off during the strikes but fled westward. As a result of the raids, North Korea had an almost complete electrical blackout for two weeks. Despite frenzied repair efforts, the North Koreans had lost 90 percent of electrical power capacity. This also caused a loss of 23 percent of northeast Red China's electrical power needs.

The campaign resulted in no visible movement by the communist negotiators at the peace talks. There was also a storm of protest in Britain over the raids. It appears that the loss of electrical power was not a body blow to the economy of North Korea and that the British reaction encouraged the communists in their tough stance.

References. Mark Clodfelter, *The Limits of Air Power: The American Bombing of North Vietnam*, 1989. Futrell, *USAF in Korea*. James T. Stewart, ed., *Airpower: The Decisive Force in Korea*, 1957.

KOREAN IRRIGATION DAMS TARGET SYSTEM

In 1953, the Far East Air Forces (FEAF) studied the North Korean irrigation dams as a possible target with which to pressure the enemy to make concessions in the ongoing Korean War* armistice negotiations. The evidence indicates this campaign succeeded.

Some 80 dams retained water needed for rice production. Breaching the dams would cause both flooding and a reduction in the rice crop. A test attack was made by F-84s* on 13 May on Toksan dam, which was selected because flood waters from it would cut enemy lines of communication. The results were excellent and, on 16 May, Chasan dam was hit by F-84s with similar success. Next, B-29s* bombed Kuwonga dam, but, by the time the attack was finished, the North Koreans had lowered the water level. Thus, the enemy could save their rail and road lines, but at a cost of rice production.

Indicative of the effectiveness of the strikes was the shrillest enemy hate propaganda campaign of the war. Masses of laborers were soon at work rebuilding the dams. The communists yielded to United Nations terms for an armistice on 8 June 1953. There were no other direct events in Korea at that time. Therefore, there are grounds to believe the dams campaign precipitated the enemy's willingness to conclude an armistice. If so, this marked the second special bombing campaign by the USAF* that ended a war, the first being the atomic bomb raids of World War II.*

The Korean raids had further consequences. They created a belief by some in the USAF that food was an Achilles' heel of a communist economy, an idea already held by some economists and historians. However, in the Vietnam War,* the North Vietnamese food supply was not hit, and the USAF was forbidden from striking at dikes. The dikes prevented flooding and helped the growth of rice. Some aversion to such a target system came from within the USAF itself. Some USAF leaders believed these were "civilian" and not "military" targets. This is strange, because cutting off an enemy's food has a long and accepted tradition in military history, particularly with blockades and sieges. Since interdiction is an aerial form of blockade, the food supply should be a legitimate target. The North Vietnamese were soon aware of the U.S. reluctance, and the dikes became a favorite site for air defense weapons.

References. Mark Clodfelter, *The Limits of Air Power: The American Bombing of North Vietnam*, 1989. Futrell, *USAF in Korea*. James T. Stewart, ed., *Airpower: The Decisive Force in Korea*, 1957.

KOREAN WAR (1950–1953)

After the invasion of the Republic of Korea (ROK) by the People's Democratic Republic of Korea in 1950, the USAF's* initial involvement was the evacuation of U.S. nationals. This resulted in the first USAF* combat of the war; transports* were protected and three Yak fighters* were shot down. The USAF precipitated the end of the war with its strategic operations* campaign against the Korean irrigation dams system.*

Early on, the USAF, as part of United Nations (UN) forces, was directed to conduct attack* operations for the ROK Army operating south of the 38th parallel. This order was then expanded to include the north, and the North Korean army air force was soon obliterated. Tactical operations* were then limited to Korean soil despite support of the enemy from Red China and the USSR. As the North

Korean army columns moved southward, their massed formations presented ideal targets for nuclear weapons.* President Harry S Truman* (HST) feared that the invasion was the opening Soviet blow in a World War III and that the U.S. use of nuclear weapons might precipitate that terrible prospect. HST decided against their use. The USAF was satisfied with that decision. It had too few nuclear weapons for a war with the USSR and considered readiness for such a contingency as having the highest priority. The decision not to use nuclear weapons made their future use less likely.

Once the UN Pusan perimeter was secure, strategic operations against North Korean industry began. They were finished in September, and no more were contemplated as there was a view that such operations could only be directed successfully at an industrialized state.

When the Inchon amphibious landings were made, the USAF provided tactical and airlift operations* in the UN advance to the Yalu River. In November, Red China entered the war, and the first all-jet air battle took place. It resulted in the first victory over a MiG-15. From then to the end of the war, an inconclusive air struggle raged over the Korean side of the Yalu River because political air superiority* was given to the enemy. The area for this struggle was called "MiG Alley,"* where clashes occurred between MiGs and USAF F-86s.* Over the rest of North Korea, the USAF kept complete air superiority despite enemy efforts to gain it. Enemy operations over U.S. lines were limited to harassing night raids by biplanes called "Bedcheck Charlie," which mainly disturbed sleep.

Once the bloody ground war of attrition ended, the land effort became one simply to hold roughly the original South Korea. It was left to the USAF and naval air power to pressure the enemy so peace would be negotiated. This effort began as mainly interdiction. There was a limit to its effectiveness because there was no ground pressure on the enemy to use up supplies. Also the political limits of the war inhibited interdiction because the enemy was given areas of sanctuary. Even so, the airmen limited the supplies reaching the front to 10 percent of those sent forward. Next the airmen attacked, under restraints, the Korean electrical power target system* in strategic operations without gaining the desired effects.

Finally, the Korean irrigation dams target system was hit and President Dwight D. Eisenhower* threatened to conduct a USAF strategic operations campaign against Manchuria. These actions provided incentives for both North Korea and China to agree to UN terms. Shortly thereafter, the communists capitulated on the sticking point in the peace talks: the enemy demand that all their prisoners of war be forcibly returned to them regardless of any desire for freedom. Thus, as in World War II* and the Vietnam War,* peace followed a special bombing campaign by the USAF.

References. Mark Clodfelter, *The Limits of Air Power: The American Bombing of North Vietnam*, 1989. Futrell, *USAF in Korea*. Higham, *Air Pwr.* Robert Jackson, *Air War over Korea*, 1973. James T. Stewart, ed., *Airpower: The Decisive Force in Korea*, 1957.

KUNSAN AIR BASE

This Pacific Air Forces* (PACAF) base is at Kunsan, Korea. Before the Korean War* the Republic of Korea Air Force (ROKAF) used the field, which had been built in 1938 by the Japanese. In 1951 the base was expanded for USAF* use with a new runway. The 3rd Bombardment Wing with B-26 Invaders* moved into Kunsan, or K-8, during August. The runway was further improved in 1952, and men and F-84Es* from the 116th Fighter-Bomber Wing (FBW) at Misawa* AB, Japan, moved into Kunsan and became the 474th FBW. The unit changed designation to the 49th FBW in 1953. In 1990 Kunsan had the 8th Tactical Fighter Wing (TFW) using F-16s* with the same mission as fighter* units of the Korean War.

References. "Air War over Korea 1950–1953," a special issue of *Air Classics*, 1980, pp. 95–97. Futrell, *USAF in Korea*. "Guide to Major Air Force Installations Worldwide," *AF*, May 1990, p. 126. Roberts, *Dir. USAF*.

KUTER, GENERAL LAURENCE S. (1905–1979)

Kuter was a seminal leader in the development of U.S. strategic operations* concepts and forces. He also held an extraordinary range of senior command positions during his 35-year career.

Born in Rockford, Illinois, he graduated from the U.S. Military Academy (USMA) in 1927 and became a pilot* in 1930. In 1933 he became an alternate member of Captain Claire L. Chennault's* air demonstration team, the "Three Men on the Flying Trapeze," which was the forerunner of the Thunderbirds.* He played a leading role in the operational development of the B-9* bomber,* which illustrated his resolve to convert ideas into action. Kuter attended the Air Corps Tactical School* (ACTS) and graduated first in his class in 1935. He stayed on at the ACTS as bombardment instructor and quickly succumbed to the new orthodoxy of independent strategic daylight bombing against an enemy's vital economic centers. He believed strategic operations would make war quick and relatively bloodless.

Along with three other former ACTS instructors who championed strategic bombing, Kuter co-authored AWPD-1,* the air plan that first defined the use of strategic air power in the European theater. In February 1942, he was promoted directly from lieutenant colonel to brigadier general. At 36, he was the youngest general officer of the time. A whirlwind of choice assignments then followed: commander of the 1st Bombardment Wing of the Eighth Air Force* (8AF) (1942–1943), where he directed B-17* raids on Germany; commander of the Allied Tactical Air Forces in North Africa (1943), where he led the Tunisian air campaign; assistant chief of the Air Staff for plans and combat operations (1943–1945); and deputy commander of Army Air Forces in the Pacific, where he helped organize and operate B-29* units against Japan.

After the war, Major General Kuter midwifed infant USAF* commands into mature organizations. Early in 1948 he became the first commander of the Military Air Transport Service (MATS), now the Military Airlift Command*

(MAC). He next commanded the Air University* (AU), where he upgraded the educational quality of the Air Command and Staff School (1953–1955). Finally, as a four-star general, he commanded the Far East Air Forces (FEAF), which evolved into the Pacific Air Forces* (PACAF) while still under his control (1955–1959). He concluded his career as commander in chief of the North Atlantic Air Defense Command (NORAD) (1959–1962). After retirement from the USAF, he was a vice president of Pan American World Airways.

References. Primary: Haywood S. Hansell, Jr., "Gen. Laurence S. Kuter," *AF*, June 1980, pp. 95–97. Laurence S. Kuter, *The Great Gamble: The Boeing 747*, 1973, and "JFK and LBJ Consider Aerospace Defense," *AH*, March 1978, pp. 1–4. Secondary: DeWitt S. Copp, *A Few Great Captains: The Men and Events That Shaped the Development of U.S. Air Power*, 1980, and *Forged in Fire: Strategy and Decisions in the Airwar over Europe 1940–1945*, 1982.

Peter R. Faber

KUW-1. *See* JB-2.

L

L-1 TO L-28. *See* liaison aircraft.

L-19. *See* O-1 Bird Dog.

LABORATORY

USAF* laboratories are units like centers* except they work on research and development (R&D). Laboratories are usually named but may be numbered. An example of one is the 6570th Aerospace Medical Research Laboratory.

Reference. Ravenstein, *Org. USAF*.

LABS. *See* Low-Altitude Bombing System.

LACKLAND AIR FORCE BASE

Near San Antonio, Texas, this is an Air Training Command* (ATC) base. It began as part of Kelly* Field but was detached in 1942 as the San Antonio Aviation Cadet Center (SAACC). In 1945 it was renamed the San Antonio District of the Army Air Forces Personnel Distribution Command. In 1946 it became the Army Air Forces Military Training Center and then the Indoctrination Division of the ATC. In 1948 it was named for Brigadier General Frank D. Lackland, a military aviator from 1917 to 1942 and one-time commandant of Kelly Field's flying school. Lackland has been used mostly for basic training.

References. "Guide to Major Air Force Installations Worldwide," *AF*, May 1990, p. 126. Mueller, *AFB*. Roberts, *Dir. USAF*.

LADIES COURAGEOUS. See movies.

LAFAYETTE ESCADRILLE

This was a famed unit of Americans in World War I* which represented the essence of American idealism, patriotism, and sacrifice. Originally, it was a French squadron staffed by U.S. volunteers, except for a French commander and his assistant. Its official designation was N. 124 when flying Nieuport 28s* and S. 124 when it later flew Spad XIIIs.* Its mission was reconnaissance,* patrol, and fighter escort.* After the war, monuments to the men and achievements of the Escadrille were established in Luxeuil, in eastern France, and Paris.

The prime mover in its formation was Norman Prince of a distinguished Boston family. He was breveted a pilot* for the French in 1915 and flew Voisin bombers* until February 1916. From his arrival in France he was active in convincing French authorities of the benefits of an all-American flying unit in the French service. As a result of his enthusiasm, family contacts, the efforts of other Americans fighting for France, and the assistance of individuals in Paris, the unit was established.

The Escadrille was authorized on 21 March 1916. Its formation was delayed by French doubts about U.S. intentions and an abundance of French aviation candidates. As the war became a stalemate and French resources dwindled, the French aviation officials saw the practical and political benefits of the unit. The French officials felt, rightly, that the Escadrille would focus U.S. attention favorably on the French cause. At first it was called the "American Escadrille," but U.S. neutrality caused the change to "Lafayette." It reached the front in April 1916 and operated until February 1918, when it transferred to U.S. control as the 103rd Aero Squadron. During its existence, the Escadrille roster had 38 U.S. pilots, and nearly one-third were killed. It was credited with 37 enemy aircraft,* of which 17 fell to Raoul Lufbery.* Victor Chapman was its first pilot to die in battle, on 23 June 1916. Prince died in a night landing accident on 12 October 1916. William Thaw was the unofficial leader of the unit, but the official commander was Capitaine Georges Thenault. Well-known pilots included Kiffin Rockwell, Bert Hall, Ted Parsons, and James Norman Hall.

After the war James Norman Hall teamed with Charles Nordhoff, who had flown for the French in another unit, and they wrote *The Lafayette Flying Corps* in 1920. The Lafayette Flying Corps was an unofficial name for Americans flying for the French, so it includes more than those in the Lafayette Escadrille. Nordhoff and Hall moved to Tahiti, where they wrote *Mutiny on the Bounty* and other books.

References. Primary: Bert Hall, *"En l'Air!"* 1918. James Norman Hall, *High Adventure*, 1918. James McConnell, *Flying for France*, 1917. Edwin "Ted" Parsons, *The Great Adventure*, 1937. Secondary: Philip Flammer, *The Vivid Air: The Lafayette Escadrille*, 1981.

D. K. Vaughan

LAHM, MAJOR GENERAL FRANK P. (1877–1963)

This pioneer was the first man to get a pilot's* rating in the Aeronautics Division of the U.S. Army Signal Corps,* and he flew both airplanes and balloons. Lahm was inducted into the National Aviation Hall of Fame in Dayton, Ohio, in 1963.

Lahm was from Mansfield, Ohio, and graduated from the U.S. Military Academy (USMA) in 1901. Lahm soloed in an airplane in 1909, but he had already

helped set an endurance record of one hour and 12 minutes while flying with
Orville Wright. Lahm flew the Aeronautical Division's first cross-country flight.
He commanded balloon units in World War I* and was on the First Army General
Staff for the St. Mihiel* and Meuse-Argonne* actions. In 1926 he became
assistant chief of the Air Corps. He organized and led the Air Corps Training
Center.* He became chief of aviation for the First Army and retired in 1941.

   References. DuPre, *USAF Bio*. Samuel S. Whitt, "Frank Lahm: Pioneer Military
Aviator," *AH*, December 1972, pp. 172–77.

LAJES FIELD

This base is on Terceira Island in the Azores, Portugal, and is a Military Airlift
Command* (MAC) facility. U.S. operations began there in 1946.** Lajes was
a key base for MAC's 1973 Israeli Airlift because Portugal was the only European
country to cooperate with the United States in the effort. In 1990 its USAF*
unit was the 1605th Military Airlift Support Wing. It helped U.S. and other
authorized aircraft cross the Atlantic Ocean. It also supported U.S. Navy antisubmarine warfare activities.

   References. "Guide to Major Air Force Installations Worldwide," *AF*, May 1990,
p. 126. Charles E. Miller, *Airlift Doctrine*, 1988. Roberts, *Dir. USAF*.

   **Another airfield in the Azores was used by the USAAF* in World War II.

LAKENHEATH. *See* RAF Lakenheath.

LAMPERT COMMITTEE

   This House of Representatives committee studied U.S. aviation in 1924 and
1925. It recommended both a unified Department of Defense, which could
emphasize military aviation, and government assistance to the aviation industry.
This was based on Brigadier General William Mitchell's* belief that aviation
would be the nation's first line of defense in protecting the United States from
an enemy.

   Named for its chairman, Florian Lampert of Wisconsin, it was established to
investigate charges by Representative John M. Nelson. Nelson said the nation's
aviation development was backward because of the conservatism of U.S. Army
and Navy officers and because of the monopolistic practices of the Manufacturer's
Aircraft Association in controlling patents on aircraft and aircraft engines. The
committee held hearings on all phases of commercial and military aviation in
the United States, questioning most of the same experts the President's Aircraft
Board,* or Morrow Board, heard after September 1925.

   Reporting in the same month as the president's board, it agreed with the
Morrow Board that the government should assist the aviation industry, but, unlike
the Morrow Board, it endorsed many of Mitchell's proposals to make aviation
the first line of defense. While rejecting the concept of a separate department
of aviation, the Lampert group thought a unified defense department relying on
coastal air defenses would be the most economical means of national defense.
A unified defense agency would end the interservice bickering between the Army

and Navy in aviation affairs and define the missions of each branch. It could also give the aviation officers the autonomy they needed.

The committee's report was not acceptable to the War and Navy Departments, but it influenced congressional action in 1926. The legislation was favorable to the air industries, especially in providing for five-year military and naval airplane construction programs.

References. Primary: U.S. Congress, House, *Hearings before the Select Committee on Inquiry into Operations of the United States Air Service*, 69th Cong., 1st Sess., 1925. Lampert report is in U.S. Congress, House, *Department of Defense and Unification of the Air Services*, 69th Cong., 1st Sess., 1926. Secondary: Lester H. Brune, *The Origins of American National Security: Sea Power, Air Power and Foreign Policy, 1900 to 1941*, 1981. Futrell, *Ideas*, vol. 1. Irving Brinton Holley, Jr., *Buying Aircraft: Matériel Procurement for the Army Air Force*, 1964. John B. Rae, *Climb to Greatness: The American Aircraft Industry 1920–1960*, 1968.

Lester H. Brune

LANCER. *See* B-1; P-43.

LANGLEY, SAMUEL P. (1834–1906)

Langley's great contributions to aviation, and thus to the USAF,* were his work with powered models and the simple fact that a scientist of his reputation felt manned flight was possible at a time when most people doubted its practicality. In addition, the aircraft he worked on was paid for by, and intended for, the U.S. Army. Langley AFB,* Virginia, is named in his honor. The National Aeronautics and Space Administration's* (NASA) Langley Research Center, at the AFB, also preserves his memory. He was inducted into the National Aviation Hall of Fame in Dayton, Ohio, in 1963.

He was born in Massachusetts and never attended a college or university. His chief interest was astronomy, and his most lasting contributions were in that field. In 1867 he was appointed director of the Allegheny Observatory, near Pittsburgh, Pennsylvania, and for 20 years he served, in effect, as the United States's chief astronomer. His greatest achievements were in the field of spectral measurements of solar and lunar radiation, where his work was fundamental. In 1887 he was appointed the third secretary of the Smithsonian Institution, where he exercised great influence on late-19th-century U.S. science.

His interest turned to the problem of manned flight, and he began experiments with flying machines. In 1896 he flew a series of powered models from a houseboat anchored in the Potomac River. The longest flight was more than 4,200 feet. These were the first sustained free flights of a powered, heavier-than-air flying machine ever made. In 1898 the Army gave Langley $50,000 to create a manned airplane. His manned machines were not successful, culminating with a disastrous crash of his ''Aerodrome'' on 8 December 1903.

References. Primary: Samuel P. Langley, *Langley Memoir on Mechanical Flight*, 1908. Secondary: Charles G. Abbot, ''Samuel P. Langley,'' *Smithsonian Miscellaneous Collections*, 92, No. 3281, 22 August 1934. Tom D. Crouch, *A Dream of Wings:*

Americans and the Airplane 1875–1905, 1981. Juliette A. Hennessy, *The United States Army Air Arm April 1861 to April 1917*, 1985.

Patrick B. Nolan

LANGLEY AIR FORCE BASE

Adjacent to Hampton, Virginia, Langley is one of the oldest continuously operating AFBs in the United States. In 1916, upon the recommendation of the National Advisory Committee for Aeronautics (NACA), Congress provided for an "Aviation Experimental Station and Proving Grounds." It was named to honor Samuel P. Langley,* an aviation pioneer. Operations began by the end of 1917.

During the postwar years, training and experimentation were done on it. In 1920 NACA built the first of its wind tunnels on it. Another important event was Mitchell's bombing tests on warships,* in which the base's aircraft successfully used bombs* to sink warships. In 1922 the 2nd Bombardment Group moved in and remained for 20 years. The establishment of the General Headquarters Air Force* (GHQ Air Force) at Langley in 1935 marked a step toward an autonomous air arm. Its units' World War II* roles were training, including airborne radar* operators, coastal defense, and antisubmarine warfare.

In 1946, it became the headquarters for the Tactical Air Command* (TAC). When the Korean War* began, its 4th Fighter Wing was one of the first USAF* units to deploy. In 1953, what is now the 405th Tactical Fighter Wing (TFW) became its host unit and led in developing procedures for using tactical nuclear weapons.* In 1975 the 1st TFW arrived and became the first to be equipped with the F-15.* In 1990, the First Air Force* (1AF), responsible for the air defense of the United States, was headquartered there.

References. Primary: Robert I. Curtis et al., *Langley Field, The Early Years: 1916–1946*, 4500th Air Base Wing History Office, 1977. Official USAF History, Langley AFB, Virginia, 1TFW Public Affairs Office, 1987. TAC Historical Division, *50th Anniversary, Langley Air Force Base, Virginia*, 1966. Secondary: Brown, *Eagles*. Mueller, *AFB*. Merle Olmsted, "Langley Field 1917–1945," *AAHS Journal*, Spring 1965, pp. 3–12.

David L. Rosmer

LANPHIER, COLONEL THOMAS G., JR. (1915–1987)

For years Lanphier has been credited with having shot down, on 18 April 1943, the Mitsubishi G4M1 Hamaki, or "Betty," carrying Japanese Admiral Isoroku Yamamoto.* This credit has always been disputed.** Lanphier was also the first elected National President of the Air Force Association* (AFA), serving from 1947 to 1948.

Lanphier was born in Panama City, Republic of Panama. He graduated from Stanford University and became an aviation cadet* in 1941. He became a pilot* and officer the same year. He served in the 339th Fighter Squadron in the Pacific flying P-38s.* He flew 112 combat sorties and was credited with 5.5 victories. He left the USAAF* in 1945 and his principal employment after World War II* was with the General Dynamics Corporation (GD). He rose to become vice president and assistant to the president of the Convair Division of GD. After 1963 he ran a consulting business.

References. Primary: Burke Davis, *Get Yamamoto*, 1969. Gurney, *5 Down*. Secondary: "Aerospace World," *AF*, January 1988, p. 37. C&C, vol. 4. DuPre, *US Bio*. Carroll V. Glines, *Attack on Yamamoto*, 1990.

**The victor over Yamamoto may have been Colonel Rex T. Barber.

LANTIRN. *See* Low-Altitude Navigation and Targeting Infrared System for Night.

LAOS. *See* Barrel Roll.

LASHUP. *See* Permanent System.

LASSITER BOARD

This board was a step toward enlargement of the air arm and a shift from ground-oriented uses of military aviation to independent and concentrated operations.

Major General Charles T. Menoher,* chief of Air Service,* wanted a change in the composition of the USAAS's* types of aircraft. At the time, 1921, 40 percent of the strength was in observation aviation* and was tied to U.S. Army units. The rest was in fighter,* or pursuit, bomber,* and attack* types which were suited to independent operations. Menoher wanted the observation aircraft reduced to 20 percent. The War Department accepted the idea of the differences between the types of aircraft but did not change the status quo.

Menoher's replacement, Major General Mason M. Patrick,* proposed a reduced proportion of observation aircraft and a change of their control from division to corps level. He wanted more fighters and bombers and wanted to place those plus attack aircraft under the control of Army General Headquarters (GHQ).

Secretary of War John W. Weeks appointed a board under Major General William Lassiter, Army assistant chief of staff for operations and training, to analyze Patrick's proposals. The board wanted the USAAS enlarged with little organizational change in the operational control of aircraft. Enlargement of the USAAS required congressional action. When no proposal for legislation was made to Congress, the House of Representatives formed the Lampert Committee* in 1924. In 1925 the President's Aircraft Board* (Morrow Board) was appointed, and, finally, the Air Corps Act* of 1926 was enacted.

References. Futrell, *Ideas*, vol. 1. Goldberg, *Hist. USAF*. Maurer, *Avn. in Army*.

LAST DOGFIGHT, THE. *See* novels.

LAUGHLIN AIR FORCE BASE

This Air Training Command* (ATC) field is near Del Rio, Texas. It was first established in 1942. It was named for First Lieutenant Jack T. Laughlin, the first Del Rio resident to die in World War II* when his B-17* was shot down over Java by flak.* The field was used first as an advanced flight training* field but changed to training for the B-26 Marauder* in 1943. After the war it was used as a logistics base until 1953, when it was used for F-84* training. In 1954, pilot training in T-33s began. In 1957 it started to operate RB-57s (*see* B-57) and U-2s* in the Strategic Air Command* (SAC). In 1962 the base returned to training under the ATC. In 1990 its 47th Flying Training Wing (FTW) was conducting flight training with T-37s* and T-38s.*

References. "Guide to Major Air Force Installations Worldwide," *AF*, May 1990, p. 126. Mueller, *AFB*. Roberts, *Dir. USAF*.

LAVELLE, MAJOR GENERAL JOHN D. (1916–1979)

Lavelle became notorious for allegedly disobeying the political air superiority* limitations placed upon the USAF* in the Vietnam War:* he authorized his pilots* to shoot at the enemy before being fired upon and directed that records be falsified to conceal the fact. In 1972 he was relieved of his command, retired, and reduced in grade* from general to major general. After Lavelle was fired, the communists launched an offensive, and air power was directed to be used against them in the manner for which he was removed.

He received his wings from the aviation cadet* program in 1940 and flew combat missions in Europe. In 1946 he became deputy chief of statistical services at headquarters of the Air Materiel Command (AMC). During the Korean War* he was commander of the Tachikawa Supply Depot. From 1952 to 1956 he was commander of McGuire* AFB and a wing commander in the Military Air Transport Service (MATS). In 1956 he attended the Air War College and then spent five years at headquarters of the USAF. In 1966 he assumed command of the Seventeenth Air Force* (17AF) in Europe. After a short tour as vice commander in chief of the Pacific Air Forces* (PACAF), Lavelle was given command of the Seventh Air Force* (7AF) until his recall in 1972.

References. Air Force Pamphlet 31–1, "Roster of USAF Retired General Officers," 1987. John Morrocco, *Rain of Fire: Air War, 1969–1973*, a vol. of *The Vietnam Experience*, 1985. Office of Air Force History, *Air Interdiction in World War II, Korea, and Vietnam*, 1986. U.S. Air Force Biography, Secretary of the Air Force, Office of Public Affairs.

Steven K. Yates

LAWRENCE G. HANSCOM AIR FORCE BASE. *See* Hanscom Air Force Base.

LAY, COLONEL BEIRNE, JR. (1909–1982)

Lay was the author of important books and screenplays about the USAF.* From Berkeley Spring, West Virginia, Lay became a pilot* and officer in 1933. In World War II* he was commander of the 487th Bomb Group of the Eighth Air Force* (8AF). He was shot down over enemy territory but was not captured. Before the war he had written the novel* *I Wanted Wings*, which was made into a movie* in 1941. The movie stimulated recruiting for the USAAC.* After the war he was co-author of his main story, *Twelve O'Clock High* (1948). He wrote other stories relating to the USAF that became movies: *Above and Beyond* (1953), *Strategic Air Command* (1955), and *Toward the Unknown* (1956).

References. DuPre, *USAF Bio*. "The 40th Anniversary of the USAF," a special issue of *AH*, September 1987, pp. 207–8. Roger A. Freeman, *The Mighty Eighth: Units, Men and Machines*, 1970.

LEAD CREW

Experienced and competent leadership in the air is as necessary as in any other field. The USAAF's* Eighth Air Force* (8AF) found in World War II* that experience alone was insufficient. Leading bomber* formations needed special abilities to make masses of planes as effective as possible. Colonel Curtis E. LeMay* initiated a formal lead crew system in 1942.

In particular, a lead pilot* needed to fly smoothly and within the limits of every other plane in a formation, especially in turns and in the thin air of high altitudes. The lead navigator* needed the skills to effect the assembly of the group formations of an entire air force* into an organized column. Furthermore, navigators had to be skilled in leading the huge and clumsy masses to the target and back, giving consideration to enemy flak* defenses. The lead bombardier* was the most important man on a lead crew. He was the key to effective bombing, for all planes in a formation dropped when he did. The commander of a formation was the most important man in it, for he made the command decisions. He flew with the lead crew.

Crews were observed for competence, and promising ones were trained for the lead crew function. There were two specialties: those who bombed under visual conditions and those who bombed blindly in the Pathfinder Force* (PFF).

References. Charles D. Bright, "Navigating in the Big League," *AH*, December 1988, pp. 259–65. Roger A. Freeman, *Mighty Eighth War Manual*, 1984.

LEGAL SERVICES CENTER. *See* Air Force Legal Services Center.

LEMAY, GENERAL CURTIS E. (1906–1990)

LeMay embodied the modern USAF* and strategic operations* to the world. The United States's most successful air combat commander and one of the nation's great war commanders of any service and any time, he was chief of staff of the Air Force* from 1961 to 1965. He was the first chief who was not a graduate of the U.S. Military Academy (USMA). LeMay was inducted into the National Aviation Hall of Fame in Dayton, Ohio, in 1972.

LeMay was born in Columbus, Ohio, and graduated as a civil engineer from

Ohio State University in 1927. He became an aviation cadet* in 1928 and completed pilot* flight training* and became an officer in 1929. He was the navigator for the interception of the USS *Utah** in 1937 and the *Rex* interception* of 1938. Also in 1938 he navigated for the Goodwill Flight to South America.* Because of his experience in long-range overwater navigation, he was tasked to pioneer the ferry routes to England over the North Atlantic, and to Africa by way of South America and the South Atlantic.

In 1942, LeMay assumed command of the 305th Bombardment Group in Europe. He demonstrated the efficiency of the straight-in bombing run and initiated the lead crew* system to improve bombing accuracy. He also developed the combat box* formation of 18 aircraft, arranged to fully exploit firepower against fighters* coming in from any angle. His battle innovations were used by the USAAF* throughout the war.

In August 1942, he led a shuttle mission from England to Regensberg, Germany, landing at the end of the mission in North Africa. This was the first such mission ever flown. He was the commanding general of the 3rd Bombardment Division of the Eighth Air Force* (8AF) for his final assignment in England from 1943 to 1944.

He transferred to the China-Burma-India* (CBI) theater in 1944, where he led the XX Bomber Command which had recently received the new B-29.* In 1945 he assumed command of the XXI Bomber Command operating out of the Marianas.* He was sent to make that command effective after a period of disappointing results. Here he made the famous decision to switch the B-29s from daylight high-altitude raids to night low-level operations in the strategic campaign against Japan.* The tactic was used in the great fire strike on Tokyo of 9 March 1945.

After the war he flew a B-29 nonstop from Japan to Chicago, Illinois, to set a record. Late in 1945 he was appointed the first deputy chief of the Air Staff for research and development. In 1947 he became commander of the U.S. Air Forces in Europe* (USAFE). During this assignment he initiated the Berlin Airlift,* which countered the Soviet attempt to take the city.

In 1948, LeMay returned to the United States to become commanding general of the Strategic Air Command* (SAC). His tireless efforts to increase the combat readiness of SAC greatly improved the effectiveness and morale of the command. He inspired the highest order of faith, devotion, and loyalty in his men. U.S. foreign policy at the time depended heavily upon the nuclear weapons* capability of SAC. His final assignments were as vice chief and then chief of staff of the Air Force. When he left the USAF he had done much to make it more of a traditional military service than it had been. Because he was demanding, he was nicknamed "Iron A———." Because of his blunt way of speaking, he was given the ironic nickname of "the diplomat." This quality, together with the dominance of the U.S. Army's views with President Lyndon B. Johnson* (LBJ) and Secretary of Defense (SECDEF) Robert S. McNamara,* probably denied him the position of chairman of the Joint Chiefs of Staff (JCS).

References. Primary: Curtis E. LeMay, *Mission with LeMay: My Story*, 1965. Curtis E. LeMay and Bill Yenne, *Superfortress: The Story of the B-29 and American Air Power*, 1986. Secondary: Thomas M. Coffey, *Iron Eagle: The Turbulent Life of General Curtis LeMay*, 1986. Futrell, *Ideas*, 2 vols. Jacob Neufeld, *Ballistic Missiles in the United States Air Force 1945–1960*, 1990.
See also 94-target plan; Vietnam War.

Steven K. Yates

LEND-LEASE

Until the spring of 1940, the United States believed the British and French would surely, by themselves, defeat Germany in World War II.* The rapid and sweeping successes of Germany in western Europe changed that smug complacency into fear. The United States began to rearm in earnest and supplied munitions of war to Britain to contribute to U.S. defense.

The most critical arms of the time were aircraft. It was a difficult choice to give priority to the British when U.S. air power was minuscule and equipped mostly with obsolete aircraft, but this was not the greatest obstacle.

U.S. legislation was a serious impediment. General U.S. disenchantment with World War I,* combined with a widespread belief that wars could be caused by a free nation being armed and having an arms industry—"merchants of death" in the parlance of the 1930s—had led to stringent legislation to avoid entanglement in a war through arms sales. However, that legislation was increasingly evaded and superseded over time. When the principal remaining barrier was the ban on U.S. financing of arms shipments, a Lend-Lease Act was enacted in March 1941. In selling the act, President Franklin D. Roosevelt* (FDR) called the U.S. arms industry the "Arsenal of Democracy."

After the act's passage, the United States integrated production plans for U.S. forces with those of Britain and, when it entered the war, the USSR. In March, Congress authorized $7 billion for Lend-Lease. On the eve of Pearl Harbor,* plans were to give arms aid on the basis of 40 percent to Britain, 40 percent to the USSR, 10 percent to China, and 10 percent to others. Pearl Harbor changed the division of allocations between U.S. services and the Allies.

The programs of providing arms to Britain and others had both positive and negative effects on the buildup of U.S. air power from its parlous condition in the 1930s. It provided earlier industrial capacity for the United States and the weapons were tested in battle, but it diverted arms from the weak U.S. services later.

References. C&C, vol. 1. Goldberg, *Hist. USAF*. Irving Brinton Holley, Jr., *Buying Aircraft: Matériel Procurement for the Army Air Forces*, 1964. Warren F. Kimball, *The Most Unsordid Act: Lend-Lease, 1939–1941*, 1969.
See also Lindbergh, Brigadier General Charles A.

LEWIS GUN

This gas-operated, air-cooled machine gun was capable of firing 500 to 600 rounds per minute. A standard issue gun to the British and Americans in World War I,* it was especially useful on aircraft because it weighed only 25 pounds. Isaac Newton Lewis, a U.S. Army officer and inventor, developed it in 1911.

The aerial gun was modified from the infantry version by removing the water-cooling jacket from around the barrel. It was used by pilots,* observers,* and gunners.* The latter two liked it because its lightness permitted twin mountings. It was capable of easy mounting on the upper wing of a biplane for fighters,* which was necessary up to 1917 because the Allies had not been able to develop an interrupter gear to fire a machine gun through the propellor. The Dutch designer Anthony Fokker had developed such a device for the Germans early in the war. After the Allies had a gear to fire through the propellor and used the Vickers gun* for this, the Lewis was still used for added firepower. It was fed from flat drums holding either 47 or 96 rounds; changing drums in flight was a challenge for fighter pilots, especially during a dogfight.

References. James J. Hudson, *Hostile Skies: A Combat History of the American Air Service in World War I*, 1968. John Quick, *Dictionary of Weapons and Military Terms*, 1973. W.H.K. Smith and Joseph E. Smith, *Small Arms of the World*, 6th ed., 1960. Arch Whitehouse, *The Military Airplane: Its History and Development*, 1971.

D. K. Vaughan

LEYTE, PHILIPPINES

In Allied plans for the invasion of the Philippines in 1944, the USAAF's* initial role was planned to be only reconnaissance.* This was because of the distance of the action from USAAF bases. As soon as landing fields were available on Leyte Island, fighters* would move in, followed by attack* aircraft and, finally, bombers.* The main USAAF organization would be the Fifth Air Force* (5AF), which would be backed up by the Thirteenth Air Force* (13AF).

After the first engagements in the Battle of Leyte Gulf in October, B-24s* attacked Japanese naval units and sank a crippled light cruiser, the *Abukuma*. U.S. Navy losses from the forces they had for covering the beachhead on Leyte allowed Japanese aircraft to attack the landing areas. The carrier forces were also low on supplies and they were forced to withdraw, endangering the beachhead. Vice Admiral T. C. Kinkaid called for earlier basing of USAAF fighters as an emergency measure to cover the Navy's inability to continue air defense of the beachhead.

U.S. Army engineers and USAAF ground crews worked around the clock and under Japanese air attacks to prepare an adequate landing strip using pierced-steel planking((PSP). On 27 October, 34 P-38s* landed* and General of the Army Douglas MacArthur ordered that the Allied Air Forces assume the mission of supporting the beachhead. He ordered the Navy not to attack land targets unless they coordinated their action.

Japanese air attacks continued. On 1 November, they sank a destroyer and damaged three ships. Kinkaid asked for air help from General George C. Kenney* and Fleet Admiral Chester Nimitz. Kenney sent all the P-38s the landing facilities could handle. The Allied air forces also began a campaign of bombing the airfields the Japanese were using as staging bases for their attacks. At first, Admiral William Halsey, for Nimitz, said he would provide more ships but would not risk any aircraft carriers, but, by 5 November, Halsey felt he could risk more.

The Army had continued difficulty building airfields, and the Japanese made strenuous air and ground efforts. Slowly, through November and December, the Allied air forces achieved air superiority* and supported the Army. Leyte was a hard-won success and demonstrated the critical importance of airfields to air operations.

References. C&C, vol. 5. Goldberg, *Hist. USAF*. Ronald W. Yoshino, *Lightning Strikes: The 475th Fighter Group in the Pacific War, 1943–1945*, 1988.

LGB. *See* bombs.

LIAISON AIRCRAFT

In World War I* observation aviation* performed several tasks. Until the Battle of France in 1940, most air forces believed such aircraft would still be effective. The battle showed they could no longer live in the air.

The answer air forces found was to divide the functions of observation aircraft and give them to different specialized airplanes. The tasks of battlefield reconnaissance,* utility, and artillery spotting and correction were given to small, light planes. The USAAC* had not developed such aircraft but found that small planes built for the private market would be suitable. These planes stayed close to the ground which had hid them well from the enemy and enabled them to survive. They were called liaison aircraft. Starting in 1940 the USAAC bought the new type of aircraft and gave them the old observation designation of *O*. In 1942 they began to receive an *L* designation. They had a new function added on the battlefield: as vehicles for forward air controllers* (FAC). When the USAF* separated from the U.S. Army, the ground service kept liaison planes for its organic aircraft. When the services were ordered to adopt standard designations, the *O* designator was revived for aircraft performing the former *L* functions. Liaison aircraft as a class were nicknamed "Maytag Messerschmitts."

References. Primary: James H. Straubel, ed., *Air Force Diary: 111 Stories from the Official Service Journal of the USAAF*, 1947. Secondary: C&C, vol. 6. Swanborough, *US Mil. Airc.* "U.S. Army Air Forces," a special issue of *Flying and Popular Aviation*, September 1941, pp. 64–66, 206.

LIBERATOR. *See* B-24.

LIBERTY ENGINE

U.S. development and mass production of this truly fine high-horsepower aircraft power plant was one of the country's contributions to World War I.* During May 1917, Americans learned that Britain was manufacturing or experimenting with some 37 different service engines, and France with 46 more. Americans first considered copying one or more of those. However, a decision was made in late May to develop an original engine. It was hoped this engine would lend itself to rapid mass production and have enough power to remain serviceable for at least two years. Lieutenant Colonels E. J. Hall of Hall-Scott and J. E. Vincent of Packard Motor companies, along with a few other industrialists, designed the Liberty in just a few days.

On 4 June the design was approved by the Aircraft Production Board* and the Joint Army and Navy Technical Board. The first eight-cylinder Liberty was tested by the Bureau of Standards on 4 July and the first 12-cylinder on 25 August. All features of the Liberty were based on well-proven aeronautical and automotive engine practices. Although Americans may have been behind in airframe production in 1917, they had no superiors in the manufacture of engines. Within a short time the 12-cylinder was stepped up from 330 to 400 horsepower and was being produced by Packard, Ford, Lincoln, Nordyke & Marmon, Willys-Overland, Olds, and General Motors companies.

By the end of the war, 13,574 Liberty engines had been produced. Most of them were used on de Haviland DH-4* aircraft, so they were operational until 1932, despite becoming obsolete.

References. William E. Barrett, *The First War Planes*, 1960. I. B. Holley, Jr., *Ideas and Weapons*, 1953. James J. Hudson, *Hostile Skies: A Combat History of the American Air Service in World War I*, 1968. Theodore Macfarlane Knappen, *Wings of War*, 1920. Herschel Smith, *A History of Aircraft Piston Engines: From the Manly Balzer to the Continental Tiara*, 1986.

James J. Hudson

LIBYAN RAID

Libyan-sponsored terrorism was markedly reduced by this raid. The lessons learned were applied in the Panama incident of 1989.* This was an operation run by commanders on the scene rather than micromanaged from Washington, D.C., in accordance with the command changes made under President Ronald Reagan.*

In 1986 the United States knew that the Libyan dictator, Colonel Moammar Khadafi, was conducting terrorist operations against U.S. citizens. A decision was made to strike at the facilities in Libya that supported those operations. The raid was named Eldorado Canyon.

On the evening of 14 April some of the tankers,* KC-10s (*see* C-10) and KC-135s (*see* C-135) took off from RAF Mildenhall* and RAF Fairford,* England. This meant the British had agreed to the operations. The French, Spanish, and Italian governments refused to cooperate, so the attack* aircraft had to fly to Libya over international waters. Later F-111Fs* and EF-111s took off from RAF Lakenheath* and RAF Upper Heyford, England. The round-trip was 6,000 miles. There were three targets: the Libyan Air Force, Al Quwwat al-Jawwiya al-Libiyya, facility on Tripoli airport; Al Azziziyah barracks with a command post in Tripoli; and the Libyan Navy facility at Sidi Bilal. Also, the U.S. Navy struck simultaneously at two targets near Benghazi and provided F-14 fighters* for air superiority* purposes. The F-111s used lasar-guided bombs* in the raid. USAF* SR-71s* conducted reconnaissance* after the strike and all of the targets had been hit. One F-111 was lost in the raid. It is not known if the loss was due to enemy action.

References. Daniel P. Bolger, *Americans at War: 1975–1986, An Era of Violent Peace*, 1988. Victor Flintham, *Air Wars and Aircraft: A Detailed Record of Air Combat, 1945 to the Present*, 1990. Robert Jackson, *Strike Force: The USAF in Britain since 1948*, 1986. "USAF's Role in Libyan Raid," *AF*, November 1986, pp. 26, 29.

LIGHTER-THAN-AIR (LTA)

In this age of jets and missiles, it is difficult to believe that LTA was ever a competitive technology with heavier-than-air (HTA). In fact, the USAF* can assert it began as an organization with LTA in 1861, when Thaddeus C. Lowe was selected to organize a balloon observation unit for the U.S. Army. It was disbanded in 1863. A balloon section was formed in the Signal Corps in 1892, and one of its balloons did useful service in Cuba in the Spanish-American War. This unit was disbanded in 1899.

When the Aeronautical Division of the U.S. Army Signal Corps* was established in 1907, beginning a continuum of activity for an air organization to the present, it used both LTA and HTA. In 1908, Army Dirigible No. 1 was acquired. It was declared unsafe in 1912 and sold. A U.S. Army balloon section operated captive kite balloons for observation in World War I.* By November 1918, there were 35 U.S. balloon companies in France.

After the war, LTA operations continued using semirigid and nonrigid airships and balloons. In 1920 the semirigid *Roma* * was bought from Italy. Only difficulties attended its use, and it crashed in 1922. Several other airships were used with varying success until 1938, when the USAAC* ended its LTA operations. Two activities involved balloons in the interwar years. One was the USAAC balloonists who participated in some of the races held during those years. The other activity was scientific. The USAAC and the National Geographic Society teamed up to study the upper atmosphere. A balloon, *Explorer I*, was built and, in 1934, its flight reached 60,000 feet when its fabric tore. Major William E. Kepner, Captain Albert W. Stevens, and Lieutenant Orvil A. Anderson bailed out successfully at lower altitudes. A second balloon, *Explorer II*, with Stevens and Anderson reached 72,395 feet in 1935.

Balloon experiments were renewed after World War II.* Their crowning achievement was a parachute jump from a balloon at 102,800 feet on 16 August 1960 by Captain Joseph W. Kittinger, Jr., in project Man High.

References. Primary: Craig Herbert, "Gasbags Preferred," *AH*, Summer 1968, pp. 26, 39–51. William E. Kepner, "The Saga of Explorer I: Man's Pioneer Attempts to Reach Space," *AH*, September 1971, pp. 123–28. Secondary: Juliette A. Hennessy, *The United States Army Air Arm: April 1861 to April 1917*, 1985. *The Official Pictorial History of the AAF*, 1947. John H. Scrivner, Jr., "Our First Long Step into Space," *AF*, October 1971, pp. 58–64. Swanborough, *US Mil. Airc*.

See also Luke, Second Lieutenant Frank, Jr.

LIGHTNING. *See* P-38.

LINCOLN LABORATORY. *See* think tanks.

LINDBERGH, BRIGADIER GENERAL CHARLES A. (1902–1974)

A USAAC* Reserve and airmail pilot,* he carefully planned, raised money for, and piloted solo the first flight from New York to Paris in May 1927 with the *Spirit of St. Louis*, a single-engine plane, after others had died in similar attempts. He was an inventor, an author, and a consultant to airline companies and the USAF.* In 1967 he was inducted into the National Aviation Hall of Fame in Dayton, Ohio.

He was born in Detroit, Michigan, and graduated from the University of Wisconsin as a mechanical engineer in 1922. He enlisted in the USAAS* as a cadet in 1924 and became a pilot and an officer in 1925. After his famous transatlantic flight, the USAAC promoted him to colonel in the Reserve and decorated him with the Distinguished Flying Cross (DFC). Congress awarded him a special Medal of Honor, one of only two men so decorated in peacetime.

An instant celebrity, he turned down offers totaling $5 million to appear, speak, and act, and he donated or returned more than $2 million in gifts. Lindbergh used his notoriety, technical expertise, and high standards to help develop commercial aviation and to promote flight as a means of building goodwill among nations. He promoted and raised money for Dr. Robert Goddard's seminal work in rocketry. He invented surgical blood pumps, making several significant medical discoveries in the process. In addition, he was a technical adviser to Pan American Airways.

At the request of the U.S. military attaché in Berlin, Germany, he toured German factories and attended airshows in 1936 and debriefed his experience to U.S. military intelligence. In subsequent prewar speeches, he acknowledged German aviation superiority, an unpopular theme among U.S., British, and French officials. In addition, he spoke out against President Franklin D. Roosevelt's (FDR) ''arsenal of democracy'' thesis as unwise, considering the U.S. state of military preparedness. In so doing, he helped build pacifist isolationism, which was considered by many as unpatriotic and defeatist.

During World War II,* when Lindbergh was 42 years old, he spent four months in the South Pacific. Although he was officially a civilian, he flew F-4U Corsairs and P-38s* on 50 combat sorties of 179 hours. His main contribution was to show U.S. fighter* pilots how to get better range performance from their aircraft. He scored one aerial victory and was nearly shot down. After the war, Lindbergh served as an adviser to the USAF, contributing, among other things, to the Berlin Airlift,* the Scientific Advisory Board,* and the Strategic Air Command* (SAC) reorganization and procedures. In 1954 he was promoted to brigadier general.

Despite his contributions to the United States, some have never forgiven him for his visit to Germany and for his attempts to keep the United States out of the war before Pearl Harbor.* For example, this great U.S. hero's likeness has never appeared on a U.S. postage stamp although it has on the stamps of many other countries, while often obscure Americans have received the honor in the United States.

References. Primary: Charles A. Lindbergh, *The Spirit of St. Louis*, 1955. Secondary: DuPre, *USAF Bio.* Perry D. Luckett, *Charles A. Lindbergh: A Bio-Bibliography*, 1986. Leonard Mosley, *Lindbergh*, 1976. Ronald W. Yoshino, *Lightning Strikes: The 475th Fighter Group in the Pacific War, 1943–1945*, 1988.

See also Lend-Lease.

Thomas C. Blow II

LINDSEY AIR BASE

This facility is a converted barracks in Wiesbaden, Germany, under the U.S. Air Forces in Europe* (USAFE). Germany established it in 1897 and the USAFE moved there in 1947. As part of the occupation forces, the USAFE chose Wiesbaden, near the principal German city of Frankfurt am Main for its headquarters (HQ). Later, the HQ moved out of downtown Wiesbaden to Lindsey. The facility's name honors Darrel R. Lindsey, a World War II* bomber* pilot* killed in action in France and a recipient of the Air Force Medal of Honor.* In 1972 the HQ moved from Lindsey southwest to Ramstein* AB. This was to move the HQ west of the Rhine River in case of Soviet aggression and to save money. In 1990 the units at Lindsey were the 65th Air Division of the Seventeenth Air Force* (17AF) and the 7100th Combat Support Wing.

References. "Guide to Major Air Force Installations Worldwide," *AF*, May 1990, p. 126. Roberts, *Dir. USAF*.

LINEBACKER

Under President Lyndon B. Johnson* (LBJ) and Secretary of Defense (SEC-DEF) Robert S. McNamara,* the principal bombing operations in North Vietnam were called Rolling Thunder.* The rules followed General Maxwell Taylor's "flexible response" and "gradual escalation" concepts, giving the enemy political air superiority.* Rolling Thunder began in 1965 and failed in its goal of improving the morale of the South Vietnamese. LBJ called several bombing halts* and finally ended all bombing of the North for U.S. domestic reasons in 1968. President Richard M. Nixon ordered some limited purpose operations called "protective reaction strikes."* The experiences of these two arrangements reinforced the idea many held that aerial bombing was ineffective against a determined enemy like the North Vietnamese.

In March 1972, the North Vietnamese launched a conventional military offensive, emphasizing armor, against South Vietnam. The army of the Republic of Vietnam (ARVN) was badly defeated and most resistance rested upon the USAF* and the South Vietnamese air force (VNAF). Nixon stopped cease-fire negotiations and authorized Operation Linebacker with less political air superiority given to the enemy. This became Linebacker I. The previous targets in North Vietnam were reauthorized for raids, and, for the first time, a sea blockade with mining* was allowed. Operations began in May against an air defense system that the North had reinforced in the opportunity provided by the bombing halt.

Linebacker I put the Paul Doumer* bridge into the Red River, and other targets were hit. By the end of June, the results were evident as the ARVN began a successful counteroffensive that drove the enemy back. Instead of trying to stop a trickle of supplies for guerrillas and limited engagements, the USAF could devastate the larger quantities needed for conventional war. Peace talks began again in July. Linebacker I's punch had shown what air power could do against a conventional ground offensive. The talks seemed to be progressing satisfactorily by October, and Nixon called another bombing halt as a gesture of goodwill as LBJ had often done. As with all previous bombing halts, the enemy did not become more willing to negotiate.

When Nixon learned there were indications of preparation for a new offensive by the North, he authorized fresh bombing operations which were to be called Linebacker II. This time there was to be little political air superiority given the enemy, and the bombing would include targets in Hanoi* and Haiphong.* The target list was very close to that of the USAF's 1964 94-target plan* for a 16-day war drawn up under General Curtis E. LeMay,* and B-52s* would be used against North Vietnam itself. The targets were mostly transportation and supply, but power plants and air defense systems were also included.

Linebacker II, "The 11-Day War," began on 18 December 1972. The North Vietnamese fought back with a formidable air defense system. The raids continued for 11 days, except for a one-day break for Christmas Day. At the end of the 11 days, there were few targets left, and the North Vietnamese air defense system had collapsed.

During Linebacker II, the B-52s flew more than 700 sorties, and other aircraft flew 1,000. There were 15 B-52s and 11 other U.S. aircraft shot down. B-52 losses were heavy for the first three days because of poor tactics. Once some lessons from World War II* were reapplied, B-52 losses became small. The enemy lost eight aircraft. Of the targets, 1,600 structures and 373 pieces of rail equipment were hit. About three million gallons of petroleum were destroyed, 500 cuts were made in rail lines, and 10 airfields were damaged. Critical enemy targets which U.S. politicians had safeguarded for years were ravaged. Linebacker II's attacks on the logistics systems cut imports by North Vietnam from 160,000 to 30,000 tons per month. The blockade desired by the USAF and the U.S. Navy was much more effective than McNamara's interdiction attempts in the jungles. The USAF had tried to avoid civilian casualties. The North Vietnamese said between 1,300 and 1,600 noncombatants were killed. If true, these are quite low for intensive bombings that included targets in dense urban areas, including those casualties that resulted from North Vietnam's vigorous air defense. Linebacker did not follow Taylor's flexible response and gradual escalation. It followed the wishes of the USAF and of the former chairman of the Joint Chiefs of Staff (JCS), Army General Earle G. Wheeler (1964–1970), who had wanted a quick, strong stroke against North Vietnam. A cease-fire was signed on 23 January 1973.

Conditions were not identical for the Rolling Thunder and Linebacker operations. U.S. air power had made some significant technological improvements, including new "smart" weapons and Wild Weasel.* Nixon's rapprochement with Red China had reduced fears of provoking that nation. North Vietnam in 1972 had lost its guerrilla army and had to rely on conventional forces which required higher supply levels than did guerrillas. On the other hand, North Vietnam had greatly improved its war economy and air defenses over the years. The main difference was in the leadership in Washington, D.C., which used better strategy and tactics with Linebacker. In part, this was due to more respect for air power by Nixon and his superb manager, SECDEF Melvin R. Laird. The results obtained by Linebacker were strikingly better than those by Rolling Thunder.

References. Primary: George B. Allison, "The Bombers Go to Bullseye," *AH*, December 1982, pp. 227–38. Karl J. Eschmann, *Linebacker: The Untold Story of the Air Raids over North Vietnam*, 1989. Charles K. Hopkins, "Linebacker II—A Firsthand View," *AH*, September 1976, pp. 128–35. Secondary: Mark Clodfelter, *The Limits of Air Power: The American Bombing of North Vietnam*, 1989. Jeffrey Ethell and Alfred Price, *One Day in a Long War: May 10, 1972 Air War, North Vietnam*, 1989. John Morrocco, *Rain of Fire: Air War, 1969–1973*, a vol. of *The Vietnam Experience*, 1985.

LINK TRAINER

This pioneer in simulators was a ground trainer for pilots* used especially for instrument flying.* Edwin A. Link, Jr., invented it in 1928, and it was made by Link Aviation, Inc. Link was inducted into the National Aviation Hall of Fame in Dayton, Ohio, in 1976.

The USAAC* demonstrated little interest in it until pilots began to have trouble flying blind during the airmail flights of 1934.* After several embarrassing and fatal crashes, the USAAC ordered six Link trainers in March 1934. They proved valuable and helped reduce the number of crashes.

The trainer looked like a small, box-shaped airplane. It had a fuselage, wings, and a tail. It rested on a fixed platform and had the ability to take various positions as would a plane in flight. The hooded cockpit had a joystick, a rudder, flight instruments, earphones, and a microphone. The last items were to communicate with the instructor. The Link was designed to be unstable, thus requiring the pilot to be in control throughout his exercise. Once a pilot was inside, it soon became completely clear who the experts and novices were. The USAAC installed one or more of the Links on each of the principal flying fields in the United States and overseas. Each pilot had to prove his proficiency once a year using the Link or an aircraft.

The Link received its greatest use during World War II* and the Korean War.* The key to training a pilot to face all kinds of conditions were the controls in the hands of the instructor. The instructor could simulate various weather, air, and mechanical conditions and changes at a moment's notice. In this way the

Link was close to flying without actually leaving the ground. In addition, it allowed pilots to face crisis situations without risking their lives.

Since its original "Blue Box" trainer, the Link organization has continued to build simulators for flight and space training.

References. Primary: Edwin A. Link, Jr., "The Link Trainer," *Aeronautics*, 2 October 1940, pp. 271–86. Secondary: "Ed Link: Our Man for All Ages," *The Link Log*, September 1981, pp. 1–2. Materiel Command, *Case History of the Link Trainer*, Patterson Field, Ohio, 1945. Maurer, *Avn. in Army*. Training Aid Division, HQ AAF, *History of Link Training*, AFHRC, Maxwell Field, Alabama, 1946.

William Head and Diane Truluck

"LITTLE FRIENDS"

"Little friends" was a sobriquet for the fighter escort,* usually F-47s* and F-51s,* used in the European theater of operations in 1944–1945. Similarly, the bombers* being escorted, usually B-17s* and B-24s,* were called "big friends." The Luftwaffe called the little friends "Indianer" (Indians).

References. Primary: Harold W. Bowman, "Little Friend," *AH*, December 1983, pp. 235–39. Richard E. Turner, *Big Friend, Little Friend: Memoirs of a World War II Fighter Pilot*, 1969.

Ronald W. Yoshino

LITTLE ROCK AIR FORCE BASE

This facility was formally established in 1955 and was named for and was near Little Rock, Arkansas. It was built to be a Strategic Air Command* (SAC) base. It was the home of the 825th Air Division from 1955 to 1970, with two wings* flying B-47s* and RB-47s. In 1961 construction began on 18 Titan* II missile silos, and they became operational in 1963. In 1964, one wing with B-47s was deactivated and replaced with a wing of B-58s.* The B-58s remained at Little Rock until their unit was deactivated in 1970.

The base went under the Tactical Air Command* (TAC) in 1970. The new units included the 834th Air Division and the 64th Tactical Airlift Wing (TAW). The 314th TAW replaced the 64th in 1971 and was still at the base in 1990. The 314th was one of four stateside C-130* outfits. In 1974 TAC units were transferred to the Military Airlift Command* (MAC) as part of a major consolidation of airlift resources under a single operating agency. The 834th was inactivated, and the 314th became a primary training unit for C-130 operations. The Titan IIs were deactivated in the mid-1980s.

References. Ralph W. Doty, *History of the 314th Tactical Airlift Wing, 1942–1977*, Office of History, 314 TAW, n.d. Mueller, *AFB*. Charles A. Ravenstein, *Air Force Combat Wings: Lineage and Honors Histories, 1947–1977*, 1984.

Roger D. Launius

LITTLE VITTLES. *See* Operation Little Vittles.

LOCKHEED CORPORATION. *See* aerospace industry; C-5, C-121; C-130; C-141; F-80; F-104; P-38; SR-71; U-2.

LOFT BOMBING. *See* Low-Altitude Bombing System.

LOGISTICS COMMAND. *See* Air Force Logistics Command.

LOOKING GLASS. *See* Post Attack Command and Control System.

LOOK OF THE EAGLE. *See* novels.

LOON. *See* JB-2.

LORING AIR FORCE BASE

This Strategic Air Command* (SAC) field is near Limestone, Maine. It was activated in 1953 as Limestone AFB but renamed in 1954 for Major Charles J. Loring, Jr. He dove his disabled F-80* into a gun position in the Korean War* and was awarded the Air Force Medal of Honor.* B-36s* used the field until 1956 when B-52s* arrived. KC-97s (*see* C-97) were also there until 1957 when KC-135s (*see* C-135) arrived. The original base unit, the 42nd Bomb Wing, was still there in 1990.

References. "Guide to Major Air Force Installations Worldwide," *AF*, May 1990, p. 126. Mueller, *AFB*. Roberts, *Dir. USAF*.

LOS ANGELES AIR FORCE BASE

This facility is in El Segundo, California, within the Los Angeles metropolis. It was under the Air Force Systems Command* (AFSC) and was activated in 1960. The Space Systems Division of the AFSC was located there in 1990.

References. "Guide to Major Air Force Installations Worldwide," *AF*, May 1990, p. 126. Roberts, *Dir. USAF*.

LOUISIANA MANEUVERS OF 1941. *See* maneuvers of 1941.

LOVE, NANCY HARKNESS (1914–1976)

Love was an outstanding woman flier of the 1930s and commander of the Women's Auxiliary Ferrying Squadron* (WAFS) during World War II.* She received her private pilot's* license at the age of 16. Love was an early pioneer in the development of student flying clubs in U.S. colleges and a charter member of the Ninety-Nines. She received her transport license when she was 18 years old and her commercial license in July 1933. In 1935 the Bureau of Air Commerce hired her to participate in the air marking of the principal U.S. cities. She married Robert Maclure Love in 1936 and helped him operate their company, Inter City Aviation. She often delivered planes to their customers. In 1937 she tested and demonstrated the Gwinn air car and Hammon "safety planes" and later participated as a test pilot in the development of the tricycle landing gear, soon adopted for medium and heavy bombers.*

Love had more than 1,200 hours of flying time and 600 horsepower, instrument, and seaplane ratings when she joined the war effort. She was one of several Massachusetts women who ferried light planes, destined for Britain, to the Canadian border. In 1940 she recommended to the Plans Division of the Office of the Chief of Air Corps that 49 experienced women pilots serve as substitutes for men. On 10 September 1942, the secretary of war announced the formation of the WAFS to be stationed at New Castle Army AB, Wilmington, Delaware. On 5 July 1943, the WAFS merged with Jacqueline Cochran's* group of women aviators to become the Women Airforce Service Pilots* (WASP). Love was a rival of Cochran. Love sponsored professional women pilots, while Cochran wanted women trained to become flyers.

Love was the first woman in U.S. military aviation to fly a bomber, a B-25,* and she flew it from the West Coast to the East Coast in record time. At the end of the war, she and her husband had the unique distinction of being simultaneously awarded the Air Medal for their leadership and service in World War II.

References. C&C, vol. 7. RitaVictoria Gomez, *A History of Women in the Air Force*, forthcoming. Sally Van Wagenen Keil, *Those Wonderful Women in Their Flying Machines*, 1979. Valerie Moolman, *Women Aloft*, a vol. of *The Epic of Flight*, 1981.

RitaVictoria Gomez

LOVETT, SECRETARY ROBERT A. (1895–1986)

Lovett was assistant secretary of war for air* from 1941 to 1945. During those critical years of U.S. participation in World War II,* Lovett worked hard to increase aircraft and flying equipment production. He was instrumental to the formation of the USAAF.* He also was a strong representative and advocate for the USAAF with President Franklin D. Roosevelt* (FDR). For his contributions he received the Distinguished Service Medal (DSM).

From Huntsville, Texas, he graduated from Yale University and did postgraduate work at Harvard University. In World War I* he was a bomber pilot* in the U.S. Navy and took part in operations against Germany. He won the Navy Cross and rose to the grade of lieutenant commander. Between wars he was a banker. In 1940 he was asked to serve as special assistant to the secretary of war. He returned to banking in 1945 but was asked again to serve the United States in 1951 as secretary of defense (SECDEF) for the Korean War.*

References. C&C, vol. 6. DuPre, *USAF Bio*. Irving Brinton Holley, Jr., *Buying Aircraft: Matériel Procurement for the Army Air Forces*, 1964.

LOW-ALTITUDE BOMBING SYSTEM (LABS)

With all aircraft weapon delivery systems, the launcher runs the risk of damage from his own arms if he is too close to their impact. With nuclear weapons* this risk is greatly amplified, and the traditional methods of avoiding self-damage from one's own ordnance were inadequate. LABS, invented by John A. Ryan, Jr., was an attempt to reduce the risk. Although there are variations, the simplest LABS maneuver is to approach the target at low altitude and then to pull up sharply. The weapon is released in the pull up. The aircraft then does an Im-

melmann turn and dives away from the target at high speed. This is also called
loft, over-the-shoulder, or toss bombing.

References. Primary: John A. Ryan, Jr., "LABS," *Air University Quarterly Review*,
Spring 1957, pp. 92–97. Secondary: Alwyn T. Lloyd, *B-47 Stratojet in Detail & Scale*,
1986.

LOW-ALTITUDE NAVIGATION AND TARGETING INFRARED SYSTEM FOR NIGHT (LANTIRN)

LANTIRN is a system that the USAF* hopes will, at long last, remove the
sanctuary of night from an enemy. It should not only permit blind attack*
operations but permit night landings on unlit fields. This has revolutionary potential for air power.

LANTIRN equipment has two components. One is for navigation, providing
a "heads-up" display for pilots* to see the terrain at low altitudes at night, in
weather, and through dust and smoke. A pilot can descend to 200 feet, even
over broken terrain, and fly at speeds up to 600 miles per hour. The second
component is for target finding from miles away and delivery of traditional
weapons, laser-guided bombs,* and AGM-65s.* Future weapons developed specifically for LANTIRN may improve results further. The system magnifies the
view of the target up to 17 times. LANTIRN is made by the Martin Marietta
Corporation. It has been used on F-15s* and F-16s* and is intended for use with
A-7s,* A-10s,* AC-130s (*see* C-130), B-1s,* C-17s,* C-130s,* and the F-22
or F-23 Advanced Tactical Fighter.* Plans are to introduce color coding into
the system to make it easier to use. For example, picturing the targets in red
could ease the aircrew's task.

References. Primary: "Lantirn Provides Breakthrough in Night-Fighting Capabilities,"
AWST, 25 April 1988, pp. 34–38, 42. Secondary: James W. Canan, "Coming on and
Coming Up," *AF*, January, 1985, pp. 34–42, and "Fighting around the Clock," *AF*,
January 1987, pp. 52–53. David Fulghum, "LANTIRN, Lighting up the Night," *Air
Force Times*, 19 February 1990, pp. 22, 26. Futrell, *Ideas*, vol. 2.

LOWRY AIR FORCE BASE

This facility in Denver, Colorado, was established in 1937 and designated
Lowry Field in 1938 in honor of Lieutenant Francis B. Lowry. A native of
Denver, Lowry was an observer* killed in action near Crepion, France, in
September 1918. Flak* destroyed his Salmson* 2A-2. Lowry has a long history
of training and reflects the character of the USAF* in the nature of its work.

Armament, photo, and clerical training were transferred from Chanute* Field
to Lowry in 1938. During World War II,* training was added for B-29* crews,
bombardiers,* and other technical courses. Courses added in the Korean War*
included rocket propulsion, missile guidance, and flexible gunnery. Lowry was
temporary home to the U.S. Air Force Academy* (USAFA) from 1955 until
1958, when its permanent facility was completed. In 1966, training that included
flying ended because of Denver's urban sprawl. In the late 1960s, new training
for Titan* I and intelligence was included. In 1976 the U.S. Air Force Accounting

and Finance Center* (AFAFC) and the Air Reserve Personnel Center* (ARPC) relocated from Denver to Lowry. In 1990, besides the AFAFC and ARPC, Lowry's Technical Training Center was training students in avionics, space operations, munitions, logistics, and audiovisual fields.

References. "Guide to Major Air Force Installations Worldwide," *AF*, May 1990, p. 126. Michael H. Levy and Patrick M. Scanlan, *Pursuit of Excellence: A History of Lowry AFB, 1937–1987*, Lowry Historical Monograph, 1987. Mueller, *AFB*. Melvin F. Porter, *A Forty Year Look at Lowry AFB, 1937–1977*, Lowry Historical Monograph, 1978. Roberts, *Dir. USAF*.

Thomas A. Manning

LOYAL LOOK. *See* Corona Harvest.

LTA. *See* lighter-than-air.

LTV AEROSPACE AND DEFENSE COMPANY. *See* A-7.

"LUCKY." *See* Emmons, Lieutenant General Delos C.

LUCKY LADY

There were a string of Boeing Aircraft Company bombers* named *Lucky Lady*, three of which became famous. First, there was a B-29*-40 flown by Lieutenant Arthur M. Neal from the Marianas* Islands during World War II.* The second was a B-29A-75 flown by Neal from Davis-Monthan* AFB in Arizona. It was one of three that attempted an around-the-world flight in 1948. *Lucky Lady* and *Gas Gobbler* completed the flight, while the third crashed in the Arabian Sea.

In 1949 a B-29A-25 named *Lucky Lady II*, flown by Neal and Captain James Gallagher, made the first nonstop around-the-world flight. It used aerial refueling* from KB-29Ms. Five B-52Bs* from Castle* AFB, California, started out on another nonstop around-the-world flight in 1957. Three completed the mission, while two were planned spares. The lead B-52 was named *Lucky Lady III* and was flown by Colonel James H. Morris, who had flown on *Lucky Lady II*.

References. Walter Boyne, *Boeing B-52—A Documentary History*, 1981. James N. Eastman, Jr., "Flight of the Lucky Lady II," *AH*, Winter 1969, pp. 9–11, 33–35. Alwyn T. Lloyd, "World Circlers," *AAHS Journal*, Spring 1989, pp. 65–69.

Alwyn T. Lloyd

LUFBERY, MAJOR RAOUL G. V. (1885–1918)

Lufbery was a famous American ace,* with 17 aerial victories, and the inventor of the maneuver called the Lufbery circle.* He was born of an American father and French mother in Clermont, France. He traveled widely before World War I,* lived mostly in France, and was active in aviation from 1910 on. While visiting Saigon, French Indochina, he met the well-known flier Marc Pourpe, and signed on as a mechanic for Pourpe who flew in air shows. When France went to war, Pourpe immediately volunteered and Lufbery, after difficulties associated with his U.S. citizenship, rejoined Pourpe as a mechanic. Pourpe was killed in action in December 1914.

From that point, Lufbery determined to become a pilot,* to fly in combat against the Germans and avenge his friend's death. He obtained his wings but was not considered an especially good pilot while he was a student. His first combat unit was V.B. 106, which he left to join the Lafayette Escadrille,* the squadron of U.S. volunteers flying with the French. He won 17 victories, far more than any other member of the Escadrille.

When the Escadrille was discontinued in February 1918, he was commissioned a major in the Aviation Section of the U.S. Army Signal Corps.* He was commanding officer of the 94th Aero Squadron* when he was killed in action in 19 May 1918 while engaging a German observation aircraft. A quiet and reserved man, he was popular with his squadron mates because he possessed a fine sense of humor and with experience had become a highly skilled pilot.

References. Laurence La Tourette Driggs, *Heroes of Aviation*, rev. ed., 1927. Philip Flammer, *The Vivid Air*, 1981. James J. Hudson, *Hostile Skies: A Combat History of the American Air Service in World War I*, 1968. Quentin Reynolds, *They Fought for the Sky*, 1957. Bruce Robertson, *Air Aces of the 1914–1918 War*, 1959.

D. K. Vaughan

LUFBERY CIRCLE

This is an aerial defensive maneuver in which two or more aircraft fly in a nearly vertical, or about a 90-degree, bank. They fly in a nearly horizontal circle. This protects each other from attack by enemy planes, because any enemy that enters the circle may be easily shot at by someone behind them in the circle. It is not easy to shoot at any aircraft from outside the circle.

The maneuver was invented by Major Raoul Lufbery,* who developed it in World War I* while flying with the Lafayette Escadrille.* It has been an excellent escape device when badly outnumbered or when flying inferior airplanes against superior ones. It can be used until help arrives or until descent has been made to treetop level and a run can be made for safety. At the lowest altitudes, a superior aircraft loses some advantages. The Lufbery has gained another benefit from modern aircraft; it provides maximum sensor, such as radar,* coverage for detection of possible enemies.

References. Philip Flammer, *The Vivid Air*, 1981. John Quick, *Dictionary of Weapons and Military Terms*, 1973. Robert L. Shaw, *Fighter Combat: Tactics and Maneuvering*, 1985.

D. K. Vaughan

LUKE, SECOND LIEUTENANT FRANK, JR. (1897–1918)

Luke is the United States's most colorful and dramatic ace.* He was the first airman to earn the Air Force Medal of Honor,* and the only one to do so during World War I.* He scored the second-highest number of U.S. victories, 18, in the war. It is appropriate that the great fighter* field, Luke AFB,* is named in his honor. In 1930 a statue of him was erected in front of the Arizona State capitol. He had permanent nicknames of "The American Balloon Buster" and "The Arizona Cowboy." He was inducted into the National Aviation Hall of Fame in Dayton, Ohio, in 1975.

From Phoenix, Arizona, Luke enlisted in 1917 and became a pilot* and officer in 1918. He trained further at Issoudon,* France. In May he joined the 27th Aero Squadron at the front. Luke was an excellent pilot and a great gunner— two important strengths for an ace. At first he lacked knowledge of tactics and did not score. He soon became an outcast in his squadron because he was crude, undisciplined, vain, and boastful. He gained the nickname "The Arizona Boaster." Luke began to break the rules by leaving formation and hunting alone, a risky tactic. Another outcast made friends with Luke: First Lieutenant Joseph F. Wehner, who had been under suspicion as a German spy for months. The only grounds for the suspicion were that his parents were German immigrants.

One day, at the mess, the squadron pilots discussed shooting down German observation balloons, or *Drachen*. A pilot received a victory credit for shooting one down because it was more difficult than destroying a plane. The captive balloons were exceedingly valuable and so had intense flak* protection and usually a patrol of friendly fighters nearby. The balloons could rarely be surprised and were reeled in when under attack.* This brought them down close to the flak. Surprisingly, they were not easy to ignite with the .30-caliber bullets of the time, even when incendiary rounds were used. Finally, attacking them gave the higher defending fighter patrol a big tactical advantage over the attacker. In World War I,* less than a dozen pilots became balloon aces and only three of them survived the war.

Luke was silent at the mess, but he told Wehner afterward that they would be a team against the balloons. Luke would attack at dusk to have surprise through low visibility, while Wehner flew top cover to drop down on any defending fighters. They tried it the next day, 12 September 1918, and Luke burned a balloon. It took him three passes through the flak to get it, and it was almost on the ground when it lit. Luke's Spad XIII* was struck many times by the flak and was unrepairable. Luke lost his former nickname.

Luke and Wehner went on a rampage. In a seven-day period Luke shot down 11 balloons and two planes, while Wehner shot down four balloons and three aircraft. On 18 September, Luke shot down two balloons and three planes in a time span of ten minutes, but Wehner was shot down by a German fighter and died after the crash. Wehner's total victories were eight. Luke now had 12 victories and was the leading USAAS* ace by a five-victory margin. Lieutenant Ivan A. Roberts tried to replace Wehner, but the two were attacked by a flight of five Fokker D-VIIs and Roberts was shot down. Luke again became a loner.

On 29 September Luke took off against orders and dropped a note to U.S. balloonists. It said to watch three German balloons on the Meuse River. It was twilight, but the balloonists could watch. The three enemy balloons were burned in a span of three minutes. French villagers later said German fighters attacked

Luke and he shot down two. Then he strafed German infantry but was wounded by return fire. He landed. When approached by the infantry and ordered to surrender, he opened fire with his pistol and was killed by the soldiers.

Luke's final confirmed score was 18, with 14 of those balloons. He returned with five Spads that had so much battle damage they could not be repaired.

References. Laurence La Tourette Driggs, *Heroes of Aviation*, rev. ed., 1927. Raymond H. Fredette, "Luke: 'Watch for Burning Balloons,' " *AF*, September 1973, pp. 78–82. Norman S. Hall, *The Balloon Buster*, 1966. Hess, *Aces Album*. Quentin Reynolds, *They Fought for the Sky*, 1957.

LUKE AIR FORCE BASE

The "Home of the Fighter Pilot,"** located near Phoenix, Arizona, was activated in 1941. It is a Tactical Air Command* (TAC) field. It covers 4,197 acres and has the Barry M. Goldwater* USAF* range of 2,700,000 acres nearby at Gila Bend, Arizona. It was, appropriately, named for Second Lieutenant Frank Luke, Jr.,* one of the United States's greatest aces.*

In 1990, it had the largest fighter* training facility for the free world and was instructing in the F-15* and F-16.* Its units were the 832nd Air Division and the 405th Tactical Training Wing. The main purpose of the training was to produce air superiority* fighter pilots.* By 1985, Luke had trained 29,000 U.S. and 2,000 foreign pilots. That included 1,574 Luftwaffe pilots. The Luftwaffe had a fighter program at Luke from 1957 to 1983. Luftwaffe instruction in the F-104G* began in 1965, and there were more than 100 F-104s at Luke at the height of the program.

References. James P. Coyne, "Fighter Pilot University," *AF*, December 1985, pp. 52–58. "Guide to Major Air Force Installations Worldwide," *AF*, May 1990, p. 126. *Kaktus Starfighter Staffel I*, yearbook, 1976. Mueller, *AFB*. Barney Oldfield, "The Lukewaffe Winds It Up," *AF*, April 1983, pp. 110–11. Robert C. Sullivan, "The Luftwaffe at Luke," *AH*, June 1977, pp. 100–106.

**Nellis* AFB, Nevada, also claims to be "Home of the Fighter Pilot."

LUZON, PHILIPPINES

The reconquest of Luzon Island crowned the retaking of the Philippines, but it was a grueling, savage campaign for the USAAF* and the U.S. Army. There is a body of opinion that retaking the Philippines was unnecessary and that they could have been bypassed.

The decision on the Philippine operations was made in July 1944 at the Pearl Harbor meetings between President Franklin D. Roosevelt* (FDR) and his Pacific commanders. Leyte* Island, in the eastern Philippines, was slated first for invasion on 20 October 1944. The Leyte campaign saw hard fighting by General Walter Krueger's Sixth Army, the climactic Battle of Leyte Gulf that decimated Japanese sea power, and the advent of *Shimpu*, or kamikaze units. The United States next invaded Mindoro, just south of Luzon, in the first week of 1945.

The tenacious defense of Leyte had bought the overall Japanese Philippine commander, General Tomoyuki Yamashita, time to prepare Luzon defenses.

One of the most capable Japanese army officers, the "Tiger of Malaya" decided to give up the waterline and flat plains of Luzon, concentrating his forces in its mountains: his own *Shobu* group north and east of Lingayan Gulf; the *Kembu* group defending westerly mountains and threatening Clark* Field; and the *Shimbu* group holding hostage Manila's water supplies, principally on the Ipo dam east of the city. The plan was defensive and aimed at exacting maximum U.S. casualties.

The USAAF's* Fifth* and Thirteenth* Air Forces (5AF and 13AF) spearheaded campaign Luzon. They had fought from primitive fields on Leyte, like Tacloban and Dulag, and defended the landings from Japanese assaults. The 5AF and 13AF also struck Luzon targets to eliminate Japanese air power as a prelude to invasion of the island. The USAAF targeted Clark, a major center of Japanese air power, before, during, and after Christmas in 1944. Heavy bomber* units riddled the fields, while fighter* groups like the 49th and 475th destroyed enemy aircraft* that rose to intercept, or had been flushed, during the raids. The strikes quickly decimated the 200 Japanese airplanes allocated for Luzon's air defenses. After unopposed landings, Yamashita's men fought stubbornly. Manila fell to the U.S. Army on 3 March 1945, after a month's struggle that left it second only to Warsaw, Poland, in war damage. The USAAF's air superiority* left it free for attack* operations. By April, fighter groups began systematically to napalm* the area around Ipo, the waves of flame forcing Japanese soldiers into the open where they were killed. By May, the Ipo dam was again in friendly hands. On 4 July 1945, General of the Army Douglas MacArthur declared the Luzon campaign ended, but fighting would continue in the mountains of northern Luzon until the end of the war.

References. Primary: James H. Straubel, ed., *Air Force Diary: 111 Stories from the Official Service Journal of the USAAF*, 1947. Secondary: C&C, vol. 5. M. Hamlin Cannon, *Leyte: The Return to the Philippines*, 1954. Robert Ross Smith, *Triumph in the Philippines*, 1963. Ronald W. Yoshino, *Lightning Strikes: The 475th Fighter Group in the Pacific War, 1943–1945*, 1988.

Ronald W. Yoshino

LYNCH, LIEUTENANT COLONEL THOMAS J. (1916–1944)

With 20 aerial victories, Lynch is the 20th-ranking USAF* ace,* an honor he shares with Lieutenant Colonel Robert B. Westbrook.* He was a native of Hazelton, Pennsylvania, graduated from the University of Pittsburgh in 1940 and became an aviation cadet.* He became an officer and pilot* in 1941. Lynch joined the 39th Fighter Squadron of the Fifth Air Force* (5AF) flying P-39s* in New Guinea.* He won his first victories in May 1942 and was also shot down and parachuted to safety. The squadron* got P-38s* near the end of the year. On 8 March 1944, he crashed and died while strafing a boat in Aitape Harbor, New Guinea.

References. DuPre, *USAF Bio*. Hess, *Aces Album*.

M

M-61 VULCAN

This is a six-barreled 20mm rotary cannon developed from the 1861 patent of Dr. Richard Gatling. In 1946, the General Electric Company (GE) received a contract to design a very-high-rate-of-fire gun for use in the new jet fighters* just entering the inventory. By 1954, the first guns were installed in the F-104,* but the use of conventional ammunition feed boxes held the rate of fire to 4,000 rounds per minute (rpm). Only when a new linkless drum feed system was installed in the F-105* was the full practical 6,000 rpm realized. Now the gun is ubiquitous in nearly all U.S. battle planes. The Vulcan was only the first in a long series of rotary guns made in all calibers, from 5.56mm to 37mm. The USAF* uses them in fixed- and rotary-wing aircraft and ground mounts of all types. Thus, U.S. fighters in the 21st century will carry a gun system invented during the Civil War.

References. George M. Chinn, *The Machine Gun*, 5th ed., 1987. Paul Wahl and Don Toppel, *The Gatling Gun*, 1965.

Philip Long

MACARTHUR-PRATT AGREEMENT. *See* Army-Navy agreements of 1931 and 1938.

MCCHORD AIR FORCE BASE

This AFB was established in 1938 at what had been the Tacoma, Washington, airport, and was named for Colonel William C. McChord who was killed in an aircraft accident in 1937.

It first hosted the 17th Bombardment Group flying B-18s* and B-23s. Throughout World War II,* it was one of the nation's largest bomber* bases, using B-25s* and other types. Lieutenant Colonel James H. Doolittle* went to McChord to find experienced B-25 crews for his 1942 Doolittle raid on Tokyo.* After the war, the potential of McChord for aerial port operations for the Pacific was realized. In 1947, the 62nd Troop Carrier Group was stationed on it with the mission of supporting combat cargo movement in the Pacific. In 1950 the base was assigned to the Air Defense Command (ADC) and made the home of the 25th Air Division and the 318th Fighter Interceptor Squadron (FIS) operating F-86,* F-94, and F-106* aircraft in the air defense role.

During the Korean War,* it served as a major supply and transit point for the Far East. In the 1960s, the importance of McChord as a logistical support and airlift base was further demonstrated for Southeast Asia (SEA) operations. Its 62nd Military Airlift Wing (MAW) transported troops and equipment from nearby Fort Lewis to Vietnam. In 1966, the 62nd received its first jet transport,* the C-141,* which began replacing aging C-124s.* In 1968, the 62nd became the host unit as McChord was assigned to the Military Airlift Command* (MAC). The air defense role has since shrunken while the airlift operations* role has grown considerably. The 62nd has added a few C-130s.*

References. Brown, *Eagles.* "Guide to Major Air Force Installations Worldwide," *AF*, May 1990, p. 128. Mueller, *AFB.* "Short History of McChord AFB," Office of History, 62 MAW, n.d.

Roger D. Launius

MCCLELLAN AIR FORCE BASE

This field near Sacramento, California, was established in 1936 and is an Air Force Logistics Command* (AFLC) facility. It was originally called the Sacramento Air Depot. In 1939 it was named for Major Hezekiah "Hez" McClellan, who died in a flight test in 1936. McClellan has always provided depot maintenance* for the USAF.* In the mid–1950s it added air defense operations, but they ended in 1976. In 1990 it had the Sacramento Air Logistics Center; headquarters of the Fourth Air Force* (4AF); and the 41st Rescue and Weather Reconnaissance Wing.

References. Douglas Baldwin, "Revolution in the Hangar," *AF*, April 1990, pp. 78–82. Brown, *Eagles.* "Guide to Major Air Force Installations Worldwide," *AF*, May 1990, p. 128. Mueller, *AFB.* Roberts, *Dir. USAF.*

MCCONNELL AIR FORCE BASE

This Strategic Air Command* (SAC) base is in Wichita, Kansas. It was established in 1942 and was first named for Wichita. In 1954 it was renamed for Second Lieutenant Thomas L. McConnell and his brother, Captain Fred McConnell, Jr. Lieutenant McConnell died in a B-17 accident in 1943, and Captain McConnell died in a private plane crash in 1945. During World War II,* the field accepted aircraft built at the adjacent Boeing Aircraft Company plant. From 1946 to 1951 it was under civilian control. From 1951 to 1963, it was a B-47* crew training center. It had Titan* IIs and F-105s* beginning in 1963. The F-105s left in 1972, and the Titans in 1986. It received B-1Bs* in 1988. In 1990 its unit was the 384th Bomb Wing with B-1Bs and KC-135s (*see* C-135).

References. "Guide to Major Air Force Installations Worldwide," *AF*, May 1990, p. 128. Mueller, *AFB*. Roberts, *Dir. USAF*.

MCCONNELL, GENERAL JOHN P. (1908–1986)

McConnell was the sixth chief of staff of the Air Force* from 1965 to 1969. He was one of the chief architects of the buildup of the USAF* in Southeast Asia (SEA) during the Vietnam War,* and he presided while the USAF was losing in that war.

Born on Booneville, Arkansas, he graduated from the U.S. Military Academy (USMA) in 1932 and served in various positions in the China-Burma-India* theater (CBI) during World War II.* In postwar years he was assigned as chief of the Reserve and National Guard Division at headquarters of the USAAF,* chief of the Civilian Components Group, deputy special assistant to the chief of staff for Reserve forces, and numerous Strategic Air Command* (SAC) command positions in England and the United States. His principal assignments were as commander of the Second Air Force* (2AF) (1957–1961), vice commander in chief of SAC (1961–1962), deputy commander in chief of the U.S. European Command (1962–1964), and vice chief of staff of the USAF (1964–1965). He retired in 1969.

References. Air Force Pamphlet 31–1, "Roster of USAF Retired General Officers," 1987. DuPre, *USAF Bio*. Futrell, *Ideas* vol. 2. U.S. Air Force Biography, Secretary of the Air Force, Office of Information, 1968. U.S. Air Force Historical Study No. 91, Biographical Data on Air Force General Officers, 1917–1952, vol. 3, n.d. Bill Yenne, *The History of the US Air Force*, 1984.

James C. Hasdorff

MCCONNELL, CAPTAIN JOSEPH, JR. (1922–1954)

McConnell was the leading U.S. ace* of the Korean War,* with 16 victories. From Dover, New Hampshire, he enlisted in the U.S. Army in 1940. He became a navigator* and an officer in 1944. In 1945 he flew combat in B-24s* with the 448th Bomb Group in Europe. He became a pilot* in 1948. In 1952 he joined the 51st Fighter Interceptor Wing (FIW) in the Korean War* and flew F-86s.* After his eighth victory he was hit by flak* and had to bail out. Between 13 and 18 May, he scored six victories over MiG-15s. He flew 106 combat sorties in this war. In 1954 he was testing a newly modified F-86 in the United States and crashed and died while trying to save the plane.

Movie: The McConnell Story, 1955.

References. DuPre, *USAF Bio*. Gurney, *5 Down*. Hess, *Aces Album*.

MCCOOK FIELD. *See* Wright-Patterson AFB.

MACDILL AIR FORCE BASE

Located south of Tampa, Florida, MacDill Field was activated in 1941 and named to honor Colonel Leslie MacDill, who was killed in an airplane crash in 1936. During World War II* its mission was transitional training in B-17s* and

B-26 Marauders.* It became a Strategic Air Command* (SAC) base, and B-29* training was conducted beginning in 1948. Its facilities were converted for B-47s* and KC-97s (see C-97) in 1951. When most of its activities were planned to cease, the Cuban crisis of 1962* changed the plans, and fighters* and headquarters of the U.S. Strike Command moved onto it. By 1965 it had two F-4*-equipped wings. During the Vietnam War,* B-57s* were located on it. In 1972 the U.S. Readiness Command replaced the Strike Command. By 1982 it had F-16s* and a new training mission. Responding to the Iranian crisis and the Soviet invasion of Afghanistan, the Joint Chiefs of Staff (JCS) activated in 1981 the Rapid Deployment Joint Task Force (RDJTF) as a part of Readiness Command. In 1983 the RDJTF became a separate unified command, called the U.S. Central Command, and in 1987 Readiness Command was inactivated.

References. "Guide to Major Air Force Installations Worldwide," *AF*, May 1990, p. 126. Mueller, *AFB*. Official USAF History, 56TTW Public Affairs Office, MacDill AFB, Florida, 1989.

David L. Rosmer

MACDONALD, COLONEL CHARLES H. (1916–)

MacDonald is the fourth ranking USAF* ace* of all time, an honor he shares with Lieutenant Colonel Robert S. Johnson. He scored 27 aerial victories.

From DuBois, Pennsylvania, MacDonald graduated from Louisiana State University in 1938, and became an aviation cadet.* He became a regular officer in 1939. His unit went to Hawaii aboard the aircraft carrier USS *Enterprise*, and he was at Wheeler* Field when the Japanese raided Pearl Harbor.* In 1943 he went to New Guinea* as a P-38* pilot.* In that same year he joined the 475th Fighter Group as group executive officer, and a month later he became the commander. MacDonald flew 204 combat sorties. During the Leyte* campaign he scored three victories in one day. The 475th scored 522 victories in World War II,* with 28 planes shot down on 7 December 1944 alone. MacDonald's last assignment was vice commander and deputy chief of staff for operations (DCS Ops) of the 25th Air Division at McChord* AFB, Washington. He retired in 1961.

References. DuPre, *USAF Bio.* Hess, *Aces Album.* Edward H. Sims, *American Aces in Great Fighter Battles of World War II*, 1958. Ronald W. Yoshino, *Lightning Strikes: The 475th Fighter Group in the Pacific War, 1943–1945*, 1988.

MCDONNELL DOUGLAS CORPORATION. See aerospace industry; F-4; F-15; F-101.

MACE. See TM-61.

MCGUIRE, MAJOR THOMAS B., JR. (1920–1945)

McGuire is the second-ranking U.S. ace* of all time, with 38 victories. He won the Air Force Medal of Honor,* and McGuire AFB* in New Jersey was named in his honor.

A native of Ridgewood, New Jersey, he enlisted in 1941. He became a pilot* and officer in 1942. In 1943, he joined the 431st Squadron of the 475th Fighter Group of the Fifth Air Force* (5AF) flying P-38s.* In his first combat he shot down three Japanese aircraft over Wewak, New Guinea.* Three days later he shot down two more to become an ace. On another day he was shot down and bailed out, after scoring three victories. Once he and an enemy collided in attacking each other head-on. McGuire's aircraft was still able to fly afterward. He flew 741 combat hours. On five occasions he shot down three in one day, and five times he shot down two. He won his last four victories on 26 December 1944. On 7 January 1945 McGuire's flight* engaged a single Nakajima Ki–43 Hayabusa, or "Oscar," flown by Warrant Officer Akira Sugimoto. The Oscar got the tail of Lieutenant Douglas S. Thropp, Jr.'s P-38. McGuire turned tightly at low altitude and low airspeed to help. He stalled and died in the crash. Later in the fight, Sugimoto sustained battle damage to his plane and made a forced landing safely. Philippine guerrillas ran to his Oscar and killed him with six bullets to his chest.

References. Primary: Gurney, *5 Down*. Secondary: Carroll R. "Andy" Anderson, "McGuire's Last Mission," *AF*, January 1975, pp. 58–64. DuPre, *USAF Bio*. Hess, *Aces Album*. Ronald W. Yoshino, *Lightning Strikes: The 475th Fighter Group in the Pacific War, 1943–1945*, 1988.

MCGUIRE AIR FORCE BASE

Named for Major Thomas B. McGuire, Jr.,* Air Force Medal of Honor* recipient and ace* with 38 victories, who died in action in World War II,* this base is adjacent to the U.S. Army's Fort Dix near Wrightstown, New Jersey. Established in 1937, it was called Fort Dix Army Air Base from 1942 to 1948, when it was named for McGuire. During the war it was an air defense installation and air transportation port for Europe.

Since then many units from the Air Defense Command (ADC), Strategic Air Command* (SAC), and Continental Air Command* (CONAC) have been stationed on it. Its greatest use has been as a base for the Military Airlift Command* (MAC) and MAC's predecessor organizations.

Since 1954, it has been the home of the Twenty-First Air Force* (21AF), which has managed airlift to Europe and Southwest Asia (SWA), and the 438th Military Airlift Wing (MAW), which uses the C-141.*

References. "Guide to Major Air Force Installations Worldwide," *AF*, May 1990, p. 128. Mueller, *AFB*. Roberts, *Dir. USAF*.

Roger D. Launius

MCLUCAS, SECRETARY JOHN L. (1920–)

McLucas was the tenth secretary of the Air Force* (SAF), serving from 1973 to 1975. His short tenure was marked by adjustment to the end of U.S. support of the Republic of South Vietnam. McLucas also tried to introduce the B-1* and F-16* into the USAF,* emphasized the Total Force Policy,* and gave attention to the needs of USAF people to make the new volunteer system work.

He is a native of Fayetteville, North Carolina, and earned degrees from Davidson College in North Carolina and Tulane University in Louisiana. McLucas served in the U.S. Navy in World War II.* He received his doctorate in physics from Pennsylvania State University in 1950. An expert in electronics, he held ten patents and founded several small businesses in Pennsylvania and Massachusetts. His government service before becoming SAF was deputy director of defense research and engineering, assistant secretary general for scientific affairs at headquarters of the North Atlantic Treaty Organization* (NATO), under secretary of the Air Force for four years, and acting SAF for two months.

References. Primary: John L. McLucas, "USAF's Increasing Operational Efficiency," *AF*, May 1975, pp. 48–50, 53. Secondary: Claude Witze, "USAF's New Leaders," *AF*, September, 1973, pp. 58–59.

MCNAMARA, SECRETARY ROBERT S. (1916–)

He was secretary of defense (SECDEF) from 1961 to 1968. No other SECDEF has exercised the power in that position or influenced events as he did. His was the most important tenure as SECDEF to date.

Born in San Francisco, California, he graduated from the University of California at Berkeley. While there he was elected to Phi Beta Kappa before his junior year. He earned a master of business administration at the Harvard Business School and soon joined its faculty. He went to work as a consultant to the War Department to establish a statistical control system for the USAAF.* In 1943 he entered the USAAF as a captain and believed that USAAF generals resisted the use of statistical analysis. He left active duty in 1946 as a lieutenant colonel decorated with the Legion of Merit. He later rose to the grade of colonel in the U.S. Air Force Reserve* (USAFR). McNamara joined the Ford Motor Company and became its president in November 1960 but left to be SECDEF in 1961. He loved power and became SECDEF just after a series of legislative changes from 1949 to 1958 had enhanced the potential authority of the post. These changes had resulted from the beliefs that the most effective management results from concentrating power in one man and that detailed military affairs can be run best by civilians.

With the confidence of Presidents John F. Kennedy* (JFK) and Lyndon B. Johnson* (LBJ), he used the legal reins to implement those managerial views. He became the "super secretary" feared by the U.S. Navy's prescient objection to a unified defense department run by people unfamiliar with naval needs. McNamara made the Office of the Secretary of Defense (OSD) into a large civilian bureaucracy, making micromanagerial military as well as economic and policy decisions. At the time, these civilians were called "McNamara's Whiz Kids" or "McNamara's Band." McNamara introduced the highly effective economics approach of offsetting benefits of a proposal against its costs. In doing so, he placed heavy reliance upon the powerful tool of statistical analysis. This tool is a two-edged sword. Errors can be disastrous, and it lends itself to misuse by slanting the input data. Critics alleged that the new system did slant inputs and that McNamara knew the price of everything and the value of nothing.

McNamara's ultimate use of statistics was body counting as a measure of progress in the Vietnam War,* which was a great failure.

He changed the national strategy by drawing back from the use of nuclear weapons.* He did not believe they were militarily useful, and he was strictly against first use of them by the United States. He wanted the strategy called mutual assured destruction (MAD), which rejected deterrence through weapons superiority and the search for a defense against ballistic missiles.* His changes cast doubt that the United States would use nuclear weapons under any circumstances.

McNamara and General Curtis E. LeMay,* chief of staff of the Air Force,* did not get along. This could be said of the USAF* as a whole, because the USAF lost status in the McNamara years. Also, McNamara often said air power was ineffective. McNamara said his main military advisers were Generals Maxwell Taylor, Earle G. Wheeler, and Lyman L. Lemnitzer, all U.S. Army officers. Under McNamara, the USAF lost seven major programs and had three reduced. The Navy and Army lost one each, and the Army had one reduced. Strategic operations* forces declined from 27 percent of the defense budget in 1961 to 12 percent in 1965.

He set out to revolutionize military procurement by forcing the services to use common equipment and to get materiel without cost overruns. He succeeded with the F-4,* already in production, but the most spectacular examples were to be the F-111—for both the USAF and Navy—and fixed-cost contracts. The services preferred The Boeing Company design for the F-111, but McNamara overrode them and chose the proposal by General Dynamics Corporation and Grumman Aircraft Engineering Corporation. The F-111 never became a Navy aircraft, for it could not be made to land on an aircraft carrier. The fixed prices were to be achieved by McNamara's Total Package Procurement Concept (TPPC), which was applied to buying the C-5.* The cost overruns of both the F-111 and the C-5 became scandalous. After McNamara's term, the Department of Defense (DoD) reverted to traditional, and better, procurement methods.

He micromanaged the air war in Vietnam, called "McNamara's War" in the USAF. He faithfully followed Taylor's strategies of flexible response and gradual escalation. For years, weekly meetings of civilians at the White House selected targets, armament loads, and tactics to be used by the USAF and Navy. LBJ's frustrations with the war increased as time went on. In February 1968, LBJ moved McNamara from the DoD to the World Bank. His management of the bank did not enhance his reputation.

Much of McNamara's management style remained after he was no longer SECDEF: centralized power at the top, OSD bureaucracy, micromanagement by top civilians, and the USAF's loss of priority. Perhaps the biggest and most long term effects are "what might have been" in the Vietnam War. His example indicates the czar system of management does not work well, even with a man as brilliant as he. His example also indicates that civilians are not necessarily the best managers of military affairs.

References. Primary: Robert McNamara, *Blundering into Disaster: Surviving the First Century of the Nuclear Age*, 1986. Secondary: Thomas M. Coffey, *Iron Eagle: The Turbulent Life of General Curtis LeMay*, 1986. David Halberstam, *The Best and the Brightest*, 1969. Richard A. Stubbing, *The Defense Game*, 1986. George M. Watson, Jr., "Man in the Middle: Eugene Zuckert as Secretary of the Air Force," *Air Power History*, Summer 1989, pp. 20–29.

MCNARNEY, GENERAL JOSEPH T. (1893–1972)

After World War II* McNarney transferred to the new USAF* and, most notably, headed the Air Materiel Command, now the Air Force Logistics Command* (AFLC), as its first commander. Said to be a tough and competent staff man, he relieved General of the Army George C. Marshall of the administrative load that would otherwise have distracted him from strategic and political issues.

Born in Emporium, Pennsylvania, he graduated from the U.S. Military Academy (USMA) in 1915. He became a pilot* at the San Diego Signal Corps Aviation School* in California in 1917. In France he served in observation aircrew, staff, and command positions. Between the wars, he briefly commanded the 7th Bomb Group and flight training* units. He spent longer periods attending the Air Corps Tactical School* (ACTS), Command and General Staff School, and Army War College and spent still longer periods on the faculties of the first and the last. In 1939 he joined the War Plans Division of the War Department in Washington, D.C. He was a principal in the implementation of the Army reorganization in early 1942 and then was deputy chief of staff for most of the rest of World War II.* He went to the Mediterranean as deputy supreme commander in 1944 and succeeded General of the Army Dwight D. Eisenhower* late in 1945. He retired in 1952 and then worked for the General Dynamics Corporation.

References. DeWitt S. Copp, *A Few Great Captains: The Men and Events That Shaped the Development of U.S. Air Power*, 1980. *Generals of the Army and Air Force*, 1954. Robert McHenry, ed., *Webster's American Military Biographies*, 1978. Roger J. Spiller, ed., *Dictionary of American Military Biography*, vol. 2, 1984.

David R. Mets

MCPEAK, GENERAL MERRILL A. "TONY" (1936–)

McPeak was the 14th chief of staff of the Air Force,* taking office in 1990. He succeeded General Michael J. Dugan,* who had been fired for some of his public statements. McPeak said he wished to reorganize the USAF* to provide top readiness with quality people and first-class equipment. He intended to achieve these goals by reducing overhead in headquarters units and eliminating some separate operating agencies* (SOA) and direct reporting units* (DRU).

He graduated from the Air Force Reserve Officer Training Corps* (AFROTC) program at San Diego State College in California. A fighter* pilot,* he flew 269 combat sorties in the Vietnam War* and was with the Thunderbirds.* He rose through tactical operations* staff and command positions to commander in chief of the Pacific Air Forces* (PACAF) in 1988, and it was from there he was selected to head the USAF.

References. Primary: Julie Bird, "McPeak Stresses Need to Correct 'Misperceptions,' " *Air Force Times*, 12 November 1990, p. 14, and "Some Forward Wings Would Have a Mix of Planes, McPeak Says," *Air Force Times*, 12 November 1990, pp. 15, 76. Lee Ewing, "McPeak Outlines AF-wide Reorganization," *Air Force Times*, 5 November 1990, pp. 3, 69. Secondary: "Aerospace World," *AF*, November 1990, p. 21.

MACREADY, COLONEL JOHN A. (1887–1979)

Macready was a test pilot,* a pioneer of flight at high altitudes, and one of the pilots for the first nonstop transcontinental flight.* He won the Mackay Trophy three consecutive times. In 1968 he was inducted into the National Aviation Hall of Fame in Dayton, Ohio.

From San Diego, California, he graduated from Stanford University. He enlisted in the U.S. Army in 1917 and became a pilot and officer, but he did not go overseas in World War I.* In 1919 he was assigned to McCook Field, Ohio, as a test pilot although he was already in his 30s. In 1921 Macready showed that crop dusting with aircraft was practical. In the same year, he began his work in high-altitude flight and received his first Mackay Trophy. Most of his work was done to perfect a General Electric Company supercharger, but flying clothing and oxygen support equipment were also being developed in the process. In September 1921 he set a new world record altitude of 34,509 feet flying a supercharged LePere LUSAC-11. In 1924 he reached 35,239 feet; in 1925, 37,569 feet; in 1926, 38,704 feet. The importance of these tests was that they contributed to the USAAF's* turbosupercharged high-performance aircraft of World War II* and to adequate personal flying equipment. The development of the turbosupercharger contributed to jet engine development.

In 1922 Macready and Lieutenant Oakley G. Kelly attempted a nonstop transcontinental flight which did not succeed but which set an unofficial world endurance record of 35 hours and 18 minutes. They received a Mackay Trophy for it. The next year they succeeded in flying nonstop from Roosevelt Field, New York to Rockwell Field, California, for another Mackay Trophy. Also in 1923, Macready made the first successful parachute jump at night. In 1924 Macready teamed with Lieutenant A. W. Stevens to make the first aerial photographic survey of the United States, flying 10,000 miles and taking 2,000 photos.

Macready resigned from the USAAS* in 1926 to join the General Motors Corporation; later he worked for the Shell Oil Company and finally took up cattle ranching. He returned to active service for World War II.*

References. Maurer, *Avn. in Army*. Joseph A. Ventolo, Jr., "Col. John A. Macready," *AF*, February 1980, pp. 76–78.

MAHURIN, COLONEL WALKER M. "BUD." (1918–)

Mahurin is the ninth-ranking USAF* ace* of all time with 24.5 victories. Born in Benton Harbor, Michigan, he became an aviation cadet* in 1941 and a pilot* and officer in 1942. Mahurin served in the 63rd Fighter Squadron of the 56th Fighter Group, flying F-47s* in the Eighth Air Force* (8AF) in England.

After 17 months in battle and with 20 victories, he was shot down in March 1944. Helped by the French underground, he was able to evade capture and return. In March 1945 he went to the Pacific theater to command the 3rd Air Commando Group. He shot down one Japanese aircraft. During the Korean War,* he was commander of the 51st Fighter Group, shooting down 3.5 MiG-15s. Mahurin was again shot down in May 1952 and spent 16 months as a prisoner of war (North Korea).* He was in solitary confinement the entire time. Mahurin left the USAF* in 1956. In his service he had lost four aircraft and parachuted three times.

References. Primary: Walker M. (Bud) Mahurin, "The Day I Got My Tail Chewed Off," *AF*, March 1973, pp. 72–75. Secondary: DuPre, *USAF Bio*. Roger A. Freeman, *The Mighty Eighth: Units, Men and Machines*, 1970. Hess, *Aces Album*.

MAINTENANCE. *See* depot maintenance; field maintenance; organizational maintenance.

MAITLAND, COLONEL LESTER J. (1899–1990)

Along with First Lieutenant Albert F. Hegenberger,* Maitland was the first to fly from the continental United States (CONUS) to Hawaii. In addition, he set a world speed record in 1923.

From Milwaukee, Wisconsin, Maitland enlisted in the U.S. Army in 1917, becoming a pilot* and officer in 1918. Maitland was the first American to fly faster than 200 miles per hour. He took second place in the Pulitzer Trophy race* of 1922. He made his historic overwater flight to Hawaii in 1927 in the aircraft *Bird of Paradise*.* Maitland was stationed at Clark* Field when World War II* began. He later served in the Pacific in the Air Service Command. In 1943, he commanded the 386th Bomb Group in Europe, flying B-26 Marauders.* He retired in 1944 and became an ordained Episcopal minister.

References. DuPre, *USAF Bio*. William J. Horvat, "*Bird of Paradise*," *AH*, Summer 1968, pp. 27–31. Maurer, *Avn. in Army*.

MAJOR COMMAND (MAJCOM)

A MAJCOM is a principal subdivision of the USAF;* there were 12 MAJCOMs in 1990. Some MAJCOMs are specified commands under the Joint Chiefs of Staff (JCS). Specified commands are service units that receive orders from the president through the secretary of defense (SECDEF) with advice from the JCS. The USAF specified commands have been the Strategic Air Command* (SAC), U.S. Air Forces in Europe* (USAFE) from 1951 to 1956, Aerospace Defense Command* (ADC) from 1975 to 1980, and the Military Airlift Command* (MAC). The other MAJCOMs may be part of JCS unified commands. Unified commands are made up of parts of the armed forces. Examples of MAJCOMs in unified commands are Pacific Air Forces* (PACAF) as part of the Pacific Command and USAFE as part of the European Command.

A MAJCOM may be an operational command conducting strategic,* tactical,* or other operations or in direct support of them. Examples are SAC, the Tactical

Air Command* (TAC), MAC, PACAF, and USAFE. A MAJCOM may also be a support command providing supplies, material, education, maintenance, personnel, communications, training, and like functions. Examples are the Air Force Logistics Command* (AFLC), Air Force Communications Command* (AFCC), and Air Training Command* (ATC).

References. Ravenstein, *Org. USAF*. U.S. Air Force Fact Sheet 89–05, "Organization of the United States Air Force," February 1989.

MALE CALL. *See* Caniff, Milton.

MALMSTROM AIR FORCE BASE

This field near Great Falls, Montana, is a Strategic Air Command* (SAC) installation. It was established in 1942 and had the name Great Falls until 1955 when it was named for Colonel Einar A. Malmstrom. He died in a T-33 accident in 1954 near the base. Until 1943, bomber* crews were trained at it. Then it was used to ready Lend-Lease* aircraft for the USSR. It was an aerial port to Alaska from 1946 to 1953. From then until 1961 it was a base for interceptors* and tankers.* In 1961, it was the first USAF* base to have Minuteman* ballistic missiles.* In 1990 it had the 341st Strategic Missile Wing and the 301st Air Refueling Wing.

References. "Guide to Major Air Force Installations Worldwide," *AF*, May 1990, p. 126. Mueller, *AFB*. Roberts, *Dir. USAF*.

MANAGEMENT ENGINEERING AGENCY. *See* Air Force Management Engineering Agency.

MANEUVERS OF 1941

In 1941 the United States was desperately trying to rearm and needed realistic exercises. Two were conducted that year. In September they were held in Louisiana; in November they were held in North Carolina. The latter was called the "Battle of the Carolinas." The maneuvers took place on a large scale. Aside from training, the main result of the maneuvers was the successful introduction of pierced-steel planking* for quick runway construction. For the USAAF,* the fighters* used were P-38s,* P-39s,* P-40s,* and P-43s,* the bombers* were B-17s,* B-25s,* and B-26 Marauders;* and attack* aircraft were A-20s* and A-24s. Use of the last was influenced by the German Ju 87 Stuka. Liaison aviation* made its first appearance in these exercises.

References. *The Official Pictorial History of the AAF*, 1947. Richard K. Smith, "Marston Mat," *AF*, April 1989, pp. 84–88.

"MAORI." *See* Coningham, Air Marshal Sir Arthur.

MARAUDER. *See* B-26 Marauder.

MARCH AIR FORCE BASE

In service since 1918, March is a Strategic Air Command* (SAC) base near Riverside, California. It was named for Second Lieutenant Peyton C. March, Jr., son of the U.S. Army chief of staff, who died in the crash of his JN* Jenny.

It has usually been an important base since it was established. The base was used for pilot* flight training* until 1923 and returned to that task in 1926. In 1931, March's training function went to the new Randolph* Field, Texas, and then it got the 1st Bombardment Wing. In the 1930s it was a base for bombers* and attack aviation* with the 19th Bombardment and 17th Attack Groups on it. Heavy bomber crew training was done during World War II.* In the early 1950s it had B-47* and KC-97 (see C-97) operations, and by 1966 it had B-52s* and KC-135s (see C-135). At that time, it was SAC's largest installation. In 1990 it was the site for headquarters of the Fifteenth Air Force* (15AF) and the 22nd Air Refueling Wing with KC-10As (see C-10) and KC-135s.

References. Brown, *Eagles.* "Guide to Major Air Force Installations Worldwide," *AF*, May 1990, p. 126. Maurer, *Avn. in Army.* Mueller, *AFB*. Roberts, *Dir. USAF*.

MARIANAS ISLANDS

The Marianas have provided critical bases for the USAF* because of their geographic position 1,500 miles from Japan and 6,000 miles from Vietnam.

In 1943, the USAAF* had no intercontinental bomber* with which to reach Japan. Its most immediate possibility was the B-29,* which was ready for production. Chinese bases could put the B-29 within range, but supplying the effort over the "Hump"* would be grossly inefficient. It was tried anyway in Matterhorn.*

The only alternative was the Marianas Islands, deep within the Japanese Empire's defensive perimeter. The United States was able to reach and invade the Marianas by June 1944. In August that task, supported by the Seventh Air Force* (7AF), was completed. Construction of five great airfields for B-29s was pushed. A B-29 wing of 180 aircraft and 12,000 men were to use each field. There were two fields each on Guam and Tinian Islands and one on Saipan.

The strategic campaign against Japan* from the Marianas began in November. Daylight raids produced disappointing results. They improved when Iwo Jima Island was taken, for its airfield saved some battle-damaged B-29s and made fighter escort* possible. Iwo was roughly halfway between Japan and the Marianas. In February 1945, Major General Curtis E. LeMay* switched the assault to night incendiary raids which devastated Japan. Mining* was also done from the Marianas. By June 1945, almost 1,000 bombers* were based there. The nuclear weapon* strikes on Hiroshima and Nagasaki flew from the Marianas.

Andersen* AFB on Guam was used again in 1965 for B-52* operations in the Vietnam War.* The B-52s needed one aerial refueling* for the round-trip.

References. Primary: Haywood S. Hansell, Jr., *Strategic Air War against Japan*, 1980. Curtis E. LeMay and Bill Yenne, *Superfortress: The Story of the B-29 and American Air Power*, 1988. Secondary: C&C, vols. 4 and 5. Polmar, *SAC*.

MARK, SECRETARY HANS M. (1929–)

Mark became the 13th secretary of the Air Force* (SAF) in 1979. His distinguished scientific background joined with that of Chief of Staff of the Air Force* General Lew Allen, Jr.,* to form a complementary aerospace team at the top for the final 18 months of the Carter presidency.

Born in Mannheim, Germany, Mark emigrated to the United States in 1940 and became a U.S. citizen in 1945. He graduated with a degree in physics from the University of California, Berkeley, and earned a doctorate from the Massachusetts Institute of Technology (MIT). He was a research physicist at the University of California and Lawrence Radiation Laboratory and chairman of the university's Department of Nuclear Engineering from 1964 to 1969. Mark was then selected to be director of the National Aeronautics and Space Administration's* (NASA) Ames Research Center, where he oversaw research and application projects in aeronautics, space science, life science, and space technology. In 1977 he was appointed under secretary of the Air Force, a position he held until he became SAF.

Soon after becoming SAF, Mark set an agenda: (1) to enhance strategic forces at a level that would ensure equivalence with the USSR, (2) to enhance strategic and tactical airlift operations* so the United States could respond adequately to contingencies anywhere, and (3) to develop a doctrine and organization that would take full advantage of USAF* space technology.

Carrying out the president's policies for the modernization of the strategic deterrent forces, Mark's agenda included the cruise missile,* Peacekeeper,* advanced Strategic ALCM Launcher (SAL), and a follow-on strategic airplane called Long-Range Combat Aircraft (LRCA). A special study group was formed in 1979 to define a new transport.* The group concluded it should be able to operate in a relatively austere environment at destination and be capable of carrying outsize U.S. Army equipment. Contracting was planned for early 1981, with first flight in another three and one-half years. Expanding space capabilities included creating a Space Division in the Air Force Systems Command* (AFSC), as the focal point for integrating national security–related systems into the Space Shuttle program, and building a West Coast launch site for the shuttle at Vandenberg* AFB, California. Mark ended his term in January 1981.

References. Primary: Hans M. Mark, "Priorities and Progress," *AF*, May 1980, pp. 60, 61. Secondary: USAF Biography, "Hans M. Mark," July 1979.

Warren A. Trest

MARKET (MARKET GARDEN)

Hoping to open a quick route into western Germany, the Allies attempted to capture intact key bridges over the Rhine River between Eindhoven and Arnhem, the Netherlands, with an airborne assault from 17 to 26 September 1944. This was to expedite an overland offensive. It was called Operation Market Garden, with Market referring to the tactical airlift* portion. The number of transports* available required the airborne forces to be delivered over a three-day period. To alleviate part of the problem, the Eighth Air Force* (8AF) offered to use some of its B-24s* to drop supplies to the airborne troops.

Poor weather conditions in England delayed the airlift operations* on 17 September, but that afternoon, 1,306 airplanes and 1,152 gliders* completed the mission before dark. As promised, 246 B-24s dropped supplies to the U.S.

paratroopers. Unexpected resistance from German panzer units in the area aggravated the problems and increased the need for aerial resupply. Eventually, 36,000 airborne troops, 1,927 vehicles, 568 artillery pieces, and 5,227 tons of equipment and supplies, including gasoline, were delivered by airlift.

The inability of the Allies to deliver all the airborne troops at one time, in part due to weather, became the critical element in the failure of this operation. Other factors included the inability of ground forces to break through and poor intelligence. After Market, the Allies recognized that successful airborne operations demanded the initial airdrop to be of sufficient strength to achieve its objectives quickly. Furthermore, future airborne assaults would have to place greater emphasis on securing airfields for resupply. Larger transport aircraft, capable of delivering heavy equipment to the lightly armed airborne troops, was regarded as a necessity.

References. C&C, vol. 3. James A. Huston, *Out of the Blue: US Army Airborne Operations in World War II*, 1969.

Jeffery S. Underwood

MARTIN, GLENN L., COMPANY, AND MARTIN MARIETTA CORPORATION. *See* aerospace industry; B-10; B-26 Marauder; B-57; Martin Bomber; Titan; TM-61.

MARTIN BOMBER

In World War I* Glenn Martin, of the Glenn L. Martin Company, was asked to design a bomber* superior to Britain's Handley Page and an order was given for ten. First flight of the GMB was in August 1918. This model, which was redesignated the MB-1, and its derivative MB-2 have been popularly called the Martin bomber. Originally intended as a bomber, some MB-1s were used for observation aviation* and one as a transport.* The MB-2 variant was intended to be a night bomber, and the later ones in production received a night bomber designation of NBS-1. The first orders for MB-2 production were given in 1920, and the bombers served until they were replaced by the Keystone* bomber in the late 1920s. All eight USAAC* bomber squadrons of the time were equipped with MB-2s. In 1921, Brigadier General William Mitchell* used MB-2s in Mitchell's bombing tests on warships,* an important event in USAF* history.

Characteristics (MB-2): engines, two Libertys of 420 horsepower each; span, 74 feet; length, 43 feet; height, 15 feet; gross weight, 12,064 pounds; top speed, 99 miles per hour at sea level; service ceiling, 8,500 feet; range, 558 miles; bombs, 2,000 pounds.

References. Merle Olmsted, "The Era of the Martin Bomber," *AAHS Journal*, Fall 1962, pp. 187–94. Swanborough, *US Mil. Airc.* Wagner, *Am. Planes.*

MASSIVE RETALIATION. *See* Eisenhower, President Dwight D.

MATADOR. *See* TM-61.

MATHER AIR FORCE BASE

Established in 1918, this field near Sacramento, California, was named after Second Lieutenant Carl S. Mather, who died in the crash of his JN* while on a training flight in Texas. It was used as a pilot* training base in the final months of World War I* and was inactivated in 1922. With the exception of USAAC* maneuvers in 1930, the field remained dormant until World War II.*

It was reactivated for pilot flight training* in May 1941. Before the war was over, Mather also became the home of navigator,* observer,* and bombardier* training. Following the war, navigator training continued and expanded. In 1947, a unique school opened to train triple-rated navigators in bombardier and radar* operations. The mission grew in 1962 when electronic warfare* officer (EWO) training was relocated to Mather from Keesler* AFB, Mississippi. Three years later, undergraduate navigator training (UNT) was transferred from Carswell* AFB, Texas, to Mather. The addition of UNT consolidated all formal navigator training for the first time in USAF* history. Moreover, Mather's school was the only source of aerial navigators for the U.S. Navy, and it trained navigators of nearly 30 other nations.

Besides conducting navigator training, the 323rd Flying Training Wing (FTW) supported several tenant organizations. The largest was the Strategic Air Command's* (SAC) 320th Bombardment Wing which relocated to Mather in 1958 as part of a dispersal of the deterrent force. The navigator training aircraft included the T-43 and the T-37,* while SAC flew the B-52* and KC-135 (*see* C-135). Mather is scheduled to close in 1993, and the navigator school will move to Beale* AFB, California.

References. "Guide to Major Air Force Installations Worldwide," *AF*, May 1990, pp. 126, 128. Mueller, *AFB*. E. R. Nacey, *A History of Mather AFB*, 1963 (ATC History Office, Randolph AFB, Texas). Roberts, *Dir. USAF*. Wanda Stroud, *History of the 323d Flying Training Wing, 1973–1985*, 1985 (ATC History Office, Randolph AFB, Texas).

Thomas A. Manning

MATTERHORN

This World War II* campaign planned to use B-29s* in strategic operations* out of China against Japan. In 1943 the China and B–29 combination was the only possible quick way to hit Japan because of distance. An intercontinental bomber* was still in the early stages of development and was not available. Matterhorn failed, primarily because of vexing logistical problems. Its principal contribution to the USAAF* was the B-29 operational experience gained.

The Air War Plans Division* had determined that the Japanese iron and steel industry was a suitable target for strategic operations. From a U.S. base at Chengtu, China, B-29s could reach steel plants in Manchuria, Korea, and Kyushu

Island in Japan. Chengtu was 1,150 miles from Calcutta, India. The "Hump" Airlift* was the only means to bring supplies into China, and this was a severe limitation with the aircraft of the time. This required that Matterhorn have a limited goal. It was intended to damage Japan as a contribution toward the eventual strategic operations from the Marianas* Islands when they were seized. China's leader, Chiang Kai-shek, had bases laboriously built by hand for the B-29s. They were to support 280 B-29s and 2,000 B-24* transport* variants to provide the logistics. The British built facilities for the B-24s at the other end of the supply line in India.

On 15 June 1944, the first raid by 75 B-29s of the XX Bomber Command struck the Imperial Iron and Steel Works at Yawata, Kyushu, considered to be Japan's most important steel plant. A total of 47 B-29s bombed it and one bomber* was lost to enemy action. The bombing was totally ineffective. Other raids were well spaced and a tenth strike was not made by the command until 14 October. Meanwhile, operations began against Southeast Asia (SEA) from India, and the Marianas were invaded in June 1944. In January 1945 the B-29s began to leave China. Operations in SEA continued until the end of March. The B-29s had dropped only 800 tons of bombs* from the Chinese bases.

References. Primary: Curtis E. LeMay and Bill Yenne, *Superfortress: The Story of the B-29 and American Air Power*, 1988. Secondary: C&C, vol. 5. Haywood S. Hansell, Jr., *Strategic Air War against Japan*, 1980.

MAVERICK. *See* AGM-65.

MAXWELL AIR FORCE BASE
The Wright brothers* opened the first civilian flying school near Montgomery, Alabama, in 1910. They chose an area that was not built up and which had a favorable climate. Their school lasted only two months, but in 1918 the Aviation Section of the U.S. Army Signal Corps* liked the site well enough to construct a military airfield on it. Initially, it was a repair facility. In 1922 it was named after Second Lieutenant William C. Maxwell, who died in a flying accident in the Philippines. In the 1920s observation aviation* used the field. The Air Corps Tactical School* (ACTS) moved to it from Langley* Field in 1931. During World War II,* the base conducted flight training.* More than 100,000 aviation cadets* were trained there, as well as 2,653 B-24* and 728 B-29* crews. After the war it became the location for the Air University,* which has remained there.

References. Brown, *Eagles*. "Guide to Major Air Force Installations Worldwide," *AF*, May 1990, p. 128. Mueller, *AFB*. John H. Napier III, "The Military, Montgomery, and Maxwell," *AH*, December 1977, pp. 189–95. Juliette D. Pearce, "Maxwell: The Man and the Base," *AH*, Spring 1969, pp. 6–9.

MAYAGUEZ INCIDENT
On 12 May 1975, Cambodian Khmer Rouge communist gunboats seized the American SS *Mayaguez* in international waters in the Gulf of Thailand. It was then sailed to Koh Tang Island, Cambodia. The *Mayaguez* incident took place

two weeks after Saigon fell to North Vietnamese aggression. The defeat of the South Vietnamese ally, which the United States had betrayed to the communists, had been humiliating to Americans. The reaction of the U.S. government and the military to the Khmer Rouge bullying revived some small self-respect and pride for the United States.

The USAF* began to watch the ship on 13 May, using F-111s* and AC-130s (*see* C-130). The aircraft were fired upon but did not return fire. The communists took the ship's crew to the mainland and then to the island of Koah Rong Sam Loem. On 14 May, the USAF hit enemy gunboats and sank some. That night President Gerald Ford ordered the U.S. military to retake the *Mayaguez* and any of its crew on Koh Tang.

Six HH-53s (*see* H-53) and five CH-53s (*see* H-53) loaded 230 U.S. Marines. Some were delivered to the USS *Harold E. Holt* for boarding the *Mayaguez*. The rest were landed on Koh Tang. Little resistance was expected, but this was a gross error; two CH-53s were shot down and one of them was destroyed. Some A-7s,* AC-130s, and OV-10s* were then called in to strafe the enemy. When the *Holt* approached the *Mayaguez*, the enemy abandoned ship. The U.S. crew was recovered from a fishing boat as it sailed toward Koh Tang, for the Khmer had decided to free the men after the destruction of the gunboats. Then it became necessary to reinforce the Marines so as to withdraw all troops with minimum losses. The evacuation was done under fire. U.S. losses included 15 dead, three missing, and 50 wounded from enemy action. All those killed were lost in the first 90 minutes of the assault. Two airmen won Air Force Crosses for their heroism.

References. Daniel P. Bolger, *Americans at War: 1975–1986, An Era of Violent Peace*, 1988. Ray L. Bowers, *Tactical Airlift*, 1983. Jack Lavalle, ed., *Air War—Vietnam*, 1978. David R. Mets, *Land-Based Air Power in Third World Crises*, 1986.

MB-1 and MB-2. *See* Martin bomber.

MDAP. *See* Military Assistance Program.

MEDICAL. *See* Air Force Office of Medical Support; aviation medicine.

MEMPHIS BELLE

This movie* was a documentary made by the USAAF* and released by Paramount Studios in April 1944. It was directed by Lieutenant Colonel William Wyler. *Memphis Belle* has been the most successful movie made by the USAF or USAF antecedents.* A commercial success when it came out, scenes from it are ubiquitous in other documentaries and in fictional movies. The B-17* *Memphis Belle* has been kept as a memorial in Memphis, Tennessee, but it has already been immortalized by the movie.

The story follows the 25th sortie of an aircrew of an Eighth Air Force* (8AF) B-17F named the *Memphis Belle*. This sortie was a raid on Wilhemshaven,

Germany, and it completed the operational tour* of the aircrew. To make this color movie, 16,000 feet of film was shot on 13 combat sorties by the USAAF's First Motion Picture Unit (FMPU) commanded by Lieutenant Colonel Paul Mantz. It took 14 months to make, and one cameraman was killed in action.

In 1990 Time Warner, Inc., remade it using conventional Hollywood story formulas and a fictionalized script by Monte Merrick. It was filmed in England at RAF Binbrook airfield with British director Michael Caton-Jones and starred Matthew Modine as Captain Robert Morgan, the *Belle*'s pilot.* A co-producer was Wyler's daughter, Catherine.

References. Roger Ebert, ''Despite Cliches, 'Memphis Belle' Soars,'' *Journal American*, 12 October 1990, p. B1. James H. Farmer, *Celluloid Wings*, 1984. Monte Merrick, *Memphis Belle*, 1990. Bruce W. Orriss, *When Hollywood Ruled the Skies*, 1984.

MENOHER, MAJOR GENERAL CHARLES T. (1862–1930)

Menoher was the third chief of the USAAS* and was serving in 1921 at the onset of the controversy over Brigadier General William Mitchell.* As a nonpilot heading the USAAS from 1919 to 1921, he has been depicted as a reactionary inhibiting the development of air power in accordance with the Mitchell theories, but such a picture is overdrawn. He did advance doctrines* somewhat like the blitzkrieg theories so successful in World War II.*

He was born in Johnstown, Pennsylvania, and graduated from the U.S. Military Academy (USMA) in 1886. He led a modernization of artillery as a full-fledged combat branch of the U.S. Army and fought in Cuba in the Spanish-American War. Later he served multiple tours in the Philippines in peacekeeping operations. Arriving in France soon after the U.S. declaration of war in 1917, he set up the artillery school there and commanded the 42nd Division in the St. Mihiel* and Meuse-Argonne* campaigns. Though Menoher had experimented with the use of balloons in support of artillery from the 1880s onward and used them in the development of indirect fire doctrine and tactics, he had little experience with airplanes until the end of World War I.*

When Mitchell's report on the *Ostfriesland*'s sinking in 1921 was leaked to the press, Menoher asked the secretary of war to relieve Mitchell or himself. Mitchell survived. Major General Mason M. Patrick was chosen as the new chief of the USAAS, and Menoher was given command of the Hawaiian Department.

References. Futrell, *Ideas*, vol. 1. Maurer, *Avn. in Army*. Roger J. Spiller, ed., *Dictionary of American Military Biography*, vol. 2, 1984.

David R. Mets

MERSEBERG-LEUNA, GERMANY

This largest German synthetic oil plant was the object of 22 raids by Allied bombers* during World War II.* The Eighth Air Force* (8AF) made 20 of the raids. A total of 6,552 bombers struck the target with 18,328 tons of bombs.* Leuna was one of the major air battles of the war. The first raid was a daylight strike by the 8AF with 220 bombers and fighter escorts* on 12 May 1944, which halted production for ten days. Leuna was heavily defended by the Germans and emergency measures used by them brought rapid recuperation, hence a need for continual raids. By January 1945 the plant was producing only 15 percent of its capacity.

References. C&C, vol. 3. *The United States Strategic Bombing Survey*, vol. 1, 1976. Anthony Verrier, *The Bomber Offensive*, 1968.

Edward L. Homze

MEUSE-ARGONNE CAMPAIGN

This operation opened on 26 September 1918 and was one of the greatest conflicts in U.S. history. It lasted 47 days, with only trifling intervals of inactivity. When it began, some 450,000 of General John J. Pershing's* men went into action, but other troops were thrown in until the total of Americans engaged was about 1.2 million.

The U.S. numerical preponderance was overwhelming, and the war-weary Germans were soon in retreat. Nevertheless, the Germans knew the terrain in the Meuse River and Argonne forest area, and the Americans did not. The forest country fought over became an almost impenetrable tangle of fallen timbers, an ideal place for labyrinths of barbed wire and nests of machine guns. Consequently, U.S. forces suffered around 200,000 casualties. Nevertheless, U.S. forces managed to drive to the heights of the Sedan-Mézières railway. The campaign was ended by the surrender of Germany on 11 November.

In the last few weeks of the conflict the Allied air forces played a large role. The largest single raid of the campaign was on 9 October when Brigadier General William Mitchell* assembled more than 200 bombers,* 110 fighters,* and 50 three-place Caudrons for a strike against the German troop concentration in the Damvillers-Wavrille area. More than 300 aircraft in what was then two huge formations flew north to pound the vital German buildup. More than 30 tons of bombs* were dropped in the face of a vigorous German air defense, and the enemy's impending counterattack on the ground was disrupted. During the night, British bombers continued the attack,* and within a 24-hour period no less than 81 tons of bombs smashed into the German positions. Although the Americans did not employ large bombers, they used de Haviland DH-4s* and other two-seaters effectively. All told in the Argonne campaign, no less than 45 U.S. air squadrons were involved.

During the Meuse-Argonne campaign, Second Lieutenant Frank Luke, Jr.,* ran his victory score to 18 but was killed on 29 September. He was awarded the Air Force Medal of Honor.* Captain Edward V. Rickenbacker* pushed his score to 26 and also was awarded the Air Force Medal of Honor at a later date. All together, about 80 Americans became aces.*

References. Edward M. Coffman, *The War to End All Wars: The American Military Experience in World War I*, 1986. James J. Hudson, *Hostile Skies: A Combat History of the American Air Service in World War I*, 1968. Maurice Matloff, ed., *American*

Military History 1607–1958, 1959. Maurer Maurer, *The U.S. Air Service in World War I*, vols. 1, 2, and 4, 1978 and 1979.

                                                                    James J. Hudson

MEXICAN EXPEDITION OF 1916

Francisco "Pancho" Villa led 500 to 1,000 Mexicans in a raid on Columbus, New Mexico, in March 1916, and 17 Americans were killed. Brigadier General John J. Pershing* was sent with a force into Mexico to search for the outlaws and to secure the border. The 1st Aero Squadron* was ordered along. This was the first offensive military operation conducted against an enemy in which a USAF* antecedent took part. The 1st Aero Squadron performed well considering its equipment, and the airmen learned much about operations and logistics from the expedition. Congress soon appropriated $13 million for military aviation as a result of the problems and lessons learned.

The squadron was to conduct observation aviation* operations with eight JN3* Jennies. The planes had not been used for months but had to fly as high as 12,000 feet over the mountainous terrain and operate over long distances in winter weather of rain, hail, and snow. The JNs proved inadequate. From 15 March to 15 August, the squadron flew 540 sorties for 346 hours. By 20 April, only two of the original JNs were still operational. On that date, four new JN4s arrived, but these were unsuitable aircraft. The U.S. Army tried to censor dispatches on the expedition, but the U.S. press reported the difficulties. The Army never caught Villa.

References. James L. Crouch, "Wings South: The First Foreign Employment of Air Power by the United States," *AH*, March 1972, pp. 27–31. Juliette A. Hennessy, *The United States Army Air Arm April 1861 to April 1917*, 1985. Calvin W. Hines, "First Aero Squadron in Mexico," *AAHS Journal*, Fall 1965, pp. 190–97.

MEYER, GENERAL JOHN C. (1919–1975)

This fighter* pilot* is the seventh-ranking USAF* ace* of all time, an honor he shares with Captain Edward V. Rickenbacker.* Meyer was the top ace of the Eighth Air Force* (8AF) with 26 victories. He rose later to be the USAF's vice chief of staff from 1969 to 1972 and commander of the Strategic Air Command* (SAC) from 1972 to 1974. In 1988 he was inducted into the National Aviation Hall of Fame in Dayton, Ohio.

Born in Brooklyn, New York, he became an aviation cadet* in 1939 and a pilot and officer in 1940. He went to the 8AF in 1943 as commander of the 487th Fighter Squadron flying F-51s.* Meyer shot down 24 German aircraft and destroyed 13 on the ground in 200 combat sorties and 462 combat hours. Over Kassel, Germany, one day he alone engaged 20 enemy fighters* and shot down four of them.

He was based at Asch, Belgium, on 31 December 1944 and was scheduled for an early patrol the next day with the 487th. At the time, Meyer was deputy commander of the 352nd Fighter Group. As he began to roll down the runway in the morning, German fighters appeared. It was the German air attack of 1

January 1945.* Meyer was barely airborne when he shot down an Fw 190. Later in the dogfight he shot down another. The 487th's pilots scored 25 victories that day with no losses and received a Presidential Unit Citation for the engagement.

Meyer graduated from Dartmouth College, New Hampshire, in 1947. In 1950 he became commander of the 4th Fighter Interceptor Group. He took this unit to the Korean War.* In April 1951 he became the deputy commander of the 4th Fighter Interceptor Wing. In Korea he flew 31 sorties in F-86s* and scored two victories.

References. DuPre, *USAF Bio*. John L. Frisbee, "Four-Star Ace," *AF*, May 1989, p. 172. Gurney, *5 Down*. Hess, *Aces Album*. Edward H. Sims, *American Aces in Great Fighter Battles of World War II*, 1958.

MH-60G PAVE HAWK. *See* H-60G Pave Hawk.

MID-CANADA LINE

This was the name given to the early warning radar* line built by the Royal Canadian Air Force (RCAF) in the mid–1950s, along the 55th parallel in southern Canada. It proved to be an invaluable extension of the Permanent System* and the Pinetree Line* and served as a backup line for the distant early warning line* (DEW Line).

It coincided with U.S. efforts to strengthen continental air defense by building the DEW Line along the northern boundary of the Western Hemisphere. In January 1953, U.S. requirements for the development, installation, and testing of air defense equipment under Arctic conditions were presented to the Canadian government, along with a request for approval to carry out site surveys for a possible DEW Line. The Canadians granted conditional approval in February. One of the conditions was forming a joint study group to examine defense matters of concern to both nations. The resultant Canada–United States Military Study Group was created, and one of its first recommendations was building of the Mid-Canada Line.

In September, President Dwight D. Eisenhower* approved a policy directive for an improved air defense system for the continental United States (CONUS). It, and the National Security Council's call for an expeditious installation of a radar line across southern Canada, led to speedy approval of the 55th parallel line. After a series of delays, the Mid-Canada Line was finally completed and put into service in January 1957, at a total cost of $170 million. It was also known as the McGill Line after the scientists at McGill University, Montreal, who planned and designed it. It consisted of a chain of semi- and fully automatic radar stations along the 55th parallel from the east to west coasts of Canada.

References. "Canada: Mid-Canada Radar System," *Military Review*, October 1956, p. 72. C. L. Grant, *The Development of Continental Air Defense to 1 September 1954*,

1957. Richard Morenus, *DEW Line*, 1957. Thomas W. Ray, "A History of the DEW Line 1946–1964," Aerospace Defense Command History Office, 1965.

E. Michael Del Papa

"MIDGETMAN." *See* Small Intercontinental Ballistic Missile.

MIG. *See* enemy aircraft.

MIG ALLEY

During the Korean War,* MiG Alley was an area in northwestern Korea where communist and United Nations (UN) air forces fought for air superiority* so their attack* aircraft could influence the ground war. MiG Alley resembled a parallelogram, with the following North Korean cities forming its apices: Antung-Sinuiju, west; Suiho, north; Huichon, east; and Sinanju, south. The aerial arena took in 6,500 square miles and, if the 50,000-foot maximum operational ceiling for jets in 1952 were applied, the Alley encompassed about 65,000 cubic miles of airspace. From early 1951 through the armistice in 1953, UN fighters,* primarily F-86s,* battled the Soviet-built Chinese MiG-15s. The USAF* triumphed and, by war's end, it had shot down 792 MiGs and lost only 78.

The UN air forces, with the USAF bearing the heaviest load, labored under severe disabilities. The MiG's superior high-altitude characteristics could only be offset by the F-86's faster diving speed to carry the battle to more favorable low altitudes. The Americans were far from their South Korean bases. This limited patrol times, a situation aggravated when communist ground-controlled interception (GCI) came into operation.

However, the two greatest UN problems in the battle for air superiority were the enemy sanctuaries and a shortage of F-86s. The constant fear of Chinese and then Soviet intervention made U.S. civil leaders reluctant to fight the war aggressively. Self-imposed limits were granted communist strategic and tactical targets; the Antung airfield complex, bridges, railroads, roads, and dams were on or near the Chinese border and were granted sanctuary. The communists could loiter over their bases, hit UN aircraft under advantageous conditions, and run back to their sanctuary. The UN was deprived of the tactic of striking airfields to drive the enemy back to reduce patrol and combat time. Thus, the enemy was given political air superiority.*

The shortage of F-86s restricted the USAF to two wings, the 4th and the 51st, with a total of 115 fighters. In the spring of 1952, the Antung complex held 400 to 500 MiGs. USAF logistics were strained to supply the two wings. In January 1952, the aircraft-out-of-commission rate reached 45 percent. Hard work relieved the supply crisis by April 1952, but the F-86s still faced three- to four-to-one odds in the Alley.

The USAF won because its pilots had extensive World War II* experience and a great fighter plane. One of the veterans was Colonel Francis S. "Gabby" Gabreski.* The June 1952 introduction of the F-86F modification provided 15 percent more power, an improved wing and tail, and the A-1 radar* computed gunsight to help reduce the MiG's high-altitude advantage.

References. Futrell, *USAF in Korea*. Ray Wagner, "MiG-15," *AH*, March 1988, pp. 45–54. Bryce Walker, *Fighting Jets*, 1983.

Ronald W. Yoshino

MIG ALLEY. *See* novels.

MIGCAP

This is a combat air patrol (CAP) of U.S. fighters* deployed between a MiG or ground threat and a U.S. force to be protected. The term was used mostly in the Vietnam War* together with similar terms that meant the same thing: Barriers CAP (BARCAP), MIGSCREEN, and Rescue CAP (RESCAP). Fundamentally, the function is the same as fighter escort.*

References. Berger, *USAF in SEA*. Jack Lavalle, ed., *Air War—Vietnam*, 1978.

Frank L. Goldstein

MIGSCREEN. *See* MIGCAP.

"MIKE." *See* Dugan, General Michael J.

MILDENHALL. *See* RAF Mildenhall.

MILITARY AIRLIFT COMMAND (MAC)

Airlift operations* are a major part of U.S. power, and they are carried out by MAC, a USAF* major command (MAJCOM). MAC is headquartered at Scott* AFB, Illinois.

The USAAF* created the first U.S. military air transport unit, the Air Corps Ferrying Command (ACFC), in May 1941 to move U.S.-built planes to Britain as part of Lend-Lease.* By Pearl Harbor,* the ACFC had delivered about 1,350 aircraft to Britain and its allies. U.S. entry into World War II* greatly expanded the activities of the ACFC. It developed air routes to war theaters and acquired new transports* with greater payloads and range. The expansion prompted the USAAF to rename it the Air Transport Command (ATC) in July 1942 and to give it global responsibilities.

The most spectacular ATC operation of the war began on 1 December 1942, after Japan cut water and land access to China in June. President Franklin D. Roosevelt* (FDR) decided to resupply Allied forces in China by air. Known as "Flying the 'Hump'*" because the route crossed the dangerous Himalaya mountains, ATC's C-46,* C-54,* and C-87 aircraft and crews moved nearly 650,000 tons of supplies.

In June 1948, ATC was redesignated the Military Air Transport Service (MATS) and charged with the management of all strategic airlift operations. It included four squadrons of the Naval Air Transport Service (NATS), the Air Weather Service (AWS), the Air Rescue Service (ARS), and the Airways and

Air Communications Service (AACS). The last three had been in the command since 1946.

Only 25 days after MATS was formed, the USSR blockaded West Berlin. MATS' foremost airlift expert, Major General William H. Tunner,* led the international and historic Berlin Airlift.* Less than a year after the successful completion of that airlift, the Korean War* broke out. In the resultant Korean Airlift,* MATS operated a logistical pipeline of nearly 10,000 nautical miles and transported nearly 80,000 tons of cargo and 214,000 personnel from the United States to the Far East. Its aeromedical evacuation* airlift returned 66,536 patients to the United States.

MATS leaders realized the command needed newer aircraft. The workhorse in the 1950s had been the piston-engine C-124.* In 1965, the first jet cargo strategic airlifter, the C-141,* entered the inventory. It, and the larger C-5* which began service in 1969, have since provided effective airlift support for the nation's widespread commitments. Congress acknowledged the command's importance when it directed redesignation to Military Airlift Command (MAC) and placed MAC on a level with the other USAF combat elements in 1966.

In the same year, MAC's Eastern Air Force (EASTAF) was redesignated the Twenty-First Air Force* (21AF), responsible for airlift in the eastern half of the continental United States (CONUS) and the European area; and the Western Air Force (WESTAF) became the Twenty-Second Air Force* (22AF), serving the western CONUS and the Pacific theater. The 21AF was headquartered at McGuire* AFB, New Jersey, and the 22AF at Travis* AFB, California.

The Vietnam War* posed the greatest test of MAC's strategic airlift since World War II. From 1964 to 1973 MAC managed a Vietnam Airlift* over a complicated 10,000-mile supply route to Southeast Asia. MAC transported about two million tons of materiel and more than two million persons in this operation.

Another great challenge arose when President Richard M. Nixon called upon MAC to transport military equipment and supplies to help Israel in its war against Egypt in 1973. In a single 32-day period, MAC flew 422 missions and carried 22,395 tons of critical war materiel from 20 U.S. airports to Lod Airfield in Tel Aviv.

In 1974 MAC was directed to assume responsibility for tactical airlift* as well as strategic airlift. Thus, MAC absorbed the tactical airlift assets of the other USAF commands and was put in charge of combat and intratheater airlift operations. Recognizing the growing importance of airlift, MAC was designated a specified command* in February 1977. In 1983, MAC assumed responsibility for all remaining phases of airlift operations in the USAF. The command merged the special operations forces and rescue* operations into a new Twenty-Third Air Force* (23AF).

In the Grenada incident,* MAC airlifted 15,374 tons of cargo and 35,911 persons between 25 October and 2 November 1983. It also evacuated 709 noncombatant Americans from the island.

In 1987 the U.S. Transportation Command was activated, a unified command* under the Joint Chiefs of Staff (JCS). It comprises MAC,the Military Sealift Command, and the Military Traffic Management Command, which are air, sea, and land components. For the Iraq crisis of 1990–1991,* MAC and the Civil Reserve Air Fleet* (CRAF) flew 1.67 billion ton miles from August to the end of November. By contrast, the Berlin Airlift flew 697.5 million ton miles.

References. Primary: William H. Tunner, *Over the Hump: The Story of William H. Tunner, the Man Who Moved Anything Anywhere, Anytime*, 1964. Secondary: Ray L. Bowers, *Tactical Airlift*, 1983. "Military Airlift Command," *AF*, May 1990, pp. 76–78. Charles E. Miller, *Airlift Doctrine*, 1988. U.S. Congress, House, Committee on Armed Services, Research and Development Subcommittee, *The Posture of Military Airlift*, 1975.

Roger D. Launius

MILITARY AIR TRANSPORT SERVICE. *See* Military Airlift Command.

MILITARY ASSISTANCE PROGRAM (MAP)

As the world's most powerful air force, backed by the arsenal of democracy, the USAF* has been active in helping its allies. This began formally and in earnest with the Mutual Defense Assistance Program (MDAP), created in 1949 after the formation of the North Atlantic Treaty Organization* (NATO). The MDAP's emphasis was on training of all types and on furnishing equipment. It was renamed MAP in 1954. MAP provided extensive help to the Republic of South Vietnam. For the USAF, this began with the Farm Gate* operation. An indication of MAP's contribution is that, in 1963, 1,800 men of the South Vietnamese air force (VNAF) were students. The VNAF's total strength was 7,736 at the time. Of the 1,800, 459 were in training in the United States in 1963. USAF advisers were active in South Vietnam from 1955 to 1965, when the United States decided the advisory method had failed to blunt the rising aggression of North Vietnam.

U.S. arms are not simply given away in MAP. The gifts are usually accompanied by sales to the same countries. Arms are not given or sold unless U.S. agencies believe there is a genuine security need for them. It is not uncommon for U.S. officials to refuse to provide arms and for the requesting country to turn to other nations and get what they wish. There are critics of MAP, who resent the arms business or any giveaways. The critics do not always recognize the policy of genuine security need. Another point critics of MAP often overlook is that providing MAP can reduce the need for the United States to use its own forces in conflicts. Finally, the program enables the United States to promote peace among its clients by influence and by withholding replacement parts and other supplies, should that prove desirable.

References. Berger, *USAF in SEA*. Don Clelland, "Military Assistance Program— MAP for Security," *AF*, April 1973, pp. 68–71. Robert F. Futrell, *The Advisory Years to 1965*, 1981. Goldberg, *Hist. USAF*.

MILITARY AVIATOR RATING

This was the first U.S. Army aviator's rating and was created in February 1912. It replaced the standards of the Fédération Aéronautique Internationale (FAI) pilot certificate. Later in the year a badge was available for the uniform. The badge said "Military Aviator" on a bar with an eagle in flight suspended below. The eagle had the semaphore flags which represented the Signal Corps in its beak. The rating was given to 14 aviators then on duty. One of those men was Lieutenant H. H. Arnold.* The badge was replaced on 24 July 1917 with a new design, a winged shield which is still used.

References. Primary: H. H. Arnold, *Global Mission*, 1949. Secondary: *The Official Pictorial History of the AAF*, 1947.

MILITARY PERSONNEL CENTER. *See* Air Force Military Personnel Center.

MILLER, MAJOR (ALTON) GLENN (1904–1944)

Glenn Miller had a civilian band that was regarded as the most popular one in the United States for more than three years. He formed a special Army Air Force Band after the United States entered World War II.* He altered military music to a new style and established the tradition for the U.S. Air Force Band.* Today's "Airmen of Note" is a unit of the band that typifies the Miller style. As a passenger in a plane, Miller left England in 1944 en route to France. The plane was never found, but in 1984 some Royal Air Force (RAF) bomber* crewmen said they knew what happened. They said they had jettisoned their bombs* from an aborted sortie and the bombs accidentally struck Miller's plane.

References. Napoleon B. Byars, "From Valley Forge to Gabriel," *AF*, December 1984, pp. 74–77. "Tribute to the Major Glenn Miller AAF Band," *United States Air Force Museum Friends Bulletin*, Summer 1988, p. 8.

MINING

Perhaps the least known of the USAF's* major accomplishments and capabilities is aerial mining. Mining disrupts shipping as well as sinks or damages it. In 1945, the USAAF* performed the greatest aerial mining done in history. In 1990, the USAF was able to plant mines as part of its mission to help control the seas.

Mining was not considered a part of strategic operations* in the U.S. Army air arm until 1944, despite the aerial mine laying done by the Luftwaffe and Royal Air Force (RAF) after 1939. The usefulness of aerial mines was appreciated by the U.S. Navy, which also saw that the B-29* could deliver mines effectively. The USAAF wanted to conduct other actions and bowed reluctantly to the Navy's urging to mine. The training of USAAF crews began in February 1945 with Navy help.

The 313th Bombardment Wing (Very Heavy), based on Tinian in the Marianas* Islands, started mining operations in March 1945. A B-29 could carry six tons of mines, which were of either 1,000- or 2,000-pound sizes. By May, mines caused more shipping losses than did submarines. In four and one-half months of mining operations, the 313th conducted 1,528 sorties, laying 12,053 mines at a cost of only nine aircraft to enemy action. While it was mining, the wing's mines accounted for half of Japan's shipping tonnage lost. For the entire war, mines were credited with about 830,000 tons of Japanese ships, and the B-29s dominated the mining totals. In the Vietnam War* the USAF dropped water and land mines in Laos from 1968 to 1971.

References. Primary: Curtis E. LeMay and Bill Yenne, *Superfortress: The Story of the B-29 and American Air Power*, 1988. Secondary: Berger, *USAF in SEA*. C&C, vol. 5. Jeffrey P. Rhodes, "SAC's Sea Patrol," *AF*, October 1987, p. 48. "Strategic Air Command," *AF*, May 1990, p. 83.

MINOT AIR FORCE BASE

Named for the nearby town in North Dakota, Minot is a Strategic Air Command* (SAC) base. The citizens of Minot donated $50,000 toward the purchase of land needed by the USAF* for the field. The USAF occupied it in 1957. At first it was an air defense base with a Semiautomatic Ground Environment* (SAGE) installation. In 1963 facilities were finished for 150 Minuteman* I offensive ballistic missiles.* These were replaced by IIIs with multiple independent re-entry vehicles* (MIRV) in 1971. In 1990 it had the headquarters of the 57th Air Division, the 5th Bomb Wing with B-52s* and KC-135s (*see* C-135) and the 91st Strategic Missile Wing with Minuteman IIIs.

References. "Guide to Major Air Force Installations Worldwide," *AF*, May 1990, p. 128. Mueller, *AFB*. Roberts, *Dir. USAF*.

MINUTEMAN

Minuteman was the world's first solid-fueled intercontinental ballistic missile* (ICBM) and the mainstay of the ICBM leg of the triad.* At the peak, 1,000 Minutemen, made by The Boeing Company, were deployed in subsurface concrete silos. In 1990, there were still 950, and they were expected to be viable into the 21st century.

Minuteman was designed to make full use of the advantages of solid propellants: a smaller, simpler missile capable of instantaneous launch; a long deployment life; smaller launch and maintenance crews; cheaper to buy; and offering a variety of mobile deployment options. Minuteman reached its goals and, in addition, became the most reliable large missile of its era. Although it ended up in stationary silos, experiments were made with a rail-mobile launch system during the early 1960s.

Minuteman I, designated also as HSM-80 at first and then LGM-30A, made its first launch from Cape Canaveral on 1 February 1961 and was operational from 1962 to 1974. The first ones had a single-target capability, but they were quickly superseded by the LGM-30B with memory for two prestored targets.

Minuteman II, or LGM-30F, became operational in 1965. Outwardly it resembled the first versions of the missile and used the same first- and third-stage engines. A larger second stage, however, gave increased range and payload, and an improved guidance system provided greater accuracy and target flexibility. At full deployment, 450 Minuteman IIs stood on alert at Malmstrom* AFB, Montana; Ellsworth* AFB, South Dakota; and Whiteman* AFB, Missouri.

Minuteman III, or LGM-30G, was the final version. A larger third stage matched the diameter of the second stage and offered improved performance; a pointed-arch shroud concealed up to three warheads and completely changed the familiar "stepped" silhouette of the earlier models. The capability to deliver multiple independent re-entry vehicles* (MIRV) greatly added to the deterrent value of the Minuteman system. The deployment of 550 Minuteman IIIs made a total of 1,000. They, with 54 Titan* IIs, comprised the land-based leg of the triad.

Characteristics (Minuteman III): first stage engine, Thiokol M-55 of 210,000 pounds thrust; second stage, Aerojet General SR19-AJ-1 of 60,300 pounds thrust; third stage, Thiokol SR-73-AJ-1 of 34,400 pounds thrust; length, 60 feet; diameter of first stage, 6 feet; launch weight, 78,000 pounds; speed at burnout, 15,000 miles per hour; highest point of trajectory, 700 miles; range, more than 7,000 miles; warheads, three MIRV of about 200 kilotons rating each.

References. Roy Neal, *Ace in the Hole: The Story of the Minuteman Missile*, 1962. Jacob Neufeld, *Ballistic Missiles in the United States Air Force*, 1990. Polmar, *SAC*. Strategic Air Command Office of Public Affairs, "Minuteman Fact Sheet," April 1985. Susan H. H. Young, "Gallery of USAF Weapons," *AF*, May 1990, pp. 155–56.

Raymond L. Puffer

MISAWA AIR BASE

Near the city of Misawa in northern Japan, this is a Pacific Air Forces* (PACAF) airfield. Emperor Meiji's cavalry made the first use of the site, and the imperial Japanese army built an airfield there in 1938. The imperial navy took over in 1942. The USAAF* arrived in September 1945. About 90 percent of it had been destroyed by B-29s* and U.S. Navy aircraft. The base was rebuilt by 1946 and was used by the 49th Fighter Group with F-80s.* Since then it has been a fighter* base for the USAF.* In 1990 it had the 432nd Tactical Fighter Wing (TFW) with F-16s.* The Japanese Air Self-Defense Force also used the facility.

References. William R. (Ross) Graham, *Misawa: The Air Base and City*, 1982. "Guide to Major Air Force Installations Worldwide," *AF*, May 1990, p. 128. Roberts, *Dir. USAF*.

MISSILES. *See* ballistic missiles; cruise missiles.

MITCHEL AIR FORCE BASE

Located on an airfield in New York that predated World War I,* Mitchel AFB was an important air base. It was established as a U.S. Army field in 1918 and named for Major John P. Mitchel who died in an aircraft accident. He had been the mayor of New York City. Permanent buildings were built in the 1930s. Many famous flights involved the field, including Lieutenant James Doolittle's* first blind flight. It was the base for the 9th Bombardment Group (Medium), which was a part of the General Headquarters Air Force* (GHQ Air Force). After World War II* it had the headquarters of the Air Defense Command and U.S. Air Force Reserve* (USAFR) units. Mitchel ceased to be a USAF installation in 1963.

References. "Air Force Magazine Guide to Air Force Bases," *AF*, September 1960, p. 229. Robert F. Schirmer, "Memories of Mitchel Field," *AH*, September 1986, pp. 190–98.

MITCHELL, MAJOR GENERAL WILLIAM "BILLY" (1879–1936)

Mitchell was the leading U.S. prophet of air power. He was chief of Air Service in Europe for the American World War I* air effort, combat leader, pilot,* strategic* and tactical* operations author, first American spokesman for a separate air force, and critic of neglect of the air services. His writings incorporated others' ideas. Though his scholarship was criticized, he distinguished himself from scholars by developing theories into tactics. He was the first to show the effectiveness of aircraft against warships by sinking the battleship SMS *Ostfriesland*. His critics regarded him as an irksome, flamboyant showman and propagandist with incorrect ideas. He went over the heads of his superiors to appeal to the American public for support for air power. While he lived, the public, in love with flying, was receptive to his ideas but would not upset the existing order during the complacency of peacetime. In the dark days of defeat and enemy air dominance (1940 to 1942), he was remembered by the public who felt Mitchell had been vindicated. In 1947 to 1948, Congress posthumously compared his fate to that of Joan of Arc, promoted him to major general, and awarded him a special medal. In 1966 he was inducted into the National Aviation Hall of Fame in Dayton, Ohio.

Mitchell was born in Nice, France, the son of a U.S. senator from Wisconsin. He graduated from George Washington University in 1899 after enlisting in the U.S. Volunteers. In 1903 he became the youngest captain in the U.S. Army. In 1913 he was the youngest officer ever to be selected for the War Department general staff. At the unusually old age of 36, he learned to fly in his off-duty time at the Curtiss Company's school in Newport News, Virginia.

In World War I,* he directed the U.S. air effort in the St. Mihiel* and Meuse-Argonne* campaigns. In 1921 Mitchell became assistant to the chief of Air Service* and conducted the famous Mitchell bombing tests on warships.* Following the crash of the naval airship USS *Shenandoah*, Mitchell accused the U.S. Navy of incompetence, criminal negligence, and virtually treasonous administration. He also asserted that the War and Navy Departments were giving false information to Congress. Mitchell was court-martialed for this insubordination in 1925 and used the trial as a platform to address the public. Found guilty, Mitchell resigned his commission in 1926. An aftermath was that President Calvin Coolidge asked Dwight Morrow to be chairman of the President's

Aircraft Board* to investigate U.S. military aviation, which resulted in some improvements. One was the Air Corps Act* which elevated the USAAS* into the USAAC.*

Mitchell's main ideas were to divide offensive air power into fighter,* bomber,* and attack;* all of which he believed must work together. He wrote that the application of air power meant attaining air superiority* through air combat and then carrying the war to the enemy's heartland, that armies and navies cannot exist without air power, that air power makes war sharper and more decisive, that speed is the main characteristic of air power, and that air power is the most efficient means of defense.

Movie: The Court Martial of Billy Mitchell, 1955.

References. Primary: William Mitchell, *Our Air Force: Keystone of National Defense*, 1921, and *Winged Defense*, 1925. Secondary: Burke Davis, *The Billy Mitchell Affair*, 1967. John L. Frisbee, "Warrior, Prophet, Martyr," *AF*, September 1985, pp. 158–66. Futrell, *Ideas*, vol. 1. Alfred F. Hurley, *Billy Mitchell, Crusader for Air Power*, 1975. Isaac D. Levine, *Mitchell: Pioneer of Air Power*, rev. ed., 1958.

Thomas C. Blow II

MITCHELL. *See* B-25.

MITCHELL'S BOMBING TESTS ON WARSHIPS

In defending the United States, the U.S. Army and Navy had an overlapping capability in coastal areas. The development of the military airplane, to which the demarkation between water and land meant nothing, obviously had effects on planning and conflicts for U.S. coastal defense.

In March 1919, Brigadier General William Mitchell* proposed a test of the effectiveness of aircraft when used against ships. Mitchell believed that ships were highly vulnerable to aircraft. He did not get approval until after the Navy had conducted tests in 1920, but these did not include dropping live bombs* from airplanes. Mitchell's tests, called project B, started in 1921 under Navy rules using surrendered German warships. Mitchell's aircraft sank each ship they attacked, the destroyer G-102, cruiser SMS *Frankfurt*, and battleship SMS *Ostfriesland*. The tests made Mitchell a hero to the U.S. public, and he believed he had verified his beliefs about the effectiveness of aircraft operating against ships. The Navy downgraded the results by saying that Mitchell had good weather, the airmen did not have to search for the ships, the ships lacked crews for damage control, the ships were not defended, and the ships were not under way. A Joint Army and Navy Board claimed the tests did not make the battleship obsolete.

In September, Mitchell conducted his own tests on the USS *Alabama*, a battleship out of commission. The USAAS learned some tactics from attacking and sinking the ship. The 1921 Washington Conference for the Limitation of Armament terms provided some U.S. battleships for scrapping, and Mitchell got the USS *New Jersey* and *Virginia* for more tests. Unable to conduct the tests as he wished, Mitchell nevertheless sank both ships. These last tests had no effects upon Mitchell's military superiors or on public opinion.

References. Primary: William Mitchell, *Winged Defense*, 1925. Secondary: Maurer, *Avn. in Army*. David Nevin, *Architects of Air Power*, a vol. in *The Epic of Flight*, 1981. Dale L. Walker, "The Bombing at Virginia Capes," *AAHS Journal*, Fall 1971, pp. 170–74.

See also Bismarck Sea, Battle of the.

MITRE. *See* think tanks.

MK-20 ROCKEYE

The Rockeye cluster is one of the U.S. Navy series of "eye" weapons. Entering service in 1968, it soon became the standard antitank cluster bomb.* The Rockeye weighs 500 pounds and originally carried 247 Mk 118 antitank bomblets. In 1974, an improved version with 717 BLU-77 antipersonnel, anti-materiel (AP/AM) target-discriminating bomblets went into production.

The Mk–20 is free-dropped from high-speed aircraft. At a predetermined height the fuze functions, splitting the bomb lengthwise and releasing the bomblets. The bomblet "footprint" covers a large area, and the shaped-charge warhead will penetrate the thin top armor of any known vehicle. The BLU-77 explodes as a shaped-charge, antitank warhead if a hard target is struck; if a soft target is hit, a small charge in the front throws the body of the bomblet a few feet in the air where it explodes like an air burst fragmentation grenade.

References. Norman Friedman, *U.S. Naval Weapons*, 1983. Gunston, *Airc. Arm.*

Philip Long

MOMYER, GENERAL WILLIAM W. "SPIKE" (1916–)

Momyer was the commander of the Tactical Air Command* (TAC) from 1968 to 1973 and is the author of two books: *The Vietnamese Air Force, 1951–75: An Analysis of Its Role in Combat* (1975) and *Airpower in Three Wars* (1978). He has contributed to tactical operations* thinking and was an outspoken opponent of using helicopters* for attack.*

Born in Muskogee, Oklahoma, he graduated from the University of Washington in 1937. He then enrolled as an aviation cadet,* becoming a pilot* and officer in 1939. He was commander of the 33rd Pursuit Group in October 1942, and he led the unit in the North Africa, Sicily, and Naples-Foggia campaigns. In 1944, he returned to the United States where he became chief of combined operations for the Army Air Forces Board. He also played a major role in developing air-ground operations doctrine.

From 1946 to 1958, he served in tactical command and staff positions. From 1958 to 1961, he was first director and later deputy chief of staff for plans in TAC. From 1961 to 1964, Momyer was at headquarters of the USAF, first as deputy for plans and later as assistant deputy chief of staff for programs and requirements. From 1964 to 1966 he was commander of the Air Training Command* (ATC). From 1966 to 1968, Momyer was deputy commander for air operations of the Military Assistance Command, Vietnam (MACV), serving at the same time as commander of the Seventh Air Force* (7AF).

References. Primary: Jack Broughton, *Going Downtown: The War against Hanoi and Washington*, 1988. Richard H. Kohn and Joseph P. Harahan, eds., *Air Superiority in World War II and Korea: An Interview with General James Ferguson, General Robert M. Lee, General William Momyer and General Elwood R. Quesada*, 1983. Secondary: Futrell, *Ideas*, vol. 2. Official Histories, Tactical Air Command, 1968–73 (Unclassified Extracts). Official USAF Biography, 1 May 1971.

David L. Rosmer

MOODY AIR FORCE BASE

Located just northeast of Valdosta, Georgia, Moody originated with a plan by county business and civic leaders in 1940 to help the growing U.S. defense effort and to take advantage of its economic benefits. In 1942, Moody Field Advanced Pilot Training School began operations, using Beech Aircraft Corporation's AT-10 trainers. The field was named for Major George P. Moody, who died in testing the new AT-10.

Put on inactive status in 1946, Moody was reactivated in 1951 to train aircrews for the Korean War.* During this period, the USAF's* Instrument Pilot School and later the Instrument Pilot Instructor Flying School were at Moody. Initially, the Air Training Command* (ATC) used F-89s* and F-94s for this training but replaced them in 1957 with F-86s.* In 1960, Moody became responsible for preflight, primary, and basic flying training,* using T-33s and T-37s.* The T-38* became the main mission aircraft in 1963. The Tactical Air Command* (TAC) assumed control of the base and activated an F-4E* unit, the 347th Tactical Fighter Wing (TFW), in 1975. In 1987, the 347th began converting to F-16s,* which it still had in 1990.

References. "Guide to Major Air Force Installations Worldwide," *AF*, May 1990, p. 128. Mueller, *AFB*. Official USAF History, Moody AFB, Georgia, 347th Public Affairs Office, 1988. Roberts, *Dir. USAF*.

David L. Rosmer

MOORE, LIEUTENANT GENERAL JOSEPH H. (1914–)

Moore had a distinguished career in battle and as a tactical operations* commander. Reared in South Carolina, he was educated at Wofford and Centenary Colleges in Louisiana. He became an aviation cadet* in 1937, receiving his wings and commission in 1938. When the Japanese attacked Clark* Field, Philippines, on 8 December 1941, Lieutenant Moore was a squadron* commander and one of the few pilots* able to get into the air. By the time he evacuated to Australia in 1942, he had flown more than 100 combat hours in P-40s.* Later, he took part in the Normandy, northern France, and Rhineland campaigns. He assumed command of the 137th Fighter-Bomber Wing in 1951, and became vice chief of staff of the U.S. Air Forces in Europe* (USAFE) in 1954. He held similar commands until he became commander of the 2nd Air Division in Vietnam in 1964. The next year he was made deputy commander for air operations of the Military Assistance Command, Vietnam (MACV). When the Seventh Air

Force* (7AF) was reactivated in 1966, he became its commander. His final assignment was as commander of the Sixth Allied Tactical Air Force in Europe.

References. Official USAF Biography, 15 August 1967, updated, USAFHRC, Maxwell AFB, Alabama, 1971. David L. Rosmer, *An Annotated Pictorial History of Clark Air Base*, Thirteenth Air Force Office of History, 1986.

David L. Rosmer

MORROW BOARD. *See* President's Aircraft Board.

MOSQUITO. *See* forward air controller; T-6.

MOUNTAIN HOME AIR FORCE BASE

This Tactical Air Command* (TAC) base near the city of Mountain Home, Idaho, was established in 1942. The training of bomber* crews was conducted there in World War II.* It was inactive or partially used from the end of the war until 1949 when it became a strategic reconnaissance* field. B-47s* arrived in 1954, and it had a strategic operations* mission when Titan* Is were used from 1962 to 1964. Then the base hosted RF-4s (*see* F-4) but changed to F-111s* in 1971. In 1990 the 366th Tactical Fighter Wing (TFW) was there, using F-111As and EF-111As (*see* F-111).

References. "Guide to Major Air Force Installations Worldwide," *AF*, May 1990, p. 128. Mueller, *AFB*. Roberts, *Dir. USAF*.

MOVIES

Since movies have a significant effect upon image, they are important to USAF* history. For example, *Wings* (1927), which was about the USAAS* in World War I,* influenced favorably the recruitment of pilots.* A later movie about USAAC* flight training,* *West Point of the Air* (1935) continued this effect.

In World War II,* movies about flight training appeared first. Examples were *I Wanted Wings* (1941), *Keep 'Em Flying* (1941), *Thunderbirds* (1942), *Aerial Gunner* (1943), and *Bombardier* (1943). Later, films about battle were popular, including *Flying Tigers* (1942), *A Guy Named Joe* (1943), *Thirty Seconds over Tokyo* (1944), and the effective *Air Force** (1943). Other noteworthy movies were *Ladies Courageous* (1944) and *Winged Victory* (1944). An influential movie about air power theory was a movie version of Major Alexander P. de Seversky's* book, *Victory through Air Power* (1943).

The USAAF* itself produced some documentary films for popular consumption and recruiting including *Winning Your Wings* (1942), *The Rear Gunner* (1943), *Wings Up* (1943), *Combat America* (1943), *Memphis Belle** (1944), and *Thunderbolt* (1945).

World War II, the Korean War,* and the USAF stayed in high regard in the immediate postwar years with movies including *Command Decision** (1948), *Fighter Squadron* (1948), *Twelve O'Clock High** (1950), *Chain Lightning* (1950), *Wild Blue Yonder* (1952), *Fighter Attack* (1953), *Sabre Jet* (1953), *Flight*

Nurse (1953), *Above and Beyond* (1953), *Strategic Air Command* (1955), *Toward the Unknown* (1956), *The Hunters** (1956), *Jet Pilot* (1957), *Bombers B-52* (1957), *China Doll* (1958), *Thundering Jets* (1958), *No Time for Sergeants* (1958), *X-15* (1961), *The War Lover** (1962), and *A Gathering of Eagles** (1963).

The spirit of the 1960s saw the USAF fall from favor with Hollywood, and the movies turned unfriendly. Films reflecting this change include *Fail-Safe* (1964), *Dr. Strangelove or: How I Learned to Stop Worrying and Love the Bomb** (1964), *Catch–22** (1970), and *Sole Survivor* (1970).

After the 1960s there was some return to the traditional with *The Thousand Plane Raid* (1969), *Hanover Street* (1979), *Enola Gay* (1980), *Red Flag: The Ultimate Game* (1981), *Hanoi Hilton* (1987), *BAT-21* (1989), and the commercial *Memphis Belle** (1990).

References. James H. Farmer, *Celluloid Wings*, 1984. "The 40th Anniversary of the USAF," a special issue of *AH*, September 1987, pp. 206–13. Jim and Maxine Greenwood, *Stunt Flying in the Movies*, 1982. Bruce W. Orriss, *When Hollywood Ruled the Skies*, 1984. Lawrence H. Suid, *Guts and Glory: Great American War Movies*, 1978.

See also novels; television.

MPC. *See* Air Force Military Personnel Center.

MULTIPLE INDEPENDENTLY TARGETABLE RE-ENTRY VEHICLE. *See* multiple independent re-entry vehicle (MIRV).

MULTIPLE INDEPENDENT RE-ENTRY VEHICLE (MIRV)

MIRV, also called multiple independently targetable re-entry vehicle, is a system of putting several warheads aimed at different targets onto one ballistic missile.* MIRV has greatly enhanced the effectiveness of USAF* ballistic missiles using nuclear weapons.* MIRV became a part of the Minuteman* III intercontinental ballistic missile (ICBM), entering active service in 1970 with the 741st Strategic Missile Squadron at Minot* AFB, North Dakota.

References. Ernest J. Gentle and Lawrence W. Reithmaier, eds., *Aviation/Space Dictionary*, 6th ed., 1980. Polmar, *SAC*.

MUSEUMS

In 1987 there were 30 museums in the USAF,* which was up from around ten in 1971. The increased interest in museums illustrated by this growth was inspired by the USAF Museum Program (USAFMP) of 1982. The core museum has been the U.S. Air Force Museum* at Wright-Patterson* AFB in Ohio, a specialized unit of the Air Force Logistics Command* (AFLC). It is the oldest and largest aviation museum in the world, established in 1923. Its current name was adopted in 1956. Exhibits include more than 200 aircraft and large missiles. Other USAF museums tend to specialize. The total aircraft and large missiles for all 30 museums in 1987 was 1,509.

References. "The 40th Anniversary of the USAF," a special issue of *AH*, September 1987, pp. 214–20. U.S. Air Force Fact Sheet 86–12, "Air Force Logistics Command," April 1986.

MUSTANG. *See* F-51.

MUTUAL DEFENSE ASSISTANCE PROGRAM (MDAP). *See* Military Assistance Program.

MX. *See* Peacekeeper.

MYRTLE BEACH AIR FORCE BASE

This field is at the southern edge of the city of Myrtle Beach, South Carolina. Begun as a municipal airport in 1940, it was taken over by the federal government and designated as Myrtle Beach Army Airfield in 1943. It served as a replacement crew training center, bombing-gunnery range, and as a prisoner of war (POW) camp.

After 1945, it became a location for the Civil Air Patrol* (CAP), Air National Guard* (ANG), and U.S. Military Academy (USMA) encampments until its inactivation in 1947 and reversion to municipal control. Local businessmen succeeded in getting the USAF* to resume control of the base in 1954 and to reactivate it as a Tactical Air Command* (TAC) installation in 1956. The host unit was TAC's 354th Fighter-Day Wing, now the 354th Tactical Fighter Wing (TFW), which had been activated earlier in 1956. The 354th became fully equipped with F-100D* aircraft by the end of 1957 and participated in several major events, including the Vietnam War,* before converting to A-7Ds* in 1970. First to fly the A-7D in battle, the 354th fired the United States's last shots and dropped its last bombs* of the war on 15 August 1973.

Redeployed to Myrtle Beach by the end of 1974, the 354th began converting to A-10A* aircraft in early 1977. The conversion was completed in 1978 and the 354th was the USAF's first operational A-10 wing. In 1975 the Myrtle Beach jetport became colocated on the base, and civilian aircraft now share the base's runways.

References. "Guide to Major Air Force Installations Worldwide," *AF*, May 1990, p. 128. Mueller, *AFB*. Official USAF History, Myrtle Beach AFB, South Carolina, 354TFW Public Affairs Office, 1989. Roberts, *Dir. USAF*.

David L. Rosmer

N

NACA. *See* National Aeronautics and Space Administration.

NAGASAKI, JAPAN. *See* Hiroshima and Nagasaki, Japan.

NAKHON PHANOM ROYAL THAI AIR FORCE BASE

This field is in Thailand near the Laotian border and once based USAF*
A-1Es* and O-1 Bird Dogs* beginning in April 1967. These planes were used
in reconnaissance* and forward air controller* (FAC) action in Steel Tiger* and
Barrel Roll* missions. O-2s* later replaced the O-1s. Further changes were the
addition of B-26 Invaders* and AC-47s (*see* C-47) and their replacement by
AC-119s (*see* C-119) and AC-130s (*see* C-130). An Infiltration Surveillance
Center (ISC) was also based there. The USAF left this field in 1974. It had the
nickname in the USAF of "Naked Fanny."

References. Primary: Richard S. Drury, *My Secret War*, 2d ed., 1979. Berger, *USAF
in SEA*. John Schlight, *The War in South Vietnam: The Years of the Offensive 1965–
1968*, 1988.

"NAP." *See* Gorrell, Colonel Edgar S.

NAPALM

This is an anagram from the *na*phthenic and *palm*iyic acids used as thickeners
for the fuel. Developed by the U.S. Army in 1941 for flamethrowers, napalm
stuck to its target and burned more fiercely than straight fuel. First used during
the Marianas* campaign in 1944, the original napalm was corrosive to aluminum
and had to be mixed just before use. Modern napalm is storable and is issued
premixed. Napalm bombs* are of light metal construction similar to drop tanks*
and are fitted with white phosphorous or magnesium-teflon igniters and all-ways-
acting fuses. Napalm is very effective against field fortifications, vehicles, and
troops in the open.

References. Berger, *USAF in SEA*. C&C, vol. 5. Norman Friedman, *U.S. Naval Weapons*, 1984. Futrell, *USAF in Korea*.

Philip Long

NARSARSSUAK, GREENLAND. *See* North Atlantic air bases.

NASA. *See* National Aeronautics and Space Administration.

NATIONAL ADVISORY COMMITTEE FOR AERONAUTICS (NACA). *See* National Aeronautics and Space Administration.

NATIONAL AERONAUTICS AND SPACE ADMINISTRATION (NASA)

NASA's antecedent organization, the National Advisory Committee for Aeronautics (NACA), was created in 1915. Its charter was to keep the United States ahead technologically in aeronautics, a critical matter for aerospace power* and the USAF.*

Between World Wars I* and II,* NACA did much useful work in drag reduction, airframe structures, and stability and control. These contributed to the technological revolution in aviation. NACA's wind tunnels and research exemplified federal laboratories assisting industry. During World War II, NACA concentrated on problems associated with the existing aircraft designs to be used in the war.

When the war was over, many great advancements in aeronautics were ready for further exploitation. The jet engine was in its early stages. Even then it called for radically new shapes and structures like swept wings, delta wings, and engine locations. The big rocket engine had already produced a ballistic missile,* the German V-2, which had first penetrated into space in 1942. Electronics was also in its early stages. There were intensive research efforts to exploit these potentials by industry, the armed forces, and NACA. Sometimes the efforts were done jointly, as with the X-15.* The principal postwar contributions of NACA and NASA to the USAF has been in swept wings, the area rule,** and space operations research.

In 1957, the USSR put the first artificial earth satellite, *Sputnik*, into orbit. The United States was shocked at the Soviet lead in missiles and space vehicles. NACA was reorganized and was renamed NASA to reflect the attempt to reinvigorate it and reorient it with an emphasis on space activities. In the 1960s, the aerospace industry* and NASA had magnificent accomplishments in space, exemplified by a man's first walk on the moon in 1969. In 1986, the luster was tarnished by the loss of the space shuttle *Challenger*. NASA had other difficulties in the late 1980s, followed by the Hubble Space Telescope scandal; accusations were made that it had grown bureaucratic and inefficient. In 1990, a White House Committee led by Norman Augustine, chief executive officer of Martin Marietta Corporation, was asked to recommend corrective actions for NASA.

References. Primary: James R. Hansen, *Engineer in Charge: A History of Langley Aeronautical Laboratory, 1917–1958*, 1985. Secondary: Eugene M. Emme, *Aeronautics* *and Astronautics: An American Chronology of Science and Technology in the Exploration of Space, 1915–1960,* 1961. Futrell, *Ideas,* vol. 2. George W. Gray, *Frontiers of Flight: The Story of NACA Research,* 1948. Laurence K. Loftin, Jr., *Quest for Performance: The Evolution of Modern Aircraft,* 1985.

**The area rule, developed by Richard T. Whitcomb, changes the cross-section of airframe bodies to reduce drag. It can result in a "coke-bottle" shape for the fuselage.

See also Air Force Systems Command; astronauts; Scientific Advisory Board.

NATIONAL DEFENSE ACT OF 1916

This act of June 1916 was favorable to the Aviation Section of the U.S. Army Signal Corps.* It increased the authorized officer strength from 60 to 148. Marital and age restrictions on officers were ended, and provisions were made for a reserve corps of Aviation Section officers and men. The act was inadequate in terms of creating sufficient Army aviation for the unforeseen needs ahead, but it was a step in the right direction. It resulted in expanded manpower and training facilities.

References. Goldberg, *Hist. USAF.* Juliette A. Hennessy, *The United States Army Air Arm April 1861 to April 1917,* 1985.

NATIONAL DEFENSE ACT OF 1920

This act reorganized the U.S. Army in the light of World War I* and for the peacetime future. It resulted in a small Army designed to fight any future war with citizen soldiers. The role of aviation in this Army was to continue to be a subject of debate.

The USAAS* in 1919 performed administrative tasks, with operational control under ground-force commanders unless a unit was especially assigned to the USAAS. Such assignment was typically for exercises or special projects. Congress had been presented with alternatives. The Crowell Commission's* report sought a secretary of air to oversee all U.S. aviation, and bills were introduced to create a U.S. Air Force. None of the alternatives were chosen, and the act kept the former status of the USAAS. While the act was in effect, funding for airmen was quite low, and there were demotions. The number of air officers fell to 996 by 1926, and the number of enlisted men hit a low of 7,160 in 1921. The act was replaced by the Air Corps Act* of 1926.

References. Goldberg, *Hist. USAF,* 1957. Maurer, *Avn. in Army.*

NATIONAL EMERGENCY AIRBORNE COMMAND POST (NEACP).
See E-4; Post Attack Command and Control System.

NATIONAL SECURITY ACT OF 1947

This act provided the air force with the independence and separation from the U.S. Army* it had sought for three decades. It created the modern USAF.*

In 1946, President Harry S Truman* (HST) ordered the U.S. Army and Navy to draft a legislative proposal for the unification of the armed forces. He wanted to ensure that the experiences and lessons of World War II* would be codified.

Secretary of War Robert P. Patterson selected USAAF* Major General Lauris Norstad* to represent the War Department, and Secretary James V. Forrestal* chose Admiral Forrest Sherman for the Navy to agree on provisions for the bill. At meetings they agreed that a single theater commander would control all armed forces in his area. These would be called unified commands* and would exist for Europe and the Far East. The commanders were required to use a staff drawn from all services.

Next Patterson and Forrestal drew up draft legislation together with a proposed executive order on roles and missions. They provided for a secretary of national defense; Departments of Army, Navy, and Air Force; Joint Chiefs of Staff; War Council; Council of National Defense; National Security Resources Board; and Central Intelligence Agency. The Navy would keep its own and the U.S. Marine air forces. In the draft, the USAAF had sought centralized control and management. The Navy feared this and tried to make the unified system one of coordination. The final bill was closer to the Navy's decentralization desires than the USAAF's.

The National Security Act, Public Law 253, was signed into law by HST on 26 July 1947. At the same time, he signed Executive Order 9877.* As passed, the act created the USAF, National Security Council, National Security Resources Board, Joint Chiefs of Staff, Research and Development Board, Munitions Board, and Central Intelligence Agency. The USAF came into existence on 18 September 1947. Forrestal became the first secretary of defense (SECDEF).

Performance under the decentralized act led to dissatisfactions with it, and subsequent legislation from 1949 to 1958 created a tightly centralized department of defense (DoD). The centralization under a "super secretary" of defense was finally realized with Secretary Robert S. McNamara* in 1961.

References. "The 40th Anniversary of the USAF," a special issue of *AH*, September 1987. Goldberg, *Hist. USAF*. Herman W. Wolk, "The Birth of the US Air Force," *AF*, September 1977, pp. 68–72, 75–78, and "The Establishment of the United States Air Force," *AF*, September 1982, pp. 76–80, 83–84, 87.

NAVAHO

After World War II,* the USAAF* wanted to develop a new vehicle based upon the German V-1 and V-2. The former was a cruise* and the latter a ballistic* missile. The plan was to add wings to the V-2, substitute a ramjet for the internal rocket engine, and add a booster engine. The booster was intended to give the missile intercontinental ranges. The contractor was North American Aviation, Inc.

Testing was done with a similar vehicle, the X-10. It used turbojet engines and achieved the goals of the test program. It was first flown in 1953. Designated in 1950 the Navaho, XMS-64, and B-64, the final vehicle concept was first test flown in 1956. The flight was unsuccessful, lasting only 26 seconds. A successful flight, on the 11th try, was made in 1957. There were many difficulties with it, mainly with the engine and external power unit. It acquired the nickname "Never go, Navaho.'' The program had been changed to a cruise missile when it was canceled in 1957.

Further launches were attempted in 1958 for testing purposes. The longest flight lasted 42 minutes, and the highest speed attained was over Mach 3. The research done on the Navaho contributed to the U.S. Army's Redstone missile engine, Thor,* Atlas,* USS *Nautilus* submarine, and the U.S. Navy's A3J-1.

Characteristics: engines, two RJ47s with 20,070 pounds thrust each; span, 40 feet; length, 87 feet; gross weight, 120,500 pounds; range, 5,500 miles; warhead, 7,000 pounds. The booster weighed 169,500 pounds and produced 415,000 pounds of thrust.

References. Jay Miller, *The X-Planes*, rev. ed., 1988. Jacob Neufeld, *Ballistic Missiles in the United States Air Force 1945–1960*, 1990. Kenneth P. Werrell, *The Evolution of the Cruise Missile*, 1985. Bill Yenne, *Rockwell: The Heritage of North American*, 1989.

NAVIGATION. *See* navigator.

NAVIGATION COMPETITION. *See* competitions.

NAVIGATOR

The navigator has been an aircrew specialty in the USAF* for a half-century. Until World War II,* there was no rating for navigators. On flights requiring navigation skills, the task was done by a pilot.* In the war, it became efficient to specialize, especially when ocean crossings became frequent.

The first specialist navigation training for the USAAC* was done under contract by Pan American World Airways in Miami, Florida, with the University of Miami furnishing the classrooms and quarters. Eventually, six bases trained navigators for the war: Barksdale* Field, Louisiana; Ellington, Hondo, and Kelly* Fields, Texas; Mather* Field, California; and Turner Field, Georgia. The green navigators performed well; only a few aircraft were lost to their mistakes. Two navigators won the Air Force Medal of Honor,* Second Lieutenants Robert E. Femoyer and Walter E. Truemper.

After the war, the specialist bombardier* became unnecessary and his tasks were merged with those of the navigator. The combined job was labeled aircraft observer for a short period. In the mid–1970s navigator training for all the services became a USAF responsibility. The increased use of radar* and other electronics led to some navigators becoming weapon system officers.* At the same time, electronic warfare* became more important and this task also fell to rated navigators.

Because of these technological changes, the USAF has altered its training. Until 1986, all navigators received the same training for their rating, and it was called Undergraduate Navigator Training (UNT). In 1986, the training became Specialized Undergraduate Navigator Training (SUNT). In this program, a trainee studies in one of three systems: fighter*-attack*-reconnaissance,* tanker*-transport*-bomber,* or electronic warfare. Since the mid–1960s, the USAF has conducted all its navigator training at Mather. When Mather closes in 1993, the school is scheduled to move to Beale* AFB, California.

References. Primary: Charles D. Bright, "Navigating in the Big League," *AH*, December 1988, pp. 259–65. Monte Duane Wright, *Most Probable Position: A History of Aerial Navigation to 1941*, 1972. Secondary: Bruce D. Callander, "Navigators with a Difference," *AF*, December 1987, pp. 68–76. Jeffrey P. Rhodes, "Slam 'Em and Jam 'Em," *AF*, June 1989, pp. 50–56. Ralph R. Williams, "Navigation: From Dead Reckoning to Navstar GPS," *AF*, December 1984, pp. 62–68.

NBL-1. *See* Barling bomber.

NEACP. *See* E-4; Post Attack Command and Control System.

NELLIS AIR FORCE BASE

This Tactical Air Command* (TAC) base is near Las Vegas, Nevada. It was established in 1941 and was named for the city until 1950. Then it was named for First Lieutenant William H. Nellis, an F-47* pilot* killed in action in 1944. Nellis calls itself "The Home of the Fighter Pilot."** During World War II,* the base trained aerial gunners.* From 1947 to 1950 the field was closed. In 1950, it began training fighter* pilots in weaponry. The Thunderbirds* demonstration team moved to Nellis from Luke* AFB, Arizona, in 1956. Red Flag* operations began in 1975. In 1990 it had the USAF Tactical Fighter Weapons Center and the 57th Fighter Weapons Wing. The aircraft used were A-7s,* A-10s,* F-5s,* F-15s,* F-16s,* F-111s,* F-117s,* and T-38s.*

References. "Guide to Major Air Force Installations Worldwide," *AF*, May 1990, p. 128. George Hall, *Nellis: The Home of 'Red Flag,'* 1988. T. R. Milton, "Nellis and the Art of Airpower," *AF*, July 1987, pp. 80–85. Mueller, *AFB*. Roberts, *Dir. USAF*.

**Luke AFB also claims to be "The Home of the Fighter Pilot."

NEUTRAL COUNTRIES

World War II,* with long-range air actions and neutral countries nearby the routes, posed the possibility of conflict, mistaken identity, and internment. The largest potential problem was Switzerland, for years surrounded by Axis territory. The Swiss air force's practice of using interned aircraft aggravated the possibilities. Considering the scale of operations, U.S. incidents with neutrals were probably minimal.

In its aircraft identification sessions, the Eighth Air Force* (8AF) warned that the Swiss were operating both German and U.S. aircraft, and the Swedes were using B-17s.* Conflict was not totally avoided. In September 1944, 8AF F-51s* engaged three Bf 109s and claimed two. It turned out they were being flown by the Swiss. One of the two claims was not destroyed but was badly damaged. Fortunately, the pilot* of the Bf 109 shot down parachuted successfully. This was not the worst incident for the Swiss. In April 1944, 38 B-24s* went off course and mistakenly bombed Schaffhausen, Switzerland. The last unfortunate events occurred despite an 8AF order putting a 50-mile buffer zone around Switzerland for visual bombing and 150 miles for radar* bombing. Nevertheless, Schaffhausen was hit again in February 1945. The next month was even grimmer, because nine B-24s bombed Basle and six struck Zurich.

Internment also caused concern. The first Americans interned in Switzerland came on 17 August 1943, from the famous Schweinfurt*-Regensburg raid. Two battle-damaged B-17s landed in the neutral country. Sweden acquired bombers* over several months until 20 June 1944 when a shocking 19 B-24s and one B-17 landed there. There were reports that many had no battle damage. The number of crews interned by the end of July in Switzerland was 101 and there were 94 in Sweden. U.S. diplomats in those countries believed, on the basis of their interrogations of the crews, that there were many cases of cowardice. General Carl A. Spaatz,* commander of the U.S. Strategic Air Forces* (USSTAF), demanded that knowledgeable military officers be permitted to question the crews. The investigation was done in August and September. No cases of cowardice were confirmed. The biggest problem found was a determination of some Americans to escape from the internment.

References. Primary: Charles C. McBride, *Mission Failure and Survival*, 1990. John W. Woolnough, ed., *The Second Five Years of The 8th AF News 1980–1984*, 1985, and *Stories of the Eighth: An Anthology of the 8th Air Force in World War Two*, 1983. Secondary: C&C, vol. 3. Robert M. Foose, "USAAF Aircraft in Switzerland," *United States Air Force Museum Friends Bulletin*, Winter 1990, pp. 18–22. Roger A. Freeman, *The Mighty Eighth: Units, Men and Machines*, 1970.

NEWARK AIR FORCE BASE

This facility is near and named for Newark, Ohio. An Air Force Logistics Command* (AFLC) base, it was activated in 1962. In 1990 it had the Aerospace Guidance and Meteorology Center, a facility doing mostly repair work.

References. "Guide to Major Air Force Installations Worldwide," *AF*, May 1990, p. 128. Roberts, *Dir. USAF*.

NEW GUINEA

The USAAF* fought a long, hard attrition campaign in New Guinea from 1942 to 1944, and it was a model effort. In the spring of 1942, the rapidly expanding Japanese Empire landed forces in New Guinea, a springboard for a possible assault on Australia. In May they were moving on Port Moresby, located on the southeast coast of the island. Their fleet was turned back in May in the Battle of the Coral Sea. With their landing force repulsed, the Japanese moved on Port Moresby overland out of Buna, on the north coast, in July. By September, the Japanese had reached their high-water mark of 30 miles from Port Moresby. Major General George C. Kenney* became commander of the Allied Air Forces in the area and formed the Americans into the Fifth Air Force* (5AF).

Kenney began an air superiority* campaign. He started by attempting to take out the enemy air operations from the airfields at Buna and Lae. These fields were attacked by A-20s,* B-17s,* and B-25s.* After air superiority was gained, Kenney airlifted 4,500 soldiers in to provide the means for a counteroffensive on the ground. Then troops were moved by tactical airlift* to the vicinity of Buna, which fell in January 1943.

In March, the Japanese attempted to reinforce Lae with a 16-ship convoy. In the ensuing three-day Battle of the Bismarck Sea,* the USAAF sank all the ships except for four destroyers. The next step was to destroy Japanese air power at Wewak, to the west of Lae. On 17 and 18 August, 175 enemy aircraft* were destroyed on the ground. This done, the Japanese garrisons at Salamaua were bypassed and tactical airlift dropped soldiers to take Lae. The emphasis then switched to neutralizing the main base at Rabaul,* New Britain.

In March 1944, the immediate objective switched back to New Guinea in a campaign to take Hollandia, west of Wewak, which was to be bypassed. In the first days of April, 50 Japanese aircraft were shot down and 340 destroyed on the ground by 5AF and U.S. Navy pilots* with a loss to the USAAF of only two P-38s* and two other aircraft. Hollandia fell.

The last steps were to take the small islands of Wakde, Biak, and Noemfoor on the northwest coast, followed by taking Sansapor on the northwest tip of New Guinea. The tactics in each case were to use air power as the spearhead of the drive. In July the stepping-stone campaign that had run the length of New Guinea, more than 800 miles, ended. New Guinea was neutralized as a base for Japanese power, although 80,000 soldiers left behind had not surrendered. This field army was now useless to the Japanese except that guards over them were necessary. The Americans could then look to the Philippines.

References. C&C, vols. 1 and 4. Goldberg, *Hist. USAF*. Ronald W. Yoshino, *Lightning Strikes: The 475th Fighter Group in the Pacific War, 1943–1945*, 1988.

NEWPORT CONFERENCE. *See* Key West and Newport Conferences of 1948.

NHA TRANG AIR BASE

This airfield was located on the coast of the Republic of South Vietnam in the center of the country. USAF* occupancy began on a small scale in 1962. The first aircraft, three C-123s* and three C-47s,* arrived in 1964. Squadron*-sized units arrived in 1965 with C-123s and C-47s. In 1966, AC-47s (*see* C-47) and EC-47s (*see* C-47) were added; in 1968, AC-119s (*see* C-119) and C-130s* were added. The USAF departed the base in 1971.

References. Berger, *USAF in SEA*. Robert F. Futrell, *The Advisory Years to 1965*, 1981. John Schlight, *The War in South Vietnam: The Years of the Offensive 1965–1968*, 1988.

NIAGARA. *See* Khe Sanh, South Vietnam.

NIEUPORT 28

In World War I,* no U.S.-made fighter* reached the front, and the United States had to buy fighters made by the Allies. The Nieuport 28, made by the Société Anonyme des Establissements Nieuport, was a principal design bought from the French. The 94th* and 95th Aero Squadrons of the Aviation Section of the U.S. Army Signal Corps* were the first to use it. The first U.S. victory belonged to Lieutenant Alan Winslow while flying a 28 on 14 April 1918. Lieutenant Douglas Campbell* became the first U.S.-trained ace* in 28s. The 28 was obsolete before it was bought by the United States, and it was replaced by the French Spad XIII* as soon as possible, although some U.S. pilots* preferred the 28. The 28 was fragile and tended to shed its upper-wing fabric in a dive. The USAAS* used 297 of them.

References. Primary: Edward V. Rickenbacker, *Fighting the Flying Circus*, 1919. Secondary: Peter M. Bowers, "Nieuport 28," *AAHS Journal*, Summer 1965, pp. 108–9. Swanborough, *US Mil. Airc.* Wagner, *Am. Planes.*

NIGHT FIGHTER. *See* interceptor.

NIGHT OBSERVATION DEVICES (NOD)

The first primitive night vision devices were infrared and were used in World War II,* but they were not overly successful. It was not until the Starlight scope invented during the Vietnam War* that these devices came into wide use. Now they are very common in military and civilian use throughout the world.

They fall into two categories, thermal imaging and low-light intensifying. Thermal imaging uses the heat of an object to create a picture. It is very useful in seeing through fog, battlefield smoke, or heavy snow; most modern tank or antitank weapons have this capability. Light-intensifying sights use the ambient light available, intensify it by electronic means, and present the picture to the user. The devices are now quite small, with the most modern being no larger than a set of goggles and about as hard to use.

References. Berger, *USAF in SEA. Jane's All the World's Infantry Weapons*, 1988.

Philip Long

NINETEENTH AIR FORCE (19AF)

The 19AF was formed in 1955 at Foster AFB, Texas, as a subcommand of the Tactical Air Command* (TAC). Its headquarters moved to Seymour Johnson* AFB, North Carolina, in 1958, and it was inactivated in 1973. The mission of the 19AF was to be a mobile task force headquarters for the Composite Air Strike Force* (CASF). In a crisis it would be able to move overseas and would gain preplanned TAC units for its task. The 19AF also had the mission of conducting USAF* field training jointly with the U.S. Army.

References. Goldberg, *Hist. USAF.* Ravenstein, *Org. USAF.*

19TH BOMBARDMENT GROUP

The most famous bomber* unit of World War II,* it began as the 19th Observation Group in 1927. It became a bomb* group* in 1929. It was equipped with B-10s,* then B-18s,* and finally B-17s* before moving to the Philippines in the fall of 1941.

The group was badly mauled on the ground at Clark* Field by the Japanese on the day war began. For two weeks, and suffering heavy losses, the 19th conducted reconnaissance* and bombing operations. The 19th's aircrews moved to Australia and performed airlift operations* from there back to the Philippines. The ground personnel went into infantry units. At the end of 1941 and into 1942, the 19th conducted bombing operations out of Java, returning to Australia in March. During the same month, the group moved General Douglas MacArthur and his party from the Philippines to Australia. Later that year, the 19th took part in the Battle of the Coral Sea and in operations in Papua and New Britain. Late in 1942, the 19th returned to the United States to become a replacement training unit.

In 1944, it moved to Guam Island to be part of the Twentieth Air Force* (20AF) and began operations in 1945 with B-29s.* It received two Distinguished Unit Citations for its part in the strategic campaign against Japan.* The 19th started strategic* and tactical* operations in the Korean War* in June 1950 and continued them until 1953, still using B-29s. The group was inactivated in June 1953.

References. C&C, vol. 1. Futrell, *USAF in Korea*. Maurer Maurer, ed., *Air Force Combat Units of World War II*, 1983. W. L. White, *Queens Die Proudly*, 1943.

94-TARGET PLAN

In World War II,* the USAAF* proposed a famous plan to conduct the war, AWPD-1;* in the Vietnam War,* a 94-target plan was submitted for the same purpose. Neither plan was followed because higher priority was given to land power than to air power. Later events indicated a greater emphasis on those plans might have been a better course of action for the United States.

General Curtis E. LeMay,* chief of staff of the Air Force,* believed that, if military force was to be used, the action to take in Vietnam was an air and sea blockade of North Vietnam. To do this, he directed the design of the 94-target plan. The targets were Haiphong,* other ports, electrical power, and transportation and supply centers. To LeMay, such a campaign would force North Vietnam to stop its aggression by loss of its sinews of war. He also believed limited attack* operations, such as Rolling Thunder,* would not influence the North Vietnamese to yield anything. In August 1964, U.S. Army General Earle G. Wheeler, chairman of the Joint Chiefs of Staff (JCS), gave LeMay's 94-target plan to Secretary of Defense (SECDEF) Robert S. McNamara* with the recommendation that it be conducted in a concentrated 16-day campaign. McNamara rejected the plan on the basis that it was air power and thus could not destroy North Vietnam's ability to conduct war. McNamara used Rolling Thunder instead, which failed.

In 1972, the United States put into effect what was substantially the 94-target plan. It was called Linebacker* II. Under conditions somewhat different from 1964, the air campaign produced the desired results—peace negotiations—in 11 days.

References. Mark Clodfelter, *The Limits of Air Power: The American Bombing of North Vietnam*, 1989. Thomas M. Coffey, *Iron Eagle: The Turbulent Life of General Curtis LeMay*, 1986.

94TH AERO SQUADRON

This was the most famous U.S. Army squadron* in World War I.* When the war ended on 11 November, the 94th had 70 victories and several pilots* had become aces.*

It was organized at Kelly* Field, Texas, in August 1917; trained in the United States; and reached Issoudon,* France, early in 1918. Its 16 officers and 120 men reported in at Villeneuve on the St. Mihiel* front on 5 March 1918, equipped with unarmed Nieuport 28* fighters.*

On 3 April the fully equipped 94th, called the "Hat-in-the-Ring" squadron, began battle operations. On 14 April, Lieutenants Alan F. Winslow and Douglas Campbell* shot down two enemy aircraft.* Within the next few weeks Campbell and Edward V. Rickenbacker* became aces. Major Raoul Lufbery,* formerly of the Lafayette Escadrille,* was a member of the 94th and was killed in action on 19 May. On 29 June, the 94th was transferred to Tonquin airfield in the Chateau-Thierry sector where it, and six other squadrons, participated in halting the German drive toward Paris. In late July, it was equipped with Spad XIIIs.* The 94th and 25 other squadrons were shifted to St. Mihiel* for the four-day offensive beginning on 12 September. The Meuse-Argonne* drive began on 26 September, and the 94th played a large air superiority* role in the area. A new squadron commander, Rickenbacker, scored 26 victories and, years later, was given the Air Force Medal of Honor.*

References. Edward V. Rickenbacker, *Fighting the Flying Circus*, 1919. Secondary: William E. Barrett, *The First War Planes*, 1960. Roy F. Houchin II, "The 94th Aero Squadron's Technical Problems—1918," *AH*, September 1985, pp. 154–57. James J. Hudson, *Hostile Skies: A Combat History of the American Air Service in World War I*, 1968. Lucien H. Thayer, *America's First Eagles: The Official History of the U.S. Air Service, A.E.F. (1917–1918)*, 1983.

James J. Hudson

NINTH AIR FORCE (9AF)

The 9AF has a distinguished history in conducting tactical operations.* A small formation of B-24s,* which had been directed to fly to India, was diverted to the defense of Egypt in May 1942. In June, Major General Lewis A. Brereton* arrived in Cairo with orders to consolidate the B-24s and all other U.S. planes in Egypt into a new Middle East Air Force. It was redesignated the 9AF** in November.

Equipped with B-17s,* B-24s, and P-40s,* the 9AF supported Allied operations in North Africa, Sicily, and Italy before moving the headquarters to England in the fall of 1943. The 9AF now took over medium bombers* from the VIII Bomber Command and added F-47s,* P-38s,* and some tactical airlift* assets. The 9AF provided tactical operations support for Operation Overlord* with a strength of 3,500 aircraft. It supported the rapid advance of General George Patton's Third Army. From 23 to 27 December 1944, it flew 5,291 sorties to blunt the German offensive in the Battle of the Bulge.* Before it was inactivated in December 1945, the 9AF had become the largest tactical air force in history.

It was reactivated in March 1946 at Biggs Field, Texas, with only one combat unit. In October it moved to Greenville Army Air Base, South Carolina, and took over units which had been under the Third Air Force* (3AF). In August 1947 it moved to Langley* AFB, Virginia, and was placed under the Continental Air Command* (CONAC) to be an administrative headquarters supervising training. During the Korean War,* its training mission expanded, it moved to Pope* AFB, North Carolina, and was reassigned to the Tactical Air Command* (TAC). In 1954, the headquarters moved to Shaw* AFB, South Carolina. Since then, it has supported TAC commitments to other commands in many overseas deployments, including the Cuban crisis of 1962,* the Vietnam War,* and the Grenada incident.*

In 1979, following the Iranian Revolution and the Soviet invasion of Afghanistan, the Department of Defense (DoD) established the Rapid Deployment Joint Task Force (RDJTF), a part of Readiness Command. The 9AF was the air arm of the RDJTF, or the Rapid Deployment Air Force Forces (RDAFFOR). In 1983, the RDJTF was redesignated as a separate unified command, U.S. Central Command (USCENTCOM), and the 9AF became U.S. Central Command Air Forces* (USCENTAF). In 1990, to meet its TAC and USCENTAF commitments, the 9AF had about 41,000 active duty personnel plus 35,000 in its Air National Guard* (ANG) and U.S. Air Force Reserve* (USAFR) units. USCENTCOM was used in the Iraq crisis of 1990–1991* and the Iraq War.*

References. C&C, vol. 3. Maurer Maurer, ed., *Air Force Combat Units of World War II*, 1983. Official USAF History, Ninth Air Force, 9AF History and Public Affairs Offices, 1989. Ravenstein, *Org. USAF*. Thomas E. Wiltsey, "Ninth Air Force History, 1941–1986," 9AF History Office, n.d.

**In the confusion created by the war, the U.S. Army failed to note that another Ninth Air Force already existed, derived from the old V Air Support Command, which had been activated in September 1941.

David L. Rosmer

NOD. *See* night observation devices.

NONSTOP TRANSCONTINENTAL FLIGHT

As one of the flights made to show the military potential of the airplane, the first nonstop transcontinental flight was conducted by the USAAS* on 6 May 1923. Lieutenants Oakley G. Kelly and John A. Macready* used one of the

USAAS's two single-engine Dutch-made Fokker T-2s. It was equipped with extra fuel tanks. The pilots* flew the 2,520-mile flight from Mitchel* Field, New York, to Rockwell Field, California, in 26 hours and 50 minutes. The future head of the USAAF,* Major H. H. Arnold,* was on hand for their arrival.

References. Primary: John A. Macready, "The Non-stop Flight across America," *National Geographic Magazine*, July 1924, pp. 1–83. Secondary: Goldberg, *Hist. USAF.* Maurer, *Avn. in Army.* Len Morgan, "Kelly, Macready and the T-2," *AF*, August 1956, pp. 290–99. *The Official Pictorial History of the AAF*, 1947.

Alwyn T. Lloyd

NORAD. *See* North American Aerospace Defense Command.

NORDEN BOMBSIGHT

The Norden was a critical element in conducting high-altitude precision strategic operations* by the USAAF* in World War II* and was made a most secret device. The sight was a highly accurate precision instrument developed by Carl L. Norden, a civilian consultant, and Captain Frederick I. Entwistle, assistant research chief of the U.S. Navy's Bureau of Ordnance. In 1932, following extensive testing the previous year using outdated warships, the USAAC* ordered its own Norden bombsight.

Precision bombing required meticulous control; to accomplish this, the Norden incorporated a gyrostabilized automatic pilot. The mechanism was modified in 1941 by the Minneapolis Honeywell Company and designated the Army Type C-1 autopilot. This modification enabled a bomber* to be flown on a straight, level course, giving the bombardier* a steady platform on which to operate the bombsight during the bombing run. Also known as the "Blue Ox," the Norden could quickly calculate and correct directional changes due to wind drift. Flying at a preset altitude, it could rapidly compute the correct bomb* release angle for a constant speed of closure to the aiming point. Adjustments could be made in a fraction of a second based on data entered into the sight. Under optimal conditions on an undisturbed run, the accuracy of the device was excellent. However, any last-second changes in the attitude of the bomber at the instant of release, such as those encountered during battle, could markedly influence the accuracy of the sight.

References. Primary: Michael J. Nisos, "The Bombardier and His Bombsight," *AF*, September 1981, pp. 106–10, 113. Secondary: Bruce D. Callander, "Bombardier," *AF*, December 1990, pp. 76–80. Edward Jablonski, *Flying Fortress*, 1965. Alwyn T. Lloyd and Terry D. Moore, *B-17 Flying Fortress in Detail & Scale*, part 1, "Production Versions," 1981. Thomas Parrish, ed., *The Simon and Shuster Encyclopedia of World War II*, 1978.

Gilbert E. D'Alonzo

NORSTAD, GENERAL LAURIS (1907–1988)

Norstad was a strategic planner in World War II,* an architect of the postwar U.S. defense establishment, and a builder of the North Atlantic Treaty Organization* (NATO) nuclear weapons* strategy. He was the supreme Allied commander in Europe (SACEUR) and commander in chief of the U.S. European Command (CINCEUCOM) from 1956 to 1963.

From Minneapolis, Minnesota, he graduated from the U.S. Military Academy (USMA) in 1930 and joined the USAAC* in 1931. After graduating from the Air Corps Tactical School* (ACTS) in 1939, he was assigned to the intelligence staff of the General Headquarters Air Force* (GHQ Air Force). In 1942, he became assistant chief of staff of the Twelfth Air Force* (12AF) and greatly impressed General Dwight D. Eisenhower.* In 1943, Norstad became director of operations for the Mediterranean Allied Air Forces under Lieutenant General Ira C. Eaker.* The following year he returned to Washington, D.C., as chief of staff of the Twentieth Air Force* (20AF) and helped plan B-29* raids, including the Hiroshima* and Nagasaki missions.

He remained in planning duties after the war. Amid the controversial discussions on postwar service organization, he and Vice Admiral Forrest P. Sherman drafted the Joint Chiefs of Staff Unified Command Plan of December 1946, which was the origin of unified commands* for all theaters. He and Sherman also worked out arrangements for the national military establishment with a Department of Defense (DoD) and service roles as defined in the National Security Act of 1947.* With the creation of the independent USAF,* he became vice chief of staff for operations. In 1950 he took command of the U.S. Air Forces in Europe* (USAFE) and the next year became commander of the Allied Air Forces Central Europe. In 1953 he moved to Paris, France, as air deputy to General Matthew Ridgeway, SACEUR, and retained that post under Ridgeway's successor, General Alfred M. Gruenther. He succeeded Gruenther as SACEUR.

Norstad took responsibility for broad planning and negotiations for nuclear policy in 1957, after NATO heads of state agreed to President Eisenhower's proposal to increase Allied participation in nuclear planning and deployment. Norstad forcibly articulated a NATO strategy based on a combination of U.S. strategic operations* forces and European-based conventional and tactical nuclear forces. His planning and public statements laid much of the groundwork for the "flexible response" policies favored by President John F. Kennedy* (JFK).

After his retirement in 1963, he became president and later chairman of Owens-Corning Fiberglass Corporation, as well as a director of United Air Lines.

References. Primary: U.S. Air Force Oral History Interview K239.0512–1116, 1979, USAFHRC/OH, Maxwell AFB, Alabama. Secondary: "An Airman Boss for NATO," *Time*, 23 April 1956, p. 29. DuPre, *USAF Bio*. Futrell, *Ideas*, vol. 1. Herman S. Wolk, *Planning and Organizing the Postwar Air Force 1943–1947*, 1984.

Maurice Maryanow

NORTH AMERICAN AEROSPACE DEFENSE COMMAND (NORAD)

NORAD is a combined command between the United States and Canada. Both nations faced a threat from Soviet strategic operations* in the late 1940s and early 1950s. On 12 September 1957, NORAD was activated to provide an integrated command for the control of air defense forces of the two nations. For more than 30 years, NORAD has been an effective means for the USAF* to contribute to continental aerospace defense operations.*

U.S. and Canadian cooperation preceded NORAD. In 1954, the Pinetree Line* of radar* stations was completed. It was followed by the Mid-Canada Line* and the distant early warning* (DEW) Line, both in 1957.

In its early years, the North American Air Defense Command (NORAD) controlled fighters,* interceptors,* surface-to-air missiles* (SAM), control centers, and other facilities to defend the continent against bombers.* The command then included 250,000 Americans and Canadians. The advent of Soviet intercontinental ballistic missiles* (ICBM) and intermediate-range ballistic missiles (IRBM), which could be launched from submarines, dictated an expansion of the defenses. The United States established a space detection and tracking system to which Canada contributed. Passive defenses were also undertaken, including putting NORAD's combat operations center inside Cheyenne Mountain near Colorado Springs, Colorado. To recognize this broadening of operations, NORAD changed its name to North American Aerospace Defense Command in 1981.

In the 1980s, NORAD had a modernization program of using more airborne warning and control system* (AWACS) planes, increased use of F-15s* and F-18s, over-the-horizon-radar, and replacement of the DEW Line with better facilities called North Warning system. In 1990, the Tactical Air Command's* (TAC) First Air Force* (1AF) provided the command and control for the continental United States (CONUS) region of NORAD. The Eleventh Air Force* (11AF) did the same for NORAD's Alaskan Region, replacing the Alaskan Air Command* (AAC) in August 1990.

References. "Alaskan Air Command," *AF*, May 1990, pp. 73–74. John L. Piotrowski, "The North American Partnership," *AF*, October 1987, pp. 78–81. "Tactical Air Command," *AF*, May 1990, pp. 88–90.

NORTH AMERICAN AVIATION, INC. *See* aerospace industry; B-25; B-45; B-70; F-51; F-82; F-86; F-100; Navaho; O-47; OV-10; T-6; T-28; X-15.

NORTH ATLANTIC AIR BASES

During the first two years after World War II* began in September 1939, the administration of President Franklin D. Roosevelt* (FDR) gradually extended the meaning of hemispheric defense as far to the northeastern Atlantic as Iceland. The USAAC,* thus, took some steps in the direction of global operations early in the war. North Atlantic bases provided defense bases as well as ports for convoys during World War II. Consequently, they enabled materials from the U.S. "arsenal of democracy" to reach England and, after June 1941, the USSR. The bases also greatly assisted the North Atlantic ferry route.*

U.S. Army intelligence estimated German Heinkel bombers* could reach New York City from Norway with only one refueling near Newfoundland, and the German conquest of Norway in the spring of 1940 indicated this air route needed to be defended as far east as possible. In August 1940, the United States and Canada established a Permanent Joint Board on Defense to coordinate the defenses of North America. In March 1941, agreements were reached for the United States to protect bases in a variety of British Empire possessions, including Newfoundland.

Greenland was the next eastward step, and, in April 1941, U.S. and Danish officials agreed that the United States should guarantee Greenland's security by establishing bases there. By the end of June, Base Bluie West 1 (BW-1) at Narsarssuak became a major U.S. Army and Navy facility in Greenland. Negotiations with Iceland had begun in July 1940, but FDR was concerned because it was outside the traditional Western Hemisphere and because British and Canadian forces had occupied it in May 1940. By early 1941, however, the British wanted to shift their forces elsewhere and, as FDR ordered "neutrality patrols" in the Atlantic to support British convoys, discussions with Icelandic officials were completed. In June, FDR ordered U.S. forces to prepare protective bases in Iceland. In September, a convoy reached Iceland with 5,000 U.S. troops, the first contingents to replace the British-Canadian forces.

References. Donald F. Bittner, *The Lion and the White Falcon: Britain and Iceland in the World War II Era*, 1983. Stetson Conn, Rose C. Engleman, and Bryon Fairchild, *Guarding the United States and Its Outposts*, 1964. Stetson Conn and Bryon Fairchild, *The Framework of Hemispheric Defense*, 1960.

Lester H. Brune

NORTH ATLANTIC FERRY ROUTE

These ferry operations spurred and influenced the arrival of routine and frequent transoceanic air operations by the USAF.* After the fall of France in 1940, Britain desperately needed war supplies from the United States and placed a high priority on U.S.-built bombers.* To expedite delivery and save precious cargo space on ships, the British decided to fly these bombers across the Atlantic. In November 1940, a Canadian civil agency contracted with the British government to fly the bombers from Newfoundland to Scotland. In compliance with the Neutrality Law, American pilots* employed by the aircraft companies flew the bombers from the factories to Montreal, Canada. Then Canadian pilots took over, flying to Gander Lake, Newfoundland, and from there made the 2,100-mile flight to Prestwick, Scotland.

Improving spring weather and the passage of the Lend-Lease* Act in May 1941 increased the flow of aircraft to Britain. The larger number of planes meant the British had to take pilots out of combat units to ferry the planes. Major General H. H. Arnold* suggested in April that USAAC* pilots fly the planes. The British and President Franklin D. Roosevelt* (FDR) agreed, and, on 28 May, FDR ordered the USAAC to take responsibility for aircraft delivery to Britain.

The next day the USAAC created the Ferrying Command to carry out FDR's order. Led by Colonel Robert Olds,* it delivered more than 1,300 aircraft over the North Atlantic to Britain by Pearl Harbor.* Most of the aircraft were twin-engine Bostons and Hudsons. After the United States entered the war, the Air Transport Command (ATC) used the route pioneered by the Canadian pilots and the Ferrying Command.

References. C&C, vols. 1 and 7. Ernest K. Gann, *Fate Is the Hunter*, 1961.

See also Military Airlift Command; North Atlantic air bases.

Jeffery S. Underwood

NORTH ATLANTIC TREATY ORGANIZATION (NATO)

NATO has been a significant factor for the USAF* for 45 years. In response to Soviet aggression and the Cold War,* nations in the North Atlantic area formed a defensive alliance. The final Soviet act that precipitated it was a 1948 blockade of West Berlin, Germany, which was countered by the Berlin Airlift.* In April 1949, the alliance was founded and consisted of the United States, Belgium, Canada, Denmark, France, Iceland, Italy, Luxembourg, the Netherlands, Norway, Portugal, and the United Kingdom. The U.S. commitment to NATO was actively to help in the defense of Western Europe. Included in the U.S. commitment were USAF units stationed at sites in Europe and under the control of Supreme Headquarters Allied Powers Europe (SHAPE).

NATO started slowly but was inspired to become much more serious by the armed invasion of the Republic of South Korea by the communist Peoples Republic of North Korea. In response to NATO, the Soviet Empire formed the Warsaw Treaty Organization, popularly called the Warsaw Pact, of the USSR and its East European satellites in 1955.

NATO had one major internal crisis in the mid–1960s when France argued with its allies over the command of the forces. The outcome was that France remained in NATO but took its military forces out from under NATO's command. As part of this, the USAF was ordered to depart from its ten facilities on French soil, which was done in 1966 to 1967. Over the years, Greece, Spain, Turkey, and the Federal Republic of Germany joined NATO.

Before the 1989 anticommunist revolutions, NATO appeared to be badly outnumbered by the Pact in the air and on the ground. At that time, the Pact included the USSR, Bulgaria, Czechoslovakia, the German Democratic Republic, Hungary, Poland, and Romania. In the wake of the revolutions, the future of NATO and the Pact became uncertain. In 1990, the USSR's Mikhail Gorbachev agreed to the reunification of the Germanies and the new nation's membership in NATO. However, Soviet military capabilities remained virtually unchanged and projected to slowly withdraw to within the USSR over several years. In 1991, the Pact was scheduled to lose its military aspects later in that year.

In 1990, the commander in chief of the U.S. Air Forces in Europe* (USAFE) was also the commander of the Allied Air Forces, Central Europe (CO-MAAFCE). He commanded 2,000 tactical operations* aircraft divided into the Second and Fourth Allied Tactical Air Forces, made up of contingents from the United States, Belgium, Canada, the Federal Republic of Germany, the Netherlands, and the United Kingdom.

References. Futrell, *Ideas*, vol. 2. Goldberg, *Hist. USAF*. Robert Jackson, *Strike Force: The USAF in Britain since 1948*, 1986. Michael Skinner, *U*S*A*F*E: A Primer of Modern Air Combat in Europe*, 1988. "United States Air Forces in Europe," *AF*, May 1990, pp. 93–95.

NORTH CAROLINA MANEUVERS OF 1941. *See* maneuvers of 1941.

NORTHEAST AIR COMMAND (NEAC)

The technical advances in aviation, together with the perception of the USSR as a potential enemy after World War II,* led to a concern about transpolar air strikes on the United States. This focused attention on areas northeast of the United States.

The North Atlantic air base* and ferry route* operations in World War II had already caused a USAAF* presence to the northeast and led to an organization, the Newfoundland Base Command. This organization was under the Eastern Air Defense Command until 1946. Then it was placed under the Air Transport Command (ATC) and under the successor organization, the Military Air Transport Service (MATS).

The Newfoundland Base Command became a USAF* major command* (MAJCOM) in 1950 and was renamed NEAC. Its mission was air defense and support for Strategic Air Command* (SAC) and MATS operations through its area of control. Discharging this mission required cooperation with other concerned nations in the area, Canada and Denmark. NEAC built Thule* AB, Greenland, to help with its mission. In 1957, a reorganization discontinued NEAC and divided its resources between the Air Defense Command (ADC) and SAC.

References. Goldberg, *Hist. USAF*. Ravenstein, *Org. USAF*.

NORTON AIR FORCE BASE

Near San Bernardino, California, this base was first named after the city in 1942. The name was changed in 1950 to honor San Bernardino native Captain Leland F. Norton who was killed in action near Amiens, France, in 1944.

The USAAF* used the base during World War II* principally as an air depot, from which thousands of tons of supplies and equipment were provided to the combat forces and to which hundreds of aircraft were sent for major overhauls and maintenance. By 1943, it had on hand about 26,000 tons of supplies and was manned by almost 5,000 military and 13,000 civilian personnel. After the war, it continued to be a major logistics facility. Until its inactivation in 1966, the San Bernardino Air Materiel Area was a subordinate unit to the Air Materiel Command (AMC) and later the successor major command* (MAJCOM), Air Force Logistics Command* (AFLC). While it was an Air Materiel Area it provided maintenance and logistics support for all liquid-fuel and intercontinental ballistic missiles* (ICBM) and space booster systems.

In 1990 the host unit at Norton was the 63rd Military Airlift Wing which moved to the base in 1967. The 63rd flew C-141s* to global destinations. The

63rd's aerial port was one of four operating embarkation points for the Pacific area and Asia. Norton was scheduled to be closed in 1994.

References. "Guide to Major Air Force Installations Worldwide," *AF*, May 1990, p. 128. Mueller, *AFB*. Charles A. Ravenstein, *Air Force Combat Wings: Lineage and Honors Histories, 1947–1977*, 1984. Roberts, *Dir. USAF*.

Roger D. Launius

NOSE ART

Personalized markings on aircraft, primarily on the nose, are called nose art. A military airplane with only a serial number is merely a piece of government hardware. With unit markings, which mostly began after World War I* in the USAAS,* a sense of organizational identity came into being. When air and ground crews started naming their airplanes and adding personalized markings, the machine became special for those people and a sense of pride was enhanced. Although not strictly nose art, the practice of putting aircrewmen and ground crewmen's names on aircraft increased pride further.

The tradition* became large scale by the USAAF* in World War II* and continued during the Korean War.* By the mid–1950s, command directives forbade nose art. The tradition was revived during the Vietnam War;* however, much of the quality in the artwork was lost. With the end of hostilities, sterility in markings returned. Despite complaints from the National Organization for Women because beautiful women were favorite subjects, the commander in chief of the Strategic Air Command* (CINCSAC) endorsed nose art on aircraft in the late 1980s to reinstill the tradition and pride. While in the past, nose art ran the gamut from religion to raunch, today there are more restrictions on subjects. Many historical markings are being revived today.

References. John M. and Donna Campbell, *War Paint: Fighter Nose Art from WWII & Korea*, 1990. Roger A. Freeman, *The Mighty Eighth: Units, Men and Machines*, 1970. Alwyn T. Lloyd, "Nose Art: A USAF Tradition," *Combat Crew Magazine*, July 1988, pp. 16–19. Gary M. Valant, *Vintage Aircraft Nose Art*, 1987.**

**Valant's book has excellent photography, but it is poorly researched and documented.

Alwyn T. Lloyd

NO TIME FOR SERGEANTS. See movies.

NOVELS

Military aviation was seen for many years as adventurous and glamorous, and the USAF* has its share of fiction. The first USAF author of consequence was Elliott White Springs,* a USAAS* ace.* He wrote in the 1920s, and his fiction appeared mostly in magazines. In the 1930s, the most popular aviation fiction in the United States appeared in the pulp magazines, and it was nearly all about the USAAS in World War I.* This material was widely read, mostly by boys and young men, and influenced USAAC* and USAAF* recruiting of aircrews in World War II.*

After the war, many novels about the USAAF appeared. There was *Command*

*Decision** (1947), by William Wister Haines; *Twelve O'Clock High** (1948), by Beirne Lay, Jr.,* and Sy Bartlett; *Guard of Honor** (1948), by James Gould Cozzens; *Face of a Hero* (1950), by Louis Falstein; *Angle of Attack* (1952), by Joseph Landon; *Roll Back the Sky* (1956), by Ward Taylor; *The War Lover** (1959), by John Hersey; *Shoulder the Sky* (1959), by George Leonard; and *Skip Bomber* (1960), by Lloyd E. Olson.

While the World War II novels were still appearing, the USAF was engaged in the Korean War.* Soon there were novels about it. Some were *Don't Touch Me** (1951), by MacKinlay Kantor; *Troubling of a Star* (1952), by Walt Sheldon; *Look of the Eagle* (1955), by Robert L.Scott;* *The Hunters** (1956), by James Salter; *Turn the Tigers Loose* (1956), by Walt Lasly; *MiG Alley* (1959), by Robert Eunson; and *Air Force!* (1959), by Frank Harvey.

The first novel about future nuclear war came in 1958, with *Red Alert* by Peter Bryant. This was followed in the 1960s by stories that were often hostile to the USAF: *Catch–22** (1961), by Joseph Heller; *Fail-Safe** (1962), by Eugene Burdick and Harvey Wheeler; *Scramble!* (1962), by Mario Capelli; and *The Penetrators* (1965), by Anthony Gray. *Red Alert* was greatly altered for a movie, *Dr. Strangelove or: How I Learned to Stop Worrying and Love the Bomb* (1964). The movie script was converted to novel form and published.

After the 1960s, fiction returned to viewing the USAF in a neutral, or favorable, light. There was *The Last Dogfight* (1974), by Martin Caidin; *Eagles* (1980), by M. H. Davis; *Goodbye, Mickey Mouse** (1982), by Len Deighton; *Sweet Vietnam* (1984), by Richard Parque; *Taxi Dancer* (1985), by Joe T. Heywood; *The Wild Blue* (1986), by Walter J. Boyne and Steven L. Thompson; *Wings over Nam #2: The Wild Weasels, #3: Linebacker*, and *#5: Bird Dog* (1989–1990), by Cat Branigan.

References. "The 40th Anniversary of the USAF," a special issue of *AH*, September 1987, pp. 206–13. Eugene N. Laughridge, "The Air Force in Books about Vietnam," *AH*, December 1988, pp. 266–67. David K. Vaughan, *The Literature of Flight*, 1982.

NUCLEAR-POWERED AIRCRAFT. See X-6.

NUCLEAR WEAPONS

Nuclear weapons have multiplied enormously the striking power of the USAF* for both strategic* and tactical* operations. In addition, the advent of thermonuclear weapons made feasible long-range ballistic missiles.*

The devices cause massive explosions by the rapid release of huge amounts of energy resulting from reactions involving atomic nuclei. They are of three types: fission, fusion, and enhanced radiation.

The fission device uses a neutron to split the nucleus of an atom of uranium 235 or plutonium 239, liberating neutrons plus energy. If it is of a supercritical mass, a reaction cascades within one microsecond for an explosion equal to more than 50,000 tons of trinitrotoluene (TNT) plus massive amounts of energy in the forms of heat, light, and radioactivity. There are two methods to convert a subcritical mass to a supercritical one. One is the "gun type," with subcritical masses at both ends of a gun barrel device. An explosive charge set off behind one mass moves it to the other end, forming a supercritical mass. The other method uses an "implosion." A sphere of plutonium is surrounded by high explosives. The latter are simultaneously detonated, crushing the inner sphere into a supercritical mass. Fission weapons are used only for smaller munitions; over a certain size they are wasteful of fission material. Also, large fission weapons are very "dirty" in radioactive by-products.

The fusion type is the thermonuclear, or "hydrogen," weapon. It works by converting hydrogen atoms into helium, as the sun does. It is "cleaner" than fission types, and it is cheaper and safer because its deuterium fuel has no critical mass. By heating deuterium to 350 million degrees centigrade, or a mixture of deuterium and tritium to 45 million, the nuclei will interact in an explosion. A small fission device is used to initiate the fusion explosion. Fusion weapons are the mainstay of U.S. nuclear forces.

The enhanced radiation type, or "neutron bomb," is designed for the smallest blast and greatest neutron radiation. Its blast is similar to a high-explosive bomb.* Its burst of radiation will kill all life within a 1.25-mile diameter but leave no lingering radiation.

The USAF has many models of nuclear weapons that are much improved over those used on Hiroshima* and Nagasaki. They are much smaller, more efficient, and safer. A long series of events must occur in a precise order and at exact intervals before one is armed. A Permissive Action Link (PAL) is also used. It is a device that arms a weapon only after an individual code has been set into it. Modern weapons resist long storage, launch accelerations, the cold of outer space, and the heat of re-entry.

The weapons can be used as depth charges, free-fall, or parachute-retarded bombs or on missiles. Some have several different yields that can be dialed into the weapon to match its power to the size of the target. There are three kinds of nuclear warheads. One is a single unit and is obsolete except for cruise missiles or the Small ICBM.* A second carries several warheads on one vehicle and uses a shotgun effect to saturate a target. The third is the multiple independent re-entry vehicle* (MIRV), which has separate warheads dropped off its carrier at predetermined times to hit different targets.

References. Christopher Campbell, *Nuclear Weapons Fact Book*, 1984. Christy Campbell, *Weapons of War*, 1983. John T. Correll, "The Nuclear Crews," *AF*, February 1984, pp. 56–58. Futrell, *Ideas*, 2 vols. Bill Yenne, *The History of the US Air Force*, 1984.

Philip Long

O

O-1 BIRD DOG

The USAF* opened a competition in 1950 for a new plane for liaison aviation.* The Cessna Aircraft Company won with a version of its Model 170. The USAF designated it the L-19A, and it went into service in 1950. In 1962, it was redesignated as the O-1 when the armed forces adopted common designations.

The O-1 was used extensively in the Vietnam War* for forward air controllers* (FAC) starting in 1963. In April 1965 the USAF activated three more squadrons* of O-1s in South Vietnam. They were based at Bien Hoa* AB, Binh Tuy, Da Nang* AB, and Pleiku AB, but operated from 65 airfields. In January 1966, O-1s were put at Nakhon Phanom* Royal Thai AFB for use in Laos. O-1s were overweight, slow, underpowered with full military loads, had inadequate cockpit lighting and navigation equipment, and needed armor and armament. As the war went on, O-1 loss rates increased. The USAF lost a total of 89 O-1s in action in 1965 through 1968. The U.S. Army, Marine Corps, and the South Vietnamese air force (VNAF) also used O-1s in the war. Replacement of the O-1s with O-2s began in 1967.

Characteristics: engine, Continental O-470–11 flat four of 213 horsepower; span, 36 feet; length, 26 feet; height, 7 feet; gross weight, 2,400 pounds; top speed, 151 miles per hour; service ceiling, 18,500 feet; range, 530 miles.

References. Robert F. Futrell, *The Advisory Years to 1965*, 1981. Edward H. Phillips, *CESSNA: A Master's Expression*, 1985. John Schlight, *The War in South Vietnam: The Years of the Offensive 1965–1968*, 1988. Swanborough, *US Mil. Airc.*

O-1 FALCON

This update of the World War I* observation aviation* type was produced by the Curtiss Aeroplane and Motor Company, Inc., and accepted in 1925. It and its variants were bought up through 1933. Produced in small numbers because of the leanness of the USAAC* budget in its years, the O-1 was still an important aircraft.

Variants were mostly a result of trying different engines and included the O-11, XO-12, XO-13, XO-16, XO-18, Y10–26, and O-39. The Falcon was also an executive transport,* the XBT-4 was tested as a trainer, and the A-3 and XA-4 were built for attack.* The number of variants show the basic soundness and adaptability of the airframe.

Characteristics (O-1E): engine, Curtiss V-1150–5 of 435 horsepower; span, 38 feet; length, 27 feet; height, 11 feet; gross weight, 4,347 pounds; top speed, 140 miles per hour; service ceiling, 15,300 feet.

References. Swanborough, *US Mil. Airc.* Wagner, *Am. Planes.*

O-2 SUPER SKYMASTER

Manufactured by the Cessna Aircraft Company, the O-2A was bought to replace the O-1 Bird Dog.* It was a military variant of the Cessna Model 337 Skymaster. It entered service in 1966 and was withdrawn in 1986. A total of 346 were bought by the USAF.* The O-2, nicknamed the "Duck," was used by forward air controllers* (FAC) in the Vietnam War* for the control of close air support in attack.* It proved better than the Bird Dog for FAC and night operations but was not as good for reconnaissance.* It could not use very small fields and lacked armor. The USAF lost 23 O-2s in action in 1967 and 1968.

Characteristics: engines, two Continental IO-360-C/D of 210 horsepower each; span, 38 feet; length, 30 feet; height, 9 feet; gross weight, 5,400 pounds; top speed, 199 miles per hour; service ceiling, 19,300 feet; range, 1,060 miles.

References. Primary: Higham, *Combat Airc.*, vol. 1. Secondary: Robert W. Nicholson, Jr., "The Duck Lives," *AF*, July 1985, pp. 128–29. John Schlight, *The War in South Vietnam: The Years of the Offensive 1965–1968*, 1988. Susan H. H. Young, "Gallery of USAF Weapons," *AF*, May 1986, p. 147.

O-47

The General Aviation Company started work on a new observation aviation* design in 1934. A monoplane with a canopy, the design broke with observation tradition primarily in using three crewmen instead of the previous two. The crew stations were in tandem, consisting of pilot,* observer*-photographer, and gunner.*

When production began, in 1937, the firm had a new name, North American Aviation, Inc. The first flight was in 1938, and the O-47 became the USAAC's* standard observation model. Some were present at Pearl Harbor* during the Japanese raid. They took off but were fortunate enough not to find the enemy. They were already badly obsolete, since the Battle of France showed that observation aircraft were almost helpless in battle at that time. For the rest of their service life, the O-47s were used as trainers and tow target aircraft.

Characteristics: engine, Wright R-1820–49 of 975 horsepower; span, 46 feet; length, 34 feet; height, 12 feet; gross weight, 7,636 pounds; top speed, 221 miles per hour; service ceiling, 23,200 feet; endurance, 2.1 hours.

References. Primary: Higham, *Combat Airc.*, vol. 3. Secondary: Swanborough, *US Mil. Airc.* Wagner, *Am. Planes.*

OBOE. *See* GEE, Oboe and GEE-H.

OBSERVATION AVIATION

The first widespread military use of planes was for "observation," which meant, in World War I,* visual and photographic reconnaissance,* bombing, and artillery correction and spotting. This activity was performed from the front lines to some depth into enemy territory.

Early in the war, observation aircraft became two-seaters to provide for a specialized observer.* The pilot* usually sat forward and the observer aft, where the latter was armed with single or twin flexible light machine guns for rearward defense. The intelligence from observation aircraft was vital to the conduct of the war as early as the Battles of the Marne and Tannenberg. Fighter* aviation then developed to put out these eyes of the enemy. After the war, observation aviation received continued emphasis, while ground commanders dominated the use of aircraft. The USAAC* aircraft for this task had the *O* designation.

Until the Battle of France in 1940, it was believed that the traditional slow aircraft defended with an observer's light machine guns could function in battle. The fast and more heavily armed Luftwaffe fighters quickly swept the French observation aircraft from the skies. Since then, the tasks formerly given to observation aviation have been divided among other types of aircraft that can survive in battle. Primarily these have been fighters, bombers,* attack,* reconnaissance,* and liaison aviation.*

References. Charles D. Bright, "Air Power in World War I: Sideshow or Decisive Factor?" *AH*, June 1971, pp. 58–62. James J. Hudson, *Hostile Skies: A Combat History of the American Air Service in World War I*, 1968. Maurer Maurer, ed., *The U.S. Air Service in World War I*, 4 vols., 1978–1979. James J. Sloan, "The 12th Aero Squadron Observation (A.R.2 & Salmsons)," *AAHS Journal*, part 1, Fall 1964, pp. 179–88; part 2, Spring 1965, pp. 47–52. "U.S. Army Air Forces," a special issue of *Flying and Popular Aviation*, September 1941, pp. 64–66, 206.

OBSERVATION BALLOONS. *See* lighter-than-air.

OBSERVER

Until World War II,* aircrewmen called observers had the task of observing enemy positions and movements. They also were expected to correct artillery fire, take photographs, operate the radio, act as bombardiers, and be flexible gunners.* These tasks were usually done in a tandem two-seat aircraft, with the observer behind the pilot.*

In World War II, observation aviation* proved helpless in battle. The different tasks have since been performed by pilots, forward air controllers* (FAC), army aviation, or, in large aircraft, by specialists such as bombardiers. In the war and since, the term *reconnaissance** has usually been used instead of *observation.* Also, *navigator** has been preferred to *observer* because the Russian language does not have a term equivalent to *observer*, and in translation *spy* could be used.

References. Royal D. Frey, "Setting the Record Straight, the First of Many American Air-to-Air Victories," *AH*, September 1974, pp. 156–59. James J. Hudson, *Hostile Skies: A Combat History of the American Air Service in World War I*, 1968. Maurer Maurer, ed., *The U.S. Air Service in World War I*, 4 vols., 1978–1979. Lucien H. Thayer, *American's First Eagles: The Official History of the U.S. Air Service, A.E.F. (1917–1918)*, 1983. "U.S. Army Air Forces," a special issue of *Flying and Popular Aviation*, September 1941, pp. 64–66, 206.

ODLUM, COLONEL JACQUELINE COCHRAN. *See* Cochran, Colonel Jacqueline.

O'DONNELL, GENERAL EMMETT "ROSIE," JR. (1905–1972)

O'Donnell was commander in chief of the Pacific Air Forces* (PACAF) from 1959 to 1963. One of the most colorful USAF* commanders and generals, he led the first B-29* raid on Tokyo, Japan, in 1944.

He was born in Brooklyn, New York, and graduated from the U.S. Military Academy (USMA) in 1928. He led a squadron* of B-17s* across the Pacific to Manila in September 1941. It was the first mass flight of land planes to fly the western Pacific from Hawaii to the Philippines. When World War II* began in December, his B-17s fought in the Philippines and later supported the infantry until forced to withdraw to Bataan and then to Mindinao. He and his group later moved to Java to continue air operations. He returned to the United States, trained a B-29* wing,* and led it to the Marianas.*

During the Korean War,* O'Donnell took a nucleus of his Fifteenth Air Force* (15AF) staff to Japan to organize and command the Far East Bomber Command. His B-29 units were the first to arrive from the United States, and in less than two months all industrial strategic operations* targets north of the 38th parallel were neutralized by his forces.

Besides PACAF, his major assignments included deputy chief of staff for personnel at headquarters of the USAF, (1953–1959); commanding general of the 15AF (1951–1952); commanding general of the Far Eastern Bomber Command (Provisional) (1950–1951). His retirement in 1963 took place in a special White House ceremony.

References. Air Force Pamphlet 31–1, "Roster of Retired General Officers," 1987. DuPre, *USAF Bio*. U.S. Air Force Historical Study No. 91, Biographical Data on Air Force General Officers, 1917–1952, vol. 3, n.d.

James C. Hasdorff

OFFICE OF MEDICAL SUPPORT. *See* Air Force Office of Medical Support.

OFFICE OF SECURITY POLICE. *See* Air Force Office of Security Police.

OFFICE OF SPECIAL INVESTIGATIONS. *See* Air Force Office of Special Investigations.

OFFICER CANDIDATE SCHOOL (OCS)

With the enormous expansion of the USAAF* in World War II,* an increasing administrative burden was placed on officers, especially the few fliers. The solution was a major historic program, the OCS, which trained masses of staff officers. OCS produced a total of more than 41,000 officers, a great contribution to the USAF.*

In 1942, Lieutenant General H. H. Arnold* ordered the establishment of OCS. Major General Walter R. Weaver, head of the Technical Training Command, quickly opened the OCS at several Miami Beach, Florida, hotels. Candidates were either eliminated aviation cadets* or warrant officers and enlisted men. Candidates had to be 18 to 36 years old, demonstrate a capacity for leadership, and score at least 110 on the U.S. Army general classification test. Initially,the uniform curriculum course lasted 12 weeks. In January 1943, it was divided into two phases. The first was military indoctrination and leadership, and the second was specialized in a particular field. This required an extension of the course to 16 weeks in June 1943. In June 1944, the school moved to the San Antonio Aviation Cadet Center, now Lackland* AFB, Texas. During the war, OCS graduated 29,000 men.

Although only a shell of its former self, the postwar school graduated Reserve officers at a rate of 300 to 600 per year for 17 years, except for an expansion during the Korean War.* The curriculum changed little, though the course was extended to 24 weeks. At first, only warrant officers and enlisted men were eligible. In 1947, civilians and, in 1948, women were admitted. In 1955, an eligibility change required a year of active duty. In the late 1950s, OCS began to send about half of its graduates to preflight school as the need grew for aircrews. Further expansion was needed in 1959, and the USAF opened Officer Training School* (OTS). With this, OCS's days were numbered. For more than 21 years, OCS had given airmen the opportunity to earn a commission. Faced with the USAF's increased emphasis on college graduates as officers, and the establishment of OTS and the Airman Education and Commissioning Program (AECP) in 1960, OCS was ended on 1 July 1963.

Movie: *Wings Up*, 1943.

References. C&C, vol. 6. Goldberg, *Hist. USAF*. History, Air Training Command, January 1963–June 1963; History, Army Air Forces Training Command, 1 January 1939–V-J Day, vol. 5, n.d.; History, Army Air Forces Training Command, 1 September 1945–1 December 1945, vol. 1, n.d.; (ATC History Office, Randolph AFB, Texas).

Thomas A. Manning

OFFICER TRAINING SCHOOL (OTS)

In the late 1950s, there were four officer sources for the USAF:* the U.S. Air Force Academy* (USAFA), Air Force Reserve Officer Training Corps (AF-ROTC), Officer Candidate School* (OCS), and direct commissioning. These four were not producing the desired mix of skills, especially in technical, engineering, and scientific fields. In addition, the new USAFA and the old AFROTC were slow to respond to changing needs. The USAF was reluctant to use direct commissioning as a solution. The action taken was to tap a significant pool that previous methods had largely ignored: graduating college seniors who had not participated in AFROTC.

For training, the USAF resurrected a concept tried briefly in World War II,* an OTS. It was activated in November 1959 at Lackland* AFB, Texas. The concept gave college graduates a shorter, more intense course than OCS. OTS would take three months instead of the OCS' six. At the same time, to tap the airmen resource and to provide motivation, the Airman Education and Commissioning Program (AECP) was established.

OTS had several advantages over OCS. It was a more expeditious and responsive procurement system, and training costs per graduate were less. More important to the USAF, OTS met the desire to make a college degree the minimum educational standard for officers. In its first three years, OTS had a tenfold increase in production. It outgrew its facilities and moved to Medina Base, two miles west of Lackland. With the growth of OTS and the establishment of the AECP, OCS was ended in July 1963.

OTS soon became the major supplier of officers. The Vietnam War* increased officer requirements, but its unpopularity on college campuses resulted in large drops in AFROTC enrollment. OTS took up the slack. In the 1980s, as reenlistment rates rose and the military became more accepted on campuses, the ratio between AFROTC and OTS reversed and AFRTOC became double or triple OTS production.

However, OTS remains the most flexible source for officers. Through 1988, OTS had produced more than 90,000 officers. In fiscal year 1989, OTS produced 1,236 officers.

References. "Air Training Command," *AF*, May 1990, pp. 68–69. History, Air Training Command, July–December 1959, January–June 1963; Edgar P. Sneed, Special Study, Air Force Military Training Center History Office, "Initial Training of Officers for the Air Force, September 1941–July 1973," 10 February 1989; (ATC History Office, Randolph AFB, Texas). Gene E. Townsend, "Lead, Motivate, Then Evaluate," *AF*, August 1980, pp. 72–77.

Thomas A. Manning

OFFUTT AIR FORCE BASE

This AFB is near Omaha, Nebraska, and is a Strategic Air Command* (SAC) field. Previously a U.S. Army post, use of it for balloons began in 1918 and for airplanes in 1924. It was named in 1924 for First Lieutenant Jarvis J. Offutt who died in an SE-5 crash in France in World War I.* Offutt was used for reserve flying training and airmail flights until 1935, when it became inactive. During World War II,* it supported heavy and medium bomber* production by the Glenn L. Martin Company. It was used for administrative purposes from 1946 to 1948, when headquarters of the SAC moved to it. KC-135 (*See* C-135) aircraft began operations in 1959. Atlas* D ballistic missiles* were there from 1959 to 1970. E-4s* began operations there in 1975.

In 1990 it had the headquarters of the SAC, the 55th Strategic Reconnaissance

Wing (SRW), 544th Strategic Intelligence Wing, 1st Aerospace Communications Wing, and the Strategic Communications Division. E-4 and C-135 variants were based there, as was a museum.

References. "Guide to Major Air Force Installations Worldwide," *AF*, May 1990, p. 128. Mueller, *AFB*, Roberts, *Dir. USAF*.

OKINAWA ISLAND, RYUKYU ISLANDS

Okinawa is an important geographic location for the global USAF.* After the U.S. return to the Philippines, the next stepping-stone for an invasion of Japan was Okinawa, the main island in the Ryukyus. An invasion of it began on 1 April 1945 with air operations conducted by aircraft carriers. On 7 April, units of the Seventh Air Force* (7AF) and U.S. Marine air elements began attack* operations on the island. As soon as possible, airfield construction began for support of an invasion of Japan. By July, a large force of fighters* and bombers* of the Fifth Air Force* (5AF) were ready. Their missions were air superiority,* control of the seas, raiding land communications and military forces in Kyushu and western Honshu Islands, reconnaissance,* protection of U.S. Navy units, and targets in China and Korea. In August, before the raids on Hiroshima* and Nagasaki, the pilots* reported that Japanese civilians were waving white flags. In this short period, while a buildup was still in progress, the Okinawa units of the USAAF* had flown 6,435 sorties and lost only 43 aircraft.

U.S. forces stayed on Okinawa after World War II.* On 5 July 1950, in response to the aggression of communist North Korea against the Republic of Korea (ROK), the Strategic Air Command* (SAC) sent B-29s* to Okinawa. Bombing operations began on 13 July. The airfields at Kadena* and Naha were built up and used as bomber bases throughout the Korean War.* Okinawa was valuable in a third war as a base for B-52* Arc Light* missions in Vietnam. Also KC-135s (*See* C-135) operated out of Okinawa to support B-52s and tactical operations.*

References. Berger, *USAF in SEA*. C&C, vol. 5. Futrell, *USAF in Korea*. Goldberg, *Hist. USAF*.

OLDS, MAJOR GENERAL ROBERT (1896–1943)

Olds contributed greatly to the U.S. development of bombers* and was a disciple of Brigadier General William Mitchell.* Born in Woodside, Maryland, Olds began his career by enlisting in the Aviation Section of the U.S. Army Signal Corps* as an aviation specialist in 1916. He began flying as an enlisted pilot* and had earned promotion to captain in France by 1918. He commanded the 2nd Bomb Group before World War II,* leading the Goodwill Flights to South America* in 1938 and 1939. For these, he received the Mackay and Harmon Trophies. This command was significant for developing strategic operations* concepts and the B-17.* He organized and commanded the ferrying service in 1941, which evolved into the Aircraft Ferrying Command under him. He briefly commanded the III Bomber Command at MacDill* Field, Florida, in

1942 before assuming command of the Second Air Force* (2AF) at Ft. George Wright, Washington, from 1942 until 1943, when he was relieved for illness.

References. Primary: Harold L. George, "The Most Outstanding Leader," *AH*, Summer 1968, pp. 4–7. Secondary: Air Force Pamphlet 31–1, "Roster of USAF Retired General Officers," 1987. DeWitt S. Copp, *A Few Great Captains: The Men and Events That Shaped the Development of U.S. Air Power*, 1980. Futrell, *Ideas*, vol. 1. Maurer, *Avn. in Army*.

Steven K. Yates

OLDS, BRIGADIER GENERAL ROBIN (1922–   )

Robin Olds is noteworthy as a World War II* ace* who also scored four aerial victories in the Vietnam War.* From Beverly Hills, California, he graduated from the U.S. Military Academy (USMA) in 1943 where he had been an All-American tackle. He entered combat in England with the 479th Fighter Group flying first P-38s* and later F-51s.* He flew 107 sorties and shot down 13 enemy aircraft* and destroyed another 11 on the ground. After World War II, he flew on the first jet aerobatic team and won second place in the Thompson Trophy Race (Jet Division) in 1946. He flew in the first one-day, dawn-to-dusk transcontinental round-trip flight in June 1946. Olds flew in the first F-80* jet squadron. In 1948, he served as commander of the No. 1 Fighter Squadron, flying Gloster Meteors at RAF Tangmere, in the USAF-Royal Air Force (RAF) exchange program.

With the 8th Tactical Fighter Wing, he earned distinction as an innovative and resourceful wing commander during the Vietnam War. He flew 152 sorties in F-4s* and participated in Operation Bolo.* He shot down two MiG-21s in Bolo. Later in 1967 he shot down another two MiG–17s. He got these four victories with an AIM-7* and AIM-9s.* Olds served as the U.S. Air Force Academy (USAFA) commandant of cadets from 1967 to 1971 and then was director of aerospace safety until he retired in 1973.

References. Primary: Robin Olds, "Forty-Six Years a Fighter Pilot," *AAHS Journal*, Winter 1968, pp. 235–39. Secondary: Air Force Pamphlet 31–1, Roster of USAF Retired General Officers," 1987. R. Frank Futrell, *Aces & Aerial Victories: The United States Air Force in Southeast Asia 1965–1973*, 1976. Hess, *Aces Album*. Edward H. Sims, *Fighter Tactics and Strategy 1914–1970*, 1972.

Steven K. Yates

ONIZUKA AIR FORCE BASE

This Air Force Space Command* (AFSPACECOM) base is at Sunnyvale, California. It was activated in 1959 as Sunnyvale Air Force Station (AFS) and was renamed for Lieutenant Colonel Ellison S. Onizuka who died in the 1986 space shuttle *Challenger* accident. In 1990, it had units of the 2d Space Wing stationed on it.

References. "Guide to Major Air Force Installations Worldwide," *AF*, May 1990, p. 128. Roberts, *Dir. USAF*.

OPERATIONAL COMMAND

Major commands* (MAJCOM) that include strategic, tactical, defense units, or which conduct flying activities directly in support of such organizations, are operational commands. Examples are the Military Airlift Command* (MAC) and the Strategic Air Command* (SAC).

Reference. Ravenstein, *Org. USAF*.

OPERATIONAL TEST AND EVALUATION CENTER. *See* Air Force Operational Test and Evaluation Center.

OPERATIONAL TOUR

Also called tour of operations, this is a combat assignment with a length determined by the number of sorties flown. The purpose of such a tour is to set a level of combat that is physically sustainable and that gives the knowledge of an ultimate end. For example, the operational tour in the Eighth Air Force* (8AF) bombers* was originally set at 25 sorties, often erroneously called "missions." The B-17F* *Memphis Belle** became famous because its crew was the first in the 8AF to complete an operational tour. The length was extended to 35 sorties after the USAAF* gained air superiority* over the Luftwaffe in 1944.

References. Roger A. Freeman, *The Mighty Eighth: Units, Men and Machines*, 1970. Woodford Agee Heflin, ed., *The United States Air Force Dictionary*, 1956.

OPERATION BABYLIFT

Operation Babylift was another demonstration of the power of the USAF* to conduct humanitarian missions.* In 1975, when the North Vietnamese invaders of the South neared final success, President Gerald R. Ford ordered the evacuation of 2,000 Vietnamese orphans to the United States. Unfortunately, the first aircraft in the operation, a C-5,* crashed shortly after takeoff from Tan Son Nhut* AB on 4 April 1975. Of 314 on board the C-5, 138 died. The rest of the operation proceeded smoothly until its end on 9 May 1975. The number of Vietnamese and Cambodian children airlifted away from communist tyranny totaled 2,678.

References. John L. Frisbee, "The Lady Was a Tiger," *AF*, June 1986, p. 115. James S. Olson, ed., *Dictionary of the Vietnam War*, 1988.

OPERATION BOLO

A resounding success, Bolo was the largest aerial victory to that point in the Vietnam War.* At the end of 1966 the MiG threat over North Vietnam had settled into a deadly pattern. U.S. fighters* held a decisive edge in air combat, having downed 23 MiGs (19 by USAF* crews) against a loss of nine (five of them USAF) during 1966. North Vietnam's air tactics were becoming better coordinated and more aggressive after it introduced a new ground-controlled interception* (GCI) system and newer model MiG-21s armed with Atoll infrared-homing air interceptor missiles* (AIM). Not only were they becoming more menacing, but the MiGs were disputing U.S. attack* forces by causing them to jettison their bombs* before reaching their targets. When U.S. fighters sought to engage, the MiGs retreated from battle to their political sanctuaries.

Since existing rules of engagement, or political air superiority,* prohibited hitting the MiG bases, the Seventh Air Force* (7AF) commander and his staff devised a deceptive fighter sweep nicknamed "Operation Bolo" to lure the MiGs into the air and to destroy them in aerial combat.

Led by Colonel Robin Olds,* the 8th Tactical Fighter Wing carried out the fighter sweep on 2 January 1967. Composed of F-4* fighters, accompanied by F-105* Wild Weasel* surface-to-air missile* (SAM) suppression aircraft, the sweep was designed to appear as a normal F-105 attack mission. Simultaneous sweeps were planned to enter the target area from Laos and from the Gulf of Tonkin, but the Gulf force had to abort its mission because of weather. The MiGs rose to challenge a daily attack force of "F-105s" but found instead, to their surprise, F-4s spoiling for a fight. The North Vietnamese had been outwitted and now were outgunned. Within minutes, Olds and his pilots* shot down seven MiGs without a single loss. Olds was personally credited with two of the kills.

References. Berger, *USAF in SEA*. R. Frank Futrell, *Aces & Aerial Victories: The United States Air Force in Southeast Asia 1965–1973*, 1976. William W. Momyer, *Air Power in Three Wars*, 1985.

Warren A. Trest

OPERATION BOOTSTRAP

Fathered by General Curtis E. LeMay,* Operational Bootstrap was one of the educational programs supervised from headquarters of the USAF.* It aimed to raise the general educational level of USAF officers and airmen by enabling them to attend college on permissive temporary duty (TDY). It dovetailed with the volunteer off-duty education program. The latter, however, offered tuition assistance, where the first named did not.

Bootstrap began in the late 1940s and came at a time when about 25 percent of USAF officers did not have college degrees. LeMay wanted that statistic revised, hence his interest in the program. From 1950 to 1955, a relatively small number took advantage of the opportunity. Beginning in 1956 and continuing until about 1970, enrollments totaled about 1,000 officers and airmen annually. This number dropped drastically to around 500 from 1970 to 1972, partially because of the volunteer program mentioned earlier. TDY lasted from six to nine months, and the schools involved numbered around 50. By 1988, the total enrollment in Bootstrap was 250 officers and enlisted yearly.

References. Air Training Command Pamphlet 190–1, *History of the USAF*, 1961.** Goldberg, *Hist. USAF*. Telephone interview with Mr. Gill and Chief Master Sergeant Miskelly, HQ USAFE/MPPE, 22 April 1988. USAF Regulation 213–1, 31 March 1988.

**This is in error. It has confused the program with the volunteer off-duty education effort.

Lloyd H. Cornett, Jr.

OPERATION COBRA. *See* St. Lo, France.

OPERATION CROSSROADS

Conducted in the summer of 1946 at Bikini Atoll in the Marshall Islands, this was the first post–World War II atmospheric nuclear weapon* test series. President Harry S Truman's* (HST) approval in January 1946 to use three nuclear bombs, half of the country's stockpile, underscored the importance of Crossroads. Although not a weapons development test, the significance of Crossroads was that it collected valuable scientific nuclear weapons effects data that previously was unavailable from the Trinity test or the Hiroshima* and Nagasaki bombings.

The tests measured the hostile environment created by a nuclear detonation to include static, or crushing, and dynamic, or blast, pressure; heat; and fallout radiation. In addition, they determined the effects on animals and military equipment such as ships, aircraft, tanks, trucks, artillery, medical equipment, and radar;* and on supplies such as aircraft parts, ammunition, petroleum, field stoves, and clothing. The results were to be used to define the nature, range, and duration of radiation danger; to assist in the design of naval vessels to improve protection against nuclear weapons; and to shape naval tactics for the nuclear age.

Crossroads consisted of two detonations. "Able" took place on 1 July 1946, and "Baker" took place on 25 July. Each weapon had a yield equal to 23,000 tons of TNT and were of the same design used on Nagasaki, Japan. For Able, a USAAF* B-29,* named *Dave's Dream*, dropped the bomb* which burst 520 feet above the target fleet anchored in Bikini lagoon. Baker detonated in a waterproof container 90 feet below the water surface. A third and deeper underwater shot named "Charlie" had been planned but was canceled after Baker. At the time, Crossroads was the largest U.S. peacetime military operation conducted, involving 42,000 people, 251 ships, and 156 aircraft. A specially convened Joint Task Force One, made up of U.S. Army, Navy, and civilian representatives, and commanded by Vice Admiral William H. P. Blandy was responsible for the tests. The target fleet consisted of three surrendered German and Japanese warships, surplus U.S. cruisers, destroyers, submarines, two aircraft carriers, and a large number of auxiliary and amphibious craft.

Able sank five ships, yet radiation levels allowed boarding most ships within a day. Baker inflicted more damage than Able, sinking eight ships. It also produced high levels of radiation contamination resulting in a two-week waiting period before the target ships could be boarded to recover instrumentation.

References. L. Berkhouse, Frank W. McMullan, et al., DNA (Defense Nuclear Agency) Report Number 6032F, "Operation Crossroads: 1946," 1 May 1984. Lloyd J. Graybar, "The 1946 Atomic Bomb Tests: Atomic Diplomacy or Bureaucratic Infighting?"

Journal of American History, March 1986, pp. 888–907. Kenneth L. Moll, "Operation Crossroads," *AF*, July 1971, pp. 62–69.

Robert W. Duffner

OPERATION EAGLE CLAW. *See* Iran hostage rescue mission.

OPERATION JUST CAUSE. *See* Panama incident of 1989.

OPERATION KINGPIN. *See* Son Tay prison raid.

OPERATION LINEBACKER I AND II. *See* Linebacker.

OPERATION LITTLE VITTLES

During the Berlin Airlift* of 1948 to 1949, Operation Little Vittles, named by the fliers, was an especially important contribution to the morale of those associated with the airlift. It was a *tour de force*; a success beyond anyone's expectations and a means of ensuring Allied cooperation.

First Lieutenant Gail S. Halvorsen, an airlift pilot,* decided to supplement the Berlin,* Germany, children's meager supply of candy by dropping some to them by parachute from his airplane. In July 1948, he was struck by the thought that, unlike other European children he had met, those of Berlin did not ask him for gum or candy when he was on the street. He handed out some sweets anyway to a large number of children gathered at the Tempelhof* AB fence and promised to bring more the following day. Accordingly, the next day Halvorsen dropped three handkerchief "parachutes" with candy attached from the flare chute of his aircraft; thereafter, he made daily drops.

At first, Halvorsen was concerned that Major General William H. Tunner,* Berlin Airlift Task Force* commander, might disapprove; but Tunner immediately grasped the morale benefit of the action for both aircrews and the Berlin people. Tunner institutionalized the Little Vittles airdrops by establishing collection points for candy and handkerchiefs and by arranging special flights for Halvorsen to circle the city dropping candy during his approach to Tempelhof, even to children in the Soviet Zone of occupation. Within a few months the operation had taken on massive proportions as U.S. businesses and citizens contributed candy. At one point the American Confectioners' Association shipped 6,500 pounds of candy for Little Vittles.

References. Primary: Gail S. Halvorsen, *The Berlin Candy Bomber*, 1990. *Oral History with Col. Gail S. Halvorsen*, Scott AFB, Illinois, Office of MAC History, 1988. William H. Tunner, *Over the Hump: The Story of General William H. Tunner, the Man Who*

Moved Anything Anywhere, Anytime, 1964. Secondary: Harold Nufer, "Uncle Wiggly Wings," *Air Power History,* Spring 1989, pp. 26–29.

Roger D. Launius

OPERATION MARKET GARDEN. *See* Market.

OPERATION NEUTRALIZE

This action demonstrated the capability of air power in reconnaissance* and attack* against a conventional ground offensive. In the summer of 1967 the North Vietnamese army (NVA) massed 37 battalions just north of the Demilitarized Zone (DMZ) in preparation for an invasion of the Republic of South Vietnam. In response, the United States and its allies reinforced a line of defensive positions south of the DMZ. Shelling by the NVA became heavy, about 1,000 rounds per day, especially on the U.S. Marine Corps base at Con Thien. The Seventh Air Force* (7AF) devised a plan to upset the NVA, called Operation Neutralize. Besides the 7AF, U.S. Navy aircraft and shipboard and Marine artillery would try to disrupt the NVA artillery and mortars. Neutralize began on 12 September 1967 and lasted for 49 days.

At the start there were coordination problems within the Neutralize forces. By the end of September, informal arrangements between the services greatly reduced those difficulties. In the operation, the USAF* flew 2,220 sorties, of which 820 were by B-52s.* The Marines flew about 1,600. Of the sorties, 916 used Combat Skyspot* radar* direction. The NVA artillery was hurt badly and its activity dwindled to the point that Con Thien was no longer considered under siege. The NVA invasion had been blocked.

References. Berger, *USAF in SEA.* John Schlight, *The War in South Vietnam: The Years of the Offensive 1965–1968,* 1988.

OPERATION NIAGARA. *See* Khe Sanh, South Vietnam.

OPERATION OVERLORD

This was the Allied code for the World War II* cross-Channel invasion of German-held Europe on "D-Day." During the initial weeks, Allied air superiority* was nearly absolute and proved to be the key aspect of success against a most capable force. The ability to provide attack* for friendly forces and to interfere decisively with the movement of German reserves made possible both the successful invasion and subsequent rapid drives to the German border.

Led by General Dwight D. Eisenhower,* supreme commander of the Allied Expeditionary Force, the primary objectives were to gain a secure foothold in France and then drive across the Seine River toward Germany. Preparations involved a massive accumulation of forces in Britain, including 39 battle divisions, 15,800 aircraft of all types, and more than 6,000 vessels. German defenses, commanded by Generalfeldmarschall Gerd von Rundstedt, included 58 divisions of varying quality, and only 160 serviceable aircraft of all types. These forces were scattered among fortifications along the European west coast from southern

France to Norway. The Germans recognized the dominance of Allied air power, so they hoped to prevent a serious buildup of an invasion by containing it at the beachhead.

In April and May 1944, Eisenhower combined strategic* and tactical* operations in an effort to isolate the invasion area by destroying German air capabilities and transportation networks in France, especially the bridges across the Oise, Seine, and Loire Rivers. Then, on the morning of 6 June, five infantry divisions of the U.S. First and British Second Armies, preceded by three airborne divisions dropped inland by tactical airlift* to protect the Allied flanks, invaded the Normandy Peninsula between Caen and Carentan. Strategic and tactical air units flew more than 14,600 sorties the first day, providing combat air patrol (CAP) and attack for both naval and land elements.

Due to weather and a lack of aerial reconnaissance,* the Germans were caught by surprise. Their response was further slowed by Adolf Hitler's refusal to release sufficient reserves and by the air superiority of the Allies. The latter was crucial. Allied air forces had ruined the French roads and railways, and they now relentlessly attacked German divisions moving to reinforce the battle zone. Even if units managed to reach the front, the need to disperse, the heavy loss of materiel en route, and the continuing Allied ground offensive precluded timely massing for significant counterattacks or realistic attempts to contain the Allied lodgement. The Allies quickly secured their beachhead, made slow and inexorable progress across Normandy, and finally broke out across central France on 31 July.

References. Primary: Dwight D. Eisenhower, *Crusade in Europe*, 1948. Laurence S. Kuter, "D-Day: June 6, 1944," *AF*, June 1979, pp. 96–101. Secondary: W. W. Rostow, *Pre-Invasion Bombing Strategy: General Eisenhower's Decision of March 25, 1944*, 1981. Hilary St. George Saunders, *The Fight Is Won*, vol. 3 of *Royal Air Force 1939–1945*, 1954. Herman S. Wolk, "Prelude to D-Day: The Bomber Offensive," *AF*, June 1974, pp. 60–65. Humphrey Wynn and Susan Young, *Prelude to OVERLORD*, 1983.

See also Zuckerman, Professor Solly.

                                                                                        Richard L. Davis

OPERATION POINTBLANK. *See* Combined Bomber Offensive.

OPERATION RANCH HAND

Crop dusting was the origin of releasing chemicals from aircraft. In World War II,* Royal Air Force (RAF) Hurricanes sprayed a valley in Burma with D.D.T. in advance of the British army to suppress malaria. In the communist rebellion in Malaya, the British struck the rebels a heavy blow by spraying insurgents' crops. In 1959, herbicides that could improve the visibility for military operations were developed.

In 1961 defoliants were provided to the Republic of South Vietnam to help it secure its borders. The next step was to use the chemicals along communication routes to suppress guerrilla ambushes. In January 1962, four chemical-spray C-123s* arrived at Ton Son Nhut* AB, South Vietnam, for the project called

Operation Ranch Hand. After the first year of operations, the number of ambushes declined markedly. In 1962, President John F. Kennedy* (JFK) approved the destruction of enemy crops by the Vietnamese air force (VNAF). In 1964, the USAF* C-123s started crop destruction. The success of these operations led to the addition of three more C-123s for the mission in 1965. Ranch Hand reached its zenith in 1967 with 1,687,758 acres sprayed. Of this, 85 percent was for defoliation and the rest was for crop destruction. The force then had 19 UC-123s. In the same year, some people in the United States began to object to the operation on moral and ecologic grounds.

In 1968, with the military effectiveness of Ranch Hand well established, President Nguyen Van Thieu of South Vietnam asked that the program be reduced. He did this because he believed North Vietnam gained more from propaganda about Ranch Hand than it lost in physical damage. This, combined with the beginnings of U.S. retreat, acted to reduce Ranch Hand operations. The same year, the Herbicide Policy Review Committee, appointed by the U.S. ambassador to South Vietnam, Ellsworth D. Bunker, released its report. It said the use of Agents White, Blue, and Orange should not cause concern. In 1969, U.S. press and public pressure to stop the use of herbicides increased greatly. They were joined by U.S. scientists, antiwar activists, and enemy propaganda. In 1970 Ranch Hand operations were ended. The effects of its chemicals on people and the ecology have been disputed ever since. The dispute may only be resolved by studies after the passage of many more years.

References. Berger, *USAF in SEA*. William A. Buckingham, Jr., *Operation Ranch Hand: The Air Force and Herbicides in Southeast Asia 1961–1971*, 1982. John Lewallen, *Ecology of Devastation: Indochina*, 1971. John Schlight, *The War in South Vietnam: The Years of the Offensive 1965–1968*, 1988.

OPERATION ROLLING THUNDER. *See* Rolling Thunder.

OPERATIONS PLAN 34A

This plan evolved from Secretary of Defense (SECDEF) Robert S. McNamara's* visit to the Republic of South Vietnam in December 1963. He was concerned with the situation there and adopted plans by the commander in chief Pacific (CINCPAC), Admiral Harry D. Felt.

The idea was for extensive covert sabotage raids on North Vietnam by troops of the Republic. They were to put psychological pressure on the North. The USAF* would contribute reconnaissance* with U-2s.* McNamara persuaded President Lyndon B. Johnson* (LBJ) to approve the plan on 31 December. In February, U-2s of the Strategic Air Command* (SAC) flew one to two sorties every day. The intelligence, together with that from other sources, indicated the North Vietnamese would invade the South through Laos. On 30 July, South Vietnamese navy commandos raided Hon Me and Hon Ngu Islands in North Vietnam. These islands had facilities that supported North Vietnamese infiltration of the South by sea. In response, the North's navy may have sent torpedo boats into the Gulf of Tonkin to strike at the destroyer USS *Maddox*.USAF and U.S. Navy aircraft retaliated. The action had escalated beyond Plan 34A.

References. David A. Anderton, *History of the U.S. Air Force*, rev. ed., 1989. Robert F. Futrell, *The Advisory Years to 1965*, 1981.

OPERATION STEEL TIGER. *See* Steel Tiger and Tiger Hound Operations.

OPERATION STRANGLE

Strangle was conducted from 19 March to 11 May 1944 by the Mediterranean Air Forces under Lieutenant General Ira C. Eaker* and was an aspect of the Allied campaign to capture Rome, Italy. This World War II* campaign taught the Allies much about low-level interdiction attack.* The lessons contributed directly to the tactical operations* for and after Operation Overlord,* especially the destruction of bridges along the Loire and Seine Rivers in France. It, and Operation Diadem, showed that interdiction aimed at supply denial is most effective when combined with ground action.

The Allied Fifteenth Army Group, commanded by General Sir Harold Alexander, landed in Italy in September 1943. Skillful delaying actions and stubborn defense by Luftwaffe Generalfeldmarschall Albert Kesselring's Army Group Southwest stopped the Allied advance at the Gustav line, a defensive installation, just north of Naples. An amphibious assault at Anzio in January 1944, intended to outflank the Germans, stalled without result. Thus a decision was made to use interdiction in an attempt to break the deadlock.

The objective of Strangle was to concentrate all types of Allied aircraft against enemy transportation and communication lines to make German supply operations impossible. The Allies flew 65,006 sorties and dropped 33,104 tons of bombs,* losing 365 aircraft to the German's 296. Strangle failed to force a retreat by itself because of the German ability to effect countermeasures. German withdrawal from the Gustav was finally forced in a second interdiction campaign, Diadem, begun in conjunction with a massive ground drive on 11 May 1944.

Movie: *Thunderbolt*, 1945.

References. Primary: John Slessor, *The Central Blue: Recollections and Reflections*, 1956. Secondary: C&C, vol. 3. Eduard Mark, "A New Look at Operation STRANGLE," *Military Affairs*, October 1988, pp. 176–184. James Parton, *"Air Force Spoken Here": General Ira Eaker and the Command of the Air*, 1986. F. M. Sallagar, *Operation "STRANGLE" (Italy, Spring 1944): A Case Study of Tactical Air Interdiction*, 1972.

Richard L. Davis

OPERATION TALLY HO

This 1966 campaign in the Vietnam War* was a special effort to stop supplies moving south to frustrate a North Vietnamese buildup for an offensive to seize Quang Tri Province in the Republic of South Vietnam. The interdiction belt ran north for 30 miles from the Demilitarized Zone (DMZ), so it was in Route Package* 1 of the Rolling Thunder* operation. Despite some problems, the

North Vietnamese offensive was abandoned, so Tally Ho achieved its goal. It was a foretaste of what would be done in Linebacker* I.

Tally Ho was to be conducted by the USAF* and the U.S. Marines. The USAF requested a coordinated effort, but the Marines balked, preferring independent operations. General William C. Westmoreland, commander of the U.S. Military Assistance Command, Vietnam (MACV), ruled in favor of the Marines. Action began on 20 July 1966 with the USAF using F-4s,* B-57s,* and O-1 Bird Dogs* based in South Vietnam. Not until 24 July was the USAF permitted to attack* inside the DMZ, despite the long-standing and extensive military use of the zone by the North Vietnamese. In the campaign, the North Vietnamese could move only by night because of USAF effectiveness by day. The volume of supplies and the enemy's inability to move by day forced it to use supply dumps and caches, and these were hit by the airmen.

Tally Ho destroyed much ammunition, 70 trucks, 1,200 structures, 80 watercraft, and 90 flak* locations by November. The USAF believed results would have been better had there been more coordination between the services. The U.S. Army selected the targets, causing the USAF to believe that some lucrative targets for air power were ignored. Also, some targets escaped greater danger because the Army ordered the ordnance and it was inappropriate. Sometimes artillery use prevented air support. The USAF reduced the effectiveness of attack by not giving flight* commanders more latitude in decisions. The USAF also found in this operation that the enemy had obtained enough flak to drive away the O-1s.

References. Berger, *USAF in SEA*. John Schlight, *The War in South Vietnam: The Years of the Offensive 1965–1968*, 1988.

OPERATION TIDAL WAVE. *See* Ploesti, Romania.

OPERATION TORCH

This campaign began with Allied landings in Algeria and Morocco on 8 November 1942 and was the first large-scale combined U.S.-British operation of World War II.* The Allies planned to cut off German forces in North Africa, secure the Mediterranean lines of communication, relieve some German pressure on the USSR, and open up southern Europe for strategic operations* from air bases in North Africa. The move would also force the French to declare their position in the war, a risky but possibly beneficial result.

The Americans created the Twelfth Air Force* (12AF) with 1,244 aircraft and the mission to guard against possible hostile Spanish or German reaction through the Iberian Peninsula. The British contributed the Royal Air Force Eastern Air Command with 454 aircraft, plus carrier-based attack* aircraft. To support invasion preparations, Allied air units hit U-boat pens on the French coast, provided bases and support in England and Gibraltar, conducted reconnaissance* and antisubmarine warfare, shepherded convoys, mined and bombed Italian ports, and kept track of the French, Spanish, and Italian navies.

Torch started well, and the Allies readily advanced to within 40 miles of Tunis by the ninth day. Then rapid German reinforcement and counterattacks effectively stopped the Allies until mid-December, when winter rains mired operations in mud. The Allies did not regain the initiative until the following spring. The Germans held throughout the winter, finally evacuating Tunisia in May 1943.

The requirements of Torch drew off much of the forces from the build up in England. This hampered both the strategic operations against Germany and delayed Operation Overlord* until 1944. The supporting bombing raids in Italy, however, disorganized and demoralized the Italians and may have contributed to the Italian surrender the following year. Torch was the first fruit of the U.S.-British combined strategy and thus set the pattern for Allied cooperation for the rest of the war.

Torch taught some important lessons to the USAAF.* It showed the value of accurate intelligence, the utility of indivisible use of air assets, and the importance of air bases close to the front lines. Most important, the Americans learned that a centralized command structure was essential to the use of air power's flexibility. During the campaign, the lack of a unified air component command had resulted in heavy losses, an inability to mass air assets effectively, and a failure to obtain air superiority* over Tunisia quickly.

References. C&C, 7 vols. Denis Richards and Hilary St. George Saunders, *Royal Air Force 1939–1945*, 1954. John Slessor, *The Central Blue: Recollections and Reflections*, 1956.

See also Coningham, Air Marshal Sir Arthur; Palm Sunday Massacre.

                                                                    Richard L. Davis

OPERATION URGENT FURY. *See* Grenada incident.

OPERATION VITTLES. *See* Berlin Airlift.

OPERATION VULTURE

When the French were beleaguered at Dien Bien Phu, Indochina, in 1954, the United States considered military action to relieve them. The USAF* and the U.S. Navy believed that B-29* strikes would help. The U.S. Army thought only ground forces would be effective. President Dwight D. Eisenhower* and Senator Lyndon B. Johnson* opposed using soldiers. Eisenhower reluctantly agreed to the use of air strikes, code-named Operation Vulture, but on the condition of agreement and support for such action from U.S. allies. There was none, and the idea was abandoned.

References. David A. Anderton, *History of the U.S. Air Force*, rev. ed., 1989.

"OPIE." *See* Weyland, General Otto P.

ORGANIZATION

The organization of the USAF's* antecedents underwent rapid change until 1946 when the modern form was established. The 1916 organization of the Aviation Section of the U.S. Army Signal Corps* consisted of the 1st Aero

Squadron* with the Mexican expedition of 1916,* the San Diego Signal Corps' Aviation School* in California, and the 1st Company of the 2nd Aero Squadron in the Philippines. The section had 46 officers, 243 enlisted men, and 23 aircraft. On the eve of the U.S. entry into World War I,* there were plans for seven squadrons. After war began, several divisions were created in the section, and reliance was placed on assistance from the National Advisory Committee for Aeronautics (NACA) and the Aircraft Board.*

Organization was better in the American Expeditionary Force (AEF). At first, the airmen were divided into a Zone of Advance for operations and a Zone of Interior for support. Late in 1917, the staff was organized into a number of parts: Policy, Administration, Technical, Training and Organization, Operations, Balloons, Personnel, and Supply.

In 1920, the USAAS* had four departments called groups: Administrative, Information, Training and Operations, and Supply. With the formation of the USAAC* in 1926 there became five units: the Air Corps Training Center* for flight training,* Technical School, Balloon and Airship School, Tactical School, and Materiel Division.

The first air force,* the General Headquarters Air Force* (GHQ Air Force) of 1935, was not part of the USAAC but was placed under the War Department chief of staff. This was done for operational reasons, but it caused problems because the USAAC was still responsible for materiel and personnel. In 1939 the GHQ Air Force was placed under the USAAC.

When the huge expansion took place for World War II,* the organization had to become more specialized. In the USAAF* of March 1942, there were six agencies in its Operating Staff. There were eight major commands* (MAJCOM): Proving Ground, Technical Training, Flying Training, Materiel, Air Service, Ferrying, Second Air Force* (2AF), and Third Air Force* (3AF). A year later, the main headquarters staff consisted of Personnel; Intelligence; Training; Materiel Maintenance and Distribution; Operations, Commitments, Requirements; and Plans. In addition, there were six special staff agencies. This organization lasted, generally, through most of the war.

When General Carl A. Spaatz* succeeded the General of the Army H. H., Arnold* in February 1946 as head of the USAAF, he reorganized it along the lines he anticipated a USAF would need. In March, the beginnings were made with the creation of 13 MAJCOMs. There were the Strategic Air,* Tactical Air,* and Air Defense Commands; five support commands;* and five overseas commands aligned into the pattern of theater of war commands. This structure became that of the USAF when independence was achieved. The basic concept of functional organizations has not changed since.

In 1990, the USAF had 12 MAJCOMs: Air Force Communications,* Air Force Logistics,* Air Force Space,* Air Force Systems,* Air Training,* Electronic Security,* Military Airlift,* Strategic Air, and Tactical Air Commands; Air University;* Pacific Air Forces;* and U.S. Air Forces Europe.* The USAF also had 16 separate operating agencies* (SOA), 11 direct reporting units*

(DRU), the Air National Guard* (ANG), and the U.S. Air Force Reserve* (USAFR).

References. C&C, vols. 1 and 6. Goldberg, *Hist. USAF.* Juliette A. Hennessy, *The United States Army Air Arm April 1861 to April 1917*, 1985. James J. Hudson, *Hostile Skies: A Combat History of the American Air Service in World War I*, 1968. Maurer, *Avn. in Army.* U.S. Air Force Fact Sheet 89–05, "Organization of the United States Air Force," February 1989.

ORGANIZATIONAL MAINTENANCE

This is maintenance that an operating unit does on its equipment. For example, it includes servicing, adjustment, inspection, cleaning, and minor repair. Originally, the unit doing this for aircraft was a flying squadron.* In the 1960s it was decided that aircraft had become too complicated for this arrangement. The operating unit became a wing* which had an Organizational Maintenance Squadron for all the wing's flying squadrons.

References. Primary: James R. McCarthy, "A Quarter Century of Air Force Maintenance," *AH*, March 1982, pp. 48–55. James H. Straubel, ed., *Air Force Diary: 111 Stories from the Official Service Journal of the USAAF*, 1947. Secondary: Woodford Agee Heflin, ed., *The United States Air Force Dictionary*, 1956.

ORPHAN. *See* Aphrodite.

ORR, SECRETARY VERNE (1916–   )

Orr was the 14th secretary of the Air Force* (SAF) serving from February 1981 to December 1985, which was longer than any other. Orr wanted to be remembered for being a caring person, and he succeeded. He was one of the USAF's* most popular secretaries and led the service through one of its most progressive periods. The Air Force Association* established an annual award in his name to recognize the unit or individual making the most effective use of human resources.

Like others in the presidency of Ronald Reagan,* Orr was new to the Washington, D.C., scene. He was a successful California businessman who had an outstanding civic service record and who had held important state posts when Reagan was governor. A U.S. Navy officer during World War II,* he had no USAF service. That proved no handicap.

Orr's leadership was people-oriented, emphasizing USAF families and their needs. He was proud to report at the end of his watch that there had been large pay raises for the military and quality-of-life enhancements like new dormitories, family housing, and commissaries at many bases.

Nevertheless, readiness of the force was paramount. Upon taking office, Orr declared the B-1* to be his number-one priority. Killed by the Carter administration, it was restored by Reagan as a high-priority program. Orr was "privileged" to fly on the first B-1B delivered to the Strategic Air Command* (SAC) before he left office. Shortly after SAC had its first B-1B, the first C-5B* rolled out. Orr could also boast the USAF had 650 more fighters* than in 1981, with modern F-15s* and F-16s* the principal ones. The Air Force Space Command* (AFSPACECOM) was born in Orr's term, and ground was broken for the Consolidated Space Operations Center in Colorado and the USAF Shuttle Launch Facility in California. Testing of the Peacekeeper* ballistic missile* continued, and Orr reported the C-17* and the Advanced Tactical Fighter* (ATF) dreams were within reach. He also approved changes at the Air University* (AU) that were designed to make it the premier professional military education school.

References. Primary: Verne Orr, "The Air Force Family—Our Most Essential Resource," *AF*, May 1981, pp. 72, 73; and "Finishing the Firsts," *AF*, February 1985, pp. 85–89. Secondary: Ron Fuchs, "Saying Goodbye," *Airman*, November 1985, pp. 8–11. Futrell, *Ideas*, vol. 2. USAF Biography, "Verne Orr," November 1983.

Warren A. Trest

OSAN AIR BASE

This Pacific Air Forces* (PACAF) field is 38 miles south of Seoul, Republic of Korea. The USAF* activated it in 1952 as K-55. In 1956 it was named for a nearby village. The field was built to serve jet fighters* in 1952 and was the only base built entirely new for the Korean War.* It received the 18th Fighter-Bomber Wing, initially with F-51s,* but with F-86s* later. In 1990 it had headquarters of the Seventh Air Force* (7AF) and the 51st Tactical Fighter Wing (TFW) with F-16s.*

References. Futrell, *USAF in Korea*. "Guide to Major Air Force Installations Worldwide," *AF*, May 1990, p. 128. Roberts, *Dir. USAF*.

OSI. *See* Air Force Office of Special Investigations.

OV-10 BRONCO

This aircraft was developed for both the USAF* and the U.S. Marine Corps and started as the North American Aviation, Inc., NA-300. It was part of Secretary of Defense (SECDEF) Robert S. McNamara's* drive for aircraft in use with more than one service, or "commonality." It was selected for further development in a design competition in 1964. The competition was with the General Dynamics Corporation's Charger. The Charger had similar performance but had been built as a private venture at one-fifth the cost of the NA-300. Some people believed the NA-300 was selected only out of embarrassment because of the government time and money sunk into it.

The USAF wanted such an aircraft primarily for forward air controllers* (FAC). The first flight took place in 1965. It entered active service in the Vietnam War* in 1968, and the USAF sent 126 for duty there. Originally, it was unarmed, but four M60C .30-caliber machine guns and high-velocity aircraft rockets* (HVAR) were added. In 1970 another addition to 15 OV-10s was intended to equip them for night FAC operations. This equipment, called Pave Nail, included a night sight, laser rangefinder, and target illumination device.

The OV-10 was built with insufficient power and, as a commonality aircraft, with compromises. Its performance has been disappointing. The USAF bought

157, and it was still in active service in 1990. Its nickname was "Double-Breasted Hummingbird."

Characteristics: engines, two Garrett-AiResearch T76-G-10/132 turboprops of 715 horsepower each; span, 40 feet; length, 40 feet; height, 15 feet; gross weight, 14,444 pounds; top speed, 281 miles per hour; service ceiling, 28,800 feet; range, 450 miles.

References. Primary: Henry S. Bartos, "The OV-10: USAF's Battling Bronco," *AF*, April 1973, pp. 36–40. Higham, *Combat Airc.*, vol. 1. Secondary: Swanborough, *US Mil. Airc.* Wagner, *Am. Planes.*

OVERLORD. *See* Operation Overlord.

OVER-THE-SHOULDER BOMBING. *See* Low-Altitude Bombing System.

OX-5. *See* Curtiss OX-5.

P

P-1, P-3, P-5, P-6, and P-23

The Curtiss Aeroplane and Motor Company, Inc., provided the main USAAC* fighters in the later 1920s with its "Hawk" series. Curtiss called them Hawks, but the USAAS* and USAAC did not. The P-1 of 1925 was derived from an earlier USAAS Curtiss fighter,* the PW-8. The PW-8 had been based upon the Curtiss R-6 racer, which took first and second place in the 1922 Pulitzer Trophy Race.* The liquid-cooled engines of the P-1 were replaced by radials in the P-3. The P-5 and P-6 returned to liquid cooling. The P-6 took first and second places in the 1927 National Air Races. The winner flew at 201 miles per hour. At the time, the P-6E was called the most beautiful fighter plane in history.

A final model was the XP-23, a redesigned P-6. It had an all-metal monocoque fuselage and metal tail surfaces. Total production for the USAAS and USAAC was 25 PW-8s and 253 P-1s through the XP-23.

Characteristics (P-6E): engine, Curtiss V-1570C of 700 horsepower; span, 32 feet; length, 23 feet; height, 9 feet; gross weight, 3,436 pounds; top speed, 193 miles per hour; service ceiling, 23,900 feet; range, 244 miles.

References. Primary: Ross G. Hoyt, "The Curtiss Hawks," *AF*, October 1966, pp. 68, 69. Secondary: Peter M. Bowers, *Curtiss Aircraft 1907–1947*, 1979. Swanborough, *US Mil. Airc.*

P-12

This single-seat Boeing Airplane Company biplane was known as the F4B in the U.S. Navy and Boeing Model 100 for export. There was little of innovation in the plane; however, it was highly popular and was produced in large numbers for its time: 586. The P-12 was the last biplane fighter* to be introduced in numbers in the USAAC* inventory. It first flew in 1929. Later P-12Bs added a cowl ring to reduce drag and so to increase speed. A flyable example is on display at the Museum of Flight in Seattle.

Characteristics (P-12E): engine, Pratt & Whitney R-1340–17 of 500 horsepower; span, 30 feet; length, 20 feet; height, 9 feet; gross weight, 2,690 pounds; top speed, 189 miles per hour at 7,000 feet; service ceiling, 26,300 feet.

References. Primary: Mark Bradley, "The Boeing P-12E," *AH*, December 1985, pp. 239–45. S. L. Wallick and Peter M. Bowers, *Flying the P-12*, 1982. Secondary: Peter M. Bowers, *Boeing Aircraft since 1916*, 1989. Swanborough, *US Mil. Airc.*

Alwyn T. Lloyd

P-26

This was the first monoplane fighter* and first all-metal airplane produced for the USAAC.* It was a low-wing type, externally braced with wires, and was equipped with a cowl ring and wheel pants to reduce drag. Nicknamed "Peashooter," it first flew in 1932. The Boeing Division of the United Aircraft and Transport Corporation built 184.

Characteristics (P-26A): engine, Pratt & Whitney R-1340–27 of 500 horsepower; span, 28 feet; length, 24 feet; height, 10 feet; gross weight, 2,955 pounds; top speed, 234 miles per hour at 7,500 feet; service ceiling, 27,400 feet; range, 360 miles.

References. Primary: Higham. *Combat Airc.*, vol. 2. Secondary: Peter M. Bowers, *Boeing Aircraft since 1916*, 1989. Edward T. Maloney, *Boeing P-26 "Peashooter,"* 1973. Swanborough, *US Mil. Airc.*

Alwyn T. Lloyd

P-35

The Seversky Aircraft Corporation built two fighters* with their own funds, and one flew first in 1935. The USAAC* asked it be redesigned and accepted the changed model as the P-35 in 1937. An order was given for 77 of them. When this production ended, the renamed Republic Aviation Corporation designed an export version. Sweden bought 100 in 1940. In late 1940, President Franklin D. Roosevelt* (FDR) requisitioned all 60 undelivered aircraft, and they were designated as P-35As. When the United States entered World War II,* there were 48 P-35As in the Philippines. Most were lost on the ground when the Japanese achieved surprise in a raid.

Characteristics (P-35A): engine, Pratt & Whitney R-1830–45 of 1,050 horsepower; span, 36 feet; length, 27 feet; height, 10 feet; gross weight, 6,723 pounds; top speed, 290 miles per hour at 12,000 feet; service ceiling, 31,400 feet; range, 950 miles.

References. Edward T. Maloney, *Sever the Sky: Evolution of Seversky Aircraft*, 1979. Swanborough, *US Mil. Airc.* Wagner, *Am. Planes.*

P-36

The first product of Curtiss-Wright Corporation's chief designer, Donovan Berlin, was the Model 75. It had a sturdy airframe powered by a radial engine which did not do it justice. It failed the competition to choose the United States's first 300-mile-per-hour fighter,* but, in 1938, an improved version won a contract for 210 planes—the largest order yet placed by the USAAC.* As the P-36, this fast, aluminum-skinned monoplane served as the United States's frontline fighter for the next two years and saw service at Pearl Harbor* and Clark* Field in December 1941. Most USAAC models had only two nose guns, but wing guns were added at the request of the British, and up to six were in the P-36G. British Commonwealth, Dutch, and French pilots* fought valiantly in P-36s but to little effect in 1940 to 1941. From India, Royal Air Force (RAF) Mohawks, as they were called by the British, fought over Burma as late as June 1942. Under license, China built a cheaper, less powerful version with fixed landing gear that was a principal weapon of its air force from 1937 to 1942, often with mercenary pilots.

Characteristics (P-36G): engine, Wright R-1820–95 of 1,200 horsepower; span, 37 feet; length, 29 feet; height, 10 feet; gross weight, 5,750 pounds: top speed, 323 miles per hour at 15,100 feet; service ceiling, 32,700 feet; range, 650 miles.

References. Primary: Higham, *Combat Airc.*, vol. 2. Secondary: Gerry Beauchamp, *Mohawks at War*, 1988. Peter M. Bowers, *Curtiss Aircraft 1907–1947*, 1979. Joe Christy and Jeff Ethell, *P-40 Hawks at War*, 1980. Murray Rubenstein and Richard Goldman, *To Join with the Eagles*, 1974.

Daniel Ford

P-38 LIGHTNING

The P-38 was a twin-engine, twin-boom fighter* produced by the Lockheed Aircraft Corporation in response to a USAAC* Circular Proposal for a high-altitude interceptor.* Unable to meet requirements with one of the power plants available, H. L. Hibbard's design staff opted for two engines, each housed in a boom, with a central nacelle between the booms containing armament, landing gear, and pilot.* Lieutenant Benjamin S. Kelsey* flew the prototype XP-38 in January 1939 and, despite a crash upon landing, the USAAC ordered 13 more planes. They were the first of an eventual 9,923 P-38s delivered by August 1945.

It was the first modern USAAC fighter of World War II* and saw action in the 1942 Operation Torch* with inconsistent results. Combat often took place below the P-38's optimum altitudes and a slow adaption to appropriate tactics reduced results. In Europe, the heavy fighter had difficulties with more maneuverable enemy aircraft* even though the Germans called it *Der Gabelschwanz Teufel*, "fork-tailed devil."

In the Pacific, P-38s became the premier U.S. fighter. With proper tactics, heavy firepower, and long range, it helped decimate Japanese air power. The two top-scoring USAF* aces* of all time, Majors Richard I. Bong* and Thomas B. McGuire, Jr.,* flew P-38s in the Pacific. It was a P-38 that shot down Japanese Admiral Isoroku Yamamoto.*

Before ending active service, the P-38 claimed several U.S. fighter firsts: twin-engine fighter, speed of more than 400 miles per hour, compressibility effects, full-scale production with turbosupercharger, ferry the Atlantic, aerial victory after U.S. entry into World War II.

Characteristics (P-38L): engines, two Allison V-1710–111/113 of 1,475 horsepower each; span, 52 feet; length, 38 feet; height, 10 feet; gross weight, 21,600 pounds; top speed, 414 miles per hour at 25,000 feet; service ceiling, 44,000 feet; range, 450 miles.

References. Primary: Martin Caidin, *Fork-Tailed Devil: The P-38*, 1971. Higham, *Combat Airc.*, vol. 1. Secondary: Warren M. Bodie, *The Lockheed P-38 Lightning*, 1990. R. L. Foss and Roy Blay, "From Propellors to Jets in Fighter Aircraft Design," *Lockheed Horizons*, April 1987, pp. 3–9. Le Roy Weber, "The Lockheed P-38J-M Lightning," *Profile*, n.d., pp. 3–10.

Ronald W. Yoshino

P-39 AIRACOBRA

The Bell Aircraft Corporation submitted a proposal for this fighter* in 1937, and a contract for a prototype was made. The first flight was in 1939, and a production contract followed. In 1940, Britain ordered production of a modified version. The British used only one squadron of P-39s in battle and shipped 212 of theirs to the USSR. The USAAF* reclaimed 253 from Britain after Pearl Harbor.* USAAF P-39s went into action in New Guinea* and western Europe in 1942. They soon proved inadequate as air superiority* fighters because of poor rate of climb and high-altitude performance. In Europe, P-39s were relegated to attack* tasks. In early 1944, the USAAF had 2,150, but the numbers declined as it was replaced by the superior F-47s,* F-51s,* and P-38s.* However, production continued to supply the USSR and Portugal. A total of 9,585 were built, of which 4,773 went to the USSR.

Characteristics (P-39N): engine, Allison V-1710–85 of 1,200 horsepower; span, 34 feet; length, 30 feet; height, 12 feet; gross weight, 8,200 pounds; top speed, 399 miles per hour at 9,700 feet; service ceiling, 38,500 feet; range, 750 miles.

References. Primary: Higham, *Combat Airc.*, vols. 1 and 3. Secondary: Swanborough, *US Mil. Airc.* Wagner, *Am Planes*.

P-40 WARHAWK

This versatile Curtiss-Wright Corporation fighter,* with its shark-mouthed profile, resulted from mating the P-36* airframe with an Allison in-line engine. Lacking a supercharger, the hybrid had to do most of its fighting below 20,000 feet. At medium altitude, however, even the early P-40 could engage such enemy aircraft* as the Bf 109, Ki–43 Hayabusa ("Oscar"), and A6M Reisen ("Zero"), if the pilots* used sound tactics and exploited its high diving speed. Its large-caliber nose guns and ability to absorb great punishment were most helpful.

Adapted from an existing airframe, the P-40 had the additional advantage that it could be rushed into production a year earlier than superior fighters. From 1940 to 1941, Curtiss built 524 of the Tomahawk version for the USAAC* and 1,180 for the Royal Air Force (RAF). Some of the latter were sold to China and saw service with the American Volunteer Group* (AVG). The more powerful Warhawk with six .50-caliber wing guns became a mainline fighter in 1942.

The RAF called it the Kittyhawk. Altogether, 13,700 P-40s were accepted by the USAAF* before production ended in 1944.

Characteristics (P-40N): engine, Allison V-1710–81 of 1,360 horsepower; span, 37 feet; length, 33 feet; height, 12 feet; gross weight, 8,850 pounds; top speed, 378 miles per hour at 10,500 feet; service ceiling, 38,000 feet; range, 240 miles.

References. Primary: Robert W. Fausel, *Whatever Happened to Curtiss-Wright?* 1990. Higham, *Combat Airc.*, vol. 3. Secondary: Peter M. Bowers, *Curtiss Aircraft 1907–1947*, 1979. Joe Christy and Jeff Ethell, *P-40 Hawks at War*, 1980. Murray Rubenstein and Richard Goldman, *To Join with the Eagles*, 1974.

Daniel Ford

P-43 LANCER**

The Seversky Aircraft Corporation's last P-35* produced had a turbosupercharger, and tests of it in 1939 led to an improved airplane in 1940 which was designated YP-43. The manufacturer had by then been renamed Republic Aviation Corporation. A production order for 54 was placed, and deliveries began in 1941. Additional orders followed, and some aircraft were given to the Chinese air force and to the Royal Australian Air Force (RAAF). Early in production, information from the war in Europe showed the P-43 would be unsatisfactory in battle. Its significance is that it was an important step toward the F-47.*

Characteristics: engine, Pratt & Whitney R-1830–47 of 1,200 horsepower; span, 36 feet; length, 29 feet; height, 14 feet; gross weight, 7,935 pounds; top speed, 349 miles per hour at 25,000 feet; service ceiling, 38,000 feet; range, 800 miles.

References. Edward T. Mahoney, *Sever the Sky: Evolution of Seversky Aircraft*, 1979. Swanborough, *US Mil. Airc.*

**The B-1* was also named Lancer.

P-47. *See* F-47.

P-51. *See* F-51.

P-59 AIRACOMET

This was the United States's first jet aircraft and was developed by the Bell Aircraft Corporation as a result of a 1941 request by the USAAF.* The first fight was in 1942. Its engines were General Electric Company–developed British Whittle's. The successful development of the superior F-80* stopped production after 30 P-59s had been built. Moreover, the Airacomet's performance was poor, being both below those of the F-47* and P-38.* It was an unstable gun platform.

Characteristics (P-59B): engines, two General Electric J31-GE-5 of 2,000 pounds thrust each; span, 46 feet; length, 39 feet; height, 12 feet; gross weight, 13,700 pounds; top speed, 413 miles per hour at 30,000 feet; service ceiling, 46,200 feet; range, 525 miles.

References. Ronald D. Neal, "The Bell XP-59A Airacomet: The United States' First Jet Aircraft," *AAHS Journal*, Fall 1966, pp. 155–78. Swanborough, *US Mil. Airc.* Wagner, *Am. Planes.*

P-61 BLACK WIDOW

The Luftwaffe's night raids on England in 1940 spurred the USAAC* to seek a night interceptor.* In November, Northrop Aircraft, Inc., offered a plan for one that could carry radar.* It was to be the first USAAC plane designed specifically for the task. The first flight was in 1942. For its night operations, the P-61 was painted black, which led to its name. It became operational in the South Pacific in 1944, and its first victory came on 7 July. One variant was the F-15A Reporter for reconnaissance.* The F-15As were redesignated RF-61Cs in 1948. A total of 732 were built, and they ended active service in 1952.

Characteristics (P-61B): engines, two Pratt & Whitney R-2800–65s of 2,000 horsepower each; span, 66 feet; length, 50 feet; height, 15 feet; gross weight, 29,700 pounds; top speed, 366 miles per hour at 20,000 feet; service ceiling, 33,100 feet; range, 3,000 miles in ferrying.

References. Bill Gunston, *Night Fighters: A Development & Combat History*, 1976. Swanborough, *US Mil. Airc.* Wagner, *Am. Planes.*

P-63 KINGCOBRA

Based upon the P-39* Airacobra, its first flight was in 1942. The Bell Aircraft Corporation's P-63 entered active service the next year, but most of those built were given to the USSR and France. A total of 3,303 were built. A variant was unique in the history of aviation. It was meant to be used as a target for machine guns using frangible bullets. A thickened skin was used, and hits on the aircraft caused a red light to blink like a pinball machine's lights. This model was designated RP-63A and was, naturally, nicknamed "Pinball."

Characteristics (P-63A): engine, Allison V-1710–95 of 1,325 horsepower; span, 38 feet; length, 33 feet; height, 13 feet; gross weight, 8,800 pounds; top speed, 408 miles per hour at 24,450 feet; service ceiling, 43,000 feet; range, 390 miles.

References. John D. Edgar, "The Texas Pinball Machine," *AF*, August 1976, pp. 57–61. E. F. Furler, Jr., "Pinball: The Story of Bell's Armored P-63," *United States Air Force Museum Friends Bulletin*, Winter 1987–1988, pp. 44–47. Swanborough, *US Mil. Airc.* Wagner, *Am. Planes.*

P-80. *See* F-80.

P-82. *See* F-82.

P-84. *See* F-84.

P-86. *See* F-86.

PACAF. *See* Pacific Air Forces.

PACCS. *See* Post Attack Command and Control System.

PACE-FINLETTER MEMORANDUM OF 4 NOVEMBER 1952

After USAF* separation from the U.S. Army,* the latter continued to learn the advantages of air power and steadily increased the amount of its aviation. This concerned the USAF and acrimony grew in turf battles over Army aerospace power.* The Pace-Finletter memorandum was one of many efforts to try to resolve the issue. It had little effect upon the Army's recognition of the effectiveness of aerospace power and the strong desire for much more of it under direct Army control.

The memorandum represented the completion of agreements worked out in 1951 to 1952 between Secretary of the Army Frank Pace and Secretary of the Air Force* Thomas K. Finletter.* It limited Army fixed-wing aircraft to 5,000 pounds weight and tried to define better the attack* responsibilities between the services. Essentially, the Army's air power was limited to liaison aircraft,* observation aviation,* airlift operations,* and aeromedical evacuation.*

References. Futrell, *USAF in Korea*. Goldberg, *Hist. USAF*.

See also A-7; C-7; flak; Howze Board; Jupiter; Key West and Newport Conferences of 1948; surface-to-air missiles; and Wilson memorandums.

PACIFIC AIR FORCE/FEAF (REAR)

This named air force* was activated as the Pacific Air Force in 1954 at Hickam* AFB, Hawaii. It was assigned to the Far East Air Forces (FEAF). It was redesignated Pacific Air Force/FEAF (Rear) in 1956. This air force was established to control USAF* operations in the Pacific theater while the move of FEAF was made from Japan to Hawaii. It was inactivated in 1957.

Reference. Ravenstein, *Org. USAF*.

PACIFIC AIR FORCES (PACAF)

This major command* (MAJCOM) serves as the USAF* component of the Pacific Command (PACOM), a unified command.* Its headquarters is at Hickam* AFB, Hawaii, and is responsible for planning, coordinating, and conducting USAF operations within PACOM. Its area of responsibility covers 65 percent of the earth's surface, from the west coast of the United States to the east coast of Africa.

PACAF's long history began in 1912 with the establishment of a flying school at Fort William McKinley in Manila, Philippines. The National Defense Act of 1916* established air units which included the 2nd Aero Squadron in the Philippines and the 6th Aero Squadron in Hawaii. In 1931, the first central air service headquarters was established to manage the units in Hawaii.

In November 1941, the Far East Air Force** was formed in the Philippines. The units that had escaped the advancing Japanese were merged into the Fifth Air Force* (5AF) in Australia in September 1942. The Thirteenth Air Force* (13AF) was activated in New Caledonia in 1943. A new MAJCOM, Far East Air Forces (FEAF), was formed over the 5AF and the 13AF and was the direct precursor of PACAF. In 1942, the Hawaiian Air Force was redesignated the

Seventh Air Force* (7AF) and was assigned to FEAF in 1945. FEAF was headquartered in Tokyo, Japan, in 1945. FEAF directed USAF operations during the Korean War,* and in 1957 it was redesignated as PACAF and moved to Hickam. During the Vietnam War,* PACAF operated about 1,700 aircraft in the Pacific theater. After the end of the war, PACAF's inventory fell to about 200 aircraft in 1976.

During the early 1980s, PACAF began to modernize and expand by adding A-10s,* F-15s,* and F-16s.* This buildup was prompted by an increased Soviet presence in Southeast Asia (SEA) and the Soviet Far East Military District, as well as a realization that the Pacific region had become increasingly vital, economically and geopolitically, to the United States. In 1990, PACAF had four numbered air forces* and the 313th Air Division. The Eleventh Air Force* (11AF) was at Elmendorf* AFB, Anchorage, Alaska; the 5AF was at Yokota* AB, Japan; the 7AF was in Seoul, Republic of Korea (ROK); and the 13AF was at Clark* AB in the Philippines.

References. James P. Coyne, "PACAF's Global Perspective," *AF*, August 1985, pp. 42–48. "Pacific Air Forces." *AF*, May 1990, pp. 81–82. Ravenstein, *Org. USAF*. Tactical Air Command Manual 2–1, "The United States Pacific Command," 15 April 1978.

**The Far East Air Force was not the same organization as the Far East Air Forces (FEAF).

George W. Hawks, Jr.

PACUSAN DREAMBOAT

In 1945 and 1946, with World War II* over, the USAAF* thought it was necessary to maintain public interest in air power. A way to do this was to demonstrate the capability of aircraft, a technique used often between the world wars. The improved aircraft available after the last war offered a new means to do this.

A B-29* named *Dreamboat* flew nonstop from Guam to the District of Columbia in 1945. The distance of 8,198 miles was flown in 35 hours and five minutes, a new record. Other, shorter flights were made in other B-29s to set records. A second long flight was made in 1946 with a B-29 named the *Pacusan Dreamboat*. The name *Pacusan* was derived from Pacific Air Command, *U.S. Army*, with a letter *n* added. In October the plane took off from Honolulu, Hawaii, with 12,892 gallons of gasoline, giving the plane a gross weight of 148,477 pounds. The flight went over Alaska, the Arctic, Greenland, and on to Cairo, Egypt, approximating a great circle route of 10,925 miles. It took 39 hours and 36 minutes. Both *Dreamboat* flights were under the command of Colonel C. S. "Bill" Irvine.

In addition, the *Pacusan Dreamboat* demonstrated the vulnerability of the United States to long-range bomber* strikes in the air age.

References. James M. Boyle, "This Dreamboat Can Fly!" *AH*, Summer 1967, pp. 85–92. Alwyn T. Lloyd, *B-29 Superfortress in Detail & Scale*, part 2, "Derivatives," 1987.

PALM SUNDAY MASSACRE

Luftwaffe airlift operations* never recovered from the debacle of the Palm Sunday Massacre and campaign. The massacre shows the absolute need for air superiority* in conducting an airlift.

By April 1943, supply of the German Afrika Korps in Tunisia depended upon airlift operations using Ju 52s, SM-82s, and Me 323s. These Axis aircraft were operating out of Naples and Palermo, Italy, to Sidi Ahmed and El Aouina, Tunisia. About 500 transports were involved and the fighter escort* and for any particular group was usually 12 aircraft.

The Allies deliberately did not strike in order to wait for the opportunity of a large kill. On 5 April the first Allied effort was made. It was called Operation Flax. A convoy of 50 to 70 Ju 52s, 20 Bf 109s, six Ju 87s, four Fw 190s, and one Fw 187 was intercepted by 26 P-38s.* The USAAF* lost two P-38s and claimed 11 Ju 52s, two Bf 109s, two Ju 87s, and the Fw 187. More operations were conducted on succeeding days.

On 18 April a large Luftwaffe convoy flew into Tunisia without battle. About 100 Ju 52s with German and Italian fighters* in close escort attempted to return. Four P-40* squadrons with some British Spitfires caught them in what is now known as the Palm Sunday Massacre. German losses were 51 Ju 52s and 16 other aircraft: Bf 109s, Me 110s, and Me 202s. Allied losses were six P-40s and one Spitfire.

After the massacre, the Germans had the greatest difficulty in operating at sea but continued their airlift despite catastrophic losses because the situation of the Afrika Korps was desperate. By 22 April their losses could no longer be sustained.

References. C&C, vol. 2. Goldberg, *Hist. USAF.*

PANAMA INCIDENT OF 1989

The U.S. invasion to oust General Manuel Antonio Noriega, the dictator of Panama, was called Operation Just Cause. It was the biggest U.S. night airdrop in combat since Operation Overlord.* The USAF* role was to spearhead the night attack,* suppress the defenses, and provide tactical airlift* for U.S. Army Rangers.

Two F-117As* led the attack by striking the flak* at Rio Hata, a key Panamanian military base 50 miles southwest of Panama City. They evidently succeeded, for the fixed flak battery did not operate. However, mobile flak did open fire on the 15 C-130s* conducting the tactical airlift. The first C-130s dropped paratroopers who secured the field for landings. Four C-130s dropped Rangers onto Torrijos-Tocumen International Airport near Panama City. After the initial landings, C-130s and C-141s* brought in reinforcements. Eleven C-130s were damaged by small arms fire. The operation was influenced by the Grenada incident* and the Libyan raid.*

References. David Fulgham, "The Air Force Role in Panama," *Air Force Times*, 8 January 1990, pp. 14–16. David Hughes, "Night Airdrop in Panama Surprises Noriega's

Forces." *AWST*, 1 January 1990, pp. 30–31. Edward Luttwak, "Operation Just Cause: A Look at What Went Right, Wrong," *Air Force Times*, 8 January 1990, pp. 21, 61. John D. Morrocco, "F-117A Fighter Used in Combat for First Time in Panama," *AWST*, 1 January 1990, pp. 32–33.

PAN AMERICAN FLIGHT OF 1926

As one of the spectacular flights performed to demonstrate the capability of aircraft, the USAAC* sent five AO-1As** to the Panama Canal Zone and then around the coast of South America. Under the command of Major Herbert A. Dargue, they departed in December 1926 and returned by May of 1927. Despite maintenance problems and accidents that claimed two lives, they were celebrated upon their return.

References. Primary: Ira C. Eaker, "The Air Corps's 1926 Pan American Flight," *AF*, September 1976, pp. 114–24. Secondary: Maurer, *Avn. in Army*. James Parton, *"Air Force Spoken Here": General Ira Eaker and the Command of the Air*, 1986.

**These aircraft were observation amphibians built by the Loening Aeronautical Engineering Corporation and should not be confused with the O-1 Bird Dog* or O-1 Falcon.*

PANTELLERIA, ITALY

This island in the Pelagie group, between Tunisia and Sicily, was in a strategic location in World War II.* It had been called the "Gibraltar of the Central Mediterranean." In the possession of the Axis powers, it was a threat to an invasion of Sicily. It had an airfield and radar* and could service enemy U-boats and torpedo boats. A neighboring island, Lampadusa, was a lesser threat. A decision was made to try to force Pantelleria to surrender by bombardment from air and sea in Operation Corkscrew.

The Allies' air strength for the attempt was 1,000 aircraft, and the enemy had available about 900. Corkscrew was scheduled for 18 May to 11 June 1943. On 8 June USAAF* fighters* dropped messages demanding unconditional surrender. Then bombers* dropped leaflets saying resistance was useless. There was no response from the island. An amphibious landing force was then made ready to invade. The island ran up a white flag and radioed a request to surrender, and Axis resistance ceased before any landings were made. The air raids shifted to Lampadusa, and after one day the island showed white flags.

These events were to be the first case of surrender to air operations. Two factors strongly favored the result. Pantelleria was not well prepared to resist air assault, and the main forces, Italians, had low morale.

References. C&C, vol. 2. Goldberg, *Hist. USAF*.

"PAPPY." *See* American Volunteer Group; Gunn, Colonel Paul I.

PARRISH, BRIGADIER GENERAL NOEL F. (1909–1987)

Parrish was the white director of training and commander of black pilots* at Tuskegee Army Air Field, Alabama, during World War II.* His other major assignments included deputy secretary of the Air Staff* (1948–1951), air deputy of the North Atlantic Treaty Organization* (NATO) Defense College (1954–1956), deputy director of the Military Assistance Division of the U.S. European Command (EUCOM) (1956–1958), assistant for coordination to the deputy chief of staff of plans and programs (1958–1962), and director of the Research Studies Institute (1962–1964). After retirement in 1964, he earned a Ph.D. in history from Rice University. He taught military history at Trinity University, Texas, and the Air War College, Maxwell* AFB, Alabama.

References. Primary: U.S. Air Force Oral History Interview K239.0512–744, 10–14 June 1974, USAFHRC/OH, Maxwell AFB, Alabama. Secondary: Air Force Pamphlet 31–1, "Roster of Retired General Officers," 1987. Alan L. Gropman, *The Air Force Integrates, 1954–1964*, 1978. Department of the Air Force, Office of Information Services, Public Information Division, 1956.

James C. Hasdorff

PARTRIDGE, GENERAL EARLE E. "PAT" (1900–1990)

Partridge was commander in chief of the Continental Air Defense Command (CONAD) and its USAF* component, the Air Defense Command (ADC), from 1955 to 1959.

Born in Winchendon, Massachusetts, he was a U.S. Army enlisted man in France in 1918, graduated from the U.S. Military Academy (USMA) in 1924, and then received flight training.* He served at the Air Corps Tactical School* (ACTS), assisted in the buildup of the USAAC* before World War II,* participated in the North African campaign and the air war over Europe, and had an active role in the Korean War.* He was commander of the Far East Air Forces (FEAF) (1954–1955), deputy chief of staff for operations at headquarters of the USAF (1953–1954), commander of the Air Research and Development Command (ARDC) (1951–1953), and commander of the Fifth Air Force* (5AF) (1948–1951). He retired in 1959.

References. Primary: Richard H. Kohn and Joseph P. Harahan, eds., *Air Interdiction in World War II, Korea, and Vietnam*, 1986. U.S. Air Force Oral History Interview K239.0512–729, 23–25 April 1974, USAFHRC/OH, Maxwell AFB, Alabama. Secondary: Air Force Pamphlet 31–1, "Roster of USAF Retired General Officers," 1987. DuPre, *USAF Bio*. U.S. Air Force Biography, Secretary of the Air Force, Office of Information, 1957.

James C. Hasdorff

"PAT." *See* Partridge, General Earle E.

PATHFINDER FORCE (PFF)

Pathfinder operations in World War II* were the use of electronic means to bomb when clouds or night obscured the target. Attention was first given by the USAAF* in England in late 1942 to British systems, GEE, Oboe, and GEE-H.* Difficulties with these systems led to a switch in emphasis to H2S in March 1943.

H2S was British also, a self-contained airborne radar* set which was in short supply. The USAAF turned to the Massachusetts Institute of Technology (MIT) for help. By September 1943, 12 sets of H2X, the U.S. and improved version of H2S, were available.

The first plan for its use was to make the 482nd Bomb Group with B-17s* into a pathfinder unit, with one squadron using H2S and two using H2X. Individual crews and their planes of this PFF would fly as lead crews with regular groups.* The regular bombers* would drop their bombs* upon a signal from the PFF plane. Later the pathfinders were integrated into regular groups.

Although PFF operations enabled bombing to be conducted through clouds, the results were much less accurate than visual aiming. On balance, the USAAF liked H2X, and the demand exceeded the supply. The Eighth Air Force's* (8AF) goal was two bombers from each regular group to be pathfinders by the end of 1944. Seventy-eight percent of the goal was reached. The Fifteenth Air Force* (15AF) also adopted H2X. In the last quarter of 1944, about 80 percent of 8AF and 70 percent of 15AF operations included some blind-bombing devices. These units continued to believe that blind bombing was better than no bombing.

References. C&C, vols. 2 and 3. Roger A. Freeman, *Mighty Eighth War Manual*, 1984.

PATHFINDER RADAR (H2X). *See* Pathfinder Force.

PATRICK, MAJOR GENERAL MASON M. (1863–1942)

Patrick was the fifth and last chief of the USAAS* and the first chief of the USAAC,* serving from 1921 to 1926 in those capacities. He sought to moderate the more ardent complaints of Brigadier General William Mitchell* and other air power enthusiasts to obtain a gradual evolution of the U.S. Army air arm under War Department auspices. The most notable result of his attitude and efforts was the Air Corps Act* of 1926 which created the USAAC and had a five-year aircraft construction program.

Patrick was born in Lewisburg, West Virginia, and graduated second in the class of 1886 at the U.S. Military Academy (USMA). A classmate of General John J. Pershing,* he was academically inclined and first gained attention when Pershing appointed him air chief of the American Expeditionary Forces (AEF) in France in 1918. Pershing wanted to keep two airmen with personality clashes separate and operating at their best: Brigadier General Benjamin D. Foulois* and Mitchell.

In 1921, Pershing became Army chief of staff and appointed Patrick as chief of Air Service, passing over Mitchell who had been serving as assistant to Chief of Air Service Major General Charles T. Menoher.* During the next five years, Patrick led the USAAS transition to the USAAC and tried to channel Mitchell's aviation enthusiasm into constructive channels where other military brass would not be irritated. Mitchell was sent on inspection tours to both Europe and the Pacific, but he could not be silenced even after Patrick "exiled" him to a Texas station in early 1925.

Judging from Patrick's testimony to such groups as the Lampert Committee*
and the President's Aircraft Board,* he agreed with Mitchell that air power
would eventually become a vital element of national defense. Patrick's style,
however, was to marshal strong evidence of aviation's potential and the lagging
development of U.S. aviation to maintain good relations with superiors and
Congress. Thereby, he believed, the orderly growth of air power would be obtained.

Thus, while Mitchell irritated and prodded officials to investigate aviation
needs, Patrick swept up what crumbs of funding and authorization for aviation
could be garnered. As early as 1924, Patrick suggested organizing offensive air
units into a General Headquarters Air Force* (GHQ Air Force), but his proposal
was not realized until 1934. Patrick praised Mitchell's foresight and prophecy,
but accepted whatever practical steps might be taken to advance aviation. Historically, Patrick served a role contrasting with, but as vital as, Mitchell's colorful, charismatic role in promoting air power. By the time Patrick retired in
1927, the USAAC was a separate Army unit and Congress had approved an
assistant secretary of war for air* as well as the five-year aircraft program.

References. Primary: Ira C. Eaker, "As I Remember Them: Air Chiefs Patrick and
Fechet," *AH*, June 1973, pp. 57–59. Mason M. Patrick, *Military Aircraft and Their Use
in Warfare*, 1923, and *The United States in the Air*, 1928. Secondary: DeWitt S. Copp,
*A Few Great Captains: The Men and Events That Shaped the Development of U.S. Air
Power*, 1980. Futrell, *Ideas*, vol. 1.

Lester H. Brune

PATRICK AIR FORCE BASE

This Air Force Systems Command* (AFSC) field is near Cocoa Beach, Florida.
The USAF* gained it in 1948 and first called it the Joint Long Range Proving
Ground but renamed it in honor of Major General Mason M. Patrick,* a head
of the USAAS* and USAAC,* in 1950. With USAF occupancy, the field was
expanded and rehabilitated for use with the ballistic missile* ranges running
10,000 miles southward. In 1961 it added facilities for project Mercury and
Saturn launchings. In 1990, it had the Eastern Space and Missile Center and
had supported more than 3,000 launches since 1950 from Cape Canaveral.

References. "Guide to Major Air Force Installations Worldwide," *AF*, May 1990,
p. 128. Mueller, *AFB*. Roberts, *Dir. USAF*.

PAUL DOUMER BRIDGE

This rail and highway bridge at the edge of Hanoi,* Vietnam, was a main
bottleneck in North Vietnam's transportation system. It had 19 spans across a
flood plain. It was 8,467 feet long and rested on 18 huge concrete piers. The
bridge was not only vital logistically, it was of psychological importance to the
North Vietnamese. It illustrates what interdiction can do against strong defenses.

The strategy of gradual escalation meant the bridge was not targeted by Secretary of Defense (SECDEF) Robert S. McNamara* until the summer of 1967.
Then it was attacked by three USAF wings* from Thailand using F-105s.* In

the attack,* one rail and two highway spans were dropped, and two F-105s were damaged. By 3 October the bridge had been repaired. Weather prevented an attack until 25 October when another span was dropped. By 20 November it was again repaired and then cut again on 14 and 18 December. This time repairs were not completed until 14 April 1968. When the bridge was out, the North used a ferry. A bombing halt* was ordered by President Lyndon B. Johnson* (LBJ) on 31 March. In the 1967 to 1968 missions, the F-105s flew 113 sorties against the bridge. The air defenses had 84 surface-to-air missile* (SAM) sites, 300 flak* guns, and 24 MiG-17s and MiG-21s were used. A total of 109 SAMs were fired. Two F-105s were lost to flak and 15 were damaged.

When Linebacker* I started, the bridge was again a target. It was struck on 10 May 1972 using guided bombs.* This strike dropped 29 bombs and got 12 direct hits. The bridge became unusable. The air defenses were intense, with 160 SAMs fired and 41 MiGs committed. No U.S. aircraft were lost. The next day, four F-4s* dropped eight bombs and three more spans went into the river. The bridge was out of service for months.

References. Berger, *USAF in SEA.* John L. Frisbee, "A Place Called the Doumer Bridge," *AF*, February 1988, p. 100. Jack Lavalle, ed., *Air War—Vietnam*, 1978.

See also Thanh Hoa bridge.

PAVE LOW. *See* H-53.

PAVEWAY I, II, AND III LASER-GUIDED BOMBS (LGB)

The Paveway series are Mark (Mk) 82, 83, and 84 general-purpose (GP) bombs* that are combined with guidance and control kits at the using base. The target is illuminated with a laser designator and the bomb dropped. A microprocessor controls the guidance fins and guides it to the target. Paveway bombs are cheap, require no modifications to the carrying aircraft, and are widely used throughout the world.

The 540-foot-long bridge at Thanh Hoa,* North Vietnam, was called the "Dragon's Jaw." By 1972, 871 sorties of the USAF* and the U.S. Navy had been flown in attacks* on this heavily defended bridge, and 11 aircraft were lost. In 1972 the bridge was dropped by four USAF F-4s* in one strike using Paveway I bombs. None of the F-4s was lost.

Paveway II was redesigned to be cheaper and has folding wings to extend the glide. Paveway III, or GBU-24, or low-level, laser-guided bomb (LLLGB), is the latest improved version. It has quick-fold wings, a new microprocessor, and greater ability to guide through clouds and other forms of low visibility.

References. Berger, *USAF in SEA.* Christopher Campbell, *Air Warfare: The Fourth Generation*, 1984. Gunston, *Airc. Arm.* Jack Lavalle, ed., *Air War—Vietnam*, 1978. Jeffrey P. Rhodes, "Improving the Odds in Ground Attack," *AF*, November 1986, p. 48.

Philip Long

PEACEKEEPER (MX)

The MX is a four-stage intercontinental ballistic missile* (ICBM) designed to deliver ten re-entry vehicles to targets at ranges of about 6,000 miles.

Its program began in the late 1970s as a project to supplement the aging

Minuteman* force and to make use of the latest advances in guidance technology. It consists of three solid-fuel stages which boost it to about 700,000 feet. Stage IV is fueled by a bipropellant liquid mixture that guides the post-boost vehicle (PBV) and deploys the re-entry vehicles. The guidance and control (G&C) unit within the PBV includes an innovative floating Advanced Inertial Reference Sphere.

The MX represents dramatic advances in three areas of missile technology: accuracy, size of payload, and basing versatility. The ten multiple independent re-entry vehicle* (MIRV) warheads allow a single ICBM to put up to ten targets at risk. The MX has a new and fully self-contained inertial guidance and navigation system that nearly doubles the accuracy of earlier systems. Its greatest advance, however, is its great potential for mobility. The missile is "cold launched" by steam pressure from a highly portable canister. The canister serves the functions of storage container, carrying case, and launch pad. The MX can be deployed and launched from anywhere the canister can be transported and erected. Thus, many basing options can be used: rail, truck, underground tunnel, ship, submarine, aircraft, and airship.

Peacekeeper first flew in 1983, followed by 16 other flights over the next four years. Seventeen successes and no failures is a rate unmatched by any other ICBM system in the world. Following lengthy studies and proposals for suitable basing, the decision was made to base the first 50 in converted Minuteman silos at the Francis E. Warren* AFB in Wyoming. Initial operational capability (IOC) was reached in 1986 when the first ten went on alert.

Characteristics: length, 71 feet; diameter, 92 inches; gross weight, 195,000 pounds.

References. Ballistic Missile Office, "Peacekeeper Missile Fact Sheet," June 1986. *From Snark to Peacekeeper: A Pictorial History of Strategic Air Command Missiles*, Office of Historian, SAC, Offutt AFB, Nebraska, 1990. Futrell, *Ideas*, vol. 2. Headquarters, Strategic Air Command, "Peacekeeper ICBM Program Fact Sheet," May 1986. Polmar, *SAC*.

Raymond L. Puffer

PEARL HARBOR, HAWAII

The Japanese attack* at Hawaii on 7 December 1941 was two-pronged. One struck the U.S. Navy; the other hit the USAAF* to prevent interference with the raid. It was an utter defeat for the surprised USAAF units.

At 0755 hours, 28 bombers* with fighter escort* raided Hickam* Field and the Hawaiian Air Depot. This strike lasted ten minutes. After a 15-minute lull, there was another raid, and a final one at 0900. A few minutes after the strike on Hickam, about 25 dive bombers hit Wheeler* Field. The initial attack lasted for 15 minutes, and the field was strafed after 0900. Nine Japanese fighters* shot up Bellows Field after 0900. For the rest of the day, the USAAF conducted reconnaissance* for the Japanese fleet without success.

Contributing to the ruin at the USAAF fields was the circumstance that the planes were massed to protect them from sabotage. This not only made them vulnerable, it made takeoffs more difficult. Only four P-40s* and two P-36s* got into the air from Wheeler. Five fighters took off from an auxiliary field at Haleiwa, and one of the pilots,* Lieutenant George S. Welch, claimed four victories. The outclassed P-36s shot down two enemy aircraft* with the loss of one. Twelve unarmed B-17s* arrived during the battle. They were en route to the Philippines from California; one was lost and three were heavily damaged. Of the USAAF's 231 aircraft, 64 were destroyed and 88 severely damaged. Casualties were 163 killed, 43 missing, and 336 wounded.

Movie: Tora! Tora! Tora! 1970.

References. Primary: Harold S. Kaye, "Hickam Field, 7 December 1941—The First U.S. Army Air Corps [sic] Flying Fortress (B-17D) Combat Mission in World War II," *AH*, December 1966, pp. 218–27. Henry C. Woodrum, "Cloak of Darkness," *AH*, December 1988, pp. 281–91. Secondary: C&C, vol. 1.

PENETRATORS, THE. *See* novels.

PERMANENT SYSTEM

This was the name given to the first true aircraft control and warning* (AC&W) radar* network for the air defense of the continental United States (CONUS), built between 1949 and 1953. The initial Permanent System was a foundation, but extensive improvements were required to provide an adequate air defense for the CONUS.

As early as 1945, leaders of the USAAF,* including its commander, General of the Army H. H. Arnold,* had warned that any future war would probably be initiated by a surprise air strike on the CONUS. Primary responsibility for countering such a raid rested with the USAAF.

In the fall of 1947, the new USAF* submitted to Congress its requirement for an AC&W radar network, nicknamed "Project Supremacy." Congress refused to act on it, and the USAF submitted a Modified Program for a minimum network. Approved by Congress in March 1949, it was called a Permanent System of 85 radar stations and 11 control centers, which included ten radars and one center in Alaska. To provide for the immediate threat, the USAF built a temporary system called Lashup. This was 44 radar sites on government-owned lands in California, the Northeast, and the Northwest. It was in operation by mid-1950. Lashup was dismantled as the Permanent System came into operation.

Construction of the Permanent System began in the winter of 1949, and it was in operation by 1953. Because it was a minimum system, it had serious defects. Skilled personnel, equipment, and spare parts were scarce. In addition, the system was manually operated, which was slow and inefficient. Finally, serious gaps existed in low-altitude radar coverage, early warning capability, and data-handling capacity.

References. Goldberg, *Hist. USAF*, 1957. C. L. Grant, "The Development of Continental Air Defense to 1 September 1954," Air University, Maxwell AFB, Alabama, 1957.
See also Pinetree Line.

E. Michael Del Papa

PERSHING, GENERAL OF THE ARMIES JOHN J. (1860–1948)

Pershing was commander in chief of the American Expeditionary Forces (AEF) from 1917 to 1919. He contributed to the success of U.S. Army aviation in France through his insistence that U.S. forces, including the air, should operate independently of, but in coordination with, Allied units and not be attached to them. He was quick to grasp the full range of possible applications of air power of the time and encouraged his air commanders, like Brigadier Generals Mason M. Patrick* and William Mitchell,* to use their forces to best advantage.

Pershing was a graduate of the U.S. Military Academy (USMA) in 1886. Before serving with the AEF, he compiled an impressive career in Indian campaigns, against insurgents in the Philippines, and against Pancho Villa on the Mexican border. He retired in 1924 after being Army chief of staff.

References. A. N. Marquis, *Who Was Who in America*, vol. 2, 1950. Maurer Maurer, ed., *The U.S. Air Service in World War I*, 4 vols., 1978 and 1979. Frank E. Vandiver, *The Life and Times of John J. Pershing*, 2 vols., 1985.

D. K. Vaughan

PERSIAN GULF WAR. *See* Iraq War.

"PETE." *See* Aldridge, Secretary Edward C., Jr.; Quesada, Lieutenant General Elwood R.

PETERSON AIR FORCE BASE

This Air Force Space Command* (AFSPACECOM) base is near Colorado Springs, Colorado. It became a USAAF* base in 1942. It was named in 1943 for First Lieutenant Edward J. Peterson who crashed in an F-4, an F-51* variant, on takeoff from the field in 1942. The base first conducted photoreconnaissance training, then bomber* training in 1943, fighter* training in 1944, and instructor pilot* training in 1945. It was inactivated in 1945, reactivated in 1947, and inactivated again in 1948. It was part of Ent AFB from 1951 to 1975 and then became a primary facility again. In 1990 it had the headquarters of AFSPACECOM, and the 1st Space Wing on it.

References. "Guide to Major Air Force Installations Worldwide," *AF*, May 1990, pp. 128, 130. Mueller, *AFB*. Roberts, *Dir. USAF*.

PFF. *See* Pathfinder Force.

PGM. *See* bombs.

PHAN RANG AIR BASE

This airfield was constructed as part of the USAF* buildup for the Vietnam War.* It was on the coast in the midsection of the Republic of South Vietnam. The AB was opened in March 1966 but did not have an adequate runway until

October. Its first aircraft were a squadron* of F-4s* which left when a wing* of F-100s* and a squadron of B-57s* arrived in late 1966. Three squadrons of C-123s* arrived in 1967. The USAF moved out in 1972.

References. Berger, *USAF in SEA*. John Schlight, *The War in South Vietnam: The Years of the Offensive 1965–1968*, 1988.

PHANTOM II. *See* F-4.

PHILIPPINES INCIDENT OF 1989

In 1989, when Philippines President Corazon Aquino faced her sixth attempt at a coup, she asked President George Bush for military assistance. It was given.

The leader of the coup attempt was Colonel Gregorio B. "Gringo" Honasan who was part of the 1986 coup that overthrew President Ferdinand Marcos. Honasan also attempted a coup against Aquino in 1987, after which he said he failed because he lacked air power. In the 1989 attempt, Honasan had control of some T-28s.* Philippine assets were nine F-5s,* 30 T-28s, and 20 attack* helicopters.* On 1 December, T-28s struck the presidential palace in Manila. The USAF* used F-4s* from Clark* AB to patrol over rebel airfields to prevent further rebel air operations despite the Philippines' F-5s which sided with Aquino. No other U.S. forces were used. Just after the coup failed, popular opinion in the Philippines credited the USAF with the most important role in its defeat.

References. Julie Bird, "Clark AB F-4s Answer Philippine Call for Help," *Air Force Times*, 11 December 1989, p. 6. Matt Miller, "Aquino Survives Coup Attempt But Hold on Philippines Weakens," *The Wall Street Journal*, 4 December 1989, p. A12.

PHOTORECONNAISSANCE. *See* reconnaissance.

PHU CAT AIR BASE

This airfield was near the coast in the northerly central part of the Republic of South Vietnam. The decision to build it was made in February 1966. It was occupied by C-7s* in January 1967 before it was finished. By May, F-100s* were being used there also. The USAF* left in 1971.

References. Berger, *USAF in SEA*. John Schlight, *The War in South Vietnam: The Years of the Offensive 1965–1968*, 1988.

PIERCED-STEEL PLANKING (PSP)

PSP is metal plank, first made of steel, ten feet long and 15 inches wide with flanged round holes punched in it. It has hooks and eyes for joining one piece with another. PSP can be quickly locked together to produce a surface of any size. In place, a mat of PSP can support aircraft that weigh up to 60,000 pounds and move up to 90 miles per hour. It was first called "Marston Mat" and was invented in 1940 by Gerald G. Greulich of the Carnegie Illinois Steel Company. It caused an aviation revolution because it provided a quick means to build runways, taxiways, and hardstands on bare ground. It could be called "instant airfield." It enabled the USAAF* rapidly to build airfields around the world and as the war situation changed. In the Vietnam War,* aluminum mats were introduced. The mat is still an efficient tool for its purpose.

References. Futrell, *USAF in Korea. The Official Pictorial History of the AAF*, 1947. Richard K. Smith, "Marston Mat," *AF*, April 1989, pp. 84–88.

PILOT

A pilot is a person who has the directional controls of an aircraft or spacecraft and who is in the vehicle. In the USAF* it is an aeronautical rating, and the commander of an air or space vehicle must be a pilot.

References. Ernest J. Gentle and Lawrence W. Reithmaier, eds., *Aviation/Space Dictionary*, 6th ed., 1980. Woodford Agee Heflin, ed., *The United States Air Force Dictionary*, 1956, and *The Second Aerospace Glossary*, 1966.

PILOT TRAINING. *See* flight training.

PINETREE. *See* High Wycombe, England.

PINETREE LINE

This was the nickname given to the Radar Extension Program for the Permanent System* of air defense agreed upon and built in the early 1950s by the USAF* in conjunction with the Royal Canadian Air Force (RCAF). As anticipated, the Pinetree Line filled many radar* and early warning gaps in the Permanent System.

The Permanent System for the continental United States (CONUS) had deficiencies. Radar coverage was shallow, early warning was lacking for the most vital approaches from the north and from the Atlantic and Pacific Oceans, and there were gaps in the low-altitude coverage. Complete radar coverage was deemed economically infeasible, so the USAF adopted a "double perimeter." This was two lines of radar around the most important target areas, requiring mobile and gap-filler radars, more automation of data, and extension of the early warning line northward and seaward. In 1949, the U.S. Joint Chiefs of Staff (JCS) approved the Canada–United States Emergency Defense Plan calling for joint high-level air defense planning. In 1950 the USAF directed the Continental Air Command* (CONAC), in conjunction with the RCAF, to prepare a plan for the Pinetree Line. The plan was submitted in July. Deliberations between the nations then took place until approval of the Radar Extension Program in February 1951.

The Pinetree Line called for 33 aircraft control and warning (AC&W) sites, 22 to be financed by the United States and 11 by Canada. Ten would be manned by the Northeast Air Command* (NEAC), eight by the Air Defense Command (ADC), and the other 15 by the RCAF. Delays in construction slipped Pinetree's target completion date from 1952 to 1954. By the end of June 1954, all of Pinetree Line's sites were fully operational.

References. Goldberg, *Hist. USAF*. C. L. Grant, "The Development of Continental Air Defense to 1 September 1954," Air University, Maxwell AFB, Alabama, 1957.

                                                                              E. Michael Del Papa

PLATTSBURGH AIR FORCE BASE

This base is named for the nearby city in New York. It is a Strategic Air Command* (SAC) field and is the second-oldest active facility in the United States, being established in 1814.** Before the USAF* moved there in 1955, it was Plattsburgh Barracks. The first USAF planes there were KC-97s (*see* C-97) and B-47s* in 1956. In 1962 Atlas* ballistic missiles* became operational. In 1966 it got B-52s* and FB-111s (*See* F-111) in 1972. In 1990 it had the 380th Bomb Wing with FB-111s and KC-135s (*See* C-135).

References. "Guide to Major Air Force Installations Worldwide," *AF*, May 1990, p. 131. Mueller, *AFB*. Roberts, *Dir. USAF*.

**The oldest is the U.S. Military Academy (USMA).

PLOESTI, ROMANIA

Eight oil refineries ringed the city of Ploesti and supplied the Third Reich with ten million tons of oil fuel annually, meeting one-third of the Luftwaffe's and Panzer Corps' needs. It was part of the German oil industry target system* which the USAAF* hoped to destroy with strategic operations.* A raid of 1 August 1943 was the only single action in World War II* in which as many as five Air Force Medals of Honor* were awarded.

That raid, code-named Operation Tidal Wave, was painstakingly planned by Colonel Jacob Smart as a low-level assault to minimize the need for a restrike. Led by Brigadier General Uzal G. Ent, 178 B-24Ds* took off from Libya to make the strike. The raid was plagued by several unfavorable events. A "don't shoot" radio message to Allied naval units was promptly deciphered by German intelligence, who alerted Colonel Alfred Gerstenberg's defenders of Ploesti. Crossing the mountains of Albania, clouds and wind shear separated the formations. A navigation error diverted two of the five formations toward Bucharest; although the error was eventually corrected, the new flight path brought the B-24s over the densest flak* corridor.

Intense flak erupted from camouflaged emplacements; barrage balloon cables and 52 enemy fighters* brought down more of the raiders. The boxcars of a speeding train dropped their sides and, at pointblank range, fired on B-24s on the final approach. That approach was followed by what was, for most B-24s, a bloody, smoke-and-flame–filled bomb* run requiring precision bombing of targets enclosed by concrete blast walls. After the bomb runs, 125 fighters took an additional toll of the bombers.*

Tidal Wave incapacitated about 42 percent of Ploesti's refining machinery for six months; unfortunately, this was surplus capacity, and delivery rates for refined crude were unaffected. Only 92 B-24s made it back to Benghazi, and most were badly shot up. These losses, with shifts in the battle front, delayed a restrike until 5 April 1944, when high-level attacks were primarily used. The Germans used smoke screens on these raids. In 19 missions, Ploesti's capacity was reduced by 80 percent. It was overrun by Soviet ground forces on 30 August 1944.

References. Tom Blow, "The First Raid on the Ploesti Oil Fields," *Annals of War*, January 1988, pp. 46–51. C&C, vols. 2 and 3. James Dugan and Carroll Stewart, *Ploesti: The Great Air-Ground Battle of 1 August 1943*, 1962. Barrie Pitt, ed., *The Military History of World War II*, 1986. Leon Wolff, *Low Level Mission*, 1957.

Thomas C. Blow II

POINTBLANK. *See* Combined Bomber Offensive.

POLITICAL AIR SUPERIORITY

This refers to battle advantages and sanctuaries awarded to an enemy by U.S. politicians in an effort to limit perceived risks of escalation, reduce the effectiveness of air power, to raise friendly power morale, or to convince a hostile power of U.S. goodwill, humanity, and peacefulness. It is unknown how accurate these perceptions were or whether the goals were achieved. It seems clear that the immediate cost to the United States of giving political air superiority to an enemy has been U.S. blood and treasure.

In the Korean War,* the USAF* was forbidden to cross the Yalu River, giving the enemy a sanctuary in Manchuria although Red China had entered the war. The enemy could remain free of interference when north of the Yalu until it was advantageous to cross and attack.* This also enabled the enemy to break off action by retreating across the barrier. His vulnerable bases across the Yalu were made immune to attack, and battle was, therefore, confined to MiG Alley.*

It has been contended that this situation was actually of military advantage to the USAF as well, for the Chinese did not commit to risk their large air forces because of the sanctuary. In addition, the argument goes, the political air superiority caused the reciprocity of limiting China's actions to Korea itself. On the other hand, China may have feared to expand the war, in which case the sanctuary was, basically, disadvantageous to the United States.

A disadvantage for the USAF's future was that it set a precedent; in addition, the facts that the political air superiority granted to China did not prevent the USAF from achieving air superiority south of MiG Alley or from achieving U.S. war goals obscured the disadvantages of the policy. It was easy to overlook heavier losses of men and equipment in a war. Consequently, political air superiority was reapplied in the Vietnam War.*

The restrictions applied in Vietnam under President Lyndon B. Johnson* (LBJ) were more comprehensive than those in Korea. There was to be no blockade at sea, and a sizeable sanctuary was created along the Chinese border. The principal cities of Hanoi and Haiphong, and their military installations, were put off-limits. In areas where interdiction was allowed, only specific military resources were put at risk. Few or no attacks were permitted on targets of high value to the enemy's war effort: electrical power, shipping, arms industries, the transportation network, airfields, military training centers, oil facilities, flak,* surface-to-air missile* (SAM) sites, and the food system. Much fewer restrictions were applied under President Richard M. Nixon for the Linebacker* operations.

References. Primary: Jack Broughton, *Going Downtown: The War against Hanoi and Washington*, 1988. Secondary: Larry Berman, *Lyndon Johnson's War: The Road to Stalemate in Vietnam*, 1989. John Morrocco, *Rain of Fire: Air War, 1969–1973*, a vol. of *The Vietnam Experience*, 1985. George E. Tormoen, " 'Political Air Superiority' in the Korean Conflict," *Air University Quarterly Review*, Winter 1953–54, pp. 78–84.

See also Broughton, Colonel Jacksel M.; Lavelle, Major General John D.

POLTAVA, USSR

During World War II,* the USAAF* was interested in flying over enemy territory to a friendly base and landing there rather than making a round-trip flight from the home field. The advantages of these shuttle flights were seen as hitting targets otherwise out of range, forcing the dilution of air defenses through expansion of operational areas, and, in the case of the USSR, to show U.S. vigor in prosecuting the war and the advantages of strategic operations.* Shuttle missions to the USSR were called Operation Frantic.

Joseph Stalin, the Soviet dictator, agreed to support 200 USAAF aircraft on six bases the Soviets would prepare. On 2 June 1944, the first flight was made with 130 B-17s* and 70 F-51s* from the Fifteenth Air Force* (15AF) in Italy. Led by Major General Ira C. Eaker,* they bombed Debrecen, Hungary, and landed at Poltava after losing one B-17. On the return, another B-17 was lost.

On 21 June, the Eighth Air Force* (8AF) sent 114 B-17s and 70 F-51s to bomb near Berlin,* Germany, and then fly on to Poltava. The USAAF had not calculated on the lack of air superiority* on the eastern front. Shortly after midnight, the Luftwaffe raided Poltava, destroying 43 and damaging 26 B-17s, while 15 F-51s were lost. The USAAF's munition dumps and 450,000 gallons of gasoline were blown up. One American and 25 Soviets died. This Luftwaffe victory greatly cooled the enthusiasm for Frantic, although more missions were flown with the last on 18 September.

It was found that the Frantic operations could have been conducted with less cost by regular round-trip flights. The Luftwaffe did not shift its air defense resources because of the shuttle flights. The Soviets were not impressed. Frantic was a failure.

References. Primary: Marvin S. Bowman, "Stopping Over at Ivan's Airdrome," *AF*, April 1972, pp. 51–55. James H. Staubel, ed., *Air Force Diary: 111 Stories from the Official Service Journal of the USAAF*, 1947. Secondary: C&C, vol. 3. Glenn B. Infield, "Shuttle Raiders to Russia," *AF*, April 1972 pp. 46–50.

POPE AIR FORCE BASE

Near Fayetteville, North Carolina, this base was established as Camp Bragg Flying Field in 1919. In the same year it was renamed for First Lieutenant Harley H. Pope who was killed in a crash nearby. The USAAS* used it for aircraft and balloons in its early years. Later it was a base for test operations for the Keystone* bomber. In the 1930s Pope underwent a far-ranging expansion program. The improvements were put to good use in World War II* when Pope became a center for tactical airlift* training. C-46s,* C-47s,* and gliders* used the field, training with the U.S. Army's 82nd and 101st Airborne Divisions.

In 1950 it became a Tactical Air Command* (TAC) base. During the Korean War* it had the headquarters for the Ninth Air Force* (9AF) and had fighter,* fighter-bomber, and photoreconnaissance elements. In 1954 the 9AF moved out, and the 464th Troop Carrier Wing moved in. The 464th worked closely with the Army's XVIII Airborne Corps at adjacent Fort Bragg. In 1971, the 464th deactivated and the 317th Tactical Airlift Wing, with C-130s,* moved to it from Europe. In 1974 the 317th and Pope were transferred from TAC to the Military Airlift Command* (MAC) when the USAF* consolidated all airlift into MAC. In 1990 the 317th and C-130s were still there.

References. Brown, *Eagles.* "Guide to Major Air Force Installations Worldwide," *AF*, May 1990, p. 131. Mueller, *AFB.* "Pope Air Force Base, 1919–1979: Sixty Years of Leadership and Service to Country," Office of MAC History, Scott AFB, Illinois. Roberts, *Dir. USAF.*

Roger D. Launius

POPEYE. *See* AGM-142.

"POP-UP" MANEUVER

This is a technique used in attack* and tactical operations.* The target is approached at a low level. The attacker pulls up, or "pops up," in time to reach an altitude and position that is desirable for target identification and to launch weapons.

References. Ernst J. Gentle and Lawrence W. Reithmaier, eds., *Aviation/Space Dictionary*, 6th ed., 1980. Bill Gunston and Lindsay Peacock, *Fighter Missions*, 1989.

"POSSUM." *See* Hansell, Major General Haywood, S., Jr.

POST ATTACK COMMAND AND CONTROL SYSTEM (PACCS)

If the Strategic Air Command* (SAC) Command Post at Offutt* AFB were destroyed, an alternate means of command exists in PACCS and National Emergency Airborne Command Post (NEACP). This system was continuously airborne from 1961 until 1990, flying randomly over the United States to be invulnerable. In those 29 years, it flew 275,000 hours without a major accident. Beginning in 1990, it flew randomly timed sorties and otherwise was on quick reaction ground alert. Also called Looking Glass, the system used EC-135* (*See* C-135) and E-4B* aircraft.

References. "Strategic Air Command," *AF*, May 1990, p. 83. Bill Yenne, *S*A*C: A Primer of Modern Strategic Airpower*, 1981.

POWER, GENERAL THOMAS S. (1905–1970)

Power was a major figure in strategic operations* and was commander in chief of the Strategic Air Command (CINCSAC) from 1957 to 1964. He was born in New York City, New York, and enlisted in the USAAC* in 1928. He became a pilot* and officer in 1929. He had various operational assignments in the United States and the Philippines before World War II.* He began combat as the executive and deputy commander of the 304th Bomb Wing in Europe with B-24s* from January to August 1944. Then he returned to the United States to command the 314th Bomb Wing at Colorado Springs, Colorado, a B-29* unit he led to Guam, Marianas* Islands. He helped Major General Curtis E. LeMay* change the tactics of the B-29s from high-altitude daylight bombing to low-level night fire-bomb raids against Japan. From Guam, he led the first large-scale bombing raid on Tokyo, Japan, when 334 B-29s, the largest and most deadly such raid, struck on 9 March 1945. Such assaults included not only Tokyo but Osaka, Nagoya, Yokohama, and other industrial cities. General Carl A. Spaatz* moved Power on 1 August 1945 to his staff as deputy chief of operations for the U.S. Strategic Air Forces* in the Pacific.

In 1946 he became assistant deputy task force commander for Air Task Force No. 1, or Operation Crossroads,* on Bikini Atoll in the Pacific Ocean. In 1948 he became vice commander of the Strategic Air Command* (SAC). From 1954 to 1957, he commanded the Air Research and Development Command. After his tour as CINCSAC, he retired.

References. Primary: Thomas S. Power, *Design for Survival*, 1964. Secondary: Department of Air Force, Office of Information, Biography, "General Thomas Sarsfield Power," n.d. DuPre, *USAF Bio*. War Department, Biography, "Thomas Sarsfield Power," 20 April 1945.

Lloyd H. Cornett, Jr.

PRATT & WHITNEY (P&W) ENGINES

The Pratt & Whitney Aircraft Company, a division of United Technologies, has been a leading manufacturer of aircraft engines for the USAF* for longer than any other U.S. firm.

Frederick B. Rentschler was the founder of the company. In the early 1920s he was employed by the Wright Aeronautical Corporation. He decided that the engine of the future was "air cooled" and not "liquid cooled." All piston engines are air cooled, but the liquid-cooled engine uses an intermediate medium to carry the heat to the air. Because the medium is a liquid, it is heavy and subject to leaking. Eliminating the intermediate step can raise efficiency. Rentschler clashed with some people at Wright, and he left it in 1924 to convert P&W to an aircraft engine manufacturer.

His first design was the Wasp R-1340—R for radial—with 1,340 cubic inches of displacement, finished on Christmas Eve 1925. The Wasp had a new design for the crankshaft, master rod, and cylinder head. The engine weighed less than 650 pounds and produced 425 horsepower (HP) with nine cylinders. This was a fine 1.5 pounds per HP. The Wasp was efficient and reliable. About 100 types of aircraft used it, and it stayed in production until 1960. At the end of production, its HP had been raised to 600. Wasps built in the 1920s were still in service in the 1980s. The Wasp was used by the USAAC* in the A-17,* P-3A, P-12,* P-26,* and T-6.*

New engines were quickly developed, the larger R-1690 Hornet and R-985 Wasp Jr. Thus a product line was developed. The Hornet was used by the USAAC in the YB-9 (*See* B-9), the B-12 version of the B-10,* and the Keystone* bomber. It was also used in the famous German Junkers Ju 52 transport.* The Wasp Jr. was used in the C-45 and BT-13.* In 1929, P&W became a division of the United Aircraft Transport Corporation. The firm was changed again to United Aircraft Corporation in 1934.

In the 1930s, proponents of the air-cooled engine and the liquid-cooled engine still argued, and P&W suffered when the USAAC decided that the liquid-cooled engine was the engine of the future for fighters.* At the same time, P&W floundered with indecision and pursued too many design possibilities. Progress was finally made by a campaign to focus development efforts on new radials with a second bank of cylinders for more HP. One was the R-1830 Twin Wasp with 1,350 HP. More Twin Wasps were built—173,618—than any other aircraft engine in history. It powered many World War II*–era aircraft, including the B-24,* C-47,* P-35,* P-36,* and P-43.* A variant R-2000 powered the C-54.*

Another superb and, in the opinion of some pilots,* the greatest piston engine ever built was the next design, the Double Wasp R-2800 with 18 cylinders and 2,000 HP. With a turbosupercharger and water injection it produced more than one HP per cubic inch displacement. The USAAF* aircraft using it included the B-26 Invader,* B-26 Marauder,* C-46,* C-82,* C-123,* F-47,* P-61,* and T-29.* It was not until the R-2800 that P&W fully recovered from its malaise of the 1930s.

P&W's last piston engine was its largest, the R-4360 Wasp Major of 4,300 HP. It had 28 cylinders in four banks, a trend showing obvious technological limits for the piston engine. It powered the B-35,* B-36,* B-50,* C-97,* C-119,* and C-124.* P&W's piston engines were famous for reliability and ruggedness.

The arrival of jet power handicapped P&W because the government wanted the natural association of jets with companies already experienced in building turbines. An example was the General Electric* (GE) and Westinghouse companies. In this second major crisis for P&W, the firm resolved to do better than the competition and built the Andrew Willgoos Turbine Laboratory. Its first jet engine used by the USAF was the J48 Turbo-Wasp of 1950 producing 6,250 pounds of thrust. It was used in the F-94. P&W also developed a turboprop, the T34 of 7,500 HP, which was used in the C-133.*

P&W's first highly successful jet was the J57 turbojet of 10,000 pounds thrust. It was used in the B-52,* B-57,* C-135,* F-100,* F-101,* F-102,* and U-2.* Of great help to the firm in the jet age has been P&W's success in getting its engines used in airliners. In 1975, P&W became a division of United Technologies Corporation. The firm's F100 turbofan has 25,000 pounds of thrust and was chosen for the USAF's F-15* and F-16.* Technical and labor problems with the F100 led to "the great engine war" with P&W's main U.S. competitor, General Electric. This struggle led to P&W and GE sharing the market for the F-16. The competition proved so productive that the USAF has tried to spur it. The struggles are now with GE's YF120 and P&W's YF119 as competing engines for the Advanced Technology Fighter* (ATF).

References. F. Clifton Berry, Jr., "The Push for Fighter Engines," *AF*, January 1990, pp. 74–79. Robert W. Drewes, *The Air Force and the Great Engine War*, 1987. *The Pratt & Whitney Aircraft Story*, 1950. Robert Schlaifer, *Development of Aircraft Engines: Two Studies of Relations between Government and Business*, 1950. Herschel Smith, *Aircraft Piston Engines: From the Manly Balzer to the Continental Tiara*, 1981.

PRECISION BOMBING. *See* Norden bombsight.

PRECISION-GUIDED MUNITIONS (PGM). *See* bombs.

PREDDY, MAJOR GEORGE E., JR. (1919–1944)

Preddy is the sixth-ranking USAF* ace* of all time with 26.83 victories. He was the first U.S. fighter* pilot* to score six victories over Luftwaffe aircraft in a single day.

From Greensboro, North Carolina, he became an aviation cadet* in 1940 and a pilot and officer in 1941. He went to Australia in 1942 and was in the 49th Fighter Group. In July he had a midair collision, was hospitalized, and returned to the United States. One year later he joined the 352nd Fighter Group of the Eighth Air Force* (8AF) flying F-47s.* In December he shot down his first plane. A month later, after his second victory, he was hit by flak* and bailed out over the English Channel. In the spring of 1944 his group* exchanged its F-47s for F-51s.* On 6 August he shot down six Bf 109s while on a fighter escort* mission. Soon after that he returned to the United States. In November he rejoined the 352nd. On Christmas Day 1944 he shot down two Bf 109s near Koblenz, Germany, and later gave chase to an Fw 190. Over Belgium, U.S. flak gunners aimed at the Fw 190 and hit Preddy, who died in the crash of his plane.

References. John R. Beaman, Jr., "The Unknown Ace," *AAHS Journal*, Winter 1969, pp. 242–44. DuPre, *USAF Bio*. John L. Frisbee, "The Complete Fighter Pilot," *AF*, December 1987, p. 106. Hess, *Aces Album*. Joseph W. Nah, *Wings God Gave My Soul: The Story of George E. Preddy, Jr., American Fighter Pilot, World War II*, 1974.

PRESIDENTIAL AIRLIFT

The first U.S. president to fly was Theodore Roosevelt,* who went up in a Wright Type B in 1910 after his administration had ended. The aerial transport of presidents and other very important persons (VIPs) was controversial when it began in 1943, because flying was still considered risky. President Franklin D. Roosevelt (FDR) did it first with his flight from Miami, Florida, to Casablanca,

Morocco. An important argument for it was the capability of the U-boats. The flight was made in a commercial aircraft under contract to the U.S. Navy, a Boeing Aircraft Company Model 314 named *Dixie Clipper*.

The success of the trip led to "Project 51," a USAAF* C-54* built especially for presidential airlift. It included modifications for FDR's crippled condition. It was officially named *The Flying White House*, but reporters called it the "Sacred Cow" and the nickname stuck despite official attempts to suppress it. FDR did not like to fly, and he used the *Cow* only once, for the Yalta Conference. As with subsequent presidential airlift, there was much use of the plane by other VIPs. The *Sacred Cow* was retired in 1947 as the presidential aircraft. President Harry S Truman* (HST) enjoyed flying and visited 51 nations by way of air. The *Sacred Cow* had flown 431,000 miles, of which presidents had used 10 percent. It continued to fly with the 1,254th Air Transport Squadron, better known as the Special Air Missions (SAM) squadron for flying government officials.

The next presidential airplane was a Douglas Aircraft Company DC-6, designated as a C-118. It was named the *Independence* for HST. It was briefly called "Sacred Cow II," but this time the name did not stick. It went into service in 1947 and changed to being a SAM aircraft in January 1953. When it was expected that Thomas E. Dewey would become president in 1949, a Lockheed Aircraft Corporation C-121* Constellation was prepared for him, and it was to be named *Dewdrop*. It was assigned to SAM and received the name after Dwight D. Eisenhower* became president. While commander of the Supreme Headquarters Allied Powers Europe (SHAPE), Eisenhower had a C-121 at his service. He named it *Columbine*. When he became president, a second C-121 was made the presidential aircraft and named *Columbine II*. A Super-Constellation became *Columbine III* in 1954. It was used frequently by Eisenhower until the end of his administration. Eisenhower also had Aero Design and Engineering Company Aero Commanders assigned for his use for trips to his Gettysburg, Pennsylvania, farm. They were designated L-26s at first, and later as U-4s.

President John F. Kennedy* (JFK) chose a Douglas VC-118A, or DC-6A. JFK did not name the USAF* presidential aircraft, and it was called by its serial number, 3240. Beginning in 1959, presidents used SAM VC-137As (*See* C-137), or Boeing Model 707–153s. These aircraft from the SAM pool of planes were not named but were known by their radio call sign "Air Force One," when the president was aboard. In 1990 the two VC-137s were replaced with two VC-25As (*See* C-25), or Boeing 747–200Bs. One is a primary Air Force One, and the second is a backup. The C-137s used 17 in their aircrew and carried 46 passengers. The VC-25's aircrew is 23; it carries 70 passengers and has 85 telephones, 19 television sets, and 11 videocassette recorders.

The extensive use of USAF airlift by government executives and congressmen has aroused the ire of some critics who allege it is an abuse. The USAF has reported that its airlift costs six times those of a commercial flight per passenger. Congressional aides have disputed the USAF figures, asserting that the true costs are only double the commercial ones.

References. Jeffrey H. Birnbaum, "Schroeder Tour of Europe to Collect Data on Spending Cuts Is Costly for Taxpayers," *The Wall Street Journal*, 8 September 1988, p. 56. Robert C. Mikesh, "Presidential Aircraft," *AAHS Journal*, Summer 1963, pp. 79–96, and "Air Force One before the 'Sacred Cow,' " *Air Power History*, Winter 1990, pp. 15–22. Susan H. H. Young, "Gallery of USAF Weapons," *AF*, May 1990, pp. 151–52.

PRESIDENT'S AIRCRAFT BOARD

Also known as the Morrow Board, this commission was appointed by President Calvin Coolidge in September 1925 to study the status of U.S. aviation. This group aided the development of aviation by recommending government encouragement of commercial aviation and congressional authorization of a five-year aircraft construction program for the U.S. Army and Navy.

Appointing Dwight W. Morrow as chairman, the president formed this commission in response to national publicity about William Mitchell's* charges of "almost treasonable" action by Army and Navy officers in neglecting aviation. Mitchell's charges followed two naval aviation disasters in early September: (1) a Navy plane downed in the Pacific Ocean while flying from California to Hawaii and (2) the deaths of 14 men when the Navy's USS *Shenandoah* airship crashed during a severe thunderstorm while flying over Ohio. Although Mitchell faced a court-martial for his accusations, Coolidge appointed this board.

After hearing testimony from aircraft manufacturers, as well as Army, Navy, and USAAS* officers, including Mitchell, the board reported in December 1925. It rejected Mitchell's proposal to make aviation the primary element of national defense and his charges against Army and Navy officers. It did, however, urge government action to underwrite development of the aviation industry. It recommended a five-year military contract program to enhance aircraft manufacturing, federal regulations for aviation, and creation of assistant secretaries of the War, Navy, and Commerce Departments to promote the growth of aviation.

The board's hearings paralleled those of the congressional Lampert Committee,* whose December 1925 report was comparable to that of the Morrow Board.

References. Primary: U.S. Congress, House; *Aircraft Hearings before the President's Aircraft Board*, 4 vols., 68th Cong., 2d sess., 1925. U.S. Congress, Senate; *Report of the President's Aircraft Board*, Senate Document 18, 69th Cong. 1st sess., 1925. Secondary: Lester H. Brune, *The Origins of American National Security: Sea Power, Air Power and Foreign Policy, 1900 to 1941*, 1981. Futrell, *Ideas*, vol. 1. Clark G. Reynolds, "John H. Towers, the Morrow Board and the Reform of the Navy's Aviation,"*Military Affairs*, April 1988, pp. 78–84.

Lester H. Brune

PRESIDENT'S AIR POLICY COMMISSION

In the years immediately following World War II,* the U.S. aircraft industry, a vital part of U.S. air power, faced a crisis as it did following World War I.* Research and development (R&D) costs of producing the new jet aircraft and reduced military orders threatened much of the industry with bankruptcy. Reacting to public concern over the threat to the nation's aviation preparedness, President Harry S Truman* (HST) appointed this commission in July 1948 to examine the situation and provide advice on a national aviation policy. This paralleled the establishment of the President's Aircraft Board* of 1925. Under the leadership of Thomas K. Finletter, and often called the Finletter Commission, the board took several months of testimony from military, government, industry, and scientific leaders. It released its report in early 1948.

The commission concluded that air power was the key to the security of the United States. It recommended the development of modern air forces to deter any aggressor through threat of retaliation and to defend against any attack should one take place. Using 1953 as a target date for potential aggressors to have nuclear weapons,* the commission supported an immediate increase in the size of the USAF* with a target completion date in 1952. However, the recommendations reflected the continuing interservice strategic and funding controversies. Though it recommended a 70-group air force,* the commission also supported an expansion in naval air strength. Support for the aircraft industry would be a by-product of this research and procurement effort.

Though the commission directed public attention to air power and called for an expanded USAF, in reality it accomplished little. Funds for the USAF expansion were reduced in the 1948 budget and only with the Korean War* did they rise. The commission's call for across-the-board expansion dodged difficult questions concerning overall strategy and procurement emphasis. The commission also avoided criticism of the Joint Chiefs of Staff (JCS) for failing to provide a coherent plan for the defense of the United States.

References. Primary: President's Air Policy Commission, *Survival in the Air Age*, 1948. Secondary: Futrell, *Ideas*, vol. 1. Higham, *Air Pwr*.

Budd A. Jones, Jr.

PRISONERS OF WAR (POW), GERMANY

Large numbers of U.S. Army aviators were POWs of the Germans in World Wars I* and II.* German treatment of them was humane and in accord with international conventions. In World War I nearly 500 were POWs. In World War II, 35,621 USAAF* airmen were captured in the West. A factor in the good treatment was that the Luftwaffe ran the prison camps for airmen in World War II. In fact, treatment of prisoners while in the hands of flying units in both wars was sometimes comradely because of the affinity of aviators for each other.

On 4 July 1942, the first USAAF aircrews to become POWs were lost while flying RAF Boston IIIs, a variant of the A-20.* The last was an F-47* pilot* captured on 8 May 1945. These, and thousands of others, were placed in a Stammlager Luft, Stalag Luft for short, a POW camp of the Luftwaffe. From their point of capture, prisoners were sent to "The Center," seven miles northwest of Frankfurt am Main, or to Durchgangsler Fuer Luftwaffe, Dulag Luft for short, within the city. After a stay of one to four weeks, during which they were interrogated and processed, they were moved to one of five Stalag Lufts or to a smaller camp in Germany or an occupied East European country. Conditions at all these camps ranged from adequate to privation and starvation in relation to Germany's fortunes of war.

Prisoners taken measured the intensity of the air war. From a handful in early 1942 raids, those taken rose to 392 on 17 August 1943 during the battles of Schweinfurt* and Regensburg, Germany, and 415 during the 6 March 1944 strike on Berlin,* Germany. Among the thousands of POWs were such notable USAAF personalities as Lieutenant John C. Morgan, Air Force Medal of Honor* winner; Colonel Hubert A. "Hub" Zemke,* captured on 30 October 1944, who became the senior U.S. officer at Stalag Luft I, Barth, Germany; and Lieutenant Colonel Francis S. "Gabby" Gabreski,* captured on 25 July 1944, also held at Stalag Luft I. At the end of hostilities in May 1945, most USAAF POWs were repatriated through Camp Lucky Strike, France, and then via troopship or airlift to the United States.

References. Primary: Maurer Maurer, ed., *The U.S. Air Service in World War I*, vols. 1 and 3, 1978 and 1979. Secondary: Martin W. Bowman, *Home by Christmas? The Story of U.S. Airmen at War*, 1987. Philip M. Flammer, ed., "Dulag Luft: The Third Reich's Prison Camp for Airmen," *AH*, June 1972, pp. 58–61. Royal D. Frey, 'Poets Laureate of Stalag I," *AH*, Winter, 1969, pp. 16–18. William R. Larsen, *Hell Above and Hell Below*, 1985. Raymond Toliver, *The Interrogator*, 1978.

Roger M. Fox

PRISONERS OF WAR (POW), JAPAN

The nations of the West faced, in Japan, a nation that believed its fighting men should not allow themselves to be disgraced by being taken prisoner. The obvious implication was that the Japanese would not be inclined to take prisoners and would treat those captured with contempt. Generally, this proved to be the case. The Japanese record in the treatment of POWs was vicious and disgraceful, but they were not signatories to the Geneva Convention. There were 5,436 USAAF* airmen captured by Japan.

The most famous USAAF POWs of the Japanese were two aircrews from the Doolittle raid on Tokyo,* Japan. U.S. inquiries about them through the Swiss resulted in a Japanese reply in February 1943 that it was intended to put all U.S. POWs on trial and some would be executed. Two airmen had died in the crash of their B-25.* The other eight men were captured in China, tortured, and then taken to Tokyo. There they were mistreated. They were then removed to Kiangwan, China, tried, and sentenced to death for allegedly bombing or strafing nonmilitary targets. Lieutenants Dean E. Hallmark and William Farrow and Sergeant Harold A. Spatz were executed on 15 October 1942. The other five were given "mercy," and the sentences were commuted to life imprisonment. On 1 December 1943, Lieutenant Robert J. Meder died of malnutrition, dropsy, dysentery, and beri-beri. He normally weighed 175 pounds but was about 110 when he died. After his death, conditions improved for the others. After the war, four Japanese officers were tried under international law for the trials of the raiders. One received a sentence of nine years; the others received five.

After the war, B-29s* were tasked to airlift supplies to the POW and internee camps until the inmates could be evacuated. In August and September 1945, 154 camps were supplied with food, clothing, and medical kits by airdrop. The B-29s flew 900 sorties and dropped 4,470 tons to about 63,500 prisoners. Eight aircraft and 77 casualties were the cost of the operation. One B-29 was attacked by Soviet fighters* and damaged so much it crash-landed.

References. C&C, vol. 5. Carrol V. Glines, *Doolittle's Tokyo Raiders*, 1964.

PRISONERS OF WAR (POW), NORTH KOREA AND RED CHINA

In its second war in Asia in a decade, the USAF* faced another brutal enemy. Like the Japanese and North Vietnamese, the North Koreans were vicious and inhumane. In the North Korean POW camps, USAF fliers were beaten, starved, and tortured with brainwashing to elicit false confessions of conducting germ warfare.

After the first year of the Korean War,* the USAF knew of only three of its men who were POWs, although 412 were missing in action (MIA). The end of the war found 220 USAF POWs repatriated, but a known 35 were not released. By 1990, the United States still had 8,172 MIAs and 389 POWs unaccounted for. Of these, 999 MIAs were from the USAF. In 1990, the first U.S. remains, five, were returned since 1954.

No USAF men succeeded in escaping from POW camps that were deep inside North Korea. Anyone escaping was handicapped by being highly visible in a hostile population and difficult terrain. In addition, communist countries had not signed the Geneva Convention and killed anyone trying to escape. There were three USAF pilots* who escaped after being captured. Captain William D. Locke escaped in the chaos of a North Korean retreat while en route to a camp. First Lieutenant Melvin J. Shadduck also escaped en route to a camp. The most remarkable was the escape of Captain Ward Millar. When he was shot down, he had bailed out and broken both ankles upon landing. He made his first escape from his military hospital on his hands and knees but returned undetected because travel was impractical. After three months in the hospital, he made his final escape by walking with his bones unhealed. He eventually signaled a United Nations (UN) plane which got a rescue* helicopter* for him. He was assisted in the last part of his escape by a defecting North Korean army sergeant who also rode the helicopter to freedom.

The USAF's most famous POW in this war was Colonel Walker M. "Bud" Mahurin,* an ace* with 24.5 victories, who was shot down by ground fire on 13 May 1952. Several USAF airmen who bailed out landed across the Yalu River in Manchuria. The Red Chinese refused to agree they were POWs and held them prisoners in China until the late 1950s.

References. Primary: Ward Millar, *Valley of the Shadow*, 1955. Secondary: Clay Blair, Jr., *Beyond Courage*, 1955. Futrell, *USAF in Korea*.

PRISONERS OF WAR (POW), NORTH VIETNAM

The most publicized, longest, and most traumatic USAF* POW experience was when airmen again faced a brutal and communist Asiatic enemy. North Vietnam signed the Geneva Convention in 1957 but claimed its captives were not POWs for there had been no declaration of war. Inconsistently, it also said the men were war criminals who should be prosecuted under the Nuremburg rules. When it said this, some U.S. senators threatened severe retaliation and no trials were held.

There was a complex of prisons in Hanoi,* Vietnam, and in its outskirts. The main one was Hoa Lo, or "Hell Hole" in Vietnamese, nicknamed the "Hanoi Hilton" by Americans. There were also some jungle camps. Starting in 1965, systematic torture was applied to the POWs. It was not designed to extract information but to break the POWs so they would betray comrades or contribute to enemy propaganda. The torture included beatings to a pulp with rubber belts, being tied in ropes until shoulders were dislocated or ribs broken, starvation, dehydration, solitary confinement, and being chained to a slab for days with never a release for any reason. The worst punishment was meted out to Brigadier General John P. Flynn; Colonels George E. "Bud" Day, Lawrence N. Guarino, James H. Kasler, and Robinson Risner;* and Lieutenant Colonel Ronald E. Storz. It is believed Storz was tortured to death. In 1966, 52 POWs were paraded through Hanoi so mobs could stone and beat them. Despite intense North Vietnamese efforts to prevent it, the POWs set up a military organization. To communicate they were forced to devise several signal codes.

In February and August 1968, North Vietnam released each time three USAF pilot* POWs to U.S. antiwar activists. The purpose was to deter future U.S. bombing. In July 1969, another three were released, one USAF officer and two U.S. Navy men. The naval officer was warned that, if he told the truth about POW treatment, the North Vietnamese would take revenge against those still held. This did not deter him, and he related the conditions.

Conditions improved after the death of the dictator Ho Chi Minh in September 1969. In 1970, because of the Son Tay prison raid,* all POWs were taken to the Hanoi Hilton. In 1972, Jane Fonda visited some selected POWs. She did not believe the accounts of mistreatment before or after her visit. That incident, combined with an antiwar broadcast to U.S. soldiers and a visit to an enemy flak* position where she waxed enthusiastic, led to her nickname of "Hanoi Jane." Conditions improved for the POWs when the guards were frightened and impressed by the Linebacker* II raids.

The peace settlement of January 1973 resulted in the release of 318 USAF men from Vietnam and six from Laos. The North Vietnamese said 16 died in captivity. In 1990, there were still 2,300 Americans unaccounted for from the war.

Movie: *The Hanoi Hilton*, 1987.

References. Primary: George E. Day, "Escape in Vietnam," *AF*, September 1976, pp. 84–86, 89. Larry Guarino, *A POW's Story: 2801 Days in Hanoi*, 1990. Robinson

Risner, *The Passing of the Night*, 1973. Secondary: Berger, *USAF in SEA*. William P. Schlitz, "The POWs Return," *AF*, April 1973, pp. 25–29.

PRISONER OF WAR (POW), USSR. *See* Cold War.

PROBE AND DROGUE

The probe-and-drogue method of aerial refueling* in the USAF* was developed from a British system and was first installed on the YKB-29T (*see* B-29). This was a modified KB-29M incorporating a three-point refueling system—a pair of wingtip-mounted hose and drogue pods and a single reel located in the aft unpressurized fuselage compartment.

After testing, the system was put on 137 KB-50Js (*see* B-50) in 1957. They refueled fighters* and attack* planes for both the Tactical Air Command* (TAC) and the Pacific Air Forces* (PACAF) until aircraft deterioration and high maintenance costs resulted in retirement in 1964. A hose-and-drogue adapter was developed for attachment to the flying boom* on KC-135s* (*see* C-135) so that the Strategic Air Command* (SAC), by then the single tanker* task force manager for the USAF, could refuel TAC's B-66s* and F-100s.* The adapter was kept after those models were retired for USAF refueling of U.S. Navy and Marine aircraft.

Long-range rescue* operations during the Vietnam War* matched HC-130H, HC-130N, and HC-130P (*see* C-130) aircraft equipped with underwing refueling probe-and-drogue pods with HH-3Es (*see* H-3) and HH-53B (*see* H-53) helicopters.* The HC-130H was introduced in 1965, and its largest inventory was 72 in 1970 and 1971. This system was used in the first nonstop transatlantic helicopter flight in 1967 and the first such transpacific flight in 1970. A team of two HC-130Ps, an HH-3, and five HH-53s was used in the Son Tay prison raid.* Combinations of HC-130s and HH-53s flew in Operation Eagle Pull, the removal of the last 15 U.S. military persons from Phnom Penh, Cambodia, on 12 April 1975; Operation Frequent Wind, the evacuation of 362 persons from Saigon, Vietnam, to the USS *Midway* on 29 April 1975; and the *Mayaguez* incident* in May 1975.

References. Knaack, *US Airc.*, vol. 2. Donald L. Little, "Aerospace Rescue and Recovery Service 1946–1981," MAC History Office, 1983. Alwyn T. Lloyd, *B-29 Superfortress in Detail & Scale*, 1987.

Alwyn T. Lloyd

PROCUREMENT

Procurement consists of determining specifications, standards, financing, and administering purchase contracts. The USAF* has been the most capital-intensive service of the armed forces, so the function of procurement has been critical to it. There have been constant, intense pressures to obtain equipment on the cutting edge of technology because that is necessary in air battle, to get it at a reasonable cost, and to be able to use and maintain it in the field. There have also been continuous and savage external pressures and criticism, often resulting from a common U.S. belief that government procurement officials are incompetent and wasteful. It has been easy for politicians and the media to capitalize on these basic beliefs.

These external views had some validity in World War I.* Lacking experience in the procurement of aircraft, mistakes were made on a large scale. In the rush to get production during war, waste occurs. The contracts used had the formula of cost plus percentage of cost (CPPC) to arrive at a fair profit and total payment. These contracts encouraged waste by paying a profit for it. Unrelated to those contracts, production goals were not met in World War I, a tempting basis for finding fault. A large problem for future procurement was that manufacturers were encouraged to expand using private financing, and then they were sacrificed at the end of the war when contracts were simply ended with no consideration for the catastrophic effects on business.

Between the wars, little equipment was bought, and the peacetime plans for mobilization were hopelessly inadequate for the needs of mature air power in World War II.* It proved most fortunate that Britain and France rearmed before the United States. They had massive procurement problems of their own in rearming their air services and turned to the United States for help. Nevertheless, they had underestimated needs also. The early battle experiences of the war showed the vastly increased ability of air power and the need for better equipment.

In World War II, knowledge of the mistakes of the earlier war produced much more effective planning and management. Red tape was cut and the government financed the aircraft industry's expansion. Contracts used cost plus fixed fee (CPFF) for determining a fair profit, which did not encourage waste. At the end of the war, contracts were terminated with consideration of shutdown costs for business. The procurement record of this war was a huge success.

After the war, the USAF centralized procurement. In its separation from the U.S. Army,* it could get no arsenals, a blessing in disguise. The USAF had to rely entirely on private manufacturers, historically the most efficient system for procurement in aviation.

The fine record of World War II should have resulted in better procurement for the Korean War.* Mistakes were repeated. However, some problems came from the fact that it was a different kind of war and one that happened after the technological revolution resulting from the development of the jet engine. Rapid obsolescence and a new revolution, the advent of ballistic missiles,* meant expensive crash programs again. In response, the USAF tried concurrent procurement. Tooling and production was set up before designs were finished or tested. Sometimes this worked and saved time, but it usually caused horrendous costs for redesign and retooling. There had to be a return to development by steps.

The biggest change in procurement in the postwar period was the adoption of the "weapon system" concept,* first developed by the Germans. Previously, different items of equipment, such as guns and radios, were purchased and then issued to airframe manufacturers for inclusion in new designs. The new concept treated all aspects of a new airplane, or other equipment, as a system in which all components were especially created for the best fit.

Secretary of Defense (SECDEF) Robert S. McNamara* introduced radical new concepts to reduce costs. He introduced statistical analysis to reduce stocks and had shortages as one result. He took final procurement decisions away from the USAF, which caused great trouble in getting the F-111.* He tried to prevent cost overruns with a fixed-price contract even on new technological developments. It was called Total Package Procurement Concept (TPPC). TPPC proved infeasible and led to higher cost overruns. After McNamara, experiments in new procurement devices slowed down. There was a return to the proven method of duplicate designs with one selected on the basis of tests, called ''fly before you buy.''

A principal, and probably the largest, problem with all military procurement in the United States is that the public swings from complacency to fear. This is reflected in a cycle of procurement stretchouts, cutbacks, or cancellations followed by expensive crash programs. This is an extremely wasteful process, but it is probably inevitable with politics in a free country.

References. Charles D. Bright, *The Jet Makers: The Aerospace Industry from 1945 to 1972*, 1978. Woodford Agee Heflin, ed., *The United States Air Force Dictionary*, 1956. Irving Brinton Holley, Jr., *Buying Aircraft: Matériel Procurement for the Army Air Forces*, 1964. Bernard J. Termena et al., *Logistics: An Illustrated History of AFLC and Its Antecedents 1921–1981*, 1981.

PROJECT B. *See* Mitchell's bombing tests on warships.

PROJECT BIG BELLY. *See* Arc Light.

PROJECT CONTEMPORARY HISTORICAL EXAMINATION OF CURRENT OPERATIONS. *See* Contemporary Historical Examination of Current Operations.

PROJECT CORONA HARVEST. *See* Corona Harvest.

PROTECTIVE REACTION STRIKES

This was a euphemism used for political reasons. In November 1968, President Lyndon B. Johnson* (LBJ) stopped all Rolling Thunder* bombing operations in North Vietnam in hopes of ending the Vietnam War* through negotiation. There was an understanding with the North that reconnaissance* operations would continue without interference.

Evidently there was insufficient discipline in the North, for occasionally the planes were fired upon. By February 1970, President Richard M. Nixon decided something must be done about these incidents. He authorized retaliatory attacks* on the North's air defenses. To justify them, they were called ''protective reaction strikes.'' The first ones were fairly limited in scope, but, from 1 to 4 May, 500 sorties were flown by the USAF* and U.S. Navy against flak* and surface-to-air missile* (SAM) sites. This larger effort was called "reinforced protective reaction."

References. David A. Anderton, *History of the U.S. Air Force*, rev. ed., 1989. Berger, *USAF in SEA*.

PROUD SHIELD. *See* competitions.

PROVIDER. *See* C-123.

PSP. *See* pierced-steel planking.

PT-1

The Consolidated Aircraft Corporation built the primary trainers (PTs) for the USAAS* and USAAC* in the 1920s and 1930s. The firm was formed in 1923. It acquired from the Dayton-Wright Company its chief designer, design rights to a TW-3 primary trainer, and a TW-3 contract. Dayton-Wright had been a subsidiary of General Motors Corporation (GMC), and GMC shut the firm down. The PT-1 was a modified TW-3, and 171 were built. Further changes resulted in the PT-3 and PT-5. The PT-3 was altered to become the O-17. The PT-3 was also improved to the PT-11, and the latter was altered to become a basic trainer, the BT-7.

Characteristics (PT-3A): engine, Wright R-790-AB of 220 horsepower; span, 35 feet; length, 28 feet; height, 10 feet; gross weight, 2,481 pounds; top speed, 102 miles per hour; service ceiling, 14,000 feet; endurance, 3.7 hours.

References. Swanborough, *US Mil. Airc.* Wagner, *Am. Planes.* John Wegg, *General Dynamics Aircraft and Their Predecessors*, 1990.

PT-13 KAYDET

This plane was the most successful piston-engine trainer. A Stearman Aircraft Company design, it started as a private venture in 1934. The first USAAC* order was for 26 PT-13s in 1936. More orders followed nearly every year. In 1942 the USAAF* and U.S. Navy decided to standardize their trainers, and they chose the PT-13D. In 1940 the airframe with a different engine became the PT-17. It was the most used of the rugged and dependable series. A shortage of engines early in World War II* resulted in the fitting of a different engine to become the PT-18. A final variant, the PT-27, was built for the Royal Canadian Air Force (RCAF).

Kaydets were also used by the Royal Air Force (RAF). Nearly 5,000 were built for the USAAC and USAAF; many more were built for the Navy and export for a grand total of 8,429. Many, about 2,200 were still flying in 1988. After World War II more than 2,000 had been used for crop dusting. Others were used for airshow acrobatics. After new crop dusters were designed in the 1950s, the Stearmans became favorites for sport flying. Stearman was acquired by the Boeing Airplane Company in 1934 and the name "Stearman" should have died. However, the surviving planes are still called "Stearmans" and not "Kaydets" or "Boeings."

Characteristics (PT-17): engine, Continental R-670–5 of 220 horsepower; span, 32 feet; length, 25 feet; height, 10 feet; gross weight, 2,635 pounds; top speed, 135 miles per hour; service ceiling, 13,200 feet; endurance, 3.9 hours.

References. Peter M. Bowers, *Boeing Aircraft since 1916*, 1989. Swanborough, *US Mil. Airc.*

PT-16

When the USAAC* mobilized in 1940, it ordered a version of the Ryan Aeronautical Company's Model S-T for primary training (PT). As the YPT-16, it was the first monoplane used for flight training.* Variants were the PT-20, PT-21, and PT-22. The PT-22s, named Recruit, were used at civilian primary flight training* schools. Ryan PTs were built for export as well as USAAF* use. Production of the PT-22 ended in 1942. Its nickname was "Maytag Messerschmitt," because it sounded like a washing machine; it was an allusion to students being "washed out," or failing.

Characteristics (YPT-16): engine, Menasco L-365–1 of 125 horsepower; span, 30 feet; length, 22 feet; height, 10 feet; gross weight, 1,600 pounds; top speed, 128 miles per hour; service ceiling, 15,000 feet; range, 350 miles.

References. Primary: Don J. Armand, "Pilot Training—WWII: Primary Training 21 May 1943–29 July 1943," *Friends Journal*, Fall 1990, pp. 40–45. Swanborough, *US Mil. Airc.*

PT-19

In 1940 the M-62 design for a monoplane primary trainer by the Fairchild Engine and Airplane Corporation was bought by the USAAC* for the mobilization and designated PT-19. Fairchild could not expand enough to fill all the orders and many were built by Aeronca, Fleet, Howard, and St. Louis Aircraft Corporations. Variants were an uncowled PT-23 and canopied PT-26. The latter was for the Royal Canadian Air Force (RCAF). Fairchild built 4,626; Aeronca, 620; Fleet, 1,057; Howard, 150; and St. Louis, 204. When enough PT-13* Kaydet biplanes were available, the monoplanes, PT-16* and PT-19, were retired because the Stearmans produced pilots with higher skills.

Characteristics (PT-19A): engine, Ranger L-440–1 of 175 horsepower; span, 36 feet; length, 28 feet; height, 11 feet; gross weight, 2,545 pounds; top speed, 132 miles per hour; service ceiling, 15,300 feet; range, 400 miles.

Reference. Swanborough, *US Mil. Airc.*

PUFF, THE MAGIC DRAGON. *See* gunship.

PULITZER TROPHY RACES

The USAAS* regarded air racing as a golden opportunity to test new equipment. One of the races entered was for the Pulitzer Trophy, which the USAAS won five out of the six years it entered. The sixth, and last, was flown in 1925 at Mitchel* Field, New York. The U.S. Army and Navy agreed to buy three Curtiss Aeroplane and Motor Company's R3C-1 racers, at a price of $250,000, for a joint effort in trying to recapture the 1924 record from the French. On 12 October, the USAAS' First Lieutenant Cyrus Bettis won the speed portion by averaging 248.975 miles per hour. Lieutenant L. H. Dawson won the pylon portion of the race, giving the USAAS a clean sweep. In 1926, neither the USAAS nor Navy entered, nor did any international competitors, and the Pulitzer was stopped.

References. Maurer, *Avn. in Army*. Lowell Thomas and Edward Jablonski, *Doolittle— a Biography*, 1976.

Alwyn T. Lloyd

PURSUIT AVIATION. *See* fighter.

PUSAN PERIMETER

This area saw some of the most intense and successful attack* operations in the history of air warfare. Caught ill-prepared and unaware by the North Korean aggression in June 1950, the U.S. Eighth Army and Republic of Korea (ROK) forces retreated south to a line about 50 miles from the city of Pusan, Korea. Here they made a desperate stand from July to September.

The principal support for the ground forces was Lieutenant General Earle E. Partridge's* Fifth Air Force* (5AF). Partridge, a veteran of World War II's* North African and European campaigns, worked quickly to create an attack system. Working against shortages of trained people, 5AF placed Tactical Air Control Parties (TACP) with Army regiments as soon as they could. Forward air controllers* (FAC) worked in T-6* and L-6 aircraft. This proved vitally important as most sorties originated in Japan and so had limited loiter time. With as little as 20 minutes loiter with an F-80,* correct targeting decisions and identification were necessary. Overcoming communication and operational difficulties, U.S. Navy and Marine aircraft from Task Force 77 (TF77) were successfully integrated into the effort.

When the North Koreans began their final push to force the U.S. and ROK forces out of Korea in August and September, the USAF* responded. The Far East Air Forces (FEAF) flew 7,397 close air support (CAS) sorties in August, an average of 238 a day, and air power's flexibility and firepower contributed mightily to the perimeter's successful defense. In addition to the CAS missions, the FEAF began an interdiction campaign to slow the flow of supplies from the North. Also, B-29s* carried out carpet, or area, bombing operations at the perimeter.

Following the successful defense, General Walton H. Walker, Eighth Army commander, said that air support by the 5AF was necessary for the Army to stay in Korea. The CAS system developed at Pusan and the close cooperation between the air and ground forces set the tone for the rest of the Korean War.*

References. Futrell, *USAF in Korea*. Edwin P. Hoyt, *The Pusan Perimeter*, 1984. David Rees, *Korea: The Limited War*, 1964.

Budd A. Jones, Jr.

PYROTECHNICS

These are military fireworks used for signaling, screening, and countermeasures. Aviation uses include tracer ammunition, flare, and smoke signaling devices. Warplanes also carry flares to decoy enemy heat-seeking missiles. Reconnaissance* planes, such as the RF-4C (*see* F-4), carry photoflash cartridges for night photography.

Reference. K.J.W. Goad and D.H.J. Halsey, *Ammunition*, vol. 3 of *Battlefield Weapons Systems & Technology*, 1982.

Philip Long

Q

QUAIL. *See* ADM-20.

QUARLES, SECRETARY DONALD L. (1894–1959)

Quarles was the fourth secretary of the Air Force* (SAF), from 1955 to 1957, a period of turbulence after the advent of fusion nuclear weapons.* Born in Van Buren, Arkansas, he graduated from Yale University, Connecticut, in 1916. He enlisted in the U.S. Army in World War I,* serving two years in the Field Artillery and rising to the grade of captain. Before reentering government service he worked for Bell Telephone Laboratories and rose to be vice president. Quarles became assistant secretary of defense for research and development from 1953 to 1955. In this time he also served as the first chairman of a reorganized Air Navigation Development Board and as a member of the National Advisory Committee for Aeronautics (NACA). After he was SAF, he was deputy secretary of defense until his death.

References. DuPre, *USAF Bio.*** Marion E. Grambow and Wayne W. Parrish, eds., *Who's Who in World Aviation and Astronautics*, vol. 2, 1958. Jacob Neufeld, *Ballistic Missiles in the United States Air Force 1945–1960*, 1990.

**Cites incorrect dates for Quarles' tenure as secretary of the Air Force.

Lloyd H. Cornett, Jr.

QUESADA, LIEUTENANT GENERAL ELWOOD R. "PETE" (1904–)

Quesada led tactical operations* for Operation Overlord* and the Allied advance into Germany in World War II.* He also, along with Major Carl A. Spaatz,* Captain Ira Eaker,* and a fourth pilot,* flew in the *Question Mark*'s* famous aerial refueling* flight of 1929.

Born in Washington, D.C., he enlisted in the USAAS* as a flying cadet in 1924. He became a pilot* and officer in 1925. His assignments included flying aide to Major General James E. Fechet* (1926–1930) and to the assistant secretary of war for air* (1932–1933), technical adviser to the Argentine air force

(1938–1940), commanding general of the IX Fighter Command in England (1943–1944), commanding general of the Tactical Air Command* (TAC) (1946–1948), and commander of the Joint Task Three in Eniwetok (1950–1951). He retired in 1951 and entered the business world. He was administrator of the Federal Aviation Agency in the 1950s.

References. Primary: Richard H. Kohn and Joseph P. Harahan, eds., *Air Superiority in World War II and Korea: An Interview with General James Ferguson, General Robert M. Lee, General William Momyer, and Lieutenant General Elwood R. Quesada,* 1983. Secondary: John L. Frisbee, ed., *Makers of the United States Air Force,* 1987. Office of Air Force History, *Condensed Analysis of the Ninth Air Force in the European Theater of Operations,* 1984. Official Biography, USAFHRC, Maxwell AFB, Alabama.

David L. Rosmer

QUESTION MARK

On 1 January 1929, Major Carl A. Spaatz,* Captain Ira C. Eaker,* and three other crewmen took off in an American Aircraft Corporation Fokker C-2 named the *Question Mark.* The purpose was to test both the practical value of aerial refueling* and crew and aircraft endurance. It was to be one of the great flights made by the USAAC.*

The plane took off from and recovered at the Los Angeles Metropolitan Airport in Van Nuys, California. The refueling track was flown between San Diego and Santa Monica. A pair of Douglas Aircraft Company C-1s with three crewmen each were the tankers. After some engine trouble, the *Question Mark* landed on 7 January, having flown more than 150 hours. A total of 43 contacts were made in which 5,700 gallons of gasoline were transferred by dangling a hose from one aircraft to the other. Oil, food, and other items were also transferred. The *Question Mark*'s crew was awarded the Distinguished Flying Cross (DFC) for this achievement.

References. Primary: Ross G. Hoyt, "Reflections of an Early Refueler," *AF*, January 1974, pp. 55–59. Secondary: Vincent A. Giroux and David W. Harvey, *Seventy Years of Strategic Air Refueling 1918–1988: A Chronology,* Strategic Air Command History Office, Offutt AFB, Nebraska, 1990. Maurer, *Avn. in Army.* L. I. Wilson, "Thanks, Tank . . . ," *AH*, June 1976, pp. 65–70.

Alwyn T. Lloyd

R

RABAUL, NEW BRITAIN

Rabaul was the main Japanese bastion in the southwest Pacific and it was a cover for the base at Truk. Near the city were five airfields that could accommodate 166 bombers* and 265 fighters.* There were also 367 flak* guns. Airfields on nearby islands could support Rabaul's defenses.

On 12 October 1943, the Fifth Air Force* (5AF) began an air campaign against Rabaul. Bases gained in the New Guinea* campaign had put Rabaul within the reach of the Allies. B-25s* strafed and bombed, B-24s* bombed, and P-38s* were used for air superiority.* The first raid achieved surprise and was highly successful. Weather permitted another strike on 18 October. On 2 November a famous attack* was made by 75 B-25s and 57 P-38s. Japanese sources after World War II* indicated three cargo ships totaling 8,000 tons, a minesweeper, and two small boats were sunk. A 10,000-ton tanker was damaged. The 5AF claimed 94 enemy aircraft* shot down or destroyed on the ground or on the sea. The USAAF* lost eight B-25s and nine P-38s in the air. More had unrepairable battle damage. The heaviest one-day loss of the campaign for the 5AF was 45 men killed or missing. On 5 November a joint attack was made with U.S. Navy carrier aircraft. The campaign ended on 11 November with Rabaul no longer an important threat to the Allies.

References. Steve Birdsall, "Target: Rabaul," *AF*, September 1975, pp. 108–13. C&C, vol. 4. Ronald W. Yoshino, *Lightning Strikes: The 475th Fighter Group in the Pacific War, 1943–1945*, 1988.

RADAR

Radar, short for *R*adio *D*etection *a*nd *R*anging, uses radio beams and their reflections for finding objects and measuring distances to them. Radar revolutionized air warfare and became ubiquitous. Offensively, it has enabled aircraft with airborne radar to navigate and find targets in night and poor weather.

Defensively, both airborne and surface radar have found aircraft in similar conditions and beyond visual or aural detection.

Before radar, navigating and finding targets at night and in poor weather was difficult at best. Defenders' warning of an air raid depended upon sound detectors and visual sightings, which were not able to provide timely identification. Defenders were, therefore, forced into wasteful patrols to provide reasonable defense probabilities.

Radar was one of those inventions that occurred in pieces in different countries nearly simultaneously. Christian Huelsmeyer, a German engineer, demonstrated radar detection of ships and obtained a patent in 1904. In the United States, Dr. A. Hoyt Taylor of the U.S. Naval Research Laboratories observed the reflection capacity of radio signals in 1922. Work on the phenomenon proceeded, and the U.S. Army Signal Corps was informed in 1932. From then on, cooperation took place through a joint Army and Navy board. In 1933, the German navy decided to find targets by radar. From its system, the Freya ground radar was developed to detect enemy aircraft. By May 1940, Germany had a chain of Freyas which were technically superior to the British radar, but German organization to use the information derived was inferior. At the same time, the Luftwaffe had completed its Wuerzburg radar for its flak.* R. Watson-Watt in Britain proposed radar for air defense in 1935, and, by 1937, 20 radar stations were in operation. By 1939, Britain had a continuous watch over the North Sea. In 1940, the British began working with the United States to help it catch up with them. Later, the British development of microwave radar was a major breakthrough and helped greatly to win the air war against the U-boats.

The USAAF* developed its H2X, or AN/APS-15, airborne radar for navigation and bombing, nicknamed "Mickey," in 1943 after access to information on the British H2S system. By 1945, with the AN/APS-10, a specialized radar was no longer needed and weight had been reduced by 80 percent.

Since then, radar has been much improved and refined, especially over-the-horizon equipment. Radar has also become organic in some bombs* and missiles. Attempts today include, as a partial countermeasure to radar effectiveness, "stealth"* technology as in the B-2* and F-117.*

References. C&C, vols. 1–6. Richard S. Friedman et al., *Advanced Technology Warfare*, 1985. David Pritchard, *The Radar War: Germany's Pioneering Achievement 1904–1945*, 1989. Milton Rhodes, "RADAR: Wartime Development—Postwar Application, AN/APS-10," *AH*, December 1981, pp. 231–40. Konrad F. Schreier, "American Radar," *United States Air Force Museum Friends Bulletin*, Spring 1989, pp. 14–19.

See also aerospace defense; Airborne Warning and Control System; Ballistic Missile Early Warning System; chaff; College Eye; Combat Skyspot; Ground-Controlled Approach; ground-controlled interception; identification friend or foe; interceptor; Pathfinder Force; Side-Looking Airborne Radar.

RADIO PROXIMITY FUZES

These fuzes were developed during World War II* to burst accurately bombs,* missiles, and shells at a specific altitude. Early time fuzes used a mechanical clockwork or powder train time system that had to be set just before firing to burst the munition at a specific time, resulting in built-in problems. Proximity fuzes use a small radar* in the nose to sense the target. When the radar tells the fuze it is within a specified distance from the target, the fuze detonates. These fuzes were first used on flak* shells but were soon applied to bombs. They are now widely used for cluster bombs, general-purpose bombs, rockets, missiles, and other purposes.

Reference. Gunston, *Airc. Arm.*

Philip Long

RAF ALCONBURY

This Royal Air Force (RAF) facility is near Huntington, England, and the first U.S. use was by the USAAF* in 1942. B-24s* of the Eighth Air Force* (8AF) used it in World War II.* After modernization, the USAF* returned to it in 1955 with B-45s.* RB-66s (*see* B-66) moved there in 1959 after the French ordered out U.S. nuclear weapons.* The base was reequipped with RF-4Cs (*see* F-4) in 1965. In 1990 it had the 10th Tactical Fighter Wing of the U.S. Air Forces in Europe* (USAFE) with A-10As* and the 17th Reconnaissance Wing of the Strategic Air Command* (SAC) with TR-1As.

References. "Guide to Major Air Force Installations Worldwide," *AF*, May 1990, p. 131. Robert Jackson, *Strike Force: The USAF in Britain since 1948*, 1986. Colleen A. Nash, "A Moving Experience at Alconbury," *AF*, December 1990, pp. 74, 75. Roberts, *Dir. USAF*.

RAF BENTWATERS AND RAF WOODBRIDGE

These are twin Royal Air Force (RAF) facilities near Eyke and Woodbridge, 90 miles northeast of London, England. Bentwaters became a USAF* base in 1951 and Woodbridge in 1952. They are operated as one base. Bentwaters has based F-86As,* F-84Fs,* F-101s,* and F-4s.* Woodbridge has had F-84Gs, F-100s,* and F-4s. In 1990, this was the home of the 81st Tactical Fighter Wing (TFW) of the U.S. Air Forces in Europe* (USAFE) with F-16s* and A-10s.*

References. "Guide to Major Air Force Installations Worldwide," *AF*, May 1990, p. 131. Robert Jackson, *Strike Force: The USAF in Britain since 1948*, 1986. Roberts, *Dir. USAF*.

RAF CHICKSANDS

This Royal Air Force (RAF) facility is near Bedford, England, and is named for its soil. The USAF* moved onto it in 1978. In 1990, it was a U.S. Air Forces in Europe* (USAFE) base and the home of the 693rd Electronic Security Wing of the Electronic Security Command* (ESC).

References. "Guide to Major Air Force Installations Worldwide," *AF*, May 1990, p. 131. Robert Jackson, *Strike Force: The USAF in Britain since 1948*, 1986. Roberts, *Dir. USAF*.

RAF FAIRFORD

This Royal Air Force (RAF) facility is near Swindon, England, and is named for a town. The USAF* began to use it in 1951. Over the years up to 1964, B-29s,* B-50s,* B-36s,* B-47s,* and RB-47s (see B-47) operated from it. In 1990 it had the 7020th Air Base Group of the U.S. Air Forces in Europe* (USAFE) and squadrons* of the 11th Strategic Group of the Strategic Air Command* (SAC). It was part of the European Tanker Task Force with KC-135s (see C-135).

References. "Guide to Major Air Force Installations Worldwide," *AF*, May 1990, p. 131. Robert Jackson, *Strike Force: The USAF in Britain since 1948*, 1986. Roberts, *Dir. USAF*.

RAF GREENHAM COMMON

Near Newbury and 47 miles southwest of London, England, this Royal Air Force (RAF) facility is named for the tract of land it is on. A USAF* presence began in 1951. In 1953, after rebuilding, it was used by B-47s.* In 1956, KC-97G (see C-97) tankers* arrived. From 1964 to 1983, it was used sporadically. In 1990 it had a U.S. Air Forces in Europe* (USAFE) unit, the 501st Tactical Missile Wing (TMW) using BGM-109Gs.* Greenham Common is famous for being unpopular with the local population and with unilateral disarmament partisans who have vigorously protested use of the base by either aircraft or missiles. The USAF nickname for it, "Stalag Greenham," arose when the RAF Regiment security forces encircled the field with concertina wire in the early 1980s.

References. "Guide to Major Air Force Installations Worldwide," *AF*, May 1990, p. 131. Robert Jackson, *Strike Force: The USAF in Britain since 1948*, 1986. Roberts, *Dir. USAF*.

RAF LAKENHEATH

This has been one of the most important of USAF* fields. The Royal Air Force (RAF) facility is 25 miles from Cambridge, England, and is named for a nearby village. B-29s* arrived in 1948 because of the Berlin Airlift* crisis, followed in 1949 by B-50As* and KB-29M tankers. Strategic Air Command* (SAC) deployments to it have included B-36Ds* and B-47s.* In 1954, B-47s were based there. The USAF vacated the field from 1956 to 1960. Since then, it has been used by F-100Ds* and F-4s.* In 1986, F-111s* took off from it for the Libyan raid.* In 1990 it had the U.S. Air Forces in Europe's* (USAFE) 48th Tactical Fighter Wing (TFW) with F-111s.

References. "Guide to Major Air Force Installations Worldwide," *AF*, May 1990, p. 131. Robert Jackson, *Strike Force: The USAF in Britain since 1948*, 1986. Roberts, *Dir. USAF*.

RAF MILDENHALL

Used by the U.S. Air Forces in Europe* (USAFE), this facility is 63 miles northeast of London, England. The Royal Air Force (RAF) opened the base in 1934. A U.S. presence began in 1950, and the 1950s had Strategic Air Command* (SAC) bomber,* reconnaissance,* and tanker* units serving rotational duty to it. Since 1972 it has hosted headquarters of the Third Air Force* (3AF); since 1966 the U.S. European Command's (USEUCOM) airborne command post, or Silk Purse Control Group, aboard USAFE EC-135s (*see* C-135); since 1959 Military Airlift Command* (MAC) units; and now the 313th Tactical Airlift Group with C-130s* on rotational duty.

References. 513th Combat Support Group, "RAF Mildenhall Golden Jubilee 1934–1984," 1984. "Guide to Major Air Force Installations Worldwide," *AF*, May 1990, p. 131. Robert Jackson, *Strike Force: The USAF in Britain since 1948*, 1986. Eric Minton, "RAF Mildenhall: Gateway to the United Kingdom," *The Retired Officer*, March 1988, pp. 42–44, 46. Roberts, *Dir. USAF*.

Jeffrey C. Benton

RAF UPPER HEYFORD

This Royal Air Force (RAF) facility dates from 1916, is 13 miles from Oxford, England, and is named for the nearby town. The USAF* began use of it in 1950 as a base for Strategic Air Command* (SAC) B-47s,* B-50s,* KC-97s (*see* C-97) and KC-135s (*see* C-135). The tankers* were tenants on a 90-day rotational basis. In 1965, operations were transferred from SAC to the U.S. Air Forces in Europe* (USAFE). In 1966, RF-101Cs (*see* F-101) moved to it from Laon AB, France. In 1969, some of these aircraft were replaced by RF-4Cs (*see* F-4). In 1970, the RF-4Cs were replaced by F-100s.* In 1986, F-111s took off from Upper Heyford for the Libyan raid.* In 1990, it had the 20th Tactical Fighter Wing (TFW) with F-111s.*

References. "Guide to Major Air Force Installations Worldwide," *AF*, May 1990, p. 131. Robert Jackson, *Strike Force: The USAF in Britain since 1948*, 1986. Roberts, *Dir. USAF*. Ricky Ryan, "From Grass to Concrete," *AH*, December 1974, pp. 206–9.

RAM. *See* competitions.

RAMSTEIN AIR BASE

This U.S. Air Forces in Europe* (USAFE) base is at Ramstein, near Kaiserslautern, Federal Republic of Germany. It was one of the U.S. bases built as a gift for France in the Rhineland in 1953 after the North Atlantic Treaty Organization* (NATO) was created. Originally, it was a twin base with Ramstein used for headquarters and administration and Landstuhl AB used for operations. From its beginning it has had the 86th Tactical Fighter Wing (TFW), with fighters* from the 1950s' F-84* to 1990s' F-16s.* In 1990 it also had headquarters of the USAFE, headquarters of the Allied Air Forces Central Europe (AAFCE), headquarters of the 316th Air Division, headquarters of the European Electronic Security Division, headquarters of the 7th Air Division, the 322nd Airlift Division, the 2nd Weather Wing, and the 7455th Tactical Intelligence Wing.

References. "Guide to Major Air Force Installations Worldwide," *AF*, May 1990, p. 131. Roberts, *Dir. USAF*. Michael Skinner, *U*S*A*F*E: A Primer of Modern Air Combat in Europe*, 1988.

RANCH HAND. *See* Operation Ranch Hand.

RAND CORPORATION. *See* think tanks.

RANDOLPH AIR FORCE BASE

Known for many years as the "West Point of the Air" and then as the "Show Place of the Air Force," Randolph Field was dedicated on 20 June 1930 as a flight training* base. Lieutenant Harold L. Clark, then in the Kelly* Field motor pool, designed the unique layout. Borrowing from the local architecture of San Antonio, Texas, he designed his "Air City" in Spanish mission style, highlighted by the "Taj Mahal," the administration building that encloses a 500,000-gallon water tank.

Randolph's concept began in 1926 when the Air Corps Act* permitted a five-year growth program for the USAAC.* The USAAC outgrew its flying training fields at Brooks* and Kelly* Fields in Texas and wanted an "Air Corps Training Center."* After the site was selected, a committee was appointed to select a name. One of the committeemen, Captain William M. Randolph, was killed on 17 February 1928 in a flying accident, and the base was named for him. The first class of cadets began training in 1931. All primary and basic flying training was done at Randolph, while advanced training remained at Kelly. This pattern was followed until 1939 when the expansion of the USAAC caused Randolph units to teach just basic flying. Aviation cadet* training continued until 1943 when the Central Instructor School was established to train instructor pilots. In 1945, only B-29* pilot* training was done on it.

From 1945 to 1948, primary and basic training returned. Primary ended in 1948, and basic continued until 1951. In the 1950s Randolph had crew training for B-29s, B-57s,* C-119s,* and KC-97s (*see* C-97). From 1960 to 1967, it primarily had instructor pilot training again. In 1967 the new "undergraduate pilot training" (UPT) system reached Randolph. In 1971, another of the frequent changes occurred when instructor pilot training was done again. In 1990, it was home of the headquarters of the Air Training Command* (ATC), Air Force Military Personnel Center* (AFMPC), Air Force Management Engineering Agency* (AFMEA), Air Force Civilian Personnel Management Center* (AFCPMC), and the 12th Flying Training Wing using T-37s* and T-38s.* It is an ATC base.

Movies: *West Point of the Air*, 1935. *I Wanted Wings*, 1941.

References. Brown, *Eagles*. "Guide to Major Air Force Installations Worldwide," *AF*, May 1990, p. 131. Thomas A. Manning, "The Origins of Randolph AFB," February 1987 (ATC History Office, Randolph AFB, Texas). Mueller, *AFB*. Roberts, *Dir. USAF*.

Thomas A. Manning

RANKS. *See* grades.

RAPID DEPLOYMENT JOINT TASK FORCE (RDJTF). *See* U.S. Central Command Air Forces.

RAPIER

This surface-to-air missile* (SAM) provides defense for seven USAF* installations in Britain and two in Turkey. It was battle-tested in the Falklands War and is a short-range, line-of-sight system assisted by radar* for all-weather capability. It is made by British Aerospace Corporation. In 1980, the United States agreed to buy 32 Rapier units, and the British agreed to provide manning by the Royal Air Force Regiment. The U.S. Army is charged with surface-to-air base defense for the USAF, and this Rapier arrangement was the result of British efforts to offset the costs of buying the U.S. Trident missile. The Rapier missile first went into active service for the USAF in 1984.

Characteristics: engine, IMI two-stage solid rocket; span, 15 inches; length, 7 feet; diameter, 5 inches; weight, about 94 pounds: top speed, more than Mach 2; range, 4 miles.

References. Christopher Campbell, *Air Warfare: The Fourth Generation*, 1984. *Defense Marketing Services Market Intelligence Reports, Missiles*, January 1988. Lon O. Nordeen, Jr., *Air Warfare in the Missile Age*, 1985. "Rapier: Combat Proven Point Defence," *Defence Update International*, 1938, pp. 54–61. Susan H. H. Young, "Gallery of USAF Weapons," *AF*, May 1990, p. 158.

Jeffrey C. Benton

RAVEN. *See* F-111.

RAWLINGS BOARD

The 1956 USAF* Educational Conference board's chairman was General Edwin W. Rawlings, commander of the Air Materiel Command (AMC). It reviewed the USAF's programs and made significant recommendations because it shifted the service toward more formal education for officers.

In 1956 slightly less than half of all officers held baccalaureate degrees, and the report recommended the degree should be a prerequisite for a regular commission. In addition, it advocated the following: postgraduate work should take place early in an officer's career, the Air University* (AU) should coordinate the curricula of all precommissioning programs, projections of quantitative and qualitative officer requirements should be the basis of long-range education and training goals, and the USAF should create a missile-oriented officer corps.

References. Goldberg, *Hist. USAF*. *Report of the USAF Educational Conference of 18–19 October 1956*, Maxwell AFB, Alabama, 8 November 1956. Billy Joe Tolson, *A History of Air University*, unpub. doctoral diss., University of Oklahoma, 1983.

Jeffrey C. Benton

RAZON. *See* AZON, RAZON, and TARZON.

RDC. *See* Air Force Systems Command.

RDJTF. *See* U.S. Central Command Air Forces.

REAGAN, PRESIDENT RONALD (1911–   )

By 1980, the demoralizing effects of the Vietnam War* and President Jimmy Carter's budget cutting had left the U.S. armed forces in a dolorous condition. Candidate Reagan made this a campaign issue and won, although incumbent

Carter said he would change his ways on defense. The former movie star and governor of California had served in the USAAF* in World War II.* As president, Reagan achieved weapons modernization, a recovery in military pay, and better funding for training and operations. Some people credit Reagan's rearmament and Strategic Defense Initiative* (SDI) as causing the final strains on the USSR's economy that precipitated the troubles and collapse in the Soviet Empire in 1989. There can be little doubt that Reagan's revitalization of the armed forces should get most of the credit for the great U.S. victory in the Iraq War.* Such revitalization takes years to achieve.

Yet the revitalization cost much less than the impressions given by a hostile and angry media and some politicians. In the last year, 1960, of Dwight D. Eisenhower's* presidency, Department of Defense (DoD) spending was 8.3 percent of the gross national product (GNP). In 1970, at the end of the John F. Kennedy* (JFK) and Lyndon B. Johnson* (LBJ) eras, it was 8 percent. In 1980, the end of Carter's presidency, it was 5.2 percent. In 1984, after the Reagan restoration of defense, it had revived to 6.5 percent.

For the USAF* Reagan restored the B-1* program, got the Peacekeeper* into production, revitalized USAF forces overseas, and started the SDI. He also reduced the micromanagement from Washington of forces in action.

References. Edward N. Luttwak, *The Pentagon and the Art of War: The Question of Military Reform*, 1985. Richard A. Stubbing, *The Defense Game*, 1986.

RECONNAISSANCE, OR "RECCE"

Recce investigates enemy areas or electromagnetic radiations to produce information for intelligence. It is done by visual, photographic, and electronic means from the ground, air, or space. It has proven decisive for military operations time and time again.

The earliest U.S. air recce was the use of observation balloons in the Civil War. Recce was the first military mission for aircraft and was an early one for space vehicles. It was used visually from airplanes as soon as World War I* began and made allied victory possible at the Battle of the Marne in September 1914. The successes and value of aerial recce from aircraft and lighter-than-air* (LTA) vehicles, then called observation aviation,* led to vigorous countermeasures, including the development of flak* and the fighter* type of aircraft. Soon photoreconnaissance was adopted and became the dominant technique. The British took more than a half million photos during the war.

Between World Wars I and II,* recce continued to be emphasized, and the USAAC* made significant advances in photoreconnaissance through the inventions of Dr. Sam M. Burka, Major James W. Bagley, Captain Albert W. Stevens, and First Lieutenant George W. Goddard.*

Observation aviation proved obsolete when World War II began. Its aircraft were too slow and nearly defenseless. Yet recce had to be done, and the task was transferred mostly to fighters adapted for the role and liaison* aircraft. Goddard's inventions were made even more useful by these developments. The increased use of electromagnetic devices in the war caused electronic recce to receive emphasis. Armed recce was used much in World War II and since. This is recce by an aircraft armed to destroy the targets it finds.

With the Cold War* and advanced weaponry, recce remained a critical function as shown by President Dwight D. Eisenhower's* famous Open Skies proposal. Other outstanding examples were the role of the U-2* in recce over the USSR and in the Cuban crisis of 1962.* The airplane was soon supplemented by orbiting satellites, and Goddard's inventions continued to be used in space-based recce.

In the Vietnam War* and with the follow-on forces attack* (FOFA) strategy, recce with all types of sensors increased in importance with real-time intelligence a need. There are four recent new systems. One is side-looking airborne radar* (SLAR), a standoff system with links to a ground facility to receive data immediately. A second is the tactical electronic reconnaissance (TEREC) system, which collects electromagnetic transmission information in any weather and transmits it to a ground facility. The third is the quick strike reconnaissance (QSR) system, which is for armed recce, providing means other than visual to find the target. The fourth is strike control and reconnaissance (SCAR), which is the use of recce aircraft as pathfinders to mark targets for attack.*

References. Primary: John P. Kelly, "Tac Recce: A Different Breed of Cat," *AF*, February 1979, pp. 60–62. Secondary: Charles D. Bright, "Air Power in World War I: Sideshow or Decisive Factor?" *AH*, June 1971, pp. 58–62. C&C, vol. 6. Glenn B. Infield, *Unarmed and Unafraid: The Complete History of the Men, Missions, Training and Techniques of Aerial Reconnaissance*, 1970. Maurer, *Avn. in Army*.

RECONNAISSANCE AIR MEET. *See* competitions.

RECRUIT. *See* PT-16.

RED ALERT. *See Dr. Strangelove or: How I Learned to Stop Worrying and Love the Bomb*.

RED BARON STUDIES. *See* Red Flag.

RED FLAG

After World War I* the USAAC* downgraded the air superiority* fighter* in the belief that bombers* could be built that could attain air superiority. World War II* showed this idea was not feasible with piston engines. After the war, an effort was made to accomplish the concept with jet engines. Also, a belief arose that the jet was so fast it had ended the possibility of the dogfight.

The Korean War,* the afterburner, and the air interceptor missile* (AIM) proved the bomber was still vulnerable and the dogfight very much alive. There was a resurgence of emphasis on air superiority aircraft and tactics after the USAF's* shock in Korea. The F-104* was built and air combat maneuvers (ACM) were emphasized in training. As Korea faded in memory, the F-104 was phased out, and ACM was progressively cut back to favor increased training in attack,* especially in tactical nuclear weapons* delivery. For the first time, missile partisans pushed the idea that the dogfight and the gun were finally obsolete.

When the USAF entered the Vietnam War,* it lacked air superiority fighters except for a handful of remnant F-104s. Its F-4s* lacked guns. The USAF also lacked the fighter pilot* experience that had helped so much in battling the superb MiG-15 in Korea. The Vietnam War was another air superiority shock for the USAF. The obese F-4 had to be redesigned for an internal gun, and its performance against the MiG-21 was disappointing. The USAF's difficulties did not all arise from having given the enemy political air superiority.* Only one USAF pilot, Captain Richard S. Ritchie,* became an ace* in the entire war. The North Vietnamese claimed to have gained 13 aces, but there is reason to believe this claim is inflated.

During the war, the USAF conducted an analysis of its air superiority operations. It was called "Red Baron" and looked at all the dogfights. The study found that USAF aircrews were (1) often caught by surprise, (2) had inadequate training, and (3) lacked knowledge of the enemy. It was back to the drawing board to get a successor to the F-104, the F-15.*

It was also back to the training skies. General Robert S. Dixon, commander of the Tactical Air Command* (TAC) from 1973 to 1978, reinstated realistic training, or "flag" as it is now called, in 1975. One training program, Red Flag, is intended to prevent the USAF from having to again reinvent the wheel of air superiority. In World War II it was an axiom that most mistakes were made in a pilot's first five combat sorties. In Vietnam, the opinion was that it was the first ten. Red Flag attempts to give a pilot a synthetic equivalent of those ten sorties. The training is done out of Nellis* AFB, Nevada. Some USAF men play the role of Soviet fighter pilots, called "Aggressors." They have been flying the F-5,* because its nimbleness resembles that of the excellent Soviet fighters such as the MiG-21. Thus, Red Flag includes dissimilar aerial combat tactics* (DACT). Computers score the "victories" in the training. Red Flag and its U.S. Navy counterpart, Top Gun, have become famous.

Other "flags" are Black for maintenance, Blue for control and communications, Checkered for overseas deployments, Copper for air defense, Green for electronic warfare,* and Silver for support elements such as law enforcement and medical services.

Movie: *Red Flag: The Ultimate Game*, 1981.

References. "Air War Vietnam," a special issue of *Air Progress*, 1981, pp. 45–49, 72–74. F. Clifton Berry, Jr., "Think and Fly Like the Enemy," *AF*, April 1982, pp. 36–41. Quinn G. Johnson, "Range Wars," *AF*, December 1987, pp. 78–82, 85. T. R. Milton, "Nellis and the Art of Airpower," *AF*, July 1987, pp. 80–85.

RED FLAG: THE ULTIMATE GAME. *See* movies.

REED, SECRETARY THOMAS C. (1934–   )

Reed was the 11th secretary of the Air Force* (SAF), serving from January 1976 to April 1977. Like some other SAFs, he made people his primary concern. He believed the way to control personnel costs was to control the quantity and quality of people. He also emphasized weapon system technology and the management of USAF* procurement.*

He was a distinguished Air Force Reserve Officer Training Corps* (AFROTC) graduate from Cornell University, New York, in 1956. On active duty from 1956 to 1961, he served initially with the Ballistic Missile Division as a project officer for the Minuteman* Re-entry Vehicle System. He earned a master of science degree in electrical engineering from the University of Southern California during his off-duty hours. He was engaged in thermonuclear weapons physics at the Lawrence Radiation Laboratory from 1959 to 1961. Reed rejoined the laboratory as a civilian in 1962 and then continued as a consultant until 1967. During this period, he also organized and retained interest in two companies. He became an assistant to the secretary of defense (SECDEF) in 1973 and was appointed director of Telecommunications and Command and Control Systems in 1974.

References. Futrell, *Ideas*, vol. 2. USAF Biography, "Thomas C. Reed," May 1976. Claude Witze, "Thomas C. Reed, USAF's New Secretary," *AF*, February 1976, pp. 32, 33.

Warren A. Trest

REESE AIR FORCE BASE

At Lubbock, Texas, Reese is an Air Training Command* (ATC) field. It became a USAAF* base in 1941 and was named then for the city of Lubbock. In 1949 it was renamed in honor of First Lieutenant Augustus F. Reese, Jr., who was killed in action in Sardinia flying a P-38* in 1943. In World War II* the field was a site for advanced flight training.* It was inactive from 1945 to 1949. TB-25s (*see* B-25) were used in flight training from 1955 to 1959, T-33s from 1958 to 1963, followed by T-38s* and then T-41s in 1965. In 1990 it had the 64th Flying Training Wing (FTW) training pilots* with T-37s* and T-38s.

References. "Guide to Major Air Force Installations Worldwide," *AF*, May 1990, p. 131. Mueller, *AFB*. Roberts, *Dir. USAF*.

REGENSBURG-SCHWEINFURT. *See* Schweinfurt.

REGION. *See* areas and regions.

REINFORCED PROTECTIVE REACTION STRIKES. *See* protective reaction strikes.

REMOTELY PILOTED VEHICLES. *See* unmanned aerial vehicles.

REPORTER. *See* P-61.

REPUBLIC AVIATION CORPORATION. *See* aerospace industry; A-10, F-47; F-84; F-105; P-43.

RESCAP. *See* MiGCAP.

RESCUE

An important humanitarian mission* of the USAF* is the use of its resources to rescue people, military and civilian, from danger in peace or war. Aircraft have the ability to operate at high speed over any surface feature, which gives them a unique ability in searching for and rescuing people. In all, USAF rescue had helped save the lives of almost 23,000 persons by the end of the 1980s.

Before World War II,* U.S. rescue efforts were left to the U.S. Coast Guard or were improvised, as in the 1937 effort to protect and find Amelia Earhart. In the USAAF* in World War II, the first rescue aircraft were amphibians originally developed for the U.S. Navy. Most were OA-10s from the Consolidated Aircraft Company, called Catalinas. Dissatisfied with the OA-10's range, the USAAF adapted B-17s* and B-29s* as SB-17s and SB-29s. These landplanes performed rescue at sea by carrying lifeboats for airdrop. The boats had provisions and a 500-mile range at eight knots.

Obviously the early development had emphasized rescue from the sea. However, there had always been a need for land recovery from wilderness areas or from disasters, or to prevent the capture of downed aircrews. This need first became critical for the operations over the jungles and mountains of the China-Burma-India* (CBI) theater. The helicopter* was part of the answer to these problems, but the first USAAF helicopter rescue squadron* was not formed until 1945. It played little role in rescuing the 5,000 USAAF aircrewmen saved in World War II.

Today's Aerospace Rescue and Recovery Service was established in 1946 under the Air Transport Command (ATC). After the war, the U-16* amphibian became a mainstay of the service.

Despite the successes of World War II, rescue only became truly recognized for its value in the Korean War.* Initially pressed into service for aeromedical evacuation* (MEDEVAC) of U.S. Army casualties to mobile Army surgical hospitals (MASH), USAF helicopters were so successful that the U.S. Army adopted MEDEVAC helicopters on a large scale. For the USAF, the war showed the great usefulness of saving downed aircrews, especially from capture. This was often done far behind the front line because the USAF had air superiority.* Of 1,690 USAF men who went down inside enemy territory, 170 were rescued and 255 were taken prisoner. The USAF also rescued 84 downed airmen from other U.S. and United Nations (UN) services. Of the 40 USAF aces* from this war, four were rescued including the top one, Captain Joseph C. McConnell, Jr.*

Vietnam War* rescue became even more important, for 3,883 U.S. and Allied aircrewmen were rescued from jungles, mountains, and the seas. Of these, 1,201 were USAF men. The USAF aircraft proved unsatisfactory at first, but in November 1965 an improved helicopter arrived, the HH-3 (*see* H-3). The ranges used in this war led to USAF development of an aerial refueling* capability for helicopters. The HC-130P (*see* C-130) was the tanker* used for this function. Capability was improved again with the more powerful HH-53 (*see* H-53). It was used in the attempted rescue in the Son Tay prison raid.* The price the rescuemen paid for their huge contribution was 71 killed and 45 aircraft lost. All rescue aircraft are nicknamed "Dumbo."

References. Berger, *USAF in SEA*. Earl H. Tilford, "The Development of Search and Rescue: World War II to 1961," *AH*, December 1977, pp. 228–39. U.S. Air Force Fact Sheet 87–30, "Aerospace Rescue and Recovery Service," July 1987.

RESCUE COMBAT AIR PATROL. *See* MiGCAP.

RESEARCH AND DEVELOPMENT COMMAND. *See* Air Force Systems Command.

RESERVE FORCES BILL OF RIGHTS AND VITALIZATION ACT. *See* U.S. Air Force Reserve.

RETARDED BOMBS

When bombs* are dropped at low altitude they may require some form of retardation to keep them from damaging the releasing aircraft in the explosion. In and after World War II,* retardation devices such as parachutes had been used, but not generally, except for the 23-pound fragmentation bomb. It was not until the late 1950s that manufacture of a series of low-drag, general-purpose (LDGP) bombs included the "snakeye" retard fin developed by the U.S. Navy. This device replaces normal fins with a cylindrical one that can be dropped closed as a normal bomb. At the pilot's option, four large spoiler plates open up on release, slowing down the bomb. A new type of retard device, the MAU-91, has been developed by the Goodyear Company. It uses a combination balloon-parachute, or ballute, to achieve safe separation, and is coming into wide use.

References. Berger, *USAF in SEA*. Norman Friedman, *U.S. Naval Weapons*, 1988. Robert L. Shaw, *Fighter Combat: Tactics and Maneuvering*, 1985.

Philip Long

"REVOLT OF THE ADMIRALS." *See* B-36 controversy.

REX INTERCEPTION

On 12 May 1938, the USAAC* demonstrated that its bombers* could carry out the coastal defense mission hundreds of miles at sea against a hostile fleet. Three B-17s* departed Mitchel* Field, New York, at 0830 hours to intercept the SS *Rex*, an Italian liner 725 miles at sea. The commander was Major Vincent J. Meloy, and the navigator was Lieutenant Curtis E. LeMay.* Also aboard were members of the National Broadcasting Company's (NBC) news staff and reporters from the *New York Herald Tribune*. Despite adverse weather, the ship was successfully intercepted at 1225 hours. Appropriate radio announcements were made, and Meloy talked with the ship's captain as photographs were taken of two B-17s over the *Rex*.

Evidently, the airmen proved their point. Brigadier General H. H. Arnold* thought some U.S. Navy man contacted the U.S. Army General Staff. The War Department ordered all activities of the USAAC to be confined to a 100-mile distance from the U.S. shoreline unless authority for greater distances was requested in advance. Only four years later, the USAAF* would be conducting operations against the German and Japanese navies over most of the Atlantic and Pacific Oceans.

References. Primary: H. H. Arnold, *Global Mission*, 1949. Curtis E. LeMay, *Mission with LeMay: My Story*, 1965. Secondary: Maurer, *Avn. in Army. The Official Pictorial History of the AAF*, 1947. A. D. Turnbull and C. L. Lord, *History of U.S. Naval Aviation*, 1949.

See also Army-Navy agreements of 1931 and 1938; interception of the USS *Utah*.

Alwyn T. Lloyd

RHEIN-MAIN AIR BASE

This has been one of the most historical of USAF* bases. After April 1959, within the planning framework of the North Atlantic Treaty Organization* (NATO), Rhein-Main became the main supply and support base for the U.S. Air Forces in Europe* (USAFE), providing the air logistical support for the U.S. military forces in Europe.

It got its name from its location at the confluence of the Rhein and Main Rivers, near Frankfurt am Main, Federal Republic of Germany. The field began operation in 1936 as a commercial airdrome. From it the two giant airships, LZ 127 *Graf Zeppelin* and LZ 129 *Hindenburg*, began their regular nonstop transatlantic flights, taking an average of 60 hours. The Luftwaffe used it for attack* operations late in World War II.* It was captured in March 1945 and, in the last weeks of the war, USAAF* attack sorties were flown from it. After the war, it quickly became a primary facility for the USAAF.

For 15 months of the Berlin Airlift,* C-47s* and C-54s* flew into the divided city from Rhein-Main and other bases in West Germany. On one day alone, its tower logged 635 takeoffs and landings.

To meet Rhein-Main's obligations as the primary arrival and departure point for all U.S. military personnel in Europe, a large Aerial Port Transient Facility was built in 1956. Within 12 months of its construction it handled nearly 30,000 people a month.

Since the Berlin Airlift, planners of maneuvers and NATO military exercises have frequently used Rhein-Main as a main logistical nexus because of its airlift capability and strategic location. The largest exercises, such as REFORGER I/

CRESTED CAP 1980, which involved the airlifting and deployment of 17,000 USAF and U.S. Army people to bases and training areas in Western Europe, proved the base's capability as a supply and support center. Rhein-Main moved from the control of USAFE to the Military Airlift Command* (MAC) in 1975. Since then it has had the primary mission of providing tactical, aeromedical, and administrative airlift within the European theater. MAC's unit there in 1990 was the 435th Tactical Airlift Wing with C-130E* aircraft.

References. "Guide to Major Air Force Installations Worldwide," *AF*, May 1990, p. 131. Patricia Parrish, *Forty-Five Years of Vigilance for Freedom: United States Air Forces in Europe, 1942–1987*, Ramstein AB Office of USAFE History, 1987. Roberts, *Dir. USAF*.

Roger D. Launius

RIBOT, PREMIER ALEXANDER (1842–1923)

On 26 May 1917, Ribot, the premier of France, sent President Woodrow Wilson a detailed cable requesting that the United States provide 4,500 aircraft, 5,000 pilots,* and 50,000 mechanics for the war by 1918. These figures were highly influential on the future of the U.S. Army's airmen. This request more than doubled the 12 April estimate by the National Advisory Committee for Aeronautics (NACA). An Army committee, headed by Colonel Benjamin D. Foulois,* recommended figures higher than NACA's, perhaps using Ribot's cable. The final numbers approved in the Appropriations Act of 24 July 1917 were based on the Foulois committee's figures, and those were the numbers that the Aircraft Board* hoped U.S. production efforts could achieve.

References. I. B. Holley, Jr., *Ideas and Weapons*, 1953. *Webster's Biographical Dictionary*, 1964.

D. K. Vaughan

RICE, SECRETARY DONALD B. (1939–   )

Rice became the 19th secretary of the Air Force* (SAF) in 1989. From Frederick, Maryland, he graduated as a chemical engineer from the University of Notre Dame, Indiana, in 1961. He also had two degrees from Purdue University, Indiana, an M.S. in industrial administration and a Ph.D. in management and economics. He served in the Department of Defense (DoD) from 1967 to 1970, ending as the deputy assistant secretary of defense for resource analysis. From 1970 to 1972 he was assistant director in the Office of Management and Budget (OMB) in the Executive Office of the President. In 1972 he became president and chief executive officer of the RAND Corporation. He also was a member of the Defense Science Board (1977–1983), a member of the Trilateral Commission, and director of the Secretary of Defense and President's Defense Resource Management Study (1977–1979). Rice's background has caused some turbulence in his relations with Congress.

References. Primary: Donald B. Rice, "AF's Future Strategy: 'Punch Hard and Terminate Quickly,' " *Air Force Times*, 26 March 1990, pp. 23, 68. Secondary: Julie Bird, "Wave of AF Leadership Changes Still Causing Ripples," *Air Force Times*, 7 January

1991, pp. 8–9. Andy Pasztor, "Air Force Secretary Donald Rice Is under Fire from Lawmakers Who Question His Strategy," *The Wall Street Journal*, 9 July 1990, p. A12. *Supplement to Who's Who in America*, 45th ed., 1989.

RICKENBACKER, CAPTAIN EDWARD V. (1890–1973)

The United States's ace* of aces in World War I* with 26 victories, Rickenbacker is the seventh-ranking U.S. ace of all time, an honor he shares with General John C. Meyer. He was inducted into the National Aviation Hall of Fame in Dayton, Ohio, in 1965.

Born Edward Rickenbacher in Columbus, Ohio, he anglicized his last name by changing the *h* to *k* and made his name fancier by adding a middle name of Vernon. His first vocation was racing car driver, and he became one of the best. He enlisted in the Signal Corps in 1917. In France, he became General John J. Pershing's* driver and rose to sergeant first class. He asked to learn to fly and was permitted to, graduating in October as a pilot* and first lieutenant. He was then assigned as an engineering officer at Issoudon,* under Major Carl A. Spaatz.* Rickenbacker repeatedly asked for combat duty, but Spaatz refused until March 1918.

He was assigned to the 1st Pursuit Group's 94th Aero Squadron,* the "Hat-in-the-Ring-Squadron," under Major Raoul Lufbery.* His first victory came on 25 April, and he was an ace by 30 May. In the summer of 1918, he was hospitalized for two months with a mastoid infection. He returned to the 94th as its commander. He scored six victories in September and 14 in October. Rickenbacker received an Air Force Medal of Honor* in 1930 for an action on 25 September 1918, when he attacked five fighters* that were protecting two observation planes. He shot down one fighter and one observation plane.

After the war he started the Rickenbacker Motor Company and served as vice president and director of sales. He intended his car to be the most advanced from an engineering standpoint and to be made with fine workmanship. Production began in 1922 and the car was an initial success. The 1924 model had the first four-wheel brakes. Competitors claimed four-wheel brakes were extremely dangerous, and the public believed them. The company failed in 1927 and Rickenbacker was $250,000 in debt. He went back to auto racing and became president of the Indianapolis Speedway. In 1929 he was promoted to colonel in the Reserve. After five years he gave it up, saying he wanted to be remembered as a captain. In 1934 the General Motors Corporation asked him to run a troubled subsidiary, Eastern Air Lines. It was soon running profitably. In 1938 he raised enough money to buy the airline and was president of a successful company until he was nearly 70 years old. He was critically injured in an Eastern crash in 1941.

During World War II,* he traveled the world visiting USAAF* units, especially those with fighters. Once his plane, a B-17,* went down at sea in the South Pacific. He and the crew, save one, survived a terrible 24 days in open rafts with little water and food before being found. The old survivor died of heart failure at age 83 and was saluted at his funeral by a flight* of F-4s* from the 94th Tactical Fighter Squadron of MacDill* AFB, Florida.

References. Primary: Edward V. Rickenbacker, *Fighting the Flying Circus*, 1919, and *Rickenbacker*, 1967. Secondary: DuPre, *USAF Bio*. Finis Farr, *Rickenbacker's Luck: An American Life*, 1979. Raymond H. Fredette, "Rickenbacker: 'Most Natural Leader I Ever Saw,' " *AF*, April 1974, pp. 65–71.

RISNER, BRIGADIER GENERAL (JAMES) ROBINSON (1925–   )

A veteran of three wars, Risner made his greatest mark in the third. He had unique accomplishments as a leader while a prisoner of war (POW), North Vietnam.* The Risner Trophy has been established in his honor to recognize the outstanding graduates of the Tactical Fighter Weapons School at Nellis* AFB, Nevada.

From Oklahoma City, Oklahoma, he became a pilot* in World War II,* but served in the minor location of Panama flying P-38s* and P-39s.* He returned to civilian life in 1946, starting an auto parts store and parking garage. His Air National Guard* (ANG) squadron was federalized during the Korean War.* Flying F-86s* he became an ace* with eight victories in 109 sorties in that war. In 1957 he was chosen to fly an F-100* named *Spirit of St. Louis II* from New York to Paris as the Charles Lindbergh Memorial Flight.

In February 1965, he went to Korat Royal Thai* AFB, Thailand, to command the 67th Tactical Fighter Squadron flying F-105s.* He was shot down on a Rolling Thunder* sortie in April but succeeded in reaching the Gulf of Tonkin and ejecting. He was rescued by a U-16.* Then he was shot down a second time and captured. Risner was sent to Hoa Lo, the vicious "Hanoi Hilton." He was the senior prisoner and immediately set about establishing an effective POW organization. When the guards became aware of his progress, he was severely tortured. He persisted as leader and was effective. He spent over seven years as a POW.

References. Primary: John L. Frisbee, "Surviving in Hanoi's Prisons," *AF*, June 1973, pp. 32–33. Jon A. Reynolds, "The Eagle in the Hilton," *AF*, February 1983, pp. 82–85. Robinson Risner, *The Passing of the Night*, 1973. Secondary: John L. Frisbee, ed., *Makers of the United States Air Force*, 1987.

RITCHIE, LIEUTENANT COLONEL RICHARD S. "STEVE" (1942–)

Ritchie is the only USAF* fighter* pilot* to become a Vietnam War* ace.* He is also the only American who has shot down five MiG-21s.

Born in Reidsville, North Carolina, Ritchie graduated from the U.S. Air Force Academy* (USAFA) in 1964. He finished at the top of his flight training* class at Laredo AFB, Texas. On his second tour in the Vietnam War he scored his first victory on 10 May 1972. His fifth came on 28 August. Ritchie left active service in 1974. He was a candidate for Congress. He has been president of Steve Ritchie Associates, Inc., speaking and consulting for a free enterprise economy.

References. Primary: R. Frank Futrell et al., *Aces & Aerial Victories: The United States Air Force in Southeast Asia 1965–1973*, 1976. Steve Ritchie, "An Eagle for All Arenas," *AF*, November 1983, pp. 43–49. Secondary: Sisco Deen, "How Steve Ritchie Got His Fifth MIG [sic]," *AF*, October 1972, pp. 328–29. Hess, *Aces Album*.

ROBBINS, LIEUTENANT GENERAL JAY T. (1919–   )

With 22 victories, Robbins is the 11th-ranking USAF* ace* of all time, an honor he shares with Colonels Gerald R. Johnson* and Neel E. Kearby.* He was one of the most decorated USAF officers.

Robbins was born in Coolidge, Texas, and graduated from Texas A&M University in 1940 with a Reserve commission. In 1942 he joined the 8th Fighter Group of the Fifth Air Force* (5AF), flying P-38s.* He scored four victories on each of two sorties. On one of these occasions he was in a formation of 12 P-38s that engaged 50 Japanese fighters.* Robbins damaged an enemy besides the four shot down, but his own plane was badly hit, including the loss of one engine. Robbins returned to the United States at the end of 1944 after 181 combat sorties lasting 607 hours. After World War II,* Robbins became a regular officer and made the USAF his career.

References. DuPre, *USAF Bio*. Hess, *Aces Album*, 1978. Edward H. Sims, *American Aces in Great Fighter Battles of World War II*, 1958.

ROBINS, BRIGADIER GENERAL (AUGUSTINE) WARNER (1882–1940)

Robins is regarded as the father of modern USAF* logistics. When he was chief of the USAAC* Materiel Division in the 1920s he developed an important system of cataloging. Robins* AFB, Georgia, is named in his honor. He was born in Gloucester County, Virginia, and graduated from the U.S. Military Academy (USMA) in 1907. He became a pilot* in 1918. In the 1920s he developed USAAS* and USAAC supply procedures and continued in logistics until 1939 when he became commandant of the Air Corps Training Center* at Randolph* Field, Texas. He died there in his quarters.

References. DuPre, *USAF Bio*. Bernard J. Termena et al., *Logistics: An Illustrated History of AFLC and Its Antecedents, 1921–1981*, 1981.

ROBINS AIR FORCE BASE

Near Macon, Georgia, this Air Force Logistics Command* (AFLC) field is named for Brigadier General Warner Robins,* former commander of the Materiel Division from 1935 to 1939. Robins is generally recognized as the father of modern USAF* logistics. Robins Field and the Warner Robins Army Air Depot were dedicated in 1943.

Base personnel have played a key role in the maintenance of important weapon systems and supply functions through three wars and numerous international crises. In World War II,* they maintained numerous warplanes and trained and dispatched more than a quarter-million maintenance, supply, and logistics experts to every theater of the war. During the Korean War,* its 3,900 workers swiftly fitted hundreds of mothballed B-29s.* In the 1960s and 1970s Robins had an important role in the "pipeline" sending critical men and material to the Vietnam War.*

Originally the field had 3,000 acres and its construction cost $20 million. Today it covers 8,790 acres with nine million square feet of facilities worth nearly $890 million. In 1990 it had the Warner Robins Air Logistics Center (WR-ALC), headquarters of the U.S. Air Force Reserve (USAFR), and the 19th Air Refueling Wing (19 AREFW). The mission of the WR-ALC is management of more than 200,000 aircraft and avionics items. It also manages the Foreign Military Sales (FMS) program for 55 countries involving about $2.6 billion annually. Its maintenance responsibility is for the F-15,* C-130,* and C-141.*

References. "Electronic Warfare," a special edition of *AWST*, 11 September 1989, pp. 103–6. William Head, *A Chronological History of the Warner Robins Air Logistics Center and Robins Air Force Base, Georgia, 1936–1986*, WR-ALC History Office, 1987. Mueller, *AFB*. Roberts, *Dir. USAF*. Robins Air Force Base Heritage Committee, *A Pictorial History of Robins Air Force Base*, 1982.

William Head and Richard W. Iobst

ROCKET-ASSISTED TAKEOFF (RATO, JATO)

RATO are small rocket boosters, usually with solid fuel, used to give extra thrust to heavily laden aircraft or to reduce the length of the takeoff roll. Auxiliary jet engines were similarly used, so the term *JATO* referred to "jet" instead of "rocket." Often RATO units were erroneously called JATO. These devices were in common use after World War II* and before the advent of the afterburner.

References. Ernest J. Gentle and Lawrence W. Reithmaier, eds., *Aviation/Space Dictionary*, 6th ed., 1980. Woodford Agee Heflin, ed., *The United States Air Force Dictionary*, 1956.

ROCKEYE. *See* MK-20.

ROCKWELL INTERNATIONAL CORPORATION. *See* aerospace industry; B-1; OV-10.

ROLL BACK THE SKY. *See* novels.

ROLLING THUNDER

This operation was the USAF* and U.S. Navy air power campaign used against the North in the Vietnam War* from 1965 to 1968. President Lyndon B. Johnson's* (LBJ) goals for Rolling Thunder were to (1) create a viable state in South Vietnam, (2) prevent armed conflict with the USSR or Red China, and (3) prevent the U.S. public from becoming concerned about the air campaign. Secretary of Defense (SECDEF) Robert S. McNamara's* objectives in support of LBJ's were to (1) raise morale in the Republic of South Vietnam and (2) make the infiltration of men and materiel from the North to the South too expensive for North Vietnam.

The original strategy was to interdict the flow southward under U.S. Army General Maxwell Taylor's strategy of "flexible response" and "graduated escalation.'' The attacks* would begin at the southernmost part of North Vietnam and be expanded northward and in intensity if the initial efforts did not produce the desired results. This plan led to the operation's name. This strategy had two serious problems. First, it betrayed contempt for the enemy, which led to come-uppance. An enemy should be treated with the utmost respect. Second, the strategy was self-defeating. It automatically gave the enemy the time to organize defenses and countermeasures to offset the telegraphed punch of the next es-calation. Besides those flaws, political air superiority* was to be given to the enemy in the hope it would show a desire to negotiate and to achieve LBJ's second goal. Enemy losses in men were to be minimalized although it was known this would increase U.S. casualties, and it was incongruous with the strategy of bloody attrition being followed in South Vietnam.

Before the start of Rolling Thunder, the USAF's leading combat commander, General Curtis E. LeMay,* was retired on 31 January 1965. The previous summer LeMay had recommended a vigorous, sudden, and hard-hitting air assault, the 94-target plan,* and LeMay had strong differences of opinion in general with McNamara. LeMay was replaced with General John P. McConnell* who stayed on the JCS throughout Rolling Thunder. McConnell did not have much battle leadership experience and, in contrast to LeMay, did not challenge McNamara.

Rolling Thunder began in February 1965. Command and control was exercised by the SECDEF and the civilians in the Office of the SECDEF (OSD) and was approved or disapproved by LBJ. This group determined targets, ordnance loads, and tactics. The Joint Chiefs of Staff (JCS) made recommendations that were seldom followed but did have some influence. By December it had dropped 40,000 tons of bombs. A bombing halft* began that month in hopes the North would negotiate. While Rolling Thunder had raised morale in the South and there was no battle action by the USSR or Red China, it had failed in its other objectives.

The JCS persuaded LBJ and McNamara to escalate the operation by a campaign against the North's oil. This lasted until August 1966, when it had obviously failed. This failure, together with the Jason Division* report, which recom-mended Igloo White* instead of Rolling Thunder, convinced McNamara the campaign would not succeed.

In October 1966, the JCS proposed to attack the North's industry, power system, ports, and locks and dams. McNamara did not object, but LBJ approved attacking only industry and the power system. This phase lasted until May 1967. Then lack of progress with both Rolling Thunder and Igloo White led to paralytic indecision, and Rolling Thunder was continued at a steady level. By the end of 1967, LBJ had lost confidence in McNamara. The Tet offensive of 1968 surprised and shook LBJ. He appointed a new SECDEF, Clark M. Clifford, who rec-ommended withdrawal from Vietnam. LBJ decided to deescalate the war and halted Rolling Thunder at the end of March 1968 as he faced a fall election.

Rolling Thunder was a tragic failure. It had dropped 643,000 tons of bombs, 90 percent of which had been directed at transportation, yet the USAF's big punch, heavy bombers,* had never been used. The campaign never restricted the flow of supplies enough to hurt the small needs of the guerrilla army operating in the South. Its attacks on the minor industries of the agricultural nation did not disrupt the war economy because imported goods were allowed to flow freely into the seaports and overland from Red China. As Rolling Thunder dragged on, it proved unable to sustain the morale of the South which it had achieved earlier. The only goal attained, if indeed it was ever a factor, was that the USSR and Red China did not intervene with their own forces.

References. Primary: Jack Broughton, *Going Downtown: The War against Hanoi and Washington*, 1988. Secondary: Berger, *USAF in SEA*. Larry Berman, *Lyndon Johnson's War: The Road to Stalemate in Vietnam*, 1989. Mark Clodfelter, *The Limits of Air Power: The American Bombing of North Vietnam*, 1989. Futrell, *Ideas*, vol. 2. James Clay Thompson, *Rolling Thunder: Understanding Policy and Program Failure*, 1980.

See also Linebacker, route package.

ROMA

The *Roma* was a semirigid airship of the USAAS* that had a major accident. This accident caused a permanent changeover from hydrogen to helium gas in U.S. airships. The use of any airships by the USAF's* antecedents was never again given much thought, as the U.S. Army and Navy had already agreed that only the Navy would develop rigid airships.

Brigadier General William Mitchell* proposed in 1920 that the *Roma* be bought from Italy. It had a gas capacity of 1.1 million cubic feet. When the USAAS* first flew it in 1921, the ship was found to be underpowered. Its six Ansaldo engines were replaced with Liberty engines.* On its first flight after the change, in 1922, it dived suddenly from 600 feet, hit a high-tension wire, and exploded. Thirty-four died in the flames and 11 survived.

References. Maurer, *Avn. in Army. The Official Pictorial History of the AAF*, 1947. Swanborough, *US Mil. Airc*.

ROOSEVELT, PRESIDENT FRANKLIN D. (FDR) (1882–1945)

In the late 1930s, FDR helped create awareness of the new role of aviation in national defense, often surprising even air power advocates by proposing figures for aircraft in the tens of thousands. He did this to help Americans understand that German air power had the potential to strike at the Western Hemisphere. While the development of U.S. aviation would have inevitably taken place, FDR's backing and support for air power greatly enhanced the USAAC* and USAAF* after 1938.

In 1933 and 1934, FDR gave some attention to building naval ships and aircraft, but the services did not get what they would require later. Not until his reelection in 1936 did FDR give much attention to the world situation. There is little doubt he took steps indicating he had a broader conception about threats to the nation than those in the War, Navy, and State Departments. However, until 1938 FDR believed flak* would stop air operations, so he had little interest in the nation's air services.

Late in 1938, reports on German aviation, actions in the Spanish Civil War, the air raid scare preceding the Munich Conference of September 1938, and the extensive buying of U.S. aircraft by the British and French made FDR aware that U.S. aviation required special attention in preparing the nation's defenses. At a White House conference in November, FDR told military officers they should plan for 20,000 aircraft. Roosevelt's message to Congress of 12 January 1939* adjusted down this figure for political reasons. Although it was a dramatic psychological figure and not a realistic one for the time, the rhetoric stimulated debate that helped get some aerial arming including, finally, long-range bombers.*

In the Roosevelt message of 16 May 1940,* FDR called for, not 20,000 planes, but a production capacity of 50,000 planes a year. In 1941, FDR exchanged U.S. naval destroyers for U.S. rights to build naval and air bases in British imperial possessions on the Atlantic coasts. Also in 1941, FDR approved the creation of the USAAF* with a separate air staff to prepare the plans that became AWPD-1* in August.

References. Lester H. Brune, *The Origins of American National Security: Sea Power, Air Power and Foreign Policy, 1900 to 1941*, 1981. Wayne S. Cole, *Roosevelt and the Isolationists, 1933–1945*, 1983. Futrell, *Ideas*, vol. 1. Irving Brinton Holley, Jr., *Buying Aircraft: Matériel Procurement for the Army Air Forces*, 1964. William Langer and S. Everett Gleason, *The Challenge to Isolation*, 1952.

See also presidential airlift.

Lester H. Brune

ROOSEVELT, PRESIDENT THEODORE "TEDDY" (1858–1919)

Roosevelt is noteworthy for urging his secretary of war, William H. Taft, to investigate buying an aircraft for military use. The result was a call for bids for an aircraft capable of carrying two people at a speed of 40 miles per hour for a distance of 125 miles. The bids were called for in December 1907; the only successful respondents were the Wright brothers,* who delivered their aircraft in February 1908.

Roosevelt was the first president to fly. His son, Quentin, joined the Aviation Section of the U.S. Army Signal Corps* as a pilot,* flew with the 95th Aero Squadron, and was killed in action in July 1918.

References. Goldberg, *Hist. USAF*. Juliette A. Hennessy, *The United States Army Air Arm April 1861 to April 1917*, 1985, A. N. Marquis, *Who Was Who in America*, 1943.

D. K. Vaughan

ROOSEVELT MESSAGE OF 12 JANUARY 1939

In this speech President Franklin D. Roosevelt* (FDR) took a giant step in building the USAAC* for the crisis ahead. He asserted that the United States could not wait for attack to prepare for war and that the new range and speed of the offensive required new thinking about aircraft to defend the Western Hemisphere. His message was not a complete surprise because of the Munich Conference in September 1938.

After consultations with the War and Navy Departments, FDR asked in the message for at least 3,000 airplanes, at a cost of $300 million, and another $32 million to enable the aircraft industry to prepare for quantity production. In addition, FDR asked for $21 million for naval aircraft and $10 million to train civilian pilots who could be called up.

The request for 3,000 planes was a ploy. FDR wanted 6,000, with 5,500 for fiscal year 1939. After asking for the 3,000, he permitted the chairman of the House Military Affairs Committee to introduce a bill in February for 6,000 planes. By framing his request in terms of hemispheric defense, FDR gained approval from isolationists such as Senator William E. Borah* who favored more aircraft for coastal defense. By May, the legislation passed the Senate with only eight nays and the House with only 15 nays.

References. Primary: Roosevelt's speech is in *Congressional Record*, 12 January 1939, pp. 218ff. Secondary: Stetson Conn and Bryon Fairchild, *The Framework of Hemispheric Defense*, 1960. Irving Brinton Holley, Jr., *Buying Aircraft: Matériel Procurement for the Army Air Forces*, 1964.

See also act of 3 April 1939; Woodring directive of 1938.

Lester H. Brune

ROOSEVELT MESSAGE OF 16 MAY 1940

This speech was another enormous step forward in the building of the USAAC's* air power. As dictator Adolf Hitler's blitzkrieg was rolling westward, President Franklin D. Roosevelt* (FDR) told Congress that millions of dollars must be spent for defense and emphasized a production goal of 50,000 aircraft a year. FDR noted that the power of the services had greatly improved but that air combat conditions had changed rapidly.

FDR said the oceans were no longer barriers because air power might bring raids from Greenland to New England, from the Azores to the eastern seaboard, from the West Indies to Florida, and from West Africa to Brazil. FDR said he wanted to attack an aggressor at his bases and on the flight routes. He asked for an immediate $896 million and an additional authorization for contracts for $286 million more. These funds would go for increasing aircraft production, flak,* and training.

As Irving Brinton Holley, Jr., has said, FDR's request for 50,000 aircraft was an imaginative and psychological figure in response to the dramatic success of the Germans. The figure gained public attention and moved the country toward essential goals.

References. Primary: Roosevelt's speech is in *Congressional Record*, 16 May 1940, pp. 6244ff., and *Vital Speeches*, 1 June 1940, pp. 482–84. Secondary: Irving Brinton Holley, Jr., *Buying Aircraft: Matériel Procurement for the Army Air Forces*, 1964.

Lester H. Brune

"ROSIE." *See* O'Donnell, General Emmett.

ROUNDEL. *See* insignia.

ROUND-THE-CLOCK BOMBING. *See* Combined Bomber Offensive.

ROUND-THE-WORLD FLIGHT OF 1924

In the early 1920s the chief of the USAAS,* Major General Mason M. Patrick,* was determined his airmen would be the first to fly around the world. He hoped the flight would bring back information on long-distance navigation and worldwide flying conditions that would be useful in establishing global air routes. In addition, he believed such an historic accomplishment would increase public and congressional support for the USAAS in an era of growing isolationism and shrinking military budgets. The famous flight achieved Patrick's goals.

The project was a team effort. Supplies and information on foreign operating conditions came from U.S. companies with overseas offices. The U.S. Navy, Coast Guard, and Bureau of Fisheries supported the overwater portions of the flight and helped the USAAS establish and maintain advanced bases along each major leg of the trip. The Douglas Aircraft Company designed and built the World Cruisers. The subcontractor list for the planes reads like a "Who's Who" of America's young aviation industry. Powered by 400-horsepower Liberty engines,* the sturdy two-seat biplanes had a top speed of 103 miles per hour and an 830-mile range. Major Frederick L. Martin was to lead the expedition.

Christened *Boston*, *Chicago*, *New Orleans*, and *Seattle*, the planes departed Seattle, Washington, on 6 April 1924. Martin's *Seattle* crashed into an Alaskan mountainside, and First Lieutenant Lowell Smith assumed command. The route was Japan, Shanghai, Hong Kong, Bangkok, Rangoon, Calcutta, Karachi, Constantinople, Paris, and London. *Boston* made an emergency landing on the transatlantic leg and sank during recovery efforts. A new plane, *Boston II*, was added in Nova Scotia. The three aircraft arrived in Seattle on 28 September, after 27,553 miles in 175 days and 371 hours and 11 minutes flying time.

References. Primary: Alva Harvey, "*Seattle* Has Crashed in Alaska," *AF*, September 1974, pp. 104–7. Leigh Wade, "The World Flight: An All-American Venture," *AF*, March 1974, pp. 60–61. Secondary: Aeronautical Chamber of Commerce of America, *Aircraft Yearbook, 1925*, 1925. Joe Christy, "That First Round-the-World Flight," *AF*, March 1974, pp. 52–59. Maurer, *Avn. in Army*.

John R. Reese

ROURKE, SECRETARY RUSSELL A. (1931–)

Rourke served the shortest term of any secretary of the Air Force.* He took the post as the 16th secretary in December 1985 and resigned for personal reasons only four months later, in April.

He entered government service in 1960, leaving a law firm to be a congressional assistant. In 1976 he became a special assistant to President Gerald R. Ford. From 1981 to 1985, he was assistant secretary of defense for legislative affairs.

Rourke said he had five challenges as USAF secretary: (1) increase readiness through restoring public and congressional confidence in defense management, (2) maximize defense growth by more precisely defining weapons requirements,

(3) emphasize the value of compensation and retirement programs to the maintenance of a high-quality force, (4) institutionalize the process for meeting the threat of terrorism and low-intensity war, and (5) continue a strong USAF space program.

References. Primary: Russell A. Rourke, "Five Challenges," *AF*, May 1986, p. 70. USAF Biography, "Russell A. Rourke," February 1986.

Warren A. Trest

ROUTE PACKAGE (RP)

The USAF* and U.S. Navy were unable to cooperate in Rolling Thunder* operations and competed vigorously. This intolerable situation led to dividing North Vietnam into zones of operation. An Air Force–Navy Coordinating Committee established six zones, or target areas, in the North in November 1965. The zones were called "route packages," or RPs, "Packs," or "Paks." The original plan was for each service to have three packages and exchange them every three weeks. This was soon changed to monthly exchanges.

Admiral U. S. Grant Sharp, commander in chief of the Pacific Command (CINCPAC), ordered permanent package assignments in April 1966. In addition, he created seven packages by dividing RP 6. The allocation gave the Seventh Air Force* (7AF) RPs 5 and 6A. These were the northerly areas containing Hanoi* and the Northwest Railroad. Carrier Task Force 77 (CTF 77) had RPs 2, 3, 4, and 6B. These areas extended from the 18th parallel to Red China and included Haiphong and part of the Northeast Railroad. The U.S. Military Assistance Command, Vietnam (MACV), received RP 1, which was the one immediately north of the Demilitarized Zone (DMZ). This would also be a USAF responsibility.

The USAF's Lieutenant General Joseph H. Moore,* commander of the 2nd Air Division (2nd AD), believed in cooperation and not the zoning. He also believed the permanent division was inequitable to the USAF because the 2nd AD got the most heavily defended areas. He protested, but Sharp overruled him. Sharp's decision did not end the unproductive competition.

References. Primary: G. I. Basel, *Pak Six: A Story of the War in the Skies of North Vietnam*, 1982. U.S.G. Sharp, *Strategy for Defeat, Vietnam in Retrospect*, 1978. Secondary: Berger, *USAF in SEA*. Mark Clodfelter, *The Limits of Air Power: The American Bombing of North Vietnam*, 1989.

RPV. *See* unmanned aerial vehicles.

RUNWAY CRATERING MUNITIONS

These are specialized munitions made to crater and render unusable an enemy runway or parking apron. Airfields are very well defended targets, and normally only one bombing pass at low altitude can be made safely. Regular "iron" bombs* dropped under such conditions tend to bounce from thick concrete, so a special bomb is used. In 1986 the USAF* adopted the Durandal "dibber" bomb made by Matra S. A. of France. Upon release from an aircraft, a parachute deploys and orients the bomb nose downward. A rocket engine then accelerates the 453-pound bomb, which can penetrate 15.75 inches into reinforced concrete. Detonation pushes up a large area, rendering the runway unusable until it is repaired. Successors to Durandal are the Direct Airfield Attack Combined Munition (DAACM) weapons. They are smaller and lighter than Durandal, but they are as effective.

References. Gunston, *Airc. Arm.* Edgar Ulsamer, "The Steady Evolution in Armaments," *AF*, December 1985, pp. 80–81.

Philip Long

RYAN, JOHN D. (1864–1933)

Ryan was director of Air Service and second assistant secretary of war from 27 August 1918 to the end of World War I.* This was an important post designed to end organizational turmoil in the new USAAS.*

Ryan resigned his position as president of the Anaconda Copper Mining Company in 1917 to serve on the war council of the American Red Cross. On 21 May 1918, President Woodrow Wilson transferred the air arm away from the U.S. Army Signal Corps to two new agencies under the secretary of war. One was the Division of Military Aeronautics, responsible for training and operations, under Major General William L. Kenly.* The other was the Bureau of Aircraft Production,* chaired by Ryan. It was given complete control over production of planes, engines, and aircraft equipment. On 29 May the two agencies were made a part of the new USAAS. Sharp differences of opinion over aircraft types, engines, and equipment soon developed between the builders and the fliers. Wilson's August appointment of Ryan was intended to coordinate the two agencies. Ryan's prestige and authority ended the turmoil. When the war was over, he returned to his business interests.

References. Primary: H. H. Arnold, *Global Mission*, 1949. Benedict Crowell, *America's Munitions: 1917–1918*, 1919. Secondary: Goldberg, *Hist. USAF*. James J. Hudson, *Hostile Skies: A Combat History of the American Air Service in World War I*, 1968.

James J. Hudson

RYAN, GENERAL JOHN D. "THREE-FINGER JACK" (1915–1983)

Ryan was the seventh chief of staff of the Air Force,* serving from 1969 to 1973. The most striking event in his tenure was the relief of General John D. Lavelle,* commander of the Seventh Air Force* (7AF), for falsifying information on targets in the Vietnam War.*

Ryan was a 1938 graduate of the U.S. Military Academy (USMA) and saw combat in Italy in World War II.* After the war, he participated in the nuclear weapons* tests of Operation Crossroads* at Bikini Atoll. He was commander in chief of the Strategic Air Command* (CINCSAC) (1964–1967), commander in chief of the Pacific Air Forces* (CINCPACAF) (1967–1968), and USAF* vice chief of staff (1968–1969). He retired in 1973.

References. Primary: Jack Broughton, *Going Downtown: The War against Hanoi and Washington*, 1988,. U.S. Air Force Oral History Interview K239.0512–1123, 15–17 May

1979, USAFHRC/OH Maxwell AFB, Alabama. Secondary: Air Force Pamphlet 31–1, "Roster of USAF Retired General Officers," 1987. Futrell, *Ideas*, vol. 2. U.S. Air Force Biography, Office of Information, 1973.

                                                                    James C. Hasdorff

S

SA-2 GUIDELINE

This Soviet surface-to-air missile* (SAM) became famous when used fairly successfully against the USAF* in the Vietnam War.* The Soviet designation was V75 Dvina. The North Vietnamese fired about 9,000 of them, and they shot down about 150 U.S. aircraft. It has been the most widely used SAM except for the man-portable types. In 1990, the SA-2 was one of a family of 28 Soviet SAMs in service or development.

It was designed to shoot down bombers* at high altitudes. It had a two-stage rocket engine and was guided by a radar* controller. Its USAF nickname was "Flying Telephone Pole." Its first success was shooting down Gary Powers in his U-2* flight over the USSR in 1960. It is believed a salvo of SA-2s was fired; shot down at the same time was a Soviet MiG-19 that was also attempting an interception.

The Vietnam War gave the USSR an opportunity both to battle test the SA-2 and to aid the North Vietnamese. Americans knew when the construction of SA-2 sites began, but the existing political air superiority* prevented preemptive action. One reason for the restraints was the belief that 1,000 Soviets were SA-2 advisers to the North. The SA-2's first victory was over a USAF F-4.*

When allowed to defend themselves, the USAF's pilots* found that the North moved the missiles often and massed flak* around the sites. The USAF response was Wild Weasel* aircraft that detected the guidance signals and sent AGM-45s* or AGM-75s* to "ride" the emissions down to their source. Then fighters* would use bombs* to destroy the rest of the site. Countermeasures progressively reduced the effectiveness of the SA-2. Its victory rate was 5.7 percent of firings in 1965, 3 in 1966, 1.8 in 1967, and 0.9 in 1968. Its usefulness became similar to that of flak, to reduce the effectiveness of air strikes.

Characteristics (SA-2): span, 6 feet; length, 35 feet; diameter, 20 inches; launch weight, 5,040 pounds; top speed, Mach 3.5; effective ceiling, 90,000 feet; slant range, 22 miles.

References: James D. Crabtree, "DVINA...Guide Line over Vietnam," *United States Air Force Museum Friends Bulletin*, Fall 1989, pp. 36–38, 45. Larry Davis, *Wild Weasel: The SAM Suppression Story*, 1986. Futrell, *Ideas*, vol. 2. "Gallery of Soviet Aerospace Weapons," *AF*, March 1990, pp. 87–88. Lon O. Nordeen, Jr., *Air Warfare in the Missile Age*, 1985.
   See also Rapier.

SA-16. *See* U-16.

SABRE. *See* F-86.

SABRE JET. *See* movies.

SAC. *See* Strategic Air Command.

SAGE. *See* Semiautomatic Ground Environment.

ST. LO, FRANCE

Operation Cobra, the successful air and land effort to break out of the Normandy beachhead, took place at St. Lo on 25 July 1944. Seven weeks after the landings of Operation Overlord,* the Allied armies were still less than 20 miles from the original invasion beaches and were mired in mud and hedgerows. Lieutenant General Omar N. Bradley, commander of the U.S. First Army, decided to drive on a narrow front southwest of St. Lo against German defenders under Generalfeldmarschall Gunther von Kluge.

The assault was preceded by a massive air attack* similar to coordinated bombing raids used earlier against the Germans around Caen. Fighters* destroyed bridges on the left and right flanks, and bombers* blasted a 14-square-mile "carpet" in front of the advance. Like the Caen raids, the bombing turned terrain into rubble that slowed Allied progress. In addition, the raids only temporarily disorganized the Germans, who were able partially to rally afterward to try to counter the assault. However, the carpet bombing had destroyed 50 percent of the German forces lost in the battle and insured victory. Cobra also succeeded because of direct communication between individual tanks and fighters, which allowed highly effective reconnaissance* and attack. The momentum of the drive allowed the Allies quickly to capture Avranches and subsequently envelop the German left flank.

References. C&C, vol. 3. J. F. C. Fuller, *The Decisive Battles of the Western World*, vol. 2, 1970. Richard P. Hallion, *Strike from the Sky: The History of Battlefield Air Attack 1911–1945*, 1989.

Richard L. Davis

ST. MIHIEL CAMPAIGN

The first great battle test of an antecedent to the USAF* was at the St. Mihiel salient in France.

The salient was created in 1916 by German Generalfeldmarschall Eric von

Falkenhayn's attempt to take the French fortress town of Verdun. The salient was about 24 miles across the base and 14 miles deep. General John J. Pershing's* American First Army prepared to wipe out the salient in September 1918.

For several weeks in advance, the airmen made ready for the assault by limiting German reconnaissance* and performing their own without arousing suspicion of a concentration. The Americans had 26 squadrons,* and British, French, and Italian units were involved. The Allied air forces had some 1,481 pursuit, bomber,* and observation aviation,* while the Germans had 295 planes. The commander, Brigadier General William Mitchell,* had one of the largest aggregation of planes that had ever been engaged in one operation on the western front.

The ground assault began on 12 September, but the airmen were slowed by rain. The Germans began to shift some of their best pursuit squadrons to the battle. With better weather on 14 and 15 September, Mitchell was able to put his plans fully into motion. About 500 observation and pursuit planes did attack* operations on the front, while the remainder struck behind German lines to strafe troops and bomb installations and communication centers. The Allied units suffered heavy losses but inflicted great damage on the German air service. The overall results for the Allied airmen were favorable, because the Germans were kept on the defensive and most of the action had been behind the German lines.

The end of the offensive came on 15 September. Many of the U.S. pursuit pilots had pushed their victory scores to the ace* level. Clearly, U.S. forces had won the St. Mihiel campaign.

References. R. Ernest and Trevor N. Dupuy, *The Encyclopedia of Military History from 3500 BC to the Present*, 1970. Goldberg, *Hist. USAF*. Richard P. Hallion, *Strike from the Sky: The History of Battlefield Air Attack 1911–1945*, 1989. James J. Hudson, *Hostile Skies: A Combat History of the American Air Service in World War I*, 1968.

James J. Hudson

SAIPAN. *See* Marianas Islands.

SALERNO, ITALY

The main thrust in the invasion of Italy was the amphibious landing at Salerno, code-named Avalanche. Salerno had been selected because air cover was deemed a requirement, and Allied fighters* lacked range to operate beyond it. With overwhelming air superiority,* the USAAF* operations in support of the invasion went close to the planning.

Prior to the invasion, Allied bombers* struck at enemy airfields and land communications. The weak Axis, with only 380 fighters available, had obsoleteness and maintenance problems. The Allies had 670 fighters and interceptors.* Landings were made on 9 September 1943, and the Luftwaffe launched only 82 air superiority and 26 attack* sorties in hit-and-run actions. By contrast, Allied aircraft flew 2,700 sorties on 10 and 11 September. The main German counterattack on 13 and 14 September failed in large part because of air attacks that included heavy bombers. The beachhead was secured by 15 September.

From 1 to 15 September, Allied aircraft flew around 17,500 sorties, of which two-thirds were by the USAAF. The Allies dropped 10,000 tons of bombs,* of which the USAAF dropped 7,500. The enemy lost 221 planes, the Allies 89. USAAF aircraft had 80 percent of the victories and 66 percent of the losses.
References. C&C, vol. 2. Goldberg, *Hist. USAF*.

SALMSON 2A-2

This French observation aviation* airplane, built by the Société des Moteurs Salmson, was used by the U.S. Army air arm when the de Haviland DH-4* was not yet available. It was similar to the Breguet 14* and was a standard airplane for the French. It was unusual in that it lacked a fin and the pilot's* cockpit was forward of the biplane's wings. The Americans received 705 of them. In the Meuse-Argonne* campaign, observation aircraft claimed to have shot down 26 enemy aircraft,* and 17 of these claims were from Salmsons.
References. James J. Hudson, *Hostile Skies: A Combat History of the American Air Service in World War I*, 1968. Swanborough, *US Mil. Airc.* Wagner, *Am. Planes*.

SAM. *See* presidential airlift; surface-to-air missiles.

SAN DIEGO SIGNAL CORPS AVIATION SCHOOL

This field was important to early U.S. Army flight training.* In 1911, Glenn H. Curtiss* founded a flying school and test operation on North Island in San Diego, California. In November 1912, Lieutenant Harold Geiger arrived to set up a Signal Corps school at Curtiss's invitation. Geiger and four other lieutenants, eight enlisted men, and three Curtiss airplanes began operations in December. By 1915, the school had 30 officers, 185 enlisted men, 12 civilians, and 13 airplanes. It continued to expand thereafter. The Army paid Curtiss $25 per month for the use of the field and hangar space. Accidents were common at the school, although the climate was ideal for training. The Army moved out of the facility, which had been named Rockwell Field, at the end of World War I.*
References. Goldberg, *Hist. USAF*. Juliette A. Hennessy, *The United States Army Air Arm April 1861 to April 1917*, 1985. *The Official Pictorial History of the AAF*, 1947.

"SANTY." *See* Fairchild, General Muir S.

SAN VITO DEI NORMANNI AIR BASE

This U.S. Air Forces in Europe* (USAFE) base is near Brindisi, Italy. It is named for a nearby village. Americans have been there since 1960. In 1990, the 7275th Air Base Group was there to provide logistics and air base management.
Reference. "Guide to Major Air Force Installations Worldwide," *AF*, May 1990, p. 131.

SAVILLE, MAJOR GENERAL GORDON P. (1902–1984)

Saville rose to be deputy chief of staff of development in the Air Staff* from 1950 to 1951. He was an outspoken advocate of a strong air defense system for the United States after serving in several positions dealing with the matter.

Saville was born in Macon, Georgia, and was appointed a second lieutenant in the Infantry Reserve in 1923. He became a cadet in the USAAC* and graduated as a pilot* in 1927. He held various fighter* positions until his first assignment in air defense in 1940. From 1943 to 1944, he was commanding general of the XII Fighter Command. He was deputy commander of the Air Transport Command (ATC) (1945–1947) and commanding general of the Air Defense Command (ADC) (1948–1949). He later became director of requirements in the Office of the Deputy Chief of Staff for Operations in the headquarters of the USAF.* He retired in 1951.

References. Primary: U.S. Air Force Oral History Interview K239.0512–1322, 26–29 March 1973, USAFHRC/OH, Maxwell AFB, Alabama. Secondary: Air Force Pamphlet 31–1, "Roster of USAF Retired General Officers," 1987. Futrell, *Ideas*, vol. 1. Kenneth Schaffel, "A Minority of One (Major General Gordon P. Saville)," *AAHS Journal*, Summer 1987, pp. 104–9. U.S. Air Force Historical Study No. 91, Biographical Data on Air Force General Officers, 1917–1952, vol. 4, USAF Historical Division, 1953.

James C. Hasdorff

SAWYER, K. I., AFB. *See* K. I. Sawyer AFB.

SCHILLING, COLONEL DAVID C. (1918–1956)

With 22.5 victories in World War II,* Schilling is the 10th-ranking USAF* ace* of all time. He also pioneered transoceanic flights by fighters.* The Air Force Association* (AFA) named him the outstanding aviator of 1952 for his transpacific flight. Schilling AFB in Salina, Kansas, was named in his honor.

He was born in Leavenworth, Kansas, and graduated from Dartmouth College in 1939. He became an aviation cadet* and graduated as a pilot* and officer in 1940. He went to England in 1943, joined the 56th Fighter Group, and rose to be its commander. On 23 December 1944, he and his group* attacked 250 German fighters and downed 37 with the loss of one F-47.* Schilling's score that day was three Bf 109s and two Fw 190s. In combat he flew 350 hours in 132 sorties with F-47s.

In July 1948, Schilling planned and led 16 F-80s* in a flight from Selfridge* AFB, Michigan, to Germany. This was the first time a group of jet aircraft had crossed the Atlantic Ocean. In 1950 he and another pilot flew F-84s* nonstop from RAF Manston, England, to Mitchel* AFB, New York, with aerial refueling* from KB-29s (*see* B-29). This was the first nonstop transatlantic flight by a jet fighter, and Schilling received the Harmon International Trophy for his feat. In 1952, as commander of the 31st Strategic Fighter Wing, he started to lead his wing* of F-84s on a transpacific flight from Turner AFB, Georgia, to Yokota* AB, Japan, via Hawaii. Schilling was delayed for a maintenance problem in Hawaii, but his wing completed the history-making flight. Schilling died in an automobile accident.

References. DuPre, *USAF Bio.* Gurney, *5 Down.* Hess, *Aces Album.*

SCHNEIDER CUP RACE OF 1925

First Lieutenant James H. Doolittle* won this race spectacularly and became a national hero. Jacques Schneider, a French engineer and pilot,* offered his cup, nicknamed the "Flying Flirt," because he felt seaplanes and flying boats were the future best hope for transoceanic flight but were being neglected. La Coup d'Aviation Maritime Jacques Schneider resulted in 12 seaplane and flying boat races between 1913 and 1931 and ended with the British getting permanent possession by achieving the prescribed three wins in five years. The races did much for aviation development and not just for seaplanes and flying boats. Americans entered five races, but the USAAS* entered only in 1925.

The Curtiss Aeroplane and Motor Company's R3C-1 racer used by First Lieutenant Cyrus Bettis to win the Pulitzer Trophy Race* of 1925 was outfitted with pontoons to become the R3C-2 for the Scheider race held 24 October at Bay Shore Park near Baltimore, Maryland. The USAAC* was pitted against competitors from the U.S. Navy, Britain, and Italy. The Navy entered two R3C-2s. Doolittle had observed the Pulitzer race and determined that speed was lost during the pylon turns. He changed the place of turn entry and dived into the turns from above, thereby holding his speed for the straightaway. On the straightaway, Doolittle found it was best to fly low into the wind and high when with it. In these changes, Doolittle made use of his doctoral studies and dissertation at the Massachusetts Institute of Technology (MIT). Using his new techniques, Doolittle dramatically shaved the pylons in his turns, won, and set a seaplane record of 245.713 miles per hour.

References. Ralph Barker, *The Schneider Trophy Races*, 1974. Tony Gwynn-Jones, "Winning in the Turns," *AF*, January 1985, pp. 84–87. Maurer, *Avn. in Army.* Lowell Thomas and Edward Jablonski, *Doolittle—a Biography*, 1976.

Alwyn T. Lloyd

SCHRIEVER, GENERAL BERNARD A. (1910–)

Schriever was the father of the USAF* ballistic missile* program. He was a visionary who also commanded the Air Force Systems Command* (AFSC). He developed an entire family of new aerospace systems, set the groundwork for future missiles, and gave the National Aeronautics and Space Administration* (NASA) the engines ultimately to send Americans to the moon. He did these things by introducing novel management and engineering practices still used today. Schriever was inducted into the National Aviation Hall of Fame in Dayton, Ohio, in 1980.

Born in Bremen, Germany, he graduated from Texas A&M University in 1931 and entered the Field Artillery. He completed flight training* in 1933. After a lapse in service, he returned to active duty as a regular officer in 1938 to be an engineering officer and test pilot. He earned a master's degree in aeronautical engineering from Stanford University in California in 1942. During World War II,* he flew 63 combat sorties in B-17s* in the southwest Pacific.

After the war, with the help of Dr. Theodore Von Karman,* Schriever forged bonds between the scientific community and the USAF that still exist. As head of the USAF Development Planning Office, he oversaw and encouraged the early analyses of the RAND Corporation. His goal was to push technology forward, and he did this brilliantly in the development of ballistic missiles. He became the USAF intercontinental ballistic missile (ICBM) program manager in 1954. His nature and ability to convince others of his views led to the creation of the Atlas,* Minuteman,* Thor,* and Titan* missiles in record time. As a hedge against failure by a contractor, he ensured there was a second firm for each major component. He insisted on maximum interchangeability between the subsystems of different missiles. He developed a system where ground and static tests became basic ingredients of programs to avoid costs. Another innovation was "concurrency": developing the subsystems so components were delivered at roughly the same time. He championed solid, rather than liquid, rocket engines. Finally, he pioneered using data automation to manage programs.

He retired in 1966 in reaction to what he saw as Secretary of Defense (SEC-DEF) Robert S. McNamara's* autocratic style and hostility toward the search for new technology.

References. John L. Frisbee, ed., *Makers of the United States Air Force*, 1987. Futrell, *Ideas*, 2 vols. Jacob Neufeld, *Ballistic Missiles in the United States Air Force*, 1990. Ernest G. Schwiebert, "A History of the U.S. Air Force Ballistic Missiles," *AF*, May 1964, pp. 51–166.

Peter R. Faber

SCHWEINFURT, OR REGENSBURG-SCHWEINFURT, GERMANY

This was the largest and one of the costliest daylight air battles, fought on 17 August 1943. The dual targets were the ball bearing plants at Schweinfurt and the Messerschmitt aircraft complex at Regensburg. It was part of the Combined Bomber Offensive* (CBO), initiated with the Combined Chiefs of Staff directive of 10 June 1943, which aimed at the destruction of German air power through strategic operations.* Strategically, the raids on Schweinfurt were important in forcing the Germans to disperse their ball bearing industry and important for the Allies in realizing that further deep raids were impossible without long-range air superiority* fighters.* The long-range F-51s* became available in March 1944.

The dual mission was the deepest penetration of German territory to date with the largest force ever dispatched by the Eighth Air Force* (8AF). A force of 376 B-17s* was escorted by 18 squadrons* of F-47s* from the VIII Fighter Command and 16 squadrons of Royal Air Force (RAF) Spitfires. Unfortunately, most of the fighters did not have drop tanks* for fuel so their range was limited. The original plan was for the 3rd Bombardment Division, with 147 B-17s, to hit Regensburg and the 1st Bombardment Division, with 230 B-17s, to raid Schweinfurt ten minutes later. Bad weather over the 1st's bases caused a takeoff delay, which was lengthened to three and one-half hours to allow the fighter escort* time to land and refuel.

The Luftwaffe organized a maximum effort to meet the first wave just outside of escort range. Relays of single- and twin-engine fighters tore into the B-17 formations using cannon, machine guns, and rockets. Despite the ferocity of the battle, the bombers* got excellent results on the target and surprised the Germans by heading south to bases in North Africa. The Schweinfurt wave met similar defenses, and heavy damage to the factories was achieved even with inaccurate bombing. U.S. losses were severe. The Regensburg force lost 36 and the Schweinfurt force lost 24—16 percent of the bombers dispatched. Many more bombers received heavy damage, and about one-third of the attacking force was either downed or damaged. German records indicate 25 fighters lost, although U.S. crews claimed 288.

A second heavy raid on Schweinfurt was made on 14 October, and it was nearly a disaster. A force of 291 B-17s met the best-organized Luftwaffe defenses to date. German defenders flew some 500 sorties in what was described as an unprecedented assault in terms of its planning and execution. It cost 60 B-17s destroyed, 17 with major damage, and 121 with reparable damage. This battle earned the nickname "Black Thursday." German losses were 38 fighters destroyed and 20 damaged.

References. Martin Caidin, *Black Thursday*, 1960. C&C, vol. 2. Thomas M. Coffey, *Decision over Schweinfurt: The U.S. 8th Air Force Battle for Daylight Bombing*, 1977. Alfred Price, *Battle over the Reich*, 1973. Anthony Verrier, *The Bomber Offensive*, 1968.

Edward L. Homze

SCIENTIFIC ADVISORY BOARD (SAB)

The SAB started with a request from General of the Army H. H. Arnold* to Dr. Theodore von Karman* in 1944 to forecast the broad and distant future, based upon the state of aeronautical science. Von Karman formed a team called the Scientific Advisory Group (SAG). SAG's report recommended intensive scientific research and development (R&D) in support of air power and a specialized USAAF* organization to do so. This philosophy has been followed by the USAF;* in 1947 it set up the SAB and established the Air Research and Development Command (ARDC).

The SAB was such a success that many other government agencies copied the USAF and created special units of scientific and engineering (S&E) experts. There came to be so many imitators that the available S&E talent became highly diluted. By the 1960s, the SAB could no longer achieve what it had before. In addition, the Department of Defense (DoD) bureaucracy expanded and preempted funding for the S&E teams.

This process was such that the USAF's SAB lost the role and means to conduct significant studies. This decline led, in the 1980s, to focusing on details of minor subjects for the immediate future. Its traditional role had been mostly replaced by "think tanks."*

References. Goldberg, *Hist. USAF*. Michael H. Gorn, *Harnessing the Genie: Science and Technology Forecasting for the Air Force. 1944–1986*, 1988.
See also Air Force Systems Command; National Aeronautics and Space Administration.

SCORCHY SMITH. *See* Caniff, Milton.

SCORPION. *See* F-89.

SCOTT AIR FORCE BASE

This field, near Belleville, Illinois, is a Military Airlift Command* (MAC) installation and was occupied in 1917. It was promptly named for Corporal Frank S. Scott, the first enlisted man to die in a military air accident. Scott AFB is the only base named in honor of an enlisted person. In World War I* it was used for flight training* and for instruction of ground crews and mechanics. By November 1918, more than 500 pilots* had received primary training and hundreds more men had mechanical instruction.

In 1921, Scott was made the USAAS's* major lighter-than-air* (LTA) base with its Air Service Balloon and Airship School. LTA activities ended in 1937. The field was rebuilt for the General Headquarters Air Force* (GHQ Air Force), but World War II* interrupted the plans. In the war, Scott was known as the "Communications University of the Army Air Forces." It trained radio operator-mechanics to man and repair aircraft radios and provide command and control communications. By war's end, the graduates, including foreign students, numbered more than 77,000.

In 1949 the headquarters of the Air Training Command* (ATC) moved to it. During the Korean War,* the primary mission remained communications training but expanded to include courses in personnel. In 1957, control of the base was turned over to the Military Air Transport Service (MATS). Soon headquarters of MATS moved in and the base's primary mission became serving the support needs of several major organizations. In 1990, it had headquarters of MAC, headquarters of the Air Force Communications Command* (AFCC), and headquarters of the U.S. Transportation Command.

References. Brown, *Eagles*. "Guide to Major Air Force Installations Worldwide," *AF*, May 1990, p. 131. B. R. Kennedy, *An Illustrated History of Scott Air Force Base, 1917–1987*, Scott AFB, Illinois, Office of MAC History, 1987. Mueller, *AFB*. Roberts, *Dir. USAF*.

Betty Raab Kennedy

SCOTT, BRIGADIER GENERAL ROBERT L., JR. (1908–   )

Scott is famous for his best-selling autobiography *God Is My Co-Pilot*, 1943, which became a movie in 1945, and other writings. He was born in Macon, Georgia, and graduated from the U.S. Military Academy (USMA) in 1932. He finished flight training* in 1933 and flew in the airmail flights of 1934.* In early 1942 he was executive and operations officer for the Assam-Burma-China Ferry Command in the "Hump" Airlift,* from which he went to command the 23rd

Fighter Group. This unit had earlier been the American Volunteer Group* (AVG), or "Flying Tigers." With them for a little more than a year, Scott scored 13 aerial victories flying 925 combat hours in 388 sorties. He went home for a few months and then returned to the war against Japan, experimenting with new rocket arms for fighters.* Most of his post–World War II assignments were in command of fighter units. He retired in 1957. Scott also wrote *Damned to Glory* (1944), *Boring a Hole in the Sky* (1953), *Look of the Eagle* (1955), *Tiger in the Sky* (1959), *Flying Tiger: Chennault of China* (1959), and *The Day I Owned the Sky* (1988).

References. DuPre, *USAF Bio.* Gurney, *5 Down.* Hess, *Aces Album.*

SCRAMBLE! See novels.

SEAMANS, SECRETARY ROBERT C., JR. (1918–   )

As the ninth secretary of the Air Force* (SAF), from 1969 to 1973, Dr. Seamans worked on many projects that had a major effect upon the USAF.* Included were the A-10,* B-1,* C-5,* F-15,* F-111,* V/STOL technology, and electronic warfare* devices. He was also intimately familiar with minority issues, including projects Transition and 100,000. He served during a critical phase of the Vietnam War.*

Born in Salem, Massachusetts, he graduated from Harvard College in 1949. He earned two advanced degrees from the Massachusetts Institute of Technology (MIT) in 1951 and 1952. He stayed at MIT for 15 years and was active in the fields of missiles and aeronautics and worked under Charles Stark Draper, the father of inertial guidance. Seamans served on various technical committees for the National Advisory Committee for Aeronautics (NACA) and served on and was a member of the Scientific Advisory Board* (SAB) of the USAF. In 1960 he became associate administrator for the National Aeronautics and Space Administration* (NASA), and later he was deputy administrator of NASA.

References. Primary: Oral History Interview Number 687, 24–27 September 1973, 239.0512–687, USAFHRC/OH, Maxwell AFB, Alabama. Secondary: USAF Biography, "Dr Robert Channing Seamans, Jr: Secretary of the Air Force," 1 September 1971.

Lloyd H. Cornett, Jr.

SEARCH AND RESCUE. *See* rescue.

SECOND AIR FORCE (2AF)

The 2AF started as the Northwest Air District in 1940. It was redesignated as the 2AF in early 1941, the year its mission was air defense and training. After 1942 it conducted training for Heavy and later for Very Heavy Bombers.* It was inactivated in March 1946. In June 1946 it was reactivated and assigned to the Air Defense Command (ADC). It was inactivated again in 1948. In 1949 it was reactivated and assigned to the Strategic Air Command* (SAC), where its mission was to train men for strategic operations.* Its headquarters was at

Barksdale* AFB, Louisiana, until it was inactivated in 1975. Its famous commanders were Major Generals Robert Olds* and Frank A. Armstrong, Jr.*

References. Maurer Maurer, ed., *Air Force Combat Units of World War II*, 1983. Ravenstein, *Org. USAF*.

SECOND AVIATION OBJECTIVE**

Formulated by the USAAC* on 26 April 1941, this important planning revised the First Aviation Objective* of May 1940 by calling for 84 groups* based on a potential U.S. aircraft production of 36,500 planes per year. Of this number, the USAAC expected it could obtain only 18,641 planes by 1 July 1942. During World War II,* objectives were continually revised upward as air power became more effective and important. On 7 January 1942, the goal became 115 groups; on 31 December 1943, it became 224 groups.

References. C&C, vol. 1. Irving Brinton Holley, Jr., *Buying Aircraft: Matériel Procurement for the Army Air Forces*, 1964.

**This should not be confused with "second aviation strength" which, during World War II, meant the normal number of planes for a combat group ("first aviation strength") plus one additional squadron for each group.

Lester H. Brune

SECORD, MAJOR GENERAL RICHARD V. (1932–   )

Secord was deputy assistant secretary of defense for international security affairs (Near East, Africa, and South Asia) from 1981 to 1983. In 1990 the U.S. District Court found him guilty of lying to Congress about buying a home security system for U.S. Marine Corps Lieutenant Colonel Oliver North. Secord was sentenced to two years of probation.

Secord was a 1955 graduate of the U.S. Military Academy (USMA). His major assignments included chief of the Air Force Section of the Military Assistance Advisory Group in Iran (1975–1978), director of military assistance and sales in the Office of the Deputy Chief of Staff for Logistics and Engineering (1978–1979), and director of international programs in the Office of the Deputy Chief of Staff for Programs and Evaluation (1979–1981). Following retirement in 1983, Secord teamed up with arms dealer Albert Hakim, an Iranian-born businessman, and formed Stanford Technology Trading Group International. His close friendship with North led to a congressional investigation of his involvement in the "Iran-Contra" affair during the administration of President Ronald Reagan.*

References. "The Secret World of General Secord," *Newsweek*, 11 May 1987, pp. 20–22. "A Shadowy Figure behind the Scenes," *Newsweek*, 9 February 1987, p. 27. U.S. Air Force Biography, Secretary of the Air Force, Office of Public Affairs, 1982.

James C. Hasdorff

SECRETARY OF THE AIR FORCE (SAF)

This position came into being with the passage of the National Security Act of 1947.* The first SAF was Stuart Symington;* there had been 19 by 1990.

By law, service secretaries are appointed by the president. They serve under the secretary of defense (SECDEF) but have direct access to the president and the director of the budget. The secretaries are not directly concerned with operations. Rather, they administer their departments as an individual executive department. They manage matters relating to funds, procurement, and legal plans and programs.

The SAF's duties were further defined in the Air Force Organization Act of 1951.* The SAF became responsible for all USAF* matters and had the authority and assistants to carry out the duties. The SAF could set up commands and organizations when necessary and could consolidate or abolish three major commands—Strategic Air,* Tactical Air,* and Air Defense—or establish new ones in times of emergency or war. In short, the act gave the SAF more flexibility.

References. Air University, *Basic Data Handbook about the US Air Force*, 1975. Futrell, *Ideas*, vol. 1. Goldberg, *Hist. USAF*.

See also McNamara, Secretary Robert S.; Zuckert, Secretary Eugene M.

John F. Farrell

SELFRIDGE, FIRST LIEUTENANT THOMAS E. (1882–1908)

Selfridge was the first military officer of any nation to make a solo flight and the first person to die in a powered airplane crash. Selfridge* Air National Guard* Base was named in his honor. He was inducted into the National Aviation Hall of Fame in Dayton, Ohio, in 1965.

He was born in San Francisco, California, and graduated from the U.S. Military Academy (USMA) in 1903. He distinguished himself as a troop commander during the 1906 San Francisco earthquake but had already decided his future lay in aeronautics. In 1907 he was detailed to work with Alexander Graham Bell and Glenn H. Curtiss* in the newly formed Aerial Experiment Association (AEA). The AEA designed and built several flying machines. On 19 May 1908, and again on 2 and 3 August 1908, Selfridge flew the "White Wing" at Hammondsport, New York. These flights constitute the first solo flights made by a military officer anywhere in the world. Immediately following these flights, Selfridge was sent to Fort Myer, Virginia, as an official observer at the acceptance trials of the Wright Flyer, which was being considered for purchase by the Signal Corps. On 17 September 1908, with Orville Wright piloting and Selfridge as a passenger, the plane crashed. A propellor had broken, damaging the rudder. The Flyer went out of control and dived into the ground. Selfridge was killed and Wright was seriously injured.

References. Tom D. Crouch, *The Bishop's Boys: A Life of Wilbur and Orville Wright*, 1989. Juliette A. Hennessy, *The United States Army Air Arm April 1861 to April 1917*, 1985. Cecil R. Roseberry, *Glenn Curtiss: Pioneer of Flight*, 1972.

Patrick B. Nolan

SELFRIDGE AIR NATIONAL GUARD BASE

This airfield in Michigan was founded in 1917 and was named for First Lieutenant Thomas E. Selfridge.* He was the first military officer to fly an airplane. He was flying as a passenger of Orville Wright when he was killed, the first person to die in a powered airplane crash. Selfridge Field did training in World War I* and was a fighter base after that war. In 1971 it was transferred from the USAF* and the Aerospace Defense Command* (ADC) to the Michigan Air National Guard* (ANG). In 1990 the 127th Tactical Fighter Wing (ANG) was based there.

References. Brown, *Eagles*. "Guide to ANG and AFRES Bases," *AF*, May 1990, p. 137. Jane S. Ketchum, "Selfridge Field (1917–1978)," *United States Air Force Museum Friends Bulletin*, Summer 1988, pp. 10–23.

SEMBACH AIR BASE

Nine miles from Kaiserslautern, Germany, this is a U.S. Air Forces in Europe* (USAFE) AB. The USAF* began to use it in 1953. It is named for a community alongside it. In 1990, it had the headquarters of the Seventeenth Air Force* (17AF). It was the home of the 66th Electronic Combat Wing, which has a mission of electronic warfare* in the European theater flying EC-130H (*see* C-130) Compass Call aircraft, and the 601st Tactical Control Wing.

References. "Guide to Major Air Force Installations Worldwide," *AF*, May 1990, pp. 131–32. Roberts, *Dir. USAF*.

SEMIAUTOMATIC GROUND ENVIRONMENT (SAGE)

SAGE was the pioneering air defense system that used electronic controls. It was deployed in the late 1950s and early 1960s. SAGE was characterized by large numbers of powerful small radars,* rapid data transmission between radars and direction centers/combat centers (DCs/CCs) via telephone lines, and centralized data processing by means of large digital computers. It served efficiently and effectively as the ground electronic environment of the air defense network for the continental United States (CONUS) for more than 20 years.

Its origin was in the recommendations of the Air Defense Systems Engineering Committee (ADSEC), or Valley Committee, named for its chairman, Massachusetts Institute of Technology (MIT) physicist Dr. George E. Valley, Jr. The committee was formed in December 1949 by the Scientific Advisory Board* (SAB) to study post–World War II* air defense requirements. Within months, the committee concluded the existing system of a few large radars and manual methods of data processing was totally inadequate. In July 1951, responsibility for implementing the recommendations of the committee was assumed by the Lincoln Laboratory. Lincoln was established at Hanscom* Field, Massachusetts, as an air defense advance research and development (R&D) think tank* operated by MIT with support from the military services.

In 1953, Lincoln called for a Lincoln Transition System of a centralized combination of MIT's high-speed digital computer with radar data transmission equipment from the Air Force Cambridge Research Center (AFCRC). The USAF* decided to use this system rather than the Air Defense Integrated System (ADIS) developed by the University of Michigan's Willow Run Research Center. In 1954, the Lincoln Transition System was renamed SAGE. SAGE's first direction center (DC) was operational at McGuire* AFB, New Jersey, by July

1958. Full deployment of SAGE in 22 air defense sectors in the United States and one in Canada was achieved in 1963. In 1983, SAGE ceased operations when its replacement, the Joint Surveillance System* (JSS), achieved full operational capability.

References. Primary: George E. Valley, Jr., "How the SAGE Development Began," *Annals of the History of Computing*, July 1985, pp. 196–226. Secondary: E. Michael Del Papa and Mary P. Warner, "A Historical Chronology of the Electronic Systems Division 1947–1986," Hanscom AFB, Massachusetts, History Office, 1987. C. L. Grant, *The Development of Continental Air Defense to 1 September 1954*, 1957. John F. Jacobs, "SAGE Overview," *Annals of the History of Computing*, October 1983, pp. 323–29. Charles J. Smith, "SAGE: Background and Origins," Hanscom AFB, Massachusetts, History Office, 1964.

E. Michael Del Papa

SENTRY. *See* E-3.

SEPARATE OPERATING AGENCY (SOA)

SOAs are a type of organization that are immediately subordinate to headquarters of the USAF.* They are assigned highly specialized and restricted missions under close control from a functional part of the Air Staff.* Examples are the Air Force Audit Agency* and the Air Force Inspection and Safety Center.*

References. Ravenstein, *Org. USAF*. U.S. Air Force Fact Sheet 89–05, "Organization of the United States Air Force," February 1989.

SEPARATION FROM THE U.S. ARMY

President Harry S Truman* (HST) approved the National Security Act* on 26 July 1947, authorizing a separate air service. The USAAF* officially became the USAF* on 18 September 1947 and was designated a coequal arm with the U.S. Army and Navy in the defense establishment. World War II* had proven the rationale for independence convincingly, despite opposition.

The Navy feared it would lose its air power to a USAF, and problems arose after independence. The Key West* Agreement, a collection of compromises, was approved by HST in 1948. Disputes and incongruities continued. For example, the USAF was made responsible for air defense, but the Army was given flak* and, later, surface-to-air missiles* (SAM). The Army would yield no arsenals, but this was a blessing in disguise as the USAF had to rely upon the more efficient procurement* means of contracting with private firms. Adjustments continue to be made.

The physical separation of the USAF from the Army took almost two years, based upon 200 Army-USAF agreements. The first order transferring military and civilian personnel of the USAAF to the Department of the Air Force* was approved by Secretary of Defense (SECDEF) James V. Forrestal* on 26 September 1947. However, the final transfer orders were not signed until 22 July 1949. By then, all areas of personnel, training, administration, operations, and supply were the USAF's responsibility.

References. Arnold Brophy, *The Air Force*, 1956. Futrell, *Ideas*, vol. 1. Goldberg, *Hist. USAF*.

John F. Farrell

SERVICE

This is a type of organization that has a mission of providing a service to the entire USAF* and, if ordered, to external agencies. For example, the USAF Recruiting Service of the Air Training Command* (ATC) works strictly for the USAF, but the Air Weather Service (AWS) of the Military Airlift Command* (MAC) helps the U.S. Army and works with other weather organizations internationally.

References. Woodford Agee Heflin, ed., *The United States Air Force Dictionary*, 1956. Ravenstein, *Org. USAF*.

SEVENTEENTH AIR FORCE (17AF)

The 17AF was established in 1953 as part of the U.S. Air Forces in Europe* (USAFE). Originally it was located at Rabat-Sale, French Morocco. It moved to Wheelus AB, Libya, in 1956; to Ramstein* AB, Germany, in 1959; and to Sembach* AB, Germany, in 1972. In 1990, the 17AF controlled USAF* tactical operations* forces in Germany.

References. Ravenstein, *Org. USAF*. "United States Air Forces in Europe," *AF*, May 1990, pp. 93–95.

SEVENTH AIR FORCE (7AF)

This organization began as the Hawaiian Air Force in 1940 but was redesignated the 7AF in 1942. Initially, its mission was the air defense of Hawaii, but in mid–1943 it began combat in the central and western Pacific Ocean. Its famous commanders in World War II* were Major Generals Clarence L. Tinker* (1941–1942) and Thomas D. White* (1945–1946).

The 7AF returned to Hawaii in 1946. It was redesignated the Pacific Air Command in 1947 and discontinued in 1949. It was reactivated as the 7AF in Hawaii in 1955 and assigned to the Far East Air Forces. Again it was inactivated in 1957. It was reactivated in March 1966 to replace the 2nd Air Division and was located at Tan Son Nhut* AB, South Vietnam. It moved to Nakhon Phanom Royal Thai* AFB, Thailand, in 1973 and was inactivated in 1975. Its famous commanders in the Vietnam War* were Lieutenant General Joseph H. Moore* (1966), General William W. Momyer* (1966–1968), General George S. Brown* (1968–1970), General Lucius D. Clay, Jr.* (1970–1971), General John D. Lavelle* (1971–1972), and General John W. Vogt, Jr.* (1972–1973). In 1986, the 7AF was reactivated to conduct tactical operations* relating to the Republic of Korea (ROK) and was located in 1990 at Osan* AB, Korea. It was assigned to the Pacific Air Forces* (PACAF).

References. Berger, *USAF in SEA*. Futrell, *Ideas*, vol. 2. Maurer Maurer, ed., *Air Force Combat Units of World War II*, 1983. "Pacific Air Forces," *AF*, May 1990, pp. 81–82. Ravenstein, *Org. USAF*.

70-GROUP AIR FORCE

The post–World War II* USAAF* calculated that its peacetime size should be composed of at least 70 groups.* Such a force could only conduct extensive strategic operations.* The 70-group or wing* concept was never truly reached or used, but the concept was useful for planning. The reality in 1946 was 48 operational groups. The number did rise to 70 wings in 1948 during the Berlin Airlift* emergency. Thereafter the number of wings declined again to 48 by 1950. The Korean War,* another emergency, eventually led to 134 wings by 1956.

By 1956 there were new needs not envisioned in 1946: imminent practical ballistic missiles,* readiness for a limited war using tactical operations,* support for the North Atlantic Treaty Organization* (NATO), the demonstrated usefulness of airlift operations,* aerial refueling,* and the need for aerospace defense operations.* The 70-group idea had become obsolete.

Reference. Charles D. Bright, *The Jet Makers: The Aerospace Industry from 1945 to 1972*, 1978. Goldberg, *Hist. USAF*.

SEVERSKY AIRCRAFT CORPORATION. *See* de Seversky, Major Alexander P.; P-35; P-43.

SEYMOUR JOHNSON AIR FORCE BASE

In 1942 the Headquarters Technical School was established at this field near Goldsboro, North Carolina. The base was named for U.S. Navy Lieutenant Seymour A. Johnson, a Goldsboro native who died in an aircraft crash. During World War II,* it also conducted training of replacements for overseas. The field was inactivated in 1946 and turned over to the city, but it reverted to USAF* control in 1952. The first new unit was the 83rd Fighter-Day Wing, followed in 1957 by the 4th Fighter-Day Wing, today the 4th Tactical Fighter Wing. In the mid–1960s the 4th received F-4s* and was the first unit to receive the new F-15E* in 1989. In 1990 this Tactical Air Command* (TAC) base still had some remaining F-4Es as well as F-15Es. Besides the 4th, it had the 68th Air Refueling Wing of the Strategic Air Command* (SAC) with KC-10As (see C-10).

References. "Guide to Major Air Force Installations Worldwide," *AF*, May 1990, p. 132. Mueller, *AFB*. Official USAF History, Seymour Johnson AFB, North Carolina; 4TFW Public Affairs Office, 1988. Roberts, *Dir. USAF*.

David L. Rosmer

SHAPED-CHARGE WARHEADS

These are munitions that focus the explosive energy of a warhead into a narrow jet burst so as to penetrate armor. Detonated at a specific distance—called the "standoff"—from the target, it will penetrate a foot or more of armor. The critical distance demands a super-quick fuze or a nose-actuated base fuze. Air-launched antitank guided missiles such as the AGM-65* have massive shaped-charge warheads capable of penetrating any tank. Shaped-charge "bomblets" such as the Mk–20* are common payloads in submunitions dispensers. Shaped-charge warheads should be a common air munition as long as tanks exist.

References. K. J. Goad and D. H. J. Halsey, *Brassey's Battlefield Weapons Systems & Technology*, vol. 3, 1982. USAF Technical Order 11A-1-34, *Military Explosives*, 1967.

Philip Long

SHARP, SECRETARY DUDLEY C. (1905–1987)

The sixth secretary of the Air Force* (SAF), Sharp dealt with numerous problems in his years from 1959 to 1961. These were the budget, interservice rivalry, and the USAF* in transition from aircraft to a mixture of aircraft and missiles. During his era, the USAF was also striving to develop a nuclear-powered aircraft, the X-6,* and fought for a mission in space.

Born in Houston, Texas, Sharp graduated from Princeton University, New Jersey, in 1928. In World War II,* he was in the Navy's Office of Procurement and Materiel in Washington, D.C. He left the service in 1945 and became the president of Mission Manufacturing. As a businessman, he engaged in applied physics and manufacturing and was a special consultant on machine tools for the USAF's Air Materiel Command (AMC). Sharp's relationship with President Dwight D. Eisenhower* led to his appointment as assistant secretary of the Air Force for materiel, serving from 1955 to 1959. Then he became under secretary of the Air Force in 1959 under Secretaries Donald L. Quarles* and James H. Douglas.*

References. Primary: Oral History Interview by Dr. James C. Hasdorff, 6–7 June 1979, Transcript K239.0512–1128, USAFHRC/OH, Maxwell AFB, Alabama. Secondary: DuPre, *USAF Bio*.

Lloyd H. Cornett, Jr.

SHAW AIR FORCE BASE

This Tactical Air Command* (TAC) field near Sumter, South Carolina, was named for a Sumter native, First Lieutenant Erwin D. Shaw, a reconnaissance* pilot* who was shot down over France in 1918. During World War II,* flight training* was conducted on it.

After the war Shaw became home for the 20th Fighter Group with F-51s.* In 1951, the 363rd Tactical Reconnaissance Wing arrived. In the 1960s and early 1970s, TAC's Tactical Air Reconnaissance Center had its headquarters at Shaw. In 1954, the headquarters of the Ninth Air Force* (9AF) moved to Shaw and has remained there ever since. Also in 1954, the 507th Tactical Control Group (later Wing) relocated to Shaw where it remains. In 1979, the 363rd began converting from RF-4Cs (*see* F-4) to F-16s* and became a fighter* wing* in 1981. Also in 1981, headquarters of the 9AF became the air arm of the Rapid Deployment Force (RDF), which became the U.S. Central Command Air Forces* (USCENTAF) in 1983.

References. "Guide to Major Air Force Installations Worldwide," *AF*, May 1990, p. 132. Mueller, *AFB*. Official USAF History, Shaw AFB, South Carolina, Hq 9AF Office of History, 1989. Roberts, *Dir. USAF*.

David L. Rosmer

SHEMYA AIR FORCE BASE

This Pacific Air Forces* (PACAF) base, at the western tip of the Aleutian* Islands, is most famous as the airfield with the world's worst weather. It is barren and bleak, and a long-standing joke has been to cultivate an imported tree and call it the "Shemya National Forest." The international date line has been bent west around it so the local date is the same as for the rest of the United States. The field, activated in 1943, is named for the island. Shemya was built to be a B-29* base. In 1990 it had the 5073rd Air Base Group to make it a forward operating base for F-15s.* It also had a phased-array radar* for the Air Force Space Command* (AFSPACECOM).

References. "Guide to Major Air Force Installations Worldwide," *AF*, May 1990, p. 132. Mueller, *AFB*. Roberts, *Dir. USAF*.

SHEPPARD AIR FORCE BASE

By Wichita Falls, Texas, this is an Air Training Command* (ATC) base. It was activated in 1941 and named for U.S. Senator Morris E. Sheppard who died shortly before the activation. Sheppard had struggled vainly for a militarily prepared United States. The field was inactivated between 1946 and 1948. Throughout its existence, Sheppard has been used for training. Skills taught on it have included basic training, mechanics, building trades, ballistic missiles,* helicopters,* medical services, and pilot* flight training* for U.S. allies. In 1990, the Sheppard Technical Training Center had the 3700th Technical Training Wing, 3790th Field Training Wing, 3785th Field Training Wing, and the 80th Flying Training Wing (FTW). The 80th conducted flying training and instructor pilot training for 12 nations in the Euro-NATO Joint Jet Pilot Training Program with T-37s* and T-38s.*

References. "Guide to Major Air Force Installations Worldwide," *AF*, May 1990, p. 132. Mueller, *AFB*. Roberts, *Dir. USAF*.

SHOOTING STAR. *See* F-80.

SHORAN

This is a form of radar* for precision location, derived from *short-range navigation*. It can be used for either navigation or bombing. In the bombing mode, it is a guide to the correct position for bomb* release.

References. Ernest J. Gentle and Lawrence W. Reithmaier, eds., *Aviation/Space Dictionary*, 6th ed., 1980. Woodford Agee Heflin, ed., *The United States Air Force Dictionary*, 1956.

SHORT-RANGE ATTACK MISSILE (SRAM). *See* AGM-69.

SHOULDER THE SKY. See novels.

SHRIKE. *See* A-12; AGM-45.

SIDE-LOOKING AIRBORNE RADAR (SLAR)

Used since the 1950s, SLAR is an immobile radar* mounted in the side of a carrier aircraft or pod. It uses a linear antenna to project the radar beam sideways thus observing an area without flying toward it. It is widely used for radar mapping, sea surface search, and observation of aircraft movements in one country using aircraft flying parallel to the border over another country. In the 1970s, SLAR was integrated with a ground receiving station to speed exploitation of the information that it generated.

References. David A. Anderton, *History of the U.S. Air Force*, rev. ed., 1989. John P. Kelly, "Tac Recce: A Different Breed of Cat," *AF*, February 1979, pp. 60–61. Bruce D. Nordwall, "Signal Processing and VHSIC Transforming Reconnaissance," *AWST*, 7 September 1987, pp. 68–69.

Philip Long

SIDEWINDER. *See* AIM-9.

SIKORSKY AIRCRAFT DIVISION *See* H-3; H-19; H-53; H-60.

SINANJU AND YONGMIDONG, KOREA

This USAF* operation was intended to control a surface area by air power alone. The area was 100 miles north of U.S. Army control and was two by four miles in size. In it were bridge complexes over the Chongchon and Taeryong Rivers at Sinanju and Yongmidong. Through this bottleneck area with the strongest flak* concentration in North Korea passed supply lines critical to the communists. The campaign showed air power could, at great effort, temporarily control fully a small enemy land area against strong resistance with the conventional weapon means available in the early 1950s. Those means did not make the effort worthwhile but indicated that superior weapons might do so.

The USAF used 2,292 sorties from 10 to 15 January 1953 to attack* the bridges, flak, and rail yards in the area. It was done around-the-clock. For six days thereafter supplies did not move through the area. Then repairs began and supplies flowed again. Harassment of the area became easy for a while, and the attacks made the communists risk daylight supply movements at great cost to themselves. Communist supplies at the front became low, and repairs to the area were costly.

References. Futrell, *USAF in Korea*. James T. Stewart, *Airpower: The Decisive Force in Korea*, 1957.

SIXTEENTH AIR FORCE (16AF)

Originally this numbered air force* was a separate operating agency* (SOA) called the Joint U.S. Military Group, Air Administration (Spain). It was established in 1954 at Madrid, Spain. In 1956 it was redesignated as the 16AF. In 1957 it was assigned to the Strategic Air Command* (SAC), and it moved to Torrejon* AB, Spain, in 1958. It was reassigned in 1966 to the U.S. Air Forces in Europe* (USAFE). In 1990 it was still in the USAFE and at Torrejon, with three wings* under it.

References. Ravenstein, *Org. USAF*. "United States Air Forces in Europe." *AF*, May 1990, pp. 93–95.

SIXTH AIR FORCE (6AF)

This numbered air force* began in 1940 as a named one, the Panama Canal Air Force. It was redesignated as the Caribbean Air Force in 1941 and as the 6AF in 1942. Its missions were defense of the Panama Canal and antisubmarine operations. In 1946 it lost its air force status and became the Caribbean Air Command. It was based at Albrook Field in the Canal Zone. It had one famous commander, Major General Frank M. Andrews,* from 1940 to 1941.

References. Maurer Maurer, ed., *Air Force Combat Units of World War II*, 1983. Ravenstein, *Org. USAF*.

SKIP BOMBER. See novels.

SKIP BOMBING

This is an attack* technique in which a plane flies level just above the sea or land surface and releases one or more bombs.* A bomb will then slide or glance along the surface as a flat stone will until it reaches its target. The technique results in hits like a torpedo on a ship's waterline. It penetrates structures from the side. It also permits running bombs between the rails and into railroad tunnels. Properly done, skip bombing can bounce bombs into revetments. The U.S. Navy developed dive bombing as a ship-killing system, and the USAAF* developed skip bombing for the same purpose. A main contributor to its development was Colonel Paul I. "Pappy" Gunn,* and the technique was used to great effect against sea and land targets thereafter. It is most famous for its use in the Battle of the Bismarck Sea.*

References. Lawrence Cortesi, *The Battle of the Bismarck Sea*, 1967. John L. Frisbee, "Skip-Bombing Pioneer," *AF*, December 1990, p. 87. Ernest J. Gentle and Lawrence W. Reithmaier, eds., *Aviation/Space Dictionary*, 6th ed., 1980. Woodford Agee Heflin, ed., *The United States Air Force Dictionary*, 1956.

SKYBOLT

The Skybolt missile, or GAM-87A, was derived from the Bold Orion air-launched ballistic missile* program used to develop the concept. It was designed for carriage by both B-52Hs* and Royal Air Force (RAF) Vulcan bombers; it was to be a two-stage, inertially guided hypersonic vehicle with a range of 1,000 miles. Its cancellation led to diplomatic turmoil with Britain.

The Douglas Aircraft Company was awarded an advanced design study contract for it in 1959, but it suffered politically, which impacted its work technically. Skybolt bore the brunt of media dislike of defense programs. It underwent three demonstration programs, five separate test requirements, and 37 manufacturing proposals. Its first flight was in 1961. Ironically, on 22 December 1962, the press carried two stories, side-by-side. One was President John F. Kennedy's* (JFK) formal cancellation of the program; the other was a report on its successful launch from a B-52G over the Atlantic Test Range by the program manager, Brigadier General David C. Jones.* Skybolt was one of eight USAF* programs that Secretary of Defense (SECDEF) Robert S. McNamara* cancelled, reduced, or phased out. The reasons he gave for Skybolt's end were cost increases and low performance.

The cancellation caused a messy political crisis with Britain, which wanted Skybolt to replace its Blue Streak missile. Britain's status as a nuclear power had been committed to Skybolt alone. The British saw the cancellation both as a U.S. violation of a solemn agreement and as an effort to deprive Britain of an independent nuclear deterrent. JFK saved face for the British by selling them Polaris fleet ballistic missiles, but this was still a bitter pill for them. They had earlier chosen Skybolt in preference to Polaris.

References. Walter J. Boyne, *Boeing B-52—A Documentary History*, 1981. James A. Dewar, "Britain and the Skybolt Affair," *AH*, September 1971, pp. 129–34. Futrell, *Ideas*, vol. 2. SAC Missile Chronology 1939–1988, Office of the Historian, Strategic Air Command, Offutt AFB, Nebraska, 1990. Richard A. Stubbing, *The Defense Game*, 1986.

Alwyn T. Lloyd

SKYMASTER. *See* C-54.

SKYRAIDER. *See* A-1.

SKYTRAIN. *See* C-47.

SLANG

Even a casual reading of this dictionary will show that the everyday language of the USAF* is heavily spiced with acronyms. Slang is also used frequently. Some of the slang is assimilated from the outside, but much has been generated internally. The following is a very brief sampling of the slang, from World War I* to the present.

ack ack: flak*

archie: flak

bounce or jump: a fighter* attacking an aircraft

brown bar, or second balloon: second lieutenant

buy the farm, or go west: to die

buzz, or buzz job: to fly just above the ground at high speed

BX ribbons: cheap decorations

Chinese Air Force: too many cheap decorations

clooge: makeshift repair

controller mouth, Porky Pigging: radio chatterbox

fighter jock, jock, driver: fighter pilot*

first john: first lieutenant

flap jockey: copilot

fox 1: long-range missile attack

fox 2: short-range missile attack

fox 3: use fighter guns

fox 4: midair collision

full bull, bird colonel, or chicken colonel: colonel

gadget: cadet

gate: full speed, in afterburner

golden BB: lucky hit

ground pounder, or gravel agitator: nonflyer

hot rock, Ace of the Base, Steve Canyon: an egotistical pilot

I&I: intoxication and intercourse (used instead of the official term R&R, or rest and
    recuperation)

light, or telephone, colonel: lieutenant colonel

mae west: a life preserver

meatball: a Japanese (because of flag and aircraft insignia)

mink farm: area that complains of aircraft noise

needle, ball, and ripcord: instrument flying*

nylon descent or letdown: to parachute

pucker factor: being shot at

punch out: use ejection seat

quick turn burn: refuel and reload

SACumsized: completely indoctrinated by the Strategic Air Command*

seagull: a staff person (in other words, a parasite)

Seattle Air Command: Strategic Air Command (from the heavy use of Boeing Company
    aircraft)

sierra hotel: the best

target-rich environment: Iraq

throttle jockey: bomber* or transport* pilot

thunderbumper: thunderstorm

tub: a two-seat aircraft

wing weenie: wing staff member

References. Michael Skinner, *U*S*A*F*E: A Primer of Modern Air Combat in Europe*, 1988. Bob Stevens, *"There I Was . . . Flat on My Back,"* 1975, and *If You Read Me, Rock the Tower*, 1980. Joseph F. Tuso, *Singing the Vietnam Blues: Songs of the Air Force in Southeast Asia*, 1990.

SLAR. *See* side-looking airborne radar.

SMALL INTERCONTINENTAL BALLISTIC MISSILE (SICBM)

The SICBM, or MGM-134A, is the newest strategic missile system under development for the USAF.* It is to be a product of Martin Marietta Corporation. It is designed to complement the Peacekeeper* system and modernize the nation's strategic operations* forces and offer increased survivability. It has been called "Midgetman" by the media and Congress.

The SICBM was developed on the recommendation of the President's Commission on Strategic Forces, or the Scowcroft Commission, in 1983. The commission called for a new ballistic missile,* smaller than Peacekeeper, with a single re-entry vehicle, and light enough in weight to be easily based in a highly mobile manner. The single warhead would cause a potential enemy to regard the SICBM as a less threatening and destabilizing weapon system. In addition, its extreme mobility would make it more difficult to hit, thus enhancing deterrence. It features an advanced guidance system. Each SICBM is to be deployed with a hard mobile launcher (HML) vehicle under development by The Boeing Company. The HML is a large all-terrain truck just over 100 feet long, five and one-half feet wide, and 14 feet high, with a gross vehicle weight of more than 200,000 pounds. Upon receipt of warning, the HML would move at high speed on- or off-road, thereby spoiling an enemy's aiming point. The SICBM could be based at many locations in the western United States. The first cold launch of the SICBM was in 1989 and was unsuccessful.

Characteristics: engines, three stages of solid-propellant rockets; length, 53 feet; diameter, 46 inches; weight, 37,000 pounds; range, 6,835 miles.

References. U.S. Air Force Ballistic Missile Office, Hard Mobile Launcher Fact Sheet, March 1987, and Small Intercontinental Ballistic Missile Fact Sheet, May 1987. Susan H. H. Young, "Gallery of USAF Weapons," *AF*, May 1990, p. 156.

Raymond L. Puffer

"SMART BOMBS." *See* bombs.

SNARK

This cruise missile,* *SM–62* for "strategic missile," was designed to be an intercontinental cruise missile (ICM). It was the only missile of its type fully developed in history, being intercontinental and ground-launched. Germany had started one, its A-10, during World War II.*

The USAAF* asked for an ICM in 1945. In 1946 the Northrop Aircraft Corporation began work on the Snark, named for the Lewis Carroll creation. It was to fly similarly to the bombers* of that time. Its first flight was in 1951, and it entered active service in March 1961. Test failures caused firing-range men to speak derisively of "Snark-infested waters." In June 1961 it was taken out of service. A total of 30 had been built. Snark's advantages were to have been low cost production and maintenance, an ability to carry a large warhead, no crew, no need for aerial refueling,* and it was difficult for radar* to find. Its disadvantages were high vulnerability in the air because it was a subsonic vehicle flying at high altitude, complexity, and inaccuracy. The ballistic missile* was seen in 1961 as a superior vehicle.

Characteristics: engines, one Pratt & Whitney J57-P-17 turbojet of 9,500 pounds thrust, and two solid-fuel rocket boosters of 130,000 pounds thrust each; span, 42 feet; length, 67 feet; height, 15 feet; launch weight, 49,000 pounds; top speed, 524 miles per hour; range, about 6,000 miles.

References. Charles D. Bright, *The Jet Makers: The Aerospace Industry from 1945 to 1972*, 1978. Jacob Neufeld, *Ballistic Missiles in the United States Air Force 1945– 1960*, 1990. Polmar, *SAC. From Snark to Peacekeeper: A Pictorial History of Strategic Air Command Missiles*, Office of Historian, SAC, Offutt AFB, Nebraska, 1990. Kenneth P. Werrell, *The Evolution of the Cruise Missile*, 1985.

SOESTERBERG AIR BASE

This field is unique as one established not for military or political reasons but for social ones. Disappointed when Americans failed to ask for a military base on their soil, the Dutch approached the USAF* and asked for one. Instead of "Yank go home," it was "Yank, make your home here." This Royal Netherlands AB is three miles from Zeist and 26 miles from Amsterdam. It was established in 1913, and the USAF moved there in 1954. The USAF has maintained fighters* there ever since. The U.S. area of the base is called Camp New Amsterdam. In 1990, the 32nd Tactical Fighter Group of the U.S. Air Forces in Europe* (USAFE) was based there flying F-15s.*

References. "Guide to Major Air Force Installations Worldwide," *AF*, May 1990, p. 132. Roberts, *Dir. USAF*.

SOLE SURVIROR. *See* movies.

SOLOMON ISLANDS. *See* Guadalcanal.

SONGS

Songs have played an important role in the morale and tradition* of the USAF* since World War I.* The songs reflect the ardor, skepticism, humor, satire, and pride not only of a military service but of the youth, optimism, verve, and spirit of adventure of aviators.

The USAF has a famous rousing official song, "The U.S. Air Force Song,"* and dozens of unofficial songs. Many have several versions, sometimes modified by time. They are joyful, plaintive, boisterous, vulgar, prurient, and prideful. Some are native USAF, but others have been adopted from other services or nations, including the spoils of war. A sampling of the songs are:

World War I

"A Poor Aviator Lay Dying."

World War II

"The Air Force Has Gone to Hell"

"Bless Them All"

"Cats on the Rooftop"

"The Copilot's Lament"

"Early Abort"

"Give Me Operations"

"Glory Flying Regulations"

"The Harlot of Jerusalem"

"Into the Air"

"Into the Air, Junior Birdmen"

"I Wanted Wings"

"Let's Have a Party"

"Lili Marlene"

"The Man behind the Armor-plated Desk"

"Roll Me Over"

"Save a Fighter* Pilot's* Ass"

"Scotch [sic] Wedding" ("The Ball of Kerrymuir")

"The Sexual Life of the Camel"

"She Was Poor but She Was Honest"

"Sweet Violets"

"There Are No Fighter Pilots in Hell"

"Wingman's Lament"

Korean War*

"Cigarettes and Sake and Wild, Wild Jo-Sans"

"Did You Go Boom Today?"

"The Goddamned Reserves"

"Itazuke Tower"

"Mary Ann Burns"

"The Prettiest Plane"

"Seoul City Sue"

"Sidi Slimane"

"You'll Never Mind"

Vietnam War*

"Cruising over Hanoi"

"Don't Send Me to Hanoi"

"Doumer Bridge Blues"

"F-4* Serenade"

"Falsies in Brassieres"

"I'm a Young Ranch Hand"

"In-flight Refueling"

"MiG-19"

"O Little Town of Ho Chi Minh"

"Where Have All the Old Heads Gone?"

"The Yellow Rose of Hanoi"

References. C. W. "Bill" Getz, ed., *The Wild Blue Yonder: Songs of the Air Force*, 2 vols., 1981 and 1986. Bob Stevens, *There I Was . . . Flat on My Back,"* 1975. Joseph F. Tuso, *Singing the Vietnam Blues: Songs of the Air Force in Southeast Asia*, 1990.

SON TAY PRISON RAID

In the summer of 1970, the Joint Chiefs of Staff (JCS) planned to rescue more than 100 U.S. prisoners of war (POWs) in North Vietnam* from the Son Tay prison 23 miles west of Hanoi.* It was named Operation Kingpin. President Richard M. Nixon had been receiving reports that the POWs were dying from torture and ill-treatment, and he believed a raid to rescue them could only be considered humanitarian. In addition, it would boost U.S. morale, which was low from the Vietnam War.*

Among Kingpin planners was USAF* Brigadier General Leroy J. Manor, overall raid commander. The plan entailed a helicopter* assault on the prison with a 56-man force. The first helicopter was to crash-land inside the compound and eliminate most of the guards. The other helicopters would land outside the prison with men to prevent reinforcement by nearby North Vietnamese troops and with assault forces to breach the walls. Several helicopters would be empty for the POWs. To divert the enemy, USAF and U.S. Navy aircraft would pretend to attack Haiphong.* The raid was to last no more than 30 minutes so the enemy would not have the time to respond with overwhelming force.

Designated Joint Contingency Task Force (JCTF) Ivory, the 56 men selected were Special Forces and Ranger volunteers. They trained for six months and had three months of rehearsal at Eglin* AFB, Florida. Intelligence was from SR-71* high-altitude and drone low-altitude photos. The intelligence did not confirm the continued presence of POWs at the prison. After the raid, it was found the POWs had been moved on 14 July 1970 because of severe flooding.

The raid was on the night of 20–21 November 1970. The raiders flew out of Thailand and arrived at the prison a little after 0200 hours on 21 November. There were few problems. The one mistake proved fortuitous; the helicopter with the support group landed in the wrong compound. It had been identified as a "secondary school" but actually contained Soviet or Chinese troops who were training the North Vietnamese in air defense. The Americans engaged this force before it could get organized. As a measure of the planning and execution, the Americans suffered but one casualty. One man was slightly injured in the crash-landing. The greatest disappointment came when the raiders found the POWs were gone.

Kingpin produced positive results in spite of no rescue. The conditions for POWs improved. POWs who had been scattered throughout the countryside were concentrated in the prison called the "Hanoi Hilton." This move improved prisoner morale for they could now encourage their fellows to persevere under the desperate conditions. Finally, the raid caused concern among the North Vietnamese and their allies because it showed vulnerability to this kind of operation.

References. Berger, *USAF in SEA.* John Morrocco, *Rain of Fire: Air War, 1969–1973*, a vol. of *The Vietnam Experience*, 1985. Benjamin F. Schemmer, *The Raid*, 1976.

Roger D. Launius

SPAATZ, GENERAL CARL A. "TOOEY" (1891–1974)

Spaatz** was the last commanding general of the USAAF* and the first chief of staff of the Air Force.* As such he established the initial institutions of the new USAF.* He was second only to General of the Air Force H. H. Arnold* as a father and founder of the independent USAF. Spaatz was more than an organizer; he was one of the great combat leaders in the defeat of Germany, noted for his integrity and pragmatism. He was inducted into the National Aviation Hall of Fame in Dayton, Ohio, in 1967.

He was born in Boyertown, Pennsylvania, and graduated from the U.S. Military Academy (USMA) in 1914. He became a pilot* and immediately was posted to the 1st Aero Squadron in the Mexican expedition of 1916.* He served in France as commander of the 3rd Aviation Instruction Center at Issoudon.* He served at the front for the last three weeks of the war and was credited with two victories. He became a close associate of Brigadier General William Mitchell.* He held many important command assignments in fighters* and bombers* between the wars. He was commander of the record-breaking *Question Mark** in its 1929 experiment in aerial refueling.*

In the summer of 1940 he went overseas to observe the Battle of Britain. Shortly after Pearl Harbor,* he was made the USAAF's main combat commander. He presided over the buildup for the Eighth Air Force* (8AF) and its first months of battle. He was General Dwight D. Eisenhower's* air commander for the African, Sicilian, and Italian campaigns. Eisenhower brought Spaatz back to England for Operation Overlord.* Spaatz was in command when air superiority* was achieved over the Luftwaffe, and he is credited with persistence in favor of the decisive offensive against the German oil industry target system.* Immediately after the collapse of Germany, he was transferred to command the B-29s* in the strategic campaign against Japan.* He supervised the nuclear weapons* raids on Hiroshima and Nagasaki.* Spaatz retired in 1948.

References. Primary: H. H. Arnold, *Global Mission*, 1949. Ira Eaker, "Memories of Six Air Chiefs, Part II, Westover, Arnold, Spaatz," *AH*, December 1973, pp. 194–96. Dwight David Eisenhower, *Crusade in Europe*, 1948. Secondary: Michael Carver, *The War Lords: Military Commanders of the Twentieth Century*, 1964. David R. Mets, *Master of Airpower: General Carl A. Spaatz*, 1988.

**Spaatz was born Carl Spatz. The name was changed in 1938 to simplify pronunciation for English-speaking people.

David R. Mets

SPACE COMMAND. *See* Air Force Space Command.

SPAD XIII

The favorite airplane of USAAS* pilots* in World War I* was the French-built Spad XIII, and it became famous in the United States. It was one of the foreign aircraft bought to equip the USAAS because U.S. fighter* aircraft were not available. Spad is an acronym for the manufacturer's name, Société pour Aviation et ses Dérivés.

When the Lafayette Escadrille* entered U.S. service, it was flying XIIIs. It was July 1918 before other U.S. units had the XIII. For many it was a welcome replacement for the Nieuport 28s* previously in use, but some U.S. pilots preferred the more agile 28. The XIII was flown by Captain Edward V. Rickenbaker* and Second Lieutenant Frank Luke, Jr.* The Spad was a sturdy fighter that could dive faster than 200 miles per hour, an attractive quality for a wood and cloth airplane. Its main problem was engine failure. The USAAS bought 893 Spads. When the war was over, 435 were shipped to the United States but were not used for long. The XIII remained in the popular memory of U.S. airmen, and, in the Vietnam War,* they nicknamed the ancient A-1* "Spad."

Characteristics: engine, Hispano-Suiza 8BEc of 235 horsepower; span, 26 feet; length, 20 feet; height, 8 feet; gross weight, 1,811 pounds; top speed, 138 miles per hour; service ceiling, 22,300 feet; endurance, 2.5 hours.

References. Primary: Higham, *Combat Airc.*, vol. 3. Edward V. Rickenbacker, *Fighting the Flying Circus*, 1919. Secondary: Wagner, *Am. Planes*.

SPANGDAHLEM AIR BASE

This U.S. Air Forces in Europe* (USAFE) base is eight miles east of Bitburg, Germany. The field was activated in 1953 as one of the bases built after the North Atlantic Treaty Organization* (NATO) was formed. It is named for a nearby town. In 1990 it had the 52nd Tactical Fighter Wing (TFW) on it flying F-4s* and F-16.* It was the only USAFE Wild Weasel* base.

References. "Guide to Major Air Force Installations Worldwide," *AF*, May 1990, p. 132. Roberts, *Dir. USAF*.

SPARROW. *See* AIM-7.

SPECIAL AIR MISSIONS. *See* presidential airlift.

SPECIAL OPERATIONS. *See* Twenty-Third Air Force.

SPECIAL WEAPONS COMMAND

Atomic, or nuclear, bacteriological, and chemical military means were once called ABC, or special weapons. In 1949, the USAF* formed a Special Weapons Command as a major command* (MAJCOM). It was to supervise the units that possessed such arms. Because many of the units had research and development (R&D) missions, the Special Weapons Command was absorbed into the Air Research and Development Command (ARDC) in 1952 and lost MAJCOM status. It was redesignated as the Air Force Special Weapons Center. The center* was inactivated in 1954.

References. Goldberg, *Hist. USAF*. Ravenstein, *Org. USAF*.

SPECIFIED COMMAND

This important designation gives to one military service control over all joint forces within a "specified command." The Office of the Secretary of Defense (OSD) has direct operational control of the specified command itself. An example of a USAF*-specified command is the Strategic Air Command* (SAC).

References. Woodford Agee Heflin, ed., *The United States Air Force Dictionary*, 1956. Edward N. Luttwak, *The Pentagon and the Art of War: The Question of Military Reform*, 1985.

SPECTRE

This was the call sign and nickname of the AC-130 (*see* C-130) gunships* flown by the 16th Special Operations Squadron from Ubon* Royal Thai AFB, Thailand. From 1969 to 1973, Spectre flew attack,* MiGCAP,* and perimeter defense missions in Laos, South Vietnam, and Cambodia. At night and in marginal weather conditions, no other weapon system could provide such highly accurate firepower. Its ability to find targets, accurate and effective firepower, long loiter time, and large ordnance capacity made for a potent and versatile weapon system.

A close relationship between the AC-130 developers and users insured that innovation continuously improved effectiveness. Although few AC-130s were lost, its vulnerability to ground fire was a constant concern. Spectre's reputation is based on night interdiction along the Ho Chi Minh trail.* The AC-130 was considered to be the most successful and economical truck killer used on the trail, damaging or destroying tens of thousands of trucks. Gunships also provided effective close support; those missions flown in South Vietnam from April to June 1972 were especially important.

References. Primary: Richard A. Lehnert, "The Ghost Rider in the Sky," *AF*, September 1973, pp. 118–22. Secondary: Jack S. Ballard, *Development and Employment of*

Fixed-Wing Gunships 1962–1972, 1982. Ross E. Hamlin, "Side-Firing Weapon Systems," *Air University Review*, January-February 1970, pp. 76–88.

Jeffrey C. Benton

"SPIKE." *See* Momyer, General William W.

SPOOKY. *See* gunship.

SPOT PROMOTION

This is USAF* temporary promotion of an officer intended to provide the authority needed for the job. The system has caused much dissension with allegations that it has been a means to advance favoritism. It has also caused pain to the holder when there has been reversion to a lower grade than the spot grade.

References. Woodford Agee Heflin, ed., *The United States Air Force Dictionary*, 1957. Dennis K. McDaniel, "The B-47 from the Back Seat, SAC from the Bottom— One Pilot's Account," *AH*, March 1987, pp. 42–43.

SPRINGS, LIEUTENANT COLONEL ELLIOTT WHITE (1896–1959)

A World War I* ace,* Springs is one of the USAF's* main authors. His writings probably early influenced U.S. opinion about military flying. He ranked 15th as a U.S. ace in his war, an honor he shares with four others. He had 12 victories.

Born in Lancaster, South Carolina, he started to learn to fly for the U.S. Army while still a student at Princeton University. After graduation he finished his flight training* in England. Then he was sent to France to fly combat in S.E.5s with No. 85 Squadron of the British Royal Air Force (RAF). By the end of June 1918 he had four victories and had been shot down and injured in the crash. He returned to combat in August, flying Sopwith Camels in the USAAS's* 148th Aero Squadron.

After the war, Springs did test flying and barnstorming. He took up writing and produced *War Birds* (1926), *Nocturne Militaire* (1927), *Leave Me with a Smile* (1928), *Contact* (1930), *In the Cool of the Evening* (1930), *Rise and Fall of Carol Burke* (1931), *Pent Up on a Penthouse* (1931), *Warbirds and Ladybirds* (1931), and three other books. *War Birds* was a spectacular success. However, Springs' father was unhappy about the writing. Springs stopped writing in 1931 and became president of the family business, the Springs Cotton Mills. In the years he ran the business he increased his personal wealth by $200 million in this tough industry, despite the Great Depression. In World War II* he served the USAAF* as executive officer of Charlotte AB in North Carolina. Springs became famous again after this war by preparing his own titillating advertising for his Springmaid brand fabrics.

References. Burke Davis, *War Bird: The Life and Times of Elliott White Springs*, 1987. Gurney, *5 Down*. Hess, *Aces Album*. Quentin Reynolds, *They Fought for the Sky*, 1957.

SQUADRON

This type of USAF* unit is subordinate to a group* and superior to a flight.* Squadrons are numbered, and Arabic numbers are always used. There is one exception, the USAF Demonstration Squadron, known as the Thunderbirds.*

References. Woodford Agee Heflin, ed., *The United States Air Force Dictionary*, 1956. Ravenstein, *Org. USAF*.

SR-71

Built by the Lockheed Corporation, the SR-71 had the highest performance of any aircraft for nearly 30 years. It has been the only Mach 3 aircraft in the USAF.*

It was a product of Lockheed's "Skunk Works" and another design triumph of Clarence L. "Kelly" Johnson. For example, Mach 3 flight raised airframe temperatures so high that 93 percent of its structure had to be made of titanium alloy. Originally called the A-11, its first prototype was designed to be an interceptor and was designated YF-12A. The first flight was in 1962. The YF-12 was canceled in 1967, but a reconnaissance* prototype had been produced in 1964. Designated the SR-71, it entered USAF service in 1966, and more than 32 had been built when production ended in 1968. The SR-71 could survey more than 100,000 square miles in one hour while at Mach 3 and above 80,000 feet altitude. In 1976 it set an absolute world speed record of 2,193.167 miles per hour and an altitude record of 85,069 feet. Many people believe it had not been flown at its top performance for these marks. It was retired in 1990 to save money. When the Iraq War* began in 1991, the retirement was criticized. Its nicknames were "Blackbird" (for its color), "Habu" (an Okinawan snake), and "Lead Sled."

Characteristics (SR-71A/B) (estimated): engines, two Pratt & Whitney JT11D-20B (J58) turbojets with 34,000 pounds thrust each; span, 56 feet; length, 107 feet; height, 18 feet; gross weight, 170,000 pounds; top speed, over Mach 3; ceiling, above 80,000 feet; range (unrefueled) at Mach 3, 3,000 miles.

References. Primary: Patrick J. Halloran, "SR-71 at Mach 3.0 Cruise," *AF*, September 1971, pp. 62–68. Secondary: Michael A. Dornheim, "U.S. Reconnaissance Weakened by SR-71 Program Termination," *AWST*, 22 January 1990, pp. 38–41. René J. Francillon, *Lockheed Aircraft since 1913*, 1987. Swanborough, *US Mil. Airc*. Susan H. H. Young, "Gallery of USAF Weapons," *AF*, May 1989, p. 138.

SRAM. *See* AGM-69.

STALAG LUFT. *See* prisoners of war (POW), Germany.

STANDARD ARM. *See* AGM–78.

STAPP, COLONEL JOHN PAUL (1910–   )

Stapp had a distinguished record in USAF* medical research. He performed the highly dangerous experiment on the effects of acceleration and deceleration on the human body. He proved a person could withstand ejections from aircraft at high speeds and high altitudes.

He was born in Bahia, Brazil; graduated from Baylor University, Texas, in 1931; and received his master's degree there in 1932. He earned a Ph.D. from the University of Texas in 1940 and an M.D. from the University of Minnesota in 1944. Stapp graduated from the School of Aviation Medicine at Randolph* Field, Texas, in 1945. In 1954 he rode a rocket-powered sled on rails to a speed of 632 miles per hour in five seconds, and then stopped in 1.4 seconds. This was a deceleration force of 40 times that of gravity. He received the Cheney Award for this work in 1954.

References. DuPre, *USAF Bio*. John L. Frisbee, "The Track to Survival," *AF*, May 1983, p. 64.

STARFIGHTER. *See* F-104.

STARLIFTER. *See* C-141.

STEALTH

This term is a collective one for the technology of avoiding detection, primarily by radar.* Escaping radar detection is done by adopting shapes that are less conducive to reflection, as in the B-2* and F-117,* reducing the metallic content of an aircraft, and using radar-absorbing materials. Other techniques, usually decoys or misleading methods, are used to reduce detection by infrared, lasers, television cameras, noise, and electronic emissions.

Enhancing detection, now called counter-stealth, involves the new and un-developed technology of radar systems called ultra-wideband. The most important element in these systems is impulse radar, transmitting short pulses over a wide spectrum of frequencies. Another possibility for counter-stealth is to expand radar networks and to increase greatly computer analysis and processing of the resultant information.

References. David F. Bond, "Radar Networks, Computing Advances Seen as Keys to Counter Stealth Technologies," *AWST*, 4 December 1989, p. 41. Jay H. Goldberg, "The Technology of Stealth," *Technology Review*, May/June 1989, pp. 32–40. William B. Scott, "UWB Radar Has Potential to Detect Stealth Aircraft," *AWST*, 4 December 1989, pp. 38–41.

See also electronic warfare; follow-on forces attack strategy.

STEARMAN. *See* PT-13.

STEEL TIGER AND TIGER HOUND OPERATIONS

These were identical operations but covered different geographic areas. Steel Tiger ran from the Mu Gia pass, Laos, south to the 17th parallel. Tiger Hound ran from Tchepone, Laos, south to Cambodia. Steel Tiger began in April 1965 and Tiger Hound in December in an effort to stop the communist infiltration, which at that time was estimated at 4,500 men and 300 tons of supplies per month, into South Vietnam through Laos. U.S. and Laos officials agreed to concentrate more air power on that portion of the Ho Chi Minh trail* closest to South Vietnam. The operations ended in April 1973 and were not successful.

The operations required more resources than the USAF* had used in Laos up to that time. The first aircraft used were C-47s,* later replaced by C-130s.* USAF O-1 Bird Dogs* and A-1Es* were also used, along with Royal Laotian air force (RLAF) T-28s* which served forward air controllers* (FAC). RF-101s (*see* F-101) and RF-4Cs (*see* F-4) were employed with their new infrared and side-looking airborne radars* (SLAR). UC-123s (*see* C-123) sprayed defoliant to suppress jungle growth along primary trails. Attack* planes included B-57s,* F-100s,* F-105s,* and AC-47 gunships.* The U.S. Army provided 0-1 and OV-1 Mohawk aircraft which also had SLAR. Tiger Hound flew many missions at night, and to facilitate the destruction of targets the rules of political air superiority* were less stringent than elsewhere in Laos and Vietnam. An attack by B-52s* on 11 December on the Mu Gia pass marked their first use, and by mid–1966 they had flown 400 sorties in support of Tiger Hound. By April 1967, U.S. aircrews were flying 2,900 to 3,400 sorties per month. However, in the first six months of Tiger Hound, 22 U.S. aircraft were downed by hostile fire.

References. Berger, *USAF in SEA*. René J. Francillon, *Vietnam: The War in the Air*, 1987. John Morrocco, *Rain of Fire: Air War, 1969–1973*, a vol. of *The Vietnam Experience*, 1985.

Frank L. Goldstein

STETSON, SECRETARY JOHN C. (1920–   )

Stetson was picked from the private sector to be the 12th secretary of the Air Force* (SAF), serving from 1977 to 1979. He focused on long-range planning to deal with his expectation that there would be raw material shortages, fewer military-qualified youths, and expanding Soviet military capabilities. He believed in decentralized decisions and saw his principal role as assisting the USAF* to get the people, equipment, and funds it needed. His management philosophy produced close working relationships with the two chiefs of staff of the Air Force* who served under him, Generals David C. Jones* and Lew Allen, Jr.* He resigned in 1979 to return to business.

Before his appointment, Stetson was president of A. B. Dick Company. Before that he had been a partner in the consulting firm of Booz, Allen and Hamilton and had experience in the aviation industry. He had been a structural engineer with the Douglas Company before becoming a naval officer in World War II.* In his consultant work, he dealt closely with large aviation firms on programs for new military and commercial aircraft. He consulted for major oil companies in Iran and Kuwait, which prepared him to deal with one of the USAF's major problems in the 1970s: managing the shortage and inflationary costs of fuels.

References. Primary: John C. Stetson. "Broadening the Strategic Planning Process," *AF*, May 1979, pp. 58, 59. Secondary: "Secretary of the Air Force John C. Stetson Resigns," *AF*, June 1979, p. 32. USAF Biography, "John C. Stetson," June 1978.

Warren A. Trest

"STEVE." *See* Ritchie, Lieutenant Colonel Richard S.

STEVE CANYON. *See* Caniff, Milton.

STEWART, BRIGADIER GENERAL JAMES "JIMMY" (1908–   )

Stewart was a movie actor who proved himself in battle and as a leader. He used his acting skills to help the USAF* uniquely through two films: *Winning Your Wings* (1942) and *Strategic Air Command* (1955). Already a famous Hollywood movie star when World War II* began, Stewart enlisted as a private in 1941. He became a pilot* and took a B-24* bomber* squadron* to England as its commander. He flew 35 sorties in the war. After the war, Stewart went back to acting and stayed in the U.S. Air Force Reserve* (USAFR). In 1959, after congressional debate about it, he was promoted to brigadier general. As an actor he won two Oscars and had five Academy Award nominations.

References. DuPre, *USAF Bio.* Arthur Hyland, "A Real Hero," *AF*, March 1988, p. 108.

STRANGLE. *See* Operation Strangle.

STRATEGIC AIR COMMAND (SAC)

From its establishment on 21 March 1946, SAC had the mission of being prepared to conduct strategic operations* in any part of the world. Although SAC's nuclear weapons* capabilities were virtually nonexistent in 1946, its long-range bombers* were viewed from the outset as a deterrent to the start of another unlimited war. The role was not a credible one, though, until after the USAF* brought Lieutenant General Curtis E. LeMay* back from Europe to build up SAC and after President Harry S Truman* (HST) officially adopted a national policy of nuclear deterrence in 1949. As the principal deterrent force, SAC can claim possible credit for the long peace without a major war since then.

During the 1950s, SAC was made solely responsible for land-based ballistic missiles,* and it had its strategic operation missiles before the end of the decade. Today, its bombers and missiles form two-thirds of the nuclear triad,* so its readiness posture remains a primary deterrent to an assault against the United States and its allies.

As shown in the Korean* and Vietnam* Wars, SAC's bombers remained a vital part of nonnuclear U.S. power as well. B-29s* provided the United Nations (UN) forces with heavy air power to keep pressure on the North Korean and Chinese armies, and their presence helped prevent a widening of the war. A few years later, B-52s* were used extensively in battle in Southeast Asia (SEA).

SAC began equipping with its B-36* intercontinental bombers* before the Korean War, but they never saw combat. The B-36 was replaced by the B-52 in the mid–1950s, and the new bombers began a continuous airborne nuclear alert. Today's strike force of more than 400 aircraft is comprised mostly of B-52s and F-111s,* which entered the inventory during the SEA conflict. SAC also has B-1s* now. Its intercontinental ballistic missiles by 1990 totaled 1,000 Minuteman* II and III, and the new Peacekeeper.* A lesser-known mission of SAC, which results from its global reach, is to help control the seas. This includes attacking enemy ships, mining,* and reconnaissance.*

Throughout SAC's history, reconnaissance has been vital for the entire mission. Marked by such successes as the U-2* photos proving the Soviet missile buildup before the Cuban missile crisis of 1962,* SAC's reconnaissance forces today include U-2s, TR-1s, and RC-135s (see C-135).

Since receiving its initial tankers* in 1948, SAC has made aerial refueling* an indispensable element in its operations. The KC-135s (see C-135) proved valuable in supporting B-52s and attack* aircraft in the Vietnam War.* A few new KC-10s (see C-10) have improved SAC's role as the single manager of tanker operations.

In 1990, SAC had two historical air forces* under it, the Eighth Air Force* (8AF) headquartered at Barksdale* AFB, Louisiana, and the Fifteenth Air Force* (15AF) at March* AFB, California.

There was a general understanding when SAC was formed that it would respond to the Joint Chiefs of Staff (JCS), but it was not until the Key West and Newport Conferences of 1948* that it officially became a specified command* tasked directly by the JCS. Officially, it was not given the mission of strategic operations by the JCS until 1949. It has now had that mission for four decades.

Movies: Strategic Air Command, 1955. A Gathering of Eagles,* 1963. Dr. Strangelove or: How I Learned to Stop Worrying and Love the Bomb,* 1964.*

References. Futrell, *Ideas*, 2 vols., and *USAF in Korea*. J. C. Hopkins, *The Development of Strategic Air Command, 1946–1981 (A Chronological History)*, Offutt AFB, Nebraska, 1982. Jacob Neufeld, *Ballistic Missiles in the United States Air Force 1945–1960*, 1990. "Strategic Air Command," *AF*, May 1990, pp. 83–85.

Warren A. Trest

STRATEGIC AIR COMMAND

This 1955 movie* was written by Beirne Lay, Jr.,* and Valentine Davis. It depicts the Strategic Air Command* (SAC) as an institution through the experiences of the central character, Lieutenant Colonel Robert R. "Dutch" Holland, played by James Stewart.* The experiences relate to SAC's mission, concepts, recruiting, retention, and the stresses on its married personnel. At the time, the last two were severe problems in the command.

Reference. "The 40th Anniversary of the USAF," a special issue of *AH*, September 1987, p. 210.

STRATEGIC AIRLIFT. *See* airlift operations; strategic operations.

STRATEGIC BOMBARDMENT. *See* strategic operations.

STRATEGIC BOMBING SURVEY. *See* U.S. Strategic Bombing Survey, The.

STRATEGIC CAMPAIGN AGAINST JAPAN

The USAAF's* B-17s* and B-24s* had the range to conduct strategic operations* from England, Africa, and Italy against Europe. With the advent of the B-29* and the conquest of the Marianas* Islands, the means were at last available to assault Japan by air. To avoid the dispersion of effort from strategic to tactical operations,* as had occurred in Europe, a new organization was formed in April 1944. It was the Twentieth Air Force* (20AF), and it was commanded from Washington, D.C., by General of the Army H. H. Arnold.* It was an important event in U.S. history.

It had first been the USAAF's intention to conduct the campaign from China, designated Matterhorn,* and bases were built for this purpose. This campaign had to be supplied by airlift operations* over the "Hump,"* and these were inadequate. The decision was made to operate from the Marianas. Under Brigadier General Haywood S. Hansell, Jr.,* the Marianas effort did not go well. It began on 24 November 1944 and encountered the previously unknown phenomenon of the jet stream, which adversely affected high-altitude bombing. The Norden bombsight* had not anticipated the speeds of the stream combined with a plane like the fast B-29. This problem was overcome by lowering the altitude of operations, but this improved the effectiveness of Japanese air defense. The weather over Japan had more cloud cover than expected. This proved intractable to high-altitude operations on the scale needed.

By the end of January, Arnold was dissatisfied with results. He replaced Hansell with Major General Curtis E. LeMay.* LeMay began with an analysis of the situation. He found the main problems were the weather undercasts which frustrated visual bombing, the troublesome B-29 engines which did not perform well at high altitudes, the small bomb loads resulting from high-altitude operations, and the effectiveness of the Japanese day air defenses. LeMay also believed incendiary bombs should be used instead of high explosives.

LeMay changed the target priority from the airframe and engine industries to (1) aircraft engines and (2) aircraft assembly and the cities. He also switched the tactics to low-altitude raids at night. His solutions avoided all the big problems, though they violated the USAAF's aversion to hitting civilians. The first strike with LeMay's innovations was on Tokyo on 9 March. It killed 84,000, injured 41,000, and burned one-fourth of the city, making one million homeless. These results were greater than either of the nuclear weapons* raids on Hiroshima* and Nagasaki and were the biggest city fire in history. There had been 334 B-29s launched and 14 lost.

By 19 March the supply of incendiaries was exhausted and the B-29s were diverted for tactical operations to support the Okinawa* invasion. Also the B-29s began their highly effective blockade operations of mining.* In mid-May the use of incendiaries was resumed and day operations were practical. In July, LeMay had such an upper hand he informed the Japanese in advance of targets to be hit.

By 14 August, the B-29s had dropped 159,862 tons of bombs; 91 percent, by weight, of the bombs fell on the homeland; Japan's cities and industries were badly damaged; and its food and oil distribution systems were not working. It is believed that 900,000 Japanese died, 1,300,000 were injured, and 9,200,000 were made homeless. There had been 147 B-29s lost, at a rate of 0.47 percent by sorties, to achieve this.

On 6 and 9 August, the two nuclear weapons were dropped. On 14 August, V-J Day, Japan conditionally surrendered after this special bombing campaign and without any land assault while it still had 2.5 million battle-ready soldiers.

References. Primary: Leslie R. Groves, *Now It Can Be Told: The Story of the Manhattan Project*, 1962. Haywood S. Hansell, Jr., *Strategic Air War against Japan*, 1980. Curtis E. LeMay and Bill Yenne, *Superfortress: The Story of the B-29 and American Air Power*, 1988. Secondary: C&C, vol. 5. Richard G. Hewlett and Oscar E. Anderson, Jr., *The New World: A History of the United States Atomic Energy Commission, 1939–1946*, vol. 1, 1990.

STRATEGIC DEFENSE INITIATIVE (SDI)

In March 1983, President Ronald Reagan* announced a plan, the SDI, to protect civilians from nuclear weapons* delivered by ballistic missiles.* SDI was to consist of a space-based array of vehicles that would destroy incoming missiles in the suborbital phase. This proposal aroused vigorous dissent from the proponents of the mutual assured destruction (MAD) policy, which has sought to avoid superpower war by holding populations hostage to the ballistic missile forces. The media generally sided with MAD supporters and labeled SDI as "Star Wars" in an attempt to cast it as too futuristic and unworkable.

The administration's budget requests for SDI were not granted by Congress, but some research was funded. This eliminated the possibility of developing the original proposal, which used directed-energy weapons (DEW). The research has instead pursued kinetic energy weapons (KEW). Two KEW means have been under consideration. One was "smart rocks," or nonnuclear warheads in orbit aboard spacecraft. The other was "brilliant pebbles," or small spacecraft to strike on command.

SDI has had two major problems. One is launch capability and the related costs. The other is the complexity required of the computers involved in detecting enemy warheads and directing the defenses at an effective level.

There has been much skepticism about the feasibility of SDI within the United States. Should SDI prove practical, the USSR would lose much of its superpower status. It is understandable, then, that the USSR has taken SDI as a serious, feasible threat and has vigorously tried to induce the United States to abandon the program. The USSR also worked on its own SDI program, and some people in the West have ventured the idea that SDI was an added burden that contributed significantly to the Soviet internal economic reverses which reached crisis proportions in 1989.

There have been many people in the United States who regarded SDI as a useful defense only against the USSR, which still possessed a virtually undiminished nuclear missile force in 1990. Others believed it is needed against even minor nations possessing nuclear weapons and ballistic missiles. Regardless of these opinions, it appeared in 1990 that politically motivated defense cuts rather than technical feasibility would scrap this costly program.

References. Frank Barnaby, *The Automated Battlefield*, 1986. David Bellin and Gary Chapman, eds., *Computers in Battle—Will They Work?* 1987. Richard S. Friedman et al., *Advanced Technology Warfare*, 1985. John Rhea, "The Scaled-Down Look of Star Wars," *AF*, October 1989, pp. 60–63. Edgar Ulsamer, "The Battle for SDI," *AF*, February 1985, pp. 44–53.

STRATEGIC OPERATIONS

Strategic operations are actions designed to project aerospace power against the weak links of a whole nation; in other nations they are called grand strategy. Their primary purpose, for the United States, is to pose such retaliatory force that a potential aggressor will be deterred from acting. Failing that, their purpose is the use of power to end the enemy's ability to conduct war. Strategic airlift* and strategic reconnaissance* operations are means to support strategic operations or national policy.

Strategic operations can be directed against an enemy's population, military forces, or economy; or combination thereof. With civilians, the object is to cause such population losses or distress and despair as to disrupt the fabric of the society. As applied against the USSR, this was called mutual assured destruction (MAD), which acknowledges massive losses also among U.S. civilians. Strategic operations against military forces—land, sea, or air—is called counterforce. It envisions neutralizing the enemy's military power.

Such operations against a nation's economy are designed to end its capability to make war. The economic approach is considered the most efficient, because all economies have targets that are difficult to protect, critical bottlenecks, vital supplies, or other vulnerable systems. The most effective passive defense against strategic operations aimed at an economy is dispersal of the critical elements. It is not a wholly satisfactory answer, however, for dispersal can take time and it has two results: markedly reduced efficiency and dependence upon a transportation system that may be or become inadequate or vulnerable.

The concepts of strategic operations are roughly as old as aviation, but a common mistake is to believe that they are only directed at civilians. Strategic operations were not done by the USAAS* in World War I,* but the ideas and early attempts by other nations impressed U.S. airmen. Between the world wars, the Air Corps Tactical School* (ACTS) developed doctrine* based upon conducting strategic operations with large bombers,* primarily against an enemy's economy. During World War II,* the USAAF* tried strategic operations, under restraints, against the enemy. The AWPD-1* was the blueprint for the assault on Germany, targeting the electric, oil, and transportation industries. The strategic campaign against Japan* first targeted the aircraft industry.

After the war, the USAAF and USAF* believed that the U.S. Strategic Bombing Survey* had shown the efficacy of strategic operations and that those lessons, together with nuclear weapons,* continued to give the doctrine primacy. It was believed by the USAF that an ability to use these methods successfully against the strongest enemy would assure victory against lesser powers as well. An important new tool was added to the arsenal with the ballistic missile* in 1958.

The Korean War* showed that the U.S. government would shrink from the full application of modern strategic operations, conventional or nuclear, in limited wars because of their terrible power. Nevertheless, strategic operations were used in abridged fashion in that war and in the Vietnam War.* As a result, some people have believed that the campaigns against the Korean irrigation dams target system* in 1953 and Linebacker* II in 1972 showed the true potential of strategic operations against unindustrialized nations in limited wars.

Like everything else, strategic operations are neither a panacea nor impotent. They are directed at an entire society. Societies have more similarities than differences: they are complex, responsive, intelligent and resilient. They have strengths and weaknesses, physically and psychologically. They can be compared to a locked house that one can break into with least effort or destruction with a single key or combination. The task for strategic operations is to find the correct key or combination that will force entry and shatter the psychology or physical resources that sustain the household. That can be done with any society with the correct keys and means. No society is immune to psychological or economic upset. If there is a lack of either the key or the means, the effort will fail.

There now is some historical evidence on strategic operations. It seems evident that, with Germany in World War II, only annihilation would bring an end to the war because of insistence upon unconditional surrender. The USAAF's experience, then, indicates that strategic operations can bring annihilation only with nuclear weapons. The experience with Japan, North Korea, North Vietnam, and Iraq indicates that strategic operations can induce a peace with terms.

Movie: Victory through Air Power, 1943.

References. Primary: H. S. Hansell, "Strategic Air Warfare," *AH*, Winter 1966, pp. 153–60. Secondary: David A. Anderton, *Strategic Air Command: Two-thirds of the Triad*, 1974. Futrell, *Ideas*, 2 vols. Higham, *Air Pwr*. D. MacIsaac, *Strategic Bombing in World War II: The Story of the U.S. Strategic Bombing Survey*, 1976.

See also German aircraft industry target system; German ball bearing industry system; German oil industry system; German transportation target system.

STRATOFORTRESS. *See* B-52.

STRATOFREIGHTER. *See* C-97.

STRATOJET. *See* B-47.

STRATOLIFTER. *See* C-135.

STRATOTANKER. *See* C-135.

SUB PENS. *See* U-boat bases and yards.

SUI-HO. *See* Korean electrical power target system.

SUPERFORTRESS. *See* B-29; B-50.

SUPER JOLLY. *See* H-53.

SUPER SABRE. *See* F-100.

SUPPLY

The function of supply in the USAF* is to procure, store, and distribute materiel. It may also include salvage. In modern war it is an indispensable function for millions of items. Supply is especially critical for the United States because (1) a great industrial nation possesses a great military advantage if it uses its productive power and (2) Americans believe in expending materiel and not blood. As the most technical military service, supply is most important to the USAF.

The U.S. Army already had a system for supplies when it entered into aviation. In World War I* the airmen used it and established 14 air depots across the United States. Each depot had around a dozen officers and several hundred men, and they supplied the airfields.

When the USAAC* was formed, it created a Materiel Division at McCook Field, Ohio, which moved to nearby Wright Field in 1927. The creation of the USAAF* provided another organizational opportunity and the need to create supply functions appropriate to explosive growth and a huge service. Thus was created the Air Service Command (ASC), headquartered in Washington, D.C. By the fall of 1942, the ASC had more assets and manpower than the General Motors Corporation, and they were needed. After a few months of modern war, supply shortages grounded 40 percent of the USAAF's planes. A prime reason was the new problems in forecasting demand for supplies in the expansion to a global force.

In 1946, supply became part of the new Air Materiel Command (AMC), a major command* (MAJCOM). At first it had a disposition problem as the USAAF demobilized. Soon an about-face was needed for the demands of the Berlin Airlift* and the Korean War.* Reassessment after that war resulted in dissatisfaction with surface logistics, the older communications systems, and record-keeping. The solutions were the Logistical Airlift (LOGAIR) system of airlifting supplies and adopting the computer, both activated in 1954. Because the USAF was a global organization, the AMC was extended to worldwide status to use its solutions fully.

In 1961 the AMC was transformed into the current Air Force Logistics Command* (AFLC). This nearly coincided with the new Defense Supply Agency (DSA). The DSA was intended to be a single organization to rationalize the military services' supply function by having single managers for military supply items common to more than one service.

References. Primary: Fred J. Dau, "Air Force Supply—1952–1959," *AH*, March 1982, pp. 26–30. Secondary: Woodford Agee Heflin, ed., *The United States Air Force Dictionary*, 1956. Bernard J. Termena et al., *Logistics: An Illustrated History of AFLC and Its Antecedents, 1921–1981*, 1981.

See also Robins, Brigadier General (Augustine) Warner.

SUPPORT COMMAND

A support command does not conduct operations. It provides supplies, services, maintenance, transportation, administration, training, education, or similar functions. Examples are the Air Force Logistics Command* (AFLC) and the Air University* (AU).

Reference. Ravenstein, *Org. USAF*.

SURFACE-TO-AIR MISSILES (SAM)

These are guided missiles used against aircraft. They are composed of a rocket or ramjet main engine and booster, control surfaces, warhead, fuzing and firing section, and guidance and control section. They originated in German research during World War II.* The U.S. Army was given the SAM mission by one of the Wilson memorandums,* despite the fact that the USAF* is responsible for air defense. The first effective one was the Army's Nike Ajax of the 1950s. The USSR soon followed with the SA-2* used in the Vietnam War.* Since then, SAMs have proliferated.

SAMs can be differentiated by their guidance system. The earliest system was command; an automatic ground link controlled the SAM by radio. But this was and is very susceptible to electronic countermeasures (ECM), or jamming, as shown by the performance of SAMs in the Linebacker* II raids.

Another form of guidance is optical. This is similar to antitank systems; indeed, antitank missiles can be used against aircraft flying slowly. The target is acquired optically or by radar.* An optical or laser designator is placed on the target, and the SAM is fired. These SAMs are usually limited to clear weather use.

Radar or "beam rider" guidance works by placing a signal on the target, and the SAM flies up the beam. As with all radar-controlled SAMs, it is vulnerable to ECM. Radar guidance may also be used by on-board equipment. Ground operators place a launched missile on course, and the on-board radar takes over to home on the target. The equipment requires a large SAM, and it is still subject to jamming.

A final guidance form is infrared (IR). These SAMs are small, sometimes shoulder-fired, are short-ranged, and home on the engine or on the surface skin heat generated by supersonic flight. Early versions were called revenge weapons, for they were useful only against the tailpipes of retreating jet aircraft. The IR also tended to chase the sun and was easily spoofed by IR flares. Second generation IR SAMs have a much more sensitive seeker with two frequencies. They are less liable to diversion. These have "fire-and-forget" capability and lack radar, so they are popular with users.

References. Frank Barnaby, *The Automated Battlefield*, 1986. Shelford Bidwell, ed., *Brassey's Artillery of the World*, 1977. Larry Davis, *Wild Weasel: The SAM suppression Story*, 1986. Lon O. Nordeen, Jr., *Air Warfare in the Missile Age*, 1985. Robert L. Shaw, *Fighter Combat: Tactics and Maneuvering*, 1985.

Philip Long

SWEDEN. *See* neutral countries.

SWEET VIETNAM. *See* novels.

SWITZERLAND. *See* neutral countries.

SYMINGTON, SECRETARY STUART (1901–1988)

Symington was the first secretary of the Air Force* (SAF), serving from 1947 to 1950, so he exerted great influence upon both the establishment and nature of the USAF.* In 1953 he became a U.S. senator and served for 24 years in this capacity. He never lost an election.

Born in Amherst, Massachusetts, he graduated from Baltimore City College in 1918 and then enlisted in the U.S. Army. He became a second lieutenant at the age of 17. By 1938 he was president of the Emerson Electric Company. In 1941, the War Department sent him to England to study aircraft gun turrets. Returning to St. Louis, Missouri, his company built a factory to manufacture turrets.

In 1946 he was appointed assistant secretary of war for air.* From that job he became SAF. In these positions he was a strong influence for an independent air force, air power, and a strong USAF. He stood up for the USAF against the U.S. Navy and Secretary of Defense (SECDEF) James V. Forrestal.* As secretary, he focused on organization, people, and attitudes. He instituted comptrollers and pushed for full racial integration in the USAF. He resigned in April 1950 as a protest against the level of defense spending, which he believed was too low. Within three months, the Korean War* began and proved him right.

References. Primary: Stuart Symington, "Symington Remembers," *AF*, July 1984, pp. 92–93. Eugene M. Zuckert, "Stuart Symington, 1901–1988," *Air Power History*, Spring 1989, p. 57. Secondary: James P. Coyne, "Standing up for Airpower," *AF*, September 1986, pp. 159–60, 163. DuPre, *USAF Bio*. "The 40th Anniversary of the USAF," a special issue of *AH*, September 1987, pp. 185–89.

SYNTHETIC APERTURE RADAR (SAR)

SAR and inverse synthetic aperture radars (ISAR), developed in the late 1980s, make possible excellent images of objects that are at a distance. The addition of a computer and data links can transmit those images in real time to ground facilities.

   Reference. Bruce D. Nordwell, "Signal Processing and VHSIC Transforming Reconnaissance," *AWST*, 7 September 1987, pp. 68–69.
See also E-8; follow-on forces attack strategy.

SYSTEMS COMMAND. *See* Air Force Systems Command.

T

T-6 TEXAN

A classic design still flying after more than a half-century, the T-6 has been one of the most useful and popular aircraft in history. Intended as a trainer to introduce aviators to combat flying, it has since served to train pilots* and gunners* and has been used in battle by forward air controllers* (FAC). It has been very popular in civil life for sport, racing, sky writing, and for making movies as radial-engine aircraft or as impersonating Japanese aircraft, especially the A6M Reisen, or "Zero."

Conceived by North American Aviation, Inc., as a trainer with the equipment and characteristics of a fighter,* the NA-26 was originally designated the BC-1, or Basic Combat Trainer, in 1937. The first flight was in 1938. A BC-2 followed, and in 1940 it was redesignated the AT-6, an advanced trainer, and the T-6 in 1948. The USAAF* bought more than 8,000 during World War II* and kept more than 2,000 in the postwar period. Its battle service with FACs was in the Korean War.*

The T-6 is a versatile, stable, aerobatic, and easy airplane to pilot, except for its strong tendency to ground loop. From World War II on, it has been said there are two kinds of T-6 pilots: those who had ground looped and those who were going to. Its nicknames were "Awful Terrible Six" and "Mosquito" (for FAC duties).

Characteristics (T-6A): engine, Pratt & Whitney R-1340–49 of 600 horsepower; span, 42 feet; length, 29 feet; height, 12 feet; gross weight, 5,155 pounds; top speed, 210 miles per hour; service ceiling, 24,200 feet; range, 629 miles.

References. Primary: Higham, *Combat Airc.*, vol. 2. Walt Ohlrich and Jeff Ethell, *Pilot Maker: The Incredible T-6*, 1983. Secondary: Swanborough, *US Mil. Airc.* Bill Yenne, *Rockwell: The Heritage of North American*, 1989.

T-28 TROJAN

The USAF* and North American Aviation, Inc., had high hopes for this trainer, which was intended to combine the latest in piston engine aeronautics with the ease of a trainer. It proved to be disappointing as a user-friendly trainer, and its concept underrated the superiority of the jet engine.

In 1948 the USAF sought to buy a single airplane for both primary and basic flight training.* North American's Model NA-159 won the competition and was designated the BT-28. The first flight of the redesignated T-28 was in 1949. It entered active service in 1950. It soon was a disappointment, and the USAF bought the T-34 and went back to two trainer types. The T-28 began to be replaced by the jet T-37A* in 1957. The partisans of slow, piston-engine attack* aircraft led to the T-28's adoption for use against guerrillas, starting in 1962. It was ready for this duty, because it had been designed for training in armament. The attack T-28s were designated AT-28Ds. An attack version with a turboprop engine was tested but not adopted. The T-28 was not considered a success in the attack role either, because it was vulnerable to ground fire.

Characteristics (T-28A): engine, Wright R-1300-1 of 800 horsepower; span, 40 feet; length, 32 feet; height, 13 feet; gross weight, 6,365 pounds; top speed, 283 miles per hour at 5,900 feet; service ceiling, 24,000 feet; range, 1,000 miles.

References. Robert F. Futrell, *The Advisory Years to 1965*, 1981. Swanborough, *US Mil. Airc.* Bill Yenne, *Rockwell: The Heritage of North American*, 1989.

See also A-1; Farm Gate.

T-29

The Consolidated-Vultee Aircraft (Convair) Corporation's highly successful 240, 340, and 440 airliners were adopted by the USAF* for trainers and transports.* The first flight of the T-29, a navigator* trainer, was made in 1949. Active service began in 1950. Variants were the VT-29, for staff transport; AT-29C or ET-29C, an aircraft to check airways; and ET-29, for electronic warfare.* The principal variant was the transport C-131A, or MC-131A, Samaritan for aeromedical evacuation.* It entered service in 1954. Versions of this airplane were the C-131B, for electronics testing; JC-131B, for finding missile cones after re-entry; VC-131s, for staff transport; RC-131s, for charting; and RC-131, for checking airways. A few C-131s were modified for turboprop engines, as were some airliner cousins. In 1990 a few C-131s were still in service with the Air National Guard* (ANG).

Characteristics (T-29B): engines, two Pratt & Whitney R2800–97s of 2,400 horsepower each; span, 92 feet; length, 75 feet; height, 27 feet; gross weight, 43,575 pounds; top speed, 296 miles per hour; service ceiling, 23,500 feet; range, 1,500 miles.

References. Primary: Higham, *Combat Airc.*, vol. 3. Secondary: Swanborough, *US Mil. Airc.* John Wegg, *General Dynamics Aircraft and their Predecessors*, 1990.

T-33. *See* F-80.

T-37 TWEET

In 1952, the USAF* decided to use a jet for primary flight training.* The Cessna Aircraft Company won the design competition, and its T-37 was first flown in 1954. Service use began in 1957. In the 1960s a variant, the A-37, was developed for light attack* work in the Vietnam War.* The current designation of this aircraft is OA-37B Dragonfly. It is used for forward air controllers* (FAC) and rescue.* By 1990, the T-37 had been training pilots* for 33 years, so it has proven to be an outstanding trainer. More than 1,000 were built, and more than 600 remain in service. It was affectionately nicknamed "Tweety Bird," "Converter" (converts fuel into noise), "Hummer," and "World's Largest Dog Whistle."

Characteristics: engines, two Continental J69-T-25 turbojets of 1,025 pounds thrust each; span, 34 feet; length, 29 feet; height, 9 feet; gross weight, 6,600 pounds; top speed, 426 miles per hour at 25,000 feet; service ceiling, 35,100 feet; range, 870 miles.

References. Primary: Danny Piper and Dan McCauley, "The Trail of the T-37," *AF* April 1975, pp. 65–69. Secondary: Bill Gunston, *An Illustrated Guide to USAF: The Modern US Air Force*, 1986. Swanborough, *US Mil Airc.* Susan H. H. Young, "Gallery of USAF Weapons," *AF*, May 1990, p. 154.

T-38 TALON

The T-38 is a supersonic aircraft used for USAF* flight training.* In service since 1961, its success and place in USAF history is assured as it continues into the 1990s. A related design was the F-5.*

Built by the Northrop Aircraft Corporation, production had reached 1,187 when it ceased in 1972. Other purchasers were the U.S. Navy, the National Aeronautics and Space Administration* (NASA), and the German Luftwaffe. It is one of the most thrilling aircraft to fly because of its excellent maneuverability and favorable thrust-to-weight ratio. It was designed with the pilot* in mind, with all controls and switches placed in logical, easily accessible positions. It was designed to ease the transition of pilots into modern, high wing loaded, fighters.* Proof that it has done so is its lowest accident rate of any trainer in USAF history. Its longevity has been possible through modification programs. One is the AT-38 variant, used for weapons training. Its nickname is "White Rocket."

Characteristics (T-38A): engines, two General Electric J85-GE-5A turbojets of 3,850 pounds thrust each with afterburner; span, 25 feet; length, 46 feet; height, 13 feet; gross weight, 11,761 pounds; top speed, 805 miles per hour at 36,089 feet; service ceiling, 45,000 feet; range, 860 miles.

References. Primary: David R. "Rich" Croft, "I Fly the T-38," *AF* August 1971, pp. 36–41. Secondary: *Jane's All the World's Aircraft. 1971–72*, 1974. Herbert Molloy Mason, Jr., *The New Tigers*, 1967. Swanborough, *US Mil. Airc.*

George W. Hawks, Jr.

T-39 SABRELINER

The T-39 was produced by North American Aviation, Inc., to meet several utility and training needs of the USAF* and U.S. Navy. It was produced in two versions for the USAF: the T-39A for pilot* proficiency and administrative support and the T-39B radar* trainer. The first flight was in 1958, and active service began in 1960. The T-39 was used for instrument flying* and systems test and evaluation at the Instrument Pilot Instructor School (IPIS) at Randolph* AFB, Texas, during the 1960s and until the school was closed in 1976. The aircraft was initially dispersed among the various major commands* (MAJCOM) for use as utility airlift and proficiency trainer aircraft. In 1975 the Military Airlift Command* (MAC) became the USAF single manager for airlift and consolidated the T-39s at central locations. At the same time the USAF reduced proficiency flying, increasing the T-39's availability for utility and staff airlift. The T-39s were retired in 1984.

Characteristics (T-39A): engines, two Pratt & Whitney J60-P-3 turbojets of 3,000 pounds thrust each; span, 44 feet; length, 44 feet; height, 16 feet; gross weight, 17,760 pounds; top speed, 595 miles per hour at 36,000 feet; service ceiling, 39,000 feet; range, 1,725 miles.

References. *Jane's All the World's Aircraft, 1973–74*, 1976. Swanborough, *US Mil. Airc.*

George W. Hawks, Jr.

TACC. *See* Tactical Air Control Center.

TACTICAL AIR COMMAND (TAC)

This major command* (MAJCOM) was established in 1946 as part of the postwar reorganization by General Carl A. Spaatz.* It was activated at Tampa, Florida, but moved in two months to Langley* Field, Virginia, where it has remained. The move signified the USAAF's* desire to work closely with the U.S. Army and Navy in ground and amphibious operations. TAC's mission was and is to train and equip air units for tactical operations* anywhere. It has responded to crises around the world, notably the Korean War;* the Lebanon and Formosa* crises of 1958; the Berlin, Germany, crisis of 1961; the Cuban crisis of 1962;* the Vietnam War;* the Iraq crisis of 1990–1991;* and the Iraq War.

In the 1950s, TAC had the Composite Air Strike Force* (CASF), which tailored extremely mobile forces with different levels of firepower to respond to any and all contingencies. While the CASFs disappeared, the mission remained and took the guise of support to a series of joint, unified,* and specified* commands. Thus TAC provides the USAF* components of U.S. Atlantic Command (USLANTCOM), U.S. Central Command (USCENTCOM), and U.S. Southern Command (SOUTHCOM).

Its mission otherwise has changed. Once TAC had tactical airlift* and participated in numerous humanitarian missions,* such as feeding drought-stricken areas in Chad, Mali, and Mauritania. Its airlift was transferred to the Military Airlift Command* (MAC) in 1974. Two years later, TAC added an airborne warning and control (AC&W) capability. In 1979, the assets of the Aerospace Defense Command* (ADC) went to TAC along with the responsibility for aerospace defense operations.* TAC's special operations forces transferred to MAC in 1983.

TAC conducts its operations from three numbered air forces:* the First Air Force* (1AF) at Langley; the Ninth Air Force* (9AF) at Shaw* AFB, South Carolina; and the Twelfth Air Force* (12AF) at Bergstrom* AFB, Texas. TAC's immediate reporting units include the USAF Tactical Fighter Weapons Center at Nellis* AFB, Nevada; the USAF Tactical Air Warfare Center at Eglin* AFB, Florida; and the 28th Air Division at Tinker* AFB, Oklahoma. The 12AF has a Southern Air Division at Howard* AFB, Panama, which is responsible for the joint defense of the Panama Canal. Training is done under a series of "Flag" programs, such as Red Flag.* Its assets include A-10s,* EC-130s (see C-130), EC-135s (see C-135), E-3s,* F-4s,* RF-4s, F-15s,* F-16s,* and F-111s.*

References. Futrell, *Ideas,* 2 vols. Lineage and Honors, Tactical Air Command, prepared by USAFHRC, Maxwell AFB, Alabama. "Tactical Air Command," *AF,* May 1990, pp. 88–90. U.S. Air Force Fact Sheet 88–8, "Tactical Air Command," March 1988.

Lloyd H. Cornett, Jr.

TACTICAL AIR CONTROL CENTER (TACC)

TACC directs all tactical operations* for a forward area. Thus, it exercises centralized control, usually for an air force.* The components of this control are local air support centers, radar* posts, forward air controllers* (FAC), and attack* planes. The concept is to use USAF and U.S. Army officers side-by-side at each level of command up to the TACC, so that optimum use of the firepower of both services will be attained. The officers cooperate as peers.

This system, developed in World War II,* was repeated for the Korean War.* However, in late 1951, Lieutenant General James A. Van Fleet, commander of the Eighth U.S. Army, asked for a return to decentralized control of attack by putting it back under army corps control. General Mark W. Clark, commander of the Army Forces Far East, rejected the request after learning the costs of the plan. It required a great increase in the number of aircraft. At the end of the war, a conference of Army, Navy, USAF, and Marine Corps officers endorsed the continued joint integration of the services for attack work.

In the Vietnam War,* there was the formality of centralized control, with the TACC located at Tan Son Nhut* AB, South Vietnam, under the Military Assistance Command, Vietnam (MACV). It was not centralized in practice. Tactical operations were, in fact, conducted separately by the USAF, Navy, Army,

Marines, and Vietnamese air force (VNAF). Also, the USAF members of the MACV were seldom given decision-making positions. The USAF in 1990 still cannot believe U.S. air power resources were used efficiently in the war since control was fragmented. There was centralized control in the Iraq War.*

References. Primary: Laurence S. Kuter, "Goddammit, Georgie!" *AF*, February 1973, pp. 51–56. Robert D. Russ, "The Eighty Percent Solution," *AF*, January 1991, pp. 60–62. Secondary: Futrell, *USAF in Korea*. Woodford Agee Heflin, ed., *The United States Air Force Dictionary*, 1956. John Schlight, *The War in South Vietnam: The Years of the Offensive 1965–1968*, 1988.

See also Coningham, Air Marshal Sir Arthur

Frank L. Goldstein contributed to this essay.

TACTICAL AIR FORCES. *See* tactical operations.

TACTICAL AIRLIFT

Tactical airlift is the term presently used by the USAF* in place of past terms such as *troop carrier*, *combat cargo*, *airborne force*, *airborne infantry*, and *airborne troops*. Tactical airlift is the deployment, airborne assault, aeromedical evacuation,* rescue,* or supply in the vicinity of an enemy. Therefore, it is an important subdivision of airlift operations.*

The USAAS* considered dropping parachutists on Metz, then in Germany, in 1918. The idea was a natural one, and, in the interwar years, Germany and the USSR investigated this vertical envelopment technique. Luftwaffe success with the concept in the spring of 1940 led to serious preparation of the capability within the USAAC* and USAAF.* The USAAF first dropped paratroopers in the second of the two maneuvers of 1941.* The first USAAF battle use was against the French at La Senia airport in Algeria on 7 November 1942. Supply and aeromedical evacuations in North Africa began in the same month. The first large-scale USAAF use of tactical airlift was in the invasion of Sicily in July 1943. More use was made for the invasion of Italy in September.

These early operations were eclipsed by the huge vertical envelopment for Operation Overlord* in June 1944. More than 13,000 paratroopers were dropped, and gliders* were also used. The following day 156 tons of supplies were dropped by parachute from 148 planes. Tactical airlift was also used in the invasion of southern France in August. Then a large airlift was used to supply Lieutenant General George S. Patton's armored blitzkrieg across France. Tactical airlift was a main part of the attempt to cross the Rhine River, called Market,* in September. This was the largest Allied airborne assault, using 5,000 tactical airlift transports* and 2,400 glider sorties involving 35,000 men. The final airborne assault in Europe was a successful crossing of the Rhine near Wesel, Germany, in 1945.

Instead of airborne assault, tactical airlift in the Pacific theater was more logistical. The forbidding terrain of New Guinea* forced heavy reliance upon airlift capabilities from 1942 until the campaign was over in 1944. This reliance continued through the Philippines* campaign from November 1944 to June 1945.

The difficult terrain of the China-Burma-India* (CBI) theater likewise caused emphasis on logistics rather than airborne assault starting in 1942. U.S. Army Lieutenant General Joseph W. Stillwell's drive to retake Myitkyina, Burma, from October 1943 to May 1944, relied on tactical airlift. By April, the tonnage delivered was up to 7,309. Forty-two percent of all tonnage delivered was airdropped, 38 percent was parachuted, and only 20 percent was landed. The tonnages included heavy construction equipment and 155mm artillery. In the Japanese drive to take Imphal, India, from March to June 1944, the USAAF* supported the defenses with 20,000 tons and 12,000 men while continuing to supply 58,000 Allied troops in Burma. The Allied victory drive from October 1944 to May 1945, when Rangoon, Burma, fell, was supported by 155,000 tons delivered by the Tenth Air Force* (10AF) in conjunction with the Royal Air Force's (RAF) Air Command for Southeast Asia.

After World War II,* restricted budgets resulted in unpreparedness of tactical airlift for the demands of the Korean War.* After that conflict began, there was an immediate great demand for airlift. Insatiable demands for supplies by the ground forces and poor land transportation were normal in the first year of the war. Along with other shortages, there were inadequate airfields. This resulted in a heavy reliance upon airdrops. The Combat Cargo Command (CCC) of the Far East Air Forces was established at Ashiya AB, Japan, in August 1950. The CCC flew tactical airlift for the Inchon invasion, the subsequent Eighth Army drive north, the 187th Airborne Regiment's assault on Sukchon, and the deployment of the Fifth Air Force* (5AF). When Red China entered the war in late 1950, CCC C-47s* landed on makeshift runways near Chosin* Reservoir with nearly 300 tons of supplies for entrapped U.S. Marines. Then 4,684 wounded Marines were evacuated. CCC C-119s* airdropped a bridge to enable the Marines to break out with their vehicles. CCC used a fleet that averaged only 210 aircraft, flew 210,343 sorties, and carried 307,804 patients in aeromedical evacuation,* 2,605,591 passengers, and 391,763 tons of cargo. CCC used centralized control of its resources.

By the Vietnam War,* the USAF* had its best tactical airlifter ever, the wonderful C-130.* To manage the tactical airlift, an 834th Air Division was established at Tan Son Nhut* AB, South Vietnam, in 1966. The forces available for tactical airlift in 1968 were 13 C-130, six C-7,* and four C-123* squadrons.* Tactical airlift operations peaked in 1969 at 82,500 tons. C-130 airfields were used as hubs for U.S. Army search-and-destroy actions. Tactical airlift was indispensable for the garrison at Khe Sanh,* South Vietnam, which was supplied by air for 11 weeks in 1968.

In 1990, tactical airlift was the responsibility of the Military Airlift Command* (MAC), and the core of the force was still the classic C-130. USAF airmen nickname tactical airlift airplanes as "trash haulers" and "trash carriers."

References. Primary: John G. Martin, *It Began at Imphal: The Combat Cargo Story*, 1988. U.S. Congress, House, Committee on Armed Services, Research and Development Subcommittee, *The Posture of Military Airlift*, 1975. Secondary: Ray L. Bowers, *Tactical*

Airlift, 1983. Futrell, *Ideas*, 2 vols. Charles E. Miller, *Airlift Doctrine*, 1988. Annis G. Thompson, *The Greatest Airlift: The Story of Combat Cargo*, 1954.

Coy F. Cross II contributed to this essay.

TACTICAL NUCLEAR WEAPONS. *See* nuclear weapons.

TACTICAL OPERATIONS

Tactical operations by an air service are conducted against hostile armed forces and may be done in cooperation with friendly surface or air arms. Cooperation is best effected through a joint headquarters with commanders of equal authority, the Tactical Air Control Center* (TACC). The function is made up of five tasks: air superiority,* interdiction, close air support, tactical airlift,* and reconnaissance.* The second and third tasks are considered to be attack* aviation.

The USAF* considers air superiority to have first priority in tactical operations, because attack, airlift, or reconnaissance cannot be done effectively without control of the air. Air superiority includes both the offensive and defensive. Fighters* conduct both the offensive and defensive roles, while interceptors* can provide air defense against aircraft other than fighters. Fighters may employ fighter escort* and fighter sweeps on the offensive. With fighter sweeps, fighters aggressively seek out and destroy enemy aircraft* in the air and on the ground in an area. Achieving air superiority has the same effect that control of the seas had for sea power before the advent of air power. Over land, it is the equivalent of a ground breakthrough, for it opens the enemy's rear to exploitation so that interdiction, the second priority, can proceed effectively.

Aerial interdiction can be deep in the enemy's rear, or near the battlefield. Interdiction means blockading or isolating the battlefield from resources, be they supplies, reinforcements, communications, or movement. Interdiction with close air support, is siege warfare. Interdiction can be done by fighters or attack planes. Some targets, usually fixed ones such as bridges, can be planned for strikes in advance. In the past, mobile targets, such as trains, vehicles, and men, were found visually by pilots* on sorties called armed reconnaissance, or "armed recce," and then struck. Aircraft such as the E-8* may also find targets for the fighters and attack planes.

The third priority is close air support, or direct support, which is an attack on enemy soldiers engaging or close to friendly troops. This is usually done by fighters or attack planes, but it can also be done by bombers,* usually in mass strikes called "carpet bombing." The reason interdiction takes priority over close support is productivity. Along a battlefront, enemy resources are dispersed, hardened, hidden, and defended to a high degree. For a given effort, results are less than in interdiction.

Interdiction targets, behind a front, are usually much more concentrated as in supply dumps and on trains, exposed when being moved, and less protected and defended. In a sense, interdiction targets are bottlenecks. Thus, for a given effort, more can be accomplished.

Just as an army prefers to exploit the enemy rear through breakthrough rather than make a direct assault on strong points, an air force desires to exploit the softness and weakness of rear areas rather than hit at the enemy's strongest points on the battlefront.

By extension of this reasoning, hitting the economy or military facilities by strategic operations* can be more effective than interdiction. Each element of an economy has optimum-sized facilities for particular tasks. For example, it is most inefficient to refine petroleum or make steel on a small scale. Thus, an economy has bottlenecks in some industries, and they are often difficult to harden, hide, or defend. If one or more industries are essential to a war economy, and there is a bottleneck, maximum effectiveness can be achieved by striking at that point. An enemy's only nonmilitary defense is to disperse the bottleneck operation, creating inefficiency and increased dependence upon transportation. Thus dispersion may create high costs and difficulties, and the shift to transportation can make land or sea communications vulnerable. Sometimes nonindustrial factors, such as food or water, may be more productive targets.

Thus, the rationale for priorities leads to strategic operations, and there is no sharp boundary between it and tactical operations. In addition, strategic and tactical operations, as envisioned by the USAF, exemplify B. H. Liddell Hart's concept of the indirect approach.

References. Futrell, *Ideas*, 2 vols. Richard P. Hallion, *Strike from the Sky: The History of Battlefield Air Attack, 1911–1945*, 1989. Woodford Agee Heflin, ed., *The United States Air Force Dictionary*, 1956. Jeffrey P. Rhodes, "Improving the Odds in Ground Attack," *AF*, November 1986, pp. 48–52. Albert F. Simpson, "Tactical Air Doctrine: Tunisia and Korea," *Air University Quarterly Review*, Summer 1951, pp. 4–20.

See also Coningham, Air Marshall Sir Arthur; doctrine.

TAKHLI ROYAL THAI AIR FORCE BASE

The USAF* started to use this base in south central Thailand in 1962 with F-100s.* It became one of the USAF's main fields in Thailand with the 355th Tactical Fighter Wing (TFW) using F-105s* in 1965. The 355th was inactivated in 1970. In June 1970, the 366th TFW arrived with F-4s,* and it left in November. Other aircraft that had used Takhli included EB-66s (*see* B-66), F-111s,* and tankers.*

References. Primary: Jack Broughton, *Going Downtown: The War against Hanoi and Washington*, 1988. Secondary: Berger, *USAF in SEA*. Robert F. Futrell, *The Advisory Years to 1965*, 1981.

TALBOTT, SECRETARY HAROLD L. (1888–1957)

Third secretary of the Air Force,* from 1953 to 1955, Talbott originated and supported many measures to elevate the personal stature, pay, housing, and other advancements for USAF* members.

Born in Dayton, Ohio, he graduated from Yale University in 1911. He was closely associated with several aviation enterprises, including the Dayton-Wright Company, where he was president and Orville Wright* was vice president. That company produced more aircraft than any other in World War I.* Most of the production was of de Haviland DH-4s.* In 1918, Talbott received a commission as major in the USAAS* and was tasked to manage maintenance and repair of aircraft in France, but the war ended before he assumed his duties. After the war he stayed with Dayton-Wright for five years after it became part of the General Motors Corporation. In the 1930s he served as chairman of the board for North American Aviation, Inc. In World War II* he was director of aircraft production for the War Production Board.

References. American Aviation Publications, *Who's Who in World Aviation—1955*, 1955. DOD/OPI Press Branch, "Harold E. Talbott, Secretary of the Air Force," 1953. DuPre, *USAF Bio*. Jacob Neufeld, *Ballistic Missiles in the United States Air Force 1945–1960*, 1990.

Lloyd H. Cornett, Jr.

TALLY HO. *See* Operation Tally Ho.

TALON. *See* T-38.

TANKER

This is now an aerial refueling* vehicle. It has made possible a global USAF* equipped with high-performance aircraft. The USAF gives tankers the prefix *K* as in KC-135 (*see* C-135).

Tankers were originally conceived as airshow stunts in which a man climbed from one aircraft to another with a five-gallon can of gasoline strapped to his back. The first air-to-air hose refuelings were conducted in 1923. This was followed by the famous endurance flight of the *Question Mark** in 1929. During World War II,* some transports* were used as tankers for cargo purposes only. The USAAF* used stripped CB-24s (*see* B-24), B-29s,* and C-109s, a B-24* variant, to haul fuel over the "Hump"* from India to China. Transports also supplied the fuel for Lieutenant General George S. Patton's armored blitzkrieg across France.

A British company, Flight Refueling Limited, developed a practical method of hose refueling, the probe and drogue,* in the 1940s. This allowed dramatic increases in range and endurance of airborne planes. The USAF and Boeing Aircraft Company teamed to adapt this system to B-29 and B-50* aircraft. This system has also been used for helicopter* refueling by KC-130s (*see* C-130). Subsequently, the Boeing flying boom* was developed. The boom was used on the KB-29P (*see* B-29), KC-97 (*see* C-97), KC-10 (*see* C-10), and KC-135. The Tactical Air Command* (TAC) pursued the probe-and-drogue method, and the Strategic Air Command* (SAC) chose the boom. There is an adapter for the boom to permit refueling of aircraft equipped with a probe. Besides the mechanical means of transferring fuel, an important step in the history of the tanker was the creation of jet-powered refuelers. Until they became available, there was a mismatch in refueling speeds and altitudes between the piston-engine tankers and jet operational aircraft.

References. Alwyn T. Lloyd, *B-29 Superfortress in Detail & Scale*, part 2, "Derivatives," 1987, and *Liberator—America's Global Bomber*, forthcoming. *Seventy Years* *of Strategic Air Refueling 1918–1988*, Office of the Historian, SAC, Offutt AFB, Nebraska, 1990.

Alwyn T. Lloyd

TAN SON NHUT AIR BASE

Located at Saigon, South Vietnam, this base was important to the USAF* during the Vietnam War.* It was the principal airport in the country. USAF personnel first arrived in November 1961. The 2nd Air Division arrived in June 1962 and became the Seventh Air Force* (7AF) in April 1966. From 1966 to 1972, the 834th Air Division was based there. Other principal units included the 315th Air Commando Wing and the 460th Tactical Reconnaissance Wing (TRW). In 1973 the USAF moved out.

References. Berger, *USAF in SEA*. Robert F. Futrell, *The Advisory Years to 1965*, 1981. John Schlight, *The War in South Vietnam: The Years of the Offensive 1965–1968*, 1988.

TARGET-MARKING MUNITIONS

An accurate strike on any target presupposes the ability to identify it. Marker munitions were developed as an aid for the Pathfinder Force* (PFF) in World War II.* Markers consist of bombs,* rockets, artillery shells, or grenades with a filler such as colored smoke, white phosphorus or "Willy Peter," or some other pyrotechnic mixture. Target markers have been used by the PFF, forward air controllers* (FAC), artillery, and ground observers.

References. Berger, *USAF in SEA*. Futrell, *USAF in Korea*. John Schlight, *The War in South Vietnam: The Years of the Offensive 1965–1968*, 1988. Donald K. Schneider, *Air Force Heroes in Vietnam*, 1979.

Philip Long

TARZON. *See* AZON, RAZON, and TARZON.

TASK FORCE ALPHA

This was a targeting analysis unit at Nakhon Phanom* AB, Thailand. The unit checked photographic reconnaissance,* corrected coordinates for mapping errors, and gathered information needed for air missions using Loran navigation. It had great success in rescue* operations. The most famous mission was the exemplary rescue of a crew member from "Bat–21." An EB-66 (*see* B-66) was shot down on 2 April 1972, with the sole survivor being Lieutenant Colonel Iceal E. Hambleton, the navigator.* The rescue evolved into a dramatic 12-day struggle between the successful USAF* and the North Vietnamese.

Movie: BAT-21, 1989.

References. William C. Anderson, *BAT-21*,** 1980. Berger, *USAF in SEA*. Jack Lavalle, *Air War—Vietnam*, 1978. Earl H. Tilford, *Search and Rescue in Southeast Asia, 1961–1975*, 1980.

**This is an account that has been fictionalized partially for security reasons.

Frank L. Goldstein

TAXI DANCER. *See* novels.

TECHNICAL APPLICATIONS CENTER. *See* Air Force Technical Applications Center.

TECHNICAL TRAINING AIR FORCE (TECH TAF)
This named air force* conducted preofficer, basic, and technical training. It was established in April 1951 as part of the Air Training Command* (ATC). It was headquartered at Gulfport, Mississippi, until it was inactivated in 1958. Its contemporaries in the ATC were the Crew Training* and Flying Training* Air Forces.

References. Goldberg, *Hist. USAF*. Ravenstein, *Org. USAF*.

"TEDDY." *See* Roosevelt, President Theodore.

TELEVISION
Television is a highly influential medium, and there have been two successful series about the USAF.* The first, and most significant, was *Twelve O'Clock High*,* the classic story of the USAF. It began in 1964 and ran a few seasons. Robert Lansing first played the lead; then Paul Burke did. The second series was 20 years later after two decades of much antipathy toward the military services. In 1984 there was a resurgence of patriotism in the United States. The new series about the USAF, *Call to Glory*, began in that summer and, obviously, tried to capitalize commercially on the new feelings. The main character was Colonel Raynor Sarnac, played by Craig T. Nelson. The series' plots were laid in the 1960s and expressed the agenda of the rebels of that decade but wrapped in the flag. It was hardly compatible with the true USAF and had inherent contradictions. It ran two seasons, and its schizophrenia probably explains why it was a short-lived success.

Aside from series, television has influenced the status and image of the USAF with its news reports and documentaries. The USAF has been helped by the glamour of aviation but hindered by great ignorance of the service by those in television and other media. Additional hindrances resulted until after the Iraq War* from a general media antipathy to the armed forces. The balance has probably been unfavorable.

References. Martha Bayles, "Super-Dad Joins the Air Force," *The Wall Street Journal*, 13 August 1984, p. 12. "The 40th Anniversary of the USAF," a special issue of *AH*, September 1987, pp. 212–13.

TEMPELHOF CENTRAL AIRPORT AIR STATION

The significance of this German field to the USAF* is that it was one of the primary unloading sites during the Berlin Airlift* of 1948–1949. The Wright brothers* used it for landing in 1908 to demonstrate their airplane to the German military. In 1922 it became a full-time airport and was soon one of the world's busiest. Construction of a gigantic complex was begun before World War II* and never finished. Its plan was unique, designed to resemble an eagle in flight, with the "wings" being a huge overhanging mile-long roof to permit aircraft parking out of the weather. Behind was the bird's "body," a series of administrative buildings and billets. Covered corridors and overhanging walkways connected it all, and there were underground tunnels in the area below the terminal and hangar.

Americans occupied it in July 1945 and replaced its sod strip with pierced-steel planking* (PSP). The PSP could not take the traffic of the airlift. Two new runways were built without interrupting the air bridge operations. By the end of the airlift there were three parallel runways, improved communications, and very high intensity approach lighting. From 1949 to 1990, it was a commercial field although the urban location became increasingly more difficult for operations as · aircraft improved. It had a small USAF presence in those years because Berlin was still a zone of military occupation. Its housekeeping unit, the 7350th Air Base Group, was part of the U.S. Air Forces in Europe* (USAFE).

References. Lowell Bennett, *Berlin Bastion: The Epic of Post-War Berlin*, 1951. "Guide to USAF's Minor Installations," *AF*, May 1990, p. 133. Robert Jackson, *The Berlin Airlift*, 1988. Roberts, *Dir. USAF*. "A Special Study of Operation VITTLES," *Aviation Operations*, vol. 11, April 1949, pp. 2–120.

Roger D. Launius

TENTH AIR FORCE (10AF)

This numbered air force* was activated in 1942 and served in the China-Burma-India* (CBI) theater until 1943. Then it operated in India and Burma until it moved back to China in July 1945. It was inactivated in January 1946 and reactivated in May. It was put in the Air Defense Command (ADC) until 1948 and then moved to the Continental Air Command* (CONAC) where it supervised U.S. Air Force Reserve* (USAFR) and Air National Guard* (ANG) activities. It was inactivated again in 1960. It was reactivated in 1966 and assigned again to the ADC and again inactivated in 1969. It was reactivated in 1976, assigned to the USAFR, and headquartered at Bergstrom* AFB, Texas. In 1990 it was still at Bergstrom with seven wings* under it.

References. "Air Force Reserve," *AF*, May 1990, pp. 112–13. Maurer Maurer, ed., *Air Force Combat Units of World War II*, 1983. Ravenstein, *Org. USAF*. Herbert Weaver and Marrin Rapp, *Tenth Air Force, 1942*, 1977.

TERRY AND THE PIRATES. *See* Caniff, Milton.

TET OFFENSIVE. *See* Khe Sanh, South Vietnam; Vietnam War.

"TEX." *See* Hill, Colonel David L.

TEXAN. *See* T-6.

TEXAS TOWERS

This was the name of radar* platforms constructed in the late 1950s on shoals off the northeast coast of the United States. They got their name because they resembled the oil-well drilling rigs in the Gulf of Mexico. These sea-based platforms, along with airborne early warning (AEW) aircraft and radar-equipped picket ships, were the three elements of the Seaward Extension of the Permanent System* of air defense.

The idea for them originated at the Lincoln Laboratory, a think tank,* in 1952. A study of the picket ships showed they were expensive, were limited to medium-power radars, and did not provide stable platforms even when anchored. The laboratory proposed the 60-by-120 foot platforms, at a cost of $1 million each. Shoal locations between Nova Scotia and New Jersey were suitable for sites, and the platforms would provide coverage seaward for 200 to 300 miles.

In 1953, the USAF* approved five towers shaped as equilateral triangles of 210 feet per side. The first tower was occupied in 1955. Improved coverage by AEW flights caused two proposed towers to be dropped from the program in 1956. The three towers built had crews of 85 to 100 men. In a storm of 15 January 1961, Tower No. 4, 80 miles southeast of New York City, New York, collapsed, claiming 28 lives—14 USAF and 14 contract repair workers. The tragedy, and the advent of automatic long-range input (ALRI) systems on the AEW planes, led to a 1963 decision to inactivate the other two towers.

References. C. L. Grant, "The Development of Continental Air Defense to 1 September 1954," Maxwell AF Base, Alabama, 1957. Thomas W. Ray, "A History of Texas Towers in Air Defense 1952–1964," Aerospace Defense Command History Office, Peterson AFB, Colorado, 1965. Evan McLeod Wylie, "Farewell to the Iron Bastards," *Life*, 26 July 1963, pp. 7–9.

E. Michael Del Papa

TFX. *See* F-111.

THANH HOA BRIDGE

This bridge, spanning the Song Ma River, was a bottleneck in the flow of supplies south out of Hanoi, North Vietnam, to support the aggression against South Vietnam. A rail and road bridge, it was finished in 1964 after a crash construction program. It was built to be sturdy and was 540 feet long, 56 feet wide, and 50 feet above the river. The North Vietnamese named it Ham Rung, or "Dragon's Jaw."

The first USAF* attack* was on 3 April 1965. Other attacks followed, with the bridge made temporarily unusable until repaired. In November, the USAF and U.S. Navy agreed that the area would be attacked by the Navy. The Navy's operations produced similar results, and the enemy built pontoon bridges nearby.

In addition, the enemy concentrated flak* and surface-to-air missiles* (SAM) around the bridge and used MiG fighters* to defend it. A difficulty for the Americans was the weather, which allowed only two to four attacks in some months. On 28 January 1968, the USAF and Navy launched a combined strike with 44 aircraft. Again the bridge remained standing and was only temporarily unusable. On 31 March 1968, President Lyndon B. Johnson* (LBJ) halted all attacks north of the 19th parallel. This protected the bridge for four years, and it was repaired for heavy traffic and was able to channel men and supplies south.

When the North Vietnamese mounted their conventional ground offensive of 30 March 1972, U.S. interdiction resumed as Linebacker* I. By this time, Paveway* I bombs* had been developed. An attack was made with them by the USAF on 27 April 1972, which damaged the bridge. Another strike on 13 May finally dropped the bridge into the river. Until President Richard M. Nixon's bombing halt* of October 1972, repairs and strikes continued.

References. Berger, *USAF in SEA*. Jack Lavalle, *Air War—Vietnam*, 1978.

THINK TANKS

Since World War II,* a new class of corporations has strongly influenced the direction taken by the USAF.* Formally known as Federal Contract Research Centers (FCRC), they are usually called "think tanks." They are independent nonprofit companies that contract with the federal government and do not compete with other types of businesses. Their products are ideas and analyses, which are expected to be objective.

General of the Army H. H. Arnold,* like other USAF officers, fully appreciated the technological basis for aerospace power.* This led him not only to form the Air Force Scientific Advisory Group under Theodore von Karman,* but Project RAND as well. An acronym for *research and development*, RAND was formed in 1946 and was designed to perform the idea parts of those activities. RAND's first study was *Preliminary Design of an Experimental World-Circling Spaceship* (SM-11827) in 1946. At its founding, RAND was an organ of the Douglas Aircraft Company, but the potential conflict of interest in such an arrangement led to a spin-off in 1948. RAND, now a corporate entity itself, relocated to Santa Monica, California.

In the succeeding years, RAND has held contracts with agencies other than the USAF. The studies it has done for the USAF have covered a wide range of topics which have considered political, economic, and social factors, as well as technical ones. A famous study that illustrates this breadth of interest, and which the USAF adopted, recommended greater reliance on aerial refueling* and less on overseas basing.

RAND's success led to the formation of other think tanks. In 1950, General Hoyt S. Vandenberg* asked Dr. James R. Killian, Jr., president of the Massachusetts Institute of Technology (MIT), to design a modern air defense system. The result was Lincoln Laboratory, located at Hanscom* AFB, Massachusetts, and established in 1951. Lincoln's work led to the Semiautomatic Ground Environment* (SAGE) system. By 1958, when the first SAGE center had become operational, Lincoln wished to avoid such close association with system implementation. Yet Lincoln has since continued to work on aerospace defense operations,* including ballistic missile* defense, communications, and sensor technologies.

When Lincoln ended its direct connection with the SAGE system, that work was picked up by a corporation, MITRE, formed for that purpose. The new firm went on from SAGE to work on command and control systems. It has also been involved with the Airborne Warning and Control System* (AWACS), the Joint Tactical Information Distribution System* (JTIDS), and over-the-horizon (OTH) radars.*

A fourth organization, the Aerospace Corporation, was established in 1960. It has provided systems engineering and integration support for ballistic missiles* and other space vehicles. Examples of the latter are the Defense Meteorological and Defense Communications Satellites.

References. Merton E. Davies and William R. Harris, *RAND's Role in the Evolution of Balloon and Satellite Observation Systems and Related U.S. Space Technology*, R-3692-RC, 1988. Alexander H. Flax, "High Tech Trailblazers," *AF*, August 1984, pp. 66–70. Futrell, *Ideas*, vol. 1. Jacob Neufeld, *Ballistic Missiles in the United States Air Force 1945–1960*, 1990. Bruce L. Smith, *The Rand Corporation: Case Study of a Non-profit Advisory Corporation*, n.d.

E. Michael Del Papa contributed to this essay.

THIRD AIR FORCE (3AF)

This numbered air force* originated as the Southeast Air District in 1940. It was redesignated the 3AF in 1941 and headquartered for five years in Tampa, Florida. It trained units, crews, and individuals for bombers,* fighters,* and reconnaissance.* It conducted antisubmarine operations from 1941 to 1942. In 1946 it was assigned as a troop carrier, or tactical airlift,* unit to the Tactical Air Command* (TAC) and inactivated the same year. It was reactivated in 1951 and assigned to the U.S. Air Forces in Europe* (USAFE). Its headquarters was in South Ruislip, England. It moved to RAF Mildenhall,* England, in 1972. In 1990, it had six wings* assigned to it.

References. Robert Jackson, *Strike Force: The USAF in Britain since 1948*, 1986. Maurer Maurer, ed., *Air Force Combat Units of World War II*, 1983. Ravenstein, *Org. USAF*. "United States Air Forces in Europe," *AF*, May 1990, pp. 93–95.

THIRTEENTH AIR FORCE (13AF)

This numbered air force* was nicknamed "The Jungle Air Force" because of its island-hopping in World War II* and because its headquarters never was located in a metropolitan area during the war. It was activated on New Caledonia in January 1943. In the following two and one-half years, its units operated from more than 40 islands, using B-24s* and P-38s,* and participated in campaigns in New Guinea,* Solomon Islands, Admiralty Islands, Morotai, and the Philippines.

Located briefly on Okinawa* Island after the war, its headquarters moved to Clark* Field, Philippines, where it has remained. During the Korean War,* the 13AF served as a logistics hub and kept several bases thereafter in the Republic of China (ROC) on Taiwan. The 13AF had responsibility for all USAF operations in the Vietnam War* until 1965, when the Seventh Air Force* (7AF) was reactivated. At its zenith, the 13AF had seven combat wings,* nine major bases, 11 smaller installations, and 31,000 personnel. The 13AF and 7AF had an unusual arrangement. The 13AF had responsibility for the logistics and administration for the bases in Thailand, while the 7AF directed those units' operations; this arrangement was criticized.

Since 1976, the 13AF has been based only in the Philippines. Its mission is to provide tactical operations* to support U.S. goals in the west southern Pacific Ocean area (WESTPACSOUTH) from the east coast of Africa to Hawaii and to train Pacific Air Forces* (PACAF) aircrews.

References. Maurer Maurer, ed., *Air Force Combat Units of World War II*, 1983. "Pacific Air Forces," *AF*, May 1990, pp. 81–82. Ravenstein, *Org. USAF*. David L. Rosmr, *An Annotated Pictorial History of Clark Air Base: 1898–1986*, 13AF Office of History, 1986.

David L. Rosmer

30MM GUN. *See* GAU-8.

THOR

This missile, designated SM-75 and later PGM-17, was a single-stage, liquid propellant, intermediate-range ballistic missile* (IRBM). It was designed as a stopgap to meet pressing military needs while the first generation of large intercontinental ballistic missiles (ICBM) was being developed. After a brief deployment abroad, it served a long and useful career as a booster for space vehicles.

In late 1955, there was concern about the USSR's development of IRBMs. Thor was seen as an interim quick-fix, using state-of-the-art technology of the Atlas* ICBM. The USAF's* Ballistic Missile Division chose the Douglas Aircraft Company as its prime contractor. Thor's first flight was in 1957. After a spectacularly successful test launch series, it became one of the United States's most reliable missiles. In 1958 an agreement was reached with Britain, and overseas deployment began immediately. By late 1959, some were in place in England, with Royal Air Force (RAF) insignia and manned by RAF crews. However, the USAF kept custody of the nuclear warheads.* By the end of 1963, the last squadron* was inactivated.

Thor was selected for a role in the U.S. space program. In 1958 it boosted the USAF Thor-Able I launch vehicle on the first lunar probe mission. Thereafter it boosted many National Aeronautics and Space Administration* (NASA) space vehicles. It served the USAF in testing nosecones, guidance systems, and other ICBM programs.

Characteristics: engine, Rocketdyne LR-79 of 150,000 pounds thrust; length,

61 feet; diameter, 8 feet; gross weight, 55 tons; top speed, 11,000 miles per hour; range, 1,650 miles.

References. *From Snark to Peacekeeper: A Pictorial History of Strategic Air Command Missiles*, Office of Historian, SAC, Offutt AFB, Nebraska, 1990. Julian Hartt, *The Mighty Thor: Missile in Readiness*, 1961. Jacob Neufeld, *Ballistic Missiles in the United States Air Force 1945–1960*, 1990. Polmar, *SAC*. Space and Missile Systems Organization, *Chronology: 1954–1979*, 1980.

Raymond L. Puffer

THOUSAND PLANE RAID, THE. *See* movies.

"THREE-FINGER JACK." *See* Ryan, General John D.

THULE AIR BASE

This facility is on the northwest coast of Greenland and is an Air Force Space Command* (AFSPACECOM) base. It was activated in 1952. In 1990 the main unit was the 1012th Air Base Group, and it had a Ballistic Missile Early Warning System* (BMEWS) radar.*

References. Christopher Gierlich, "Arctic Sentinels," *AF*, December 1989, pp. 94–96. "Guide to Major Air Force Installations Worldwide," *AF*, May 1990, p. 132. Roberts, *Dir. USAF*.

THUNDERBIRDS

This is the popular name for the USAF* Air Demonstration Squadron; a unit with the mission of assisting in morale, recruitment, and retention, while showing professional competence to enhance public confidence in the USAF.

Originally it was the 3600th Air Demonstration Team, formed at Luke* AFB, Arizona, in 1953. The Thunderbirds were successors to earlier teams, which started with Captain Claire L. Chennault's* "Three Men on a Flying Trapeze" flying P-12s.* Chennault's planes were tied together with short cables and flew as one. The Thunderbirds' airshows consist of about 35 maneuvers flown in 30 minutes. They perform variations on the basic aerobatics of loops, rolls, and Immelmanns done solo and in formation. In addition, they fly high-speed passes. The acts in their performance are done between 200 and 15,000 feet altitude. The team usually puts on 85 shows a year and has performed in each state and more than 50 foreign countries. Over the years, the aircraft used by the team have been F-84Gs,* F-84Fs, F-100Cs,* F-100Ds, F-105s,* F-4Es,* T-38As,* and F-16s.* The team was based at Nellis* AFB, Nevada, in 1990.

References. Martin Caidin, *Thunderbirds!* 1961. Jon R. Donnelly, "Remounted and Ready," *AF*, September 1984, pp. 196–200. Michael B. Perini, "Curtain up on the 1983 Thunderbirds," *AF*, February 1983, pp. 52–54. U.S. Air Force Fact Sheet 87–41, "Thunderbirds," October 1987.

See also Four Horsemen, The.

THUNDERBIRDS. *See* movies.

THUNDERBOLT. *See* A-10; F-47.

THUNDERBOLT

This was an excellent documentary movie produced by the USAAF* in 1944–1945 and released in 1947. It describes the activities of the men and F-47* Thunderbolts of the 65th Fighter Squadron operating out of Alto AB, Corsica. The squadron* was conducting attack* operations in Italy, and the commentary, scenes, and photography were superb.

References. James H. Farmer, *Celluloid Wings*, 1984. Bruce W. Orriss, *When Hollywood Ruled the Skies: The Aviation Film Classics of World War II*, 1984.

THUNDERBOLT II. *See* A-10.

THUNDERCHIEF. *See* F-105.

THUNDERING JETS. *See* movies.

THUNDERJET. *See* F-84.

THYNG, BRIGADIER GENERAL HARRISON R. (1918–1983)

Thyng is one of only six men in the world who became an ace* in both piston- and jet-engine fighters.* From Laconia, New Hampshire, he graduated from the University of New Hampshire in 1939 and immediately became an aviation cadet.* He became a pilot* and officer in 1940. In World War II,* he commanded the 309th Fighter Squadron flying Spitfires. He scored victories over six Germans, one Frenchman, and one Italian. In Europe he flew 162 combat sorties. He became a colonel at age 26 and commanded the 413th Long Range Fighter Group flying fighter escort* in F-47s* for B-29s* out of Ie Shima, Okinawa.* He shot down one Japanese. In the Korean War,* he commanded the 4th Fighter Wing and shot down five MiG-15s in 114 combat sorties. Some say the character of Colonel Dutch Imil in James Salter's *The Hunters** reminds them of Thyng. In 1966, as a brigadier general, he flew a few sorties in the Vietnam War,* testing missiles. Thyng retired from the USAF* that year. He ran for the U.S. Senate but lost. He was president of a junior college and the American Fighter Aces Association.

References. John L. Frisbee, "A Thyng of Valor," *AF*, January 1989, p. 111. Gurney, *5 Down*. Hess, *Aces Album*.

TIBBETS, BRIGADIER GENERAL PAUL W., JR. (1915–   )

Tibbets was given what was probably the most important task ever for a man of his grade when he was a lieutenant colonel. He organized and trained the 509th Composite Group and then dropped the first nuclear weapon.*

He joined the USAAC* in 1937 and became a pilot* in 1938. As commander of the 340th Bomb Squadron he flew an operational tour* in B-17s* in the Eighth Air Force* (8AF). In September 1944, he was tasked to command the USAAF's* operations and training for the use of the atomic bomb;* he selected Wendover Airfield, Utah, as the test and training site. From Wendover, the 509th went to Tinian Island in the Marianas.* On 5 August 1945, Tibbets, flying the B-29* *Enola Gay*,* made the strike on Hiroshima,* and it went just as he had planned it. After the war, he was commander of the 308th Bomb Wing from 1956 to 1959 and of the 6th Air Division from 1959 to 1961. He retired in 1966.

Movies: The Beginning or the End, 1947. *Above and Beyond*, 1953. *Enola Gay*, 1980.

References. Primary: Paul W. Tibbets, Jr., "Training the 509th for Hiroshima," *AF*, August 1973, pp. 49–55. Paul W. Tibbets, Jr., et al., *The Tibbets Story*, 1978. Secondary: C&C, vol. 5. DuPre, *USAF Bio*. Gordon Thomas and Max Morgan Witts, *Enola Gay*, 1977.

TIDAL WAVE. *See* Ploesti, Romania.

TIGER. *See* F-5.

TIGER HOUND. *See* Steel Tiger and Tiger Hound Operations.

TINIAN. *See* Marianas Islands.

TINKER, MAJOR GENERAL CLARENCE L. (1887–1942)

Tinker was the first U.S. general lost in action in World War II,* and Tinker AFB,* Oklahoma, was named in his honor. He was the highest-ranking officer of Indian ancestry, a one-eighth Osage, in the U.S. Army.

He entered military service as a third lieutenant in the Philippine Constabulary and took flight training* in 1921. He earned the Soldier's Medal for saving the life of a comrade after their plane crashed and burned. During the 1930s, he commanded fighter* and bomber* units. Shortly after Pearl Harbor,* he became commander of the air forces in Hawaii and was ordered to reorganize the air defenses of the central Pacific. On 7 June 1942 he led a formation of LB-30s, an early B-24* type, to strike Japanese ships retreating toward Wake Island, and his plane fell out of control into the sea.

References. James L. Crowder, *Osage General: Major General Clarence L. Tinker*, Office of History, Tinker AFB, Oklahoma, 1987. DuPre, *USAF Bio*.

James L. Crowder

TINKER AIR FORCE BASE

In 1941 some farsighted businessmen and civic leaders in Oklahoma City, Oklahoma, acquired land and offered it to the federal government. It became Tinker AFB, a logistics depot now under the Air Force Logistics Command* (AFLC). Of the base's land, 54 percent was donated by the community. It became the largest single employer in Oklahoma. It was named to honor Major General Clarence L. Tinker,* who died in action near Wake Island in 1942.

In World War II,* it repaired B-17s* and B-24s* and outfitted B-29s.* In the Korean* and Vietnam* Wars, it performed comparable logistics support. In recent years it had the Oklahoma Air Logistics Center managing ten types of aircraft, four missile types, and 16 engine families. It has overhauled more jet engines than any other facility in the free world and has more than 300,000 stock items. It is also the home of the 28th Air Division with E-3As.*

References. "Guide to Major Air Force Installations Worldwide," *AF*, May 1990, p. 132. Mueller, *AFB*. Roberts, *Dir. USAF*. *Tinker Air Force Base: A Pictorial History*, Office of History, Tinker AFB, Oklahoma, 1982.

James L. Crowder

TITAN

This was the United States's second and largest intercontinental ballistic missile* (ICBM). It was developed nearly in tandem with the Atlas* and greatly exceeded the other in size, accuracy, and sophistication. Until it was retired in 1986, 54 Titan IIs stood on strategic alert in silos in Arizona, Arkansas, and Kansas. Titan variants are heavy space launch vehicles expected to serve into the next century.

The Ballistic Missile Division of the USAF's* Air Research and Development Command* (ARDC), now the Air Force Systems Command* (AFSC), supervised its development by the Martin Marietta Corporation. The project had been recommended by the Strategic Missiles Evaluation Committee, headed by Dr. John von Neumann, in 1955. It was to be a two-stage ICBM, big enough to carry the largest possible payload over the greatest distance and taking advantage of the rapidly unfolding missile technology coming from the Atlas. Titan I's first successful test launch was in 1959.

The liquid-fueled Titan Is were deployed in silo-lift launchers in California, Colorado, Idaho, South Dakota, and Washington. In only four years, Titan I was replaced by Titan II. Titan II used an inertial guidance system and a storable propellant mixture. This allowed instantaneous launch from an underground silo, eliminating the need to raise the missile to the surface and then fuel it before liftoff. A new fuel mixture of 50 percent by weight of hydrazine and unsymmetrical dimethylhydrazine and an oxidizer of nitrogen tetroxide increased thrust. A Titan II so fueled was first launched in 1962.

Characteristics (Titan II): first-stage engine, Aerojet General LR87 rocket of 430,000 pounds thrust; second-stage engine, Aerojet General LR91 rocket of 100,000 pounds thrust; length, 103 feet; diameter, 10 feet; weight, 330,000 pounds; payload, RV Mk-6 of about 10 megatons; range, 9,300 miles.

References. David A. Anderton, *Strategic Air Command: Two-thirds of the Triad*, 1974. Jacob Neufeld, *Ballistic Missiles in the United States Air Force 1945–1960*, 1990. Polmar, *SAC*. Ernest G. Schwiebert, *A History of the U.S. Air Force Ballistic Missiles*, 1964. USAF Office of Public Affairs, "Titan II LGM-25C Fact Sheet," June 1983.

Raymond L. Puffer

TM-61 MATADOR AND MACE

The TM-61A and TM-61C Matador was an air-breathing, turbojet-powered, surface-to-surface cruise missile* built by the Glenn L. Martin Company for the Tactical Air Command* (TAC) on a 1945 USAAF* requirement. The unsuccessful first flight was in 1949. TM-61s cost $60,000 each and were deployed to Sembach* AB, West Germany, from 1955 to 1962. These missiles had a guidance system that limited them to 250 miles and that could be jammed.

New guidance systems were adopted, resulting in the TM-61B Mace, also designated as the TM-76A. Mace also differed from the Matador in having shorter, folding wings, longer fuselage, and more weight. Mace had more than its share of problems in development, production, engine, and guidance systems. It had a final cost of $250,000 each. A contract for the Mace was made in mid-1954, but it was renegotiated many times for frequent design changes. For example, one change was the adoption of two guidance systems, so it had an interchangeable nose section that used either a Goodyear Aircraft Company guidance system labeled Automatic Terrain Recognition and Navigation (ATRAN) or the AC Spark Plug firm's Inertial Guidance System (IGS). ATRAN compared radar* photographs with earth features to orient itself and was difficult to jam. IGS had prelaunch-programmed navigation and could fly more than 1,000 miles with an evasive course and no contact with its launch point. It, too, was difficult to jam. The TM-61B was deployed to Europe from 1959 to 1966 and to Okinawa* Island from 1961 to 1969.

Characteristics (TM-61B): engines, General Electric J33-A-41 of 5,200 pounds thrust and a launch booster of 97,000 pounds thrust; span, 29 feet; length, 47 feet; height, 10 feet; gross weight, 18,750 pounds; payload, 3,000 pounds; top speed, Mach 0.85 at 42,000 feet; range, 1,288 miles at high altitude.

References. Frederick I. Ordway III and Ronald C. Wakefield, *International Missile and Spacecraft Guide*, 1960. Bernard J. Termena, "History of the Matador and Mace Guided Missiles 1951–1957," Air Materiel Command Historical Study No. 317, unpub. ms. Kenneth B. Werrell, *Evolution of the Cruise Missile*, 1985.

Lloyd H. Cornett, Jr.

TOKSAN DAM. *See* Korean irrigation dams target system.

TOKYO, JAPAN. *See* Doolittle raid on Tokyo; strategic campaign against Japan.

TOM-TOM

Officially project MX-1018, this was a fighter* range-extension idea. During World War II,* the USAAF* soon learned in Europe that fighter protection was essential to bomber* penetration. After the war some fresh ideas to provide fighter range were evaluated, because the fuel-hungry jets could not use piston-engine methods satisfactorily. One idea led to the XF-85 Goblin, a jet fighter designed to be carried as a parasite of a bomber. The XF-85 had a hook to attach it to its mother ship. A B-29* was developed with a trapeze to catch and hold the XF-85's hook in tests of the idea. It was intended if successful, to use the F-85 with the B-36.* This was reminiscent of the U.S. Navy's F9C Sparrowhawk fighter carried within the airships USS *Los Angeles, Akron,* and *Macon.* Capturing the XF-85 on the trapeze was not fully successful in the tests and the F-85 was abandoned. However, the idea led to the GRB-36F and GRF-84F (*see* F-84) fighter conveyor* (FICON) system, which was used to a limited degree in 1955.

Another idea, Tom-Tom, or "the floating wing," was conceived by Dr.-Ing. Richard Vogt, former head of design of Germany's Abteilung Flugzeugbau der Schiffswerft Blohm und Voss. His designs included the BV 141, BV 222, and BV 238. For Tom-Tom in 1953, an ETB-29A and two F-84Bs were modified to grasp each other at their wingtips. Thus the fighters were extensions of the bomber's wings. In addition, a B-36 was adapted to carry a pair of F-84Fs. Tests showed that Vogt's calculations for fuel economy were correct, but wingtip vortices made the release of the fighters extremely dangerous. In one test, an F-84B flipped over onto its back and struck the ETB-29A, requiring all three planes to land. A similar oscillation problem occurred with the B-36, and the project was canceled. The best idea was aerial refueling.*

References. Primary: Richard Vogt, *Weltumspannende Memoiren eines Flugzeug-Konstrukteurs,* n.d. Secondary: Jay Miller, "Project Tom-Tom," *Aerophile,* December 1977, p. 161. Swanborough, *US Mil. Airc.*

Alwyn T. Lloyd

"TONY." *See* McPeak, General Merrill A.

"TOOEY." *See* Spaatz, General Carl A.

TORCH. *See* Operation Torch.

TORNADO. *See* B-45.

TORREJON AIR BASE

Near Madrid, Spain, this U.S. Air Forces in Europe* (USAFE) base was activated in 1957. It is named for the nearby village of Torrejon de Ardoz. In 1990 it had the headquarters of the Sixteenth Air Force* (16AF) and the 401st Tactical Fighter Wing (TFW) flying F-16s.* Its mission was to support the North Atlantic Treaty Organization's* (NATO) Southern Region. Torrejon is scheduled to close in 1991.

References. "Guide to Major Air Force Installations Worldwide," *AF,* May 1990, p. 132. Roberts, *Dir. USAF.*

TOSS BOMBING. *See* Low-Altitude Bombing System.

TOTAL FORCE POLICY

Total Force Policy integrates the active and reserve forces into a homogenous whole so that the latter comprise the initial and primary augmentation of the active forces in contingencies or war. The impetus for this policy came out of the Vietnam War.* The military services had then been forced to rely upon Selective Service for augmentation, because President Lyndon B. Johnson* (LBJ) refused to mobilize the reservists. In 1966, in the midst of the war, the USAF* devised a modified total force concept incorporating the U.S. Air Force Reserve* (USAFR) and Air National Guard* (ANG) into daily operations.

In 1970, seeking to cut costs, Secretary of Defense (SECDEF) Melvin R. Laird directed the concept be applied to all aspects of planning, programming, manning, equipping, and employing the reserves. In 1973, SECDEF James R. Schlesinger elevated the concept to a policy of full integration. He directed the service secretaries to produce Selected Reserve units that would meet the readiness standards for wartime and declared that strong management and high readiness levels in the Selected Reserve were among the Department of Defense's (DoD) highest priorities. A DoD review of the policy in 1975 found the application of it in the USAF was so successful that no additional guidance needed to be made. The USAF incorporated the policy into a revision of USAF Basic Doctrine in 1975.

References. Primary: Air Force Manual 1–1, "United States Air Force Basic Doctrine," 15 January 1975. *Air Reserve Forces 2000: Supplement to Air Force 2000, Air Power Entering the 21st Century*, 1983. Melvin R. Laird memo, "Support for Guard and Reserve Forces," 21 August 1970. James R. Schlesinger memos, "Readiness of the Selected Reserve," 23 August 1973, and "Total Force Program Guidance," 2 June 1975. Secondary: Charles Joseph Gross, *Prelude to the Total Force: The Air National Guard 1943–1969*, 1985. "The Total Force," A special issue of *AF*, October 1981, pp. 1, 5, 7, 20, 28, 35, 39, 45, 52, 60, 71.

Gerald T. Cantwell

TOUR. *See* operational tour.

TOURS, FRANCE

This base was the home of the 2nd Aviation Instruction Center from November 1917 until shortly after the Armistice. As such it was a main factor in the U.S. Army air effort in World War I.*

The first U.S. cadets arrived at Tours as early as August 1917, where they hoped to begin training at the French flight training* school then in operation. However, little training was conducted until the following spring, primarily because the French aircraft were obsolete and fragile. In January 1918 a school for observers* was opened, but again progress was slow because the French required most of the facility for their flight training and the observation aviation* planes were unsuited to U.S. purposes. The observation school proceeded more smoothly after suitable aircraft arrived—Breguets,* Salmsons,* and U.S.-built de Haviland DH-4s.*

During the spring of 1918, a school in basic flight instruction was established to accommodate a large number of cadets who had arrived in the winter with no previous instruction. By the end of the spring, 839 of these cadets had completed their training, and the facilities were then devoted to other schools, including gunnery, radio, and photography. In August a further expansion enabled Tours to accommodate more than 900 officers and 2,500 men. By the end of the war, 555 observers had been trained and another 426 were under instruction.

References. James J. Hudson, *Hostile Skies: A Combat History of the American Air Service in World War I*, 1968. Maurer Maurer, ed., *The U.S. Air Service in World War I*, 4 vols., 1978–1979. Lucien H. Thayer, *America's First Eagles: The Official History of the U.S. Air Service, AEF (1917–1918)*, 1983.

See also Issoudon, France.

D. K. Vaughan

TOWARD THE UNKNOWN. *See* movies.

TR-1. *See* U-2.

TRADITION

The U.S. Army airmen's struggle for independence led them to be upstarts against tradition. In those years of rebellion, with debates over doctrine* and rapid technological progress, it could almost be said the airmen's only tradition was to deny tradition. With independence, the rebelliousness to service traditions ended and USAF traditions have become more conventional.

A tradition was established as early as World War I* of decorating aircraft, such as the "Hat-in-the-Ring" painted on the fuselages of the 94th Aero Squadron* planes. This tradition flourished in World War II,* mostly taking the form of nose art* which originated with the USAAF.* Nose art has been suppressed at times, but it revived in the 1980s because it was seen as a factor in morale.

The main effort in the years of struggle was rebellion centered on the uniform.* The airmen sought distinction and independence in uniform when denied it in organization. For example, a prime device for distinction by officers was in the visored hat. It was unrealistic to keep the stiffening grommet in the hat when wearing a radio headset. The answer was to remove the grommet; this led to efforts to wear the hat that way when away from the flight line. During World War II, the hat was also artificially aged, and, without the grommet, was revered as having a "50-mission crush." World War II, in addition, gave birth to a proud tradition that has continued, that the USAF* has never been turned back from a target because of enemy action.

Reference. "The 40th Anniversary of the USAF," a special issue of *AH*, September 1987, pp. 199–205.

TRAINING. *See* Air Training Command; flight training.

TRANSPORT

This type of plane is indispensable for a global, mobile, hard-hitting projection of air power. A pipeline of spare parts, munitions, support equipment, and people is required to sustain air warfare. Transports provide this logistical support rapidly through airlift operations* and tactical airlift.* Airlift means not only speed but lower inventories and related costs. The United States has long triumphed and led the world in transport design and manufacture, a synergic product of the USAF,* U.S. aerospace industry,* and airlines.* The transport well demonstrates these bases for aerospace power.*

Transports have a large fuselage able to carry either cargo or people. Early military transports were adaptions of standard commercial aircraft, many with big doors added to the side of the fuselage for cargo access. The main example of them was the C-47.* Transports in the USAF have had the designator *C* for "cargo." The first cargo plane specifically designed as a military transport was the USAAF's* C-82.* Its innovative features were a truckbed-height cargo floor and a fuselage end loading ability. The C-82 became primarily a developmental design. Its more successful successor, the C-119,* performed yeoman service in the Korean War.*

The USAAF appreciation of the value of possessing many transports resulted in commandeering airliners and the conversion of entire factories to produce more of them for military use during World War II.* In addition, Pan American World Airways and Transcontinental & Western Air (TWA) did logistical support for the USAAF and pioneered air routes around the world. Consolidated Vultee Aircraft Corporation (Convair) established its Consairways for operations in the Pacific Ocean area. The "Hump"* was the USAAF's great airlift in the war. After the war, the Berlin Airlift* (1948–1949) was a masterpiece of airlift. In 1953, the U.S. Air Forces in Europe* (USAFE) began its Air Logistic Service, operated both by USAFE and allied air forces.

Under contract, civil airlines supplemented the USAF's Korean* and Vietnam* airlifts. In 1954, in the United States, the USAF Logistic Airlift (Logair) began operations. The Civil Reserve Air Fleet* (CRAF), started in 1951, was first activated for the Iraq crisis of 1990–1991.

References. Peter W. Brooks, *The Modern Airliner: Its Origins and Development*, rev. ed., 1982. Higham, *Air Pwr*. Charles E. Miller, *Airlift Doctrine*, 1988. Ronald Miller and David Sawers, *The Technical Development of Modern Aviation*, 1970. U.S. Congress, House, Committee on Armed Services, Research and Development Subcommittee, *The Posture of Military Airlift*, 1975.

Alwyn T. Lloyd

TRAVIS AIR FORCE BASE

Located east of Fairfield, California, this base was established in 1941 and activated in 1943. It was originally named Fairfield-Suison Army Air Base but was redesignated in 1950 in honor of Brigadier General Robert F. Travis, who was killed that year in a B-29* accident. It is a Military Airlift Command* (MAC) base. It has been used since its activation mostly for airlift operations* to the Pacific area and has had a large aerial port operation for this purpose. Since 1958 it has been the headquarters for the Twenty-Second Air Force* (22AF), which manages airlift to the Pacific area and Asia. It also has had, since the 1950s, the 60th Military Airlift Wing. The 60th is the only USAF* unit with squadrons* of both C-5* and C-141* transports.

References. "Guide to Major Air Force Installations Worldwide," *AF*, May 1990, p. 132. Mueller, *AFB*. Roberts, *Dir. USAF*.

Roger D. Launius

TRENCHARD, MARSHAL OF THE ROYAL AIR FORCE LORD HUGH M. "BOOM" (1873–1956)

Trenchard has been called the father of the Royal Air Force (RAF). He was the first chief of the Air Staff of the RAF, commander of the Independent Force RAF, and commander of the predecessor of the RAF, the Royal Flying Corps (RFC). Of importance to the USAF,* he had a lasting influence on the U.S. service.

He was hard-hitting and had the affectionate nickname of "Boom" which came from his voice. He learned to fly at his own expense only a few days before his 40th birthday. He commanded the RFC in France during most of the years through 1917. He never became a skilled pilot but was tireless in administration and command. He was callous about the lives of his aircrews, and the resultant wastage was immortalized in the 1938 movie *Dawn Patrol*.

In retaliation for the bombardment of London and some other English cities by German zeppelins and bombers,* the British government in the spring of 1918 decided upon strategic operations* of its own. The result was the formation of the Independent Force RAF commanded by Trenchard. The Independent Force accomplished all he said it would, although he was given only four of the 60 squadrons he requested. The Independent Force never had more than ten squadrons. The Force went into action in June. By the war's end it had dropped 540 tons of bombs,* flown 12,000 hours, and destroyed 150 enemy aircraft in the air. It lost 111 machines. There were plans to give Trenchard the 60 squadrons in 1919. Brigadier General William Mitchell* strongly supported Trenchard's operations, and General John J. Pershing* had begun to appreciate the Independent Force. It is likely the USAAS* would have supported the effort in 1919.

References. William E. Barrett, *The First War Planes*, 1960. Barry D. Bowers, *Strategy without Slide Rule*, 1976. James J. Hudson, *Hostile Skies: A Combat History of the American Air Service in World War I*, 1968. Neville Jones, *The Origins of Strategic Bombing*, 1973. Alan Morris, *First of the Many*, 1968.

James J. Hudson

TRIAD

This word describes the U.S. nuclear weapon* strategic operations* deterrent made up of three "legs," or forces. Two are the Strategic Air Command's* (SAC) bombers* and intercontinental ballistic missiles* (ICBM). The third is the U.S. Navy's fleet of ballistic missile submarines. When fission bombs* were large and heavy, only SAC's B-29s* could deliver nuclear weapons. The development of compact thermonuclear weapons made it economic to incorporate them into missiles in useful numbers, and both land- and submarine-based missiles were developed to add to the certainty of deterrence. When using all three systems, or the triad, they (1) increase an enemy's problem in locating U.S. forces, (2) complicate through dispersal the timing and effectiveness of an enemy first strike, (3) force the enemy to prepare more complex defensive reactions, and (4) reduce the risk of one system becoming obsolete. The disadvantages are possible duplication of the forces needed and higher costs.

References. David A. Anderton, *Strategic Air Command: Two-thirds of the Triad*, 1974. Futrell, *Ideas*, vol. 2. Bill Yenne, *S*A*C: A Primer of Modern Strategic Airpower*, 1981.

TROJAN. *See* T-28.

TROOP CARRIER. *See* tactical airlift.

TROUBLING OF A STAR. *See* novels.

TRUMAN, PRESIDENT HARRY S (HST) (1884–1972)
The 33rd president, HST respected air power and was sympathetic to the aspirations of the USAAF* for independence. He also wanted unification of the armed forces. It is possible that he was an indispensable ingredient in creating the USAF.*

On 19 December 1945, he proposed that the armed forces be placed in a single department and that air power receive parity with land and sea services. This message specifically suggested the U.S. Navy keep its shipborne and water-based air arms and asked for universal military training (UMT). Most opposition came from the Navy, which feared for its future. However, in June 1946, in negotiations with HST, the Navy agreed to an independent USAF and a single department in exchange for keeping land-based air power in the naval air arm. By January 1947, Secretary of War Robert Patterson and Secretary of the Navy James V. Forrestal* had agreed on a new defense structure, and HST accepted it although it had less change than he desired. HST signed the National Security Act of 1947* and issued Executive Order 9877* in July 1947, and a separate USAF came into being in September.

References. "The 40th Anniversary of the USAF," a special issue of *AH*, September 1987, pp. 176–84. Futrell, *Ideas*, vol. 1. Herman S. Wolk, "The Birth of the US Air Force," *AF*, September 1977, pp. 71–72, 75–78, and "The Establishment of the United States Air Force," *AF*, September 1982, pp. 83–84, 87.

See also presidential airlift.

TRUMAN'S MESSAGE TO CONGRESS OF 19 DECEMBER 1945. *See* Truman, President Harry S.

"TUBBY." *See* Westover, Major General Oscar.

TUNNER, GENERAL WILLIAM H. (1906–1983)

Tunner and the concepts and management of airlift operations* will always be associated. Called "Mr. Airlift," he led the "Hump"* and Berlin* Airlifts and was commander of the Military Air Transport Service (MATS).

He graduated from the U.S. Military Academy (USMA) in 1928 and went to flight training.* In 1942, the Air Transport Command (ATC) was formed with Tunner as the commander of the Ferrying Division. He built it into an efficient delivery system of 50,000 people. Two of his innovations were the Women Airforce Service Pilots* (WASP) to fly airplanes from the factories to a staging area, and a flying safety program patterned after insurance company practices to investigate and prevent aircraft accidents. The flying safety program became a pattern for other USAAF* commands and was especially important to the "Hump" operations. Tunner assumed command of the India-China Division and the "Hump" Airlift in August 1944. His management doubled the tonnage and reduced the accident rate to less than 10 percent of what it had been and improved living conditions and morale.

The 1948 Berlin Airlift was a month old when he became commander of the Combined Airlift Task Force* (CATF). He began to organize for an extended operation. He refined loading and unloading procedures, planned regular maintenance* and overhauls, and scheduled flights until the airlift resembled an efficient conveyor belt hauling food, coal, and other needs to the determined Berlin people. On Easter 1949, Tunner staged the "Easter Parade," an all-out effort for 24 hours to achieve the greatest tonnage possible in a safe operation. His C-54s* carried an amazing 12,941 tons of coal that day into the blockaded city. The Soviets announced the end of their failed blockade a short time later.

During the Korean War* he helped establish the Combat Cargo Command (CCC) for tactical airlift,* and it was the only true supply line to the quickly assembled United Nations (UN) forces. During the first massive Red Chinese offensive, the CCC airlifted a huge portable bridge to help 20,000 Marines escape a trap at the Chosin Reservoir,* besides other airlift aid to them. Tunner pioneered the ideas of modern aeromedical evacuation* in World War II* and perfected the practices in Korea.

Tunner made some of his greatest contributions to airlift during his tenure as commander of MATS from 1958 to 1960. Congressional budget cutters, other USAF commands trying to protect their interests, and civil airlines all sought to reduce airlift. Tunner fought to keep MATS' capability. To emphasize his belief that the United States needed more and not less airlift, he conceived a dramatic joint exercise with the U.S. Army. In "Operation Big Slam," 21,030 soldiers flew from the continental United States (CONUS) to Puerto Rico and back, proving the United States needed more airlift capability. The exercise helped win congressional support for a larger, jet strategic airlifter, the C-141.* Tunner retired in 1960.

References. Primary: William H. Tunner, *Over the Hump: The Story of General William H. Tunner, the Man Who Moved Anything Anywhere, Anytime*, 1985. Secondary: C&C, vol. 7. Futrell, *Ideas*, 2 vols., and *USAF in Korea*.

Coy F. Cross II

TURKESTAN INCIDENT. *See* Broughton, Colonel Jacksel M.

TURN THE TIGERS LOOSE. *See* novels.

TUY HOA AIR BASE
This field was on the coast of South Vietnam in the upper middle third of the nation. In late 1965 the USAF* decided it needed more airfields, and Tuy Hoa was picked as one site. The AB was built by Walter Kidde Constructors, Inc., under USAF contract in 275 days after approval and without a cost overrun. Its principal unit, the 31st Tactical Fighter Wing (TFW) with F-100s,* moved onto it in December 1966. The 31st departed Tuy Hoa in October 1970.

References. Berger, *USAF in SEA*. John Schlight, *The War in South Vietnam: The Years of the Offensive 1965–1968*, 1988.

TWELFTH AIR FORCE (12AF)
This numbered air force* was activated at Bolling* Field, District of Columbia, in 1942 and moved to England and from there to the Mediterranean area for Operation Torch.* It stayed there until inactivation in August 1945. It was reactivated at March* Field, California, and was assigned to the Tactical Air Command* (TAC) until 1948. Then it was reassigned to the Continental Air Command* (CONAC) at Brooks* AFB, Texas, and tasked to serve the U.S. Air Force Reserve* (USAFR) and Air National Guard* (ANG). It was discontinued in 1950. In 1951 it was organized again at Wiesbaden, West Germany, and assigned to the U.S. Air Forces in Europe* (USAFE). It moved to Ramstein* AB, West Germany, in 1953. In 1958 it moved to Waco, Texas, absorbing the Eighteenth Air Force* (18AF) and was assigned again to TAC. It moved to Bergstrom* AFB, Texas, in 1968. In 1990 it was still at Bergstrom and had five air divisions* and five separate wings* under it.

Movie: Thunderbolt, 1945.

References. Maurer Maurer, ed., *Air Force Combat Units of World War II*, 1983. Ravenstein, *Org. USAF*. Kenn C. Rust, *Twelfth Air Force Story—In World War II*, 1975. "Tactical Air Command," *AF*, May 1990, pp. 88–90.

TWELVE O'CLOCK HIGH
This is perhaps the best novel* about the USAF.* In it, Beirne Lay, Jr.,* and Sy Bartlett tell the story of the revival of a losing bomber* group* through an effective commander's leadership. The story is based upon actual events in two bomb groups in England in World War II* and the commander, Colonel Frank

A. Armstrong, Jr.* A highly successful movie* of the same name followed the book and starred Gregory Peck. It was nominated for four Oscars and won two. A long-running television* series, again with the same name, made its debut in 1964. The lead was first played by Robert Lansing, who was followed by Paul Burke.

References. James H. Farmer, *Celluloid Wings*, 1984. "The 40th Anniversary of the USAF," a special issue of *AH*, September 1987, pp. 207–8. Brent L. Gravatt and Francis H. Ayers, Jr., "The Fireman: *Twelve O'Clock High* Revisited," *AH*, September 1988, pp. 204–8. Bruce W. Orriss, *When Hollywood Ruled the Skies*, 1984. David K. Vaughan, *The Literature of Flight*, 1982.

TWENTIETH AIR FORCE (20AF)

This numbered air force* was the first U.S. unit to achieve the goal of a global strategic operations* organization under the direct control of an airman, General of the Army H. H. Arnold.* It was activated in April 1944. Some of its combat units moved from the United States to India and China in the summer and operated against Japan, Formosa, Thailand, and Burma. In the same year, other units moved from the United States to the Marianas* Islands. In 1945, those units based in India also moved to the Marianas. From there the 20AF conducted the strategic campaign against Japan* and dropped nuclear weapons* on Hiroshima* and Nagasaki, Japan. The 20AF's headquarters moved from Washington, D.C., to Harmon Field, Guam, in the Marianas in July 1945. After World War II,* the 20AF did not move until 1949 when it went to Kadena* AB, Ryukyu Islands. It was assigned to the Pacific Air Command in December 1945, which became the Far East Air Forces (FEAF). At the beginning of the Korean War,* it conducted operations but was later changed to an air defense and logistical support organization. It was inactivated in 1955.

References. Primary: H. H. Arnold, *Global Mission*, 1949. Curtis E. LeMay, *Mission with LeMay: My Story*, 1965. Curtis E. LeMay and Bill Yenne *Superfortress: The Story of the B-29 and American Air Power*, 1988. Secondary: C&C, vol. 5. Maurer Maurer, ed., *Air Force Combat Units of World War II*, 1983. Ravenstein, *Org. USAF*.

20MM GUNS

This size, about .80-caliber, is a world standard. The USAF* and its antecedents have used three basic types, the M-1 to M-24, M-39, and M-61.* The U.S. Army began testing a model from the Société Française Hispano-Suiza in 1938, but it took four years of modifications before the M-3 version emerged as a reliable belt-fed gun. By that time, the USAAF* was well satisfied with the Browning* M-2 .50-caliber machine gun, and the M-3 to M-24 never served more than a minor role. The M-39 was a single-barreled, four-chambered revolver cannon developed from the German Mk213C of 1945. Its high rate of fire, 1,800 rounds per minute, suited the USAF needs, and it armed some post–Korean War aircraft: the B-57,* F-100,* and F-101.* The standard today is the M-61, a six-barreled Gatling gun style.

References. George M. Chinn, *The Machine Gun*, 1st ed., 1951, and 5th ed., 1987.

Philip Long

TWENTY-FIRST AIR FORCE (21AF)

The 21AF has always been an important airlift unit. This numbered air force* began as the 23rd Army Air Forces (AAF) Ferrying Wing in June 1942 at Presque Isle, Maine, assigned to the AAF Ferrying Command. In February 1944, it became the North Atlantic Wing of the Air Transport Command (ATC). It was redesignated as the North Atlantic Division in June. Again redesignated, it became the Atlantic Division in September 1945 when it moved to Fort Totten, New York.

When the USAF* was created it was assigned to the Air Transport Service (ATS). In October 1947, it moved to Westover Field, Massachusetts. In June 1948 its assignment was to the new Military Air Transport Service (MATS). It moved to McGuire* AFB, New Jersey, in 1955, and was redesignated as a named air force, the Eastern Transport Air Force, in 1958. In 1966, it became the 21AF. In 1990 it was still at McGuire, and was assigned to the Military Airlift Command* (MAC). Its mission was both strategic airlift operations* and tactical airlift.*

References. "Military Airlift Command," *AF*, May 1990, pp. 76–78. Ravenstein, *Org. USAF*.

TWENTY-SECOND AIR FORCE (22AF)

The 22AF has always had an important airlift mission. This numbered air force* was established as the Domestic Division of the Air Corps Ferrying Command in December 1941, based in Washington, D.C. It was redesignated as the Domestic Wing of the Air Corps Ferrying Command in February 1942. In the next month it was the Domestic Wing of the Army Air Forces Ferry Command, which was changed to be the Army Air Forces Ferrying Command. Three months later it became the Ferrying Division of the Air Transport Command (ATC). In February 1943, it moved to Cincinnati, Ohio. In February 1946 it was redesignated the Continental Division of the ATC. Then it was discontinued in October. It was organized in July 1948 under the Military Air Transport Service (MATS) at Kelly* AFB, Texas. It moved in June 1958 to Travis* AFB, California, and was redesignated as a named air force, the Western Transport Air Force. It became the 22AF in January 1966.

In 1990 its mission was both strategic airlift operations* and tactical airlift* under the Military Airlift Command* (MAC); it was still headquartered at Travis.

References. "Military Airlift Command," *AF*, May 1990, pp. 76–78. Ravenstein, *Org. USAF*.

TWENTY-THIRD AIR FORCE (23AF)

The 23AF is the last numbered air force* organized, and its mission involves some of the last developed aerial tasks: special operations, rescue,* and some specialized airlift functions. It was established in February 1983 under the Military Airlift Command* (MAC) and was headquartered at Scott* AFB, Illinois.

Special operations were once called air commando operations, or shock units, usually intended for hit-and-run raids against an enemy. USAF* special operations began as air support operations for guerrillas in World War II.* The concept was expanded when the 1st Air Commando Group was formed under Colonel Philip G. Cochran* to support British Brigadier Orde Wingate's raids into Burma. After the war, the function was discontinued until 1951. Then it was restarted and called air resupply and communications (ARC), but was discontinued again in 1956.

President John F. Kennedy's* (JFK) concerns about guerrilla war caused another revival in 1961 in the USAF as the 4400th Combat Crew Training Squadron. A detachment of this squadron* became the Farm Gate* operation in the Vietnam War.* In 1962, the USAF's effort was expanded with the establishment of the Special Air Warfare Center at Hurlburt* Field, Florida. One product of this work was the development of the gunship,* an idea conceived for the C-47* by USAF pilot* Captain Ronald W. Terry. Commando and infiltration missions were further aided by the development of the MC-130E (*see* C-130) Combat Talon aircraft. This type was fitted with a yoke on the nose and some other equipment to snatch up agents or downed crewmen from behind enemy lines. The Son Tay prison raid* and the Israeli raid on Entebbe, Uganda, illustrate special operations work.

In the niggardly defense atmosphere of the Carter administration, special operations got a low priority. However, the debacle of the Iran hostage rescue mission* showed the need to revitalize such U.S. forces. Under President Ronald Reagan* the USAF formed the 23AF and established the U.S. Special Operations Command (USSOCOM), a unified command,* in 1987. In 1990, the 23AF was headquartered at Hurlburt and had five wings* and the USAF Special Operations School.

References. James L. Cole, Jr., "USAF Special Operations Forces: Past, Present, and Future," *AH*, December 1980, pp. 218–26. "Military Airlift Command," *AF*, May 1990, pp. 76–78. Jeffrey P. Rhodes, "Any Time, Any Place," *AF*, June 1988, pp. 68–75. P. A. Towle, *Pilots and Rebels: The Use of Aircraft in Unconventional War 1918–1988*, 1989.

TWINING, GENERAL NATHAN F. (1897–1982)

Twining was the fourth chief of staff of the Air Force,* from 1953 to 1957, and he was the first USAF* officer to be chairman of the Joint Chiefs of Staff (JCS), serving from 1957 to 1960. For two decades after his retirement, he voiced opinions on defense issues, including support for an antiballistic missile system (ABM) and an objection to the United States's prolonged involvement in the Vietnam War.* He was inducted into the National Aviation Hall of Fame in Dayton, Ohio, in 1976.

Born in Monroe, Wisconsin, he graduated from the abbreviated course at the U.S. Military Academy in 1918 and became a pilot* in 1923. His interwar experience was in fighter* and attack* aviation, and he attended the Air Corps Tactical School* (ACTS). Beginning in 1942, he had a series of war commands in the Pacific and European theaters, including the commands of three numbered air forces.* In February 1943, his B-17* was shot down in the Pacific and he spent six days on a life raft before rescue.* His wartime experience, including directing raids on Ploesti,* Romania, and seeing nuclear weapon* devastation, gave him skills for joint operations and a belief in strategic operations.* In 1950 he became vice chief of staff of the USAF.*

While he was chief of staff, President Dwight D. Eisenhower's* emphasis on strategic operations, called the New Look, gave Twining the funds for conversion of the USAF to jet aircraft. He also instituted programs to develop ballistic missiles.* He supported the use of nuclear weapons to help the French at Dien Bien Phu, French Indochina. His agreement with Eisenhower on strategic operations and his ability to compromise led to his chairmanship of the JCS. However, he resigned because he could not accept the new ideas called ''flexible response.''

References. Primary: Interviews with John T. Mason (1965) and the Air Force Academy Faculty (1967), Albert F. Simpson Historical Research Center, Maxwell AFB, Alabama. Nathan F. Twining, *Neither Liberty nor Safety*, 1966. Secondary: DuPre, *USAF Bio*. John L. Frisbee, ed., *Makers of the United States Air Force*, 1987. Futrell, *Ideas*, vol. 1.

Budd A. Jones, Jr.

TYNDALL AIR FORCE BASE

This Tactical Air Command* (TAC) field is near Panama City, Florida. It was activated in 1941 and named for First Lieutenant Frank B. Tyndall, a World War I* fighter* pilot* who died in the crash of his P-1* in 1930. In World War II,* the base conducted gunner* training. After the war it was used for training interceptor* crews and aircraft controllers. In 1967 the Air Defense Weapons Center was established on it. In 1990 it still had the center* and had the 325th Tactical Training Wing (TTW) using F-15s.* Its units train pilots, maintenance* personnel, and weapons controllers.

References. ''Guide to Major Air Force Installations Worldwide,'' *AF*, May 1990, p. 132. Mueller, *AFB*. Roberts, *Dir. USAF*.

U

U-2

This is one of the most controversial airplanes to serve with the USAF.* The designation *U* for "utility," was used to disguise the real purpose of the airplane. The Central Intelligence Agency (CIA) used it until stopped by President Dwight D. Eisenhower* in 1960, after Gary Francis Powers' U-2 had been shot down near Sverdlovsk, USSR. It did photographic, electronic, and communications intelligence gathering by overflying the USSR and its satellite countries. The USAF has used it for weather and other reconnaissance,* upper atmospheric particulate and gas sampling, mapping, and geodetic and natural resource surveying. The U-2 was important for reconnaissance in the Cuban crisis of 1962,* the Vietnam War,* and the Middle East.

The Lockheed Corporation began work on it in 1954, and the design evolved from the concept of an F-104* with exceptionally long wings. It was to be launched from a dolly and land on skids, but the lightweight landing gear installed for training was so successful it became standard. The first flight was reportedly in 1955. The first production was for the CIA and then for the Strategic Air Command* (SAC) and for research and development (R&D) at Edwards* AFB, California. The latter were used for tracking and recovery of space capsules and R&D for equipment for Midas and Samos earth satellites.

A complete redesign, in 1966, incorporating many improvements, was designated the U-2R. It was sometimes redesignated as TR-1 to avoid the politically unacceptable "U-2." The TR-1 was designed for standoff reconnaissance at high altitudes, using the Precision Location Strike System (PLSS) which finds enemy radars* and can direct attacks* on them by aircraft or missiles.

Characteristics (U-2A): engine, Pratt & Whitney J57-P31 turbojet of 11,200 pounds thrust; span, 80 feet; length, 50 feet; height, 13 feet; gross weight, 20,000 pounds; top speed, 528 miles per hour; ceiling, over 70,000 feet; range, more than 4,600 miles. Contrary to popular opinion, pilots* did not shut off the engine and glide to save fuel.

References. Primary: Richard M. Bissell, Jr., "Origins of the U-2," *Air Power History*, Winter 1989, pp. 15–24. Robert Gaskin, "Flying the U-2," *AF*, April 1977, pp. 66–71. Secondary: Swanborough, *US Mil. Airc.* Susan H. H. Young, "Gallery of USAF Weapons," *AF*, May 1990, p. 147.

Joe M. Jackson

U-16 ALBATROSS

When the Albatross amphibian first flew in 1947, the USAF* soon ordered some. It had been developed, starting in 1946, by the Grumman Aircraft Engineering Corporation for the U.S. Navy. It entered USAF service in 1947 as a rescue* aircraft in the Military Air Transport Service's (MATS) Air Rescue Service. It was first designated the SA-16, with the *S* standing for search and rescue and the *A* standing for amphibian. In 1962, with the adoption of a common service system, the *A* was dropped from SA-16As, and HU-16 became the new designation for SA-16Bs. The SA designation led to its nickname of "Slobbering Albert." A dependable and versatile aircraft, the Albatross served the USAF for 26 years, a testament to its usefulness. The USAF bought 302.

Characteristics (HU-16): engines: two Wright R-1820–76As of 1,425 horsepower each; span, 97 feet; length, 61 feet; height, 26 feet; gross weight, 32,000 pounds; top speed, 236 miles per hour at 18,800 feet; range, 3,220 miles.

References. Primary: Robert Joseph Powers, "Flying the SA-16A Albatross," *AH*, December 1985, pp. 252–60. Secondary: René J. Francillon, *Grumman Aircraft since 1929*, 1989. Swanborough, *US Mil. Airc.*

U-BOAT BASES AND YARDS

The Army Air Forces Antisubmarine Command* (AAFAC) was not the only involvement of the USAAF* in the war against the German Navy. A diversion from USAAF strategic operations* was mounted against the U-boat bases and yards which did not achieve its goals.

The U-boats were highly effective in 1942, and the VIII Bomber Command, later redesignated the Eighth Air Force* (8AF), was ordered in October to hit German submarine bases. Major General Ira C. Eaker* believed that ten bomber* groups* could eliminate five U-boat bases on the Bay of Biscay, but Lieutenant General Carl A. Spaatz* thought the bombers could better be used against strategic operations targets. There was knowledge that the bombs* of the USAAF would not penetrate the U-boat pen roofs. However, officials expected that damage to the rest of the bases would achieve the same goal. Despite a long and intense struggle, the campaign was evaluated as a failure.

The day after the order to bomb, Lorient-Keroman, France was hit. The results were not encouraging because three bombers of the 90 dispatched were lost. In November, bombing was tried from lower altitudes, 7,500 to 10,000 feet, in an attempt to improve results. However, three more bombers were lost and 22 damaged out of 31 trying the tactic on St. Nazaire, France. In addition, bomb accuracy was poor. This tactic was not tried again. A return to altitudes of 17,500 to 22,000 feet resulted in better bombing and in bomber losses of 5 percent, which was acceptable. The raids in October and November proved disruptive to the German Navy, with much work moved to inside the pens. No raids were made in December, however, and the bases were repaired. Strikes were resumed in January 1943 and continued until June.

Assessments of the results of the entire campaign were pessimistic at the end of 1943. It became apparent that bombing the bases and yards was much less effective than aerial operations against the U-boats at sea. These assessments were confirmed after the war. It is possible that raids in greater strength might have improved results. That is considered unlikely, for the pens, which contained most of the facilities needed for U-boat maintenance, were impervious to U.S. bombs of the time. Nor could B-17s* carry the larger British bombs.

References. C&C, vol. 2. DeWitt S. Copp, *Forged in Fire: Strategy and Decisions in the Air War over Europe 1940–1945*, 1982. Roger A. Freeman, *The Mighty Eighth: Units, Men and Machines*, 1970.

UBON AIR BASE

In 1962, the USAF* moved radar* equipment to this field in Thailand. It provided a location for excellent coverage of the air over Cambodia, Laos, and South Vietnam. Ubon also provided a forward base for College Eye's* EC-121D (*see* C-121) airborne radar and control aircraft. The 8th Tactical Fighter Wing (TFW), flying F-4s,* was organized at the field in December 1965 and stayed there until 1974.

References. Berger, *USAF in SEA*. Jack Lavalle, ed., *Air War—Vietnam*, 1978.

UDORN ROYAL THAI AIR FORCE BASE

This Thai field was close by the Laotian capital of Vientiane. In 1964, the deputy commander of the 2nd Air Division (2AD) of the Thirteenth Air Force* (13AF) moved in to command USAF* operations in Thailand and Laos. By 1965, a squadron* of F-105s* arrived to operate in the Laotian panhandle. The 432nd Tactical Reconnaissance Wing (TRW), flying RF-101s (*see* F-101) and RF-4s (*see* F-4), was organized at Udorn in September 1966. The commander of the 2AD became the deputy commander of both the Seventh Air Force* (7AF) and the 13AF. He reported operationally to the 7AF and logistically and administratively to the 13AF. The USAF moved out in 1973.

References. Berger, *USAF in SEA*. John Schlight, *The War in South Vietnam: The Years of the Offensive 1965–1968*, 1988.

UNIFICATION BILL OF 1946 (S2044)

This bill, sometimes called the Common Defense Act, was in response to President Harry S Truman's* (HST) message to Congress of 19 December 1945. He said air power had responsibilities equal to land and sea power, and administrative parity was necessary. The bill did not pass, but it proved to be an important step toward independence for the USAF.*

The bill was drafted in April 1946 by the Senate Committee on Military Affairs, under Senator Elbert D. Thomas. It provided for a Department of Common

Defense, under a civilian secretary. The three armed forces would each have a civilian secretary and a military commander. There would be a military chief of staff of common defense superior to the service commanders. In addition, there would be a Council of Common Defense, a National Security Resources Board, and a Central Intelligence Agency. There were no provisions for either an Army or Navy air force.

The Senate Committee on Naval Affairs objected to a single "super secretary" with sole access to the president, to a chief of staff of common defense, and to the omission of a Navy air force. The differences were so great that the bill could not pass, but HST would not tolerate continuation of the old system and went back to negotiating a solution. He succeeded with the National Security Act of 1947* which formed the basis for the current defense establishment.

References. "The 40th Anniversary of the USAF," a special issue of *AH*, September 1987, pp. 169–71. Goldberg, *Hist. USAF*. Herman S. Wolk, "The Establishment of the United States Air Force," *AF*, September 1982, pp. 79, 83–84.

See also Executive Order 9877, 27 July 1947; Key West and Newport Conferences of 1948.

UNIFIED COMMAND

This form of organization is composed of more than one U.S. armed force and may also include the forces of an allied power. The secretary of defense (SECDEF) directs the unified commands with the advice of the Joint Chiefs of Staff (JCS). Two USAF* major commands* (MAJCOM) are part of unified commands. The U.S. Air Forces in Europe* (USAFE) is part of the European Command (EUCOM), and the Pacific Air Forces* (PACAF) is part of the Pacific Command (PACOM).

References. Woodford Agee Heflin, ed., *The United States Air Force Dictionary*, 1956. Edward N. Luttwak, *The Pentagon and the Art of War: The Question of Military Reform*, 1985. Ravenstein, *Org. USAF*.

UNIFORMS

The uniforms worn by the antecedents of the USAF* were as important as those of the modern air force to those in service. Lacking the desired independence, the airmen tried to distinguish themselves through dress.

The first distinguishing element was a series of aviator's badges, introduced in 1913. During World War I,* the fliers adopted the open lapel coat and abandoned the choke collar. They were copied in this by the rest of the U.S. Army in 1925, and the airmen were no longer so different in dress. A cadet uniform for flight training* provided another opportunity and a slate gray uniform was adopted. Aside from insignia, the airmen again felt the need to look independent. The Sam Browne sword belt was dropped in favor of a leather belt. As the airmen were again copied by the rest of the Army, cloth replaced the leather. The cloth belt was sometimes replaced by a cloth strip sewn around the coat and the buckle abandoned. The visored cap was made as floppy as officers dared, and flying clothes were worn as much as possible away from the flight line. The importance of these measures is shown in the current revival of the USAAC's* popular A-2 leather flying jacket for USAF aircrews.

When independence was achieved, a search began for a unique uniform. Some Army officers predicted it would be garish and more suited to musical comedy than a military service. The actual proposal was conservative. It was basically the Army uniform in a new blue shade, copied from and close to the Royal Air Force (RAF) color, and with some different insignia. For example, oxidized silver was substituted for Army brass. General Hoyt S. Vandenberg* made the final decisions in detail on the proposed uniform. It was approved and accepted by the secretaries of the Army and Navy in 1949. It had replaced Army uniforms by 1951. The changes since then have been minor and have paralleled some of those of the other services.

References. Bruce D. Callander, "They Wanted Wings," *AF*, January 1991, pp. 80–83. "The 40th Anniversary of the USAF," a special issue of *AH*, September 1987, pp. 199–205.

See also tradition.

UNITED NATIONS COMMAND (UNC) IN KOREA

The UNC was essentially a U.S. Army command from July 1950 to 1 January 1953, when it gained a joint staff. The land war orientation of this supervisory command until 1953 inhibited the use of air and naval power by the USAF* and U.S. Navy.

When the United Nations (UN) decided to fight North Korean aggression, the question of command had to be resolved. The United States proposed that it be the UN's executive agent in Korea, and this was approved by the UN Security Council on 7 July 1950. The next day, President Harry S Truman* (HST) named General of the Army Douglas MacArthur as the commander in chief (CIN-CUNC). MacArthur established the UNC on 24 July. Army General Mark W. Clark succeeded Army General Matthew B. Ridgeway as CINCUNC on 28 April 1952. Clark soon believed the structure of the staff was inadequate. In August he noted that the Korean War* had shifted from a land to an air war. The land effort had failed to annihilate the enemy or gain a negotiated settlement and was just holding ground. Clark, determined to reorganize the top, put a new staff into operation on 1 January 1953, with 91 Army, 48 USAF, and 43 Navy officers. This improvement came too late to influence the war greatly, and the UNC still suffered from a lack of unity between USAF and Navy air efforts.

The truly biggest change was in the presence of Clark himself, who not only changed the staff but sought to use air power more vigorously to force the enemy to terms with strategic operations* campaigns against the Korean electrical power target system* and Korean irrigation dams target system.* It was the latter that appears to have done the job.

Reference. Futrell, *USAF in Korea*.

UNMANNED AERIAL VEHICLES (UAV)

UAVs are as old as World War I,* and the ideas for them are even older. The possibility of eliminating aircrews offers tantalizing advantages, especially in saving lives and cutting costs. UAVs should be ideal for "dangerous, dirty, and dull" tasks. They have been called "flying bombs," "cruise missiles,"* "standoff weapons," and "remotely piloted vehicles" (RPV). Currently, the USAF* uses the terms *RPV* and *UAV*, but *UAV* should be the term of the future, as it is the most general.

In World War I an attempt was made with the Army-Kettering Bug of 1918. It was developed by Charles F. Kettering, inventor of the automobile self-starter and later a vice president of General Motors Corporation. Others also tried, but the technology of the time would not work satisfactorily. In World War II,* the USAAF* tried the Aphrodite* radio-controlled worn-out airplanes. But it was the Luftwaffe that built the first practically designed UAV, the V-1. By the Vietnam War,* technological progress enabled the USAF to fly 3,400 RPV sorties over Southeast Asia (SEA), but the results were mixed. The Israeli air force had more success in their wars of 1973 and 1982 with U.S.-built UAVs, but desert conditions are highly favorable for their use because of few clouds.

The practicality of UAVs depends heavily upon avionics and the computer state of the art. Continuous and great progress in these fields since World War II has kept increasing the potential for UAVs. The principal missions for UAVs are seen to be bombing, suppressing aerospace defense* systems, communications relay, reconnaissance,* decoys, and target drones. They may make one-way or round-trips. Currently UAVs are considered close-range if they operate up to 20 miles; short-range, for up to 200 miles; and medium-range for up to 450 miles. Today they do not show they can displace manned vehicles, but they may do some tasks better and thus complement aircrewed missions.

The principal RPV that has been in service with the USAF is the BQM-34 Firebee, made by the Teledyne Ryan Aeronautical Company. The BQM-34 was developed in the late 1950s and more than 6,000 have been used for research and as targets. In development for the USAF and U.S. Navy by Teledyne Ryan is a medium-range UAV, designated UAV-MR as an unmanned air reconnaissance system (UARS). It is intended for either air or ground launching. Its first flight was in 1988, and it is scheduled for service beginning in fiscal year 1994.

Characteristics (BQM-34A): engine, General Electric J85-GE-7 turbojet of 2,450 pounds thrust; span, 13 feet; length, 23 feet; diameter, 3 feet; launch weight, 2,500 pounds; top speed, 690 miles per hour at 6,500 feet; operating altitude, 20 to over 60,000 feet; range, 796 miles. UAV-MR: engine, Teledyne CAE 382–10 turbofan; span, 11 feet; length, 18 feet.

References. James W. Canan, "On the Horizon: Unmanned Aerial Vehicles," *AF*, October 1988, pp. 84–88, 91–92. John J. Fialka, "Toy Soldiers, No, but Model Planes and Such Are Military Idea Whose Time May Have Come," *The Wall Street Journal*, 29 November 1989, p. A18. Kenneth P. Werrell, *The Evolution of the Cruise Missile*, 1985. Susan H. H. Young, "Gallery of USAF Weapons," *AF*, May 1990, p. 160.

UPPER HEYFORD. *See* RAF Upper Heyford.

URGENT FURY. *See* Grenada incident.

USAAC. *See* U.S. Army Air Corps.

USAAF. *See* U.S. Army Air Forces.

USAAS. *See* U.S. Army Air Service.

USAF. *See* U.S. Air Force.

USAFA. *See* U.S. Air Force Academy.

USAF AIR DEMONSTRATION SQUADRON. *See* Thunderbirds.

USAFE. *See* U.S. Air Forces in Europe.

USAFR. *See* U.S. Air Force Reserve.

U.S. AIR FORCE (USAF)

The three decades-long dream of the U.S. Army airmen was realized on 18 September 1947, when the USAF came into being. In the 43 years to 1990, the service evolved as world politics and technology changed, but the basic mission has remained unchanged.

The USAF began with a functional structure devised in the USAAF* through General Carl A. Spaatz* in anticipation of independence. It had 14 major commands* (MAJCOM), five of which still exist today with the same names: Air Training Command* (ATC), Strategic Air Command* (SAC), Tactical Air Command* (TAC), Air University* (AU), and U.S. Air Forces in Europe* (USAFE). Three changed substantially and have new names: Air Materiel Command (AMC) into Air Force Logistics Command* (AFLC), Air Transport Command (ATC) into Military Airlift Command* (MAC), and Far East Air Forces (FEAF) into Pacific Air Forces* (PACAF). The six MAJCOMs that became obsolete in status or organization have been the Air Defense Command (ADC), Bolling Field Command, Air Proving Ground Command,* Alaskan Air Command* (AAC), Caribbean Air Command, and Seventh Air Force* (7AF). The other MAJCOMS of 1990 that reflect changes and were created over the years are the Air Force Communications Command* (AFCC), Air Force Space Command* (AFSPA-CECOM), Air Force Systems Command* (AFSC), and Electronic Security Command* (ESC).

In 1947 there were 305,827 people in the USAF. This increased in peace and the Korean War* to a high of 977,593 in 1953, and then receded to 814,213 in 1960. Another war, the Vietnam War,* raised it to 904,759 in 1968. Another decline to 557,969 came in 1980, followed by a rise to 608,199 in 1986. In 1990 it was 545,000 and was expected to decline below this level with the possible end of the Cold War.* With the same fundamental mission throughout its existence, it appears there has been too much turbulence and instability for the efficient use of personnel in years extending over about 1.5 times a person's military career.

In 1947 the USAF had about 25,000 aircraft, but in 1990 only 6,860. With the Total Force Policy,* it should be noted that the U.S. Air Force Reserve* (USAFR) had 529 aircraft and the Air National Guard* (ANG) had 1,749 aircraft in 1990. There has been a huge improvement in the productivity of individual aircraft during the intervening years. In the Berlin Airlift* of 1948–1949, 697.5 million ton miles were flown. In the airlift for the Iraq crisis of 1990–1991,* 1.67 billion ton miles were flown from August through November. This is an increase of 2.4 times as much in a little over one-third the time.

There is no sign of the end either of war or of technological progress despite the premature declarations in Congress in 1990 that history had ended with the Cold War. A view back of 43 years shows titanic change, and more is to be expected. The USAF should be able to continue to adapt, if it is not made too small. In 1990, its officer force had 1.45 percent with doctoral and professional degrees, 43.6 percent with master's degrees, and 54.9 percent with baccalaureate degrees. Its enlisted force had 3.4 percent with baccalaureate or higher degrees and 59.8 percent with some college work.

References. David A. Anderton, *History of the U.S. Air Force*, rev. ed., 1989. "The 40th Anniversary of the USAF," a special issue of *AH*, September 1987, pp. 146–220. Futrell, *Ideas*, 2 vols. Goldberg, *Hist. USAF*. "State of the Force: The 1990 USAF Almanac," *AF*, May 1990, pp. 37–160.

U.S. AIR FORCE ACADEMY (USAFA)

The USAFA is a direct reporting unit* (DRU) and is located near Colorado Springs, Colorado. Its mission is to provide cadets with the education, character, and motivation for a leadership career in the USAF.*

After the USAF became independent, a board of civilian and military educators met to study the academy needs of the new service. They reported this need could best be met by a new academy, and President Dwight D. Eisenhower* authorized one in 1954. The first class of 306 cadets entered in July 1955, at a temporary location at Lowry* AFB, Colorado. In August 1958, the current complex was completed. The first class graduated in 1959. In 1964, Congress authorized an expansion of the USAFA from 2,529 to 4,417 cadets. In 1975, Congress authorized women to attend and they entered in 1976. Appointments to the USAFA can be made by a congressional sponsor or by meeting eligibility requirements in other competitive methods.

The USAFA has nearly 600 on its faculty, most of whom are USAF officers. One-fourth have doctoral degrees. The core curriculum is made up of basic science, engineering, humanities, and social sciences. The four years for a cadet averages 167 semester hours. There is also military education that includes military organization, drill, ethics, honor, physical training, the USAF, communication, and military thought and operations. There are also courses in pilot* training, navigation, parachuting, survival, escape, evasion, and resistance. By June 1988, it had 21,600 graduates, and about 70 percent were still in the service. The class of 1959 had contributed 14 second-generation graduates. Honor code scandals occurred in 1965, 1972, and 1984. These have been the USAFA's greatest periods of trial.

References. Paula Lee Potts, "The U.S. Air Force Academy: Aiming for Excellence," *The Retired Officer*, June 1989, pp. 42, 44–45, 46, 48–49. Roberts, *Dir. USAF*. "United States Air Force Academy," *AF*, May 1990, p. 120. U.S. Air Force Fact Sheet 88–29, "United States Air Force Academy," December 1988. Bill Wallisch, "Four Pillars of Excellence," *AF*, April 1984, pp. 94–97.

U.S. AIR FORCE ACCOUNTING AND FINANCE CENTER (AFAFC)

This separate operating agency* (SOA) has the responsibility for pay service to USAF* military personnel, for accountability for all USAF appropriated monies, for assistance in the accounting and finance tasks of other USAF units, and for control of funds for foreign military sales. The center* opened in 1951, a result of difficulties encountered in initially relying on U.S. Army support. At first it handled only finance, but the accounting function was included in 1956. The center is located at Lowry* AFB, Colorado.

References. Primary: E. W. Rawlings, "The Air Force Finance Service," *AH*, March 1983, pp. 50–51. Secondary: "Air Force Accounting and Finance Center," *AF*, May 1990, p. 98. Roberts, *Dir. USAF*. U.S. Air Force Fact Sheet 86–31, "U.S. Air Force Accounting and Finance Center," September 1986.

U.S. AIR FORCE BAND

This band is stationed at Bolling* AFB, District of Columbia, and is one of 20 USAF* bands that provide official musical support. The bands are spread geographically to get optimum coverage, and 18 are located in the United States. The earliest known band to support an antecedent of the USAF was in France in September 1917. It had 14 members and its instruments had been bought with its lieutenant's own money.

References. Napoleon B. Byars, "From Valley Forge to Gabriel," *AF*, December 1984, pp. 74–77. U.S. Air Force Fact Sheet 88–2, "Air Force Bands," February 1988. *See also* Miller, Major (Alton) Glenn.

U.S. AIR FORCE HISTORICAL RESEARCH CENTER (AFHRC)

Collocated with the Air University* (AU) at Maxwell* AFB, Alabama, the AFHRC is the repository for USAF* historical documents. This center* is a primary source for historical information about the USAF, and it offers a variety of historical services to government agencies and the public. This includes providing research facilities for professional military education students, the faculty, and visiting scholars.

The center's collection was begun during World War II* as part of the service's historical program. In 1949, the Air Historical Office moved with the collection from Washington, D.C., to Maxwell to support the newly formed AU. At one time it was named the Albert F. Simpson Historical Research Center. Renamed the Historical Division, it remained part of AU until July 1979 when headquarters of the USAF established the center as a direct reporting unit* (DRU).

Center holdings comprise more than 60,000,000 pages, consisting mostly of periodic organizational histories and supporting documents dating from 1942. The center has also amassed special collections dating from the early days of military aviation. These include personal papers, oral history interviews, aircraft records, and a variety of historical studies and documents. The center accessions about 6,000 documents of all kinds annually and records those on microfilm with copies deposited at the National Archives and Records Service in Washington, D.C., and at the Office of Air Force History at Bolling* AFB, D.C. The center is also responsible for the lineage and honors of USAF units, the records of the Air Force Seal and Flag, and the records of unit and establishment emblems and flags. It determines aerial victory credits.

References. Brochure, "Information for Researchers," U.S. Air Force Historical Research Center: "USAF Historical Research Center," *AF*, May 1990, p. 119.

Warren A. Trest

U.S. AIR FORCE MUSEUM

This is a specialized organization under the Air Force Logistics Command* (AFLC) and is located at Wright-Patterson* AFB (W-P AFB), Ohio. It is not the only museum in the USAF,* but it is the biggest and oldest aviation museum in the world with more than 200 aircraft and large missiles. It also has more than 20,000 aircraft components, personal effects, photographs, and a piece of lunar ground. It has more than one million visitors each year. It began at McCook Field, Ohio, in 1923, and moved to Wright Field, Ohio, in 1927. The collection was stored during World War II* and reopened at W-P AFB in 1954. Its current building opened in 1971 and was paid for by public donations to the nonprofit Air Force Museum Foundation, established in 1960. The building was doubled in size in the 1980s with public and private monies. This museum has operated the USAF Museum Program (USAFMP) since 1983. The USAFMP is responsible for ensuring that there is a coherent structure for all the museums throughout the USAF.

References. "The 40th Anniversary of the USAF," a special issue of *AH*, September 1987, pp. 214–20. U.S. Air Force Fact Sheet 86–12, "Air Force Logistics Command," April 1986. Lois E. Walker and Shelby E. Wickham, *From Huffman Prairie to the Moon: The History of Wright-Patterson Air Force Base*, 1982.

U.S. AIR FORCE RESERVE (USAFR)

The USAFR is both a component of the USAF* and a separate operating agency* (SOA) within its management structure. In the Total Force Policy,* the USAFR forms a substantial, effective, and economic portion of the USAF's air power.

As a component, the USAFR originated in the National Defense Act of 1916,* when a Reserve Corps of 2,300 officers and men was authorized. It continued through the organizational changes of the USAF's antecedents until it was confirmed in the Army and Air Force Authorization Act of 1950.* The Continental Air Command* (CONAC) administered the USAFR under policies established by headquarters of the USAF. In 1 December 1948, the Reserve program was put in the Office of the Special Assistant to the Chief of Staff for Reserve Forces. It was renamed the Assistant Chief of Staff for Reserve Forces in October 1953.

Secretary of Defense (SECDEF) Robert S. McNamara* was never satisfied with the composition and organization of the U.S. Army Reserve Components, believing their structure was too rigid to allow flexible use of the reservists. By late 1963 the Army was planning a reorganization of its reserves and tending toward eventual merger of them. Rejecting McNamara's unilateral moves, Congress asserted its Constitutional power "to regulate the militia" and passed the Reserve Forces Bill of Rights and Vitalization Act in 1967. It called for the creation of offices of chiefs of the Reserve components in each of the armed services and guaranteed the separate existence of Reserve and Guard components. The new offices were headed by major generals called to extended active duty as the primary advisers to their service chiefs on the respective Reserves.

The USAFR became an SOA on 1 August 1968, which ended CONAC as the agency responsible for administering, commanding, and training the Reserve. In March 1972, the second chief of the Air Force Reserve, Major General Homer I. Lewis, secured authority from the vice chief of staff of the Air Force to assume command of headquarters of the USAFR in the field while retaining his Air Staff* role. This action unified the functions of policy and command in one person.

The next major reorganization of the USAFR was in 1976 when the chief of staff of the Air Force* authorized the third chief of the Air Force Reserve, Major General William Lyon, to reinstate numbered air forces* in place of Air Force Reserve regions in the management structure. Manned primarily by reservists, the regions, which had replaced CONAC's numbered air forces in a 1960 reorganization, never had the authority or the stature to conduct the middle management role. In October 1976, the USAFR activated the Fourteenth Air Force* (14AF) at Dobbins AFB, Georgia; the Tenth Air Force* (10AF) at Bergstrom* AFB, Texas; and the Fourth Air Force* (4AF) at McClellan* AFB, California. These three air forces command USAFR units in the field. Part of the USAFR was used in the Iraq crisis of 1990–1991.

References. Primary: *Army and Air Force Authorization Act of 1949, 64 Stat 323 (1950).* Army Circular 103/Air Force Letter 35–124, "Air Force Reserve and Air Force Honorary Reserve," 14 April 1948. Department of the Air Force Special Orders AA-371, 3 March 1972. Headquarters Continental Air Command Special Orders G-46, 16 July 1968. *National Defense Act of 1916 39 Stat. 166 (1916). Reserve Forces Bill of Rights and Vitalization Act 81 Stat 521 (1968).* Secondary: "Air Force Reserve," *AF,*

May 1990, pp. 112–13. Sloan R. Gill, "Evolution to Partnership," *AF*, September 1984, pp. 88–90.

See also Air Reserve Technician Program; U.S. Air Force Reserve (USAFR) flying force.

Gerald T. Cantwell

U.S. AIR FORCE RESERVE (USAFR) FLYING FORCE

The USAFR's flying force has progressed from being a "flying club" to a modern, effective part of U.S. air power. In the earliest post–World War II period, the USAFR flying units were designated "heavy bombardment," "troop carrier," and the like. These were "flying club" days, however, for these were essentially paper units flying T-6,* T-7, and T-11 trainers. Conditions improved in 1947 with the assignment of B-26 Invaders,* C-46s,* and C-47s,* but it was not until the promulgation of the fiscal year 1950 USAFR program in May 1949 that the force truly began to take shape. The program included 20 tactical airlift* wings,* with C-46s and C-47s, and five light bomber* wings with Invaders. All these units were mobilized for the Korean War.*

By 1957, the USAFR had evolved to two bomber wings with Invaders; nine fighter* wings which had progressed through F-80s* and F-84Es to the F-86H;* 13 tactical airlift wings of C-46s, except for one with C-119s;* and five rescue* squadrons* with U-16s.*

As a result of President Dwight D. Eisenhower's* economies and revised war plans, the flying force was reorganized in 1958. The fighter mission was moved to the Air National Guard* (ANG). Then there were 15 tactical airlift wings and the five rescue squadrons. One wing got C-123s* in 1959, and C-124s* began to arrive in 1961. Two rescue squadrons received HC-97s (*see* C-97). This pattern lasted until 1968.

In the eight years after 1968, the flying force changed constantly. One reason was the phasedown of the USAF* following the Vietnam War,* making more modern aircraft available to the USAFR. The new aircraft included A-37s,* C-130s,* F-105s,* and CH-3s (*see* H-3). The other reason was that the Military Airlift Command* (MAC) could no longer use or support the USAFR's C-124s. MAC developed the associate unit concept in which the USAFR units flew and maintained C-141s* and C-5s* assigned to collocated USAF units.

Another sweeping round of conversions began in the latter half of 1975, as the USAFR acquired new missions and more modern equipment. The new missions included using gunships,* weather reconnaissance,* the Airborne Warning and Control Systems* (AWACS), and aerial refueling.* Those missions brought in AC-130s, WC-130s, ECC-121s (*see* C-121) and KC-135s (*see* C-135). Modernization continued with A-10s,* C-130Hs, F-4s,* and F-16s.* The KC-10 (*see* C-10) was put into the associate mode. In 1985 and 1986, the USAFR acquired C-5s and C-141s. By October 1987, it had 13 tactical airlift squadrons, 13 airlift operations* squadrons, three rescue squadrons, 12 fighter squadrons, three aerial refueling squadrons, two special operations squadrons, and a flight* flying weather reconnaissance. There were also four units in associated airlift, three associate squadrons in aerial refueling, and an aeromedical evacuation* associate squadron with C-9s.*

References. "Air Force Reserve," *AF*, May 1990, pp. 112–13. Charles Joseph Gross, *Prelude to the Total Force: The Air National Guard 1943–1969*, 1985. William P. Schlitz, "The C-5 Team at Dover," *AF*, August 1983, pp. 62–67.

Gerald T. Cantwell

U.S. AIR FORCES IN EUROPE (USAFE)

For more than four decades, USAFE has been dedicated to the security of Western Europe. It was activated on 7 August 1945, as a direct successor to the mightiest of the USAAF's* wartime commands, the U.S. Strategic Air Forces* (USSTAF). Formed at St. Germain-en-Laye, France, from USSTAF resources, USAFE headquarters moved in September 1945 to Wiesbaden, West Germany, where it shared occupation duties and soon dwindled to the size of an administrative support force in the great demobilization after the war. It began to regain some of its former strength after the Berlin Airlift* in 1948 and the birth of the North Atlantic Treaty Organization* (NATO) in 1949 signaled the onset of the Cold War.* U.S. leaders became convinced that rebuilt and long-term U.S. air power in Europe was essential to Western security. The headquarters remained in Wiesbaden for nearly 30 years, finally moving in March 1973 to Ramstein* AB, West Germany, so it would be collocated with the headquarters of NATO's Allied Air Forces Central Europe (AAFCE) which was to be formed in June 1974. USAFE's commander has a dual responsibility as commander of the AAFCE.

Since the NATO crash buildup of the early 1950s, USAFE has managed an array of combat units stationed in and around the continent, and the makeup has varied over the years. The Third Air Force* (3AF), established in England in 1951, is still there. The Strategic Air Command* (SAC) bomber* units, which the 3AF supported, have long since departed, but for many years 3AF tactical operations* wings* have supported NATO from England. The Twelfth Air Force* (12AF) was also formed in 1951 in Germany to command all USAFE tactical operations units on the continent. It was replaced by the Seventeenth Air Force* (17AF), which today is headquartered in Germany. The 17AF was first organized in 1953 and was responsible for the Mediterranean and North African areas. The Mediterranean flank is guarded today by units of the Sixteenth Air Force* (16AF), headquartered at Torrejon* AB, Spain.

Of the many changes since the NATO buildup, none was more drastic than that caused by the French ultimatum in 1966 that foreign forces be withdrawn from French soil by April 1967. This required closing nine major and 78 minor USAFE installations in France, with relocations to Britain, West Germany, and the United States. Coupled with the drain on tactical operations forces to meet the demands for protracted battle in the Vietnam War,* the withdrawal from France influenced a decision to base dually some USAF squadrons in the United

States for rapid deployment to specified European bases to meet NATO wartime needs. These and other Tactical Air Command* (TAC) forces were rotated overseas periodically to train in the European environment and were ready to deploy at a moment's notice.

In keeping with President John F. Kennedy's (JFK) flexible response policy of the early 1960s, USAFE has since focused on upgrading conventional war capabilities, as well as maintaining the nuclear weapons* alert posture, in support of NATO. USAFE's modernized conventional capabilities were ably demonstrated by its F-111s* which operated out of England for the Libyan raid* of 1986. There is a wide variety of modern aircraft in USAFE, including the A-10s,* F-4Es,* F-111E/Fs, F-15C/Ds,* and F-16s.* USAFE's strike forces have been bolstered also by the BGM-109G* missile, a highly survivable, mobile, nuclear weapon designed for tactical operations.

While USAFE's forces are pledged to NATO and come under control of NATO in a war, the command is also a component of the American European Command (EUCOM), a unified command.* As such, USAFE responds to U.S. military plans and operations in the European area.

References. Goldberg, *Hist. USAF*. Robert Jackson, *Strike Force: The USAF in Britain since 1948*, 1986. Patricia Parrish, *Forty-Five Years of Vigilance for Freedom: United States Air Forces in Europe 1942–1987*, Ramstein AB, 1988. Roberts, *Dir. USAF*. Michael Skinner, *U*S*A*F*E: A Primer of Modern Air Combat in Europe*, 1988. "United States Air Forces in Europe," *AF*, May 1990, pp. 93–95.

Warren A. Trest

U.S. AIR FORCE SONG, THE

In its eight decades, the USAF's* people have sung many songs,* but its rousing official song is special with its famous lyrics about the wild blue yonder.

For the first three of those decades the independence-minded leadership of the U.S. Army air arm had sought a song to establish identity and separateness. In 1937, Brigadier General H. H. Arnold* suggested to Major General Oscar Westover,* chief of the USAAC,* that a competition for one be held. Unfortunately, the Army controlled the USAAC budget. Fortunately, Bernarr MacFadden, publisher of *Liberty* magazine, offered a $1,000 prize for the winner.

A committee chaired by Mildred Yount, wife of Brigadier General Barton K. Yount of the USAAC, reviewed the 650 entries which included one from Meredith Wilson and two from Irving Berlin. Berlin's songs eventually were included in Moss Hart's musical *Winged Victory*.

A last-minute entry, on 13 July 1939, was Robert Crawford's "The Army Air Corps Song." Crawford was 40 years old, a graduate of Princeton University, a civilian pilot,* and a professional singer known as "The Flying Baritone." The competition was no contest. On 15 July, Crawford's song was selected by the committee. Promotion began with Crawford singing it each day at the Cleveland, Ohio, air races in September. Arnold used his chief of Air Corps petty cash fund to pay for its distribution to military bands. This was not enough, and the song was commercially copyrighted and published.

"The Army Air Corps Song" was quickly a success, but it had to be modified through the years for organizational changes to "The Army Air Forces Song" and to its current title. In the 1950s an unsuccessful attempt was made to replace it with "Air Force Blue." Crawford died in 1964 on the 25th anniversary of presenting his song in Cleveland.

References. C. W. "Bill" Getz, ed., *The Wild Blue Yonder: Songs of the Air Force*, vol. 1, 1981. Murray Green, "Off We Go into the Wild Blue Yonder . . . ," *The Retired Officer*, July 1987, pp. 38–41.

U.S. AIR FORCES SOUTHERN COMMAND

When aviation units for the Canal Zone area expanded in 1940, the Panama Canal Air Force was activated as a major command* (MAJCOM) in November. It was redesignated the Caribbean Air Force in August 1941, the 6th Air Force in February 1942, the Sixth Air Force* (6AF) in September 1942, the Caribbean Air Command in July 1946, and the U.S. Air Forces Southern Command in July 1963. The organization was inactivated in January 1976, and most of its mission and resources went to the Tactical Air Command* (TAC). TAC created the 830th Air Division for the tasks, and it has its headquarters at Howard* AFB, Panama. The 830th's assignment was to the Twelfth Air Force* (12AF) in 1990.

References. Goldberg, *Hist. USAF*, 1957. Ravenstein, *Org. USAF*. "Tactical Air Command," *AF*, May 1990, pp. 88–90.

U.S. ARMY AIR CORPS (USAAC)

The Air Corps Act* established this organization on 2 July 1926 as a means to improve and expand the air arm. In contrast to the previous USAAS,* the air arm now had an assistant secretary of war for air,* Air Sections in the General Staff, and a five-year plan for expansion. F. Trubee Davison was appointed as assistant secretary, serving until 1932. President Franklin D. Roosevelt* (FDR) did not appoint a successor.

The initial organization had five subordinate agencies: Training Center, for flight training;* Technical School; Balloon & Airship School; Tactical School; and Materiel Division. The division had an Engineering School, Depots, Procurement Planning Representatives, and Plant Representatives.

The USAAC started with 919 officers, 8,725 men, and 1,254 airplanes. It expanded slowly but steadily until 1939, when it had 23,455 men. With war in Europe it then expanded rapidly to more than 150,000 in 1941, when it was replaced by the USAAF.* The first true increase in aircraft numbers was not realized until 1938 when the USAAC had 1,719, and then in 1939 when there were 2,177. These were almost microscopic numbers considering the tasks ahead in World War II.* However, much of aviation's technological revolution—such as changing from wood and cloth to metal; adopting flaps, retractable landing gear, variable pitch propellors, and high octane fuel—is concealed within the numbers. These improvements, which were collateral with and dependent upon increases in engine power, had greatly improved quality beyond mere numbers.

Yet the United States had fallen behind other great powers and had only one effective battle plane when rearmament started: the B-17.* The USAAC's share of U.S. Army military appropriations rose from 5.7 to 15.7 percent during 1939, an amount that was lower than it should have been.

The USAAC continued the USAAS's efforts to develop air power. Some of the things it did were the Pan American flight of 1926,* the first flight from California to Hawaii using the *Bird of Paradise** in 1927, the 1929 endurance flight of the *Question Mark*,* the Alaskan flight of 1934,* and the 1938 Goodwill Flight to South America.*

The most important work done by the USAAC for the development of air power was its preparation for strategic operations.* This required doctrine,* organization, and equipment. The doctrine was developed by the Air Corps Tactical School,* and the needed centralized organization was established in embryonic form in the General Headquarters Air Force* (GHQ Air Force) in 1935. The equipment was dramatically improved with the development of the B-17 and the Norden bombsight.* Unfortunately, the USAAC wanted 206 B-17s but was allowed the pitifully few 13 it had until war broke out in Europe. Then approval was given for a paltry 42 more. During the war, the USAAF* was to lose at times that many or more bombers* in a day's fighting. The USAAC had one major disaster that turned out to be a blessing in disguise. Its involvement in the airmail flights of 1934* made obvious the sorry state of equipment and some training needs.

It was still as the USAAC that the airmen began to expand into a large modern air force to fight in a total, global war. The USAAC's organization after creation of the GHQ Air Force shows how great this challenge would be. Kept under ground officer operational control was observation aviation* assigned to corps areas and all aircraft in overseas departments. Under the USAAC were the schools and the Materiel Division. By 1939, fortunately, the GHQ Air Force had been removed from the Army chief of staff and was under the chief of the Air Corps. The USAAC became the USAAF* in June 1941. The airmen's response to the challenge of World War II shows there was much of merit within the old USAAC and more handicaps imposed on them than the airmen deserved.

References. C&C, vol. 1. DeWitt S. Copp, *A Few Great Captains: The Men and Events That Shaped the Development of U.S. Air Power*, 1980. Goldberg, *Hist. USAF*. Maurer, *Avn. in Army. The Official Pictorial History of the AAF*, 1947.

U.S. ARMY AIR FORCES (USAAF)

When the threat of German air power dominated the Munich Conference of 1938, the United States faced the first of a series of shocks that would transform U.S. Army aviation. The USAAC* had increased in size only slightly on an absolute basis by the beginning of World War II* in Europe in September 1939, but it more than doubled during the "Phoney War" or "Sitzkrieg" after Poland fell. Then, in 1940, more traumas took place. In April 1940, the Luftwaffe controlled Norway and its sea communications, and then its tactical operations* in the Battle of France was part of a crushing blitzkrieg. Congress's reaction was to give the USAAC a blank check.

From 1940 to 1941, the USAAC tripled in size, an enormous achievement for a technical organization after a year of doubling. Seemingly endless problems existed in converting a World War I*–style observation aviation* air arm to one for strategic* and tactical* operations. USAAC planners looked forward in 1940 to an eventual force of 2,165,000 men. It was evident that the air arm's status as a minor appendage was over. A new organization and status was needed for air power having come of age. Army Regulation 95–5,* issued on 20 June 1941, created the USAAF. The rest of the Army was divided into the Army Ground Forces, Army Service Forces, Defense and Theater Commands.

There was a new internal organization for the nascent USAAF. It had two subordinate organizations: the Combat Command, to conduct air operations and to succeed the General Headquarters Air Force* (GHQ Air Force); and the Air Corps (AC). The AC had two subcommands: Materiel, and Training and Operations. The latter had four subordinate organizations: Technical Schools, Southwest Training, Gulf Training, and Southeast Training. This organization was designed to build an air force—the necessary first task—and not to fight a war.

Within six months, the USAAF had to fight a war anyway. In its first year, it quintupled to 764,000 men and tripled again in another year. In 1944, it reached 2,372,292, the all-time high for the USAF* and a credit to the USAAC planners of 1940. It represented 31 percent of Army strength. The improvised USAAF of 1944 was organized to fight a global war under controls containing little adjustment for an independent air force. The ten major commands* (MAJCOM) in the continental United States (CONUS) were: Training, I Troop Carrier, Air Transport, Materiel, Air Service, and Proving Ground Commands; and First,* Second,* Third,* and Fourth* Air Forces. Besides the commands there were eight agencies: AAF Board, Tactical and Redistribution Centers, Army Airways Communications System and Weather Wings, School of Aviation Medicine, First Motion Picture Unit, and Aeronautical Chart Plant. Oversea organizations used air forces* subordinate to theater of operations command.

By 1944, the USAAF was finally trained and equipped to fight the air war it had envisioned, although the emphasis had already begun to shift from training to operations in 1943. The annual rate of aircraft production reached 110,000 in March 1944, and these were modern planes with emphasis on four-engine bombers,* a massive contrast to the observation aviation of the USAAC. In mid–1944, the USAAF mustered 78,757 aircraft, of which 445 were Very Heavy and 11,720 were Heavy Bombers. It had a maximum of 269 groups.*

By February 1944, the USAAF had the air superiority* fighter escorts* needed to support strategic operations against the German aircraft industry target system,* but much of the effort was diverted to tactical operations for Operation Overlord.* Before the bombers could be fully relieved of this diversion, a strategic campaign against the German oil industry target system* was launched in May and then switched to the German transportation target system* in 1945 as Germany was annihilated.

On the other side of the world in the Pacific, the USAAF had the bases in the Marianas* Islands to begin its strategic campaign against Japan* in October 1944. By August 1945, air and submarine blockade and bombing had reduced Japanese production by 75 percent. The USAAF and the U.S. Navy believed the war could be ended without a land invasion, but the U.S. Army disagreed. The special bombing campaign with nuclear weapons* against Hiroshima* and Nagasaki made the argument moot as Japan's government accepted terms.

After the war, the USAAF imploded in a great demobilization. The only forces left outside CONUS were in occupied Germany and Japan. In December 1946, there were only two combat-ready groups left in the USAAF. The number of personnel had shrunk to 303,000 by May 1947. By the end of the demobilization, the USAAF had 63 wings* and 25,000 aircraft. However, it had begun to restructure toward a true air force in March 1946 when the Strategic Air,* Tactical Air,* and Air Defense Commands were established as MAJCOMs.

References. *AAF: A Directory, Almanac, and Chronicle of Achievement*, 1944. C&C, 7 vols. Goldberg, *Hist. USAF*. "U.S. Army Air Forces," a special issue of *Flying and Popular Aviation*, September 1941. "U.S. Army Air Forces at War," a special issue of *Flying*, October 1943.

U.S. ARMY AIR SERVICE (USAAS)

Despite competent men, the Aviation Section of the U.S. Army Signal Corps* was inadequate organizationally for its tasks in World War I.* It had too few men knowledgeable about aviation, and the existing organization resulted in confusion over authority and responsibility. The focus of dissatisfaction by the spring of 1918 was on lagging aircraft production.

On 21 May 1918, President Woodrow Wilson took aviation away from the Signal Corps, putting it directly under the secretary of war and thus creating the USAAS. In the new arrangement it was divided into two agencies: the Bureau of Aircraft Production and the Division of Military Aeronautics. Thus procurement and operations were no longer in a single organization, and confusion remained. On 27 August, Wilson finally solved the problem, putting both agencies under John D. Ryan,* whose title became second assistant secretary of war and director of the Air Service. After the war, Congress passed the National Defense Act of 1920,* giving legal recognition to the past status of the USAAS and confirming it as an arm under the Army.

After World War I,* the USAAS's first task was to demobilize its 190,000 men. By June 1919 it had 27,000 remaining, or 14 percent of the previous force, but only 5 percent of its officers. The USAAS stopped procurement and training and got rid of many facilities and much equipment.

Its organization was divided in 1920 into four principal subordinate units, called groups: Administrative, Information, Training and Operations, and Supply. It was authorized two wings,* seven groups,* 27 squadrons,* and 42 companies for lighter-than-air* (LTA). Forty percent of this force was devoted to observation aviation.* The USAAS could now attend to regular duties instead of demobilization. A principal task was flight training,* which resumed in January 1920, as did other aircrew, technical, and professional training. Another task was protecting the border with Mexico. Procurement began again for bombers,* attack* planes, and fighters.* The USAAS tried to improve its equipment and techniques and to demonstrate the potential for air power.

Manning fluctuated within the range of 9,000 to 11,600 in the years 1920 to 1926. In 1924 the USAAS had 1,364 aircraft, but only 754 were in commission. The warplanes were 457 observation, 78 fighter, 59 bomber, and eight attack aircraft.

There was much discontent in the USAAS over its status. It sought independence from the Army; it wanted more bombers, fighters, and attack aircraft and less observation; it tried to demonstrate the changes in power relationships with surface forces by Mitchell's bombing tests on warships;* and it wanted to be larger and have modern equipment. The aircraft industry was also in a dismal state. The upshot was the Air Corps Act* which ended the USAAS on 2 July 1926 and created the USAAC.* The airmen's status was raised to corps level, and a five-year expansion and procurement program was scheduled, but independence was denied.

References. Goldberg, *Hist. USAF*. James J. Hudson, *Hostile Skies: A Combat History of the American Air Service in World War I*, 1968. Maurer Maurer, *Avn. in Army*. Maurer Maurer, ed., *The U.S. Air Service in World War I*, 4 vols., 1978–1979.

U.S. CENTRAL COMMAND AIR FORCES (USCENTAF)

USCENTAF is the air component of the U.S. Central Command, formed in 1983 and intended to deal with crises in a 19-nation area in Southwest Asia, the Persian Gulf, and the Horn of Africa. The Command was used in the Iraqi crisis of 1990–1991* and Iraq War.*

In the early days of the Cold War,* the United States was not faced with the urgency of projecting its power quickly wherever needed in the world. It had its forces in advanced positions for deterrence and containment of the Soviet Empire; the British and French Empires were still in existence with some military strength; there was a large, self-sufficient U.S. Navy; and there were residual bases in the Philippines and from post–World War II occupations. Therefore, speedy deployment was not a problem. Over the years, the Soviet Empire expanded with satellites or client governments in Asia, Africa, and the Western Hemisphere. The British and French Empires collapsed, and their forces shrank to basically a capability in Europe. At the same time, the military power and belligerency of other nations, particularly in the Middle East, grew.

The need for an enhanced capability to have a global fire-fighting force to protect U.S. interests became so evident that pacifistic President Jimmy Carter requested the means for one. In October 1979, the Rapid Deployment Force (RDF) was established with units from within the U.S. Army, Navy, Air Force, and Marines. The Iranian Revolution and Soviet invasion of Afghanistan in 1979 added pressure for the need. In 1980 the Rapid Deployment Joint Task Force

(RDJTF) was established with headquarters at MacDill* AFB, Florida, to replace the RDF. Its mission was to plan and jointly train forces ready to deploy anywhere in the world. It was controlled by the Joint Chiefs of Staff (JCS). In 1983, the RDJTF was replaced by the U.S. Central Command.

To a high degree, the USAF had been prescient to the need for such a force, and truly rapid deployment today can only be done by airlift operations.* The USAF formed its Composite Air Strike Force* (CASF) in 1955 to project air power globally and rapidly. The Nineteenth Air Force* (19AF) was created for that purpose. Although the 19AF was disbanded to save money in 1973, the USAF interest continued. Also the development of heavy airlift capability, beginning with the C-124,* demonstrated the USAF's long-time interest in providing rapid deployment.

The USAF has designated the Ninth Air Force* (9AF) to become the US-CENTAF in a contingency. The forces able to respond include A-10s,* B-52s,* C-5s,* KC-10s, C-130s,* EC-130s, EC-135s (see C-135), C-141s,* E-3s,* F-15s,* F-16s,* and F-111s.* The C-17,* under development, should be a significant addition to capability.

References. David Eshel, *The U.S. Rapid Deployment Forces*, 1985. Futrell, *Ideas*, vol. 2. "Tactical Air Command," *AF*, May 1990, pp. 89–90.

USSTAF. *See* U.S. Strategic Air Forces.

U.S. STRATEGIC AIR FORCES (USSTAF)

The U.S. Strategic Air Forces in Europe (USSAFE) was a headquarters organization established in November 1943 to coordinate the activities of the Eighth* and Fifteenth* Air Forces (8AF and 15AF) in war and was an antecedent to the U.S. Air Forces in Europe* (USAFE).

On 4 February 1944, its name changed to the USSTAF. The headquarters was put together during January 1944 at Bushey Park,* code-named Widewing, outside London, England. Bushey had been the headquarters of the 8AF, which moved to High Wycombe,* England, the former home of the disbanded VIII Bomber Command. Lieutenant General Carl A. Spaatz* was put in command of USSTAF and was responsible to the Combined Chiefs of Staff (CCS) through the chief of the Air Staff, Marshal of the Royal Air Force Lord Portal of Hungerford. Spaatz reported to General Dwight D. Eisenhower* in the latter's capacity as supreme Allied commander for Operation Overlord.* Through two deputy commanders, Major General F. L. Anderson, operations, and Brigadier General Hugh J. Knerr,* administration, Spaatz exercised operational control over the 8AF in England, under Major General James H. Doolittle,* and the 15AF in Italy under Major General Nathan F. Twining.* Spaatz exercised administrative and logistical control over the 8AF and Ninth Air Force* (9AF), the U.S. component of the Allied Expeditionary Air Force (AEAF) and under Air Marshal Sir Trafford Leigh-Mallory.

USSTAF's primary functions for the remainder of the war involved strategic planning, target selection, the setting of policies for combat crew operational tour* lengths, and the movement of personnel and missions between the 8AF and the 15AF.

References. C&C, vol. 2 and 3. Futrell, *Ideas*, vol. 1. W. A. Jacobs, "Air Command in the United Kingdom, 1943–44," *Journal of Strategic Studies*, March 1988, pp. 51– 78.

David MacIsaac

U.S. STRATEGIC AIR FORCES IN EUROPE. *See* U.S. Strategic Air Forces.

U.S. STRATEGIC BOMBING SURVEY, THE

This was a commission established by President Franklin D. Roosevelt* (FDR) in 1944 at the instigation of USAAF* officers in Washington, D.C., and London, England. The airmen argued an impartial, civilian-dominated commission should direct an evaluation of the strategic operations* in Europe. The results are still disputed.

General of the Army H. H. Arnold* cleared the idea with General Carl A. Spaatz,* commanding the U.S. Strategic Air Forces* (USSTAF), and his colleagues on the Joint Chiefs of Staff (JCS). In October, FDR appointed Franklin D'Olier, president of the Prudential Insurance Company, to act as chairman. Before the war was over, more than 1,000 people were assigned to the Survey, as it came to be called. A third of them, including most of the decision makers, were civilians: experts in such fields as structural damage, economic planning, manufacturing, transportation, and psychology. The Survey's top echelon included many who would later become famous in their own right: Henry Clay Alexander, George W. Ball, John Kenneth Galbraith, and Paul H. Nitze.

Divided into teams essentially on the basis of particular industries, the Survey set to work both in England and on the continent well before hostilities ended. Many were shot at; five were killed in the line of duty. They measured effects, interviewed survivors at the highest and lowest levels, impounded records, and even had disputes with the Soviets in Berlin, Germany. Returning to England and later Washington, D.C., they sifted and cross-checked evidence, argued occasionally among themselves, but eventually came to the consensus that air power was decisive in the war in Western Europe.

Their charter was extended by President Harry S Truman* (HST) and they went to Japan in the fall of 1945. It was the middle of 1947 before the task was finally completed, the Survey dissolved, and its records turned over to the National Archives to become Record Group 243.

The Survey completed 321 reports, 212 on Europe and 109 on the Pacific. Seventy-eight, 23 for Europe and 55 for the Pacific, were offered for sale by the superintendent of documents, the remainder being restricted to limited distribution within the government. Of the reports, only six, numbers 1 to 3 for both Europe and the Pacific, bear the formal stamp of the Office of the Chairman;

all the others are technically supporting documents and should, although some do not, bear a disclaimer to that effect. There was a similar British Strategic Bombing Survey.

References. Primary: Garland Publishing's 10-volume series of 1976 contains the 31 most important reports, a general introduction to the Survey and the postwar controversies over strategic bombing, and background notes for each reproduced report. Complete sets of the 321 reports are now rare but may be found in the Library of Congress, U.S. Army Center for Military History, the Air University Library, and the USAF Academy Library. Secondary: Futrell, *Ideas*, vol. 1. David MacIsaac, *Strategic Bombing in World War II: The Story of the U.S. Strategic Bombing Survey*, 1976, and "What the Bombing Survey Really Says," *AF*, June 1973, pp. 60–63.

David MacIsaac

UTAH, USS. *See* interception of the USS *Utah*.

U-TAPAO ROYAL THAI AIR FORCE BASE

USAF* operations at U-Tapao Royal Thai AFB, Thailand, began in August 1966, as the 4258th Strategic Wing conducted aerial refueling* operations with 20 KC-135s (*see* C-135). More tankers* were added later. Beginning in 1967, the tankers supported only fighters.* In April 1967, Arc Light* B-52* operations began from the field. U-Tapao provided two advantages over conducting Arc Light from Guam in the Marianas* Islands. One was it cut en route time from 12 to five hours, or even two hours, and eliminated the need for aerial refueling. The second was relief for overloaded facilities on Guam. When Arc Light operations were reduced in the early 1970s, all of them were then done from U-Tapao, and the number of tankers there fell to 30. Activity rose for Linebacker* I and II, requiring 45 tankers. The 4258th was redesignated the 307th in 1970; the USAF departed U-Tapao in 1973.

References. Berger, *USAF in SEA*. Jack Lavalle, ed., *Air War—Vietnam*, 1978. John Schlight, *The War in South Vietnam: The Years of the Offensive 1965–1968*, 1988.

V

VALIANT. *See* BT-13.

VALKYRIE. *See* B-70.

VANCE AIR FORCE BASE

Near Enid, Oklahoma, Vance is an Air Training Command* (ATC) field. It was activated in 1941 to provide pilot* flight training.* It was named Enid until 1949, when it was renamed for Lieutenant Colonel Leon R. Vance whose aeromedical evacuation* plane vanished between Iceland and Newfoundland. Vance had, earlier in 1944, won the Air Force Medal of Honor* for ditching his crippled B-24,* while wounded, in the mistaken belief one crewman had been unable to bail out. After World War II,* its units had the same mission flying B-25s,* then T-33s, and, finally, T-38s.* In 1990 its unit was the 71st Flying Training Wing (FTW) with T-37s* and T-38s.

References. "Guide to Major Air Force Installations Worldwide," *AF*, May 1990, p. 132. Mueller, *AFB*. Roberts, *Dir. USAF*.

VANDENBERG, GENERAL HOYT S. (1899–1954)

The second chief of staff of the Air Force,* from 1948 to 1953, Vandenberg played an important part in shaping military policy after 1945. Most important, he implemented the U.S. national strategy of deterrence. Vandenberg was a main participant in some other significant events of his time: unification of the armed forces and formation of an independent USAF,* the establishment of the USAF as an on-going concern after separation from the U.S. Army,* the formation of the Strategic Air Command* (SAC), the Berlin Airlift,* the B-36 controversy,* the development of fusion nuclear weapons,* and the Korean War.* Under the stringent fiscal policies of Harry S Truman* the air power needed was simply not available at first. Vandenberg called it a "shoestring air force." When he retired, the understrength USAF had changed into the cornerstone of U.S. military policy.

He was born in Milwaukee, Wisconsin, and graduated from the U.S. Military Academy (USMA) in 1923. For the next decade he was a fighter* pilot,* becoming an outstanding flier and junior officer who was recognized as such throughout the USAAC.* During World War II,* he served on the Air Staff* in Washington, D.C., as an air planner for Operations Torch* and Overlord;* was a diplomat in Moscow, USSR; was deputy commander of the Allied Expeditionary Air Force (AEAF) for Overlord; and was commander of the Ninth Air Force* (9AF). He was able to adapt and persevere; while others were competent in staff, planning, or command, he excelled at all three.

After the end of the war in Europe, he was instrumental in founding SAC. General of the Army and Chief of Staff Dwight D. Eisenhower* made him War Department intelligence chief, and he reorganized the function in a scant three months. President Truman appointed him director of the Central Intelligence Group, forerunner of the Central Intelligence Agency (CIA). After one year, Vandenberg became deputy commander of the USAAF* and was the second-youngest American to achieve the grade of general. When the USAF was created, he became its first vice chief, and, one year later, its chief.

Vandenberg's concept of air power was crucial to his success because he struck a balance between the strategist and the tactician, advocating the primacy of strategic operations* as a deterrent to war and a potentially decisive weapon, but never forgetting the need for tactical operations.* His technical expertise as a pilot, combined with his managerial ability, dynamic personality, and aggressive leadership, made him a dominant and respected figure in the early Cold War* era. His early death, and his reticence to commit his innermost thoughts to paper, have caused his significance to be largely overlooked.

References. Primary: Noel F. Parrish, "Vandenberg: Rebuilding the 'Shoestring Air Force,' " *AF*, August 1981, pp. 88–93. Secondary: John L. Frisbee, ed., *Makers of the United States Air Force*, 1987. Phillip S. Meilinger, *Hoyt S. Vandenberg: The Life of a General*, 1989. Jon A. Reynolds, "Education and Training for High Command: Hoyt S. Vandenberg's Early Career," Ph.D. diss., Duke University, 1980.

Phillip S. Meilinger

VANDENBERG AIR FORCE BASE

This Air Force Space Command* (AFSPACECOM) base is near Lompoc, California. It began in 1941 as the U.S. Army's Camp Cooke. The USAF* took over in 1957 and renamed it in honor of General Hoyt S. Vandenberg,* second chief of staff of the Air Force.* It has been used for ballistic missile* launching, crew training, research, and testing. It has also been used for polar-orbit satellite launching. In 1990 its main units were headquarters of the 1st Strategic Aerospace Division (1stSTRAD), the Western Space and Missile Center of Air Force Systems Command* (AFSC) and the center's* Western Test Range, and the 4392nd Aerospace Support Wing.

References. John T. Greenwood, "The Air Force Ballistic and Space Program, 1954–1974," *AH*, December 1974, pp. 190–205. "Guide to Major Air Force Installations Worldwide," *AF*, May 1990, p. 132. Mueller, *AFB*, Roberts, *Dir. USAF*.

VC-25. *See* C-25.

VC-137. *See* C-137 and VC-137.

VICKERS GUN

The Vickers-Berthier .303-caliber Mk I aircraft machine gun was developed by the English firm of Vickers in 1917. Originally intended for infantry use, it was modified for use on Allied aircraft through removal of its water-cooling jacket. It became the aerial fixed gun used by Americans in World War I.* The Vickers used the belt-fed machine gun system invented by Hiram Maxim and was an advance over the earlier drum-fed Lewis* gun because of a higher rate of fire, 750 to 900 rounds per minute, and greater firing capacity. The ammunition feed at first used a canvas belt, which often deteriorated in battle conditions and caused jams. It was replaced with an aluminum link system. After the British developed an interrupter gear, it could be fired through a rotating propellor. Many Allied pilots* continued to use a Lewis mounted on a biplane's top wing in tandem with one or two Vickers mounted on the fuselage.

References. John Quick, *Dictionary of Weapons and Military Terms*, 1973. W.H.B. Smith and Joseph E. Smith, *Small Arms of the World*, 6th ed., 1960. Arch Whitehouse, *The Military Airplane: Its History and Development*, 1971.

D. K. Vaughan

VICTORY THROUGH AIR POWER. See de Seversky, Major Alexander P.

VIETNAM AIRLIFT

When the large-scale deployment of military forces for the Vietnam War* began in 1965, the Military Airlift Command* (MAC) was tasked to provide urgent transportation. Airlift operations* stemmed from the necessity of projecting forces over long distances in a short period of time and from the inability of U.S. Navy and merchant transports to move people and supplies as quickly to the other side of the world.

It was a staggering challenge. The USAF saw traffic to Southeast Asia (SEA) grow from a monthly average of 33,779 to 65,350 passengers and 9,123 to 42,296 tons of cargo from fiscal 1965 to 1967. In addition, thousands of combat troops were flown to Honolulu, Hawaii, and nine other cities in the Pacific area for rest and recuperation (R&R) leaves. R&R grew from 14,970 passengers in fiscal 1966 to 521,496 in 1967 and 774,386 in 1968. To expedite the flow, MAC developed intercontinental routes, each with well-equipped and efficiently managed personnel and equipment-handling facilities. Its fastest service guaranteed shipment within 24 hours of receipt at an aerial port.

On several occasions, MAC was asked to deploy major U.S. Army units. The first, designated Operation Blue Light, was in late 1965 when it moved the 3rd Brigade of the 25th Infantry Division from Hawaii to Pleiku, Vietnam, to counter a communist forces buildup. In 26 days, 231 sorties moved 3,000 troops and 4,700 tons of equipment the 6,000 miles.

Within SEA, the USAF* used tactical airlift.* The first four C-47* transports* arrived in November 1961. They supported other USAF aircraft, airdropped Vietnamese paratroopers, and conducted night flare operations. Their most demanding task was to resupply Army Special Forces detachments at remote locations in South Vietnam. These tasks gradually shifted to 16 larger C-123s* sent to Vietnam in December 1961, although they were considered obsolescent. Until 1965 these aircraft were the principal airlift within Vietnam. In 1965, C-130s began to dominate tactical airlift there. A C-130 could move about three times as much as a C-123, and by April C-130 operations had become routine. By December the force had grown to 32 C-130s, and by February 1968 there were 96 of them. Meanwhile, in April 1966, the Army transferred its C-7* transports to the USAF so all fixed-wing, land-based transports would be under USAF control.

Airlift played key roles in virtually all SEA operations. Perhaps the greatest test came in the 1968 Tet offensive, which started eight days after operations to support Khe Sanh* began. Early enemy strikes at Tan Son Nhut* AB, and many of the northerly airstrips, temporarily dislocated the airlift system. Yet the transport crews managed to fly many emergency troop and supply missions on behalf of hard-pressed garrisons. By 3 February, the fourth day of the offensive, the tactical airlift had regained full capability, and resupply played a critical role in the defeat of the communist effort. Between 1962 and 1973, USAF tactical airlift delivered more than seven million tons of passengers and cargo within South Vietnam. By comparison, U.S. and British transports carried slightly more than two million tons in the great Berlin Airlift,* and the USAF about 750,000 tons during the Korean War.* USAF C-130 losses in SEA were 53, with more than half in 1967 and 1968. C-123 losses were also 53, and C-7s were 20. Of these, 61 were lost to enemy action, including 17 by sapper or shelling. The others were lost to accidents, usually at the difficult forward airstrips.

In 1969 withdrawal began with 25,000 troops to be removed by September. The MAC airlift redeployed the forces through a series of operations called Keystone. As U.S. participation phased out, MAC devoted much strategic airlift to equipment for the South Vietnamese forces. After the peace agreements in January 1973, MAC turned its attention to withdrawal of the remaining U.S. personnel and equipment from Vietnam. This task involved several thousand tons of equipment and more than 20,000 personnel.

References. Berger, *USAF in SEA*. Ray L. Bowers, *Tactical Airlift*, 1983.

Roger D. Launius

VIETNAM WAR (1965–1973)

Although "Vietnam War" is the name most commonly used, it is an inappropriate designation as the war was fought both throughout former French Indochina and a wider area. The USAF* more properly refers formally to the war as the Southeast Asia (SEA) War, and informally to the reality of two separate wars: "in-country" and "out-country." "Country" refers to the Republic of South Vietnam. The war was called "McNamara's War" by many in the USAF.

North Vietnam made substantial gains in its subversion of the South in the early 1960s, and this led to increasing U.S. involvement to prop up the South. This was a reversal by President John F. Kennedy* (JFK) of President Dwight D. Eisenhower's* policies regarding both involvement and military strategy. JFK ended the USAF dominance of defense with its nuclear weapons* and quick, hard-strike strategy for war. Replacing it was U.S. Army dominance, with its belief that land war alone is decisive, using Army General Maxwell Taylor's flexible response and graduated escalation strategy. Taylor convinced JFK this strategy would be especially effective in countering guerrillas. There was also a new Army air force to provide attack* and tactical airlift* operations organically under ground commanders—the airmobile division of the Howze Board.*

The situation in Vietnam provided the Army with an opportunity to prove its concepts and capability; to show what modern land power, including massive subordinate air power, could do. Before the end of the war, the Army's organic air power would become the world's third largest air force.

In the early 1960s, it was believed that a necessary preliminary to defeating guerrillas was to blockade any external logistical support. If true, South Vietnam would prove a severe test of land power and the Army's air force. It was a long, narrow country with sea on one side and jungle on the other. Consequently, blockade of the South alone would be difficult at best. Aside from those conditions, use of the Army in Vietnam would violate the old axiom that the United States should not engage in a land war on the Asian mainland, a concept reinforced by the Korean War.*

When war came in 1965 under President Lyndon B. Johnson* (LBJ), the Army strategy was an offensive campaign of attrition in an Asian land war, with progress measured by "body counts." A war of attrition is always risky because it tends to be bloody for the offensive as well as for the defensive, and the U.S. people have not been inclined to support high casualty rates when there is little evidence of progress toward ending the war. This factor helped end the Army's "killer offensives" in the Korean War.* Thus in Vietnam the Army had to pin its hopes on the correctness of its strategy, on its eagerness and high morale, on its new air force to overcome the "land war in Asia" problem, and on the hope that ground commanders' common belief that they can conduct a low-casualty, clever campaign would be realized. Unfortunately, the use of Selective Service provided the Army with abundant cheap manpower. Commonly, leaders will respond to these economics by making a war labor intensive with excessive staffing and less concern for casualties. Important to the strategy was the role of the USAF. It, not the Army, was asked to impose a blockade in a most difficult area, the long western land border. There the vital North Vietnam logistical Ho Chi Minh trail* pierced that border.

The Army fought almost entirely in-country. The USAF's role, besides the land blockade, was to provide attack and tactical airlift support under the Military Assistance Command, Vietnam (MACV). There were only a handful of USAF officers in MACV who had any power of decision. The Army, through MACV, ran the in-country war. Thus, wielding air power there was done the Army way.

In the in-country war, the USAF had 11 percent, 58,000, of the military personnel there. It flew 1,250,000 sorties in support of the Army with a peak inventory of 1,085 aircraft or about 19 percent of the USAF's total. From 1966 to 1971, the Army's air force flew 36,000,000 sorties and had, at one time, 3,500 more aircraft than the USAF in the war. The USAF supported 73 big Army offensives, and it was satisfied with the overall effectiveness of its support.

By 1968, the Army thought it was making progress in attrition of the guerrillas, but it was taking casualties that made an unfavorable impression throughout the United States as the bodies and wounded came home. The blockade of the western border, called Rolling Thunder,* was ineffectual because it could not stop the trickle of supplies the guerrillas needed. In the 1968 Tet offensive, the North had its guerrillas come out in the open to try to spark a general revolt in 105 cities. In not a single city did a popular revolt join the guerrillas, and the U.S. Army's counteroffensive ruined the guerrilla army which took 40,000 casualties. The Army had achieved its attrition goal because of Tet. Yet the enemy was not willing to surrender unconditionally or seek terms. Although the North's advance elements in the South were no longer capable of significant operations, the North's ability to make war from its political sanctuaries were hurt but not incapacitated. The land war had failed despite the airmobile formations.

The Tet offensive was a turning point. During Tet, U.S. journalists, incredibly, decided the war was being lost despite the fact that the U.S. Army and the army of the Republic of Vietnam (ARVN) were everywhere clearly victorious. In addition, the journalists decided the South Vietnamese wanted the North to win despite the fact that nowhere did the people join the guerrilla offensive. The journalists' view of and attitudes on the war, repulsive as war always is at the worm's-eye level, appeared graphically every night on television* in U.S. homes. Combined with Hanoi's fifth column in the United States, this led to popular revulsion with the war.

After Tet, a new secretary of defense (SECDEF), Clark Clifford, asked the Joint Chiefs of Staff (JCS) how and when the war would end. They could not answer these questions to Clifford's satisfaction and asked for more men and weapons despite having grossly excessive staff and support personnel in South Vietnam. They did not suggest the only other alternatives, a land invasion of the North or air strategic operations* combined with a blockade of the North, both of which LBJ had rejected before. Clifford recommended to LBJ that he abandon the war. LBJ stayed on as a lame duck, peace negotiations began, the United States went over to the defensive, and the Army became dispirited.

President Richard M. Nixon withdrew the U.S. Army and wanted to defend the South with the ARVN and USAF, U.S. Navy, and Vietnamese air force (VNAF) air power; or "Vietnamization."

The out-country war was fought over Laos, Cambodia, and North Vietnam. The operations in Laos were directed against communist forces and called Barrel Roll.* They continued from 1964 to 1973. Although they were generally successful there was much acrimony, because detailed operational control of the USAF was given to the U.S. ambassador to Laos. The Cambodian operations* were attack and tactical airlift used against North Vietnamese troops in Cambodia and against communist rebels from 1969 to 1973. The operations were successful while they lasted, but Congress decided against continuing them.

When a major commitment in SEA was being considered in 1964, the USAF drew up the 94-target plan,* a proposal for a swift, hard, strategic operations campaign against the North at a time when there was little air defense there. The plan was supported by the JCS, but it was rejected by SECDEF Robert S. McNamara* in favor of Rolling Thunder.

Rolling Thunder's goal was the support of the morale of the South's people and government. This was to be achieved by the blockade of the Ho Chi Minh trail and followed the policy of flexible response and gradual escalation while giving political air superiority* to the enemy. It was micromanaged by the civilian leadership in Washington, D.C. Thus the USAF had no power of decision in any part of the SEA war during the presidency of LBJ.

The logistics went down the Ho Chi Minh trail to the South, a route that lent itself, some in the USAF argued, to nuclear weapons* for civil engineering acts to block the passes and destroy tree canopies with little loss of life. Fear of Soviet or Red Chinese entry into the war, despite the disarray of the Cultural Revolution, and revulsion at using nuclear weapons in any way meant this option was not employed. The USAF had to use attack aircraft and electronic warfare* on the trail. Rolling Thunder failed to stop the trickle of supplies needed by the guerrillas, and, when the effort stretched into years, it began to have a negative effect on morale in the South. After Tet, the campaign was stopped in the hope its abandonment would lead to peace negotiations. There had been 6,162,000 tons of bombs dropped on the North for this slap on the wrist. In contrast, in 1944–1945, the Japanese economy had been made into a shambles with 502,000 tons. The difference was in target selection.

Lacking its big lost guerrilla army, the North tried an invasion using conventional armored land forces in 1972. The North achieved tactical surprise and initially made progress against the ARVN. However, the necessary reliance on armor, 600 tanks, and other heavy equipment made the North Vietnamese army (NVA) highly vulnerable to air power. The USAF, Navy, and VNAF responded when Nixon authorized interdiction of the logistical train, no longer a trickle for guerrillas, all the way back to the North through the port of Haiphong. Nixon also granted less political air superiority to the enemy. This was Linebacker* I, and it smashed the NVA's offensive, costing the North 100,000 men and all its drive's heavy tanks and artillery. Peace negotiations, which had begun in 1968 but broken off, resumed.

Renewed truculence by the North in the peace talks in the fall of 1972 caused

Nixon to launch Linebacker II. It was similar to the 94-target plan. At its end, negotiations resumed and were soon completed. As in the wars with Japan and North Korea, a special bombing campaign had led to a negotiated peace.

There is an argument that Linebacker II failed because the terms were the same as those demanded by the North in the fall of 1972. This is a strong argument, but three factors should be noted. One is that the North was not talking until Linebacker II. Another is that Nixon believed Congress intended unilaterally to surrender in January or February 1973. The third is that Nixon believed he could repeat Linebacker I if there was renewed aggression, but this was a forlorn expectation for Congress would not permit this action when the next invasion occurred in 1975.

There is a general belief that the North defeated the United States. If so, it was a political, and not a military, defeat. Yet, it can also be asserted it was a political victory for the United States. In 1964, the threat of communist takeovers was pandemic in SEA and the western Pacific area. By 1973, no dominoes outside of Indochina had fallen, and the threat had greatly receded in the area and has continued to retreat. U.S. action in Vietnam may have contributed greatly to this change despite the final betrayal of the South.

If the North won the war, it lost the peace. It imposed a harsh tyranny and a communist basket-case economy on Vietnam. Some weakening of communist dogma and inroads of Western culture were evident in Vietnam in 1990, so the results of the war may someday be reversed.

References. Primary: Jack Broughton, *Going Downtown: The War against Hanoi and Washington*, 1988. Vo Nguyen Giap and Van Tien Dung, *How We Won the War*, 1976. Nguyen Cao Ky, *How We Lost the Vietnam War*, 1978. Secondary: Berger, *USAF in SEA*. Larry Berman, *Lyndon Johnson's War: The Road to Stalemate in Vietnam*, 1989. Mark Clodfelter, *The Limits of Air Power: The American Bombing of North Vietnam*, 1989. George C. Herring and Kevin Simon, *The Vietnam War: Lessons from Yesterday for Today*, 1988. John Schlight, *The War in South Vietnam: The Years of the Offensive 1965–1968*, 1988.

See also Jason Division; Joint Chiefs of Staff memorandum of 22 January 1964; Korean irrigation dams target system.

VITTLES. *See* Berlin Airlift.

VOGT, GENERAL JOHN W., JR. (1920–)

Vogt was commander of the Allied Air Forces Central Europe (AAFCE) and commander in chief of the U.S. Air Forces in Europe* (USAFE) from 1974 to 1975. He was responsible for USAF* air operations in Southeast Asia (SEA) for the last 18 months of U.S. combat activity. Following the cease-fire in Vietnam, he commanded the U.S. Support Activities Group (USSAG) in Thailand, which conducted all U.S. air activities in Laos and Cambodia until combat ceased in August 1973. He served as commander in chief of the Pacific Air Forces* (PACAF) from 1973 to 1974 and as commander of the Seventh Air Force* (7AF) from 1972 to 1973. He retired in 1975.

References. Primary: Richard H. Kohn and Joseph P. Harahan, eds., *Air Interdiction in World War II, Korea, and Vietnam*, 1986. U.S. Air Force Oral History Interview K239.0512–1093, USAFHRC/OH, Maxwell AFB, Alabama. Secondary: Air Force Pamphlet 31–1, "Roster of USAF Retired General Officers," 1987. Futrell, *Ideas*, vol. 2. U.S. Air Force Biography, Secretary of the Air Force, Office of Information, 1974.

James C. Hasdorff

VOLL, COLONEL JOHN J. (1922–)

Voll was the top-scoring ace* of the Fifteenth Air Force* (15AF) and was, with Lieutenant Colonel George A. Davis, Jr., and Colonel William T. Whisner, Jr., the 16th-ranking USAF* ace of all time with 21 victories. He was born in Cincinnati, Ohio, and became an aviation cadet* in 1943 and was assigned to the 308th Fighter Squadron. In one action he scored three victories without firing a shot. The three enemies had been chasing him. Two collided, and Voll dived at the ground and pulled out, but the third enemy hit the ground. In his last action, in November 1944, he single-handedly chased a Ju 88 into a formation of 12 German fighters.* In five minutes he had four victories, two probables, and two damaged. He ended World War II* serving in the headquarters of the Chinese American Composite Wing. He left the USAAF* in 1945 but was recalled to active duty in 1948.

References. DuPre, *USAF Bio*. Gurney, *5 Down*.

VON KARMAN, DR. THEODORE (1881–1963)

Von Karman was a world leader in aeronautics, astronautics, and rocketry. As such, he had an enormous impact upon the United States and the USAF.* In 1963, he received the first National Medal of Service from President John F. Kennedy* (JFK). In 1983, he was inducted into the National Aviation Hall of Fame in Dayton, Ohio.

A native of Hungary, von Karman emigrated to the United States in 1929 and took up citizenship. He became director of the Guggenheim Aeronautics Laboratory at the California Institute of Technology (GALCIT). Under him, GALCIT became a world leader in aeronautics in the 1930s, and it contributed to the rise of the aircraft industry in southern California. In 1938 Major General H. H. Arnold* asked von Karman to join a committee of the National Academy of Sciences to review science projects of potential value to the USAAC.* This began two decades of direct influence upon the USAF.

Von Karman's success in developing small rocket engines for the USAAC led to his founding of the Aerojet General Corporation. In 1944, GALCIT became the famous Jet Propulsion Laboratory (JPL) for the purpose of developing tactical ballistic missiles* for U.S. Army Ordnance.

Also in 1944, von Karman became Arnold's scientific adviser. Then he became the first head of the Air Force Scientific Advisory Group, which became the Air Force's Scientific Advisory Board* (SAB). The group's first reports were *Science, the Key to Air Supremacy* and *Toward New Horizons*, completed in 1945. The SAB spurred aerospace research and development (R&D) to greater efforts than ever before, speeding the feasibility of supersonic aircraft and intercontinental ballistic missiles (ICBM). Later, von Karman's JPL became a significant factor in U.S. astronautics. Von Karman's close association with the USAF ended in 1949, when he also retired from Caltech.

References. Primary: T. F. Walkowicz, "Von Karman's Singular Contributions to US Aerospace Power," *AF*, May 1981, pp. 60–69. Secondary: Futrell, *Ideas*, vol. 1. Michael H. Gorn, *Harnessing the Genie: Science and Technology Forecasting for the Air Force, 1944–1986*, 1988. R. Cargill Hall, "Theodore Von Kármán 1881–1963," *AH*, December 1981, pp. 253–58.

VOODOO. *See* F-101.

VOUGHT DIVISION. *See* A-7.

VULCAN. *See* M-61.

VULTEE AIRCRAFT INC. *See* BT-13.

VULTURE. *See* Operation Vulture.

W

WADE, MAJOR GENERAL LEIGH (1896–)

Wade did important flight test work and set many records. He was the pilot*
of one of the planes of the Round-the-World Flight of 1924,* for which he
received the Distinguished Service Medal (DSM). He was inducted into the
National Aviation Hall of Fame in Dayton, Ohio, in 1974.

He was born in Cassopolis, Michigan, and enlisted in the National Guard in
1916. Wade then became an aviation cadet,* and a pilot and officer in 1917. In
France he was an instructor pilot and test pilot. After the war he worked in
aircraft procurement.* Wade left the service in 1926 for Consolidated Aircraft
Corporation but returned in 1941. He then held a series of commands, including
that of Batista Field, Cuba, from 1942 to 1946. He also held staff positions.
His last office was chief of the Air Section of the Joint Brazil-U.S. Military
Commission. He retired in 1955.

References. *Biographical Study of USAF General Officers, 1917–1952*, vol. 2, n.d.
DuPre, *USAF Bio.*

WAF. *See* Women in the Air Force.

WAFS. *See* Women's Auxiliary Ferrying Squadron.

WAR DEPARTMENT REORGANIZATION OF 1942

This action established a command structure that moved the young USAAF*
toward virtual autonomy. It had its origins in the airmen's drive for independence.
Difficulties in the mobilization before the U.S. entry into World War II* had
also convinced the Army chief of staff, General George C. Marshall, that the
War Department's feudal bureaucratic structure had to be modified to meet the
demands of a global war. The reorganization plan strove for centralized planning
and decentralized execution. The chief of staff, aided by the War Plans Division,
later called Operations Division, of the General Staff, would direct activities in

the wartime theaters of operations. Within the continental United States (CONUS), or Zone of the Interior (ZI), responsibility for raising, training, equipping, supplying, and transporting troops was divided among three equal services: Army Ground Forces under Lieutenant General Leslie J. McNair, Army Air Forces under Lieutenant General H. H. Arnold,* and Services of Supply (SOS) under Lieutenant General Brehon Somervell. Each commander reported directly to the chief of staff.

The USAAF, created in 1941, achieved something less than the full independence desired by interwar air advocates. Nevertheless, reorganization gave airmen some freedom, not present under the former ground-dominated command structure, to exploit what they saw as the unique capabilities of the air arm.

References. C&C, vol. 1. Russell F. Weigley, *History of the United States Army*, 1967.

John R. Reese

WARHAWK. *See* P-40.

WAR LOVER, THE

John Hersey's 1959 novel,* important in USAF* fiction, was set in the Eighth Air Force* (8AF) in World War II.* Intended as an antiwar and a psychological novel, its plot is the story of a war lover, William S. "Buzz" Marrow, in battle. Hersey's thesis is that Marrow is not an uncommon type of man and that such men make war more terrible. *The War Lover* became a best-seller. The novel was made into a movie* in 1962. Steve McQueen played the lead with the character name changed to "Buzz" Rickson. Although well done, the movie fell far short of the novel in influence.

References. "The 40th Anniversary of the USAF," a special issue of *AH*, September 1987, pp. 208–9. Bruce W. Orriss, *When Hollywood Ruled the Skies*, 1984.

WARREN, FRANCIS E., AFB. *See* Francis E. Warren AFB.

WASHINGTON NAVAL CONFERENCE, 1921 TO 1922

Called by President Warren Harding, this conference placed limitations on naval vessels, especially battleships, but its Aviation Subcommittee failed to agree on rules to govern aerial bombardment. It did, however, agree to limit the number of aircraft carriers.

Because of wide publicity on an impending naval race between Britain, Japan, and the United States, politicians such as William E. Borah* stirred sufficient public interest to persuade the president to call for a disarmament conference. A variety of treaties on naval arms and the Far East situation resulted from the conference, and aviation played two minor roles. First, aircraft carrier tonnage was limited at a ratio giving Britain and the United States three carriers each and Japan two carriers. Second, the Aviation Subcommittee concluded that affinity of commercial and military aviation might preclude the development of commercial transportation if aircraft were restricted. The subcommittee recommended a special committee of experts to study rules governing aircraft in future wars. This Jurist Hague Commission to regulate aerial warfare* met in December 1922.

References. Lester H. Brune, *The Origins of American National Security: Sea Power, Air Power and Foreign Policy, 1900 to 1941*, 1981. Harold and Margaret Sprout, *Toward a New Order of Sea Power*, 1940.

Lester H. Brune

WASP. *See* Women Airforce Service Pilots.

WEAPON SYSTEM CONCEPT

The weapon system concept treats a combat unit, such as an airplane or missile, as an entity from its design to use. Thus, a unit should have its concept as an instrument of war, with integrated design, fabrication, test, logistics, training, and maintenance. For example, the point of view is not of the B-1* as an airplane but as a consistent weapon system.

In the USAF's* antecedent organizations, the method for procuring new equipment had been for the service to buy engines, machine guns, radios, and other equipment and ask an aircraft maker to use these components in its design. These components were called "government-furnished equipment" (GFE). Manufacturers, therefore, installed equipment in their designs from "off-the-shelf." There are great advantages in this method: standardized equipment, cost reduction through volume purchasing, and contractual relationships which could push federal socioeconomic goals through more companies. Over time, this method became less efficient. Aircraft and missiles became denser, resulting in degradation of performance as designs were altered to accommodate standard components.

The alternative weapon system method was conceived in Germany, and the USAAF's Scientific Advisory Group suggested it be adopted. This did not occur, however, until advances in avionics increasingly led to difficulties in using GFE. In 1950, the USAF let its first partial weapon system contract for the F-102* and its first complete one for the B-58* in 1952. The transition was not a problem for the aerospace industry,* which was already using it for commercial products. The weapon system concept worked so well that the U.S. Army and Navy followed the USAF's lead.

References. Charles D. Bright, *The Jet Makers: The Aerospace Industry from 1945 to 1972*, 1978. Woodford Agee Heflin, ed., *The United States Air Force Dictionary*, 1956. Bernard J. Termena et al., *Logistics: An Illustrated History of AFLC and Its Antecedents, 1921–1981*, 1981.

WEAPON SYSTEM OPERATOR (WSO)

After World War II* avionics advanced rapidly. A controversy developed in fighters* as a result: was a second crewman now necessary? Those who thought so argued a single pilot* could no longer effectively control the aircraft while operating the myriad of avionics efficiently. Those who disagreed said avionics were, inherently, capable of being automated, that the heavy penalties in performance from added weight, volume, and structure would outweigh the value of a second crewman in an air superiority* fighter. Both single- and dual-seat fighter types were built for the USAF.*

A second crewman, called a WSO, keeps electronic "silence" until advised by ground-controlled interception* (GCI) to "unmask," or use his radar* to search for the enemy. When the enemy aircraft* is located, the pilot tries to gain the most advantageous position for attack.* The WSO sets up a target sequence and approach for his computer, selects the missile ordnance to be used, and activates the missile systems. When the WSO determines it is time to launch a missile, he informs the pilot who fires it. At first, the USAF hoped to have only pilots in its two-man crews, but this proved wasteful and extremely unpopular with pilots. Consequently, navigators* came to be used as WSOs.

In the Vietnam War,* the air superiority* task fell to the two-seat F-4.* At first, victories were divided by a crew, much as they were divided between two or more fighter pilots in earlier wars when each contributed to a victory. Later, in Vietnam, as air superiority results proved disappointing to the USAF, it decided to award a full victory credit to both men of a crew. This change was made retroactive and added substantially to scores. In the war, the USAF gave credit as aces* to three men. One was a pilot, Captain Richard S. "Steve" Ritchie.* Two were WSOs, Captains Charles B. DeBellevue, with credit for six, and Jeffrey S. Feinstein with five. The American Fighter Aces Association, and other people, do not recognize WSOs or gunners* as aces. WSOs have been nicknamed "Ace of Gages," "Backseater," "Bear," "Fightergator" (a blend of fighter-navigator), "'Gator," "Guy in Back" or "GIB," "Pitter," "Prisoner of the Pit," and "Whizzo."

In the 1980s, it appeared the single-seat concept was best for fighters, and the dual was satisfactory for interceptors.*

References. R. Frank Futrell et al., *Aces & Aerial Victories: The United States Air Force in Southeast Asia 1965–1973*, 1976. Bill Gunston and Lindsay Peacock, *Fighter Missions*, 1989. Mike Spick, *The Ace Factor: Air Combat & the Role of Situational Awareness*, 1988.

WEARY-WILLIE. *See* Aphrodite.

WEHNER, FIRST LIEUTENANT JOSEPH F. *See* Luke, Second Lieutenant Frank, Jr.

WELCH, GENERAL LARRY D. (1935–)
Welch was the twelfth chief of staff of the USAF,* serving from 1986 to 1990, and was commander in chief of the Strategic Air Command* (CINCSAC) from 1985 to 1986. As chief, Welch's accomplishments included negotiations on the Intermediate-Range Nuclear Forces Treaty signed with the USSR, a strengthening of USAF* relationships with Latin America, improving officer development, and reducing the strength of the USAF.

Born in Guymon, Oklahoma, he enlisted in the 161st Armored Field Artillery of the Kansas National Guard in 1951. Welch became an aviation cadet* in 1953 and a pilot* and an officer in 1955. His undergraduate education was in business administration with the University of Maryland, and he had a master's degree in international relations from George Washington University in Washington, D.C. For the most part he served in fighter* units until he flew combat from 1966 to 1967 in F-4s* in the Vietnam War.* From 1972 to 1981, Welch had important staff and command positions in the Tactical Air Command* (TAC). From 1981 to 1982, he was commander of the Ninth Air Force* (9AF) and of the USAF part of the Rapid Deployment Joint Task Force (RDJTF). He became vice chief of staff of the USAF in 1984.

Welch was considered the leading candidate to replace Admiral William J. Crowe, Jr., as chairman of the Joint Chiefs of Staff (JCS) in 1990. However, he angered Secretary of Defense (SECDEF) Richard B. Cheney in a discussion on ballistic missiles* with Congress and was retired at the end of his standard term.**

References. John Ginovsky, "AF Pulls Out All the Stops for Welch Send-off," *Air Force Times*, 9 July 1990, p. 16. Steve Weber, "Welch Acknowledges He'll Retire in June," *Air Force Times*, 19 February 1990, p. 3.

**Less than two months after Welch retired, Cheney fired his successor, General Michael J. Dugan,* for discussions with the press about the Iraq crisis of 1990.*

WESTBROOK, LIEUTENANT COLONEL ROBERT B. (1917–1944)

Westbrook and Lieutenant Colonel Thomas J. Lynch* share the honor of ranking 20th of all USAF* aces.* Born in San Antonio, Texas, he served with the California National Guard and the Infantry from 1938 to 1942. In January 1942, he became an aviation cadet* and in August was a pilot.* He then joined the 44th Fighter Squadron flying P-38s* and P-40s* in the southwest Pacific. In September 1943 he became the 44th's commander and had seven victories. In January 1944 he joined headquarters of the Thirteenth Air Force* (13AF). In March 1944, he led four risky missions and, on one of them, he and his men fought eight A6M Reisens ("Zeros"). Westbrook shot down three. In November he strafed airfields near Makassar, Celebes. He strafed freighters and gunboats on the return flight, lost an engine, and had to ditch in the sea. He did not survive.

References. DuPre, *USAF Bio.* Hess, *Aces Album.*

WESTERN AIR DEFENSE FORCE

This named air force* was established in 1949 at Hamilton AFB, California, and was assigned to the Continental Air Command* (CONAC). Its mission was the air defense of the western part of the continental United States (CONUS). In 1951, it was reassigned to the Air Defense Command (ADC). It was discontinued in 1960.

Reference. Ravenstein, *Org. USAF.*

WESTERN TRANSPORT AIR FORCE. *See* Twenty-Second Air Force.

WESTOVER, MAJOR GENERAL OSCAR "TUBBY" (1883–1938)

Westover was the fourth head of the USAAC,* serving from 1935 to 1938. In 1932, when he became assistant to the chief of Air Corps, he planned for U.S. air defense, and this led to the General Headquarters Air Force* (GHQ Air Force) in 1935. As chief, Westover emphasized flight training,* worked to save the B-17* from its enemies, and promoted aviation. Westover AFB at Chicopee Falls, Massachusetts, was named for this chief who was noted as able, conscientious, and honest.

Westover was born in Bay City, Michigan, and graduated from the U.S. Military Academy (USMA) in 1906. He then spent ten years in the Infantry before transferring to the Aviation Section of the U.S. Army Signal Corps.* He became rated for airplanes, balloons, and airships as a pilot* and observer.* From 1920 to 1922 he was executive to the chief of the Air Service.* In 1922 he won the elimination free-balloon race. From then until 1928 he was director of aircraft production. Westover died in an aircraft accident while he was chief.

References. Primary: Ira Eaker, "Memories of Six Air Chiefs, Part II: Westover, Arnold, Spaatz," *AH*, December 1973, pp. 189–91. Secondary: DeWitt S. Copp, *A Few Great Captains: The Men and Events That Shaped the Development of U.S. Air Power*, 1980. DuPre, *USAF Bio*. Futrell, *Ideas*, vol. 1.

WEST POINT OF THE AIR. See movies.

WETMORE, LIEUTENANT COLONEL RAY S. (1923–1951)

With 21.25 aerial victories, Wetmore ranks 15th among USAF* aces* for all time. From Madera, California, he enlisted in the USAAF* in 1941. At first he was an armorer but became a pilot* and officer in 1943. He saw battle in Europe with the 370th Fighter Squadron flying F-47s* and F-51s.* He flew 142 combat sorties for 563 hours. The Eighth Air Force* (8AF) shot down four Me 163 rocket fighters,* and Wetmore scored the last of those victories. On 2 November 1944 he attacked Bf 109s engaging bombers* and shot down one. Later, on the same sortie, he alone attacked a formation of more than 15 Bf 109s and shot down another. Flying fighter escort* on 27 November he saw about 200 Bf 109s and Fw 190s approaching. His element* attacked one formation and Wetmore scored three victories. He stayed in fighters after World War II* and was killed in a flying accident while commander of the 59th Fighter Interceptor Squadron.

References. DuPre, *USAF Bio*. Roger A. Freeman, *The Mighty Eighth: Units, Men and Machines*, 1970. Hess, *Aces Album*.

WEYLAND, GENERAL OTTO P. "OPIE" (1902–1979)

During 36 years of service, Weyland mastered tactical operations,* becoming both a theorist and practitioner of that function of air power. Born in Riverside, California, he graduated from Texas A&M University and entered the USAAS* in 1923. After becoming a pilot,* his early career was spent in fighter* and observation aviation.* Named deputy director of air support at headquarters of the USAAF,* he developed tactics, techniques, and equipment for tactical operations. In 1943 he went to Europe to lead the 84th Fighter Wing and soon commanded the XIX Tactical Air Command. In the latter position he directed fighter attack* for Operation Overlord* and then teamed with General George S. Patton to spearhead the breakout from Normandy. He introduced "armor-column liaison officers," USAAF fighter pilots riding with the lead tanks to be forward air controllers* (FAC). Additionally, he perfected battlefield air interdiction (BAI) tactics, permitting air power to "cover" Patton's southern flank during the blitzkrieg across France.

In July 1950, he became vice commander for operations of the Far East Air Forces (FEAF), where he coordinated the attack efforts to save the United Nations (UN) troops hemmed into the Pusan perimeter.* Later he focused USAF* efforts upon interdiction of enemy rail and communications lines in the Korean War.* In 1951 he became FEAF and UN Air Force commander. He directed the continued interdiction efforts and the air superiority* struggles in "MiG Alley."* He also directed the strategic operations* campaigns against the Korean electrical power target system* and the Korean irrigation dams target system.* After the Korean War, he reorganized Japan's air defense and aircraft industry.

After he returned to the United States in 1954, he battled for tactical operations in a USAF dominated by the Strategic Air Command* (SAC). He became commander of the Tactical Air Command* (TAC), where he introduced the Composite Air Strike Force* (CASF). He retired in 1959.

References. Primary: James C. Hasdorff and Noel F. Parrish, U.S. Air Force Oral History Interview, Albert F. Simpson Historical Research Center, Air University, Maxwell AFB, Alabama, 1974. Secondary: DuPre, *USAF Bio*. Futrell, *USAF in Korea* and *Ideas*, vol. 1.

John T. Farquhar

WHEELER AIR FORCE BASE

A Pacific Air Forces* (PACAF) base located near the center of Oahu Island, Hawaii, Wheeler was activated in 1922. It was named for Major Sheldon H. Wheeler, commanding officer of Luke Field, Hawaii, who died in an aircraft accident. It is alongside the U.S. Army's famous Schofield Barracks and is the oldest active air base in Hawaii.

At the time of the Pearl Harbor* raid, the 15th and 18th Pursuit Groups were stationed on it, with one squadron* away at Haleiwa Airfield. About 25 Japanese dive bombers attacked Wheeler Field at 0800 hours. After the raid, P-36s* and P-40s* took off in pursuit of the enemy aircraft* and flew 25 sorties. Some sorties were flown from Haleiwa, and Lieutenant George S. Welch claimed four victories. Only one U.S. fighter* was lost in the air, believed to be a victim of U.S. flak.* In 1990, Wheeler had the 6010th Aerospace Defense Group and U.S. Army helicopter* training based upon it.

References. Primary: Henry C. Woodrum, "Cloak of Darkness," *AH*, December 1988, pp. 281–91. Secondary: C&C, vol. 1. "Guide to Major Air Force Installations Worldwide," *AF*, May 1990, p. 132. Roberts, *Dir. USAF*.

WHISNER, COLONEL WILLIAM T. (1923–1989)

Whisner ranks 16th among USAF* aces* of all time along with Lieutenant Colonel George A. Davis, Jr.,* and Colonel John J. Voll.* He had 21 victories.

He was born in Shreveport, Louisiana, became an aviation cadet* in 1942, and graduated as a pilot* in 1943. Assigned to the 487th Fighter Squadron of the Eighth Air Force* (8AF) in England, he became a wingman to Major George E. Preddy, Jr.* Flying F-47s* and, later, F-51s,* he scored 15.5 aerial victories in World War II.* On 21 November 1944, while flying fighter escort,* Whisner and his flight* attacked 100 German aircraft. Whisner claimed seven Fw 190s in this dogfight, but his gun camera film ended after his sixth victory. During the German air attack of 1 January 1945,* Whisner shot down four in one day.

After the war, he left the USAAF* but was recalled one year later for fighter* assignments. He flew F-86s* with the 4th Fighter Group in the Korean War,* where he shot down 5.5 MiG-15s. Thus, Whisner achieved the distinction of becoming an ace in two wars. For the rest of his USAF career he filled command and staff assignments.

References. DuPre, *USAF Bio*. Roger A. Freeman, *The Mighty Eighth: Units, Men and Machines*, 1970. Hess, *Aces Album*.

WHITE, GENERAL THOMAS D. (1901–1965)

White was the fourth chief of staff of the Air Force,* serving from 1957 to 1961. He is remembered as the advocate in USAF* headquarters of ballistic missiles* and space efforts.

Born in Walker, Minnesota, he graduated from the U.S. Military Academy (USMA) in 1920 as a first lieutenant. At first he was in the Infantry but switched to the USAAS* and became a pilot* in 1925. In the late 1920s he compiled a Chinese-English dictionary of military nomenclature while a student of the Chinese language. He served in air attaché posts in the USSR, Italy, and Greece until 1935. White was fluent in the Chinese, Greek, Italian, Portuguese, Russian, and Spanish languages. After schools and more attaché work, he became chief of staff of the Third Air Force* (3AF) in 1942. White became deputy commanding general of the Thirteenth Air Force* (13AF) in 1944 and commanding general of the Seventh Air Force* (7AF) the next year. Later he headed the Fifth Air Force* (5AF). In 1951 he went to headquarters of the USAF to stay. By 1953 he was vice chief of staff. After his retirement he was a frequent writer for *Newsweek* magazine.

References. DuPre, *USAF Bio*, and "The Chiefs of Staff of the United States Air Force," *AF*, September 1967, pp. 190, 193. Futrell, *Ideas*, 2 vols. Bill Yenne, *The History of the United States Air Force*, 1984.

WHITEHEAD, LIEUTENANT GENERAL ENNIS C. (1895–1964)

Whitehead was second only to General George C. Kenney* in leading the USAAF* against Japan in the southwest Pacific. During World War II* he commanded the Fifth Air Force* (5AF) and the Far East Air Forces (FEAF).

From Westphalia, Kansas, he became a flying cadet in 1917. After becoming a pilot* he was an instructor pilot at Issoudon,* France. He graduated from the University of Kansas in 1920 and became a regular officer. Until 1926 he had flying duties; then he graduated from the Air Service Engineering School at McCook Field, Ohio. He participated as a pilot and engineering officer in the Pan American Flight of 1926.* Thereafter he continued in maintenance for a few years. In the 1930s he had a variety of command and staff positions. In 1942 he joined the 5AF as deputy commanding officer. He was aggressive, and the Japanese called him "Ennis the Menace" and "The Butcher of Moresby." After serving in the Far East, he commanded the Continental Air Command* (CONAC) and the Air Defense Command (ADC). After retirement he became highly active in the Air Force Association* (AFA) and wrote articles for publication.

References. *Biographical Study of USAF General Officers 1917–1952*, n.d. C&C, vols. 4 and 5. DuPre, *USAF Bio*.

WHITEMAN AIR FORCE BASE

This base, near Sedalia, Missouri, is a Strategic Air Command* (SAC) installation. It was activated in 1942 and named for the city until 1955 when it was renamed for Second Lieutenant George A. Whiteman, of Sedalia, the first pilot* killed in action during the Pearl Harbor* raid. He was flying a P-40.* The field began as a glider* school but mainly trained transport* pilots during World War II.* It became inactive in 1946 but was reactivated in 1951 for B-47s* and KC-97s (*see* C-97). They moved out in 1963, and Minuteman* IIs arrived in 1964. In 1990 the 351st Strategic Missile Wing (SMW) was there with Minuteman IIs. It was scheduled to receive B-2s* in the 1990s.

References. "Guide to Major USAF Installations Worldwide," *AF*, May 1990, p. 132. Mueller, *AFB*. Roberts, *Dir. USAF*.

WILD BLUE, THE. See novels.

WILD BLUE YONDER. See movies.

WILD WEASEL

This is a class of aircraft that conducts a form of electronic warfare* designed to reduce the effectiveness of an enemy's air defenses. They find and destroy an enemy's surface-to-air missiles* (SAM) and the associated radars.* They use radar identification equipment and missiles that can home on SAM guidance and control signals. In the Vietnam War,* the main USAF* Wild Weasel aircraft used were F-4s,* F-100s,* and F-105s.* In 1991 the USAF used the F-4G

Advanced Wild Weasel in the Iraq War.* The aircraft's armament includes the AGM-45* and AGM-88.*

References. Berger, *USAF in SEA*. Thomas M. Cleaver, "Wild Weasels Smash the Vermin," *AF*, July 1982, pp. 80–82. Larry Davis, *Wild Weasel: The SAM Suppression Story*, 1986. Jeffrey P. Rhodes, "Slam 'Em and Jam 'Em," *AF*, June 1989, pp. 50–56. Susan H. H. Young, "Gallery of USAF Weapons," *AF*, May 1990, pp. 143, 157, 158.

Frank L. Goldstein contributed to this essay.

WILLIAMS AIR FORCE BASE

Near Chandler, Arizona, this is an Air Training Command* (ATC) field. It was activated in 1941 and was first known as Mesa or Higley for nearby towns. It was renamed in 1942 for First Lieutenant Charles L. Williams who died in a PW-9A crash near Fort DeRussy, Hawaii, in 1927. Because of its location and climate, it has been one of the most popular USAF* bases, affectionately called "Willy Air Patch." The field has always been used for training, first in twin-engine, then in single-engine beginning in 1943, and finally in four-engine aircraft in 1944. Fighter* pilot* training began in 1945, then flight training,* and fighter gunnery in the mid–1950s. In 1961 it returned to flight training which has continued to today. In 1990 it was the largest flight training base for the USAF with its 82nd Flying Training Wing (FTW) flying T-37s* and T-38s.* It also had the Human Resources Laboratory of the Flying Training Division doing research on flight simulators.

References. "Guide to Major Air Force Installations Worldwide," *AF*, May 1990, p. 132. Mueller, *AFB*. Roberts, *Dir. USAF*.

WILLIAM TELL. *See* competitions.

WILSON, MAJOR GENERAL WINSTON P. "WIMPY" (1911–)

Wilson is the single most important figure in the history of the Air National Guard* (ANG). Under his dynamic leadership, the ANG was transformed from glorified, government-sponsored flying clubs into a first-rate component of the USAF.*

He was born in Arkadelphia, Arkansas, and enlisted as a mechanic in the Arkansas National Guard in 1929. He became a pilot* in 1940, entered active federal duty, and was soon separated from his Guard unit. His World War II* service in a variety of assignments convinced him that Guard units must never again be carved up to serve as individual replacements for the regular service. He believed Guard units should retain their cohesion and unique identities.

Wilson returned to the ANG in 1946. It was badly neglected by the USAF after the war. Wilson knew it would not survive unless it got true war missions and had the same standards as the regular force. Despite skepticism and even outright hostility from the regulars, he was able to begin reform when he was recalled to active duty for the Korean War.* Assigned to the National Guard Bureau (NGB) in the Pentagon, he became acting chief of its Air Force Division in 1953, then deputy chief of the NGB in 1955, and chief in 1963. He was the only ANG member to hold that assignment on a permanent basis in the Army-oriented NGB.

Wilson was a skilled manager, political and bureaucratic infighter, and publicist. He got true war missions with training under the active force. In 1953, he won grudging USAF approval of a test where two ANG fighter* squadrons* augmented the Air Defense Command's (ADC) runway alert forces for training. The experiment was highly successful. It was widely expanded and paved the way for the Total Force Policy* of the 1970s, because it demonstrated that properly prepared Reserves could train for war while actively supporting the regulars.

Wilson was able, in time, to diversify the ANG's mission, increase manning, and modernize aircraft. After years of effort by Wilson and others, the secretary of the Air Force* (SAF) approved the gaining command concept in 1960. That forced commanders of the major commands* (MAJCOM) that would gain ANG and U.S. Air Force Reserve* (USAFR) units in war to be responsible for their peacetime training.

He had a strong reputation for honesty and reliability. His folksy and straight-forward style won many friends in Congress, the states, and the USAF. He was a man of action and a quick thinker who never delegated authority and knew when to ignore a chain of command. Although friendly and outgoing, he would fight for the interests of the ANG. He remained active in ANG affairs following his retirement.

References. Primary: Interview of Major General Winston P. Wilson, ANGUS (Retired), Forrest City, Arkansas, December 17–18, 1978, with Charles J. Gross, *Air Force Logistics Command Oral History Program Interview #19*. Secondary: Charles J. Gross, *Prelude to the Total Force: The Air National Guard, 1943–1969*, 1985, and "From Jennies to Jets: Maj. Gen. Winston P. Wilson and the Air National Guard," *AH*, December 1986, pp. 257–64.

Charles J. Gross

WILSON MEMORANDUMS

The Pace-Finletter memorandum of 4 November 1952,* on the extent of U.S. Army air power, did not last in the environment of acrimony between the USAF* and the Army on this issue. The Army placed heavy emphasis on helicopters* which were permitted without limit under Pace-Finletter, and it sought the ballistic missile* mission. Then, after the Korean War,* the USAF cut back on its plans for tactical airlift* wings.* Adding to the rancor in the 1950s was the Army's perception that it was being neglected by the Department of Defense (DoD) and Congress because strategic priority went to the USAF. Army General Maxwell D. Taylor called the period the "Babylonian Captivity" of the Army.

Secretary of Defense (SECDEF) Charles E. Wilson sought a resolution to the disagreements. In his memorandum of 26 November 1956, Wilson suggested a study of how much guided missiles could substitute for USAF attack* operations. He also gave the Army a monopoly on surface-to-air missiles* (SAM) to parallel that of all flak.* Wilson gave control of intermediate-range ballistic missiles

(IRBM) and intercontinental ballistic missiles (ICBM) to the USAF. In a memorandum of 18 March 1957, he said the Army's air force could operate in a zone of 100 miles on either side of a front line to perform liaison, observation, tactical airlift, and aeromedical evacuation.* Army fixed-wing aircraft and helicopters could not exceed 5,000 and 20,000 pounds empty respectively. Wilson's efforts cooled but did not end the disagreements.

References. A. J. Bacevich, *The Pentomic Era: The US Army between Korea and Vietnam*, 1986. Frederic A. Bergerson, *The Army Gets an Air Force: The Tactics of Insurgent Bureaucratic Politics*, 1980. Goldberg, *Hist. USAF*.

See also A-7; C-7; Howze Board; Jupiter; Kennedy, President John F.; Key West and Newport Conferences of 1948; separation from the U.S. Army; Vietnam War.

"WIMPY." *See* Wilson, Major General Winston P.

WING

This USAF* unit is subordinate to the division* level and superior to the group.* It is normally the USAF's basic, self-sufficient unit. Wings, designated by Arabic numerals, are predominantly of three kinds: operational, support, and air base. An operational wing will have, for example, fighters,* tankers,* or trainers. A support wing is like the 6940th Security Wing. An air base wing is one responsible for operating a base. The USAF's strength can be quickly and roughly, but reasonably, measured by counting the operational wings. Usually, a wing will have four groups under it. In the USAF's antecedents the equivalent organization was usually called a group. Wings in those organizations were roughly equal to today's divisions.

References. Woodford Agee Heflin, ed., *The United States Air Force Dictionary*, 1956. Ravenstein, *Org. USAF*.

WINGMAN. *See* element.

WINGS. *See* movies.

WINGS OVER NAM. *See* novels.

WINNING YOUR WINGS. *See* movies.

WOLFE, LIEUTENANT GENERAL KENNETH B. "K.B." (1896–)

Wolfe did the invaluable service of supervising the USAAF* side of the development of the B-29* and its flight tests, and he organized the plane's first raid on Japan. He was born in Denver, Colorado, and enlisted in the Aviation Section of the U.S. Army Signal Corps* in January 1918. By July he was a pilot* and officer and then served as an instructor pilot. In 1920 he was promoted to first lieutenant and stayed in that grade for 14 years. During the peacetime years he had varied assignments and attended the Air Corps Engineering School in 1931. In 1937, Wolfe became USAAC* representative to the Douglas Aircraft

Company, and, in 1939, chief of the Production Engineering Section at Wright Field. There he headed the B-29 Special Project Staff. In June 1943, he became commanding general of the 58th Bomb Wing at Smoky Hill Field, Kansas. Wolfe then organized the XX Bomber Command, trained it, and led it as it moved to India and China and delivered the first B-29 raids on Japan.

Then he returned to Wright Field for more procurement* duties. In October 1945, he took command of the Fifth Air Force* (5AF) to supervise it as an occupation unit in Japan. In 1948 he returned to Wright Field to be director of procurement and industrial mobilization planning in the Air Materiel Command (AMC). The next year he went to the Air Staff* as deputy chief of staff for materiel. He retired in 1951.

References. Steve Birdsall, *Saga of the Superfortress: The Dramatic Story of the B-29 and the Twentieth Air Force*, 1980. Thomas Collison, *The Superfortress Is Born: The Story of the Boeing B-29*, 1945. DuPre, *USAF Bio*. Irving Brinton Holley, Jr., *Buying Aircraft: Matériel Procurement for the Army Air Forces*, 1964. Curtis E. LeMay and Bill Yenne, *Superfortress: The Story of the B-29 and American Air Power*, 1988.

WOMEN AIRFORCE SERVICE PILOTS (WASP)

In 1939, Jacqueline Cochran* publicly suggested recruiting and training women to fly military aircraft and perform a variety of noncombat flying tasks. While military leaders debated the need for and practicality of women pilots,* Cochran recruited 25 U.S. women volunteers for Britain's Air Transport Auxiliary.

On 7 October 1942, Lieutenant General H. H. Arnold,* facing a growing need for men combat pilots, directed the inauguration of a flight training* program to produce 500 women ferry pilots. On 15 October, Cochran was appointed director of Women's Flying Training. By 18 October, 50 women had been interviewed and 40 accepted and sent for training at Howard Hughes airport in Houston, Texas. By November, Arnold wanted all future training to qualify women pilots for most noncombat flying jobs. This meant even larger numbers of women trainees; in February 1943, a new school for women pilots opened at Avenger Field, Sweetwater, Texas. In June, Cochran was appointed special assistant and director of women pilots within the USAAF.* In August the new official title for all women pilots serving with the USAAF became Women Airforce Service Pilots (WASP).

The WASP attracted more than 33,000 women applicants. Of those selected, 1,074 graduated. Most were excellent pilots. During the program there were 402 airplane accidents, about one fatality for every 16,000 hours of flight. Every bomber* and transport* ferried by a WASP was safely delivered to its destination without a single mishap. The planes flown by WASP included training planes AT-7, AT-10, AT-11, and BT-13;* transports C-47,* C-54,* C-64, and C-78; attack* planes A-24 and A-25; bombers* B-25,* TB-26,* and B-34. At least one WASP learned to fly the B-24* and P-63.* The WASP flew more than 75 million miles, five million miles per month, with each woman averaging more than 14 flying hours per month. In October 1944 the USAAF, citing the changing combat situation, announced the WASP would be deactivated in December. The WASP's appeal for veterans' status was ignored until 1978 when Congress finally granted benefits to the 850 surviving WASP.

References. Primary: Ann R. Johnson, "The WASP of World War II," *AH*, Summer–Fall 1970, pp. 76–82. Secondary: C&C, vol. 6. Victor K. Chun, "The Origin of the WASPs," *AAHS Journal*, Winter 1969, pp. 259–62. RitaVictoria Gomez, *A History of Women in the Air Force*, forthcoming. Sally Van Wagenen Keil, *Those Wonderful Women in Their Flying Machines*, 1979. Valerie Moolman, *Women Aloft*, a vol. of *The Epic of Flight*, 1981.

See also Love, Nancy Harkness; Women's Auxiliary Ferrying Squadron.

RitaVictoria Gomez

WOMEN IN THE AIR FORCE (WAF)

On 1 July 1943, President Franklin D. Roosevelt* (FDR) signed a bill permitting women to join a Women's Army Corps (WAC). By September, there were 20,000 WAC in the USAAF.* In time they were stationed at 158 airfields and worked in 201 duty specialties, the bulk of them clerical, communication, and motor transport jobs. But women also worked in nontraditional jobs such as Link trainer* operators, weather observers, and flight control tower operators. By January 1945, 42,181 women were serving with the USAAF, 7,000 of whom were stationed overseas.

On 12 June 1948, President Harry S. Truman* (HST) signed the Women's Armed Services Integration Act. Women were now permitted to join the USAF,* and Geraldine Pratt May was appointed the first director of WAF. In increments of 100 inductees monthly, the first WAF reported for basic training in September at Lackland* AFB, Texas. Except for quarters and facilities, the WAF received identical treatment and training as men airmen. They worked and served in almost all career fields, with warrant officers serving only in the cryptographic fields; no women performed flying duties in the USAF except flight nurses.* This ended in 1958, when women were no longer allowed to enter fields such as intelligence, information, weather, certain maintenance fields, and control tower operation.

By 1965, enlisted women were found in only 36 of 61 noncombatant occupational fields in all the services. Nearly 70 percent were in clerical and administrative work and 23 percent in medical facilities. Opportunities were likewise limited for officers. More than 75 percent of women line officers held administrative, personnel, information, and similar desk jobs. In November 1964, the number of WAF was further curtailed to 5,000 women and 700 officers.

A turning point came in the spring of 1966; the USAF and other services agreed to a small expansion in their women's programs. This was the first major change in the attitude toward military women since the Korean War.* On 8 November 1967, President Lyndon B. Johnson* (LBJ) signed Public Law 90–130 which removed restrictions on the career ceilings for women officers. It also removed the 2 percent restrictions on regular line officer and enlisted strengths.

During the 1970s WAF numbers expanded. In June 1976, the office of WAF director was dissolved as women became integral members of the USAF.

References. C&C, vol. 7. RitaVictoria Gomez, *A History of Women in the Air Force*, forthcoming. Edwin J. Kosier, "Women in the Air Force," *AH*, Summer 1968, pp. 18–23.

RitaVictoria Gomez

WOMEN'S AUXILIARY FERRYING SQUADRON (WAFS)

Nancy Harkness Love,* a well-known aviator of the 1930s, proposed to the USAAF* Ferrying Command that 21- to 35-year-old women possessing high school diplomas, U.S. citizenship, a commercial pilot's* license, 500 hours of logged and certified flying time, and a 200 horsepower rating be hired as military ferry pilots. They would ferry primary trainers and liaison aircraft for a $250 monthly salary plus a $6 per diem for any time spent away from their assigned bases.

Major General H. H. Arnold,* chief of the USAAC,* rejected the proposal, but, in September 1942, facing increasing shortages of men pilots, he reconsidered and approved formation of a women's ferrying squadron.* In the same month, the secretary of war announced the founding of the WAFS. The majority of the original squadron members, 21 out of 25, had superior qualifications. All were proficient flyers, many were flying instructors, and one had 2,500 hours flying time and ran her own airport. The WAFS was based at the Second Ferrying Group, New Castle Army Air Base, Wilmington, Delaware. Love was appointed its director; however, no squadron was ever formally activated.

The WAFS was nothing more than a convenient, albeit unofficial, designation for these women pilots. In reality, they were "civil pilots" with no distinction between themselves and civilian men ferry pilots. They followed the same mixture of USAAF* regulations, Civil Aviation Agency (CAA) rules, and Ferry Instructions as men pilots did. In recognition of their gender, they were organized into a separate and distinct organization of 50 women under Love. During late 1942 and early 1943, there were only 23 WAFS performing ferrying duties, yet these women ferried an average of 49 planes per month and logged more than 21 flying hours per woman per month.

The success of this program influenced Arnold's decision to substitute women pilots for most noncombat flying. This meant the need for larger numbers of women pilots. In February 1943, a new training school for women pilots opened at Avenger Field in Sweetwater, Texas. The WAFS was ordered to merge with these new women pilots. In August the new official title for all women pilots serving with the USAAF became Women Airforce Service Pilots* (WASP).

References. C&C, vol. 7. RitaVictoria Gomez, *A History of Women in the Air Force*, forthcoming. Sally Van Wagenen Keil, *Those Wonderful Women in Their Flying Machines*, 1979.

RitaVictoria Gomez

WOODBRIDGE. *See* RAF Bentwaters and RAF Woodbridge.

WOODRING DIRECTIVE OF 1938

In May 1938, Secretary of War Harry H. Woodring issued a directive that showed why the USAAC* was a neglected service in the 1930s and unprepared for modern war. The directive told the USAAC to confine its requirements for fiscal year 1940 to attack* aircraft, that the B-17* had no mission, and that no further contracts for B-17s would be let. The timing of these views was poor, for the Munich agreement was on the horizon and it would drastically change President Franklin D. Roosevelt's* (FDR) attitudes on air power.

Woodring had been governor of Kansas and wanted to be secretary of agriculture and not of war. He was not interested in the War Department and hoped it would be an interim post. He had no qualifying background for the war position and knew nothing about aviation. He was parsimonious, and his natural inclination was to buy more small airplanes rather than fewer larger ones. Finally, Woodring had to consider the U.S. Army's General Staff, which regarded air power as a minor auxiliary to land power, and thus opposed large airplanes with the capability of strategic operations.* The directive represented the General Staff's views exactly. The directive was reversed with Roosevelt's message to Congress of 12 January 1939.* Symbolic of the change also was the reappointment of Henry L. Stimson as secretary of war when FDR faced the possibility of a war.

References. Primary: H. H. Arnold, *Global Mission*, 1949. Secondary: DeWitt S. Copp, *A Few Great Captains: The Men and Events That Shaped the Development of U.S. Air Power*, 1980. Goldberg, *Hist. USAF*.

WORKHORSE. *See* H-21.

WORLD WAR I (1914–1918)

This war brought on the adolescence of air power and the USAF.* When the war began, both were in their infancy, but the pressures of war resulted in a growth spurt.

Before the war, airmen and some others had anticipated armed aircraft and airships for attack* and strategic operations,* but the brass envisioned only reconnaissance.* The last function was used immediately in the war and influenced the early and critical Battles of the Marne and Tannenberg. Yet the first long-range strategic operation was carried out as early as November 1914 by three British Avro 504As, when they raided the airship sheds at Friedrichshafen, Germany. The 504A, representative of the aircraft of its time, had one engine of 80 horsepower (HP), a top speed of 95 miles per hour (MPH), and carried a payload of 80 pounds of bombs. Extensive reconnaissance quickly became necessary to prevent surprise in ground operations, and the fighter* was developed to put out these eyes of the enemy. The first true fighter was the German Fokker E I, introduced in August 1915. In the same year, German naval airships conducted strategic operations against Britain.

By the time the United States entered the war, April 1917, European aircraft had made much technological progress. The German Albatross D III was so effective that the month was called "Bloody April" by the British. The D III had 160 HP and a top speed of 103 MPH. Air power was no longer in its infancy in Europe, but it still was in the United States. The U.S. Army had 350 obsolete aircraft on order in that April, but, as a war participant, the plans were upgraded to 22,000 aircraft by July 1918. U.S. plans were not achieved, but the importance of air power in the war is illustrated by British war production of 52,440 aircraft.

By the end of the war, air superiority,* attack, and strategic operations had all been explored. The best fighter of the war, the Fokker D VII, had 160 HP and a top speed of 117 MPH at 3,280 feet. The British were building the Handley-Page V/1500 to raid as far as Berlin,* Germany, in strategic operations. It had four engines with 375 HP each, a top speed of 103 MPH, an endurance of 14 hours, and a payload of 10,000 pounds of bombs for a range of 400 miles. Many of the technological advances realized in World War II* had been tried at least experimentally.

The airmen of all nations were impressed with the results of their operations and had the expectations of greatly increased capability as aviation technology advanced. Air power had been highly successful at the defensive operation of reconnaissance but had made mostly tentative and experimental efforts at the vital tasks of the offensive. The successes of aerial reconnaissance had acted to prolong the war substantially by reducing the ability to achieve surprise. Although the upper hand switched back and forth between the Allies and the Germans on the western front, air superiority was never fully achieved. This was to result in downgrading the air superiority fighter between the wars. The feeble efforts at attack and strategic operations proved only promising.

The airmen came out of the war believing they should take the offensive, and this would change air power from an auxiliary to at least parity with surface forces. Independence from the ground commanders had been first achieved by the formation in May 1918 of the British Independent Force RAF (Royal Air Force). The RAF itself had replaced the British Army's Royal Flying Corps (RFC) and the Royal Naval Air Service (RNAS) in April 1918. The postwar interpretation of what an independent RAF meant would give the American airmen a dream, example, and encouragement. The USAAS* had a battle-proven air commander, Brigadier General William Mitchell,* and the combat experiences of the St. Mihiel* and Meuse-Argonne* campaigns reinforced their faith in the future capability of air power. Other powerful and favorable factors for the USAF resulting from the war were a fine legacy of excellent airfields, the lessons of production mistakes which would be remembered and usefully applied in the period of rearmamental instability for World War II, and U.S. public support for the airplane and air power created by World War I.

References. Charles D. Bright, "Air Power in World War I: Sideshow or Decisive Factor?" *AH*, June 1971, pp. 58–62. Higham, *Air Pwr*. James J. Hudson, *Hostile Skies: A Combat History of the American Air Service in World War I*, 1968. Maurer Maurer, ed., *The U.S. Air Service in World War I*, 4 vols., 1978–1979. Lucien H. Thayer,

America's First Eagles: The Official History of the U.S. Air Service, A.E.F. (1917–1918), 1983.

WORLD WAR II (1939–1945)

Air power and aviation came of age in this war. During the 1930s, there was a general fear of strategic operations* in the West. This had several bases. One was the awareness of the great strides forward in aviation capability because of the completed technological revolution to metal construction, retractable landing gear, flaps, and so on. Another was the belief that strategic operations would be directed against civilians to terrorize populations, based upon the experiences of World War I* and the Spanish Civil War. Associated with that was the assumption that incendiary and poison gas bombs* would be the most effective and likely ones used. These fears affected the Munich Conference of 1938 because German dictator Adolf Hitler possessed his apparently overpowering Luftwaffe.

The Luftwaffe had many aircraft for the time, had impressed the world with its operations in Spain, and was an "independent" air force, which implied strategic operations. That was not reality. The Luftwaffe's brilliant proponent of strategic operations, General der Flieger Walter Wever, died in 1936, and the service was taken over by advocates of tactical operations.* The Luftwaffe became an auxiliary in fact to the German army. It downgraded air superiority* and had a force of only one-fifth fighters.* The rest were attack* and tactical airlift* aircraft.

The British independent Royal Air Force (RAF) believed in strategic operations and expected bombers* to be able to live in the air. Fortunately for the RAF and Britain, this belief in the bomber led to the best air defense system of its time with interceptors* that turned out to be superb air superiority fighters. The RAF also had many attack aircraft but in 1934 had essentially reached the perfection of 1917. The nominally independent French l'Armée de l'Air was captive to World War I concepts. France's socialist government had nationalized the aircraft industry in 1936, which ruined it. The minor air arm of the U.S. Army, starved for funds and dominated by observation aviation* and attack outlooks of the ground force, had nothing truly modern except 13 B-17s.*

When war came, the Luftwaffe quickly overwhelmed the outnumbered Polish air arm which was an auxiliary to the army. The British evacuated their children from London and braced for the expected mass aerial gas attack. In the fall of 1939, the RAF's new bomber crews quickly learned they could not operate in daylight against air superiority fighters.

In the spring of 1940, the Allies were planning operations in Norway when the Germans preempted them. Winston Churchill believed, as did most naval people of the time, that navies could operate in the face of enemy air superiority. Churchill called the German expedition a strategic error and promised the House of Commons to sink all German ships moving through the Skagerrak and Kattegat on the necessary sea communications lane to Norway. German air superiority over the routes trumped this promise. The Allies were then able to operate in northern Norway until the Luftwaffe's short-range aircraft had moved to advanced bases, forcing Allied evacuations.

The Battle of France followed, opened by effective tactical airlift for vertical envelopment behind the defense lines. L'Armée de l'Air and the small RAF Advanced Air Striking Force (AASF), with only two squadrons* of air superiority fighters, were routed as the Luftwaffe had a turkey shoot with the Allied attack and observation aircraft. With control of the air, Germany's attack forces made a blitzkrieg possible. The air and land rout ended at Dunkirk. The Luftwaffe had moved only four air superiority fighter Geschwader, or wings,* to advanced bases within range of the port. In addition, Dunkirk was within range of the RAF's main force of air superiority fighters in England, and this allowed the "miracle" evacuation of Dunkirk. There was now a pause in the Battle of France which was partly from the Luftwaffe moving up its short-range aircraft to advanced bases.

Churchill then said Germany would have to break Britain on its island or lose the war, and this time he was right. At the beginning of the Battle of Britain, which ran from July to September 1940, the opposing air superiority fighter forces were equal in numbers and quality. The Germans had far superior tactics but had to operate at the limit of their radius of action, a crippling factor. Another factor was that the British were producing more air superiority fighters at this time—three times more in the critical month of August. The Luftwaffe tried to conduct strategic operations with its attack air force, and the RAF fighters had many field days. RAF adoption of the Luftwaffe fighter tactics; the German range problem; the fact that the battle was fought over England and that shot down but unhurt British, but not Germans, could be returned to the fray; and higher British production of air superiority fighters and new fighter pilots* for them defeated the Germans and turned the course of the war. The British Fleet Air Arm, using Swordfish biplanes, or "Stringbags," devastated the Italian navy at the Battle of Taranto in November 1940, providing a preview of Pearl Harbor* and underlining the Norwegian campaign's example of the air's dominance of the sea.

The air power triumphs of the spring and summer of 1940 destroyed the old order. The USAAC* would have to reequip almost entirely, and its size would have to grow from a dwarf to a giant.

The German drive to the Mediterranean in 1941 was made in surges followed by pauses, while the Luftwaffe took time to move to advanced bases. The German surge-and-pause pattern was necessarily repeated for its short-range air force in the invasion of the USSR, giving the Red Army breathing times to reorganize and regroup. The Luftwaffe's lack of long-range aircraft for strategic operations left vital Soviet resources out of its reach and lost the U-boat war for Germany. A feeble effort by the Luftwaffe converted a four-engine airliner design to a handful of long-range reconnaissance-bomber Fw 200 Condors. The potential effectiveness of Germany's lost opportunity with such craft was shown by Churchill's calling Condors the "scourge of the Atlantic."

In 1942, in Operation Torch,* the Allies worked out an effective organization for tactical operations. The RAF, under cover of night, conducted strategic operations against German civilians. The USAAF* began daylight strategic operations intended to strike at the German economic capacity to make war. In 1943, the Luftwaffe's interceptors played havoc with the RAF, and its air superiority fighters did the same against USAAF bombers. The USAAF bowed to necessity and dropped its erroneous dogma of the ability of bombers to operate against fighters. It built long-range air superiority fighters which wrecked the Luftwaffe fighters and interceptors, achieving air superiority over the heart of Germany in March 1944. Huge Allied tactical operations and tactical airlift supported the land invasions of Europe in the summer of 1944 and helped crush the German army. Necessary to this result was the triumph of titanic U.S. production of aircraft and thorough training of a vast "instant" global air force.

In the Pacific, the Japanese used air power as auxiliary to their surface forces. In 1940 they had attack aircraft and the best air superiority fighter of the time, the long-range A6M Reisen, or "Zero." Its naval air arm smashed the U.S. Navy's battleships at Pearl Harbor. Japanese planes quickly sank HMS *Prince of Wales* and *Repulse* while they were under way off Malaya, in a demonstration that the critics of Mitchell's bombing tests against warships* were in error.

Range was even more important to air power in the Pacific than in Europe. The great emptiness of that ocean required air power of the time to be staged from aircraft carriers. In the spring of 1942, the Navy's carrier forces turned back the Japanese thrust into the southwest Pacific in the Battle of the Coral Sea and into the central Pacific at the Battle of Midway. The U.S. counteroffensive in the central Pacific was primarily with carrier aviation. In a war of attrition in the southwest Pacific, land-based air power of the USAAF, U.S. Navy, and their Allies chewed up Japanese air power and surface forces with air superiority fighters, tactical airlift, and attack planes. The Japanese had failed to build an adequate airfield system and faced increasingly improved aircraft types. Japanese production of pilots and even of the older types of aircraft could not replace the losses.

When bases close enough were won in the Marianas Islands* in the summer of 1944, the strategic campaign against Japan* began in the autumn with a greatly advanced bomber, the B-29,* with double the B-17's weight and speed. Initially, daylight precision bombing of war economy targets was tried and was ineffective largely because of the previously unknown jet stream phenomenon. The USAAF switched to night bombing of civilians and conducted extensive mining* operations. After the first nuclear weapons* were dropped on Hiroshima* and Nagasaki in a special bombing campaign, the Japanese, already brought to their knees by bombing and blockade, accepted peace terms.

To a much greater extent than in World War I, there were giant leaps forward in technology. Possibilities that had existed but had not been fully exploited were developed, such as tactical airlift, rescue,* and aeromedical evacuation.* Besides those improvements, which should include the B-29's exploitation of existing technology, the revolutionary jet engine, radar,* ballistic missiles,* nuclear weapons, helicopters,* and electronics were introduced. Essential to victory was the prodigious achievement of the U.S. aircraft industry, a reversal of World War I results. In 1944, the United States produced more than 96,000 airplanes with a weight of almost one billion pounds, while Germany's production was 40,000 airplanes of less than 200,000 pounds. The enemy was crushed under the weight of U.S. production, illustrating a role of industry in aerospace power. The USAAF became a global air force due in part to prodigies of airfield construction, especially using pierced-steel planking* (PSP), or "instant airfield."

One of the continuing controversies of the war concerns the effectiveness of strategic operations. The RAF said it was given only a fraction of the resources it had predicted it needed to "win the war." The RAF's strategic operations received 7 percent of Britain's war resources. The USAAF leaders believed their concepts had been validated even though it had been given limited resources also; strategic operations in Europe had received $27 billion in resources, or only 11 percent of the U.S. war effort by 31 December 1944. In addition, the USAAF believed the series of diversions of its operations meant there was not a true test in Europe. Its strategic operations resources were diverted to the Mediterranean theater, to strike the U-boat bases and yards,* to the V-weapon launching sites, and to Operation Overlord.*

Critics say strategic operations got a fair trial and results showed it alone "cannot win a war." They have maintained that the German war was won by land power, and the end of the war with Japan was a surprise and fluke because of nuclear weapons that will never be repeated.

The question needs more analysis than simply "what won the war." One must ask what that means. Is it a point in time when it is realized a war is won or lost? Reichsmarschall Hermann Goering, head of the Luftwaffe, said he knew in March 1944 that Germany had lost the war. That was at the time the USAAF won air superiority over central Germany. General der Jagdflieger Adolf Galland said he knew it in the spring when the USAAF was allowed to begin its strategic operations against the German oil industry target system.* Because of the same operations, Albert Speer, German munitions minister, said he knew that Germany's armament production would become finished. Had Germany lost the war before Operation Overlord? If so, it was air power, strategic operations, which won the war, and not land power.

Or does "win the war" mean the end of the war? And does the "end of the war" mean annihilation or an agreement to stop fighting? If one chooses annihilation, then, certainly, land power "won" World War II in Europe. Strategic operations, with nuclear weapons, can certainly "win" war this way. In Europe, nuclear weapons were not used, and the German expression of late in the war— "Our walls break, but not our hearts"—indicates strategic operations without nuclear weapons cannot annihilate.

Annihilation results from policies such as President Franklin D. Roosevelt's* (FDR) insistence on unconditional surrender. Germany, told it faced a Carthaginian peace, fought on to annihilation. Another German saying of the time was, "Enjoy the war, the peace will be dreadful." A functioning German government never surrendered unconditionally. And that was true no matter how desperate the land war situation was. The "surrender" papers were signed by some phantoms in uniform who controlled only fragments of armed forces. Consequently, it can be said that, short of annihilation, land power cannot "win a war" either unless there is a peace with terms.

Terms, of course, is how the war ended with Japan. Before the war ended, Japan, probably a more fanatical enemy than Germany, lacked sea power, was crippled in the air, but still had main armies that were undefeated. It was hoarding a large kamikaze air force for the expected invasion. It was even making spears for its women to use to help defend the landing beaches. It seems evident they would have fought to annihilation rather than surrender unconditionally. In July 1945 a new president, Harry S Truman* (HST), was prepared to offer terms, and it was on conditions that the Japanese government made peace on 14 August.

The experience of World War II and of the Korean,* Vietnam,* and Iraq* Wars indicates strategic operations can "win a war" if nuclear weapons are used. In addition, strategic operations can "win a war" with conventional weapons if there is to be a negotiated peace and not the annihilation that may accompany unconditional surrender.

In 1949, Churchill said armies and navies were still necessary, but they had become ancillary to air power. This was far from his beliefs in April 1940 and a great tribute to air power in World War II.

References. Primary: H. H. Arnold, *Global Mission*, 1949. Adolf Galland, translated by Mervyn Savill, *The First and the Last: The Rise and Fall of the German Fighter Forces, 1938–1945*, 1954. Masatake Okumiya and Jiro Horikoshi, *Zero!* 1956. Secondary: C&C, 7 vols. Higham, *Air Pwr*. R. J. Overy, *The Air War 1939–1945*, 1981.

See also Eighth Air Force.

WRIGHT BROTHERS

Orville Wright (1871–1948) and Wilbur Wright (1867–1912) were the co-inventors of the airplane, perhaps the most important invention of the 20th century. Working together, they discovered the basic elements of aircraft control and built and flew the first powered, controlled, man-carrying, heavier-than-air flying machine. All modern airplanes are descended from the original Wright Flyer. The Wright brothers built the first airplane owned by the U.S. government and thus the direct ancestor of the USAF.* The Wrights were the first persons inducted into the National Aviation Hall of Fame, which is in their home city of Dayton, Ohio.

They were raised in Dayton and did not graduate from high school or attend college. Instead, they embarked on business careers, first as printers and publishers of a newspaper. Later they opened bicycle shops where they sold and repaired bicycles and later began to manufacture their own brands. The cycle business prospered and provided them with the income to sustain their aeronautical research.

They first became interested in human flight in 1899, following the death of the German experimenter Otto Lilienthal. At first they built a kite to test their theories of control but soon decided a man-carrying glider was necessary for proper experimentation. The wide-open sand dunes and strong winds of Kitty Hawk, North Carolina, were chosen as the testing place. From 1900 to 1902 they built and flew a series of gliders, each more successful than the last. They perfected their system of control, which involved twisting or bending the wingtips for lateral balance, a horizontal elevator for fore-and-aft control, and a moveable vertical tail, linked with the "wing warping" for turning.

This system, patented in 1906, forms the basis for all modern aircraft control and is the source for successful powered flight. Ailerons later replaced the wing-warping technique, but the Wright patent was repeatedly upheld in court. The Wrights also were the first to produce reliable tables of lift and pressure and the proper shape of airfoils, derived from tests conducted in a wind tunnel of their own design.

On 17 December 1903 at Kitty Hawk, they successfully flew a powered machine. It was based on their glider prototypes, a biplane with a forward, or canard, elevator, and a rear, vertical rudder. Equipped with an engine and propellors of their own design, the Wright Flyer made four successful flights, the longest of 852 feet in 59 seconds, demonstrating beyond all doubt that the machine was capable of free, sustained, and controlled flight.

The next several years were spent in perfecting the airplane and arranging for its sale to governments and private corporations. On 10 February 1908, they negotiated a contract for the sale of a "heavier-than-air flying machine" to the U.S. Army Signal Corps. The flight trials were held at Fort Myer, Virginia, from 29 June to 30 July 1909 and at their conclusion the plane was accepted as Signal Corps Number 1. After Wilbur's premature death in 1912, Orville retired from the aviation business. However, he remained active on the National Advisory Committee for Aeronautics (NACA) and thus contributed substantially to later advances in aviation.

References. Primary: Marvin W. McFarland, ed., *The Papers of Wilbur and Orville Wright*, 1953. Secondary: Harry Coombs, *Kill Devil Hill: Discovering the Secrets of the Wright Brothers*, 1979. Tom D. Crouch, *The Bishop's Boys: A Life of Wilbur and Orville Wright*, 1989. Fred Howard, *Wilbur and Orville*, 1987. John E. Walsh, *One Day at Kitty Hawk*, 1975.

Patrick B. Nolan

WRIGHT ENGINES

The ratio of weight to power is critical to flight. In successfully flying first, the Wright brothers* mastered this in their engine design. Their engine had four cylinders, was in-line, had 200 cubic inches of piston displacement, generated 12 horsepower (HP) at 1,040 revolutions per minute (RPM), and weighed 179 pounds, or 14.9 pounds per HP.

The Wrights formed the Wright Company, Inc., which built engines as well as airplanes. In 1915 Orville, the surviving brother, sold his interest in the company. It merged with the Glenn L. Martin Company to become Wright-Martin Aircraft Corporation in 1916. The name was changed to Wright Aeronautical Corporation in 1919. It merged with the Curtiss Aeroplane and Motor Company in 1929 to become Curtiss-Wright Corporation (C-W).

During World War I* the company built 5,816 engines. In 1921, Charles L. Lawrance, with a small firm, produced a nine-cylinder radial called the J-1, which had 180 HP. Lawrance's company lacked money and merged with Wright, and the J-1 became the great Wright J-5 Whirlwind. The engine was revolutionary in its reliability. Charles A. Lindbergh* chose it and a single-engine airframe for his 1927 transatlantic flight to show that a reliable aircraft engine had been created and aviation had a great future. The J-5 had 220 HP at 1,800 RPM, 788 cubic inches of piston displacement, and 2.16 pounds weight per HP.

Lawrance left Wright and joined with Frederick B. Rentschler to form Pratt & Whitney* (P&W) Aircraft Company in 1924. In response, Wright developed the larger Cyclone, with 525 HP at 1,900 RPM, 1,750 inches of displacement, and 1.4 pounds per HP. The Cyclone became a great engine, and its R-1820 version stayed in production for 25 years. The R-1820 powered the B-17,* a historic combination of engine and airframe.

Until 1932, in the strong competition that arose between Wright and P&W, Wright used smaller cylinders. After 1932, the reverse was true. In the 1930s, also, the radials grew to double banks of cylinders for increased power. Wright's entry in the double bank engine competition was the R-2600, launched in 1939 with 14 cylinders and 1,500 HP at 2,300 RPM, and 1.3 pounds per HP. Engines of this size made transatlantic crossings commonplace. The R-2600 was used in the A-20* and B-25.* During World War II,* the HP was increased to 1,800.

In 1941, Wright produced its R-3350 with 2,800 HP and 18 cylinders. It reached the old dream of aviators of less than one pound per HP, with a ratio of 0.99. Unfortunately for C-W, the R-3350 had overheating problems that were never solved in the B-29.* Evidently, the fault lay with the airframe, for the R-3350 was free of these difficulties when used in the Lockheed Aircraft Corporation's L-1049 Super Constellation. After World War II, the R-3350 incorporated an exhaust-driven turbine which increased HP to 3,400. It was called the Turbo-Compound engine, and C-W's hopes that it could compete with turbojet engines were soon lost. After the war, Wright also produced the Cyclone 7, a seven cylinder with 800 HP and 1,300 cubic inches of displacement. It was tried with T-28s,* but the older R-1820 proved a better fit.

Wright had emerged from the war with modern production facilities. Its officers planned to enter the turbojet engine business. In the process, C-W stayed with the R-3350 for too long and then tried to get into jets quickly by adapting the British Armstrong-Siddeley company's Sapphire engine to USAF specifications. This could not be done as quickly as expected, and C-W's J65 did not appear until 1953. It was used in the F-84F* and RF-84F, and C-W built 11,000 of them. However, C-W managerial decisions had inadequately provided for the research and development (R&D) required to compete on a long-term basis, and inadequate R&D is a death knell in the aerospace industry.

C-W remained an aviation company, but by 1968 had stopped producing any new airframes or engines. It was a sad event for one of the major firms in U.S. history and one started by important pioneers and developers.

References. Primary: Robert W. Fausel, *Whatever Happened to Curtiss-Wright?* 1990. Secondary: Robert Schlaifer, *Development of Aircraft Engines: Two Studies of Relations between Government and Business*, 1950. Herschel Smith, *Aircraft Piston Engines: From the Manly Balzer to the Continental Tiara*, corrected ed., 1986.

WRIGHT FIELD. *See* Wright-Patterson AFB.

WRIGHT-PATTERSON AIR FORCE BASE (W-P)

Wright Field, Ohio, was established in 1927 and named for the Wright brothers.* Patterson Field was originally Wilbur Wright Field, established in 1917. It was renamed in 1931 for First Lieutenant Frank S. Patterson, who was killed in the crash of a de Haviland DH-4* in 1918. In 1948 the fields were merged. Previous names of component facilities which today make up W-P total 13, including McCook Field. The Wrights did much flying on Huffman Prairie, now part of W-P which is an Air Force Logistics Command* (AFLC) base. W-P has always been one of the most important, if not the most important, air installations since it was activated.

The work done there has always been materiel and engineering, including research and logistics. The first practical free-fall parachute was invented in 1918 at McCook by J. Floyd Smith. Between 1919 and 1925 pilots* from McCook set 27 significant aviation records. It was at McCook that the logistical planning was done for the Round-the-World Flight of 1924.* This was the USAF's* first global planning, and it included six advance party officers. The meticulous work paid off. The Boeing Aircraft Company's Model 299, the prototype of the B-17,* was tested at Wright Field and crashed there through no fault of the plane.

Enemy aircraft* captured in World War II* were studied at Wright, and Germany's research and development (R&D) literature was indexed, abstracted, and put on microfilm. The material was useful to 2,500 private and governmental organizations. In the 1950s, W-P processed aircraft out of storage and for the Korean War,* began computer operations, and expanded facilities. The emphasis in the 1970s was on economics and environmental considerations in W-P's vast installations.

In 1990, its units included headquarters of the AFLC, the Air Force Institute of Technology, and the U.S. Air Force Museum.* The total of USAF and other government agencies on the base was more than 90. W-P employed more people, 35,000, than any other AFB, and the payroll was $899 million.

References. "Guide to Major Air Force Installations Worldwide," *AF*, May 1990, pp. 132–33. Mueller, *AFB*. Roberts, *Dir. USAF*. Lois E. Walker and Shelby E. Wickham, *From Huffman Prairie to the Moon: The History of Wright-Patterson Air Force Base*, 1982. Charles G. Worman, "McCook Field: A Decade of Progress," *AH*, Spring 1970, pp. 12–15, 34–36.

WSO. *See* weapon system operator.

WURTSMITH AIR FORCE BASE

This Strategic Air Command* (SAC) field is near Oscoda, Michigan. It was established as Camp Skeel in 1924 and began to be called Oscoda in 1942. In 1953 it was named in honor of Major General Paul B. Wurtsmith who was a commander of the Thirteenth Air Force* (13AF) in World War II.* Wurtsmith died in a B-25* crash in 1946. The field was used for exercises from 1924 to 1944. After 1927 it was also used for aerial gunnery. B-52s* and KC-135s (*see* C-135) arrived in 1960, and in 1990 the 379th Bomb Wing operated from it using the same aircraft types.

References. "Guide to Major Air Force Installations Worldwide," *AF*, May 1990, p. 133. Mueller, *AFB*. Roberts, *Dir. USAF*.

X

X-1

The X-1 is one of the most famous airplanes in history. Before it, there were doubts that an airplane could be built that could penetrate the "sound barrier" and fly faster than Mach 1, the speed of sound, because airflows behave differently above that speed. The X-1 not only attained supersonic speed but proved to be one of the most successful test vehicles in history.

In 1945, the USAAF* contracted with the Bell Aircraft Corporation to build the XS-1 to investigate transonic and supersonic flight. The lack of knowledge of the time is illustrated by the aerodynamic shape of the X-1; it was formed in the shape of a bullet, a shape that had exceeded the speed of sound. The first X-1 was finished in late 1945.

Designed with limited fuel, the X-1 had to be staged, with the first stage being a B-29.* Its first flights on its own were glides. Next, powered flights up to Mach 0.8 were made. On 14 October 1947, Captain Charles E. "Chuck" Yeager,* flying the first X-1, named *Glamorous Glennis* for his wife, achieved Mach 1.06 without difficulty. The brand new USAF* tried to keep its achievement a secret, but *Aviation Week* reported it in December. The X-1s continued to be used for testing into 1951. Four variants were built, the X-1A, X-1B, X-1D, and X-1E. They were intended for research at speeds greater than Mach 2 and altitudes above 90,000 feet. The two surviving X-1s are displayed at the National Air and Space Museum in Washington, D.C., and at Edwards* AFB in California.

Characteristics (X-1): engine, Reaction Motors, Inc., bifuel XLR11-RM-3/5 rocket of 6,000 pounds thrust; span, 28 feet; length 31 feet; height, 11 feet; gross weight, 12,000 to 14,751 pounds; top speed (estimated), Mach 2.44; highest altitude, above 70,000 feet; endurance 5 minutes.

References. Primary: Frank K. Everest, Jr., *The Fastest Man Alive*, 1958. Chuck Yeager and Leo Janos, *Yeager: An Autobiography*, 1985. James O. Young, ed., *Supersonic Symposium: The Men of Mach 1*, AFFTC History Office, Edwards AFB, California.

Secondary: Richard P. Hallion, *Test Pilots: The Frontiersmen of Flight*, 1981, and *On the Frontier: Flight Research at Dryden 1946–1981*, 1984. Jay Miller, *The X-Planes*, rev. ed., 1988.

X-2

In 1945, the USAAF* and the National Advisory Committee for Aeronautics (NACA) wanted an X-1* to exploit and extend German research on swept wings. They found a complete redesign was necessary, which became the X-2 made by the Bell Aircraft Corporation. Although this was a troubled design, the airplane contributed to the advancement of aerodynamics. The first flight was in 1950. Like the X-1, it was staged, but with the B-50.* In 1953, one of the two that had been built exploded while attached to its B-50, killing the pilot* and one crewman on the carrier aircraft. The program was delayed three years by instability problems. In July 1956, it set a speed record of Mach 2.87 at 68,000 feet, flown by Captain Frank K. "Pete" Everest, Jr.* In the same year, Captain Iven C. Kincheloe* set an altitude record in it of 125,907 feet. Only 20 days later, Captain Milburn Apt lost control of it and died.

Characteristics: engine, Curtiss-Wright XLR25-CW-1/3 rocket of 15,000 pounds thrust; span, 32 feet; length, 45 feet; height, 12 feet; gross weight, 24,910 pounds; top speed, Mach 3.196; endurance, almost 11 minutes.

References. Primary: Frank K. Everest, Jr., *The Fastest Man Alive*, 1958. Secondary: Richard P. Hallion, *Test Pilots: The Frontiersmen of Flight*, 1981, and *On the Frontier: Research at Dryden 1946–1981*, 1984. Jay Miller, *The X-Planes*, rev. ed., 1988.

X-5

In 1948 the Bell Aircraft Corporation proposed an interceptor* using in-flight, variable-sweep wings, inspired by the German Messerschmitt P 1101. The P 1101 had variable-sweep wings set on the ground. The USAAF* was not interested in the interceptor, but it and the National Advisory Committee for Aeronautics (NACA) did sponsor the X-5 for investigations of variable-sweep wings.

Two X-5s were built, closely resembling the P 1101. The first was completed in 1951 and flew that year. After 149 flights, the X-5s were retired in 1955. They were the first aircraft ever to fly with in-flight variable-geometry wings. They had instability problems and severe spin tendencies which discouraged immediate exploitation of the idea. A practical aircraft using the concept later was the F-111.*

Characteristics: engine, Allison J35-A-17A turbojet of 4,900 pounds thrust; span, 21 to 34 feet; length, 33 feet; height, 12 feet; gross weight, 9,875 pounds; top speed, about 705 miles per hour; highest altitude, about 42,000 feet; range, about 750 miles.

References. Richard P. Hallion, *Test Pilots: The Frontiersmen of Flight*, (1981), and *On the Frontier: Flight Research at Dryden 1946–1981*, 1984. Jay Miller, *The X-Planes*, rev. ed., 1988.

X-6

The USAF* and the Atomic Energy Commission (AEC) believed in 1951 that nuclear propulsion was feasible for aircraft. A contract was given to the General Electric Company to develop a nuclear turbojet engine and to the Consolidated-Vultee Aircraft Corporation (Convair) to adapt two B-36Hs* for the project. The obvious advantage of such an engine would be a revolution for aircraft; unlimited range, endurance, and cruise flight at supersonic speeds.

In 1953, advisers in the new administration of President Dwight D. Eisenhower* declared that a nuclear-powered airplane would have no military usefulness. The X-6 project was not canceled outright, but funds were cut deeply. The designation was also changed to NB-36H. One of these made flights from 1955 to 1957, testing parts of a nuclear engine. In 1955, the program encountered three severe technical problems. First, the radiation shielding was overweight. Second, existing materials could not withstand the required temperatures and thrust. Third, chemical engines were required for some functions, and the chemical fuel added to the weight problem. These problems were not overcome when the project was canceled. From 1956 on, funding became more restrictive, and the administration of President John F. Kennedy* (JFK) canceled the project in the early 1960s.

References. "Air Force Nuclear Propulsion," a special issue of *Air University Quartely Review*, Fall and Winter, 1959. Jay Miller, *The X-Planes*, rev. ed., 1988.

X-13

In 1947 the U.S. Navy asked the Ryan Aeronautical Company to explore the feasibility of a fighter* that could takeoff and land vertically (VTOL). The Navy lost interest, and the USAF* adopted the project as the X-13 in 1953. Two were built, and testing began with temporary conventional landing gear. In 1956 testing began with the intended nose hook and trapeze to put the X-13 in a vertical position for takeoff and recovery. The hook was successfully used by 1957. The X-13s flew satisfactorily, proving the concept. However, the feasible payloads were small. The X-13 is considered to have been ahead of its time, and the Navy uses today the more successful vectored thrust system for a VTOL of the British-developed AV-8A Harrier.

Characteristics: engine, Rolls Royce Avon RA.28–49 turbojet of 10,000 pounds thrust; span, 21 feet; length, 23 feet; height with landing gear, 15 feet; gross weight, 7,313 pounds; top speed, 483 miles per hour; highest altitude, about 30,000 feet; range, 192 miles.

References. Richard P. Hallion, *Test Pilots: The Frontiersmen of Flight*, 1981. Jay Miller, *The X-Planes*, rev. ed., 1988.

See also zero launch.

X-15

The X-15 was a true aerospace plane that made huge contributions to hypersonic aerodynamics and space research. In 1952, Robert J. Woods of the Bell Aircraft Corporation, who was an important contributor to the X-1,* X-2,* and

X-5,* proposed to the National Advisory Committee for Aeronautics (NACA) a hypersonic research vehicle. Woods endorsed a plan drawn up by Bell engineer Walter Dornberger, former commander at the Peenemuende, Germany, facility which developed the V-2 ballistic missile.* In 1954 the USAF's* Scientific Advisory Board* (SAB) made a similar recommendation. In 1954 the U.S. Navy also joined as a sponsor.

In 1955 the winner of the design competition for the X-15 was North American Aviation, Inc., and three were ordered. The B-52* was chosen to be the first-stage vehicle. The first flight was in 1959. In 1960, new speed and altitude records of 2,196 miles per hour and 136,500 feet altitude were set. In 1966 an X-15 was modified to be an X-15A-2 with improved performance, and it set records of Mach 6.33, or 4,250 miles per hour, and 354,200 feet altitude. The 199th, and last, X-15 flight was made in 1968. The U.S. Air Force Museum* has an X-15A-2 and the National Air and Space Museum has an X-15 on display.

Characteristics: (X-15A-2): engine, Reaction Motors, Inc., XLR99 of 50,000 pounds thrust; span, 22 feet; length, 52 feet; height, 12 feet; gross weight, 56,130 pounds; range, 175 miles.

Movie: X-15, 1961.

References. Martin Caidin, *X-15: Man's First Flight into Space*, 1959. Richard P. Hallion, *Test Pilots: The Frontiersmen of Flight*, 1981, and *On the Frontier: Flight Research at Dryden 1946–1981*, 1984. Jay Miller, *The X-Planes*, rev. ed., 1988.

X-15. See movies.

X-20 DYNA-SOAR

This experimental project was intended to study the military use of space and controlled reentry from earth orbit to landing. The research done on the X-20 proved useful to later projects such as the X-15* and the space shuttle.

The concepts originated in World War II* with Drs. Eugen Saenger and Irene Bredt in Germany. They were seeking an intercontinental bomber* that would achieve its range by skipping along on the earth's atmosphere as a flat stone skips along a pond surface.

The X-20 program, conducted by the Boeing Airplane Company, started formally in 1959. It was a single-seat glider that was to be boosted into space. The administration of President John F. Kennedy* (JFK) found the X-20's potential for the military use of space to be uncomfortable and an obstruction to diplomatic negotiations. The project was canceled in 1963 before any flights were made.

References. Roy F. Houchin II, "The Diplomatic Demise of Dyna-Soar: The Impact of International and Domestic Political Affairs on the Dyna-Soar X-20 Project, 1957–1963," *AH*, December 1988, pp. 274–80. Jay Miller, *The X-Planes*, rev. ed., 1988.

XB-15. *See* B-15.

XB-19. *See* B-19.

XB-35. *See* B-35 and B-49.

XB-70. *See* B-70.

Y

YALU BRIDGES

The Yalu River forms the border between North Korea and Manchuria, and it is a major river. In November 1950, when Red China attacked United Nations (UN) forces in Korea, its huge armies used all six of the river bridges. General of the Army Douglas MacArthur asked for air attacks* on the bridges, and permission was granted with the political air superiority* restriction that Manchurian territory not be violated. This greatly inhibited the interdiction effort, and, with other factors, resulted in a futile attempt.

When U.S. attack aircraft approached the Yalu, Chinese fighters* took off and climbed to altitudes above those the UN planes would use for their strikes. The Chinese would cross the river to hit with a firing pass and then flee to their political sanctuary. The Chinese also fired flak* from their side of the river.

The Yalu bridges, built by the Japanese, were sturdy. One, at Namsan-ni, was in a bend of the river, and there was no way to approach it except over Manchuria. The normal winds in the area meant extreme crosswinds at up to 140 miles per hour at B-29* operating altitudes.

USAF* and U.S. Navy attacks cut half of the bridges and damaged others. In this period, the Chinese added four pontoon bridges. The attacks were abandoned in late November as the river began to freeze so solidly that railroads could be built across it, as had been done in earlier years. The Yalu bridges effort also was partly a case of closing the barn door after the horse was out; later intelligence showed that four Chinese field armies, each the same size as a U.S. army corps, had already crossed the river by 26 October.

Reference. Futrell, *USAF in Korea*.

YAMAMOTO, ADMIRAL ISOROKU (1884–1943)

Yamamoto was a leading builder of the World War II* Imperial Japanese navy (IJN), its air power, and he was the architect of Japan's attack* on Pearl Harbor,* Hawaii. He entered the IJN in 1897 and rapidly rose through the ranks.

Attracted early to naval air power, he was considered the foremost authority on it and its tactical applications by 1923. He lent much prestige to the design of first-rate naval fighters* and bombers,* emphasizing adapting aircraft carriers to their fighters.

Yamamoto, cautious because of U.S. industrial might, spoke out against the Axis Tripartite Pact which he feared would antagonize the United States. In 1941, he attempted to dissuade Japan's leaders from carrying out the September decision to begin planning a war against the United States. Defeated, he argued against the conventional view of a climatic, conventional naval battle, positing, instead, a surprise air raid against the heart of the U.S. Navy at Pearl Harbor. The December strike's success incapacitated the battleships of the U.S. Pacific Fleet and catapulted a united America into war.

The retaliatory Doolittle raid on Tokyo* stung Yamamoto into moving ahead his plan to invest Midway Island to seal off easterly approaches to Japan. The subsequent Battle of Midway broke the IJN's back with four carriers and its most experienced pilots* lost.

From August 1942 to April 1943, Yamamoto attempted to check increasing U.S. successes in the southwest Pacific. After fighting coalesced around Guadalcanal* and the Solomon Islands, he decided on an inspection tour of Japanese airfields in southern Bougainville. As at Midway, U.S. code-breakers intercepted his itinerary and plans were drawn up for an aerial ambush. On 18 April 1943, 18 P-38s* of the Thirteenth Air Force* (13AF) caught his bomber just short of Kahili Field, Buin. Captain Thomas G. Lanphier, Jr.,* was credited** with the victory over Yamamoto's G4M, or "Betty," which crashed and burned in the jungle. Japan never recovered from his loss.

References. Hiroyuki Agawa, *The Reluctant Admiral: Yamamoto and the Imperial Navy*, 1979. Burke Davis, *Get Yamamoto*, 1969. Carroll V. Glines, *Attack on Yamamoto*, 1990. Terry Gwynn-Jones, "In Search of Yamamoto," *AF*, April 1985, pp. 120–25. John Dean Potter, *Yamamoto: The Man Who Menaced America*, 1965.

**This credit has long been disputed. Colonel Rex T. Barber may be the true victor.

Ronald W. Yoshino

YEAGER, BRIGADIER GENERAL CHARLES E. "CHUCK" (1923–)

Yeager gained lasting fame when, on 14 October 1947, he became the first man to exceed the speed of sound, Mach 1, while flying the X-1.* He was inducted into the National Aviation Hall of Fame in Dayton, Ohio, in 1973.

He enlisted in the USAAF* in 1941 and served as an aircraft mechanic until 1942 when he entered flight training.* By late 1943, he was flying combat out of England in F-51s* for the 363rd Fighter Squadron. He was shot down over France in March 1944 and evaded capture, returning to his unit. He became an ace* with 13 victories, including five on one sortie.

In 1945, he was assigned to the Fighter Test Branch at Wright Field, Ohio. Considered a superb "stick-and-rudder man," he was selected as project pilot* for the X-1 which was to explore transonic and supersonic flight. From August

1947, at Edwards* AFB, California, he proceeded in gradual, carefully planned steps to his historic flight in October.

During his tour as a test pilot at Edwards, from 1947 to 1954, he flew virtually every prototype and experimental aircraft then undergoing flight test. On 12 December 1953 he made his final flight, taking the X-1A to a record speed of Mach 2.44. He nearly lost his life as he was one of the first to encounter the phenomenon of "inertial coupling," or high-speed instability. Successfully landing, he was awarded the 1953 Harmon International Trophy for his achievement on this flight.

From 1954 to 1961 he commanded operational units in Europe and California. Then he took command of the USAF Test Pilot School at Edwards where he served until 1966. As commander of the 405th Fighter Wing at Clark* AB in the Philippines from 1966 to 1967, he flew 127 sorties in the Vietnam War.* Mostly command assignments followed until his last as director of the Air Force Inspection and Safety Center from 1973 to 1975, from which he retired.

Movie: The Right Stuff, 1983.

References. Primary: Chuck Yeager and Leo Janos, *Yeager: An Autobiography*, 1985. Secondary: Richard P. Hallion, *Supersonic Flight: The Story of the Bell X-1 and Douglas D-558*, 1972, *Test Pilots: The Frontiersmen of Flight*, 1981, and *On the Frontier: Flight Research at Dryden, 1946–1981*, 1984. Tom Wolfe, *The Right Stuff*, 1979.

James O. Young

YOKOTA AIR BASE

West of Tokyo, Japan, this is a Pacific Air Forces* (PACAF) field. The base was originally established in 1940 as Tama Army Air Field, and the USAF* has been there since World War II.* It has been an important base for the USAF since that war.

When the Korean War* began, Yokota had combat-ready units on it flying F-80Cs,* F-82s,* and RF-80As. These planes were soon used in the war. In July 1950, the headquarters of the Far East Air Forces Bombing Command was formed at the base for strategic operations* in the war. Soon B-29s* of the 98th Bombardment Group moved onto it as a base for raids and conducted the first on the fifth day after leaving the United States. Later, the 92nd Bomb Group came to the base, causing severe congestion of the facilities. In the Vietnam War,* Yokota was a main airlift operations* base, and a passenger terminal able to process 35,000 people per month opened in 1969. Yokota also had a major aeromedical evacuation* redistribution center for the war. In 1990, Yokota had the headquarters of U.S. Forces in Japan, headquarters of the Fifth Air Force* (5AF), the 475th Air Base Wing (ABW), the 374th Tactical Airlift Wing (TAW), and an aerial port. The aircraft on the base were C-21s, C-130s,* and UH-1Ns.

References. Berger, *USAF in SEA*. Futrell, *USAF in Korea*. "Guide to Major Air Force Installations Worldwide," *AF*, May 1990, p. 133. Roberts, *Dir. USAF*.

YONGMIDONG, KOREA. *See* Sinanju and Yongmidong, Korea.

Z

ZARAGOZA AIR BASE

This field, located near Zaragoza, Spain, last became a USAF* field in 1970. It is assigned to the U.S. Air Forces in Europe* (USAFE). In 1990, the mission of its 406th Tactical Fighter Training Wing (TFTW) was to conduct attack* and air superiority* training for USAFE's Central Region fighter* units.

References. "Guide to Major Air Force Installations Worldwide," *AF*, May 1990, p. 133. Roberts, *Dir. USAF*.

ZELL. *See* zero launch.

ZELMAL. *See* zero launch.

ZEMKE, COLONEL HUBERT A. "HUB" (1914–)

Zemke was the commander of the 56th Fighter Group, which scored the most aerial victories, 665.5, of a USAAF* unit in the European theater. He was a tactician whose innovations contributed to that score. He himself was an ace* with 17.75 victories. He was credited with another 8.5 on the ground. Zemke was called the "fightingest" fighter* commander in Europe because he led his group* into battle so frequently.

Born in Missoula, Montana, he graduated from the University of Montana in 1936 and then entered the USAAC.* He became a pilot* and officer in 1937. In 1942 he took over the 56th and took it to England in 1943. In the summer, the 56th pioneered USAAF fighter escort* with F-47s.* His group had 300 victories before it lost an ace in battle. At that time, group losses had been 50. In August 1944 he took command of the 479th Fighter Group flying P-38s.* Later the group flew F-51s.* In October 1944 he bailed out in violent weather and became a prisoner of war (POW) in Germany.*

References. Primary: Gurney, *5 Down*. Hub Zemke, *Zemke's Wolf Pack*, 1988. Secondary: Roger A. Freeman, *The Mighty Eighth: Units, Men and Machines*, 1970. Hess, *Aces Album*.

ZERO LAUNCH

Zero launch, zero length launch (ZELL), or zero length launch and mat landing (ZELMAL) was an experimental program to explore the possibility of fighter* takeoffs from trucks. Zero launch worked in tests, but it was concluded that it was impractical for field use.

When World War II* began, fighters could use grass fields. As weights increased rapidly with new model fighters, runways became necessary. When jets were developed with their long takeoff rolls, grave concerns arose over the vulnerability of airfields with long, paved runways.

In the 1950s, several alternatives were explored to solve the problem. There were vertical takeoff and short takeoff and landing programs, or V/STOL. A program in 1954 tested the launching of a fighter from a rack on the back of a truck. The heavy F-84G* was used in the tests, and a droppable booster rocket engine accelerated the plane far enough and high enough for its jet engine to sustain flight.

The 1961 success of the British Hawker Siddeley P. 1127 using vectored engine thrust proved to be the best solution for current technology. It has evolved into today's Harrier plane.

References. Goldberg, *Hist. USAF*. Richard P. Hallion, *Test Pilots: The Frontiersmen of Flight*, 1981. Knaack, *US Airc.*, vol. 1.

See also X-13.

ZUCKERMAN, PROFESSOR SOLLY (1904–)

Zuckerman was a scientific adviser on the staff of the Deputy Supreme Allied Air Commander Air Chief Marshal Sir Arthur Tedder in World War II.* He was the author of a controversial interdiction attack* plan for Operation Overlord.*

He was a physician and biology researcher and studied animal behavior. He analyzed the effects of bombing on Tripoli, Libya, and Sicily. In addition, he participated in planning the operations against Pantelleria,* Italy. These experiences convinced him that raids on rail yards and shops were more efficient than those on bridges and tunnels.

In January 1944, he convinced General Dwight D. Eisenhower,* and the British air commanders other than Air Chief Marshal Sir Arthur T. "Bomber" Harris, of his idea. He maintained that Overlord required intensive and extensive raids on French and German rail yards near France by the Eighth Air Force* (8AF) and Royal Air Force (RAF) Bomber Command. His plan was his alone, was not done in collaboration with British military transportation experts, and downgraded the importance of air superiority* for Overlord. In February the RAF, in support of the plan, proposed diverting all 8AF efforts to the rail yards. This meant taking them away from the struggle for air superiority which included the German aircraft industry target system.* General Carl A. Spaatz* of the USAAF* was outraged. He believed air superiority was critical for Overlord and could not be won at the last minute. In addition, he believed the raids on the rail system would not be as effective as Zuckerman thought. He believed strategic operations* on the German oil industry target system* would be more productive. Zuckerman accused Spaatz of having a motive of interservice rivalry. At a meeting on 25 March, Eisenhower decided against Spaatz.

As time passed, circumstances altered the situation. The Luftwaffe had been hurt worse in February and March than the Allies first believed. In addition, Spaatz's objections had shrunk Zuckerman's 90-day plan to 60 days. In May, Eisenhower relented on his stand enough for Spaatz to conduct some highly successful raids on German oil. In May, experiments made at the suggestion of Air Marshal Sir Arthur Coningham* indicated that fighters* would be more productive than bombers* in striking bridges. On 24 May, the Ninth Air Force* (9AF), a tactical operations* unit, began a campaign on the bridges which was regarded as a complete success.

References. Primary: Lord Arthur Tedder, *With Prejudice: War Memoirs*, 1966. Solly Zuckerman, *From Apes to Warlords*, 1972. Secondary: DeWitt S. Copp, *Forged in Fire: Strategy and Decisions in the Airwar over Europe 1940–1945*, 1982. David R. Mets, *Master of Airpower: General Carl A. Spaatz*, 1988. W. W. Rostow, *Pre-Invasion Bombing Strategy: General Eisenhower's Decision of March 25, 1944*, 1981. Charles Webster and Noble Frankland, *Victory*, vol. 3 of *The Strategic Air Offensive against Germany 1939–1945*, 1961.

ZUCKERT, SECRETARY EUGENE M. (1911–)

As seventh secretary of the Air Force* (SAF), serving from 1961 to 1965, Zuckert was engaged in several USAF* lost causes such as the B-70,* Manned Orbiting Laboratory, and Skybolt.* More successful from his term were the Atlas,* F-4,* Minuteman,* and Titan* projects.

He was born in New York City, New York, and graduated from Yale University in 1933. He practiced law, was attorney for the Securities and Exchange Commission (SEC), and taught at the Harvard Graduate School of Business (HBS), becoming assistant dean. HBS started his relationship with the USAF as he was a consultant in the development of the service's statistical controls. In World War II,* he served in the U.S. Navy.

SAF Stuart Symington* brought Zuckert into his office as a special assistant; after the USAF became independent, he was appointed assistant secretary of the Air Force on 26 September 1947. This put him in the midst of the battle to integrate racially the armed forces. He found himself in the throes of intense service rivalry until the strife was reduced by compromises such as the Key West and Newport Conferences.* He left the USAF in 1952 for the U.S. Atomic Energy Commission (AEC) until 1954 and then returned to private practice.

Zuckert always believed his role was a mixed one: interpreting to the service the administration while also being the advocate of his service. Zuckert had the greatest difficulty in reconciling the relatively minor position of SAF under the autocratic Secretary of Defense (SECDEF) Robert S. McNamara* with the secretary's status when he was assistant secretary in 1947 to 1952.

References. Primary: USAFHRC Oral History Interviews K239.0512–674, April 1973, no author, and K239.0512–763 by Colonel John L. Frisbee, 1 September 1965, USAFHRC/OH, Maxwell AFB, Alabama. Secondary: DuPre, *USAF Bio.* USAF Biography, "Eugene M. Zuckert, Secretary of the Air Force," 30 September 1965. George M. Watson, Jr., "Man in the Middle: Eugene Zuckert as Secretary of the Air Force," *Air Power History,* Summer 1989, pp. 20–29.

Lloyd H. Cornett, Jr.

ZWEIBRUECKEN AIR BASE

This U.S. Air Forces in Europe* (USAFE) base is south of Ramstein* AB, Germany, and is named for a nearby city. The AB dates from 1953, but the USAF* presence began in 1969. In 1990, the 26th Tactical Reconnaissance Wing was based upon it with RF-4Cs (*see* F-4). The USAF is scheduled to move out in 1993.

References. "Guide to Major Air Force Installations Worldwide," *AF,* May 1990, p. 133. Roberts, *Dir. USAF.* Terence Roth, "Some Germans Fear U.S. Military Pullout," *The Wall Street Journal,* 10 May 1990, p. A10.

INDEX

ABOUT THE EDITOR AND CONTRIBUTORS

DAVID H. ANDERSON, Engineer, Product Development, The Boeing Company. Lieutenant Colonel, USAF Retired, command pilot. Formerly Editor, Pilot's Flight Handbooks for C-97, C-135, and all variants thereof.

ROGER A. BEAUMONT, Professor of History, Texas A&M University. Eight books.

LAWRENCE R. BENSON, Director of Research Services, Air Force Operational Test and Evaluation Center, Kirtland AFB, New Mexico.

JEFFREY C. BENTON, Colonel, USAF, Commander, 3360th Technical Training Group, Chanute AFB, Illinois. Formerly Military Doctrine Analyst, Air Power Research Institute, Maxwell AFB, Alabama.

THOMAS C. BLOW II, Major, USAF, Chief, Contingency Plans Branch, 9th Strategic Reconnaissance Wing, Beale AFB, California. Formerly Military Doctrine Analyst, Air Power Research Institute, Maxwell AFB, Alabama.

CHARLES D. BRIGHT, Lieutenant Colonel, USAF Retired. Formerly Chairman, Business Administration, Mount St. Clare College, Iowa. Command pilot, lead navigator. *The Jet Makers: The Aerospace Industry from 1945 to 1972*, 1978.

LESTER H. BRUNE, Professor of History, Bradley University, Illinois. *The Origins of American National Security: Sea Power, Air Power and Foreign Policy, 1900 to 1941* (1981). Three other books.

GERALD T. CANTWELL, retired. Formerly Director of Historical Services, USAFR, Robins AFB, Georgia.

LLOYD H. CORNETT, JR., retired. Formerly Director, USAF Historical Research Center, Maxwell AFB, Alabama.

COY F. CROSS II, Senior Master Sergeant, USAF Retired. Historian, History Office, Western Space and Missile Center, Vandenberg AFB, California.

JAMES L. CROWDER, Historian, Oklahoma City Air Logistics Center, Tinker AFB, Oklahoma. *Osage General: Major General Clarence L. Tinker*, Tinker AFB Office of History (1987).

GILBERT E. D'ALONZO, Major, USAFR Retired. Formerly lead bombardier.

RICHARD L. DAVIS, Lieutenant Colonel, USAF. Air Attaché, Republic of Zaire. Formerly Military Doctrine Analyst, Air Power Research Institute, Maxwell AFB, Alabama.

E. MICHAEL DEL PAPA, Chief, History Office, Electronic Systems Division, Hanscom AFB, Massachusetts.

ROBERT W. DUFFNER, Chief, History Office, Phillips Laboratory, Kirtland AFB, New Mexico.

PETER R. FABER, Major, USAF. Doctoral student, Yale University, Connecticut. Formerly Instructor in Military History, USAF Academy, Colorado.

JOHN T. FARQUHAR, Captain, USAF. Doctoral candidate, Ohio State University. Formerly Instructor in Military History, USAF Academy, Colorado.

JOHN F. FARRELL, Captain, USAF. Assistant Professor, USAF Academy, Colorado.

DANIEL FORD, writer specializing in aviation and World War II. *Flying Tigers: Claire Chennault and the American Volunteer Group* (forthcoming). Three novels.

ROGER M. FOX, helicopter pilot, KOMO Radio and Television, Seattle, Washington. Formerly Captain, Army of the United States, and Battalion Assistant Operations Officer.

FRANK L. GOLDSTEIN, Lieutenant Colonel, USAF, U.S. Special Operations Command, MacDill AFB, Florida.

RITAVICTORIA GOMEZ, Instructor, Ann Arundel Community College, Maryland. Major, USAFR. *A History of Women in the Air Force* (forthcoming).

CHARLES J. GROSS, Historian, Office of History, Air Force Systems Command, Andrews AFB, District of Columbia. *Prelude to the Total Force: The Air National Guard 1943–1969* (1985).

JAMES C. HASDORFF, Adjunct Instructor in History, Auburn University, Alabama. Formerly Deputy Chief, Oral History Division, USAF Historical Research Center, Maxwell AFB, Alabama.

GEORGE W. HAWKS, JR., Boeing 727 First Officer, Delta Air Lines. Lieutenant Colonel, USAF Retired, command pilot.

WILLIAM HEAD, Historian, Warner Robins Air Logistics Center Office of History, Robins AFB, Georgia. *Yenan* (1989). Five other books.

CHARLES G. HIBBARD, Chief Master Sergeant, USAF Retired. Formerly Chief, Office of History, Ogden Air Logistics Center, Hill AFB, Utah.

ROBIN HIGHAM, Professor of History, Kansas State University. Editor Emeritus, *Aerospace Historian*. Formerly Royal Air Force Volunteer Reserve pilot. *Air Power: A Concise History*, 3d ed. (1988). Numerous other books in aviation history.

IRVING BRINTON HOLLEY, JR., Professor of History, Duke University, North Carolina. Major General, USAFR, Retired. *Buying Aircraft: Matériel Procurement for the Army Air Forces* (1964). *Ideas and Weapons* (1953).

EDWARD L. HOMZE, Professor of History, University of Nebraska—Lincoln. *Arming the Luftwaffe: The Reich Air Ministry and the German Aircraft Industry 1919–1939* (1976).

JAMES J. HUDSON, Professor Emeritus of History and former Dean, Graduate School, University of Arkansas, Arkansas. Formerly First Lieutenant, USAAF, pilot. *Hostile Skies: A Combat History of the American Air Service in World War I* (1968).

RICHARD W. IOBST, Chief, Office of History, Warner Robins Air Logistics Center, Robins AFB, Georgia. *The Bloody Sixth* (1989).

JOE M. JACKSON, Air Force Medal of Honor. Colonel, USAF Retired, command pilot.

W. A. JACOBS, Professor of Political Science, University of Alaska, Anchorage.

BUDD A. JONES, JR., Major, USAF. Assistant Professor and Director, Military History, USAF Academy, Colorado.

BETTY RAAB KENNEDY, Staff Historian, Military Airlift Command, Scott AFB, Illinois. Formerly Staff Sergeant, USAR. *Anything, Anywhere, Anytime: An Illustrated History of the Military Airlift Command 1941–1991* (Office of MAC History, 1991).

MICHAEL A. KIRTLAND, Military Doctrine Analyst, Air Power Research Institute, Maxwell AFB, Alabama. Formerly Associate Editor, *Airpower Journal*. Editor, *Air University Review Index 1947–1987*.

ROGER D. LAUNIUS, Chief Historian, National Aeronautics and Space Administration, NASA Headquarters, Washington, D.C. *Joseph Smith III: Pragmatic Prophet* (1988). Five other books.

ALWYN T. LLOYD, Editor, *Boeing Airliner Magazine*. *B-17 Flying Fortress in Detail & Scale*, part 1, "Production Versions" (1981). Seven other books on aircraft types.

PHILIP LONG, graduate student in military history, Kansas State University. Master Sergeant, USAF Retired. Formerly explosive ordnance disposal technician.

DAVID MACISAAC, Associate Director, Air Power Research Institute, Maxwell AFB, Alabama. Lieutenant Colonel, USAF, Retired. *Strategic Bombing in World War II: The Story of the United States Strategic Bombing Survey* (1976).

THOMAS A. MANNING, Command Historian, Air Training Command, Randolph AFB, Texas. *The World Is Our Classroom* (USAF Historical Program, 1987).

MAURICE MARYANOW, Doctoral student in English, Auburn University, Auburn, Alabama. Lieutenant Colonel, USAF Retired. Formerly Chief, Oral History Division, USAF Historical Research Center, Maxwell AFB, Alabama. Editor, *Catalog of USAF Oral History Collection* (USAF Historical Research Center, 1989).

PHILLIP S. MEILINGER, Lieutenant Colonel, USAF, Air Operations Staff Officer, Headquarters USAF, Washington, D.C. Formerly Associate Professor and Deputy Head, History Department, USAF Academy, Colorado. *Hoyt S. Vandenberg: The Life of a General* (1989).

DAVID R. METS, Professor of Technology and Innovation, School of Advanced Air Power Studies, Maxwell AFB, Alabama. Lieutenant Colonel, USAF Retired, command pilot, navigator. *Master of Airpower: General Carl A. Spaatz* (1988).

BRIAN J. NICHELSON, Training Specialist, Exxon Products Research Co., Houston, Texas. Formerly Major, USAF, and Assistant Professor, History Department, USAF Academy, Colorado.

PATRICK B. NOLAN, Executive Administrator, Center for the History of Business, Technology, and Society, Hagley Museum and Library, Wilmington, Delaware. *Kitty Hawk and Beyond: The Photographic Legacy of the Wright Brothers* (1990). One other book.

RAYMOND L. PUFFER, Chief Historian, Ballistic Missile Organization, Norton AFB, California.

JOHN R. REESE, Captain, USAF, Associate Professor of History, USAF Academy, Colorado.

DAVID L. ROSMER, Chief, Office of History, 9AF/USCENTAF, Shaw AFB, South Carolina. Doctoral candidate, University of South Carolina. *An Annotated Pictorial History of Clark Air Base: 1898–1986* (13AF Office of History, 1986).

WARREN A. TREST, Senior Historian, USAF Historical Research Center, Maxwell AFB, Alabama. *Evolution of Air Force Roles and Missions* (forthcoming).

DIANE TRULUCK, Historical Clerk and Editorial Assistant, Office of History, Warner Robins Air Logistics Center, Robins AFB, Georgia.

JEFFERY S. UNDERWOOD, Historian, Air Defense Weapons Center, Tyndall AFB, Florida. *Wings of Democracy: The Army Air Corps under Franklin D. Roosevelt, 1933–1941* (forthcoming).

D. K. VAUGHAN, Assistant Professor of Technical Communications, Air Force Institute of Technology, Wright-Patterson AFB, Ohio. Major, USAF Retired, command pilot. *An American Pilot in the Skies of France* (forthcoming).

P. SUSAN WEATHERS, retired. Formerly Historian, Office of History, Ogden Air Logistics Center, Hill AFB, Utah.

STEVEN K. YATES, Major, USAF Retired. Formerly Chief, Oral History Division, USAF Historical Research Center, Maxwell AFB, Alabama.

RONALD W. YOSHINO, Assistant Professor of History, Riverside Community College, Riverside, California. *Lightning Strikes: The 475th Fighter Group in the Pacific War, 1943–1945* (1988).

JAMES O. YOUNG, Chief Historian, Air Force Flight Test Center, Edwards AFB, California. *Black Riders of the Thirties* (1973). Two other books.